Department of Social Policy and Social Work
University of Oxford
Barnett House
32 Wellington Square
Oxford OX1 2ER
England

HANDBOOK OF
Mixed
Methods
IN SOCIAL &
BEHAVIORAL
RESEARCH

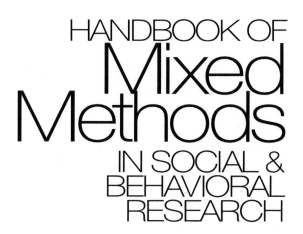

HANDBOOK OF
Mixed
Methods

IN SOCIAL &
BEHAVIORAL
RESEARCH

EDITORS

ABBAS TASHAKKORI
Florida International University

CHARLES TEDDLIE
Louisiana State University

SAGE Publications
International Educational and Professional Publisher
Thousand Oaks ▪ London ▪ New Delhi

For information:

Sage Publications, Inc.
2455 Teller Road
Thousand Oaks, California 91320
E-mail: order@sagepub.com

Sage Publications Ltd.
6 Bonhill Street
London EC2A 4PU
United Kingdom

Sage Publications India Pvt. Ltd.
M-32 Market
Greater Kailash I
New Delhi 110 048 India

Printed in the United States of America

Library of Congress Cataloging-in-Publication Data

Tashakkori, Abbas.
   Handbook of mixed methods in social and behavioral research /
Abbas Tashakkori, Charles Teddlie.
      p. cm.
   Includes bibliographical references and index.
   ISBN 0-7619-2073-0 (alk. paper)
      1. Social sciences—Research—Methodology—Handbooks, manuals, etc.
I. Teddlie, Charles. II. Title.
      H62 .T244 2002
300′.7′2—dc21   2002005206

This book is printed on acid-free paper.

03 04 05 06 10 9 8 7 6 5 4 3 2 1

Acquisitions Editor:	C. Deborah Laughton
Editorial Assistant:	Veronica K. Novak
Copy Editor:	D. J. Peck
Production Editor:	Diane S. Foster
Typesetter:	Tina Hill
Proofreader:	Scott Oney
Indexer:	Terri Greenberg
Cover Designer:	Michelle Lee

CONTENTS

SECTION TWO
METHODOLOGICAL AND ANALYTICAL
ISSUES FOR MIXED METHODS RESEARCH

SECTION THREE
APPLICATIONS AND EXAMPLES OF MIXED
METHODS RESEARCH ACROSS DISCIPLINES

PREFACE

The methodology of social and behavioral research has undergone several dramatic changes over the past 30 years. These changes have had an impact on the purposes, worldviews, and methods of studying behaviors, programs, and social interactions. During most of the 20th century, social and behavioral research was dominated by "quantitative methods," with positivism (and variants thereof such as postpositivism) as its dominant worldview. Value neutrality was widely expected of researchers, and methods of studying behaviors and social interactions relied heavily on "objective" measures. Basic research was predominantly valued.

During the last two decades of the century, qualitative methodology emerged with a worldview associated with variants of constructivism. Qualitative research was seen as a reaction against the dominant (received) quantitative methodology of the time, and it became immensely popular among those who were dissatisfied with the established methodological "order." Other shifts that were occurring around this time included a movement toward more socially and culturally sensitive research and a greater emphasis on applied, as opposed to basic, research. The qualitative approach to research promoted a more subjective, culture-bound, and emancipatory approach to studying individual behaviors and social phenomena, and it introduced innovative new research methods for answering questions.

Despite their obvious merits, each of the two basic approaches to research has been criticized by proponents from the other orientation. Although much of the controversy has focused on paradigm or worldview (i.e., the "paradigm wars" [Gage, 1989]), each camp has also criticized the other's methods of study, the rigor of its procedures, and the validity of its outcomes. The field of mixed methodology, which we call the "third methodological movement," has evolved as a result of these discussions and controversies and as a pragmatic way of using the strengths of both approaches.

An examination of recent social and behavioral research reveals that mixed methods are being used extensively to solve practical research problems. Most investigators using these methods have not been interested in delving deeply into the philosophical orientations that supposedly underlie the application of their research studies. This is why the paradigm wars that occurred during the 1970s, 1980s, and early 1990s did not affect many of the researchers working with mixed methods; these authors simply were more interested in the research questions they were studying than in discussions of complex philosophical issues.

This practical orientation may explain why mixed methods research has not emerged sooner and more forcefully as the third methodological movement. Authors working in the quantitative and qualitative traditions have seldom referred to mixed methods. Similarly, writings on the philosophical underpinnings for social and behavioral research seldom include pragmatism, the paradigm most often associated with mixed methods (e.g., Howe, 1988). There appears to be a bias that mixed methods designs are simply combinations of qualitative and quantitative techniques and that it is debatable whether these types of designs are truly the proper way in which to conduct research. As for pragmatism, many dismiss it as a "naive" or even "vulgar" orientation that simplifies highly complex philosophical issues into "what works."

It is the intent of this handbook to demonstrate that mixed methods research has evolved to the point where it is a separate methodological orientation with its own worldview, vocabulary, and techniques. Mixed methods designs incorporate techniques from both the quantitative and qualitative research traditions yet combine them in unique ways to answer research questions that could not be answered in any other way. In Chapter 26 of this handbook, we (the editors) argue that this combination (a whole or gestalt) is more than the sum of its qualitative or quantitative components. We believe that

mixed methods designs will be the dominant methodological tools in the social and behavioral sciences during the 21st century.

Mixed methods research is still in its adolescence, and we will see much more development during the years to come. We hope that one impact of such development will be the creation of bridges between the qualitative and quantitative camps.[1]

◆ Defining the Third Methodological Movement

This handbook presents, in a single volume, the diverse theoretical and methodological applications of mixed methods research in the social and behavioral sciences. In Chapter 1, we present a historical analysis of its evolution as a separate type of methodology that is clearly distinct from the quantitative and qualitative approaches. Our historical analysis led us to the conclusion that mixed methods research has yet to be recognized for the unique nature of its designs and has yet to be accorded the separate status that it deserves as the third methodological movement.

Eminent social and behavioral scientists conducted mixed methods research throughout the 20th century, but it was only during the last decade of that century that researchers began giving unique names to their designs. It is argued throughout this handbook that mixed methods designs evolved from the notion of "triangulating" the information from different data sources, a technique that emerged first from psychology (Campbell & Fiske, 1959) and sociology (Denzin, 1978) but that reached its fullest application in applied research areas such as evaluation (e.g., Patton, 1990) and nursing (e.g., Morse, 1991).

In our previous book (Tashakkori & Teddlie, 1998), we endeavored to present the unique aspects of mixed methods research. That book built on previous writings regarding the feasibility and practicality of mixed method and mixed model designs. We demonstrated that a relatively large number of studies in the social and behavioral sciences have used mixed methods by employing designs that included both qualitative and quantitative data and their related analyses. We also demonstrated that many of the investigators did not identify their research designs as being mixed methods in nature. We further demonstrated that mixed approach studies are frequently more complex and advanced than simple combinations of the two basic types of approaches. We proposed that a truly mixed approach methodology (a) would incorporate multiple approaches in all stages of the study (i.e., problem identification, data collection, data analysis, and final inference) and (b) would include a transformation of the data and their analysis through another approach. We used the label "mixed model design or study" to identify these studies.

The current handbook carries these themes even further. Philosophical orientations, design issues, analysis issues, and inference issues are examined and debated in several chapters of this handbook. This examination and debate among mixed methods experts is illustrative of the ongoing emergence of mixed methods as the third methodological movement in the social and behavioral sciences.

◆ The Structure of the Handbook

The handbook is divided into four parts plus a Glossary. The four parts are as follows:

I. The Research Enterprise in the Social and Behavioral Sciences: Then and Now (Chapters 1-5)

II. Methodological and Analytical Issues for Mixed Methods Research (Chapters 6-16)

III. Applications and Examples of Mixed Methods Research Across Disciplines (Chapters 17-23)

IV. Conclusions and Future Directions (Chapters 24-26)

The first section discusses many of the philosophical and theoretical issues in the use of mixed methods research. This section addresses controversial paradigm issues, with an overview in Chapter 1 (Teddlie & Tashakkori), a presentation of the pragmatist position in Chapter 2 (Maxcy), and a portrayal of the transformative-emancipatory perspective in Chapter 5 (Mertens). Also, Greene and Caracelli (Chapter 3) present the "dialectic" stance, which does not advocate one paradigm over others but rather sees mixed methods research as intentionally engaging a multiple set of paradigms and their assumptions. The value of using mixed methods in exploring cultural diversity issues is discussed in Chapter 4 (Moghaddam, Walker, & Harré).

The second section of the handbook presents detailed coverage of methodological issues in mixed methods research and provides a variety of data collection, data analysis, and inference techniques. The 11 chapters in this section follow the mixed methods research process from the development of research questions (Newman, Ridenour, Newman, & DeMarco, Chapter 6) through the development of the research design (Chapters 7-9), through sampling (Kemper, Stringfield, & Teddlie, Chapter 10), through data collection (Johnson & Turner, Chapter 11), through data analysis and presentation (Chapters

12-14), and finally through the inference process (Chapters 15 and 16).

The design of mixed methods research is a major topic of this handbook; therefore, the inclusion of three chapters specifically devoted to the topic is appropriate. Morse (Chapter 7) updates her typology of mixed methods research designs, which includes notations and abbreviations that many scholars have adopted (e.g., qual, quan, simultaneous design, sequential design). Creswell, Plano Clark, Gutmann, and Hanson (Chapter 8) present four criteria that then become the foundation for the development of six specific types of mixed methods research designs. Finally, Maxwell and Loomis (Chapter 9) present an "interactive model" for mixed methods research design in which the components of research design are in a network or web rather than in a linear progression.

The three chapters on data analysis and presentation address somewhat different issues. In Chapter 12, Sandelowski discusses the challenges associated with writing mixed methods studies. Onwuegbuzie and Teddlie (Chapter 13) present a variety of ways in which to analyze mixed methods data, including several techniques for determining effect sizes from qualitative data. Bazeley (Chapter 14) discusses the use of computerized data analysis in mixed methods research. Finally, both Miller (Chapter 15) and Erzberger and Kelle (Chapter 16) discuss issues associated with drawing inferences in mixed methods.

The third section of the handbook includes chapters by scholars from several different disciplines, thereby demonstrating the interdisciplinary appeal of mixed methods research. Contributions in this section come from evaluation research (Rallis & Rossman, Chapter 17), management and organizational research (Currall & Towler, Chapter 18), health sciences (Forthofer, Chapter 19), nursing research (Twinn, Chapter 20), psychology (Waszak & Sines, Chapter 21), sociology (Hunter & Brewer, Chapter 22), and education (Rocco, Bliss, Gallagher, Perez-Prado, Alacaci, Dwyer, Fine, & Pappamihiel, Chapter 23).

The final section of the handbook provides conclusions and future directions. It addresses two very practical issues: how to teach mixed methods research (Creswell, Tashakkori, Jensen, & Shapley, Chapter 24) and how to effectively collaborate on mixed methods research studies (Shulha & Wilson, Chapter 25). The final chapter (Tashakkori & Teddlie, Chapter 26) revisits six major issues identified by the co-editors of the handbook in Chapter 1 and derives conclusions and future directions for each of these issues.

The Glossary contains approximately 150 terms and their definitions. We asked the authors to designate and define a few terms from each of their chapters in the handbook. We then compiled the terms to create the Glossary. There are alternative definitions for several of the Glossary terms, and we believe that these alternative definitions indicate that different authors may disagree about exactly what a term means but nevertheless think the term is important. The Glossary also includes terms whose definitions are more or less agreed on by different scholars or seem to have a great potential for generating such agreement. We tried in Chapters 1 and 26 and the Glossary to create bridges by incorporating components from both the quantitative and qualitative traditions and by using conceptual frameworks offered by different scholars in the field of mixed methods.

◆ *The Major Issues*
  Addressed in the Handbook

While we initially had certain themes in mind for the handbook, others emerged during the process of writing and editing it. After reading and rereading all of the chapters, we identified six major unresolved issues and controversies in the use of mixed methods in the social and behavioral sciences. We discussed each of these issues in both Chapters 1 and 26. In fact, these issues are discussed throughout the handbook and serve as one of the major ways in which content is integrated throughout the volume.

The six issues are as follows:

1. The nomenclature and basic definitions used in mixed methods research

2. The utility of mixed methods research (why do we do it?)

3. The paradigmatic foundations for mixed methods research

4. Design issues in mixed methods research

5. Issues in drawing inferences in mixed methods research

6. The logistics of conducting mixed methods research

Because these issues are discussed throughout the handbook, we do not summarize them here. Instead, we advise readers of the handbook to focus on these issues and to examine the variety of opinions stated regarding each one.

◆ The Authors of the Handbook

We were very fortunate to have recruited a diverse and accomplished group of authors to write this handbook. Our own appreciation of the complexity and potential for mixed methods has been greatly enhanced by reading their writing and by interacting with them.

The authors varied on at least three important dimensions. First, some are new to the field and make interesting new contributions by addressing topics in ways that have not been addressed before. Other authors have been writing in the field for several years, and their contributions reflect original insights plus a mature appreciation of the evolution of the field.

Second, as noted earlier, the authors come from throughout the spectrum of the social and behavioral sciences. There are more than 50 contributors to the handbook. Their backgrounds include anthropology, sociology, several branches of psychology (e.g., school, social, industrial, organizational), nursing, education, management, evaluation research, counseling, community and family health, and communication disorders, among others.

Third, the authors are truly an international group, bringing with them perspectives from a rich variety of cultural and national backgrounds. While most chapters were written by individuals from the United States, there were contributors from five other countries: Australia, Canada, Germany, Hong Kong, and the United Kingdom. We were also pleased to discover that among the authors from the United States, several have been raised abroad and/or have extensive research in cross-cultural issues. This diversity of perspectives has been refreshing and points to the fact that further internationalization of the field is a welcome trend.

It may be interesting to note that the co-editors of the handbook come from backgrounds that led us naturally to the use of mixed methods. Teddlie was trained as an experimental social psychologist but has worked extensively in university and government environments where practical research questions had to be answered. During his career, he has taught both statistics and qualitative research methods. Tashakkori is also a social psychologist with interest and experience in cross-cultural research that is naturally amenable to mixed methods. We both have had extensive experience in program evaluation involving mixed methods and have taught courses from the mixed methods perspective. Thus, we both were trained in the quantitative tradition, have used qualitative methods extensively in our own research, and end up advocating for the use of mixed methods because they are the most practical and useful tools to answer the most complex research questions in the social and behavioral sciences.

◆ Acknowledgments

This handbook would not have been possible without the hard work of our contributors. We were fortunate to have had an accomplished and diverse group of scholars working with us, and we appreciate all of the contributions that they have made to the handbook and to our further understanding of mixed methods. This handbook would not have materialized without the constant encouragement of our editor at Sage Publications, C. Deborah Laughton. She worked with us extensively in outlining the handbook and in lining up the roster of authors, and she then continued to work with us on each step of the lengthy editing process. The initial plan for the handbook was critiqued and improved by a group of insightful reviewers. We appreciate their willingness to share their ideas with us. Among them, we are specifically grateful for the advice we received from Rosaline S. Barbour, Department of General Practice, University of Glasgow; Cheryl Tatano Beck, School of Nursing, University of Connecticut, Storrs; H. Russell Bernard, Department of Anthropology, University of Florida, Gainesville; Linda B. Bourque, School of Public Health, University of California, Los Angeles; Pamela Brink, Faculty of Nursing, University of Alberta; Lynne M. Connelly, Department of Nursing Science, Army Medical Department Center & School; Benjamin F. Crabtree, Department of Family Medicine, University of Medicine & Dentistry of New Jersey; John W. Creswell, Department of Educational Psychology, University of Nebraska–Lincoln; Steven C. Currall, Jesse H. Jones Graduate School of Management, Rice University; Arlene Fink, Department of Public Health, University of California, Los Angeles; Roxie Foster, School of Nursing, University of Colorado-Denver; Marcel Fredericks, Department of Sociology and Anthropology, Loyola University–Chicago; Jennifer C. Greene, Department of Educational Psychology, University of Illinois, Urbana-Champaign; Christine Griffin, School of Psychology, University of Birmingham, UK; Alice M. Hines, Alcohol Research Group; Nancy Hoffart, School of Nursing, University of Kansas; Ann Chih Lin, School of Public Policy, University of Michigan; Mark W. Lipsey, Department of Psychology and Human Development, Vanderbilt University; Mark Litwin, Department of Urology, University of California, Los Angeles; Donna M. Mertens, Department of Educational Foundations and Research, Gallaudet University; Steven I. Miller, School of Education, Loyola University-Chicago; John Modell, Department of Sociology, Brown University; Fathali M. Moghaddan, Department of Psychology, Georgetown University; David L. Morgan, Institute on Aging, Portland State University; Pauline Pearson, Department of Primary Health Care, University of Newcastle; Michael Quinn Patton, The Union Institute, Utilization Focused Evaluation; Keith F. Punch, Graduate School of Education, University of Western Australia; Sharon F. Rallis, Neag School of Education, University of Connecticut; Daryl G. Smith,

School of Educational Studies, Claremont Graduate Uni- versity; Nick L. Smith, School of Education, Syracuse University; Robert E. Stake, Department of Educational Psychology, University of Ilinois, Urbana Champaign; Deborah L. Tolman, Center for Research on Women, Wellesley College; Sheila Twinn, Nethersole School of Nursing, The Chinese University of Hong Kong; Marja J. Verhoef, Department of Community Health Sciences, University of Calgary; Paul Vogt, College of Education, Illinois State University; Cindy Waszak, Family Health International.

In addition, the complete manuscript was reviewed by a group of dedicated and helpful researchers whose advice we found useful in shaping this book. We would like to thank: Sharlene Hesse-Biber, Boston College; Gerald K. LeTendre, Penn State University; John Gaber, University of Nebraska-Lincoln; and, Michael Quinn Patton, The Union Institute, Utilization-Focused Evaluation.

■ Note

1. "Bridges," a Web site devoted to this purpose, is already established (www.fiu.edu/~bridges).

■ *References*

Campbell, D., & Fiske, D. W. (1959). Convergent and discriminant validation by the multitrait-multimethod matrix. *Psychological Bulletin, 54*, 297-312.

Denzin, N. K. (1978). The logic of naturalistic inquiry. In N. K. Denzin (Ed.), *Sociological methods: A sourcebook*. New York: McGraw-Hill.

Gage, N. (1989). The paradigm wars and their aftermath: A "historical" sketch of research and teaching since 1989. *Educational Researcher, 18*(7), 4-10.

Howe, K. R. (1988). Against the quantitative-qualitative incompatibility thesis or dogmas die hard. *Educational Researcher, 17*(8), 10-16.

Morse, J. M. (1991). Approaches to qualitative-quantitative methodological triangulation. *Nursing Research, 40*(2), 120-123.

Patton, M. Q. (1990). *Qualitative evaluation and research methods* (2nd ed.). Newbury Park, CA: Sage.

Tashakkori, A., & Teddlie, C. (1998). *Mixed methodology: Combining the qualitative and quantitative approaches*. Thousand Oaks, CA: Sage.

The Research Enterprise in the Social and Behavioral Sciences: Then and Now

1

MAJOR ISSUES AND CONTROVERSIES IN THE USE OF MIXED METHODS IN THE SOCIAL AND BEHAVIORAL SCIENCES

◆ Charles Teddlie
Abbas Tashakkori

This chapter answers two basic questions related to the *Handbook of Mixed Methods in Social and Behavioral Research* (hereafter referred to as the handbook):

1. Why do we need a handbook in this field at this point in time?

2. What major issues and controversies does this handbook address?

As the editors of this handbook, it is our opinion that the area of mixed methods research has reached a critical point in its development that allows for the publication of a handbook. We agree that the field is just entering its "adolescence" and that there are many unresolved issues to address before a more mature mixed methods research area can emerge. Nevertheless, we also believe that the handbook, with its explicit recitation of important issues and its presentation of differing points of view regarding these issues, will stimulate greater maturity in the field.

Mixed methods research is still in its adolescence in that scholars do not agree on many basic issues related to the field. It may be that scholars will ultimately agree to disagree on some of these issues; for instance, they may decide that there are several viable ways to categorize mixed methods research designs such that more than one competing typology will be widely recognized and used by scholars in different contexts. It is not the resolution of the basic issues that is important; rather, it is the presentation and discussion of the differing viewpoints that is crucial at this time.

We have identified six major unresolved issues and controversies in the use of mixed methods in the social and behavioral sciences:

1. The nomenclature and basic definitions used in mixed methods research

2. The utility of mixed methods research (why do we do it)

3. The paradigmatic foundations for mixed methods research

4. Design issues in mixed methods research

5. Issues in drawing inferences in mixed methods research

6. The logistics of conducting mixed methods research

These issues are discussed throughout the handbook and serve as one of the major ways in which content is integrated throughout. In each of the sections in this chapter, we (a) define the problem and why it is a major issue in mixed methods research, (b) briefly state our position with regard to the issue, and (c) introduce the positions of others in the handbook.

In their chapter on mixed methods design, Maxwell and Loomis (Chapter 9, this volume) state that they are not taking an adversarial or polemic stand toward other approaches. That is our position

throughout this chapter: We are presenting different points of view on several important issues so as to stimulate further dialog. Ultimately, the better ideas should prevail as the field matures.

◆ The Evolution of the Research Enterprise in the Social and Behavioral Sciences

THREE METHODOLOGICAL MOVEMENTS IN THE SOCIAL AND BEHAVIORAL SCIENCES

The historical analysis that follows describes how the field of mixed methods has developed to the point where a handbook is now necessary. Currently, researchers in the social and behavioral sciences can be roughly categorized into three groups: (a) quantitatively oriented researchers (QUANs)[1] working within the postpositivist tradition and primarily interested in numerical analyses, (b) qualitatively oriented researchers (QUALs) working within the constructivist tradition and primarily interested in analysis of narrative data, and (c) mixed methodologists working within other paradigms (e.g., pragmatism, transformative-emancipatory paradigm) and interested in both types of data. (For a discussion of pragmatism, see Maxcy, Chapter 2, this volume. For a discussion of the transformative-emancipatory paradigm, see Mertens, Chapter 5, this volume.)

The first two groups need no introduction to readers. The dominant and relatively unquestioned methodological orientation (with the exception of anthropology and sociology in some cases) during the first half of the 20th century was quantitative methods and the positivist paradigm. This orientation was transformed during the 1950-1970 period as postpositivists responded to some of the more obvious difficulties associated with positivism, yet the methods stayed quantitative. QUALs refer to this as the "received" paradigm.

Qualitatively oriented researchers (e.g., Eisner, Geertz, Lincoln & Guba, Stake, Wolcott) wrote several popular books during the 1970-1985 period that were critical of the positivist orientation and proposed a wide variety of qualitative methods. The most common name given to the paradigm that was associated with the qualitative research position during this period was constructivism. This qualitative research movement gained widespread acceptance, as described by Denzin and Lincoln (1994):

> Over the past two decades, a quiet methodological revolution has been taking place in the social sciences. . . . The extent to which the "qualitative revolution" has overtaken the social sciences and related professional fields has been nothing short of amazing. (p. ix)

Recent theoretical work in the qualitative research movement (e.g., Lincoln & Guba, 2000; Schwandt, 2000) has led to the conclusion that multiple paradigms (and not just constructivism and its variants) are applicable to qualitative research. This point is discussed later in this chapter because it represents an interesting change in perspective from a group that has historically tied particular methods to particular paradigms.

Mixed methodologists need more of an introduction because they have been neither the traditionalists (quantitatively oriented researchers) nor the revolutionaries (qualitatively oriented researchers) over the past 30 years. Despite this, researchers have employed mixed methods throughout the 20th century and into the 21st century, as described throughout this chapter. Before the paradigm wars, there was no need for mixed methodologists to bring attention to their distinct orientation. Before the incompatibility thesis (i.e., stating that it was inappropriate to mix quantitative and qualitative methods), researchers who used mixed methods to answer their research questions were mostly unaware that they were doing anything out of the ordinary.

These three methodological "movements" continue to evolve simultaneously throughout the social and behavioral sciences. While one may be more in ascendance for some period of time, all three methodological orientations are practiced concurrently. This handbook focuses on the *third methodological movement*, which is just now explicitly developing.

A HISTORICAL ANALYSIS OF THE EMERGENCE OF MIXED METHODS

Denzin and Lincoln (1994) defined five "moments" in the history of qualitative research: the traditional (1900-1950), the modernist or Golden Age (1950-1970), blurred genres (1970-1986), the crisis of representation (1986-1990), and postmodern or present moments (1990-present). These broad historical periods agree to a substantial degree with our previous analysis (Tashakkori & Teddlie, 1998) of the evolution of mixed methods research, although we have divided the periods somewhat differently (1900-1950, 1950-1970, 1970-1990, and 1990-present). This section describes what was happening in mixed methodology research as the qualitative research world was going through its first five moments.[2]

The "traditional" 1900-1950 period actually saw a substantial degree of important mixed methods research ongoing with little methodological controversy. Maxwell and Loomis (Chapter 9, this volume) contend that there was less orthodoxy in methodology during this time period than later in the century. While there had been some debate since the mid-19th century (especially in sociology during the 1920s and 1930s) about the relative merits of quantitative and qualitative research (e.g., Hammersley, 1992), this debate did not have the rancor that accompanied the later paradigm wars.

Classic mixed methods studies from this period are described in this handbook from the field of sociology (Hunter & Brewer, Chapter 22, this volume). These works include the Hawthorne studies (Roethlisberger & Dickson, 1939) and the studies of "Yankee City" (Warner & Lunt, 1941). For example, there was extensive use of both interviews and observations in the overall research program in addition to the famous experimental studies associated with the "Hawthorne" effect.

The time period labeled "modernist" or "Golden Age" (1950-1970) by Denzin and Lincoln was marked in the history of mixed methods research by two major events: (a) the debunking of positivism and (b) the emergence of research designs that began to be called "multimethod" or "mixed." While a distinct field of mixed methods had not emerged by this time, numerous important studies using mixed methodologies occurred, especially in the field of psychology (see the chapters in this volume by Maxwell & Loomis [Chapter 9] and Waszak & Sines [Chapter 21]). These studies included the Festinger, Riecken, and Schachter (1956) research on end-of-the-world cults, the Robber's Cave Experiment by Sherif, Harvey, White, Hood, and Sherif (1961), and Zimbardo's (1969) simulated "prison" studies of deindividuation. For example, Sherif, et al. (1961) made extensive use of qualitative participant observation data to explain quantitative results from the field experiment used in the Robber's Cave Experiment.

Positivism was discredited as a philosophy of science after World War II (e.g., Howe, 1988; Reichardt & Rallis, 1994). Dissatisfaction with the axioms of positivism (e.g., ontology, epistemology, axiology)[3] became increasingly widespread throughout the 1950s and 1960s, giving rise to postpositivism, the intellectual heir to positivism. Landmark works of postpositivism (e.g., Hanson, 1958; Popper, 1935/1959) gained widespread credibility during the late 1950s. Tenets of postpositivism include value-ladenness of inquiry (research is influenced by the values of investigators), theory-ladenness of facts (research is influenced by the theory that an investigator uses), and the nature of reality (our understanding of reality is constructed). These beliefs are widely held by mixed methodologists.

The other important development of this period was the emergence of the first explicit multimethod designs, which inevitably led to studies that mixed quantitative and qualitative methods. Campbell and Fiske (1959) proposed their "multitrait-multimethod matrix," which used more than one quantitative method to measure a psychological trait. They did this to ensure that the variance in their research was accounted for by the trait under study and not by the method that was employed to measure it (e.g., Brewer & Hunter, 1989; Creswell, 1994).

The periods described by Denzin and Lincoln as "blurred genres" (1970-1986) and "crisis of representation" (1986-1990) coincide with what we (Tashakkori & Teddlie, 1998) have called "the ascendance of constructivism, followed by the paradigm wars." Several significant events for mixed methodology occurred during the 1970-1990 period such as (a) qualitative methods and constructivism grew quite rapidly in popularity, (b) the paradigm wars were launched based largely on the incompatibility thesis, (c) mixed methods studies were introduced in conjunction with writings on triangulation, and (d) important mixed methods studies and syntheses appeared.

The discrediting of positivism resulted in the increasing popularity of paradigms more "revolutionary" than postpositivism. These paradigms have several names (e.g., constructivism, interpretivism, naturalism), with constructivism being the most popular.[4] Theorists associated with these paradigms borrowed from postpositivism but then added dimensions of their own (e.g., Denzin, 1992; Gergen, 1985; Hammersley, 1989; Lincoln & Guba, 1985). Some of these theorists argued for the superiority of their own paradigm so as to overcome the biases associated with the deeply embedded traditions of positivism or postpositivism (i.e., the "received" paradigm).

For example, Lincoln and Guba (1985) set up contrasts between positivism and naturalism (constructivism) on basic issues: ontology, epistemology, axiology, the possibility of generalizations, and the possibility of causal linkages. Given such contrasts, it was inevitable that paradigm wars would break out between individuals convinced of what Smith (1994) called the "paradigm purity" of their own position. Paradigm "purists" further posited the incompatibility thesis with regard to research methods: Compatibility between quantitative and qualitative methods is impossible due to the incompatibility of the paradigms underlying the methods. According to these theorists, researchers who combine the two methods are doomed to failure due to the differences in underlying systems.

Scholars criticized the incompatibility thesis by noting that, among other points, mixed methods were already being used in many fields (e.g., Brewer & Hunter, 1989; Greene, Caracelli, & Graham, 1989; Patton, 1990). For example, Greene et al. (1989) presented 57 studies that employed mixed methods and described their design characteristics.

Progress was also made during this period on the explicit specification of mixed methods research designs. Denzin (1978) introduced the term "triangulation," which involved combining data sources to study the same social phenomenon. He discussed four types, including data triangulation (the use of multiple data sources) and methodological triangulation (the use of multiple methods). Jick (1979) discussed triangulation in terms of the weaknesses of one method being offset by the strengths of another method. He also discussed "across methods triangulation," which involved quantitative *and* qualitative approaches.

The period described by Denzin and Lincoln (1994) as "postmodern or present moments" (1990-present) coincides with what we have called the emergence of "pragmatism and the compatibility thesis." Two significant events for mixed methodology that occurred during this period were that (a) the pragmatist position was posited as a counterargument to the incompatibility thesis and (b) several seminal works appeared aimed at establishing mixed methods as a separate field.

On a philosophical level, mixed methodologists had to counter the incompatibility thesis, which was predicated on the link between epistemology and method. To counter this paradigm-method link, Howe (1988) posited the use of a different paradigm: pragmatism. A major tenet of Howe's concept of pragmatism was that quantitative and qualitative methods *are compatible*. Thus, because the paradigm says that these methods are compatible, investigators could make use of both of them in their research. This position has been questioned by several scholars writing within the mixed methods literature, and this debate is discussed in a later section of this chapter.

A short list of influential mixed methods works that appeared during this time period includes Creswell (1994), Greene and Caracelli (1997), Morgan (1998), Morse (1991), Newman and Benz (1998), Patton (1990), Reichardt and Rallis (1994), and Tashakkori and Teddlie (1998). These works include several typologies of mixed methods designs, enumeration of key words with both consistent and inconsistent definitions, different paradigm formulations, and so on.

WHY A HANDBOOK NOW?

The previous historical analysis yields several reasons why this is a good time to produce a handbook:

1. The requisite elements for the field of mixed methods now exist: basic terms and definitions thereof, typologies of research designs, arguments for the use of paradigms, and the like.

2. Many scholars would like to see greater consistency across the terms and definitions.

3. The handbook can be used as another piece of evidence for the overall legitimacy of mixed methodology as a separate methodological movement.

4. That which is unique about mixed methods can be displayed in distinction to purely quantitative or purely qualitative methods.

5. The handbook and specific chapters can be used as a pedagogical tool for professors teaching courses in the area.

6. The handbook presents a third alternative for researchers in the social and behavioral sciences as an overall method for doing research.

◆ The Nomenclature and Basic Definitions Used in Mixed Methods Research

The development of a nomenclature that is distinctly associated with mixed methods is both extremely important and overdue. As this book was being produced, we asked the authors to designate and define a few terms, which they considered essential, from their various chapters. In this handbook, we present a Glossary that consists of the terms and definitions that our authors designated to be important.

There are multiple definitions for several of the Glossary terms, and these point out disagreements among the authors. We believe that these alternative definitions are a sign of strength in a field that is still in its adolescence because it indicates that different authors disagree about exactly what a term means but nevertheless think the term is important. Hopefully, these differences of opinion regarding the basic terminology of the field will be resolved over time, and the publication of the Glossary may serve as a catalyst in this resolution.

An interesting distinction exists between the QUAL and QUAN traditions with regard to the issue of common nomenclature and definitions. Traditional quantitative definitions of basic constructs and designs have been long established in classic texts (e.g., Cook & Campbell, 1979) and in the annals of statistics and measurement journals. While there is slow evolution in the QUAN methodological research area,[5] no one expects large changes in the basic paradigm, constructs, or research designs associated with this worldview.

Common definitions of qualitative constructs and designs, on the other hand, have been slow to develop.[6] Part of the reason for this is that many of the leading figures in qualitative research do not believe that such codification is either possible or even productive.

A reasonable question for mixed methodologists at this point in time is "Do we want a common nomenclature with a set of terms and definitions?" We believe that the answer from the majority of authors contributing to this handbook is yes. Part of the reason for this is that the lack of an overall system of terms and definitions has led to confusion and imprecision in the presentation of research findings, as noted by Datta (1994) and others.

This section on nomenclature in mixed methods is concerned with issues related to a common nomenclature for mixed methods research. It is divided into four parts:

1. Commonalities across the definitions of terms associated with mixed methods

2. Inconsistency in basic definitions (using *multimethod* as an example)

3. The choice of bilingual or common nomenclature (using *validity* as an example)

4. Differences across disciplines in terms of nomenclature

COMMONALITIES ACROSS THE DEFINITIONS OF TERMS ASSOCIATED WITH MIXED METHODS

Some of the terms uniquely associated with mixed methods have been defined consistently across a number of authors. These terms are found in the Glossary with no alternative definitions.

An interesting case in point is the term *data transformation* with its two sub-processes that are defined in the Glossary as follows:

◆ *Qualitized data:* Collected quantitative data types are converted into narratives that can be analyzed qualitatively.

◆ *Quantitized data:* Collected qualitative data types are converted into numerical codes that can be statistically analyzed.

These definitions were first derived by Miles and Huberman (1994), who coined the term "quantitize" in a sourcebook for qualitative data analysis. We (Tashakkori & Teddlie, 1998) then applied the same process to the transformation of quantitative data (qualitize). These terms are specific enough to be presented consistently in a number of sources (e.g., Boyatzis, 1998), including six chapters of the current handbook (Chapters 1, 12, 13, 14, 21, and 23).

For instance, Sandelowski (Chapter 12, this volume) describes her use of quantitizing techniques in a study where she transformed narrative interview data into numerical data that were then analyzed using Fisher's exact probability test (Sandelowski, Harris, & Holditch-Davis, 1991). In her qualitizing example, she discusses taking quantitatively derived clusters of numerical data and transforming those into distinct qualitatively described "profiles" using grounded theory.

Other examples of terms with widely accepted meanings are some of the basic mixed methods designs such as equivalent status designs, dominant-less dominant designs, sequential designs, and simultaneous or concurrent designs. Creswell, Plano Clark, Gutmann, and Hanson (Chapter 8, this volume) interestingly take some of these basic designs and cross them with other design components to create unique mixed model designs such as the "sequential explanatory" and "concurrent transformative" design types.

Another contribution of the Glossary is the introduction of some innovative new terms to the mixed methods lexicon. For instance, several new terms for mixed methods data analysis are included from Onwuegbuzie and Teddlie (Chapter 13, this volume), including qualitative contrasting case analysis, qualitative residual analysis, qualitative follow-up interaction analyses, and qualitative internal replication analysis. Another example is fused data analysis (an integrated analysis in which the same sources are used in different but interdependent ways) from Bazeley (Chapter 14, this volume).

INCONSISTENCY IN BASIC DEFINITIONS

As the field of mixed methods has evolved, there has been inconsistency in the manner in which certain terms have been defined. The Glossary attests to this in its alternative definitions of some basic terms. For several years, the terms *multimethod design* and *mixed methods design* have been confused with one another. There seems to be a particular issue with the term *multimethod design,* which has been defined quite differently by different authors:

◆ Campbell and Fiske (1959) introduced the term "multitrait-multimethod" matrix to connote the use of more than one quantitative method to measure a personality trait.

◆ Morse (Chapter 7, this volume) defines multimethod design as "qualitative and quantitative projects that are relatively complete but are used together to form essential components of one research program."

◆ Hunter and Brewer (Chapter 22, this volume) define the multimethod strategy as "the use of multiple methods with complementary strengths and different weaknesses in relation to a given set of research problems. But these criteria don't imply that one must always employ a mix of qualitative and quantitative methods in each project. This may sometimes be the case, but some research problems might be better served by combining two different types of quantitative methods . . . or of qualitative methods."

Thus, the term multimethod design has been used to describe the following:

◆ the use of two quantitative methods;

◆ the use of relatively separate quantitative and qualitative methods; and

◆ the use of both QUAN and QUAL methods or the use of two different types of either QUAL or QUAN methods (QUAL/QUAL or QUAN/QUAN).

Throughout this volume, we are more interested in the consistent use of the term *mixed methods,* but this difficult term *multimethod* (research or strategy or design or whatever) must also be addressed to create a common nomenclature. We recently (Tashakkori & Teddlie, in press) proposed a typology of research designs that incorporates both mixed and multimethod designs in a consistent manner. The following is an outline for that typology together with definitions for the key terms:

I. Multiple Method Designs (more than one
   method or more than one worldview)

   A. Multimethod designs (more than one
      method but restricted to within
      worldview [e.g., QUAN/QUAN,
      QUAL/QUAL])

      1. Multimethod QUAN studies

      2. Multimethod QUAL studies

   B. Mixed methods designs (use of
      QUAL and QUAN data collection
      procedures or research methods)

      1. Mixed method research (occurs in
         the methods stage of a study)

      2. Mixed model research (can occur
         in several stages of a study)

We (Tashakkori & Teddlie, in press)
have defined multiple method designs as
research in which more than one method
or more than one worldview is used. At
least three broad categories of these multiple method designs have been identified in
the literature: (a) multimethod research,
(b) mixed method research, and (c) mixed
model research.

In *multimethod research* studies, the research questions are answered by using
two data collection procedures (e.g., participant observation and oral histories) or
two research methods (e.g., ethnography
and case study), each of which is from the
same QUAL or QUAN tradition. This was
the type of design first proposed by Campbell and Fiske (1959) for QUAN applications only.

We suggest *mixed methods* (plural) *designs* as a cover term for mixed method
and mixed model research. *Mixed method
research* studies use qualitative and quantitative data collection and analysis techniques in either parallel or sequential
phases. This mixing occurs in the methods

section of a study. For example, this is the
type of research in which a qualitative *and*
a quantitative data collection procedure
(e.g., a personality inventory and a focus
group interview) or research method (e.g.,
an ethnography and a field experiment)
are used to answer the research questions.
Although mixed method studies use both
qualitative and quantitative data collection and analysis, they are often marginally mixed in that they are frequently either qualitative or quantitative in the type
of questions they ask and the type of inferences they make at the end of the studies.

Mixed model research (Tashakkori &
Teddlie, 1998), by contrast, is mixed in
many or *all* stages of the study (questions,
research methods, data collection and
analysis, and the inference process). It is
obvious, from the preceding discussion,
that mixed model research has to meet a
much more stringent set of assumptions
than does multimethod or even mixed
method research. For example, mixed
model research might have multiple research questions, each rooted in a distinct
paradigm (what Greene & Caracelli,
1997, called "dialectic"), and might make
multiple inferences corresponding to different worldviews. Therefore, one of the
assumptions of such research is that it is
indeed possible to have two paradigms, or
two worldviews, mixed throughout a single research project.

This typology of multiple method designs is an effort to provide some consistency in the literature, especially with regard to the misuse of the *multimethod*
term and the introduction of the mixed
model concept. We invite others to refine
(or reject and replace with something
better) our typology. A later section of this
chapter presents much more information
on typologies of research designs in mixed
methods and how these typologies are
similar and different.

THE CHOICE OF BILINGUAL
OR COMMON NOMENCLATURE

One of the major decisions that mixed methodologists have to make concerning nomenclature is whether to

◆ use a bilingual nomenclature that employs the QUAL, QUAN, or a combination of QUAL and QUAN terms for issues such as validity and sampling or

◆ create a new language for mixed methodology that gives a common name for the existing sets of QUAL and QUAN terms.

We believe that mixed methodologists should adopt a common nomenclature transcending the separate QUAL and QUAN orientations when the described processes (QUAL and QUAN) are highly similar and when appropriate terminology exists. Currently, the decision to use either bilingual or common nomenclature must be made separately for each of the large-component parts of research methodology (e.g., sampling, validity) because the terminology in each is so varied.

For instance, although sampling has well-defined and entrenched QUAL and QUAN techniques, it is possible to develop a common terminology. Sampling may be conceptualized on a continuum with probability samples (from QUANs) on one side and purposive samples (from QUALs) on the other (see Tashakkori & Teddlie, 1998). Different sampling strategies may be placed on such a continuum. As an example, in such a classification, QUAN's quota sampling is classified as purposive, next to QUAL's sequential sampling.[7] Kemper, Stringfield, and Teddlie (Chapter 10, this volume) demon-strate numerous ways in which these probability and purposive sampling strategies may be combined in mixed methods studies.

Another reason to develop a common nomenclature pertains to situations in which the existing QUAL and QUAN terms have been overly used or misused. Probably the best example is that of the current use of the term *validity* in the QUAN and QUAL traditions.

Lincoln and Guba (1985) attempted to set up a system in which there were equivalent QUAL terms for existing QUAN validity types. For instance, they equated credibility with internal validity and equated transferability with external validity (p. 300).

This attempt at bilingualism in the QUAN and QUAL communities was criticized by many, including Maxwell (1992). Terms that the critics believed were more appropriate (e.g., understanding, authenticity) were put forth to replace validity, with the result being an explosion in the number of validity (or authenticity) types proposed from the QUAL community over the past 10 years. This increase in the variants of QUAL validity types mirrors an already long list of QUAN validity types that include both design and measurement constructs.

Table 1.1 lists 35 types of validity, and this list is not exhaustive. With so many types of validity, the term has lost meaning. This is a good example of a situation in which mixed methodologists may want to create their own terminology to simplify matters and to give greater meaning to the processes being described.

This section on nomenclature is closely linked with a later section on quality of inferences. In that section, we propose the use of terms associated with "inference" as the mixed methodology equivalent of validity.

**TABLE 1.1   Types of Validity in Qualitative and
Quantitative Research**

Quantitative	*Qualitative*
Internal validity (causal, relationship definitions)	Catalytic validity
	Crystalline validity
Statistical conclusion validity	Descriptive validity
External validity	Evaluative validity
Population	Generalizability validity
Ecological	Interpretive validity
Construct validity (causal)	Ironic validity
Consequential validity	Neopragmatic validity
Validity (measurement)	Rhizomic validity
Face	Simultaneous validity
Content	Situated validity
Criterion related	Theoretical validity
Predictive	Voluptuous validity
Concurrent	Plus terms associated with authenticity
Jury	Educative
Predictive	Ontological
Systemic	Catalytic
Construct validity (measurement)	Tactical
Convergent	
Discriminant	
Factorial	

SOURCES: These types of validity were compiled from several sources, including Cook and Campbell (1979); Cohen, Manion, and Morrison (2000); Lincoln and Guba (2000); Lather (1993); Maxwell (1992); Messick (1995); and Tashakkori and Teddlie (1998).

DIFFERENCES ACROSS DISCIPLINES IN TERMS OF NOMENCLATURE

A final nomenclature issue that deserves some attention concerns the fact that several different fields in the social and behavioral sciences have contributed to mixed methods and that they use somewhat different terms. For instance, we have contributions in this handbook from evaluation research (Rallis & Rossman, Chapter 17), management and organizational research (Currall & Towler, Chapter 18), health sciences (Forthofer, Chapter 19), nursing research (Twinn, Chapter 20), psychology (Waszak & Sines, Chapter 21), sociology (Hunter & Brewer, Chapter 22), and education (Rocco & colleagues, Chapter 23). Some obvious differences exist among these chapters in terms of nomenclature.

For instance, Twinn (Chapter 20, this volume) concludes from her review of nursing research that the term *triangulation* was used much more than the terms *mixed methods* and *multimethod design*. Indeed the term *triangulation* is featured highly in two other chapters in this handbook written by authors from the nursing research field: Morse (Chapter 7) and Sandelowski (Chapter 12). Sandelowski (Chapter 12, this volume) concludes that the term *triangulation* has been used so much that it has no meaning at all. The term *triangulation* does occur in each of the other six separate "discipline" chapters noted previously, but primarily as a historical artifact rather than as a currently dominant term.

All of the individual "disciplines" in this handbook also use different typologies to organize the studies in their field except for two that use no typology at all (Forthofer, Chapter 19, and Hunter & Brewer, Chapter 22). This variety in typologies used exemplifies the diversity of approach across the different fields and the fact that all of the reviewers selected typologies close to their own disciplines.

For instance, Rallis and Rossman (Chapter 17, this volume), writing in the field of evaluation research, chose a typology developed by others working in evaluation (Greene & Caracelli, 1997). Currall and Towler (Chapter 18, this volume), writing in the field of management and organizational research, chose a typology developed by Creswell (1994), who has a background in educational psychology. Twinn (Chapter 20, this volume), writing in the field of nursing research, uses a basic nursing research text in evaluating and categorizing mixed methods research in her field (Polit & Hungler, 1999). Waszak and Sines (Chapter 21, this volume), writing in the field of psychology, classify their research studies by type of research design, which is certainly appropriate for

that field of study. Rocco and colleagues (Chapter 23, this volume), writing in the field of education, classify their research studies by paradigmatic orientation (pragmatic or dialectical), which is appropriate for the discipline that spawned the paradigm wars and the incompatibility thesis.

These differences in terminology and typology can be expected at this time in the development of the field. As mixed methods research evolves and more common terms appear, these differences should diminish.

◆ The Utility of Mixed Methods Research

The utility of mixed methods research concerns "why" we do them. With the plethora of research methods associated with either the QUAL or the QUAN tradition, why would we go to the bother of combining them, or of generating new techniques, to do mixed methods research?

The ultimate goal of any research project is to answer the questions that were set forth at the project's beginning. Mixed methods are useful if they provide better opportunities for answering our research questions. Also, mixed methods are useful if they help researchers to meet the criteria for evaluating the "goodness" of their answers (e.g., Tashakkori & Teddlie, 1998) better than do single approach designs.

There appear to be three areas in which mixed methods are superior to single approach designs:

◆ Mixed methods research can answer research questions that the other methodologies cannot.

◆ Mixed methods research provides better (stronger) inferences.

◆ Mixed methods provide the opportunity for presenting a greater diversity of divergent views.

MIXED METHODS RESEARCH CAN ANSWER RESEARCH QUESTIONS THAT THE OTHER METHODOLOGIES CANNOT

One dimension on which quantitative and qualitative research is said to vary is the type of question answered by each approach. Some authors have suggested that QUAL research questions are exploratory, while QUAN research questions are confirmatory. Erzberger and Prein (1997) and Tashakkori and Teddlie (1998, in press) have disagreed with this dichotomization of research questions. Erzberger and Prein (1997) labeled it "a Cinderella position view of qualitative research" (p. 143) in that it "restricts the use of qualitative methods to preliminary phases of social research where quantitative techniques could not (yet) be employed" (p. 142).

Punch (1998) provided another argument against this dichotomization:

> Quantitative research has typically been more directed at theory verification, while qualitative research has typically been more concerned with theory generation. While that correlation is historically valid, it is by no means perfect, and there is no necessary connection between purpose and approach. That is, quantitative research can be used for theory generation (as well as verification), and qualitative research can be used for theory verification (as well as generation). (pp. 16-17)

We agree with this statement, yet we also believe that most QUAN research is confirmatory and involves theory verification, while much QUAL research is exploratory and involves theory generation. What happens when you want to do both? *A major advantage of mixed methods research is that it enables the researcher to simultaneously answer confirmatory and exploratory questions, and therefore verify and generate theory in the same study.*

Many of the research projects that we supervise are doctoral dissertations where the students want to simultaneously accomplish two goals: (a) demonstrate that a particular variable will have a predicted relationship with another variable and (b) answer exploratory questions about how that predicted (or some other related) relationship actually happens.

An example is a recent dissertation by Stevens (2002). In this study, the student wanted to examine and describe the changes that occurred in a set of middle schools as a result of the introduction of an external change agent, a distinguished educator (DE), through a new state school accountability program. It was hypothesized that teachers in schools with the DE would perform better on measures of teacher effectiveness than would teachers in schools without the DE.[8]

The study's quantitative quasi-experimental design confirmed the hypothesis: Teachers in the schools with the DEs had significantly higher rates of effective teaching than did teachers in the schools without the DEs. While this result was important, the doctoral student also wanted to know how this had occurred. Simultaneously to gathering the quantitative data, she conducted case studies in each of the schools using qualitative techniques such as observations, interviews, and document analysis. The DEs were perceived as having a positive influence on teacher collaboration and sharing, on the expectations of both teachers and students for student learning, and on the quality of instruction. These positive school and teacher effectiveness processes led to the higher rates of effective teaching.

This mixed model study could not have been conducted exclusively within either the quantitative or the qualitative tradition. The mixed model design allowed the doctoral student to simultaneously confirm a quantitatively derived hypothesis and explore in greater depth the processes by which the relationship occurred.

MIXED METHODS RESEARCH PROVIDES BETTER (STRONGER) INFERENCES

Several authors (e.g., Brewer & Hunter, 1989; Greene & Caracelli, 1997; see also Creswell et al., Chapter 8, this volume) have postulated that using mixed methods can offset the disadvantages that certain of the methods have by themselves. Johnson and Turner (Chapter 11, this volume) refer to this as the *fundamental principle of mixed methods research:* "Methods should be mixed in a way that has complementary strengths and nonoverlapping weaknesses." A classic case involves using case studies in conjunction with mailed surveys. One method gives greater depth, while the other gives greater breadth; hopefully, together they give results from which one can make better (i.e., more accurate) inferences.

Further support for the usefulness of mixed methods came from Greene et al. (1989), who proposed five functions for such methods: triangulation, complementarity, development, initiation, and expansion. The first two functions of mixed methods (triangulation and complementarity) are related to the fact that mixed methods lead to multiple inferences that confirm or complement each other. The other three functions (development, initiation, and expansion) are more related to mixed methods studies in which inferences made at the end of one phase (e.g., QUAL) lead to the questions and/or design of a second phase (e.g., QUAN).

Also, complex social phenomena such as the DE intervention described earlier (Stevens, 2002) require different kinds of methods so as to best understand and make inferences about these complexities (Greene & Caracelli, 1997). Such social phenomena cannot be fully understood using either purely qualitative or purely quantitative techniques. We need a variety of data sources and analyses to completely understand complex multifaceted institutions or realities. Mixed methods can provide that.

MIXED METHODS PROVIDE THE OPPORTUNITY FOR PRESENTING A GREATER DIVERSITY OF DIVERGENT VIEWS

One of the agreements against mixed methods is related to the final conclusions or inferences. What happens if the QUAN and QUAL components lead to two totally different (or contradictory) conclusions? Erzberger and Prein (1997) asked and answered the question eloquently:

> What happens if the two perspectives do not fit together . . . ? The idea that qualitative and quantitative findings always relate to different aspects of *one* research object does not automatically mean that a coherent picture can be depicted. It even has to be expected that this type of "peaceful coexistence" between methodological paradigms will be rather infrequent. . . . Research findings can converge, which can be seen as an indicator of their

validity; secondly, they can generate a new comprehension of the phenomenon by forming complementary parts of a jigsaw puzzle, or, thirdly, they can produce unexplainable divergence leading to a falsification of previous theoretical assumptions. (pp. 146-147)

According to this view, divergent findings are valuable in that they lead to a reexamination of the conceptual frameworks and the assumptions underlying each of the two (QUAL and QUAN) components. Johnson and Turner (Chapter 11, this volume) state that one of the major reasons for following the fundamental principle of mixed methods research is to "elucidate the divergent aspects of a phenomenon." Further analyses of the data in the form of possible transformation of data types to each other, internal validity audits (Tashakkori & Teddlie, 1998), and design of a new study or phase for further investigations (Rossman & Wilson, 1985) are three outcomes of such reexamination.

Deacon, Bryman, and Fenton (1998) summarized the advantages of this reexamination:

Whatever short-term inconvenience this may cause, in many cases the reappraisal and re-analysis required can reap long term analytical rewards: alerting the researcher to the possibility that issues are more multifaceted than they may have initially supposed, and offering the opportunity to develop more convincing and robust explanations of the social processes being investigated. (p. 61)

The different inferences from mixed methods research often reflect different voices and perspectives. Such diversity of opinion is welcome in mixed methods research (for an extended discussion of the ramifications of the divergence of qualitative and quantitative findings in mixed methods research, see Erzberger & Kelle, Chapter 16, this volume).

◆ The Paradigmatic Foundations for Mixed Methods Research

A continuing issue in mixed methods research concerns the manner in which paradigms are used in the development of the field. Researchers have had at least six different positions on the issue of how paradigms are to be used in the development of mixed methods research:

1. Some scholars believe that methods and paradigms are independent of one another; therefore, the epistemology-method link is not an issue, and it is permissible to do mixed methods research (a-paradigmatic thesis).

2. Some researchers agree with the tenets of the incompatibility thesis and conclude that mixed methods research is impossible (e.g., Smith & Heshusius, 1986).

3. Some scholars believe that mixed methods are possible but that they must be kept separate so that the strengths of each paradigmatic position (e.g., postpositivism, constructivism) can be realized (Brewer & Hunter, 1989; Morse, 1991; see also Morse, Chapter 7, this volume). We label this point of view the "complementary strengths" thesis.

4. Some researchers believe that a single paradigm should serve as the foundation for mixed methods research.

a. Some advocate that pragmatism serve as the foundation for mixed methods research (e.g., Datta, 1997; Howe, 1988; Patton, 1990; Tashakkori & Teddlie, 1998; see also chapters in this volume by Maxcy [Chapter 2], Bazeley [Chapter 14], Rallis & Rossman [Chapter 18], Forthofer [Chapter 19], and Rocco et al. [Chapter 23]).

b. Some advocate that the transformative-emancipatory paradigm serve as the foundation for mixed methods research (see, e.g., Mertens, Chapter 5, this volume).

5. Some scholars propose the "dialectic" stance, which does not advocate one paradigm above others but rather sees mixed methods research as intentionally engaging a multiple set of paradigms and their assumptions (e.g., Greene & Caracelli, 1997; see also Greene & Caracelli, Chapter 3, this volume). According to these theorists, all paradigms are valuable, but only partial, worldviews. To think dialectically means to examine the tensions that emerge from the juxtaposition of these multiple diverse perspectives.

6. Some scholars believe that multiple paradigms may serve as the foundation for doing research in the social and behavioral sciences. This position has been explicitly applied to qualitative research (e.g., Lincoln & Guba, 2000; Schwandt, 2000), but it is also applicable to mixed methods research (see, e.g., Creswell et al., Chapter 8, this volume). A difference between this position and the dialectic stance is that the multiple paradigm theorists believe that one type of paradigm is best used when one is doing one type of study, while another paradigm is best used if one is doing another type of study. Those advocating the dialectical stance reject the selection of one paradigm over another.

The remainder of this section contains more detailed discussions of these six points of view.[9]

THE A-PARADIGMATIC STANCE

Some scholars see the epistemology-methods link as distracting or unnecessary and simply ignore it, continuing to work as they always have worked, using whatever methods seem appropriate for the question at hand. This is often the stance of scholars working in applied fields such as evaluation, nursing, and the health sciences.

In a book where he also discussed the connection between paradigms and what he called "mixed form" designs, Patton (1990) made the following commonsense statement:

> In short, *in real world practice, methods can be separated from the epistemology out of which they emerged.* One can use statistics in a straightforward way without doing a literature review of logical-positivism. One can make an interpretation without studying hermeneutics. And one can conduct open-ended interviews or make observations without reading treatises on phenomenology. (p. 90, italics in original)

THE INCOMPATIBILITY THESIS AND MIXED METHODS RESEARCH

As noted throughout this chapter, the incompatibility thesis states that compatibility between quantitative and qualitative methods is impossible due to the incompatibility of the paradigms that underlie the methods. This thesis was argued during the time period labeled by some (e.g., Gage, 1989) as the paradigm wars. Theorists writing primarily during the paradigm wars of the 1980s (e.g., Guba, 1987; Smith, 1983; Smith & Heshusius, 1986) indicated that researchers who try to combine the two methods are doomed to failure due to the inherent differences in the philosophies underlying them. For example, Guba (1987) stated that one paradigm precludes the other "just as surely as the belief in a round world precludes belief in a flat one" (p. 31).

Denzin and Lincoln (1994), in the first edition of the *Handbook of Qualitative Research,* were explicit in their description of the separateness of the qualitative and quantitative methodologies:

> The five points of difference described above . . . reflect commitments to different styles of research, different epistemologies, and different forms of representation. Each work tradition is governed by a different set of genres. . . . Qualitative researchers use ethnographic prose, historical narratives, first-person accounts, still photographs, life histories, fictionalized facts, and biographical and autobiographical materials, among others. Quantitative researchers use mathematical models, statistical tables, and graphs. (p. 6)

The incompatibility thesis has now been largely discredited, partially because scholars demonstrated that they had successfully employed mixed methods in their research. Smith (1996) lamented the success of the compatibilists' point of view:

> In 1986 I published an article . . . (Smith & Heshusius, 1986) that, be-

cause of its early reception, I thought would prevent for some time to come a closing down of the conversation about the compatibility-incompatibility of the approaches. . . . I was overly optimistic to say the least, because by 1990 or so the issues were decided in favor of the compatibilists. This happened not because they had the better arguments, but because educational researchers in general lost whatever interest they may have had in the discussion. I remember the editor of a major journal writing to me saying that most researchers had become bored with philosophical discussions and were more interested in getting on with the task of doing their research. (pp. 162-163)

Even though the incompatibility thesis per se is not held by many researchers today, it has influenced some other more popular positions (e.g., the complementary strengths thesis, the dialectical thesis).

THE COMPLEMENTARY STRENGTHS THESIS AND MIXED METHODS RESEARCH

Some researchers believe that mixed methods are possible but that they must be kept as separate as possible so that the strengths of each paradigmatic position (e.g., postpositivism, constructivism) can be realized (Brewer & Hunter, 1989; Morse, 1991; Stern, 1994). For example, Morse (Chapter 7, this volume) reminds readers of "the edict that the researcher must retain the assumptions of each paradigm." She views the "ad hoc" mixing of methods as a serious threat to the validity of mixed methods research.

Similarly, Brewer and Hunter (1989) suggested that a multimethod approach to research is superior to a monomethod approach because it provides grounds for data triangulation. Brewer and Hunter disfavored what they labeled "composite" methods research, which is composed of "elements borrowed from the basic styles" (p. 80). While acknowledging the strengths of composite methods, these authors concluded that the basic methods lose some of their strengths when incorporated into competing methodologies. In addition, they contended that this methodological eclecticism does not provide enough data for proper "cross-method comparison."

On the other hand, Maxwell and Loomis (Chapter 9, this volume) do not believe in uniform purely qualitative and purely quantitative research paradigms. Citing several sources, these authors argue convincingly that each of these two generic positions has a large number of separate and distinct "components." They argue further that these quantitative and qualitative components can be put together in multiple legitimate ways. Because the two research paradigms are not "pure" to begin with, researchers lose little when they mix them up in a variety of often creative ways.

A reading of this handbook indicates that most of its authors are comfortable with mixing their methods and are, in general, not very concerned with the purity of the underlying paradigms being maintained.

THE SINGLE PARADIGM THESIS AND MIXED METHODS RESEARCH

Another result of the paradigm wars was the search by individuals using mixed methods for a paradigm to support their methodological predilection. The single paradigm/methodology link was initiated by Lincoln and Guba (1985) with their equation of the two single links between

postpositivism-quantitative methods and constructivism-qualitative methods. Because the qualitative and quantitative positions had their own epistemologies, scholars using mixed methods began looking for a paradigm to support their methodology.

Several scholars (e.g., Howe, 1988) posited a link between pragmatism and mixed methods. Later, other scholars (e.g., Mertens, 1998, 1999) discussed the transformative-emancipatory paradigm as a philosophical underpinning for mixed methods. The remainder of this subsection contains brief presentations of these two philosophical positions and their association with mixed methods.

Pragmatism as the Foundation for Mixed Methods Research. Several authors (e.g., Datta, 1997; Howe, 1988; Patton, 1990; Rossman & Wilson, 1985; Tashakkori & Teddlie, 1998) have proposed that pragmatism is the best paradigm for justifying the use of mixed methods research. For example, Rallis and Rossman (Chapter 17, this volume) present what they call a "pragmatic framework" for the use of mixed methods in evaluation research.

Maxcy (Chapter 2, this volume) presents an extended discussion of the link between pragmatism and the use of mixed methods in the social and behavioral sciences. In his chapter, he traces the development of pragmatism from the early philosophers (e.g., Charles Sanders Peirce, William James, John Dewey, George Herbert Mead, Arthur F. Bentley) through more contemporary voices (e.g., Cleo Cherryholmes, Richard Rorty). The work of Cherryholmes (1992, 1999) is singled out as an example of important current writing in the area of "critical pragmatism."

Tashakkori and Teddlie (1998, pp. 22-30) made a number of points regarding pragmatism and mixed methods:

◆ Pragmatism supports the use of both qualitative and quantitative research methods in the same research study and within multistage research programs. Pragmatism rejects the incompatibility thesis.

◆ Pragmatist researchers consider the research question to be more important than either the method they use or the paradigm that underlies the method. We refer to this as the "dictatorship of the research question."

◆ Pragmatists also reject the forced choice between postpositivism and constructivism with regard to logic, epistemology, and so on. In each case, pragmatism rejects the either/or of the incompatibility thesis and embraces both points of view (or a position between the two opposing viewpoints).[10]

◆ Specific decisions regarding the use of mixed methods or qualitative methods or quantitative methods depend on the research question as it is currently posed and the stage of the research cycle that is ongoing.

◆ Pragmatism avoids the use of metaphysical concepts (e.g., "truth," "reality") that have caused much endless (and often useless) discussion and debate (e.g., Howe, 1988).

◆ Pragmatism presents a very practical and applied research philosophy.

Tashakkori and Teddlie suggested, "Study what interests and is of value to you, study it in the different ways that you deem appropriate, and utilize the results in ways that can bring about positive consequences within your value system" (p. 30).

See our Chapter 26 in this handbook for more discussion of pragmatism and mixed methods.

The Transformative-Emancipatory Paradigm as the Foundation for Mixed Methods Research. In Mertens's chapter in this handbook (Chapter 5; see also Mertens, 1998, 1999), she presents the transformative-emancipatory paradigm as a third alternative to the positivist-postpositivist and interpretive-constructivist paradigms. She concludes that the underlying philosophical assumptions and methodological implications of the transformative-emancipatory paradigm can be used fruitfully within the discussion of mixed methods in research.

Mertens advocates the creation of a more just and democratic society as the ultimate goal for conducting research. She believes that this goal should permeate the entire research process, from problem formulation through the drawing of conclusions and into the use of the results. The following are some tenets of the transformative-emancipatory paradigm, according to Mertens (Chapter 5, this volume):

◆ The paradigm places central importance on the experiences of individuals who suffer from discrimination or oppression.

◆ Researchers working within the transformative-emancipatory paradigm are aware of power differentials in the context of their research and use their research to promote greater social equity and justice.

◆ With regard to ontology, Mertens states that the transformative-emancipatory viewpoint is to describe reality within its multiple contexts (e.g., cultural, political, economic, historical).

◆ With regard to epistemology, Mertens states that interaction between the researcher and the participants is essential and that this interaction requires understanding and trust.

◆ Mertens concludes that from a methodological point of view, mixed methods offer especially promising ways to address the concerns of diverse groups in an appropriate manner.[11]

See our Chapter 26 in this handbook for more discussion of the transformative-emancipatory paradigm and mixed methods.

THE DIALECTICAL THESIS AND MIXED METHODS RESEARCH

The dialectic stance assumes that all paradigms have something to offer and that the use of multiple paradigms contributes to greater understanding of the phenomenon under study. Greene and Caracelli (1997; Chapter 3, this volume) are the foremost proponents of this position, which has also been adopted by other writers in this handbook (e.g., Maxwell & Loomis, Chapter 9).

Greene and Caracelli (1997; Chapter 3, this volume) reject the continued search for the single best paradigm as a relic of the past and the paradigm wars. Instead, they believe that multiple diverse perspectives are important because they are required to explain the complexity of an increasingly pluralistic society.

An important component of this position is the ability to think dialectically. This involves consideration of opposing viewpoints and interaction with the "tensions" caused by their juxtaposition. These tensions come from the differences in the assumptions of the different paradigms. There are several other points about conversations/dialogues in dialectic inquiry, including the following (Greene & Caracelli, Chapter 3, this volume):

◆ These conversations/dialogues are not typically about philosophical issues but rather about the phenomena that are the subject of the research.

◆ Historical dualisms (such as those featured in the paradigm wars) are not of particular importance in dialectical inquiry. There are no endless discussions of induction versus deduction, subjectivity versus objectivity, and so on.

◆ Greene and Caracelli list some dichotomies that are important in dialectical inquiry: value-neutrality and value-commitment, emic and etic, particularity and generality, social constructions and physical traces, and so on.

THE MULTIPLE PARADIGM THESIS AND MIXED METHODS RESEARCH

Some scholars believe that multiple paradigms may serve as the foundation for mixed methods research. For instance, Creswell and colleagues (Chapter 8, this volume) present six advanced mixed methods designs and then argue that no single paradigm applies to all of the designs. Referencing Denzin and Lincoln (2000), Creswell and colleagues conclude that multiple paradigms may be applied to diverse mixed methods designs. Researchers have to decide which paradigm is best given their choice of a particular mixed methods design for a particular study.

Creswell and colleagues give several examples: Postpositivism might be the best paradigm for a sequential-explanatory design using quantitative methods, interpretivism might be the best paradigm for a sequential-exploratory design using qualitative methods, several paradigms may serve as the framework for a triangulation design, and so on.

This multiple paradigm perspective stems at least partially from recent writings in qualitative research methodology. The editors of the second edition of the *Handbook of Qualitative Research* (Denzin & Lincoln, 2000) drew the following conclusion:

> A complex, interconnected family of terms, concepts, and assumptions surround the term *qualitative research.* These include the traditions associated with foundationalism, positivism, postfoundationalism, postpositivism, poststructuralism, and the many qualitative research perspectives and/or methods connected to cultural and interpretive studies. (p. 2)

Later in the same chapter of their book, Denzin and Lincoln (2000) concluded that there are four major paradigms that structure qualitative research: positivist-postpositivist, constructivist-interpretive, critical (e.g., Marxist, emancipatory), and feminist-poststructural (pp. 19-20).

In the same volume, Schwandt (2000) concluded that there were three epistemological stances for qualitative research: interpretivism, hermeneutics, and social constructionism:

> Thus qualitative inquiry is more comprehensible as site or arena for social scientific criticism than as any particular kind of social theory, methodology, or philosophy. . . . I focus on the site as an arena in which different epistemologies vie for attention as potential justifications for doing qualitative inquiry. (p. 190)

THE EVOLUTION IN THOUGHT REGARDING PARADIGMS AND RESEARCH METHODS

The preceding discussion has presented six different positions on the issue of how paradigms can be used in mixed methods research. Some of these positions are directly related to seminal works in the field of qualitative research, and they represent important aspects in the evolution of thought in that area regarding the paradigm-method link. Consider the following three "snapshots" from that evolution:

1. Lincoln and Guba (1985) presented their paradigm table contrasting the positivist and naturalist positions on five dimensions and arguing for the superiority of the naturalist position. Naturalism was posited as the paradigm that supported qualitative research methods, while positivism underlay the use of quantitative methods. During this time period, the incompatibility thesis was postulated.

2. In the first edition of the *Handbook of Qualitative Research*, the position of the qualitative research theorists softened a bit. Guba and Lincoln (1994) protested the use of the term "paradigm wars" and opened the door to possible reconciliation:

    > The metaphor of paradigm wars described by Gage (1989) is undoubtedly overdrawn. Describing the discussions and altercations of the past decade or two as wars paints the matter as more confrontational than necessary. A resolution of paradigm differences can occur only when a new paradigm emerges that is more informed and sophisticated than any existing one. That is most likely to occur if and when proponents of these

several points of view come together to discuss their differences. (p. 116)

However, in the same volume, Denzin and Lincoln discussed five points of difference between qualitative and quantitative research, indicating that they were "governed by a different set of genres" (p. 6). (See the extended quote earlier in this section.)

3. In the second edition of the *Handbook of Qualitative Research,* the position of the qualitative research theorists changed even more, as indicated by the quotes from both Guba and Lincoln (2000, p. 2) and Schwandt (2000, p. 190). Now, it was determined that multiple paradigms (including positivism-postpositivism) could be used to support qualitative research.

There appear to be three reasons for the evolution in the position of the qualitative research theorists over time:

◆ Initially, the qualitative research theorists believed that they had to demonstrate the supremacy of their ideology and method to that which they called the "received" view of science (positivism-postpositivism). As it turned out, however, the ready acceptance of qualitative research by many in the social and behavioral sciences over the decade from 1985 to 1995 made further attacks on the received tradition unnecessary.

◆ Coincidentally, there was an explosion in the number of paradigms to be discussed. The initial two-column paradigm table (naturalism and positivism) in Lincoln and Guba (1985) became a four-column paradigm table (positivism, postpositivism, critical theory, and constructivism) in Guba and Lincoln (1994), which then became a five-

column paradigm table (with the addition of the participatory-cooperative paradigm) in Lincoln and Guba (2000). In addition, there was a particularly large explosion in paradigms associated with qualitative research methods. There are six chapters in the second edition of the *Handbook of Qualitative Research* devoted to different paradigms. With so many paradigms to choose from, it made sense to advocate the multiple paradigm stance as opposed to the single paradigm/methodology viewpoint.

◆ There is evidence that the qualitative research theorists were uncomfortable in their perceived role as originators of the paradigm wars. The previous quote from Guba and Lincoln (1994, p. 116) indicates that they did not like the "confrontational" components of the paradigm debate.[12] The multiple paradigm stance is much less confrontational.

Thus, the increased legitimacy of qualitative research methods, the increase in the number of paradigms that could be associated with qualitative research methods, and the unpopularity of the paradigm wars all were factors that led to the current advocacy of the multiple paradigms perspective.

THE RESIDUES OF THE WARS

So, what does this historical analysis have to do with mixed methods at the current point in time? There are ongoing consequences of the paradigm wars—some positive and some negative. As noted throughout this chapter, the paradigm wars (and particularly the incompatibility thesis) were a major catalyst in the development of the mixed methods as a distinct third methodological movement.

The paradigm wars and the discussions that are still ongoing point out the continuing importance of paradigms to researchers (including mixed methods researchers) today. At least nine of the chapters in this handbook (Chapters 1, 2, 3, 4, 8, 9, 17, 23, and 26) contain lengthy discussions about paradigms and mixed methods. These discussions and debates will continue to help define mixed methodology as a separate research movement.

Nevertheless, there are some negative residuals of the paradigm wars. There are still many graduate programs in various disciplines across the country that consider themselves and their students to be QUALs or QUANs. Students often identify themselves as QUANs or QUALs and never again will (if they ever did before) darken the door of a lecture hall where the opposing methodology is being presented. Therefore, we are raising a generation of scholars, many of whom do not know what a standard deviation is, on the one hand, or what a constant comparative analysis is, on the other.

Schwandt (2000) commented on this issue:

> So the traditional means of coming to grips with one's identity as a researcher by aligning oneself with a particular set of methods (or by being defined in one's department as a student of "qualitative" or "quantitative" methods) is no longer very useful. If we are to go forward, we need to get rid of that distinction. (p. 210)

◆ Design Issues in Mixed Methods Research

Many individuals writing in the field of mixed methods have proposed their own typologies of mixed methods research designs. Indeed, several contributors to this handbook present original or revised typologies (e.g., Morse, Chapter 7; Creswell et al., Chapter 8; Tashakkori & Teddlie, Chapter 26) or have had their typologies described by others in this volume (e.g., Greene & Caracelli, 1997; Greene et al., 1989).

This section describes issues related to typologies of mixed methods research designs that are discussed throughout the handbook. We examine seven of these issues in this chapter:

1. Are typologies of mixed methods designs necessary? Why?

2. Can we expect a typology to be exhaustive?

3. What are the major typologies of mixed methods research designs presented in this handbook?

4. What criteria can a researcher use to select the best mixed methods design for his or her research project?

5. Is there an alternative way to discuss different kinds of mixed methods designs other than using typologies?

6. What are points of agreement regarding design issues in mixed methods research?

7. What are continuing points of controversy regarding design issues in mixed methods research?

ARE TYPOLOGIES OF MIXED METHODS DESIGNS NECESSARY? WHY?

Scholars writing in the field of mixed methods research have presented typologies of mixed designs from the time the field emerged. For instance, Greene et al. (1989) examined a large number of mixed methods studies and developed a typology for the designs used in those studies based on purpose and design characteristics.

Why did Greene et al. (1989) want to develop a typology of mixed methods research designs, and why have so many of their colleagues followed suit? Following are five reasons why typologies have been used in classifying mixed methods designs:

1. Typologies of mixed methods designs help to provide the field with an organizational structure. For instance, the Greene et al. (1989) analysis indicated that there were at least five distinct types of mixed methods designs. At this point in time, given the wide range of typologies, it is more accurate to say that such typologies provide the field with multiple competing organizational structures.

2. Typologies of mixed methods designs help to legitimize the field because they provide examples of research designs that are clearly distinct from either quantitative or qualitative research designs. For instance, the basic mixed methods designs proposed by Morse (1991) were different from the designs found in either quantitative or qualitative research methods. No one before had ever used names such as "simultaneous triangulation" and "sequential triangulation" in describing quantitative or qualitative research designs.

3. Typologies of mixed methods research designs are useful in helping to establish a common language for the field. Again, using the work of Morse (1991; Chapter 7, this handbook) as an example, her typologies of mixed methods research designs included notations and abbreviations that many scholars still use today (e.g., simultaneous design, sequential design).

4. Typologies help researchers to decide how to proceed when designing their mixed methods studies. Typologies pro-

vide a variety of paths that may be chosen to accomplish the goals of researchers' studies. They may include particular mixed methods research designs that are most appropriate for the goals of particular research projects.

5. Typologies are useful as a pedagogical tool. Presenting a variety of mixed methods research designs to students helps familiarize them with the criteria underlying the designs and gives them prototypes on which to model their own research. A particularly effective teaching technique is to present competing design typologies and then have the students discuss their strengths and weaknesses.

CAN WE EXPECT A TYPOLOGY TO BE EXHAUSTIVE?

We often expect that a typology will be exhaustive; that is, we expect that the typology will include all of the elements within the universe of elements for that particular quality. This expectation is based on the presumed thoroughness of typologies of elements found in the physical world.

Such an expectation is not reasonable with regard to a typology of mixed methods research designs.[13] Maxwell and Loomis (Chapter 9, this volume) point out the very obvious fact that "the actual diversity in mixed methods studies is far greater than any typology can adequately encompass."

Mixed model designs can be distinguished on a number of different dimensions (e.g., purpose, underlying paradigm), and developing a typology that would encompass all of those dimensions would be impossible. What is more, even if we could list all of the mixed methods designs at one point in time, the types of designs would continue to evolve, thereby making the typology no longer exhaustive.

The best one can expect is to adopt a typology of mixed methods research designs that includes the most important criteria to the individual researcher. Indeed, the best typology of mixed methods designs for a researcher might change later if the context within which the researcher is operating changes.

WHAT ARE THE MAJOR TYPOLOGIES OF MIXED METHODS RESEARCH DESIGNS PRESENTED IN THIS HANDBOOK?

Morse (1991; Chapter 7, this volume) and Morgan (1998) Typologies. Morse (1991), writing in the applied field of nursing, authored an important article on approaches to qualitative-quantitative methodological triangulation. In that article, she presented a notational system that is also found in her chapter in this handbook (Chapter 7). While some of Morse's definitions do not currently agree with those of others writing in the field (see subsection on points of controversy later), her basic terminology and notational system is still widely employed today. Her notational system is the standard currently used in the mixed methods research area.

Components of this system include the following:[14]

◆ Use of the abbreviations QUAN for quantitative and QUAL for qualitative

◆ Use of the plus sign (+) to indicate that data are collected simultaneously (e.g., QUAN + qual)

◆ Use of the arrow to indicate that data collection occurs sequentially (e.g., QUAL → quan)

◆ Use of uppercase to denote more priority given to that orientation (e.g., QUAN)

We discuss the criteria used in developing typologies of mixed methods research designs throughout this chapter. These criteria are used to differentiate between research designs within the typology and to express important underlying assumptions. In Morse's typology, there are two obvious criteria that distinguish between the designs: the sequence in which data are collected and the priority assigned to one orientation or the other (dominant, less dominant).

Following Creswell's (1994) distinction between dominant and less dominant approaches in mixed methods studies, Morgan (1998) presented a "Priority-Sequence Model" consisting of a set of decision rules for combining qualitative and quantitative data collection in a study. Decision rules consist of (a) deciding the priority of either the qualitative or the quantitative method and (b) deciding on the sequence of the two by identifying the order of conducting the complementary method (either a preliminary or a follow-up phase). The four basic designs that result from these two decisions are qualitative preliminary (qual-QUAN), quantitative preliminary (quan-QUAL), qualitative follow-up (QUAN-qual), and quantitative follow-up (QUAL-quan) (p. 367). This typology of designs includes multiphase studies and does not impose any limitation on the order of QUAL and QUAN phases of the study.

Greene and Caracelli (1997; see also Greene et al., 1989) Typologies. Greene et al. (1989) presented a typology of mixed methods designs based on their function or purpose, as noted earlier in this chapter. There were five designs in their initial typology. A later revision

(Greene & Caracelli, 1997) included two types of designs with a total of seven distinct mixed methods designs: component designs (triangulation, complementary, and expansion) and integrated designs (iterative, embedded or nested, holistic, and transformative).

Other scholars (e.g., Creswell, 2002, chap. 17; McMillan & Schumacher, 2001) have developed typologies of mixed methods designs that include some of these functions.

Creswell (2002, chap. 17; see also Creswell et al., Chapter 8, this volume). Incorporating the Greene et al. (1989) purposes, while also taking the sequence of QUAL and QUAN components, Creswell (2002) classified mixed methods designs in three types: triangulation, explanatory, and exploratory. In the triangulation mixed methods design, the investigators "collect both quantitative and qualitative data, merge the data, and use the results to best understand a research problem" (pp. 564-565). The explanatory design consists of "collecting quantitative data and then collecting qualitative data to help explain or elaborate on the quantitative results" (p. 566). The exploratory design has an opposite sequence consisting of "first gathering qualitative data to explore a phenomenon, and then collecting quantitative data to explain relationship found in the qualitative data" (p. 567). The emphasis in this typology is on type of data.

In the triangulation design from Creswell's (2002, chap. 17) typology, the QUAL and QUAN components proceed in a simultaneous or parallel manner (Tashakkori & Teddlie, 1998). The other two designs are sequential. The explanatory design has a QUAN-QUAL sequence, while the exploratory design has a QUAL-QUAN sequence.

By contrast, McMillan and Schumacher (2001) adopted three types from Greene et al. (1989): complementary, developmental, and expansion designs. Their complementary design is parallel (they use the term *simultaneous*), while the other two are sequential. However, unlike Creswell's sequential designs, the order of the QUAL and QUAN phases are not predetermined (i.e., each might start with a QUAL or a QUAN phase).

The design chapter by Creswell and colleagues in this handbook (Chapter 8) demonstrates both progress toward a convergent model and a divergence of ideas. After an insightful review of the current typologies, Creswell and colleagues identify four criteria (dimensions) for conceptualizing a mixed methods design (see Table 8.3 in their chapter). They then propose six types of mixed methods design: sequential explanatory, sequential exploratory, sequential transformative, concurrent triangulation, concurrent nested, and concurrent transformative. Criteria used in the Creswell and colleagues classification include the sequence in which data are collected, the purpose of the study, and theoretical perspective (transformative or not).

Tashakkori and Teddlie (1998). We (Tashakkori & Teddlie, 1998) developed a typology of mixed method and mixed model designs based on "procedure" or method of study rather than on priority of orientation, purpose of study, theoretical perspective, and so on. In this subsection, we review our 1998 typology, revising it slightly with regard to terminology. In Chapter 26 of this handbook, we extend the typology by expanding on what we called parallel mixed model designs and sequential mixed model designs in the 1998 typology. The following are a series of points that describe our 1998 typology of mixed method and mixed model designs:

◆ First, we distinguished between mixed method and mixed model designs.

Mixed method designs are those that combine the qualitative and quantitative approaches into the research methodology of a single study or a multiphased study. These methods are further subdivided into five specific types of designs: sequential studies, parallel/simultaneous studies, equivalent status designs, dominant-less dominant studies (Creswell, 1994), and "designs with multilevel utilization of approaches in which researchers utilize different types of methods at different levels of data aggregation" (Tashakkori & Teddlie, 1998, p. 18).

◆ Mixed model studies are considerably different. These are studies that "combine the qualitative and quantitative approaches within different [stages] of the research process" (Tashakkori & Teddlie, 1998, p. 19). Extending the work of Patton (1990), we classified three stages of the research process: exploratory versus confirmatory nature of the investigation, quantitative and qualitative data/operations, and statistical analysis/inference and qualitative analysis/inference.[15] Mixed methods relate to the data collection/operations stage only, while mixed model studies concern all three stages.

◆ A shortcoming of this classification is that it does not clearly differentiate between the data analysis stage and the nature of the final inferences that are made on the basis of the data analysis results. The main reason for this lack of differentiation in the typology of designs is that we, like many other writers, believe that all inferences in social/behavioral research have *some* degree of subjectivity and value in them (see Moghaddam, Walker, & Harré, Chapter 4, this volume). Also, regardless of type of analysis, we usually go beyond the "results" by offering more abstract/

general explanations for events/behaviors and the like in the conclusion of a report. In other words, following both types of data analysis, inferences vary in degree of qualitative and quantitative approaches. Instead of being a dichotomy (constructivist/subjectivist vs. objectivist/value-neutral [see Crotty, 1998; Greene & Caracelli, Chapter 3, this volume]), multiple inferences are made at the end of the study, each varying in generality, subjectivity, cultural orientation, political ideology, value orientation, and so on. Therefore, adding type of inference to our proposed typology is not necessary or even possible. Figure 1.1 depicts this relativity of inferences following QUAL and QUAN data analysis.

◆ In an extension of our earlier work, we now distinguish between monostrand and multistrand mixed model studies, using the word *strand* in the sense that Maxwell and Loomis do in this handbook (Chapter 9). A monostrand mixed model design is a study with a single method for answering either QUAL or QUAN research questions. The data may be transformed from QUAL to QUAN (or vice versa) and analyzed to reach either a QUAL or a QUAN inference. The monostrand studies are mixed across stages of the research process such that one stage is different (in QUAL or QUAN orientation) from the other two stages. These monostrand mixed model studies are the building blocks of the more common multistrand mixed model studies.

◆ Eight designs emerge from the combination of the three research stages noted (a graphic presentation of these designs may be found in our Chapter 26 in this volume). They are presented in Table 1.2 (e.g., Mixed Type IV, which is an exploratory investigation, with qualita-

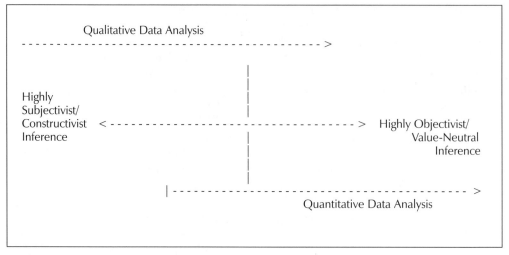

Figure 1.1. Dimensions of Data Analysis and Inference in Tashakkori and Teddlie's Monostrand Mixed Model Typology

tive data collection and operations and statistical analysis/inference). Two are classic single approach designs (pure QUAN and pure QUAL). The other six designs[16] are monostrand mixed model designs in that there is a switching of the approach (e.g., from QUAL to QUAN) in one of the stages of the study. For example, the Mixed Type IV design is a predominantly exploratory study in which the data are quantitized and analyzed statistically.

◆ Multistrand mixed model studies were referred to as parallel mixed model designs (Type VII) and sequential mixed model designs (Type VIII) in the Tashakkori and Teddlie (1998) typology. In a multistrand mixed model design (what Creswell, 1994, called a two-phase design), there are multiple types of questions (QUAL and QUAN) and both types of data and data analysis techniques. The inferences that are made on the basis of the results are both subjectivist/constructivist (QUAL

[Crotty, 1998]) or objectivist (QUAN) in approach. This type of design may be sequential or parallel.

◆ Chapter 26 in this handbook contains an extension of Tashakkori and Teddlie (1998) in that several specific parallel and sequential multistage mixed model designs are presented.

WHAT CRITERIA CAN A RESEARCHER USE TO SELECT THE BEST MIXED METHODS DESIGN FOR HIS OR HER RESEARCH PROJECT?

We have argued that typologies of mixed methods research designs are important for several reasons, including helping the researcher select a particular design for his or her study. The process of selecting the best mixed methods research design for a project is a complex one involving several steps (both assumptions and actions). The details for much of this

TABLE 1.2 Tashakkori and Teddlie's (1998) Classification of Single Strand Mixed Model Designs

| Confirmatory Investigation | | | | Exploratory Investigation | | | |
| Quantitative Data/Operations | | Qualitative Data/Operations | | Quantitative Data/Operations | | Qualitative Data/Operations | |
Statistical analysis and inference	Qualitative analysis and inference	Statistical analysis and inference	Qualitative analysis and inference	Statistical analysis and inference	Qualitative analysis and inference	Statistical analysis and inference	Qualitative analysis and inference
Pure quantitative	Mixed Type V (rare)	Mixed Type I	Mixed Type II	Mixed Type III	Mixed Type VI (rare)	Mixed Type IV	Pure qualitative

process were derived from Morgan (1998) and Creswell and colleagues (Chapter 8, this volume):

1. There are a number of typologies of mixed methods research designs, as noted previously.

2. None of these typologies is exhaustive, as argued in a previous section.

3. The researcher wants to select the best research design for his or her particular study and assumes that one of the published typologies includes the best design for the project.

4. Typologies may be differentiated by the criteria that are used to distinguish among the research designs within them (Morgan, 1998; Creswell et al., Chapter 8, this volume). These criteria identify the important assumptions of the typology.

5. The criteria that each typology uses may be determined through an analysis of the designs within the typology. We did this for several of the typologies previously described in this section. Both Morgan (1998) and Creswell et al. (Chapter 8, this volume) identified two basic criteria in the designs presented by Morse (1991) and others: These designs vary in terms of the sequence in which the QUAN and QUAL data collection procedures are implemented, and they vary in terms of the priority given to each type of data (QUAN or quan, QUAL or qual).

6. These criteria may be listed by the researcher, who then may select the criteria that are most important to him or her. Creswell and colleagues (Chapter 8, this volume) list four such criteria and then assess their six mixed methods designs according to those criteria. In addition to order of implementation

and priority, Creswell and colleagues distinguish two other criteria: stage of integration and theoretical perspective. The stage of integration criterion comes from Tashakkori and Teddlie's (1998) typology that suggests that integration of the QUAL and QUAN perspectives can occur at different stages of the research process (research question, data collection, data analysis, or data interpretation). The theoretical perspective criterion comes from the writing of Greene and Caracelli (1997), who included a transformational, action-oriented dimension to their research. The presence or absence of this theoretical perspective constituted the fourth of Creswell and colleagues' (Chapter 8, this volume) criteria for distinguishing among research designs. Of course, other criteria may apply. For instance, it is obvious that the purpose of the study plays a large role in the two typologies of Greene and Caracelli (1997; see also Green et al., 1989). Also, number of strands (monostrands or multistrands) is an important criterion in Tashakkori and Teddlie's update of their 1998 typology. Of course, it is up to the researcher to select the particular criteria that are important to him or her.

7. The researcher may then apply the selected criteria to potential designs, ultimately selecting the best research design for his or her study.

8. To do this, the researcher must determine which of the research designs is most in accordance with the desired qualities on the selected criteria. For example, if the researcher believes that qualitative research will play the predominant role in his or her study, then the researcher should select a design in which that is the case.

9. In some cases, the researcher may have to develop a new mixed methods design because no one best design exists for his or her research project. Also, some designs may change over the course of the study. This might occur, for instance, if one type of data becomes more important as the study develops.

IS THERE AN ALTERNATIVE WAY TO DISCUSS DIFFERENT KINDS OF MIXED METHODS DESIGNS OTHER THAN USING TYPOLOGIES?

Some readers may tire of the different typological approaches to mixed methods research designs and seek another, more dynamic point of view. Maxwell and Loomis (Chapter 9, this volume) present an alternative approach to conceptualizing mixed methods designs. Instead of presenting another typology of designs, they introduce what they call an "interactive model" for research design in which the components of research design (purpose, conceptual framework, research question, methods, and validity) are components in a network or web rather than in a linear progression (e.g., from purpose to method to inference). The authors then apply this interactive model to mixed methods research, demonstrating how the different components of real mixed methods studies are integrated. Furthermore, in each of these five components, the investigators use quantitative or qualitative lenses/approaches for different conceptualizations.

Maxwell and Loomis's conception of the differences between quantitative and qualitative research is also different. Their analysis concerns what they call variance theory and process theory.

Maxwell and Lomis see their approach as complementary to the more typical ty-pological approaches and suggest that we should combine both strategies when analyzing mixed methods research designs. Their contribution to the handbook (Chapter 9) is highly creative and should generate friendly debate.

WHAT ARE POINTS OF AGREEMENT REGARDING DESIGN ISSUES IN MIXED METHODS RESEARCH?

Creating a systematic and more uniform conceptualization of mixed methods now appears more possible than ever before because the requisite "elements" are largely in place due to the high-quality contributions that have emerged over the past 10 years. These elements are demonstrated throughout this handbook, which we also hope will serve as a stimulus for further development and unification. It is useful to look at the points of commonality that we now have with regard to mixed methods research design:

◆ Scholars agree that it is possible to use both QUAL and QUAN methods to answer objective-value neutral AND subjective-constructivist questions.

◆ Scholars agree, to different degrees, that it is possible to have both inductive/exploratory questions and deductive/confirmatory ones in the same study.

◆ Scholars agree, more or less, that different orientations may be mixed in the statement of purposes/questions of the study (e.g., exploration, explanation, confirmation, political/social transformation), methods (e.g., QUAN and QUAL sampling, data collection procedures, data analysis), and/or inferences/conclusions.

◆ Scholars agree that research questions do not emerge in a vacuum. Rather, they emerge or are influenced by the culture of the investigator as well as through social and political agendas. This point of view is reflected in several chapters in this handbook (Moghaddam et al., Chapter 4; Mertens, Chapter 5; Newman, Ridenour, Newman, & De-Marco, Chapter 6).

◆ There is basic agreement on the terms and notations used in describing mixed methods research designs.

◆ Many scholars recognize that there are many research questions that can be answered only with a mixed methods design.

◆ Most agree with Creswell and colleagues (Chapter 8, this volume) that a mixed methods study involves the collection of both quantitative and qualitative data in a single study, in which the data are collected concurrently or sequentially, and involves the integration of the data at one or more stages in the process of research.

WHAT ARE CONTINUING POINTS OF CONTROVERSY REGARDING DESIGN ISSUES IN MIXED METHODS RESEARCH?

While we are closer than ever before to the development of a uniform and systematic classification of mixed methods design, there is still great divergence of ideas among the scholars in the field, as readers will notice throughout this handbook:

◆ Different criteria are used by different scholars in defining their typologies of mixed methods research designs.

◆ There is confusion between the descriptions of data analysis and the interpretation of the results (what we call "inferences").

◆ There is divergence in nomenclature, with the same design being labeled differently by different scholars (e.g., simultaneous, concurrent, or parallel). This extends to some basic terms such as mixed methods designs (see, e.g., Morse, Chapter 7, this volume).

◆ Triangulation, complementarity, and expansion are used by some scholars to represent types of *design*. As demonstrated by Erzberger and Kelle (Chapter 16, this volume), they are possible outcomes of research; therefore, it is not always possible to predict which of the three might occur at the end of a mixed methods study.

◆ Erzberger and Prein (1997) criticized limiting exploratory designs to a QUAL-QUAN sequence. They argued that is it possible to have an exploratory QUAN study with a QUAL phase to confirm/disconfirm the inferences that were made in the first phase.

◆ Miller (Chapter 15, this volume) argues that researchers should give priority to QUAN inferences in QUAN-QUAL designs. Onwuegbuzie and Teddlie (Chapter 13, this volume) counterargue that the overall research purpose should determine which inference is given primacy.

◆ *Issues in Drawing Inferences in Mixed Methods Research*

Much of the literature on mixed methods has been devoted to issues of research design or paradigm. Although these discussions have led to the identification of a large variety of design and paradigm issues, they have distracted us from the most important component of any research project: the inference (see Miller, Chapter 15, this volume).

We believe that the ultimate advantage of using mixed methods is in the quality of inferences that are made at the end of a series of phases/strands of study. As such, we differentiate the "results" of a study from the "inferences" that are made from that study. Results are the outcomes of data collection and data analysis (e.g., data reduction by creating themes or numerical indicators, establishing the degree of relationship between two categories). Inferences are based on the investigators' interpretations and expansions of such results. As discussed by Moghaddam and Hare (1995), inferences are always made in the cultural context. Hence, the same results might lead to different interpretations by different investigators in two different cultural contexts.

This section on inferences in mixed methods begins with some basic definitions, including inference, inference quality, design quality, interpretive rigor, and inference transferability. We then discuss three basic challenges related to the issue of inference in mixed methods research, with an emphasis on inference quality. Finally, we discuss issues related to inference transferability.

BASIC DEFINITIONS OF INFERENCE AND INFERENCE-RELATED MATTERS IN MIXED METHODS RESEARCH

The Definition of Inference: One Common Term for QUALs and QUANs. Consistent with the writings of some of the authors in this handbook (e.g., Miller, Chapter 15; Erzberger & Kelle, Chapter 16), we (Tashakkori & Teddlie, in press) defined "inference" elsewhere as

an umbrella term to refer to a final outcome of a study. The outcome may consist of a conclusion about, an understanding of, or an explanation for an event, [a] behavior, [a] relationship, or a case (e.g. in qualitative research). We use the term "inference" as a mixed methods term because it may take a variety of meanings ranging between a purely qualitative connotation to a purely quantitative connotation. The dictionary definition of "infer" (the root word for inference) is central to our decision to use the term broadly. The definition is as follows: "to bring or carry in; cause; induce" (Webster's New World Dictionary, 3rd Edition, p. 691), or "to draw a conclusion , as by reasoning" (Webster's Universal College Dictionary, 1997, p. 418). Thus, the dictionary definitions for infer include making conclusions, as well as both the term "cause," which is associated with the quantitative orientation, and the term "induce" (the root word for induction), which is associated with the qualitative orientation.

This is also consistent with Angeles's (1981) *Dictionary of Philosophy,* in which inference is defined as "a conclusion reached," a "deduction from premises that are accepted as true," or an "induction" by "deriving a conclusion from factual statements taken as evidence for the conclusion" (p. 133). Therefore, inference is a term that can be used by QUALs and QUANs alike because it refers to the inductively or deductively derived conclusions from a study.

Use of the Term Inference Quality *Rather Than* Validity.[17] We also use the umbrella term *inference quality* to refer to issues such as internal validity (QUAN term) or credibility (QUAL term). Cook and Campbell (1979) defined internal validity as the "approximate validity with which we infer that a relationship between two variables is causal or that the absence of a relationship implies the absence of cause" (p. 37). More recent definitions of internal validity include noncausal relationships. For example, Krathwohl (1993) defined it as "the power of a study to support an inference that certain variables in it are *linked* in a relationship (p. 271, italics in original). According to this expanded definition, internal validity is the degree to which alternative plausible explanations of the results are ruled out, controlled for, or eliminated. Lincoln and Guba (1985) proposed credibility as the QUAL equivalent for internal validity and proposed several techniques to produce it (e.g., prolonged engagement, persistent observation) (p. 300).

Alternatively, we propose the term *inference quality* as the mixed methods term for the accuracy with which we have drawn both our inductively and our deductively derived conclusions from a study. There are two basic reasons for proposing a new mixed methods term to replace the traditional QUAN and QUAL terms. First, we believe that mixed methods researchers should adopt a common nomenclature that transcends the QUAL and QUAN orientations when the described processes are highly similar and when appropriate terminology exists. Second, we especially believe that a common nomenclature is necessary when the existing QUAL and QUAN terms have been overly used or misused.

The concepts of internal validity and credibility appear to be highly similar because both processes involve determining the degree to which a researcher believes that his or her conclusions accurately de-scribe what actually happened in the study. In one case, the researcher rules out alternative explanations through research design and logic. In the other case, the investigator uses a variety of techniques, the most important of which is to ascertain whether the research participants find the investigator's conclusions "credible" (i.e., member checks).

Fortunately, an appropriate alternative term exists for internal validity/credibility in the form of *inference quality*. We have demonstrated how inference takes into consideration both the QUAL (inductively derived) and QUAN (deductively derived) concepts of coming to conclusions. Quality is a straightforward word connoting degree of excellence. Because quality has seldom been used in research methodology, it has not been overly used or misused.

The second reason for proposing a new mixed methods term is when the existing QUAN or QUAL terms have been overly used or misused. As we concluded in a previous section of this chapter on nomenclature, "validity" has been used in such diverse and imprecise ways that it has lost its meaningfulness as a distinct term connoting either internal or external validity, or catalytic or ironic validity, or any of the other 35 types of validity found in Table 1.1.

The pioneers who proposed the original use of the term *validity* in research and measurement (e.g., Campbell & Stanley, 1963; Cook & Campbell, 1979) made seminal contributions to our understanding of design and measurement issues in quantitative research methodology. However, we believe that validity has become a catchall term that is increasingly losing its ability to connote anything. When a term is used with other words to connote so many meanings, it essentially has none. As Lincoln and Guba (2000) concluded, "Radical reconfigurations of validity leave researchers with multiple, sometimes conflicting, mandates for what constitutes rigorous research" (p. 178).

It should be reiterated at this point that we are not suggesting that QUANs stop using the term *internal validity* in their research studies or that QUALs stop using the term *credibility*. Instead, we are suggesting that when researchers use mixed methods, *inference* and *inference quality* are better terms to use when describing the mixed (QUAL and QUAN) results.

Terms Associated With Inference Quality. In determining the authenticity of findings from qualitative research, Lincoln and Guba (2000) suggested that there are two basic criteria: rigor in the application of method and rigor in interpretation. We now apply these concepts with regard to mixed methods and inference quality. We contend that mixed methods nomenclature should include two important aspects of inference quality. The first we call *design quality*, which comprises the standards for the evaluation of the methodological rigor of the mixed methods research, and the second we call *interpretive rigor*, which comprises the standards for the evaluation of the accuracy or authenticity of the conclusions.

With regard to design quality, we can assemble a whole set of criteria from both the quantitative and qualitative orientations to determine whether our study adheres to commonly accepted best practices. If, for example, we coupled a small-scale quasi-experimental study together with extensive interviews and observations of participants, then a variety of criteria could apply such as the following. Were the participants selected in accordance with the best sampling criteria available? Was the treatment consistent with the definition provided in the statement of purpose? Was there prolonged engagement with and persistent observation

of the participants? Was a dependability audit undertaken?

The issue of *interpretive rigor* is more difficult to assess. Lincoln and Guba (2000) defined the concept as follows: "Are we *interpretively* rigorous? Can our cocreated constructions be trusted to provide some purchase on some important human phenomenon?" (p. 179).

How might this interpretive rigor be determined? There have been a number of attempts in qualitative research to further analyze what we are calling interpretive rigor, including the Guba and Lincoln (1989) description of five authenticity criteria (fairness, ontological authenticity, educative authenticity, catalytic authenticity, and tactical authenticity). Indeed, attempts to further refine the "internal validity" of qualitative research findings have led to the further proliferation of different kinds of validity or authenticity.

A more productive manner for handling this issue of interpretive rigor might be to describe a process whereby the accuracy, or authenticity, of our conclusions/interpretations is assessed. We offer such a process in a later subsection of this chapter.

Inference Transferability. While inference quality is emphasized in this chapter, we also need to consider the generalizability of our results—or what the QUANs have called external validity or what the QUALs have called transferability of results. Although the controversies regarding external validity or transferability are easier to deal with than issues of inference quality, they still pose a challenge to mixed methods researchers.

We propose to use the term *inference transferability* as an umbrella term that refers to both the QUAN term *external validity* and the QUAL term *transferability*. As with inference quality, we believe that a common nomenclature should be adopted when the described QUAL and QUAN processes are similar and when appropriate terminology exists.

The concepts of external validity and transferability are similar because both processes involve determining whether our conclusions may be extrapolated beyond the particular conditions of the research study. When introducing transferability as the qualitative equivalent of external validity, Lincoln and Guba (1985) referred to transferability of the results from the sending context to the receiving context. One had to know the characteristics of both contexts to know how transferable the results were. Therefore, thick descriptions of the contexts are required. The quantitative concept of external validity encompasses populations, settings, and times.

Again to avoid some of the confusions surrounding the term *validity*, we propose replacing it with *transferability*, borrowed from qualitative research literature. Like the terms *inference* and *quality*, transferability seems appropriate for use in both the QUAN and QUAL contexts and has not been overly used or misused. *Inference transferability* can be used as an overall umbrella term, while other terms may refer to more specific types of transferability:

◆ Transferability might refer to contexts other than the ones studied (*ecological transferability*).

◆ Transferability might refer to individuals/groups or entities (e.g., texts, artifacts) other than the ones studied (*population transferability*).

◆ Transferability might refer to other time periods (*temporal transferability*).

◆ Transferability might refer to other modes/methods of measuring/observing the variables/behaviors (*operational transferability*).

Summary of Definitions of Inference-Related Matters in Mixed Methods Research. We used the term *inference* to refer to an outcome of a study, whether it is derived inductively or deductively. We used the term *inference quality* to refer to a process that encompasses both internal validity and credibility. We then defined two aspects of inference quality: design quality and interpretive rigor.

We also defined inference transferability as a term that encompasses external validity and transferability. Other important concepts related to inference transferability include ecological transferability and population transferability.

The labels that we proposed throughout this chapter were constructed through combining what we consider to be the best nomenclature from the current research methodology literature (e.g., inference, quality, transferability) and avoiding overused or misleading terminology. We hope that other mixed methods scholars refine these terms further as we move toward a more unified nomenclature.

THREE BASIC CHALLENGES RELATED TO THE ISSUE OF INFERENCE IN MIXED METHODS RESEARCH

There is much inconsistency between and within the QUAL and QUAN orientations with regard to the issue of inference or what others refer to as validity. Mixed methodologists face at least three challenges with regard to the issue of inference:

1. confusion between the quality of data/ observations and the quality of inferences that are made on the basis of the analysis of such data;

2. controversies regarding standards for evaluating inference quality (what we call design quality and interpretive vigor); and

3. creating bridges or superordinate standards for evaluating the quality of inferences in mixed methods research.

In the following subsections, we summarize our positions regarding these three issues.

Confusion Between the Data Quality and the Quality of Inferences Based on That Data. We have noted before (Tashakkori & Teddlie, 1998, in press) that there is a need for differentiating data quality from inference quality. There is no doubt that the quality of *measures/observations* affects the quality of the *inferences* that are made at the end of the study; that is, bad measures/observations will lead to inaccurate conclusions regardless of the design. But assuming acceptable measures/observations, the quality of inferences is largely independent of the quality of data; that is, inaccurate conclusions may be made on the basis of good data. Inference quality has to be evaluated separately from data quality, and the standards for evaluating them are not the same (Tashakkori & Teddlie, 1998).

Obviously, the fundamental principle of data quality in mixed methods research should be the following: "If the data do not represent the theoretical phenomena or the attributes under study, then nothing else in the design of the study matters." In other words, nothing good emerges from bad data. In QUAN research, this is known as the GIGO (garbage in, garbage out) principle. Data quality affects what Cook and Campbell (1979) called the "construct validity of putative causes and effects" (p. 59). In Cook and Campbell's terms,

> For persons interested in theory testing, it is almost as important to show that the variables involved in the research are constructs A and B (construct validity) as it is to show that the relationship is causal and goes from one variable to the other (internal validity). (p.83)

Similarly, a person involved in studying a phenomenon qualitatively must be sure that the data represent the phenomenon of interest. The investigator must follow certain established procedures, such as prolonged engagement, to be sure that he or she is examining the correct phenomenon. As we noted elsewhere,

> It is important that investigators spend an adequate amount of time in the field to build trust, learn the "culture," and test for misinformation either from informants or [from] their own biases. . . . The purpose of prolonged engagement is to provide "scope" for researchers by making them aware of the multiple contextual factors and multiple perspectives of informants at work in any given social scene. (Tashakkori & Teddlie, 1998, p. 90)

Controversies Regarding Standards for Evaluating Inference Quality. One major issue under this challenge is a matter of definition: Sometimes QUAL and QUAN researchers define the same concept differently. If a mixed methodologist wanted to establish that a certain type of validity existed with a research study, then such a conflict in definition would make the establishment of validity impossible. For example, both QUALs and QUANs (e.g., Liebert & Liebert, 1995; Maxwell, 1992) have used the term *theoretical validity*. In QUAL research, it has been used to represent "the degree that a theoretical explanation developed from a research study fits the data" (Johnson & Christensen, 2000, p. 210). In other words, do the inferences of the study (emergent theory) fit the data? By contrast, in QUAN research, *theoretical validity* has been used as the degree to which the interpretation of the findings is consistent with the theories and known knowledge in the field. In other words, does the inference fit the present knowledge and theories outside of the study? Obviously, the two questions asked by the term *theoretical validity* are very different from each other.

Of course, we have suggested that a more global term, *inference quality,* be used to assess the accuracy with which we have drawn both inductively and deductively derived conclusions from a mixed methods study. By using a common term to assess both the internal validity and the credibility of a study, we avoid some of the problems that practitioners of the two orientations have in interacting with one another.

In both traditions, the strategies for evaluation and for improvement of inferences may generally be placed along four evaluation dimensions: consistency within the design of the study, consistency of multiple conclusions with each other, consistency of interpretations across people, and distinctiveness of the interpretations from other plausible ones.[18] These four dimensions lead to four types of criteria for evaluation that are not necessarily exhaustive (there might be others) or mutually exclusive (one does not preclude the others). These four dimensions are (a) within-design consistency, (b) conceptual consistency, (c) interpretive agreement (or consistency), and (d) interpretive distinctness.

The remainder of this subsection provides examples of questions that might be asked in the evaluation of the inference quality of our research, which is a function of both design quality and interpretive rigor. In the examples that follow, the criterion of within-design consistency is related to what we call design quality. What we call interpretive rigor is related to the other three criteria.

1. *Within-design consistency* is the consistency of the procedures/design of the study from which the inferences emerged:

    Is the design consistent with the research questions/purpose?

    Do the observations/measures have demonstrated quality?

    Are data analysis techniques sufficient/appropriate for providing answers to research questions?

    Do the results happen the way the investigator claims they did? Do they have the necessary magnitude/strength or frequency to warrant the conclusions (*demonstrated results* in QUAL research, *magnitude of effect* in QUAN research)?

    Are the inferences (e.g., emergent theory or explanations) consistent with the results of data analysis? Do they strongly "follow" the findings?

    Are the inferences consistent with the research questions/purposes? Are the inferences obtained in each of the two strands (QUAL and QUAN) consistent with the corresponding research questions/purposes?

2. *The conceptual consistency* dimension consists of the degree to which the inferences are consistent with each other and with the known state of knowledge and theory. It incorporates explanation credibility and credible results audits from QUAL research.

2a. Consistency of inferences with each other within a study (cross-inference consistency):

    Are answers to different aspects of the research question/purpose consistent with each other?

Is the final (global) inference consistent with the ones obtained on the basis of QUAL and QUAN strands of the study? As Erzberger and Kelle (Chapter 16, this volume) suggest, inconsistent inferences obtained from phases/strands of a mixed methods study (e.g., dissonance, complementarity) should lead to a different higher order inference than should consistent inferences (e.g., triangulation, expansion).

2b. Consistency of inferences with current state of knowledge and theory (theoretical consistency):

Do the inferences take the current literature into consideration?

Are the inferences consistent with the state of knowledge? If not, do the inferences offer explanations (theory) for the inconsistency?

3. *Interpretive agreement* (or *consistency*) is consistency of interpretations across people (e.g., consistency among scholars, consistency with participants' construction of reality):

Do other scholars agree that the inferences are the most defensible interpretation of the results?

If participants' construction of the events/relationships is important to the researcher, do the interpretations make sense to participants of the study?

4. *Interpretive distinctiveness* includes the degree to which the inferences are distinctively different from other possible interpretations of the results and the rival explanations are ruled out (eliminated):

Are the inferences distinctively superior to other interpretations of the same findings? This is consistent with the criteria for evaluating internal validity in QUAN research where the

final inferences are the strongest and the most defensible to other scholars and are clearly distinct from other plausible interpretations of the results. Also, it is consistent with the "rival explanations eliminated" in QUAL research.

Are there other plausible explanations for the findings?

We believe that in evaluating the quality of inferences in mixed methods research, the issue of dominance or priority of one methodological approach (e.g., QUAL-quan, qual-QUAN) over another is not very important. Therefore, we have not included it in the preceding criteria/questions.

At the end of each strand/phase of the designs, inferences are made that are either qualitative (predominantly inductive, subjective, constructivist, emic, etc.) or quantitative (predominantly deductive, objective, value-neutral, etic, etc). These inferences either (a) follow each other, separated by a study (i.e., an inference points to the necessity of further data collection and analysis, which is followed by new inferences), or (b) are combined/contrasted to achieve a fuller picture of a phenomenon. The first type of inference is achieved in sequential designs, while the second is achieved in concurrent and transformational designs discussed in an earlier section of this chapter.

Strategies for integrating these inferences and the role of each (e.g., exploratory or confirmatory, triangulation or expansion, etc., as discussed by Miller [Chapter 15], Erzberger & Kelle [Chapter 16], and others in this volume) are more crucial than the dominance of one approach over another. One of the difficult tasks facing mixed methodologists has been in the formulation of such strategies. Erzberger and& Prein's (1997) "rules of integration" are expanded and discussed in detail in this handbook by Erzberger and Kelle (Chapter 16). Miller (Chapter 15) skillfully discusses a variety of issues regarding the term *inference* (as a process and as a product), and suggests "rules" for integrating inferences obtained from QUAL and QUAN phases.

Creating Bridges (Superordinate Standards) for Evaluating the Quality of Inferences in Mixed Methods Research. There appear to be four ways to create superordinate standards for evaluating the quality of inferences in mixed methods research:

1. Identify terms that are the same or similar in both traditions.

2. Borrow terms from the QUAL orientation that have potential for representing concepts in both.

3. Borrow terms from the QUAN orientation that have potential for representing both.

4. Construct totally new terms.

We have used all four of these techniques (in some combination) throughout this chapter to create a common nomenclature for inference in mixed methods. For example, the term *inference* means about the same in both traditions because it has been used very rarely (in definitions) in either one. We borrowed the term *transferability* from the QUAL literature to construct *inference transferability* as a common term for *external validity* and *transferability*. We took terms such as *population* from the QUAN literature to help denote certain types of transferability (e.g., population transferability). *Inference quality* is a good example of a constructed term.

SOME FURTHER COMMENTS ON INFERENCE TRANSFERABILITY

We have previously suggested (Tashakkori & Teddlie, 1998) that inference transferability is relative. That is, no research inference in social and behavioral sciences is fully transferable to *all* (or even most) settings, populations (of entities, people, texts, etc.), or time periods. On the other hand, we believe that any inference has *some* degree of transferability to other settings, populations, or times.

How do we determine the range of transferability of mixed methods inferences? A number of the scholars in this handbook (e.g., Kemper et al., Chapter 10; Johnson & Turner, Chapter 11) suggest that mixed methods inferences are more transferable than the inferences of either the QUAL or QUAN component. This assumption is based on the *gestalt principle* that the whole is bigger than the sum of its parts.

Finally, we believe that although inference transferability and quality might be improved by mixed methods, mixing two or more (QUAL and QUAN) strands/phases with poor inferences will not improve the otherwise poor quality of inferences that are made on the basis of each. The literature is littered with QUAN studies in which interpretations are made on the basis of small correlations or small magnitudes of differences between groups. The results of such studies are readily amenable to multiple inferences, some of which are more plausible than the ones made by the investigators (see, e.g., Ratner, 1997, p. 35; Tashakkori & Ropers-Huilman, 2000). On the other hand, the literature also includes QUAL studies in which a collection of isolated observations and personal opinions is used to make inferences that claim to represent others' perceptions and realities. Combining such poor quality inferences into global mixed methods inferences will not improve the rigor of the conclusions.

Our Chapter 26 in this handbook contains more details comparing our position on inferences to those of the authors of two other chapters: Miller (Chapter 15) and Erzberger and Kelle (Chapter 16). This is another of those areas in mixed methods research where there is lively debate but no consensus at this point in time. The discussion in Chapter 26 points out areas of agreement and contention with regard to the use of inferences in mixed methods.

◆ *The Logistics of Conducting Mixed Methods Research*

The issue of the logistics (i.e., organization and implementation) of mixed methods research is probably the least discussed of the major issues presented in this chapter. From our viewpoint, logistics involves both pedagogy (teaching people how to do mixed methods research) and collaboration (researchers working together in mixed methods research projects). Although little doubt is expressed regarding the usefulness of mixed methods for answering many research questions, it is also widely acknowledged that implementing mixed methods requires more time and effort than does implementing single approach studies (e.g., Creswell, 2002, chap. 17; McMillan & Schumacher, 2001). On the other hand, applied researchers in health, behavioral, and social sciences are increasingly expected to use mixed methods to answer increasingly complex and multifaceted research questions (Tashakkori & Teddlie, in press).

While there has been steady progress in the development of mixed methods over the past 10 to 15 years, there are still very few university courses available that are specifically devoted to mixed methods research (Tashakkori & Teddlie, in press; see also Creswell, Tashakkori, Jensen, & Shapley, Chapter 24, this volume). Part of the reason for this is that the current cohorts of professors teaching research methods never took a course in mixed methods themselves because it was not a recognized research topic when they were in graduate school. This lack of formal courses in the area obviously causes problems for the implementation of mixed methods research projects because all of the researchers involved are essentially self-taught.

Mixed methods research (especially in large-scale projects) is an area that is facilitated by collaboration or the team approach (Shulha & Wilson, Chapter 25, this volume). As suggested by others (Hafernik, Messerschmitt, & Vandrick, 1997; Miller & Crabtree, 2000), collaboration research not only is necessary for answering complex research questions but also enriches the experiences and competencies of the researchers who are involved.

THE FAILURE OF PEDAGOGY

As noted in the paradigm section earlier in this chapter, there are still many professors in graduate programs across the country who consider themselves and their students to be either QUALs or QUANs. These professors might not actively discourage their students from taking courses in the other research tradition, but they certainly do not encourage them. The minimum educational requirement for doing mixed methods research is to have taken courses in both the QUAL and QUAN research traditions or to be self-taught (which requires years of experience).

As Creswell and colleagues (Chapter 24, this volume) conclude, now is the time for attention to be paid to the teaching of mixed methods research courses. Articles and chapters on teaching qualitative methods are readily available (e.g., Stallings, 1995; Webb & Glesne, 1992), but the first two publications (of which we are aware) on teaching mixed methods have just appeared in 2002 (Creswell et al., Chapter 24, this volume; Tashakkori & Teddlie, in press). Fortunately, these two publications both contain a sample syllabus and a listing of a set of modules together with readings for the courses. Creswell and colleagues (Chapter 24, this volume) list more than 20 books, chapters, and articles, thus indicating the wide range of available high-quality sources for a mixed methods course.

It is good that such sources exist because an examination of most current general research methodology textbooks in the social and behavioral sciences would verify that some of them (e.g., psychological research methods) are still lacking even a systematic coverage of qualitative methods. When both approaches to research are presented, they are typically presented in a binary manner, completely separated from each other in different chapters. Currently, there are very few textbooks that cover mixed methods (e.g., Creswell, 2002; McMillan & Schumacher, 2001). The new edition of Johnson & Christensen's (2000) text is also expected to include a chapter on mixed methods.

THREE MODELS FOR PROFESSIONAL COMPETENCY AND COLLABORATION

There are three current models for professional competency and collaboration. According to one model, to find the best answers to research questions, a researcher should be able to fully use methods from both traditions. One of the concerns often expressed in this respect is that it might be impossible for a single researcher to have the necessary competencies in *both* qualitative and quantitative methods.

A second model solves the problem of dual competency by proposing a team approach to research. According to this model, research teams may consist of researchers with competency in one of the two traditions. Such a model is not uncommon in large-scale studies, especially in health sciences. A research team in such projects consists of one or more qualitative and one or more quantitative researchers. How do these team members conceptualize different aspects of the question, plan and implement data collection and analysis, and integrate the obtained inferences in a consistent and fully integrated manner? Mixed methods research is not a simple collection of two strands of data collection and analysis. The strength of the mixed methods designs is in using a systemic approach to integrate multiple types of questions that are answered by multiple types of data and an analysis procedure that ultimately leads to an integrated set of inferences.

A third model (Newman & Benz, 1998; Tashakkori & Teddlie, in press) calls for a *minimum* competency in both qualitative and quantitative designs on the part of all researchers in the project, together with a highly specialized set of competencies in one of the two designs. Large-scale studies and/or those studies that require highly specialized competencies in *both* traditions can achieve this goal by using a team approach consisting of predominantly qualitative and quantitative researchers (see Shulha & Wilson, Chapter 25, this volume).

While the team approach solves the problem of a single researcher having to know both types of research, it also creates new problems. Although this would alleviate the problem of requiring multiple competencies, it does not alleviate the problem in smaller scale studies, or in doctoral dissertations, where only one investigator has to conduct the study from the conceptualization phase to the inference phase. Another problem with the team approach is that, without a minimum competency in *both* types of research, the team members are not able to efficiently communicate and coordinate the research activities. Without some familiarity with *both* traditions, integrating the inferences that are drawn by different team members might be difficult. In our experience, even when a team includes qualitative and quantitative researchers working together, communication between them is hampered by this lack of familiarity with the methods of the other tradition.

For the team members to understand each other, some common language is needed. For this reason, we believe that the third model just presented (the minimum competency model) is a necessary prerequisite for the second one (the team approach). Investigators' "methodological bilingualism" (at least a minimum degree of familiarity with both types of methods) is necessary for effective mixed methods teams. This points to the need for fundamental change in the teaching of research methods in our graduate programs in social, behavioral, and health sciences.

◆ **Summary: The Third Methodological Movement**

This chapter has reviewed six major issues in the use of mixed methods research in the social and behavioral sciences. These issues are discussed in more detail throughout this handbook and are re-examined in our Chapter 26. It is through the intensive examination and resolution of these (and other) controversial issues that the *third methodological movement* (mixed methods research) will be firmly established alongside the other two.

■ *Notes*

1. Morse (1991) introduced the abbreviations QUAN and QUAL to stand for the respective quantitative and qualitative stages of a mixed-methods research design. We have extrapolated the terms QUANs and QUALs to apply to researchers who are quantitatively and qualitatively oriented.

2. While two other moments were noted in the second edition of the *Handbook of Qualitative Research* (Denzin & Lincoln, 2000), we believe that the original five moments are more appropriate for this comparison.

3. Ontology refers to the nature of reality, epistemology refers to the relationship of the knower to the known, and axiology refers to the role of values in inquiry.

4. We use the term *postpositivism* to refer to a family of paradigms that also includes positivism and empiricism. We use the term *constructivism* to refer to a family of paradigms that also includes interpretivism and naturalism.

5. Examples include recent criticisms of the abuse of statistical significance (e.g., Thompson, 1998) and the shift toward emphasis on reporting effect sizes in the *Publication Manual of the American Psychological Association* (American Psychological Association, 2001).

6. That is not to say that such sources are unavailable; rather, they are more rare in the QUAL world than in the QUAN world. For example, see Schwandt (1997) for a dictionary of terms used in QUAL inquiry.

7. As another example, probability samples require a random selection of a relatively large number of units. Randomly selecting 5 hospitals from a total of 200 does not provide a probability (cluster) sample. The result of such sampling strategy may be classified somewhere in the middle of the continuum between

probability and purposive sampling (for further discussion, see Tashakkori & Teddlie, 1998, p. 72).

8. All schools had some assistance from the state in the form of a District Assistance Team; the experimental schools in the study also had the DE.

9. Greene and Caracelli (Chapter 3, this volume) describe four stances on mixing methods and mixing paradigms that are similar to the six points of view described in this chapter.

10. See Tashakkori and Teddlie (1998, pp. 20-30) for an extended comparison of pragmatism with positivism, postpositivism, and constructivism.

11. Qualitative or quantitative methods may also be used in research associated with the transformative-emancipatory paradigm so long as the ideological perspective described in this section shapes the research.

12. Guba (1996) expressed being concerned about his colleague Dan Stufflebeam's criticism of the paradigm tables as having "introduced a major schism into the profession" (p. 46).

13. This problem of the exhaustiveness of the typology is not restricted to mixed methods designs. Campbell and Stanley (1963) introduced the nonequivalent control group design as a single design type (i.e., the untreated control group design with pretest and posttest). More than a decade later, Cook and Campbell (1979) presented a family of "generally interpretable nonequivalent control group designs" with eight members. Quasi-experimental work ongoing between these two books had led to the invention or discovery of several new members of the family of designs.

14. Some of the definitions given here are related to current use of the symbols. For instance, the use of uppercase letters to express priority or dominance (see Creswell et al., Chapter 8, this volume) is different from Morse's preferred terms of thrust and drive (see Morse, Chapter 7, this volume).

15. The confirmatory versus exploratory dimension distinguishes between predominantly deductive (hypothesis-testing) questions and predominantly inductive questions. A clear QUAN-QUAL distinction is not offered on this dimension. Instead, it is suggested that QUAN questions are predominantly hypothetico-deductive, while QUAL questions are predominantly inductive. In any study, QUAL or QUAN has elements of both inductive and deductive components.

16. Examples of all six of these designs were taken from the Louisiana School Effectiveness Study (Teddlie & Stringfield, 1993) and presented in Tashakkori and Teddlie (1998).

17. Interestingly, Cronbach (1982) also made extensive use of the terms internal *inference* (conclusion) and external *inference* (extrapolation) in his theory of how to do evaluations of educational and social programs. He used the terms *internal validity* and *external validity* to refer to the "trustworthiness" of the internal or external inferences. His distinctions are similar to our use of the terms *inference* (he also used the term *inference*) and *inference quality* (he instead used the term *validity*).

18. Our conceptualization of these four dimensions was inspired by theories of social perceptions such as Kelley's (1967) attribution theory.

■ *References*

American Psychological Association. (2001). *Publication manual of the American Psychological Association*. Washington, DC: Author.

Angeles, P. A. (1981). *Dictionary of philosophy*. New York: Barnes & Noble.

Boyatzis, R. E. (1998). *Transforming qualitative information: Thematic analysis and code development*. Thousand Oaks, CA: Sage.

Brewer, J., & Hunter, A. (1989). *Multimethod research: A synthesis of styles*. Newbury Park, CA: Sage.

Campbell, D., & Fiske, D. W. (1959). Convergent and discriminant validation by the multitrait-multimethod matrix. *Psychological Bulletin, 54,* 297-312.

Campbell, D. T., & Stanley, J. (1963). *Experimental and quasi-experimental design for research*. Chicago: Rand McNally.

Cherryholmes, C. C. (1992). Notes on pragmatism and scientific realism. *Educational Researcher, 21*(6), 13-17.

Cherryholmes, C. C. (1999). *Reading pragmatism*. New York: Teachers College Press.

Cohen, L., Manion, L., & Morrison, K. (2000). *Research methods in education* (5th ed.). New York: Routledge/Falmer.

Cook, T. D., & Campbell, D. T. (1979). *Quasiexperimentation: Design and analysis issues for field settings*. Boston: Houghton Mifflin.

Creswell, J. W. (1994). *Research design: Qualitative and quantitative approaches*. Thousand Oaks, CA: Sage.

Creswell, J. W. (2002). *Educational research: Planning, conducting, and evaluating quantitative and qualitative research*. Upper Saddle River, NJ: Merrill Prentice Hall.

Cronbach, L. J. (1982). *Designing evaluations of educational and social programs*. San Francisco: Jossey-Bass.

Crotty, M. (1998). *The foundations of social research: Meaning and perspective in the research process*. Thousand Oaks, CA: Sage.

Datta, L. (1994). Paradigm wars: A basis for peaceful coexistence and beyond. In C. S. Reichardt & S. F. Rallis (Eds.), *The qualitative-quantitative debate: New perspectives* (pp. 53-70). San Francisco: Jossey-Bass.

Datta, L. (1997). A pragmatic basis for mixed-method designs. In J. C. Greene & V. J. Caracelli (Eds.), *Advances in mixed-method evaluation: The challenges and benefits of integrating diverse paradigms* (pp. 33-46). San Francisco: Jossey-Bass.

Deacon, D., Bryman, A., & Fenton, N. (1998). Collision or collusion? A discussion of the unplanned triangulation of quantitative and qualitative research methods. *International Journal of Social Research Methodology, Theory, and Practice, 1*, 47-64.

Denzin, N. K. (1978). The logic of naturalistic inquiry. In N. K. Denzin (Ed.), *Sociological methods: A sourcebook*. New York: McGraw-Hill.

Denzin, N. K. (1992). *Symbolic interactionism and cultural studies*. Cambridge, UK: Basil Blackwell.

Denzin, N. K., & Lincoln, Y. S. (1994). Introduction: Entering the field of qualitative research. In N. K. Denzin & Y. S. Lincoln (Eds.), *Handbook of qualitative research* (pp. 1-18). Thousand Oaks, CA: Sage.

Denzin, N. K., & Lincoln, Y. S. (2000). Introduction: The discipline and practice of qualitative research. In N. K. Denzin & Y. S. Lincoln (Eds.), *Handbook of qualitative research* (2nd ed., pp. 1-28). Thousand Oaks, CA: Sage.

Erzberger, C., & Prein, G. (1997). Triangulation: Validity and empirically based hypothesis construction. *Quality & Quantity, 2*, 141-154.

Festinger, L., Riecken, H. W., & Schachter, S. (1956). *When prophecy fails*. Minneapolis: University of Minnesota Press.

Gage, N. (1989). The paradigm wars and their aftermath: A "historical" sketch of research and teaching since 1989. *Educational Researcher, 18*(7), 4-10.

Gergen, K. J. (1985). The social constructionist movement in modern psychology. *American Psychologist, 40*, 266-275.

Greene, J. C., & Caracelli, V. J. (Eds.). (1997). *Advances in mixed-method evaluation: The challenges and benefits of integrating diverse paradigms* (New Directions for Evaluation, No. 74). San Francisco: Jossey-Bass.

Greene, J. C., Caracelli, V. J., & Graham, W. F. (1989). Toward a conceptual framework for mixed-method evaluation designs. *Educational Evaluation and Policy Analysis, 11*, 255-274.

Guba, E. G. (1987). What have we learned about naturalistic evaluation? *Evaluation Practice, 8*, 23-43.

Guba, E. G. (1996). What happened to me on the road to Damascus. In L. Heshusius & K. Ballard (Eds.), *From positivism to interpretivism and beyond: Tales of transformation in educational and social research* (pp. 43-49). New York: Teachers College Press.

Guba, E. G., & Lincoln, Y. S. (1989). *Fourth generation evaluation*. Newbury Park, CA: Sage.

Guba, E. G., & Lincoln, Y. S. (1994). Competing paradigms in qualitative research. In N. K. Denzin & Y. S. Lincoln (Eds.), *Handbook of qualitative research* (pp. 105-117). Thousand Oaks, CA: Sage.

Hafernik, J. J., Messerschmitt, D. S., & Vandrick, S. (1997). Collaborative research: Why and how? *Educational Researcher, 26*(9), 31-35.

Hammersley, M. (1989). *The dilemma of qualitative method: Herbert Blumer and the Chicago tradition.* London: Routledge.

Hammersley, M. (1992). *What's wrong with ethnography.* London: Routledge.

Hanson, N. R. (1958). *Patterns of discovery: An inquiry into the conceptual foundations of science.* Cambridge, UK: Cambridge University Press.

Howe, K. R. (1988). Against the quantitative-qualitative incompatibility thesis or dogmas die hard. *Educational Researcher, 17*(8), 10-16.

Jick, T. D. (1979). Mixing qualitative and quantitative methods: Triangulation in action. *Administrative Science Quarterly, 24,* 602-611.

Johnson, B., & Christensen, L. (2000). *Educational research: Quantitative and qualitative approaches.* Boston: Allyn & Bacon.

Kelley, H. H. (1967). Attribution theory in social psychology. In D. Levine (Ed.), *Nebraska Symposium on Motivation.* Lincoln: University of Nebraska Press.

Krathwohl, D. R. (1993). *Methods of educational and social science research: An integrated approach.* New York: Longman.

Lather, P. (1993). Fertile obsession: Validity after poststructuralism. *Sociological Quarterly, 34,* 673-693.

Liebert, R. M., & Liebert, L. L. (1995). *Science and behavior: An introduction to methods of psychological research.* Englewood Cliffs, NJ: Prentice Hall.

Lincoln, Y. S., & Guba, E. G. (1985). *Naturalistic inquiry.* Beverly Hills, CA: Sage.

Lincoln, Y. S., & Guba, E. G. (2000). Paradigmatic controversies, contradictions, and emerging confluences. In N. K. Denzin & Y. S. Lincoln (Eds.), *Handbook of qualitative research* (2nd ed., pp. 163-188). Thousand Oaks, CA: Sage.

Maxwell, J. A. (1992). Understanding and validity in qualitative research. *Harvard Educational Review, 62,* 279-300.

McMillan, J. H., & Schumacher, S. (2001). *Research in education: A conceptual introduction* (5th ed.). New York: Longman.

Mertens, D. M. (1998). *Research methods in education and psychology: Integrating diversity with quantitative and qualitative approaches.* Thousand Oaks, CA: Sage.

Mertens, D. M. (1999). Inclusive evaluation: Implications of transformative theory for evaluation. *American Journal of Evaluation, 20*(1), 1-14.

Messick, S. (1995). Validity of psychological assessment. *American Psychologist, 50,* 741-749.

Miles, M., & Huberman, M. (1994). *Qualitative data analysis: An expanded sourcebook* (2nd ed.). Thousand Oaks, CA: Sage.

Miller, W. L., & Crabtree, B. J. (2000). Clinical research. In N. K. Denzin & Y. S. Lincoln (Eds.), *Handbook of qualitative research* (2nd ed., pp. 607-631). Thousand Oaks, CA: Sage.

Moghaddam, F. M., & Harre, R. (1995). But is it science? Traditional and alternative approaches to the study of social behavior. *World Psychology, 1,* 47-78.

Morgan, D. (1998). Practical strategies for combining qualitative and quantitative methods: Applications to health research. *Qualitative Health Research, 8,* 362-376.

Morse, J. M. (1991). Approaches to qualitative-quantitative methodological triangulation. *Nursing Research, 40*(2), 120-123.

Newman, I., & Benz, C. R. (1998). *Qualitative-quantitative research methodology: Exploring the interactive continuum.* Carbondale: University of Illinois Press.

Patton, M. Q. (1990). *Qualitative evaluation and research methods* (2nd ed.). Newbury Park, CA: Sage.

Polit, D. F., & Hungler, B. P. (1999). *Nursing research principles and methods* (6th ed.). Philadelphia: J. B. Lippincott.

Popper, K. R. (1959). *The logic of scientific discovery.* New York: Basic Books. (Original work published 1935)

Punch, K. F. (1998). *Introduction to social research: Quantitative and qualitative approaches.* Thousand Oaks, CA: Sage.

Ratner, C. (1997). *Cultural psychology and qualitative methodology: Theoretical and empirical considerations.* New York: Plenum.

Reichardt, C. S., & Rallis, S. F. (1994). Qualitative and quantitative inquiries are not incompatible: A call for a new partnership. In C. S. Reichardt & S. F. Rallis (Eds.), *The qualitative-quantitative debate: New perspectives* (pp. 85-92). San Francisco: Jossey-Bass.

Roethlisberger, F. J., & Dickson, W. J. (1939). *Management and the worker.* Cambridge, MA: Harvard University Press.

Rossman, G. B., & Wilson, B. L. (1985). Numbers and words: Combining quantitative and qualitative methods in a single large scale evaluation study. *Evaluation Review, 9,* 627-643.

Sandelowski, M., Harris, B. G., & Holditch-Davis, D. (1991). Amniocentesis in the context of infertility. *Health Care for Women International, 12,* 167-178.

Schwandt, T. A. (1997). *Qualitative inquiry: A dictionary of terms.* Thousand Oaks, CA: Sage.

Schwandt, T. A. (2000). Three epistemological stances for qualitative inquiry: Interpretivism, hermeneutics, and social constructionism. In N. K. Denzin & Y. S. Lincoln (Eds.), *Handbook of qualitative research* (2nd ed., pp. 189-214). Thousand Oaks, CA: Sage.

Sherif, M., Harvey, O. J., White, B. J., Hood, W. R., & Sherif, C. W. (1961). *Intergroup conflict and cooperation: The Robber's Cave Experiment.* Norman: University of Oklahoma, Institute of Intergroup Relations.

Smith, J. K. (1983). Quantitative versus qualitative research: An attempt to clarify the issue. *Educational Researcher, 12*(2), 6-13.

Smith, J. K. (1996). An opportunity lost? In L. Heshusius & K. Ballard (Eds.), *From positivism to interpretivism and beyond: Tales of transformation in educational and social research* (pp. 161-168). New York: Teachers College Press.

Smith, J. K., & Heshusius, L. (1986). Closing down the conversation: The end of the quantitative-qualitative debate among educational researchers. *Educational Researcher, 15*(4), 4-12.

Smith, M. L. (1994). Qualitative plus/versus quantitative: The last word. In C. S. Reichardt & S. F. Rallis (Eds.), *The quantitative-qualitative debate: New perspectives* (pp. 37-44). San Francisco: Jossey-Bass.

Stallings, W. M. (1995). Confessions of a quantitative educational researcher trying to teach qualitative research. *Educational Researcher, 24*(3), 31-32.

Stern, P. N. (1994). Eroding grounded theory. In J. Morse (Ed.), *Critical issues in qualitative research methods* (pp. 214-215). Thousand Oaks, CA: Sage.

Stevens, J. G. (2002). *Differential modes of external change agent support in diffusion of innovation.* Unpublished doctoral dissertation, Louisiana State University.

Tashakkori, A., & Ropers-Huilman, B. (2000). Methodological and conceptual issues in research on gender and ethnicity [review of *Gender, Culture, and Ethnicity: Current Research About Women and Men*]. *Contemporary Psychology, 45,* 170-174.

Tashakkori, A., & Teddlie, C. (1998). *Mixed methodology: Combining the qualitative and quantitative approaches* (Applied Social Research Methods, No. 46). Thousand Oaks, CA: Sage.

Tashakkori, A., & Teddlie, C. (in press). Issues and dilemmas in teaching research methods courses in social and behavioral sciences: A U.S. perspective. *International Journal of Social Research Methodology.*

Teddlie, C., & Stringfield, S. (1993). *Schools make a difference: Lessons learned from a 1-year study.* New York: Teachers College Press.

Thompson, B. (1998, April). *Five methodology errors in educational research: The pantheon of statistical significance and other faux pas.* Invited address presented at the annual meeting of the American Educational Research Association, San Diego.

Warner, W. L., & Lunt, P. S. (1941). *The social life of a modern community* (Yankee City

Series, Vol. 1). New Haven, CT: Yale University Press.

Webb, R. B., & Glesne, C. (1992). Teaching qualitative research. In M. LeCompte, W. Milroy, & J. Preissle (Eds.), *The handbook of qualitative research in education* (pp. 771-814). San Diego: Academic Press.

Zimbardo, P. G. (1969). The human choice: Individuation, reason, and order versus deindividuation, impulse, and chaos. In W. T. Arnold & D. Levine (Eds.), *Nebraska Symposium on Motivation* (Vol. 17, pp. 237-307). Lincoln: University of Nebraska Press.

2

PRAGMATIC THREADS IN MIXED METHODS RESEARCH IN THE SOCIAL SCIENCES: THE SEARCH FOR MULTIPLE MODES OF INQUIRY AND THE END OF THE PHILOSOPHY OF FORMALISM

◆ Spencer J. Maxcy

For the past 30 years, there has been a growing concern that "the scientific method" and the general school of social scientific thought termed "formalism" (i.e., positivism, logical positivism, and logical empiricism) have properly served social science inquiry. Recently, the so-called "paradigm wars" in educational research found sides drawn by "quantitative" and "qualitative" researchers hoping to stem this assault on social science. The resulting stalemate yielded instead a greater diversity in research methods in education and a further departure from formalism.[1]

The softening of deeply entrenched positions that linked social science to the hard sciences through a monochromatic method and singular framework valorizing only a narrow band of research studies has given way to a search for a common ground in which differing methods of inquiry may be mixed and matched in new ways. In spirit, the "naturalization" of investigative techniques has opened the social sciences to engagement with social issues over the historical posture of detachment (Wolfe, 1999).

For social science researchers wishing to bridge the gap between the singular scientific method and structuralist orientation of old-line research and the new, more freewheeling inquiry approaches of the naturalists, one answer has been found in historical contributions of the philosophy of pragmatism to the changing conceptions of research methodology. It may be argued that the currently popular mixed methods, multiple methods, and serial methods employed by more liberal social scientists constitute a kind of practical revolution that has changed the face of social science research. Beginning with the works of Charles Sanders Peirce, John Dewey, and Arthur F. Bentley, and punctuated by the more recent writings of the neo-pragmatists, mixed or multiple methods support a new philosophy of science and have underwritten an array of pluralistic genderized, racial, and ethnic studies. Such research products have added depth and richness to our understanding of research methodology as well as of our social and cultural conditions and problems.

Pragmatism offers historical strands and warrants for the new discourse of social science research, which embraces plurality of method and multiple methods philosophies. Furthermore, this revolution in technique (which is the topical center of this handbook) has moved researchers away from sole considerations of knowledge and knowns to a discourse centered on consequent knowings and meanings. It is noteworthy that this shift is not without its challenges, as it has spun off a variety of pseudo-pragmatic efforts to ground social science research on a platform of old-fashioned logical positivism, naive realism, and radical relativist assumptions about the nature of the world,

experience, research, and reporting. This chapter seeks to increase social scientists' vigilance of both traditional and nontraditional research for nonpragmatic schemes, standards, and values.

This chapter begins by tracing the contributions of Charles Sanders Peirce, William James, John Dewey, George Herbert Mead, and Arthur F. Bentley, and then later neo-pragmatism and mixed methodology, to social science. It concludes with comments about the latest and most current strands of pragmatism operating within the social science research environment today.

This chapter draws on sources in philosophy, postmodern theory, research theory, and research methodology in an effort to describe and explain the current arguments and proposals regarding the use of mixed methods in social science research.

◆ Historical Sources of Pragmatic Thinking in Social Science Inquiry

Pragmatism is a philosophical movement begun during the latter decades of the 19th century by the American philosopher Charles Sanders Peirce (1839-1914). This distinctly American philosophy was elaborated on by William James (1842-1910), John Dewey (1859-1952), George Herbert Mead (1863-1931), and Arthur F. Bentley (1870-1957) along with countless other academics and nonacademics over the past century. They were in fundamental agreement in their rejection of certain traditional assumptions about the nature of knowledge and truth and about the nature of inquiry. There was a sympathetic challenging by these pragmatists of the singular notion that social science inquiry was able to access the "real world" solely by virtue of a single "scientific method." A uniform method with accompanying assumptions regarding the language of descriptions and the unbridled penchant for classification, which viewed such statements as equivalent to "truth," was completely rejected by the founders of American pragmatism. There was a search for meaning and an accompanying mood of social reform.

Meaningful research for these early pragmatists began not with a single method or set of methods but rather with ordinary experience and the desire for a better world (Wolfe, 1999). Once launched, inquiries were aimed at refined and enriched experience. The early pragmatic philosophical insights into questions of inquiry methods and their relationship to one another and phenomena must be teased out of the writings of these pragmatists.

Pragmatism entered the arena of research methodology, probably around 1861 or 1862, when Peirce introduced a "triadic scheme" to scientific research, no doubt influenced by his future wife's encouraging him to convert to the Trinitarian-based Episcopalian faith (Fisch, 1982, pp. i-ii). Essentially, this scheme suggested that science dealt with the world at three levels: the observed object; the working scientist; and the signs the scientist used to understand, describe, and explain this world. Peirce went on to refine his notions of method and science, yet his work had little influence on the larger course of pragmatism. James, a Harvard University colleague, converted this Peircean pragmaticism of science into a series of subjective and introspective investigations of psychological and paranormal phenomena. While James was read, particularly by educators interested in his stress reduction ideas, his influence tended to direct pragmatism toward a personalistic philosophy rather than a refined social science research. The pragmatist Mead, a colleague

of Dewey's at the University of Chicago, influenced psychologists and social scientists through his "social behaviorism," his development of the notion of "the act," and his presentism or belief that what is real is what is occurring now. Bentley, a disaffected academic turned apple farmer, made major contributions to social science, in particular political science, by introducing the conception of government as a "process."

Perhaps owing to Dewey's long career and broad range of writings, he contributed the most to the ongoing debates surrounding scientific research during the first half of the 20th century. It remained for Dewey to reinterpret and reattach the threads of pragmatic thinking to serious social science investigation through his conception of the social. Unlike his fellow pragmatists, Dewey sought to invest social science with more objective methods within the larger concerns of people as they formed communities.

INFLUENCES ON THE PRAGMATISTS

It is possible to divide pragmatism into two historical periods: the early period (1860-1930) and a later period starting up again during the 1960s. With World War I and the financial depression in America during the 1930s, pragmatism was displaced as a university study and gradually replaced by analytical philosophy (Dickstein, 1999). However, a neo-pragmatic period began during the late 1960s and fueled a wholly new way of thinking about pragmatism and its place in philosophy, science, and life, making pragmatism as much a philosophy and method of research as it is a political, religious, and aesthetic statement.

Early American pragmatist leaders, such as Peirce, James, Dewey, and Bentley, were affected by key traditions in British and Continental philosophy as well as by the science of the day. These writers influenced social scientists and philosophers until a new wave of pragmatic thinking emerged with Richard Rorty's book *Philosophy and the Mirror of Nature* (Rorty, 1979). What we may mean by pragmatism today is in part attached to certain features of this historic pragmatism as well as to the more contemporary writings of the neo-pragmatists.

The later neo-pragmatic period draws in part from the work of Peirce, James, Dewey, Mead, and Bentley but seriously reconceptualizes it. Thinkers such as Abraham Kaplan, Richard Rorty, Richard Bernstein, Richard Shusterman, Karl Otto Apel, Cornel West, and Hilary Putnam have constructed "strands" or veins of a new pragmatism, contributed to the debates regarding the methods and forms of social science, and redefined the relationships between the earlier work of Peirce, James, Mead, Dewey, and Bentley and Continental and British philosophy, American transcendentalism, analytical philosophy, and the traditions of democracy. As such, neo-pragmatists have continued to have an impact on social science methods and the philosophy of science. Sharing in some of the fundamentals of older pragmatic thought, neo-pragmatism is a more recent set of versions of pragmatism that builds on current cultural conditions (some have called these "postmodern"), stresses the importance of richer modes of inquiry, elevates new means of communicating, attempts to secure more progressive forms of common experience, and advocates the growing of more democratic and vital forms of living. In its essentials, pragmatism operates in a critical mode as a critique of critiques and in a postliberal mode as a reconstruction of individual and communal life.

The philosophical tradition we know as pragmatism was an indigenous philosophy to America; it has no parallels in American history. Sleeper (1986) defined it as follows: "Pragmatism . . . is a philosophy rooted in common sense and dedicated to the transformation of culture, to the resolution of the conflicts that divide us" (pp. 8-9).

The extent to which early pragmatists addressed the inquiry into social problems of their day versus confining their techniques to scientific explication situates their discourse in either social reconstructive or theoretical paths. There certainly are vast differences in the pragmatisms of Peirce, James, Dewey, Mead, and Bentley as well as in those of Rorty, Bernstein, and Shusterman today. What is vital is to see the common sources and the historical directions pragmatism claims and takes— and, for our purposes, to see how pragmatism, particularly in the hands of Dewey and his followers, was "irenic" in the sense that he sought to overcome the isolation of philosophy from the natural and social sciences (Boisvert, 1988, p. 212).

There is a relationship between the American frontier mentality, attached to the westward movement, and pragmatism. It may be said that these historical and cultural conditions set the tone for the development of American pragmatic thinking. However, although it is unique in its philosophical point, American pragmatism did not emerge from nothing. Pragmatism was fueled by the philosophical traditions of Britain and Europe. Pragmatists in America read and were influenced by post-Kantian thought, British empiricism, utilitarianism, biological evolutionary theory, the new realism, Descartes's ideas, and the philosophies of Kant and Hegel. If we read Peirce, James, Dewey, Mead, and Bentley carefully, we find them either accepting or rejecting major streams of this theorizing.

Post-Kantian Thought. Built on the ideas of Immanuel Kant (1724-1804), post-Kantian thought found its way into pragmatism via Peirce and Dewey. Peirce stated that the term "pragmatic" was suggested to him by his study of Kant's works. Both Peirce and Kant were interested in establishing laws of practical reason within the domain of the a priori. Following Kant's lead, Peirce constructed a doctrine of the universalizability of concepts that set the arena for experience.

Early in his career, Dewey was influenced by the Kantian tradition, and only later did he move to a more Hegelian approach to science and method. "In Kant, Dewey encountered a profound clarification of philosophical problems, an exciting epistemology which emphasized the activity rather than the passivity of mind, and an ethical theory which internalized the moral law by identifying it with the law of human reason" (Rockefeller, 1991, pp. 55-56).

British Empiricism. British empiricism made a deep impression on James. His take on science and the methods of psychological introspection, the impact of Peirce's scientific philosophy on his thought, and his many trips to Britain all furnished his pragmatism with an empirical temper. Dewey was more sanguine regarding the tradition of Hobbes to Hume. Whereas the British empiricists tended toward establishing dualisms, Dewey would have none of them. He was critical of the psychology grounding of the British view. In the final analysis, he believed that inquiry began and ended in experience (Rockefeller, 1991).

Inquiry for pragmatists was empirical, but not in the same way that the British empiricists believed it to be empirical. Dewey pointed out that British empiricism was retrospective in being focused on antecedent phenomena, while pragmatism

was interested in the consequent phenomena (Muelder, Sears, & Schlabach, 1960).

Empiricism forced the issue of the primary unit of analysis and description: experience. By rejecting metaphysics and embracing empirical phenomena, the pragmatists redirected the course of philosophy away from continental idealism and New World romantic transcendentalism and toward commonsense practical thinking.

Utilitarianism. The concern of Jeremy Bentham (1748-1832), James Mill (1773-1836), and John Stuart Mill (1808-1873) with social issues and the practical decision-making processes attached to improving social problems appealed to the pragmatists. James dedicated his book *Pragmatism* to John Stuart Mill. The principle of utility, or "the greatest good for the greatest number," is the ethical basis for democracy in the hands of the pragmatists. While there are strong utilitarian elements in Dewey's ethics, in the end he would have found them foreign (Welchman, 1995), preferring instead to allow each community to adjudicate the soundness of solutions to problems.

Evolutionary Theory. The early pragmatists Peirce, James, Dewey, and Bentley were strongly influenced by Chevalier de Lamarck (1744-1829), Charles Darwin (1809-1882), and the theory of evolution. The idea of the contingency of nature and the irreducible individuality of humans provided a touchstone for the investigation of the human adventure (Wiener, 1949/1965). Peirce accepted Lamarckian evolutionary theory, while Dewey and James were followers of Darwin's theory. Evolution was the most important idea for Dewey. This theory explained natural development and provided a foundation for pragmatic psychology, particularly linguistic development. Evolution may be defined as "the transformation of development." The theory forced the belief in a dynamic rather than a static universe without acceding to absolutes such as chaos and order. Organisms adapted and interacted as well as interacted and adapted. Cultures evolved, but not through a "survival of the fittest," as Herbert Spencer had said. Rather, following the kinder, gentler version of social evolutionary theory, Dewey and his followers saw cooperation and conjoint behavior marking successful social and cultural development.

The New Realism. Each of the key leaders of the pragmatic movement reacted to idealism and moved toward the "new realism" dominant in American literature and philosophy during the latter decades of the 19th century and early decades of the 20th century. Peirce was deeply affected by "Scottish commonsense realism." James claimed his philosophy to be a "radical realism."

What realism offered was a more solid purchase on the social conditions of the times. Dewey in particular focused on the ills in society. For example, he joined forces with Jane Addams to help rescue immigrants through social worker experiments. His University of Chicago "Laboratory School" represented an effort to rebuild public education in America through experimentation and the exporting of vital new ways of teaching throughout the United States.

The Philosophy of René Descartes (1596-1650). The pragmatists all reacted to the "Cartesean legacy." Peirce was critical of Descartes's method, believing instead that the pragmatic method was evolving toward more reasonableness. Recently, Bernstein (1983) cautioned fellow pragmatists against embracing a Cartesean point of view. Objectivism and relativism are the twin conditions that devolve from taking Descartes too seriously.

Georg Wilhelm Friedrich Hegel (1770-1831). From Kant came the regard for reason and value, while Hegel provided the process. Peirce's pragmatism is indebted to Kant. For Peirce, the notion of "abduction" replaced Kant's idea of "understanding" and "reason." Peirce stressed "practical consequences," while Kant claimed that differences between claims arise from understanding and reason. Peirce found Kant's distinction between regulative and constitutive principles to be unsound. Peirce rejected the distinction in Kant between reason and understanding (Davis, 1972).

Hegel informed the foundations of Dewey's instrumentalist philosophy. Pragmatism was looking for a theory of process that would take seriously the historical changes in culture while at the same time yielding a meliorism. Societies change, but the need was for humans to control such changes in the future. Hegel allowed pragmatists to jettison determinism in the face of powerful forces of science and business, which seemed to reveal this as impossible.

Each of these historical sources of American pragmatism dealt with the problem of inquiry and the need to establish a posture toward knowing which path to take in a problematic situation. Pragmatism was a theory of inquiry and research with different faces, depending on which of the founders of the movement one read.

FORCES TO WHICH THE PRAGMATISTS RESPONDED

As a distinctly American philosophy, pragmatism responded to a number of currents and popular conceptions in science and social science. The key challenges to the success of any pragmatic invasion of traditional social science research were and still are formalism, foundationalism, supernaturalism, constructivism, coherentism, operationalism, causationism and effectivism, and naive realism and radical relativism.

Formalism. From the start, pragmatism rejected the philosophy of formalism or the belief that there was one "scientific method," one framework underwriting science, and a collection of "scientists" whose practice of this method would result in indisputable knowledge (Dewey, 1927). This formalism continues today under a number of guises (e.g., structuralism, restructuring, systems theory, functionalism) and continues to argue that only research based on a single scientific method and strictly followed procedures of validation is appropriate to the practice of social science.

Foundationalism. Pragmatists following the lines of Dewey did not accept the view that there are certain "forms" that categorize or lump together human experiences, nor did they believe, like Rorty, that there were no foundations whatsoever (Boisvert, 1988; Margolis, 1986). Dewey, unlike Rorty, rejected both the correspondence theory of truth and the coherence theory of truth. The researcher is not invested in the task of discovering the correspondence of language to prior existent objects, Dewey stated. Yet he did believe that the enterprise of inquiry could result in the "grounding" of the methods of investigation in the world (Boisvert, 1988, p. 206).

The conduct of inquiry for pragmatists such as Dewey need not rest on the "quest for certainty" or on any desire to establish or rely on any given "foundations" of knowledge. Dewey did not believe that the forms existed prior to experience; rather, he posted three factors involving the methods of inquiry: (a) the fact of primary or

"had" experiences that is wider and deeper than the cognitive reflection; (b) the fact that all experiences grow out of transactions; and (c) the notion that the forms, structures, frameworks, paradigms, networks, and so on are realized out of inquiry and not merely discovered (Boisvert, 1988, p. 206).

The consequence of Dewey's and later pragmatists' contributions to the debate on the subject of foundations was to relieve contemporary pragmatists of the necessity of resorting to some a priori set of conditions and categories by which new "data" must be known. No such external vocabularies with their categories exist except in the constructive minds of the researchers, and there is no need for us to look to them in our research.

Supernaturalism Versus Naturalism. "Naturalistic" has been conceptualized in two ways by philosophers of science and social science. For the advocates of logical empiricism and its varieties, naturalistic refers to the view that social sciences are like the physical sciences (Phillips, 1987). The clarion call to "naturalize" methods of inquiry is thus conceived of as reattaching human questioning skills to the structural and functional system of the social sciences as modeled on physics.

However, naturalism in another sense is also embraced by the pragmatists, and here it refers to an empirical theory of knowledge (particularly held by Dewey) that is a reconstruction of the traditional realist doctrine of natural kinds (Sleeper, 1986) and instrumentalist ontology (Boisvert, 1988). Naturalism with this face also refers to the biological (evolutionary) take on the universe. Finally, naturalism in the hands of pragmatists, and of Dewey in particular, has strong affiliations with American transcendentalism and the writings of Emerson and Thoreau.

It was Dewey who contrasted naturalism with supernaturalism. He believed that the major problem facing anyone interested in adopting a critically pragmatic attitude is the school of thought that assumes a wholesale cosmic condition (whether chaotic or orderly) of a supernatural kind. The effort to seek cover under the comfortable umbrella of a super-organic entity turns out to be a reinvestment in metaphysics and an abandonment of modern science. Evolution continues to be central to any critical pragmatic stance, but the thrust is downward into nature and experience rather than upward into a metaphysics. The mechanisms whereby nature moves genera and species is the template for considering all versions of experience, Dewey asserted.

Furthermore, the question as to whether there is an absolute understanding of the cosmic condition has plagued humanity for centuries. However, two polar positions have secured popular imagination. On the one hand, there are some that would propose that we inhabit a "chaos," the nature of which is revealed and revealing itself sui generis. Humans have neither the knowledge of, nor the capacity to interfere with, the eternal laws of cosmic development. Beneath the discord and mess is to be found sublime order, which develops according to mechanisms imbedded within. Scientists embracing theories of chaos of this type find such "complexity" everywhere, from the mind of a child to a supernova. Scientists are set outside the phenomena, cast as cautious observers, while the mechanisms move inexorably toward the unknown future.

Researchers are exposed to such chaos thinking by advocates of the "garbage can" theory of organizations. Here, organizations such as schools, for example, are deemed disorderly systems, or virus-infected organisms, that can be neither understood nor cured. The strategy proposed is to backward-map vision and purpose. Administration is filling in reports

and forms, which rationalize what is already in disarray. Sublimely meaningless, teaching is transformed into "managing chaos." At its most vicious, chaos thinking becomes an anarchistic strategy for introducing disorder and the mechanism of redemption.

At the other pole on the chaos-order continuum is to be found the camp favoring rational systems. Here, the assumption is that the cosmos is a natural logical machine, something like our modern computer, that operates precisely and with efficiency. This view was made popular by Descartes and continues to hold sway today. God is the "Great Geometer," and God's universe is a neat collection of cause-effect relations that may be studied and reported using a single scientific method, albeit backed with computers and graphics.

The impact of such "systems thinking" for organizations, such as corporations, hospitals, and schools, is to stress for managers and accountants the necessity for control over causes and the testing of effects relative to techniques that generate "causal" reports. "Effectiveness" is the only goal of organizations perfectly understood as orderly efficient machines. Human collectivities "run" like well-oiled automobiles. The rational-technical mind-set is vindicated by the exercise of effect.

In the end, as Dewey put it, the contest is between systems of thinking that are "supernatural" and those that are "natural." The former serve as part of absolute idealism, while the latter are rooted in an empirical naturalism that takes advantage of an evolutionary take on the world. Dewey offered a strong ontology of Darwinian "nature" with the entailed methods of empirical science.

Constructivism. "Constructivism" is frequently used to designate an increasingly popular research orientation used in the sciences and social sciences. Phillips (2000) called it a "magic word" because it gives the user a sense of certainty as well as a sense of fellowship while discouraging analysis of its meanings (p. 1). Steffe and Gale (1995) located six meanings or "core paradigms": "social constructivism, radical constructivism, social constructionism, information-processing constructivism, cybernetic systems, and sociocultural approaches to mediated action" (p. xiii).

Vanderstraeten and Biesta (1998) argued that there are but two classifications of constructivism—individualistic (subjective) and sociological (intersubjective)—and then challenged the notion that constructivism is a new epistemology on the grounds that constructivism is caught on the horns of a dilemma: If the constructivist theory of knowledge holds that knowledge does not represent the world, then how are plural realities accounted for by the theory? And if, on the other hand, the practice of constructivist research has yielded "convincing evidence" for its realism (which it has in their judgment), then how can it not be faulted for generating a theory of knowledge? Dewey's pragmatism was offered as a way to reconcile this dilemma. Dewey worked aggressively, the authors maintained, to show that humans live in a common world that is nevertheless nonobjective. Humans do not bring to their experience of this world any set of structures or a priori knowns. It is through social transactions that we come to understand the existence of multiple subjective realities while at the same time seeking agreement via action (Vanderstraeten & Biesta, 1998). Such agreement in action calls for a coordination of differing individual perspectives but does not require that such differing views become identical.

Given this view of Dewey as a constructivist, we may see that mixed methods of social science research are warranted by a Deweyan pragmatism. Dewey rejected traditional epistemological foundations along with his fellow constructivists and moved the dialogue regarding knowledge and reality to the area of the meanings-action connection. Dewey and Bentley presented a transactional theory of knowing, which attacks the presumption that there is a dualism between knowing, on the one hand, and reality, on the other. It is perfectly logical for researchers to select and use differing methods, mixing them as they see the need, and to seek to apply their findings to a reality that is at once plural and unknown.

It should be noted that a viable pragmatic constructivism must become a reconstructionism through its rejection of the dualisms invoked by traditional research between the knower and the known, subjectivity and objectivity, and knowledge and reality—all with the purpose of meaningful understanding of the characters and events that make up our praxis.

Coherentism. Pragmatism has embraced holism and continuity; however, coherentism as a philosophy has not been a central theme. For the coherentist, what counts is to what extent the mixture of theories or methods "cohere" or not. "Coherence" is taken to be either a kind of congealed social common sense or an algorithmic or positivist mechanism for theory and method choice (Putnam, 1995, pp. 14-16). Historically, pragmatism has favored the former meaning, while the logical empiricists have favored the latter. When Dewey was called a "coherentist" by Pepper (1939, p. 379), Dewey (1939a) responded by saying that certain schools of philosophy had borrowed "coherence" from aesthetic experience and that the term was not meant to be applied or "illegitimately extended" as a category of the universe at large (p. 553).

Some writers seek to mistakenly tag this drive for coherency as "pragmatic." However, unlike pragmatic theories of choice that pride themselves in avoiding the empty engagement with theory building and the valorizing of privileged vocabularies, coherency theorists are dedicated to the logical empiricist world of their forefathers. A pragmatic criterion for theory selection shifts from using a correspondence theory of truth, setting theories against one another relative to their fruitfulness in knowledge production. Historically, verifiability had been the major concern of research methodologists. That theory is best which produces the most truthful account of the states of affairs. But this view was taken to be naive. In its place appeared the pragmatic criterion in the shape of coherency.

What has emerged is the belief that the best theory was the one that cohered or pulled together truth claims and argued that research in educational administration calls for a pragmatic perspective (Evers & Lakomski, 1991). Finally, both the theoretical pragmatist and the methodological pragmatist assume logic to be the generic trait of existence, which Dewey and his followers never did (Sleeper, 1986). Methodologists who seek to adjudicate research schemes based on the final arbiter of technique run the risk of thinking that singular operations have a kind of ontological oversight status that they share with objects under investigation. All inquiry methods engage in a kind of transformation in which old objects are changed into new ones. For the pragmatist, all discourse is transformational, whether it be statistical or Latin, as experience immediately had is made into objects of knowing and meaning for the purposes of future action.

Operationalism. "Operationalism" has often been used interchangeably with the word "pragmatism." Originating in physics, this program sought to purge research of all terms not defined with respect to "operations." P. W. Bridgman, a Nobel Prize winner in physics, is credited with fathering this philosophical view. In the hands of the social scientists, the call for "operational definitions" to be specified within research studies signaled the criterion of meaningfulness of concepts to be tagged to concrete observable conditions. This specification soon became meaningless; what self-respecting scientist would use theoretical terms which held no sway over the experiences being investigated? Today, operationalism continues to be used in educational research, perhaps owing to the fact that this research arena is fairly insulated from philosophical critique.

There is no relationship between the demand for observable referents for terms of research language and the pragmatic theory of truth. As a part of physicalism and behaviorism, the former impulse is in stark contrast to the pragmatist call for "truth happening to an idea" and the reflexive nature of inquiry itself.

Causationism and Effectivism. The fundamental contribution of the strands of pragmatism has been the development of arguments illustrating the most serious defects of the Aristotelian theory of reality and the mechanism of causation. Pragmatists have historically rejected the notion that a vocabulary has an elevated status such that it may mirror the processes of reality to such an extent that "truth" comes to name the logical relations of concepts within its reporting sentences. Nor do such sentences necessarily depict the states of affairs in some real world. Dewey, in his critique of the "correspondence theory of knowledge," and Rorty, in his use of "language games," challenged the notion that there is a structured way in which the ontological status of characters and events is somehow hooked to numerical or linguistic symbols in unambiguous ways.

Ironically, despite widespread commonsense use of the idea, there appears to be no scientific way to prove causality. That is, no experiments may be conducted to prove the universal nature of causality. Beyond this, it is decidedly suspicious when researchers invest causal efficacy (power) in certain matters and then claim that such power explains the relationship between the cause and its effect. And the claim that causes and effects are somehow necessarily connected in a unidirectional and temporal manner is philosophically questionable.

The twin of the causationist argument is the "effectivist" argument. Distilled from Aristotelianism and valiantly challenged by philosopher David Hume, effectivism assumes that "effects" are linked linguistically to "causes." There appear to be two forms of effectivism practiced. First, methodological effectivism argues that the method or method set is best which has the *best* effects (findings). Here, best findings may be matters of simplicity, least cost, fecundity, richness, generation of the most possibilities for future research, and so forth. Second, normative effectivism in social science assumes that when one or more causes of one or more matters are perceived, that cause or group of causes must lead to, or result in, certain larger effects. From the perspective of methodology, the view is that a method ought to be causal relative to its effects, whereas such effects occur on the margins of or outside of the study itself. Normative effectivism looks to the social and cultural impacts of research studies, for example, with an interest in improving participants' lives and futures.

A fallacy comes into play as a qualitative judgment is introduced relative to the effect of any cause, which moves the

effects status to the category of "prized." The mechanism of justification is summarily drawn into the equation. When the discourse on cause-effect is fixed at the level of method, the results are as follows: On the grounds that one method or method set satisfies the investigator over other methods, in terms of the criterion attached to best or better findings, that method or method set is valued as "effective." What is presumed is that (a) there is a correspondence not between theory and the world but rather between vocabularies about methods and research findings and that (b) the researcher description of such a state of affairs is a "true" report of his relation as a valuable relation.

The idea that there is a necessary connection between cause and effect, as Hume pointed out, is a piece of metaphysics and not research. The notion of causal efficacy as differentiating a cause from its effect is even more of a wonderment! Common sense wishes to attach a power or force that moves or directs something. The first event leads to the next state of affairs, which is thus named an "effect." However, most events and linguistic reports of their logical relations certainly are linked so tightly that it is difficult, if not meaningless, to pull them apart intellectually and then name them as prior cause or subsequent effect. Given this view, effects change into causes, and the latter transform into effects, ad infinitum. Oddly, variables and variability relations were introduced to correct for just this naïveté of causationist and effectivist explanations of meaning in social science research. They remain unheeded of late.

Finally, Donald Davidson told us that the languages of belief and justification are intertwined yet must be disentangled. We believe that the logical relation exhibits a real relation; therefore, we believe it. Belief is buffered by justification claims. We are a species that embraces beliefs and engages in the justification of them; however, no special techniques or methods are necessary for us to do so (Rorty, 1999, p. xxvii). As Putnam put it, "Elements of what we call 'language' or 'mind' penetrate so deeply into reality that the very project of representing ourselves as being 'mappers' of something 'language-dependent' is fatally compromised from the start" (cited in Rorty, 1999, p. xxvii). Causationism and effectiveness assume law-like behavior of causes and effects, separation and distinctness of the two, temporality, sequence, uniformity of nature, and an engine to power the transfer (efficacy). Hence, while causationism and effectivism are employed at the level of common sense, they pose a very real challenge to the research methodologist and challenge the use of pragmatic criteria for meaningfulness in the conduct of serious intellectual inquiry.

Naive Realism and Radical Relativism.
Two other challenges to pragmatic social inquiry are to be labeled "naive realism" and "radical relativism." Pragmatists, it is frequently claimed, are nothing but short-sighted practical people with little regard for ideals and values. On the other hand, pragmatism has often been equated with a kind of radical relativism in which anything goes.

In the name of social activism, the radicalism of social scientists has been known to be reduced to the claim that groups may possess their own "rationality," which is impossible for outsiders to understand, let alone critique. Meanwhile, the more inclusive "scientific" model for social science is deemed false on the grounds that it is insensitive to the vocabularies of particular groups. At the same time, members of certain interest groups (e.g., feminists, ethnics) are encouraged to critique the larger (false) discourse of realist research science from their particular perspectives

in a kind of archaeological manner toward the end of emancipating these groups.

What is involved is a "practical inter-subjectivity" wherein the only significant criterion for identity in meaning is in the agreement in action (Biesta, 1994). This is what we mean by collaboration, joint tenancy, or partnership and is what the outcome may mean in social action. Hence, "understanding is basically a practical matter" (p. 315). The error is in assuming that the research and methods of some ideal and abstract social science remain fixed, while individual groups shift and change in their absolutely rational yet relative efforts to fight their repressions and obsessions. An appeal to a transcendental argument for a framework of all frames is as anti-pragmatic as the quest for certainty through absolute vocabularies (Maxcy, 1995). Pragmatists seek to "move beyond relativism and absolutism" (Bernstein, 1983) by embracing processes of inquiry along with multiple tools or methods of achieving settlement of doubt.

◆ The Founders

All of the founders of pragmatism were the products of rural America. During their lifetimes, all saw the settlement of the West and the rise of science and technology. All felt as though they were in a period of rapid social and cultural change. All saw the attempt to create a new nationalism as a defining moment in American history. All of these pragmatists had confidence in America and human nature. All believed in the capacity of humans to improve their condition through intelligent action. And finally, all of these leaders of the pragmatic movement had an impact on social science philosophy and research methodology.

From the "fathers" of pragmatism, we may locate distinct versions of pragmatism: Peirce's scientific realist version (called "pragmaticism"), James's individualist and radical empiricist variety of "pragmatism," Dewey's "instrumentalism," and Bentley's "process pragmatism." Recent writers have developed their own strands of pragmatism; Richard Rorty has provided an elaboration of James's radical empiricism, Richard Bernstein has adopted a Deweyan social reconstructionist position, and Richard Shusterman has identified himself with Dewey's aesthetic and emancipatory pragmatism.

As a group, pragmatists are convinced that human thought is intrinsically linked to action. Theory was joined with practice. Ideas operate as instruments rather than ideals. Reality is in process, undergoing change at every turn of events. The universe is seen as evolving rather than static. External forces do not determine humans; rather, through intelligence, humans are capable of shaping experience. The faith is lodged in ordinary people who can develop the necessary social institutions and standards to guide their futures (Childs, 1956).

From the expanding western frontier, pragmatists gleaned the fact that experience was all there was. As Dewey discovered, experience was something one could lay back on. The westward expansion had taught the nation the virtue of mobility. Americans became oriented toward the future and not the past. Persons were to be judged on what they did, and not on their ancestors or social class (Childs, 1956).

The democratic way of life became the way of living for pragmatists. Pragmatism acquired the values of democracy, fusing them with their mode of inquiry. At the same time, pragmatists were critical of American life and sought to improve on it via "reconstruction." Schooling became one of the areas in which it was believed that critical pragmatic thinking could be exercised. Pragmatism's founders offered a template for contemporary excursions into pragmatism that is more artistic than political and is more interested in qualitative inquiry than in scientific determination.

CHARLES SANDERS PEIRCE'S THEORY OF INQUIRY

The "Father of Pragmatism" is Charles Sanders Peirce. In a series of articles for *Popular Science Monthly* in 1877 and 1887, he borrowed the term "pragmatic" from Kant and, supported by his own pioneering work as a researcher, set the tone for a new understanding of scientific investigation.

Peirce contributed to research methodology in two ways. He was a practicing scientist (geodesist, astronomer, chemist, and physicist) who conducted benchtop and field-based investigations into a number of problems in science. He also contributed substantial insights into the study of research methodology itself. His "doubt-belief theory of inquiry," in which he drew on Darwinian biological evolutionary principles, set the stage for the pragmatists who followed. A set of triadic categories and relationships marked a series of "systems" that Peirce worked out to explain the processes of thought and inquiry and the nature of phenomena investigated.

Essentially, Peirce proposed that a human seeking to survive would develop habits of thought and action to satisfy his or her needs. Peirce termed these behaviors "habits." Once such habits are in place, they achieve the status of "beliefs." A human possessing beliefs actually knew how to satisfy his or her wants. To hold these beliefs is therefore fruitful. In addition, such beliefs are both settled and satisfying states to the individual. In short, "doubt" can be considered the initiation of inquiry (Hausman, 1993), and belief can be considered its terminus.

If the belief is disturbed by doubt and uncertainty develops relative to satisfying one's desires, then the individual will seek to escape this unpleasant condition. The first impulse is to flee the problematic situation. However, if one decides not to run away from the difficulty, then a method or set of methods for seeking to restore belief will be set into motion. Now, "belief" may be understood as logical, psychological, and referring to a state or condition of being (Hausman, 1993, p. 25). Following the psychologist Sir Russell Bain, Peirce (1931/1966, hereafter CP) believed that "belief" should be defined as "that upon which a man is prepared to act" (CP, 5.12). More fully, if a person has a belief, then he or she is disposed to act in a certain way with regard to the anticipated results of holding that particular belief. Beliefs, then, are habits.

There were two foundations for the sciences: mathematics and phenomenology. Peirce held that mathematics was foundational for the hard sciences, while phenomenology was foundational for the normative sciences (Hausman, 1993, p. 115). In his list of "categories," Peirce offered three "modes of being": (a) firstness or "qualitative possibility" (that which will govern the future), (b) secondness or the dependency of a thing on other things (e.g., causality), and (c) thirdness or the category of intelligible meaning that provides disclosure of continuity and the sense of anticipation of future results (Hausman, 1993, pp. 120-139). Each and every mode of inquiry must take into consideration the foundations of the science pursued and the three categories attendant to all human problem solving.

For Peirce, there were many modes or methods of inquiry aimed at restoring be-

lief. However, he identified the four major methods of settling belief as (a) the method of tenacity, (b) the method of authority, (c) the method of discussion (a priori method), and (d) the pragmatic method (CP, 5.358-5.387). The method of tenacity, Peirce stated, develops a strong and determined will (a characteristic of the successful person). The method of authority produces intellectual slaves but offers security. The method of discussion makes thought a comfortable and delightful process. Only the pragmatic method assures us that we may determine "truth" (Buchler, 1939, p. 68; CP, 5.358-5.387).

We must note that any individual researcher could combine or mix two or more of these four methods and that not every investigation would necessarily exclude any one of the others. However, the preferred method of inquiry for Peirce was the pragmatic method (CP, 5.358-5.387). Peirce wished to rename the "scientific method" the "experiential method" and to make it a piece of his pragmatism (Buchler, 1939, p. 67). Unlike his pragmatist followers James and Dewey, Peirce continued to rely on the view that the proper method of inquiry must be grounded in the belief that a workable method of inquiry is one that is connected to "our external permanency." Peirce was a thoroughgoing scientific realist.

Peirce drew on his understanding of human nature and psychology to provide the key insight that from an "irritation of doubt" flows inquiry. Inquiry leads to belief. Belief forms habit. There is a strong sense in which the method of pragmatism was a fuller route to such clarity. Ideas become clear, he reasoned, to the extent that we are aware of the acts they prescribe. The pragmatic test of meaning for Peirce was simple. In a letter to Lady Welby in 1903, he wrote, "It seems to me that the objections that have been made to my word 'pragmatism' are very trifling. It is the doctrine that truth consists in future serviceableness for our ends" (cited in Wiener, 1949/1965, p. 381). For Peirce, pragmatism was a method leading to the solution of the problem of meaning, where the meaning of an idea was interpreted through conduct—all the more reason, he believed, that our goal should be to locate clear and distinct ideas (CP, 5.388-5.410).

Perhaps most important for our discussion of multiple and mixed methods of inquiry, it is vital to see that Peirce's pragmatic method of science posited an a priori "social impulse" in inquiry. This is an idea he derived from Darwin's notion of social feeling in animals and humans (Hausman, 1993, p. 32). Peirce would argue that the alternative methods of tenacity, authority, and discussion would not win out over scientific method on the grounds that it could be observed empirically that these other methods did not suffice. In addition, Peirce believed that reasoning was like a cable with many strands that could be numerous and intimately connected. The function of the social impulse was tied to the demand that doubt be settled in as stable a way as possible. The social impulse was a part of Peirce's ontology, which held that there was a habit or human disposition to move from fragmentation and chaos, toward consistency and lawfulness, and ultimately to a state of "evolutionary love" (Hausman, 1993).

For Peirce, there were certain unquestionable conditions of reality that may be publicly ascertainable (Buchler, 1939). Inquirers must use the method of science because through this method alone, the "ultimate conclusion of every man shall be the same" (Hausman, 1993, p. 34). Hence, quite early on, pragmatism came to be associated with the public character of procedures of inquiry and open disputations over findings. In addition, Peirce believed that the inquirer used not only deductive and inductive means of investigation but also "abduction" (or "retroduction"). By the latter, he had in mind

what today we would term the "logic of discovery" or "problem finding." Thus, for Peirce, scientists were employing logic in the doubting process as readily as they were in the traditional inductive and deductive phases of inquiry. The method of abduction was added to, and mixed in with, the two other historical methods of inquiry so that scientists could actively engage in the rational discovery of new and worthwhile problems.

For Peirce, the method of science pursues evidence, while inquiry fixes or establishes belief. For Peirce, it would be incorrect to see science as a "guide to conduct" or an "instrument for a practical end"; rather, he called these moral or ethical concerns, and they have no place in free inquiry. Science in the abstract or set methods of inquiry ought not to set us up to inquire in particular ways. Rather, Peirce believed that doubt differed from belief in the practical.

In contrast to Marx, Peirce's experiments led him to believe in "the method of residual phenomena." Peirce wrote,

> The so-called "method of residual phenomena" is so simple that it hardly calls for any remark. At any given stage of science when there are few observations of a given matter, and those rough ones, a law is made out which, when the observations come to be increased in number and made more accurate, is found not to hold exactly. The departures from this law are found themselves to follow a law, which may now be shown to be true. But at a later date it is found that this law again is interfered with, that there are still more minute departures from it, and these departures are again found to follow a law. All the successive laws so found may be real, or they may be merely empirical formulae. (CP, 1.98)

Finally, Peirce's so-called "pragmatic maxim" sought to provide a theory of meaning that could be used to settle doubt and restore belief. He wrote, "Consider what effects, that might conceivably have practical bearings, we conceive the object of our conception to have, then, our conception of these effects is the whole of our conception of the object" (CP, 5.409). His classic example amounted to the clarification of the claim "a diamond is hard." By this statement, we mean that if we were to avoid scratching or rubbing it on any other substance, the meaning would be empty. "Propositions . . . , like that about a diamond being hard when it is not pressed, concern much more the arrangement of our language than they do the meaning of our ideas" (CP, 5.409). Thus, Peirce called for experiential testing of meanings as they form the parts of the doubt-inquiry process. Long before the analytical philosophy movement, Peirce was proposing that we "make our ideas clear."

The "scientific method," or as Peirce termed it the "experiential method," assumed the fundamental characteristic of this method to be the public nature of truth. Beneath this method was the following belief:

> There are Real things, whose characters are entirely independent of our opinions about them; those Reals affect our senses according to regular laws, and, though our sensations are as different as are our relations to the objects, yet, by taking advantage of the laws of perception, we can ascertain by reasoning how things really and truly are; and any man, if he [has] sufficient experience and he reasons enough about it, will be led to the one True conclusion. (Buchler, 1939, p. 69)

Even though Peirce favored this experiential method to all others, he knew that other methods were employed in determining truth and, moreover, that they operated simultaneously with the best one. The interplay of the method of tenacity, the method of authority, and the discussion method could go on unconsciously or consciously. The mixture could compromise the experiential method, whose one goal was the pursuit of evidence, with these other less rigorous methods. Truths, which are not doubted, are often the result of this interaction in methods.

For Peirce, his pragmatism and his doubt-belief theory meant that belief was best when it was a product of inquiry as well as a match with the laws of science. Methodology, or the study of the best methods for arriving at beliefs, was at the heart of his system. Yet the metaphysician in Peirce allowed him to conceive of an entire system of science, categories, and relationships that were prompting human inquiry toward an ultimate good or fusion between evolutionary perfection and love.

Peirce focused on induction and the role of hypothesis in inference that led to truth. He held that given sufficient time and the conscious application of methods, humanity would arrive at the truth. This assertion could not be proved but could be assumed. If inquiries went on forever, then eventually they would converge. Belief is fixed or established by inquiry, with the form of inquiry most adequate to the task being the method of science. However, Peirce argued that there were two kinds of belief: theoretical and practical. The first method of science is aimed at discovering whether a hypothesis has been confirmed such that it affects living and practical affairs.

Peirce believed that pragmatism was the method for fixing belief that was far more significant than other methods. His pragmatic theory of meaning asserts that what the concept of an object means is simply that set of all habits (conditionals) involving the behavior of that object under all conceivable conditions. Peirce further refined his definition of pragmatism in terms of belief being the willingness to act and abandoned "pragmatism" for a new term "pragmaticism" (Apel, 1981).

Thus, Peirce's contribution to research methodology was made as part of his gift of pragmaticism. There are three ingredients to his position: (a) the acceptance of reality; (b) the role of the future as the space within which things may be known; and (c) a purport, or a commitment to purposive action, following a plan with an end or highest good (what Peirce called "evolutionary love") (Hausman, 1993, p. 52). Peirce accepted mathematics and phenomenology as foundations for his science. And he believed that logic could aid, via abduction, the methods of scientific deduction and induction in characterizing problems, reasoning, and resolving doubt. His method of residual phenomena allowed him to hold tentative any law that served to support evidence. For Peirce, his faith in his new science convinced him that given sufficient time, all methods of inquiry would mix and eventually converge into a final opinion (Murphy, 1961).

WILLIAM JAMES'S EXPERIMENTS AND GEORGE HERBERT MEAD'S PHILOSOPHY

Pragmatism seemingly was publicly launched by William James in a speech titled "Philosophical Conceptions and Practical Results," given before the Philosophical Union of the University of California, Berkeley, in August 1898 (Fisch, 1986). James acknowledged Peirce's influence on pragmatism by mentioning Peirce's 1878 publication of "How to Make Our Ideas Clear." Over the years, pragmatism had come to mean something different from Peirce's original conception for James as James explored the regions of psychology and religion.

It is often overlooked that James conducted a vast array of psychological experiments into the characteristics of the human mind and paranormal experience using a variety of methods, including carefully recorded observations, drug-conditioned introspection, biography, history, hypnosis, seances, and textual analysis. He even allowed Edward L. Thorndike's dissertation experiments into chicken intelligence to be conducted in the basement of his home. In his seminal two-volume text, *Psychology*, James (1890) delineated competing theories of mind and its categories—carefully defined concepts of sensation, habit, will, instinct, reasoning, and so forth. In addition, it is clear that James used both qualitative and quantitative methods as well as mixtures of methods in his psychology inquiries.

In the second volume of *Psychology*, James (1890) divided the sciences into two groups: the natural sciences and the pure sciences. While the natural sciences depended primarily on the techniques of observation and introspection, James proposed that the pure sciences used the methods of classification, logic, and mathematics. The latter provided structure through the mechanisms of resemblance and difference as well as discrimination and comparison. James argued that the fundamental distinction between the two sciences was that the first relied on experience, whereas the second did not.

Perhaps the most stunning example of James's strenuous engagement in research was his text *Varieties of Religious Experience: A Study in Human Nature* (James, 1902). His methodology for this study involved careful definition of key concepts, perceptual and sensory considerations, and the development of procedures to be used in gathering data and information. He examined "personal documents," reports, literary accounts, and histories in his research. James seemed to move between differing methods with ease. James began with religious experiences and accounts of mystical states, trances, ghosts, and so forth. Each account was checked against the medical and scientific explanations available. His experiments with drugs and dedication to psychical research were controversial and criticized (Myers, 1986). "For James, research into telepathy, clairvoyance, mediumship, and even demonic possession was simply an extension of abnormal psychology" (p. 10). His effort to approach each instance from a pragmatic perspective led him to conclude that it was impossible to establish definite hypotheses based on "so-called experimental data" (Myers, 1986).

James employed the method of "radical empiricism," which was a scientific attitude that admitted a variety of techniques and tools into the social scientist's methodological tool chest. James's book *Pragmatism* appeared in May 1907. Dewey read it approvingly (Perry, 1935, Vol. 2). The book enunciated a theory of meaning as well as a theory of inquiry. It stood in stark contrast to Peirce's ideas, if only by the fact that it was so readable an account. James came to his pragmatism through more than 30 years of thinking and experimenting. It is possible to see the evolution of this philosophy in his writings during these years. However, James was quick to point out that he had not invented the ideas set out in *Pragmatism*.

According to Bird T. Baldwin, James's book *Talks to Teachers on Psychology* (James, 1899/1939), along with his earlier book *The Principles of Psychology* (James, 1890, Vols. 1-2), attempted to establish the method of introspection on a scientific basis (Myers, 1986). His *Talks* applied the methods and techniques of physiological psychology to teaching with particular reference to the concepts such as "interest" that James had developed in his earlier work. As Edward L. Thorndike, the "Father of Educational Measurement," put it, "[*Talks*] prepared the way for the factual studies of intelligence, learning, and the like" (cited in Myers, 1986, p. 11).

George Herbert Mead advanced beyond James's individualist psychology into the realm of the social. Interestingly, he had lived in Cambridge, Massachusetts, with James and even tutored James's children, yet Mead appeared not to develop a deep relationship with the family. Like many intellectuals of his day, Mead traveled to Europe to study. He was influenced by Darwin's writings, Wundt's psychology of the gesture, and G. Stanley Hall. Mead was also influenced by James Tufts at the University of Chicago. Perhaps the most profound friendship, however, was that between Mead and Dewey, whom he first linked up with at the University of Michigan in 1891. Later, as a member of the Chicago School of Pragmatism, and as a colleague of Dewey's from 1894 at the University of Chicago until Dewey's hasty departure for Columbia University in 1904, Mead made significant contributions to social psychology (Rockefeller, 1991). Today, much of the qualitative research in sociology and social psychology has been influenced by theorists close to pragmatism such as Mead and his students (who took notes on Mead's lectures that were turned into the book *Mind, Self, and Society*) (Wolfe, 1999).

For Mead, scientific method involved solving problems, reconstructing ends, and finding new means to achieve them. Science looked at the means-ends relationship. Like Peirce, Mead was concerned with the categories used by social scientists in their work. He sought to redefine and explain the relationships between the individual's "mind," "self," and "act" with "language," "society," and "the world." The focal point of Mead's work was not the relationship between the individual's volition and will but rather the interrelationship between thought and action as viewed from a sociological and social-psychological point of view (Miller, 1973). Like Bentley, Mead felt that all reality was in process and viewed in multiple ways. There was no single agreed-on "objective" perspective on phenomena. Once the passage is the consideration, the social scientist must shift to considering "adjustment," "novelty," and "creativity" (p. 209).

For Mead, perception and thought are derived from action rather than image. His study of "the act" allowed Mead to conclude that meaning is not the result of perspective but rather the result of "proposed or actual ways of acting" (Miller, 1973, p. 211). Different methods of securing an objective are really differing ways of acting. While Mead continued to embrace "the scientific method," it is clear from the focus of his research on the social-psychological relationships of what were largely personalistic concepts linked to acts that he was willing to do two things. First, after conducting a thorough historical study of science from the 5th century B.C. to modernity, he was willing to jettison the theory of causation. Mead (1936) argued, "Science, in its more dogmatic phase, set up a universal law of cause and effect. Every effect must have a cause, every cause, a like effect. The scientist found, however, that an attempt to define causes was most difficult—finally impossible" (p. 176). In the place of a theory of causation, Mead willingly adopted a theory of probabilities.

Second, Mead removed the obligation of the social scientist to indemnify theories and validate scientific laws. Mead (1936) wrote, "Science, then, is not simply an advance from one theory to another, is not the erecting of a structure of laws simply to pull them down the next moment. Science is an expression of the highest type of intelligence, a method of continually adjusting itself to that which is new" (p. 290). He went on, "The process of intelligence, then, is one of conduct which is continually adjusting itself to new situations. Therefore, it is continually changing its technique" (p. 290). Mead's pragmatism allowed for a mixture of methods that the social scientist found helped to adjust oneself to a new situation. If there were no new situations, then scientific method would be mere habit and consciousness would disappear. "Conscious beings are those that are continually adjusting themselves, using their past experiences, reconstructing their methods of conduct" (p. 290).

In summary, James reshaped Peirce's "pragmatism" and by so doing prompted the latter to shift to the term "pragmaticism." For James, pragmatism was the natural purposiveness of the stream of consciousness as it was directed rationally in the cause of making certain an idea was right. The search or method of inquiry was conceived of as looking at what followed and not toward some ideal or some historical precedent. James wrote, "Ideas [which themselves are but parts of our experience] become true just insofar as they help us to get into satisfactory relation with other parts of our experience" (cited in Barzun, 1983, p. 86). "True" is equated with what is helpful or fruitful in a given situation. Highly individualistic, James came to see pragmatism as a common sort of device, psychological in nature, for describing how we think. This ordinary process wove together abstract and concrete elements, obvious and not so obvious, known and imagined, into a tentative truth we can live by. James provided unusual methods of research into psychological phenomena that were often interspersed. He expanded inquiry in psychology to domains that had historically been considered outside the social scientist's concern.

Mead contributed to the extension of personal and individual psychology to that of the social-psychological sources of action. His contribution was less as a bench scientist and more as a conceptualizer of domains of research in sociology and the development of the new social psychology. His shift from the locus of the person to sources in community and society influenced generations of social scientists to conduct their inquiries along social scientific lines.

JOHN DEWEY'S
THEORY OF INQUIRY

After Peirce and James, it was left to John Dewey to reestablish a link not to the hard sciences but rather to the social and behavioral aspects of experience. Dewey profited from the ideas of Peirce, yet he did not continue in the scientific realism tradition of his teacher. Dewey, always interested in providing unique approaches to questions, traced the development of inquiry in history through four stages or periods of inquiry whereby humans moved from the notion that ideas were fixed to seeing them as unfixed. The first stage was that of the idea. Next came the age of discussion and reflection. This was followed by a historical period dominated by reasoning or proof. Finally, in the final stage, modern thought was characterized by inductive and empirical science (thought in the form of inference).

The main features of sound inquiry method began and ended in experience for Dewey. The investigator starts with a problematic situation, which is directly a part of ordinary experience. The investigator, in seeking a solution to the problem, may use imagination, reasoning, or statistical calculation at this point. Whatever techniques are used, this reflection must be turned back on directly experienced matters, where they are to be tested and verified (Rockefeller, 1991).

When Dewey turned his attention to values, he sought to apply his pragmatic method of inquiry through the following procedures. First, we encounter conflicting desires and alternative apparent goods. Next, we ask, "What is the right course of action to take?" Then, we inquire by observing details of the situation, analyzing different factors, clarifying the obscure, discounting insistent and vivid traits, tracing the consequences of various modes of action, and finally regarding the decision as hypothetical and tentative until the expected consequences (which led us to adopt our solution) are squared with actual consequences (Dewey, 1948).

In the preface of his book *Logic: The Theory of Inquiry*, Dewey (1938) confessed that the term "pragmatism" did not occur in the text. He stated, "Perhaps the word lends itself to misconception. At all events, so much misunderstanding and relatively futile controversy have gathered about the word that it seemed advisable to avoid its use." Yet he went on to give a general definition or proper interpretation of "pragmatic" as "namely the function of consequences as necessary tests of the validity of propositions, provided these consequences are operationally instituted and are such as to resolve the specific problem evoking the operation" (pp. iii-iv). This gesture tells us two things. First, Dewey was aware that the term "pragmatism" had lost much of its earlier precision. Second, it was time to speak of pragmatism in instrumental terms as "tests" of meaning.

Dewey was born the year Charles Darwin's *Origin of Species* was published (1859), and this book had a fundamental impact on his conception of scientific inquiry (Wiener, 1949/1965). For Dewey, inquiry is the controlled transformation (by the use of symbols—propositions, terms, and relations) of a problematic situation into one in which the relevant elements are so ordered with respect to each other that the initial difficulty is resolved (Hook, 1939, p. 94).

Dewey's theory of scientific inquiry was the same as that of ordinary investigation or "problem solving." Social scientific research was merely a refinement on this type of reflective thought. Hans Reichenbach, the premier philosopher of science of Dewey's day, explained Dewey's scientific method in this way:

> In an instructive analysis of some simple examples, such as the explanation of dew and the investigation of the malaria disease, Dewey illustrates this deep insight into the logical structure of modern scientific method. He uses the comprehensive term "inductive methods" for the various procedures which lead from observational data to hypothetical assumptions; by deductive methods, inversely new observational predictions are inferred from the hypothesis the experimental test of which confirms or disproves the hypothetical assumption. Scientific inquiry is thus hypothetical-deductive. (Reichenbach, 1939, p. 183)

Dewey specifically rejected the "objectivist" stance or the view that there was a possible validity of objective phenomena over subjective experience. This view assumed that the researcher could drop all theories, hypotheses, values, passions, and motives—and merely record a collectivity of independent facts with total impartiality (Marshall, 1984). On the other hand, Dewey was unwilling to accept the view of the "subjectivist" or "radical relativist," a position that observations and findings of social inquiry were simply relative to the individual's or group's psyche and/or context.

In the place of objectivism and relativism, Dewey proposed a pragmatist or instrumentalist view that scientific and social scientific method is naturalistic and fluid. In 1929, the publication of Dewey's book *The Quest for Certainty* became the strongest statement against the formalism of his day. In that book, Dewey took on two outdated ideas that were stumbling blocks to the new experimentalism he supported: "that knowledge is concerned with the disclosure of the characteristics of antecedent existences and essences, and that the properties of value found therein provide the authoritative standards for the conduct of life" (Dewey, 1929, p. 71). These traits of inquiry are the result of "the quest for certainty" that dominated life for centuries. Dewey proposed that, rather than looking backward toward old fixed ideas and categories, "practical activity," or the actions that actually change existence, must be looked to.

A second seminal moment in Dewey's battle against a logical positivist or logical empiricist version of unified science came with the publication of his *Theory of Valuation* (Dewey, 1939b/1966). Dewey was invited by editor Otto Neurath to publish a monograph in *International Encyclopedia of Unified Science* (Neurath, 1938). His contribution found him departing from the intentions to foundationalize science by adopting the biases of logical positivism and logical empiricism. Dewey had worked out his own unity of science as early as 1892, when he proposed that science include the subject matter of ethics and aesthetics. While Neurath and his friends had sought to develop a concept of a single science growing out of the logical syntax of the language of science—one that informed all of the other monographs in the *Encyclopedia*—Dewey replaced the backward look of logic and science with the forward look of art. "[Dewey] offered a reconstruction of the notion of science in which the distinctly normative character of judgment is as integral to the methodology as the descriptive function" (Sleeper, 1986, p. 173). Such a move radically influenced social science research and paved the way for the use of multiple methods of inquiry.

Regarding knowledge and its acquisition, Dewey argued that the knowing subject affected the object of knowledge. Radical relativism failed on the grounds that it did not prevent an objective stance toward knowledge. Dewey was an empiricist. He readily admitted to the fact of a reality. Out of these insights, Dewey came to the conclusion that research methodology was already mixed insofar as it contained both inductive and deductive methods. Following Peirce, Dewey left room for the method of discovery, or what Peirce had termed "retroduction," yet he refused to adopt Peirce's narrow realism.

While Peirce believed logic to be the method of science, Dewey opted for a naturalized scientific method more like common sense. As Reichenbach (1939) described Dewey's quest,

> It is the basic idea of Dewey that the method of modern science becomes understandable only if we drop the conception of science as a system of absolute truths. If the scientific work of Antiquity and of the Middle Ages seems so inefficient in comparison with the science of Modern Times, the reason is to be found in the fact that the science of the ancients was a search for necessities and essences, a "quest for certainty." (p. 182)

Finally, we must not overlook one of the greatest experiments in pragmatism ever conducted: the University of Chicago "Laboratory School" (sometimes called the "Dewey School"). When Dewey was hired as the chairman of the University of Chicago's Department of Philosophy, Psychology, and Pedagogy in 1894, he also accepted responsibility for developing the new Laboratory School on the campus. Using what might be termed "action research" today, Dewey quickly set about investigating what function the school ought to have relative to the conditions of society in Chicago at the time. He teamed up with teachers in the school; University of Chicago social scientists such as Thorstein Veblen, Albion Small, Edward W. Bemis, Frederick Starr, and W. I. Thomas; and social activists such as Jane Addams of Hull House and Francis Wayland Parker of Cook County Normal School to discover what his school could provide for children and youths on the South Side of the city (Rockefeller, 1991).

The result of Dewey's and fellow progressive social scientists' inquiry was to conceive of a teaching method as the "arrangement of subject matter which makes it most effective in use" (Garrison, 1998). Such an arrangement may be according to the logic of the discipline of which it is a part or the "developmental" method based on the prior experience of the student. The latter was Dewey's choice, and he arranged the subjects in the Laboratory School according to the interests, needs, and abilities of his pupils (Garrison, 1998).

Dewey's philosophy fastened on the goal of "growth" and held that pedagogy was to foster student inquiry over the traditional memorization and recitation of facts. In true pragmatic fashion, pupil inquiry would begin with real and living doubt and proceed to problem resolution. Classes in the Laboratory School were taught from this inquiry perspective and amounted to group projects and active constructions of solutions to real-life matters such as traffic problems on the University of Chicago campus and achieving better means of moving products from farm to home. Social science and its methods of data collection were central to these projects, and students became experts in investigative techniques. Until his leave-taking from the University of Chicago in 1904, arising out of a fight with the president of the university over Dewey's wife's running of the Laboratory School, Dewey's progressive ideas spread across the nation. He wrote two of his seminal pieces on education during this time, *My Pedagogic Creed* (Dewey, 1897) and *School and Society* (Dewey, 1899), and became the most famous spokesman for education in American history.

By 1916, Dewey was writing in his *Democracy and Education* that democracy meant we must have faith in the individual and intelligence (or the "experimental method") (Dewey, 1916). He took to task the first scientist of education, Johann Friedrich Herbart (1776-1841), pointing out the fallacies associated with the notion that teachers must make students interested in subject matter. Dewey argued that this was artificial and counterproductive. Each child had his or her own interests, which must be appealed to as the starting point of inquiry. Thus, he extended his model of experimental method to even the youngest child.

Dewey's commitment to methodological liberalism allowed him to break through rigid structures of educational

and social science research. He was perhaps the most significant force in redirecting social scientific and educational research toward a qualitative model.

ARTHUR F. BENTLEY AND PROCESS

Arthur F. Bentley, an idiosyncratic thinker and former banker turned apple farmer, exercised considerable pragmatic influence on political science research. Bentley's (1908/1969) text, *The Process of Government: A Study of Social Pressures*, revolutionized how political scientists regarded government and its study. Bentley saw the traditional study of forms of government as an investigation of their branches (i.e., legislative, executive, and judicial) as static and unrepresentative rather than as representations of what governing entailed. Bentley's study of government as "process" reoriented inquiry to the behaviors engaged in by governing officials, lobbyists, and the like, thus transforming political science into a scholarly behavioral science.

During the 1930s, Bentley joined forces with Dewey in the latter's battles against the logical positivists and logical empiricists such as Rudolph Carnap and Charles Morris. By the end of the 1930s, Bentley was to regard his work as the next stage, after Dewey, in the development of pragmatism (Ward, 1984, p. 202).

Bentley's philosophy of social science may be characterized as "behavioral naturalism," as it accepts the position that behavior (not "experience" as Dewey claimed) is the fundamental category of existence and "nature" is the horizon of all inquiry; there is no comfort to be drawn from extra-natural logic or theories. His philosophy of science was "transactional" in the sense that he focused on relational factors between the knower and the known. Rather than static relations, Bentley was interested in investigating "action." "Transaction" signified the knowing-known relationship not as a static state but rather as a process gone through before any "knowing" may be had. As such, the transaction was the basic unit of social science analysis for Bentley (1954). He was quick to distinguish his (and Dewey's) notion of transaction from the traditional philosophy of science idea that social scientists must study the "interactions" among things. The latter led practice to a mechanistic theory of inquiry in which only the causal interconnections among things counted (Ward, 1984, pp. 207-208). This theory had been generated by Newtonian physics but was widely accepted among social scientists by the 20th century.

In 1949, Bentley coauthored *Knowing and the Known* with Dewey (1949). The Bentley-Dewey correspondence leading up to this book, as well as Bentley's increased interest in the writings of Peirce, provoked the analysis of the terms used in social science research (e.g., "judgment," "meaning," "name," "fact," "knowledge"). The pair challenged the view held by the logical positivists that formal logic provided the foundation for inquiry. The views expressed in this book by Bentley are similar to those of W. V. O. Quine, a student of Dewey's, who wrote, "With Dewey, I hold that knowledge, mind, and meaning are part of the same world that they have to do with, and that they are to be studied in the same empirical spirit that animates natural science. There is no place for a prior philosophy" (cited in Ward, 1984, p. 206).

Quantification proved to be an insignificant issue for Bentley. He did not debate the merits or demerits of statistical procedures as methodological tools in the social sciences. He did criticize the "mensurators" for restricting methodological issues

to controversies surrounding the use of measurement or statistics. Instead, Bentley simply refused to believe that measuring the relations among data or quantification was the sole foundation of social science or any science for that matter (Ward, 1984, p. 130). His stand on the single foundation thesis also found Bentley rejecting the "operationalism" of his contemporaries. For Bentley, the idea that social science concepts could or should be defined in terms of "operations," or types of measurement, was fundamentally confused (p. 130).

By rejecting the metaphysical assumption that abstract, symbolic mathematical objects populate the world, Bentley placed himself in the anti-Cartesean camp. For Bentley, social scientific methods of inquiry were entirely too tied up with a pre-scientific worldview.

Bentley (1935) wrote, "Knowledge, whether regarded as the wisdom of the individual or as the accumulated intellectual treasure of the many, is always in some sense the behavior of men" (p. v). "Behaviors survey behaviors," he wrote (p. 376). He continued,

> The investigator cannot place himself outside of the field of behaviors in which he is undertaking behavioral investigation. He is within society as a participant in its activities when he studies it. What he learns he must permit to appear as the template of his own learning. His own background, his own setting, his own localization must come into the account. (p. 376)

Bentley believed that even when researchers were theorizing, they were practicing. When they were observing, they were doing so within their theoretical frame. When they reported the findings of their work, their reports were of facts construed within their own socially situated and "thoroughly practical activity of observing" (p. 377). Bentley refused to assume a distinction between the practical and the theoretical on the grounds that it was in error and because it bred inefficiency and ignored the time-bound nature of our facts/behaviors.

Bentley's contributions to a pragmatic understanding of mixed methods in social science research must begin with his rejection of foundationalism. He believed that no academic discipline or theoretical framework named the essential ground on which research operated. His fundamental discovery was that the inquiry process is hidebound by a set of prescientific assumptions about the nature of the world and social life that are outdated and misleading, thereby leading him to assert a pragmatic theory of action and "naturalized behaviorism." Bentley's embrace of a naturalized inquiry mode allowed for the use of multiple methods of investigation if directed at the realm of action and behavior. Tools and techniques of inquiry were subservient to the task of identifying the transactions between the knower and the known.

For Bentley, methods may be mixed within any research strategy so long as the outcome results in researcher behaviors accounting for participant behaviors and the recognition that transactions are going on between them all of the time.

◆ The Neo-Pragmatists of the 20th Century

There were three fundamental points at which the relevance of pragmatism to social science research methods was to surface during the second half of the 20th century: epistemological, meta-methodological, and methodological.

EPISTEMOLOGICAL PRAGMATISM

As we have seen, the earliest expressions of pragmatism occurred as a result of a decisive encounter with a variety of "-isms" that dominated the vocabulary of social scientists and philosophers. Peirce, James, Mead, Dewey, and Bentley sought to define truth not in terms of descriptions of matches between ideas and things but rather in terms of predictions. Pragmatists took issue with the logical empiricist belief that unless a proposition originated or came from either the sensations or reflective thought about the relationships among ideas, it was in error. Pragmatists looked not at the origins of the idea but instead to its destination. What counted was not where you had been with an idea but rather where it took you.

As Abraham Kaplan pointed out, "It is not that the pragmatist is seeking a logic of discovery rather than a logic of proof, but rather that he refuses to identify the formalist reconstruction of scientific method with the procedures of discovery and of proof that the scientist actually employs" (Kaplan, 1964, p. 33). This "naturalizing" of inquiry has continued to have a profound effect on the conduct of scientific and social scientific research, and it accounts for the ready acceptance of "qualitative" methods today.

Philosophers of science, and later of social science, began to seriously consider that practitioners had been obsessed with grounding scientific knowledge on logical proper names. Next, scientists shifted to examining propositions, statements, and descriptions in the form of sentences as the epistemological unit on which to rest empirical knowledge. Following this period, science shifted to the consideration of conceptual schemes or frameworks as the proper unit of epistemology. Finally, the focus has been directed to conflicting theories, paradigms, research programs, and the like (Bernstein, 1983).

Throughout most of its history, science had been in the business of grounding its processes and products on some network foundation or set of interwoven beliefs. Pragmatists argued that there could be no transcendental rules or algorithms such as "scientific method" or "rationality" in guiding inquiry. Knowledge was constructed through an exercise of thought on experience, catalyzed by doubt and a desire to seek some kind of resolution or closure to a problem (Bernstein, 1983).

For most of its history, pragmatism had been interested in knowledge and how to use it. It is therefore no surprise that when we search the literature in social science and education, we find pragmatism first and most often being cited as a theory of knowledge.

META-METHODOLOGY AND PRAGMATISM

One position emerged that underscored the view that the pragmatist can provide insight into the ways in which pragmatism helps us to understand the problems and issues within research methodology (i.e., the study of research methods). We may regard this as the "meta-methodological position" relative to the place of pragmatism in general inquiry. (Some writers prefer to also regard this view as the "philosophical" take on methodology [Popp, 1998].)

Pragmatists claim that their meta-methodology is neither a "system" nor a fully formed "philosophy." In fact, understanding pragmatics is limited if one adopts a "framework" or "school of thought" perspective. Pragmatists are anti-foundations of any sort, including frames, platforms, and other "worked-out-in-advance" templates of belief. For ideas to be more than simply airy theories,

they must be connected to action. And because actions are manifestations of beliefs, examining ideas that may work turns out to be the essence of inquiry.

From the 1920s until the 1950s, the dominant philosophy of social science was variously termed "positivism," "logical positivism," and "logical empiricism." Essentially, this philosophy and its mutations built on the French philosopher Auguste Comte's hierarchical structuring of the sciences and search for "positive knowledge" using relatively simple methods while fueling the search for precision and certainty. The most popular offshoot was logical empiricism. Logical empiricists believed that Comte's philosophy of history was not science but rather metaphysics and, as such, was unacceptable. They differed with Comte's project when they refused to accept his arrangement of the sciences and social sciences. For these Vienna Circle thinkers, the laws and language of the "higher sciences" could be used in the lower sciences as well, thus fixing once and for all the problem of what constitutes "scientific method" (Evers & Lakomski, 1991; Outhwaite, 1987).

Beginning during the 1950s, social science researchers began looking at alternative philosophies and methodologies to the orthodox view of inquiry commonly known as "logical empiricism" (Outhwaite, 1987). A number of candidates emerged: analytical philosophy, hermeneutics, critical theory, and pragmatism. Each of these philosophies had been around for quite a number of years, but the last half of the 20th century found them redefined in terms of a reaction to logical empiricism and its tenets. Hermeneutics sought to approach reality from a textual model of successive approximations and thresholds or horizons of understanding. Critical theory and critical social science attempted to raise consciousness of social conditions and emancipate individuals from their situations via critical methods of inquiry (Fay, 1987). (Mertens's chapter in this volume [Chapter 5] centers on a discussion of what she calls the "transformative-emancipatory perspective," which is her umbrella term for many of the orientations currently subsumed under "critical theory.") We shall not dwell on analytical philosophy. Suffice it to say that this movement sought to redefine key concepts in discourse, with the aim of clarity of inquiry. We would like to direct attention to pragmatism and the issues it provoked in the dialogues regarding social science inquiry and its rejection of logical empiricism or "formalism."

A long-standing argument, typically associated with logical positivism and logical empiricism, had marginalized philosophers from the discourse regarding scientific inquiry until the middle of the 20th century. With the publication of Peter Winch's book, *The Idea of a Social Science and Its Relation to Philosophy,* in which Winch (1958) argued that philosophy had indeed something to say about social scientific research methodology (but nothing to add to our understanding of the particular methods used by the different social sciences), the discussion regarding social science inquiry became open once again.

Winch (1958) moved the discourse of science and its methods from within the fields of the physical and social sciences out into the arena of intellectual combat. He showed that sense could be made of the relevance of philosophy to a broader understanding of science and methods, and as such he restored the meta-methodological conversation.

Abraham Kaplan

The revival of pragmatism and the emergence of "neo-pragmatism" as a challenge to the narrow empiricism that had dominated the social sciences since their inception emanated from the writings of Abraham Kaplan (1918-1993) in his book *The Conduct of Inquiry: Methodology for Behavioral Science* (Kaplan, 1964), and Richard Rorty in his book *Philosophy and the Mirror of Nature* (Rorty, 1979).

Kaplan (1964) offered a pragmatic study of the methods of social science. Kaplan began by calling "methodology" the study of methods while recognizing that common usage also slips in by referring to any method as a methodology. Hence, given Kaplan's distinction, he would honor methodology as the study or use of methods of inquiry, mixed or singular.

Kaplan (1964) found the key difficulties in methodology to lie elsewhere. He distinguished a number of uses of "methodology." First, he found the term used to identify "techniques" or the specific procedures used in a given science or scientific context. Examples would be Freud's use of the technique of free association to locate the meaning of experiences one has had. Second, methodology is often taken to be synonymous with "scientific method." In this meaning, methodology is honorific and a prologue to something else, conferring that something with status. A third meaning of methodology is often indistinguishable, Kaplan tells us, from epistemology or the theory of knowledge or philosophy of science. In this sense of the term, methodology deals with what can be said about a science or sciences. For example, the problem of the justification of induction, the problem of the counterfactual conditional, or the logical positivist's thesis of physicalism would be grist for the methodologist's mill.

Kaplan (1964) wrote, "Methods are techniques sufficiently general to be common to all sciences, or to a significant part of them. Alternatively, they are logical or philosophical principles sufficiently specific to relate especially to science as distinguished from other human enterprises and interests" (p. 23). For Kaplan, the aim of methodology is to "describe and analyze these methods, throwing light on their limitations and resources, clarifying their presuppositions and consequences, relating their potentialities to the twilight zone at the frontiers of knowledge" (p. 23). The aim of methodology is to help us understand the process of scientific inquiry. Kaplan quickly admitted, by citing Max Weber, that methodology thus understood is no more the precondition of fruitful intellectual work than the study of anatomy is the precondition for correct walking! Yet bringing attention to methods can improve what is done in inquiry.

Kaplan (1964) identified the "myth of methodology" as the promise that if we but locate the one best method, we will progress rapidly toward our goals in research. Following David Riesman, he cautioned not to become excessively preoccupied with technique (method). Kaplan cautioned against a conception of the methodologist as the baseball commissioner writing the rules or the umpire throwing a player or coach out of the game. Rather, the methodologist is better cast as a coach, "and the merit of his recommendations rests entirely on what the play of the game shows to be effective" (p. 25).

Kaplan (1964) warned, "The more realistic danger is that some preferred set of techniques will come to be identified with scientific method as such. The pressures of fad and fashion are as great in science, for all its logic, as in other areas of culture" (p. 28). Following R. A. Fisher, Kaplan argued that a brilliant achievement on which attention is focused may give the method used prestige, even for applications for which it has no appropriate use. Kaplan called this "the law of the instrument"; if you give a small child a hammer, then everything the child encounters will need pounding! Scientists are not free from this tendency, Kaplan asserted.

Mixed methods are to be supported over a single monolithic method. Following Peirce, Kaplan (1964) told us that sometimes the method must be ridden as hard as it can be, letting others hold back within proper limits. In other words, "What is objectionable is not that some techniques are pushed to the utmost, but that others, in consequence, are denied in the name of science" (p. 29). Kaplan added, "I believe it is important that training in behavioral science encourage appreciation of the greatest possible range of techniques [methods]" (p. 29). With respect to method adoption, we must be aware of "defensive incorporation" and "inclusion" in the forms "everybody ought to work on . . ." and "nobody ought to . . ." (p. 29).

The reason why multiple and mixed methods are to be embraced is warranted by logic, but not the logical positivist version of logic as "hypothetical-deductive method." For Kaplan, and for a number of other pragmatists, there is no reason to exclude discovery of hypotheses and the search for methods from the actual logic of inquiry itself. Following Dewey, Kaplan told us that there are many "logics-in-use" and a large number of "reconstructed logics." Historically, it was believed that logic dealt only with the context of proof. Kaplan, following Peirce, pointed out that logic also deals with the context of discovery.

Driven by a search for universality and necessary truth, methodologists have focused on what they deem practical or effective. Social science becomes the exercise of certain methods tested relative to their outcomes and effects. This concern is deemed "practical." But what is practical in one set of circumstances might not be in another. Hence, "practical" and "effective" must be treated as unknowns until tested, and then once they are tested and found to be effective, they might not be included in the next go-around.

Finally, another trend that saw an infusion of philosophy into research thinking during the 1980s was that of the "qualitative research" thrust, found principally in education. The influential Lincoln and Guba (1985) book, *Naturalistic Inquiry,* provided armaments to those who sought to contest the sole use of quantitative methods in social science research during the mid-1980s. Education, in particular, seemed to feel the contention most seriously, with rival camps fighting out their disagreements in the pages of the *Educational Researcher,* the principal organ of the large American Educational Research Association. The so-called "paradigm wars" pitted the historical advocates of a worldview, in which it was assumed that the fundamental and detailed aspects of the world could be observed and recorded using sophisticated quantitative techniques of "data collection," against these new "naturalistic researchers." (Once gathered, these data could then be translated into linguistic reports buffered by charts and tables of a statistical nature.) The so-called "naturalistic inquiry" reported on by Lincoln and Guba illustrated a new trend in social science and educational inquiry that jettisoned the once popular "data-based" research method of the logical empiricists. This book touched off a widespread reform in social science research called "qualitative research." This orientation has been most responsible for introducing diverse methods such as biographical and autobiographical, hermeneutic, constructivist, naturalistic, and phenomenological studies.

A safe haven between the two camps of quantitative and qualitative researchers came to be that of pragmatism. Howe (1988) suggested that a compatibility thesis (justified from a pragmatic perspective) could be held that melded quantitative and qualitative methods. Tashakkori and Teddlie (1998) argued that pragmatism

offered a justification for the use of research method pluralism by moving outside of the methodological confines of their disciplines to solve social scientific puzzles. Pragmatism seems to have emerged as both a method of inquiry and a device for the settling of battles between research purists and more practical-minded scientists.

Richard Rorty

No one was more important in the reintroduction of pragmatism into the American research vocabulary than Richard Rorty. In his book, Philosophy and the Mirror of Nature, Rorty (1979) introduced "neo-pragmatism" to a larger audience, challenging the assumption that the search for the foundations of knowledge, with their frameworks and rules, was fruitful. Researchers and all the rest of us were better off giving up the "quest for certainty" by embracing an anti-foundationalist pragmatism such as the one that he saw Dewey championing. Rorty proposed that rather than dividing the world into thought and objects, or mind and behavior, one needed to think of language and context. The search for a meta-vocabulary to describe and explain objects was inappropriate to a moving universe comprising of numerous persons and multiple contexts. In his text *Objectivity, Relativism, and Truth,* Rorty (1991) wrote,

As one moves along the spectrum from habit to inquiry—from instinctive revision of intentions through routine calculation toward revolutionary science or politics—the number of beliefs added to or subtracted from the web increases. At a certain point in this process it becomes useful to speak of "recontextualization." (p. 94)

Operating as a "strong poet" in the sense that he saw "method" in the hands of the ordinary social science researcher as mistakenly presupposing a privileged vocabulary, Rorty's recontextualizing device was aimed at removing the security of this mistaken relationship. By focusing on the necessity of a willingness to talk and a renewed interest in community, Rorty's metacritique of standard methodologist beliefs resulted in the blinders being taken off of inquirers. Like Winch (1958), Rorty sought to show the conceptual confusion involved in thinking that an object, methods, and the aim of social science inquiry are on the same line of the same page or an isomorph of the natural sciences (Bernstein, 1983).

Having poeticized social-behavioral science and converted the pragmatic method of science à la Peirce and Dewey into a "recontextualization," it may be claimed that Rorty is "anti-methodological" in the sense that he prefers telling stories or engaging in narratives. His agenda amounts to avoiding old vocabularies with their dualisms of absolute-relative, truth-error, and rational-irrational. He is comfortable in using metaphors and seeing talk of scientific method and the methods of the social and physical sciences as "vocabularies" and "language games." He recognized early on that meta-methodology had been used to legitimize vocabularies and scientific knowledge, insulating these from critique and test.

Clearly the historicist, Rorty began with the Enlightenment in his historical critique of the press of the ideal of a scientific rationality on the West. He called for new vocabularies that can get us what we want. Pragmatism comes to be a literary approach dedicated to illustrating how vocabularies are contingent to social and physical sciences seen as "disciplines." In this light, "methods" of inquiry are vocab-ularies that do not support social science disciplines so much as they form ways in which to achieve the effects that members of these communities desire.

Rorty's readings of Dewey and James have provoked many scholars. Richard Bernstein, Robert Westbrook, and Hilary Putnam have put forth vigorous contrary views. The current dialogue among scholars is heated and has led to new threads and veins of investigation into how pragmatism may influence social science inquiries. One interesting thread is "feminist pragmatism," which traces the historical role that women such as Jane Addams, of Hull House, and Ella Flagg Young, superintendent of schools in Chicago, played in operationalizing pragmatic ideals in the helping professions (Seigfried, 1996).

In the face of the "modernist" social science of the past, Rorty proposed a new postmodern bourgeois liberal science. Rorty's version is that "a new stage of creative and scholarly work on pragmatism and the several pragmatists" has emerged recently (Brodsky, 1982, p. 333). As such, Rorty himself has made a number of changes in the traditional interpretation of historical pragmatism, all of which lead to a more aestheticized methodology of inquiry.

Rorty draws for his support on Dewey. For Dewey, "Art . . . is nothing else than the quest for concretely embodied meaning and value in human existence" (Alexander, 1987, p. 269). As such, art conceived of as a mixture of methods deployed on a problematic situation ought to appropriate the ideal possibilities of the current situation to aid action. The action is then aimed at filling out and enriching human experience in the future. Democracy becomes the more viable context and ideal within which to make this happen: Democracy is not just a political system but rather an entire way of thinking such that inquiry is free from autocratic controls and its findings are free to be disseminated to the community.

METHODOLOGICAL PRAGMATISM

The third view, methodological pragmatism, proposes that pragmatism itself be conceived either as (a) a method for selecting inquiry methods or (b) a method of inquiry itself, broadly conceived. As such, methodological pragmatism has a weaker and stronger version.

This first sense of pragmatism as method profited from the opening up of the discourse concerning research and its methods during the latter half of the 20th century. It was reasoned that pragmatism, with its eye to effects and consequences, could be used as a way to examine problems within the social sciences and their fit to particular methods of resolution. At this juncture in history, the numbers of pragmatic methodologists are few, but their number may grow for the reason that qualitative research, as a social science researcher movement, has opened the door to new (and older) techniques that differ from the quantitative camp's tools. Thus, pragmatism fits the bill where it confronts the essential quantitative assumptions about the nature of the world and the limits to knowledge of it.

D. C. Phillips's long-awaited book, *Philosophy, Science, and Social Inquiry* (Phillips, 1987), sought to apply philosophy to and explain methodological issues in the derivative fields of nursing and education and to set the record straight regarding the play of theory over the social sciences. Although it may be argued that his postpositivism retained too much of the original mind-set for the new qualitative researchers to come, Phillips did nudge the dialogue away from specific technical methods toward a consideration of mixed forms of social scientific inquiry. The arena of social science was fraught with archaic and meaningless gestures within the specific disciplines and subfields, and no one was listening to anyone else.

Rescher (1977) had earlier called for a "methodological pragmatism" for research. In Rescher's view, the role of the philosopher of science was to move researchers from a quest for a pragmatic solution to the knowledge question to an embrace of pragmatism as a criterion for method acceptance. Competing methods of inquiry were to be tested by how well they achieved their purported goals.

In social-behavioral research, methodologists have begun to move toward a pragmatic criterion for method acceptability. It is reasoned that the best method or mix of methods is the one that produces the most "effectiveness" (Tashakkori & Teddlie, 1998). The suggestion calls for "mixed methods" research strategies that combine quantitative and qualitative approaches in regulated fashion. Effectiveness (rather than correspondence of findings to some "true" condition in the real world) functions to justify the method or methods mix employed.

Speaking for social science at large, Rescher (1977) had earlier advanced the view that also rejected epistemological pragmatism and embraced methodological pragmatism in its place. He asserted,

> It is thus clear that, with particular regard to methodology at any rate, the pragmatists were surely right: There can be no better or more natural way of justifying a method than by establishing that "it works" with respect to the specific appointed tasks that are in view for it. (p. 3)

A method is appropriate if and only if it achieves its purposes. In fact, for Rescher, method and purpose are used interchangeably. It follows for this group of methodological pragmatists that a method may be evaluated in rational terms if it succeeds.

Effectiveness of method is logically related to its causal power. Findings logically link backward to method used to cause the valued findings. Dewey, in his psychological works, critiqued this Aristotelian argument in his treatment of the "reflex arc" concept. Methodological pragmatism in its current iteration once again lodges practicalism within the realm of decision, but no longer at the level of theory. By focusing on the logical link between a pluralistic set of research tools (lumped into two gross paradigms of inquiry: quantitative and qualitative) and a pragmatic choice matrix and criterion of "effectiveness," tools of research are voted up or down based on their results, conceived of as "findings."

Methodological pragmatism of this sort is an improvement on empistemological pragmatism. Rather than embracing a system based on a ratio of perceived description of the "real world," Rescher moved dangerously close to an aesthetic pragmatism in which he valorized the shape of research outcomes. No emphasis was placed on operationalizing such ventures; rather, the desire was to restore a kind of research elegance to what has become somewhat messy after the infusion of qualitative methods in the research study. Decision making is retained, in this case in "methods" of investigation, but the theories attached to such methods are no longer important or involved in the selection process.

Rescher did not justify the research enterprise by exercising criteria of theory correspondence or coherence. He instead sought to avoid the paradigm wars—real or unreal. However, what we get is an atheoretical practicalism driven by a cross-methodological selection matrix in which justification for method acceptance is rooted in combinational moves taken as a priori more valuable than any individual technique. That is, to keep the peace, and to satisfy members of the qualitative researcher camp, such methods will be introduced into a decision model, as yet un-worked out, at the level of method. However, the ultimate arbiter remains that of a quantitative and essentially logical positivist summary account of acceptance resting on fecundity. (That method is most effective which yields the most [richest] linguistic-numerical statements corresponding with actually perceived states of affairs.)

The second sense of "methodological pragmatism" is far more encompassing. Social scientists are increasingly concerned about the place of the researcher (embodiment) in the investigation of problems within a social or cultural system. Here, owing to its acceptance of the situating of the researcher within the context under investigation and the context as part-and-parcel of investigator values and beliefs, pragmatism may be used to uncover the meanings that certain social science methods have for their contribution to the larger life of the community (of both inquirers and participants). A rich interest in social justice in terms of gender, racial, and ethnic dimensions of society and culture can thus be surfaced and dealt with within social science research without fear of taint of "bias" or "subjectivity." Moreover, whereas the first sense of methodological pragmatism continues in the tradition of logical empiricism, the second sense of the phrase is invested in the fuller range of abductive, inductive, and deductive intellectual moves, as reflexive on the sociocultural values and practices under scrutiny. The tools and techniques of investigation are thus themselves open to reconstruction and reappropriation based on their workability.

Insofar as mixed or multiple methods of social science research are concerned, clearly the first pragmatism (epistemological pragmatism) sought to cast a light on the meaning and point of competing, interspersed, sequential, and other methods combinations adopted within social science research programs with respect to the aim of establishing knowledge. Metamethodological pragmatism, as the study of research methods, has expanded the problem of inquiry and technique. Here, pragmatists came to see the task to be the discovery of the place of consequences and test, as they are attached to using any research method. Finally, the methodological pragmatism perspective, which is interested either in constructing a decision calculus regarding the selection of the most coherent, cost-efficient, or effective method or in finding what method or set of methods is best (valuable), reflects back on issues relative to the larger "way of life." The questions are of the order of "What possible difference can these methods in combination and mixture make for the meanings of the research questions raised in the initial plan of investigation?" Mixed and multiple methods would rise or fall in significance and meaning as they were tested out in experience. Allied questions may include the effects of these mixed methods on researcher expectations and their reference back to the original queries. Certainly, theories and leading concepts would be open to investigation as part of this pragmatic approach.

Richard Bernstein, Cornel West, and Cleo Cherryholmes

Richard Bernstein has attempted to link pragmatism and certain European philosophies such as hermeneutics and critical theory (Bernstein, 1983). His efforts have led to a poly-methodological solution in the face of the quest for method rigor.

Harvard professor Cornel West has written eloquently on the place of pragmatism in the development of faith and race in America (West, 1989). West has used historical methods to trace the importance of William James, W. E. B. Du Bois, and others to the generation of "prophetic pragmatism" in the United States.

Curriculum theorist Cleo Cherryholmes, strongly influenced by pragmatist philosophers John Dewey, W. V. O. Quine, and Donald Davidson, has drawn an elegant bead on "reading pragmatism" (Cherryholmes, 1999). Cherryholmes has argued that social scientists must read research and that when they do so, they are better off reading it with a pragmatic consideration of how truth and meanings are "constructed" in research studies. Adapting the "deconstruction" methods of the French to a "critical pragmatism," Cherryholmes has offered us a way to read research studies with a consideration of what they draw on and what they foretell.

◆ Recent Excursions Into Aesthetic Pragmatism

Peirce argued that all inquiry began with quality and would evolve in the end into agape (love). Dewey agreed that every inquiry was sourced in quality and added that it should end in a richer reconstructed experience. By beginning and ending with value, and adding art and aesthetics to scientific modes of investigation, Peirce and Dewey completely mixed methods of social science inquiry. More currently, Thomas Alexander and Richard Shusterman have given us a pragmatism strongly based in an aesthetics built from Dewey's (1934) *Art as Experience*

(Alexander, 1987; Shusterman, 1992). This pragmatist strain introduces new methods of inquiry into the search for meaning that overshadow the older logical empiricist singular vision of methodology. Pragmatists within social educational research, such as Philip W. Jackson in his *John Dewey and the Lessons of Art* (Jackson, 1998); Jim Garrison in his *Dewey and Eros: Wisdom and Desire in the Art of Teaching* (Garrison, 1997); Gert J. J. Biesta in his "Education as Practical Intersubjectivity: Towards a Critical-Pragmatic Understanding of Education" (Biesta, 1994); and my own works *Educational Leadership* (Maxcy, 1991), *Postmodern School Leadership* (Maxcy, 1994), and *Democracy, Chaos, and the New School Order* (Maxcy, 1995), have sought to reintroduce an aesthetic pragmatism into educational thought as plural in its methods and multiple in its techniques.

Richard Shusterman, in his book *Pragmatist Aesthetics* (Shusterman, 1992) (no doubt influenced by Alexander, 1987), drew on Dewey to form a strand of pragmatism that emphasized all of the arts as forms of inquiry. As Shusterman (1992) viewed it, "Dewey, though intensely appreciative of science and its gifts to civilization, could not help but regard scientific experience as thinner than art" (p. 11). Shusterman went on to say that "Dewey's privileging of art over science on a fundamentally naturalist and empiricist philosophical base was both a brave and a therapeutic gesture in an increasingly technological world whose dominant cultural hero was the scientist" (p. 11). As a mode of inquiry, "aesthetic inquiry" was "hard thinking" and as valued as scientific inquiry. In addition, science itself dealt with aesthetic quality, for science could provide a satisfying emotional experience for the scientist resulting from internal integration and a fulfillment resulting from ordered and organized processes. Thus, there were deep similarities between science and art for Dewey. Dewey wrote that "science itself is but a central art auxiliary to the generation and utilization of other arts" (cited in Shusterman, 1992, p. 12). For Shusterman, humans inquire into their cultural conditions via drama, music, sculpture, painting, and other arts widely defined. For example, he believes that rap music is a culture form that penetrates into the problematics of contemporary youths and cultural conditions.

Pragmatism of a Deweyan artistic kind illustrates how children and adults might live their lives better as a result of art. Focusing on Dewey's concept of experience, Jackson (1998) fashioned a philosophy of inquiry that is at once critical of today's "psychobabble" and driven by a thirst for quality. What controls an artist's processes of selection and rejection, and the coherency that results in a compressed and intensified qualitative whole, provides a model for the scientist as well. The entire project is one aimed at a coherent and integrated individual arising out of the quest for quality (rather than certainty). Jackson quoted Dewey:

> To gain an integrated individual, each of us needs to cultivate his own garden. But there is no fence about this garden; it is no sharply marked off enclosure. Our garden is the world, in the angle at which it touches our own manner of being. By accepting the . . . world in which we live, and by thus fulfilling the precondition for interaction with it, we, who are also parts of the moving present, create ourselves as we create an unknown future. (pp. 163-164)

◆ Conclusion

PRAGMATIC STRANDS AND MULTIPLE AND MIXED METHODS OF RESEARCH

Historically, pragmatists have contributed to the rebuilding of the social sciences, at times directly through their writings and at other times indirectly through their experiments. The essays and books of Peirce, James, Dewey, Mead, and Bentley influenced the conduct of social scientists in the most subtle of ways, broadening their lenses and practicalizing their research goals.

James's support of Thorndike's chicken experiments, as well as personal experimentation with drugs and altered states, opened up methods and refined investigative tools. Dewey's University of Chicago "Laboratory School" was one of the great examples of what pragmatism could achieve for social inquiry and institutional improvement in a society.

Since the 1960s, pragmatism has become even more of a kaleidoscope of views, with some emphasizing it as a route to knowledge; others emphasizing it as a means of clarifying method; another group stressing the role and point of theory; others stressing its religious side; another group stressing its literary, dramatic, and poetic face; and yet another group stressing its reformist and aesthetic perspectives. Each view has had a special place during the past six decades.

While some older and some newer strands of pragmatism lend credence to a methodology warranting the use of multiple and mixed methods in social science research, certain warnings need to be heeded as we begin the 21st century. Much of current philosophy of social science is two-dimensional (syntactic and semantic) rather than three-dimensional, as called for by Peirce. As the prophet of a cybernetic technological future, Peirce pointed out the dangers of an "instrumental reason" that excludes consideration of the transcendental and hermeneutic side of the idea of the community of inquirers constituting a communication community (Apel, 1981).

Following Bernstein (1983), what is needed is mixed or multiple methods of social science inquiry that interlace "techne," or the technical skills of the research viewed as a craft (rather than routines of observation and enumeration where research is seen as a mechanical process); "phronesis," or ethical know-how in which human researchers seek to understand human subjects and their actions from a practical moral perspective; and "praxis," or the mechanisms of deliberation, choice, and decision making regarding what ought to be done—all relative to the concrete problematic situations in which humans find themselves.

What is healthy about a pragmatic social science of mixed and multiple methods is the fact that this effort has opened up the languages of social science. It allows a number of projects to be undertaken without the need to identify invariant prior knowledges, laws, or rules governing what is recognized as "true" or "valid." Only results count! Nor do we require a single foundational discourse of "research methodology" to warrant our activities. "Rationality" need not be affixed to a single overarching method of inquiry, nor do we require that the belief in any method or mixture of methods requires "justification" for the pragmatic interest to win out.

It is vital to see methods of inquiry, whether single or multiple, as necessarily best employed in a "reflexive" manner (Alvesson & Skoldberg, 2000). Mixed and multiple methods have value as they open up the interpretive dimensions of social science research and lay bare the assumptions about the nature of reality, the human mind, and the tools that investigators employ in research. Good research is, given the infusion of the new pragmatic pluralism in research method, not the consequence of increased sophistication at the technical level but rather the consequence of the freeing of the investigative impulses toward a natural and practical refining and reconstruction of the tools of inquiry in light of the larger communal meanings achieved (Campbell, 1992). That such an enterprise is aesthetic is not without significance, for it is rooted in larger purposes, "ways of life," or "traditions" of research as the final arbiters, which themselves must undergo pragmatic refinement or else become nonviable (Smith, 1978).

To its credit, this kind of pragmatic approach to social-behavioral research is prospective. What matters is not the origin of ideas as they have been sensed and reported in research studies but rather the outcomes yet to be realized and yet to be measured (Kaplan, 1964). Pragmatism is not as interested in explanations of anomalous cause-effect cases as in the ways in which practical intelligence may push toward full and free settlement of chaos and discord (Maxcy, 1995). Pragmatic-oriented social-behavioral researchers join hands with rationalists as they seek better reasons for educational policies and arguments. On the other side, they link with empiricists who support a "real world" and some matters as "given." Their unique contribution is to open up inquiry to all possibilities while tying that search to practical ends.

James challenged the mono-methodological idols of research when he wrote, "The truth of an idea is not a stagnant property inherent in it. Truth happens to an idea. It becomes true, is made true by events. Its validity is the process of its validation" (cited in Dickstein, 1998, p. 7). It would be unfortunate during this era of new methodological pluralism to seek to reattach the free spirit of inquiry to the old-line thinking of previous decades. Methodological liberalism needs to be coupled with a free and open philosophy of social-behavioral science and research in which, to paraphrase Peirce, we must "let no method stand in the way of inquiry."

■ Note

1. Philosophy of social science recognizes that, within the literature, the term "methodology" is sometimes used interchangeably for techniques of research, for the so-called "scientific method," for the study of research methods, and for the analysis and understanding of the entire enterprise of social science research. In this chapter, such confusion is made less unbearable by frequent cautionary stipulation.

■ References

Alexander, T. M. (1987). *John Dewey's theory of art, experience, and nature: The horizons of feeling.* Albany: State University of New York Press.

Alvesson, M., & Skoldberg, K. (2000). *Reflexive methodology: New vistas for qualitative research.* Thousand Oaks, CA: Sage.

Apel, K. (1981). *Charles S. Peirce: From pragmatism to pragmaticism* (J. M. Krois, Trans.). Amherst: University of Massachusetts Press.

Barzun, J. (1983). *A stroll with William James.* New York: Harper & Row.

Bentley, A. F. (1935). *Behavior knowledge fact.* Bloomington, IN: Principia Press.

Bentley, A. F. (1954). *Inquiry into inquiries: Essays in social theory* (S. Ratner, Ed.). Boston: Beacon.

Bentley, A. F. (1969). *The process of government: A study of social pressures* (edited with an introduction by P. H. Odegard). Cambridge, MA: Harvard University Press. (Original work published 1908)

Bernstein, R. J. (1983). *Beyond objectivism and relativism.* Philadelphia: University of Pennsylvania Press.

Biesta, G. J. J. (1994). Education as practical intersubjectivity: Towards a critical-pragmatic understanding of education. *Educational Theory, 44,* 299-317.

Boisvert, R. D. (1988). *Dewey's metaphysics.* New York: Fordham University Press.

Brodsky, G. (1982, Fall). Rorty's interpretation of pragmatism. *Transactions of the Charles S. Peirce Society, 18*(4), 311-337.

Buchler, J. (1939). *Charles Peirce's empiricism.* New York: Harcourt, Brace.

Campbell, J. (1992). *The community reconstructs.* Urbana: University of Illinois Press.

Cherryholmes, C. C. (1999). *Reading pragmatism.* New York: Teachers College Press.

Childs, J. L. (1956). *American pragmatism and education.* New York: Henry Holt.

Davis, W. H. (1972). *Peirce's epistemology.* The Hague, Netherlands: Martinus Nijhoff.

Dewey, J. (1897). My pedagogic creed. *The School Journal, 54*(3), 77-80.

Dewey, J. (1899). *School and society.* Chicago: University of Chicago Press.

Dewey, J. (1916). *Democracy and education.* New York: Macmillan.

Dewey, J. (1927). *The public and its problems.* New York: Henry Holt.

Dewey, J. (1929). *The quest for certainty: A study of the relation of knowledge and action.* New York: Putnam.

Dewey, J. (1934). *Art as experience.* New York: Minton, Balch.

Dewey, J. (1938). *Logic: The theory of inquiry.* New York: Henry Holt.

Dewey, J. (1939a). Experience, knowledge, and value: A rejoinder. In P. A. Schillp (Ed.), *The philosophy of John Dewey* (pp. 517-608). New York: Tudor.

Dewey, J. (1948). *Reconstruction and philosophy.* Boston: Beacon.

Dewey, J., with Bentley, A. F. (1949). *Knowing and the known.* Boston: Beacon.

Dewey, J. (1966). Theory of valuation. In O. Neurath (Ed.), *International Encyclopedia of Unified Sciences* (Vol. 2, No. 4). Chicago: University of Chicago Press. (Original work published 1939b)

Dickstein, M. (Ed.). (1998). *The revival of pragmatism: New essays on social thought, law, and culture.* Durham, NC: Duke University Press.

Evers, C., & Lakomski, G. (1991). *Knowing educational administration: Contemporary methodological controversies in educational administration research.* Oxford, UK: Pergamon.

Fay, B. (1987). *Critical social science: Liberation and its limits.* Ithaca, NY: Cornell University Press.

Fisch, M. H. (Ed.). (1982). *Writings of Charles S. Peirce: A chronological edition: Vol. 1. 1857-1866.* Bloomington: Indiana University Press.

Fisch, M. H. (1986). *Peirce, semiotic, and pragmatism.* Bloomington: Indiana University Press.

Garrison, J. W. (1997). *Dewey and eros: Wisdom and desire in the art of teaching* (Advances in Contemporary Thought Series, Vol. 19). New York: Teachers College Columbia Press.

Garrison, J. W. (1998). John Dewey's philosophy of education. In L. A. Hickman (Ed.), *Reading Dewey: Interpretations for a postmodern generation* (pp. 63-81). Bloomington: Indiana University Press.

Hausman, C. R. (1993). *Charles S. Peirce's evolutionary philosophy.* Cambridge, UK: Cambridge University Press.

Hook, S. (1939). *John Dewey: An intellectual portrait.* New York: John Day.

Howe, K. R. (1988). Against the quantitative-qualitative incompatibility thesis or dogmas die hard. *Educational Researcher, 17,* 10-16.

Jackson, P. W. (1998). *John Dewey and the lessons of art.* New Haven, CT: Yale University Press.

James, W. (1890). *Psychology* (Vols. 1-2). New York: Henry Holt.

James, W. (1902). *Varieties of religious experience: A study in human nature.* New York: Longmans, Green.

James, W. (1907). *Pragmatism: A new name for some old ways of thinking*. New York: Longmans, Green.

James, W. (1939). *Talks to teachers on psychology* (Rev. ed.). New York: Henry Holt. (Original work published 1899)

Kaplan, A. (1964). *The conduct of inquiry: Methodology for behavioral sciences*. San Francisco: Chandler.

Lincoln, Y. S., & Guba, E. (1985). *Naturalistic inquiry*. Beverly Hills, CA: Sage.

Margolis, J. (1986). *Pragmatism without foundations: Reconciling realism with relativism*. Oxford, UK: Blackwell.

Marshall, J. D. (1984). John Dewey and educational research. *Journal of Research and Development in Education, 17*(3), 66-77.

Maxcy, S. J. (1991). *Educational leadership: A critical pragmatic perspective*. New York: Bergin & Garvey.

Maxcy, S. J. (Ed.). (1994). *Postmodern school leadership*. Westport, CT: Praeger.

Maxcy, S. J. (1995). *Democracy, chaos, and the new school order*. Thousand Oaks, CA: Corwin.

Mead, G. H. (1936). *Movements of thought in the nineteenth century* (M. H. Moore, Ed.). Chicago: University of Chicago Press.

Miller, D. L. (1973). *George Herbert Mead: Self, language, and the world*. Chicago: University of Chicago Press.

Muelder, W. G., Sears, L., & Schlabach, A. V. (1960). *The development of American philosophy*. Boston: Houghton Mifflin.

Murphy, M. G. (1961). *The development of Peirce's philosophy*. Cambridge, MA: Harvard University Press.

Myers, G. E. (1986). *William James: His life and thought*. New Haven, CT: Yale University Press.

Neurath, O. (Ed.). (1938). *International encyclopedia of unified science* (Vols. 1-2). Chicago: University of Chicago Press.

Outhwaite, W. (1987). *New philosophies of social science: Realism, hermeneutics, and critical theory*. New York: St. Martin's.

Peirce, C. S. (1966). *Collected papers of Charles Sanders Peirce* (Vols. 1-6, C. Hartshorne & P. Weiss, Eds.; Vols. 7-8, Arthur Burks, Ed.). Cambridge, MA: Belknap Press of Harvard University Press. (Original work published 1931)

Pepper, S. C. (1939). Some questions on Dewey's asthetics. In P. A. Schillp (Ed.), *The philosophy of John Dewey* (pp. 371-389). New York: Tudor.

Perry, R. B. (1935). *The thought and character of William James* (Vols. 1-2). Boston: Little, Brown.

Phillips, D. C. (1987). *Philosophy, science, and social inquiry: Contemporary methodological controversies in social sciences and related applied fields of research*. Oxford, UK: Pergamon.

Phillips, D. C. (Ed.). (2000). *Constructivism in education: Opinions and second opinions on controversial issues* (Part 1). Chicago: National Society for the Study of Education.

Popp, J. A. (1998). *Naturalizing philosophy of education: John Dewey and the postanalytic period*. Carbondale: Southern Illinois University Press.

Putnam, H. (1995). *Pragmatism: An open question*. Oxford, UK: Blackwell.

Reichenbach, H. (1939). Dewey's theory of science. In P. A. Schilpp (Ed.), *The philosophy of John Dewey* (pp. 157-192). New York: Tudor.

Rescher, N. (1977). *Methodological pragmatism: A systems-theoretic approach to the theory of knowledge*. New York: New York University Press.

Rockefeller, S. C. (1991). *John Dewey: Religious faith and democratic humanism*. New York: Columbia University Press.

Rorty, R. (1979). *Philosophy and the mirror of nature*. Princeton, NJ: Princeton University Press.

Rorty, R. (1991). *Objectivity, relativism, and truth: Philosophical papers* (Vol. 1). Cambridge, UK: Cambridge University Press.

Rorty, R. (1999). *Philosophy and social hope*. London: Penguin.

Seigfried, C. (1996). *Pragmatism + feminism*. Berkeley: University of California Press.

Shusterman, R. (1992). *Pragmatist aesthetics: Living beauty, rethinking art*. Oxford, UK: Blackwell.

Sleeper, R. W. (1986). *The necessity of pragmatism: John Dewey's conception of philosophy.* New Haven, CT: Yale University Press.

Smith, J. E. (1978). *Purpose and thought: The meaning of pragmatism.* Chicago: University of Chicago Press.

Steffe, L. P., & Gale, J. (Eds.). (1995). *Constructivism in education.* Hillsdale, NJ: Lawrence Erlbaum.

Tashakkori, A., & Teddlie, C. (1998). *Mixed methodology: Combining qualitative and quantitative approaches* (Applied Social Research Methods, No. 46). Thousand Oaks, CA: Sage.

Vanderstraeten, R., & Biesta, G. (1998, August). *Constructivism, educational research, and John Dewey.* Paper presented before the World Congress of Philosophy, Boston.

Ward, J. F. (1984). *Language, form, and inquiry: Arthur F. Bentley's philosophy of social science.* Amherst: University of Massachusetts Press.

Welchman, J. (1995). *Dewey's ethical thought.* Ithaca, NY: Cornell University Press.

West, C. (1989). *The American evasion of philosophy: A genealogy of pragmatism.* Madison: University of Wisconsin Press.

Wiener, P. P. (1965). *Evolution and the founders of pragmatism.* New York: Harper & Row. (Original work published 1949)

Winch, P. (1958). *The idea of a social science and its relation to philosophy.* London: Routledge & Kegan Paul.

Wolfe, A. (1999). The missing pragmatic revival in American social science. In M. Dickstein (Ed.), *The revival of pragmatism: New essays on social thought, law, and culture* (pp. 199-206). Durham, NC: Duke University Press.

3

MAKING PARADIGMATIC SENSE
OF MIXED METHODS PRACTICE

◆ Jennifer C. Greene
Valerie J. Caracelli

W anda Jenkins hurried out of her office building so that she could catch the 1:10 No. 32 bus uptown. On the bus, she reviewed her schedule for the afternoon. Wanda planned to meet with the director of the Brookfield Community Action Agency at 2:30 and then with several members of the Magnolia Tenants Association at 3:30. These were both long-term community organizations, and Wanda hoped that their members could help to fill in local neighborhood history. At 4:30, she planned to drop by the Center Street Youth Alliance and continue her conversations and interactions with the children and youths who spend their after-school and some weekend time in sports and recreational activities there. This youth center was a recently revitalized neighborhood organization that was providing the very heart and soul of Wanda's ethnographic study of under-resourced urban neighborhoods. Wanda's ethnography was focusing on the meanings of racial/cultural/ethnic identity for contemporary urban youths of color and how those identity meanings intersected with the political and economic

AUTHORS' NOTE: The opinions expressed in this chapter represent those of the authors and should not be construed as the policy or position of the U.S. General Accounting Office. The authors thank Leslie J. Cooksy, George Julnes, Robert A. Johnson, and Donna M. Mertens for their insightful and substantive comments on this chapter.

boundaries and relationships that demarcated the youths' communities from the larger society.

Wanda's study was relying on traditional observation and interview methods of ethnographic fieldwork. These methods were invaluable in helping her to understand, interpret, and contextualize youths' cultural/racial/ethnic identities. What being a person of color meant to these contemporary youths was rooted in complex interactions of local history, family heritage, and ever-changing dynamic peer cultures.

Wanda was also experimenting with the integration of geographic information systems (GIS) methodology and data sources into her ethnography. With GIS, she could generate visual aerial maps of her study's neighborhoods and then—in the manner of a walking tour of a neighborhood—insert ethnographic fieldnotes at various spots. More substantively, these GIS maps offered various spatial representations of neighborhoods—highlighting demographic characteristics, public and private resources, health and welfare profiles, patterns of crime and violence, and more—all of which could be studied historically or in comparison with surrounding neighborhoods or other parts of the city. These spatial representations of neighborhoods were enabling Wanda to probe and understand the meanings of political and economic boundaries and relationships—one neighborhood with another and especially marginalized neighborhoods with more mainstream ones—in markedly different ways than was her fieldwork. The combination was potentially very powerful.

◆ Sam Wood hit the "save" key on his computer, pushed his chair away from his desk, and heaved a huge sigh, mixing fatigue with deep satisfaction. He had just completed a first draft—but a very solid and strong first draft—of a paper from his recent study on the "compliance" of medical patients with physician-prescribed special diets and medications. Sam was a junior researcher. His Ph.D. in health services research was 3 years old, and this was his second postdoctoral study. But previously Sam had been a nurse for 10 years, he had worked with hundreds of people on special diets and medications, and he had struggled with the nature and meaning of "compliance" both in his practice and then throughout his graduate education. The conventional wisdom about patient compliance had seemed superficial to Sam, and he had long wondered what else was going on here. His research had engaged this question.

And his recent study had begun to offer some understandings of compliance that Sam believed were superior to prior work. Building on an interaction of both survey work and targeted case studies, Sam believed that these understandings of compliance were *both* meaningfully contextual and respectful of diversity *and* more broadly generalizable and descriptive of patterned regularities in social behavior. Sam was particularly intrigued by the political dimensions of "compliance" revealed in this recent study—dimensions such as the importance of challenging rather than simply accepting expert authority and the valuing of good citizenship and obeying the law. These are complexities of patient compliance long suspected (at least by Sam) but first revealed in such compelling form in Sam's recent study. Perhaps the need to integrate diverse data sources, and (more profoundly) different ways of making sense of the social world, contributed to the big steps forward in the understanding of patient compliance that Sam's study had achieved.

◆ The state's new chancellor of education had decided to mandate annual standardized achievement testing of all students in Grades 3 to 12 (anticipating passage of President George W. Bush's federal educational policy initiative). And Sarah Moore, as director of the state Office of Educational Evaluation, had the difficult job of developing an evaluation plan for her boss's new mandate. While an independent research firm or university was likely to actually do the evaluation, the state wanted to set forth its purposes and directions.

Among the challenges of this task were the many differences that existed among the state's schools, teachers, and classrooms. Any state policy would clearly be implemented and thus experienced differently in the different regions and corners of the state. An evaluation needed to respect and account for this diversity while also providing information at the state level. Another challenge was how the evaluation could meaningfully engage the considerable literature on the merits and limitations of standardized achievement tests as indicators of student learning and of teacher or school "performance" or "effectiveness." Still another challenge was to contend with the complex politics of such a policy initiative. The evaluation had to be positioned delicately so as to engage these political debates while remaining impartial.

Sarah had two thoughts for how to respond to this challenging evaluation context. She could send an owl to Harry Potter and ask for some magic, or she

could think expansively and inclusively about evaluation approaches, methods, and designs.

These applied inquiry scenarios well illustrate the complexities of human activities and the considerable challenges of endeavoring to understand these activities. Developing meaningful stories or finding discernible patterns of regularity amid the infinite variety, contextuality, and contingency of human behavior is indeed a daunting challenge. These applied inquiry scenarios further suggest that one important response to this challenge is to intentionally engage multiple perspectives, diverse ways of knowing and understanding, and varied ways of studying and representing human phenomena. Wanda Jenkins engaged the diverse perspectives offered by ethnographic fieldwork and GIS spatial mapping. Sam Wood juxtaposed the structured, researcher-defined representations of human phenomena generated by surveys with the emergent, contextually defined representations of the same phenomena generated by case studies. And Sarah Moore knew that the acute political sensitivities and far-reaching contextual diversity of her evaluation context mandated a mix of methodological responses.

These researchers were responding to the complexities of their inquiry contexts and problems of practice with a mixed methods approach and, more important, with *a mixed methods way of thinking* (Greene, Benjamin, & Goodyear, 2001). They were openly inviting diverse ways of thinking, knowing, and valuing into their studies toward better understandings of the phenomena of interest. To achieve such understandings, mixed methods inquiry should include not just more valid and credible inferences but also understandings that are broader, deeper, and wiser as well as more multiplistic, more accepting of difference, and more tolerant of uncertainty.

So far, this portrayal of applied social inquiry and of the merits of mixing methods is uncontroversial. Many applied researchers and evaluators today routinely mix methods in their inquiry practice as one valuable way to generate better understandings of inquiry problems. This handbook itself attests to the popularity of mixing methods and to the concomitant need for discussion and guidance on how to conduct mixed methods inquiry in a thoughtful and defensible manner (see also prior work by Brewer & Hunter, 1989; Bryman, 1988; Creswell, 1994; Greene & Caracelli, 1997a; Mark & Shotland, 1987; Ragin, 1989, 1994; Reichardt & Rallis, 1994; Tashakkori & Teddlie, 1998). This chapter then takes up one issue within the continuing discussion on just what constitutes thoughtful and defensible mixed methods inquiry. This issue concerns the nature and role of inquiry paradigms in mixed methods practice. Specifically, when multiple diverse methods are mixed so as to generate better understandings, are paradigmatic assumptions also mixed? And should they be? Is mixed paradigm inquiry sensible, logical, and worthwhile?

Our discussion first elaborates on what we have called *the paradigm issue* in mixed methods social inquiry. Looking at mixed methods practice through the conceptual lens of theory, we set forth several different stances on this issue that represent both support for and opposition to the importance of philosophical assumptions in mixed methods inquiry practice. We illustrate this conceptual discussion with instances of practice. We then shift lenses and look at mixed methods theory through the concrete lens of practice. We share what selected practitioners say and do about paradigms and practice and then use their insights to reframe the paradigm issue in mixed methods inquiry. Directions for future work are also charted.

◆ Considering the Paradigm Issue in Mixed Methods Social Inquiry

As noted, the paradigm issue in mixed methods inquiry refers to the sensibility of mixing paradigms while mixing methods. When a social inquirer uses *both* a survey and a set of case studies in the same study—as does Sam Wood in the earlier vignette—is he or she also using *both* the realist, objectivist, value-neutral perspectives *and* the constructivist, subjectivist, value-engaged perspectives that are characteristic of the survey and case study researcher, respectively? And *should* the mixed methods inquirer mix such paradigmatic assumptions, particularly key assumptions regarding (a) the nature of the social world we endeavor to understand; (b) the nature of the knowledge we can have about that world, including the relationship between the knower and the known; and (c) the purpose and role of social inquiry in society?

There are numerous facets of this issue that have been the subject of much debate in the philosophical and methodological literatures. These facets include the very nature of a paradigm (sparked by Kuhn's [1962] multiple uses of the term within his own revolutionary work), in particular, whether the various attributes or dimensions of a paradigm necessarily cohere. The commensurability or compatibility of different paradigms has also been intensely debated (Guba, 1990; Lincoln, 1991; Sechrest, 1992), as has the requisite binding of philosophy to methodology and thereby to particular methods, for example, postpositivism to experimentation and quantitative methods or interpretivism to case study and qualitative methods (Bednarz, 1985; Howe, 1988, 1998; Reichardt & Cook, 1979). These debates continue, fueled recently by postmodern critiques of both postpositivist and interpretivist inquiry for their misplaced faith in rationalism (Stronach & MacClure, 1997).

This chapter, however, is not intended to further engage these debates. Rather, for purposes of our discussion, we agree with many that paradigms are indeed socially constructions, historically and culturally embedded discourse practices, and therefore neither inviolate nor unchanging. At the same time, we believe that there is some value in considering historically different paradigms and in thinking about each as having its own coherent set of assumptions and stances but not intrinsically bound to a particular set of methods or techniques. Multiple methods can be used, and indeed are strongly encouraged, within most paradigms. We further reject both the continued search for the one best paradigm and the assumed incommensurability of different paradigms as relics of a past era. We are committed instead to the acceptance of difference and the importance of multiple diverse perspectives. The complexity and the pluralism of our contemporary world demand such a commitment.

So, the discussion in this chapter concentrates on how to think about the interface between philosophy and methodology in mixed methods practice. What do we do with our philosophical assumptions and stances when we mix different methods? Some in the mixed methods literature have referred to this set of questions as mixing inquiry models (Tashakkori & Teddlie, 1998), designs (Creswell, 1994), styles (Brewer & Hunter, 1989), or strategies or approaches (Niglas, 2000), as distinct from mixing methods. Again, there is no debate at the technical level of method;

method mixes are welcome in most domains of social research and evaluation. There remains debate, however, at the more conceptual levels of epistemology and philosophy. This chapter reviews and attempts to advance this debate.

Why does it matter? What difference does it make whether or not epistemological and philosophical assumptions can be sensibly and defensibly mixed in inquiry practice? We believe that this constitutes a critical issue for two main reasons. First, we believe that all inquirers approach their work with some set of assumptions about the social world, social knowledge, and the purpose of social research. Whether these assumptions form a formal philosophical paradigm or more of a "crude mental model" (Phillips, 1996; Smith, 1997), the activity of social inquiry requires an image of the situation. Writing about evaluation, Smith (1997) argued,

> It is a useful principle of symbolic interactionism . . . that action is impossible unless one has constructed a mental model, image, or definition of the situation. This claim pertains to the act of inquiry no less than any other social action. A particular evaluation rests on the evaluator's mental picture of what the world is like, what evaluations ought to be, and what counts as knowledge. Because evaluation is social action, an act of inquiry rests also on expectations for what standards the relevant community will likely apply to it. (p. 73)

So, philosophy or crude mental models are an inevitable part of the inquiry process. The question of mixing paradigms or models cannot be avoided. Second, as Smith noted, mental models include "what counts as knowledge" and what standards or warrants are relevant to this determination. The power to determine

TABLE 3.1   Stances on Mixing Paradigms While Mixing Methods

Issue	Stance
Yes, paradigms do matter significantly when making inquiry decisions . . .	
• . . . and all paradigms are valuable and have something to contribute to understanding; use of multiple paradigms leads to better understandings.	Dialectic
• . . . and newer paradigms are superior to older historical paradigms because they invite multiplism in methods and perspectives (e.g., scientific realism, critical social science).	New paradigm
No, paradigms are not critically important in the making of inquiry decisions . . .	
• . . . rather, what matters most is responsiveness to the demands of the inquiry context.	Pragmatic or context driven
• . . . rather, what matters most is conceptual or theoretical congruence, such that inquiry decisions best enable study of the phenomena of interest.	Concept driven

warrantable knowledge claims from unwarrantable ones should never go uncontested. Perhaps the inclusion of disparate warrants, as well as the concept of warrantability, helps to ensure that the voices of the minority are heard—that the claims of the usually silent are voiced.

◆ *Stances on Mixing Paradigms While Mixing Methods*

In previous work, we have delineated several distinct stances on the meaningfulness of mixing paradigms while mixing methods (Greene & Caracelli, 1997b; Greene et al., 2001). In this chapter, we update and again illustrate these stances.

The stances are importantly differentiated along two dimensions. First, do paradigms or mental models or other forms of philosophical assumptions matter in making inquiry decisions? If so, then what about paradigms most importantly matters, and how does it matter? Second, if not, then what else matters in making inquiry decisions? These aspects of this issue are presented in Table 3.1. In the discussion that follows, each of our four stances is elaborated and briefly illustrated.

THINKING DIALECTICALLY ABOUT MIXING METHODS AND PARADIGMS

To think dialectically is to invite the juxtaposition of opposed or contradictory ideas, to interact with the tensions invoked by these contesting arguments, or to engage in the play of ideas. The arguments and ideas that are engaged in this dialectic stance emanate from the assumptions that constitute philosophical paradigms—assumptions about the social world, social knowledge, and the purpose of science in society. In a dialectic stance, these assumptions matter. They importantly guide inquiry activities and frame what sense is made from inquiry findings. Because different paradigms are intentionally included in dialectic mixed methods inquiry, there are contradictory oppositional ideas and forces to contend with. This does not mean that the conversations or dialogues in dialectic inquiry are necessarily *about* philosophical assumptions; rather, these conversations are more productively about the phenomena being studied. But the contradictions, tensions, and oppositions that characterize these conversations are rooted in, and thereby reflect, different ways of knowing and valuing.

Proponents of this dialectic stance thus privilege philosophical assumptions, crude mental models, or ways of seeing and knowing as key influences on inquiry decisions. Methods are selected and other inquiry decisions are made so as to actualize or enact identified sets of assumptions or models. These dialectic proponents, however, do not privilege any one particular set of assumptions or any one mental model or way of knowing. Rather, all are viewed as offering a partial but valuable lens on human phenomena. And dialectic mixed methods inquiry is envisioned as a way of intentionally engaging with multiple sets of assumptions, models, or ways of knowing toward better understanding.

Moreover, the process of reaching this better understanding is dialectical. This is because different paradigms do indeed offer different, and sometimes contradictory and opposing, ideas and perspectives. In dialectic mixed methods inquiry, these differences are valued precisely for their potential—through the tension they invoke—to generate meaningfully better understandings. "It is in [this] tension that the boundaries of what is known are most generatively challenged and stretched" (Greene & Caracelli, 1997b, p. 12). However, the differences that are highlighted in this frame for mixed methods inquiry are *not* historical dualisms that continue to bedevil philosophers, notably subjectivity-objectivity, induction-deduction, relativism-realism, and holism-reductionism. These historical differences are still viewed by many as incommensurable, and they are unlikely to be reconciled in our lifetimes. Instead, the paradigmatic differences that matter in mixed methods inquiry must be "characteristics that importantly define [different] inquiry traditions and therefore warrant our attention and respect, but also that are not logically irreconcilable when juxtaposed with contrasting characteristics" (p. 12)—features such as emic and etic, particularity and generality, social constructions and physical traces, even value-neutrality and value-commitment.

A 3-year evaluation of a controversial science reform in a local high school illustrates the dialectic stance on mixing paradigms while mixing methods (Greene, 2000; Greene & others, 1998). Program goals of this science reform included fostering scientific literacy and developing scientific reasoning, and program activities emphasized hands-on work with content relevant to students' lives. The program also included a "de-tracking" change, merging the high school's two college-bound tracks into one. The pedagogical changes in this program were widely accepted by the Grandview community. However, the de-tracking component of the program met with considerable controversy. A vocal group of opponents to the change was concerned that children would not be adequately challenged in the merged classes or competitively prepared for admission to exclusive colleges and universities. Another group of less vocal supporters was committed to upgrading the educational opportunities for poor children and children of color in the school system. For this group, de-tracking was viewed as an essential reform.

The mixing of methods in the Grandview High School science evaluation was intentionally designed primarily to engage the political controversy surrounding this program. Deliberatively invoking multiple paradigms, program implementation was conceptualized in this evaluation as both fidelity to program design and meaningfulness of experience, as both intellectual challenge/rigor and affirmation of each student's potential to be a scientist, and as both explicable via patterned regularities of pedagogy and understood only in its contextual particularity. Program outcomes were conceptualized comparatively and normatively as well as at the levels of individual and program performance.

The plan was to use the varied results of the diverse methods as a forum for dialogue about differences, especially differences in the underlying value commitments represented by the various methods and results. The methods were chosen to reflect these different conceptualizations. The basic intention of the design was to invite philosophical and methodological difference into the evaluative study as a way to engage the value-based differences that mattered in this contentious context.

The dialogues in this evaluation were not actualized as intended, and the reasons were largely related to values and politics. Differences in value stances and political beliefs were centrally featured in this evaluation, in part because of the intentional mixing of paradigms/belief systems implemented via a mixing of methods. Specifically, methods and results from alternative perspectives (paradigms) were not welcomed into the conversation by those who believed they had the most to lose and thereby rigidly closed their minds to all but their own predispositions. Dialogues were blocked by arguments about methods—arguments that were really proxies for differences in value commitments and priorities (see Greene, 2000). So, although unsuccessfully dialogic, this evaluation does illustrate the dialectic potential of mixed paradigm inquiry.

USING A NEW, MORE EXPANSIVE AND INCLUSIVE PARADIGM AS A FRAMEWORK FOR MIXING METHODS

As noted, we view paradigms as social constructions and thereby as highly mutable and dynamic. A given set of assumptions about reality and knowledge is not sacrosanct; rather, it can be modified, expanded, or constricted—altered to fit changing social understandings and needs. And paradigms do indeed change over time and place. The recent explosion of paradigmatic alternatives in social science clearly substantiates this claim. These alternatives include a reclamation of scientific realism (House, 1991) and of various genres of hermeneutics (Schwandt, 1997), more politically engaged ways of knowing such as feminisms (Olesen, 2000) and critical social science (Fay, 1996), and various accounts of American pragmatism (Bernstein, 1983; Rorty, 1979) as well as the challenging, and sometimes nihilistic, perspectives of postmodernist and poststructuralist thought.

Common to many of these alternatives is a privileging of paradigmatic or philosophical assumptions as important influences on inquiry practice, much like the dialectic stance. While the nature of these influences—and indeed the inquiry decisions themselves—vary widely across the paradigmatic spectrum, many do share a centering of social inquiry around our beliefs and assumptions about the social world and social knowledge.

Relevant to the current discussion, some of these newer paradigms intentionally incorporate a broader set of beliefs and assumptions, and thereby welcome a more diverse set of methods, than do their ancestors. These belief systems endeavor to get beyond old dualisms and incommensurabilities by redefining the nature of social reality and knowledge. One such paradigm is commonsense or scientific realism (Putnam, 1990). In commonsense realism, social reality is *both* causal and contextual, and social knowledge is *both* propositional and constructed. To respect all facets of realism, multiple methods are not only welcomed but actually required.

Proponents of commonsense or emergent realism view its epistemological and ontological foundations as providing a potential rapprochement to the paradigm wars. The key to its encompassing stance is the dual emphasis placed on sensemaking and value probing, with both of these understood as part of a naturalized epistemology. The dictum of a naturalized epistemology is that to understand how we should make sense of our world, it is important first to study how humans actually do make sense of the world. For example, by appreciating the developments of research in cognitive psychology, we recognize that we have multiple ways of understanding causality. As such, rather than accepting only the formal techniques prescribed by one of the competing paradigms, social inquirers can select multiple methods in support of the multiple natural sensemaking capacities of humans. More generally, emergent realism recognizes the contextual complexity and hierarchical structure of the social phenomena that so-

cial inquirers aim to understand. Multiple and mixed methods are used in the service of this framework for the purposes of discovering underlying causal mechanisms, elaborating our understandings by multiple-level analysis, and providing credible evidence for these activities (Julnes & Mark, 1998).

An important instance of a new theory grounded in these tenets of commonsense realism is the sensemaking evaluation theory recently advanced by Mark, Henry, and Julnes (2000). This realist evaluation theory seeks to broaden the range of questions that evaluators ask and thereby the methods that are needed to answer these questions. Qualitative methods are seen as an essential complement to quantitative methods because the factors that determine program success or failure are often far from transparent, and these factors may be hidden or seriously distorted by the simplifying assumptions that are used in formal theories. Both quantitative and qualitative approaches need to recognize that the underlying mechanisms affecting the success or failure of a program may operate at multiple levels of analysis— such as the levels of school, classroom, and the individual student in educational evaluations—and that both mechanisms and outcomes evolve over time as participants, administrators, and others adapt to changing realities. Most important, realist evaluation encompasses the study of values as well as of facts. There is a "dual focus between sensemaking and valuing" (Henry, Julnes, & Mark, 1998). As with other pragmatic approaches, the question of values cannot be avoided because value presuppositions influence the language that evaluators and others use to describe reality. The question of which program outcomes constitute improvements is inherently a question of values, and the answer is often far from obvious. Evaluators, program participants, stakeholders, and others in a community may attach very different valuations to any set of outcomes that might be attained by a program.

Consistent with its emphasis on understanding context, realist evaluation is itself contextual in that the particular methods selected for a particular evaluation will depend on contextual factors such as the purpose of the evaluation and the information needs of stakeholders. As an example, consider an evaluation of a substance abuse treatment program that is proposed as an alternative to the imprisonment of convicted drug offenders in State A. A conventional quantitative evaluation might feature a before-treatment/after-treatment comparison of the extent of drug use and related outcome measures such as criminal behavior, health, and employment—a design that has been frequently applied in this field (see, e.g., Gerstein & Johnson, 2000). A contemporary realist evaluation would go beyond the conventional approach in several respects. First, the evaluation would not be restricted to variables measured at the level of program participants because the mechanisms that are likely to affect program outcomes are likely to operate on a number of levels such as the group of patients who are treated by the same counselor, the service delivery unit (i.e., the location where treatment is administered), and the community within State A. Evaluation designs need to be fashioned to measure mechanisms and outcomes at these different levels, and appropriate analytical methods (e.g., hierarchical linear modeling) should be deployed. Second, the alternative to imprisonment may critically affect the families of convicted drug offenders. In-depth qualitative interviews with family members of program participants seem essential to understand these program effects. Finally, the valuation of the outcomes of the alternative to imprisonment involves complex trade-offs such

as the trade-off between the lower cost of substance abuse treatment and the greater security afforded by imprisonment. The valuations of all persons potentially affected by such trade-offs are highly relevant to meaningful interpretation and use of the evaluation results. A sample survey of residents of State A is one means of improving knowledge about these value dimensions of the problem.

As an example in a different context, the commonsense realist approach to evaluation has been used to design a mix of methods in promoting better policies for supporting the disabled in entering or reentering the workforce. The primary mechanism for informing policy has been the establishment of participatory action research (PAR) groups composed of all relevant stakeholders, including administrators, disabled consumers, employers, service providers, and evaluators. These groups engage in spirited dialogues with different views of current policy obstacles and possible solutions. But recognizing the inherent limitations of sensemaking based only on firsthand experiences, these PAR groups are supported with quantitative data from surveys and from administrative data records. Such data have the potential to confirm or refute some of the groups' conclusions and can even suggest more effective policy solutions. In this case, as well as in others, the methods are not mixed in accordance with a formula or a foundational value. Rather, the concern is with selecting methods that meet the particular information needs of relevant stakeholders in the specific context.

BEING PRAGMATIC ABOUT APPLIED SOCIAL INQUIRY

To the practical pragmatist, all of this philosophical mumbo-jumbo does not get the job done (Miles & Huberman, 1994).

And the hallmark of the philosophical pragmatist is to eschew the "tyranny . . . of the epistemological over the practical, of the conceptual over the empirical," insisting instead on "a mutual adjustment between the two such that practice is neither static nor unreflective nor subject to the one-way dictates of a wholly abstract paradigm" (Howe, 1988, p. 13). In lieu of such dictates, the pragmatic mixed methods inquirer attends to the demands of the particular inquiry context and makes inquiry decisions so as to provide the information needed and maximize desired consequences—"get the job done."

To adopt a pragmatic position means to believe that

> *the essential criteria for making design decisions are practical, contextually responsive, and consequential.* "Practical" implies a basis in one's experience of what does and does not work. "Contextually responsive" involves understanding the demands, opportunities, and constraints of the situation in which the [inquiry] will take place. "Consequential" [means] . . . that the truth of a statement consists of its practical consequences, particularly the statement's agreement with subsequent experience. (Datta, 1997b, p. 34, emphasis in original)

> Pragmatists supplant coherence and correspondence [as criteria for the truth of their knowledge claims] with criteria such as accuracy, scope, simplicity, consistency, and comprehensiveness. (Howe, 1988, p. 15)

And pragmatists characteristically mix different kinds of methods because the complexity of the contexts in which they work demands multiple methods.

Over the past decade, Lois-ellin Datta has offered elegant examples of and reflections on pragmatic mixed methods inquiry in the field of program evaluation. One such example is a 1988 U.S. General Accounting Office (GAO) evaluation on the H-2A Farmworkers Protection program (Datta, 1997a, 1997b). This program was intended to enable farmers to bring in foreign workers willing to work for low wages so as to keep food prices low while still protecting the interests and welfare of resident workers. Datta presented this example as one that meaningfully integrated a full case study (within the tobacco industry) with other methods such as historical analysis of policy documents and administrative records, economic analysis of secondary data on costs and wages, and on-site observations and interviews. With respect to the findings of this mixed methods evaluation, Datta (1997a) maintained,

> Reliance on the interviews, surveys, economic data, and documents would have shown a program with some flaws in reporting that essentially was working as intended. . . . The ethnographic studies showed, however, a more complex picture . . . [in which the resident] local workers believed the farmers did not want them. If they were nominally hired, working conditions would be such as to "run them off the farm." For example, one worker hired in response to an ad for tobacco leaf loaders was told to muck out cow barns, whereas the workers hired under H-2A opportunities were assigned relative lighter work. . . . With regard to nonlocal U.S. workers, the conditions of farmwork were not sufficiently attractive to bring in a reliable labor force to less populated rural areas. . . . [Moreover,] farmers often had well-established arrangements to bring in workers from villages in Central American countries. The villagers

expected to make the yearly trek to the United States . . . , [and they] offered a reliable, docile, and relatively easy-to-access labor force. Further, they were more productive than the mostly older, mostly female U.S. workers who lasted the season. . . . [In short,] without access to special-permit immigrant workers . . . , farmers would have had to change working conditions to attract the largely unskilled labor force from the urban areas, plus take on different supervisory and training responsibilities. The costs of attracting, training, and supervising the larger U.S. unskilled labor pool might raise prices too high, even with federal price supports, for some of the industries using the H-2A program to compete with imported products. (pp. 349-351)

While this evaluation example clearly attests to the value of mixed methods approaches, Datta did not present mixed methods approaches as a panacea to the challenges of complex empirical work. Instead, she drew lessons from this and other examples to recommend the particular conditions under which a mix of methods will add important value or have superior consequences to a monomethod study. This concerted and thoughtful emphasis on consequences is indeed the defining characteristic of the pragmatic stance on mixing methods in applied social inquiry.

More recently, ethnographic methods are being called on in situations where the study of the culture of an organization—understanding the assumptions, beliefs, values, attitudes, and expectations shared by an organization's members (GAO, 1992)—is necessary to fostering change and innovation in that organization. The GAO (1992, 2000a) has identified barriers to culture change as a problem facing federal agencies endeavoring to become high-performance organizations. One planned mixed methods initiative will use case study ethnographies and quantitative survey data to study two Veterans Administration (VA) Medical Centers as they implement patient safety initiatives. The ethnographies will include participant observation, in-depth interviews, and focus groups. The survey will address some of the same questions covered in the interviews and will be distributed to a random sample of center staff. In prior studies, the GAO (2000b) has identified the VA's existing organizational culture as a challenge to its efforts to improve patient safety. The major cultural shift required is to encourage staff to look beyond the blame of the individual and toward system-related solutions to problems. The new initiatives are moving the VA toward a culture of safety (e.g., confidential adverse event reporting), but a more detailed understanding of organizational culture is needed to aid this cultural change and assist in the diffusion of the initiatives. This understanding is viewed as best obtained through ethnographic methods that include multiple and mixed methodologies.

Today, the adaptive stance of the pragmatist position may include features of "futures studies." Although not a discipline per se, this "futures"-based interest in knowledge has emerged in response to a complex set of challenges—societal, technological, economic—that have become apparent with the advent of the 21st century. On the basis of past and present studies, assessments of the future are made and are intended to serve as a basis for societal planning and decision-making activities, including citizens' input. These studies require multidisciplinary theoretical and empirical contributions. For example, developments such as "chaos theory" (Gleick, 1987) and the science of complexity (Waldrop, 1992) provide "new perspectives and possibilities to create new methodologies and use the old ones in a new framework" (Mannermaa, 2000, p. 5).

The pragmatist is theoretically unencumbered by an allegiance to any one specified framework that fits with the idea that futurist studies need to be conceptually broader than any one discipline. Mannermaa (2000) described futurist interest in knowledge with Habermas's old categories: technical, hermeneutic, and emancipatory. The technical refers to the attempt to find invariances and regularities for forecasting and use in rational planning and decision making. The hermeneutic aspects of future studies look toward communication and understanding among people and the creation of a subjective understanding of social reality. The emancipatory interest of knowledge is aimed at establishing a theoretical basis for futures studies through alternative subjective and objective premises. For example, forecasts on objective possibilities are supplemented with studies concerning subjective premises that serve as counterpoints that further support or weaken the forecasted possibilities. The emancipatory study is the most relevant from a mixed methods and pragmatic perspective because it can be used to "not simply study 'probable' developments or increase common understanding, but [such a study also] searches for 'deviating' alternatives and criticizes even strongly dominant beliefs in order to give space to new ideas" (p. 6).

PUTTING SUBSTANTIVE UNDERSTANDING FIRST

Our final stance on mixing paradigms in mixed methods inquiry, like the pragmatic stance, also eschews the restrictions imposed by strict adherence to epistemology. In this final stance, inquiry decisions are made not for their congruence with particular sets of philosophical assumptions but rather for their ability to further the substantive agendas of the inquiries. In this stance, the nature of the concepts being studied leads the inquirer's field decisions.

Now, it is important to note that an inquirer's views of the concepts that she or he is studying are entangled with the inquirer's philosophical understandings and beliefs, for example, beliefs about the intentional or mechanistic character of human behavior, about the socially constructed or externally explicable nature of human meanings and motivations, or about the intertwinement or separability of facts and values. An inquirer must have some "theory" about the problem and program so as to conduct a meaningful study, and this may be the case in more than one of the stances we are illustrating. The inquirer's theory certainly includes epistemological and ontological beliefs. So, the distinction being made here is acknowledged to be somewhat subtle.

In practice, however, the distinction can be marked. It involves the difference between making inquiry decisions so as to honor broad philosophical assumptions *or* to enhance understanding of a particular set of concepts in a particular context. It involves the difference between making inquiry decisions so as to minimize error variance due to differences across study contexts (or, alternatively, to fully understand the complexities and contingencies of each study context) *or* to make better sense of the concepts being studied. In a study of the meanings of racial/cultural/ethnic identity for contemporary urban youths of color, such as Wanda Jenkins's study in the opening vignette, inquiry decisions could be based on the inquirer's philosophical beliefs about all human phenomena as endurable patterned regularities or as contextually constructed, temporary understandings as well as the in-quirer's general beliefs about the place of values in social knowledge claims. *Or,* Wanda could locate the particular phe-nomenon of *minority youth identity* as the central nexus of inquiry decisions. Identity viewed as a developmental, psychological process of becoming might require one set of methods, while identity viewed as a po-litically shaped, culturally shared sense of individual and collective efficacy might in-voke a different set of methods. Identity viewed as complex and multilayered might well demand a mix of different kinds of methods. Again, acknowledg-ing that this difference might be a small one in theory—as one's understandings of concepts are entangled with one's social philosophy or mental model—we main-tain that the difference in practice can be substantial.

Among adherents, leading with theory (both of the problem and of the program) is viewed as advantageous in providing a framework for improving design and in-terpreting results. The theory, however, must be explicit given that different in-quirers use different conceptual frame-works (Lipsey, 1993; Popper, 1979). The reason is that making theories explicit ex-poses the underlying assumptions and value premises to the maximum risk of be-ing uncovered, debated, and tested by oth-ers. Explicit theorizing is simply a tool of communication—a means toward the goal of public awareness. Program theory can provide a structure for integrated ho-listic evaluations using qualitative and quantitative methods (Chen, 1997). For example, the explication of the theory, through the use of a logic model, can serve as a framework for integrating disparate methods, meanings, and understandings (Cooksy, 1999).

Cooksy, Gill, and Kelly (2001) illus-trated how such a framework can be used through the depiction of a multimethod evaluation of Project TEAMS, a middle school curriculum delivery program. The program was intended to integrate into regular classroom activities, active learn-ing strategies, computer access, and inter-disciplinary instruction. The logic model served to focus and organize a diverse set of data collection activities (review of pro-gram documents, teacher and student sur-veys that also included open-ended ques-tions, and parent surveys). As important, the logic model allowed for the interpreta-tions of data from multiple methods and sources within an integrative framework.

In terms of advantages for mixed meth-ods designs, the logic model allowed for evidence from different data sources and data collection methods to be organized by program element rather than by meth-ods per se. Thus, triangulation among sources intended to address a particular program element was facilitated, and con-sistency of findings from different sources and methods could be examined. The logic model also integrated data collection and analysis by allowing evidence on a program element to be viewed in terms of its expected relationships, that is, its an-tecedents and consequences. Last, the logic model served to enrich data interpre-tation by revealing patterns across the middle schools being evaluated. For ex-ample, incongruencies are highlighted rather than suppressed, as illustrated by inconsistent reports about acquisition of computer skills from students, teachers, and parents across schools. More specifi-cally, teachers rated all outcomes highly despite differences in program implemen-tation across schools and discrepancies with student self-assessments of their own skills. Because antecedent conditions such as program implementation issues were taken into account, discrepant out-comes across schools could be observed. Thus, the logic model allowed for a more complete assessment of the value of the evidence. Ultimately, the evaluation was able to identify concerns with program operations and to suggest avenues for program improvement more in line with the theory of how the program was expected to operate.

◆ *What Practitioners Do: Enlightening Theory With Practice*

It is time to turn to the field and ask whether practitioners, particularly mixed methods practitioners, actually use any of these stances in their work. Is mixed methods practice well-characterized by these various stances on the sensibility of mixing paradigms while mixing methods, or is mixed methods practice different in some significant ways? What important light can mixed methods practice shed on this aspect of mixed methods theory?

Studies that address these questions are not plentiful but are provocative. Datta (1994) found that evaluation studies identified as exemplars of "qualitative" and "quantitative" paradigms "seem actually to be mixed models . . . [in part because] people who do a lot of evaluations find out that the world is a complex place, where even an apparently simple question has subtle overtones" (p. 67). So, in practice, "already . . . we merge, combine, mix, and adapt, using the implicit standards in theory to help establish explicit standards for practice" (p. 67). Datta went on to suggest that evaluators need a new paradigm that better captures the actual mixing that goes on in practice so that, pragmatically, paradigms and practice are more in harmony with and reciprocally supportive of one another.

In a small interview study of the inquiry decisions of evaluation practitioners,[1] preliminary findings suggested that philosophical assumptions play a small role at best in evaluation practice decisions, at least on a conscious level. Most respondents offered a pragmatic or responsive portrait of their practice in which they developed evaluation questions, designs, methods, samples, and (later) analyses and interpretations so as to best address the context at hand within the available resources. When pressed, some respondents acknowledged that their understandings of their own practice might well be rooted in their graduate training, in the influences of a key mentor, and even in a philosophical or crude mental model of the world. These influences, however, did not operate at a conscious level for most of the respondents.

As background for her own empirical study, Niglas (1999) referred to several other studies of mixed methods practice.[2] These studies either reviewed published work or interviewed active social researchers to assess the relationship between paradigms and practice. Study findings indicated that applied social inquiry practice was not readily sorted into distinct, conceptually pure paradigmatic stances. Rather, practice was most commonly characterized by blends or mixes of paradigmatic positions, by the absence of explicit or clear relationships between philosophical beliefs and practice decisions, or by the absence of philosophy altogether.

Niglas's (1999) own empirical study sought to examine *"whether particular studies follow clearly only one of two broad methodological approaches [qualitative-interpretivist or quantitative-postpositivist] or do they combine these approaches or mix aspects from both of them in the framework of one study"* (p. 7, emphasis in original). Niglas reviewed all empirical studies (*n* = 46) from the *British Educational Research Journal* for 3 years (1997-1999) and classified six selected aspects of these studies: research aims; overall strategy; sample type; methods for data gathering, recording, and analysis; validation methods; and types of claims— either as clearly "qualitative" or "quantitative" or as "mixed" or "other" (not clear/may be both/not reported). She was particularly interested in whether these inquiry characteristics could be clearly ascertained as derived from a "qualitative" or "quantitative" paradigm and whether there was paradigmatic consistency among these six aspects of inquiry practice.

Among Niglas's (1999) intriguing findings were the following:

◆ The research aims of nearly one half (44%) of the studies, the overall strategy of three fourths (76%), and the sampling of three fourths (74%) could be clearly categorized as qualitative or quantitative. There were 9 studies with mixed research aims, only 2 studies with mixed strategies, and only 4 studies with mixed sampling approaches. The remaining studies were categorized as unclear on these inquiry aspects.

◆ Similar proportions, or from one half to three quarters of the studies, had clear quantitative or qualitative methods of data collection (47%), recording (63%), and analysis (72%). And by contrast, most of the rest— approximately one third—had mixed data gathering, recording, and analysis methods. *That is, there was more clear mixing of methods than of research intentions and overall strategies (and sampling) in these studies.*

◆ Relatedly, Niglas found moderate correlations (around .50) among categorizations of research aims, strategy, sampling, and methods as well as much stronger correlations (around .90)

among methods of data gathering, recording, and analysis.

◆ Cluster analysis yielded four distinct clusters of studies: (a) 11 studies that were qualitative in all aspects; (b) 16 studies that were quantitative in all aspects; (c) 11 studies based on qualitative research strategies, namely case study approaches, used nonrandom sampling methods, but also used mainly quantitative data handling methods; and (d) 8 studies based on quantitative strategies, namely experiments and small-scale surveys, also incorporating some qualitative data and analysis from interviews or open-ended questions on the surveys. These latter two clusters might well represent Creswell's (1994) "dominant-less dominant" mixed inquiry designs in that the overall inquiry strategy is of one type and the specific methods are of a different type.

Niglas (1999) concluded that in this sample, research practice is as likely to commonly blend or mix features of different paradigmatic traditions as it is to use features from only one tradition. Thus, from the viewpoint of inquiry practice, paradigms are not incommensurable. Moreover, it appears to be

> the concrete research problem rather than philosophical position which determines the methodology (or overall strategy) of the study. . . . In addition, within each strategy there is a possibility either to use data gathering methods usually associated with the same approach or to combine the techniques of both types. And finally, there is a possibility to use both quantitative and qualitative data within each study regardless of the overall strategy of the research or the concrete data gathering techniques. (pp. 15-16)

Niglas thus disrupted the idea of necessary coherence among paradigmatic beliefs by suggesting some independence of inquiry decisions regarding design, sampling, methods, and analysis and interpretation. Both qualitative and quantitative alternatives remain available at each decision point, in many cases regardless of prior decisions. This is congruent with House (1994), who noted that even when methods are distinct, "the findings from them blend into one another in content" (p. 17), so that quantitative findings contain qualitative interpretations even if they are not apparent and vice versa.

Yet, citing cautions by Hammersley (1995), Niglas (1999) concluded by critiquing "methodological eclecticism where the primary concern is *fitness for purpose*" (p. 17, emphasis in original). Such an approach to inquiry practice ignores critical differences in underlying worldviews and value commitments, both between major traditions such as interpretivism and postpositivism and within them.

◆ *Conclusion*

In theory, paradigms can matter in mixed methods inquiry. Social inquirers can mix not only different ways of gathering, representing, and analyzing data but also different inquiry strategies or designs along with different philosophical assumptions about the social world, our knowledge of it, and our place within it. In theory, deeper and broader mixes can lead to more generative, insightful understandings. In theory, mixed methods inquiry can be a means for exploring differences; a forum for dialogue; or an opportunity to better understand different ways of seeing, knowing, and valuing.

Based on the small sampling of social research reviewed herein, however, it ap-

pears that paradigms are not the primary organizing framework for mixed methods practice. Rather, applied social inquirers appear to ground inquiry decisions primarily in the nature of the phenomena being investigated and the contexts in which the studies are conducted. Inquiry decisions are rarely, if ever, consciously rooted in philosophical assumptions or beliefs. It further appears that mixed methods social inquirers choose from the full repertoire of methodological options at multiple points in the inquiry process—inquiry purpose, overall design, methods and sampling, data recording, and analysis and interpretation. Many different kinds of mixes are the result (see the multiple, diverse mixed models offered by Tashakkori & Teddlie, 1998), signaling both creativity and a view that paradigm characteristics are not intrinsically bound to particular methods or techniques. Rather, methods and techniques can be crafted and used within multiple, diverse paradigmatic positions.

What does this discrepancy between theory and practice imply? We suggest two implications, both offered as invitations for further conversations among theorists and practitioners alike. First, we express concern that by attending too little to philosophical ideas and traditions, mixed methods inquirers are insufficiently reflective and their practice is insufficiently unproblematized. There is merit in different paradigmatic traditions in that each has something valuable to offer to our understanding of our complex social world. If such differences are not attended to in practice, then the full potential of mixed methods inquiry will remain unfulfilled. We believe that paradigms, mental models, or some other representations of philosophical beliefs and values *should* matter in mixed methods inquiry. The second implication leads us to suggest that it is time to reframe the key issue at hand, from deliberations about the nature and role of inquiry paradigms in mixed methods practice to questions about the legitimate bases for inquiry practice decisions. Advocating for the importance of philosophical beliefs in inquiry practice does not imply a rejection of the importance of context, substantive theory, practical resource constraints and opportunities, and political dimensions of social research as equally important bases for practice decisions. We believe that it is time to examine more closely why and how these various grounds for practice decisions become salient, important, legitimized, and even mixed. It is time to balance the philosophical, conceptual, practical, and political considerations so relevant to our inquiry.

■ Notes

1. This study is being conducted by graduate students at the University of Illinois at Urbana-Champaign under the leadership of Jennifer Greene.

2. Niglas (1999) reviewed empirical work by Firestone (1987), Friedheim (1979), Platt (1986), and Snizek (1975, 1976).

■ References

Bednarz, D. (1985). Quantity and quality in evaluation research: A divergent view. *Evaluation and Program Planning, 8*, 289-306.

Bernstein, R. J. (1983). *Beyond objectivism and relativism: Science, hermeneutics, and praxis.* Oxford, UK: Blackwell.

Brewer, J., & Hunter, A. (1989). *Multimethod research: A synthesis of styles.* Newbury Park, CA: Sage.

Bryman, A. (1988). *Quantity and quality in social research.* London: Unwin Hyman.

Chen, H-T. (1997). Applying mixed methods under the framework of theory-driven evaluations. In J. C. Greene & V. J. Caracelli (Eds.), *Advances in mixed-method evaluation: The challenges and benefits of integrating diverse paradigms* (New Directions for Evaluation, No. 74, pp. 61-72). San Francisco: Jossey-Bass.

Cooksy, L. J. (1999). The meta-evaluand: The evaluation of project TEAMS. *American Journal of Evaluation, 20*(1), 123-136.

Cooksy, L. J., Gill, P., & Kelly, P. A. (2001). The program logic model as an integrative framework for a multimethod evaluation. *Evaluation and Program Planning, 24,* 119-128.

Creswell, J. W. (1994). *Research designs: Qualitative and quantitative approaches.* Thousand Oaks, CA: Sage.

Datta, L. (1994). Paradigm wars: A basis for peaceful coexistence and beyond. In C. S. Reichardt & S. F. Rallis (Eds.), *The qualitative-quantitative debate: New perspectives* (New Directions for Evaluation, No. 61, pp. 53-70). San Francisco: Jossey-Bass.

Datta, L. (1997a). Multimethod evaluations: Using case studies together with other methods. In E. Chelimsky & W. R. Shadish (Eds.), *Evaluation for the 21st century* (pp. 344-359). Thousand Oaks, CA: Sage.

Datta, L. (1997b). A pragmatic basis for mixed-method designs. In J. C. Greene & V. J. Caracelli (Eds.), *Advances in mixed-method evaluation: The challenges and benefits of integrating diverse paradigms* (New Directions for Evaluation, No. 74, pp. 33-46). San Francisco: Jossey-Bass.

Fay, B. (1996). *Contemporary philosophy of social science.* Oxford, UK: Blackwell.

Firestone, W. (1987). Meaning in method: The rhetoric of quantitative and qualitative research. *Educational Researcher, 16*(7), 16-22.

Friedheim, E. A. (1979). An empirical comparison of Ritzer's paradigms and similar metatheories. *Social Forces, 58*(1), 59-66.

Gerstein, D. R., & Johnson, R. A. (2000). Nonresponse and selection bias in treatment follow-up studies. *Substance Use and Misuse, 35,* 971-1014.

Gleick, J. (1987). *Chaos: Making a new science.* New York: Penguin.

Greene, J. C. (2000). Challenges in practicing deliberative democratic evaluation. In K. R. Ryan & L. DeStefano (Eds.), *Evaluation as a democratic process: Promoting inclusion, dialogue, and deliberation* (New Directions for Evaluation, No. 85, pp. 13-26). San Francisco: Jossey-Bass.

Greene, J. C., Benjamin, L., & Goodyear, L. (2001). The merits of mixing methods in evaluation. *Evaluation, 7*(1), 25-44.

Greene, J. C., & Caracelli, V. J. (Eds.). (1997a). *Advances in mixed-method evaluation: The challenges and benefits of integrating diverse paradigms* (New Directions for Evaluation, No. 74). San Francisco: Jossey-Bass.

Greene, J. C., & Caracelli, V. J. (1997b). Defining and describing the paradigm issue in mixed-method evaluation. In J. C. Greene & V. J. Caracelli (Eds.), *Advances in mixed-method evaluation: The challenges and benefits of integrating diverse paradigms* (New Directions for Evaluation, No. 74, pp. 5-17). San Francisco: Jossey-Bass.

Greene, J. C., & others. (1998, June). *Evaluation of the new science program at Grandview High School: Final report.* Report prepared for the Grandview School District, Grandview, NY.

Guba, E. G. (Ed.). (1990). *The paradigm dialog.* Newbury Park, CA: Sage.

Hammersley, M. (1995). Opening up the quantitative-qualitative divide. *Education Section Review, 19*(1), 2-15.

Henry, G. T., Julnes, G., & Mark, M. M. (Eds.). (1998). *Realist evaluation: An emerging theory in support of practice* (New Directions for Evaluation, No. 78). San Francisco: Jossey-Bass.

House, E. R. (1991). Realism in research. *Educational Researcher, 20*(6), 2-9.

House, E. R. (1994). Integrating the quantitative and qualitative. In C. S. Reichardt & S. F. Rallis (Eds.), *The qualitative-quantitative debate: New perspectives* (New Directions for Program Evaluation, No. 61, pp. 13-22). San Francisco: Jossey-Bass.

Howe, K. R. (1988). Against the quantitative-qualitative incompatibility thesis or dogmas die hard. *Educational Researcher, 17* (8), 10-16.

Howe, K. R. (1998). The interpretive turn and the new debate in education. *Educational Researcher, 27*(8), 13-20.

Julnes, G., & Mark, M. M. (1998). Evaluation as sensemaking: Knowledge construction in a realist world. In G. T. Henry, G. Julnes, & M. M. Mark (Eds.), *Realist evaluation: An emerging theory in support of practice* (New Directions for Evaluation, No. 78, pp. 33-52). San Francisco: Jossey-Bass.

Kuhn, T. (1962). *The structure of scientific revolutions.* Chicago: University of Chicago Press.

Lincoln, Y. S. (1991). The arts and sciences of program evaluation. *Evaluation Practice, 12*(1), 1-7.

Lipsey, M. W. (1993). Theory as method: Small theories of treatments. In L. B. Sechrest & G. G. Scott (Eds.), *Understanding causes and generalizing about them* (New Directions for Program Evaluation, No. 76, pp. 5-38). San Francisco: Jossey-Bass.

Mannermaa, M. (2000). Multidisciplinarity, methodologies, and futures studies. *Futures Research Quarterly, 16*(2), 5-20.

Mark, M. M., Henry, G. T., & Julnes, G. (2000). *Evaluation: An integrated framework for understanding, guiding, and improving public and nonprofit policies and programs.* San Francisco: Jossey-Bass.

Mark, M. M., & Shotland, R. L. (Eds.). (1987). *Multiple methods in program evaluation* (New Directions for Evaluation, No. 35). San Francisco: Jossey-Bass.

Miles, M. B., & Huberman, A. M. (1994). *Qualitative data analysis: A sourcebook of new methods.* Thousand Oaks, CA: Sage.

Niglas, K. (1999, September). *Quantitative and qualitative inquiry in educational research: Is there a paradigmatic difference between them?* Paper presented at the European Conference on Educational Research, Lahti, Finland.

Niglas, K. (2000, September). *Combining quantitative and qualitative approaches.* Paper presented at the European Conference on Educational Research, Edinburgh, Scotland.

Olesen, V. L. (2000). Feminisms and qualitative research at and into the millennium. In N. K. Denzin & Y. S. Lincoln (Eds.), *Handbook of qualitative research* (2nd ed., pp. 215-255). Thousand Oaks, CA: Sage.

Phillips, D. C. (1996). Philosophical perspectives. In D. C. Berliner & R. C. Calfee

(Eds.), *Handbook of educational psychology*. Old Tappan, NJ: Macmillan.

Platt, J. (1986). Functionalism and the survey: The relation of theory and method. *Sociological Review, 34*, 501-536.

Popper, K. R. (1979). *Objective knowledge* (2nd ed.). Oxford, UK: Oxford University Press.

Putnam, H. (1990). *Realism with a human face*. Cambridge, MA: Harvard University Press.

Ragin, C. C. (1989). *The comparative method: Moving beyond qualitative and quantitative strategies*. Berkeley: University of California Press.

Ragin, C. C. (1994). Introduction to qualitative comparative analysis. In T. Janoski & A. M. Hicks (Eds.), *The comparative political economy of the welfare state* (pp. 299-319). Cambridge, UK: Cambridge University Press.

Reichardt, C. S., & Cook, T. D. (1979). Beyond qualitative versus quantitative methods. In T. D. Cook & C. S. Reichardt (Eds.), *Qualitative and quantitative methods in evaluation research* (pp. 7-32). Beverly Hills, CA: Sage.

Reichardt, C. S., & Rallis, S. F. (Eds.). (1994). *The qualitative-quantitative debate: New perspectives* (New Directions for Evaluation, No. 61). San Francisco: Jossey-Bass.

Rorty, R. (1979). *Philosophy and the mirror of nature*. Princeton, NJ: Princeton University Press.

Schwandt, T. A. (1997). Evaluation as practical hermeneutics. *Evaluation, 3*(1), 69-84.

Sechrest, L. (1992). Roots: Back to our first generations. *Evaluation Practice, 13*(1), 1-7.

Smith, M. L. (1997). Mixing and matching: Methods and models. In J. C. Greene & V. J. Caracelli (Eds.), *Advances in mixed-method evaluation: The challenges and benefits of integrating diverse paradigms Snizek, W. E. (1975). The relationship between theory and research: A study in the sociology of sociology. Sociological Quarterly, 16*, 415-428.

Snizek, W. E. (1976). An empirical assessment of "Sociology: A Multiple Paradigm Science." *The American Sociologist, 11*, 217-219.

(New Directions for Evaluation, No. 74, pp. 73-85). San Francisco: Jossey-Bass.

Stronach, I., & MacClure, E. (1997). *Educational research undone: The postmodern embrace*. Buckingham, UK: Open University Press.

Tashakkori, A., & Teddlie, C. (1998). *Mixed methodology: Combining qualitative and quantitative approaches* (Applied Social Research Methods, No. 46). Thousand Oaks, CA: Sage.

U.S. General Accounting Office. (1992). *Organizational culture: Techniques companies use to perpetuate or change beliefs and values* (GAO/NSIAD-92-105). Washington, DC: Author.

U.S. General Accounting Office. (2000a). *Managing in the new millennium: Shaping a more efficient and effective government for the 21st century* (GAO/T-OCG-00-9). Washington, DC: Author.

U.S. General Accounting Office. (2000b). *VA patient safety: Initiatives promising but continued progress requires culture change* (GAO/T-HEHS-00-167). Washington, DC: Author.

Waldrop, M. M. (1992). *Complexity: The emerging science at the edge of order and chaos*. New York: Simon & Schuster.

4

CULTURAL DISTANCE, LEVELS OF ABSTRACTION, AND THE ADVANTAGES OF MIXED METHODS

◆ Fathali M. Moghaddam
Benjamin R. Walker
Rom Harré

Two progressive trends in research have converged and are crossing paths at the beginning of the 21st century. The first is a greater concern to incorporate cultural diversity in social science research, toward the identification of etic (universal) and emic (local) features of human behavior, and the second is a concern to incorporate methodological diversity in the social sciences (for related discussions, see Gubrium & Holstein, 1997). However, this fortunate crossing of paths can prove fruitful in the long term only if careful attention is given to at least three

fundamental issues. The first concerns the consequences for methodology of the admission of cultural considerations into the foundations of psychology and of social science research in general. The second concerns the methodological consequences of taking levels of abstraction into account. The third concerns the apparent dichotomy between a natural science methodology, based on publicly observable data, and a phenomenological methodology, based on reports of personal experience. In examining these issues, our main focus is on the discipline of psychology, and our references to positivism or postpositivism as the "traditional paradigm" is in the context of psychology.

The first issue is complicated by the fact that not only have "anthropological" matters been imported into psychology, qualifying the traditional universalistic presuppositions, but mainstream psychology has come to be seen as one culture among others (e.g., the "three worlds" of psychology [Moghaddam, 1987]). Attention to culture has led to different mixtures of methods needed to do justice to the scope of phenomena we now presume to be the proper domain of psychology.

The second issue is related to the first in that there is a methodological tension between seeking knowledge at the highest levels of generality and the rich material that is revealed by research methods that pay close attention to the concrete and lowest levels of abstraction. Similarly, attention to cultural factors limits the scope of research domains from all people at all times and places to those that are local and historically situated.

The third issue is related to both the first and second issues in that the natural science paradigm is deeply interwoven into the culture of mainstream psychology. Paradoxically, the most advanced natural science methodology, brain scanning, depends absolutely on the verisimilitude of participants' reports of their personal experiences.

This chapter has three major sections and is organized around the three themes just noted. Thus, in the first section, we explore the methodological consequences of attending to cultural matters in research. After reviewing the concept of culture and the cultural turn in psychology, we introduce the concept of *cultural distance,* the gap between the culture of researchers and participants, so as to highlight the crucial importance of attending to culture. An in-

tegral feature of the culture of traditional psychology, as well as much research in other major social sciences, is the causal model, which we argue is flawed because it excludes cultural factors. We conclude the first section by considering the specific research domain of aggression and how the addition of qualitative methods contributes to our understanding of the meaning of behavior.

In the second section, we argue for the need to pay greater attention to the issue of levels of abstraction of explanation because it has important implications for the type of methodology most appropriate for a particular study (see also Morse, Chapter 7, this volume). We elaborate this point through more detailed discussions of levels of abstraction in single and multiple cultural domains, paying particular attention to Hardcastle's (1999) concept of functional explanation.

In the third section, we explore an intriguing turn of events: that the cultural biases in traditional psychology, which have meant greater and greater focus on new "hard science" technologies, have in some ways made the discipline more reliant on subjective reports and qualitative methods. Using examples from research in auditory perception and cognitive neuroscience, we argue that the cultural bias toward more "objective" technologies, such as new brain imaging techniques, have made it more important that qualitative methodologies assessing subjective perceptions also be incorporated into the research design. This demonstrates the advantages of mixed methodologies, albeit in unexpected ways.

Our discussions lead to five *interim conclusions* and five *proposals for mixed methods,* designed to bring our discussions to more concrete conclusions. Building on previous discussions concerning scientific criteria, culture, and mixed methods (see Moghaddam & Harré, 1995), these conclusions and proposals underline the proposition that mixed methods have strong advantages that can be realized when the role of culture is explicitly taken into consideration in science.

ON THE MEANING OF "MIXED METHODS"

At the outset, it is important that we clarify our particular approach to the meaning of "mixed methods." Perhaps the dominant approach has been to distinguish between quantitative and qualitative methods and to define as mixed methods any study that incorporates both. Although this distinction may appear simple to apply, in practice many complexities arise. For example, consider a standard laboratory experiment on the impact of heat on aggression in which the level of temperature in a laboratory (independent variable) is manipulated to measure its impact on the level of aggression (dependent variable) a participant shows toward another participant. Such experiments routinely involve interviews with participants and the gathering of qualitative data, sometimes as a check to see how well the experimental manipulations worked. Given that the qualitative data do feed back into the results in one way or another, is this type of experiment mixed methods? While some would answer "no," others would agree the answer is "to some extent." But what threshold has to be passed before such a study is accepted as mixed methods? We raise these questions to point out that even the "simple" interpretation of mixed methods as involving quantitative and qualitative methods employed in the same study can

be problematic (see Teddlie & Tashakkori, Chapter 1, this volume).

An additional, rather than a competing, interpretation of mixed methods is that it involves a variety of quantitative and qualitative methods adopted by *different* researchers in *different* studies but focusing on the *same* research phenomena and questions. Thus, for example, we discuss the case of aggression as an area in which this is taking place, and we point out that the recent addition of qualitative (discursive) methods to the traditional quantitative ones, albeit by different researchers, holds the promise that we will arrive at a better idea of *meaning* in relation to aggressive acts.

This second interpretation of mixed methods takes as the unit of analysis the whole body of research addressing a particular research question rather than just a single study. Thus, the question becomes "Are researchers *as a group* studying aggression using mixed research methods?" rather than just "Were mixed methods used in this single study?" We believe that the alternative "group-based" interpretation of mixed methods is also essential because the research enterprise is a collective one, which generates a view of some aspect of the world through multitudes of contributions. It is of great value if these contributions adopt a variety of quantitative and qualitative methods, even if any given single contribution is not adopting mixed methods in and of itself. This "holistic" interpretation of mixed methods is also more in line with the cultural perspective we adopt, with culture itself involving collective, shared, and collaboratively constructed processes. Thus, in discussing the advantages of mixed methods in relation to culture, we have in mind a wider interpretation of mixed methods, one that considers the methods mix of a whole research literature as well as single studies.

◆ Methodological Consequences of Attending to Cultural Matters

THE CULTURAL TURN IN PSYCHOLOGY

An important development in psychology since the 1970s has been the increasing importance of culture in how we see the scope of psychological research. This is clearly indicated by the enormous number of publications that espouse a cultural perspective (see Moghaddam, 1998). Even mainstream texts in psychology typically now have special boxes inserted in strategic places, highlighting "cultural cases" and discussing aspects of life outside of Western (typically American) White middle-class urban culture. Culture has to be taken into account. Parallel to this movement, there is more acknowledgment that research itself takes place in a cultural context.

What Is Culture? For a working definition of culture, we presume that a culture is a normative system, integral to which are norms, rules, and other indicators of how people should "behave" in particular roles and particular places. For example, in the United States, the normative system indicates how Joan Smith, a professor, and Jim James, a student, should interact in the classroom. Here, it is clear that the culture influences what the people do as to what it is proper or desirable to do. If Mr. James wants to ask Dr. Smith a question in class, there are particular ways he should behave. He should put up his hand, wait to be called on, and then ask a question. There are other ways he should not behave. He should not shout and interrupt Dr. Smith while she is talking with another student. The normative system of another culture would endorse a different pattern of classroom behavior. For example, in some Islamic countries, it would not be appropriate for a male student to be taught by a female professor. If male and female students sit in the same class, a curtain would separate them.

The Culture and the Individual. By its very nature, culture is social, shared, continually changing, collaboratively constructed, and collaboratively sustained (Moghaddam, 2002). Individuals appropriate cultures as they grow up in a society. Not only do they behave in ways demanded by local norms, but they come to have culturally distinctive subjective and private experiences. For example, how a sound is heard will depend on all sorts of cultural matters, including the local musical conventions.

The cultures people appropriate are already there when people are born into the world, and they will be there when people leave. The cultures of the Amish in Pennsylvania, the White Anglo-Saxon Protestants in Philadelphia, and the Irish in Boston continue to survive the comings and goings of particular individuals. Shaping individuals, cultures are shaped by individuals. This is the pervasive phenomenon that Giddens (1984) called "double structuration." Cultures continually change. They are sustained in being by the very people whose actions they influence, just in the doing of those very actions, albeit never in exactly the same manner.

Scientific Paradigms as Cultures. Nothing stands outside of culture, not even the scientists or the scientific methods adopted in science. Cultural meaning systems allow scientists to develop and use research methods as well as to recognize and interpret data. At the same time, as paradigms, such meaning systems constrain the scope of what is acceptable as science. This means that both the research psychologists and the persons being studied are in important ways influenced by culture. How, then, can psychologists come to an accurate understanding of the persons they are studying given that the psychologists themselves see the world through a cultural lens?

Accommodating Culture in Science. How should we blend cultural matters into a scientific research methodology? In addressing this important question, we put forward two main propositions. First, we propose that in collecting evidence and interpreting findings, researchers should give full and serious consideration to the role of *cultural distance,* which refers to the difference between the culture of the researchers and that of the participants in the research projects on which the investigators are embarked. Second, we show how researchers can better cope with the opportunities and limitations imposed by the recognition of the role of culture in the realm of human thought and action through adopting mixed methodologies.

Although the concept of cultural distance is our innovation, we believe that this concept has been implicit in various critical discussions about the shortcomings of mainstream psychology and particularly the methods used therein (e.g., Cole, 1996; Fox & Prilleltensky, 1997).

CULTURAL DISTANCE BETWEEN PSYCHOLOGISTS AND PARTICIPANTS

Since the 1980s, there has been increasing criticism of the "wholesale" exportation of psychological science from Western to non-Western societies (Moghaddam, 1987). One basis for this critical attack is the ethnic gap between researchers, who are for the most part White, middle-class Western males living in affluent urban centers of industrial societies,

and the majority of the people in non-Western societies, who are relatively more rural, illiterate, materially poor, and religious (Moghaddam & Taylor, 1985). This line of criticism is coupled with attempts to develop "indigenous psychologies" that are more in line with local needs (Sinha, 1997).

This is a striking example of the fact that both the culture of respondents and the culture of researchers and research disciplines need to be taken into consideration. Researchers select and approach research topics from particular cultural perspectives and are influenced by the normative systems of their own cultures. The research topics they select, as well as the research methods they adopt, are selections from an indefinitely extensive repertoire of possibilities influenced by their own cultures.

Three Examples of Cultural Distance. In the 21st century, it is very popular to examine brain activity and to try to explain behavior as a function of such activity. This approach is an aspect of Western assumptions about the relation between brain processes and patterns of behavior as well as the particular stage of technological development reached in the West. People in other cultures, such as the Yanomamo in northern Brazil and the Bahktiaris in Iran, or people in medieval Europe would find it very strange that discovering the sites of brain activity, as indicated by functional magnetic resonance imaging (fMRI), and correlating this with types of behavior should tell us anything about why humans do what they do. Many such peoples explain what people do by reference to social situations and sometimes supernatural causes. Even within Western social sciences, there are subcultural differences in presuppositions, such as the number of respondents it is "correct" to include in a study, as well as broader methodological differences between those adopting nomothetic generalizing approaches and those adopting idiographic individualizing approaches.

Cultural distance between researchers and participants was also highlighted by feminist psychologists and continues to be a major theme of feminist critical writing (e.g., Wilkinson, 1996). Most famously, Bem (1974) argued that measures of gender roles developed by men are not a valid technique for "measuring" androgyny, and Gilligan (1982) argued that tests of moral development constructed by Kohleberg and other men do not accurately reflect moral thinking in women. Mertens (Chapter 5, this volume) cites other examples from feminist scholars as well as examples from minority scholars and scholars with disabilities.

In a recent study demonstrating the importance of the cultural distance between psychologists and participants, Weinfurt and Moghaddam (2001) explored how six groups of respondents (English Canadians, French Canadians, Jews, Greeks, Indians, and Algerians) answered questions on the Bogardus Social Distance Scale. This technique has a long history (Bogardus, 1925). Respondents are asked to indicate the extent to which they are willing to have a member of a different group (e.g., Jews, Indians, Algerians, English) (a) marry into their group, (b) be a close friend to them, (c) be a next-door neighbor, (d) work in the same office, (e) be a speaking acquaintance, (f) be a visitor to their nation, and (g) be barred from their nation. The answers are supposed to indicate the degree to which members of different social categories are socially distant from one another.

One of the assumptions of the Bogardus scale is the ordering assumption: that the relative ordering of the seven categories in terms of social distance is the same for all respondents in all cultures.

Like most such scales, the Borgardus scale tested its assumptions in a particular cultural context, specifically the United States—an individualistic industrial society with a long history of immigration and high geographical mobility. In such a society, the interpretation of "family," "neighbor," and so on would be very different from how such terms are interpreted in more traditional societies with more static populations. Weinfurt and Moghaddam (2001) discovered that the closer the culture of the respondents to the culture of the researchers and the original samples, the more they shared the same assumptions. When the respondents were from a culture that was a greater distance from the culture of the researchers (i.e., Algerian and Indian), their responses tended more to reflect different assumptions.

Of course, these are just a few recent examples of a well-established problem: how to take account of a cultural distance. When tests developed by Western researchers using one set of samples are assessed in non-Western contexts with non-Western samples (for other examples, see Tashakkori, Barefoot, & Mehryar, 1989; Tashakkori & Kennedy, 1993), the test may bear little relation to psychological reality.

The idea that research methods and instruments are influenced by cultural distance is not new, nor is it novel to assert that researchers from a particular culture will tend to share certain assumptions about the world that are different from assumptions of people in other cultures. Cross-cultural researchers have taken some steps to try to bridge such differences, using back-translation procedures, developing culturally equivalent questions, using more elaborate sampling methods, and so on (see Moghaddam, 1998, chap. 2). The effect of these moves is to obscure the deep problem of cultural distance in psychological phenomena as created in the interpretations of Western psychologists and as lived by indigenous participants who may be radically different. The cultural distance between the researchers who construct measures and conduct a study and the respondents who are studied still tends to be neglected, even though it is of fundamental importance.

Can mixed methods offer a solution? In examining this question, it is important to realize that mainstream psychology is not a benchmark from which other cultures diverge and to which they must be accommodated. Cultural distance is a symmetrical relation. Middle-class American culture, of which the culture of mainstream psychology is but a species, is as distant from Buddhism and its dependent psychology as Buddhist psychology is from middle-class American culture.

MAINSTREAM PSYCHOLOGY AS ITSELF AN INDIGENOUS CULTURE

Cultural distance between psychologists and the participants in their studies is maintained and exaggerated by the peculiarities of the culture of mainstream psychology. Implicit norms are maintained through the participation of individuals in regular social practices. Consider, for example, just two norms within this culture. One concerns the setting of the criteria for statistical significance as $p < .05$ and $p < .01$. The other specifies the "correct" number of respondents that a research study must include to be an acceptable contribution to "science."

In nearly all psychological journals, it has become customary for researchers to report findings as "statistically significant" if the probability of their findings is computed to be less than .05 and to (wrongly) treat them as "highly significant" if it is less than .01. Even though these cutoff points are arbitrary (after all,

there is no objective reason why the cutoffs should not be .075 and .015 or any other of an infinite set of possibilities), they are collaboratively maintained through an array of social practices involving "data gathering," "report writing," "journal publishing," and so on. Interestingly, $p < .05$, $p < .01$, and $p < .001$ all are answers to one question: "Has this phenomenon come about by chance?" They provide no information about the magnitude of effects, about the relationships between the conditions and the observed outcome, or about the nature of the psychological process that has brought them about. "Highly significant" and "significant" are cultural constructions.

Consider another pervasive norm in psychology. It concerns the number of respondents that "must be" included in a participant panel for a psychological study to be considered "correct." The number considered correct varies considerably across subdisciplines. In social psychology, a sufficient number is typically taken to be 80 to 100 or more. In developmental psychology, the sufficient number is taken to be 10 to 15 or more. Why this difference? Why should it not be 500 or more in social psychology and 1,000 or more in developmental psychology? Clearly, these numbers are scientifically arbitrary. They are not based on objective criteria. Rather, they have evolved out of social conventions and demands of practicality and convenience. Naturally such social conventions can and often do evolve to be different in each subdiscipline. For example, it is relatively easy for academic researchers to involve 80 to 100 students in their research, so social psychologists typically include at least this number of respondents in their studies. On the other hand, 10 to 15 infants is a convenient number to get ahold of, so this is the number considered to be satisfactory for studies in developmental psychology. On the

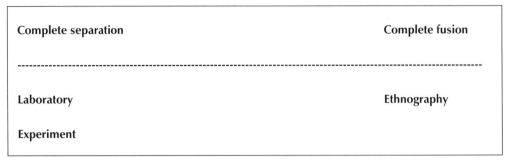

Figure 4.1. The Traditional View of Culture and Research, as Depicted by a Continuum Showing Two Extremes of Complete Exclusion of Culture From Research Methods to Complete Fusion of Culture and Research Methods

basis of objective criteria, one may well argue that the number of respondents required in developmental studies should not be any different from the number required in social-psychological studies.

There were about 6.5 billion humans at the last count. So, a sample of 50 or 200 or more is scientifically worthless unless one already believes in a deep cultural and biological uniformity across the whole of humankind. If one has this belief, then there is no point in studying 50 rather than 1!

The origins of these culture-defining norms have been traced by Danziger (1990). They have their roots in extra-scientific exigencies such as the needs of army recruitment and mass education policies.

HOW MAINSTREAM RESEARCH METHODS EXCLUDE INDIGENOUS CULTURES

For convenience, we use the expressions "local culture" and "exotic culture" in referring to the foundations of mainstream psychology and to the norms of other cultural systems, respectively.

Human Sciences Distinguished by Degree of Inclusion of Explicit Cultural Factors.

An important goal in traditional research has been to include only very small and controlled aspects of exotic culture in research methods when studying human behavior. That is, typically all of the "variables" are controlled except for the independent variable(s), and in this way indigenous culture is automatically kept out while the culture of researchers is included, even in the very idea of psychological research. We can conceptualize this as a range of possible ways of interpreting the intrusion of "cultural context" to research methods, with "complete separation" at one extreme of the continuum and "complete fusion" at the other extreme (Figure 4.1).

According to the traditional view, either culture is completely excluded or only one or two elements of culture are included in the research context, and this allows for an isolation of cause-effect relations. In essence, except for the selected aspects of culture that are included to serve as independent variables, the rest of culture becomes a group of "nuisance" variables that have to be controlled and excluded from the study. We have pointed out that the traditional view focuses exclusively on the culture of the respondents and neglects the culture of the research discipline and the researchers themselves.

An alternative approach encourages us to think more critically about the various cultures of participants and researchers when considering various research methodologies (see Maxcy's discussion of "methodological pragmatism" in Chapter 2 of this volume).

Interim Conclusion 1

Realizing that cultural distance is symmetrical throws doubt on the current hegemony of Western research methods and the associated psychological concepts because these are themselves culture bound. Is there a way in which a fruitful balance between local and exotic cultures could be struck?

Mixed Methods Proposal 1

The common distinction between quantitative and qualitative methods does not apply to the resolution of the problems posed by the recognition of the ubiquity and symmetry of cultural distance. The traditional Western methods of research presume an *etic* or abstract, culture-free, and therefore universal conceptual system, which we now see as local and culture bound or actually *emic*. The problem is to devise a way of integrating two or more emic systems for analyzing, categorizing, and explaining psychological phenomena.

Catherine Lutz's deservedly famous study of an exotic emotion system (Lutz, 1988) could serve as an exemplar of how to achieve a mixing of methods considered as indigenous cultures. She presented the American emotionology as it would be expressed (with difficulty) in the concepts of the Ifaluk system and presented the Ifaluk emotionology as it would be expressed (with difficulty) in the concepts of American English. By studying both presentations, the English-speaking reader arrives at an intuitive understanding of "how the Ifaluk system goes." By the same token, if the whole text were in Ifaluk, then an Ifaluk speaker could get an intuitive grasp of "how the American system goes."

THE CAUSAL PARADIGM EXCLUDES CULTURAL FACTORS

Consider the following methodological advice:

> Whether you use a randomized laboratory experiment or any other technique, you must satisfy three criteria if you are to infer that one variable (smiling at others) causes a change in another variable (others helping you). Specifically, you must establish covariation, temporal precedence, and control of irrelevant factors. (Mitchell & Jolley, 1992, p. 367)

The preceding statement is quoted from the text *Research Design Explained*, but it could have been derived from any one of hundreds of other social science texts on research design published during the past half century that follow a traditional positivist view of causation in human behavior. In discussions of research methods, it is commonly understood that experimental designs are the only designs that may provide the opportunity for causal inference. But this understanding is often set aside in practice through correlational studies being incorporated in discussions of causal models of behavior. Even in traditional social psychology, the goal of research is stated as the discovery of the causes of behavior (see Moghaddam, 2002), and correlational studies are cited and appropriated, albeit indirectly, as part of the causal model.

The traditional assimilation of a correlational finding to a causal account has persisted in psychology despite the fact that this specification of causality does not represent the way this notion is used in the natural sciences or how it is used in the management of everyday life. There would need to be a good working hypothesis—or, best of all, a good working model—of the intervening productive process by which the effect event or state was generated on the occasion of the occurrence of the cause event or state for a correlation even to *indicate* the possible existence of a causal process. The rule or convention a person is following consciously cannot be the cause of what that person does. For a start, it does not necessitate the action. Rules, unlike causal processes such as gravity, can be disobeyed, ignored, disrespected, flouted, and so on (Wittgenstein, 1953).

It is commonplace that cultures differ in the rules that are in play in maintaining the orderliness of the actions of the members. If causation displaces rule following as the ubiquitous paradigm of psychological explanation, then cultures as systems of rules, customs, and conventions are thereby excluded.

There are cultural differences between the *contexts* in which orderly behavior occurs as well as between the processes by which such behavior is controlled and monitored. This neglect is in spite of at least passing reference to "cultural context" in discussions of research methodology and design.

LOGICAL LIMITATIONS ON THE CREATION OF VARIABLES

To get correlational results, we must create variables—attributes that take different values in different circumstances in the same person, different values in different circumstances in different people, and so on. Variables are not given. They are constructed by analysis of patterns of be-

havior and the nature of the circumstances in which it occurs. The initial identification of psychological aspects of a situation must be in the vernacular.

Any attempt to detach features of the antecedent conditions of human actions and thoughts from the complex environment in which they occur, or to partition that environment into elements that could serve as independent variables, must pay strict attention to Vygotsky's Rule (Vygotsky, 1962, 1978). The rule forbids the partitioning of a psychologically relevant situation or a psychologically meaningful pattern of behavior into units that drop below the level of meaning of the whole. The idea of internal relations between the parts of a complex is not new. In modern times, we owe to Hegel the idea that any phenomenon derives parts of its characteristics to the context in which it exists. More recently, Gestalt psychologists popularized the edict that "the whole is more than the sum of its parts," proposing that behavior must be studied in relation to context. In the developmental domain, Vygotsky made the issue more explicit. To accomplish the plan for the kind of experimental design described previously, one must be able to partition the actual situation into components that could serve as independent and dependent variables. In accordance with Vygotsky's Rule, these components must retain their original significance and efficacy when detached from the structural totality in which they usually exist, or else the original phenomenon is not being studied. The topic of research, perhaps some aspect of remembering, is defined only relative to some such totality. These structural totalities, such as a legal trial in which a certain kind of remembering is demanded, are cultural objects. It follows that if we continue to be constrained by Vygotsky's Rule, the components manipulated in an experiment are relative to the culture in which the original structure is a meaningful phenomenon.

For example, in the debate between van't Hoof and Leach on the nature of smiling (see Hinde, 1972), van't Hoof tried to partition smiles into kinds depending on the musculature involved in their production. This gave him two kinds of smiles. Experimental smile research might involve using this two-member set as the independent variable. Leach argued that smiles cannot be partitioned into kinds independently of the cultural context in which they occur. He conjectured that, given the cultural context, there are probably at least 59 kinds of smiles if we admit cultural context into the domain of the study.

Interim Conclusion 2

Admitting cultural factors into research design puts the correlational method and the associated causal hypotheses of mainstream psychology into question. Is there a way of fruitfully mixing causal and normative or rule-following explanation formats?

Mixed Methods Proposal 2

Clearly, neither explanation format can be reduced to a species of the other. However this is just the kind of situation in which we can invoke the concept of complementarity from quantum physics to suggest a way forward. Wave analysis and particle tracking are two radically different research methods. Niels Bohr showed how they can be mixed fruitfully. Any human activity has three aspects apropos of our coming to understand the sources of its orderliness. There is a causal aspect, for example, the cough reflex. There is a conventional or customary aspect, for example, the use of the cough to discreetly attract someone's attention. And there is the habitual aspect, for example, the nervous cough that derived originally from consciously clearing one's throat to conform to the norm of clear speech. The totality of the field of phenomena denoted by "the cough in human life" can be captured only by the juxtaposition of three *complementary* explanatory modes. In just this way, the totality of the domain of the phenomena denoted by "electron-matter interactions" can be captured only by juxtaposing two complementary explanatory modes: the one based on the particle model and the other one based on the wave model of the nature of electrons.

AGGRESSION: A RESEARCH DOMAIN ALREADY USING A VARIETY OF METHODS

What Is the Domain of the Term Aggression? What do we mean by aggression? At first consideration, this seems like a typical academic question, prodding us to provide a definition of a term. For example, this question could lead us to visit a traditional definition such as "Aggression is behavior intended to harm another person." However, when we ask the question "What is aggression?" in cultural context, we are confronted by a more complex picture, in part because of the complexities involved in deciding intent. How exactly do we know that Person A intended to harm Person B?

Consider the case of Salman Rushdie, the author of *The Satanic Verses*. Rushdie, a Pakistani author living in England, was accused by the Iranian leader Ayotollah Khomeini of blasphemy and attempting to harm Islam. Millions of Muslims in Islamic countries, and thousands in Western societies, demonstrated in support of the death sentence issued by the Ayotollah against the author. From their viewpoint, Rushdie had committed an unforgivable act of aggression. However, from the perspective of Western democracies and supporters of fundamental human rights such as freedom of expression, it was the Ayotollah who was the aggressor. By inciting demonstrators who burned books and shouted "death to Rushdie," the cleric was intending to harm an author who was simply exercising his basic rights as stipulated in the *Universal Declaration of Human Rights*. Such cases clearly show that even though we might adopt specific definitions of aggression such as "behavior intended to harm others," what we identity as aggression depends on our cultural viewpoint.

The Variety of Methods in Use. The topic of aggression is particularly suitable for demonstrating the advantages of mixing quantitative and qualitative methods because each approach provides an interesting but incomplete picture. For our purposes, it is useful to contrast traditional quantitative methods with alternative qualitative methods. Quantitative methods are far better known and have already been discussed extensively, including neurophysiological ones focusing on chromosomal abnormality and aggression (Witkin et al., 1976), "aggression centers" in the brain (Moyer, 1976), the biochemistry of the body and aggression (Nelson et al., 1995), genetic similarity (Chagnon, 1992; Daly & Wilson, 1990), and heat and aggression (Anderson, Anderson, & Deuser, 1996). A wide range of quantitative social-psychological methods have also been employed, focusing on explanations in terms of conflicts of interests over resources (Sherif, 1966), explanations by reference to a "culture of honor" (Nisbett & Cohen, 1996), and a search for a more positive social identity (Tajfel & Turner, 1979). These studies adopting quantitative methods attempt to attain a high level of objectivity and detachment, but they

nearly completely neglect the issue of meaning: How do participants interpret the situation, and what meaning do they give to actions? The issue of meaning is more directly addressed through qualitative research, which has received far less attention than it deserves in psychology.

Discursive Analyses in Terms of the Meanings of Aggressive Acts. Billig (1978) and others have shown that a critical involvement with the participants themselves can be more fruitful. In his study of the National Front (an extremist right-wing paramilitary organization in the United Kingdom), Billig demonstrated that it was not enough to used standardized questionnaire procedures and rating scales that yielded "objective" numbers because members of the National Front would intentionally deceive the researcher. To really understand what the participants were up to, it was necessary for Billig to conduct interviews from a critical perspective and rely on qualitative data, which then had to be interpreted in context and with reference to the larger political situation.

According to the methodology of discursive psychology, the job of the psychologist is to find the meanings of actions and to classify them according to some plausible model. That done, it is possible to try to discern the norms that are effective in regulating the action.

Among the qualitative approaches that have attempted to adopt this more critical approach are studies in discursive psychology such as the research into the nature of football hooliganism in the United Kingdom (Marsh, Rosser, & Harré, 1978). Each Saturday afternoon, literally thousands of young men take part in large-scale aggressive displays. The study was based on the analytical method, recording and analyzing many examples of these complex events. The research was aimed at solving three problems. The first concerned the meaning of the aggressive or seemingly aggressive acts to the participants, to the bystanders, and to members of the general public who encountered these acts only in newspaper descriptions. The second concerned the explanation of the regularity and precision of the repetition of extremely complex sequences of acts on occasion after occasion. The third concerned the social order that was both required and created by these events.

The overall model was dramaturgical, taken from Burke (1969) and Goffman (1959). Riots were viewed as if they were the staging of dramas, with actors, costumes, scenes, directors, audiences, and scripts. Within this general frame, another more fine-grained model was inserted: the model of ritual. These acts rarely resulted in serious physical injury but were highly effective in transforming the social rankings of those engaged. Honor played a very large part in the interpretation of the performance of any of the many young men engaged in ritual combat. The ancillary model of a medieval joust also proved useful.

Interim Conclusion 3

Understanding social phenomena in-depth inevitably involves research into the meanings of social actions for the participants themselves. In the case of aggression, a combination of research into the physical and physiological conditions of propensities to aggression with studies that lead to an understanding of the particular social forms and social motivations of aggressors is indispensable.

Mixed Methods Proposal 3

The distinction between the conditions under which a psychological phenomenon occurs and the particular form it takes provides a natural unity between the use of quantitative methodologies and discursive analyses of meanings. The form can reveal everything from economic conditions, to the state of the material environment, to the genetic makeup of people prone to aggression. The form of the social phenomenon highlights the structure of actions and their social consequences. Both should be part of the standard repertoire of social psychologists in particular.

◆ Mixing Methodologies at Different Levels of Abstraction

LEVELS OF ABSTRACTION AND ATTENTION TO CULTURE

In addition to the *type* of explaining one wants to accomplish when crafting an explanation of a phenomenon—causal or normative—one should also be concerned with the level of abstraction of that explanation. At a high level of abstraction, culture is irrelevant. This is the domain of etic studies. For example, brain laterality is an etic property of the human organism. At the more concrete level of the distinction between left- and right-handedness, cultural factors are relevant as well. For example, the explanation of the proportion of left-handed people in a population needs to take account of local attitudes to sinistrality. The type of explaining changes as one moves from one level of abstraction to another. Any change in explanation type requires additional supporting evidence for the new hypotheses (see Morse's discussion of the "triangulation of results" in Chapter 7 of this volume).

At higher levels of abstraction, we create universal generalizations that encompass the broadest domain of the phenomenon in question. Explanations at this level are usually correlational and therefore scientifically weak. To explain the phenomenon at lower levels of abstraction, we need to create more complex and more concrete and realistic explanatory models. As we step through the levels of analysis to ever decreasing degrees of abstraction, models of the explanatory mechanisms become ever more concrete and detailed. The "mechanisms" invoked may be based on very different processes from those to be observed in the phenomena they are used to explain. For example, differences in colors are explained by reference to wavelengths of electromagnetic radiation and ultimately by the physics of photons. We must use additional methodology that examines the phenomenon from tangential viewpoints. Information gathered from these additional methods gives our models increased explanatory power.

This point can be illustrated by the search for explanations of cognitive skills by reference to brain function in the neurosciences. At the highest levels of abstraction, the claim can be made that brains are for thinking in general. It was not always obvious to biologists that this was generally so. But species of thinking, such as calculating, are cultural artifacts. For example, Australian Aboriginals used only the first five integers, thereafter treating all larger aggregates as numerically equivalent. We may claim that a particular brain nucleus is for some generic function such as "remembering." At this level of abstraction, we can compare this claim across individuals, cultures, or even species so long as a nervous system exists in each on which to make the comparisons.

LEVELS OF ABSTRACTION WITHIN A SINGLE CULTURAL DOMAIN

We have already pointed out how each scientific discipline can be viewed as an indigenous culture in its own right. When we move to less abstract levels of analysis in the field of neurosciences alone, we be-

gin to ask "how" questions such as "How is this particular brain nucleus involved in remembering?" To get at the answers to questions such as these, we need to increase the number of different experimental methods used, exploring the viability of more concrete and hence more local models.

Learning and Memory: The Role of the Hippocampus. For example, to explore the role of the hippocampus in learning and memory at a fairly high level of abstraction, we need only assert the highly abstract claim that hippocampi are used for learning and memory. This could be tested by comparing the capacities of people with intact hippocampi to the capacities of those with hippocampal damage such as the exemplary patient "H. M." (see Moghaddam, 2002, chap. 10). At this level of abstraction, we could also compare the processes of animals with rudimentary nervous systems with those of animals with more complex ones on some behavioral memory task. This is the rationale behind Kandel's Nobel Prize-winning experiments with the sea snail *Aplysia californica* (Kandel & Schwartz, 1982). Hardcastle (1999) termed this level of abstraction the "functional explanation." The role of this explanatory level is to capture abstract patterns and relations between otherwise diverse phenomena. At this level of abstraction, we can easily describe the similar functioning of brains or brain areas across species and ignore any interspecies variations.

The general rule at the most abstract level of analysis is that the explanation is less complex than what is being explained.

To move to subsequent levels of abstraction or analysis, we begin to seek explanations with increasing restricted analytical approaches and with less abstraction. At these levels of analysis, we need to approach the "how" questions (or *explanations of origins or causes*) from different angles and directions. This is required because we will now have to account for the parameters we whittled away to create the generalizations at the functional level of analysis. It is important to note that these additional parameters require multiple methods to explain them because they are often of different forms.

LEVELS OF ABSTRACTION WITHIN A MULTIPLE CULTURAL DOMAIN

The higher the level of abstraction, the more cases that will be covered but the less content the explanation will have. The more concrete and detailed the content of the explanation, the more convincing it will be but the fewer cases it will cover.

Now, we can see how cultural considerations assume more and more importance as the level of explanation moves from the abstract to the concrete. The more concrete the explanation, the more detail that is required in the content and the more likely it is that local cultural considerations will be playing a greater and greater part.

In addition to the cultural relevance for what is being explained, allowance must be made for the cultural consideration of the researcher. As we move from the abstract to the concrete, the theories we use to support and generate the experiments to explain the phenomenon are more culturally based. The categories of "learning" and of "memory" are cultural categories, not natural ones. Therefore, we should be concerned not only with the cultural perspective of the phenomenon being explained but also the cultural perspective of the researcher. This is particularly important in neuropsychology. The assumption that neural processes or brain function is universal across cultures, or universal across the entire subpopulation being examined, is crucial. The idea that fMRI results might have relevance to defi-

cits in mental functioning is a Western cultural assumption.

Interim Conclusion 4

All sciences develop research programs at both high and low levels of abstraction. At high levels of abstraction, it is possible, but not necessary, that some universals across the whole domain of concern may be revealed. Only at lower levels of abstraction are the generative mechanisms and processes by which phenomena are produced able to be studied in concrete conditions.

Mixed Methods Proposal 4

The use of mixed methods in light of these considerations is relevant for two additional reasons:

1. Using mixed methods from across cultural biases (albeit human cultures or experimental cultures) keeps the connection to the general (abstract) phenomenon. It ensures that we do not violate Vygotsky's Rule as we move through the levels of abstraction from abstract to concrete.

2. Diversity in methodologies, with each having its own cultural bias, makes it less likely that one would be relying on any *one* set of cultural assumptions so as to explain some well-defined psychological phenomenon.

◆ Phenomenology and Neurophysiology and Anatomy

AUDITORY PERCEPTION: PHENOMENOLOGY AND PHYSIOLOGY IN TANDEM

Perception is an active process that starts with a stimulus in the environment and then consists of transducing that stimulus into a type of energy that can be read by the nervous system. From there, neuronal processing occurs, and then finally the act of perception takes place. However, for most perception researchers, the journey does not stop there; the perceptual processes continue to include recognition of that environmental stimulus and finally some action or behavior by the perceiver. This is an active process because the information at each step is constantly changing. For example, we are rarely standing completely motionless while perceiving (via any of our senses) an object that is also completely motionless. In reality, the stimulus is often moving in relation to us, or we are moving in relation to it, or both. Therefore, our brains are constantly updating the information from the stimulus that is being transduced from one energy form to another. This, in turn, constantly alters the perception, recognition, and/or action to that stimulus.

To study this complex process, perception researchers focus on relationships among the various steps in the perceptual process via a variety of methodological approaches. By examining the link between the stimuli in the environment and the perception that stimulus creates, the behavioral-phenomenological approach to perception focuses on presenting objects to participants and recording the perceptions that the objects cause. To do this, a number of methods are used that fall into two categories: *phenomenological methods* and *psychophysical methods*. Phenomenological methods consist of simply presenting a stimulus to participants and asking them to describe what is perceived. For example, in a color-naming experiment, a color is shown and the participants are asked to name the color. However, as expected, this type of data is usually very qualitative. To counter this subjectivity and to provide a more quantitative connection between the stimulus

and the perception, researchers employ psychophysical methods. These methods consist of presenting a stimulus, with varying intensities, multiple times to participants to record the *threshold*, or just detectable, level of perception. In these methods, distinct stimulus intensity-perception relationships can be drawn.

To explore the link between the stimulus and the amount of neural firing, however, the physiological approach is used. Physiological methods usually consist of using an animal model of the sensory system under study and applying a stimulus of a known intensity while recording changes in neuronal properties directly from the nervous system. Via these techniques, stimulus strength (action potential number, neurotransmitter release amounts, or ionic conductance relationships) can be calculated. These techniques can also demonstrate which brain systems are activated during presentation of environmental stimuli and which physical features of these stimuli activate particular aspects of these brain systems. Examples of this use are Hubel and Wiesel's (1970) experiments with vision during the 1960s. In addition, experiments that examine the correlation between stimulus intensity and thresholds for neuronal firing can also be conducted using the physiological approach to perception. However, neither the behavioral approach nor the physiological approach can entirely explain the complexity of sensory *perception*. Therefore, a combination of methods is often used to "fill in the gaps" of perceptual knowledge.

This combination of both the phenomenological and physiological approaches has recently emerged as the field of cognitive neuroscience. This field of research consists of using brain-imaging techniques such as fMRI and positron emission tomography (PET) scanning. By using these noninvasive mapping techniques in addition to a perceptual or cognitive task, such as listening to the tone of a specific frequency or reading silently, researchers are able to "watch" the brain in action. One should note, however, that these scanning techniques are coarse-grained, picking out regions of the brain each of which may contain millions of neurons. These pictures of the brain can then be combined with the psychophysical assessments of the task from the participants. Examples for the need to use such a variety of methodologies so as to uncover the complexity of sensory perception can be drawn from the study of auditory perception.

THE PERCEPTION OF PITCH

The complexity of our sense of hearing can be illustrated by the following old query: "If a tree falls in the woods and there is no one there to hear it, does it make a sound?" Most would answer "yes," assuming that sounds exist in our world even in the absence of detectors or perceivers (some of our students have used the fact that animals or insects would be there to hear it as a rationale for their answer). Alternatively, some philosophers would argue "no," suggesting that they could conceive of a wood totally devoid of *any* perceivers and that in this case in this barren wood, no *sounds* would be emitted. The answer we give, much to the dissatisfaction of our students (at first), is "it depends." It all depends on what definition of the word "sound" one is using. In some contexts and to some people, sound refers to the physical properties of the pressure wave of air (or other medium) that is created when two or more things collide. In this case, we can say "yes," the tree has created a moving pressure wave in the air as it moved through it (on its way down) and also when it struck the surrounding trees and ground after it fell.

These physical properties would be present even if no one (animals and insects included) were around. However, we can also define sound as the *perception or experience of hearing* (Goldstein, 1999). In this case, even in the presence of the pressure waves just described, if there is no one in the woods to perceive or have the experience of these physical stimuli, then the answer is "no," the tree has made no sound.

With these definitions in place, it is easy to see that in order to hear a sound, we need *both* the sound stimulus and some psychological representation of the stimulus. It is here that information derived from mixed methods has yielded dividends. For example, experiments derived from the physical sciences have revealed properties of the physical characteristics of the pressure or sound wave. They have shown us that the sound stimulus can resemble a sine wave that can be described in terms of the number of cycles of pressure changes per second, or *frequency,* measured in units called hertz (named after the 19th-century German physicist Heinrich Hertz). The sound stimulus can also be described in terms of the longitudinal size of a single sound wave. These measurements, termed the *wavelength,* give additional information about the frequency of the pressure wave because there is an inverse relationship between frequency and wavelength. Additional experiments have described complex sound stimuli in terms of their *harmonics,* or the various combinations of sound waves that have merged to create the complex stimulus (Fourier analysis), and the relative strength of the stimulus, or *amplitude,* as measured by the height of the pressure wave.

Knowledge of these physical sound stimulus properties is required to study how we hear sounds. Researchers who examine the perceptual experience caused by sounds are analyzing how the characteristics of the stimulus combine with the anatomy of the hearing system so as to be translated into a particular sound. Specifically, the amplitude, frequency, and harmonics of the sound stimulus give rise to the psychological perception of *loudness, pitch, and timbre* of the sound. Determining how this is accomplished is one of the goals of auditory perception research. The complexity of this endeavor can be best illustrated by pitch perception. Experiments in pitch perception can be divided into two groups: physiological and psychophysical.

Physiological Approach. Physiological theories for how the auditory system codes for pitch were proposed as early as the beginning of the 20th century. One early theory, called resonance theory and proposed by Herman von Helmholtz, stated that the sound stimulus entered the ear and vibrated specific fine fibers of the basilar membrane (the membrane running through the cochlea hearing organ in the inner ear) similarly to a piano string. The particular frequency of the stimulus directly caused a particular fiber to vibrate the most, which corresponded to the particular pitch of the sound. Later work by von Bekesy (1960) demonstrated that the basilar membrane vibrates as a whole as a traveling or rolling wave (similar to when a person holds a rope tight and snaps one end of it, sending a wave rolling down the length of the rope). Bekesy concluded that different frequencies of the stimulus created a rolling wave at different points along the membrane and that the pitch of the sound was related to where along the membrane this wave was created.

These results confirmed earlier electrophysiological work by Culler, Coakley, Lowy, and Gross (1943) that examined the electrical responses of the neuronal cells in the inner ear to stimuli of varying frequencies. This work revealed that low frequencies excited neuronal cells toward the tip of the membrane, while high frequencies stimulated cells toward the base of the membrane. Work by Russell and Sellick (1978) demonstrated that each neuron responded to a specific narrow range of frequencies of the stimulus. These results suggest that both the place on the membrane that was activated and the frequency of the stimulus are related to neuronal firing. However, psychophysical experiments were needed to make the link between the frequency of the stimulus and neuronal firing and the perception of pitch.

Psychophysical Approach. Experiments that used this approach for the perception of pitch demonstrated that the pitches that are perceived rely on the sound stimulus activating a specific population of auditory neurons. During the 1950s, Egan and Hake conducted a series of sound-masking experiments in which the thresholds of hearing a range of pitches were measured (see Goldstein, 1999). After this measurement, a sound stimulus of white noise (masking sound stimulus) was delivered to the auditory system, and the pitch thresholds were remeasured. The results showed that the threshold for hearing test tones closely tuned to the range of frequencies covered by the masking sound stimulus (365-455 Hz, centered at 410 Hz) increased, thus masking the perception of these test tones. The frequencies of the test tones closest to the range of the masking stimulus were masked more strongly than test frequencies farther away from the frequency range of the masking stimulus. The explanation for this effect, which relates back to the physiological experiments discussed previously, is that the masking stimulus activated the same group of auditory neurons as did the test tones. Once these neurons were already "occupied" with the masking stimulus, it took more test tone stimulus to enable the detection of that specific frequency.

The utility of using *both* of the preceding approaches is quickly realized when we consider that at times having data from only one of these gives a confusing picture of behavior. Specifically, when discussing pitch perception as it relates to stimulus frequency and neuronal firing patterns, we soon realize that this cannot explain the phenomenon. We can detect and identify pure tone frequencies that are higher than any neuron can repeatedly fire. Therefore, if detection of high frequencies were dependent on the absolute firing rate of neurons in the auditory system, we would be able to perceive tones only up to 1,000 Hz. Because humans can detect frequencies near 7,000 Hz, something else needs to account for pitch perception.

Early in the 20th century, the "volley principle," which states that high-frequency neuronal firing can be achieved if neurons work as functional groups, was proposed by Wever and Bray (see Goldstein, 1999). According to this theory, a collection of neurons would fire at every fifth cycle of the sound wave. In this fashion, the summed response of a sufficient number of neurons could be perceived as high-frequency information, even though each neuron is limited by its refractory period. Later researchers discovered evidence for this idea and termed it "phase locking" (Rose, Brugge, Anderson, & Hind, 1967). Therefore, high-frequency pitch perception is dependent on the activity of specific neurons in the inner ear *and* the perceptual machinery.

The realization that hearing is often more than *just* the working of the neuroanatomical components of the auditory system brings us back to the issue of causation. Does the function of the auditory system *cause* us to hear? The answer would have to be "no" because the use of a variety of experimental methods has demonstrated that we can still perceive and derive meaning from a complex stimulus in the absence of a completely detected physical stimulus. However, this is not to suggest that hearing could occur in the complete absence of a functioning auditory system. Some input into the system *is* required, but the complete experience of hearing occurs only when physical and nonphysical components of the system work in tandem.

The relationship between *musical* experience and perception of auditory stimuli is also complex. Here is an example of how phenomenological analysis and cognitive hypotheses both are required to begin to understand an important facet of *music* as perceived and music as produced.

THE PERCEPTION OF RHYTHM

Music comes to us as a mode of auditory and kinesthetic experience. It has a distinctive phenomenology. The problems for the psychologist of music are presented in those terms. How is felt tension created in a melody? How are expectations, technically the pitch vectors of notes, brought into being? What is the character of the experience of unity or coherence in a melody? And so on. There would scarcely be a psychology of music if the psychologist were confined to measuring frequencies and tracking the vibrations from tympanum to cochlea to auditory cortex.

However, once one sets out on a deeper analysis, hypotheses about abstract structures seem to be required. These are the Schenkerian structures—major triads and perfect fifths—on which the whole of Western music and some Oriental music is based. This discovery seems to lead straight to computer modeling of the processes of structural cognition. One would say that the processes proposed, extending far beyond the simple four laws of gestalt apprehension, must be realized in the human brain. It seems natural to use artificial intelligence (AI) simulations as the basis for a further level of hypotheses as to what corresponds to machine processing in the auditory cortex. So far, the results of experiments on hypotheses developed along these lines have proved very disappointing.

Here is an example. A beat progression at a certain rate is established, and musicians are asked to perform two tasks: one perceptual and one performative. The perceptual task is set up as follows. After several beats, a tap is introduced a certain fraction of a beat after one of the established beats. The participants are asked to name the fraction, eighth note, quarter note, or whatever seems to be right to them. They consistently choose a name for a longer interval than has objectively—that is, physically—been produced. They overestimate the temporal span. In the second experiment, after the beat sequence has been established, the participants are asked to tap or, using their usual musical instrument, to indicate when an eighth beat or a quarter beat or whatever the experimenter asks has elapsed. They consistently come in early with respect to the time elapsed that would be physically defined by the note name, consistently underestimating the temporal span. This effect persists for however many trials each participant undergoes. The degree of over- and underestimates is specific to the performer.

How, then, can an orchestra ever play together and satisfy an audience? There are various cognitive hypotheses "on the table," so to speak. They share the problem of accounting for the apparent difference between time estimation in perception and performance of rhythms. Feedback will not do because the effect is independent of the number of trials. The

most likely suggestion is that performers share a common virtual beat, while the audience members share a different but common virtual beat. In this way, there could be a coordinated performance and a coordinated appreciation, each running on a different time scheme. The only problem with this is the role of the conductor who is both performing and auditing. There is other work that suggests that bodily movement dominates rhythm apprehension. So long as the conductor goes on beating with the baton, all will be well.

Clearly, we have here a mixed methods project. Phenomenology of musical experience sets the problem and determines whether a satisfactory answer has been achieved. Cognitive science provides tentative answers by using the AI-neural process link to propose hypotheses about unobservable mechanisms.

Interim Conclusion 5

Because there could be no way in which the relevant physiological mechanism could be identified without participants' phenomenological reports of personal experience, cognitive neuroscience necessarily requires the mixing of methods. The relevance of this example to our general theme is that the recent history of mainstream psychology reveals a transformation—as yet incomplete—of its cultural foundations. The admission of personal data into the scientific domain is a cultural event of the greatest significance for the future of this hybrid discipline.

Mixed Methods Proposal 5

One must acknowledge that psychology is a hybrid discipline and that the understanding of the processes of behavior, such as those involved in the perception of sound and rhythm, demands a combination of quantitative and qualitative methods—cross-checking and cross-validating experimenter assumptions. Advances in technology that allow for increasingly detailed measures of biological processes must be accompanied by increased accuracy in capturing subjective experiences in cultural context.

◆ Concluding Comments

We have argued that research methods not only are intimately interwoven with cultural practices, they *are* cultural practices. They are not independently justifiable or even intelligible in the absence of explicit reference to the cultural context in which they are used. Consequently, research methods tend to reflect cultural biases, although this might not be easy to see. However, there is some variation in the particular cultural biases reflected by different research methods. Not all methods reflect the same biases to the same degree. For example, the natural science paradigm, combined with phenomenological individualism, is influential to a greater degree in certain brain imaging methods used in neuroscience than it is in observational field research.

Psychology espouses the ambition to become a science of human behavior. But it is debatable whether to achieve this goal, psychology must search for universals in behavior. If this were a sine qua non of scientific status, then many studies, such as geology, would be ruled out of the catalog of sciences. This quest necessarily means that psychology must explore similarities in cognitive procedures—patterns of social behavior and the relevant neural mechanisms—across many cultural groups. This involves the issue of levels of abstraction. Universality is bought at the cost of adopting a high level of abstraction. To achieve anything like the kind of detailed understanding of the generation of psy-

chological phenomena that we find in the natural sciences, we must drop to lower levels of abstraction. Inevitably, this requires the adoption of a multimethods approach.

Even when biological universals are involved, culture can play a powerful role in how such biological characteristics become manifest in behavior. The most exciting examples of current research clearly demonstrate this point. For example, it has been known for some time now that there is a strong genetic component in dyslexia, a language disorder that creates difficulties in reading and writing. However, it has also been argued that there is a cultural component because the rate of identified dyslexia varies considerably across cultures. About twice as many individuals are recognized as dyslexic in the United States as in Italy. Using PET scans, researchers showed that British, French, and Italian adults identified as dyslexic showed lower neural activity in the same part of the brain identified as vital for reading (Paulesu et al., 2001). However, because the lexicography and pronunciation conventions of written English and French are more complex than those of written Italian, people find it harder to overcome their difficulties in recognizing word forms if they are trying to read English and French than if they are trying to read Italian.

This research illustrates very clearly the point about levels of abstraction. At the furthest distance from the actual practice of reading and writing in one's mother tongue are the brain mechanisms normally used by skilled users of language. Not surprisingly, the method appropriate to that level of analysis is the one that involves the least role for the intentional or meaningful qualities of the material on which the subject is working, namely PET scans of activated brain regions. The most concrete situation occurs when someone is using his or her mother tongue for some purpose for which the meaning of the forms of words is paramount. There, the cultural aspect comes to the fore. In this experimental program, we have the whole story of culture and its relation to non-cultural aspects of human functioning perfectly portrayed.

There is a basic methodological principle that we can now state or restate firmly: In using any neuroscience methodology to study the brain mechanisms people use for various tasks, we must give priority to the subjective realm so as to identify the relevant brain processes. Any psychologically relevant use of fMRI or PET techniques requires the participant to perform tasks that are always defined in terms of that participant's skills and subjective experience. If someone is doing a PET scan to try to find a lesion that is suspected to exist, the participant will be asked to try to perform the task or think the thoughts that are thought to be related to activities in characteristic regions of the brain. Disordered thoughts or disruption of normal skills is related to brain defects "top-down." One could not possibly study brain science unless one took for granted the phenomenology of psychologically relevant experience. Phenomenological analysis of experience and neuroscience need one another. In this domain, the mixing is not just a matter of practical technique but also a matter of logic. The identification of relevant brain states and processes depends on the ability of participants to identify their subjectively presented mental states and processes efficiently and adequately.

■ *References*

Anderson, C. A., Anderson, K. B., & Deuser, W. E. (1996). Examining an affective ag-gression framework: Weapon and temperature effects on aggressive thoughts, affects, and attitudes. *Personality and Social Psychology Bulletin, 22,* 366-376.

Bem, S. L. (1974). The measurement of psychological androgyny. *Journal of Consulting and Clinical Psychology, 42,* 155-162.

Billig, M. (1978). *Fascists: A social psychological view of the National Front.* London: Academic Press.

Bogardus, E. S. (1925). Measuring social distance. *Journal of Applied Sociology, 9,* 299-308.

Burke, K. (1969) *A grammar of motives.* Berkeley: University of California Press.

Chagnon, N. A. (1992). *Yanomamo* (4th ed.). San Diego: Harcourt Brace Jovanovich.

Cole, M. (1996). *Cultural psychology: A once and future science.* Cambridge, MA: Harvard University Press.

Culler, E. A., Coakley, J. D., Lowy, K., & Gross, N. (1943). A revised frequency map of the guinea-pig cochlea. *American Journal of Psychology, 56,* 475-500.

Daly, M., & Wilson, M. (1990). Killing the competition: Female/female and male/male homicide. *Human Nature, 1,* 81-107.

Danziger, K. (1990). *Constructing the subject.* Cambridge, UK: Cambridge University Press.

Fox, D. R., & Prilleltensky, I. (Eds.). (1997). *Critical psychology.* Thousand Oaks, CA: Sage.

Giddens, A. (1984). *The constitution of society: Outline of the theory of structuration.* Oxford, UK: Polity.

Gilligan, C. (1982). *In a different voice.* Cambridge, MA: Harvard University Press.

Goffman, E. (1959). *The presentation of self in everyday life.* New York: Doubleday.

Goldstein, E. B. (1999). *Sensation and perception* (5th ed.). Pacific Grove, CA: Brooks/Cole.

Gubrium, J. F., & Holstein, J. A. (1997). *The new language of qualitative methods.* New York: Oxford University Press.

Hardcastle, V. G. (1999). Understanding functions: A pragmatic approach. In V. G. Hardcastle (Ed.), *Where biology meets psy-*

chology (pp. 27-43). Cambridge, MA: MIT Press.

Hinde, R. A. (Ed.). (1972). *Non-verbal communication*. Cambridge, UK: Cambridge University Press.

Hubel, D. H., & Wiesel, T. N. (1970). The period of susceptibility to the physiological effects of unilateral eye closure in kittens. *Journal of Physiology, 206,* 419-436.

Kandel, E. R., & Schwartz, J. H. (1982). Molecular biology of learning: Modulation of transmitter release. *Science, 218,* 433-443.

Lutz, C. (1988). *Unnatural emotions*. Chicago: Chicago University Press.

Marsh, P., Rosser, E., & Harré, R. (1978). *The rules of disorder*. London: Routledge & Kegan Paul.

Mitchell, M., & Jolley, J. (1992). *Research design explained* (2nd ed.). San Diego: Harcourt Brace Jovanovich.

Moghaddam, F. M. (1987). Psychology in the three worlds. *American Psychologist, 47,* 912-920.

Moghaddam, F. M. (1998). *Social psychology: Exploring universals in social behavior*. New York: Freeman.

Moghaddam, F. M. (2002). *The individual and society: A cultural integration*. New York: Worth.

Moghaddam, F. M., & Harré, R. (1995). But is it science? Traditional and alternative approaches to the study of social behavior. *World Psychology, 1,* 47-78.

Moghaddam, F. M., & Taylor, D. M. (1985). Psychology in the developing world: An evaluation through the concepts of "dual perception" and "parallel growth." *American Psychologist, 40,* 1144-1146.

Moyer, K. E. (1976). *The psychobiology of aggression*. New York: Harper & Row.

Nelson, R. J., Demas, G. E., Huang, P. L., Fishman, M. C., Dawson, V. L., Dawson, T. M., & Snyder, S. H. (1995). Behavioral abnormalities in male mice lacking neuronal nitric oxide synthase. *Nature, 378,* 383-386.

Nisbett, R. E., & Cohen, D. (1996). *Culture of honor: Violence and the U.S. South*. Boulder, CO: Westview.

Paulesu, E., Demonet, J. F., Fazio, F., McCroy, E., Chanoine, V., Brunswick, N., Cappa, S. F., Cossu, S. F., Habib, M., Frith, C. D., & Frith, U. (2001). Dyslexia: Cultural diversity and biological unity. *Science, 291,* 2165-2167.

Rose, J. E., Brugge, J. F., Anderson, D. J., & Hind, J. E. (1967). Phase locked response to low frequency tones in single auditory nerve fibers of the squirrel monkey. *Journal of Neurophysiology, 30,* 769-793.

Russell, I. J., & Sellick, P. M. (1978). Intracellular studies of hair cells in the mammalian cochlea. *Journal of Physiology, 284,* 261-290.

Sherif, M. (1966). *Group conflict and cooperation: Their social psychology*. London: Routledge & Kegan Paul.

Sinha, D. (1997). Indigenizing psychology. In J. W. Berry, Y. H. Poortinga, & J. Pandey (Eds.), *Handbook of cross-cultural psychology* (Vol. 1, pp. 129-169). Boston: Allyn & Bacon.

Tajfel, H., & Turner, J. C. (1979). An integrative theory of intergroup conflict. In W. G. Austin & S. Worchel (Eds.), *The social psychology of intergroup relations* (pp. 33-47). Pacific Grove, CA: Brooks/Cole.

Tashakkori, A., Barefoot, J., & Mehryar, A. H. (1989). What does the Beck Depression Inventory measure among college students? Evidence from a non-Western culture. *Journal of Clinical Psychology, 45,* 595-602.

Tashakkori, A., & Kennedy, E. (1993). Measurement of self-perception in multicultural context: Psychometric properties of a Modified Self-Description Questionnaire. *British Journal of Educational Psychology, 63,* 337-348.

von Bekesy, G. (1960). *Experiments in hearing*. New York: McGraw-Hill.

Vygotsky, L. S. (1962). *Thought and language*. Cambridge, MA: MIT Press.

Vygotsky, L. S. (1978). *Mind in society*. Cambridge, MA: Harvard University Press.

Weinfurt, K., & Moghaddam, F. M. (2001). Culture and social distance: A case study of methodological cautions. *Journal of Social Psychology, 141,* 101-110.

Wilkinson, S. (Ed.). (1996). *Feminist social psychologies: International perspectives*. Buckingham, UK: Open University Press.

Witkin, H. A., Mednick, S. A., Schulsinger, F., Bakkestrm, E., Christiansen, K. O., Goodenough, D. R., Hirschhorn, K., Lundsteen, C., Owen, D. R., Philip, J., Rubin, D. B., & Stocking, M. (1976). Criminality in XYY and XXY men. *Science, 193,* 547-555.

Wittgenstein, L. (1953). *Philosophical investigations.* Oxford, UK: Blackwell.

5

MIXED METHODS AND THE POLITICS OF HUMAN RESEARCH: THE TRANSFORMATIVE-EMANCIPATORY PERSPECTIVE

◆ Donna M. Mertens

Researchers in social and behavioral sciences work within and as part of human society and thus are confronted with the full complexity of that society including issues of pluralism and social justice. Historically, research methods texts did not concern themselves with the politics of human research and social justice. However, changing conditions outside and inside of the research world have brought increased attention to the need to address these issues in such work. In society at large, trends in demographics and increased social pluralism increase the importance of recognizing cultural differences and injustice based on those cultural differences. Inside the world of research, the emergence of scholars from diverse ethnic/racial groups, people with disabilities, and feminists has contributed to the conversation by explicating a paradigmatic view of research known as the transformative-emancipatory paradigm. More broadly, the research community has increased its recognition of the importance of the role of values in research. These themes are explored in this chapter to illustrate the potential importance, underlying philosophical assumptions, and methodological implications of the transformative-emancipatory paradigm within the discussion of mixed methods in research.

◆ Demographic Trends and Social Justice

The increase in diverse ethnic/racial groups in the United States has tipped the balance such that those who were termed minority groups in the past are now in the majority in several urban areas, and the projection is that by the year 2020, 70% of all beginning first-grade students will be from non-White groups (Booth, 2000; U.S. Bureau of the Census, 2000). The presence of people with disabilities is also increasing in the United States such that current population estimates indicate that more than 50 million citizens have disabilities (McNeil, 1997), thus suggesting that most research study samples will include people with disabilities even if their disabilities are invisible to the researcher.

The relationship between knowledge about diversity within communities and implications for social justice and equity for diverse groups provides another layer of understanding for researchers. For example, more than 45% of Hispanic youths ages 18 to 24 years are high school dropouts as compared with only 18% of White youths. The dropout rate for Black youths is about 26% (U.S. Bureau of the Census, 1997). Graduation rates have improved for students with disabilities following the passage of the Americans With Disabilities Act and the Individuals With Disabilities Act and its amendments (Horn & Berktold, 1999). However, students with disabilities, especially students with learning disabilities, leave secondary school with dim prospects. They tend to be undereducated and underemployed. Yet if students with disabilities graduate from 4-year colleges and get jobs, their income level is as competitive as that of their nondisabled peers. Worldwide, increased schooling is associated with increased literacy and employment and with decreased poverty and infant mortality (Grant, 1993).

Hill Collins (2000) described the challenges facing U.S. Black women as follows: "Despite differences of age, sexual orientation, social class, region, and religion, U.S. Black women encounter societal practices that restrict us to inferior housing, neighborhoods, schools, jobs, and public treatment" (p. 25). Stanfield (1999) acknowledged the lower economic, employment, and educational opportunities available to many people of color while at the same time cautioning researchers to be mindful of a tendency to "negatively romanticize people of color" (p. 421). The consequence may be studying only negative questions about Black experiences and not asking questions that might shed a more positive light on Black people.

◆ Scholarly Roots of the Transformative-Emancipatory Paradigm

Despite Descartes's attempt to separate science and values during the Age of Enlightenment, current philosophers of science have recognized that science, while an empirically based tradition, is also influenced by values. Thus, scientists cannot ignore the powerful influence of values.

> What counts for or against a claim or theory is how it is integrated in a larger theory or set of theories, and how well these interconnected claims and theories collectively predict, explain, and integrate the firings of our sensory receptors. All of this seems to invite, or

at least allow, the inclusion of value claims, or value laden claims, within science. (J. Nelson, 1996, p. 65)

House and Howe (1999) examined tensions between the notion of value-free science and value recognition in social research by raising the questions of values in terms of whose values, which values, and the role of the researcher within the context of values. While Teddlie and Tashakkori argue (Chapter 1, this volume) that pragmatism represents an alternative paradigm that underlies the choice of mixed methods, House and Howe (1999) view the use of practicality as the value basis for a researcher's choices as unsatisfactory in that practicality by itself does not answer the question "Practical for what?" Writing within the context of program evaluation, they stated, "Something could be practical for bad ends. Using practicality as the primary criterion . . . means evaluators (researchers) may serve whatever ends clients or policy makers endorse. Evaluation should be premised on higher social goals than being useful to those in power" (p. 36). Furthermore, the researcher has an important role in documenting the goals and values of programs and policies and in critically examining the goals and values of the interventions under investigation. House and Howe concluded their argument by asserting that subjectivities are important; social arrangements are irremediably interest laden, power laden, and value laden; and the goal of research and evaluation should be a more just and democratic society. Thus, there is an explicit recognition of an important value that should be part of social and behavioral research and evaluation.

Several groups have extended the thinking concerning the place of values in research, including feminists, members of diverse ethnic/racial groups, and people with disabilities. Feminist philosophers of science recognize that there are two kinds of evidence for individual theories, research projects, methodologies, and claims (L. Nelson, 1996). One of these is observation (data), and the other is a body of accepted methods, standards, and theory. L. Nelson (1996) contended that both of these kinds of evidence are social in nature and are thus influenced by the values of the scientist and the scientific community. Feminist epistemologists hold that it is a mistake to ask for value-free science (Tuana, 1996). Rather, it is important for good science to focus attention on the dynamics of gender and oppression in the theories and methods of science.

FEMINIST SCHOLARS

Feminist views on research take many different forms, but all are premised on the knowledge of women's oppression and the vision of social justice for women through research as one of a range of strategies (Olesen, 2000; Ribbens & Edwards, 1998; Truman, Mertens, & Humphries, 2000). Feminists have made a unique contribution by exposing the centrality of male power in the social construction of knowledge. They have also challenged some of the fundamental binaries of traditional approaches such as objectivity and distance from the participants and hierarchies among researchers and the researched. Yet Black and Third World women (e.g., Bhavnani, 1991; Hill Collins, 2000; Mohanty, 1991) and lesbian and disabled feminists (e.g., Dockery, 2000; Mertens, 2000b) have criticized the "White," able-bodied, heterosexual feminist movement as not adequately representing their viewpoints. Hill Collins (2000) argued that human solidarity and social justice are the values that underlie transformative-emancipatory research. However, she also recognized the need to take into account the uniqueness of the Black women's experience when she stated,

> While U.S. Black women's experiences resemble others, such experiences remain unique. The importance of Black women's leadership in producing Black feminist thought does not mean that others cannot participate. It does mean that the primary responsibility for defining one's own reality lies with the people who live that reality, who actually have those experiences. (p. 35)

Stanfield (1999) discussed the implications of living in a racist society that is dominated by White supremacy so pervasive that no one can escape its touch in terms of socialization, including social and behavioral scientists. He defined racialism as "attitudes and actions of stereotyping, exclusive practices, and the creation and maintenance of unequal access to resources, education, gainful employment markets, investment capital, the polity, and natural resources" (p. 420). He contrasted racialism with racism, which is a more blatant or covert bigotry against racialized out-groups in attitudes and/or behavior. Racialism is more insidious in some ways as it may masquerade as a more benign effort on the part of researchers to study Black people, but with inappropriate processes or pursuing overly negative questions. Researchers need to be cognizant of the historical background of people of color, the racialist nature of society, and the impact of these forces on their choice of methods and the substance of the questions they investigate. Contemporary conventions of social science research on people of color commonly are based on assumptions of individual or cultural deficits in the Black community and discour-

age empowerment epistemologies, theories, methods, and intervention strategies.

DISABILITY SCHOLARS

People with disabilities have been viewed through various lenses throughout history. Gill (1999) described the moral model and the medical model of disability (Longmore, 1994). The moral model suggests that the disability results as a punishment for sin or as a means of inspiring or redeeming others. The medical model sees the disability as a problem or a measurable defect located in the individual that needs a cure or alleviation that can be provided by medical experts. In the disability community, Seelman (1998) described a shift away from the medical model that essentially focused on the impairment as a sickness and the role of the professional in treating this malady. Gill (1999) recognized a more progressive stance in the rehabilitation model where the goal is to help the individual regain as much normal independent functioning as possible.

Seelman (1998) described a new paradigm of service and opportunities that shifts the location of the problem from within the individual to the environmental response to the disability. This paradigm that evolved from the efforts of scholars, activists with disabilities, and their nondisabled allies departs from these former models in terms of its definition of disability problems, the scope of potential solutions, and the values underlying both the definition of the problems and solutions (Gill, 1999). The new paradigm frames disability from the perspective of a social, cultural minority group such that disability is defined as a dimension of human difference and not a defect (Gill, 1999; Mertens, 1998, 2000b). Within this paradigm, the category of disability is recognized as being socially constructed such that its meaning is derived from society's response to individuals who deviate from cultural standards. Furthermore, disability is viewed as one dimension of human difference. According to Gill (1999), the goal for people with disabilities is not to eradicate their sickness but instead to celebrate their distinctness, pursue their equal place in American society, and acknowledge that their differentness is not defective but rather valuable.

CRITICAL THEORY

Critical theory has contributed to the understanding of oppression and discrimination primarily on the basis of socioeconomic status and class (Humphries, Mertens, & Truman, 2000; Kellner, 1997; Kincheloe & McLaren, 2000). Critical theorists share concerns with feminists, people of diverse ethnic/cultural backgrounds, and people with disabilities in terms of power differentials and a search for a more egalitarian and democratic social order. With a specific focus on the political nature of institutions, critical theorists analyze power interests and how research can be used to either challenge or support the status quo. While current critical theorists have expressed an understanding that there are multiple forms of power, including race, gender, and sexual orientation, there is still a core belief that economic factors can never be separated from other axes of oppression (Kincheloe & McLaren, 2000).

◆ Paradigmatic Assumptions of the Transformative-Emancipatory Paradigm

A paradigm is a conceptual model of a person's worldview, complete with the assumptions that are associated with that view. Three major paradigms are oper-

ating in the research community today. The positivist-postpositivist paradigm is associated with traditional research approaches such as experimental or quasi-experimental designs and causal comparative and correlational research approaches. The interpretive-constructivist paradigm is associated with many qualitative approaches to research such as ethnography, case studies, and phenomenological investigations. The third is the transformative-emancipatory paradigm, which is described as follows:

> Transformative scholars assume that knowledge is not neutral but is influenced by human interests, that all knowledge reflects the power and social relationships within society, and that an important purpose of knowledge construction is to help people improve society (Banks, 1993, 1995). Transformative theory is used as an umbrella term that encompasses paradigmatic perspectives such as emancipatory (Lather, 1992; Mertens, 1998), anti-discriminatory (Humphries & Truman, 1994; Truman, Mertens, & Humphries, 2000), participatory (Reason, 1994; DeKoning & Martin, 1996; Whitmore, 1998), and Freirian approaches (McLaren & Lankshear, 1994) and is exemplified in the writings of feminists (Alcoff & Potter, 1993; Fine, 1992; Hill Collins, 2000; Reinharz, 1992), racial/ethnic minorities (Stanfield, 1999; Stanfield & Dennis, 1993; Madison, 1992), people with disabilities (Gill, 1999; Oliver, 1992; Mertens & McLaughlin, 1995), and people who work on behalf of marginalized groups. (Mertens, 1999, p. 4)

The transformative paradigm is characterized as placing central importance on the lives and experiences of marginalized groups such as women, ethnic/racial minorities, members of the gay and lesbian communities, people with disabilities, and those who are poor. The researcher who works within this paradigm consciously analyzes asymmetric power relationships, seeks ways to link the results of social inquiry to action, and links the results of the inquiry to wider questions of social inequity and social justice (Mertens, 1998; Mertens, Farley, Madison, & Singleton, 1994; Truman et al., 2000).

According to researchers, there are three defining questions that determine our worldview (Guba & Lincoln, 1994; Mertens, 1998). The ontological question asks, "What is the nature of reality and, by extension, truth?" The epistemological question asks, "What is the nature of knowledge and the relationship between the knower and the would-be known?" The methodological question asks, "How can the knower go about obtaining the desired knowledge and understanding?" Each question is answered differently by scholars who align themselves with the three respective paradigms. After a brief explanation of how these three questions are answered for each of the three major paradigms, a more in-depth explanation is provided for the transformative-emancipatory paradigm and accompanying implications for the use of mixed methods research approaches within that context.

ONTOLOGY

The postpositivist paradigm's ontological view holds that there is one reality—one truth—that can be known within a certain level of probability (Mertens, 1998). The interpretive-constructivists have argued for the recognition of multiple socially constructed realities. One simple example is that many fairy tales end with the phrase "They all lived happily

ever after." But as can be seen in the tale of Little Red Riding Hood, it depends on whose viewpoint is being used to tell the story. Do you think that if the wolf told the story, he would end it that way? This is not meant to imply that a postpositivist scholar would reach such an overly simplistic conclusion that everyone lived happily ever after. However, there might be a tendency to focus on a reductive assessment of how happy the characters were at the end, expressed in quantitative terms with plus or minus some degree of error. Because the interpretive-constructivist scholars would tend to focus on a credible description of the multiplicity of viewpoints (the wolf, Little Red Riding Hood, and the grandmother), these researchers have been subjected to the criticism that they are mired in absolute relativism such that no one perspective is any truer than any other perspective.

The transformative-emancipatory ontological assumption holds that there are diversities of viewpoints with regard to many social realities but that those viewpoints need to be placed within political, cultural, historical, and economic value systems to understand the basis for the differences. And then, researchers need to struggle with revealing those multiple constructions as well as with making the decisions about privileging one perspective over another.

For example, there are many concepts that are socially constructed, including what are appropriate gender roles. Clearly, there are diverse opinions as to how to define this concept, ranging from a submissive compliant doormat to a self-determined empowered woman who can think clearly and act decisively when the situation requires it. In investigating gender roles, the transformative-emancipatory researcher would ask, "When we as a society teach girls to be passive and subservient, what are the consequences of that in terms of their physical safety, earnings, and mental health?" While this question could be asked by researchers from all paradigms, it would be inescapable and of central importance for the transformative-emancipatory researcher.

EPISTEMOLOGY

In epistemological terms, the issue of objectivity is salient, along with implications for the nature of the relationship between the researcher and the researched (Mertens, 1998). In the postpositivist paradigm, objectivity is considered to be paramount and is thought to be achieved by observing from a somewhat distant and dispassionate standpoint. In the interpretive-constructivist paradigm, interaction between the researcher and the participants is felt to be essential as they struggle together to make their values explicit and create the knowledge that will be the results of the study.

In transformative terms, objectivity is valued in the sense of providing a balanced and complete view of the program processes and effects such that bias is not interjected because of a lack of understanding of key viewpoints. However, to obtain this depth of understanding, it is necessary for the researcher to be involved in the communities affected by the service, program, or policy to a significant degree. This epistemological assumption underscores the importance of an interactive link between the researcher and the participants, with sensitivity given to the impact of social and historical factors in the relationship between the researcher and the participants as well as the impact of those variables on the construction of knowledge.

Feminists have rejected the "view from nowhere" conception of objectivity and suggested that an alternative notion of objectivity might be more appropriate (Harding, 1993; Mertens, 1999; Tuana, 1996). One common tenet is that objectivity be redefined as the reduction of bias because of adequate representation of diverse groups to ensure objectivity. This requires a closeness in terms of interactions between the researchers and members of diverse groups. As Tuana (1996) wrote from the feminist perspective,

> It should be no surprise that it is feminist philosophers of science and epistemologists who are vociferously rejecting the Cartesian model of the isolated knowing subject and replacing it with models that emphasize the centrality of our relationships with others to the process of knowing. (p. 31)

And Stanfield (1999) pragmatically asked, "How ethical is it to view oneself as an authority in the study of the racialized oppressed, when one has had marginal or no contact with or real interest in the lives of the people involved?" (p. 429).

METHODOLOGICAL ASSUMPTIONS

Finally, in methodological terms, the postpositivist paradigm is characterized as using primarily quantitative methods that are interventionist and decontextualized (Mertens, 1998). The interpretive-constructivist paradigm is characterized as using primarily qualitative methods in a hermeneutical and dialectical manner. The transformative paradigm might involve quantitative, qualitative, or mixed methods, but the community affected by the research would be involved to some degree in the methodological and programmatic decisions. Mixed methods designs that use both quantitative and qualitative methods can be used in any paradigm; however, the underlying assumptions determine which paradigm is operationalized.

These philosophical assumptions provide the foundation for guiding methodology for transformative research. The research is conducted with involvement of all relevant communities, especially the least advantaged. The research conclusions are data based, but the data are generated from an inclusive list of persons affected by the research, with special efforts to include those who have been traditionally underrepresented. It does not exclude those who have been traditionally included in the research process, that is, the decision makers, program administrators and staff, and funding agency representatives. It does explicitly recognize that certain voices have been absent, misrepresented, or marginalized and that inclusion of these voices is necessary for a rigorous research study. Conclusions are based on the collection, analysis, and interpretation of inclusive data and are not forgone conclusions. Qualitative, quantitative, or mixed methods can be used; however, contextual and historical factors must be described, with special sensitivity given to issues of power that can influence the achievement of social justice and avoidance of oppression.

◆ Implications of the Transformative-Emancipatory Paradigm for Mixed Methods Research

The most fundamental principle of the transformative-emancipatory paradigm in terms of methodology is that it has a pervasive influence throughout the research process. This section contains explanations of the implications of recognition and implementation of paradigmatic assumptions from the transformative-

emancipatory paradigm, with examples of implications drawn from a variety of studies. The following aspects of a mixed methods research design are discussed and illustrated: (a) defining the problem and searching the literature; (b) identifying the research design; (c) identifying data sources and selecting participants; (d) identifying or constructing data collection instruments and methods; and (e) analyzing, interpreting, and reporting results.

DEFINING THE PROBLEM AND SEARCHING THE LITERATURE

Who researchers talk to, what literature they read, and whose opinions are given privilege in the formulation of the research problem and approach have an impact on their ability to address an issue that has relevance to the least advantaged populations and to accurately represent the diverse voices of research participants. Conducting a literature review is typically considered one of the first steps for researchers to begin formulating a research question (Mertens, 1998). Researchers can direct the literature search to be inclusive of quantitative, qualitative, and mixed methods approaches. They can also deliberately search for literature that addresses the concerns of diverse groups and issues of discrimination and oppression. However, they should be aware of at least three biases in traditional mainstream literature sources. First, quantitative research continues to dominate most journals in the social and behavioral sciences, either because of choice of the researchers or because of the gatekeepers who decide which articles will be published. Second, it is uncommon to find articles that directly address issues of discrimination and oppression within the context of research variables. Third, published literature represents an elite perspective that may well be different from that found in the streets and communities where the less powerful groups live.

Literature reviews are excellent ways to gather information related to the historical and contextual issues of importance to the population of concern. Buchanan's (1999) historical study, *Illusions of Equality*, provides an example of both the benefits of literature for gaining historical perspective and the limitations of this approach with respect to marginalized groups. Buchanan conducted a historical study of the working lives of deaf men and women in the United States from the mid-19th century to the establishment of an industrial-based working class during World War II. Using both quantitative and qualitative data, he explained the varied factors within the deaf community and U.S. society at large that have alternatively restrained and advanced the fortunes of deaf workers. Because his study was primarily based on organized state and national associations, he acknowledged that it focused on the most highly educated and professionally successful White males. The study was not centered on deaf women, deaf individuals of color, or marginally schooled and employed deaf adults because they are not generally represented in official documents.

Meadow-Orlans (2002) presented a picture of the complex terrain in the area of deafness research by explaining the impact of social change and conflict in that context. She reviewed quantitative and qualitative research in the area of sign language and achievement, and she traced its impact to policy changes in educational practices with deaf children. While Meadow-Orlans chronicled positive changes, she also noted that bitter skirmishes and conflicts have accompanied nearly every positive change. For example, a contemporary controversy emanates from the emerging use of cochlear implants to improve hearing. The medical community and some hearing parents describe the cochlear implant as a modern miracle of biotechnology (Lane, 1993). Yet many members of the deaf community (those who consider themselves to be culturally deaf) object to the surgical procedures as the "work of the devil" that the medical community is using to try to stamp out their cultural community. Any researcher who wants to work in a marginalized community should carefully explore the historical background and be well-versed in the historical and cultural conflicts, such as those described in this paragraph for the deaf community, that can affect the research process.

Thus, a literature review is an important step in formulating the research problem and questions, but it is not sufficient to define the problem adequately. Scholars in the field of participatory research have long recognized the importance of allowing the problem definition to arise from the community of concern (Kemmis & McTaggart, 2000; Whitmore, 1998). In keeping with the transformative-emancipatory paradigm, a problem can be defined through a synergistic relationship with the important participants, with a special sensitivity to issues of power. Stanfield (1999) criticized research questions and approaches that function at a distance from the populations under study. He wrote, "In many research areas, research can be done in the comforts of the library, computer lab, or Internet. Correspondingly, it has become increasingly easy to do research on human beings without talking to a single person representative of a population or community" (p. 418). He described researchers who are reluctant to venture out into a poor non-White neighborhood to have conversations with people representative of those in their impersonal secondary data sets.

Stanfield (1999) recommended that investigators who are specializing in research on the poor and/or on people of color spend quality time with the people about whom they claim professional authority. They may find that many of their academic ideas about the population on which they are supposedly authoritative are irrelevant, obsolete, or popular (but biased) "folk wisdoms." Stanfield called for "relevance validity" and defined that as "data that fit the realities of the people it supposedly represents" (p. 419). Steps toward achieving the definition of a problem by spending quality time with people may require the researcher to apply a mixed methods approach in the definition of the problem. Observation, interviewing, review of demographic and other statistical data, and sometimes preliminary surveys are mixed methods strategies that can be brought to problem definition.

Spending quality time with the population of concern can ameliorate several biases, specifically (a) building trust, (b) using an appropriate theoretical framework, (c) developing balanced questions, and (d) developing questions that might lead to transformative answers.

Building Trust. Stanfield (1999) claimed that researchers who do research without firsthand contact tend to view those studied as commodities or objects, while those who are studied in such circumstances tend to view the researcher as an exploiter who is only interested in extracting data and then disappearing. Cohen-Mitchell's (2000) study of an economic development program for disabled women in El Salvador illustrated the strategy of using firsthand quality contact time with the women in the study as a way to set a research agenda that was geared toward social change. By focusing her research design on the women's social reality, Cohen-Mitchell was able to create research questions that were geared toward documenting the impact of the women on creating development programs that would potentially affect their lives. She wrote,

> Before I could begin with interviews, it was necessary to build an environment of trust and confidence with the women I would be inviting to work on a collaborative research effort for the next five months. . . . Since people were constantly streaming in and out of the office and the ceramics workshop, my presence there and willingness to engage in spontaneous conversation was important. This allowed the women to sound me out and decide for themselves whether or not I was someone they felt comfortable inviting into their lives. (p. 150)

Theoretical Framework. As discussed in the introductory section of this chapter, various theoretical frameworks have been used to explain the poor academic performance or social conditions in the lives of women, people of color, people with disabilities, and other marginalized groups. The medical model of disability has been used to frame research in terms of how to "fix" the problem in disabled persons. Theoretical frameworks used with people of color have either blamed the individuals (genetic inferiority) or blamed the culture. Such deficit models lead to framing the problem of poverty and underachievement of children in poor urban or rural schools in terms of social deficiency or cultural deficits rather than in terms of the marginal resources of their schools and the racialized politics of local, state, and federal governments (Mertens, 1998, 1999; Stanfield, 1999; Villegas, 1991). The transformative paradigm frames gender, race/ethnicity, disability, sexual orientation, and other bases of diversity from the perspective of a social, cultural minority group such that the defining characteristic is viewed as a dimension of human difference and not a defect (Gill, 1999; Mertens, 1998, 2000b). Within this paradigm, the category of diversity is recognized as being socially constructed such that its meaning is derived from society's response to individuals who deviate from cultural standards.

For example, Cohen-Mitchell (2000) rejected the deficit model that had shaped previous economic development research on women with disabilities in El Salvador and other countries. Instead of focusing on a preset agenda of rehabilitation and vocational skill training, she engaged in dialogue with the women to determine their own views of themselves as disabled women and the need to reframe that perception according to their own needs, desires, and possibilities.

Balanced Questions. Stanfield (1999) indicated that researchers are socialized to ask negative questions about Black experiences, ignoring questions that might shed a more positive light on Black people. He wrote,

> For instance, while we may ask community residents about the needs of their community, we rarely ask questions about strengths. In some quarters, perhaps including evaluation, this is changing. But the focus of many interventions on social problems sustains the tendency to focus on negatives. While we may ask questions about why Black youth or adults get into trouble with the law, we rarely try to find the good kids and grown-ups with sterling moral characters and ask them how and why is it they maintain their impeccable moral characters in high risk environments. (pp. 421-422)

Thus, Stanfield recommended that researchers balance their research questions so as to be inclusive of both positive and negative aspects of the phenomena under study.

Social Transformation. To follow this strand of thinking to the next step, if a transformative theoretical framework guides the study and balanced questions are asked, then what is the nature of the questions that will facilitate a link between the study's findings and social transformation? How can the questions be molded to get at what is needed for social transformation? The overall research questions need to be framed to acknowledge that it is not the individual's psychological, physical, or cultural deficits that are the focus of the questions. Rather, the focus should be on structural frameworks of authority and relations of power in institutions and communities.

This is the perspective adopted by Bowen and Bok (1998) in *The Shape of the River*, a study of how race-sensitive admissions policies work and their effects on students of different races. They asked questions such as the following:

◆ How much do race-sensitive admissions increase the likelihood that Blacks will be admitted to selective universities?

◆ How well do Black students perform academically in comparison to their White classmates, and what success do they have in their subsequent careers?

◆ How actively do Black graduates participate in civic and community affairs?

◆ How do graduates of selective universities perceive the contribution of having been part of a diverse study body to their capacity to live and work with people of other races?

The authors concluded by asking what the effect of terminating such race-sensitive policies would be on the lives of both

Black and White people and on the communities in which they live. Thus, they framed their questions on the broader structural frameworks of authority in the institutions that have the power to influence national policy on this issue.

IDENTIFYING THE RESEARCH DESIGN

Traditional quantitative approaches to research include experimental, quasi-experimental, causal comparative, correlational, and surveys. Qualitative approaches include focus groups, case studies, ethnographic research, and participatory models of research. Within the assumptions associated with the transformative-emancipatory perspective, several of these approaches could be combined in a mixed methods design. However, several ethical issues associated with different design choices arise from this perspective.

Truman (2000) addressed several ethical issues that arose in an emancipatory study of safe sex and health issues among the gay community in Manchester, England. She selected a mixed methods design, combining qualitative and quantitative methods, based on the needs of her client (an activist group of gay men) and her own emancipatory philosophical beliefs. The client wanted her to conduct a needs assessment that the group could then use to approach funding agencies to support a program of materials distribution on the topic of safe sex. She described the decision to adopt a quantitative design as follows: "The group believed that a large-scale quantitative survey for gay and bisexual men would provide the 'factual evidence' for this need. Thus, a quasi-positivist framework for the conduct of the study was required to meet this criteria" (p. 30). However, she understood that a purely quantitative approach would not

sufficiently capture the complexity of the problem. Therefore, she enlisted the help of members of the gay community to provide a qualitative review of the instrument as a part of the pilot-testing.

Bowen and Bok (1998) chose a complex quantitative-qualitative design to study the long-term consequences of considering race in college and university admissions. They chose a causal comparative quantitative design that allowed comparisons to be made between the academic performance of more than 80,000 Black and White college students who were included in the *College and Beyond* database. The database contains information from students who had matriculated at 28 academically selective colleges and universities during the fall of 1951, the fall of 1976, and the fall of 1989. The study was designed to allow comparisons of Black-White differences as well as differences in subgroups of students based on gender, low-high Scholastic Aptitude Test (SAT) scores, college majors, and level of terminal degree (bachelor's degree or graduate education). Further quantitative comparisons were designed into the study through the use of a comparison group of students who did not attend the selective colleges and universities in the *College and Beyond* database. To supplement the quantitative data and aid in the interpretation of the results, they included a qualitative component that involved follow-up interviews with a subsample of the larger sample. The interviews were designed to be "free-flowing rather than structured" (p. 301). The comments from the interviews were carefully described as not being intended for scientific analysis, but they seemed to be useful to illustrate trends identified in the empirical analysis or to offer possible explanations for the findings.

Delk and Weidekamp (2000) used a mixed methods design to determine the effects of the Shared Reading Project, a program designed to provide hearing parents and caregivers with visually based strategies to read books to their deaf and hard-of-hearing children. It targets the families of deaf and hard-of-hearing children from birth through 8 years of age. David Schleper, Jane Fernandes, and Doreen Higa first began the Shared Reading Project at the Hawai'i Center for the Deaf and the Blind in 1993. Subsequently, the program was implemented at the Kendall Demonstration Elementary School on the Gallaudet University campus. During 1997-1998, the project was expanded to include five other sites: an urban center school for the deaf, a residential school with satellite programs in a rural state, an urban public school program, and two not-for-profit organizations serving families with deaf and hard-of-hearing children in urban and rural areas.

Hopson, Lucas, and Peterson (2000) chose a mixed methods design to examine the effects of a community-based HIV/AIDS prevention and intervention program based on an inclusive participatory philosophy. Their beliefs led them to emphasize the importance of listening to what program people said about their understandings and valuing what the disease meant to those who were infected with and affected by the disease. A sociolinguistic framework allowed the researchers to explore the meanings of those infected with and affected by the disease during the early stages of the study so as to design more appropriate data collection strategies and interventions. They supported their choice of a mixed methods design as follows: "When language meanings of program beneficiaries reveal how they align or perceive themselves in the context of HIV/AIDS, evaluation and program planners might use this to structure more valid instruments or design interventions that are appropriate and meaningful" (p. 31).

One of the most serious criticisms raised by many feminists and other ethicists in terms of research designs refers to the use of control groups in experimental studies (Mertens, 1998). An ethical problem emerges with the use of control groups in that the experimental group receives the treatment but the control group does not. Feminists raise the following question: Is it ethical to deny "treatment" to one group on a random basis? Many times, school or social agency policies prevent the random assignment of people to conditions, and thus a true experimental design is not possible.

The major professional associations in the human sciences, such as the American Educational Research Association, the American Psychological Association, and the American Evaluation Association, all have ethical guidelines that are designed to protect the welfare of human participants in research. Nevertheless, controversies arise in the use of random assignment in blind clinical trials to test the effectiveness of new drugs (Stephens, 2000). Drug companies are turning to Third World countries more and more to test new drugs because, compared with the United States, the restrictions are not as stringent, costs are lower, and the patients they need for the testing are plentiful and more naive (Flaherty, Nelson, & Stephens, 2000). While some researchers support the use of placebos (inert dummy medicines) to be given to the control group, the *Declaration of Helsinki* (an international medical document on ethics in research) was revised to state that "experimental therapies always should be tested against 'best current' treatments" and that "placebos should be used only when no treatment exists" (Okie, 2000, p. A3).

While all researchers recognize the need to protect human participants, the transformative-emancipatory researchers have raised additional ethical issues related to design choices and have suggested alternative approaches. Consideration can be given to designs that do not involve denial of treatment such as time-series designs, use of a known alternative treatment, comparison with an extant group whose members have similar characteristics but who are not in a position to access the intervention, or comparison with a larger statistical base in terms of known levels of incidence (Mertens & McLaughlin, 1995). For example, in the Shared Reading Project, plans for comparison groups might include young deaf children of deaf parents because their literacy has typically been higher than that of deaf children of hearing parents.

IDENTIFYING DATA SOURCES AND SELECTING PARTICIPANTS

Many issues arise within the context of identifying data sources and selecting participants, including the following questions. Who is in the target group? What are the implications of different choices for labeling the target group? What are the implications of diversity within the target group? What can be done to improve the inclusiveness of the sample to increase the probability that traditionally marginalized groups are adequately and accurately represented?

Members of the Target Group. Inherent in the choice to work within the transformative-emancipatory paradigm is the need to define groups based on the characteristics that are associated with greater discrimination and oppression. In simplistic terms, these could be listed as race/ethnicity, sex/gender, disability, sexual orientation, and economic status. However, researchers must delve into these categories in such a way that they can meaningfully select people who are representative of diverse groups to be included in their studies. This is not a simple task.

Take race and ethnicity as examples. Race is defined as "a biological grouping within the human species with shared physical characteristics and genetic material" (Walsh, Smith, Morales, & Sechrest, 2000, pp. 1-3). Ethnicity is defined as "an individual's identification as a member of a social group with a common background, usually racial, national, tribal, religious, or linguistic" (pp. 1-3). Choices for identifying someone's race or ethnicity such as self-identification, third-party identification, and use of a government protocol such as the census categories are problematic. Even the use of the category "multiracial" is problematic in that it might include those of German-Irish descent as well as those of Hispanic-African descent.

Typically, transformative-emancipatory researchers are interested in studying those characteristics thought to be associated with acts of prejudice and discrimination, such as racial phenotypes (e.g., skin color, facial features), rather than establishing a genetic link between a particular race and a societal impact. Walsh et al. (2000) acknowledged that the race variable is used as a proxy for other variables that are known or believed to correlate with race. However, they recommended that researchers be explicit about which variables they believe have a substantial causal role in their studies and then be explicit about those and measure them more directly. Writing within the context of mental health research, they provided a list of possible ecological variables that might be asserted as possible influences on mental health service use and outcomes such as level of acculturation or availability of coping strategies, comfort with ethnic and cultural differences, communication and language skills, age-related issues, attitudes toward mental health and illness, education and literacy, group identification, gender-related issues, and support networks.

Rather than relying on a simplistic categorization of race/ethnicity as explanatory variables, researchers should strive to identify those variables that are theoretically linked to program use and impact. For example, in mental health research, they should consider including variables such as perceived stigma of mental disorder, availability of other mental health services, insurance status, social class, beliefs about treatment efficacy, and trust in providers (Walsh et al., 2000). A further discussion of how overly simplistic reliance on racial categories as explanatory variables can be is provided later in the subsection on analyzing, interpreting, and using research findings (Agar, 2000).

Impact of Labeling Target Groups. Two research studies have struggled with strategies for operationalizing their sample definitions in the context of youths who are homeless or labeled "at risk" in ways that did not put the young people at greater risk because of negative connotations associated with the sample definition (Madison, 2000; Rheaume & Roy, 2000). Rheaume and Roy (2000) studied street youths from diverse cultural groups of recent immigrants to Canada who were residents of community-supported housing. The authors began with the concept that they were studying street kids but changed their focus in midstream when they realized that they were studying youths in serious trouble, perhaps suffering from family problems. Once they reframed the definition as troubled youths who had sought community support voluntarily, the social construction of the categories influenced the research design in many other ways. The focus of the intervention shifted to identifying legal interventions that could be used to place the youths in safer housing and identifying social services that could help to reintegrate the youths with their families.

Madison (2000) also challenged the label used to identify participants as "at-risk" youths in developing and evaluating social programs. In a study of a statewide youth program, she reported that *at-risk youth* was used as a label for low-income African American, Latino, and Asian youths and thus served as a stereotypical sociopolitical label. Madison argued,

> The term *at-risk youth* was coined to inter-changeably describe both the problem and the youth. Some use the term primarily to describe a category of young people who are a problem to society. This language not only provides social group identity to this category of youth, but the contextual meaning of the language stigmatizes the youth as undesirable rather than the social situation responsible for placing them at risk. (p. 20)

The at-risk label led to negative self-images on the part of the youths and blaming of parents who were struggling economically and were thus unavailable to their children. She recommended reframing the definition of the program participants in terms of youths who were growing up without adults to guide and nurture them through the critical adolescent development stage. Thus, the focus of interventions could change to the provision of a safe environment to engage youths in productive activities supervised by adults during the nonschool hours. And the study addressed the broader policy implications for addressing the educational inequities and structural unemployment that create the economic deprivation that contributes to the parents' inability to be available to their children.

Diversity Within the Target Population.
One of the major contributions that has come from transformative scholars is exploration of the myth of homogeneity, that is, that all members of a minority group share the same characteristics (Stanfield, 1993, 1999). As Seelman (1999) noted about the demographics within the disability community, there is great diversity within the 20% of the national population who have disabilities. The diversity includes not only severity and types of disabilities but also functional limitations, limitations in performance of activities and instrumental activities of daily living, use of assistive devices, and receipt of certain benefits associated with disabilities. Demographic variations are also important. Women have higher rates of severe disabilities than do men (9.7% vs. 7.7%), while men have slightly higher rates of nonsevere disabilities. Considering both sex and race, Black women have the highest rate of severe disabilities (14.3%), followed by Black men (12.6%). Rates of severe disabilities for men and women who are American Indian, Eskimo, or Aleut are nearly as high; persons who are American Indian have the highest rates of nonsevere disabilities. Researchers who undertake research with these populations need to be knowledgeable about the diversity within the community.

In preparing a sample design for a study of court accessibility for deaf and hard-of-hearing people in the United States, Mertens (2000a) worked with an advisory board that included people who preferred a variety of communication modes and represented different aspects of the judicial system. The sample design was constructed to represent the diversity of communication modes in the deaf and hard-of-hearing communities, including highly educated deaf users of American Sign Language (ASL); deaf adults with limited education and reading skills, some of whom communicated with sign language, gestures, and pantomime; deaf/blind adults who used interpreters at close range; highly educated hard-of-hearing adults who used personal assistive listening devices; deaf adults who used Mexican Sign Language (MSL); and deaf adults who relied on oral communication (reading lips and print English). In addition to the diversity in terms of communication preference, the groups were selected to be diverse in terms of gender, race/ethnicity, and status with the court (e.g., juror, witness, victim).

The Canadian Research Institute for the Advancement of Women (1996) suggested that researchers consider the following questions to guide them in determining whether they have been inclusive in their sampling strategies:

◆ Are we including people from both genders and diverse abilities, ages, classes, cultures, ethnicities, families, incomes, languages, races, disabilities, and sexualities?

◆ What barriers are we erecting to exclude a diversity of people?

◆ Have we chosen the appropriate data collection strategies for diverse groups, including providing for preferred modes of communication?

Thus, the transformative-emancipatory perspective prods the researcher to go beyond consideration of sample size to examine the barriers that might be impeding the full inclusion of diverse groups.

IDENTIFYING OR CONSTRUCTING DATA COLLECTION INSTRUMENTS AND METHODS

The combination of both quantitative and qualitative data collection methods is not unusual. For example, the Shared

Reading Project collected both quantitative and qualitative data—a mixed methods approach—to address its evaluation questions. The questions that call for a quantitative analysis included wording such as "To what extent . . . ?" and "Did they read more?" The qualitative data consisted of about 50 interviews with site coordinators, parents, and their tutors. They were designed to obtain information about the processes that were successful or unsuccessful in the project.

Scholars working within the transformative-emancipatory paradigm have raised the following issues-related choices about data collection strategies: (a) consideration of how the data collection process and outcomes will benefit the community being studied; (b) credibility of the research findings to that community; (c) the appropriateness of communication methods, knowledge about those methods, and resources to support and willingness to engage in effective communication methods; (d) knowledge about response tendencies within the community and sensitivity to culturally appropriate ways to ask questions; and (e) tying the collection of data to transformation either by influencing the design of the treatment intervention or by providing avenues for participation in the social change process. This section examines these issues.

Benefits and Credibility. Truman (2000) demonstrated her commitment to ensure that research money was spent within the gay community in a study of gay and bisexual men's needs for information about safe sex practices. She did not hire interviewers from within the university where she was employed, as is typically done. Rather, she recruited interviewers from within the gay community to undertake face-to-face interviews. She described the benefits of this choice of data collection methods as follows:

> Apart from the direct benefits of receiving payment for their work, our interviewers received training and experience of research work, thus enhancing their skills. . . . From the gay community's perspective, it was involvement in the research that was important since involvement could contribute to the greater good. (p. 32)

The choice of this data collection strategy highlights two aspects of transformative-emancipatory work. First, there were benefits to members of the community of concern in terms of payment for services and enhancement of research skills. Second, the credibility of the study was enhanced for the participants when they saw that the study was being done "with" them rather than "on" them.

Involving members of marginalized groups can be one strategy that will lead to better data collection instruments (Chelimsky, 1998; Oliver, 1992). Oliver (1992) identified questions from the Office of Population Census and Surveys in Great Britain that represented a "blame the victim" theory, including those suggesting that it was the people's fault that they could not open a door by themselves, communicate with others, or attend the school of their choice. He suggested that questions written from a transformative perspective would ask about the aspects of the social and physical environment that were serving as barriers to full access or personal freedom rather than locating the problem of disability within the individual.

Cohen-Mitchell (2000) started with interview questions about the problems experienced by disabled women in El Salvador. However, she reported that when women were asked directly about the problems they faced as disabled women in El Salvador, many of them were unable to answer. Cohen-Mitchell changed her introductory question by asking the women to describe their disabilities and then to explain their lives in relation to them. By using this sequence of questions, she was able to obtain data about what had gone right for the women as well as some of the broader problems they had experienced.

Chelimsky (1998) described one study in which the evaluators at the U.S. General Accounting Office used such a strategy that involved surveying disabled people before conducting a survey to determine the effectiveness of the Americans With Disabilities Act:

> We used their responses in construct-ing both the design and the survey in-struments, recognizing—based on what we had learned from them—the need to ask probing questions of busi-ness owners and operators not just about observable barriers, but also about invisible ones, such as whether a blind person with a guide dog might be refused entry to a cafe or restau-rant. (USGAO/PEMD, 1993, cited in Chelimsky, 1998, p. 47)

This practice of basing questions on the lives of those with personal insights and experience about the problems is in keep-ing with the tenets of transformative theory.

Appropriate Communication Strategies. Another consideration in data collec-tion strategies, particularly with diverse groups, is arranging for appropriate com-munication to occur. With the court access project mentioned previously (Mertens, 2000a), different configurations of techni-cal support were needed to facilitate effec-tive communication. For example, in the group in which the individuals had a low level of language functioning, the staff in-cluded hearing and deaf co-moderators;

an ASL interpreter who signed for the hearing moderator and voiced for the deaf participants; a deaf relay interpreter who translated the ASL signing into a combina-tion of signs, pantomime, and gestures for one individual whose language function-ing was too low to understand a pure ASL presentation; and a deaf-blind interpreter who signed into the hands of one visually impaired woman in the group. In addi-tion, a court reporter observed the group and entered the comments of everyone into a written transcript that ran as real-time captions across two television screens that were strategically situated in the room.

In the focus group in which the partici-pants used MSL, the communication loop consisted of a hearing focus group moder-ator who voiced in English; his words were translated into ASL by a hearing in-terpreter, and the hearing interpreter's signs were interpreted into MSL by a deaf interpreter who knew both ASL and MSL. This process was reversed for the focus group moderator to understand what the participants were saying.

One obvious challenge in trying to start off thought from marginalized lives as Harding (1993) suggests is the need for in-depth knowledge of how to facilitate that participation for these cultural groups, ac-cess to resources to cover the expense of providing for meaningful participation, and patience to handle the added com-plexity of ensuring that those with the least power can meaningfully participate in the provision of data. The staff and the focus group moderator expressed frustra-tion about the communication; it seemed slow and difficult to control. One could guess that the reaction of court personnel to this type of communication system might be similar. This, in itself, was a valu-able insight that was shared with court system personnel to elucidate the potential for cultural conflicts emanating from different expectations concerning language use.

Data collection strategies for the Shared Reading Project were modified to accommodate both quantitative and qualitative data collection in light of the needs of hearing and deaf participants (Delk & Weidekamp, 2000). On-site videotaping, however, would be difficult to arrange and expensive to analyze. After much discussion, the Shared Reading Project staff and evaluators decided on a different strategy for the tutor interviews after recognizing the special needs of diverse audiences. For example, the evaluators originally intended to conduct end-of-year interviews with tutors by phone using a telecommunications device for the deaf. This strategy was based on the assumption that all of the tutors hired by the expansion sites would be fluent in English as well as in ASL, so that an English-based interview would not be an impediment to clear communication. Several of the site coordinators reported, however, that some of the tutors they hired were strong ASL users and had excellent interpersonal skills with parents but were less fluent in English. One of the deaf site coordinators strongly recommended that the tutor interviews be conducted face-to-face using sign language. The Shared Reading Project staff concurred and also recommended that these interviews be conducted by a deaf interviewer and that they be audiotaped given that the evaluators wanted to have a verbatim record.

A deaf interviewer fluent in ASL was trained and traveled with an interpreter to each of the sites to interview the sample of tutors, as recommended by the site coordinators. Each interview was audiotaped, using an interpreter to voice into the tape recorder for both the interviewer and the interviewee. In this way, each interview was conducted in a manner conducive to clear and direct communication, and a verbal record of the interview was obtained for analysis.

Lee (1999) raised interesting issues concerning the validity of data collected in research with people with mental health disabilities. She contrasted her experience in asking about satisfaction with health services for people who have private insurance and transportation with that for people whose access to housing, rent subsidies, and medications necessary for life and perhaps sanity comes from one agency that is within reach by public transportation and Medicaid. She suggested that the chances are very good that people's responses will be influenced if they have already learned to settle for less when it comes to medical care or if they are unwilling to risk criticizing the programs of those who hold so much power in their hands, no matter how much the respondents are assured of anonymity. English (1997) suggested that people who are dependent on mental health services feel the threat of potential sanctions and that this has an influence on their cooperation with researchers. Mayberg (1997) reported that people with serious mental illnesses who are hospitalized do not feel they have a choice and thus will tend to report the data that they believe the researcher wants to hear.

Cultural Sensitivity. Agar (2000) identified a number of pitfalls that occurred when cultural sensitivity in the data collection process was not sufficiently present. He described the difficulties that community health workers experienced in a study of a tuberculosis (TB) screening project in an inner-city urban area. The study included both quantitative and qualitative components in the data collection plan. However, interviewers were instructed to stand at the door and speak from a standard protocol. The questions involved areas such as income, prison, drug and alcohol use, and sexual practices that were seen as too personal and intimate by most of the respondents. Some of the answers called for time line estimates that simply did not map onto the way respondents thought about their activities. Agar wrote,

> People were often suspicious—some slammed the door—and they wondered why they had to be interviewed when they had no interest in being tested. And, finally, the neighborhood selected for community screening is a serious crack area. Needless to say, crack houses and crack users are not known for their predisposition to discuss income and hours per day spent at work with community health workers. (p. 98)

Agar concluded that the data collection problem emanated from a contradiction between the scientific requirement for acquiring the data in a certain way and the communicative norms of the situation in which the interviewing was done.

Ryen (2000) provided yet another, somewhat amusing example of the results of asking culturally insensitive questions. A Norwegian researcher in Tanzania asked a local man for directions. He phrased his question as follows: "Is this the way to Arusha?" The man answered "yes." The Norwegian drove many miles before he realized that he was indeed heading in the wrong direction. This story illustrates the importance of understanding cultural codes. The European man viewed the Tanzanian as stupid and untrustworthy. However, the Tanzanian man was answering the question in accordance with local norms. He was showing politeness toward the European by avoiding opposing the guest. The way the question was worded left the Tanzanian man with no options. The European could have learned the correct direction by rewording

his question as follows: "Which way is Arusha?"

Integrating Data Collection and Social Action. A final point in data collection relates to integration of the data collection strategies with the transformative goals of the research. Hopson et al. (2000) addressed this issue in their study in the HIV/AIDS community where they conducted 75 ethnographic interviews as well as used 40 semistructured questionnaires about respondents' sociodemographics, daily routines, drug use profiles, knowledge of HIV/AIDS risks, and drug and sexual sociobehavioral characteristics. In addition, 35 participants completed open-ended interviews that explored themes related to perceptions and meanings assigned to HIV/AIDS, how the disease was affecting them and their support systems, and other discourse and attitudes surrounding the disease. Hopson et al. analyzed these data to be used as a basis for developing interventions and preventions that were relevant to the predominantly African American context.

Another aspect of transformative-emancipatory data collection involves designing the data collection that opens up avenues for participation in the social change process. In the study of court access for deaf and hard-of-hearing persons (Mertens, 2000a), the data collection strategies were designed with an eye toward facilitating transformative change. As part of the training programs for judges and other court personnel, deaf and hard-of-hearing people and their advocates were invited to attend the training workshops with representatives of the court systems in their state. The final session of the workshop involved small groups from each state working together to complete an action plan so that state-level teams could assess their current status in terms of court accessibility and make plans for future actions. Each item on the action plan form was the topic of a plenary session prior to the planning session so that the participants would have the most up-to-date information available on the topics to use in their planning discussions. The idea of planning together as a team with court personnel and representatives of the deaf and hard-of-hearing communities was emphasized repeatedly. Through the action plan process, participants were asked to reflect on actions that were not limited to appropriate use of interpreters and technology but also included legislation and attitudes as they influence achievement of equal justice.

ANALYZING, INTERPRETING, REPORTING, AND USING RESULTS

Typically, qualitative data are used to help explain quantitative results, as illustrated in three studies reviewed in this section (Agar, 2000; Bowen & Bok, 1998; Delk & Weidenkamp, 2000). However, this is not the only use of the findings, and other issues arise in analysis, interpretation, reporting, and using results from the transformative-emancipatory paradigm, including (a) raising hypotheses concerning the dynamics that underlie the quantitative results, (b) conducting subgroup analyses to look at the differential impact on diverse groups in the study, (c) improving understanding of the results from the perspective of power relationships, and (d) reporting the results in such a way as to facilitate social change.

Raising Hypotheses Concerning Dynamics. The analysis choices for the Bowen and Bok (1998) study of race-based college admissions was largely quantitative. They presented tabulations, cross-tabulations, and bar charts and other figures. They used statistical techniques such

as multivariate regression to disentangle the many forces that jointly affect student performance in college, receipt of advanced degrees, and later-life outcomes. In addition, they used the qualitative comments from a subgroup of students to illuminate the findings and interpretations. For example, based on a regression analysis that controlled for other student and institutional characteristics, they reported that the typical Black *College and Beyond* graduate earns more than do most holders of bachelor's degrees in the United States. They hypothesized that graduation from an elite university might open doors that help Black graduates to overcome negative stereotypes that might otherwise restrict their earnings potential. They supported this hypothesis with a quotation from one of the qualitative interviews in which the respondent reported,

> "I worked in the corporate auditor's office through some Yale [University] connection and got to see the workings of a corporation from an inside—and interesting—position as opposed to doing some sort of scut work. . . . It wasn't that any of these people knew me. They knew the association I belonged to at Yale—one of the secret societies. . . . I earned my way and got the job. But it was these connections that got me the introduction." (p. 131)

Subgroup Analyses. The Shared Reading Project evaluation resulted in a complex multilevel data set. The quantitative analysis was used to answer questions such as "To what extent . . . ?" and "Did they read more?" For these questions, descriptive and inferential statistics were calculated using the SPSS program. The characteristics of the children, families, and tutors were tabulated and reported as numbers and percentages to describe the different groups of stakeholders participating in the evaluation. For example, the evaluators found that 87% of the participating deaf and hard-of-hearing children belonged to one or more of the traditionally underserved groups. The average age of these children was between 4 and 5 years.

Another measure of reading frequency was the number of times families shared books during their participation in the Shared Reading Project, which parents recorded on the "family reading records." Book-sharing events were tabulated by week for each family, and average reading rates were computed for each week of the project. The families reported that they shared books an average of five times a week while participating in the project.

These data were also subjected to repeated-measures analysis of variance to determine whether there was a statistically significant increase in the number of book-sharing events during the project. Surprisingly, this analysis showed that as soon as the tutors started working with the families, parents and other family members started sharing books frequently with their children and continued doing so until the end of the tutoring sessions. This analysis did not reveal anything, however, about how the families were sharing books, only that they were sitting down with the books together and doing something.

Here is where the qualitative data collected through in-person, on-site interviews helped to explain what was happening. Parents described how they began to improve their sign language, how they gained confidence, how they began to understand better the questions their children were asking about the books, and how they learned to use more facial and body expressions to make the stories more interesting to their children. The interviews with the parents, tutors, and site coordinators also revealed that, while many of the parents increased their book-sharing abilities during the 20-week intervention, they still had more to learn and still struggled with different aspects of the story-reading process. Many of the parents asked their tutors and site coordinators if they could continue with the Shared Reading Project the following year.

Comparison of the mean number of book-sharing events for different groups yielded other interesting results. There was no significant difference in the average number of book-sharing events per week for children who were or were not members of traditionally underserved groups. This indicated that children who have not traditionally had access to the same educational services as other children were being read to just as often as children who have traditionally had more access to educational services—a good example of a negative statistical result that has a positive interpretation.

Elucidating Power Relationships. Agar (2000) was hired to conduct a qualitative follow-up to a quantitative study that suggested that a TB screening program in an urban community had not been successful. He found that interviews with the community health workers provided data that, in their view, the program had been successful. He also explored reasons why the partnership between the university medical professionals and the community church representatives had failed. The ethnographic data from the community health workers revealed that they viewed the TB screening project as an opportunity to show that they cared about the people in the program even if the people did not choose to have the TB screening procedure. The workers knew that the program clients were people who often suffer from multiple life problems, including racism, violence, poverty, dysfunctional families, drug and alcohol abuse, and other health problems. From their point of view, the workers were successful if they could demonstrate that they cared about the clients in relation to any of the these problems, and they did not view the clients' lack of interest in TB screening as a failure. Agar concluded that the medical model offered too narrow a definition of success by focusing only on the numerical count of how many people participated in TB screening when in fact the people in the community faced many complex problems and TB was not necessarily the most salient issue for them.

Another interesting finding based on the ethnographic portion of the study related to the breakdown in the relationship between the White university researcher and the Black minister who initiated the project in the community. The university researcher was frustrated by her inability to bridge the differences between the medical culture and the community. She concluded that "the country may not be ready for successful black/white partnerships because of the magnitude and subtlety of the difference" (Agar, 2000, p. 103). The minister framed the problem as one of inequitable power relations and control of resources in that the control stayed in the hands of the university representative. A third person was interviewed who was also a minister but who worked for the university as a liaison to the community. He suggested that the problem reflected a history of distrust between the community and the university as well as clashes between two strong personalities with divergent interests. Agar cautioned against an overly simplistic interpretation of the dissolution of this relationship based solely on Black-White differences. His collection of additional qualitative data supported the hypothesis that the relationship foundered because of strong personalities, changing directions, control over resources and process, and the church-science divide. In addition, historical relationships between the university and the community had to be considered. He concluded, "The demographics of race clearly define the context of the program, but the way those demographics played out locally link them to more general issues of organizational process" (p. 109).

Brown (2000) raised interesting issues related to power relationships in terms of male-female contributions in focus groups by using both quantitative and qualitative analysis of the transcripts. She counted the number of contributions made by men and women in focus groups during time that was structured by the moderator (i.e., the moderator went around the group asking each person to respond) and during unstructured time (i.e., anyone could speak as he or she wanted). During the structured time, Brown found that the men and women made an equal number of contributions based on number of lines in the transcript attributed to each subgroup. During the unstructured time, the balance shifted to 60% of the comments being made by men and 40% being made by women. However, Brown also looked at the length of the responses for males and females. This revealed that the majority of minimal responses and supportive one-word lines were made by women, thus inflating the actual quantitative contribution of the women in the counts.

To determine who contributed more content, Brown (2000) conducted a qualitative analysis of strategies for taking the floor and topic raising. She reported,

> The overriding themes that emerged from the data show that men and women used language in quite different ways to take the floor. Men were very assertive: when they desired the floor, they often took it through interruption. Men regularly used verbal means for taking the floor, which simply meant that they began to speak and

state their fact or opinion. Women, on the contrary, typically used nonverbal means of obtaining the floor. They made signals—raising a hand, raising eyebrows, and so on—as a means of conveying a desire to speak. Afterward they patiently waited for the moderator to call on them to speak. (p. 63)

Brown also reported that men introduced new topics and women tended to play a supportive role, building on the topics that men raised. When women did raise topics, either they were ignored or the men reintroduced the topics and took credit for them by claiming the ideas as their own.

From this quantitative and qualitative analysis, Brown (2000) concluded that men contributed more concrete data to the focus group study. She suggested that researchers' recognition and understanding that language differences exist between the sexes is crucial to the reliability and validity of a good research study. Differences may exist in contributions to content based on other characteristics as well. Moderators of focus groups must be assertive to ensure that specific voices are not silenced. If the study warrants, it might be best to use homogeneous groups based on salient characteristics such as race/ethnicity, sex, and disability.

Reporting Research to Facilitate Action. Mienczakowski (2000) described a way of presenting results from a research study that would facilitate the use of the information for the purpose of social change. Having conducted ethnographic studies of alcohol detoxification centers and psychiatric settings that serve people with schizophrenia, Mienczakowski sought ways to present the information that would go beyond the typically small audiences for academic reports. He developed critical ethno-dramas based on each study that

consisted of two-act, full-length performance pieces. He wrote, "The guiding principle leading this critical theory-based ethnographic approach is to attempt to accurately give voice to groups of health consumers who otherwise consider themselves to be disempowered or disenfranchised in some way" (p. 129).

The ethno-dramas are performed for health professionals, students in health-related training programs, and the general public. Following each performance, the researcher conducts a discussion forum in which the audience questions and debates the representations made on stage with the actors, the health care provider and consumer informants, and the project writers and directors. By these means, the data in the productions continue to evolve and integrate diverse reactions to the portrayals of alcohol dependency and schizophrenia. Throughout the process, the audience's perceptions of people served by mental health programs and their understandings of people with these two diseases are challenged and expanded. "Critical ethno-drama seeks to emancipate audiences and informants from stereotypical and oppressive understandings of illness, and in so doing [to] free informants from the historified perceptions of their health constraints" (p. 133).

Despite the fact that Mienczakowski's (2000) data were qualitative, the approach he used for the reporting of the information could be adapted to a mixed methods research study as well. Audience members are provided with the transcripts of the plays as well as with health education materials relevant to the topic. Researchers could consider including relevant statistics portrayed in graphics that could communicate the quantitative results as well. The important principle is the portrayal of valid data that represents the voices of the disempowered, as well as the professionals who serve them, in such a way that it engages the audience in discussions of strategies for change.

◆ Conclusions: Summary, Optimism, and Concerns

Changing conditions inside and outside of the research community have brought increased attention to the need to address the politics of human research and issues of social justice. Trends in demographics that have resulted in increased social pluralism and scholarly writers from the transformative-emancipatory paradigm have addressed the importance of the role of values in research. Teddlie and Tashakkori argue in this handbook (Chapter 1) that pragmatics provides a potential underlying paradigm that supports the choice of mixed methods. Transformative-emancipatory researchers suggest caution on basing methodological choices solely on pragmatics. The value of pragmatics that drives the desire to adopt a mixed methods stance in research is seen as inadequate and unexamined because it does not answer the question "Practical for whom and to what end?" (House & Howe, 1999). Transformative-emancipatory scholars recommend the adoption of an explicit goal for research to serve the ends of creating a more just and democratic society that permeates the entire research process, from the problem formulation to the drawing of conclusions and the use of the results (Mertens, 1998).

The transformative-emancipatory paradigm places central importance on the lives and experiences of those who suffer oppression and discrimination, whatever the basis of that is—be it sex, race/ethnicity, disability, sexual orientation, or socioeconomic status. Researchers working within this paradigm are consciously aware of power differentials in the research context, and they search for ways to ameliorate the effects of oppression and discrimination by linking their research activities to social action and wider questions of social inequity and social justice. Ontologically, reality is described within a historical, political, cultural, and economic context. Epistemologically, interaction between the researchers and the participants is essential and requires a level of trust and understanding to accurately represent viewpoints of all groups fairly. Methodologically, mixed methods offer avenues to address the issues of diverse groups appropriately.

In defining the research problem, a literature search can be used to establish the boundaries of published knowledge about an issue. However, this is seldom sufficient because of biases inherent in the nature of literature that is published. In addition, the research problem requires spending time with members of the population of interest to build trust. Methods that might supplement literature review include observation, interviewing, reviewing demographic and other statistical data, and sometimes using preliminary surveys. The reader should also be aware of prevailing theoretical frameworks that have depicted members of marginalized groups or their cultures as deficient. Questions can ask about positive and negative experiences in a study and can be linked to policy or social actions that can lead to societal transformation.

A mixed methods research design framed within the transformative-emancipatory paradigm might include the use of both qualitative and quantitative methods for the purpose of capturing the complexity of a situation, raising hypotheses about the reasons why a result is found, or providing insights into the development of more valid data collection instruments or program interventions. One ethical concern that has been raised by this approach is the choice of denying treatment to a group so as to have a true experimental design. Options include comparing the new treatment to the best known treatment, using a time-series design, making comparisons with an extant group with similar characteristics, and using a larger statistical base in terms of known levels of incidence.

Many issues have been raised with regard to the sample identification and selection in the transformative-emancipatory literature. Of particular importance is the beginning step of specifying who is in the target group along with the use of a theoretical framework that delineates the variable thought to be associated with the outcomes of interest. Caution is necessary to avoid labeling groups in such a way that it negatively affects both their self-concepts and the development of appropriate interventions. In addition, the diversity within groups must be acknowledged, whether that be in terms of severity of disability or experience with the relevant institution such as the courts. Steps must be taken to ensure that the diversity within groups is attended to by means of how individuals are invited and the support that is given to them once they have agreed to participate in the study.

Data collection issues include consideration of how the data collection process and outcomes will benefit the community being studied in terms of opportunities to contribute to the collection of more valid data as well as in terms of increasing the skills and expertise of members of the targeted community in the research process itself. Such steps can lead to an increase in the credibility of the results of the study for members of that community. However, demands are placed on researchers to achieve appropriate communication methods and resources to support the use of more complex communication strategies. As always, cultural sensitivity will mean the difference between quality data and inaccurate or irrelevant findings. Finally, the link between data collection and social change can be built into the data collection process itself by including mechanisms for the marginalized groups to influence plans for future actions based on the study's outcomes, influencing the development of additional data collection instruments or interventions, and providing information to policy-making bodies.

The ways in which data are analyzed, interpreted, reported, and used are also influenced by the transformative-emancipatory paradigm. The qualitative data can be used to test hypotheses concerning how certain dynamics affect the results that are evidenced in the quantitative data. Subgroup analyses can indicate when differential outcomes are indicative of more or less success with various subpopulations. One very interesting use is to examine the dynamics within the research study itself to determine the effects of different value systems and power relationships on the study's outcomes and the relationships among the participants in the study. This is particularly important in cross-cultural studies that pose challenges both in terms of the social problem being addressed and in terms of the relationships among the researchers and participants. Reporting results should also follow the personal and political tendencies seen in the other parts of the research study. Engaging the readers in a way that presents the results such that the full human impact is felt and understood is a challenge. Yet strategies such as ethno-drama provide such a mechanism for addressing complex social problems in this way (Mienczakowski, 2000). To increase use of research findings, the researchers need to be aware of the networks of relationships that must be established and nurtured. Finding ways to really listen and understand is a big challenge. However, it will mean more credible information that can be used to inform policies that are needed to address the inequities in the world. The social conditions and the politics within the research community can work to either impede or foster further developments of mixed methods approaches based on the transformative-emancipatory paradigm.

■ *References*

Agar, M. (2000). Border lessons: Linguistic "rich points" and evaluative understanding. In R. Hopson (Ed.), *How and why language matters in evaluation* (New Directions in Evaluation, No. 86, pp. 93-110). San Francisco: Jossey-Bass.

Alcoff, L., & Potter, E. (Eds.). (1993). *Feminist epistemologies.* New York: Routledge.

Banks, J. A. (1993). The canon debate, knowledge construction, and multicultural education. *Educational Researcher, 22*(5), 4-14.

Banks, J. A. (1995). The historical reconstruction of knowledge about race: Implications for transformative teaching. *Educational Researcher, 24*(2), 15-25.

Bhavnani, K. K. (1991). What's power got to do with it? Empowerment and social research. In I. Parker & J. Shotter (Eds.), *Deconstructing social psychology.* London: Routledge.

Booth, W. (2000, August 31). California minorities are now the majority. *Washington Post,* p. A1.

Bowen, W., & Bok, D. (1998). *The shape of the river: Long-term consequences of considering race in college and university admissions.* Princeton, NJ: Princeton University Press.

Brown, C. L. (2000). Sociolinguistic dynamics of gender in focus groups. In R. Hopson (Ed.), *How and why language matters in evaluation* (New Directions in Evaluation,

No. 86, pp. 55-68). San Francisco: Jossey-Bass.

Buchanan, R. M. (1999). *Illusions of equality: Deaf Americans in school and factory, 1850-1950.* Washington, DC: Gallaudet University Press.

Canadian Research Institute for the Advancement of Women. (1996). *Feminist research ethics: A process.* Ottawa, Ontario: Author.

Chelimsky, E. (1998). The role of experience in formulating theories of evaluation practice. *American Journal of Evaluation, 19* (1), 35-56.

Cohen-Mitchell, J. B. (2000). Disabled women in El Salvador reframing themselves: An economic development program for women. In C. Truman, D. M. Mertens, & B. Humphries (Eds.), *Research and inequality* (pp. 143-176). London: Taylor & Francis.

DeKoning, K., & Martin, M. (Eds.). (1996). *Participatory research in health.* London: Zed Books.

Delk, L., & Weidekamp, L. (2000). *Shared Reading Project evaluation.* Washington, DC: Gallaudet University, Laurent Clerc National Deaf Education Center.

Dockery, G. (2000). Participatory research: Whose roles, whose responsibilities? In C. Truman, D. M. Mertens, & B. Humphries (Eds.), *Research and inequality* (pp. 95-110). London: Taylor & Francis.

English, B. (1997). Conducting ethical evaluations with disadvantaged and minority target groups. *Evaluation Practice, 18*(1), 49-54.

Fine, M. (Ed.). (1992). *Disruptive voices.* Ann Arbor: University of Michigan Press.

Flaherty, M. P., Nelson, D., & Stephens, J. (2000, December 18). The Body Hunters: Overwhelming the watchdogs. *Washington Post,* pp. A1, A16-A17.

Gill, C. (1999). Invisible ubiquity: The surprising relevance of disability issues in evaluation. *American Journal of Evaluation, 20*(2), 279-287.

Grant, J. P. (1993). *The state of the world's children: 1993.* New York: Oxford University Press.

Guba, E. G., & Lincoln, Y. S. (1994). Competing paradigms in qualitative research. In N. K. Denzin & Y. S. Lincoln (Eds.), *The handbook of qualitative research* (pp. 105-117). Thousand Oaks, CA: Sage.

Harding, S. (1993). Rethinking standpoint epistemology: What is strong objectivity? In L. Alcoff & E. Potter (Eds.), *Feminist epistemologies* (pp. 49-82). New York: Routledge.

Hill Collins, P. (2000). *Black feminist thought: Knowledge, consciousness, and the politics of empowerment.* New York: Routledge.

Hopson, R. K., Lucas, K. J., & Peterson, J. A. (2000). HIV/AIDS talk: Implications for prevention, intervention, and evaluation. In R. Hopson (Ed.), *How and why language matters in evaluation* (New Directions in Evaluation, No. 86, pp. 29-42). San Francisco: Jossey-Bass.

Horn, L., & Berktold, J. (1999). *Students with disabilities in post-secondary education: A profile of preparation, participation, and outcomes* (NCES 1999-187). Washington, DC: U.S. Department of Education, National Center for Education Statistics.

House, E. R., & Howe, K. R. (1999). *Values in evaluation and social research.* Thousand Oaks, CA: Sage.

Humphries, B., Mertens, D. M., & Truman, C. (2000). Arguments for an "emancipatory" research paradigm. In C. Truman, D. M. Mertens, & B. Humphries (Eds.), *Research and inequality* (pp. 3-23). London: Taylor & Francis.

Humphries, B., & Truman, C. (Eds.). (1994). *Re-thinking social research.* Aldershot, UK: Avebury.

Kellner, D. (1997). Critical theory and cultural studies: The missed articulation. In M. McGuigan (Ed.), *Cultural methodologies* (pp. 12-41). Thousand Oaks, CA: Sage.

Kemmis, S., & McTaggart, R. (2000). Participatory action research. In N. K. Denzin & Y. S. Lincoln (Eds.), *Handbook of qualitative research* (2nd ed., pp. 567-606). Thousand Oaks, CA: Sage.

Kincheloe, J. L., & McLaren, P. (2000). Rethinking critical theory and qualitative research. In N. K. Denzin & Y. S. Lincoln (Eds.), *Handbook of qualitative research* (2nd ed., pp. 279-314). Thousand Oaks, CA: Sage.

Lane, H. (1993). Cochlear implants: Their cultural and historical meaning. In J. V. Van Cleave (Ed.), *Deaf history unveiled: Interpretations from the new scholarship* (pp. 272-291). Washington, DC: Gallaudet University Press.

Lather, P. (1992). Critical frames in educational research: Feminist and poststructural perspectives. *Theory Into Practice, 31*(2), 1-13.

Lee, B. (1999). The implications of diversity and disability for evaluation practice: Commentary on Gill. *American Journal of Evaluation, 20,* 289-293.

Longmore, P. K. (1994, August). *History of people with disabilities.* Keynote presentation of the Leadership Development Institute for Post-Secondary Students With Disabilities, Minneapolis.

Madison, A. M. (1992). *Minority issues in program evaluation* (New Directions for Program Evaluation, Vol. 53). San Francisco: Jossey-Bass.

Madison, A. M. (2000). Language in defining social problems and in evaluating social programs. In R. Hopson (Ed.), *How and why language matters in evaluation* (New Directions in Evaluation, No. 86, pp. 17-28). San Francisco: Jossey-Bass.

Mayberg, S. (1997, April). *The future for quality in managed care.* Paper presented at Outcomes Conference, Tampa, FL.

McLaren, P. L., & Lankshear, C. (Eds.). (1994). *Politics of liberation.* New York: Routledge.

McNeil, J. M. (1997, August). Americans with disabilities: 1994-95. *Current Population Reports,* pp. 61-70.

Meadow-Orlans, K. (2002). Social change and conflict: Context for research on deafness. In M. D. Clark, M. Marschark, & M. Karchmer (Eds.), *Context, cognition, and deafness* (pp. 161-178). Washington, DC: Gallaudet University Press.

Mertens, D. M. (1998). *Research methods in education and psychology: Integrating* diversity with quantitative and qualitative approaches. Thousand Oaks, CA: Sage.

Mertens, D. M. (1999). Inclusive evaluation: Implications of transformative theory for evaluation. *American Journal of Evaluation, 20*(1), 1-14.

Mertens, D. M. (2000a). Deaf and hard of hearing people in court: Using an emancipatory perspective to determine their needs. In C. Truman, D. M. Mertens, & B. Humphries (Eds.), *Research and inequality* (pp. 111-125). London: Taylor & Francis.

Mertens, D. M. (2000b, January). *Researching disability and diversity: Merging paradigms.* Paper presented at the meeting of the National Institute for Disability and Rehabilitative Research, Washington, DC.

Mertens, D. M., Farley, J., Madison, A. M., & Singleton, P. (1994). Diverse voices in evaluation practice: Feminists, minorities, and persons with disabilities. *Evaluation Practice, 15*(2), 123-129.

Mertens, D. M., & McLaughlin, J. (1995). *Research methods in special education.* Thousand Oaks, CA: Sage.

Mienczakowski, J. (2000). Ethnography in the form of theatre with emancipatory intentions. In C. Truman, D. M. Mertens, & B. Humphries (Eds.), *Research and inequality* (pp. 126-142). London: Taylor & Francis.

Mohanty, C. T. (1991). Cartographies of struggle: Third World women and the politics of feminism. In C. T. Mohanty, A. Russo, & L. Torres (Eds.), *Third World women and the politics of feminism.* Bloomington: Indiana University Press.

Nelson, J. (1996). The last dogma of empiricism? In L. H. Nelson & J. Nelson (Eds.), *Feminism, science, and the philosophy of science* (pp. 59-78). Boston: Kluwer Academic.

Nelson, L. H. (1996). Empiricism without dogmas. In L. H. Nelson & J. Nelson (Eds.), *Feminism, science, and the philosophy of science* (pp. 95-120). Boston: Kluwer Academic.

Okie, S. (2000, November 24). Health officials debate ethics of placebo use. *Washington Post,* p. A3.

Olesen, V. (2000). Feminisms and qualitative research at and into the millennium. In N. K. Denzin & Y. S. Lincoln (Eds.), *Handbook of qualitative research* (2nd ed., pp. 215-256). Thousand Oaks, CA: Sage.

Oliver, M. (1992). Changing the social relations of research production? *Disability, Handicap, & Society, 7*(2), 101-114.

Reason, P. (Ed.). (1994). *Participation in human inquiry.* London: Sage.

Reinharz, S. (1992). *Feminist methods in social research.* New York: Oxford University Press.

Rheaume, J., & Roy, S. (2000). Defining without discriminating? Ethnicity and social problems—The case of street youth in Canada. In C. Truman, D. M. Mertens, & B. Humphries (Eds.), *Research and inequality* (pp. 236-247). London: Taylor & Francis.

Ribbens, J., & Edwards, R. (Eds.). (1998). *Feminist dilemmas in qualitative research.* Thousand Oaks, CA: Sage.

Ryen, A. (2000). Colonial methodology? Methodological challenges to cross-cultural projects collecting data by structured interviews. In C. Truman, D. M. Mertens, & B. Humphries (Eds.), *Research and inequality* (pp. 220-235). London: Taylor & Francis.

Seelman, K. (1998, March). *Change and challenge: The integration of the new paradigm of disability into research and practice.* Paper presented at the National Council on Rehabilitation Education Conference, Vancouver, WA.

Seelman, K. (1999). *Testimony to the Commission on Advancement of Women and Minorities in Science, Engineering, and Technology.* Washington, DC: National Institute on Disability and Rehabilitation Research.

Stanfield, J. H., II (1993). Methodological reflections: An introduction. In J. H. Stanfield & R. Dennis (Eds.), *Race and ethnicity in research methods* (pp. 3-15). Newbury Park, CA: Sage.

Stanfield, J. H., II (1999). Slipping through the front door: Relevant social scientific evaluation in the people-of-color century. *American Journal of Evaluation, 20,* 415-432.

Stanfield, J. H., & Dennis, R. (Eds.). (1993). *Race and ethnicity in research methods.* Newbury Park, CA: Sage.

Stephens, J. (2000, December 17). The Body Hunters: As drug testing spreads, profits and lives hang in balance. *Washington Post,* p. A1.

Tuana, N. (1996). Revaluing science: Starting from the practices of women. In L. H. Nelson & J. Nelson (Eds.), *Feminism, science, and the philosophy of science* (pp. 17-35). Boston: Kluwer Academic.

Truman, C. (2000). New social movements and social research. In C. Truman, D. M. Mertens, & B. Humphries (Eds.), *Research and inequality* (pp. 24-36). London: Taylor & Francis.

Truman, C., Mertens, D. M., & Humphries, B. (Eds.). (2000). *Research and inequality.* London: Taylor & Francis.

U.S. Bureau of the Census. (1997). *Statistical abstracts of the United States, 1997.* Washington, DC: Government Printing Office.

U.S. Bureau of the Census. (2000). *Resident population estimates of the United States* (NP-T5-C). Washington, DC: Government Printing Office.

Villegas, A. M. (1991). *Culturally responsive pedagogy for the 1990's and beyond.* Princeton, NJ: Educational Testing Service.

Walsh, M., Smith, R., Morales, A., & Sechrest, L. (2000). *Ecocultural research: A mental health researcher's guide to the study of race, ethnicity, and culture.* Cambridge, MA: Human Services Research Institute.

Whitmore, E. (Ed.). (1998). *Framing participatory evaluation.* San Francisco: Jossey-Bass.

SECTION TWO

Methodological and Analytical Issues for Mixed Methods Research

6

A TYPOLOGY OF RESEARCH PURPOSES AND ITS RELATIONSHIP TO MIXED METHODS

◆ Isadore Newman
Carolyn S. Ridenour
Carole Newman
George Mario Paul DeMarco, Jr.

Issues of validity of social science research have never been more central. The expanding array of methodologies that are accepted as pathways to new knowledge and understanding seems nearly limitless. To the questions "What counts as research?" and "What counts as 'data' or 'representation'?," there are increasingly diverse answers. Confirming the validity of one's research, however, is no less important. In fact, establishing validity is even more consequential as methodological choices expand. Researchers strengthen validity (e.g., legitimacy, trustworthiness, applicability) when they can show the consistency among the research purposes, the questions, and the methods they use. Strong consistency grounds the credibility of research findings and helps to ensure that audiences have confidence in the findings and implications of research studies. These audiences may range from practitioners, to policy makers, to the public. In this chapter, we discuss the links among purpose, methods, and implications of study findings. We suggest a tool for thinking through the consistency of those connections.

Much has been written about systematically approaching the "what" of social science research, that is, systematically looking at the questions we ask and the methods we use. Very little has been written about systematically approaching the "why" of social science research, that is, systematically considering the purposes or reasons for carrying out the studies we conduct. These considerations are necessary to truly understand the questions and the most appropriate method(s) for answering them.

A CIRCUITOUS ROUTE TO THE TYPOLOGY OF PURPOSE

Our original goal in writing this chapter was to present a typology of research questions. Pursuing that goal led us through several winding pathways to an unintended end result: not a typology of research *questions* but rather a typology of research *purposes*. We found that without a clear understanding of the purpose behind the questions, we were inhibited when identifying the most appropriate methods to investigate those questions. Even though we ended up at a quite different place from where we originally planned to go, we were convinced that understanding this typology of purposes is necessary for the researcher to be able to identify and collect relevant data. Because purposes are often complex, the research questions frequently require multiple methods that adequately reflect this complexity. We discovered that there is a logical link among what are often complex research purposes, the questions that are necessary to reflect those purposes, and the potential need for mixed methods.

At the outset, we anticipated that our contribution would be a model of types of questions with links to suggested methodologies. For example, one might pose the question "Is Teaching Strategy A (lecture and discussion) a better choice for the general math class in a middle school than Teaching Strategy B (computer-based problem solving)?" This appears at first glance to be a fairly simple question that immediately conjures up an image of experimental or quasi-experimental design.

However, there are many purposes that might drive a question such as this. One underlying purpose might be to raise students' performance on standardized tests. Another underlying purpose might be the need to meet various learning styles of students. Still another underlying intent might be to diversify the representation of ethnic cultures in classroom activities. We failed to draw a direct link to methods.

As we struggled to create the typology of questions, each question led us to a dead end. We took a detour, then, in our pursuit of a typology of research questions. Realizing that the question with which one begins potentially comes from one or more purposes, we abandoned our original direction. Without having one's purpose (or purposes) clarified, and without time to reflect on that purpose, one cannot have a question that will directly dictate the research methodology. The researcher must understand the purpose of his or her study in all its complexity so as to make appropriate methodological choices. The research question alone will not produce links to methods unless the question is thought through seriously, as well as iteratively, and becomes reflective of purpose. In other words, we concluded that the research question is necessary but not sufficient to determine methodology. By considering the question and purpose iteratively, one can eventually get to a design or set of designs that more clearly reflect the intent of the question.

OBJECTIVE OF THIS CHAPTER

The objective of this chapter is to demonstrate that there is a link between understanding the purpose of one's research and selecting the appropriate methods to investigate the questions that are derived from that purpose. We argue that there is an iterative process between considering the research purpose and the research question. Out of this iterative process are decisions about methods made. We make the case that when the purpose is complex (as it often is), it is necessary to have multiple questions, and this frequently necessitates the use of mixed methods.

We explain how the typology of purpose can help social scientists in forming research questions and in making logical decisions about the ways in which they plan and conduct their studies. We suggest that, logically, in addition to qualitative methods and quantitative methods, mixed methods are frequently aligned with purposes. After providing a professional, academic, and historical context for this typology, we present the typology itself.

The typology is roughly hewn, tentative, fluid, and flexible. There is a risk that this typology will be interpreted as a "model" or a rigid framework that boxes in and limits the researcher. We are adamantly opposed to that; this is a tool intended not to limit but rather to help researchers organize their thinking so that they can more effectively develop appropriate research designs that will achieve their intended purposes. This schema is meant as a tool for thinking through research problems, it is a tool that will free researchers from dichotomous qualitative/quantitative thinking, and it is a tool

through which researchers can test assertions. In other words, it is clearly a "starting" place and not a "stopping" place for researchers' thinking.

We are familiar with research situations such as the following hypothetical example where insufficient attention was given to the "why." A study was designed to examine the impact of laser disc technology on science achievement among middle school students. Bypassing any focus at all on why the study was being done (or the purpose for it), the researcher embarked on designing what would undoubtedly be seen as a scientifically strong and rigorous study. Samples were selected, valid and reliable instruments were created, and data were collected and analyzed—all accomplished by following rigorous protocols. Only when the results failed to serve the actual purpose of the study did the researcher pause to consider what the actual purpose was. The purpose was indeed to measure student learning gains, but the study was also conducted to solicit community support and to obtain comparative costs of the two curricula. Reporting findings in the form of test scores to the board of education failed to provide all the board needed to know about cost and parental support. Simply, but systematically, exploring the purpose (or purposes) of a research study is the intent of what we suggest in this chapter. If this researcher had systematically studied the purposes of the research, then the design, data collection, analysis, results, and implications would have fulfilled the purposes more effectively.

We attempt to show how the typology is an expansion of an earlier framework we developed, the qualitative-quantitative interactive continuum (Newman & Benz, 1998). Qualitative and quantitative research makes up a false dichotomy, we contended in that book. Debating their comparative worth is pointless because multiple research perspectives enable social science researchers to approach questions of interest within a wide variety of ways of knowing. There are many right ways to approach research, not only one right way. One's purpose provides a way to determine the optimal path to studying the research question. Along the continuum are entry points through which a researcher can locate himself or herself and the study. An ethnographic interview and a holistic way of knowing will not empower the researcher interested in measuring heart rates, lung volume, and weight loss in a study of wellness education. Neither will a standardized paper-and-pencil test help a researcher to uncover what it means to a second-grader to learn math. Here, we suggest that the typology might lead to both a process of developing good research questions (purposefully grounded) and making subsequent effective methods decisions.

◆ Background

Over the past 30 years, a debate has taken place between two groups of researchers in the social sciences: those who are trained to use *quantitative* research methods and advocate their use as most appropriate and those who are trained to use *qualitative* research methods and advocate their use as most appropriate. These two groups of researchers claim different views of reality.

The term *quantitative* refers to a research paradigm designed to address questions that hypothesize relationships among variables that are measured frequently in numerical and objective ways. The term *qualitative* refers to a research paradigm designed to address questions of meaning, interpretation, and socially con-

structed realities. Furthermore, mixed methods refer to using perspectives of both at particular points in a research project (Tashakkori & Teddlie, 1998).

More than 15 years ago, we (Benz & Newman, 1986) began examining our own work and the writings of other research methodologists in light of our discomfort with such a fragmented view of inquiry. Searching for a different way of conceptualizing social science research, we believed strongly in the unity of science. The research question, we strongly believed, was the key; understanding the centrality of the question guided the researcher in all other decisions during a research project. Through feedback from our students, we constructed the "interactive continuum" (Newman & Benz, 1998), which is one way of presenting mixed methods. We found that such a model helped students to understand research questions and methods in a coherent way. They became comfortable in how to design a study, how to let the research question lead the design, and how to assess the quality of the studies they read in journals.

In our model ("an interactive continuum," not a dichotomy between qualitative and quantitative [see Figure 6.1]), we emphasized four major principles:

1. The research question dictates the selection of research methods.

2. The assurance of "validity" of research—both measurement validity and design validity—is central to all studies.

3. The interactive continuum model is built around the place of "theory."

4. Consistency between question and design is the standard criterion for planning studies of high quality and scientific value. (Newman & Benz, 1998)

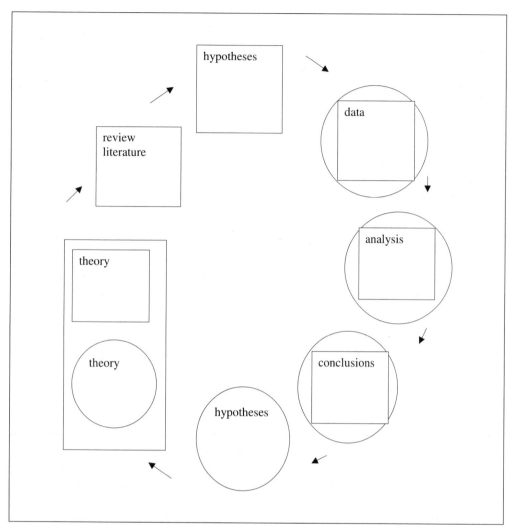

Figure 6.1. Qualitative-Quantitative Interactive Continuum of Research

SOURCE: Newman and Benz (1998).

With these four principles as a backdrop, in this chapter we set out to expand on that model. We begin by extending our discussion of the fourth principle with a focus on the researcher's *purpose* as even more fundamental than the researcher's question—our bottom line in previous work. Our circuitous journey from failed attempts to develop a typology of questions has led us to a typology of purposes.

In this chapter, we argue that the quality and indeed the meaningfulness of research to the public are enhanced if purposefulness is clearly a part of the researcher's thinking. We argue that a way of systematically ordering one's thinking about purpose can be a valuable tool for researchers to accomplish the linkages among their research questions, why they intend to carry out their studies, their methods, and their interpretations of findings. Traditionally, researchers have focused on research design. Less focus has been placed on the reasons for conducting the study, the consequences of the findings, and the potential audiences for the study. We want to shed light on that dynamic—the dynamic of purpose—in this chapter.

Altheide and Johnson (1994) captured the spirit of why we think *purpose* has gained ground over the past several decades as central to the researcher's work. They claimed that prior to the current vast array of legitimized "ways of knowing," there was more unity regarding the fact that research was knowledge. That unity no longer exists. Altheide and Johnson stated,

> What has changed is the purpose of research, and what those standards for assessing the purpose might be. Research is no longer coupled with knowledge, but has been given multiple choices (such as liberation, emancipation, programmatic politics, expressive "art"). Depending on one's choice, research is defined accordingly. (p. 487)

In other words, over the past few decades, the role that social science research plays has become broader and virtually unbounded. During the 1960s, we might have been taught that the role of social science research was prediction and control. By the year 2000, the role of research was not so easily and simply categorized. When a common unified understanding of purpose becomes a thing of the past, a typology of contemporary purposes seems justified.

Not only have the purposes of research in general expanded over the past four decades, but also researchers increasingly are open to the fact that the purposes of a particular study may be multiple and may change as the study unfolds. During the era when positivism dominated, researchers resisted such flexibility and openness; the research hypothesis served not only to focus the study but also to build boundaries around it. The researcher typically followed the hypothesis with the data collection, analysis, and conclusions in a linear fashion, deliberately avoiding being "sidetracked" and ignoring distractions along the way.

Contemporary researchers, on the other hand, tend to appreciate the fact that research projects are not linear but instead twist and turn and sometimes lead in unforeseen directions. Purposes drive the research question, but purposes can change over the course of the study. Purpose changes lead to question changes, which can lead to methods changes. Delgado-Gaitan (2000), in her study of family literacy in a Latino community, described how her purpose changed during the study itself: "At that point, I began to notice a shift in my research focus from concerns with literacy activities and processes in home and school to the process of empowerment" (p. 397). Such acquiescence to the natural unveiling of phenomena as they are being studied is not surprising; this is the essence of naturalistic inquiry (qualitative research) itself (Lincoln & Guba, 1985). Historically, the dominance of positivism was antithetical to naturalistic assumptions; it was built on assumptions of variable control. Moreover, researchers aspired to conditions of stronger control for better internal validity; the tighter the control, the less likely fluctuating purposes would be tolerated, let alone recognized.

◆ Research Purposes

The obvious purpose of research from any epistemological perspective is to answer questions. But stopping here, we realize now, avoided dealing with deeper and more complex intentions and purposes that go beyond mere "questions." The deeper purpose of a research study is the *reason* for doing it. The research question does not provide the reason for addressing it. The first benefit for the researcher who moves beyond considering only the research question is to decide, first of all, whether the study is worth pursuing at all.

Haller and Kleine (2001) provided an example of purpose and the important role it plays in thinking through a research project. They referred to a study by Finn and Achilles (1990) in which the research question was "What is the effect of making a substantial reduction in class size on student achievement?" They characterized this as the research problem, but Haller and Kleine (2001) noted that the purpose was not actually about class size. They stated,

> The problem of their study is not class size. The problem is that many primary children are not learning to read and do arithmetic as well as they should. Reducing class sizes in the primary grades is a possible solution to that problem of low achievement. (p. 285)

The fact that children were not achieving is why the study was needed. Testing the relationship between classroom conditions (in this case, class size) and academic achievement was the research study. If the researchers found a relationship between reduced class sizes and increased test scores, then the need would be beginning to be filled. While one never can show a complete causal relationship, the researcher can support an impact (or fail to support it) in accounted for variance. If the relationship was not confirmed, then researchers could move to other potential

ideas to fulfill the need to identify those dynamics that might affect student achievement. To accomplish this overall purpose very frequently requires mixed methods.

When a research study has a purpose, there is a reason for carrying it out. The purpose for a social science research study is rooted in the unique conceptualization in the researcher's thinking about the study. The purpose is not the question. Purpose is not design. Purpose is not methodology. Purpose is not data collection or analysis. Purpose is not categories of research questions (Janesick, 2000), nor is it categories of types of studies (e.g., ethnography, life history, case study). Purpose is focus on the reasons why the researcher is undertaking the study. And purpose should not be kept disconnected from the research question and the methods, as it often is. Researchers should not be blind to the purpose (or purposes) of their work.

Given these definitions, perhaps the "purpose" of the research study should be able to be written as the "rationale" of the research study, the "aim" of the research study, or the "objective" of the research study. The word "intention" implies that the research study has intent—that there is a "reason" (or those reasons) for it to be done. The researcher should make that intention visible. That reason (or reasons) should describe why the researcher is conducting the study.

Within a written research proposal, the purpose is sometimes reflected in the section called the "justification for the study" or the "importance of the study." Thoroughly considering the purpose of the study helps the researcher in other ways. For example, it links to the study's implications. That is, purposefulness is revealed later when the researcher discusses what the study results "mean." After the analysis and interpretation are completed, results are documented. Drawing implications from those results becomes the final

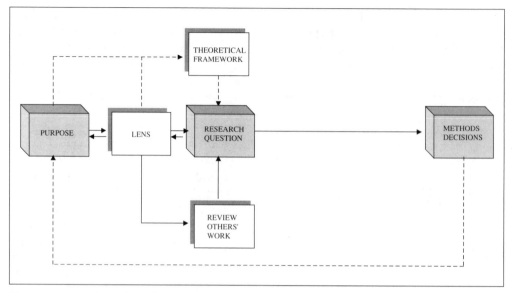

Figure 6.2. Thinking Through the Research Process

step. Knowing the purpose returns to the researcher's aid. The implications of the findings flow from the original purpose—ideas that can be consistent with the original purpose, resistant to the original purpose, or even contrary to the original purpose.

For example, in the Finn and Achilles (1990) study, the authors drew implications from their study and its findings because the study had a purpose (failure of students to learn reading and math) supporting it or a reason for conducting it. Their results can be crafted to meet the needs of those who are obligated to organize school environments that might best be related to student achievement.

◆ Thinking That Leads to the Research Question and Methods

Studying the notion of purpose, we began to believe that there could be a typology of purposes or an ordering of purposes for social science research. A typology might be helpful for researchers as they are thinking through the research process, which might be portrayed as having at least six components as depicted, in a general way, in Figure 6.2.

In Figure 6.2, we show that the purpose initiates the research study. There is intent, a reason, and a need. That purpose is identified through the lens of the researcher. How does the researcher experience the world vis-à-vis that need or that intent? Researchers' lenses are their autobiographies, who they are, their lives—all of the factors about them, including their values, beliefs, experiences, age, and gender as well as their social, psychological, and spiritual development. Their perspectives (or lenses) are what screens or filters, clouds, or magnifies their views as they think through theoretical frameworks (if applicable) that relate to their purpose. The metaphor of "lens" could include the construct of "filter" as well. The lens provides the focus, and simultaneously the filter blocks out what detracts from that focus. The lens is coherent. Only one lens at a time works to the researcher's advantage. More than one simultaneous lens leads to fuzzy vision or potentially falling down the stairs of good research intent.

At the same time, the researcher's lens views this purpose through the work of others who might have studied the topic. This dialogic process assists the researcher in forming a research question that not only "gets answered" but does so with answers that fulfill the purpose that originated his or her thinking. Because the research purpose and the research question are considered iteratively, the arrows between the two go both ways. The researcher may consider a purpose and then a question. The question may generate another possible purpose. That purpose feeds back into a new question. From this iterative process are decisions made about research methods that might be appropriate.

While Figure 6.2 is portrayed neatly and linearly, research is never linear. Faithfully reproducing on paper a messy and dynamic process is impossible. The sequence, as suggested, is intellectually logical, but the six events in the figure overlap and feed back on one another. The researcher could begin a study with a certain "justification" (or purpose) but conclude the study with newly found implications (or meanings). In other words, the purpose at the end of the study could very well be different from that at the beginning. Hunter and Brewer (Chapter 22, this volume) raise our awareness that the theoretical frame from which the researcher operates needs careful attention, particularly in mixed methods research. Within the same study, they argue that theory might be *both* constructed *and* tested. All of these concerns do not take away from the responsibility of the researcher to articulate up front what the purpose is. Implications of the findings flow from the detours and reconceptualizations through which the original purpose has traversed. That initial purpose does not disappear, but the fact that the results shift the purpose in itself might be *the important* finding or implication.

◆ Typology of Research Purpose

The nine categories listed in the next paragraph make up the typology of purpose, as we have tentatively structured it at this point in time. We recognize the limitations of this claim at the outset. The only intent here is to provide a framework through which researchers could move to clarify their thinking most effectively. We do not claim that this typology is either exhaustive or of further value beyond its use as a thinking tool here. Like the interactive continuum of qualitative and quantitative research that we designed several years ago as a conceptual tool, so too is this typology.

The full typology appears in Table 6.1. There is overlap in these specific categories. For example, "Inform constituencies" logically encompasses "Examine the past." The nine general purposes for social science research could be categorized as follows:

1. Predict.

2. Add to the knowledge base.

3. Have a personal, social, institutional, and/or organizational impact.

4. Measure change.

5. Understand complex phenomena.

6. Test new ideas.

7. Generate new ideas.

8. Inform constituencies.

9. Examine the past.

TABLE 6.1   A Typology of Research Purposes

1. PREDICT.
   a. Build general laws.

2. ADD TO THE KNOWLEDGE BASE.
   a. Confirm findings.
   b. Replicate others' work.
   c. Reinterpret previously collected data.
   d. Clarify structural and ideological connections between important social processes.
   e. Strengthen the knowledge base.

3. HAVE A PERSONAL, SOCIAL, INSTITUTIONAL, AND/OR ORGANIZATIONAL IMPACT.
   a. Deconstruct/reconstruct power structures.
   b. Reconcile discrepancies.
   c. Refute claims.
   d. Set priorities.
   e. Resist authority.
   f. Influence change.
   g. Promote change.
   h. Promote questioning.
   i. Improve practice.
   j. Change structures.
   k. Set policy.

4. MEASURE CHANGE.
   a. Measure consequences of practice.
   b. Test treatment effects.
   c. Measure outcomes.

5. UNDERSTAND COMPLEX PHENOMENA.
   a. Understand phenomena.
   b. Understand culture.
   c. Understand change.
   d. Understand people.

6. TEST NEW IDEAS.
   a. Test innovations.
   b. Test hypotheses.
   c. Test new ideas.
   d. Test new solutions.

7. GENERATE NEW IDEAS.
   a. Explore phenomena.
   b. Generate hypotheses.
   c. Generate theory.
   d. Uncover relationships.
   e. Uncover culture.
   f. Reveal culture.

(Continued)

TABLE 6.1   (Continued)

---

8. INFORM CONSTITUENCIES.
   a. Inform the public.
   b. Heighten awareness.
   c. Public relations.
   d. Enlighten.
   e. Hear from those who are affected by treatment/program.
   f. Describe the present.
   g. Comply with authority.

9. EXAMINE THE PAST.
   a. Interpret/reinterpret the past.
   b. Acknowledge past misunderstandings.
   c. Reexamine tacit understandings.
   d. Examine social and historical origins of current social problems.

From these broad categories, we have delineated more specific purposes, as can be seen in Table 6.1. Each of the categories of purposes is briefly described in this section. (Figure 6.4 later demonstrates conceptually the iterative process between the purpose and the research question that helps the researcher to determine which methods to employ.)

We offer these brief descriptions to show a general way of thinking about a variety of purposes, similar in conceptualization to what one of the most well-regarded research methodologists, Fred Kerlinger, constructed years ago as he described "science" in more than one way (Kerlinger, 1964). We are defining what Kerlinger might call science in nine different categories of purpose. (He loosely conceptualized four ways of thinking about scientists: the individual in the laboratory, the brilliant thinker "aloof from the world" (Kerlinger, 1964, p. 8), the person working to improve humankind's lot with technological progress, and the person attempting to build theory to explain phenomena.)

Nearly 40 years ago, Kerlinger, a traditional quantitative methodologist, described the researcher's struggle with questions and purpose. As he wrote about social science research, he acknowledged science as process and as product. He was unwittingly supporting the holistic nature of science and, with us, showed that qualitative and quantitative research are not antithetical to one another. Every research study has elements of both qualitative and quantitative assumptions (Newman & Benz, 1998). Moreover, we believe that Kerlinger (1964) was describing some of this same phenomena in the following description of the "scientist" as he also brought in ideas of Dewey:

The scientist will usually experience an obstacle to understanding, a vague unrest about observed and unobserved phenomena, and a curiosity as to why something is as it is. His first and most important step is to get the idea out in the open, to express the problem in some reasonable manageable form.

Rarely or never will the problem spring full-blown at this stage. He must struggle with it, try it out, and live with it. Dewey says, "There is a troubled, perplexed, trying situation, where the difficulty is, as it were, spread throughout the entire situation, infecting it as a whole." Sooner or later, explicitly or implicitly, he states the problem, even if his expression of it is inchoate and tentative. Here he intellectualizes, as Dewey puts it, "what at first is merely an emotional quality of the whole situation." In some respects, this is the most difficult and most important part of the whole process. Without some sort of statement of the problem, the scientist can rarely go further and expect his work to be fruitful. (pp. 13-14)

We suggest that Kerlinger's "getting it out in the open" is part of the path to exploring the reasons for pursuing the study. Kerlinger's description here is one of the researcher deep in thought and study, not one of the researcher automatically or superficially approaching his or her research. His warning that the research problem does not "spring full-blown" is a warning about relying on routine, automatic, and superficial shortcuts. Research questions also do not spring full-blown but rather require reflective thinking. This process often leads to a mixed methods approach, as multiple purposes are frequently driving one's study. Once again, Kerlinger was known as a quantitative researcher, and his writing was in that genre. However, his sensitivities to science and social science research were more holistic than most might recognize. It is to increase the likelihood that the researcher's work will be "fruitful," in Kerlinger's word, that we suggest this typology.

The nine categories in the typology are not independent; they may be interdependent and overlapping. We present each one with an explanation.

1. *Predict.* Social science research can serve the needs of explaining social and behavioral phenomena by testing theory. Struggling with a lack of understanding about teaching and learning, for example, the researcher can empirically test tentative relationships that might explain their success or effectiveness. Fulfilling the purpose of testing relationships helps to build general laws of human interactions that allow us to predict what is yet to happen. Kerlinger (1964), nearly 40 years ago, discussed this view of science as his preference for social science research in the field of education.

2. *Add to the knowledge base.* Social science researchers investigate phenomena to add to what is known—knowledge that has intrinsic value. Researchers conduct studies to strengthen the knowledge base. Clarifying what is known as well as correcting faulty knowledge drives some researchers' work. The knowledge base undergirds many decisions that determine public policy. The knowledge base about schooling, for example, becomes a reservoir accessible to many audiences.

3. *Have a personal, social, institutional, and/or organizational impact.* Breaking down policies and practices to reveal how they work drives research that has a purpose of subsequently rebuilding them to enhance their properties of equity and justice. In educational research, for example, schooling practices can produce discrepant outcomes in different constituencies; studies can reveal and lead to altering such differences. Strategic planning research assists organizational groups in structuring their work from high- to low-priority areas. Furthermore, those at the margins of schooling or their advocates examine their own experience as it is juxtaposed to

the dominant discourse. Some critical researchers, for example, study with an intent to influence and change that which is being studied. Researchers pursue lines of inquiry that analyze both current status and future potential of organizations. Researchers can engage inductively in examining institutions so as to generate questions about them.

4. *Measure change.* Researchers design studies that aim to link treatments to their effects. We use the word *measure* here to mean "to quantify." Researchers construct instruments to measure the outcomes of behavioral innovations. For example, a researcher may construct a performance assessment tool for professionals in training and obtain validity and reliability estimates on it. Changes in policy, changes in professional practice, and changes in the demographics of constituencies that professionals in any field serve are often the purposeful targets of researchers.

5. *Understand complex phenomena.* Research intended to achieve understanding is made up of studies that delve below the surface of the phenomena, that is, investigations that have the goal of interpreting the meaning of phenomena. In other words, rather than measuring phenomena, the purpose of studies within this category is to understand the meaning of the phenomena. In addition, research that seeks to explicate the behaviors, rituals, language, symbols, values, and social structures of a particular group of people intends to understand the culture of that group of people.

6. *Test new ideas.* Researchers formulate statements of relationships among variables and then collect data on those variables to test the probability of the relationships occurring. Researchers aid innovators by designing studies to assist these

entrepreneurs in assessing the extent to which their ideas might be supported. Researchers can design studies to examine whether or not constituents' needs are being met. Researchers can be commissioned as members of problem-solving teams.

7. *Generate new ideas.* Researchers, in addition to testing new ideas, can be part of a process of exploring ideas. For example, naturalistic researchers participate in the life of a social group, open to whatever might be revealed to them. Without hypotheses, such research is done for the purpose of allowing new ideas to be generated. Without formal restrictions on one's lenses, the researcher maintains a welcoming openness to what processes unfold naturally. These emerging ideas, then, can be subsequently tested (Newman & Benz, 1998), but their emergence is the purpose of the studies included here.

8. *Inform constituencies.* Researchers carry out studies that serve accountability needs. Publicly accountable agencies are obligated to serve the needs of the public in a democracy. Employees in these agencies are public employees, working in organizations that are accountable to that public. Researchers can be involved in reporting results of studies of these public programs. Nonpublic agencies are accountable to other governance structures; research can serve accountability purposes here as well. Similarly, societal institutions can serve professional needs by being accredited by professional organizations. Researchers serve as investigators to provide the data needed.

9. *Examine the past.* Researchers can study the historical origins of current social dynamics, patterns, and problems. Examining what has occurred before is the purpose of many studies that aim to interpret or reinterpret the history of social life.

◆ Application of the Typology

We intend this typology as an aid to researchers to think through the "why" of their research as systematically and rigorously as they have traditionally thought through the "what." With experience, routine ways to think about one's work are developed; this is natural for any expert in his or her field. The researcher develops some automatic responses and shortcuts in his or her work as well. These ways of thinking lend efficiency to the researcher's work. To the extent that automatic thinking attenuates the thoughtfulness that is needed to consider the purpose for which one is doing a study, it can lead to misguided research. Simply put, we want to suggest that serious thinking is always needed to clarify the reasons for the study; this thinking is as important as the thinking that goes into the design of the study. In fact, it may be more important. There are inherent advantages to questioning one's purposes even after they are articulated. Thinking about research before conducting it is, we suggest, the bottom line.

We use the following example, "A Study of the Public's Knowledge of Science," to suggest how using the typology can help researchers to probe their own thinking. We show how the typology, as a "thinking tool," helps investigators to formulate research questions and make design decisions most effectively because they take "purpose" into account. In this situation, researchers are interested in pursuing the public's understanding of science.

A Study of the Public's Knowledge of Science

Scientists were interested in public understanding of scientific advancements. How does the public become knowledgeable about science?

To explore this phenomenon, the researcher gathered evidence from the popular media for the 6-month period of time from January 1, 2000, to June 30, 2000: every issue of the *New York Times* and *USA Today;* transcripts of all ABC, NBC, and CBS evening news broadcasts; transcripts of every 1-hour CNN *Headline News* summary from 10 to 11 p.m.; and all issues of *Time, Newsweek,* and *U.S. News and World Report.*

In the first phase of coding, the researcher binary coded each individual story item according to the following:

Scientific topic is the
    major theme   yes/no
Scientific topic is the
    secondary theme   yes/no

In the second phase of coding, the researcher selected only those story items that were coded "yes." This data set was made up of all news stories in which science was either the primary or the secondary theme.

For each of these data units, the researcher coded on the following dimensions:

Science category	Physics
	Chemistry
	Medicine
	Biology
	Zoology
	Astronomy
	Other science areas
Message	Report research findings
	Announce a new study
	Apply scientific findings
	Refute earlier findings

Alert public to
danger
Biography of
scientist
Other message

Author   Scientist
Journalist
Educator
Other

The researcher used descriptive statistics (frequency counts) to portray the proportion of scientific stories that are reported in the various media: newspapers, television, and magazines. Subcategories within these larger groups were displayed as well. Three research hypotheses were tested. First, the extent to which the sources of scientific information differed across the various media was tested. Second, the extent to which the public is exposed to various branches of science (e.g., physics, chemistry) was tested. Third, the content of the messages in the stories was tested.

Having this brief overview, we might think through this study's potential purposes as though we were contemplating such an investigation. What was the purpose (or what were the purposes) for examining the question "How does the public become knowledgeable about science?" Before designing the study, we could use the typology as a checklist, checking our intent against potential purposes in these nine categories. Moving from the question to possible purposes— and back and forth again—would be an iterative process. Proceeding in this way is a good way to understand the typology but admittedly a very bad way to conceptualize authentic research logic due to a chronology problem that is hard to avoid.

Applying the checklist a posteriori is inconsistent with the chain of reasoning depicted in Figure 6.2 (p. 174). Because we are applying the typology here for illustrative purposes, we can explain that disconnect and justify disrupting it.

The logic shown in Figure 6.2 indicates that the purpose of a research study (the shaded box labeled "PURPOSE") has an impact on the researcher's perspective on the study (the box labeled "LENS") and affects the focus of the inquiry—the question itself (the shaded box labeled "RESEARCH QUESTION"). Because the process is iterative, the question can have an impact on the purpose as well (thus the reverse arrows between the research question and the purpose). Therefore, we are *retrospectively* considering what potential purposes for this study *might have been.* In actuality, the researcher would think through his or her intent first. Yet proceeding through the checklist in this way remains a potential way to grasp its value as a thinking tool when planning a study.

To return to this process, we ask what the purpose (or purposes) was (or were) for a study investigating the question "How does the public become knowledgeable about science?" We begin traversing through the typology, testing possible intentions and possible reasons why we might be contemplating this study. On the left side of the in-text table that follows is the typology, and on the right side of the table are possible purposes we might test out in our thinking. The comments on the right side are *merely example* questions and comments that the researcher might have asked himself or herself; they are not exhaustive and are only presented as possibilities. While proceeding through this "thinking tool," the researcher can make notes and raise questions and think through the question "What is the one purpose (or what are the several purposes) that might be driving the study?"

Typology of Purpose	Application of the Typology to One Example: Studying the Public's Knowledge of Science
1. Predict. a. Build general laws.	Do we want to be able to explain how the public uses science? Do we want to be able to predict from which sources they glean information? Why do we want to do this?
2. Add to the knowledge base. a. Confirm findings. b. Replicate others' work. c. Reinterpret previously collected data. d. Clarify structural and ideological connections between important social processes. e. Strengthen the knowledge base.	Have there been other studies we want to confirm or disconfirm? Are we invested in only added knowledge without specific practical application? If so, which knowledge base? What knowledge? The knowledge of the market? The knowledge of science? We may go back to No. 1 at this point, especially probing "why." This may tell us what literature to go to. Do we want to critique the literature for gaps? Do we want to review methods used in prior studies to determine where weaknesses are? Based on that type of review, we would design our study differently.
3. Have a personal, social, institutional, and/or organizational impact. a. Deconstruct/reconstruct power structures. b. Reconcile discrepancies. c. Refute claims. d. Set priorities. e. Resist authority. f. Influence change. g. Promote change. h. Promote questioning. i. Improve practice. j. Change structures. k. Set policy.	Are there social, institutional, or organizational dynamics we want to influence? Are there power structures in the media we want to challenge? Are television networks gaining too much authority at the expense of newspapers? Are we interested in influencing the regulation of the telecommunications industry? Are we curious about the racial and gender demographics of public policy decision makers? Do we intend to use our data to lobby for change? Are we disturbed that families at low income levels have less access to and knowledge of science that could improve their lives? Each of the preceding questions could generate a separate study. Each question signals a different set of stakeholders, audiences, methods (qualitative, quantitative, or mixed), and data sources. In the beginning, one simple study can, through the typology, illuminate a possible "thematic research agenda." Each segment of research (metaphorically like a periodic table of the elements) gets "filled in."
4. Measure change. a. Measure consequences of practice. b. Test treatment effects. c. Measure outcomes.	Are we curious about trends in the media's coverage of science? Do we have comparative data from an earlier era? Do we want to measure the comparative use of television over newspapers in a search for statistic differences? Why are we interested in this type of change? Why these trends? How good are our data likely to be? These probes help us to identify variables, measures, possible data sources, and limitations.
5. Understand complex phenomena. a. Understand phenomena. b. Understand culture.	Do we intend to be able to reveal the story of how individuals access science through the media? Are we interested in detailed descriptions of people's lives vis-à-vis the media and science? Because both science and the media are dominant in contemporary life, do we want to contextualize their role in the wider culture? Do we

Typology of Purpose	*Application of the Typology to One Example:* *Studying the Public's Knowledge of Science*
c. Understand change. d. Understand people.	want to understand the "meaning" of science in everyday life and the "meaning" of media in providing a scientific understanding to specific people? Would illuminating a case of incurable disease or global warming tell the story best? What stakeholders are we concerned about?
6. Test new ideas. a. Test innovations. b. Test hypotheses. c. Test new ideas. d. Test new solutions.	Is the relationship of people's scientific knowledge to contemporary media a new idea that we want to test? Do we have some intent to ameliorate scientific misunderstanding by testing an innovative idea that popular media may play a role in debunking scientific myths? Do we want to test a new way to teach science to adults? How is our thinking different from No. 1? This purpose appears quantitative but has heuristic aspects that may be inductive.
7. Generate new ideas. a. Explore phenomena. b. Generate hypotheses. c. Generate theory. d. Uncover relationships. e. Uncover culture. f. Reveal culture.	Is our investigation an exploratory one? Do we intend to take No. 5 a step further? In addition to enhancing our understanding of science and media, can we go further and generate a theory and hypotheses about their relationship? Do we want to incorporate what we learned from No. 5 and obtain another perspective? Do we want to be completely open to these phenomena until their meaning is naturally revealed to us?
8. Inform constituencies. a. Inform the public. b. Heighten awareness. c. Use public relations. d. Enlighten. e. Hear from those who are affected by treatment/ program. f. Describe the present. g. Comply with authority.	Is our intent to heighten the public's awareness about how scientific knowledge is dispersed? Do we want to hear from the members of the public about how science influences their lives to raise their awareness about what they know and do not know? Are we complying with some agency that accredits us, that is, an organization that regulates us and demands that we show that we serve the public appropriately?[1]
9. Examine the past. a. Interpret/reinterpret the past. b. Acknowledge past misunderstandings. c. Reexamine tacit understandings. d. Examine social and historical origins of current social problems.	Are we interested in examining how science and the media have related in the past? Are we intending to show how the public gleaned scientific understanding during the history of the United States up to the present day? Are we interested in showing how the public became knowledgeable about medicine during the late 1800s, for example? Are we interested in how members of the public view the teaching of evolution and creationism in public schools, for example, so as to understand the changes over time in their scientific points of view?

Having proceeded through the typology, one can see that this simple research question—"How does the public become knowledgeable about science?"—can be embedded within a myriad of purposes. While some questions in the analysis that has just been presented might not be new, they are usually considered haphazardly, if at all. The advantage of the typology is that it is systematic. The research question alone is insufficient to substantially fuel the decisions a researcher faces in designing the study. The very nature of asking questions from various "purposeful perspectives" sensitizes the researcher to make good design decisions, including selecting the most relevant variables and knowingly facing limitations and underlying assumptions. If the researcher's purpose is to "measure change" in the ways the public obtains scientific information, then the methodology would be quite different from what it would be if the purpose is needing deeper understanding about the public's view of science, that is, "understanding complex phenomena." As a heuristic, the typology is generative; the categories and questions here can elicit more categories and more questions, and frequently they will lead to mixed methods. As we have claimed repeatedly, the concept is a way of thinking, the typology is tentative, and the process is one that will strengthen the researcher's thinking (Newman & Ridenour, 2000).

The typology might help to clarify other concerns as well. Researchers can easily launch a study down one path toward data and answers that do not satisfy the real purposes they have failed to consider. The typology begins to force researchers to think in multiple dimensions; they have to think of possibilities or options. Methodologies then become substantive, safe, and trustworthy because the purposes they are to serve are better grounded. Debates over the past decade have raged around the question "Is it re-

search?" as scholars consider what have emerged as nontraditional representations of research in the forms of novels, poems, or photographs. But such a question is the wrong question. The answer to "Is it research?" comes from asking whether or not it serves research purposes. If it does, then the answer is "yes." The dramatic reading may indeed "be research," and the double-spaced typed report filled with data and graphs might not "be research." It is impossible to tell when considering only the form of the representation. Labeling something "research" requires knowing what purposes it serves.

The typology has advantages for the research consumer. It may be a tool that sensitizes the critical reader, first, to identify more clearly what *is* research and, second, to understand why the researcher conducted the study. Readers may approach research reports in a deeper and more thoughtful way; they will be more enlightened about the truth value of researchers' work and whether there are strong links between the studies and their implications. The circle of a study is complete when purpose (the genesis) links with implications (the conclusions).

Two other ways to conceptualize the typology of purpose are, first, through a loosely constructed *iterative flow* of ideas (Figure 6.3). In this figure, one purpose flows into, overlaps with, and generates other purposes. The *iterative flow* represents the thinking process. On the one hand, we suggest the utility of the typology in linking ideas together in a coherent and holistic research pattern from "examining the past," "discovering" and "testing" and "understanding new knowledge," on through all nine categories to "prediction" as shown in Figure 6.3. This figure shows the typology from a distance, representing the "big" ideas at each level and how they might be connected. Researchers who create a thematic research agenda or a program of studies in an area

1. Predict	using all the things we know in this knowledge "base" to explain a field and what might yet unfold in the future (so that the historians can describe these things later; return to #1)
2. Add to the knowledge base	organizing all the things we know into a "base" of knowledge
3. Have a personal, social, institutional, and/or organizational impact	struggling with the complex environments we experience; particularly when we know that some things we know and experience are not just, fair, and in keeping with our ethical or professional purpose
4. Measure change	measuring what happens when we change things
5. Understand complex phenomena	understanding what things we now experience and know
6. Test new ideas	testing these new things
7. Generate new ideas	discovering some new things
8. Inform constituencies	telling what things we know to those who need to know them
9. Examine the past	what things we already know from the past

Figure 6.3. Conceptualizing the Typology as Categories That Flow and Connect

frequently build a research base that might be represented in this way. Questions vary in purpose across one's research career. One's area of expertise might be the American family, for example, building a base of studies on this topic—a base that began by inquiring into variables related to income levels. Then, perhaps questions guided by a purpose to test public policies related to welfare are investigated. And deeper and more varied purposes continue the agenda. Figure 6.3 attempts to depict this larger perspective.

In Figure 6.4, a second conceptualization of the typology is presented. Columns 1 and 2 are meant to show the iterative nature of considering the research question and the research purpose. This iterative process results in decisions about methods, depicted in columns 3 and 4.

In column 3, we attempt to show that traditionally research intents have been aligned with research paradigms in a one-to-one fashion. Contemporary apprecia-

tion of the complex nature of social science research (multiple purposes and multiple stakeholders) continues to move away from this segmented framework and toward column 4, where a more holistic appreciation of the link between purpose and methods leads, in some cases, to methods beyond the traditional ones.

These two conceptualizations (Figures 6.3 and 6.4) are heuristics; they merely demonstrate other frameworks that explain the typology and other steps that might help a researcher to think through the purposes or the reasons why he or she is conducting a study.

◆ **Relationship Between the Typology of Purpose and Mixed Methods**

Any one study may be conceived of from a variety of perspectives. By using the

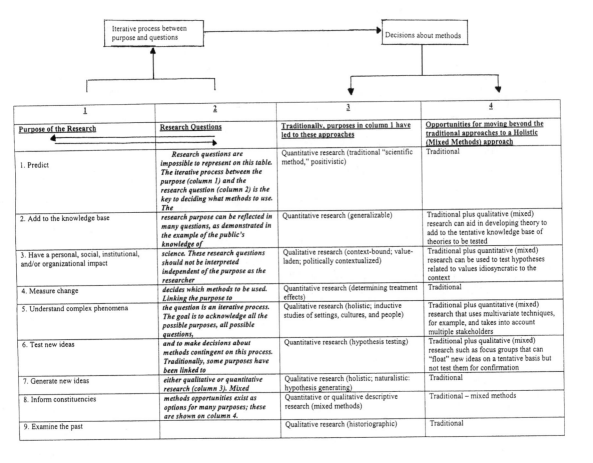

Figure 6.4. The Iterative Process Between Research Purpose and Research Question as a Prerequisite to Research Methods

NOTE: See the research example ("The Public's Knowledge of Science") in the narrative, which demonstrates that this is an idiosyncratic process for each research study.

typology, a researcher can initiate sets of questions about his or her purposes in a systematic fashion, which will facilitate the analyses of the research question under investigation (i.e., studying the question by moving through the typology to see where it might fit and whether it might fit into more than one category). This systematic process helps to identify both the types of information needed for the study and the most appropriate strategies (research methods) to use in gathering that information.

The process entails first studying the research question and then refining the question at a deeper and more substantive and purposeful level, with a greater awareness of potential multiple purposes. The more complex the purposes, the more likely that mixed methods will be necessary. By making the researcher aware of these considerations, he or she may choose to design, carry out, and interpret the research study for one purpose from the multiple purposes that exist. We are not assuming that there are right answers;

rather, we are assuming that asking appropriate questions will improve the likelihood of doing research that has greater meaning and is more apt to lead to valuable implications.

We can return now to our first example: "Is Teaching Strategy A (lecture and discussion) a better choice for the general math class in a middle school than Teaching Strategy B (computer-based problem solving)?" To determine what research methods are appropriate, one needs to know the purpose or to ask the following questions. A better choice based on what? Parent satisfaction? Teacher expertise? Student test scores? Cost of materials? Let us assume that, in moving through the typology with the stakeholders, we determine that two purposes drive this question: the need to raise students' performance on standardized tests (No. 4) and the need to diversify the curriculum away from solely Eurocentric materials (No. 3). To fulfill the first purpose, we might design an experimental study, collecting pretest and posttest quantitative data in the form of students' test scores before and after the implementation of these two instructional treatments. In addition, to fulfill our second need, we might plan to conduct a textual analysis of the materials used in both strategies for their ethnic representations and to interview parents from various ethnic backgrounds after they review the materials to determine their satisfaction with the ethnic content. This question, then, has led us to use mixed methods to conduct our investigation. Delving even deeper, our study might make use of the power of computer programs to incorporate qualitative "data" into our quantitative analysis. For example, according to Bazeley (Chapter 14, this volume), we might then cross-index the satisfaction levels of parents from different ethnic groups with student test scores.

Discourse about purpose is challenging. Thinking through the reasons for carrying out a study helps to form the question itself. Novice researchers frequently ask how to write a research question and want to know ways of identifying "good" research questions. The best response to this need is to take these researchers through the process of thinking through issues of purpose such as the following. Why are you doing this? Who needs to know what happens from your investigation if you carried it out? What has been done by others who have explored the same terrain? Who cares what you might or might not find? Struggling with these quandaries helps these researchers, first, to structure the question and, second, to write a clear rationale or justification for their research.

At the same time, clarifying the lens, or the perspective, through which the researcher will conduct research is important to his or her thinking logically, coherently, and scientifically. The researcher is a dynamic component of the research study. Perspectives and perceptions might shift as the study progresses. How vigilant is the researcher in attending to these shifts? Serendipity, unanticipated outcomes, and unplanned events all can affect the study process. The purpose can change, the question can change, and the methods can change. But the researcher must initiate each study with a singular lens and a clear purpose—an intent that is grounded and rooted in meaning.

We end this chapter where we began. Within that rapidly changing and turbulent context, social science researchers need to reinforce purposefulness in their research so that the needs of all stakeholders—children, families, professionals, and the policy audiences—are best served. In so doing, the complex nature of research becomes apparent, and it becomes clear that no one methodological approach is sufficient. We need to train a new generation of researchers who are comfortable in looking beyond a single technique. We need researchers who are competent in applying mixed methodology when the purpose and questions reflect the need. We believe that the position presented in this chapter demonstrates that even questions that appear to be simple must be examined in terms of the typology of purpose, which may clarify the complexity of the questions and indicate the need for using mixed methods.

■ Note

1. This concept is not too dissimilar from the concept of "multiple stakeholders" (Weiss, 1984) in the program evaluation literature. In this body of literature, evaluations tend to be sensitive to the different needs (or purposes) of various stakeholders—groups that have a vested interest in the program being evaluated. Different types of information must be gathered to answer different questions of different stakeholders. Potentially, different methodologies are employed for meeting those different stakeholder needs.

■ References

Altheide, D. L., & Johnson, J. M. (1994). Criteria for assessing interpretive validity in qualitative research. In N. K. Denzin & Y. S. Lincoln (Eds.), Handbook of qualitative research (pp. 485-499). Thousand Oaks, CA: Sage.

Benz, C. R., & Newman, I. (1986). Qualitative-quantitative interactive continuum: A model and application to teacher education evaluation. Resources in Education. (ERIC Clearinghouse on Tests, Measurements and Evaluation ED 269 405)

Delgado-Gaitan, C. (2000). Researching change and changing the researcher. In B. M.

Brizuela, J. P. Stewart, R. G. Carrillo, & J. G. Berger (Eds.), Acts of inquiry in qualitative research (pp. 389-410). Cambridge, MA: Harvard Educational Review.

Finn, J. D., & Achilles, C. M. (1990). Answers and questions about class size: A statewide experiment. American Educational Research Journal, 27, 557-577.

Haller, E. J., & Kleine, P. F. (2001). Using educational research: A school administrator's guide. New York: Longman.

Janesick, V. J. (2000). The choreography of qualitative research design: Minuets, improvisations, and crystallization. In N. K. Denzin & Y. S. Lincoln (Eds.), Handbook of qualitative research (2nd ed., pp. 379-400). Thousand Oaks, CA: Sage.

Kerlinger, F. N. (1964). Foundations of behavioral research: Educational and psychological inquiry. New York: Holt, Rinehart & Winston.

Lincoln, Y. S., & Guba, E. G. (1985). Naturalistic inquiry. Newbury Park, CA: Sage.

Newman, I., & Benz, C. R. (1998). Qualitative-quantitative research methodology: Exploring the interactive continuum. Carbondale: Southern Illinois University Press.

Newman, I., & Ridenour, C. S. (2000, November). Typology of purposes: A tool for thinking that leads to research questions, design, methods, and implications. Paper presented at the meeting of the Association for the Advancement of Educational Research, Ponte Vedre, FL.

Tashakkori, A., & Teddlie, C. (1998). Mixed methodology: Combining qualitative and quantitative approaches (Applied Social Research Methods, No. 46). Thousand Oaks, CA: Sage.

Weiss, C. H. (1984). Toward the future of stakeholder approaches in evaluation. In R. F. Connor, D. G. Altman, & C. Jackson (Eds.), Evaluation studies review annual (Vol. 9). Beverly Hills, CA: Sage.

7

PRINCIPLES OF MIXED METHODS AND MULTIMETHOD RESEARCH DESIGN

◆ Janice M. Morse

The goal of social science research is to understand the complexity of human behavior and experience. The researcher's task—to understand, describe, and explain the reality of this complexity —is limited by our research methods. But most of all, it is restricted by the methodological repertoire of each researcher and his or her knowledge and skill in using these research methods.

While specific research methods enable us to describe, understand, and explain the complexity of living by providing us with various perspectives, different methods are best designed for, and used to answer, particular types of questions. They provide us with different perspectives that enable us to best answer individual questions. By combining and increasing the number of *research strategies* used within a particular project, we are able to broaden the dimensions and hence the scope of our project. By using more than one *method* within a research program, we are able obtain a more complete picture of human behavior and experience. Thus, we are better able to hasten our understanding and achieve our research goals more quickly.

Research is a process—a puzzle-solving process. We come to understanding piece by piece, one step at a time. The researcher's

AUTHOR'S NOTE: This research was funded by an MRC Scientist and AHFMR Health Scholar Award.

BOX 7.1
Terminology

Core: This is the base project into which the other data, strategies, or projects fit.

Dominance: This is the method that leads or directs inquiry at *any* particular point. Thus, within a qualitatively-driven research program, a quantitative method may be dominant at some particular stage or vice versa in a quantitatively-driven project.

Methodological integrity: This is the *rigor* of a project, maintained by adherence to the assumptions, strategies, data appropriateness, adequacy, and so forth that are consistent with each particular method.

Methodological triangulated design: This is a project that is composed of two or more subprojects, each of which exhibits methodological integrity. While complete in themselves, these projects fit to complement or enable the attainment of the overall programmatic research goals.

Mixed method design: This is the incorporation of various qualitative or quantitative strategies within a single project that may have either a qualitative or a quantitative theoretical drive. The "imported" strategies are supplemental to the major or core method and serve to enlighten or provide clues that are followed up within the core method.

Multimethod design: This is the conduct of two or more research methods, each conducted rigorously and complete in itself, in one project. The results are then triangulated to form a comprehensive whole.

Sensitizing strategy: This is a single project in which multiple strategies are used. One or more strategies form the major mode of data collection. Sensitizing strategies are those strategies of data collection that supplement the major mode and may be either qualitative or quantitative strategies. They are not used as a stand-alone project but rather are used to generate clues that are confirmed within the project using another strategy.

Sequential triangulation: These are projects conducted one after another to further inquiry, with the first project informing the nature of the second project. These may or may not use a method different from the first project.

Simultaneous triangulation: These are projects conducted at the same time, with the results compared or contrasted on completion.

Supplemental data: These are data that are collected to enrich or confirm the original data.

Theoretical drive: This is the overall direction of the project as determined from the original questions or purpose and is primarily inductive or deductive. While quantitative inquiry may be placed within a project with an inductive quantitative drive, the theoretical drive remains inductive. The converse is also true for a deductive theoretical drive.

Triangulation: This is the combination of the results of two or more rigorous studies conducted to provide a more comprehensive picture of the results than either study could do alone. It was originally applied to qualitative inquiry by Goffman in 1974 (see Goffman, 1989).

comprehension of the phenomenon increases as data unfold, discrepancies are resolved, concepts are understood, and interconnections are made. In this way, the theory develops. Analysis, whether qualitative or quantitative, provides us with a progressive or an incremental understanding of reality. Knowledge is attained as pieces of information from various projects verify each other, or contradict earlier findings and demand further attention, thereby extending the developing model. These units of understanding may be part of a single project or part of several linked but self-contained projects that fit under the rubric of one general problem, topic, or research program.

In this chapter, I discuss the process and procedures for combining research strategies both within a single project (with methods to answer a particular question) and among different research projects as a series of complementary projects or a research program aimed at addressing one overall topic. In this context, when *strategies* derived from qualitative and quantitative methods are used within a single project, it is referred to as a *mixed methods design*. Qualitative and quantitative projects that are relatively complete, but are used together to form essential components of one research program, are referred to as a *multimethod design*.

We must, however, remain aware that the ad hoc mixing of strategies or methods (i.e., "muddling methods" [Stern, 1994]) may be a serious threat to validity as methodological assumptions are violated. Thus, the purpose of this chapter is to discuss the principles of, and the strategies for, conducting research with either the mixed methods or multimethod design. Major terms are defined in Box 7.1. Using examples, the process is explored in a step-by-step manner, and the strengths and weaknesses of each design are examined. Finally, these designs are explicated by dis-

secting published research to examine how the *theoretical drive* and qualitative or quantitative methods were used in comparison with the knowledge required and the *pacing* of the methods and how results were *combined* to answer the research question.

◆ Mixed Methods Design

We first discuss the process of incorporating into a single project strategies that do not normally form a part of a particular research method.[1] It may be necessary to import these strategies, not normally described in basic texts as a component of a particular method because of the nature of the phenomenon being studied, the context, or special circumstances for participants.

When using mixed methods, it is important that methodological congruence be maintained, that is, that all of the assumptions of the major method be adhered to and that components of the method (such as the data collection and analytical strategies) be consistent. When speaking of mixed methods design, we are not talking about mix-and-match research (with strategies liberally selected and combined); rather, we are talking about using supplemental research strategies to collect data that would not otherwise be obtainable by using the main method and incorporating these data into the base method.

QUALITATIVE INQUIRY AND MIXED METHODS DESIGN

Mixed methods design is a standard part of the method in each of the major qualitative research designs. Ethnography, for example, consists of fieldwork (informal interviews and participant observation), formal interviews (unstructured, open-ended, or semistructured interviews, surveys, and techniques of componential analysis), and a diary (researcher's reflections/interpretations). It also includes "other" data, defined as any other sources that the ethnographer sees fit such as documents, psychometric tests or scales, biological measurements, analysis of food, time-motion studies, and whatever will help the ethnographer to answer the research question.

Although grounded theory is fast becoming a method based only on interview data, Benoliel (1996) recently made a plea for observational data to be reincorporated as a standard data collection strategy. Even more broadly, Glaser (1978) stated that "all is data," following Goffman's (1989 [published posthumously]) example to give concepts the broadest application (see Fine & Smith, 2000). In phenomenology, the primary data are derived from conversations or interviews, and these data are then reflected from the phenomenological literature and other experiential accounts, including fiction, poetry, film, and one's own experience (van Manen, 1990).

QUANTITATIVE INQUIRY AND MIXED METHODS DESIGN

Quantitative projects, on the other hand, appear to be better delineated and more focused than qualitative methods; they are more reliant on a single method and less likely to be used with additional data collection strategies. Occasionally, single methods will be bolstered with the simultaneous use of focus groups or an observational component or, sequentially, with an instrument developed, for instance, from interview data. These projects are described as having triangulated

designs (Breitmayer, Ayres, & Knafl, 1993). However, because of the interdependency of these different data collection strategies, it is preferable to consider these studies as one method—albeit a mixed method. Because these "supplementary" data provide only a glimpse of another perspective, and are confirmed and verified in the base project and not independently from the main study, triangulation is an inappropriate term.

Mixed methods design, therefore, is a term that is applied when research strategies are used that are *not normally* described as a part of that design. For instance, in quantitative inquiry, it may be the incorporation of an observational component (a non-numerical fieldwork component) or supplementary open-ended questions at the end of a Likert scale; in qualitative inquiry (e.g., in grounded theory), it may involve the incorporation of strategies from ethnography to add a cultural dimension or the addition of quantitative measures.

What is the role of these supplemental strategies in the project? In both quantitative and qualitative research, these strategies increase the scope and comprehensiveness of the study. In a *quantitative* study, these strategies then aid in the interpretation of data in the core project, providing explanations for unexpected findings or supporting the results. In a *qualitative* study, the supplementary strategies serve one of the three functions. First, they may be used to identify notions, ideas, or concepts that are then incorporated into the main study. Second, they may provide different information or insights as to what is happening in the data as well as different explanations or ideas about what is going on—ideas that are subsequently verified within the data or used to guide subsequent interviews or the collection of additional information to verify emerging theory. Third, they may be used to reexamine a category in the main study from a different perspective.

It is important to remember that, in both qualitative and quantitative studies, the supplemental data sets are mutually interdependent. For instance, in qualitative research, if the main method used was grounded theory, then the unstructured or open-ended interviews may be supplemented by one or two focus groups. Data from these focus groups are not saturated and therefore cannot stand alone. These focus group data are intelligible and interpretable (and publishable) only as they are linked to the interview data from the main grounded theory project. In qualitative inquiry, supplemental data may be quantitative—the results of psychometric testing, for instance—and these results are then incorporated into the emerging model, providing a richer explanation. Similarly, to use a quantitative example, open-ended or unstructured interviews that accompany a quantitative survey are incomplete by qualitative standards and not publishable apart from the survey data. Often in quantitative inquiry, the supplemental observational or interview data may be transposed by coding from textual to numerical data so that they may be integrated more firmly into the analysis. A coding scheme may be developed to numerically code the participants' actions or the interview responses in the data.

PRINCIPLES OF
MIXED METHODS DESIGN

When using mixed methods, the major design principles to be considered are to (1) recognize the theoretical drive of the project, (2) recognize the role of the imported component in the project (i.e., how to inform the base project), (3) adhere to the methodological assumptions of the base method, and (4) work with as few data sets as possible. The *base project* is the project that provides the overall theoretical scheme into which the findings of other projects fit or which they complement.

Principle 1: Recognize the theoretical drive of the project. When conducting a single project, awareness of the theoretical drive is important. If the purpose of the research is to describe or discover, to find meaning, or to explore, then the theoretical drive will be inductive. The method most commonly used will be qualitative, and the outcome will be thick description as in phenomenological or narrative inquiry or some level of theory as obtained from ethnography or grounded theory. Quantitative methods may also be used for exploratory purposes with an inductive theoretical drive (sometimes referred to as "fishing trips") such as exploratory factor analysis or a survey. The direction of the researcher's thinking when conducting a single study might not be continuously inductive—adductive thinking may be used to verify hunches or conjectures— but overall the major theoretical drive will be inductive.

If the purpose of the research is to confirm (i.e., to test a hypothesis or a theory), or to determine the distribution of a phenomenon, then the theoretical drive is deductive and the method used is usually quantitative. Again, the direction of inquiry might not always remain deductive; induction may be used at times, but overall the theoretical drive will remain deductive.

Recognizing the direction of the theoretical drive has important ramifications for some crucial design issues such as sampling. If the researcher is working inductively with a qualitative sample, then the sample is small and purposely selected and therefore does not meet requirements of adequacy and appropriateness necessary for quantitative strategies or measures. If quantitative measures are used within a qualitative study, where does the researcher obtain the quantitative sample necessary to make sense of data? On the other hand, quantitative samples are too large and usually have been randomly selected. If the researcher decides to use a qualitative strategy, then how is a purposeful qualitative sample selected from the larger group?

Recall the edict that the researcher must retain the assumptions of each paradigm. Therefore, if the main study is qualitative, and a quantitative component is being sought, then a separate randomized sample must be added. Or, if the instruments are being administered to the qualitative sample, then external normative values must be available for the interpretation of the data. If the main project is quantitative and a qualitative component is added, then the sample must be purposefully selected from the main study. These sampling strategies are discussed later.

Principle 2: Recognize the role of the imported component in the project. In a single project, the main project forms the theoretical foundation, and information obtained from other strategies will be used to supplement or inform the main project. A researcher may, for instance, notice indications that important information is being missed if he or she adheres solely to the current data collection strategy. For example, when interviewing teachers about children's styles of learning, one teacher may describe a unique but important style. Because this phenomenon appears so rarely in the data—perhaps because the other teachers are unaware of the phenomenon—it may be necessary to introduce an observational component into the data to actually observe what the more experienced teacher was describing. Thus, the information obtained may then be ver-

ified outside the current data set using observations, or it may be verified within the core project during subsequent and more direct interviewing. Either way, the investigator must be aware of the interaction of the two components, and rigor must be maintained so that the project will not be jeopardized.

Principle 3: Adhere to the methodological assumptions of the base method. It is important to be constantly aware so as not to violate the methodological assumptions of the core method but, at the same time, to respect the assumptions that underlie the supplemental strategy being used. For example, when using qualitative data, researchers are often tempted to count—to know exactly how much or how many—which gives the appearance of rigor. But this is actually a perilous activity if assumptions are not adhered to. Ask "Were all of the participants asked the same question?" If not, then such data cannot be quantified in a meaningful way. What is the *significance* of such quantification? For instance, does knowing word length, sentence length, and the number of times a word was used add to our understanding of the research question? Is it even a sensible analytical strategy to use?

Conversely, quantitative researchers sometimes find themselves with unsolicited comments unexpectedly written in the margins of questionnaires or surveys. While conducting a content analysis of these responses is tempting, these comments are not good data; rather, they are a serendipitous indicator that something is wrong with the questionnaire. Evidently, the questionnaire was invalid and did not capture the experience or ask the right questions, so that the respondents felt compelled to use the margins to give the researcher the information they wished to convey. These comments indicate a serious problem with validity. Rather than analyzing these comments as a qualitative component, a qualitative study should be conducted to find out more accurately and comprehensively what is "going on."

Principle 4: Work with as few data sets as possible. If possible, incorporate data obtained from the supplemental strategy into the core project. If working quantitatively, this may mean transposing qualitative textual data into numerical data and incorporating them into the statistical analysis of the core project wherever appropriate.

If a quantitative project is being supplemented with qualitative data, then these data are often in the form of case studies to inform certain aspects of quantitative analysis at particular points or to illustrate the quantitative findings. They illuminate the quantitative research, often providing important context.

Summary. When using mixed methods within a single project, remember that the main analysis takes place primarily within the core of the strategy. The supplemental data—or rather the ideas generated from the supplemental data—inform the analysis that is taking place within the main strategy and are verified within the main focus of the project.

CHARACTERISTICS OF MIXED METHODS DESIGN

Recall that methodological strategies are *tools* for inquiry and that methods are cohesive collections of strategies that fit a particular perspective. To incorporate a different strategy into a study is risky and should be done with care, lest the core assumptions of the project be violated. Maintaining balance between respecting these assumptions and the respecting the assumptions underlying your supplemental strategies is delicate, for they may often

clash; consider, for instance, the previously mentioned differences in sampling. Consultation regarding this problem may be necessary.[2]

STRENGTHS AND WEAKNESSES OF MIXED DESIGNS

The major strength of mixed methods designs is that they allow for research to develop as comprehensively and completely as possible. When compared with a single method, the domain of inquiry is less likely to be constrained by the method itself. Because the supplementary data are often not completely saturated or as in-depth as they would be if they were a study in their own right, certainty is attained by verifying supplemental data with data strategies used within the core study.

On the other hand, the strengths of comprehensiveness from using mixed methods may also be perceived as weaknesses. Your research may be challenged on the grounds of being less rigorous than if a multimethod design were used. For instance, the supplemental data may be considered thin and therefore suspect. The researcher is advised to take care in describing both the methods and the way in which the less saturated data sets and complementary relationships between data sets were verified.

To summarize, the major difference between a *single study* using multiple strategies (mixed methods design) and a *research program* using multiple methods is that in the single study the less dominant strategies do not have to be a complete study in themselves. That is, the strategy may be used to develop indicators or to "test the waters" to follow a lead or hunch. If something of interest or importance is found, then this new finding may be used to complement or confirm something new or something that is already known or suspected. Within the research design, the new finding is treated as an *indicator*. As such, the new finding does not have to be completely verified itself; it does not have to be saturated or confirmed. Rather, the finding may be verified or confirmed elsewhere in another data set.

◆ Multimethod Design

Multiple methods are used in a research program when a series of projects are interrelated within a broad topic and designed to solve an overall research problem. Often—and this is more common in quantitative inquiry, where more is known about the topic and the expected findings—these projects are planned and submitted to a funding agency for program funding. Because of the role of discovery and the inability of the researcher to predict findings when working inductively, obtaining funding for a number of years and several projects is less common in qualitative inquiry.

PRINCIPLE 1: IDENTIFY THE THEORETICAL DRIVE OF THE RESEARCH PROJECT

All research projects, and particularly research *programs* or clusters of research projects on the same topic, have as an ultimate goal either discovery or testing. The primary way in which the researcher is thinking overall about a research topic is the *theoretical drive* (Morse, 1991) or the overall thrust of the entire research program. The theoretical drive may be inductive (for discovery) or deductive (for testing).

The *inductive* theoretical drive is when the researcher is working in the *discovery mode,* trying to find answers to problems such as the following: What is going on? What is happening? What are the characteristics of ____? What is the meaning of ____? The overall inductive drive does not change even if minor parts of the project are confirmatory or deductive; the researcher is interested only in the major direction of thinking used in the project as a whole. When in a research program the theoretical drive is inductive, the most important projects within the research program will probably be qualitative. As discussed later in the chapter, these studies will probably form the theoretical foundation of the research program. This does not mean that at particular times the researcher will not be testing ideas, hypotheses, or components of the emerging theory deductively; it only means that in the greater scheme of things, the agenda is one of discovery.

If the major thrust of the program is to test a theory or hypothesis, to answer questions of how much or how many, to determine relationships, and so forth, then the theoretical thrust will be *deductive*. The researcher will probably be using quantitative methods. While the research program may have components of induction or may incorporate qualitative inductive/discovery projects, the overall agenda is one of testing and the theoretical drive is deductive.

Because projects that have an inductive theoretical drive may embed minor deductive projects (and conversely, those with a deductive theoretical drive may include minor inductive projects), I prefer to use the term *drive* to refer to the direction or thrust of the overall design rather than the term *dominance* (as used by Tashakkori & Teddlie, 1998) or *priority decision* (Morgan, 1998). Because the minor components (i.e., inductive projects within the deductive program or vice versa) may be at any time to the fore, the term *dominance* may lead to confusion. It is imperative that the researcher at all times be aware of the mode of inquiry currently being used as well as how the current project fits into the overall agenda. The researcher must have a research question, and furthermore, inquiry is active; one cannot, and should not, have a blank mind when doing research. All projects have either an inductive or a deductive theoretical drive; they can neither be neutral nor be informed equally by inductive and deductive studies.[3]

PRINCIPLE 2: DEVELOP OVERT AWARENESS OF THE DOMINANCE OF EACH PROJECT

As well as being consciously aware of the thrust of the project, the researcher must also be aware of whether he or she is working inductively or deductively at any given time. This is crucial for successfully combining strategies within a single project or for conducting a research program containing two or more studies. While awareness of the thrust is essential for determining the fit of the results as *core* or *supplemental* (i.e., which project forms the core or base into which the results of the other projects are supplemental), awareness of working inductively or deductively at any given time will ensure that the assumption of each method is not violated.

Awareness of the theoretical drive is best achieved by using uppercase/lowercase notations indicating the major methods (a plus [+] sign indicating that the methods are used simultaneously or an arrow [→] indicating directions), with uppercase representing dominance and low-

ercase representing the supplemental projects (see Box 7.2).

TYPES OF MULTIMETHOD DESIGNS

We have four possible combinations with an inductive drive and four with a deductive drive. For an inductive theoretical drive, the possibilities are as follows:

1. QUAL + qual for two qualitative methods used simultaneously, one of which is dominant or forms the base of the project as a whole

2. QUAL → qual for two qualitative methods used sequentially, one of which is dominant

3. QUAL + quan for a qualitative and a quantitative method used simultaneously with an inductive theoretical thrust

4. QUAL → quan for a qualitative and a quantitative method used sequentially with an inductive theoretical thrust

For a deductive theoretical drive, the possibilities are as follows:

5. QUAN + quan for two quantitative methods used simultaneously, one of which is dominant

6. QUAN → quan for two quantitative methods used sequentially, one of which is dominant

7. QUAN + qual for a quantitative and a qualitative method used simultaneously with a deductive theoretical drive

8. QUAN → qual for a quantitative and a qualitative method used sequentially with a deductive theoretical drive

Of course, within a research program, one need not be restricted to only two projects;

BOX 7.2
Notations

The *plus* sign (+) indicates that projects are conducted simultaneously, with the uppercase indicating the dominant project.

The *arrow* (→) indicates that projects are conducted sequentially, again with the uppercase indicating dominance.

QUAL indicates a qualitatively-driven project.

QUAN indicates a quantitatively-driven project.

Therefore, we have eight combinations of triangulated designs:

Simultaneous designs:

QUAL + qual indicates a qualitatively-driven, qualitative simultaneous design.

QUAN + quan indicates a quantitatively-driven, quantitative simultaneous design.

QUAL + quan indicates a qualitatively-driven, qualitative and quantitative simultaneous design.

QUAN + qual indicates a quantitatively-driven, quantitative and qualitative simultaneous design.

Sequential designs:

QUAL → qual indicates a qualitatively-driven project followed by a second qualitative project.

QUAN → quan indicates a quantitatively-driven project followed by a second quantitative project.

QUAL → quan indicates a qualitatively-driven project followed by a quantitative project.

QUAN → qual indicates a quantitatively-driven project followed by a qualitative project.

Projects may have complex designs containing combinations of the above, depending on the scope and complexity of the research program.

---

the program itself may be any number of combinations of these projects. However, the theoretical drive, determined by the overall question and design, remains constant within each project.

The pacing of projects within the research program is crucial. Research is an evolving puzzle, and all of the pieces (projects) necessary to solve the puzzle might not be seen from the beginning. This is particularly evident when using sequential designs with an inductive drive; additional studies—even ones that are crucial to the overall validity of the project—may emerge as the analysis evolves. Therefore, as projects are added, the investigator must return for additional ethical review.

CHARACTERISTICS OF MULTIMETHOD DESIGNS

The major difference between multi-method and mixed methods designs is that in multimethod design all projects are complete in themselves. The major research question or problem drives the research program, but the program consists of two or more interrelated studies. Overall, the project retains either an inductive or a deductive theoretical drive, but projects conducted simultaneously or sequentially within the umbrella of the main project may have an inductive or a deductive drive depending on whether, at a particular point, the researcher needs to discover or confirm.

It is the *results* of each method that inform the emerging conceptual scheme as the investigator addresses the overall research question. When using a multimethod design, data are not usually combined within projects, as may occur in a mixed methods design when, for instance, textual data are transformed to numerical data and used in the analysis of a quantitative study. Rather, in a multimethod design, each study is planned and conducted to answer a particular subquestion. In qualitatively-driven mixed methods designs, these questions usually arise from the previous project and are therefore conducted sequentially; if more than one question arises, then the two projects may be conducted simultaneously. For quantitative mixed methods design, several projects designed to address one topic may be planned in advance at the proposal stage, and frequently major funded grants include several projects designed to address one topic. In this case, the results of one project are not usually dependent on the findings of earlier projects, and results are anticipated as hypotheses or as pieces in the theoretical framework. If unanticipated findings are obtained, then the

whole project has to be reconsidered as a new project, perhaps even with qualitative projects added to the research program. Thus, the results from the supplemental projects are fitted into the base project.

Simultaneous Designs. When used concurrently, one method usually drives the project theoretically. That is, one method forms the basis of the emerging theoretical scheme. This base project has more comprehensive relevance to the topic and is usually conceived at the design phase. The "supplemental" project(s) may be planned to elicit information that the base method cannot achieve or for the results to inform in greater detail about one part of the dominant project.

Sequential Designs. When used sequentially, the method that theoretically drives the project is usually conducted first, with the second method designed to resolve problems/issues uncovered by the first study or to provide a logical extension from the findings of the first study.

PRINCIPLE 3: RESPECT METHODOLOGICAL INTEGRITY

When using a multimethod design, keep each method intact. It is important not to violate the assumptions, sampling (appropriateness and adequacy of data), and so forth. Keep in mind that it is the *results* of each project that are triangulated to inform the research problem.

Specific Multimethod Designs

Designs With an Inductive Drive. The first four designs discussed in what follows are those with an inductive theoretical drive. That is, they are primarily used for developing description and for deriving meaning and interpretation of the phenomenon, thus forming the foundation of the program.

    1. QUAL + qual

This indicates that two qualitative methods are used simultaneously, one of which is dominant or forms the base of the project as a whole.

Types of Research Problems. This design is used when it is necessary to obtain more than one perspective on a research topic. One qualitative method will be dominant, with the second method used to provide additional insights.

Example. Morse was interested in the provision of nurse comforting of patients and proposed three simultaneous projects. The first project was a grounded theory project to identify the process of providing comfort, and this study formed the base of the research program. Supplementary projects included an ethnographic study to explore the context of comfort and a phenomenological study to elicit the meaning of comfort (see the proposal in Morse & Field, 1995, pp. 197-235).

Design Issues. When conducting several qualitative projects that are interrelated but separate, one project remains dominant or forms the base of the project as a whole, while the findings of the supplementary project inform or add to the results of the dominant one. For instance, a grounded theory project may form the base of a project, and a phenomenological study may inform the grounded theory, providing additional insight.

Sampling Strategies. Can the same person participate in more than one study? Perhaps—if it is feasible and appropriate. In the preceding example, different partici-

pants were used; the grounded theory used participants who had been through the experience and had been discharged from the rehabilitation hospital, whereas for the ethnographic study the participants were inpatients.

Can the same data be used for more than one study? If data are pertinent and in the right form, then they may be used. However, if data are old or perhaps do not directly address the central research topic, then it is prudent to collect new data. Or, perhaps it may be feasible to use the first data set and collect supplemental confirmatory data (Thorne, 1994). In the comfort studies mentioned previously, the data for the phenomenological study fit into the latter category. Morse and Field (1995) used some data already collected and also conducted new interviews.

Methodological Congruence. Good research is more than just using sets of data collection strategies; it is also a way of linking the philosophical foundations of the project with a particular question that will be best answered using a particular sampling strategy linked within the methodological framework. In other words, each method has a distinct way of thinking and approaching a research problem. Phenomenological research must be congruent with the assumptions and strategies of phenomenology, grounded theory research must be congruent with the assumptions and strategies of grounded theory, and so forth.

Triangulation of Results. As stated previously, it is the *results* of each separate study that inform the researcher about the topic. The base project is usually the study that is most comprehensive. In the Morse comfort study discussed previously (Morse & Field, 1995), the grounded theory study formed the base project. The grounded theory study provided information on the process; the stages of comforting; why and how comforting interactions were initiated; and how certain comforting actions were given, under what conditions, and why. The phenomenological study informed us about what it meant to experience discomfort and about different aspects of bodily comfort. The ethnographic study informed us about the nurse-patient interactions, how other patients competed for the nurses' time, how nurses decided when to give comfort, how they read patient cues, and so forth. By placing these pieces together, we could then build a midrange theory of comfort—one that was more comprehensive than the grounded theory findings alone and that provided us with information that we would not have obtained if we had used only a single method.

One warning, however, is that the results of the studies triangulated might not be on the same level of abstraction. Some studies may be more abstract, whereas others may be less so and more microanalytical. Some studies may inform only one part of the base project, whereas others may inform all aspects. For instance, the findings of the phenomenological study had broad application for many aspects of the emerging theory, whereas the ethnographic study was primarily useful for providing information during the acute care phase.

2. QUAL → qual

Two qualitative methods may be used sequentially, and one—usually the first one conducted—is dominant. These studies may use different qualitative methods, for instance, a grounded theory study followed by a phenomenological study supplementing findings in the first stage (see Wilson & Hutchinson, 1991). These stud-

ies may also use the same method but be at different levels of analysis.

Example. Wilson used grounded theory to explore the experience of caregivers of persons with Alzheimer's disease (Wilson, 1989b). She then conducted a second study, also using grounded theory, to explicate the process within one of the phases of the first study (Wilson, 1989a).

Design Issues. Both studies are independent. However, data obtained from the first study may be used in the second study if appropriate (i.e., relevant and in the correct form).

Sampling Strategies. If appropriate (i.e., if participants have had the necessary experiences), the same participants may participate in both studies. Alternatively, new participants may be sought using the principles of sampling for qualitative research.

Methodological Congruence. All procedures used in each method must adhere to, and be consistent with, the method selected.

Triangulation of Results. Clearly, the strength of sequential projects is when they can be viewed as a set. Yet despite the logical progression of these projects, because each study is self-contained, researchers frequently publish these studies separately so that the interaction between the two studies is often difficult to appreciate. Occasionally, however, a researcher does prepare a review article or a monograph fully integrating the entire research program.

3. QUAL + quan

A qualitative method used simultaneously with a quantitative method with an inductive theoretical thrust is used when some portion of the phenomenon may be measured, and this measurement enhances the qualitative description or interpretation.

Example. An ethnographic study exploring responses to parturition pain in Fijian and Fiji Indian women revealed that the response to pain varied between the two cultural groups. Interviews with traditional birth attendants provided cultural context of the interpretation of the behaviors. A paired comparisons test, comparing common painful events such as childbirth, enabled measurement of pain attribution in each culture. Thus, the study extended Zborowski's (1969) finding that pain behavior is culturally transmitted and found that the amount of pain associated with various conditions (and pain expectation) also differs between cultures (Morse, 1989).

Design Issues. Each project must be methodologically exquisite, independent, and adherent to its own methodological assumptions.

Sampling Strategies. The qualitative study necessarily uses a small purposeful sample, and the quantitative study uses a larger, randomly selected sample. Therefore, different sampling strategies must be used for each study. This begs the question: Can the same participants be used for both studies? Yes; if participants from the qualitative study are selected in the quantitative study's randomization process, then they may participate in the quantitative study.

Methodological Congruence. Again, each project is complete in itself, and it is the results of the quantitative project that inform the qualitative project.

Triangulation of Results. Once the projects have been completed, the results of the quantitative project are used to provide details for the qualitative project.

4. QUAL → quan

This design is used when a qualitative and a quantitative method are used sequentially with an inductive theoretical thrust.

Types of Research Problems. This design is most often used to develop a model or theory and then to test the theory. Note that while testing is the second quantitative component (and forms a deductive phase), the overall theoretical thrust is inductive.

Example. A research program investigating adolescents' response to menarche consisted of five projects. First, a qualitative project used semistructured questions to determine the experiences of seventh- and eighth-grade girls with menarche and to establish the dimensions of the experience (Morse & Doan, 1987). Second, using the qualitative analysis, a Likert scale was developed (Morse, Kieren, & Bottorff, 1993) using categories such as the dimensions, the textual data, and the adolescents' verbal expressions to form the scale items. This instrument was tested with 860 premenarcheal girls and 1,013 postmenarcheal girls from 49 randomly selected schools. The authors then revised the scale and obtained reliability and validity statistics and normative data (Morse & Kieren, 1993). Quantitative studies were then conducted to determine adolescents' preparation for menstruation (Kieren & Morse, 1992) and the influence of developmental factors on attitudes toward menstruation (Kieren & Morse,

1995). Regardless of the fact that most of these projects were quantitative, all of the projects rested on the first qualitative project (which is considered the core project), and the theoretical drive of the project remained inductive.

Design Issues. As with the previous categories, each project must be methodologically independent, exquisite, and adherent to its own methodological assumptions.

Sampling Strategies. The samples are distinct, with the qualitative study using a small purposeful sample and the quantitative study using a larger, randomly selected sample. Because of the time lapse between the two studies, it is unlikely that they will have participants in common.

Methodological Congruence. Each study is distinct, and each is congruent with its own assumptions.

Triangulation of Results. The qualitative study moves the research program along by confirming the earlier qualitative findings. What happens if the qualitative findings are not confirmed? Depending on the discrepancy, the researcher must regroup. If it is clear that the model or theory is incorrect, then the researcher must consider why. Perhaps another qualitative study using a different design, or another quantitative study, will have to be conducted. However, it is difficult to find examples of this problem given that a researcher's failures are rarely published and, more likely, the qualitative study will result in minor modifications of the theory.

Designs With a Deductive Theoretical Thrust

The following designs are used primarily for hypotheses or theory testing.

5. QUAN + quan

This is a research program consisting of two quantitative methods used simultaneously, one of which is dominant.

Types of Research Problems. This is the most common type of triangulation, in which a research question demands the administration of several instruments, all of which are related to, and measure different dimensions of, the same overall question. One instrument is usually more pertinent to the research question than the other(s) because it measures the concept most directly. The other instruments may be administered as a validity check to measure aspects of the concept that the first one might not include or to measure associated or allied concepts.

Example. A study of coping may also include measures of stress and measures of social support, and the participants may be given the test battery in one sitting.

Design Issues. Because all of the tests are administered to the same participants, *test burden* may be a problem. The time for testing may be lengthy, and participants may become tired.

Sampling Strategies. The battery of tests is administered to the same sample, preferably randomly selected from a defined population.

Methodological Congruence. Test and subscale scores are correlated with the most direct measure.

Triangulation of Results. Results are triangulated by determining statistical correlations between the measures.

6. QUAN → quan

This design is used when two quantitative methods are used sequentially. The first study is usually dominant, with the second study conducted to elicit further information about particular dimensions of the first study.

Example. A study to identify factors that contributed to patient falls was conducted. Data on a large number of variables thought to contribute to the risk of falling were collected from 100 patients who fall and 100 controls. Using computer modeling and discriminant analysis techniques, a scale to identify those at risk of falling was developed. This scale was subsequently tested on six patient care units (Morse, 1997).

Types of Research Problems. Quantitative research programs are usually used when considerable work has already been conducted in the area. Researchers have enough information to know the relevant variables, to be able to conduct a theoretical framework, and to make hypotheses about the expected results.

Design Issues. Because the studies are conducted at different times, if the second study is delayed and the time lapse between the two studies is prolonged, the setting or the study populations may have undergone change. This would reduce the comparability of the results.

Sampling Strategies. Samples are large, predetermined by power calculations according to expected group differences and the amount of error tolerable, and usually randomly selected.

Methodological Congruence. Quantitative methods are usually well-explicated,

and the assumptions are usually well-described.

Triangulation of Results. Again, it is usually the results of the studies that inform the researcher about the emerging model.

7. QUAN + qual

This design is used when a quantitative and a qualitative method are used simultaneously with a deductive theoretical drive.

Types of Research Problems. A theoretical model is created from the literature and previous research and is tested quantitatively. Because some of the components might not be quantifiable, or might require explanation or illustration, a qualitative study is conducted concurrently.

Example. A study of infant feeding in Fiji was conducted to determine the influence of breast- and bottle-feeding on infant health. Regression analysis was conducted on data obtained from infants. Ethnographic interviews conducted with Fijian and Fiji Indian women provided contextual data that enabled further interpretation of the quantitative data (Morse, 1984).

Design Issues. Due to the quantitative core of the project, this design has less flexibility than its qualitative equivalent.

Sampling Strategies. The main study uses a quantitative sample (large and preferably randomized). If the qualitative sample is drawn from the quantitative sample, then principles of qualitative sampling must be respected, including the qualities of a "good informant" (Spradley, 1979). How are these participants located? The sample may be selected from the participants of the quantitative study. Seek assistance from interviewers, and ask them to assist with the purposeful selection by making recommendations.

Methodological Congruence. When using this design, it is tempting not to saturate the qualitative data. Recall that both studies must be complete in themselves.

Triangulation of Results. The description is primarily from the quantitative data, with qualitative description enhancing particular aspects of the study.

8. QUAN → qual

This design is to conduct a quantitative study followed by a qualitative study. The studies are conducted sequentially using a deductive theoretical drive, although induction is used in the second project.

Types of Research Problems. This design is most frequently used when the quantitative study results are unexpected, unanticipated findings, and a qualitative study is then conducted to ascertain the reasons for the results or to find out what is going on.

Example. A survey of a small town produced some unexpected results, requiring the investigators to step back and reexamine some assumptions about certain parts of the community.

Design Issues. The two projects are independent and may even be conducted by different research teams.

Sampling Strategies. The first study uses a quantitative sample (large and randomized). For the second study, a separate purposeful qualitative sample is selected.

Methodological Congruence. The quantitative study is usually completed prior to the initiation of the qualitative study.

Triangulation of Results. The qualitative study provides explanation for particular parts of the quantitative study.

STRENGTHS AND WEAKNESSES OF MULTIMETHOD DESIGNS

The obvious strength of using a multimethod design is that it provides one with a different perspective on the phenomenon. While some authors have described this view or perspective as "having a different lens" or side (as provided by a crystal) (Sandelowski, 1995), the real strength in using multiple methods is to obtain a different level of data. For instance, one may conduct observational research and obtain information on group behavior and then conduct a microanalysis study of touching behavior. These two studies are interdependent and together provide a more comprehensive picture than either would alone.

The credence and weight that one places on the findings are important. Again, this is done with the study findings when the studies have been completed.

◆ Discussion

The pacing of the projects is important and is dictated by the theoretical drive. If the results of the first project are needed to plan the next study, then it is clear that the two projects should be conducted sequentially. If, on the other hand, the first project is lacking and incomplete without the second project, then the two projects should be conducted simultaneously. I have written about maintaining the independence of these projects until they are completed. I add a warning here that these projects should not contaminate each other—in particular, if the two projects are qualitative. Ideally, the staff for each project should be separate to prevent cross-fertilization of ideas and data.

Will the triangulation of multiple studies always work? Will it always enhance the results? An interesting question that has been raised is whether a researcher should expect convergence when exploring a phenomenon from two different perspectives using different methods. Should the phenomenon even be recognizable? Chesla (1992) noted that the difference in the methods themselves may account for the differences in the findings. She used an example of the measurement of coping with a card sort procedure (in which coping is scored according to whether it is seen as pertaining to the group, considers the work to be ordered and masterful, and approaches a problem as novel or as a repetition of past dilemmas [Chesla, 1992; Reiss, 1981]) versus qualitative findings that classified coping in couples as having identical, congruent, or conflicting coping patterns (Chesla, 1989). Chesla (1992) noted that, in such cases, the preponderance of evidence lies with the qualitative narrative data (although they were collected from a relatively small number of participants), as opposed to the quantitative data, and recognized correctly that differences in the context of data collection (e.g., public vs. private, family vs. investigator-controlled) and the degree of structure in the collection process may circumscribe findings. Rather than considering the theoretical drive, as recommended in this chapter, Chesla advised including some form of "synthesis" for weighing the evidence and resolving this dilemma, although that was not possible with her data.

Would an "armchair walkthrough" (Morse, 1999) have prevented this dilemma? Perhaps. Researchers should always be cognizant of the nature of their research findings, and what may or may not be "done" with them, even before their studies commence so that they will not be blindsided.

Some authors have considered triangulation as a form of convergent validity, somewhat resembling a test for constructing validity (Zeller & Carmines, 1980). This is a very poor reason for triangulation; two strong studies do not necessarily give a project more credence than does one study, and they require twice as much work. Nevertheless, demonstrating validity is a possible rationale for triangulated studies, but it should not be the main one. With the exception of divergent results such as those discussed in the preceding example, researchers should expect some overlap in findings, especially when using two qualitative or two quantitative methods. That overlap might not be helpful, however, as in the case of the frustrated parent who obtained divergent accounts from two children about "how the window was broken." If researchers trust their own abilities as researchers, and their own methods as valid and rigorous, then two methods should not have an advantage over one method; in fact, one could argue that using multiple methods for verification may be a waste of time and energy.

Weinholtz, Kacer, and Rocklin (1995) made a case for "salvaging" a quantitative study with qualitative case studies. They argued that quantitative studies may often be "ambiguous and misleading" if not supplemented with qualitative data; this may be true, but it is possible that poor quality of the quantitative studies must be addressed in this case. While qualitative work may often enhance quantitative studies, QUAN + qual triangulation is not a substitute for poor qualitative work.

Researchers must always be aware of the goal of inquiry, whether using qualitative or quantitative inquiry or some form of mixed methods or multimethod design. Again, research strategies and methods are only tools—tools that are only as good as the researcher's knowledge and skill. Inquiry is not a passive process but rather an active one for which the researcher—not the method, not the participants, and not the setting—is responsible for the outcome. Building one's toolbox, both qualitatively and quantitatively, aids the quality of one's research, as does thoughtful deliberate action coupled with foresight and skill.

■ *Notes*

1. While Tashakkori and Teddlie (1998) referred to *mixed methods design* to designate the combining of qualitative and quantitative strategies, in this chapter I *also include* the incorporation into a qualitative project of qualitative strategies that are not normally used with that particular method and, conversely, the incorporation into the definition of quantitative strategies that are not normally a part of that particular quantitative method. Hence, the label *mixed methods design* is still applicable.

2. Because the strategies that are incorporated are often not anticipated earlier in the project and not described in the original proposal, it is important to obtain ethical review board clearance for additional data collection strategies. Clearance is usually obtained by filing a minor change report to the university committee and the ethic review board committee that is responsible for the agency in which the research is being conducted. It may also be prudent, if you are a graduate student, to obtain the blessing for the revised research design from your supervisory committee.

3. In fact, using the preceding description of theoretical drive, the "equal status mixed methods design" presented by Tashakkori and Teddlie (1998, p. 45) is actually a project that has an inductive thrust.

■ *References*

Benoliel, J. Q. (1996). Grounded theory and nursing knowledge. *Qualitative Health Research, 6,* 406-428.

Breitmayer, B. J., Ayres, L., & Knafl, K. (1993). Triangulation in qualitative research: Evaluation of completeness and confirmation purposes. *Image: Journal of Nursing Scholarship, 25,* 237-243.

Chesla, C. A. (1989). Parent's illness models of schizophrenia. *Archives of Psychiatric Nursing, 3,* 218-225.

Chesla, C. A. (1992). When qualitative and quantitative findings do not converge. *Western Journal of Nursing Research, 14,* 681-685.

Fine, G., & Smith, G. (2000). *Erving Goffman* (Vol. 1). Thousand Oaks, CA: Sage.

Glaser, B. G. (1978). *Theoretical sensitivity.* Mill Valley, CA: Sociology Press.

Goffman, E. (1989). On fieldwork. *Journal of Contemporary Ethnography, 18*(2), 123-132.

Kieren, D., & Morse, J. M. (1992). Preparation factors and menstrual attitudes of pre- and postmenarcheal girls. *Journal of Sex Education and Therapy, 18,* 155-174.

Kieren, D. K., & Morse, J. M. (1995). Developmental factors and pre- and postmenarcheal menstrual attitudes. *Canadian Home Economics Journal, 45*(2), 61-67.

Morgan, D. L. (1998). Practical strategies for combining qualitative and quantitative methods: Applications to health research. *Qualitative Health Research, 8,* 362-367.

Morse, J. M. (1984). Breast- and bottle-feeding: The effect on infant weight gain in the Fiji-Indian neonate. *Ecology of Food and Nutrition, 15,* 109-114.

Morse, J. M. (1989). Cultural responses to parturition: Childbirth in Fiji. *Medical Anthropology, 12*(1), 35-44.

Morse, J. M. (1991). Approaches to qualitative-quantitative methodological triangulation. *Nursing Research, 40*(2), 120-123.

Morse, J. M. (1997). *Preventing patient falls.* Thousand Oaks, CA: Sage.

Morse, J.M. (1999). The armchair walk-through [editorial]. *Qualitative Health Research, 9,* 435-436.

Morse, J. M., & Doan, H. (1987). Growing up at school: Adolescents' response to menarche. *Journal of School Health, 57,* 385-389.

Morse, J. M., & Field, P. A. (1995). *Qualitative approaches to nursing research* (2nd ed.). London: Chapman & Hall.

Morse, J. M., & Kieren, D. (1993). The Adolescent Menstrual Attitude Questionnaire, Part II: Normative scores. *Health Care for Women International, 14,* 63-76.

Morse, J. M., Kieren, D., & Bottorff, J. L. (1993). The Adolescent Menstrual Attitude Questionnaire, Part I: Scale construction. *Health Care for Women International, 14,* 39-62.

Reiss, D. (1981). *The family's construction of reality.* Cambridge, MA: Harvard University Press.

Sandelowski, M. (1995). Triangles and crystals: On the geometry of qualitative research. *Research in Nursing and Health, 18,* 569-574.

Spradley, J. (1979). *The ethnographic interview.* New York: Holt, Rinehart.

Stern, P. N. (1994). Eroding grounded theory. In J. Morse (Ed.), *Critical issues in qualitative research methods* (pp. 214-215). Thousand Oaks, CA: Sage.

Tashakkori, A., & Teddlie, C. (1998). *Mixed methodology: Combining qualitative and quantitative methodology* (Applied Social Research Methods, No. 46). Thousand Oaks, CA: Sage.

Thorne, S. (1994). Secondary analysis in qualitative research. In J. M. Morse (Ed.), *Critical issues in qualitative research methods* (pp. 263-279). Thousand Oaks, CA: Sage.

van Manen, M. (1990). *Researching lived experience.* London, Ontario: Althouse Press.

Weinholtz, D., Kacer, B., & Rocklin, T. (1995). Salvaging qualitative research with qualitative data. *Qualitative Health Research, 5,* 388-397.

Wilson, H. S. (1989a). Family caregiver for a relative with Alzheimer's dementia: Coping with negative choices. *Nursing Research, 38*(2), 94-98.

Wilson H. S. (1989b). Family caregivers: The experience of Alzheimer's disease. *Applied Nursing Research, 2*(1), 40-45.

Wilson, H. S., & Hutchinson, S. A. (1991). Triangulation of qualitative methods: Heideggerian hermeneutics and grounded theory. *Qualitative Health Research, 1,* 263-276.

Zborowski, M. (1969). *People in pain.* San Francisco: Jossey-Bass.

Zeller, R. A., & Carmines, E. G. (1980). *Measurement in the social sciences.* Cambridge, UK: Cambridge University Press.

8

ADVANCED MIXED
METHODS RESEARCH DESIGNS

◆ John W. Creswell
Vicki L. Plano Clark
Michelle L. Gutmann
William E. Hanson

One approach to learning about mixed methods research designs is to begin with a mixed methods study and explore the features that characterize it as mixed methods research. Although many such studies are available in the literature, we begin here with a study in education exploring the factors associated with parental savings for postsecondary education, a topic to which many people can relate. Hossler and Vesper (1993) conducted a study examining the factors associated with parental savings for children attending higher education campuses. Using longitudinal data collected from students and parents over

a 3-year period, the authors examined factors most strongly associated with parental savings for postsecondary education. Their results indicated that parental support, educational expectations, and knowledge of college costs were important factors. Most important for our purposes, the authors collected information from parents and students on 182 surveys and from 56 interviews.

To examine this study from a mixed methods perspective, we would like to draw attention to the following:

◆ The authors collected "mixed" forms of data, including quantitative survey data and qualitative open-ended interview data.

◆ The authors titled the study "An Exploratory Study of the Factors Associated With Parental Savings for Postsecondary Education," containing words suggestive of both quantitative and qualitative approaches. The word *exploratory* is often associated with qualitative research, while the word *factors* implies the use of variables in quantitative research.

◆ The authors advanced a purpose statement that included a rationale for mixing methods: "The interviews permitted us to look for emerging themes from both the survey and from previous interview data, which could then be explored in more depth in subsequent interviews" (p. 146).

◆ The authors reported two separate data analyses: first the quantitative results of the survey, followed by the findings from the qualitative interviews. An examination of these two sections shows that the quantitative analysis is discussed more extensively than the qualitative analysis.

◆ The authors ended the article with a discussion that compared the quantitative statistical results with the qualitative thematic findings.

Based on these features, we see the authors mixing quantitative and qualitative research in this study—mixed methods research. More specifically, with information from recent literature on mixed methods research designs, the "type" of mixed methods design used by Hossler and Vesper (1993) in their study might be called a "concurrent triangulation method design," indicating a triangulation of data collection, separate data analysis, and the integration of databases at the interpretation or discussion stage of the report. Furthermore, their design gave priority to quantitative research.

To give their study a mixed methods name and to identify the characteristics of the design may not have affected whether it was accepted for publication or whether it was given enhanced status in the social science community. However, being able to identify the characteristics of the study that make it mixed methods and giving the design a specific name conveys to readers the rigors of their study. It also provides guidance to others who merge quantitative and qualitative data into a single study. If they were presenting it to journal editors, faculty committees, or funding agencies, the labeling of the design and an identification of its characteristics helps reviewers to decide the criteria and the personnel most qualified to review the study. If Hossler and Vesper (1993) had created a visual representation or figure of their procedures, it would have enhanced the study's readability to audiences not used to seeing complex and interrelated data collection and analysis procedures.

Like many other studies of its kind, the Hossler and Vesper (1993) study falls into a category of research called mixed methods designs. Although these studies are frequently reported in the literature, they are seldom discussed as a separate research design. However, with an increasing number of authors writing about mixed methods research as a separate design, it is now time to seriously consider it as a distinct design in the social sciences. To do this calls for a review of disparate literature about mixed methods research designs found in journals across the social sciences as well as in chapters, books, and conference papers.

This chapter presents a synthesis of recent literature about mixed methods research as a separate design. It creates an analysis of the discussion today and its historical roots over the past 20 years. It then reviews four criteria that have emerged during the past few years that provide guidance for a researcher trying to identify the type of mixed methods design to use in a particular study. From these criteria emerge six core designs under which many types of design currently being discussed can be subsumed. We then review three issues in implementing the designs: the use of paradigm perspectives, the data analysis procedures used with each design, and the use of expanded visualizations and procedures. We end by returning to the Hossler and Vesper (1993) study to review how it might be presented and understood as a mixed methods design.

◆ Mixed Methods Research as a Separate Design

There are a number of arguments for why mixed methods research might be considered a separate research design in the social sciences. By design, we mean a procedure for collecting, analyzing, and reporting research such as that found in the time-honored designs of quantitative experiments and surveys and in the qualitative approaches of ethnographies, grounded theory studies, and case studies. These arguments take several forms. Authors have increasingly recognized the advantages of mixing both quantitative and qualitative data collection in a single study. Numerous mixed methods studies have been reported in the scholarly journals for social scientists to see and use as models for their own studies. In addition, authors have delineated more carefully a definition for mixed methods research, although consensus has been slow to develop for a single definition recognized by all inquirers. Finally, method and methodological authors who write about mixed methods

research have identified procedures that point toward critical design elements such as a visual model of procedures, a notation system, the explication of types of designs, and specific criteria useful in deciding what type of design to employ in a given study.

A RECOGNITION OF ADVANTAGES

The collection and combination of both quantitative and qualitative data in research has been influenced by several factors. Unquestionably, both quantitative and qualitative data are increasingly available for use in studying social science research problems. Also, because all methods of data collection have limitations, the use of multiple methods can neutralize or cancel out some of the disadvantages of certain methods (e.g., the detail of qualitative data can provide insights not available through general quantitative surveys) (Jick, 1979). Thus, there is wide consensus that mixing different types of methods can strengthen a study (Greene & Caracelli, 1997). Qualitative research has become an accepted legitimate form of inquiry in the social sciences, and researchers of all methodological persuasions recognize its value in obtaining detailed contextualized information. Also, because social phenomena are so complex, different kinds of methods are needed to best understand these complexities (Greene & Caracelli, 1997).

PUBLISHED MIXED METHODS STUDIES

Given these advantages, authors writing about mixed methods research have frequently analyzed published mixed methods studies in terms of their procedures. For example, Greene, Caracelli, and Graham (1989) reviewed 57 evaluation studies so as to develop a classification scheme of types of designs based on purpose and design characteristics. Creswell, Goodchild, and Turner (1996) discussed 19 mixed methods studies about postsecondary education and illustrated steps in the studies. The "box feature" was used extensively in Tashakkori and Teddlie's (1998) book to illustrate examples of mixed methods research projects. In fact, a review of the many procedural discussions about mixed methods research [see Datta's (1994) review of 18 methodological discussions about mixed methods research from 1959 to 1992] shows references to published studies across the social science disciplines.

THE ISSUE OF DEFINITION

Finding these published studies, however, requires some creative searching of the literature. The actual terms used to denote a mixed methods study vary considerably in the procedural discussions of this design. Writers have referred to it as multitrait-multimethod research (Campbell & Fiske, 1959), integrating qualitative and quantitative approaches (Glik, Parker, Muligande, & Hategikamana, 1986-1987; Steckler, McLeroy, Goodman, Bird, & McCormick, 1992), interrelating qualitative and quantitative data (Fielding & Fielding, 1986), methodological triangulation (Morse, 1991), multimethodological research (Hugentobler, Israel, & Schurman, 1992), multimethod designs and linking qualitative and quantitative data (Miles & Huberman, 1994), combining qualitative and quantitative research (Bryman, 1988; Creswell, 1994; Swanson-Kauffman, 1986), mixed model studies (Datta, 1994), and mixed methods research (Caracelli & Greene, 1993; Greene et al., 1989; Rossman & Wilson, 1991). Central to all of these terms is the idea of combining or integrating different methods. The term *mixed methods* is perhaps most appropriate, although one of the authors of this chapter has used others (Creswell, 1994; Creswell et al., 1996; Creswell & Miller, 1997). Mixing provides an umbrella term to cover the multifaceted procedures of combining, integrating, linking, and employing multimethods.

To argue for mixed methods research as a specific research design requires not only an accepted term but also a common definition. Building on earlier definitions of mixed methods research (Fielding & Fielding, 1986; Greene et al., 1989), a mixed methods research design at its simplest level involves mixing both qualitative and quantitative methods of data collection and analysis in a single study (Creswell, 1999). A more elaborate definition would specify the nature of data collection (e.g., whether data are gathered concurrently or sequentially), the priority each form of data receives in the research report (e.g., equal or unequal), and the place in the research process in which "mixing" of the data occurs such as in the data collection, analysis, or interpretation phase of inquiry. Combining all of these features into a single definition suggests the following definition:

> A *mixed methods study* involves the collection or analysis of both quantitative and/or qualitative data in a single study in which the data are collected concurrently or sequentially, are given a priority, and involve the integration of the data at one or more stages in the process of research.

This definition, although a reasonable beginning point for considering mixed methods research designs, masks several additional questions that are developed further in this chapter. For example, this definition does not account for multiple studies within a sustained program of inquiry in which researchers may mix methods at different phases of the research. It also creates an artificial distinction between quantitative and qualitative methods of data collection that may not be as firmly in place as people think (see Johnson and Turner's detailed discussion about types of data in Chapter 11 of this volume). Furthermore, it does not account for a theoretical framework that may drive the research and create a larger vision in which the study may be posed.

THE TREND TOWARD PROCEDURAL GUIDELINES

The history of mixed methods research has been adequately traced elsewhere (see Creswell, 2002; Datta, 1994; Tashakkori & Teddlie, 1998). Central to this discussion is the development of procedural guidelines that argue for viewing mixed methods research as a separate design. The evolution of procedural guidelines for mixed methods studies is seen in the creation of visual models, a notation system, and the specification of types of designs.

Visual Models. Procedures for conducting a mixed methods study first emerged from discussions in which authors described the flow of activities typically used by researchers when they conducted this type of study. For example, Sieber (1973) suggested the combination of in-depth case studies with surveys, creating a "new style of research" and the "integration" of research techniques within a single study (p. 1337). Patton (1990) identified several forms of research as "mixed forms" such as experimental designs, qualitative data and content analysis or experimental designs, qualitative data, and statistical data.

Soon, writers began to draw procedures graphically and create figures that displayed the overall flow of research activities. A good example of these visuals is found in health education research. As shown in Figure 8.1, Steckler et al. (1992) provided four alternative procedures for collecting both quantitative and qualitative research and gave a brief rationale for the reason for combining methods. These models show both quantitative and qualitative methods (actually data collection) and use arrows to indicate the sequence of activities in the mixed methods study. Models 2 and 3 are similar except that the procedures begin with qualitative data in Model 2 and with quantitative data in Model 3.

Notation System. Models such as these provide a useful way for readers to understand the basic procedures used in mixed methods studies. Implied in these models is also the idea that a notation system exists to explain the procedures. In 1991, Morse, a nursing researcher, developed a notation system that has become widely used by researchers designing mixed methods studies (see also Morse's notation system as she discusses types of designs in Chapter 7 of this volume). As shown in Figure 8.2, Morse discussed several types of mixed methods studies and illustrated them with a plus (+) sign to denote the simultaneous collection of quantitative and qualitative data, an arrow (→) to designate that one form of data collection followed another, uppercase letters to suggest major emphasis (e.g., QUAN, QUAL) on the form of data collection, and lowercase letters to imply less emphasis (e.g., quan, qual). It is also noteworthy that the terms *quantitative* and *qualitative* were now shortened to *quan* and *qual,* respectively, implying that both approaches to research are legitimate and of equal stature.

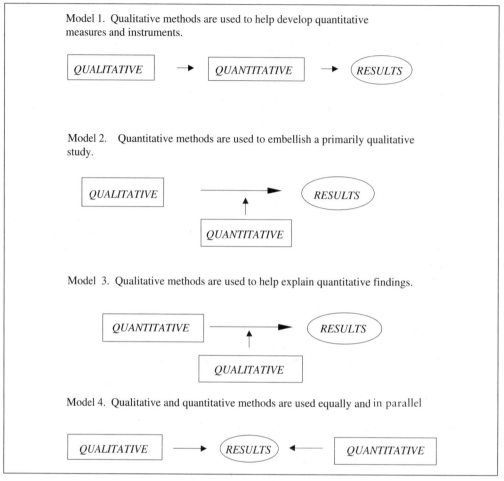

Figure 8.1. Example of Visual Presentation of Procedures

SOURCE: Steckler, McLeroy, Goodman, Bird, and McCormick (1992).

Approach	Type
QUAL + quan	Simultaneous
QUAL→quan	Sequential
QUAN + qual	Simultaneous
QUAN→qual	Sequential

Figure 8.2. Examples of Types of Designs Using Morse's (1991) Notation System

Types of Designs. As is apparent in Morse's (1991) notation system, she provided names for her approaches such as *simultaneous* and *sequential*. Terms such as these, and a few more, have now become types or variants of mixed methods designs. As shown in Table 8.1, authors from diverse discipline fields, such as evaluation, nursing, public health, and education, have identified the types of designs that they believe capture the array of possibilities. A brief review of eight studies shown in the table indicates that Morse's simultaneous and sequential labels continue to be used routinely. However, new terms have also emerged such as a mixed methods study that is based on *initiation* or *development* (Greene et al., 1989), on *complementary* designs (Morgan, 1998), or on *mixed model* designs (Tashakkori & Teddlie, 1998). Unquestionably, authors have yet to reach consensus on the types of designs that exist, the names for them, or how they might be represented visually.

◆ *Criteria Implicit in the Designs*

Although the variants of designs may be baffling, to distinguish among them is useful in choosing one to use for a study. To accomplish this requires examining the design's fundamental assumptions, a line of thinking already used by Morgan (1998). If one could understand the assumptions implicit within the designs, then a researcher could configure a procedure that best meets the needs of the problem and that includes the collection of both quantitative and qualitative data. Morgan identified two core assumptions: that the designs varied in terms of a sequence of collecting quantitative and qualitative data and that they varied in terms of the priority or weight given to

each form of data. Other assumptions can be added as well. Tashakkori and Teddlie (1998) suggested that the design contain an integration of the data in different phases such as in the statement of the research questions, the data collection, the data analysis, and the interpretation of the results. Finally, in the recent writings of Greene and Caracelli (1997), we find that some mixed methods writers include a transformational value- or action-oriented dimension to their study. Thus, we have another assumption that needs to be included in the matrix for typing and identifying forms of mixed methods designs. Four factors, as illustrated in Figure 8.3, help researchers to determine the type of mixed methods design for their study: the implementation of data collection, the priority given to quantitative or qualitative research, the stage in the research process at which integration of quantitative and qualitative research occurs, and the potential use of a transformational value- or action-oriented perspective in their study.

IMPLEMENTATION
OF DATA COLLECTION

Implementation refers to the sequence the researcher uses to collect both quantitative and qualitative data. Several authors have discussed this procedure in mixed methods research (Greene et al., 1989; Morgan, 1998; Morse, 1991). The options for implementation of the data collection consist of gathering the information at the same time (i.e., concurrently) or introducing the information in phases over a period of time (i.e., sequentially). When the data are introduced in phases, either the qualitative or the quantitative approach may be gathered first, but the sequence relates to the objectives being sought by the researcher in the

TABLE 8.1   Classifications of Mixed Methods Designs

Author	Mixed Methods Designs	Discipline/Field
Greene, Caracelli, & Graham (1989)	Initiation Expansion Development Complementary Triangulation	Evaluation
Patton (1990)	Experimental design, qualitative data, and content analysis Experimental design, qualitative data, and statistical analysis Naturalistic inquiry, qualitative data, and statistical analysis Naturalistic inquiry, quantitative data, and statistical analysis	Evaluation

Morse (1991)	Simultaneous triangulation
	    QUAL + quan
	    QUAN + qual
	Sequential triangulation
	    QUAL → quan
	    QUAN → qual
		Nursing

Steckler, McLeroy, Goodman, Bird, & McCormick (1992)	Model 1: qualitative methods to develop quantitative measures Model 2: quantitative methods to embellish quantitative findings Model 3: qualitative methods to explain qualitative findings Model 4: qualitative and quantitative methods used equally and parallel	Public health education

Greene & Caracelli (1997)	Component designs
	    Triangulation
	    Complementary
	    Expansion
	Integrated designs
	    Iterative
	    Embedded or nested
	    Holistic
	    Transformative
		Evaluation

(Continued)

TABLE 8.1	(Continued)	
Author	*Mixed Methods Designs*	*Disciplines/Field*

Morgan (1998)	Complementary designs
	  Qualitative preliminary
	  Quantitative preliminary
	  Qualitative follow-up
	  Quantitative follow-up
		Health research

Tashakkori & Teddlie (1998)	Mixed method designs
	Equivalent status (sequential or parallel)
	Dominant-less dominant (sequential or parallel)
	Multilevel use
	Mixed model designs
	  I: Confirmatory/Qual Data/Statistical analysis and inference
	  II: Confirmatory/Qual Data/Qualitative inferences
	  III: Exploratory/Quant Data/Statistical analysis and inference
	  IV: Exploratory/Qual Data/Statistical analysis and inference
	  V: Confirmatory/Quant Data/Qualitative inferences
	  VI: Exploratory/Quant Data/Qualitative inferences
	  VII: Parallel mixed model
	  VIII: Sequential mixed model
		Educational research

Creswell (1999)	Convergence model Sequential model Instrument-building model	Educational Policy

mixed methods study. When qualitative data collection precedes quantitative data collection, the intent is to first explore the problem under study and then follow up on this exploration with quantitative data that are amenable to studying a large sample so that results might be inferred to a population. Alternatively, when quantita-tive data precede qualitative data, the intent is to explore with a large sample first to test variables and then to explore in more depth with a few cases during the qualitative phase. In concurrently gathering both forms of data at the same time, the researcher seeks to compare both forms of data to search for congruent find-

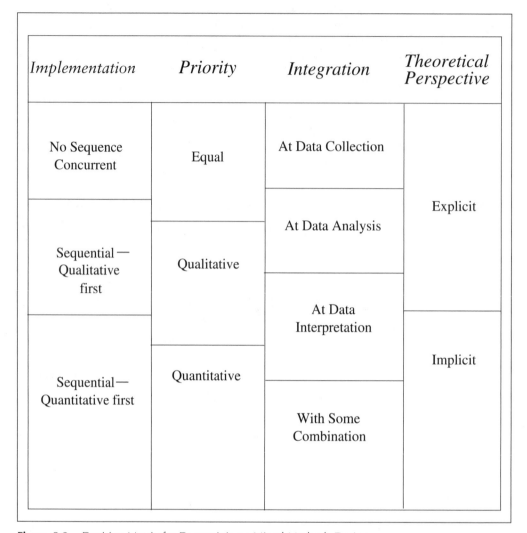

Implementation	Priority	Integration	Theoretical Perspective
No Sequence Concurrent	Equal	At Data Collection	Explicit
Sequential — Qualitative first	Qualitative	At Data Analysis	Explicit
Sequential — Quantitative first	Quantitative	At Data Interpretation	Implicit
		With Some Combination	Implicit

Figure 8.3. Decision Matrix for Determining a Mixed Methods Design

ings (e.g., how the themes identified in the qualitative data collection compare with the statistical results in the quantitative analysis).

The choice of implementation strategy has several consequences for the form of the final written report. When two phases of data collection exist, the researcher typically reports the data collection process in two phases. The report may also include an analysis of each phase of data sepa-

rately and the integration of information in the discussion or conclusion section of a study. The implementation approach also raises an issue about iterative phases of a design where a researcher may cycle back and forth between quantitative and qualitative data collection. For instance, the research may begin with a qualitative phase of interviewing, followed by a quantitative phase of survey instrument design and testing with a sample, and continued on with a third qualitative phase of exploring outlier cases that emerge from the quantitative survey. The implementation decision also calls for clearly identifying the core reasons for collecting both forms of data in the first place and understanding the important interrelationship between the quantitative and qualitative phases in data collection. These reasons need to be clearly articulated in any mixed methods written report.

PRIORITY

A less obvious issue, and one more difficult to make a decision about, is the priority given to quantitative and qualitative research in the mixed methods study (Morgan, 1998). Unlike the frame of reference of data collection in the implementation decision, here the focus is on the priority given to quantitative or qualitative research as it occurs throughout the data collection process. This process might be described as including how the study is introduced, the use of literature, the statement of the purpose of the study and the research questions, the data collection, the data analysis, and the interpretation of the findings or results (Creswell, 2002). The mixed methods researcher can give equal priority to both quantitative and qualitative research, emphasize qualitative more, or emphasize quantitative more. This emphasis may result from practical constraints of data collection, the need to understand one form of data before proceeding to the next, or the audience preference for either quantitative or qualitative research. In most cases, the decision probably rests on the comfort level of the researcher with one approach as opposed to the other.

Operationalizing the decision to give equal or unequal emphasis to quantitative or qualitative research translates is prob- lematic. For instance, the study may begin with essentially a quantitative orientation with a focus on variables, specific research questions or hypotheses, and an extensive discussion of the literature that informs the questions. Another study might convey a different priority through the length of discussions such as the inclusion of extensive discussions about the qualitative data collection with minimal information about the quantitative instruments used in the study. A project might be seen by readers as providing more depth for one method than for the other such as assessed by the number of pages given to quantitative research (e.g., as in the Hossler & Vesper [1993] article). A graduate student may of necessity delimit the study by including a substantive quantitative analysis and a limited qualitative data collection, a model referred to as the dominant-less dominant model (Creswell, 1994). A final example is that the published article provides equal emphasis on both quantitative and qualitative research as judged by separate sections of approximately equal length and treatment. Unquestionably, in each of these examples, researchers and readers make an interpretation of what constitutes priority, a judgment that may differ from one inquirer to another. On a practical level, however, we can see these different priorities in published mixed methods studies, and researchers need to make informed decisions about the weight or attention given to quantitative and qualitative research during all phases of their research.

STAGE OF INTEGRATION

Of the mixed methods design writers, it has been Tashakkori and Teddlie (1998) and Greene et al. (1989) who have emphasized the importance of considering the stage of the research process at which integration of quantitative and qualitative data collection takes place. Integration can be defined as the combination of quantitative and qualitative research within a given stage of inquiry. For example, integration might occur within the research questions (e.g., both quantitative and qualitative questions are presented), within data collection (e.g., open-ended questions on a structured instrument), within data analysis (e.g., transforming qualitative themes into quantitative items or scales), or in interpretation (e.g., examining the quantitative and qualitative results for convergence of findings). The decision that needs to be made relates to a clear understanding of the sequential model of the research process and approaches typically taken by both quantitative and qualitative researchers at each stage. (As a contrast, see the interactive model as advanced by Maxwell and Loomis in Chapter 9 of this volume.)

Examine Table 8.2, which presents four stages in the process of research and approaches researchers take in both the quantitative and qualitative areas. In quantitative research, investigators ask questions that try to confirm hypotheses or research questions, with a focus on assessing the relationship or association among variables or testing a treatment variable. These questions or hypotheses are assessed using instruments, observations, or documents that yield numerical data. These data are, in turn, analyzed descriptively or inferentially so as to generate interpretations that are generalizable to a population. Alternatively, in qualitative research, the inquiry is more exploratory, with a strong emphasis on description and with a thematic focus on understanding a central phenomenon. Open-ended data collection helps to address questions of this kind through procedures such as interviews, observations, documents, and audiovisual materials.

Researchers analyze these databases for a rich description of the phenomenon as well as for themes to develop a detailed rendering of the complexity of the phenomenon, leading to new questions and personal interpretations made by the inquirers. Although both the quantitative and qualitative processes described here are oversimplifications of the actual steps taken by researchers, they serve as a baseline of information to discuss where integration might take place in a mixed methods study.

During the phases of problem/question specification, data collection, data analysis, and interpretation, it is possible for the mixed methods researcher to integrate components of both quantitative and qualitative research. Unquestionably, the most typical case is the integration of the two forms of research at the data analysis and interpretation stages after quantitative data (e.g., scores on instruments) and qualitative data (e.g., participant observations of a setting) have been collected. For example, after collecting both forms of data, the analysis process might begin by transforming the qualitative data into numerical scores (e.g., themes or codes are counted for frequencies) so that they can be compared with quantitative scores. In another study, the analysis might proceed separately for both quantitative and qualitative data, and then the information might be compared in the interpretation (or discussion) stage of the research (see, e.g., Hossler & Vesper, 1993). Less frequently found in mixed methods studies is the integration at data collection. A good example of integration at this stage is the use of a few open-ended questions on a quantitative survey instrument. In this approach, both quantitative and qualitative data are collected and integrated in a single instrument of data collection. It is also possible for integration to occur earlier in the process of research such as in the prob-

TABLE 8.2   **Stages of Integration and Quantitative and Qualitative Approaches**

	Research Problems/ Data Questions	Data Collection/ Method	Data Analysis/ Procedure	Data Interpretation
Quantitative	Confirmatory Outcome based	Instruments Observations Documents Score oriented Closed-ended process Predetermined hypotheses	Descriptive statistics Inferential statistics	Generalization Prediction based Interpretation of theory
Qualitative	Exploratory Process based Descriptive Phenomenon of interest	Interviews Documents Observations Audiovisual Participant-determined process Open-ended process Text/image oriented	Description Identify themes/ categories Look for inter-connectedness among cate-gories/themes (vertically and horizontally)	Particularization (contextual-izing) Larger sense-making Personal inter-pretation Asking questions

lem/question stage. In some studies, the researcher might set forth both quantitative and qualitative questions in which the intent is to both test some relationships among variables and explore some general questions. This approach is seen in studies where a concurrent form of data collection exists and the researcher is interested in triangulating (Mathison, 1988) data from different sources as a major intent of the research. Finally, it should be noted that integration can occur at multiple stages. Data from a survey that contains both quantitative and qualitative data might be integrated in the analysis stage by

transforming the qualitative data into scores so that the information can be easily compared with the quantitative scores.

Deciding on the stage or stages to integrate depends on the purpose of the research, the ease with which the integration can occur (e.g., data collection integration is easier and cleaner than data analysis integration), the researcher's understanding of the stages of research, and the intent or purpose of a particular study. What clouds this decision is the permeability of the categories displayed in Table 8.2. Data collection is a good case in point. What constitutes quantitative or qualitative data collection is open to debate; indeed, LeCompte and Schensul (1999), and many ethnographers, consider both quantitative and qualitative data collection as options for field data. A similar concern might be raised about the fine distinctions being made between quantitative and qualitative research problems and questions. Many inquirers actually go back and forth between confirming and exploring in any given study, although qualitative inquirers refrain from specifying variables in their questions and attempt to keep the study as open as possible to best learn from participants. Despite these potential issues that need to be considered, the mixed methods researcher needs to design a study with a clear understanding of the stage or stages at which the data will be integrated and the form this integration will take.

THEORETICAL PERSPECTIVES

One question raised by qualitative researchers in the social sciences, especially during the 1990s (Creswell, 2002), is that all inquiry is theoretically driven by assumptions that researchers bring to their studies. At an informal level, the theoretical perspective reflects researchers' personal stances toward the topics they are studying, a stance based on personal history, experience, culture, gender, and class perspectives. At a more formal level, social science researchers bring to their inquiries a formal lens by which they view their topics, including gendered perspectives (e.g., feminist theory), cultural perspectives (e.g., racial/ethnic theory), lifestyle orientation (e.g., queer theory), critical theory perspectives, and class and social status views.

Only recently have these theoretical perspectives been discussed in the mixed methods research design literature. As recently as 1997, Greene and Caracelli discussed the use of a theoretical lens in

mixed methods research. They called such a lens the use of transformative designs that "give primacy to the value-based and action-oriented dimensions of different inquiry traditions" (p. 24). Greene and Caracelli (1997) further explicated the nature of transformative designs when they wrote,

> Designs are transformative in that they offer opportunities for reconfiguring the dialog across ideological differences and, thus, have the potential to restructure the evaluation context. . . . Diverse methods most importantly serve to include a broader set of interests in the resulting knowledge claims and to strengthen the likely effectiveness of action solutions. (p. 24)

The commonality across transformative studies is ideological, such that no matter what the domain of inquiry, the ultimate goal of the study is to advocate for change. The transformative element of the research can either be experienced by the participants as they participate in the research or follow the study's completion when the research spawns changes in action, policy, or ideology. Transformative designs are found in evaluative research as well as in health care. Issues as diverse as class, race, gender, feminist scholarship, and postmodernist thinking often inform transformative designs. To illustrate how this design might work, a researcher might examine the inequity that exists in an organization's salary structure that marginalizes women in the organization. The issue of inequity frames the study, and the inquirer proceeds to first gather survey data measuring equity issues in the organization. This initial quantitative phase is then followed by a qualitative phase in which several in-depth cases studies are developed to explore in more detail the quantitative results. These case studies might examine the issue of inequality from the standpoint of managers, middle managers, and workers on an assembly line. In the end, the researcher is interested in bringing about change in the salary structure and in using the research as evidence for needed change and to advocate for change. Also, through the research, the dialogue among organizational members is "transformed" to focus on issues of inequity.

The use of a theoretical lens may be explicit or implicit within a mixed methods study. Those espousing the transformative model encourage researchers to make the lens explicit in the study, although Greene and Caracelli (1997) were not specific about how this might be done. However, examining the use of a theoretical or an ideological lens within other studies, we can see that it often informs the purpose and questions being asked. These purposes may be to promote equity and justice for policies and practices so as to create a personal, social, institutional, and/or organizational impact (as addressed by Newman, Ridenour, Newman, & DeMarco in Chapter 6 of this volume) or to address specific questions related to oppression, domination, alienation, and inequality. A transformative model would also indicate the participants who will be studied (e.g., women, the marginalized, certain groups that are culturally and ethnically diverse), how the data collection will proceed (e.g., typically collaboratively so as not to marginalize the study participants further), and the conclusion of the study for advocacy and change to improve society or the lives of the individuals being studied. In summary, the nature of transformative mixed research methodology is such that in both perspective and outcomes, it is dedicated to promoting change at levels ranging from the personal to the political. Furthermore, it is possible to conduct any quantitative, qualitative, or mixed methods study with a transformative or advocacy purpose.

◆ Six Major Designs

The four criteria—implementation, priority, integration, and theoretical perspective—can be useful in specifying six different types of major designs that a researcher might employ. This short list of designs might not be as inclusive of types as those identified by other writers (see the types introduced in Table 8.1), but arguably, all variants of designs might be subsumed within these six types. Moreover, by identifying a small number of generic types, it can be suggested that the mixed methods researcher has the flexibility to choose and innovate within the types to fit a particular research situation. These six types build on the four decision criteria and integrate them into specific designs with a label that we believe captures the variants of the design. An overview of the types of designs by the four criteria is seen in Table 8.3. For each design, we identify its major characteristics, examples of variants on the design, and strengths and weaknesses in implementing it. In addition, a visual presentation is made for each design type and annotated with specific steps to be undertaken in the process of research. The visuals are shown in Figures 8.4 and 8.5.

SEQUENTIAL EXPLANATORY DESIGN

The sequential explanatory design is the most straightforward of the six major mixed methods designs. It is characterized by the collection and analysis of quantitative data followed by the collection and analysis of qualitative data. Priority is typically given to the quantitative data, and the two methods are integrated during the interpretation phase of the study. The steps of this design are pictured in Figure 8.4a. The implementation of this design
(Text continued on p. 227)

TABLE 8.3 Types of Designs by Four Criteria

Design Type	Implementation	Priority	Stage of Integration	Theoretical Perspective
Sequential explanatory	Quantitative followed by qualitative	Usually quantitative; can be qualitative or equal	Interpretation phase	May be present
Sequential exploratory	Qualitative followed by quantitative	Usually qualitative; can be quantitative or equal	Interpretation phase	May be present
Sequential transformative	Either quantitative followed by qualitative or qualitative followed by quantitative	Quantitative, qualitative, or equal	Interpretation phase	Definitely present (i.e., conceptual framework, advocacy, empowerment)
Concurrent triangulation	Concurrent collection of quantitative and qualitative data	Preferably equal; can be quantitative or qualitative	Interpretation phase or analysis phase	May be present
Concurrent nested	Concurrent collection of quantitative and qualitative data	Quantitative or qualitative	Analysis phase	May be present
Concurrent transformative	Concurrent collection of quantitative and qualitative data	Quantitative, qualitative, or equal	Usually analysis phase; can be during interpretation phase	Definitely present (i.e., conceptual framework, advocacy, empowerment)

Sequential Explanatory Design (8.4a)

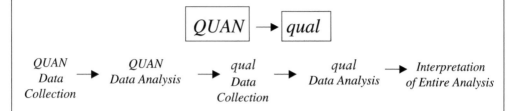

Sequential Exploratory Design (8.4b)

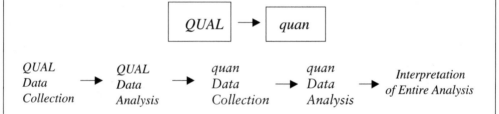

Sequential Transformative Design (8.4c)

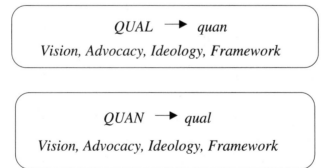

Figure 8.4. Sequential Designs
(a) Sequential Explanatory Design
(b) Sequential Exploratory Design
(c) Sequential Transformative Design

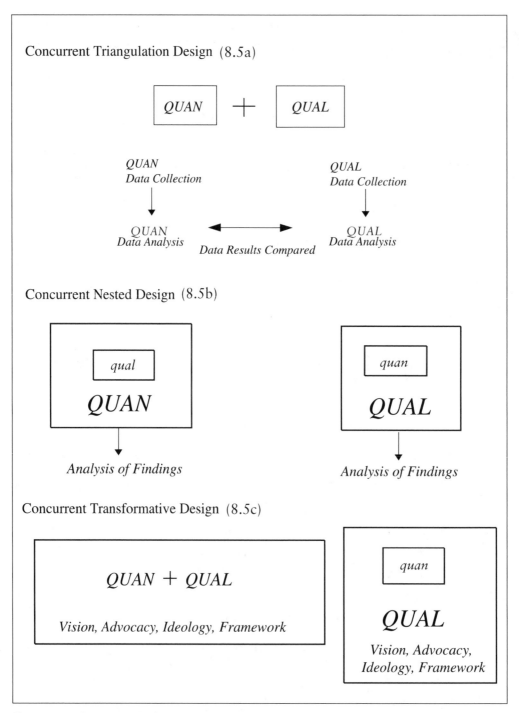

Figure 8.5. Concurrent Designs
(a) Concurrent Triangulation Design
(b) Concurrent Nested Design
(c) Concurrent Transformative Design

may or may not be guided by a specific theoretical perspective.

The purpose of the sequential explanatory design is typically to use qualitative results to assist in explaining and interpreting the findings of a primarily quantitative study. It can be especially useful when unexpected results arise from a quantitative study (Morse, 1991). In this case, the qualitative data collection that follows can be used to examine these surprising results in more detail. In an important variation of this design, the qualitative data collection and analysis is given the priority. In this case, the initial quantitative phase of the study may be used to characterize individuals along certain traits of interest related to the research question. These quantitative results can then be used to guide the purposeful sampling of participants for a primarily qualitative study.

The straightforward nature of this design is one of its main strengths. It is easy to implement because the steps fall into clear separate stages. In addition, this design feature makes it easy to describe and report. In fact, this design can be reported in two distinct phases with a final discussion that brings the results together. The sequential explanatory design is also useful when a quantitative researcher wants to further explore quantitative findings. Furthermore, the implementation of qualitative data collection and analysis within this design framework can be comfortable for quantitative researchers, and therefore it can provide an effective introduction to qualitative research methods to researchers unfamiliar with the techniques. The main weakness of this design is the length of time involved in data collection to complete the two separate phases. This is especially a drawback if the two phases are given equal priority. Therefore, a sequential explanatory design giving equal priority to both qualitative and quantitative methods may be a more applicable approach for a research program than for a single study.

SEQUENTIAL EXPLORATORY DESIGN

The sequential exploratory design has many features similar to the sequential explanatory design. It is conducted in two phases, with the priority generally given to the first phase, and it may or may not be implemented within a prescribed theoretical perspective (see Figure 8.4b). In contrast to the sequential explanatory design, this design is characterized by an initial phase of qualitative data collection and analysis followed by a phase of quantitative data collection and analysis. Therefore, the priority is given to the qualitative aspect of the study. The findings of these two phases are then integrated during the interpretation phase (see Figure 8.4b).

At the most basic level, the purpose of this design is to use quantitative data and results to assist in the interpretation of qualitative findings. Unlike the sequential explanatory design, which is better suited to explaining and interpreting relationships, the primary focus of this design is to explore a phenomenon. Morgan (1998) suggested that this design is appropriate to use when testing elements of an emergent theory resulting from the qualitative phase and that it can also be used to generalize qualitative findings to different samples. Similarly, Morse (1991) indicated that one purpose for selecting this design would be to determine the distribution of a phenomenon within a chosen population. Finally, the sequential exploratory design is often discussed as the design used when a researcher develops and tests an instrument (see, e.g., Creswell, 1999). One possible variation on this design is to give the priority to the second quantitative phase. Such a design might be undertaken when a researcher intends to conduct a primarily quantitative study, but it needs to begin with initial qualitative data collection so as to identify or narrow the focus of the possible variables. In addition, it is possible to give equal weight to the quantitative and qualitative phases, but such an approach may be too demanding for a single study due to time constraints, resource limitations, and the limitations of a researcher's experience.

The sequential exploratory design has many of the same advantages as the sequential explanatory design. Its two-phase approach makes it easy to implement and straightforward to describe and report. It is useful to a researcher who wants to explore a phenomenon but also wants to expand on the qualitative findings. This design is especially advantageous when a researcher is building a new instrument. In addition, this design could make a largely qualitative study more palatable to a quantitatively oriented adviser, committee, or research community that may be unfamiliar with the naturalistic tradition.

As with the sequential explanatory design, the sequential exploratory design also requires a substantial length of time to complete both data collection phases, which can be a drawback for some research situations. In addition, the researcher may find it difficult to build from the qualitative analysis to the subsequent quantitative data collection.

SEQUENTIAL TRANSFORMATIVE DESIGN

As with the previously described sequential designs, the transformative sequential design has two distinct data collection phases, one following the other

(see Figure 8.4c). However, in this design, either method may be used first, and the priority may be given to either the quantitative or the qualitative phase (or even to both if sufficient resources are available). In addition, the results of the two phases are integrated together during the interpretation phase. Unlike the sequential exploratory and explanatory designs, the sequential transformative design definitely has a theoretical perspective present to guide the study. The aim of this theoretical perspective, whether it be a conceptual framework, a specific ideology, or advocacy, is more important in guiding the study than the use of methods alone.

The purpose of a sequential transformative design is to employ the methods that will best serve the theoretical perspective of the researcher. By using two phases, a sequential transformative researcher may be able to give voice to diverse perspectives, to better advocate for participants, or to better understand a phenomenon or process that is changing as a result of being studied. The variations of this design would be best described by the diverse range of possible theoretical perspectives instead of the range of possible methodological choices.

The sequential transformative design shares the same methodological strengths and weaknesses as the other two sequential mixed methods designs. Its use of distinct phases facilitates its implementation, description, and sharing of results, although it also requires the time to complete two data collection phases. More important, this design places mixed methods research within a transformative framework. Therefore, this design may be more appealing and acceptable to those researchers already using a transformative framework within one distinct methodology such as qualitative research. It will also include the strengths typically found when using a theoretical perspective in other research traditions. Unfortunately, because to date little has been written on this design, one weakness is that there is little guidance on how to use the transformative vision to guide the methods. Likewise, it may be unclear how to move from the analysis of the first phase to the data collection of the second phase.

CONCURRENT TRIANGULATION DESIGN

The concurrent triangulation design is probably the most familiar of the six major mixed methods designs (see Figure 8.5a). It is selected as the design when a researcher uses two different methods in an attempt to confirm, cross-validate, or corroborate findings within a single study (Greene et al., 1989; Morgan, 1998; Steckler et al., 1992). This design generally uses separate quantitative and qualitative methods as a means to offset the weaknesses inherent within one method with the strengths of the other method. In this case, the quantitative data collection and qualitative data collection are concurrent, happening during one phase of the research study. Ideally, the priority would be equal between the two methods, but in practical application, the priority may be given to either the quantitative or the qualitative approach. This design usually integrates the results of the two methods during the interpretation phase. This interpretation either may note the convergence of the findings as a way to strengthen the knowledge claims of the study or must explain any lack of convergence that may result.

This traditional mixed methods design is advantageous because it is familiar to most researchers and can result in well-validated and substantiated findings. In addition, the concurrent data collection results in a shorter data collection time period as compared with that of the sequential designs. This design also has a number of limitations. It requires great effort and expertise to adequately study a phenomenon with two separate methods. It can also be difficult to compare the results of two analyses using data of different forms. In addition, it may be unclear to a researcher how to resolve discrepancies that arise in the results.

Other variations of this design also exist. For example, it would be possible for a researcher to integrate the two methods earlier in the research process such as during the analysis phase. This would require the transformation of the data from a quantitative to a qualitative form or from a qualitative to a quantitative form. While such transformations have been discussed in the literature (see, e.g., Caracelli & Greene, 1993; Tashakkori & Teddlie, 1998), there is still limited guidance for how to conduct and analyze such transformations in practice.

CONCURRENT NESTED DESIGN

Like the concurrent triangulation design, the concurrent nested design can be identified by its use of one data collection phase during which quantitative and qualitative data both are collected simultaneously (see Figure 8.5b). Unlike the traditional triangulation design, a nested design has a predominant method that guides the project. Given less priority, a method (quantitative or qualitative) is embedded, or nested, within the predominant method (qualitative or quantitative). This nesting may mean that the embedded method addresses a question different from that addressed by the dominant method or that the embedded method seeks information from different levels [the analogy to hierarchical analysis in quantitative research is helpful in conceptualizing these levels (see Tashakkori & Teddlie, 1998)]. The data collected from the two methods are mixed during the analysis phase of the project. This design may or may not have a guiding theoretical perspective.

The concurrent nested design may be used to serve a variety of purposes. Often, this design is used so that a researcher may gain broader perspectives from using the different methods as opposed to using the predominant method alone. For example, Morse (1991) noted that a primarily qualitative design could embed some quantitative data to enrich the description of the sample participants. Likewise, she described how qualitative data could be used to describe an aspect of a quantitative study that cannot be quantified. In addition, a concurrent nested design may be employed when a researcher chooses to use different methods to study different groups or levels within a design. For example, if an organization is being studied, then employees could be studied quantitatively, managers could be interviewed qualitatively, entire divisions could be analyzed with quantitative data, and so forth. Tashakkori and Teddlie (1998) described this approach as a multilevel design. Finally, one method could be used within a framework of the other method such as if a researcher designed and conducted an experiment but used case study methodology to study each of the treatment conditions.

This mixed methods design has many strengths. A researcher is able to simultaneously collect the data during one data collection phase. It provides a study with the advantages of both quantitative and qualitative data. In addition, by using

the two different methods in this fashion, a researcher can gain perspectives from the different types of data or from different levels within the study. There are also limitations to consider when choosing this design. The data need to be transformed in some way so that they can be integrated within the analysis phase of the research. There has been little written to date to guide a researcher through this process. In addition, there is little advice to be found for how a researcher should resolve discrepancies that occur between the two types of data. Because the two methods are unequal in their priority, this design also results in unequal evidence within a study, and this may be a disadvantage when interpreting the final results.

CONCURRENT TRANSFORMATIVE DESIGN

As with the sequential transformative design, the concurrent transformative design is guided by the researcher's use of a specific theoretical perspective (see Figure 8.5c). This perspective can be based on ideologies such as critical theory, advocacy, participatory research, and a conceptual or theoretical framework. This perspective is reflected in the purpose or research questions of the study (see Newman et al., Chapter 6, this volume). It is the driving force behind all methodological choices such as defining the problem; identifying the design and data sources; and analyzing, interpreting, and reporting results throughout the research process (see Mertens, Chapter 5, this volume). The choice of a concurrent design (whether it is triangulation or a nested design) is made to facilitate this perspective. For example, the design may be nested so that diverse participants are given a voice in the change process of an organization that is studied primarily quantitatively. It may involve a triangulation of both quantitative and qualitative data to best converge information so as to provide evidence for an inequality of policies in an organization.

Thus, the concurrent transformative design may take on the design features of either a triangulation or nested design. That is, the two types of data are collected at the same time during one data collection phase and may have equal or unequal priority. The integration of these different data would most often occur during the analysis phase, although integration during the interpretation phase would be a possible variation. Because the concurrent transformative design shares common features with the triangulation and nested designs, it also shares their specific strengths and weaknesses. However, this design also has the added advantage of positioning mixed methods research within a transformative framework, and this may make it especially appealing to those qualitative or quantitative researchers already using a transformative framework to guide their inquiry.

◆ Issues in Implementing Designs

Although there are several discussions currently under way among those writing about mixed design applications, issues related to implementation fall into three categories: whether the design needs to be lodged within a paradigm perspective; how data analysis varies by design and the use of computer programs that handle both quantitative and qualitative data; and the placement of design procedures within a study, especially the elaboration of visual presentations of the procedures.

PARADIGMS AND DESIGNS

Substantial discussion has taken place in the mixed methods literature about the "compatibility" of quantitative and qualitative research and whether paradigms of research and methods can be mixed. For example, can a qualitative philosophical perspective, such as the existence of multiple realities, be combined with a quantitative study that uses a closed-ended survey to gather data and restrict the perspectives of the participants? The linking of paradigms and methods has been referred to as the "paradigm debate" (Cook & Reichardt, 1979; Reichardt & Rallis, 1994). Although this debate has largely subsided due to the use of multiple methods regardless of paradigm perspective, the discussion helped to raise the issue of whether philosophical perspectives should be explicitly stated and acknowledged in mixed methods studies. More specifically to the point of this chapter is this question: Should a philosophical position be embraced by the author of a mixed methods study, and will this position vary by types of design? Several authors (e.g., Patton, 1990; Rossman & Wilson, 1985; Tashakkori & Teddlie, 1998) have suggested that pragmatism is the foundation for these designs. This philosophy, drawn from Deweyan ideas and most recently articulated by Cherryholmes (1992), maintains that researchers should be concerned with applications, with what works, and with solutions to problems. In light of this, the authors have called for the use of both quantitative and qualitative methods to best understand research problems.

However, as applied to the six designs advanced in this chapter, a single philosophical framework does not work with all designs. If one takes the perspective that the mixed methods researcher should be explicit about the paradigm or philosophy behind his or her design, then a number of philosophical perspectives can enter into the study. Today, multiple paradigms exist for our inquiries such as positivism, postpositivism, interpretivism, and participatory/advocacy perspectives (Denzin & Lincoln, 2000). In a sequential explanatory design, strongly based on quantitative research, the paradigm stated may be postpositivist, while in a sequential exploratory design, with the lead taken by qualitative research, the paradigm may be more interpretive or participatory/advocacy oriented. A triangulation design may use several paradigms as a framework for the study. A transformative design may employ qualitative, quantitative, or mixed methods so long as the ideological lens of advocacy or participation is a central element in shaping the purpose, the questions, the collaborative nature of data collection and analysis, and the interpreting and report of results (see Mertens's chapter in this volume [Chapter 5]). While Greene and Caracelli (1997) recommended that researchers employing mixed methods research be explicit about their paradigms, we can now extend this suggestion to a consideration of what paradigm is best given the choice of a design for the mixed methods study.

DATA ANALYSIS AND DESIGNS

Approaches to data analysis also need to be sensitive to the design being implemented in a mixed methods study. Different analysis approaches have been suggested for integrating quantitative and qualitative data that explore how the information might be transformed or analyzed for outlier cases (Caracelli & Greene, 1993). Further approaches to analyzing data are also found in Tashakkori and Teddlie (1998), Creswell (2002), and Onwuegbuzie and Teddlie's chapter in this volume (Chapter 13). When the six types of designs are considered, we see in the sequential designs that the data analysis typically proceeds independently for both the quantitative and qualitative phases. The researcher relies on standard data analysis approaches (e.g., descriptive and inferential analysis of quantitative data, coding and thematic analysis of qualitative data). Alternatively, in the concurrent designs, the analysis requires some data transformation so as to integrate and compare dissimilar databases (e.g., quantitative scales are compared with qualitative themes, qualitative themes are converted into scores). Other options exist as well, as seen in Table 8.4, which shows the relationship among data analysis approaches as well as a description of each approach and its relationship to each of the six designs.

A related issue is whether a computer program should be used in mixed methods research and what programs are amenable to the analysis of both quantitative and qualitative data (see Bazeley's discussion of computer data analysis in Chapter 14 of this volume). Several qualitative data analysis programs allow for the import and export of quantitative data in table formats (Creswell & Maietta, 2002). Programs such as ETHNOGRAPH 5, HyperRESEARCH 2.5, Classic NUD.IST Versions 4 and 5, NVIVO, ATLAS.ti, and WinMAX allow the user to move to and from quantitative and spreadsheet packages with direct links into document identification numbers. For example, it is now possible to create a numerical SPSS file at the same time that a text file is being developed and to merge the data using qualitative software computer packages.

TABLE 8.4   **Type of Mixed Methods Design and Data Analysis/Interpretation Procedures**

Type of Mixed Methods Design	Examples of Analytic Procedures
Concurrent (triangulation, nested, transformative)	• Quantifying qualitative data: Code qualitative data, assign numbers to codes, and record the number of times codes appear as numeric data. Descriptively analyze quantitative data for frequency of occurrence. Compare the two data sets. • Qualifying quantitative data: Factor-analyze the quantitative data from questionnaires. These factors then become themes. Compare these themes to themes analyzed from qualitative data. • Comparing results: Directly compare the results from qualitative data collection to the results from quantitative data collection. Support statistical trends by qualitative themes or vice versa. • Consolidating data: Combine qualitative and quantitative data to form new variables. Compare original quantitative variables to qualitative themes to form new quantitative variables. (Caracelli & Greene, 1993) • Examining multilevels: Conduct a survey at the student level. Gather qualitative data through interviews at the class level. Survey the entire school at the school level. Collect qualitative data at the district level. Information from each level builds to the next level. (Tashakkori & Teddlie, 1998)
Sequential (explanatory, exploratory, transformative)	• Following up on outliers or extreme cases: Gather quantitative data and identify outlier or residual cases. Collect qualitative data to explore the characteristics of these cases. (Caracelli & Greene, 1993) • Explaining results: Conduct a quantitative survey to identify how two or more groups compare on a variable. Follow up with qualitative interviews to explore the reasons why these differences were found. • Using a typology: Conduct a quantitative survey, and develop factors through a factor analysis. Use these factors as a typology to identify themes in qualitative data such as observations and interviews. (Caracelli & Greene, 1993)

(Continued)

TABLE 8.4   (Continued)

Type of Mixed Method Design	Examples of Analytic Procedures
Sequential (Continued)	• Locating an instrument: Collect qualitative data and identify themes. Use these themes as a basis for locating instruments that use parallel concepts to the qualitative themes. • Developing an instrument: Obtain themes and specific statements from individuals that support the themes. During the next phase, use these themes and statements to create scales and items in a questionnaire. Alternatively, look for existing instruments that can be modified to fit the themes and statements found in the qualitative exploratory phase of the study. After developing the instrument, test it out with a sample of a population. • Forming categorical data: Site-level characteristics (e.g., different ethnic groups) gathered in an ethnography during the first phase of a study become a categorical variable during a second-phase correlational or regression study. (Caracelli & Greene, 1993) • Using extreme qualitative cases: Qualitative data cases that are extreme in a comparative analysis are followed by quantitative surveys during a second phase. (Caracelli & Greene, 1993)

SOURCE: Adapted from Creswell (2002).

PROCEDURES AND DESIGNS

With the discussion of mixed methods research designs have emerged additional questions about how researchers should conceptualize and present their discussions about designs and how they can articulate them so that proposal reviewers, editorial board reviewers, and conference attendees can easily understand the procedures involved in the mixed methods discussions. With the complex features often found in these designs, it is not surprising that writers have presented figures in their studies that portray the general flow of procedures such as those advanced by Steckler et al. (1992) and shown in Figure 8.1. But such visualizations do not go far enough. Added to these visual models can also be the procedures employed by the researcher, so that readers see the visual picture and learn about the accompanying procedures involved in each step. Thus, the discussion in the mixed methods literature about visual models (see Steckler et al., 1992) and the steps in the research process (as discussed by Creswell, 1999) can be combined.

Such a combination of ideas in a single figure is illustrated in Figure 8.6. In this

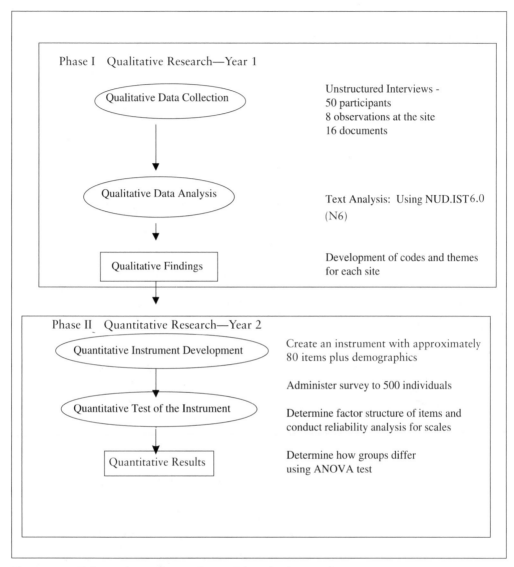

Phase I   Qualitative Research—Year 1

Qualitative Data Collection

Unstructured Interviews -
50 participants
8 observations at the site
16 documents

Qualitative Data Analysis

Text Analysis: Using NUD.IST6.0
(N6)

Qualitative Findings

Development of codes and themes
for each site

Phase II   Quantitative Research—Year 2

Quantitative Instrument Development

Create an instrument with approximately
80 items plus demographics

Administer survey to 500 individuals

Quantitative Test of the Instrument

Determine factor structure of items and
conduct reliability analysis for scales

Quantitative Results

Determine how groups differ
using ANOVA test

Figure 8.6.   Elaborated Visualization for Mixed Methods Procedures

figure, we see a two-phase mixed methods study. There are three levels introduced in the visualization of procedures. First, readers find the phases to be organized into qualitative research followed by quantitative research for each year of the project. Then, the more general procedures of data collection and analysis are presented in the circles and boxes on the left and, finally, the more specific proce-dures are identified on the right. Arrows help readers to see how the two phases are integrated into a sequential process of re-search. Although Figure 8.6 is only for the sequential exploratory model in our de-signs, one can extrapolate the basic design features to the other design possibilities and emerge with visualizations of designs that are both useful and clear to readers and reviewers of mixed methods studies.

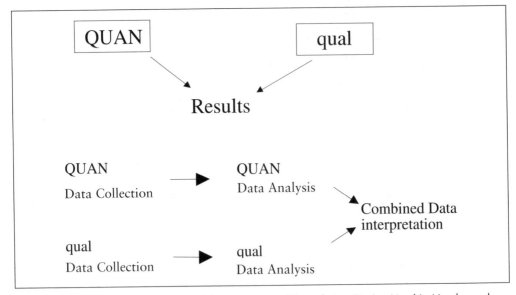

Figure 8.7. Proposed Visualization of the Concurrent Triangulation Design Used in Hossler and Vesper (1993)

◆ Returning to the Hossler and Vesper Mixed Methods Study

The Hossler and Vesper (1993) study that began our discussion can now be advanced in a visual diagram and assessed in terms of the four criteria and the six types of designs. As mentioned earlier, we can now see the Hossler and Vesper study as a concurrent triangulation design with priority given to quantitative research. The study began with quantitative questions (i.e., "To what extent are parents saving for postsecondary education? What factors are associated with parental savings? Do certain kinds of information appear to influence parental savings?" [p. 141]), but the data were collected concurrently in the form of surveys and interviews. The authors then analyzed the survey data separately from the interview data. Their intent was to triangulate the findings, which readers will find in the discussion section. They did not use a theoretical framework

to frame the study, and they did not provide a visualization of their research procedures. If they had incorporated this visualization, then it might have looked like the representation shown in Figure 8.7, where there are simultaneous quantitative and qualitative data collection and analysis and an interpretation in which they converged the data. If the data were presented in a "box text" diagram as shown in Box 8.1, as is used by writers of mixed methods research designs (e.g., see Tashakkori & Teddlie, 1998), then the essential information about the study that marks it as a mixed methods project could be illustrated through information about the methodology, aspects about the participants and data collection, the data analysis, and the discussion. Further information could be supplied about the four decision criteria made by the researchers.

This review of the Hossler and Vesper study highlights how discussions about mixed methods designs need to consider the underlying decisions that go into

BOX 8.1
Summary of the Hossler and Vesper Study

Hossler, D., & Vesper, N. (1993). An exploratory study of the factors associated with parental saving for postsecondary education. *Journal of Higher Education, 64*(2), 140-165.

This article provides an example of how qualitative and quantitative methods can be combined in educational research. As the title of the article suggests, two methodologies are used, and rationales for the use of each method are provided to readers. The primary goal of the research is to add information to the dearth of extant research in this area.

The principal methodology of this study was quantitative with a strong qualitative complement. Student and parent data garnered from a longitudinal study involving multiple surveys over a 3-year time line served as the basis for logistic regression that was used to identify the specific factors most strongly associated with parental saving for postsecondary education. Additional insights into the phenomenon of interest were gained from interviews of a small subsample of students and parents who were interviewed five times during the 3-year duration of the study. Interviews were used both to explore emerging themes in greater detail and to triangulate findings.

Components of data collection:

A total of 182 students and parents participated.
All participants completed surveys 10 times over a 4-year span.
A total of 56 students and their parents from eight high schools in the sample participated in interviews four times each year while the students were in their junior and senior years in high school.
Development of both the surveys and the interview protocols was an iterative process.

Data analysis:

Quantitative data were statistically analyzed via logistic regression, with significant discussion of coding of independent and dependent variables.

Qualitative data were analyzed via thematic analysis, with data being unitized and categorized.

Discussion and inferences:

Both quantitative and qualitative results were discussed jointly in the discussion section of the article. Significant factors identified by the logistic regression were corroborated with the theme that had emerged from the interviews. Areas of overlap between the analyses were discussed, although there was little mention of any inconsistencies in the data.

Triangulating the results from the survey and interview data allowed the authors to posit a model of parental saving.

(Continued)

BOX 8.1
(Continued)

Priority: QUANTITATIVE
Sequence: qual + QUAN simultaneously
Integration: data collection, data analysis, and inference stages
Tranformative: not present

Strengths: Combining methods of data collection and analysis allowed for the construction of more sensitive survey instruments as well as a better and broader understanding of the phenomenon of interest. Directions for intervention and policy development were identified and discussed.

Weaknesses: It was difficult to separate the quantitative and qualitative components in the discussion section. Implementing a mixed method design would be difficult if contradictory quantitative and qualitative data were found.

---

selecting a design; the type of design being used; and issues related to paradigms, data analysis, and the delineation of procedures using visuals. Undoubtedly, more issues will emerge about designing mixed methods studies, and a periodic assessment needs to provide an ongoing synthesis of the literature. In this way, we can continue to explore the methodology of mixed methods research and present additional guidelines for both novice and experienced researchers as they continue to develop, write, and publish these studies.

■ *References*

Bryman, A. (1988). *Quantity and quality in social science research.* London: Routledge.

Campbell, D., & Fiske, D. (1959). Convergent and discriminant validation by the multitrait-multimethod matrix. *Psychological Bulletin, 56,* 81-105.

Caracelli, V. J., & Greene, J. C. (1993). Data analysis strategies for mixed-method evaluation designs. *Educational Evaluation and Policy Analysis, 15*(2), 195-207.

Cherryholmes, C. H. (1992, August-September). Notes on pragmatism and scientific realism. *Educational Researcher, 21,* 13-17.

Cook, T. D., & Reichardt, C. S. (Eds.). (1979). *Qualitative and quantitative methods in evaluation research.* Beverly Hills, CA: Sage.

Creswell, J. W. (1994). *Research design: Qualitative and quantitative approaches.* Thousand Oaks, CA: Sage.

Creswell, J. W. (1999). Mixed method research: Introduction and application. In T. Cijek (Ed.), *Handbook of educational policy* (pp. 455-472). San Diego: Academic Press.

Creswell, J. W. (2002). *Educational research: Planning, conducting, and evaluating quantitative and qualitative approaches to research.* Upper Saddle River, NJ: Merrill/Pearson Education.

Creswell, J. W., Goodchild, L., & Turner, P. (1996). Integrated qualitative and quantitative research: Epistemology, history, and designs. In J. Smart (Ed.), *Higher education: Handbook of theory and research* (Vol. 11, pp. 90-136). New York: Agathon Press.

Creswell, J. W., & Maietta, R. C. (2002). Qualitative research. In N. J. Salkind (Ed.), *Handbook of social research* (2nd ed., pp. 143-184). Thousand Oaks, CA: Sage.

Creswell, J. W., & Miller, G. A. (1997). Research methodologies and the doctoral process. In L. Goodchild, K. E. Green, E. L. Katz, & R. C. Kluever (Eds.), *Rethinking the dissertation process: Tackling personal and institutional obstacles* (New Directions for Higher Education, No. 99, pp. 33-46). San Francisco: Jossey-Bass.

Datta, L. (1994). Paradigm wars: A basis for peaceful coexistence and beyond. In C. S. Reichardt & S. F. Rallis (Eds.), *The qualitative-quantitative debate: New perspectives* (New Directions for Program Evaluation, No. 61, pp. 53-70). San Francisco: Jossey-Bass.

Denzin, N., & Lincoln, Y. S. (2000). *Handbook of qualitative research* (2nd ed.). Thousand Oaks, CA: Sage.

Fielding, N. G., & Fielding, J. L. (1986). *Linking data.* Newbury Park, CA: Sage.

Glik, D. C., Parker, K., Muligande, G., & Hategikamana, D. (1986-1987). Integrating qualitative and quantitative survey techniques. *International Quarterly of Community Health Education, 7*(3), 181-200.

Greene, J. C., & Caracelli, V. J. (Eds.). (1997). *Advances in mixed-method evaluation: The challenges and benefits of integrating diverse paradigms* (New Directions for Evaluation, No. 74). San Francisco: Jossey-Bass.

Greene, J. C., Caracelli, V. J., & Graham, W. F. (1989). Toward a conceptual framework for mixed-method evaluation designs. *Educational Evaluation and Policy Analysis, 11,* 255-274.

Hossler, D., & Vesper, N. (1993). An exploratory study of the factors associated with parental savings for postsecondary education. *Journal of Higher Education, 64*(2), 140-165.

Hugentobler, M. K., Israel, B. A., & Schurman, S. J. (1992). An action research approach to workplace health: Integrating methods. *Health Education Quarterly, 19*(1), 55-76.

Jick, T. D. (1979). Mixing qualitative and quantitative methods: Triangulation in action. *Administrative Science Quarterly, 24,* 602-611.

LeCompte, M. D., & Schensul, J. J. (1999). *Designing and conducting ethnographic research* (Ethnographer's Toolkit, No. 1). Walnut Creek, CA: AltaMira.

Mathison, S. (1988). Why triangulate? *Educational Researcher, 17*(2), 13-17.

Miles, M. B., & Huberman, A. M. (1994). *Qualitative data analysis* (2nd ed.). Thousand Oaks, CA: Sage.

Morgan, D. (1998). Practical strategies for combining qualitative and quantitative methods: Applications to health research. *Qualitative Health Research, 8,* 362-376.

Morse, J. M. (1991). Approaches to qualitative-quantitative methodological triangulation. *Nursing Research, 40,* 120-123.

Patton, M. Q. (1990). *Qualitative evaluation and research methods.* Newbury Park, CA: Sage.

Reichardt, C. S., & Rallis, S. E. (1994). The relationship between the qualitative and quantitative research traditions. In C. S. Reichardt & S. F. Rallis (Eds.), *The qualitative-quantitative debate: New perspectives* (New Directions for Program Evaluation, No. 61, pp. 5-11). San Francisco: Jossey-Bass.

Rossman, G. B., & Wilson, B. L. (1985). Number and words: Combining quantitative and qualitative methods in a single large-scale evaluation study. *Evaluation Review, 9,* 627-643.

Rossman, G. B., & Wilson, B. L. (1991). *Numbers and words revisited: Being "shamelessly eclectic."* Washington, DC: Office of Educational Research and Improvement. (ERIC Document Reproduction Service No. 337 235)

Sieber, S. D. (1973). The integration of field work and survey methods. *American Journal of Sociology, 78,* 1335-1359.

Steckler, A., McLeroy, K. R., Goodman, R. M., Bird, S. T., & McCormick, L. (1992). Toward integrating qualitative and quantitative methods: An introduction. *Health Education Quarterly, 19*(1), 1-8.

Swanson-Kauffman, K. M. (1986). A combined qualitative methodology for nursing research. *Advances in Nursing Science, 8*(3), 58-69.

Tashakkori, A., & Teddlie, C. (1998). *Mixed methodology: Combining qualitative and quantitative approaches* (Applied Social Research Methods, No. 46). Thousand Oaks, CA: Sage.

9

MIXED METHODS DESIGN: AN ALTERNATIVE APPROACH

◆ Joseph A. Maxwell
Diane M. Loomis

The explicit use of both quantitative and qualitative methods in a single study, a combination commonly known as mixed methods research, has become widespread in many of the social sciences and applied disciplines during the past 25 years. Tashakkori and Teddlie (1998, p. 14) dated the explicit emergence of mixed methods research to the 1960s, with this approach becoming common by the 1980s with the waning of the "paradigm wars." They also identified a subsequent integration of additional aspects of the qualitative and quantitative approaches—not just methods—beginning during the 1990s, which they called "mixed model" studies (p. 16). Such aspects include epistemological assump-

tions, types of investigation and research design, and analysis and inference strategies.

However, the practice of mixed methods (and mixed models) research has a much longer history than the explicit discussion of the topic. In natural sciences such as ethology and animal behavior, evolutionary biology, paleontology, and geology, the integration of goals and methods that typically would be considered qualitative (naturalistic settings, inductive approaches, detailed description, attention to context, and the intensive investigation of single cases) with those that are generally seen as quantitative (experimental manipulation; control of extraneous variables; formal hypothesis testing;

theory verification; and quantitative sampling, measurement, and analysis) has been common for more than a century. In addition, many classic works in the social sciences employed both qualitative and quantitative techniques and approaches without deliberately drawing attention to this. (Several of these classic studies are analyzed in detail later in the chapter.) From this broader perspective, mixed methods research is a long-standing (although sometimes controversial) practice rather than a recent development.

Indeed, a case could be made that mixed methods research was *more* common in earlier times, when methods were less specialized and compartmentalized and the paradigm wars were less heated. Staw (1992) observed, "When the field of organizational behavior was beginning in the 1950s, there was less of an orthodoxy in method. People observed, participated, counted, and cross-tabulated. There was ready admission that each methodology was flawed" (p. 136). And Rabinowitz and Weseen (2001) argued,

> There was a time in psychology when qualitative and quantitative methods were more easily combined that they are today. Famous experimental social psychologists such as Solomon Asch, Stanley Milgram, and Leon Festinger combined both approaches in some of their most famous works, although the qualitative aspects of the pieces tend to get lost in textbook accounts of their work, as well as in the minds of many instructors and researchers. (pp. 15-16)

This widespread but relatively implicit use of methods, approaches, and concepts from both the qualitative and quantitative paradigms makes it important, in understanding mixed methods design, to investigate the actual conduct of the study (in-sofar as this can be determined from the publications resulting from the research) rather than depending only on the authors' own characterization of what they did. Kaplan (1964) coined the terms "logic-in-use" and "reconstructed logic" to describe this difference (p. 8). This issue is magnified when mixed model research is considered because aspects of the study other than methods are often less explicitly identified. It is thus important to pay particular attention to the logic-in-use of mixed methods studies in attempting to understand how qualitative and quantitative methods and approaches can be integrated.

In this chapter, we address this issue by presenting an alternative to the usual ways of thinking about mixed methods design. There are two points on which our position differs from most other approaches to mixed methods studies. First, our concept of "design" is different from that employed in most approaches to designing mixed methods studies. The authors of the latter works have typically taken a typological view of research design, presenting a taxonomy of ways to combine qualitative and quantitative methods. In this handbook, for example, the chapters on design by Morse (Chapter 7) and Creswell, Plano Clark, Gutmann, and Hanson (Chapter 8) both focus on the different *types* of mixed methods research, delineating the dimensions on which such studies can vary and identifying the possible and actual combinations of qualitative and quantitative methods.

We approach the issue of design from a fundamentally different perspective. We see the design of a study as consisting of the different components of a research study (including purposes, conceptual framework, research questions, and validity strategies, in addition to "methods" in a strict sense) and the ways in which these components are integrated with, and mutually influence, one another. We present what Maxwell (1996) called an "interactive" model for research design and apply this model to mixed methods research, showing how the different components of actual mixed methods studies are integrated. The model is termed *interactive* (*systemic* would also be appropriate) because the components are connected in a network or web rather than a linear or cyclic sequence.

The second way in which our approach is distinctive is that we base our approach to mixed methods research on a conceptual analysis of the fundamental differences between qualitative and quantitative research (Maxwell, 1998; Maxwell & Mohr, 1999; Mohr, 1982, 1995, 1996). This analysis employs a distinction between two approaches to explanation, which we call *variance theory* and *process theory*. The use of this distinction leads to somewhat different definitions of these two types of research from those found in most other works, and thus it leads to a somewhat different idea of what mixed methods research consists of.

Our purpose in this chapter is to provide some tools for analyzing such studies and for developing mixed methods designs. We begin by presenting the contrast between prevalent typological views of design and an interactive approach to research design. We develop the latter approach in detail, explaining the components of the interactive model and the systemic relationships among these components. We then turn to the nature of the qualitative-quantitative distinction, presenting an analysis of this distinction that is grounded in the contrast between two fundamentally different ways of thinking about explanation. This leads to a discussion of paradigms and of whether qualitative research and quantitative research constitute distinct or incompatible paradigms. These two analyses are then com-

bined in a presentation of the ways in which qualitative and quantitative approaches to each of the design components differ and of some of the sources of complementarity that these differences generate. Finally, we apply this approach to a variety of actual studies that combine qualitative and quantitative strategies and methods, providing an in-depth analysis of how the designs of these studies actually functioned and the strengths and limitations of the designs.

In proposing this alternative approach, we are not taking a polemical or adversarial stance toward other approaches to mixed methods design. We see our approach as complementary to others and as providing some tools and insights that other approaches might not as clearly provide. The complementarity that we see between different approaches to design is similar to the complementarity that we advocate in mixed methods research, which Greene and Caracelli (1997) called "dialectical" (p. 8), and we believe that combining typological and systemic strategies for analyzing and creating research designs will be more productive than either used alone.

◆ *Existing Approaches to Mixed Methods Design*

We stated previously that existing approaches to mixed methods design have been primarily typological. This is not to claim that issues other than typology have been ignored. We believe that these issues have generally been framed within an overall typological approach and that the *analysis* of mixed methods studies has focused on the classification of these studies in terms of a typology of mixed methods designs. For example, Caracelli and Greene (1997) identified two basic types of mixed methods designs, which they called "component" and "integrated" designs. Component designs are ones in which "the methods are implemented as discrete aspects of the overall inquiry and remain distinct throughout the inquiry," while integrated designs involve "a greater integration of the different method types" (pp. 22-23). Within these broad categories, they described seven subtypes, based largely on the purposes for combining methods. Patton (1990) presented a different typology, based on qualitative or quantitative approaches to three key stages of a study (design, data, and analysis); he used this to generate four possible mixed designs, involving a choice of qualitative or quantitative methods at each stage (not all sequences were viewed as possible by Patton). Tashakkori and Teddlie (1998) built on Patton's approach to create a much more elaborate typology. They distinguished mixed methods designs (combining methods alone) from mixed model designs (combining qualitative and quantitative approaches to all phases of the research process) and created an elaborate set of subtypes within these.

Not all work on mixed methods design has been typological. For example, Bryman (1988) focused on identifying the purposes for combining qualitative and quantitative methods, and Brewer and Hunter (1989) took a similar approach, organizing their discussion in terms of the different stages of the research. Creswell (1994) presented three models for mixed methods research but then related these models to each of his "design phases," which correspond roughly to the different sections of a research proposal.

Typologies are unquestionably valuable. They help a researcher to make sense of the diversity of mixed methods studies and to make some broad decisions about how to proceed in designing such a study. In particular, distinctions based on the sequence or order in which approaches are combined, the relative dominance or emphasis of the different approaches, whether the approaches are relatively self-contained or integrated, and the different purposes for combining methods are particularly important in understanding mixed methods design.

However, typological approaches also have their limitations. First, the actual diversity in mixed methods studies is far greater than any typology can adequately encompass; this point was emphasized by Caracelli and Greene (1997) as well as Tashakkori and Teddlie (1998, pp. 34-36, 42). In particular, the recognition of multiple paradigms (e.g., positivist, realist, constructivist, critical, postmodern) rather than only two, the diversity in the aspects of quantitative and qualitative approaches that can be employed, the wide range of purposes for using mixed methods, and differences in the setting where the study is done and the consequences of this for the design all make the actual analysis of a mixed methods design far more complicated than simply fitting it into a taxonomic framework.

Second, most typologies leave out what we feel are important components of design, including the purposes of the research, the conceptual framework used, and the strategies for addressing validity issues. All of these components are incorporated into the interactive design model presented next. Typologies also tend to be linear in their conception of design, seeing the components as "phases" of the design rather than as interacting parts of a complex whole.

Third, typologies by themselves generally do little to clarify the actual functioning and interrelationship of the qualitative and quantitative parts of a design; the typology presented by Caracelli and Greene (1997) is an exception to this criticism because that typology is based partly on the purposes for which a mixed approach is used. Similarly, Pawson and Tilley (1997, p. 154) argued that a pragmatic pluralism in combining methods leads to no new thinking and does not clarify *how* to integrate approaches or when to stop.

◆ *An Interactive Model of Design*

We believe that an interactive approach to research design can help to address these problems. Rather than seeing "design" as a choice from a fixed set of possible arrangements or sequences in the research process, such approaches (e.g., Grady & Wallston, 1988; Martin, 1982; Maxwell, 1996) treat the design of a study as consisting of the actual components of a study and the ways in which these components connect with and influence one another. This approach to design is consistent with the conception of design employed in architecture, engineering, art, and virtually every other field besides research methods in which the term is used: "an underlying scheme that governs functioning, developing, or unfolding" and "the arrangement of elements or details in a product or work of art" (Merriam-Webster, 1984). A good design, one in which the components are compatible and work effectively together, promotes efficient and successful functioning; a flawed design leads to poor operation or failure.

The interactive model presented here has two essential properties: the components themselves and the ways in which these are related. There are five components to the model, each of which can be characterized by the issues that it

is intended to address (Maxwell, 1996, pp. 4-5):

1. Purposes

What are the goals of this study? What issues is it intended to illuminate, and what practices or outcomes is it intended to influence? Why is the study worth doing? These purposes can be personal, practical, or intellectual; all three kinds of purposes can influence the rest of the research design.

2. Conceptual Framework

What theories and beliefs about the phenomena studied will guide or inform the research? These theories and beliefs may be drawn from the literature, personal experience, preliminary studies, or a variety of other sources. This component of the design contains the *theory* that the researcher has developed, or is developing, about the setting or issues being studied.

3. Research Questions

What specifically does the researcher want to understand by doing this study? What questions will the research attempt to answer?

4. Methods

How will the study actually be conducted? What approaches and techniques will be used to collect and analyze the data, and how do these constitute an integrated strategy? There are four distinct parts of this component of the model: (a) the relationship that the researcher establishes with the participants in the study; (b) the selection of settings, participants, times and places of data collection, and other data sources such as documents (what is

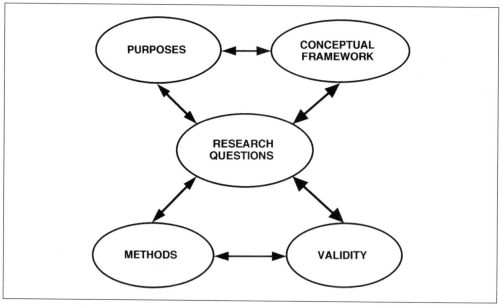

Figure 9.1. An Interactive Model of Research Design

often called "sampling"); (c) data collection methods; and (d) data analysis strategies and techniques.

5. Validity

How might the conclusions of the study be wrong? What plausible alternative explanations and validity threats are there to the potential conclusions of the study, and how will these be addressed?

These components are not radically different from the ones presented in many other discussions of research design (e.g., LeCompte & Preissle, 1993; Miles & Huberman, 1994; Robson, 1993). What is innovative is the way in which the relationships among the components are conceptualized. In this model, the components form an integrated and interacting whole, with each component closely tied to several others rather than being linked in a linear or cyclic sequence. Each of the five components can influence and be influenced by any of the other components. The key relationships among the components are displayed in Figure 9.1. In this diagram, the most important of these relationships are represented as two-way arrows. There is considerable similarity to a systems model of how the parts of a system are organized in a functioning whole.

While all of the five components can influence other components of the design, the research questions play a central role. In contrast to many quantitative models of design, the research questions are not seen as the starting point or guiding component of the design; instead, they function as the hub or heart of the design because they form the component that is most directly linked to the other four. The research questions need to inform, and be responsive to, all of the other components of the design.

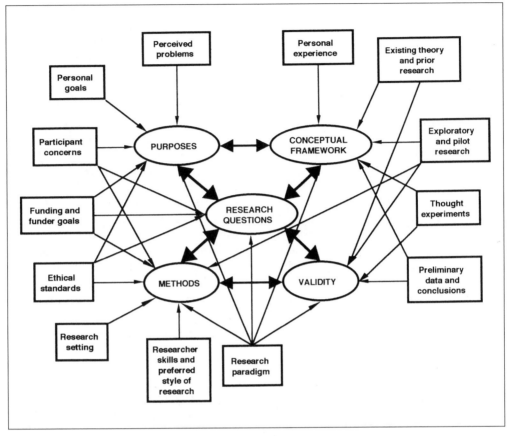

Figure 9.2. Contextual Factors Influencing a Research Design

There are many other factors besides these five components that can influence the design of a study. These include the resources available to the researcher, the researcher's abilities and preferences in methods, perceived intellectual or practical problems, ethical standards, the research setting, the concerns and responses of participants, and the data that are collected. These additional influences are best seen not as part of the design itself but rather either as part of the *environment* within which the research and its design exist or as *products* of the research (Maxwell, 1996, pp. 6-7). Figure 9.2 presents some of the factors in the environ-

ment that can influence the design and conduct of a study. The five components of this design model, by contrast, represent issues that are not external to the design of the study but rather are integral parts of it; they represent decisions and actions that must be addressed, either explicitly or implicitly, by the researcher.

One way in which this design model can be useful is as a tool or template for conceptually mapping the design of a study, either as part of the design process or in analyzing the design of a completed study. This involves filling in the boxes or circles for the five components of the model with the *actual* components of a particular study's design. We apply this technique specifically to a variety of mixed methods studies later in the chapter.

◆ The Qualitative-Quantitative Distinction

Because there are so many points of difference between the qualitative and quantitative approaches, there has been considerable variation in how the distinction between the two has been framed. Early work often based this distinction simply on the kind of data employed (textual or numerical). Creswell (1994), by contrast, saw the distinction between inductive and deductive approaches as most important, while Tashakkori and Teddlie (1998, p. 55) distinguished three different stages or dimensions for which the distinction can be made: type of investigation (exploratory or confirmatory), data collection (qualitative or quantitative), and analysis and inference (qualitative or statistical). Guba and Lincoln (1989) made the distinction at a more philosophical level, as a distinction between constructivism and positivism.

In our view, the qualitative-quantitative distinction is grounded in the distinction between two contrasting approaches to explanation, which Mohr (1982) termed variance theory and process theory. Variance theory deals with *variables* and the correlations among them; it is based on an analysis of the contribution of *differences* in values of particular variables to differences in other variables. Variance theory, which ideally involves precise measurement of differences on and correlations between variables, tends to be associated with research that employs extensive prestructuring of the research, probability sampling, quantitative measurement, statistical testing of hypotheses, and experi-

mental or correlational designs. As Mohr noted, "The variance-theory model of explanation in social science has a close affinity to statistics. The archetypal rendering of this idea of causality is the linear or nonlinear regression model" (p. 42).

Process theory, by contrast, deals with *events* and the processes that connect them; it is based on an analysis of the causal *processes* by which some events influence others. Because process explanation deals with specific events and processes, it is much less amenable to quantitative approaches. It lends itself to the in-depth study of one or a few cases or a small sample of individuals and to textual forms of data that retain the contextual connections between events. Weiss (1994) provided a concrete example of this strategy:

> In qualitative interview studies the demonstration of causation rests heavily on the description of a visualizable sequence of events, each event flowing into the next. . . . Quantitative studies support an assertion of causation by showing a correlation between an earlier event and a subsequent event. An analysis of data collected in a large-scale sample survey might, for example, show that there is a correlation between the level of the wife's education and the presence of a companionable marriage. In qualitative studies we would look for a process through which the wife's education or factors associated with her education express themselves in marital interaction. (p. 179)

Mohr (1996) has more recently extended his original distinction between process theory and variance theory to identify two conceptions of causation that he has called "factual causation" and "physical causation." Factual causation is the traditional mode of reasoning about causes in quantitative research, where the argument for causality is based on the comparison of situations in which the presumed causal factor is present or absent or has different values. Physical causation, by contrast, does not rely on such comparative logic; it is based on a notion of a mechanical connection between a cause and its effect (p. 16). Similar distinctions have been developed by realist philosophers such as Harre (1972; see also Harre & Madden, 1975) and Salmon (1984, 1989, 1998). While factual causation is an appropriate concept for comparative studies with large *N*'s, physical causation is appropriate for case studies or qualitative interview studies that do not involve formal comparisons.

Maxwell and Mohr (1999) used this distinction to identify two aspects of a study that can be productively denoted by the terms *qualitative* and *quantitative*: data and design/analysis.

> We define quantitative data as *categorical* data, with either enumeration or measurement within categories. A conceptual dimension that is itself a category subdivided by measurement, or that is divided into subcategories for enumerative or frequency data, is generally called a "variable," which is a hallmark of the quantitative approach. Qualitative data, in contrast, are typically *textual* in nature, consisting of written or spoken words, but may include video recordings and photographs as well as narrative text. (p. 2)

Categorical data lend themselves to aggregation and comparison, and they are easily quantified. Textual data, on the other hand, lend themselves to investigation of the processes by which two events or characteristics are connected.

In addition, we propose that quantitative design/analysis is research design and consequent analysis that rely in a variety of ways on the *comparison* of frequencies or measurements across subjects or across categories. Such designs focus on identifying differences between groups or correlations between variables. In contrast, qualitative design/analysis is design and analysis that rely in various ways on the treatment of focal entities as singular wholes in context, with an emphasis on the identification of meaning and process.

With these definitions of secondary terms in mind, the two fundamentally distinct ways of understanding the world can be specified as two distinct combinations of types of data on the one hand with types of design/analysis on the other. Thus, a quantitative way of understanding the world is a way that views the world in terms of categorical data, featuring the comparison of frequencies and measurements across subjects and categories. A qualitative way of understanding is a way that views the world in terms of textual data, featuring the treatment of focal entities as singular wholes in context. (p. 2)

◆ Paradigmatic Unity and Compatibility

This analysis of the qualitative-quantitative distinction reframes the nature of the qualitative and quantitative paradigms but does not address the issue of paradigmatic unity or of the compatibility of different paradigms. This unity is often assumed to be a critical issue in combining methods. For example, Patton (1980, p. 110) emphasized the "integrity" of each approach, and Morse (Chapter 7, this volume) argues,

> When using mixed methods, it is important that methodological congruence be maintained, that is, that all of the assumptions of the major method be adhered to and that components of the method (such as the data collection and analytical strategies) be consistent.

However, the need for such paradigmatic integrity cannot be assumed. McCawley (1982) examined the debate between two positions in linguistics, generative semantics and interpretive semantics, that had generally been seen as unitary paradigms. He showed that both of these approaches in fact consisted of two packages of positions on a large number of issues, with each package corresponding to the views of some prominent members of two communities of linguists. However,

> neither of these communities was completely homogeneous, no member of the community retained exactly the same set of views for very long, . . . and the relationships among the views that were packaged together as "generative semantics" or as "interpretive semantics" were generally far more tenuous than representative members of either community led people (including themselves) to believe. (p. 1)

Pitman and Maxwell (1990) similarly argued that the supposed paradigmatic unity of one area of qualitative research, qualitative evaluation, is largely illusory and that major figures in this field hold widely divergent and conflicting views on many of the fundamental issues regarding the use of qualitative approaches for program evaluation. On the quantitative side,

the recent debate over null hypothesis significance testing has revealed how the development of this approach incorporated fundamentally incompatible assumptions from different schools of statistics.

Such a position does not entail that there is *no* relationship among the different aspects of each paradigm, as Reichardt and Cook (1979, p. 18) appeared to argue. We agree with Sayer (1992) that there are "resonances" among the different components of each paradigm that "encourage the clustering of certain philosophical positions, social theories, and techniques" (p. 199). The relationship is simply not a necessary or invariant one. Each paradigm constitutes a "loosely bundled innovation" (Koontz, 1976, cited in Rogers, 1995, p. 178), and researchers often resemble the innovation adopters described by Rogers (1995), "struggling to give their own unique meaning to the innovation as it is applied in their local context" (p. 179).

Thus, we do not believe that there exist uniform, generic qualitative and quantitative research paradigms. Despite the philosophical and methodological resonances among the components of each paradigm, both of these positions include a large number of distinct and separable components, and there is disagreement even within each approach over the nature, use, and implications of some of the different components. The classic qualitative approach includes the study of natural real-life settings, a focus on participants' meanings and context, inductive generation of theory, open-ended data collection, analytical strategies that retain the textual nature of the data, and the frequent use of narrative forms of analysis and presentation. The quantitative approach includes the formulation of prior hypotheses, the use of experimental interventions, a comparison of treatment and control groups, random sampling or assignment, standardization of instruments and data collection, quantitative data, statistical hypothesis testing, and a focus on causal explanation. Each of these (and other variations too numerous to list) is a separable module with its own requirements and implications rather than an integral and inseparable part of a larger methodological and epistemological whole (Maxwell, Sandlow, & Bashook, 1986; Patton, 1990; Pitman & Maxwell, 1992). While the connections among these components are crucial to the overall coherence of a particular research design (Maxwell, 1996), the possible legitimate ways of putting together these components are multiple rather than singular and, to a substantial extent, need to be discovered empirically rather than logically deduced (Maxwell, 1990).

However, we also agree with Kidder and Fine's (1987) statement, "We share the call for 'synthesis,' but at the same time, we want to preserve the significant differences between the two cultures. Instead of homogenizing research methods and cultures, we would like to see researchers become bicultural" (p. 57). Our view of mixed methods design includes the position that Greene and Caracelli (1997) termed "dialectical" in which differences between the paradigms are viewed as important and cannot be ignored or reconciled. Bernstein (1983), in discussing the differences between Habermas and Derrida, provided a clear statement of what we advocate:

> I do not think there is a theoretical position from which we can reconcile their differences, their otherness to each other—nor do I think we should smooth out their "aversions and attractions." The nasty questions that they raise about each other's "project" need to be relentlessly pursued. One of the primary lessons of "modernity/

> postmodernity" is a radical skepticism about the possibility of a reconciliation—an *aufhebung*, without gaps, fissures, and ruptures. However, *together*, Habermas/Derrida provide us with a force-field that constitutes the "dynamic, transmutational structure of a complex phenomenon"—the phenomenon I have labeled "modernity/postmodernity." (p. 225)

From this perspective, the "compatibility" of particular qualitative and quantitative methods and approaches becomes a much more complex issue than either paradigmatic or pragmatist approaches usually suggest. Maxwell (1990) claimed that "the theoretical debate about combining methods has prevented us from seeing the different ways in which researchers are *actually* combining methods, and from understanding what works and what doesn't" (p. 507). What we want to do here is use the interactive design model to understand how qualitative and quantitative approaches can productively be combined.

◆ Qualitative and Quantitative Approaches to the Design Components

In this section, we identify the distinctive properties of the quantitative and qualitative approaches to each of the components of design described previously: purposes, conceptual framework, research questions, methods, and validity. The ways in which the two paradigms typically frame each of the components are described briefly and are summarized in Table 9.1. A more detailed discussion of each of the components, focusing mainly on qualitative research but also contrasting this with

TABLE 9.1   Possible Quantitative and Qualitative Elements of the Design Components

	Quantitative	Qualitative
Purposes	Precise measurement and comparison of variables Establishing relationships between variables Inference from sample to population	Meaning Context Process Discovering unanticipated events, influences, and conditions Understanding single cases Inductive development of theory
Conceptual framework	Variance theories	Process theories

Research questions	Variance questions
	  Truth of proposition
	  Presence or absence
	  Degree or amount
	  Correlation
	Hypothesis testing
	Causality (factual)
		Process questions
		  How and why
		Meaning
		Context (holistic)
		Hypotheses as part of conceptual framework
		Causality (physical)

Research methods		
Relationship	Objectivity/reduction of influence (researcher as extraneous variable)	Use of influence as tool for understanding (researcher as part of process)
Sampling	Probability sampling Establishing valid comparisons	Purposeful sampling
Data collection	Prior development of instruments Standardization Measurement/testing—quantitative/categorical	Inductive development of strategies Adapting to particular situation Collection of textual or visual material
Data analysis	Numerical descriptive analysis (statistics, correlation) Estimation of population variables Statistical hypothesis testing Conversion of textual data into numbers or categories	Textual analysis (memos, coding, connecting) Grounded theory Narrative approaches
Validity		
Internal validity	Statistical conclusion validity Construct validity Causal validity (control of extraneous variables)	Descriptive validity Interpretive validity Construct validity Causal validity (identification and assessment of alternative explanations)
Generalizability	External validity (comparability)	Transferability Generalizing to theory

quantitative research, is provided in Maxwell (1996).

PURPOSES

The possible purposes of a study are too numerous and disparate to list, and specific personal and practical purposes are usually not tightly linked to one or the other approach. Intellectual purposes, in contrast, do tend to segregate into qualitative and quantitative categories. Quantitative purposes include precise measurement and comparison of variables, establishing relationships between variables, identifying patterns and regularities that might not be apparent to the people in the settings studied, and making inferences from the sample to some population. Qualitative purposes include understanding the context, process, and meaning for participants in the phenomena studied; discovering unanticipated events, influences, and conditions; inductively developing theory; and understanding a single case.

CONCEPTUAL FRAMEWORK

The conceptual framework for a study consists of the theory (or theories) relevant to the phenomena being studied that inform and influence the research. The key issue for mixed methods studies, then, is the nature of these theories. Are they variance theories, process theories, some combination of these, or theories that do not fit neatly into this dichotomy? A mismatch between the conceptual framework and the research questions or methods used can create serious problems for the research; a variance theory cannot adequately guide and inform a process-oriented investigation and vice versa. Mismatches between the conceptual framework and the pur-

poses or validity strategies are less common but can also be problematic. A mixed methods study is often informed by both variance and process theories, and the main design issue is sorting out specifically how different parts of the conceptual framework are integrated with one another and how they are linked to the other design components.

RESEARCH QUESTIONS

As with conceptual frameworks, research questions can usually be categorized as variance questions or process questions. The research questions in a quantitative study typically are questions about the measurement or analysis of variation—the amount or frequency of some category, the value of some variable, or the relationship between two or more variables. Such questions are usually framed in terms of the values of key variables, and specific hypotheses are often stated. The questions and hypotheses are nearly always specifically formulated (or presented as if they were formulated) in advance of any data collection, and they are frequently framed in "operational" terms, connecting directly to the measurement or data collection strategies. In a qualitative study, by contrast, the research questions typically deal with the verbal description of some event, phenomenon, or process (What is happening here? What are the characteristics of this phenomenon?); its meaning to participants in the setting studied; or the process by which some events or characteristics of the situation influence other events or characteristics. The questions might not be explicitly stated, and when they are, they might include only the broad initial questions with which the study began and not the more focused questions that developed during the research.

METHODS

As described previously, "methods" as a design component include (a) the relationship that the researcher establishes with individuals and groups being studied; (b) the selection of sites, participants, settings, and times of data collection; (c) the methods used for data collection; and (d) the strategies used for data analysis.

Research Relationship. The relationship the researcher has with participants in the study, or with others who control access to these individuals or groups or that may influence the conduct of the study, is a key component of the research design and can have a major impact on the conduct and results of a study. This aspect of design tends to be treated very differently in quantitative and qualitative studies. Quantitative researchers tend to see the research relationship as an extraneous variable—something to be controlled. This can be done either to prevent the relationship from influencing the results or affecting the variables studied or to prevent *variance* in the relationship from introducing confounding variance in the dependent variables (e.g., standardizing survey interview procedures so that differences in procedures, either within or between interviewers, do not create an additional source of variation in the results). Qualitative studies, on the other hand, typically treat the research relationship not as a variable but rather as a process, one that can have important positive as well as negative consequences for the research. The goal is not to create a standardized relationship but rather to create a relationship that maximizes the understanding gained from each participant interviewed or each situation observed. Such a relationship is often much more personal and informal than is the case in quantitative studies.

Sampling. The two main strengths of quantitative sampling (and for experimental research, this can be extended to include assignment of participants to conditions) are to establish valid comparisons and to allow generalization from the sample to the population of interest. Some form of probability sampling (or random assignment) is usually the preferred method; in the absence of this, post hoc strategies (matching or analytical techniques such as analysis of covariance) can be used to increase comparability and generalizability. Qualitative research normally places less emphasis on formal comparisons, and the usual sampling strategy is some form of purposeful sampling. In this approach, participants are selected because they are most likely to provide relevant and valuable information or to allow the researcher to develop or test particular theoretical ideas (in grounded theory research, the latter strategy is called theoretical sampling).

Data Collection. Quantitative data collection is typically preplanned, structured, and designed to ensure comparability of data across participants and sites. The data are normally collected in numerical or categorical form, using instruments or procedures that have been designed and tested to ensure reliability and validity. Qualitative data collection is typically more open-ended, flexible, and inductive, and the data are usually textual descriptions, either written notes or recorded verbal data that are converted to textual form by transcribing (increasingly, visual means such as videotaping are being used).

Data Analysis. Quantitative analysis can be descriptive (assigning numbers or category labels to data or aggregating data on particular variables) or relational (investigating the relationship between two or more variables in the sample). Quantitative analysis can also make inferences to the population from which the sample was drawn, either estimating the values of population variables or testing hypotheses about the relationship of variables in the population. In addition, textual data can be converted into categorical or numerical form for analysis. Qualitative analysis is more diverse but typically addresses the goals listed under purposes (meaning, context, process, inductive theory development, and in-depth understanding of single cases). The analysis can involve the categorization (coding) of the textual data, but the purpose is quite different from that of quantitative categorization. Rather than being a preliminary step to counting instances of something or aggregating measurements on some variable, the function of qualitative categorization is to collect all of the instances of some type of phenomenon for further qualitative comparison and investigation. The goals of this strategy are to develop an in-depth description of this phenomenon, to identify key themes or properties, and to generate theoretical understanding. The categories are often inductively developed during the analysis rather than systematically formulated prior to the analysis. Both quantitative and qualitative analysis can be either exploratory (on exploratory quantitative data analysis, see Tukey, 1977) or confirmatory, although qualitative researchers usually do not simply test a prior theory without further developing that theory.

VALIDITY

Under validity, we include both causal (internal) validity and generalizability (external validity). Quantitative researchers, most notably Campbell and Stanley (1963) and Cook and Campbell (1979), have developed a detailed typology of validity issues, validity threats, and strategies for addressing these threats. In addi-

tion to causal validity and generalizability, Cook and Campbell identified statistical conclusion validity (the validity of inferences from the sample to the population sampled) and construct validity (the validity of the theoretical constructs employed) as distinct issues. There is less agreement on classifying validity issues in qualitative research. Maxwell (1992) distinguished four main categories of validity in qualitative research: descriptive validity (the validity of the descriptions of settings and events), interpretive validity (the validity of statements about the meanings or perspectives held by participants), explanatory (or theoretical) validity (the validity of claims about causal processes and relationships, including construct validity as well as causal validity proper), and generalizability.

Inferences about causality are controversial in qualitative research. Some researchers (e.g., Guba & Lincoln, 1989) deny that causality is an appropriate concept in qualitative research, and this view has been widely accepted. In contrast, Sayer (1992, 2000) and Maxwell (1998), taking a critical realist perspective, argue that causal explanation not only is legitimate in qualitative research but is a particular strength of this approach, although it uses a different strategy from quantitative research, based on a process rather than a variance concept of causality. Construct validity is similar for both approaches, although quantitative research may use quantitative means of assessing the construct validity of instruments. Generalizability is also similar (statistical generalization to the population sampled is included under statistical conclusion validity) and is always a matter of transferring the conclusions of a study to other situations, an inherently judgmental process; Guba and Lincoln (1989) referred to this as "transferability." However, in quantitative research, generalizability is usually seen as a matter of the results of the study being valid in other settings (replicability). Qualitative researchers, by contrast, tend to "generalize to theory" (Yin, 1984, pp. 39-40)—developing a theory and then applying that theory to other settings that may be dissimilar but that can be illuminated by the theory in question, appropriately modified (Becker, 1990).

In Table 9.1, we have tried to summarize the typical features of both quantitative and qualitative research as these involve the five design components of the interactive model.

ANALYSIS OF SELECTED EXAMPLES OF MIXED METHODS DESIGNS

Uncovering the actual integration of qualitative and quantitative approaches in any particular study is a considerably more complex undertaking than simply classifying the study into a particular category on the basis of a few broad dimensions or characteristics. It requires an understanding of each of the five components of the study's design and of the ways in which each component incorporates quantitative elements, qualitative elements, or both. In addition, as stated previously, it is important to examine the actual conduct of the study rather than simply depending on the author's assertions about the design. This issue is illustrated by Blumstein and Schwartz's (1983) study of American couples, which used both survey questionnaires and open-ended interviews. The authors described the results of their study as based entirely on the statistical analysis of the survey data, while the qualitative data were relegated to providing illustrative instances:

> we use the phrase "we find . . ." in presenting a conclusion based on statistical analysis of data from the question-

naires. . . . The interview data help us interpret our questionnaire findings, but unless we are using one of the parts of the interview that is readily quantifiable, we do not afford them the same degree of trust we grant to information derived from the questionnaires.

> The interviews serve another purpose. We use the interview materials to illustrate both majority patterns and important exceptions. (p. 23)

And the authors characterize the chapters in their book that deal with relationship histories, which are based mainly on the interviews, by stating, "In these chapters, which have nothing to do with our analysis of the data but are included only for their illustrative value . . ." (p. 22).

However, this does not explain why Blumstein and Schwartz (1983) conducted in-depth interviews, lasting 2.5 to 4.0 hours, with both partners, separately and together, for 300 couples; transcribed and coded these interviews; and followed up with questionnaires to fill in any gaps. It also seems inconsistent with the fact that, in addition to their extensive use of quotes in the thematically organized sections of the book, they devoted 213 pages, nearly half of the results section of the book, to detailed case studies of 20 couples' relationships. A closer analysis of their account reveals that triangulation of methods was an important feature of the study so as to "see couples from several vantage points" (p. 15) and that the case studies "helped to illuminate some of the ways in which money, sex, and work shape the nature of [the partners'] relationships" (p. 332). It appears that the "reconstructed logic" of the design was heavily influenced by a quantitative ideology of what counts as "results," distorting the study's logic-in-use and the actual contribution of the qualitative component.

The main purpose of this section is to present in-depth analyses of well-documented, complex examples of mixed model research, illustrating the numerous ways in which qualitative and quantitative approaches to each of the design components can be combined. We discuss these studies in terms of Caracelli and Greene's (1997) distinction between "component" and "integrated" mixed methods designs, moving from studies that resemble component designs to those that resemble integrated designs. Component designs are those in which the different methods remain discrete throughout the study and only the results of the methods are combined (p. 22). Integrated designs, by contrast, are those in which there is "a greater integration of the different method types" (p. 23); such designs involve the use not of relatively self-contained qualitative and quantitative methods modules but rather of qualitative and quantitative elements or strategies integrated within a single phase or strand of the research; the elements occur concurrently and in constant interaction with one another rather than as conceptually separate enterprises that are later linked together.

Their distinction is most useful when applied to methods; it is less meaningful when applied to the other components of a research design, and in fact the use of both qualitative and quantitative elements of components other than methods seems to have been treated by Caracelli and Greene (1997) as an "integrated" design almost by definition. In addition, Caracelli and Greene's two types are not categorically distinct; actual studies exhibit a continuum of the amount of integration of methods and also a variety of different strategies for integration. We have nonetheless organized the studies in this order for two reasons. First, doing so provides a clearer organization to this section. Second, it al-lows us to address the design features of particular *types* of mixed methods studies as well as the specific studies we describe.

A common approach to using both quantitative and qualitative methods is to use them sequentially. Sutton and Rafaeli (1992) provided an unusually detailed and candid account of such a design, a study of the relationship between expressed emotion and sales in convenience stores (see also Sutton & Rafaeli, 1988). They began their research with a well-developed theory of the expression of emotion by employees, based not only on published literature but also on informal querying of waitresses, clerks, and telephone operators. They had numerous ideas for possible empirical studies, but no actual research in progress, when they unexpectedly gained access to a quantitative data set derived from covert observations of employees and from company sales records, with detailed data on numerous control variables. Although one of the authors had considerable experience with qualitative research, this study was originally designed as a purely quantitative multiple regression analysis of this data set.

Sutton and Rafaeli's statistical analysis of this data was intended to achieve two main purposes. First, it would support their theory and further develop their scholarly agenda on expressed emotion. Second, it would advance their careers without involving all the work of collecting their own data. Unfortunately, the analysis flatly contradicted their hypotheses; expressed positive emotions had a consistently *negative* correlation with sales. They tried tinkering with the analysis, but to no avail; they could find no errors, and dozens of runs using different combinations of variables gave the same result. Their validity checks were unable to resolve the contradiction between their theory and their results. It was clear that they needed to revise their conceptual framework.

Fortunately, a colleague suggested an alternative theory, which came to be called the "Manhattan effect": that in busy stores, employees did not have time and/or were too harassed to express positive emotions. This theory was consistent with their data, and the authors' initial inclination was to simply revise their hypotheses and submit the paper for publication, having learned from experienced colleagues that this was common practice in both the natural and social sciences. There were two reasons why they did not do this. First, it would contradict their previously published theoretical work, potentially impairing their career advancement. Second, they wanted to write a paper that conveyed their actual process, believing that, although it would be harder to publish, it would be a better paper. To do this, however, they needed a clearer theoretical understanding of their findings. This led to the qualitative phase of the study, which consisted of interviews with managers and executives, four case studies, informal observations in stores, and one of the authors working for a day as a store clerk. Sutton and Rafaeli (1992) stated,

> These qualitative data proved to be essential for helping us to refine our revised conceptual perspective. For example, while we had thought about how a crowded store suppresses the display of positive emotion, we had not thought about the ways in which a slow store supports the display of good cheer. During the day that Bob spent working as a clerk, he learned that customers are an important source of entertainment, and that clerks are more friendly during slow times because they are genuinely pleased to see customers and want to encourage customers to engage in conversation. (p. 123)

Their revised and elaborated theory was used to develop a different hypothesis, which was supported by a further quantitative analysis of the original data set.

This research thus involved two cycles of induction and deduction. The first cycle was typical of quantitative research; it began with informal data collection and literature-based theorizing about how the display of positive emotion influences sales, and it ended with the statistical test of a hypothesis derived from this theory. The failure of the study to support the hypothesis forced the authors into a second cycle, beginning with a colleague's suggestion and continuing with a diverse array of qualitative data collection and analysis, which eventually led to the inductive development of a new conceptual framework that emphasized the reverse process: how store pace has a negative effect on the display of positive emotion. This conceptual framework was used to generate a new quantitative hypothesis, which was then tested statistically.

In this study, the quantitative and qualitative phases were relatively distinct. The qualitative phase was largely self-contained, and its purpose was nearly exclusively to revise and develop the conceptual framework, incorporating a process model of how the pace of work affects displayed emotion. This framework was then used to generate a variance theory hypothesis that was tested with quantitative data. Figure 9.3 provides a design map of the study.

In other component studies, rather than shifting from one approach to another in sequence, the two approaches are used concurrently, although separately, and integrated only in drawing conclusions.

Phase 1

Purposes:
support their theory
advance their careers

Conceptual Framework:
variance theory of the effect of positive
  expression of emotion on sales

Research Question:
  hypotheses derived from theory

Methods:
large quantitative data set
multiple-regression analysis

Validity:
statistical hypothesis testing

Phase 2

Purposes:
maintain consistency in work
communicate actual process of research

Conceptual Framework:
"Manhattan effect"
a more complex process theory of how
  store pace affects expression of emotion

Research Question:
revised hypothesis
what is the process by which store pace affects
  the expression of emotion?

Methods:
case studies
interviews with managers and executives
informal observations in stores
working for a day as a store clerk
large quantitative data set
multiple-regression analysis

Validity:
rich description
triangulation
statistical hypothesis testing

Figure 9.3. Design Map of Sutton and Rafaeli (1988, 1992) Study

Trend (1978/1979) gave an account of such a study, an evaluation of an experimental federal housing subsidy program involving both quantitative and qualitative data collection and analysis. Trend described the study as a "naturalistic experiment" (p. 69), but it would more accurately be called a "pre-experiment" in Campbell and Stanley's (1963) typology because it did not involve a control group. Extensive quantitative data were collected on agency activities, expenses, demographic characteristics of clients, and housing quality, mainly through surveys.

In addition, each site had an observer (usually an anthropologist) who prepared a qualitative case study of that site, using field observations, interviews, and documents. The intent was that program outcomes would be determined through analysis of the quantitative data, while the case studies would provide a holistic picture of program process (Trend, 1978/1979, p. 70).

However, this plan began to unravel when the conclusions of an observer in one site directly contradicted the results of the quantitative analysis of program outcomes in that site. While neither side doubted "the facts" produced by the other, the two interpretations of these facts differed radically. The agency conducting the evaluation sided with the quantitative results, and the observer was repeatedly told to rewrite his analysis to fit the quantitative conclusions. Finally, Trend and the observer made a sustained effort to get at what had really been going on, using both the quantitative and qualitative data. They eventually came up with a coherent process explanation for nearly all of the data that went well beyond either the quantitative or the initial qualitative conclusions and that revealed serious shortcomings in both accounts.

Although this study clearly fits into the "component" type of design in that the quantitative and qualitative data were collected and analyzed separately and were combined only in developing conclusions, it also resembles the most developed subtype of integrated design described by Caracelli and Greene (1997), the transformative design. In such designs, the value commitments of different traditions are integrated, giving voice to different ideologies and interests in the setting studied. (In the interactive design model, these value commitments can form part of both the purposes and the conceptual framework.) The quantitative ana-

lysts tended to represent the views of the program managers and funders, while the observer was an advocate for the agency staff and clients. These differing value stances, as well as the separation of the quantitative and qualitative strands of the study, led to polarization and conflict; "each side held so tightly to its own views that it was impossible to brush aside the lack of congruence" (Trend, 1978/1979, p. 84).

Trend (1978/1979) concluded that multiple methods might not lead to an easy integration of findings and that "unanimity may be the hallmark of work in which other avenues to explanation have been closed off prematurely" (p. 68). If the discrepancy between the qualitative and quantitative accounts had been discovered earlier, or if the two approaches had been more closely integrated, then it is possible that the observer would have been subtly or overtly coerced into making his conclusions fit the "hard" data (p. 84). Trend thus argued that "the proliferation of divergent explanations should be encouraged" (p. 68) but also that an effort should be made to develop an account that does justice to all of the conflicting perspectives.

A third study that initially appears "component-like," in that the quantitative and qualitative elements are conceptually distinct phases of the research, is the research described in Festinger, Riecken, and Schachter's (1956) book, *When Prophecy Fails*. This was a psychological study of an end-of-the-world cult and the consequences for cult members of the failure of its predictions. The study began with a variable-oriented theory and a hypothesis about the conditions under which disconfirmation of belief will paradoxically be followed by increased commitment. The data were collected entirely through participant observation; a number of researchers pretended to be con-

Purposes:
create generalizable knowledge about the
  phenomenon studied
test predictions of theory

Conceptual Framework:
integrated variance and process theory of the
  conditions supporting belief following
  disconfirmation, based on historical research

Research Question:
hypothesis about the conditions leading to increased
  proselytizing following disconfirmation
questions about the meaning, processes, and context
  of the events studied (implicit)

Methods:
intensive involvement of researchers in the cult
covert participant observation
narrative fieldnotes of events
categorization of members in terms of the degree
  of prior commitment and social support
determining changes in proselytizing
comparison of two groups
inferences to the meaning of events for participants
rich descriptions of situational influences and processes
case analysis of all participants

Validity:
quasi-experimental controls
ruling out alternative explanations
explaining exceptions to the predictions

Figure 9.4. Design Map of Festinger et al. (1956) Study

verts to the cult and covertly amassed detailed descriptive notes on what happened as the day of judgment approached and then passed. However, to test the hypothesis, these observational data were analyzed primarily by categorizing members in terms of the degree of prior commitment and social support (the two key independent variables) and measuring changes in proselytizing (the indicator of subsequent commitment) following disconfirmation. Figure 9.4 depicts the design of the study.

This study differs from a component study such as Sutton and Rafaeli's in that the "components" are different aspects of a single research design rather than separate quantitative and qualitative strands or phases of a larger study. At first glance, it seems to fit one of Patton's (1990) types

of "methodological mixes"—experimental design, qualitative data, and statistical analysis (p. 191)—and would thus be considered a mixed model design. The main differences from Patton's type are that the study was a "natural" experiment (more accurately, a quasi-experiment) rather than a manipulated intervention and that the analysis was hypothesis testing, variable focused, quantitative, and based on prior analytical categories but not specifically statistical due to the small number of participants. However, the design is more complex than this categorization suggests, and we want to analyze the study to reveal some of these complexities.

The purposes and explicit research questions for Festinger et al.'s (1956) study were predominantly quantitative— a goal of testing the predictions of their theory of how people with a strongly held belief respond to disconfirmation of that belief; a hypothesis, deductively generated from this theory, about the effect of social support following disconfirmation on the key measure of commitment (proselytizing); and the testing of this hypothesis, with the goal of creating generalizable knowledge. However, their conceptual framework addressed both the process by which the predicted outcome (disconfirmation leads to increased commitment) could occur and the variables that could influence this outcome, and some implicit process questions became apparent in the conclusions section.

In terms of methods, the study could be seen as a quasi-experiment, with a naturally occurring intervention, pre- and post-intervention data collection, and a comparison of two parts of the group that differed in the degree of social support. However, with the detailed qualitative data collection, the logic also resembled a qualitative case study. The research relationships and data collection involved covert participant observation, intensive involvement of the researchers in the cult, and narrative fieldnotes of events. It is unclear what formal qualitative analysis techniques, if any, were used. In the narrative of the study, the researchers made frequent inferences to the meaning of events for participants, and there were rich descriptions of situational influences and processes.

In the concluding chapter of their book, Festinger et al. (1956) first gave a case-by-case analysis of all participants in terms of the hypothesized preconditions (independent variables) and outcomes. Participants were then categorized in terms of these variables, and the authors tallied the confirmations and exceptions to the predictions and compared the two situations that differed in the key independent variable (social support). This argument is essentially quantitative. However, it is extensively supplemented by a process analysis of the sequence of events for each individual; this is used to explain apparent exceptions and to modify the hypotheses to some extent. The authors also made use of unanticipated outcomes (e.g., the persistence of predictions of disaster, the identification of visitors as spacemen) that were relevant to their conclusions.

This was a coherent and workable mixed methods design because the different components were compatible and complementary in this particular situation, not because they derived from a single paradigm or were consistent with a single set of assumptions. Testing Festinger et al.'s (1956) specific hypothesis (the primary aim of the study) would ideally have involved an experimental design. However, the nature of the phenomenon addressed by the theory made an experimental test of the hypothesis impossible. The only real alternative was a kind of "natural experiment," and one was dropped into the researchers' laps. The authors noted, somewhat apologetically, that the situation that was available to them precluded the sort of formal standardized methods that "the orthodoxy of social science" would normally require (pp. 248-249); consequently, the sampling and data collection were almost purely qualitative. These consisted mainly of the use of participant observers, who gathered whatever data they could that related to the theory and research questions—including data on the meaning, context, and process of the group's activities—and produced a detailed narrative account of the events leading up to and following the disconfirmation of the group's predictions.

The crucial links in making this a coherent design were the analysis and validity procedures employed to connect the authors' qualitative data to their research questions, hypotheses, theories, and purposes. This was accomplished in two ways. One of these involved quantifying the qualitative data to adapt these to the logical requirements of hypothesis testing. The two groups of believers, which differed in the value of the major independent variable (social support), were compared in terms of the main outcome variable (extent of proselytizing) as well as on other indicators of the strength of commitment (a key mediating variable) both before and after the disconfirmation.

If this were the entire analysis, however, the research results would have been far less convincing than they were given that the number of participants (17) on whom sufficient data existed was quite small. The study's conclusion that social support was essential to strengthened belief and proselytizing was buttressed by a second qualitative analysis that examined the data on each group member for evidence relevant to the hypothesis and constructed a "mini-case study" of each member. These cases relied heavily on inductive identification of relevant data, attention to meaning and context, and a process account that elucidated the mechanisms by which belief was strengthened or weakened—all features that are characteristic of qualitative research. In addition, most of the report was such a "case study" of the entire phenomenon, revealing in rich detail how the group developed and how it responded to the disconfirmation of its predictions. These analyses reveal (or create) a set of implicit qualitative research questions about the meaning, processes, and context of the events studied that parallel the quantitative hypothesis and connect to qualitative aspects of the authors' conceptual framework. This dual analysis was facilitated by the conceptual framework for the study, which included both variance and process aspects of the phenomenon.

The validity of Festinger et al.'s (1956) conclusions is vulnerable to the fact that

traditional experimental controls were impossible, that data were not collected in a structured way that would ensure reliability and facilitate comparison, and that the sample was quite small and self-selected. The researchers' main strategy for dealing with these validity issues was to explicitly identify plausible alternative explanations and to use their data to argue that these are not credible explanations for their results. This strategy draws on both qualitative and quantitative approaches.

We believe that few, if any, sequentially "mixed" designs of the type described by Patton (1990) maintain a complete sequential separation of the qualitative and quantitative elements of the research. As in this example, the different components tend to grow "tendrils" backward and forward, integrating both qualitative and quantitative elements into all components of the research. This is understandable given the "resonance" among the components of each approach; qualitative data collection tends to generate qualitative analysis, research questions, conceptualizations, and validity strategies, and the same is true of quantitative components, while a qualitative component of the conceptual framework tends to generate qualitative research questions and methods.

Another approach that blurs the distinction between component and integrated designs is to conduct the quantitative and qualitative data collection strands in parallel, as in the studies by Trend (1978/1979) and Festinger et al. (1956), but to embed these within an overall experimental or quasi-experimental design, one that involves a deliberate intervention as well as establishing experimental and control conditions. This sort of design has been employed by Lundsgaarde, Fischer, and Steele (1981) and by Maxwell et al. (1986), among others. Such studies are classed as integrated designs by Caracelli and Greene (1997, p. 26) and would be considered mixed model designs by Tashakkori and Teddlie (1998) because they go beyond the mixing of methods in a strict sense. However, the actual methods components can range from largely separate (as in the study by Maxwell et al., 1986) to closely integrated (as in the study by Milgram, 1974 [discussed later]). The study by Lundsgaarde et al. (1981), conducted during 1976-1977, illustrates some of the possible complexities of such designs.

These researchers, all anthropologists, carried out what they described as an "ethnographic" study of the effect of a computerized medical information system (known as PROMIS) on the functioning of a hospital ward. They did this by studying two hospital wards prior to the implementation of PROMIS and then continuing this research while PROMIS was introduced on one of the wards, using the other ward as a control group. They described this ethnographic study as one "component" of the PROMIS evaluation; it was designed to complement the other components of the evaluation, which employed a quantitative analysis of medical records to determine the impact of PROMIS on the health care delivery process. The context in which PROMIS was implemented was politically charged, and the developers of the overall evaluation strategy were concerned that variation in human and situational variables might make it difficult to interpret the overall quantitative results. The goals of the ethnographic study were to document the events surrounding the implementation of the PROMIS system, and the experiences of the health care providers using this system, using a more descriptive and inductive approach so as to characterize the context in which the system was developed and demonstrated (Lundsgaarde et al., 1981, pp. 10-11).

However, the "ethnographic" component itself involved a mix of qualitative and quantitative elements. The purposes (described previously) were mainly qualitative but included the explicit comparison of the experimental and control wards so as to determine the effects of the PROMIS implementation on the experimental ward. The conceptual framework for the study was largely drawn from innovation theory (expressed in 20 "propositions" that were a mix of variance and process statements) and the sociology of medical practice. No research questions were explicitly stated; although some process questions can be clearly inferred from the study's purposes, the overall evaluation was guided by a specific variance hypothesis about the effect of PROMIS on patient care behavior, a hypothesis that was tested by the quantitative components of the evaluation. The ethnographic component relied heavily on participant observation, informal interviewing, and document analysis, and Lundsgaarde et al. (1981) presented an explicit defense of such qualitative methods in terms of the goals of context and meaning (p. 16). However, the study also included a questionnaire, a more structured interview, and a comparative observational assessment (following the introduction of PROMIS) of the amount of time spent generating and using medical records on the two wards, using matched pairs of residents or interns observed on a randomized schedule. (The latter task was required by the funding institution [p. 11] and forced a reallocation of much of the later qualitative data collection time from participant observation to in-depth interviews.) In addition, midway through the study, the observers on the two wards switched settings so as to gain a comparative perspective and to control for biases.

Lundesgaarde et al. (1981) justified this mix of quantitative and qualitative methods as a means of triangulating data and resolving contradictions between data sources (p. 16). The concerns of the evaluation planners were well-founded; the quantitative analysis of medical records found no statistically significant advantages of PROMIS over its manual counterpart, while the ethnographic study showed that "many of the clinicians who were required to use the system were unwilling participants in the experiment and even unsympathetic to many of the goals of those who developed it" and that "many of the human and organizational problems . . . could have been avoided, or at least neutralized, if the developers had paid more attention to contextual social variables affecting system users" (p. 2). The authors stated,

> It is the unpredictability of the temporal characteristics of all innovations that presents researchers with the most thorny problems of analysis. The objective measurement of the rate of acceptance, and the estimation of the potential rate of diffusion, has proved the most difficult analytical problem in our study of the PROMIS innovation. (p. 4)

For this reason, they emphasized "the importance of a multifaceted and flexible research design for the study of the many social and operational problems created by the installation of [PROMIS]" (p. 9). The presentation of the results of the study demonstrated a close integration of the quantitative and qualitative elements in drawing conclusions and addressing validity threats. For example, their discussion of the effect of PROMIS on house staff physicians (pp. 61-91) closely integrated the data from participant observations, qualitative interviews, and the systematic time-sampling observations of residents and interns. This presentation embedded the statistical analysis of the quantitative behavioral data in a descriptive account of these activities, one that clarifies the contextual variations in, and

influences on, these behaviors. They noted that the quantitative data did not support the widespread perception on the experimental ward that residents and interns spent more time entering medical data into patients' records, and the authors devoted considerable space to discussing possible reasons for this misperception, drawing on their interviews and observations (pp. 86-90).

While this evaluation superficially resembles a component design, with separate qualitative and quantitative components of the evaluation, a detailed examination reveals a much more integrated design. Some of this integration may initially have been externally imposed but was fully incorporated into the analysis, validity procedures, and conclusions. The triangulation of different methods was the result of not only the different purposes of the evaluation but also the validity concerns that would have threatened a purely quantitative study. The presence of quantitative elements in the ethnographic part of the study was partly the result of an implicit purpose (the researchers' need to satisfy the external funder) that had little intrinsic connection to the study's conceptual framework. However, these elements were closely integrated into the study's analysis, using a validity approach based on both quantitative and qualitative concepts (experimental controls and statistical tests and a process approach to ruling out alternative explanations). Figure 9.5 provides a design map of this study.

The quantitative and qualitative elements can be even more closely integrated than in this example. Milgram's (1974) *Obedience to Authority* is a report of an experimental study (carried out between 1960 and 1963) of how people respond when they are ordered by authorities to inflict pain and possible serious harm on others. Milgram and his associates designed a series of laboratory situations in

Purposes:
determine impact of PROMIS on health care
  delivery practices
describe setting of PROMIS intervention
document events surrounding implementation and
  experiences of health care providers
document impact of PROMIS on behavior of users

Conceptual Framework:
theory on which PROMIS was based (quantitative
  component)
theory of innovation (ethnographic component)
sociological research on medical practice
  (ethnographic component)

Research Question:
hypotheses about effect of PROMIS on users' practices
  (implicit) questions about context of innovation and
  users' experiences

Methods:
2 wards, experimental and control
pre/post implementation measures
comparative behavioral observations
structured questionnaire
data from clinical records
statistical analysis
participant observation
interviews
documents

Validity:
experimental controls: pre/post control group
  design
statistical hypothesis testing
triangulation of methods and data sources
ruling out alternative explanations

Figure 9.5. Design Map of Lundsgaarde et al. (1981) Study

which participants were deceived into believing that they were part of a study of the effects of punishment on learning and were then told to give increasingly severe electrical shocks to a supposed "subject" who was actually an accomplice of the researchers and who feigned pain and eventual refusal to cooperate. Unlike Festinger et al. (1956), Milgram (1974) explicitly grounded this study in the experimental tradition in social psychology (p. xv). The researchers employed numerous different experimental conditions designed to determine the effect of different variables on the degree of obedience (the dependent variable), and they collected quantitative data about the level of shock that participants administered (the main measure of obedience) in each of the different conditions.

However, the researchers were also concerned with the *process* by which people responded to the researchers' directions: how the participants made sense of and reacted to these directions and why they complied with or resisted the orders. In introducing the individual case studies, Milgram (1974) stated,

> From each person in the experiment we derive one essential fact: whether he has obeyed or disobeyed. But it is foolish to see the subject only in this way. For he brings to the laboratory a full range of emotions, attitudes, and individual styles. . . . We need to focus on the individuals who took part in the study not only because this provides a personal dimension to the experiment but also because the quality of each

person's experience gives us clues to the nature of the process of obedience. (p. 44)

The researchers covertly recorded the participants' behavior during the experiment, interviewed some participants at length after the experiment was over to determine their reasons for compliance or refusal, and sent a follow-up questionnaire to all participants that allowed expression of their thoughts and feelings. The analysis of these data is primarily qualitative but is closely integrated with the quantitative data. The results chapters of the book present a fine-grained blending of quantitative tables and graphs with observational notes, excerpts from recorded observations and interviews, and case studies of particular participants' responses to the experimental situation.

In addition, the theoretical model developed from the study is not a pure "variance" model, restricted to the different variables that affect obedience; as in the study by Festinger et al. (1956), it incorporates extensive discussion of the social processes and subjective interpretations through which obedience and resistance to authority develop. And in discussing potential validity threats to the study's conclusions, Milgram (1974) used both the quantitative results from the experimental manipulations and qualitative data from the observations to rule out these threats. In this study, experimental intervention, laboratory controls, and quantitative measurement and analysis were integrally combined with qualitative data collection and analysis to answer both qualitative and quantitative research questions. Although Milgram himself said virtually nothing explicitly about the integration of quantitative and qualitative elements in this study, Etzioni (1968) claimed that this research "shows that the often stated opposition between meaningful, interesting humanistic study and accurate, empirical quantitative research is a false one: The two perspectives can be combined to the benefit of both" (cited in Milgram, 1974, p. 201). Figure 9.6 provides a design map of the study.

◆ Conclusions and Implications

In this chapter, we have tried to show the value of a broader and more interactive concept of research design for understanding mixed methods research. We have also argued for a broader and more fundamental concept of the qualitative-quantitative distinction, one that draws on the idea of two different approaches to explanation as well as two different types of data. Through detailed examination of particular studies, we have tried to demonstrate how these tools can be used to attain a better understanding of mixed methods research. We draw several implications from these arguments and examples.

First, the logic-in-use of a study can be more complex, and can more closely integrate qualitative and quantitative elements of the study, than an initial reading of the report would suggest. The studies by Blumstein and Schwartz (1983), Lundsgaarde et al. (1981), Festinger et al. (1956), and Milgram (1974) all involved a greater integration of qualitative and quantitative approaches than one would guess from their explicit descriptions of their methods, and the two other studies presented (Sutton & Rafaeli, 1988, 1992; Trend, 1978/1979) may be exceptions only because the authors had published candid in-depth accounts of their studies' designs and methods, including aspects rarely addressed in research reports.

Second, the interactive design model that we have presented can be a valuable tool in understanding the integration of

Purposes:
understand people's willingness to
obey immoral commands

Conceptual Framework:
mixed variance and process theory of
obedience to authority

Researach Question (largely implicit):
what effect do different variables have on obedience?
what is the process by which obedience and resistance
to authority are generated?
why do subjects comply with or resist orders?
how do they make sense of the experimental situation,
and of their obedience?

Methods:
experimental manipulation of conditions
covert observation and recording of
subjects' behavior
qualitative interviews with subjects
inferences to the meaning of events for participants
case analysis of some participants

Validity:
experimental controls
triangulation of methods
ruling out alternative explanations

Figure 9.6. Design Map of Milgram (1974) Study

qualitative and quantitative approaches and elements in a particular study. For example, the conceptual framework of a study may be largely variance theory (Sutton & Rafaeli, 1988, 1992, Phase 1), largely process theory (Sutton & Rafaeli, 1988, 1992, Phase 2), a combination of both types of theories (Trend, 1978/1979; Lundsgaarde et al., 1981), or an integration of the two in a single theory (Festinger et al., 1956; Milgram, 1974).

Third, there is considerable value in a detailed understanding of how qualitative and quantitative methods are actually integrated in particular studies. For example, the degree of integration of qualitative and quantitative elements in the conceptual framework, analysis, or validity components of a study might not correspond to the integration of data collection meth-

ods. The study by Lundsgaarde et al. (1981) has more integration in the methods and validity components than in the conceptual framework, while the study by Festinger et al. (1956) has more integration in the conceptual framework and validity than in methods. In addition, the actual integration among different components of the design is often essential to understanding how a particular combination of quantitative and qualitative elements is or is not coherent. For example, the integrated process/variance conceptual framework of Milgram's (1974) study played a key role in the integration of methods and analysis.

Fourth, we do not believe that typological models by themselves provide adequate guidance for designing mixed methods research. The examples and analyses of specific studies provided by Greene and Caracelli (1997) and by Tashakkori and Teddlie (1998) are essential complements to their typologies; these provide both a concrete realization of how the types play out in practice and an illustration of aspects of mixed methods design that are not captured in the typology.

Fifth, we also believe, however, that there is no easy generalizability or transferability of the analysis of particular studies; the actual integration of the components of a study is influenced by a wide range of conditions and factors and is not dictated by the category in which it fits. The design model that we have presented is a tool for designing or analyzing an actual study rather than a template for designing a particular *type* of study. In a sense, we are presenting a more qualitative approach to mixed methods design, emphasizing particularity, context, holistic understanding, and the process by which a particular combination of qualitative and quantitative elements plays out in practice, in contrast to a more quantitative approach based on categorization and comparison. As with quantitative and qualitative approaches in general, we advocate an integration of the two approaches.

■ References

Becker, H. S. (1990). Generalizing from case studies. In E. Eisner & A. Peshkin (Eds.), *Qualitative inquiry in education: The continuing debate* (pp. 233-242). New York: Teachers College Press.

Bernstein, R. J. (1992). *The new constellation: The ethical-political horizons of modernity-postmodernity.* Cambridge, MA: MIT Press.

Blumstein, P., & Schwartz, P. (1983). *American couples.* New York: Simon & Schuster.

Brewer, J., & Hunter, A. (1989). *Multimethod research: A synthesis of styles.* Newbury Park, CA: Sage.

Bryman, A. (1988). *Quantity and quality in social research.* London: Unwin Hyman.

Campbell, D. T., & Stanley, J. C. (1963). Experimental and quasi-experimental designs for research on teaching. In N. L. Gage (Ed.), *Handbook of research on teaching* (pp. 171-246). Chicago: Rand McNally. (Reprinted in 1966 as *Experimental and quasi-experimental designs for research*)

Caracelli, V. J., & Greene, J. C. (1997). Crafting mixed-method evaluation designs. In J. C. Greene & V. J. Caracelli (Eds.), *Advances in mixed-method evaluation: The challenges and benefits of integrating diverse paradigms* (New Directions for Evaluation, No. 74, pp. 19-32). San Francisco: Jossey-Bass.

Cook, T. D., & Campbell, D. T. (1979). *Quasi-experimentation: Design and analysis issues for field settings.* Boston: Houghton Mifflin.

Creswell, J. W. (1994). *Research design: Quantitative and qualitative approaches.* Thousand Oaks, CA: Sage.

Etzioni, A. (1968). A model of significant research. *International Journal of Psychiatry, 6,* 279-280.

Festinger, L., Riecken, H. W., & Schachter, S. (1956). *When prophecy fails.* Minneapolis: University of Minnesota Press.

Grady, K. A., & Wallston, B. S. (1988). *Research in health care settings.* Newbury Park, CA: Sage.

Greene, J. C., & Caracelli, V. J. (1997). Defining and describing the paradigm issue in mixed-method evaluation. In J. C. Greene & V. J. Caracelli (Eds.), *Advances in mixed-method evaluation: The challenges and benefits of integrating diverse paradigms* (New Directions for Evaluation, No. 74, pp. 5-17). San Francisco: Jossey-Bass.

Guba, E. G., & Lincoln, Y. S. (1989). *Fourth generation evaluation.* Newbury Park, CA: Sage.

Harre, R. (1972). *The philosophies of science.* Oxford, UK: Oxford University Press.

Harre, R., & Madden, E. H. (1975). *Causal powers: A theory of natural necessity.* Oxford, UK: Basil Blackwell.

Kaplan, A. (1964). *The conduct of inquiry.* San Francisco: Chandler.

Kidder, L. H., & Fine, M. (1987). Qualitative and quantitative methods: When stories converge. In M. M. Mark & R. L. Shotland (Eds.), *Multiple methods in program evaluation: New directions in program evaluation* (pp. 57-75). San Francisco: Jossey-Bass.

Koontz, V. (1976). Innovation: Components of bundles. *Medical Care, 7*(4).

LeCompte, M. D., & Preissle, J. (1993). *Ethnography and qualitative design in educational research* (2nd ed.). San Diego: Academic Press.

Lundsgaarde, H. P., Fischer, P. J., & Steele, D. J. (1981). *Human problems in computerized medicine* (Publications in Anthropology, No. 13). Lawrence: University of Kansas.

Martin, J. (1982). A garbage can model of the research process. In J. E. McGrath, J. Martin, & R. Kulka (Eds.), *Judgment calls in research* (pp. 17-39). Thousand Oaks, CA: Sage.

Maxwell, J. A. (1990). Response to "Campbell's Retrospective and a Constructivist's Perspective." *Harvard Educational Review, 60,* 504-508.

Maxwell, J. A. (1992). Understanding and validity in qualitative research. *Harvard Educational Review, 62,* 279-300.

Maxwell, J. A. (1996). *Qualitative research design: An interactive approach.* Thousand Oaks, CA: Sage.

Maxwell, J. A. (1998). *Using qualitative research to develop causal explanations.* Working paper, Harvard Project on Schooling and Children, Harvard University.

Maxwell, J. A., & Mohr, L. B. (1999). *Quantitative and qualitative: A conceptual analysis.* Paper presented at the annual meeting of the American Evaluation Association, Orlando, FL.

Maxwell, J. A., Sandlow, L. J., & Bashook, P. G. (1986). Combining ethnographic and experimental methods in evaluation research: A case study. In D. M. Fetterman &

M. A. Pitman (Eds.), *Educational evaluation: Ethnography in theory, practice, and politics* (pp. 121-143). Newbury Park, CA: Sage.

McCawley, J. (1982). *Thirty million theories of grammar.* Chicago: University of Chicago Press.

Merriam-Webster. (1984). *Webster's ninth new collegiate dictionary.* Springfield, MA: Author.

Miles, M. B., & Huberman, A. M. (1994). *Qualitative research design* (2nd ed.). Thousand Oaks, CA: Sage.

Milgram, S. (1974). *Obedience to authority: An experimental view.* New York: Harper & Row.

Mohr, L. (1982). *Explaining organizational behavior.* San Francisco: Jossey-Bass.

Mohr, L. (1995). *Impact analysis for program evaluation* (2nd ed.). Thousand Oaks, CA: Sage.

Mohr, L. (1996). *The causes of human behavior: Implications for theory and method in the social sciences.* Ann Arbor: University of Michigan Press.

Patton, M. Q. (1980). *Qualitative evaluation and research methods.* Beverly Hills, CA: Sage.

Patton, M. Q. (1990). *Qualitative evaluation and research methods* (2nd ed.). Newbury Park, CA: Sage.

Pawson, R., & Tilley, N. (1997). *Realistic evaluation.* London: Sage.

Pitman, M. A., & Maxwell, J. A. (1992). Qualitative approaches to evaluation. In M. D. LeCompte, W. L. Millroy, & J. Preissle (Eds.), *The handbook of qualitative research in education* (pp. 729-770). San Diego: Academic Press.

Rabinowitz, V. C., & Weseen, S. (2001). Power, politics, and the qualitative/quantitative debates in psychology. In D. L. Tolman & M. Brydon-Miller (Eds.), *From subjects to subjectivities: A handbook of interpretive and participatory methods* (pp. 12-28). New York: New York University Press.

Reichardt, C. S., & Cook, T. D. (1979). Beyond qualitative versus quantitative methods. In T. D. Cook & C. S. Reichardt (Eds.), *Qualitative and quantitative methods in* program evaluation (pp. 7-32). Beverly Hills, CA: Sage.

Robson, C. (1993). *Real world research: A resource for social scientists and practitioner-researchers.* Oxford, UK: Blackwell.

Rogers, E. C. (1995). *Diffusion of innovations* (4th ed.). New York: Free Press

Salmon, W. C. (1984). *Scientific explanation and the causal structure of the world.* Princeton, NJ: Princeton University Press.

Salmon, W. C. (1989). Four decades of scientific explanation. In P. Kitcher & W. C. Salmon (Eds.), *Scientific explanation* (pp. 3-219). Minneapolis: University of Minnesota Press.

Salmon, W. C. (1998). *Causality and explanation.* New York: Oxford University Press.

Sayer, A. (1992). *Method in social science: A realist approach.* London: Routledge.

Sayer, A. (2000). *Realism and social science.* Thousand Oaks, CA: Sage.

Staw, B. M. (1992). Do smiles lead to sales? Comments on the Sutton/Rafaeli study. In P. Frost & R. Stablein (Eds.), *Doing exemplary research* (pp. 136-142). Newbury Park, CA: Sage.

Sutton, R. I., & Rafaeli, A. (1988). Untangling the relationship between displayed emotions and organizational sales: The case of convenience stores. *Academy of Management Journal, 31,* 461-487.

Sutton, R. I., & Rafaeli, A. (1992). How we untangled the relationship between displayed emotions and organizational sales: A tale of bickering and optimism. In P. Frost & R. Stablein (Eds.), *Doing exemplary research* (pp. 115-128). Newbury Park, CA: Sage.

Tashakkori, A., & Teddlie, C. (1998). *Mixed methodology: Combining qualitative and quantitative approaches* (Applied Social Research Methods, No. 46). Thousand Oaks, CA: Sage.

Trend, M. G. (1979). On the reconciliation of qualitative and quantitative analyses: A case study. In T. D. Cook & C. S. Reichardt (Eds.), *Qualitative and quantitative methods in evaluation research* (pp. 68-86). Newbury Park, CA: Sage. (Original work published 1978)

Tukey, J. W. (1977). *Exploratory data analysis.* Reading, MA: Addison-Wesley.

Weiss, R. S. (1994). *Learning from strangers: The art and method of qualitative interviewing.* New York: Free Press.

Yin, R. K. (1984). *Case study research: Design and methods.* Beverly Hills, CA: Sage.

10

MIXED METHODS SAMPLING STRATEGIES IN SOCIAL SCIENCE RESEARCH

◆ Elizabeth A. Kemper
Sam Stringfield
Charles Teddlie

The nature of most research conducted in the social sciences lends itself to using mixed methods research procedures. Traditional disputes among scholars oriented toward qualitative versus quantitative methods have led to an artificial separation in the discussion of the use of methods, in particular sampling methods. Both sides of such disputes are often ill-matched to the practical realities of many social science research questions. Nearly any complex research question requires more than one sampling technique and often involves both probability (i.e., representative) and purposive sampling techniques.[1]

Sampling issues are inherently practical. Scholarly decisions may be driven in part by theoretical concerns, but it is in sampling, perhaps more than anywhere else in research, that theory meets the hard realities of time and resources. The purpose of this chapter is to assist fellow scholars in planning and drawing samples that will allow the use of mixed methods studies to address significant issues in their

AUTHORS' NOTE: Sam Stringfield's participation in the writing of this chapter was supported under funding from the Office of Educational Research and Improvement, U.S. Department of Education (Grant No. OERI-R-177-D-40005). However, the opinions expressed are those of the authors and do not necessarily represent the positions or policies of the U.S. Department of Education.

chosen fields. In this chapter, we do not attempt a full examination of all the issues that have evolved in the area of sampling in the social sciences and in education. For persons interested in more detailed explorations of the fascinating world of sampling theory, we recommend Jaeger's (1984) excellent *Sampling in Education and the Social Sciences* and Henry's (1990) *Practical Sampling*. The Henry book includes a discussion of the link between sampling and internal/external validity (from the quantitative perspective), an issue also elaborated on in this chapter (together with the issues of credibility/ trustworthiness and transferability from the qualitative research perspective).

Sampling issues almost invariably force pragmatic choices. Consider, for example, the 1988 reauthorization of the legislation that annually allocates more than $7 billion of federal funds to improve the education of disadvantaged children in the United States. At the time, congressional staffers were impressed with the Perry Preschool study of the long-term effects of one intervention (Schweinhart & Weikart, 1980). The staffers were particularly impressed that the study seemed to derive explanatory power through its carefully conducted longitudinal design and its carefully matched control group. The staffers wrote into the 1988 Title I legislation a requirement for a longitudinal control group study of the effects of Title I; for this 5-year study, Congress authorized $35 million.

To many of us working in the social sciences, $35 million sounds like a veritable infinity. However, by the time the requirements written into the law were at least partially met,[2] the very sophisticated sampling specialists associated with the winning bid found themselves in the awkward position of declaring that even $35 million was not enough to cover the intent of Congress. Some of the sampling issues in what

came to be called the *Prospects* study (Puma et al., 1997) and the related *Special Strategies* studies (Stringfield et al., 1997) are discussed later in this chapter. Here, the key point is that study designers are well-advised to think carefully about sampling issues before beginning their work. If sampling challenges can consume $35 million, it is easy to imagine what they can do to the much more modest budgets of most doctoral students.

In an ideal world, a researcher would have ample access to the entire target population of persons in any area of interest with no thought to cost. In such a world, concerns with ability to generalize would be moot because the characteristics of the entire target population, and the effects of any intervention on that population, would simply be known. For practical purposes, that is rarely the case. Hence, the researcher is driven to balance issues of coverage of the topic of interest with the allocation of finite resources.

The two major political parties in the United States provide superb examples of this trade-off between the desire to know "what everybody is thinking" and finite resources. On nearly a weekly basis, and sometimes on a nightly basis, both parties fund two types of information-gathering activities. They pay for quantitative polls of 500 to 1,500 "likely to vote" citizens and conduct frequent focus groups of "swing voters" and "core constituents." They sample very carefully, attempting to obtain the most accurate estimates of shifts in public perceptions and to test possible issues and "spin" on issues so as to have the greatest chance of having their issues get "traction" among the voters.[3]

Similarly, groups interested in marketing to groups ranging from "Kmart shoppers" to "the millionaire next door" (Stanley & Danko, 1997) spend tens of millions of dollars annually trying to refine their "marketing messages." Obviously, groups ranging from candidates for the presidency of the United States, to Wal-Mart, to public health researchers not only want the best possible data but also want them at the lowest practical cost. In a very practical world, they all seek to maximize their chances of getting accurate data and to get them in the most cost-efficient ways possible. Thus, the sampling scheme used in a study becomes one of the pivotal elements on which any study—whether primarily qualitative, quantitative, or mixed method—is based.

The remainder of this chapter is divided into three sections. We first consider seven broad issues that any researcher should consider in building a sampling frame and drawing a sample. Next, we discuss issues in, and provide examples from, probability and purposive approaches to sampling. Then, we discuss issues in more complex mixed methods sampling schemes, again providing examples as we go.

◆ General Issues in Sampling

There are many ways to achieve an elegant study that convincingly addresses an important question. On the other hand, there are three ways to guarantee the failure of an otherwise potentially strong study. The first is to structure a question so that it cannot be empirically addressed and/or a hypothesis that cannot be disproved (see Newman, Ridenour, Newman, & DeMarco, Chapter 6, this volume). The second is to choose measures and analytical tools that cannot provide sufficiently relevant and reliable data (see Johnson & Turner, Chapter 11, this volume). The third is to choose a sample that is (a) unlikely to allow strong (internally valid and credible) conclusions related to the initially posed questions and (b) unlikely to allow the research team to transfer/

generalize the conclusions to other desired settings or populations (e.g., Tashakkori & Teddlie, 1998).

In research, sampling is destiny.

Building on the work of Miles and Huberman (1994), Curtis, Gesler, Smith, and Washburn (2000) suggested that a sampling strategy should be based on six guidelines. Although the original intent of these recommendations was in consideration of qualitative data analysis, these standards provide excellent guidance when developing any sampling scheme, be it single method or mixed methods. The following five statements summarize the Curtis et al. guidelines; Statement 3 combines two of the original guidelines.

1. *The sampling strategy should stem logically from the conceptual framework as well as from the research questions being addressed by the study.* Is the sampling strategy in line with the conceptual ideas that underlie the study? Would the sampling frame, if achieved, logically assist in gathering data focused on the hypothesis under investigation? In short, does the sampling scheme allow at least a potentially valid means by which to answer the research questions under study?

2. *The sample should be able to generate a thorough database on the type of phenomena under study.* This item concerns the scope of the data that are to be collected. Is it adequate to answer the research questions under study? Is the sampling scheme sufficiently focused to allow a researcher to actually gather data needed to answer the research questions? If the intention of the study is purely descriptive, is the planned sample likely to provide sufficient data to produce a rich, textured, triangulated description? If the intention of the study is comparative, does the sampling scheme provide clear contrasts along the dimension(s) of interest while holding

potentially confounding variables as constant as practical?

3. *The sample should at least allow the possibility of drawing clear inferences from the data; the sample should allow for credible explanations.* From the quantitative design perspective, these inferences are referred to as internal validity or the degree to which one can be confident that changes in an outcome variable (effect) can be attributed to a preceding variable (cause) rather than to other potential causal factors (Cook & Campbell, 1979). Sampling decisions should help to eliminate other potential causal factors. For example, control and experimental samples should be drawn so that they are as similar to one another as possible so as to eliminate other possible causal factors.

Credibility is the concept that some qualitative researchers have used to substitute for internal validity, and it refers to the degree to which the researcher's reconstructions of reality are *"credible to the constructors of the original multiple realities"* (Lincoln & Guba, 1985, p. 296, italics in original).[4] Credibility is determined by a number of techniques such as "member checks" in which researchers ask study participants to assess the researchers' interpretations. The "checkers" should consist of an appropriate (representative) sample of all those who participated in the study so as to ensure that the participants do, in fact, agree with the interpretations of the researchers.

4. *The sampling strategy must be ethical.* Consideration of this element includes very important concerns as to whether participants can give informed consent regarding participation, the possible costs and benefits to the participants, and the need for absolute assurances that any promised confidentiality can be maintained.

5. *The sampling plan should be feasible.* Can the researcher actually access all of the data? Is the selected sampling method congruent with the abilities of the researcher?

We add the following two new guidelines to this list.

6. *The sampling plan should allow the research team to transfer/generalize the conclusions of the study to other settings or populations.* From the qualitative design perspective, transferability refers to the degree to which results may be applied from the sending context (where the research took place) to the receiving context (where the results are to be applied) (e.g., Lincoln & Guba, 1985; Tashakkori & Teddlie, 1998). It is analogous to the concept of generalizability (or external validity) in the quantitative design perspective; generalizability concerns whether or not the sample adequately represents the population (or elements of the population) to which results may be applied.

In research with a more qualitative focus, this guideline dictates that the researcher knows (with some confidence) "about *both* sending and receiving contexts" (Lincoln & Guba, 1985, p. 297, italics in original). In research with a more quantitative focus, this guideline would most likely be read as a recommendation to increase sample size and particularly methods of ensuring that all participants have an equal (or, in different designs, a weighted-equal) probability of participating so as to ensure a representative sample. Both quantitative and qualitative methodologists would take additional steps to ensure that the elements within the sample are the most appropriate with regard to the question under study.

7. *The sampling scheme should be as efficient as practical.* One of the ways to address several of the preceding questions is

to repeatedly expand the sample. However, every expansion of the sample requires the allocation of resources away from depth of data gathering so as to further achieve breadth. As noted previously, it is relatively easy to create a sampling frame that cannot be fulfilled for $35 million; obviously, this is not a practical solution for most researchers. Are there sampling schemes that better focus the always finite energies of the research team on the core question(s) of the study? In sampling, these are known as issues of efficiency.

Choosing a sampling scheme is seldom uncomplicated. Decisions about samples—both sample size and sampling strategies—depend on prior decisions with regard to questions asked, instruments/methods chosen, and resources available. Once a decision is made with regard to the type of sampling strategy that will be used, the ability to make inferences (internal validity/trustworthiness) and the degree of external validity/transferability of the findings can be determined. In effect, the sampling scheme sets an *upper boundary* on the internal validity/trustworthiness and external validity/transferability of the research project.[5]

The following section briefly discusses probability and purposive sampling techniques and explores the application of mixed methods research applications with regard to sampling strategies.

◆ Probability and Purposive Sampling Techniques

Sampling techniques can be divided into two types: probability sampling and purposive sampling. Purely quantitative studies typically use larger samples selected through probability techniques, while qualitative studies typically use smaller samples selected through purposive techniques. However, neither purposive nor probability sampling techniques are the sole domain of either research tradition. Any study, whether single method or mixed methods, can use any of a variety of sampling techniques or can blend probability and purposive sampling techniques to answer the research question under study.[6]

Table 10.1, derived from Tashakkori and Teddlie (1998), outlines the most frequently used sampling techniques, which are discussed in the following subsections.

PROBABILITY SAMPLING

One of the goals of research that uses probability sampling techniques is generalizability[7] (external validity) or the ability to extrapolate findings from a subset of a population or particular setting to a larger defined population of people (population validity) or settings (ecological validity). This ability rests on three assumptions: (a) that the number of selected units is large enough for the random errors to cancel each other out (Tashakkori & Teddlie, 1998); (b) that the distribution of the population under study is normal, or at least knowable, so that sampling can proceed in accordance with that distribution; and (c) that a sample can and will be drawn that is large enough to plausibly produce a reasonable estimate of the population at large. The violation of any of these assumptions will severely limit the usefulness of inferences made about the population at large.

The following subsections discuss the main approaches to probability sampling that, although typically associated with more quantitative research, could be applicable to qualitative studies and clearly have relevance to mixed methods studies

TABLE 10.1   Probability and Purposive Sampling Techniques

Probability Sampling Techniques	Purposive Sampling Techniques[a]
1. Simple random sampling	Convenience sampling
2. Systematic random sampling	Extreme/deviant case sampling
3. Stratified random sampling	Confirming/disconfirming cases and typical case sampling
Proportional	Homogeneous case sampling
Nonproportional	Stratified purposive sampling and random purposive sampling
4. Cluster random sampling	Opportunistic and snowball sampling

a. Additional purposive sampling techniques are described by Patton (1990) and include intensity sampling, maximum variation sampling, critical case sampling, criterion sampling, operational construct sampling, and sampling politically important cases.

(see Cells 1, 2, and 3 in Table 10.2 later in the chapter).

Simple Random Sampling. A *simple random sample* is one is which each person or unit in the clearly defined population has an equal chance of being included in the sample. To select a simple random sample, the technique can be as straightforward as drawing names out of a hat or as complex as using a computerized table of random numbers to draw a sample from the population at large. The advantage of this method is that the research data can be generalized from the sample to the entire population within a computable margin of error. A disadvantage of this method is that the selected units might be spread over a large geographic area, making them very difficult to reach. An example would be selecting 300 students randomly from the population of 10th-grade students in Atlanta, Georgia.

Systematic Random Sampling. Systematic *random sampling* techniques involve se-

lecting every *n*th unit of the target population from a randomly ordered list of the population. This method should be used only if the researcher is certain that the population list is not ordered in such a way that every *n*th unit results in a sample that is different from the population at large. For example, if every 10th person on a list is a group leader, then either the list should be reordered or a simple random sampling technique should be used. The advantage of employing a systematic sampling technique is that it is slightly easier to use than a simple random sampling technique; however, each member of the sample is not chosen independently because as soon as the first member is selected, the other members of the sample are determined as well.

Stratified Random Sampling (proportional and nonproportional). A *stratified random sample* is obtained by separating the population elements into groups, or strata, such that each element belongs to a single stratum. The research team then

> **BOX 10.1**
> **Nonproportional Stratified Random Sampling**
>
> Capraro, Capraro, and Wiggins (2000) conducted a study to investigate the effects of gender, socioeconomic status, race, and grades on standardized test scores. Using the National Educational Longitudinal Study of Eight Graders (NELS 88, which consists of 1,500 students), a random sample of 180 students consisting of 30 Black males, 30 Black females, 30 White males, 30 White females, 30 Hispanic males, and 30 Hispanic females was generated. This sampling logic provided the research team with equal statistical power in examining effects on three ethnic groups by two genders. Given the questions in the study, the researchers were able to sample in a way that ignored the fact that the larger population of American youths is not, in fact, so neatly divided.

independently selects a random sample from each stratum. In proportional stratified random sampling, the proportion of the units randomly selected from each stratum is the same as the proportion in the target population. In nonproportional stratified sampling, the number of units selected from each stratum is typically the same, regardless of the relative proportion in the target population (see Box 10.1).

Cluster Sampling and Multistage Cluster Sampling. Cluster sampling is most appropriate when the sampling unit is not an individual but rather a group that is naturally occurring in the population such as neighborhoods, city blocks, schools, classrooms, or families. Instead of taking a random simple within each group (as in stratified random sampling), in cluster sampling a random sample of groups within the population is first performed. *Multistage cluster sampling* allows the sample to be further reduced by selecting a random sample from the selected cluster. Several sampling stages might be carried out to select the participants ultimately chosen to participate in the sample (see Box 10.2).

PURPOSIVE (NONPROBABILITY) SAMPLING

Purposive or nonprobability samples are samples in which the researcher uses some criterion or purpose to replace the principle of canceled random errors. A list of these purposive sampling techniques was presented in Table 10.1 (and the note associated with that table). Several of these techniques are discussed in more detail in the rest of this section.

"The logic and power of purposive sampling lies in selecting information-rich cases for study in depth" (Patton, 1990, p. 169), with an underlying focus on intentionally selecting specific cases that will provide the most information for the questions under study. Researchers using random sampling techniques often seek to maximize the sample size so as to increase the probability of making accurate generalizations from the data. In contrast, researchers using purposive techniques seek to focus and, where practical, minimize the sample size, generally in nonrandom ways, so as to select only those cases that might best illuminate and test the hypothesis of the research team. Although pur-

---

BOX 10.2
Multistage Cluster Sampling

Vega, Alderete, Kolody, and Aguilar-Gaxioler (1998) used a multistage cluster sampling method in a study examining illicit drug use among Mexicans and Mexican Americans in California. The target population was Mexicans and Mexican Americans between 18 and 59 years of age in Fresno County, California. The county population is approximately 764,800, with 463,600 located in the Fresno-Clovis metropolitan area; of this, Hispanics constitute 38.3% of the total county population. From this population, 3,012 people were to be selected, stratified by urbanicity. During the first stage of the sampling process, the sampling units within each stratum (urban, rural, and town) was determined based on census blocks or block aggregates. A total of 200 sampling units within each stratum were selected with a probability proportionately based on the size of their Hispanic population. During the second stage, a quota of five households was randomly selected from each sampling unit. During the third and final stage, 1 person from each household was randomly selected to complete the survey. This resulted in a final sample of 3,012 respondents (1,006 urban respondents, 1,006 town respondents, and 1,000 rural respondents).

---

posive sampling techniques are commonly associated with qualitative methods, purposive sampling can be used within studies with either a qualitative or a quantitative orientation and are quite common in mixed methods studies (see Cells 4, 5, and 6 in Table 10.2 later in the chapter). Several of the most commonly used purposive sampling techniques are discussed in the following subsections.

Convenience Sampling. Convenience sampling, which involves drawing elements from a group (usually most appropriately regarded as a subpopulation) that is easily accessible by the researcher is one of the most commonly used purposive sampling techniques. Due to the researcher focusing on an easily accessible or volunteer population, these elements are often not the most appropriate to answer the research question under study. Although convenience samples offer relatively low cost and ease of access, such sampling very often results in spurious conclusions and

hence is rarely the sampling method of preference (see Box 10.3).

Extreme/Deviant Case and Typical Case Sampling Techniques. Extreme/deviant case sampling and *typical case sampling* are similar in that both techniques are designed to find cases that best illuminate the research question at hand. Extreme/deviant case sampling involves seeking out the most outstanding cases, or the most extreme successes and/or failures, so as to learn as much as possible about the outliers. Typical case sampling seeks those cases that are the most average or representative of the question under study.

The *Special Strategies* studies (Stringfield et al., 1997) were mixed methods research projects conducted to provide detailed case studies of schools making exemplary use of Title I funds. The study design called for the identification of reform efforts that had been implemented in multiple sites and either had prior evidence of effectiveness or were being imple-

BOX 10.3
Convenience Sampling

The famous "Kinsey Report," actually titled *Sexual Behavior in the Human Male* (Kinsey, 1948), created a sensation when it was first released to the public. In this remarkable 804-page study, Alfred Kinsey explicitly detailed results from his carefully detailed interviews of thousands of American males. The Kinsey Report appeared to demonstrate that, rather than being puritanical, the average American male of the 1940s was highly sexually active, often in quite colorful ways and with a wide range of partners. The study seemed to draw extraordinary strength from the fact that Kinsey himself had conducted hundreds of the interviews all across the country. However, as the science of sampling evolved over subsequent decades, scholars revisited Kinsey's methods and noted that he had obtained his sample through the device of taking a train into a new city and running an advertisement in the local newspapers, inviting males to be interviewed about their sexual activities. It does not require a great leap of imagination to conclude that the more than 99% of citizens in each city who did not volunteer to be interviewed were, on average, less sexually active (or, at least, with fewer partners) than the less than 1% of citizens who, self-selected through answering a newspaper advertisement asking them to talk about their sex lives, volunteered for the study. In the end, while the Kinsey Report made a major contribution to getting a nation's people to talk about the sexual aspects of their existence, it made very little contribution to scholars' understanding of the sex lives of average Americans. In spite of the considerable fiscal investment, the sample of convenience seemed unlikely to be representative of the population about which Kinsey had attempted to generalize.

mented very widely. (Note that by either definition, the sampling frame for the study would be restricted to atypical schools.) A total of 10 reform models were eventually chosen. Examples of selected reform models were Title I schoolwide projects, Success for All (Slavin & Madden, 2001), and the Coalition of Essential Schools (Sizer, 1992).

For each model, a national search was undertaken to identify very strong implementations (the design sought "exemplary" sites, not "typical" ones). Design teams, state Title I directors, regional educational laboratories, and others were asked for nominations. A total of 25 final sites (purposefully stratified so that 12 were urban and 13 were suburban or rural) were selected only after they had received multiple nominations as being exemplary implementations of their respective reforms. The sampling scheme did not allow for statements about typical schools, or even typical implementations of the various reforms, but it did enhance the possibility that the research effort would identify and study strong implementations of the various reform efforts, as specified in the federal grant (see Box 10.4).

Confirming/Disconfirming Cases Sampling Techniques. The goal of using *confirming/ disconfirming cases sampling techniques* is either to find specific sampling units that already fit into emerging patterns

---

BOX 10.4
Extreme Case Sampling

Raywid (1999) conducted a case study using extreme case sampling on a high school to examine the components and qualities that combined to make the school successful. Over the past 10 years, the school selected, Central Park East Secondary in East Harlem, New York City, had received numerous awards, had been the subject of several research articles, and had a history of unusual educational success. This school was the ideal case to examine how a school can become successful when the odds are against success. Thus, the sampling unit in this case was the school, with the number of units in the study equal to one.

---

regarding the data (confirming cases) or to seek those cases that are exceptions or provide rival explanations to the emerging patterns (disconfirming cases) (see Box 10.5).

Homogeneous Cases Sampling. Homogeneous cases sampling seeks to pick elements from a particular subgroup to study in-depth. Studies that employ focus group interviews typically use this method because the goal is usually to gather opinions from people who are demographically, educationally, or professionally similar (see Box 10.6).

Stratified Purposive (Quota) and Random Purposive Sampling Techniques. Stratified purposive sampling involves dividing the purposefully selected target population into strata (e.g., above average, average, below average) with the goal of discovering elements that are similar or different across the subgroups. *Random purposive sampling* involves taking a random sample of units in the purposefully selected target population. The logic behind using random sampling with purposive sampling is to add trustworthiness, and not generalizability, to the findings. Sample size in qualitative studies is typically too small to allow the results to be representative of an entire population, but randomization of the selection does offer an explanation as to why certain cases were excluded as well as a systematic method to make the sample manageable (see Box 10.7).

BOX 10.5
Confirming Cases

Shields and Foster (1989) used a confirming cases sampling methodology in their mixed method study exploring the emotional stereotyping of parents in child-rearing manuals. Six separate and distinct time periods were identified with regard to sociocultural conditions, and the 54 books that fit the research criteria for the study were evaluated in terms of the era in which each manual was written and whether passages pertaining to parental emotion fit into the era in which the manual was written.

BOX 10.6
Homogeneous Cases Sampling

Silverstien, Auerback, Grieco, and Dunkel (1999) conducted a study of fathers who were members of the organization "Promise Keepers" to gather data about fathering experiences. A contact within the Promise Keepers group recruited members for three of the focus groups; another contact with the National Center for Fathering in Kansas City, Missouri, supplied the names of two members in the New York City area, who in turn recruited the members for the final focus group. The final sample consisted of 22 middle-class, primarily White suburban fathers, all of whom were members of the Promise Keepers organization.

Opportunistic and Snowball Sampling. *Opportunistic and snowball sampling* techniques both involve taking advantage of circumstances and events as they arise while undergoing the data collection process. Opportunistic sampling involves taking opportunities as they come along and following up on leads as they arise within fieldwork. Snowball sampling involves using informants to identify cases that would be useful to include in the study. Both of these methods use insider knowledge to maximize the chance that the units included in the final sample are strong (highly appropriate) cases to include in the study (see Box 10.8).

◆ The Necessity of Mixed Methods Sampling Strategies

The sampling techniques that have been discussed thus far have been presented in isolation. Many of the research topics under study in the social sciences are quite complex and require a combination of sampling techniques to adequately explore the phenomena of interest. As discussed elsewhere in this volume and in other texts, the use of mixed methods sampling strategies can greatly strengthen the research design of most studies in the social and behavioral sciences.

BOX 10.7
Stratified Purposive Sampling

Ezzy, Bartos, de Visser, and Rosenthal (1998) used a stratified purposive sampling technique in their study of attitudinal, medical, and cultural correlates on the use of antiviral drugs by persons living with HIV or AIDS. A sample of 925 persons living with either AIDS or HIV was recruited through HIV/AIDS organizations, hospitals, doctors' offices, mailing lists of HIV-related materials, and a targeted advertising campaign. The participants were stratified based on their HIV/AIDS status because one of the purposes of the study was to differentiate between the perceptions of those participants who had experienced an AIDS-related illness and the perceptions of those who had not.

BOX 10.8
Snowball Sampling

Scannell-Desch (2000) conducted a study to examine the hardships faced by female nurses in Vietnam. The population under investigation consisted of female registered nurses who were able to discuss their experiences as active duty military personnel assigned to Vietnam during the Vietnam War. Because neither the Department of Defense nor veterans agencies maintain a list of Vietnam War nurses, the investigator began with 5 nurses who met the sample criteria and used them to generate lists of other potential participants. The final sample consisted of 24 nurses (9 army nurses, 8 navy nurses, and 7 air force nurses).

Mixed methods research designs often create a multifaceted view of the research questions (Minger, 2001), allow for the triangulation of data sources (Patton, 1990), and potentially facilitate the creation of stronger inferences than do single method research studies (Tashakkori & Teddlie, 1998). Mixed methods studies are becoming increasingly popular, especially because they "are often more efficient in answering research questions than either the QUAL [qualitative] or the QUAN [quantitative] approach alone" (p. 167).

Mixed methods studies frequently require mixed methods sampling procedures so as to simultaneously increase inference quality (internal validity and trustworthiness) and generalizability/ transferability. To do this, there is often a need for two types of samples: a probability sample (to increase generalizability/ transferability) and a purposive sample (to increase inference quality).

Cell 9 in Table 10.2 is the most frequently used sampling procedure (mixed methods sampling) for mixed methods studies, although Cell 3 (probability sampling only) and Cell 6 (purposive sampling only) are used occasionally to generate

mixed data. In sequential mixed methods studies, information from the first sample (typically derived from a probability sampling procedure) is often required so as to draw the second sample (typically derived from a purposive sampling procedure). For example, the selection of certain individuals (nurses) for focus group interviews may be based on an initial survey of randomly selected nurses in Chicago. The second sample (for the focus group research) is selected because there is a need to interview a certain type of nurse, who was operationally defined based on information from the survey responses from the first sample.

This combination of probability (first) and purposive (second) sampling procedures is a very powerful (and fairly common) type of mixed methods sampling strategy. It is employed often in equivialent-status sequential designs (i.e., QUAN/QUAL) in which both types of methods are given equal weight, as typically seen in dissertation research conducted in educational settings. In these studies, a probability sample is drawn first to test hypotheses based on the extant literature. Then, a purposive sample is selected from the probability sample to

TABLE 10.2 Matrix Crossing Type of Sampling Technique by Type of Data Generated

Type of Sampling Technique	Generation of Quantitative Data Only	Generation of Qualitative Data Only	Generation of Both Qualitative and Quantitative Data
Probability sampling techniques	Happens often (Cell 1)	Happens rarely (Cell 2)	Happens occasionally (Cell 3)
Purposive sampling techniques	Happens rarely (Cell 4)	Happens often (Cell 5)	Happens occasionally (Cell 6)
Mixed methods sampling strategies	Happens occasionally (Cell 7)	Happens occasionally (Cell 8)	Happens often (Cell 9)

assess research questions that go beyond what is known in the current literature.

A CAVEAT CONCERNING TYPE OF SAMPLING TECHNIQUE AND TYPE OF DATA GENERATED IN THE STUDY

Probability sampling techniques are often associated with the quantitative research tradition and, therefore, the generation of numerical data. On the other hand, purposive sampling techniques are often associated with the qualitative research tradition and, therefore, the generation of narrative data. Nevertheless, quantitative data can be generated in a study that has a purposive sampling procedure, and qualitative data can be gener-

ated in a study that has a probability sampling procedure.

Table 10.2 presents a matrix that crosses type of sampling technique (probability, purposive, or mixed) by type of data generated by the study (quantitative only, qualitative only, or mixed). This 3×3 matrix illustrates that certain types of sampling techniques are more frequently associated with certain types of data: probability samples with quantitative data (Cell 1), purposive samples with qualitative data (Cell 5), and mixed samples with mixed data (Cell 9). The diagonal cells (Cells 1, 5, and 9) represent the most frequently occurring combinations of sampling techniques and types of data generated. Despite these general tendencies, there are other conditions where sampling techniques occasionally (Cells 3, 6,

---

BOX 10.9
Combining Sampling Strategies (single method)

Morgan, Yang, and Greigo (1998) used a parallel measures approach to examine the relationship of mastery motivation to aggression and hyperactivity in preschool children. Study I used a homogeneous purposive sampling technique to recruit families of 332 3- to 5-year-old twins from a twin registry in a western state. Study II consisted of secondary analysis of the Bethesda Longitudinal Study drawn from a random sample within the database. The analysis of data from both studies was purely quantitative.

7, and 8) or rarely (Cells 2 and 4) are associated with studies that generate different types of data.

A COMPARISON OF SINGLE METHOD AND MIXED METHODS SAMPLING PROCEDURES

It is important to note that some researchers believe that the mixing of methods (QUAL, QUAN) poses a serious threat to the validity of their research because inherent assumptions of the modalities are violated when the techniques are combined (see Morse, Chapter 7, this volume). These researchers believe that they should keep their methods separate and compare across the results of single method studies. The following two research examples explore both this single method approach and the mixed methods approach (advocated throughout this chapter and most of this volume) to using both probability and purposive sampling techniques (see Boxes 10.9 and 10.10).

Study I from Box 10.9 is representative of Cell 4 in Table 10.2, while Study II is representative of Cell 1. Both studies generated quantitative data only and are, therefore, representative of single method studies. The sampling procedures and data described in Box 10.10 both are thoroughly mixed and are, therefore, representative of Cell 9 in Table 10.2.

◆ Designing Multilevel Mixed Methods Studies

Multilevel approaches are used in both qualitative and quantitative modes of inquiry. By definition, multilevel research designs use data collected from multiple levels within an organization or group so as to increase the power of inferences drawn from the data.

A multilevel study may or may not be mixed methods in design. Tashakkori and Teddlie (1998) defined "designs with a multilevel use of approaches" (p. 18) as a fifth type of mixed methods design (in addition to sequential, parallel/simultaneous, equivalent status, and dominant-less dominant designs). Sampling strategies conducted in educational settings are often "naturally" mixed because the levels of schooling are "deeply nested" (e.g., student within classroom within grade within school within district within state within country). It is likely that studies conducted within such nested settings will call for probability samples for at least one level and purposive samples for at least one level.

BOX 10.10
Combining Sampling Strategies (mixed method)

Kemper and Teddlie (2000) investigated the level of implementation of a state-mandated, site-based decision-making program in Texas. The target population of the central Texas region consisted of 111 high schools in 60 school districts. Using a nonproportional stratified random sampling procedure, the authors selected 30 schools (10 urban, 10 rural, and 10 suburban), from the target population, with a final sample of 19 schools from 15 school districts that actually participated during all stages of the study. Phase 1 of the study focused on the examination of district-level procedures (qualitative). The next two phases focused on the school level, with Phase 2 examining principal practices (using qualitative interviews) and Phase 3 examining teacher perceptions (with a quantitative survey instrument) with regard to program implementation. To select schools to be studied more in-depth, the final phase of the study used both the quantitative and qualitative data collected during the first three phases of the study to select a stratified purposive sample, identifying schools as "typical," "better," or "poor" implementers and then selecting the 6 schools from the original 19 schools (1 urban, 1 rural, and 1 suburban "typical" implementer; 1 urban, 1 rural, and 1 suburban "better" implementer) that were profiled in case studies.

The following four research examples describe a purely qualitative multilevel approach and its sampling implications, a purely quantitative multilevel approach and its sampling implications, and two multilevel mixed methods approaches and their sampling implications. *Multilevel mixed sampling* occurs when probability and purposive sampling techniques are used on different levels of the study (e.g., student, class, school, district) (see Boxes 10.11 and 10.12).

MULTILEVEL MIXED METHODS SAMPLING STUDIES, EXAMPLE 1: THE PROSPECTS STUDY

The *Prospects* study (Puma et al., 1997), briefly described in the introduction to this chapter, was an example of a complex, multilevel mixed methods effort to gather highly policy-relevant data on Title I effectiveness. To address congressional concerns about the overall effectiveness of Title I, and to provide contrasts between effectiveness in four geographic areas of the country and between effects on diverse ethnic populations, the design called for gathering 5 years of data on three cohorts of students. The first cohort began first grade during the fall of 1991 and was to be followed through fourth grade. The second cohort began fourth grade during the fall of 1991 and was to be followed through eighth grade. The final cohort began ninth grade during the fall of 1991 and was to be followed through high school graduation.

When constructing the sampling frame, the contractors, working with the U.S. Department of Education and congressional staffers, decided that every Title I (and plausible control) student in the United States had to have a statistically real chance of being selected into the study.

BOX 10.11
A Purely Qualitative Multilevel Study

Datnow and Castellano (2000) conducted a multilevel qualitative study examining two schools implementing the Success for All (SFA) school reform model. The two schools in the study were purposely selected based on a combination of predetermined sampling criteria (one school implementing SFA for 2 or more years experiencing success with program implementation and one school implementing SFA for 2 or more years experiencing difficulty with program implementation) and the recommendation of SFA trainers who work with SFA schools in a five-state region that includes California. The first level of data collection occurred at the school level, in which the principal, SFA program facilitators, and teachers at the two schools were interviewed. The second level of data collection occurred at the classroom level, in which 49 observations of English and bilingual Spanish classrooms were conducted during the 90-minute SFA reading period.

Given that there are more than 2 million children in Title I and there were to be only 25,000 children in *Prospects*, statistically real did not mean statistically likely. It did mean, for example, that every single one of the more than 800 local education authorities (LEAs) in Montana had to be kept in the sampling pool, no matter how much it would cost to visit one of them versus the cost of visiting one of 26 LEAs in Maryland. This constraint was left in even though the research team and the Department of Education oversight team all knew quite well that there were fewer children in all of Montana and Wyoming combined than in half of any borough of New York City. Congress wanted to know that every child had an at least theoretical chance of being involved in the study, and the sampling frame had to be—and was—designed accordingly.

Because Congress wanted to have regional comparisons, the first layer of sampling within *Prospects* was region, for which the nation was divided into four roughly equal quadrants. Although each student would have a different weighting for the purposes of estimating national effectiveness, for sampling purposes, equal numbers of schools and students were

---

BOX 10.12
A Purely Quantitative Multilevel Study

Twigg, Moon, and Jones (2000) employed an alternative method from traditional survey sampling to predict health-related behavior, specifically smoking and drinking indicators. The authors used routinely available data from the annual Health Survey for England ($N = 17,000$) and the decennial population census to construct a multilevel modeling approach nesting individuals within area code sectors within health authorities and focusing on the prediction of the prevalence of smoking and problem drinking as related to geographic area and health authority.

drawn from each region. The contractors next conducted a stratified sampling (by socioeconomic status) of LEAs within regions and then stratified schools within the chosen LEAs based on percentages of students receiving free or reduced-price lunch rates within schools. From the two sets of schools remaining in each district, the contractors chose one relatively high-poverty (Title I) elementary school, one relatively low-poverty elementary school, and one high school. Where possible, the high schools were chosen because they were "fed" by the elementary schools. Finally, by agreement with the Department of Education, the sampling team chose all of the students in the first, fourth, and ninth grades at the chosen schools within the chosen districts.

Within each LEA, questionnaires were completed annually by the superintendent, the Title I director, the four principals, the age cohort of students, the students' parents, and the teachers (including Title I teachers) working with the cohort of students moving through each selected school. In addition, a norm-referenced test was administered to the cohort of students as it moved through the grades. Hence, the *Prospects* research team attempted to gather quantitative data at six levels over 5 years on more than 25,000 students.

In addition, the research team faced a second congressional mandate, and that was to gather data on diverse promising programs. At the time the study was funded, the total numbers of schools engaged in various Title I-funded whole school reforms was probably in the hundreds. This means that in a national population of nearly 100,000 schools, the probability of drawing 25 schools engaged in, for example, Title I whole school projects, or the Comer School Development Program, was virtually zero. Therefore, the sample was enhanced with 25 schools drawn using the extreme case

sampling methods described earlier in the chapter. All 25 schools were followed using all of the *Prospects* quantitative measures; in addition, 3 years of intensive, qualitative case study data gathering was conducted at each site. This "sister study" was the *Special Strategies* studies described earlier in the chapter.

The result was a longitudinal, multilevel mixed methods study, with quantitative data gathered in virtually every state and qualitative data gathered at 25 sites in more than a dozen states. Not only did this effort inform subsequent reauthorizations of Title I, but the *Special Strategies* studies played an important role in Congress's decision to provide funding for thousands of schools around the nation attempting to engage in multiyear, research-based, whole school reform efforts.

MULTILEVEL MIXED METHODS SAMPLING STUDIES, EXAMPLE 2: SEEKING MAXIMUM EFFICIENCY THROUGH THE LOUISIANA SCHOOL EFFECTIVENESS STUDY

Earlier, we noted that Congress allocated $35 million for the *Prospects* study. It is unlikely that any of us will ever see the year when even one-tenth of 1% of studies in the social sciences are blessed with such large budgets. Our progress therefore lies in no small part on our ability to design intellectually and practically valuable studies on a small fraction of that budget. In the introduction to this chapter, we noted the importance of seeking efficiency in sampling. The first step toward this was the clear specification of a question in such a way that scholars could choose methods and samples to address the issue. The second was the careful choice of a design and instruments, and the third was efficient sampling.

The Louisiana School Effectiveness Study (LSES) (Teddlie & Stringfield, 1993) was a multistage effort to take those three steps so as to address a variety of clearly specified questions in the area of school effectiveness. Given limited human and fiscal resources, the study was designed to be conducted in phases. The first two phases generated completely quantitative data. A pilot study was conducted in one district to gain an estimate of whether such a study was indeed possible in Louisiana and, if so, at what cost. The team determined that questionnaires could be developed and administered and that the pilot results were, at the least, encouraging.

The second phase of the study (LSES-II) was essentially a "scaling up" of LSES-I. A sample of 76 schools that served a population that was highly representative of the state was chosen for this phase. A three-stage sampling process was undertaken to arrive at this sample. The first stage involved the decision to focus on the third grade. (This was a purposive criterion sampling decision, with the criterion being that the grade level studied in each of the 76 schools was the third grade.) The belief of the research team was that by third grade, students' scores on the state-mandated achievement test were reasonably stable. Furthermore, the state had few examples of third grade being served in a middle school, and so full years of "school effects" that were unconfounded by academic efforts from earlier grades/schools were potentially measurable by third grade. Second, a representative subset of school districts from the state was sampled. This was done so as to retain representativeness while concentrating the research team's scarce research resources within bounded areas. (This involved a combination of both cluster sampling and purposive typical case sampling, whereby 12 school districts were selected, first, because each one represented a naturally occurring group of schools and, second, because they collectively represented a good cross section of the state.) Third, the sample of 76 schools was drawn; taking care to ensure that the final sample was representative of the larger state in terms of socioeconomic status, racial makeup, and schools' histories of academic achievement. (This involved a complex, stratified random sampling technique in which each of the 270 schools with third grade classrooms in the 12 districts in the study was assigned a probability of being selected based on the stratum to which it belonged.) Thus, the sampling scheme for LSES-II was purposive at the district and grade levels, while it was probability based at the district and school levels.

One of the conclusions drawn by the research team from the second phase was that the complexity of issues determining schools' levels of effectiveness was unlikely to be fully understood through purely quantitative questionnaire-and-test methods. Therefore, LSES-III was designed as a mixed methods, extreme/deviant contrasting case study (with other purposive and probability sampling techniques embedded in the sampling procedure, as noted later). The research questions concerned the characteristics of more versus less effective elementary schools in the state. Methods included the administration of questionnaires and achievement tests, the gathering of archival data (successfully used in LSES-II), and the addition of detailed classroom observations and qualitative case studies on a smaller set of schools. Given the obvious expense (in terms of both time and money) involved in creating detailed case studies, a premium was placed on efficient sampling.

The research team was aware that there was some concern in the extant literature regarding the stability of school effects. Therefore, the sample was drawn meeting the following criteria:

1. All schools had to be outliers on third-grade achievement as measured on the state's criterion-referenced test, after controlling for free lunch percentages and school demographics. (This is an example of purposive intensity sampling.)

2. Where outliers were found, there had to be an opposite-direction outlier within the same district (or contiguous, small, rural districts). (This is an example of purposive criterion sampling.)

3. A pair of schools from a large urban school district (which had not been in the LSES-II sample) was added because it contained the largest city in the state. (This is an example of sampling politically important cases.)

4. Each school of the resulting pair had to be an extreme positive (or negative) outlier during at least 1 of the 2 prior years and at least a moderate outlier during the other of the 2 previous years. In other words, the school's "effectiveness status" had to be relatively stable. (This is an example of purposive extreme/deviant case sampling.)

5. The sample was nonproportionally stratified to include three urban, three suburban, and three rural matched pairs. (After on-site visitations began, it was later discovered that one school in one pair included an anomalous "magnet school" component that its matched school lacked, and that pair was dropped from the sample.) (This is an example of purposive nonproportional stratified sampling.)

6. Prior to making final inclusion decisions, the research team contacted local directors of testing, research, and evalu-ation to obtain triangulating confirmation of each school's and pair's status from sources who the research team presumed had access to much richer and often informal data on specific schools. Once confirmation was obtained, a pair was entered into the final sample. (This is an example of purposive confirming case sampling.)

7. One of the most important aspects of LSES-III was that it involved a teacher effectiveness study within a school effectiveness research project. Teddlie and colleagues (Teddlie, Kirby, & Stringfield, 1989; Teddlie & Stringfield, 1993) were interested in determining whether more effective teaching was actually ongoing in schools designated as more effective. To this end, they sampled third-grade classrooms performing observations of the quality of teaching ongoing in these classrooms. A total of 48 1-hour classroom observations occurred at each school during LSES-III; therefore, more than 750 hours of observation occurred during that phase of the study. A stratified random selection process was used, whereby one half of the observations occurred at the third-grade level and one half occurred at all other grade levels. Only core subjects were observed (reading, mathematics, science, and social studies). A master schedule for each school was used that contained the teaching schedule for each regular education teacher in the school. Two lists were drawn; one consisted of only the third-grade teachers and the times they taught the core subjects, while the other consisted of all the other regular education teachers and the times they taught core subjects. Classroom observations were then chosen based on a systematic random sampling technique from each list.

The eventual result of this careful sampling procedure was a low-cost, 11-year study (the study continued over two more phases following the same sample of schools) of 16 purposively chosen schools, with hundreds of hours of classroom observations based on a stratified random sampling scheme. This study is a prototype of a multilevel, mixed methods sampling strategy, with the school level employing purposive sampling techniques and the classroom level using a probability-based sampling strategy.

The study has offered more insights into the long-term impacts of school stability and change and the effects on those processes on student achievement than have studies costing more than 100 times as much. There were several features that made such contributions possible on a very modest budget, but one of them was very careful thinking about a sampling frame and very careful choice of the 16-school sample employed in LSES-III.

◆ Conclusion

This chapter has presented the most commonly employed probability and purposive sampling techniques in social and behavioral science research and provided examples of the ways in which these techniques can be used singularly (single method) or in combination (mixed method) research. Although none of the methods described here is completely without value in some circumstances, some sampling techniques are much more likely to yield reasonable intellectual and practical returns on investment than are others. The understanding of a wide range of sampling techniques in one's methodological repertoire greatly increases the likelihood of one's generating findings that are both rich in content and inclusive in scope.

Throughout this chapter, we argued for the necessity of mixed methods sampling strategies for addressing most of the sophisticated research currently conducted in the social and behavioral sciences. As noted, nearly any complex research study requires more than one sampling technique and often involves both probability and purposive sampling techniques. These mixed methods sampling strategies are particularly appropriate for mixed methods studies, which typically involve two distinct goals: (a) the testing of hypotheses based on the extant literature and (b) the assessing of research questions that push the boundaries of existing knowledge. Probability samples are typically required for the former goal, while purposive samples are most appropriate for the latter goal.

In this chapter, we reviewed seven key guidelines for sampling. A sampling strategy should be derived from the conceptual framework and research questions of the study. The sample should allow the research team to generate a thorough database on the type of phenomena under study. The sample should enhance the researchers' ability to make inferences from the data and produce credible explanations. Sampling must be done in a way that is both feasible and ethical. The sample should allow the research team to transfer/generalize the conclusions of the study to other settings or populations. Finally, attention should be paid to the efficiency of the sampling scheme.

These seven precepts can assist any research team in designing studies with the maximum chance of providing convincing evidence on any topic of interest. This is true whether the chosen methods are qualitative, quantitative, or mixed. They can make the difference between a research project that fails to reasonably test a hypothesis and one that makes a compelling case for the strength and/or limitations of a well-structured question.

Our discussion in this chapter highlighted the particular capacity of mixed model sampling strategies to address three of the seven guidelines simultaneously: (a) to enhance the inferential quality (internal validity and trustworthiness) of the research, (b) to expand the generalizability (transferability) of the results, and (c) to do this in an efficient manner. An often-stated truism from the quantitative research perspective is that as one increases internal validity, one decreases external validity (and vice versa). This inverse relationship does not have to occur with mixed methods studies employing mixed sampling strategies.

For example, sampling strategies for enhancing the external validity of the results from one phase of a sequential mixed methods study do not necessarily affect the trustworthiness of results from another phase of the study, even when both phases employ the same basic population of units. The LSES provides a worthwhile example of a preplanned multiphase study that used the same basic sample (at the district and school levels) across phases but employed different sampling procedures to yield units that could address very different hypotheses and questions. The quantitatively oriented first phase (LSES-II) employed a probability sampling technique that yielded 76 schools representative of the larger population of the state, while the qualitatively oriented second phase (LSES-III) used a purposive extreme/deviant case study sample that generated a 16-school sample of highly effective and ineffective schools.

LSES-II was a confirmatory study designed as a large-scale quantitative examination of a representative sample of schools, primarily intended to replicate and extend the results of other studies

(e.g., Brookover, Beady, Flood, Schweitzer, & Wisenbaker, 1979; Rutter, Maughan, Mortimore, & Ouston, 1979) that had concluded that manipulable school factors make a difference in student achievement. LSES-II sampling decisions focused on external validity (generalizability) issues because the internal validity (what caused the effect) of a regression study of this type is always suspect to multicollinearity problems. The researchers wanted to be sure that they could generalize their results to all schools in Louisiana and, by extension, to all schools in the United States.

LSES-III was a primarily exploratory study designed to produce tentative answers to a set of new questions related to highly effective and highly ineffective schools. This phase sampled from the same districts and the same population of schools with third-grade classrooms, yet it used a purposive extreme/deviant case sampling procedure to generate two sets of schools that were very different from one another. The emphasis in this phase was on the trustworthiness of the results; that is, would consumers of the research be persuaded that "the findings were . . . worth paying attention to, worth taking account of?" (Lincoln & Guba, 1985, p. 290). The issue of the transferability of the results from LSES-III was not as important, especially because the previous phase had addressed the overall generalizability of the research. Furthermore, in this case it is unclear what the value of extrapolating (transferring) the results to another particular set of schools (the receiving context) would be.

We believe that many contemporary studies will find mixed methods sampling strategies valuable, especially those concerned with the issues of the external validity and trustworthiness of their results. The LSES addressed both of these concerns simultaneously and in an efficient manner due to the mixed nature of its sampling scheme.

■ Notes

1. For the purposes of this chapter, a sample is defined as a "unit of observation/analysis (who or what is being studied)" such as people, groups, narrative segments, and artifacts (Tashakkori & Teddlie, 1998, p. 61). These units, of course, may be defined in either historically quantitative (e.g., probability sampling, population, sample) or qualitative (e.g., purposive sampling, whole texts, units) terms.

2. The requirements that the analysis yield regional comparisons, contrast Title I's effects on diverse racial/ethnic groups, and identify and follow a plausible control group all proved vexingly challenging. The requirement to identify and follow best practice also proved taxing.

3. In doing this, the political parties are providing strong bipartisan support for mixed methods research.

4. Lincoln and Guba (1985) used *trustworthiness* as an umbrella term that includes credibility, transferability, dependability, and confirmability. For these authors, trustworthiness is distinct from credibility in that the consumers of the research, as well as the participants in the study, find the results to be truthful: "Trustworthiness is a matter of concern to the *consumer* of inquirer reports" (p. 328, italics in original). Trustworthiness is used throughout the rest of this chapter as the substitute (in qualitative terms) for internal validity because we believe that most researchers are interested in whether or not their results appear truthful to the consumers of their research as well as to the research participants.

5. "Purpose" is important in making sampling decisions (see Newman et al., Chapter 6, this volume). If a researcher places emphasis on external validity with regard to a certain type of population (e.g., through the use of survey research or public opinion polls), then he or she needs a larger and more representative sample. On the other hand, if the researcher selects a sample to maximize the trustworthiness of the study, then critical case samples, extreme/deviant case sampling, sampling for heterogeneity, and the like are more suitable techniques to employ. Because the researcher using mixed methods may want to satisfy several purposes, he or she will probably employ several types of sampling procedures.

6. This is not to suggest that all sampling schemes are equally valuable in all research contexts; rather, it is to observe the perpetual issue of fit among the question, methods, and sampling scheme.

7. *Generalizability* and *external validity* are used interchangeably throughout this chapter. The qualitative research methodology equivalent to generalizability is *transferability*. The important criteria in transferability is the similarity between the sending and the receiving contexts and the researcher's knowledge of the different contexts.

■ References

Brookover, W. B., Beady, C., Flood, P., Schweitzer, J., & Wisenbaker, J. (1979). *Schools, social systems and student achievement: Schools can make a difference.* New York: Praeger.

Capraro, M. M., Capraro, R. M., & Wiggins, B. B. (2000, January). *An investigation of the effects of gender, socioeconomic status, race, and grades on standardized test scores.* Paper presented at the annual meeting of the Southwest Educational Research Association, Dallas, TX.

Cook, T. D., & Campbell, D. T. (1979). *Quasiexperimentation: Design and analysis issues for field settings.* Boston: Houghton Mifflin.

Curtis, S., Gesler, W., Smith, G., & Washburn, S. (2000). Approaches to sampling and case selection in qualitative research: Examples in the geography of health. *Social Science and Medicine, 50,* 1001-1014.

Datnow, A., & Castellano, M. (2000). Teachers' responses to success for all: How beliefs, experiences, and adaptations shape implementation. *American Educational Research Journal, 37,* 775-799.

Ezzy, D. M., Bartos, M. R., de Visser, R. O., & Rosenthal, D. A. (1998). Antiretroviral uptake in Australia: Medical, attitudinal, and cultural correlates. *International Journal of STD and AIDS, 9,* 579-586.

Henry, G. T. (1990). *Practical sampling.* Newbury Park, CA: Sage.

Jaeger, R. M. (1984). *Sampling in education and the social sciences.* New York: Longman.

Kemper, E. A., & Teddlie, C. (2000). Mandated site-based management in Texas: Exploring implementation in urban high schools. *Teaching and Change, 7*(2), 172-200.

Kinsey, A. C. (1948). *Sexual behavior in the human male.* Philadelphia: W. B. Saunders.

Lincoln, Y. S., & Guba, E. G. (1985). *Naturalistic inquiry.* Beverly Hills, CA: Sage.

Miles, M. B., & Huberman, A. M. (1994). *Qualitative data analysis: An expanded sourcebook* (2nd ed.). Thousand Oaks, CA: Sage.

Minger, J. (2001). Combining IS research methods: Towards a pluralist methodology. *Information Systems Research, 12*(3), 240-259.

Morgan, G. A., Yang, R. K., & Greigo, O. V. (1998, July). *Mastery motivation in preschool children: Relations to aggression and hyperactivity.* Paper presented at the National Head Start Research Conference, Washington, DC.

Patton, M. Q. (1990). *Qualitative evaluation and research methods* (2nd ed.). Newbury Park, CA: Sage.

Puma, M., Karweit, N., Price, C., Ricciuti, A., Thompson, W., & Vaden-Kiernan, M. (1997). *Prospects: Final report on student outcomes.* Washington, DC: U.S. Department of Education, Planning and Evaluation Services.

Raywid, M. A. (1999). Central Park Elementary School: The anatomy of success. *Journal of Education of Students Placed at Risk, 4*(2), 131-151.

Rutter, M., Maughan, B., Mortimore, P., & Ouston, J., with Smith, A. (1979). *Fifteen thousand hours: Secondary schools and their effect on children.* Cambridge, MA: Harvard University Press.

Scannell-Desch, E. A. (2000). Hardships and personal strategies of Vietnam War nurses. *Western Journal of Nursing Research, 22,* 526-550.

Schweinhart, L. J., & Weikart, D. P. (1980). *Young children grow up: The effects of the Perry Preschool Program on youths through age 15.* Ypsilanti, MI: High/Scope.

Shields, S. A., & Foster, B. A. (1989). Emotional stereotyping of parents in child rearing manuals, 1915-1989. *Social Psychology Quarterly, 52,* 44-55.

Silverstien, L. B., Auerback, C. F., Grieco, L., & Dunkel, F. (1999). Do Promise Keepers dream of feminist sheep? *Sex Roles, 40,* 665-688.

Sizer, T. R. (1992). *Horace's school: Redesigning the American high school.* Boston: Houghton Mifflin.

Slavin, R., & Madden, N. (2001). *One million children: Success for all.* Thousand Oaks, CA: Corwin.

Stanley, T. J., & Danko, W. D. (1997). *The millionaire next door.* Atlanta, GA: Longstreet.

Stringfield, S., Millsap, M. A., Herman, R., Yoder, N., Brigham, N., Nesselrodt, P., Schaffer, E., Karweit, N., Levin, M., & Stevens, R., with Gamse, B., Puma, M., Rosenblum, S., Beaumont, J., Randall, B., & Smith, L. (1997). *Urban and suburban/rural special strategies for educating disadvantaged children: Final report.* Washington, DC: U.S. Department of Education.

Tashakkori, A., & Teddlie, C. (1998). *Mixed methodology: Combining qualitative and quantitative approaches* (Applied Social Research Methods, No. 46). Thousand Oaks, CA: Sage.

Teddlie, C., Kirby, P., & Stringfield, S. (1989). Effective versus ineffective schools: Observable differences in the classroom. *American Journal of Education, 97,* 221-236.

Teddlie, C., & Stringfield, S. (1993). *Schools make a difference: Lessons learned from a*

10-year study of school effects. New York: Teachers College Press.

Twigg, L., Moon, G., & Jones, K. (2000). Predicting small-area health-related behaviour: A comparison of smoking and drinking indicators. *Social Science & Medicine, 50,* 1109-1120.

Vega, W. A., Alderete, E., Kolody B., & Aguilar-Gaxioler, S. (1998). Illicit drug use among Mexicans and Mexican-Americans in California: The effects of gender and acculturation. *Addiction, 93,* 1839-1850.

11

DATA COLLECTION STRATEGIES IN MIXED METHODS RESEARCH

◆ Burke Johnson
Lisa A. Turner

Authors of the previous chapters in this handbook have discussed many of the issues surrounding mixed methods research, including the philosophy of pragmatism, writing research questions, designing mixed methods studies, and sampling. Now, we move into the specific methods of data collection that are used in empirical research and how these methods can be mixed and matched in one or more research studies. We focus on the six major methods of data collection used in the social and behavioral sciences and how they may be mixed.

◆ The Data Collection Matrix

A total of 18 specific types of data collection are listed in Table 11.1. This table was formed by crossing two dimensions. The first dimension is the *research approach* dimension. Pure qualitative and pure quantitative research are the poles of this first dimension. In this chapter, *pure qualitative research* is defined as exploratory, inductive, unstructured, open-ended, naturalistic, and free-flowing research that results in qualitative data. *Pure quantitative research* is defined as confirmatory, deductive, structured, closed-ended, controlled, and linear research that results in quantitative data. The mixed anchor on the research approach dimension represents research that mixes the approaches or uses a less extreme version than the pure qualitative or pure quantitative forms.

The second dimension in Table 11.1 is the *method of data collection* dimension. This dimension is anchored with the six

TABLE 11.1   Data Collection Matrix

Method of Data Collection	Research Approach Continuum		
	Pure Qualitative	Mixed	Pure Quantitative
1. Questionnaires	1	2	3
2. Interviews	4	5	6
3. Focus groups	7	8	9
4. Tests	10	11	12
5. Observation	13	14	15
6. Secondary data (e.g., personal and official documents, physical data, archived research data)	16	17	18

major types of data collection. A method of data collection is simply a technique that is used to collect empirical research data. It is how researchers "get" their information. The six major methods of data collection are questionnaires, interviews, focus groups, tests, observation, and secondary data.

◆ Intramethod and Intermethod Mixing

The mixed categories shown in Table 11.1 are types of intramethod mixing. *Intramethod mixing* is defined as the concurrent or sequential use of a *single* method that includes both qualitative and quantitative components. The concurrent use of open- and closed-ended items on a single questionnaire and the sequential use of an open-ended questionnaire and a closed-ended questionnaire in a single research study are examples of intramethod mixing. On the other hand, *intermethod mix-*

ing is accomplished by concurrently or sequentially mixing two or more methods. The use of questionnaires and observation in a research study is an example of intermethod mixing. Intramethod mixing has also been called "data triangulation," and intermethod mixing has also been called "method triangulation" (e.g., Denzin, 1989). Intramethod mixing must include either a combination of qualitative and quantitative approaches within a single method (e.g., use of Types 4 and 6 in Table 11.1) or a method that is neither purely qualitative nor purely quantitative (i.e., the "mixed" types). The mixed types of single method data collection (i.e., intramethod mixing) are shown in the "mixed" column in Table 11.1 and, in more detail, in Table 11.2.

Intermethod mixing requires that multiple (i.e., different) methods be employed in a single study. These multiple methods can reflect only quantitative approaches (e.g., use of Types 3 and 6 in Table 11.1), only qualitative approaches (e.g., use of Types 1 and 7 in Table 11.1), only mixed

---

TABLE 11.2   Data Collection Styles for Mixed Cells

Type 2   Mixture of open- and closed-ended items on one or more questionnaires

Type 5   Mixture of depth and breadth interviewing

Type 8   Mixture of "a priori" and "emergent/flowing" focus group strategies

Type 11   Mixture of standardized open- and closed-ended pre-made tests

Type 14   Mixture of standardized/confirmatory and less structured/exploratory observation, alternating between participatory and nonparticipatory researcher roles

Type 17   Mixture of non-numeric and numeric documents; archived data based on open- and closed-ended items

---

approaches (e.g., use of Types 2 and 5 in Table 11.1), or a combination of qualitative and quantitative approaches (e.g., use of Types 6 and 10 in Table 11.1). In many cases, the mixing of qualitative and quantitative methods will result in the most accurate and complete depiction of the phenomenon under investigation (Johnson, 1995; Johnson & Christensen, 2000; Patton, 1990; Tashakkori & Teddlie, 1998).

♦ *The Fundamental Principle of Mixed Methods Research*

When conducting mixed methods research, it is important that the researcher always keep in mind what we call the *fundamental principle of mixed methods research*. According to this fundamental principle, *methods should be mixed in a way that has complementary strengths and nonoverlapping weaknesses* (Brewer & Hunter, 1989; Tashakkori & Teddlie, 1998). It involves the recognition that all methods have their limitations as well as their strengths. The fundamental principle is followed for at least three reasons: (a) to

obtain convergence or corroboration of findings, (b) to eliminate or minimize key plausible alternative explanations for conclusions drawn from the research data, and (c) to elucidate the divergent aspects of a phenomenon. The fundamental principle can be applied to all stages or components of the research process. For the purposes of this chapter, the use of the fundamental principle means that *data collection methods* should be combined so that they have different weaknesses and so that the combination used by the researcher may provide convergent and divergent evidence about the phenomenon being studied. In the next section, we outline several validity or trustworthiness issues that researchers must keep in mind when collecting data and when they mix the different methods into a single, mixed methods data collection plan.

♦ *Validity Issues in Data Collection*

When we use the term *valid* or *validity* surrounding data collection, we are simply referring to the idea of conducting high-quality research. Valid research is "plausible, credible, trustworthy, and, therefore, defensible" (Johnson & Christensen, 2000, p. 207). Our definition is pragmatic and inclusive (i.e., it can be applied to all types of research). The key issue of "research validity," in the general sense used here, is this: Do experts (e.g., academics, practitioners, or anyone else who carefully examines a research report) consider the research to be well done and worthy of readers' attention? Lincoln and Guba (1985) used the term *trustworthiness* to refer to this similar property of high-quality research. Here is the idea of trustworthiness in their words:

> The basic issue in relation to trustworthiness is simple: How can an inquirer persuade his or her audiences (including self) that the findings of an inquiry are worth paying attention to, worth taking account of? What arguments can be mounted, what criteria invoked, what questions asked, that would be persuasive on this issue? (p. 290)

We treat the terms *valid* and *trustworthy* as synonyms in this chapter. Obviously, in the mixed methods context, validity/trustworthiness issues involve all of those topics discussed in the separate quantitative and qualitative literatures under those titles plus any other issues identified through mixed methods literatures or applications. Although we focus on data collection issues in this chapter, researchers should keep in mind that every component and stage of a research study can be examined for validity or trustworthiness (e.g., design, measurement, data collection, analysis, interpretation, writing).

Obviously, there are many validity issues surrounding the conduct of good research, and we can address only a few of the issues in the space allocated here. We start with Maxwell's (1992, 1996) three

validity types that were originally developed for qualitative research. The first type, called *descriptive validity*, refers to the factual accuracy of an account as reported by the researcher. It is essential that the researcher carefully collect and corroborate descriptive information during the process of data collection to ensure its accuracy. The second type, called *interpretive validity*, refers to the degree to which the researcher accurately portrays the participants' meanings about what is being studied. In other words, the researcher must collect data that will shed light on the "emic" (or "insider" or "native") views of research participants. The goal here is to understand the research participants' (rather than the researcher's) views and ways of thinking. The third type, called *theoretical validity*, refers to the degree to which a theoretical explanation developed by the researcher fits the data (see also Glaser & Strauss, 1967; Strauss & Corbin, 1998). Some specific strategies for obtaining Maxwell's (and other) types of validity include member checking, reflexivity, negative case analysis, triangulation (method, data, investigator, and theory triangulation), extended fieldwork, persistent observation, pattern matching, peer review, referential adequacy, theoretical sensitivity, theoretical sampling, memoing and diagramming, thick description, dependability audit, confirmability audit, and use of a reflexive journal (Glaser & Strauss, 1967; Johnson & Christensen, 2000; Lincoln & Guba, 1985; Strauss & Corbin, 1998; Tashakkori & Teddlie, 1998).

The next set of validity types (i.e., internal validity vs. external validity) was introduced to the research community by Donald Campbell in 1957 (Campbell, 1957) and later elaborated by Campbell and others (e.g., Bickman, 2000; Campbell & Stanley, 1963; Cook & Campbell, 1979; Huck & Sandler, 1979; Onwuegbuzie, in press). Internal validity and external validity, and the "threats" to these, are covered in virtually every research methods textbook in the social and behavioral sciences (e.g., Babbie, 2001; Christensen, 2001; Frankfort-Nachmias & Nachmias, 2000; Johnson & Christensen, 2000). Internal validity is traditionally defined as what may be called "causal validity" or one's justification in making a causal inference from one's data. Causal validity (regardless of what it is called) can be important in quantitative, qualitative, and mixed methods research (Yin, 1994). External validity is traditionally defined as the degree to which one can generalize a research finding to other people, places, settings, and times. Stake (1990, 1995) offered a nice middle ground for generalizing when he recommended making thoughtful and "naturalistic generalizations" (i.e., generalizing based on similarity of people, circumstances, operationalizations, etc.). The concepts of internal validity and external validity were originally applied to quantitative research. Several authors, however, have discussed how these types of validity can be expanded and applied in qualitative and mixed methods research (e.g., LeCompte & Preissle, 1993; Johnson & Christensen, 2000; Onwuegbuzie, in press; Schensul, Schensul, & LeCompte, 1999; Tashakkori & Teddlie, 1998).

Although many of Campbell's threats to validity can be controlled or reduced through the use of various research designs, these threats often materialize during the collection of the data. For example, it is during data collection that *testing* effects may occur (i.e., changes occurring in respondents' scores on later administration of a test because they took the same test at an earlier time), *instrumentation* effects may occur (i.e., changes in the measurement of variables over time), and *history* effects may occur (i.e., an event other than the planned event that also occurs during data collection). Researchers

should also attempt to monitor changes taking place in research participants due to natural *maturation* as well as changes in their scores due to *statistical regression* when "extreme" groups are being studied. The point is that researchers should be cognizant of each of Campbell's threats during data collection (as well as during the other stages of research) and should attempt to minimize the influence of these threats because of their potential impact on data quality.

Another set of validity issues surrounds measurement validity (and reliability that is necessary for validity). When collecting data, researchers must consider whether they are measuring what they planned to measure. This is true when a test or standard instrument is used as well as when the researcher is the "instrument of data collection." There are several key measurement validity strategies that are covered in most research methods books (e.g., Johnson & Christensen, 2000). The first strategy is *content-related validation* (i.e., making sure the items or tasks adequately represent the domain of interest). The second strategy includes two types of criterion-related validation: *concurrent-related validation* (i.e., determining the relationship between scores on a measure and scores on a known standard measure) and *predictive-related validation* (i.e., determining the relationship between test scores and some criterion occurring at a later time). The third, and all-encompassing, strategy is *construct-related validation* (i.e., determining whether a theoretical construct can be inferred from the research operations such as from scores on a test). For specific techniques used for each of these, see Johnson and Christensen (2000) and Messick (1989).

Webb, Campbell, Schwartz, and Sechrest (1966/2000) discussed five major sources of validity problems that surround data collection and must be considered by a researcher. The first source, called *reactive effects*, refers to error resulting from the respondents' awareness that they are the targets of study. Reactive effects may include several specific types: (a) the guinea pig effect (i.e., the participants are aware that the camera is on them and react in an inaccurate, defensive, or dishonest way), (b) role selection (i.e., the participants select from "the many 'true' selves or 'proper' behaviors" [p. 16] during the study rather than acting normally), (c) measurement as change agent (i.e., the initial measurement activity can produce changes in what is being measured even when the respondents are trying to be candid), and (d) response sets (i.e., the participants tend to respond in stereotyped ways such as acquiescence and "yes-saying" or prefer extreme responses rather than moderate ones).

The second major source of error occurring during data collection is called *investigator effects* and refers to errors resulting from the investigator (Webb et al., 1966/2000). There are two specific types: (a) interviewer effects (i.e., participants are influenced by characteristics of the interviewer such as his or her age, class, and gender) and (b) change in the research instrument (i.e., changes occur when the researcher is the data collection instrument such as increases in skill or becoming tired and less accurate over time).

The third source of error identified by Webb et al. (1966/2000) is called *varieties of sampling error* and refers to inevitable errors resulting from the researcher's inability to obtain perfect samples of persons, time, or space. This includes (a) population restrictions (i.e., only certain populations are accessible for specific methods), (b) population stability over time (i.e., the accessible population is usually limited to one or a few time points and may be unstable over time), and (c) population stability over areas (i.e., the accessible population may be different in different areas).

The fourth source of error identified by Webb et al. is called *access to content* errors and refers to the researcher's inability to obtain perfect samples of relevant content. This problem includes (a) restrictions on content (i.e., some methods provide access to content not available through the use of other methods such as observation not providing direct information about motivation), (b) stability of content over time (i.e., content of collected data may vary over time due to factors not related to the research question), and (c) stability of content over area (i.e., content of data collected in different areas may vary due to factors not related to the research question).

The fifth, and last, source of error identified by Webb et al. is the *operating ease and validity checks* available for different methods. First, the dross rate (i.e., the amount of irrelevant material collected when using a particular set of data) will vary across method. For example, a closed-ended questionnaire used in a confirmatory study will tend to have a lower dross rate than will an open-ended questionnaire because the researcher is more able to direct the participants to provide only information that is known to be directly related to the research questions. Second, the ability to replicate a research study will vary across method. For example, a questionnaire is easier to replicate than is an observation.

The key point to keep in mind when thinking about the errors identified by Webb et al. (1966/2000) is that some data collection methods are more subject than others to various validity threats. It is the researcher's responsibility when doing mixed methods research to try to carefully use the fundamental principle of mixed methods research (i.e., using appropriate method mixes). It is also important to be cognizant of the potential errors during ongoing data collection. Errors may be

TABLE 11.3   Principles of Questionnaire Construction

Principle 1.	Make sure that the questionnaire items match your research objectives.
Principle 2.	Understand your research participants.
Principle 3.	Use natural and familiar language.
Principle 4.	Write items that are simple, clear, and precise.
Principle 5.	Do not use "leading" or "loaded" questions.
Principle 6.	Avoid double-barreled questions.
Principle 7.	Avoid double negatives.
Principle 8.	Determine whether an open-ended or a closed-ended question is needed.
Principle 9.	Use mutually exclusive and exhaustive response categories for closed-ended questions.
Principle 10.	Consider the different types of response categories available for closed-ended questionnaire items.
Principle 11.	Use multiple items to measure abstract constructs.
Principle 12.	Develop a questionnaire that is easy for the participants to use.
Principle 13.	Always pilot-test your questionnaire.

SOURCE: Adapted from Johnson and Christensen (2000).

compensated in a single well-designed study, or it may take many studies making up a research literature to compensate for the various errors and to demonstrate converging corroboration of a research finding. In the next section, we discuss the different methods of data collection that are commonly employed in empirical research studies.

◆ *Major Methods of Data Collection*

QUESTIONNAIRES

The first major method of data collection is the use of questionnaires. When using this method, you construct a self-report data collection instrument that is filled out by the research participants. When constructing a questionnaire, it is important to follow the 13 principles of questionnaire construction shown in Table 11.3.

Looking at the continuum for questionnaires in Table 11.1 (the data collection matrix), you can see three types. Type 1 data collection (a qualitative questionnaire) is an unstructured, exploratory, open-ended, and (typically) in-depth questionnaire. It consists of a series of open-ended questions to be answered by all or a subset of the participants in a research study. In open-ended items, respondents provide the answers in their own words. Participants may fill out the items in any order they choose, although many will tend to start with the first item and move linearly through the instrument.

Type 3 data collection (a quantitative questionnaire) is based on a completely structured and closed-ended questionnaire. All participants fill out the same questionnaire, and all of the questions or items provide the possible responses from which the participants must select. The response categories often take the form of rating scales (e.g., 4- or 5-point rating scales), rankings, semantic differentials, and checklists. Summated rating scales (i.e., Likert scales) are also common. The only exception to the "every participant fills out the same questions on a questionnaire" rule is that *contingency questions* are sometimes included to direct people to appropriate items given their personal characteristics (e.g., directing them away from inappropriate items such as about being pregnant for male participants). The use of contingency questions is generally more appropriate in interviews than in questionnaires because of the importance that a questionnaire be very simple and easily filled out by all respondents.

Type 2 data collection (a mixed questionnaire) is a self-report instrument filled out by the respondents, and it includes a mixture of completely open- and closed-ended items. In addition, a single item may also be "mixed," as shown by the set of response categories for the following item:

What is your racial identity?

a. African American

b. Hispanic American

c. Caucasian

d. Other: Please list _____

The "other" category allows respondents to fill in their answers, in their own words, in the cases where the responses provided by the researcher are incomplete or inappropriate. The researcher will need to code these other responses during data analysis.

An example of a mixed questionnaire is found in a recent study by Jones and Worthen (1999). These evaluators surveyed members of the American Evaluation Association to determine views about establishing a formal certification process within their discipline. The questionnaire employed is an example of *intramethod mixing* because it included open- and closed-ended items. The bulk of the questionnaire included closed-ended items that were easily quantified to indicate participant views on the feasibility of a certification program and the elements that should be included in the certification process. However, the open-ended questions revealed participant views of the benefits and limitations of such a process. This new information had important implications and might have been missed with completely closed-ended items. The use of open-ended questions provided Jones and Worthen with information that was not constrained by any preconceptions held by the researchers.

Questionnaires are often an important component in intermethod mixing. In a case of *sequential intermethod mixing*, Mickelson, Wroble, and Helgeson (1999) used interviews and questionnaires with the parents of children with special needs. First, 109 parents participated in exploratory telephone interviews where they were asked (through open-ended questions) what they thought caused their children's disabilities. The findings from these interviews were used to construct a quantitative questionnaire. This questionnaire consisted of 17 possible causes of disabilities (derived from the earlier open-ended interviews), and the parents were asked to rate each cause on a rating scale of 1 to 5 (indicating the degree to which they felt the cause contributed to their children's disabilities). The responses to the 17 items were factor analyzed and categorized into five more general types. The use of exploratory open-ended items to create the questionnaire helped to ensure that the views of the parents were well-represented in the final questionnaire. The researchers also structured the questionnaire and used rating scales so that responses could easily be factor analyzed. Costs were minimized by using a mail questionnaire. On the other hand, the response rate (and the representativeness of the final sample) is often suspect when based on a "mail" questionnaire.

A second example of intermethod mixing involving questionnaires can be found in a study titled "Depression and Substance Use in Two Divergent High School Cultures: A Quantitative and Qualitative Analysis," by Way, Stauber, Nakkula, and London (1994). Students in suburban and urban high schools completed questionnaires addressing depression and substance use. On discovering that depression and substance abuse were positively correlated only in the suburban sample, the authors conducted more qualitative in-depth interviews with the most depressed students from both the urban and suburban schools. In general, it appeared that the suburban students saw drugs as a way to "escape problems" more than did the urban students. In contrast, the urban students saw drug use as a cause of problems more than did the suburban students. The combination of questionnaires and in-depth interviews in this study led to a more complete and interesting depiction of the differences across the samples. The use of the in-depth interviews helped the researchers to better understand their quantitative findings.

There are several strengths and weaknesses of questionnaires that should be considered when considering this form of data collection. These strengths and weaknesses are shown in Table 11.4.

INTERVIEWS

The second major method of data collection is the use of interviews. When using this method for collecting data, the interviewer establishes rapport and asks the interviewee a series of questions. The interviewer must always remain nonjudgmental to the responses provided by the interviewee to help reduce the potentially biasing effect of the interviewer. The interviewer can probe the interviewee for clarity or for more detailed information when needed. This is an advantage of interviews as compared with questionnaires where interviewer probing is not possible. On the other hand, interviews are usually more expensive to administer than are questionnaires. Looking at the continuum for interviews in Table 11.1, you can see the three types. The first type is the pure qualitative interview. This interview is unstructured, exploratory, open-ended, and typically in-depth so that various topics can be explored effectively.

Patton (1987, 2002) provided a useful continuum of decreasingly qualitative interviews that includes *informal conversational interviews,* the *interview guide approach,* and *standardized open-ended interviewing.* The informal conversational interview is the purest qualitative form and represents Type 4 research in Table 11.1. This type of interview is completely unstructured, and the questions spontaneously emerge from the natural flow of things during fieldwork. Slightly to the right (of informal conversational interviews) on the continuum is the interview guide approach. When using this approach, the topics are prespecified and listed on an interview protocol, but they can be reworded as needed and are

TABLE 11.4   Strengths and Weaknesses of Questionnaires

Strengths:

   Good for measuring attitudes and eliciting other content from research participants

   Inexpensive (especially mail questionnaires and group-administered questionnaires)

   Can administer to probability samples

   Quick turnaround

   Can be administered to groups

   Perceived anonymity by respondents possibly high

   Moderately high measurement validity for well-constructed and well-tested questionnaires

   Low dross rate for closed-ended questionnaires

   Ease of data analysis for closed-ended items

Weaknesses:

   Need validation

   Must be kept short

   Might have missing data

   Possible reactive effects (e.g., response sets, social desirability)

   Nonresponse to selective items

   Response rate possibly low for mail questionnaires

   Open-ended items possibly resulting in vague answers

   Open-ended items possibly reflecting differences in verbal ability, obscuring the issues of interest

   Data analysis sometimes time-consuming for open-ended items

covered by the interviewer in any sequence or order.

The third type of qualitative interviewing described by Patton (1987, 2002) is called the standardized open-ended interview. This is an example of mixed interviewing (Type 5 data collection). The standardized open-ended interview is based on open-ended questions and results in qualitative data; at the same time, neither the wording nor the sequence of the questions on the interview protocol is varied, so the presentation is constant across participants. Another form of mixed interview would include open- and closed-ended items in a single interview protocol or in two separate protocols that are used in a single study.

At the right end of the interview continuum in Table 11.1 is the quantitative interview (Type 6 data collection). In this form of interviewing, a carefully written interview protocol is used in a standard way with all respondents. The interview protocol would be used like a "script" in which the interviewer simply reads the questions and records the answers. The interview items are closed-ended, with all response categories prespecified by the researcher. Any probes and/or responses to interviewee questions are preplanned. The interviewer must establish rapport; however, the only answers the interviewer gives to interviewee questions (e.g., "What do you mean by race?") are pre-established in what are sometimes called "Q by Qs" (i.e., appropriate interviewer responses are written out, question by question, by the researcher and then used by the interviewer as needed). The 13 principles of questionnaire construction shown in Table 11.3 should be carefully applied to the construction of the interview protocol.

An example of a mixed interview is found in a study titled "Analysis of Participation in an Innovative Psychiatric Rehabilitation Intervention: Supported Education" by Bybee, Bellamy, and Mowbray (2000). These researchers identified the reasons clients gave for not participating in a mental health program. In the mixed interview that included open-ended questions and a closed-ended, 14-item checklist, clients were asked to report the barriers that interfered with their participation in the mental health program. There was much agreement across the open-ended questions and the checklist, with both resulting in similar rankings for the barriers to participation. The exception was a new category (resource barriers) that was mentioned by 8% of the participants in the open-ended responses but was not included in the closed-ended rating scale. The general consistency of the responses across the two forms of questions provided corroborating evidence of the importance of the reported barriers. Furthermore, future research could be informed by the open-ended items that revealed a category of barriers that had not been anticipated by the researchers.

Interviews are often combined with other methods in intermethod mixing. In an investigation titled "Parent Involvement: Influencing Factors and Implications," Pena (2000) conducted a case study that included participant observa-tion, records, and interviews with parents and teachers. As a participant observer, Pena developed thorough knowledge of the school, enhancing her ability to conduct open-ended in-depth interviews with her participants. Also, the use of quantitative school records provided a second source of information (in addition to the parent interviews) documenting the parents' involvement with their children's school and corroborating parent report results. A major strength of the use of records is the lack of reactivity. Pena determined that language, education, social groups, family issues, and school staff attitudes all were related to parents' involvement in their children's school.

Another case of intermethod mixing, based on questionnaires and interviews, is a study titled "Relation of Attributional Beliefs to Memory Strategy Use in Children and Adolescents With Mental Retardation" (Turner, 1998). In this study, Turner (1998) measured the attributional beliefs of children with mental retardation using an open-ended interview and a closed-ended questionnaire. In each case, the students were asked to report what caused them to do well in school. For both measures, the most common (and most highly rated) cause was effort. The open-ended responses revealed how these students thought their efforts should be directed. Effort responses were coded into two categories (behavioral and cognitive), with the behavioral responses accounting for 43% of the responses of 11-year-old students and 22% of the responses of 17-year-old students. This developmental shift was not reflected in the closed-ended questionnaire data. In short, the addition of the open-ended interview helped Turner to gain insight into content that was not readily available in her stand-alone closed-ended questionnaire.

There are several potential strengths and weaknesses of interviews that should

---

TABLE 11.5   Strengths and Weaknesses of Interviews

Strengths:

Good for measuring attitudes and most other content of interest

Allow probing by the interviewer

Can provide in-depth information

Allow good interpretive validity

Low dross rate for closed-ended interviews

Very quick turnaround for telephone interviews

Moderately high measurement validity for well-constructed and well-tested interview protocols

Can use with probability sample

Relatively high response rates often attainable

Useful for exploration and confirmation

Weaknesses:

In-person interviews expensive and time-consuming

Possible reactive and investigator effects

Perceived anonymity by respondents possibly low

Data analysis sometimes time-consuming for open-ended items

Measures in need of validation

---

be considered. These strengths and weaknesses are listed in Table 11.5.

FOCUS GROUPS

The third major method of data collection is the use of focus groups. A focus group is a situation in which a group moderator keeps a small and usually homogeneous group of about 6 to 12 people focused on the discussion of a research topic or issue (Johnson & Christensen, 2000; Morgan, 1998). Focus group sessions generally last between 1 and 3 hours and allow in-depth discussion. During the conduct of a focus group, the group moderator typically facilitates group discussion on a series of about 5 to 10 open-ended items written on the moderator's "focus group interview protocol"; all of the items on the protocol are related to the focus topic. The moderator keeps the group members focused on the topic or on related issues that may lead to useful insights into the topic. The moderator must make sure that no single individual dominates the discussion, tactfully resolve any power struggles, keep the discussion moving, and keep the group "focused." Focus groups are recorded using audio- and/or videotapes that allow for later in-depth data analysis. Some useful moderator roles are the seeker of wisdom, the enlightened novice, the expert consultant, the challenger, the referee, the writer, the team member, the therapist, and the serial interviewer (Krueger, 1998). Looking at the continuum for focus groups in Table 11.1, you can see three types of focus groups.

The pure qualitative focus group (Type 7 data collection) is based on one or more research questions, but the discussion tends to be very spontaneous and the moderator does little more than bring the group back to the focus of study from time to time. This type of focus group is useful for generating ideas and impressions and for learning how participants think and interact in a relatively unstructured group situation. On the other end of the continuum is the pure quantitative focus group (Type 9), which is basically a structured group interview. In this type of focus group, the moderator does little more than interview the group using a structured protocol. In the "purely quantitative" form, the protocol items would be closed-ended, allowing little in-depth discussion. The mixed type of focus group (Type 8) is perhaps the most common type of focus group. This type of focus group may include both open- and closed-ended questions posed by the moderator. The moderator allows the group to move into related areas but also tries to keep the participants focused, bringing them back to the main topic when needed.

Focus groups are often used in intermethod mixing (i.e., along with additional methods of data collection), although they can also be used as a stand-alone method. Focus groups are often used for exploratory purposes to delve into group members' thinking on a research topic. Focus groups may be used to inform the development of questionnaires and interviews in quantitative research. Sometimes, focus groups are even used after an experiment as a "manipulation check" or to serve as a poststudy feedback or discussion session. Finally, focus groups can be used later in a sequential mixed methods research study to help researchers better understand and interpret information and findings resulting from the earlier use of other data collection methods.

In an intermethod mixing study titled "Kindergarten Teachers' Perceptions of Instructing Students With Disabilities," Vaughn, Reiss, Rothlein, and Hughes (1999) conducted focus groups with prekindergarten special education teachers to determine what these teachers thought was necessary to support the transition to kindergarten for children with disabilities. Information from the focus groups was combined with information from prior research and with consultation with other researchers in the field to develop a 56-item questionnaire that included both closed- and open-ended questions. The mixed questionnaire was then distributed to kindergarten teachers to determine what these teachers thought were desirable and feasible activities for a teacher to engage in to help children with disabilities make the transition to kindergarten. This questionnaire elicited interesting information from the teachers concerning working with children with disabilities in their classrooms. In general, teachers agreed that the activities identified in the questionnaire were desirable, but they typically rated the feasibility of the activities lower than the desirability of the activities. The use of additional, focused open-ended items would have helped the researchers to better understand the observed gap between feasibility and desirability for different activities rated by the teachers.

In a study titled "I Can Speak for Myself: Involving Individuals With Intellectual Disabilities as Research Participants," Mactavish, Mahon, and Lutfiyya (2000) found it useful to conduct individual interviews prior to focus groups. These open-ended interviews were used to gather background information and helped the researchers to develop positive relationships with the participants. The information obtained and the rapport they developed helped to set the stage for the focus groups and helped to minimize

TABLE 11.6   Strengths and Weaknesses of Focus Groups

Strengths:

    Useful for exploring ideas

    Allow good interpretive validity

    Can obtain in-depth information about exactly how people think about an issue

    Allow study of how participants react to each other

    Allow probing

    Allow most content to be tapped

    Allow quick turnaround

Weaknesses:

    Sometimes expensive

    Possible reactive and investigator effects if participants feel that they are being watched

    May be dominated by one or two participants

    Very difficult to generalize if small unrepresentative samples are used

    Focus group moderator possibly biased

    Might have high dross rate

    Measurement validity possibly low

    Usually should not be the only data collection method used in a study

    Data analysis sometimes time-consuming

later reactivity to the presence of the researchers. An unexpected outcome of the interviews was the identification of potential barriers that could have interfered with the focus groups. By gathering this individual information prior to the focus groups, the investigators were able to arrange focus groups that allowed the greatest participation from the research participants.

There are several important strengths and weaknesses of focus groups that should be considered. These strengths and weaknesses are listed in Table 11.6.

TESTS

The fourth major method of data collection is the use of tests. Tests are commonly used in quantitative research to measure attitudes, personality, self-perceptions, aptitude, and performance of research participants. *Standardized tests* are developed by psychometricians and usually include psychometric information on reliability, validity, and reference group norms. Many tests are reviewed in the *Mental Measurements Yearbook* and *Tests in Print.* For information about many tests, you can access the Buros Institute Web page (www.unl.edu.buros/). Some common types of tests are intelligence tests, personality tests, achievement tests, preschool tests, aptitude tests, and diagnostic tests (Johnson & Christensen, 2000). On the other hand, experimental researchers often generate their own tests (e.g., tests of cognitive performance, reaction time, memory, etc.).

Looking at the continuum of tests in Table 11.1, you can see three possible forms. Type 10 (pure qualitative tests) includes tests that are constructed by the researcher and include open-ended items or other tests that have been used by many researchers or practitioners such as the Rorschach inkblot test (a projective test where respondents state what they are thinking as they view inkblot pictures) and the Thematic Apperception Test (a projective test where respondents react to pictures or cartoons in an open-ended manner) (Anastasi & Urbina, 1996). Some other examples of open-ended tests are word association tasks, sentence completion tasks, essays, and unfinished scenario story completion tasks (Dillon, Madden, & Firtle, 1987).

Type 12 data collection (pure quantitative tests) is a commonly used form of data collection. These tests are standardized and completely closed-ended. When completing a paper-and-pencil test, the participants examine each item on the test and make quantitative judgments (e.g., using a rating scale such as a 5-point scale). Most nonprojective psychological tests are primarily quantitative. If a test is a cognitive or physiological performance measure, the participants may merely act and their performance will be automatically measured (e.g., response time, heart rate).

Type 11 data collection (mixed tests) is also possible. Mixed tests include a mixture of open- and closed-type items; therefore, they can provide some of the strengths of both qualitative and quantitative tests. The Scholastic Aptitude Test (SAT) (Breland, Kubota, & Bonner, 1999) is an example of a mixed test. Although the test is largely closed-ended, starting in 1994, an open-ended component was added to the SAT to provide a sample of test takers' writing skills. The authors and users of the test felt that writing was an important

skill that required some form of open-ended assessment. This writing sample is eventually quantified to reflect the judges' assessment of the quality of the product.

Tests are also frequently used in inter-method mixing. For example, in a study titled "Effects of Attitudes and Beliefs on Mathematics Achievement," Papanastasiou (2000) used intermethod mixing to provide information about what might affect mathematics achievement. Papanastasiou had students, teachers, and administrators complete quantitative questionnaires. The students also completed mathematics tests to gauge their achievement. This combination of questionnaires and tests was integral to the research question of determining the relationship of attitudes and beliefs to mathematics performance. Responses from the questionnaires were factor analyzed, and the factors were used to predict mathematics achievement (as measured by the tests).

In a similar study, Mantzicopoulos and Knutson (2000) used school records, parent interviews, teacher questionnaires, and standardized tests of achievement to determine the relationship of school and family mobility to children's academic achievement. Nonreactive school records were used to determine how often the children in this longitudinal study changed schools. Parents were interviewed to determine the parents' perceptions of the positive and negative aspects of the moves. Standardized tests were used to assess the children's performance in kindergarten and again in second grade. Results indicated that frequent school moves were related to lower performance in second grade, even when controlling for prior achievement (kindergarten tests). Again, the combination of multiple methods was virtually required by the research question of determining the role of multiple school moves in children's academic achievement. Furthermore, the standardized tests

TABLE 11.7   Strengths and Weaknesses of Tests

Strengths:
  Can provide good measures of many characteristics of people
  Strong psychometric properties (high measurement validity)
  Availability of reference group data
  Possibly can be administered to groups
  May provide "hard" quantitative data
  Allow comparability of common measures across research populations
  Instruments usually already developed
  Wide range of tests available (with most content able to be tapped)
  Response rate high for group-administered tests
  Ease of data analysis
  Researcher-designed tests possibly tailored to local needs

Weaknesses:
  Can be expensive if test must be purchased for each research participant
  Possible reactive effects (e.g., response sets)
  Possibly not appropriate for a local population
  Sometimes biased against certain groups of people
  Potential nonresponse error to selected items on the test
  Might lack psychometric data
  Psychometric data possibly do not apply to local population

provided quantitative data with good psychometric properties.

There are several important strengths and weaknesses of tests that should be considered. These strengths and weaknesses are listed in Table 11.7.

OBSERVATION

The next major method of data collection is observation. When using this method, the researcher observes participants in natural or structured environments. Observation is an important method because people do not always do what they say they do. A common problem of observation is reactivity, although reactivity may decrease significantly after the researcher has been observing for a while. In interviewing, methodologists emphasize establishing rapport; the analog in observation is to create an environment where people will act as naturally as possible without considering the researcher's presence. When observing, it is also prudent to keep in mind Goffman's (1959) point that most social behavior is *frontstage behavior* (i.e., what people want or allow us to see) rather than *backstage behavior* (i.e., what people say and do with their closest friends or when acting naturally). It is useful to consider the roles that persons being observed may be playing in response to the researcher's presence.

Three types of observation are shown in Table 11.1. On the far left of the observation continuum is pure qualitative observation (Type 13 data collection). This type of observation is sometimes called naturalistic observation because observation is done in real-world or naturalistic settings. Qualitative observation is exploratory and open-ended. The researcher takes extensive fieldnotes, and when feasible, the researcher may use audio and/or visual recording devices to establish a record of what occurred for later analysis.

The researcher doing qualitative observation may take on four different roles that roughly make up a continuum, going from more qualitative to less qualitative (Gold, 1958). The most qualitative role is the *complete participant,* where the researcher becomes a full member of the group without informing the group members that they are being observed. The next role is called the *participant-as-observer,* where the researcher spends an extensive amount of time "inside" of the group and informs the members that they are being studied. The *observer-as-participant* is the next role. When performing this role, the observer spends a limited amount of time "inside" the group and informs the members that they are being observed. The last role is the *complete observer,* where the researcher observes from the outside. Reactivity is not a problem for the two most extreme roles, but these roles may result in ethical concerns.

On the far right of the observation continuum in Table 11.1 is pure quantitative observation. In this type of observation, standardized coding instruments are used during observation. Interrater reliability (of use of the instrument) is established for all observers through training and practice with the standard instrument. Sampling procedures (e.g., time interval and event

sampling) are sometimes used. Observations are usually videotaped and coded later using a priori coding schemes. An example of a quantitative observation measure can be found in the study titled "Analysis and Treatment of Finger Sucking" by Ellingson et al. (2000). In an effort to determine the reinforcements useful in maintaining finger sucking and to test the effectiveness of several interventions to lessen finger sucking, the researchers collected observational data of a 7-year-old and a 10-year-old who regularly engaged in finger sucking. To describe the baseline behavior and to measure change in the behavior as a result of several treatments, the researchers videotaped the participants in their homes for 10- and 20-minute segments. These videotapes were then scored using a real-time recording method in which the occurrence of finger sucking was recorded for each second; this resulted in a measure of percentage of time spent finger sucking. These real-time measures of finger sucking clearly showed a dramatic decrease in finger sucking when the participants wore protective coverings on their fingers. Observational research is frequently used in operant conditioning research because of the focus on the relationship between environmental stimuli and behavior (rather than attitudes and cognition).

A researcher conducting intramethod mixed observation (Type 14 data collection) mixes the characteristics of qualitative and quantitative observation. For example, the researcher may use an a priori observation protocol but also take extensive fieldnotes during and after the observation sessions. The goal here is to capitalize on the strengths of both qualitative observation and quantitative observation. Another approach would be to separately conduct a qualitative observation session and a quantitative observation session in a single research study.

Observation is also used in intermethod mixing. By combining observations with other measures such as questionnaires, researchers are able to gather relatively "objective firsthand" information but can supplement this with self-reports from the individuals being observed or from other individuals in the setting. For example, Eisenberg et al. (1999) used observations and questionnaires in a study titled "Consistency and Development of Prosocial Dispositions: A Longitudinal Study." The research participants were followed from 4 to 20 years of age, with observational data being collected at the younger ages. During the first observations, preschoolers were observed for a minimum of 70 2-minute intervals spread over several weeks. The observers coded four types of prosocial behavior. As the participants aged, the researchers employed questionnaires that were completed by the participants, their mothers, and their friends. The early observational measures were directly related to later self- and other-reports of prosocial behaviors.

Another example of intermethod mixing using observations and interviews is Dordick's (1996) study titled "More Than a Refuge: The Social World of a Homeless Shelter." This intermethod mixing allowed Dordick to provide a relatively complete view into the lives of individuals at a homeless shelter in New York. By using participant observation, Dordick was able to see firsthand the challenges faced daily by these homeless individuals. By incorporating these insights into the development of the interviews, the researcher was able to form interview questions that connected with the important issues in the lives of these individuals. Also, the researchers' ongoing nonthreatening presence in the participants' lives contributed to the individuals' willingness to be open and candid with the researcher.

There are several important strengths and weaknesses of observational data that should be considered. These strengths and weaknesses are listed in Table 11.8.

SECONDARY DATA

Secondary data (sometimes called "existing or available data") are data that were originally recorded or "left behind" or collected at an earlier time by a different person from the current researcher, often for an entirely different purpose from the current research purpose. In other words, the researcher "uses what is already there." The researcher must, however, find these data or artifacts so as to use them in his or her research study. Secondary data may be used with other data for corroboration, or they may be the "primary" data to be used in a research study. There are several common types of secondary data that the researcher can "go find," such as personal documents, official documents, physical data, and archived research data.

Personal documents include anything written, photographed, or recorded for private purposes. These are typically Type 16 data collection (pure qualitative), including items such as letters, diaries, family videos, and pictures. Although Types 17 and 18 for personal documents are possible, they are less common. Possible examples may include an individual's income tax records and checkbook logs (recording amounts in number units).

Official documents are recorded by members acting on behalf of an organization. Some qualitative (Type 16) examples are speeches and video recordings of television shows and advertisements. Some quantitative (Type 18) examples are financial records and census data. Many official documents are probably mixed (including both qualitative and quantitative data) such as newspapers, educational journals, annual reports, minutes of school board meetings, student records, and books.

TABLE 11.8   Strengths and Weaknesses of Observational Data

Strengths:

  Allow one to directly see what people do without having to rely on what they say they do
  Allow relatively objective measurement of behavior
  Can be used with participants with weak verbal skills
  Good for description
  Can give access to contextual factors operating in natural social settings
  Moderate degree of realism (when done outside of the laboratory)

Weaknesses:

  Reasons for behavior possibly unclear
  Possible reactive and investigator effects when respondents know they are being observed
  Possibility of observer being biased (e.g., selective perception)
  Possibility of observer "going native" (i.e., overidentifying with the group being studied)
  Interpretive validity possibly low
  Cannot observe large populations
  Unable to observe some content of interest
  Dross rate possibly moderately high
  More expensive to conduct than questionnaires and tests
  Data analysis sometimes time-consuming

Physical data include any physical traces left by people as they take part in various activities. Some examples of physical data that have been used by social scientists are wear in floor tiles in museums, wear on library books, soil from shoes and clothing, radio dial settings, fingerprints, suits of armor, and contents of people's trash (Webb et al., 1966/2000). Most of these examples are primarily qualitative.

Archived research data are data that were originally used for research purposes and then stored for possible later use. The largest source for quantitative archived data is the Inter-University Consortium for Political and Social Research, based in Ann Arbor, Michigan. Many qualitative researchers are also now saving their data, and analysis of these data may become more common in the future.

Secondary data are often combined with other data collection methods in intermethod mixing. For example, in an effort to describe the availability and use of support groups, Davison, Pennebaker, and Dickerson (2000) combined the use of official records and telephone interviews in their study titled "Who Talks? The Social Psychology of Illness Support Groups." These researchers first contacted mental health agencies and requested records that might provide listings of self-help groups. All of the listed groups were then contacted to determine whether they were still functioning. This resulted in information on the availability of active support groups. Finally, interviews were conducted with a sample of the active groups to determine what their specific role was and how many people were involved in their support group meetings and activities. This sequential use of records followed by interviews proved to be an efficient and effective approach to identifying active self-help groups and obtaining detailed information about them.

Intermethod mixing was also used in a study by Berends (2000) titled "Teacher-Reported Effects of New American School Designs: Exploring Relationships to Teacher Background and School Context." Berends's research purpose was to identify factors that were related to successful implementation of schoolwide reforms in 155 schools in eight jurisdictions. He used a mixture of interviews, questionnaires, and record reviews. Interviews were conducted with principals, questionnaires were distributed to teachers, and information concerning the demographic composition of the schools was obtained from official records that were kept by the school districts. This combination of different methods allowed the researcher to consider whether the composition of the 155 schools (as determined from records) might in any way be correlated with the attitudes and opinions expressed by the teachers and administrators.

There are several important strengths and weaknesses of secondary data that should be considered. These strengths and weaknesses are listed in Table 11.9.

◆ Summary

In this chapter, we have discussed the six major methods of data collection that are used in empirical research: questionnaires, interviews, focus groups, tests, observation, and secondary data. Each of these methods can be viewed as falling along a continuum with "pure qualitative" and "pure quantitative" as the poles. The center of the continuum is anchored with the term "mixed." This continuum was used to demonstrate how each method of data collection can vary from a pure form to a mixed form. Intramethod mixing involves mixing within a single method of data collection. The inclusion of open- and closed-ended items in a single questionnaire is an example of intramethod mixing. Data collection methods can also be mixed across more than one method; this type of mixing is called intermethod mixing. An example of intermethod mixing is the use of in-depth qualitative interviews and a standardized test in a single research project. When mixing methods of data collection, researchers should be guided by the fundamental principle of mixed methods research: Methods should be mixed so that they have complementary strengths and nonoverlapping weaknesses. As shown in many examples in this chapter, the use of intramethod and intermethod mixing in a single research study often results in more thorough information, corroboration of findings, and overall a much more trustworthy research study.

■ References

Anastasi, A., & Urbina, S. (1996). *Psychological testing* (7th ed.). Englewood Cliffs, NJ: Prentice Hall.

Babbie, E. (2001). *The practice of social research*. Belmont, CA: Wadsworth.

Berends, M. (2000). Teacher-reported effects of new American school designs: Exploring relationships to teacher background and school context. *Educational Evaluation and Policy Analysis, 22*(1), 65-82.

Bickman, L. (Ed.). (2000). *Validity and social experimentation*. Thousand Oaks, CA: Sage.

Breland, H. M., Kubota, M. Y., & Bonner, M. W. (1999). *The performance assessment study in writing: Analysis of the SAT II—*

TABLE 11.9   Strengths and Weaknesses of Secondary Data

Strengths of documents and physical data:
   Can provide insight into what people think and what they do
   Unobtrusive, making reactive and investigator effects very unlikely
   Can be collected for time periods occurring in the past (e.g., historical data)
   Personal documents often unobtrusive
   Useful for corroboration
   Grounded in local setting
   Useful for exploration

Strengths of archived research data:
   Available on a wide variety of topics
   Inexpensive
   Often reliable and valid (high measurement validity)
   Can study trends
   Useful for exploration and confirmation
   Ease of data analysis
   Sometimes based on large probability samples

Weaknesses of documents and physical data:
   May be incomplete because of selective reporting or recording
   Access to some types of content possibly difficult
   Interpretive validity possibly low
   Might not apply to general populations

Weaknesses of archived research data:
   Might not apply to local population or to specific research need (content problem)
   Data possibly dated (e.g., ecological and temporal validity possibly low)
   Interpretive validity possibly low
   Many of the most important findings possibly already have been mined from the data

Writing subject test. New York: College Board.

Brewer, J., & Hunter, A. (1989). *Multimethod research: A synthesis of styles.* Newbury Park, CA: Sage.

Bybee, D., Bellamy, C., & Mowbray, C. T. (2000). Analysis of participation in an innovative psychiatric rehabilitation intervention: Supported education. *Evaluation and Program Planning, 23,* 41-52.

Campbell, D. T. (1957). Factors relevant to the validity of experiments in social settings. *Psychological Bulletin, 54,* 297-312.

Campbell, D. T., & Stanley, J. C. (1963). *Experimental and quasi-experimental designs for research.* Chicago: Rand McNally.

Christensen, L. B. (2001). *Experimental methodology.* Boston: Allyn & Bacon.

Cook, T. D., & Campbell, D. T. (1979). *Quasi-experimentation: Design and analysis issues for field settings.* Chicago: Rand McNally.

Davison, K. P., Pennebaker, J. W., & Dickerson, S. S. (2000). Who talks? The social psychology of illness support groups. *American Psychologist, 55,* 205-217.

Denzin, N. K. (1989). *The research act: A theoretical introduction to sociological methods.* Englewood Cliffs, NJ: Prentice Hall.

Dillon, W. R., Madden, T. J., & Firtle, N. H. (1987). *Marketing research in a marketing environment.* Boston: Irwin.

Dordick, G. A. (1996). More than refuge: The social world of a homeless shelter. *Journal of Contemporary Ethnography, 24,* 373-404.

Eisenberg, N., Guthrie, I. K., Murphy, B. C., Shepard, S. A., Cumberland, A., & Carlo, G. (1999). Consistency and development of prosocial dispositions: A longitudinal study. *Child Development, 70,* 1360-1372.

Ellingson, S. A., Miltenberger, R. G., Stricker, J. M., Garlinghouse, M. A., Roberts, J., Galensky, T. L., & Rapp, J. T. (2000). Analysis and treatment of finger sucking. *Journal of Applied Behavior Analysis, 33,* 41-52.

Frankfort-Nachmias, C., & Nachmias, D. (2000). *Research methods in the social sciences.* New York: Worth.

Glaser, B. G., & Strauss, A. L. (1967). *The discovery of grounded theory: Strategies for qualitative research.* New York: Aldine De Gruyter.

Goffman, E. (1959). *The presentation of self in everyday life.* Garden City, NY: Anchor.

Gold, R. (1958). Roles in sociological field observations. *Social Forces, 36,* 217-223.

Huck, S. W., & Sandler, H. M. (1979). *Rival hypotheses: Alternative interpretation of data based conclusions.* New York: Harper & Row.

Johnson, R. B. (1995). Qualitative research in education. *SRATE Journal, 4*(1), 3-7.

Johnson, R. B., & Christensen, L. B. (2000). *Educational research: Quantitative and qualitative approaches.* Boston: Allyn & Bacon.

Jones, S. C., & Worthen, B. R. (1999). AEA members' opinions concerning evaluator certification. *American Journal of Evaluation, 20,* 495-506.

Krueger, R. A. (1998). *Moderating focus groups.* Thousand Oaks, CA: Sage.

LeCompte, M. D., & Preissle, J. (1993). *Ethnography and qualitative design in educational research.* San Diego: Academic Press.

Lincoln, Y. S., & Guba, E. G. (1985). *Naturalistic inquiry.* Beverly Hills, CA: Sage.

Mactavish, J. B., Mahon, M. J., & Lutfiyya, Z. M. (2000). "I can speak for myself": Involving individuals with intellectual disabilities as research participants. *Mental Retardation, 38,* 216-227.

Mantzicopoulos, P., & Knutson, D. J. (2000). Head Start children: School mobility and achievement in the early grades. *Journal of Educational Research, 93,* 305-311.

Maxwell, J. A. (1992). Understanding and validity in qualitative research. *Harvard Educational Review, 62,* 279-299.

Maxwell, J. A. (1996). *Qualitative research design.* Thousand Oaks, CA: Sage.

Messick, S. (1989). Validity. In R. L. Linn (Ed.), *Educational measurement* (3rd ed., pp. 13-103). New York: Macmillan.

Mickelson, K. D., Wroble, M., & Helgeson, V. S. (1999). "Why my child?" Parental attributions for children's special needs. *Journal of Applied Social Psychology, 29,* 1263-1292.

Morgan, D. L. (1998). *Planning focus groups.* Thousand Oaks, CA: Sage.

Onwuegbuzie, A. J. (in press). Expanding the framework of internal and external validity in quantitative research. *Research in the Schools.*

Papanastasiou, C. (2000). Effects of attitudes and beliefs on mathematics achievement. *Studies in Educational Evaluation, 26,* 27-42.

Patton, M. Q. (1987). *How to use qualitative methods in evaluation.* Newbury Park, CA: Sage.

Patton, M. Q. (1990). *Qualitative evaluation and research methods.* Newbury Park, CA: Sage.

Patton, M. Q. (2002). *Qualitative research and evaluation methods.* Thousand Oaks, CA: Sage.

Pena, D. C. (2000). Parent involvement: Influencing factors and implications. *Journal of Educational Research, 94,* 42-54.

Schensul, S. L., Schensul, J. J., & LeCompte, M. D. (1999). *Essential ethnographic methods: Observations, interviews, and questionnaires.* Walnut Creek, CA: AltaMira.

Stake, R. E. (1990). Situational context as influence on evaluation design and use. *Studies in Educational Evaluation, 16,* 231-246.

Stake, R. E. (1995). *The art of case study research.* Thousand Oaks, CA: Sage.

Strauss, A., & Corbin, J. (1998). *Basics of qualitative research: Techniques and procedures for developing grounded theory.* Thousand Oaks, CA: Sage.

Tashakkori, A., & Teddlie, C. (1998). *Mixed methodology: Combining qualitative and quantitative approaches* (Applied Social Research Methods, No. 46). Thousand Oaks, CA: Sage.

Turner, L. A. (1998). Relation of attributional beliefs to memory strategy use in children and adolescents with mental retardation. *American Journal of Mental Retardation, 103,* 162-172.

Vaughn, S., Reiss, M., Rothlein, L., & Hughes, M. T. (1999). Kindergarten teachers' perceptions of instructing students with disabilities. *Remedial and Special Education, 20,* 184-191.

Way, N., Stauber, H. Y., Nakkula, M. J., & London, P. (1994). Depression and substance use in two divergent high school cultures: A quantitative and qualitative analysis. *Journal of Youth and Adolescence, 23,* 331-357.

Webb, E. J., Campbell, D. T., Schwartz, R. D., & Sechrest, L. (2000). *Unobtrusive measures.* Thousand Oaks, CA: Sage. (Original work published 1966)

Yin, R. K. (1994). *Case study research: Design and methods.* Thousand Oaks, CA: Sage.

12

TABLES OR TABLEAUX?
THE CHALLENGES OF WRITING
AND READING MIXED METHODS STUDIES

◆ Margarete Sandelowski

Mixed methods studies present researchers with many challenges. Not the least of these challenges, and the subject of this chapter, is how to present mixed methods studies for mixed audiences of researchers.[1] Mixed methods studies engender a "crisis of representation" (Denzin & Lincoln, 2000, p. 16) all their own as they mandate that researchers/writers communicate across entrenched divides often separating writers from readers, in general, and qualitative from quantitative writers and readers, in particular.

A major—and arguably the most important—criterion in evaluating the merits of a study lies in the ability of writers to persuade readers of its merits in their re-

search reports. Aesthetic criteria, including the sense of rightness and comfort readers experience, is crucial to the judgments they make about the validity or trustworthiness of a study (Eisner, 1985). Indeed, a judgment of trustworthiness is as much—or even more—a judgment about attractiveness and appeal as it is about objectivity or truth. But qualitative and quantitative readers have different ideas about what is appealing (Golden-Biddle & Locke, 1993). They often belong to different "interpretive communities" of writers and readers (Fish, 1980) whose members vary in their access and attunement to, knowledge and acceptance of, and participation with, for example, references and allusions in a text, the varied uses of words

◆ 321

and numbers, and various genres or conventions of writing. Qualitative and quantitative readers bring different reading backgrounds, experiences, and expectations to research reports and thus interact with these texts differently. Mixed methods studies, which entail the active engagement of highly diverse communities of qualitative and quantitative writers and readers, thus call into question which appeals will produce the most convincing texts. The production of convincing mixed methods studies lies, in large part, in how well the needs and expectations of readers representing this mix of interpretive communities have been met.

Yet, mixed methods studies are often themselves employed as appeals to validity, that is, as overcoming the shortcomings of single method studies, in general, and of quantitative and especially qualitative studies, in particular. Researchers may emphasize the quantitative research in their mixed methods studies to authorize their use of qualitative research to readers deemed likely to view qualitative work as weak scholarship. John (1992) proposed that psychologists use statistics, in large part, to confer the "epistemic authority" (p. 146) of science on psychology, a field in which the claim to science is contested. As he observed, the power of statistics lies as much in their ability to engender a "sense of conviction" (p. 147) in their "evidentiary value" (p. 144) as to provide actual evidence about a target phenomenon. In a similar but contrasting vein, researchers may emphasize the qualitative research in their mixed methods studies to authorize their use of quantitative research to readers deemed likely to view quantitative work as thin scholarship.

In this chapter, I draw from literatures on mixed methods and qualitative research, and on aesthetic modes of knowing, *rhetoric* and *representation* in science, and reader response theories (Beach,

1993) to describe the challenges of writing and reading mixed methods studies. I present mixed methods study not only as a challenge to rhetoric but also as a kind of rhetoric itself.

◆ Words and Worlds

The most important challenge to writing and reading mixed methods studies lies in the various and even bewildering uses of the words *qualitative, quantitative, mixed methods,* and *triangulation* in methodological literature about, and reports of, the findings of, mixed methods studies. The phrases *mixed methods studies* and *triangulated studies* are commonly used to refer to the use of both qualitative and quantitative approaches to inquiry within the confines of a single study. Yet in the writings about and reports of mixed methods studies, including the chapters in this handbook, there are no uniform presentations of (a) what distinguishes qualitative from quantitative research, (b) what qualitative and quantitative entities are mixed, (c) what kind of mixing is involved, and (d) why these entities are mixed at all. The consequence of this lack of uniformity is a confusing state of affairs for readers whereby mixes are claimed for studies having no mixes, for entities that cannot be mixed, and/or to resolve methodological problems that cannot be resolved by mixing.

QUALITATIVE AND QUANTITATIVE

Qualitative and *quantitative* are words that are used in a variety of ways to refer to an even wider variety of research entities, including (a) paradigms, or overarching worldviews or perspectives for inquiry, such as neo-positivism, social constructionism, and feminism; (b) kinds of data such as stories, self-reports, numbers, accounts, fieldnotes, and photographs; (c) kinds of research methods such as grounded theory and experiments; and (d) kinds of research techniques for sampling, data collection, and analysis such as random and theoretical sampling, questionnaires and in-depth interviewing, and multiple regression and qualitative content analysis. The words *qualitative* and *quantitative* are typically used to present research paradigms, methods, and/or techniques as one or the other. Mixed methods studies imply difference, as they entail the combination of entities—qualitative and quantitative—that are viewed as different from, albeit compatible with, each other.

Yet, also clear from the vast literature on the subject is that qualitative research is not an entity clearly distinguishable from quantitative research; rather, it is many things to many people. Although it seems "rhetorically unavoidable" to compare qualitative and quantitative research (Becker, 1996, p. 53), there is no consistent manner in which such comparisons are made. For some scholars, qualitative and quantitative research differ in kind, constituting entities as different from each other as cats and dogs, while for others, they differ only in degree. While some scholars emphasize and even celebrate the differences between qualitative and quantitative research, others minimize and even trivialize them. Schwandt (2000) proposed that qualitative inquiry is more appropriately viewed as a "reformist movement" (p. 189), or an "arena for social scientific criticism" (p. 190), than as any particular kind of inquiry. He suggested that qualitative research is "home" for a wide variety of scholars who appear to share very little except their general distaste for and distrust of "mainstream" (usually conceived as quantitative) research (p. 190). Indeed, these scholars are often seriously at odds with each other. Although the term *qualitative research* does manage to convey a shared "feeling tone" (Sapir, 1951, p. 308), what it signifies beyond that feeling varies with the reader and writer of qualitative research.

Accordingly, communicating the mix in mixed methods studies is complicated if only because studies might not actually include ingredients perceived by writers and/or readers as different, that is, as qualitative as opposed to quantitative. The appeal to difference fails here, thereby undermining the claim to having conducted a mixed methods study. For example, although they have been depicted as mixed methods studies, projects involving the addition of one or two open-ended questions at the end of a standardized questionnaire, a simple frequency count of topics raised by respondents in interviews, or a count of the numbers of theoretical categories created and the numbers of persons falling into those categories can hardly be considered examples of mixing qualitative with quantitative research. There are writers and readers who use the word *qualitative* as a synonym for any verbal data collected from human participants (including standardized instruments) or for any study that is not quantitative. Because mixed methods study has become somewhat of a fad, claiming to having conducted a mixed methods study becomes a way to be methodologically fashionable. Mixed methods study is used here as a rhetorical appeal not only to methodological fashion but also to methodological expertise and ecumenicism.

Adding to the confusion concerning whether anything at all is mixed in studies presented as mixed methods studies is that entities commonly conceived as qualitative, such as focus groups, are often actually implemented quantitatively. If *qualitative* refers not simply to verbal data but rather to an overarching interpretivist, hermeneutic, constructionist, or participatory perspective (Heron & Reason, 1997; Schwandt, 2000) concerning how inquiry should be conducted, there is arguably nothing qualitative about focus groups that are conducted like surveys, with highly structured interview guides allowing participants little freedom to structure responses that are, in turn, analyzed using descriptive statistics. There is nothing mixed in a purportedly mixed methods study that combines a survey tool with a focus group that is itself conducted and analyzed like a survey. Indeed, such a study is more accurately conceived as a multimethod study in which two or more like (quantitative or quantitatively informed) entities are used. A study comprised largely of focus groups treated like surveys, even if data are analyzed verbally as opposed to statistically, is at best (and depending on point of view) a *non*quantitative or *non*qualitative study.

THE MIX IN MIXED METHODS STUDIES

In addition to the lack of uniformity in presenting qualitative versus quantitative research, which calls into question whether anything has been mixed at all, is the lack of clarity concerning what qualitative and quantitative entities have been mixed and the kind of mixing involved. Writers have variously depicted mixed methods studies as mixes, mergers, blends, integrations, reconciliations, or other combinations of qualitative and quantitative paradigms, methods, or techniques. In these presentations, mergers are claimed for entities that are not exclusively either qualitative or quantitative (e.g., case studies, feminist inquiry) or are at different levels of inquiry (e.g., a hermeneutic *paradigm* and a fixed-response *data collection tool*) and for enti-

ties that cannot be merged (e.g., realist and relativist paradigms of inquiry).

What better distinguishes research entities and researchers is not whether they are qualitative or quantitative per se (as both focus groups and surveys involve verbal data and will therefore be labeled by some writers and readers as qualitative, while data from both sources can be analyzed statistically) but rather the overall attitude toward and interpretive treatment of the data collected in those studies. Methods do not by themselves signal much about the nature of inquiry; rather, it is the distinctive execution and representation of these methods that signal key differences in inquiry. Whether any mix has occurred at all is determined by ascertaining, for example, whether the interviews conducted in a study that also involves the use of questionnaires are treated like those questionnaires or as, for example, narratives of the self. In the former instance, a qualitative-quantitative mix arguably cannot justifiably be claimed, while in the latter instance, it arguably can.

The focus group, the interview, and participant observation are good examples of entities depicted at the level of both methodology and method. While some writers use the terms *methodology* and *method* synonymously, others take great pains to distinguish between them, using the term *methodology* to refer to an overall approach to inquiry regularly linked to particular theoretical frameworks (e.g., grounded theory that is linked to symbolic interactionism and pragmatism) and using the term *method* as a synonym for the techniques for sampling, data collection, and data analysis with which methodologies (e.g., grounded theory) are implemented. Some writers present the focus group, the interview, and participant observation as data collection techniques used, for example, to execute grounded theory or ethnographic studies, while others present them as wholly defining their studies (i.e., *as* methodologies), designating the studies themselves as focus group, interview, or participant observation studies. Because of the different uses to which *method* and *methodology* are put, and because the same entity may be conceived as either a method or a methodology and differently executed, the determination of what has been mixed and whether any mix has occurred at all can be difficult to make.

The determination of whether anything has been mixed is further complicated because scholars arguing for and against mixes are frequently not talking about the same mixes or claim mixes of entities that cannot be mixed. The disagreements between so-called purists and "compatibilists" (Skrtic, 1990, p. 128) over whether qualitative and quantitative research can be mixed are often not true disagreements at all; purists tend to emphasize the irreconcilability of paradigms, while compatibilists tend to emphasize the reconcilability of methods or techniques. In short, they all are ostensibly discussing the mixing of qualitative and quantitative research, but they are more often than not referring to mixes at different (paradigm, method, or technique) levels of research, conceiving the same entities differently as paradigms, methods, or techniques and/or describing different research entities as qualitative or quantitative. In addition, researchers often do not mean the same thing when they talk of any one study as a mixed methods study. To some researchers, the mixed methods study to which they are referring is one study in a program of research involving other studies (that may or may not be mixed), while to other researchers, it refers to the program of research itself. A program of research necessarily entails more than one study and may include a series of single method (qualitative and quantitative) studies, but

it is debatable whether the term *mixed methods study* ought to be used to refer to such a program of research.

Moreover, paradigms, if defined as overarching worldviews and belief systems, cannot be mixed. Paradigms, by this definition, entail competing and often contradictory views concerning the nature of reality, the proper relationship between researcher and participant, the objectives and values of inquiry, and how value is to be judged. Although paradigms are uniformly linked to neither methods nor techniques (e.g., feminist inquiry is not exclusively qualitative, nor is neo-positivist inquiry exclusively quantitative), paradigms do influence the way in which any one method or technique will be executed. Grounded theory will be differently executed and thus presented depending on whether it is informed by tenets of neo-positivism or constructivism (Annells, 1996; Charmaz, 2000). The interview will be differently conducted, and the interview data will be differently treated and presented, depending on whether researchers view the interview as an index of some external reality, such as facts or feelings (Silverman, 2000, p. 823), or as a "technology of biographical construction" (Atkinson & Silverman, 1997, p. 306). The interpretive treatment of the interview will depend on whether researchers view interview data as comprising reports of events or as public, private, moral, or other accounts of those events (Radley & Billig, 1996; West, 1990). Treatment will also depend on whether researchers view interviewees as potentially biased informants or forgetful reporters of events or as narrators or impression managers of them (Riessman, 1990). In fact, the treatment of the interview will depend on whether researchers view interviewees as fixed participants/objects of study at all. Scholars have increasingly challenged the humanist notion of a stable and individual self on which academic inquiry has been largely based (Blumenthal, 1999; Gergen & Gergen, 2000).

Accordingly, although a program of research might comprise of a series of studies that together combine two or more paradigms for inquiry, any one research project—including any one mixed methods study—can be informed by only one paradigm or viewing position. As graphic artist M. C. Escher demonstrated in his 1947 work *High and Low,* the tiled diamond entity in this work cannot simultaneously be viewed as both a ceiling and a floor (Schattschneider, 1994). Moreover, like religious beliefs, different beliefs about inquiry may be tolerated, but they are not so easily changed or exchanged by any one researcher. Any one research study, no matter what the methods or techniques used, cannot simultaneously or sequentially be informed by, for example, a belief that valid results are enhanced by a dualist and detached relationship between researcher and participant and by the opposing belief that valid results are obtained only when a fully participative relationship exists.

An excellent example of a mixed methods study in which a qualitative method (narrative analysis based on Kleinman's explanatory models framework) was used within a neo-positivist framework is the Borkan, Quirk, and Sullivan (1991) study of the relationship between elders' narrative constructions of hip fracture and functional outcomes. Borkan and his colleagues transformed and reduced the narrative data they collected into two variables so as to ascertain whether they predicted functional outcomes. The process by which this transformation took place included several sequences of interrater reliability coding, a quantitatively informed procedure reflecting the belief that truth is replicable and will elicit consensus. By contrast, researchers operating in an interpretive paradigm will treat narratives as inherently dynamic and revisionist and therefore not reducible to fixed variables in a correlation matrix or amenable to mathematized reliability testing.

An excellent example of a mixed methods study in which a quantitative technique (Spearman correlation) was used in an ethnographic/narrative framework is the Cohen, Tripp-Reimer, Smith, Sorofman, and Lively (1994) study of patient and professional explanations of diabetes. Cohen and her colleagues correlated glycosylated hemoglobin levels with interview data obtained from patients and health care professionals. They transformed these data into congruence scores, where 0 symbolized agreement (or no disagreement), 1 symbolized minor disagreement, and 2 symbolized major disagreement. The Spearman correlation coefficient showed a positive but nonsignificant relationship between explanatory model congruence and normal Hemoglobin A1c levels.

APPLE JUICE, ORANGE JUICE, AND FRUIT JUICE

Also vague from many presentations of mixed methods studies is the kind of mixing that occurred. In one kind of mixed methods study, qualitative and quantitative entities are in mixed company with each other, while in the other kind, they are actually blended.

In the first kind of mixed methods study, entities are associated with or linked to each other but retain their essential characters; metaphorically, apple juice and orange juice both are used, but they are never mixed together to produce a new kind of juice. An example of this kind of mix was the use of grounded theory and ethological observation in a study my colleagues and I conducted of the transition to parenthood of infertile couples (Sandelowski, Holditch-Davis, & Harris, 1992). We used grounded theory to describe the aspects of this transition amenable to grounded theory study, and we used ethological observation to describe those aspects amenable to ethological observation. Wolfer (1993) proposed that different aspects of reality lend themselves to different methods of inquiry. More precisely, although there is no uniform paradigm-method link, there is a method-reality link.

We used grounded theory to describe the process by which infertile couples pursued parenthood, and we used ethological observation to describe their interactions with the children they eventually parented. Both of these methods are compatible in that they are forms of naturalistic inquiry in which no a priori theoretical framework is imposed on target phenomena and no variables are manipulated. In a mixed company mixed methods study, inferences about a target phenomenon are drawn from the findings of both qualitative and quantitative data sets, each of which are separately analyzed using like-to-like techniques. That is, qualitative techniques are used to analyze qualitative data (in the case of grounded theory, constant comparison analysis), and quantitative techniques are used to analyze quantitative data (in the case of ethological observation, statistical pattern and trend analyses). Inferences may be presented in the form of theory or sets of propositions or working hypotheses that incorporate both sets of findings, for example, the proposal of a direct association between the ways couples pursued an option (identified only from the use of grounded theory) and the ways they interacted with their children (identified only from ethological observation).

In contrast to mixed company mixed methods studies are studies entailing actual blendings of two or more entities conceived as qualitative and quantitative into one entity, either qualitative or quantitative (i.e., where apple juice and orange juice are combined to create a new kind of fruit juice that is either more apple than orange, more orange than apple, or equally apple and orange). Tashakkori and Teddlie (1998) referred to the process of transforming qualitative/verbal data into quantitative/numerical data as "quantitizing" (p. 126), while Boyatzis (1998) referred to this process as "quantitative translation" (p. 129). In the transition to parenthood study, my colleagues and I transformed interview data into a display comparing the numbers of couples having and not having an amniocentesis with the number of physicians encouraging or not encouraging them to have the procedure. We then used Fisher's exact probability test, which showed a nonsignificant statistical relationship between physician encouragement and couples' decision to have an amniocentesis (Sandelowski, Harris, & Holditch-Davis, 1991).

By contrast, qualitizing is the process by which quantitative/numerical data are transformed into qualitative/verbal data. An example of this process is a study in which quantitative cluster techniques are used to identify groups of individuals distinguished from each other by their responses to a set of data collection tools. A grounded theory study is then mounted to further profile these groups theoretically—to validate that mutually distinctive groups have been identified and to explicate further the features of the individual members of these groups that make them more like each other than members of the other groups identified. The quantitatively derived clusters provide the basis for theoretical sampling and further typology development.

Yet, not all such transformations are appropriately called mixed methods studies. Rothert and her colleagues (1990) interviewed three women from each of the four groups of women they identified using quantitative cluster analysis techniques on the basis of these women's responses to eight scenarios about hormone replacement therapy. Yet as presented in the report of their study, these interviews did not constitute a fully realized qualitative study, with a clearly defined methodological approach and deliberately selected sampling, data collection, and data analysis plans. Although it is a valuable study, it is not a mixed methods study, nor did the researchers present it as one. Indeed, the interview portion of this study does not even appear in the report until the discussion section.

Similarly, although it can be called qualitizing when researchers verbally profile the participants in their studies, by designating them as largely hypertensive because 15 of 20 participants had systolic blood pressures greater than 140 or diastolic blood pressures greater than 90, this kind of qualitizing is common to all studies and not just mixed methods studies. Although it can be called quantitizing when researchers count the number of persons or events fitting into a category, such counting is inherent to the process of extracting meaning from verbal data. Meaning depends on number, just as number depends on meaning (Dey, 1993, p. 28). Moreover, most studies in the social and behavioral sciences, as well as in the practice disciplines, entail the use of more than one of something (e.g., investigators, participants, sites) for data collection. The mere use of more than one of some research entity in a study does not constitute a mixed methods study and might not even constitute a multimethod study.

CONFLICTING PURPOSES AND QUESTIONABLE APPEALS

Another persistent problem in presenting mixed methods studies concerns the depiction of the reason for mixing methods. There are two large and conflicting

purposes for combining studies: to achieve a fuller understanding of a target phenomenon and to verify one set of findings against the other. In the first instance, the goal is to achieve a kaleidoscopic or prismatic view of a target event; in the second instance, the goal is to converge on the one "true" view. In the first instance, the appeal is to comprehensive understanding; in the second, it is to validity. Arguably, only the latter purpose is appropriately referred to as triangulation, which is a process specifically aimed toward the realist goal of establishing convergent validity (Sandelowski, 1995b). Confusion arises when writers use the term *triangulated study* as if this designates a methodology itself, such as grounded theory or the randomized controlled trial, or when they use the word *triangulation* to designate the effort to ascertain multiple points of view about a target phenomenon, that is, the use of two or more investigators, sites, data sets, theories, or other research entities in a single study or the use of anything qualitative with anything quantitative. When any kind of research combination is designated as triangulation, there is no inquiry that is not triangulated. Having too much meaning, the word *triangulation* has no meaning at all. Yet the word is overused precisely because it has such diverse appeal—because mixing methods is itself a "claims making activity" (Aronson, 1984). Triangulation appears as a "near-talismanic method" (Miles & Huberman, 1994, p. 266) for democratizing inquiry and resolving conflicts between qualitative and quantitative inquiry.

Indeed, in another validation context, both mixed methods and specifically triangulated studies are depicted as necessary to offset the so-called weaknesses or limitations of single method studies. Yet methods have neither strengths nor weaknesses except in relation to particular perspectives toward and standards of inquiry.

It is not a weakness or a limitation of any qualitative study that nomothetic generalizations cannot be drawn or that samples are not statistically representative, just as it is neither a weakness nor a limitation of any quantitative study that case-bound generalizations cannot be drawn or that samples are not information rich. Rather, it is the researcher who is weak or limited who chooses inquiry approaches for the wrong reasons, executes them in the wrong way, or apologizes for method characteristics that require no apology. A rhetorical device still too often used in presenting qualitative research is to apologize for its failings relative to quantitative research and then to defend why, despite its failings, qualitative research can still contribute to the research enterprise so well-exemplified by quantitative research. While quantitative research reports seem to require the demonstration of "modesty" (Shapin, 1984, p. 494) to offset the immodesty of their claims, qualitative research reports seem to require the demonstration of contrition to offset the weakness of their claims.

Yet, what is considered a failing in one world of inquiry is often considered an advantage in another—another reason why worlds of inquiry, or paradigms, cannot be mixed. For example, participatory action researchers emphasize the necessity for nonhierarchical and engaged relationships between inquirers and participants, and they often even avoid drawing any distinction at all between researchers and participants. By contrast, neo-positivist researchers emphasize the necessity for hierarchical and dispassionate relationships between researchers and participants so as to control bias. Accordingly, the presentation of mixed methods studies as a defense against purportedly invalid research, or to offset the alleged weaknesses of specific kinds of research approaches, is a rhetorical device that masks

the assumption of a specific set of standards by which research is judged to be invalid or weak. Indeed, such defenses typically reproduce the view of qualitative research as weak and of quantitative research as strong (Blaikie, 1991).

◆ *Technologies of Persuasion*

In addition to the complicated mix of words in mixed methods studies—and of the diverse worlds they represent and create—is the challenge that lies in the very representation of the research report itself or the "write-up" (Wolcott, 1990). In quantitative research, the write-up is typically conceived as the end product of a clearly defined and sequentially arranged process of inquiry, beginning with the identification of a research problem, and research questions or hypotheses, progressing through the selection of a sample and the collection of data, and ending with the analysis and interpretation of those data (Golden-Biddle & Locke, 1993; Gusfield, 1976). The write-up is here conceived as an objective description of the activities engaged in during each phase of this process and of what was found as a result of this process. The standardization of form evident in the familiar scientific report reflects and reinforces the realist ideals and objectivist values associated with neo-positivist inquiry. Written in the third-person passive voice, separating method from findings and findings from interpretation, and representing inquiry as occurring in a linear process and findings as truths that anyone following the same procedures will also find, these "author-evacuated" texts (Geertz, 1988, p. 141) reproduce the neo-positivist assumption of an external reality apprehensible and demonstrable by objective inquiry procedures. Standardization of form is also actively sought in the belief that form ought not to confound content. Language is viewed as a neutral medium of communication by which objective scientific practices are conveyed. Readers know what to expect in the conventional science write-up, and the fulfillment of this expectation alone constitutes a major criterion by which readers will evaluate the merits of the study findings. A write-up that fails to meet readers' expectations for the write-up will jeopardize the status of a study as scientific (McGill, 1990). In the case of science reporting, familiarity breeds contentment and novelty breeds contempt or, at the very least, suspicion.

In qualitative research, the write-up is conceived less as an end product of inquiry than as inquiry in the making. The familiar components of the research process—sampling, data collection, analysis, interpretation, and representation—are in recursive and iterative relationships with each other throughout the life of any study. Decisions concerning who or what to sample next, and the means and direction for future analysis, are directed by the analysis of data collected from persons or objects already sampled. Accordingly, the qualitative write-up as an end is not easily differentiated from writing as a means of inquiry (Richardson, 2000) because writing to report findings typically leads researchers to more writing to discern (or, in a more constructivist vein, to create) findings. The embodied act of putting words on a page or on a screen to present a study to an audience usually leads researchers to see things, or things missing, in their analysis that they had not seen before. Writing up qualitative research for publication is therefore indistinguishable from analysis and interpretation; to analyze and interpret is to write. Moreover, qualitative researchers, especially those most influenced by the postmodern emphasis on language and discourse (e.g., Clifford &

Marcus, 1986), view language as itself a subject for interpretation; language is perceived less to reflect than to contribute to, create, or comprise reality. In addition, although quantitative research reports are supposed to be deliberately devoid of literary frills and of emotion in the service of reporting the "plain unvarnished truth" (Golden-Biddle & Locke, 1993, p. 597), the use of expressive language is generally highly prized among qualitative researchers.

Although there is a widely accepted genre for communicating the results of quantitative research—the "experimental" scientific report (Bazerman, 1988)—there is no one accepted genre for reporting the results of qualitative studies. "One narrative size does not fit all" (Tierney, 1995, p. 389) qualitative research. Indeed, qualitative researchers have eschewed standardization in all components of inquiry, opting for more reflexive and "confessional" (Van Maanen, 1988, chap. 4) "author-saturated" texts (Geertz, 1988, p. 141) and, to a lesser extent, for more literary, performance, and other experimental modes of presenting findings such as drama, poetry, autoethnography, and dance (Norris, 1997; Richardson, 2000). Qualitative researchers feel more acutely the lack of "innocence" in the research report (Van Maanen, 1995, p. 1). Among qualitative researchers, there is disagreement on the extent to which poetry or prose, and perspective/vision or polyphony/voice, ought to inform their writing practices (Norris, 1997; Richardson, 2000; Sandelowski, 1994a, 1995a; Schwalbe, 1995; Thorne, 1997; Tyler, 1986). Qualitative researchers have been especially concerned about writing reports, or telling "tales of the field" (Van Maanen, 1988), that communicate not only methodological rigor but also methodological flexibility and, even more important, a fidelity to and feeling for the persons and events studied. The crisis of representation for qualitative researchers involves the desires to "record" experience and to "create" it (Schwalbe, 1995, p. 395), to give voice to the voiceless and to give discourse its due (Saukko, 2000), to be truthful and to be evocative and even provocative, to be faithful and fair to the people in their studies and to be faithful and fair to the values and ideals of scholarly inquiry itself, and to create texts that are scientifically and/or ethnographically valid and that are stylish and significant. (For some ethnographers, ethnographic validity resides in being self-consciously scientific.) A consequence of these seemingly contradictory goals is that there is no one way for writers to encode and for readers to decode qualitative write-ups.

◆ *Artful Science*

This problem of encoding/decoding is further complicated in mixed methods studies where qualitative research is combined with quantitative research that generally conforms to a familiar set of rules for scientific representation. Indeed, in the qualitative researcher's desire to create something both scientific and artistic lies one of the greatest challenges to writing and reading mixed methods studies: Qualitative research lies on the "fault line" between science and art (Sandelowski, 1994a, p. 48), as both scientific and artistic traditions have influenced the conceptualization, conduct, and representation of qualitative research and as these traditions have been variously depicted as like and unlike each other. For example, Eisner (1981) emphasized differences between scientific and artistic representations in the areas of form, degree of license, and criteria for appraisal. He also viewed the "arts as paradigm cases of qualitative intelligence in action" and viewed qualitative research as evoking the "epistemic functions" of the arts (Eisner, 1991, pp. 6, 108). By contrast, Eisner (1985), in another publication, and others (e.g., Nisbet, 1976; Root-Bernstein, 1984) have emphasized the similarities between science and art in their purposes; uses of image, metaphor, and visual display; and aesthetic criteria for evaluation.

Most notable for the purposes of this chapter are discussions of the "aesthetic [as] both a subject matter and a criterion for appraising the processes used to create works of science as well as art" (Eisner, 1985, p. 27). Eisner (1985) argued that both scientists and artists "create forms through which the world is viewed" (p. 26). While artists create paintings, poems, and pottery, scientists create "taxonomies, theories, frameworks, [and] conceptual systems" (p. 26). The familiar research report and the novel both are modes of representing reality (Krieger, 1983) and "highly stylized art forms" (Krieger, 1991, p. 117). The American Psychological Association (APA, 1994) publication manual is both an official style and a "prescriptive rhetoric" (Bazerman, 1988, p. 275) for writing up the findings of scientific studies that codifies and embodies objectivist beliefs about inquiry. Here is a major reason why adherents to other than objectivist beliefs—often those conducting qualitative research—will find it hard to adhere to APA style, especially where it prescribes that results/analysis be separated from discussion/interpretation and where it proscribes ambiguity, reflexivity, and emotion. Content and form are inextricable as "formatting requirements," and "editing rules" for research write-ups constrain what can be communicated (Star, 1983, pp. 211-212). As Richardson (1990) summarized it, "*How* we are expected to write affects *what* we can write about" (p. 16, italics in original).

How we are expected to write thereby affects what and how we know.

As Shapin (1984) argued, the "production of knowledge" cannot be separated from the "communication of knowledge" by which "communities" of responsive readers are created and come to accept a study as valid (p. 481). The APA (1994) publication manual is part of a "literary technology" used to make readers "virtual witnesses" to events they have not directly seen (p. 490). As Shapin conceived it, this technology produces in readers' minds an image of a research scene that "obviates the necessity for either its direct witness or its replication" (p. 491). Indeed, the technology used to accomplish virtual witnessing is no different from the technology used to "facilitate replication." The researcher/writer "deploys the same linguistic resources in order to encourage the physical replication of experiments [as] to trigger in the reader's mind a naturalistic image of the [research] scene" (p. 491). The correlation coefficient is such a linguistic resource, that is, a numerical representation of—and appeal to—stability and consensus to those communities of scholars that will find such appeals convincing. Statistics are rhetoric, that is, "literary . . . displays treated as dramatic presentations to a scientific community" (Gephart, 1988, p. 47). Writers do not find quantitative significance so much as they participate with willing readers to create it (Gephart, 1986). Such technologies contribute to the illusion created in readers' minds that write-ups of research are reflections of reality (Shapin, 1984, p. 510).

In their influential ethnographic study *Laboratory Life*, Latour and Woolgar (1986) introduced the concept of "inscription," by which they emphasized the importance of writing not so much as a method of conveying information as a "material operation of creating order" (p. 245). As they described it, the work of science is the creation of inscriptions. What we understand to be science is wholly composed of these inscriptions or the simplifications (e.g., traces, charts, models, figures) that constitute representations of the "facts" of nature that scientists create in the process of seeking to discover them. According to Latour and Woolgar, scientists are even more "obsessed" with inscriptions than are novelists because "there is nothing but a wall of archives, labels, protocol books, figures, and papers . . . between scientists and chaos" (p. 245).

Indeed, scientific forms, like artistic ones, are judged by how well they reduce chaos. As Eisner (1985) observed, all forms are evaluated by the same aesthetic criteria, including coherence, attractiveness, and economy. Quantification and graphical displays are common ways to achieve coherence and economy in science texts (Law & Whittaker, 1988). Scientific theories are accepted because they are coherent, harmonious, and parsimonious. In short, although quantitatively oriented scientists may deny it (Lynch & Edgerton, 1988), aesthetic considerations are not confined to the arts or popular renderings of scientific findings. Rather, the aesthetic is itself a "mode of knowing" (Eisner, 1985) in science. Both scientific and artistic forms are judged by how well they confer order, make sense, and evoke sensory images of the inquiry process.

Moreover, scientific representations are no more objective or less subjective than are artistic ones. Illuminating here is Root-Bernstein's (1984) discussion of painting and scientific illustration. To counter the commonplace view that 10 painters painting the same scene will produce 10 different pictures, Root-Bernstein showed the *similarity* between two artists' resolutions of the problem of how to introduce motion into paintings. To counter the commonplace view that 10 scientists addressing the same problem will produce the same results, Root-Bernstein showed the *dissimilarity* in three graphic representations of the periodic system of elements. Root-Bernstein argued against the simplistic view that scientific representations index external and eternal truths, while artistic representations vary with the artists. Both scientists and artists working in the same tradition, with the same methods, and on the same problem will likely produce comparable forms. Scientists are no less a part of their graphic displays than artists are of their paintings. Artistic forms are as much "experiments in perception, applications of new rules, or theories . . . or concepts" (p. 113) as are scientific forms.

Art historians and social scientists have emphasized the identity between representations in science and art as stylized constructions for ordering and making sense (Gifford-Gonzalez, 1993; Law & Lynch, 1988; Nisbet, 1976; Stafford, 1991, 1994). Especially notable here are sociological and critical/cultural studies of scientific practices as exercises in rhetoric, representation, and "aesthetic judgments" (Lynch & Edgerton, 1988, p. 185). These studies suggest additional reasons why mixed methods studies present such challenges for writing and reading them in that self-consciously science-oriented inquirers will likely deny the art and craft in their work, while artistically oriented inquirers will emphasize them.

ARTFUL ASTRONOMY

In their ethnographic study of the relationship between aesthetics and science in astronomy, Lynch and Edgerton (1988) sought to reveal the "craft of visual representation . . . hidden" (p. 186) in the practices of astronomy. Describing the reliance of modern astronomers on digital representation of data and digital image processing to detect and represent astronomical phenomena, Lynch and Edgerton demonstrated the extent to which "aesthetic considerations enter into the way astronomers compose, transform, and select images for various audiences and purposes" (p. 187). They also observed astronomers' tendency to deny the influence of the aesthetic except in creating "pretty pictures" (p. 191) of astronomical findings for popular audiences. These scientists maintained a distinction between aesthetics and science, associating "false color renderings" (p. 193) with "promotion and popularization" (p. 193) but not with "doing science" (p. 195). Even more significant for the purposes of this chapter, astronomers used a familiar "quantitative/qualitative distinction" to distinguish between the "real physical quantities . . . numerical measures" revealed and the "feeling" pretty pictures evoked (p. 194). Despite the fact that the maps and graphs intended to represent the quantitatively informed science of astronomy were no less "tailored" (p. 203) than the pretty pictures intended to promote astronomy to the public, the astronomers viewed the former as a way to show natural phenomena more accurately. These scientists used digital techniques to "clean up" their data, that is, to remove "cosmetic defects" from them (p. 206). They also used colors to show phenomena, differentiating between those colors that appealed to a public audience and those colors that served as "indices of . . . objective properties" (p. 200). And they adjusted their pictures to conform to the reality they wanted to show. As Lynch and Edgerton observed, digital image processing counters the commonplace notion that captions of pictures tell readers what is in the pictures; rather, "the features of a picture can be adjusted to fit a caption" (p. 202).

Lynch and Edgerton (1988) demonstrated the extent to which aesthetic considerations are the "very fabric of [the] realism" (p. 214) scientists wish to convey. As "committed realists," the astronomers they observed sought to "endow their compositions with naturalistic adequacy" (p. 214). The work of science, and of astronomy in particular, "of composing visible coherences, discriminating differences, consolidating entities, and establishing evident relations" was accomplished by crafting and configuring them (p. 212). Although careful to separate the "appeal" of their compositions from their "representational function" (p. 216), the astronomers nevertheless drew from "currently fashionable formats and color schemes" to "package their representations" to appeal to both scientific and lay audiences (p. 213).

ARTFUL ANATOMY

Typically conceived as a "stable science" (Moore & Clarke, 1995, p. 259), human anatomy has long been of interest to artists and historians and, more recently, to a variety of social scientists and cultural critics precisely because it epitomizes the lack of stability in science and the critical role of representation in the creating of scientific knowledge. As these diverse scholars have variously demonstrated, our understanding of human anatomy is nearly wholly made up of highly stylized visual representations of the human body that reflect, reproduce, and reinforce prevailing conventions for illustration (e.g., successively peeling away the layers of the body, showing cut away sections of body parts) and cultural

prescriptions concerning normality, gender, and race. Far from being a "science that has been done," anatomy is revealed to be a "contested domain" and "key site" for the (re)production of cultural norms (pp. 256-257). Anatomical inscriptions reproduce cultural prescriptions. Most important here, anatomy is revealed to be a "kind of writing practice" that makes the body "readable" (Waldby, 2000, p. 94). As Cartwright (1998) demonstrated in her "cultural anatomy" of the Visible Human Project (a digital image library of data representing a normal adult human male and female), the way phenomena are represented will determine how and even whether we understand them. Although the Visible Human Project is intended to make human anatomy more understandable, the images detail and segment parts so minutely and arbitrarily that they preclude easy recognition and categorization. Indeed, they require an a priori textbook understanding of anatomy. A cross section of data might provide information about hearts, breasts, and bones, but this manner of offering information does not correspond to the familiar way of dividing the body by systems or organs, and the wealth of detail offered may overwhelm viewers. In short, viewers/readers have to learn new ways to view/read the body to keep the body in view, and these new ways may conflict sharply with old ways of viewing/reading it. Anatomical knowledge is thus "medium dependent" (Waldby, 2000, p. 90), changing when the medium is the printed book or cyberspace. Whether book based or virtual, anatomy does not "illustrate" bodies so much as it "demonstrates" them (p. 91). Anatomical displays are not representations of the body as it is; rather, the body we know at any one moment in time is a display. Representation is shown in these studies not to be opposed to reality but rather as constituting it.

◆ Mixed Media for Mixed Methods Studies for Mixed Audiences

Crafting convincing write-ups of mixed methods studies entails understanding that the form in which findings are shown themselves constitute those findings, recognizing the research write-up as rhetoric, and the deliberate selection and mindful use of the most convincing rhetorical tools of the trade. Reading mixed methods studies, in turn, requires an understanding of these tools and of how they convince.

Mixed methods writers have to decide whether and how to use the familiar genre of the experimental report, the ethnographic conventions of the realist or reflexive tale, or any of an array of other formats for "impression management" (Bazerman, 1988, p. 202). They have to decide how best to delineate the temporal, analytical, and interpretive relationships between the qualitative and quantitative entities in their studies. They have to decide whether to use a separate but equal sequential format to present qualitative and quantitative procedures and findings or to use a format that weaves both sets of procedures and findings together. Writers have also to decide what writing templates will give their write-ups the structure, coherence, and rhythm they seek to convey (Sandelowski, 1998). For example, the form of the write-up may reproduce the order in which researchers implemented the various phases and techniques of a study and the order in which findings were found or, instead, may reproduce the temporal flow of a life event as participants experienced it. As shown in Figure 12.1, if researchers used a sequential design format, then they may choose the conventional experimental style to describe first the procedures used and the findings produced from the initial quantitative or qualitative portion of their study and then to describe the procedures and findings from the qualitative or quantitative portion that followed. Or they may choose more ethnographically inclined formats that emphasize narratives or cases or that organize findings by methodological coding families, such as the "6 Cs" conditional matrix associated with grounded theory ("Theoretical Coding Families," 1998), or by concepts derived from established theories. Writers will also have to consider the use of devices that have different appearances, functions, and/or values in qualitative and quantitative research. Among these are visual displays, numbers, and quotes.

VISUAL DISPLAYS

Visual displays (e.g., graphs, charts, tables, lists) are familiar features of research reports. Indeed, their very familiarity paradoxically contributes to their disappearance as themselves objects of study and as powerful rhetorical devices. Yet these displays function not only "manifestly" to reduce large quantities of data into forms that can be more readily apprehended by readers but also "latently" to persuade readers of the validity of findings (McGill, 1990, p. 141). They "imply equivalence between the scientific and the tabular" or graphic (p. 136). They are components of the literary technology of science not only because they evoke images of the research that has taken place but also because they themselves constitute a visual source of information. They are part of the "iconography" of science, offering "visual assistance" to the virtual witness (Shapin, 1984, pp. 491-492).

Visual displays entail a decision (albeit often an unconscious one) to organize information in a certain way. For example, writers choose whether to construct

Mixed Methods/Design	Type	Writing Style	Temporal/Thematic Logic
Sequential design, with quantitative priority Concurrent design, with quantitative priority	QUAN > qual qual > QUAN QUAN + qual	Experimental	Research time
Sequential design, with qualitative priority Concurrent design, with qualitative priority	QUAL + qual quan + QUAL QUAL + quan	Experimental -or- Narrative Comparison of cases –Typical, deviant Perspectival/ Polyvocal Conceptual	Research time Subject/Event time -Quantitatively informed -Shared/Divergent themes Shared/Divergent views/voices -Sensitizing concepts -Theoretical framework -Coding families
Wave design Sandwich design	Quan wave 1 wave 2 wave 3 Qual ongoing fieldwork Qual > Quan > Qual Quan > Qual > Quan	Experimental -or- Narrative -Flashforward -Flashback	Research time Subject/Event time

Figure 12.1. Examples of Writing Templates for Different Mixed Methods Designs

SOURCE: The first two columns were constructed from information in Miles and Huberman (1994), Morgan (1998), and Tashakkori and Teddlie (1998).

matrices (rows and columns), networks (nodes and links), or Venn diagrams (independent and overlapping circles); what to put in the spaces in their displays (e.g., quotes, paraphrases, abbreviations, numbers, arrows, symbolic figures); and/or what to emphasize in their displays (e.g., time in a time-ordered display, event in an event-ordered display, conditions in a conditional display) (Miles & Huberman, *both for me & for pupils*

1994). The very organization of this information shapes the findings and how readers read them.[2] Quantitative research reports tend to be characterized by tables and graphs numerically profiling the demographic composition of the studied sample and showing the results of the statistical tests from which conclusions were drawn as well as by figures depicting—often in numerical form—a theoretical formulation of the relationship between variables (e.g., a path diagram). Qualitative research write-ups tend to emphasize verbal texts over visual displays.[3] Grounded theory reports often include figures of theories; indeed, some writers of grounded theory reports believe that a grounded theory cannot be conveyed without using such figures. But these figures tend also to include words as opposed to numbers. The advent of computerized text management systems for managing qualitative data has also encouraged the use of visual displays of reordered verbal text in qualitative write-ups. Indeed, these systems can be seen as important new additions to the literary technology of persuasion because they permit qualitative researchers to have printouts of data—like their quantitative counterparts—with all the veneer of scientific objectivity that such inscriptions confer. Even the purportedly "soft" data of qualitative research can become "hard" if produced by hardware (Sandelowski, 1995a).

Whether they are used in qualitative or quantitative research, tables, figures, and lists tend to fix in time and space the phenomena they portray. Visual displays give "material form" and "scientific visibility" to entities that were previously immaterial and invisible (Lynch, 1985). Their properties come to "embody" the realities they disclose (p. 43). Visual displays are "technologies of representation" that variously work by simplification, discrimination, and integration (Law & Whittaker, 1988,

p. 163). Their rhetorical effect is to create a sense of order out of chaos. In effect, they reduce the meaningfulness of information into fixed meanings; they make the potentially too meaningful more meaningless so as to establish meaning. Moreover, they rely on "discontinuity rather than continuity" (Goody, 1977, p. 81) as they remove texts from their contexts.

In these effects of displays lie reasons why qualitative researchers may avoid displays, while quantitative researchers value them. Qualitative researchers tend to want to create tableaux and graphic accounts of experience, not tables and graphs. But in these effects lies also a means for qualitative researchers to make their reports more appealing to readers wanting the boundaries, order, and "immutability" (Latour, 1988, p. 36) that such devices offer. Graphs, tables, and lists enlist readers toward a defined, linear, and/or schematic view of a set of facts or relations. In qualitative research, they can assist readers in focusing on key dimensions of a complex phenomenon that writers want to communicate. Moreover, because they convey a "sense of proximity to the data collected" by the writers (McGill, 1990, p. 130), such displays will appeal to qualitative researchers' desire to communicate that they were "there" in the field (Geertz, 1988, chap. 1).

The Breitmayer, Ayres, and Knafl (1993) analysis of their mixed methods study of family responses to a child's chronic illness shows an effective use of visual displays. Table 12.1 summarizes and clarifies the qualitative (semistructured interviews) and quantitative (structured instruments) data they collected, the family members from whom they collected these data, and the link between these data and aspects of the family management style they hoped to illuminate. Tables 12.2 and 12.3 show how mood data were analytically linked to interview data to achieve a

TABLE 12.1 Mapping Data Collection Techniques in a Mixed Methods Study

| | Domain of Interest | | | |
| | Family Management Style | | | |
Data Source	Definition of Situation	Management Behaviors	Sociocultural Context	Impact
Semistructured interviews				
Parent	X	X	X	X
Ill child	X	X	X	X
Sibling	X	X	X	X
Structured instruments				
Parent			FFFS	FFFS
				POMS
Ill child	CATIS			CBCL
				SPPC
				FSI
Sibling				CBCL
				SPPC

SOURCE: Breitmayer, Ayres, and Knafl (1993, p. 238). Used by permission of the authors and Sigma Theta Tau International.

NOTE: FFFS = Feetham Family Functioning Survey; POMS = Profile of Mood States; CATIS = Child Attitude Toward Illness Scale; CBCL = Child Behavior Checklist; FSI = Functional Status Instrument; SPPC = Self-Perception Profile for Children.

fuller understanding of family relationships and to ascertain convergent validity. The responses displayed in Table 12.2 suggest that mood can be partly explained by whether parents perceive that there is family support in managing the child's illness. The responses shown in Table 12.3 visually supported the researchers' hypothesis that parents with high mood disturbance scores would describe more difficulty in accepting a child's illness than would those with low scores.

NUMBERS

Numbers have been something of a "litmus test" (Linnekin, 1987, p. 920) of inquiry, serving in part to differentiate scientifically oriented/quantitative from humanistically oriented/qualitative research (Chibnik, 1999). Indeed, qualitative research is often simplistically defined solely by the absence and/or critique of numbers, while quantitative research is simplistically defined solely by the presence of numbers.

TABLE 12.2   Linking Instrument Scores and Quotes for Fuller Description

Profile of Mood State	Response to Interview Question on Effect of Illness on Family Relations
High mood disturbance mother	"I suppose in a way it kind of pulled us apart because it's so stressful and everything."
High mood disturbance father	"I would say in this family anything tragic pulls us together."
Low mood disturbance mother	"Probably pulled us closer."
Low mood disturbance father	"I think if anything it brought our family closer together. . . . Before, everyone went their separate ways."

SOURCE: Adapted and excerpted from Breitmayer, Ayres, and Knafl (1993, p. 240). Used by permission of the authors and Sigma Theta Tau International.

In quantitative research, the appeal to numbers gives studies their rhetorical power. Statistics, especially inferential statistics, are a naturalized and rule-governed means of producing what is perceived to be the most conclusive knowledge about a target phenomenon (John, 1992). Inferential statistics authorize studies as scientific and contribute to the "fixation of belief" whereby readers accept findings as facts and not artifacts (Amann & Knorr-Cetina, 1988, p. 85). They are a display of evidence in the "artful literary display" (Gephart, 1988, p. 63) we know as the scientific report, and they are a means to create meaning. Indeed, quantitative significance is arguably less found than created, as writers rhetorically enlist readers, with the use of words such as *high* and *substantial,* to accept their findings as significant (Gephart, 1986). Statistical meaning is not "inherent in numbers" but rather "accomplished by terms used to describe and interpret numbers" (Gephart, 1988, p. 60).

By contrast, in qualitative research, numbers are looked on with some suspicion as overly simplifying the complex. Indeed, qualitative researchers are often antagonistic toward numbers, referring to the use of numbers as number crunching and to those who use them as number crunchers and ranking numbers low in their "hierarchy of credibility" (Becker, 1967, p. 241). Wanting to move "beyond numbers" (Greenhalgh & Taylor, 1997), and committed to sampling information-rich cases, thick description, and fully rounded and grounded understanding, qualitative researchers often eschew numbers as a violation of the knowledge and ethical imperatives of qualitative research. Numbers also present a representational problem to qualitative researchers who want to satisfy both scientific and humanistic/artistic criteria in their write-ups. While quantitative researchers prize figures, qualitative researchers prize figures of speech. In short, while numbers are seen

TABLE 12.3 Linking Instrument Scores and Quotes for Convergent Validation (Triangulation)

POMS Classification	Response to Question About "Acceptance"	Response to Question About Maintaining Positive Outlook
High		
Mother	"I guess you never really accept it."	"I just keep telling myself as long as she eats the way she does and takes her insulin and checks her blood, she'll be normal."
Father	"There's nothing we can do about it."	"I try to always think in my head that they're going to figure it out soon, but I have the feeling they're not."
Low		
Mother	"We've accepted it from the beginning."	"We eat a much better diet, and it's not like we're losing anything that we need to sustain a normal life."
Father	"I think we pretty well accept it. It's a fact of life."	"[If we feel down], we just talk it out."

SOURCE: Adapted and excerpted from Breitmayer, Ayres, and Knafl (1993, p. 241). Used by permission of the authors and Sigma Theta Tau International.

to confer epistemic authority in quantitative inquiry, they may also be seen to undermine the authority, authenticity, and artfulness of qualitative work.

Qualitative researchers are especially concerned about the "dubious use" of numbers (Stern, 1989, p. 139) to authorize and legitimize qualitative work. For example, one dubious use of numbers occurs when writers become so preoccupied with providing exact numbers that they end up overcounting or counting things that cannot be counted (Sandelowski, 2001). Overcounting will seriously detract from an aesthetic presentation of findings and, even more important, can easily divert researchers away from the qualitative mandate to develop and present a fully rounded interpretation of

things. An example is when researchers emphasize the numbers of respondents falling into categories instead of detailing the qualitative nature of the categories themselves.

Another example of the dubious use of numbers is acontextual counting, whereby writers draw unsubstantiated inferences from numbers or offer no other information about participants or an event except numbers (Sandelowski, 2001). One example is when researchers offer no relevant descriptive material to contextualize a number. They might say that 40% of the children they observed were angry but offer no other information about these children. A second example is when researchers count up the number of times persons referred to a certain event and then conclude that this event was the most important event in the lives of those persons who referred to it the most. Or, researchers might count up the number of times participants used the word *angry* and conclude that people who used it more frequently were angrier than those who used it less frequently. Without some narrative or other theoretical formulation concerning talk or the salience of life events that would allow researchers to draw such conclusions, the conclusions remain theoretically invalid.

Yet, in their efforts to move beyond numbers and to avoid their dubious use, qualitative researchers might not recognize how integral numbers are in the qualitative analysis process, especially for the recognition of patterns in data and deviations from those patterns and for generalizing from data. Pattern recognition implies seeing something over and over again in one case or across a selection of cases. Finding that a *few, some,* or *many* participants showed a certain pattern, or that a pattern was *common* or *unusual* in a group of participants, implies something about the frequency, typicality, or even intensity of an event. Anytime qualitative researchers place raw data into categories or discover themes to which they attach codes, they are drawing from the numbered nature of phenomena for their analysis. Numbers are a powerful way to generate meaning from qualitative data; to document, verify, and test interpretations or conclusions; and to represent target events and experiences.

Moreover, numbers are powerful devices to show the complexity and labor of qualitative work. Qualitative writers too often apologize for their *small* sample sizes. Yet instead of showing contrition, they might show the *large* numbers of which such ostensibly small samples are often actually composed. A recently completed 17-month ethnographic study of the implementation of a computerized patient record system on a hospital unit included interviews with 20 informants totaling 325 pages of text, 124 observations of events captured in 1,162 pages of fieldnotes, and the review of documents totaling 820 pages of text (Bailey, 2000). A study of 10 participants, interviewed only once, can yield 250 pages of raw data alone. Writers of qualitative research can take advantage of the prevailing cultural belief that more is better by playing the numbers game. If this rhetorical game is played well, then there will be no doubt of the true sample size, amount of data produced from, and labor involved in even $N = 1$ studies.

The Borkan et al. (1991) report of their mixed methods study includes two effective examples of the use of numbers to document procedural and analytical moves. Figure 12.2 is intended to convey the systematic procedure used to ensure interrater reliability. Figure 12.3 is intended to convey the distribution and interpretation of the data from which the predictor variables *organic narrative* and *mechanistic narrative* were created. By counting the numbers of persons responding in each category, the researchers showed that they accounted for all of their data, did not discount any data, and noticed when they had no data. Both of these figures serve to convince readers of the tight and mindful link between the first and qualitative portion of the study and the second and quantitative portion of the study.

QUOTES

While numbers play a starring role in quantitative write-ups, quotes (from interviews and participant observations with participants) play a starring role in qualitative write-ups. The quote is arguably the

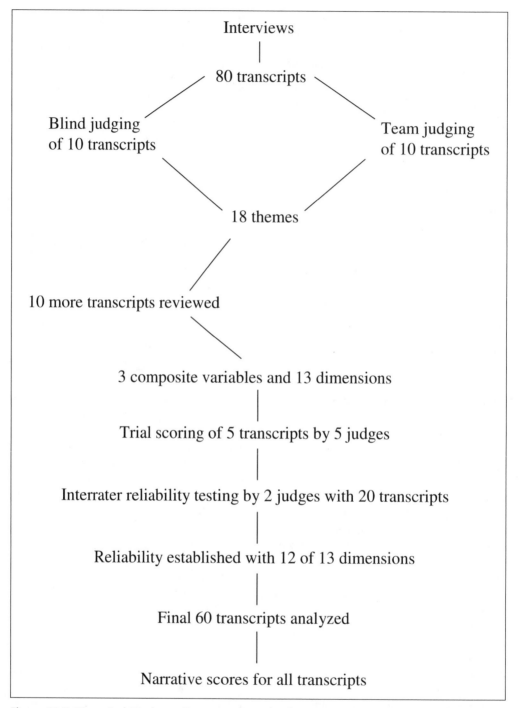

Figure 12.2. Numerical Display to Document Procedural Moves

SOURCE: Morgan, D. L. (1998). Practical strategies for combining qualitative and quantitative methods: Applications to health research. *Qualitative Health Research, 8,* 362-376. Reprinted by permission of Elsevier Science.

Poles: Organic	1-3	4	5-7	Mechanistic

Name

	Disease			Fracture
	1%	15%	49%	

Illustrative quotes:

"sickness"				"broken hip"
"osteoporosis"				"shattered bone"

Pathophysiology

	Broke and fell			Fell and broke
	10%	14%	64%	

Illustrative quotes:

"I think you break your				"I landed on my hip and
hip before you go down."				knew it was broke."

Prognosis

	Total impairment			Complete recovery
	14%	10%	70%	

Illustrative quotes:

"I might have to go to				"I'm going to recover fully."
a nursing home."				

Figure 12.3. Numerical Display to Document Analytical Moves

SOURCE: Adapted from Borkan, Quirk, and Sullivan (1991, p. 950).

analog to the number, as they are both rhetorical devices used to appeal to readers to accept findings as scientifically and/or ethnographically valid. Quotes authenticate qualitative write-ups in that they demonstrate to readers that the writer has been "there" in the field (Geertz, 1988, chap. 1), the closeness of the writer to the data and to the persons providing them (Richards, 1998), and the writer's attention to the "particularit[ies] of everyday life" (Golden-Biddle & Locke, 1993, p. 601). Whereas numbers are used in quantitative research write-ups primarily for their evidentiary power, quotes are used in qualitative research write-ups for their evidentiary power and their aesthetic value.[4] While numbers emphasize generality, quotes "privilege" individuality and "model . . . the diversity within generality" (Richardson, 1990, p. 40) that are hallmarks of qualitative research.

Quotes are used in qualitative research write-ups to validate findings and to vitalize the presentation of those findings (Sandelowski, 1994b). The function of quoting here is to offer evidence for a conclusion or claim; to illustrate an interpretive point; to represent, and facilitate understanding of, the thoughts and feelings of the persons studied; to foster in readers an identification between them and the persons quoted; to evoke certain feelings in readers; and/or to provoke action from readers (Howarth, 1990; Weiss, 1994). Like statistics and the work of statistics, quotes are rhetorical devices intended to persuade readers of the trustworthiness of a study, and quoting is a highly skilled craft that entails aesthetic and even moral choices. Writers must decide whether to quote at all; authenticity may be at stake if there are no quotes, while anonymity may be at stake if there are too many or too revealing quotes. Writers must then decide what, how, when, where, and why to quote. Such decisions include what segments of talk to quote, how to edit the

"messiness" of human talk (DeVault, 1990, p. 109) so that it speaks to the reader and for the participant, how to stage (i.e., introduce and leave) quotes, where to use quotes (e.g., interspersed throughout the text, in sets in confined sections of the text, in tabular displays), and why to use quotes (e.g., to convey the informational content or evoke the feeling tone of an experience). In short, quoting and doing statistics both entail complex efforts to persuade, but they exert their influence in different ways.

Tables 12.2 and 12.3 illustrate the use of quotes to flesh out instrument scores. The quotes are used here to link key constructs (mood, perception of effect of child's illness on family relationships, acceptance of child's illness, and strategies to maintain positive outlook) and to show their hypothesized relationship to each other.

◆ Crafting Convincing Mixed Methods Studies Texts

In conclusion, writing mixed methods studies entails both "craft and responsibility" (Schwalbe, 1995, p. 394). Writers of mixed methods studies must have the skill and motivation to permit both qualitative and quantitative readers "access" (p. 396) to their work. Writing mixed methods studies requires an understanding of differences, of how aesthetic considerations enter into the creation of convincing write-ups of both qualitative and quantitative research, and of whether and how diverse aesthetic sensibilities can be brought together. Mixed methods studies are themselves "mixed metaphors" (Wallace & Van Fleet, 1998) in that qualitative research and quantitative research are viewed as standing for different approaches to inquiry. Although there is no inherent incompatibility between numbers and words that precludes their being used together to represent the findings of a study, there is an inherent clash between, for example, the use of language and formatting styles to convey facts and express meanings or to establish a personal presence and discount one. And these differences in the look and feel of studies reflect differences between qualitative and quantitative research that cannot be overlooked. Although the emphasis on the compatibility of qualitative and quantitative research is intended to be reconciliatory and to move beyond pointless paradigm wars, it makes no sense to minimize differences that clearly exist on the "shop floor" of research (Becker, 1996, p. 60). There may very well be some overall similarities between doing statistics and doing phenomenology (cf. Dzurec & Abraham, 1986), but on the shop floor of research, they are nothing like each other. Moreover, such depictions of identity can paradoxically undermine the claim to mixed methods studies; if phenomenology and statistics are like each other, then arguably nothing has been mixed in studies using both of these modes of inquiry.

Accordingly, the question is how best to accommodate the mixes in mixed methods studies. Writers of mixed methods studies must find a "shared grammar" (Stevenson & Beech, 1998, p. 795) by which to communicate with and thereby create one community from the diverse communities reading mixed methods studies. They must "get the words right" for the purposes that they use them. As Bazerman (1988) summarized it,

> Getting the words right is more than a fine tuning of grace and clarity; it is defining the entire enterprise. And getting the words right depends not just on an individual's choice. The words are shaped by the discipline—in its communally developed linguistic resources and expectations; in its stylized identification and structuring of realities to be discussed; in its literature; in its active procedures of reading, evaluating, and using texts; in its structured interactions between writer and reader. The words arise out of the activity, procedures, and relationships within the community. (p. 47)

Crafting convincing mixed methods studies texts requires using words—especially the epistemologically and emotionally loaded terms *qualitative* and *quantitative*—in ways that will be accessible and appealing to the mixed audiences for mixed methods studies and respectful of the highly diverse communities participating in the creation of and served by mixed methods studies. Respectful use means, for example, not defining or depicting qualitative research as a nonentity (i.e., nonquantitative) and not depicting quantitative research as number crunching.

Crafting convincing mixed methods studies entails making the right appeals. There is nothing inherently more appealing about large statistically representative samples, from which nomothetic generalizations can be drawn, than smaller informationally representative samples, from which idiographic generalizations can be drawn. Rather, the one will be more appealing to the other in different writing-reading contexts. Qualitative research becomes more convincing when it is combined with quantitative research only in interpretive communities more convinced by quantitative rhetoric than by qualitative rhetoric. In short, writers of mixed methods studies must carefully consider what appeals to make and must avoid making appeals based on misunderstandings of what validity and generalizability mean in qualitative versus quantitative research. But like the failed effort to mix paradigms, the effort to mix incompatible appeals will undermine the power of any text to convince because they will cancel each other out. A writer cannot simultaneously appeal to extensive engagement with participants and controlled relations with participants to convince readers of the validity of findings.

Finally, writers and readers of mixed methods studies must develop a "rhetorical self-consciousness" (Bazerman, 1988, p. 320). They need to know how language affects us and "how we play along" (Schwalbe, 1995, p. 401). Writers and readers need to "know what each other is doing" (p. 402). Whether drawing from the power of the number or the word, from the figure or the figure of speech, or from the table or the tableaux, writers and readers must understand and play them as the "power games" (Stevenson & Beech, 1998) they are.

■ Notes

1. I consider here only researchers and not other readers such as research participants, policy makers, and other audiences for research reports.

2. Publishers may also determine the kinds of displays that will appear in research reports, but they, like writers, are influenced by prevailing conventions for how and what to display. Ironically, although so much of human knowledge is composed of the visual, publishers of science and ethnographic texts often prevail on writers to limit their displays, either for reasons of cost or because such displays may be considered more cosmetic—a "pretty picture"—than functionally necessary to show a finding. The literary title, composed of an artful phrase intended to capture the essence of a set of findings, followed by a colon and then a phrase signifying the contents of the article in more prosaic terms, often suffers the same fate in self-consciously scientific publication venues. The "flowery" title is viewed as a "frill" and a deterrent to database classification and retrieval (Levinson, 1990, p. 159).

3. Explicitly visual fields such as visual anthropology and visual sociology emphasize photographs, which constitute a complex domain of visual display not addressed here.

4. Although mathematics is an artful science (King, 1992), statistics are not deliberately and self-consciously used in quantitative research for their aesthetic qualities.

■ References

Amann, K., & Knorr-Cetina, K. (1988). The fixation of visual evidence. In M. Lynch & S. Woolgar (Eds.), *Representation in scientific practice* (pp. 85-121). New York: Kluwer Academic.

American Psychological Association. (1994). *Publication manual of the American Psychological Association*. Washington, DC: Author.

Annells, M. (1996). Grounded theory method: Philosophical perspectives, paradigm of inquiry, and postmodernism. *Qualitative Health Research, 6,* 379-393.

Aronson, N. (1984). Science as a claims making activity: Implications for social problems research. In J. W. Schneider & J. Kitsuse (Eds.), *Studies in the sociology of social problems* (pp. 1-30). Norwood, NJ: Ablex.

Atkinson, P., & Silverman, D. (1997). Kundera's *Immortality:* The interview society and the invention of the self. *Qualitative Inquiry, 3,* 304-325.

Bailey, D. (2000). *Nurse work and the computerized patient record.* Unpublished doctoral dissertation, University of North Carolina at Chapel Hill.

Bazerman, C. (1988). *Shaping written knowledge: The genre and activity of the experimental article in science.* Madison: University of Wisconsin Press.

Beach, R. (1993). *A teacher's introduction to reader-response theories.* Urbana, IL: National Council of Teachers of English.

Becker, H. S. (1967). Whose side are we on? *Social Problems, 14,* 239-247.

Becker, H. S. (1996). The epistemology of qualitative research. In R. Jessor, A. Colby, & R. A. Shweder (Eds.), *Ethnography and human development: Context and meaning in social inquiry* (pp. 53-71). Chicago: University of Chicago Press.

Blaikie, N. W. (1991). A critique of the use of triangulation in social research. *Quality & Quantity, 25,* 115-136.

Blumenthal, D. (1999). Representing the divided self. *Qualitative Inquiry, 5,* 377-392.

Borkan, J. M., Quirk, M., & Sullivan, M. (1991). Finding meaning after the fall: Injury narratives from elderly hip fracture patients. *Social Science & Medicine, 33,* 947-957.

Boyatzis, R. E. (1998). *Transforming qualitative information: Thematic analysis and code development.* Thousand Oaks, CA: Sage.

Breitmayer, B. J., Ayres, L., & Knafl, K. A. (1993). Triangulation in qualitative research: Evaluation of completeness and confirmation purposes. *Image: Journal of Nursing Scholarship, 25,* 237-243.

Cartwright, L. (1998). A cultural anatomy of the Visible Human Project. In P. A. Treichler, L. Cartwright, & C. Penley (Eds.), *The visible woman: Imaging technologies, gender, and science* (pp. 21-43). New York: New York University Press.

Charmaz, K. (2000). Grounded theory: Objectivist and constructivist methods. In N. K. Denzin & Y. S. Lincoln (Eds.), *Handbook of qualitative research* (2nd ed., pp. 509-535). Thousand Oaks, CA: Sage.

Chibnik, M. (1999). Quantification and statistics in six anthropology journals. *Field Methods, 11,* 146-157.

Clifford, J., & Marcus, G. E. (Ed.). (1986). *Writing culture: The poetics and politics of ethnography.* Berkeley: University of California Press.

Cohen, M. Z., Tripp-Reimer, T., Smith, C., Sorofman, B., & Lively, S. (1994). Explanatory models of diabetes: Patient practitioner variation. *Social Science & Medicine, 38,* 59-66.

Denzin, N. K., & Lincoln, Y. S. (2000). Introduction: The discipline and practice of qualitative research. In N. K. Denzin & Y. S.

Lincoln (Eds.), *Handbook of qualitative research* (2nd ed., pp. 1-28). Thousand Oaks, CA: Sage.

DeVault, M. L. (1990). Talking and listening from women's standpoint: Feminist strategies for interviewing and analysis. *Social Problems, 37,* 96-116.

Dey, I. (1993). *Qualitative data analysis: A user-friendly guide for social scientists.* London: Routledge.

Dzurec, L. C., & Abraham, I. L. (1986). Analogy between phenomenology and multivariate statistical analysis. In P. L. Chinn (Ed.), *Nursing research methodology: Issues and implementation* (pp. 55-66). Rockville, MD: Aspen.

Eisner, E. (1981). On the differences between scientific and artistic approaches to qualitative research. *Educational Researcher, 10,* 5-9.

Eisner, E. (1985). Aesthetic modes of knowing. In E. Eisner (Ed.), *Learning and teaching the ways of knowing: Eighty-fourth yearbook of the National Society for the Study of Education, Part II* (pp. 23-36). Chicago: National Society of the Study of Education.

Eisner, E. (1991). *The enlightened eye: Qualitative inquiry and the enhancement of educational practice.* New York: Macmillan.

Fish, S. (1980). *Is there a text in this class? The authority of interpretive communities.* Cambridge, MA: Harvard University Press.

Geertz, C. (1988). *Works and lives: The anthropologist as author.* Stanford, CA: Stanford University Press.

Gephart, R. P. (1986). Deconstructing the defense for quantification in social science: A content analysis of journal articles on the parametric strategy. *Qualitative Sociology, 9,* 126-144.

Gephart, R. P. (1988). *Ethnostatistics: Qualitative foundations for quantitative research.* Beverly Hills, CA: Sage.

Gergen, M. M., & Gergen, K. J. (2000). Qualitative inquiry: Tensions and transformations. In N. K. Denzin & Y. S. Lincoln (Eds.), *Handbook of qualitative research* (2nd ed., pp. 1025-1046). Thousand Oaks, CA: Sage.

Gifford-Gonzalez, D. (1993). You can hide, but you can't run: Representation of women's work in illustrations of paleolithic life. *Visual Anthropology Review, 9,* 23-41.

Golden-Biddle, K., & Locke, K. (1993). Appealing work: An investigation of how ethnographic texts convince. *Organization Science, 4,* 595-616.

Goody, J. (1977). *The domestication of the savage mind.* Cambridge, UK: Cambridge University Press.

Greenhalgh, T., & Taylor, R. (1997). How to read a paper: Papers that go beyond numbers (qualitative research). *British Medical Journal, 315,* 740-743.

Gusfield, J. (1976). The literary rhetoric of science: Comedy and pathos in drinking driver research. *American Sociological Review, 41,* 16-34.

Heron, J., & Reason, P. (1997). A participatory inquiry paradigm. *Qualitative Inquiry, 3,* 274-294.

Howarth, W. (1990). Oliver Sacks: The ecology of writing science. *Modern Language Studies, 20,* 103-120.

John, I. D. (1992). Statistics as rhetoric in psychology. *Australian Psychologist, 27,* 144-149.

King, J. P. (1992). *The art of mathematics.* New York: Fawcett Columbine.

Krieger, S. (1983). *The mirror dance: Identity in a women's community.* Philadelphia: Temple University Press.

Krieger, S. (1991). *Social science and the self: Personal essays on an art form.* New Brunswick, NJ: Rutgers University Press.

Latour, B. (1988). Drawing things together. In M. Lynch & S. Woolgar (Eds.), *Representation in scientific practice* (pp. 19-68). New York: Kluwer Academic.

Latour, B., & Woolgar, S. (1986). *Laboratory life: The construction of scientific facts.* Princeton, NJ: Princeton University Press.

Law, J., & Lynch, M. (1988). Lists, field guides, and the descriptive organization of seeing: Birdwatching as an exemplary observational activity. In M. Lynch & S. Woolgar (Eds.), *Representation in scientific practice* (pp. 267-299). New York: Kluwer Academic.

Law, J., & Whittaker, J. (1988). On the art of representation: Notes on the politics of visualization. In G. Fyfe & J. Law (Eds.), *Picturing power: Visual depiction and social relations* (pp. 160-183). London: Routledge.

Levinson, J. (1990). *Music, art, and metaphysics: Essays in philosophical aesthetics.* Ithaca, NY: Cornell University Press.

Linnekin, J. (1987). Categorize, cannibalize? Humanistic quantification in anthropological research. *American Anthropologist, 89,* 920-926.

Lynch, M. (1985). Discipline and the material form of images: An analysis of scientific visibility. *Social Studies of Science, 15,* 37-66.

Lynch, M., & Edgerton, S. Y. (1988). Aesthetics and digital image processing: Representational craft in contemporary astronomy. In G. Fyfe & J. Law (Eds.), *Picturing power: Visual depiction and social relations* (pp. 184-220). London: Routledge.

McGill, L. T. (1990). Doing science by the numbers: The role of tables and other representational conventions in scientific journal articles. In A. Hunter (Ed.), *The rhetoric of social research: Understood and believed* (pp. 129-141). New Brunswick, NJ: Rutgers University Press.

Miles, M. B., & Huberman, A. M. (1994). *Qualitative data analysis: An expanded sourcebook* (2nd ed.). Thousand Oaks, CA: Sage.

Moore, L. J., & Clarke, A. E. (1995). Clitoral conventions and transgressions: Graphic representations in anatomy texts, 1900-1991. *Feminist Studies, 21,* 255-301.

Nisbet, R. (1976). *Sociology as an art form.* New York: Oxford University Press.

Norris, J. R. (1997). Meaning through form: Alternative modes of knowledge representation. In J. M. Morse (Ed.), *Completing a qualitative project: Details and dialogue* (pp. 87-115). Thousand Oaks, CA: Sage.

Radley, A., & Billig, M. (1996). Accounts of health and illness: Dilemmas and representations. *Sociology of Health & Illness, 18,* 220-240.

Richards, L. (1998). Closeness to data: Goals of qualitative data handling. *Qualitative Health Research, 8,* 319-328.

Richardson, L. (1990). *Writing strategies: Reaching diverse audiences.* Newbury Park, CA: Sage.

Richardson, L. (2000). Writing: A method of inquiry. In N. K. Denzin & Y. S. Lincoln (Eds.), *Handbook of qualitative research* (2nd ed., pp. 923-948). Thousand Oaks, CA: Sage.

Riessman, C. K. (1990). Strategic uses of narrative in the presentation of self and illness: A research note. *Social Science & Medicine, 30,* 1195-1200.

Root-Bernstein, R. S. (1984). On paradigms and revolutions in science and art: The challenge of interpretation. *Art Journal, 44,* 109-118.

Rothert, M., Rovner, D., Holmes, M., Schmitt, N., Talarczyk, G., Kroll, J., & Gogate, J. (1990). Women's use of information regarding hormone replacement therapy. *Research in Nursing & Health, 13,* 355-366.

Sandelowski, M. (1994a). The proof is in the pottery: Toward a poetic for qualitative inquiry. In J. Morse (Ed.), *Critical issues in qualitative research methods* (pp. 46-63). Thousand Oaks, CA: Sage.

Sandelowski, M. (1994b). The use of quotes in qualitative research. *Research in Nursing & Health, 17,* 479-482.

Sandelowski, M. (1995a). On the aesthetics of qualitative research. *Image: Journal of Nursing Scholarship, 27,* 205-209.

Sandelowski, M. (1995b). Triangles and crystals: On the geometry of qualitative research. *Research in Nursing & Health, 18,* 569-574.

Sandelowski, M. (1998). Writing a good read: Strategies for re-presenting qualitative data. *Research in Nursing & Health, 21,* 375-382.

Sandelowski, M. (2001). Real qualitative researchers don't count: The use of numbers in qualitative research. *Research in Nursing & Health, 24,* 230-240.

Sandelowski, M., Harris, B. G., & Holditch-Davis, D. (1991). Amniocentesis in the context of infertility. *Health Care for Women International, 12,* 167-178.

Sandelowski, M., Holditch-Davis, D., & Harris, B. G. (1992). Using qualitative and quantitative methods: The transition to parenthood of infertile couples. In J. F. Gilgun, K. Daly, & G. Handel (Eds.), *Qual-itative methods in family research* (pp. 301-322). Newbury Park, CA: Sage.

Sapir, E. (1951). Culture, genuine and spurious. In D. G. Mandelbaum (Ed.), *Selected writings of Edward Sapir in language, culture, and personality* (pp. 308-331). Berkeley: University of California Press.

Saukko, P. (2000). Between voice and discourse: Quilting interviews on anorexia. *Qualitative Inquiry, 6,* 299-317.

Schattschneider, D. (1994, November). Escher's metaphors. *Scientific American,* pp. 66-71.

Schwalbe, M. (1995). The responsibilities of sociological poets. *Qualitative Sociology, 18,* 393-413.

Schwandt, T. A. (2000). Three epistemological stances for qualitative inquiry: Interpretivism, hermeneutics, and social constructionism. In N. K. Denzin & Y. S. Lincoln (Eds.), *Handbook of qualitative research* (2nd ed., pp. 189-213). Thousand Oaks, CA: Sage.

Shapin, S. (1984). Pump and circumstance: Robert Boyle's literary technology. *Social Studies of Science, 14,* 481-520.

Silverman, D. (2000). Analyzing talk and text. In N. K. Denzin & Y. S. Lincoln (Eds.), *Handbook of qualitative research* (2nd ed., pp. 821-834). Thousand Oaks, CA: Sage.

Skrtic, T. M. (1990). Social accommodation: Toward a dialogical discourse in educational inquiry. In E. G. Guba (Ed.), *The paradigm dialog* (pp. 125-135). Newbury Park, CA: Sage.

Stafford, B. M. (1991). *Body criticism: Imaging the unseen in enlightenment art and medicine.* Cambridge, MA: MIT Press.

Stafford, B. M. (1994). *Artful science: Enlightenment entertainment and the eclipse of visual education.* Cambridge, MA: MIT Press.

Star, S. L. (1983). Simplification in scientific work: An example from neuroscience research. *Social Studies of Science, 13,* 205-228.

Stern, P. N. (1989). Are counting and coding a cappella appropriate in qualitative research? In J. M. Morse (Ed.), *Qualitative nursing research: A contemporary dialogue* (pp. 135-148). Rockville, MD: Aspen.

Stevenson, C., & Beech, I. (1998). Playing the power game for qualitative researchers: The possibility of a postmodern approach. *Journal of Advanced Nursing, 27,* 790-797.

Tashakkori, A., & Teddlie, C. (1998). *Mixed methodology: Combining qualitative and quantitative approaches* (Applied Social Research Methods, No. 46). Thousand Oaks, CA: Sage.

Theoretical coding families. (1998). [Online]. Available: www.geocities.com/researchtriangle/lab/1491/gtm-i-families.html

Thorne, S. (1997). The art (and science) of critiquing qualitative research. In J. M. Morse (Ed.), *Completing a qualitative project: Details and dialogue* (pp. 117-132). Thousand Oaks, CA: Sage.

Tierney, W. G. (1995). (Re)Presentation and voice. *Qualitative Inquiry, 1,* 379-390.

Tyler, S. A. (1986). Postmodern ethnography: From document of the occult to occult document. In J. Clifford & G. E. Marcus (Eds.), *Writing culture: The poetics and politics of ethnography* (pp. 122-140). Berkeley: University of California Press.

Van Maanen, J. (1988). *Tales of the field: On writing ethnography.* Chicago: University of Chicago Press.

Van Maanen, J. (1995). An end to innocence: The ethnography of ethnography. In J. Van Maanen (Ed.), *Representation in ethnography* (pp. 1-35). Thousand Oaks, CA: Sage.

Waldby, C. (2000). Virtual anatomy: From the body in the text to the body on the screen. *Journal of Medical Humanities, 21,* 85-107.

Wallace, D. P., & Van Fleet, C. (1998). Qualitative research and the editorial tradition: A mixed metaphor. *Library Trends, 46,* 752-769.

Weiss, R. S. (1994). *Learning from strangers: The art and method of qualitative interview studies.* New York: Free Press.

West, P. (1990). The status and validity of accounts obtained at interview: A contrast between two studies of families with a disabled child. *Social Science & Medicine, 30,* 1229-1239.

Wolcott, H. F. (1990). *Writing up qualitative research.* Newbury Park, CA: Sage.

Wolfer, J. (1993). Aspects of "reality" and ways of knowing in nursing: In search of an integrating paradigm. *Image: Journal of Nursing Scholarship, 25,* 141-146.

13

A FRAMEWORK FOR ANALYZING DATA IN MIXED METHODS RESEARCH

◆ Anthony J. Onwuegbuzie
Charles Teddlie

In previous chapters of this section of the handbook, the authors have discussed various stages of the mixed methods research process. Specifically, these stages, which were presented in sequential order, included identifying the mixed methods research purpose and determining research questions that match the purpose (Chapter 6), outlining the mixed methods research design (Chapters 7-9), selecting the sample(s) (Chapter 10), and collecting data (Chapter 11).

Once data become available, the next phase of the mixed methods research process is data analysis. However, it should be noted that in mixed methods research, the data analysis stage can occur at any juncture of the data collection process. That is,

the point at which the data analysis begins and ends depends on the type of data collected, which in turn depends on the sample size, which in turn depends on the research design, which in turn depends on the research purpose.

For example, in a parallel/simultaneous mixed methods design, in which quantitative and qualitative data are collected at the same time (Tashakkori & Teddlie, 1998), the data analysis often occurs *after* all of the data (i.e., both quantitative and qualitative data) have been collected. On the other hand, in sequential mixed model studies, in which "multiple approaches to data collection, analysis, and inference are employed in a sequence of phases" (pp. 149-150), the data analysis always begins *before* all of the data are collected. Moreover, in such designs, the data collection, data analysis, and data interpretation stages are iterative. In other words, these three elements of the mixed methods research process are recursive and thus nonlinear in nature (Onwuegbuzie, 2000b).

The purpose of this chapter is to provide a framework for analyzing data in mixed methods research. The chapter begins with a definition of mixed methods data analyses or what some call "mixed analyses." Following this definition, the two major rationales for conducting mixed methods data analyses (representation and legitimation) are discussed. The chapter then presents several preanalysis considerations for mixed methods analyses. Next, it provides a model for the mixed methods data analysis process. Finally, a procedure for selecting mixed methods data-analytical techniques is presented. Throughout the chapter, examples are presented that illustrate how researchers have used quantitative and qualitative data analysis procedures together to create a bridge between these two approaches.

◆ Operational Definition of Mixed Methods Data Analyses

Before proceeding further, it is important to provide an operational definition of mixed methods research. For the purposes of this chapter, Tashakkori and Teddlie's (1998) definition of mixed methods research is adopted: "Mixed methods studies are those that combine the qualitative and quantitative approaches into the research methodology of a single study or multiphased study" (pp. 17-18). In addition, Johnson and Turner's (Chapter 11, this volume) fundamental principle of mixed methods research is applied, namely

that "methods should be mixed in a way that has complementary strengths and no overlapping weaknesses."

Throughout this chapter, it is assumed that mixed methods data analyses can stem from a variety of research designs (mixed methods, qualitative, or quantitative). In other words, mixed methods data analyses are not dependent on the particular research design that is employed. This design-independent feature of mixed methods analyses arises from the fact that epistemology and method are not synonymous (Onwuegbuzie, 2000a, in press-b). As a result, the paradigm (i.e., logic of justification) does not dictate what specific data collection and data-analytical methods should be used by researchers. Indeed, differences in epistemology between quantitative and qualitative researchers do not prevent a qualitative researcher from using procedures more typically associated with quantitative research and vice versa (Onwuegbuzie, in press-b). For example, a qualitative researcher can collect numerical information, while a quantitative researcher can collect observational or interview data. Thus, this functional independence between the logic of justification and procedure implies that mixed methods data analysis techniques should not be dictated by the underlying epistemological orientation. Rather, they should stem from the research purpose (cf. Newman, Ridenour, Newman, & DeMarco, Chapter 6, this volume).

As will be described later in this chapter, quantitative data can be subjected to both quantitative and qualitative data analysis techniques, as can qualitative data. Thus, for the purposes of this chapter, the *fundamental principle of mixed methods data analysis* is defined and adopted. According to this fundamental principle, mixed methods data analysis is defined as the use of quantitative and qualitative analytical techniques, either concurrently or sequentially, at some stage beginning with the data collection process, from which interpretations are made in either a parallel, an integrated, or an iterative manner.

◆ The Two Major Rationales for Mixed Methods Data Analyses

Two major rationales prevail for conducting mixed methods data analyses. These rationales are *representation* and *legitimation*. Representation refers to the ability to extract adequate information from the underlying data, whereas legitimation refers to the validity of data interpretation. These concepts are described in this section.

MIXED METHODS DATA ANALYSES AS A METHOD OF ENHANCING REPRESENTATION

It is argued in this chapter that a mixed methods analysis offers a more comprehensive analytical technique than does either quantitative or qualitative data analysis alone. In particular, mixed methods data analysis allows the researcher to use the strengths of both quantitative and qualitative analysis techniques so as to understand phenomena better. The ability to "get more out of the data" provides the opportunity to generate more meaning, thereby enhancing the quality of data interpretation. For instance, mixed methods data analyses permit the researcher to fulfill the five purposes of mixed methods evaluations outlined by Greene, Caracelli, and Graham (1989): (a) triangulation[1] (i.e., seeking convergence and corroboration of results from different methods studying the same phenomenon), (b) com-

plementarity (i.e., seeking elaboration, enhancement, illustration, and clarification of the results from one method with results from the other method), (c) development (i.e., using the results from one method to help inform the other method), (d) initiation (i.e., discovering paradoxes and contradictions that lead to a reframing of the research question), and (e) expansion (i.e., seeking to expand the breadth and range of inquiry by using different methods for different inquiry components).

An example of how mixed methods data analysis can enhance representation is found in an investigation by Derry, Levin, Osana, Jones, and Peterson (2000). These authors examined students' statistical and scientific thinking after taking a course in which small-group collaborative activities that stimulated complex, real-life problem solving took place regularly. The evaluation procedures involved the administration of two forms of an interview protocol (i.e., pretest and posttest measures). These protocols consisted of vignettes that allowed assessment of the students' ability to judge the credibility of correlational arguments found in naturalistic reports of uncontrolled studies and in experimental studies as well as students' understanding of random sampling and estimation.

The quantitative analysis revealed improvements (effect sizes around 1 standard deviation) in the quality of students' statistical thinking in the following three areas: correlational reasoning, scientific experimentation, and random sampling. However, Derry et al. (2000) noted that "the analysis did not capture a full range of student responses" (p. 760). Thus, the researchers developed new coding schemes. A total of 16 categories (e.g., "makes nonresearch, nonstatistical argument") for the correlational study task and 25 categories (e.g., "vague, unsupported generalization") for the experimental study task were developed. Not only did the researchers provide descriptions for these categories, but they also reported the number and percentages of students making at least one statement in each category. Thus, conducting a mixed methods analysis increased Derry et al.'s ability to extract more meaning from their data. As such, representation was enhanced.

MIXED METHODS DATA ANALYSES AS A LEGITIMATION TOOL

Most quantitative and qualitative researchers agree that rigor is needed in research (Onwuegbuzie, 2000b, in press-a). Rigor necessitates that researchers attempt to be fully accountable for their data collection, analysis, and interpretive methodologies. As noted by Onwuegbuzie (2000b), such accountability implies that researchers continually strive to assess and document the legitimacy (e.g., validity, credibility, trustworthiness, dependability, confirmability, transferability) of their findings.

Legitimation in Qualitative and Quantitative Research. In qualitative research, legitimacy has been operationalized in a myriad of ways; however, a particularly useful conceptualization of validity is that of Maxwell (1992). Specifically, he identified five types of validity in qualitative research: descriptive validity (i.e., factual accuracy of the account as documented by the researcher), interpretive validity (i.e., the extent to which a researcher's interpretation of an account represents an understanding of the perspective of the group members under study and the meanings attached to their words and actions), theoretical validity (i.e., the degree to which a theoretical explanation developed from research findings fits the data), evaluative validity (i.e., the extent to which an evaluation framework can be applied to the objects of study rather than a descriptive, interpretive, or explanatory framework), and generalizability (i.e., the extent to which a researcher can generalize the account of a particular situation or population to other individuals, times, settings, or contexts). With respect to the latter, Maxwell differentiated internal generalizability from external generalizability the former refers to the generalizability of a conclusion within the setting or group studied, whereas the latter pertains to generalizability beyond the group, setting, time, or context. According to Maxwell, internal generalizability is typically more important to qualitative researchers than is external generalizability.

In quantitative research, maximizing internal and external validity is considered essential to rigorous research. Gay and Airasian (2000) described internal validity as "the condition that observed differences on the dependent variable are a direct result of the independent variable, not some other variable" (p. 345). As such, internal validity is threatened when plausible rival explanations cannot be eliminated. Johnson and Christensen (2000) defined external validity as "the extent to which the results of a study can be generalized to and across populations, settings, and times" (p. 200). Even if a particular finding has high internal validity, this does not mean that it can be generalized outside of the study context.

The seminal works of Donald Campbell and Julian Stanley (Campbell, 1957; Campbell & Stanley, 1963) provide the most authoritative source regarding threats to validity. Campbell and Stanley identified eight threats to internal validity: history, maturation, testing, instrumentation, statistical regression, differential selection of participants, mortality, and interaction effects (e.g., selection-maturation interaction). Building on the work of Campbell and Stanley, Smith and Glass (1987) classified threats to external validity into three areas: opulation validity (e.g., selection-treatment interaction), ecological validity (e.g., experimenter effects, multiple treatment interference, reactive arrangements, time-treatment interaction, history-treatment interaction), and external validity of operations (e.g., specificity of variables, pretest sensitization).

Legitimation in Mixed Methods Research. Mixed methods data analyses offer a more comprehensive means of legitimating findings than do either qualitative or quantitative data analyses alone by allowing analysts to assess information from both data types. For example, as noted by Sechrest and Sidani (1995), "Qualitative researchers regularly use terms like 'many,' 'most,' 'frequently,' 'several,' 'never,' and so on. These terms are fundamentally quantitative" (p. 79). In fact, qualitative researchers often can generate more meaning by obtaining counts of observations in addition to their narrative descriptions (Sandelowski, 2001).

For example, Witcher, Onwuegbuzie, and Minor (2001) conducted a qualitative study to determine preservice teachers' perceptions of characteristics of effective teachers. A qualitative analysis resulted in the emergence of six characteristics of effective teaching (as perceived by the teachers). By counting the frequency of the emergent themes, these authors found that of the six identified characteristics of effective teachers, student-centeredness was the most commonly cited trait (cited by 80% of the sample). This was followed by enthusiasm for teaching (40%), ethicalness (39%), classroom and behavior management (33%), teaching methodology (32%), and knowledge of subject (32%). This example illustrates how meaning and number are inextricably intertwined

(Dey, 1993). Obtaining counts of the themes prevented the researchers from "overweighting" or "underweighting" the emergent themes (Sandelowski, 2001, p. 234).

The identification of categories, themes, typologies, and the like are based on the frequency with which a facet occurs (Miles & Huberman, 1994). In other words, every time qualitative data are reduced to categories or themes, the researcher is using the "numbered nature of phenomena for their analysis" (Sandelowski, 2001, p. 231). As noted by Miles and Huberman (1994), three rationales prevail for counting themes: (a) to identify patterns more easily, (b) to maintain analytical integrity, and (c) to verify a hypothesis. Moreover, by adding numerical precision to their descriptive accounts, Witcher et al. (2001) were able to leave an audit trail that involved a more extensive documentation of the data underlying their investigation. Interestingly, audit trails are recommended by qualitative researchers as a means of evaluating legitimation, increasing legitimation, or both (Halpern, 1983; Lincoln & Guba, 1985).

Counting themes is a manifestation of what Tashakkori and Teddlie (1998) referred to as "quantitizing" data (p. 126), in which qualitative data are converted into numerical codes that can be represented statistically. As stated by Sandelowski (2001), in quantitizing, "qualitative 'themes' are numerically represented, in scores, scales, or clusters, in order to more fully describe and/or interpret a target phenomenon" (p. 231). Also, Boyatzis (1998) referred to the counting of themes as "quantitative translation" (p. 129).

Crone and Teddlie (1995) demonstrated how emergent qualitative themes could first be quantitized and then subjected to statistical analysis. In a replication of research regarding teachers in differentially effective schools, the researchers asked teachers and principals questions using the "interview guide approach" (Patton, 1990). The open-ended data gathered through this approach were then subjected to the constant comparative technique (Lincoln & Guba, 1985), and a number of themes emerged. These themes occurred with differential frequency depending on whether or not the interviews were conducted in more or in less effective schools. One of these themes was "cohesiveness of faculty in working together on goals." The researchers then counted the different themes that emerged and subjected those data to chi-square analysis.

Subjecting quantitized data to statistical analysis aids in the interpretation of the mixed methods results. In the Crone and Teddlie (1995) study, the quantitative analysis indicated that differentially effective schools had teachers who were significantly different from one another in terms of the cohesiveness with which they worked together on their goals. The statistical analysis added greater legitimacy to the researchers' conclusions, which were based on data that were initially emergent and qualitative in nature.

Effect Sizes in Qualitative Research. Onwuegbuzie (2001) took the notion of legitimation a step further by applying the concept of effect sizes (a statistical concept) to qualitative data. According to Onwuegbuzie, the frequency of emergent themes (i.e., frequency effect size) can be determined by first "binarizing"[2] themes. Specifically, for each study participant, a score of 1 is given for a theme if it represents a significant statement or observation pertaining to that individual; otherwise, a score of 0 is given. For each sample member, each theme is binarized to a score of 1 or 0. This binarization leads to the formation of an *interrespondent matrix* (Participant × Theme matrix) and an *intrarespondent matrix* (Unit × Theme matrix).

The interrespondent matrix indicates which individuals contribute to each emerging theme, whereas the intrarespondent matrix identifies which units (statements or observations) contribute to each emerging theme. For studies that involve more than one participant, both the interrespondent matrix and the intrarespondent matrix can be used; for studies that involve only one participant, the intrarespondent matrix comes into play. The binarizing of themes allows the computation of two types of effect sizes (*manifest* and *latent* effect sizes). Onwuegbuzie (2001) developed a typology of effect sizes that are presented in Table 13.1.

Manifest Effect Sizes. Manifest effect sizes represent effect sizes that pertain to observable content. This class of effect sizes represents specific counts (or percentages) of significant statements (e.g., words, phrases, sentences, paragraphs, pages) or observations analyzed that underlie emergent themes.

Frequency (manifest) effect sizes are obtained by calculating the frequency of each theme from the interrespondent matrix. These frequencies can then be converted to percentages so as to determine the prevalence rate of each theme. *Intensity (manifest) effect sizes*, which are determined via the intrarespondent matrix, represent the frequency of each significant statement within each theme or the frequency of each theme within a set of themes. As before, intensity effect sizes can be converted to percentages. In Witcher et al.'s (2001) study described earlier, the endorsement rates pertaining to the themes underlying preservice teachers' perceptions of effective teaching characteristics were termed manifest effect sizes. Another example of manifest effect sizes is

TABLE 13.1   Typology of Effect Sizes in Mixed Methods Data Analyses

Type of Effect Size	Definition
Manifest effect size	Effect size pertaining to observable content
Frequency effect size	Frequency of theme within a sample; can be converted to a percentage (i.e., prevalence rate)
Intensity effect size	Number of units used for each theme; can be converted to a percentage (i.e., prevalence rate)
Cumulative intensity effect size	Percentage of total themes associated with a phenomenon
Raw intensity effect size	Percentage of people selecting or endorsing multiple themes (each theme is endorsed by a certain percentage of respondents)
Adjusted effect size	Effect size adjusted for time sequence and length of the unit of analysis (e.g., observation, interview, text)
Fixed-interval frequency effect size	Frequency of theme per unit of time (e.g., number of times behavior observed per hour)
Fixed-interval intensity effect size	Frequency of unit per unit of time (e.g., number of times a significant statement appears per page)
Fixed-response frequency effect size	Amount of time that elapses before theme is observed
Fixed-response intensity effect size	Amount of time that elapses before unit of analysis is observed
Latent effect size	Effect size pertaining to nonobservable underlying aspects of the phenomenon being studied
Variance-explained latent effect size	Examples include proportion of variance explained in exploratory factor analysis of themes, correlation between a theme and available or subsequent data, and canonical correlation between set of themes and set of available or subsequent data

the number and percentages of students making at least one statement in each category in the Derry et al. (2000) inquiry described earlier.

A final example of intensity (manifest) effect sizes is provided by an evaluation study of 10 Aquatic Resource Education Programs (AREPs) funded by the U.S. Fish and Welfare Service in the southeastern United States (Teddlie, 1999). One phase of the study required the program coordinators to list all activities that they had undertaken during their previous funding cycle, resulting in 1,092 activities. This information was simplified in a two-step process:

1. The 1,092 activities were reduced to 108 descriptor codes using the constant comparative method (e.g., Glaser & Strauss, 1967; Lincoln & Guba, 1985).

2. These 108 descriptor codes were further reduced to 12 generic categories, again using the constant comparative method. For example, the generic category "fishing events" was composed of the following nine descriptor codes: fishing clinics, fishing rodeos, recreational fishing, fisheries, fish identification, community fishing, urban fishing, rural fishing, and National Fishing Week. All of these descriptor codes concerned hands-on activities related to fishing programs of various types.

Table 13.2 contains the intensity effect sizes for the 12 generic categories (themes) associated with the AREP activities. The largest effect sizes were for "general education/training activities" (with an intensity effect size of 14.9%), "conservation/ ecological issues" (with an intensity effect size of 14.4%), and "fishing events" (with an intensity effect size of 11.7%).

Intensity effect sizes based on percentage of total themes associated with a phenomenon (or percentage out of 100% [Teddlie, 1999]) are different from intensity effect sizes based on numbers of people selecting multiple themes (where each theme is endorsed by a certain percentage of the individuals in the population [Witcher et al., 2001]). The former is termed *cumulative intensity effect sizes*,

whereas the latter is referred to as *raw intensity effect sizes*. The total of the cumulative intensity effects is always 100%, while it could be much higher for raw intensity effect sizes, where multiple selections by each individual are allowed. As such, comparing cumulative intensity effect sizes and raw intensity effect sizes would be misleading.

Adjusted effect sizes also can be computed where the frequency and intensity of themes are adjusted for the time sequence and length of the unit of analysis (e.g., observation, interview, text). For example, with respect to the latter (i.e., length of unit of analysis), the number of times that a theme emerges could be divided by the number of (transcribed) words/sentences/ paragraphs/pages analyzed. Such adjusted effect sizes help to reduce bias in the data sampled.

In addition, a *fixed-interval effect size index* could be estimated via the interrespondent matrix or the intrarespondent matrix, where the frequency (i.e., *fixed-interval frequency effect size*) and intensity (i.e., *fixed-interval intensity effect size*) of themes are determined as they occur within a specific period of time. For example, a researcher could investigate how many times a word is used during the first 10 minutes of a focus group. Furthermore, a *fixed-ratio effect size index* could be assessed, where a specific frequency (i.e., *fixed-response frequency effect size*) and intensity (i.e., *fixed-response intensity effect size*) of themes are specified a priori, and the amount of time that elapses before these targets are met (if they are met at all) is used as an effect size estimate.

Latent Effect Sizes. Latent effect sizes, the other class of effect sizes, represent effect sizes that pertain to nonobservable underlying aspects of the phenomenon being studied. They are more interpretive than manifest effect sizes. For example,

TABLE 13.2   Intensity Effect Sizes and Frequency Distribution for the 12 Generic Categories (Themes) Associated With the AREP Activities

Category Number	Generic Category	Number of Descriptor Codes in Each Generic Category	Frequency of Occurrence	Intensity Effect Sizes (percentage of total)
1	General education/ training activities	4	163	14.9
2	Conservation/ ecological issues	10	157	14.4
3	Fishing events	9	128	11.7
4	Special AREP strategies (e.g., Project WILD)	13	121	11.1
5	Materials	9	82	7.5
6	State sites (e.g., centers, museums)	6	79	7.2
7	Special events/exhibits	13	73	6.7
8	Other hands-on activities (not fishing)	7	54	4.9
9	School-based activities	5	51	4.7
10	Publicity/promotion efforts	8	50	4.6
11	Special needs audiences	5	47	4.3
12	All other categories (each with a frequency of less than 5% of the total)	19	87	7.9
Total	12 overall generic categories (themes)	108	1,092	100

correlational analyses could then be performed using the inter- and intrarespondent matrices to determine the relationship among the themes. Correlational analyses also could be undertaken using the *interrespondent meta-theme matrix* and the *intrarespondent thematic matrix* to determine the relationship among the meta-themes. The correlation indices contained in these correlation matrices serve as *bivariate latent effect sizes*. In addition, exploratory factor analysis undertaken on the inter- and intrarespondent matrices can be used to compute *variance-explained latent effect sizes*, stemming from the eigenvalues and the proportion of variance explained after rotation by each theme. For instance, in Witcher et al.'s (2001) inquiry described earlier, the six themes underlying preservice teachers' perceptions of characteristics of effective teachers (each binarized as 1 or 0) were correlated with a set of background and personality variables via a canonical correlation analysis. This analysis revealed that females, college-level juniors, and minority students tended to endorse teacher characteristics that were classified as ethical and teaching methodology to a greater extent than did others. They also tended to rate attributes that were associated with knowledge of subject and classroom and behavior management to a lesser degree. The canonical correlation coefficient (.44) representing this relationship served as a latent effect size.

Consistent with Onwuegbuzie's (2001) conceptualization of effect sizes in qualitative research, nearly half a century ago, Lazarsfeld and Barton (1955) advocated the use of what they coined "quasi-statistics" in qualitative research, which refers to the use of descriptive statistics that can be extracted from qualitative data. Interestingly, Becker (1970) contended that "one of the greatest faults in most observational case studies has been their failure to make explicit the quasi-statistical basis of their conclusions" (pp. 81-82). Indeed, Becker, Geer, Hughes, and Strauss (1961/1977) presented more than 50 tables and graphs in their qualitative work, which provided effect size interpretations of their qualitative data.

Using Qualitizing Techniques to Assess Legitimation. Similarly, "qualitizing" techniques, in which numerical data are converted into narrative data that can be analyzed qualitatively (Tashakkori & Teddlie, 1998), can be used to increase or assess legitimation. One way of qualitizing data is via narrative profile formation (i.e., modal profiles, average profiles, holistic profiles, comparative profiles, normative profiles), wherein narrative descriptions are constructed from quantitative data.

For example, Teddlie and Stringfield (1993) conducted a longitudinal study of eight matched pairs of schools initially classified as either effective or ineffective with respect to baseline data. Five years after the study was initiated, these investigators used eight empirical criteria to reclassify the schools' effectiveness status. These criteria were (a) norm-referenced test scores, (b) criterion-referenced test scores, (c) time-on-task in classrooms, (d) scores on quality of classroom instruction measures, (e) faculty stability, (f) student attendance, (g) changes in socioeconomic status (SES) of the schools' student bodies, and (h) measures of school "climate." Teddlie and Stringfield converted these quantitative data (i.e., qualitized them) into the following four qualitatively defined school profiles: (a) stable more effective, (b) stable less effective, (c) improving, and (d) declining. These school profiles were then used to add more meaning to the researchers' longitudinal evolving perspectives on the schools.

Another example of profile formation involves the AREP evaluation described earlier. AREPs are typically administered by one of two types of professionals: educators trained in aquatic resource issues or marine biologists with a modicum of educational training. The programs run by these two types of professionals are typically quite different, and an analysis of the frequency of activities employed in their AREPs generated two distinct profiles. One profile (of educators trained in aquatic resource issues) emphasized conservation/ecological issues, specific AREP educational strategies using national curricula (e.g., Project WILD), state sites (e.g., education centers, museums), other hands-on activities (not fishing), and school-based activities. The other profile (of marine biologists with some educational training) emphasized a different set of activities: fishing events, general education/training activities developed locally, special events/exhibits (e.g., state fairs), publicity/promotion efforts (for the fishing events), and special needs audiences (i.e., fishing events for these audiences). (See Table 13.2 for the generic set of activity categories.)

Similarly, Daley and Onwuegbuzie (in press) investigated male juvenile delinquents' causal attributions for others' violent behavior and the salient pieces of information they use in arriving at these attributions. These researchers developed the Violence Attribution Survey, a 12-item questionnaire designed to assess attributions made by juveniles for the behavior of others involved in violent acts. Each item consisted of a vignette followed by three possible attributions (i.e., person, stimulus, and circumstance) presented in multiple choice format and an open-ended question asking the juveniles their reasons for their choice of response. Participants were 82 male juvenile offenders, selected via an a priori power analysis, who were drawn randomly from the population of juveniles incarcerated at a correctional facility in a large southeastern state. These investigators employed what they called a six-stage concurrent mixed methodological analysis, which used both mixed methods data-analytical techniques. A phenomenological analysis (Stage 2) revealed the following seven themes that arose from juveniles' reasons for their causal attributions: self-control, violation of rights,

provocation, irresponsibility, poor judgment, fate, and conflict resolution. Daley and Onwuegbuzie conducted an ipsative/cluster analysis on these themes and identified three distinct profiles of delinquents.

With respect to Maxwell's (1992) components of the validity of qualitative findings, as noted by Sandelowski (2001), "Counting is essential to ensuring descriptive (getting the 'facts' of the case right), interpretive (getting participants' interpretations of events right), and/or theoretical (developing an interpretation that fits these facts) validity" (p. 234). Counting also helps researchers to assess the internal generalizability of their qualitative data (Onwuegbuzie, 2000b). Similarly, qualitizing helps analysts to assess the internal validity of numerical data by enabling them to rule in (or out) rival explanations. Because qualitative data analyses represent more *descriptive precision,* whereas quantitative data analyses provide more *numerical precision,* the use of mixed methods analyses offers the possibility of combining descriptive precision and numerical precision within the same interpretation. As such, legitimation is enhanced.

◆ Preanalysis Considerations in Mixed Methods Data Analyses

Because quantitative data-analytical procedures (e.g., *t* tests) tend to be standardized, they are usually easy to replicate. However, while dissemination of analytical techniques is a strength of numerically oriented research studies, interpretation of findings is a relative weakness. In particular, quantitative researchers tend to be more preoccupied with results than with their interpretations.[3] In other words, quantitative researchers in the social and behavioral sciences tend to emphasize figures over figures of speech, tables over tableaux, graphs over graphical accounts, visual over verbal (see Sandelowski, Chapter 12, this volume), and measurement over meaning.

On the other hand, a strength of qualitative research reports is that they typically represent an attempt to ensure that the results are as meaningful as possible. Moreover, qualitative researchers tend to discuss their findings in a sociocultural context to a greater degree than do their quantitative counterparts. However, while providing meaning to a set of results is a particular strength of qualitative research, delineating information about the analytical techniques used and the major features of the analysis is a weakness. As noted by Constas (1992), unless methods for examining rival hypotheses in qualitative research are developed, "the research community will be entitled to question the analytical rigor of qualitative research" (p. 255), where rigor is defined as the attempt to make data and categorical schemes as public and replicable as possible (Denzin, 1978).

Mixed methods research, then, offers the opportunity to address these relative weaknesses of quantitative and qualitative research by paying attention to issues related to both data analysis and interpretation. Because the mixed methods paradigm is still evolving, the onus is on mixed methods researchers to provide detailed procedural and interpretational information to their readers. However, before researchers can furnish such information, they must be aware of the important considerations that underlie their data analyses.

The researcher should consider the following 12 decisions before undertaking a mixed methods data analysis: (1) the purpose of the mixed methods research, (2) whether a variable-oriented or a case-oriented analysis should be undertaken, (3) whether to use exploratory or confirmatory data-analytical techniques or both, (4) which data types should be used, (5) what the relationships are between quantitative and qualitative data types if both types are used, (6) what data-analytical assumptions underlie the analyses, (7) what the source of typology development is, (8) what the nomination source for typology development is, (9) what the verification source for typology development is, (10) what the temporal designation for the data-analytical procedures is, (11) whether computer software should be used to analyze the data, and (12) what process of legitimation should be used. Each decision is discussed in what follows.

DECISION 1: THE PURPOSE OF THE MIXED METHODS RESEARCH

As noted earlier, Greene et al. (1989) presented five purposes for mixed methods research (triangulation, complementarity, development, initiation, and expansion). The purpose selected affects many aspects of the data-analytical process. For example, if the purpose for conducting a mixed methods study is triangulation, specifically between-method triangulation (Denzin, 1978), then clearly both qualitative and quantitative data types are needed (Decisions 1, 2, and 4), a parallel mixed analysis (Tashakkori & Teddlie, 1998) is most likely appropriate (Decision 5), both the quantitative and qualitative data collection techniques should attempt to measure the same phenomenon (Decision 6), and so on. If the purpose of the mixed methods research is initiation, then both qualitative and quantitative data types should be used (Decisions 2 and 4), and a sequential mixed analysis (Tashakkori &

Teddlie, 1998) is most likely appropriate (Decision 5).

DECISION 2: VARIABLE-ORIENTED VERSUS CASE-ORIENTED ANALYSIS

According to Miles and Huberman (1994), "The variable-oriented approach is conceptual and theory-centered from the start, casting a wide net . . . over a (usually large) number of cases. The 'building blocks' are variables and their intercorrelations, rather than cases" (p. 174). Thus, the variable-oriented approach is more consistent with quantitative methodologies or with qualitative methodologies with large samples (Decisions 1, 4, and 6). Conversely, "a case-oriented approach considers the case as a whole entity, looking at configurations, associations, causes, and effects *within* the case—and only then turns to comparative analysis of a (usually limited) number of cases" (p. 174, italics in original). As such, case-oriented analyses pertain more to qualitative analysis. Thus, whether the researcher is more interested in a variable- or case-oriented approach affects which data types will be used (Decision 4), whether the quantitative or qualitative approach will be dominant (Decision 5), what data-analytical assumptions underlie the analyses (Decision 6), and the process of legitimation (Decision 12).

DECISION 3: EXPLORATORY VERSUS CONFIRMATORY DATA-ANALYTICAL TECHNIQUES

In quantitative research, the use of both exploratory and confirmatory data analysis techniques is well-established (Onwuegbuzie, 2001; Tashakkori & Teddlie, 1998), as is the use of exploratory data analysis techniques in qualitative research. However, confirmatory data analysis is not as commonly associated with qualitative research designs. In fact, many qualitative researchers (e.g., Lincoln & Guba, 1985) believe that confirmatory techniques have no place in qualitative research because realities are not replicable. However, we contend, as do others (e.g., Patton, 1990; Sandelowski, 2001; Tashakkori & Teddlie, 1998), that qualitative data can be used to test hypotheses. For example, Minor, Onwuegbuzie, and Witcher (in press) replicated Witcher et al.'s (2001) study discussed earlier. In the follow-up study, the same six themes were confirmed, with an additional theme (personableness) emerging. The confirmation of the six themes helped to increase the credibility of the results from the initial study.

Table 13.3 presents a typology of exploratory/confirmatory data analysis techniques for quantitative/qualitative data. Deciding whether an exploratory or a confirmatory analysis technique is needed is an important preanalysis decision to make in mixed methods research.

DECISION 4: WHICH DATA TYPES TO USE

This decision relates to whether quantitative data, qualitative data, or both should be employed in the mixed methods data analysis. Clearly, this decision depends on the research purpose (cf. Newman et al., Chapter 6, this volume), the purpose of the mixed methods research (Decision 1), and whether a variable-oriented or a case-oriented analysis is the major focus (Decision 2). If only one type of data is gathered, then for the data analysis to be considered mixed, either (a)

TABLE 13.3   Data Analysis Matrix: Typology of Quantitative and Qualitative Data Analysis Techniques as a Function of Data Analysis Purpose

Exploratory Data Analysis		Confirmatory Data Analysis	
Quantitative Data	Qualitative Data	Quantitative Data	Qualitative Data
Descriptive statistics Exploratory factor analysis Cluster analysis Multidimensional scaling Configural frequency analysis	Exploratory (a posterior) thematic analysis Profile analysis Effects matrices Iterative thematic analysis Cross-case analysis Manifest content analysis Latent content analysis Conceptually ordered matrices Case-ordered matrices Time-ordered matrices Meta-matrices Latent content analysis Constant-comparative analysis Developmental research sequence	Correlational analyses t test Chi-square analysis Multiple regression analysis Logistic regression analysis ANOVA ANCOVA MANOVA MANCOVA Discriminant analysis Confirmatory factor analysis Canonical correlation analysis Path analysis Structural equation modeling Internal replication analysis	Confirmatory thematic (a priori) analysis Negative/discrepant case analysis Confirmatory case study Iterative thematic analysis Cross-case analysis Predictor-outcome matrices Simple valence analysis Manifest content analysis

a concurrent analysis of the same qualitative data must take place or (b) a concurrent analysis of the same quantitative data must take place. The former type of analysis involves the transformation of the qualitative data to a numerical form or quantitizing the data (Tashakkori & Teddlie, 1998).

On the other hand, the latter type of concurrent analysis necessitates the qualitizing of quantitative data (Tashakkori & Teddlie, 1998). It should be noted that if only one type of data is used in the data analysis process and no transformation takes place (no quantitizing or qualitizing), then the result will be either a traditional quantitative data analysis if the single data type is quantitative or a qualitative data analysis if the single data type is qualitative.

DECISION 5: RELATIONSHIPS BETWEEN QUANTITATIVE AND QUALITATIVE DATA TYPES

If, on the other hand, both quantitative and qualitative data types are used, then two decisions emerge. First, the data analyst must decide whether the quantitative and qualitative approaches will be used approximately equally (i.e., *equivalent status design*) or whether either the quantitative or the qualitative techniques should be dominant (i.e., *dominant-less dominant design*) (Creswell, 1994; Tashakkori & Teddlie, 1998). Clearly, this decision depends on the research purpose (see Newman et al., Chapter 6, this volume), the purpose of the mixed methods research (Decision 1), and whether a variable-oriented or a case-oriented analysis is the major focus (Decision 2).

The second decision relates to the extent to which the quantitative and qualitative data analyses inform each other during the data analysis process. Specifically, if (a) both sets of data analyses occur separately, (b) neither type of analysis builds on the other during the data analysis stage, and (c) the results from each type of analysis are neither compared nor consolidated until *both* sets of data analyses have been completed, then the researcher is undertaking what Tashakkori and Teddlie (1998) referred to as a "parallel mixed analysis" (p. 128).

Examples of Parallel Mixed Analyses. In parallel mixed analyses, once both sets of analyses have been conducted and verified, the researcher has the option of interpreting and writing up the two sets of findings separately or in some integrated manner. For instance, Onwuegbuzie and DaRos-Voseles (2001) investigated the effectiveness of cooperative learning (CL) in a graduate-level research methodology course comprised of 81 students enrolled in sections wherein CL groups were formed to undertake the major course requirements and 112 students enrolled in sections wherein all assignments were undertaken individually (IL). The quantitative portion of the analysis revealed an ordinal interaction between groups (CL vs. IL) and examination types (midterm vs. final examination), with IL groups obtaining higher scores on both in-class examinations but the difference between the two groups being statistically significantly higher at the midterm stage. The qualitative component of the inquiry, involving analyses of reflexive journals, revealed eight themes that represented positive experiences (e.g., enhanced positive interdependence, increased levels of self-efficacy). Six negative themes also emerged (e.g., difficulty in holding CL group meetings outside of the class). Nevertheless, most students (70%) tended to have positive overall attitudes toward their CL experiences.

Onwuegbuzie and DaRos-Voseles (2001) could have written up the two sets of findings separately, but they decided to integrate them into a more coherent whole. Consolidating these findings led to the initial conclusion that the two sets of results were in conflict because the statistical analyses revealed that CL techniques had led to decrements in performance, whereas the qualitative results suggested that CL was liked by the majority of the class. However, at the legitimation stage (i.e., member checks, weighting the evidence, making contrasts/comparisons, peer debriefing, assessing rival explanations), the researchers concluded, "The fact that students appear to like cooperative learning techniques despite not experiencing increases in their levels of performance . . . suggest[s] that, for some students, the non-cognitive outcomes may be as important as subject matter achievement" (p. 72). The researchers also noted that "a few students, particularly the weaker ones, seemed to have liked cooperative learning for reasons that are not compatible with the instructional objectives of this method" (p. 72).

The decision to use parallel mixed analysis techniques is influenced by the purpose of the mixed methods research (Decision 1). In particular, parallel mixed analyses may be used if the purpose of the mixed methods research is triangulation, complementarity, initiation, or expansion. Parallel mixed analyses routinely are used by pharmaceutical companies in clinical trials for complementarity or expansion purposes.

With respect to data collection methods, survey research is increasingly leading to some form of parallel mixed analyses. Such analyses can occur when the self-report instrument used contains both open-ended and closed-ended items. Johnson and Turner (Chapter 11, this volume) refer to this as a "Type 2" (mixed) data collection method (cf. Table 11.1 in their chapter), whereby the instrument contains a "mixture of completely open-ended and closed-ended items" and/or one or more items that are mixed. In most cases, such "mixed" self-report instruments lead to separate analyses, from which the findings are integrated after both sets of analyses have been undertaken.

Data "Correlation" in Mixed Methods Research. Surprisingly, the trend in mixed self-report data has been to conduct separate analyses of the quantitative and qualitative responses. Yet even more information can be extracted by correlating these responses to the data or producing a "data correlation." Daley and Onwuegbuzie's (in press) study mentioned earlier provides an example of how responses to the

closed-ended items can be correlated to responses to the open-ended items. As noted earlier, seven themes emerged from the open-ended responses. The researchers binarized each theme by assigning a score of 1 or 0 for each sample member, depending on whether the theme was represented by that individual, which led to the formation of an interrespondent matrix. Daley and Onwuegbuzie then correlated scores from this matrix to the scores on the closed-ended items of their Violence Attribution Scale. The authors found that "juveniles who endorsed the self-control theme tended to make *less* violence attributional errors than did their counterparts" (p. 18, italics in original), with an extremely large effect size reported. Correlating the responses to the qualitative and quantitative responses led to much more meaning being extracted from the data than would have been the case otherwise.

Collins's (2000) study provides another example of a study in which quantitative responses were correlated with qualitative responses. Specifically, Collins examined the relationship between elementary teachers' beliefs concerning National Council of Teachers of Mathematics recommendations and the extent to which teachers believe it is possible to implement these recommendations in their classrooms. Also examined was the degree to which teacher personal efficacy and outcome expectancy is influenced by students' regulatory styles and the degree to which teachers' perceptions of the effectiveness and practicality of grouping strategies is influenced by students' self-regulatory styles. The correlations of both data sources led to the conclusion that self-regulatory styles associated with learning disabilities affect teachers' levels of personal self-efficacy and outcome expectancy as well as their beliefs about the effectiveness of grouping strategies.

Sequential Mixed Analysis. Instead of analyzing quantitative and qualitative data concurrently, data from some studies are analyzed in a certain order, leading to what Tashakkori and Teddlie (1998) termed *sequential qualitative-quantitative analysis* and *sequential quantitative-qualitative analysis*. In the former case, an initial qualitative data analysis leads to the identification of groups of individuals who are similar in some respect to each other. These identified groups are then compared with each other using either existing quantitative data or data that are collected after the initial qualitative data analysis. For example, in Daley and Onwuegbuzie's (in press) study mentioned earlier, the three profiles of delinquents that emerged from the juvenile delinquents' violence attribution reasons were significantly different (moderate effect size) with respect to age.

Other forms of sequential qualitative-quantitative analysis include (a) quantitative extreme case analysis and (b) quantitative negative case analysis. Quantitative extreme case analysis involves undertaking a qualitative data analysis (e.g., thematic analysis), followed by a legitimation analysis (Onwuegbuzie, 2000b) so as to determine the extreme cases. In the second phase, new quantitative data are collected on all cases, followed by a quantitative analysis (e.g., *t* test) of the newly collected data, comparing extreme and nonextreme cases, in an attempt to determine why the former cases were so extreme in the first phase.

Quantitative negative case analysis involves undertaking a qualitative data analysis (e.g., thematic analysis), followed by a legitimation analysis so as to determine negative cases (i.e., cases that do not fit the interpretation or initial theory). In the second phase, new quantitative data are collected on all cases, followed by a quantitative analysis (e.g., *t* test) of the

newly collected data, comparing negative and non-negative cases, in an attempt to determine why the former did not fit the model in the first phase.

Similarly, sequential quantitative-qualitative analysis involves "forming groups of peoples/settings on the initial basis of [quantitative] data and then comparing the groups on [qualitative] data (subsequently collected or available)" (Tashakkori & Teddlie, 1998, p. 135). An example of this is Taylor and Tashakkori's (1997) study, in which teachers were classified into four groups based on their quantitative responses to measures of (a) efficacy (low vs. high) and (b) locus of causality for student success (internal vs. external). These four groups were then compared with respect to obtained qualitative data.

The following four additional types of sequential quantitative-qualitative analyses have been identified: (a) qualitative contrasting case analysis, (b) qualitative residual analysis, (c) qualitative follow-up interaction analysis, and (d) qualitative internal replication analysis. Qualitative contrasting analysis involves first conducting a quantitative descriptive (i.e., noninferential) data analysis (e.g., total, *z* score) on some construct (e.g., reading achievement) and then identifying a proportion (e.g., 10%) or a specific number of those who obtained the lowest and highest scores on the numerical measure. In the second phase, new qualitative data (e.g., interviews, observations) are collected on the lowest- and highest-scoring groups, followed by a qualitative analysis (e.g., thematic analysis) of the newly collected data, in an attempt to determine why the two groups were so discrepant. An example of this is Onwuegbuzie (1997), who examined the anxiety experienced by graduate students from nonstatistical disciplines who wrote research proposals in an introductory research methodology course. These students were divided into low, middle, and high groups based on their research proposal scores, and the lowest-achieving third of these students were contrasted with the highest-achieving third with respect to statements made in their reflexive journals concerning their levels of anxiety. Similarly, Sheumaker (2001), using an instrument she developed called the Technology and Teaching Practices Survey, identified teachers and administrators with the lowest and highest levels of constructivist beliefs. These educators were then subsequently interviewed to determine (a) what qualitative factors contributed to their beliefs being so extreme and (b) whether these beliefs stemmed from a constructivist-based staff development program for technology training in the state of Georgia.

Qualitative residual analysis involves undertaking a general linear model (GLM) analysis (e.g., multiple regression), followed by a residual analysis on the selected model so as to determine outliers. In the second phase, new qualitative data are collected on the outlying cases, followed by a qualitative analysis of the newly collected data, in an attempt to determine why these cases did not fit the chosen model. For example, several researchers (e.g., Teddlie & Stringfield, 1993) have classified schools into ineffective and effective groups based on the residual scores from a multiple regression analysis of standardized test scores.

According to Onwuegbuzie (in press-a), many researchers neglect to assess the presence of interactions when testing hypotheses. By not formally testing for interactions, researchers may be using a model that does not honor the nature of reality that they want to study, thereby providing a threat to internal validity. Because many analysts fail to disaggregate their data, they often incorrectly assume that their findings are invariant across all subsamples in their study. Onwuegbuzie termed this *non-interaction-seeking bias*. Researchers should use *condition-seeking* methods, whereby they "seek to discover which, of the many conditions that were confounded together in procedures that have obtained a finding, are indeed necessary or sufficient" (Greenwald, Pratkanis, Leippe, & Baumgardner, 1986, p. 223). Such condition-seeking methods would generate a progression of research questions that, if addressed in future studies, would provide increasingly accurate and generalizable conclusions.[4]

The development of school effectiveness research (SER) has involved the use of such questions, which have been employed in a sub-area of SER known as the "context of school effects" (Teddlie, Stringfield, & Reynolds, 2000). Initially, a set of effective school "correlates" were derived from case studies of highly effective schools that were supposed to be generic to all effective schools. Researchers soon began questioning the generalizability of these effective schools correlates across different school contexts, asserting that there were interactions between effectiveness status and basic school characteristics. "Contextually sensitive" studies of school effects emerged, the first of which compared effective schools that served students from lower SES environments as opposed to middle SES environments (e.g., Hallinger & Murphy, 1986; Teddlie & Stringfield, 1993). While some of the characteristics across these schools were the same, others were quite different (e.g., type of leadership, curricular emphasis). Later studies examined other context variables such as community type (urban, suburban, or rural), grade level configuration (elementary or secondary), and school size.

A final type of sequential mixed analysis (qualitative internal replication analysis) involves undertaking a GLM analysis (e.g., multiple regression), followed by an internal replication analysis on the selected model (i.e., jackknife analysis) so as to determine *internal replication outliers* (i.e., cases that unduly affect the internal replication analysis). In the second phase, new qualitative data are collected on the outlying cases, followed by a qualitative analysis of the newly collected data, in an attempt to determine why these cases did not fit the chosen model.

Rather than conducting either a concurrent analysis or a sequential mixed methods data analysis, the researcher may choose to invoke iterative data analysis techniques. An example of an iterative data analysis is what Li, Marquart, and Zercher (2000) termed *cross-tracks analysis*. This analysis is characterized by a concurrent analysis of both qualitative and quantitative data such that the data analysis oscillates continually between both data sets throughout various stages of the data analysis process.

DECISION 6: DATA ASSUMPTIONS

In mixed methods research, investigators should be cognizant of and should check the assumptions underlying their data analysis techniques. For quantitative analysis, the assumptions can be found in any standard statistics textbook. Because many quantitative inferential analyses can be classified as belonging to the GLM family (Cohen, 1968; Knapp, 1978; Thompson, 1998), the majority of statistical techniques are bounded by GLM assumptions (e.g., normality, independence, homogeneity of variance). Onwuegbuzie and Daniel (2002, in press) provided a comprehensive review of assumptions and best practices for most of the common statistical techniques, from correlational analysis to hierarchical linear modeling. Keselman

et al. (1998) also provided a discussion of statistical assumptions.

With respect to the qualitative data analysis portion of mixed methods data analyses, there are fewer generally recognized assumptions to consider. However, perhaps the most important assumption (often overlooked by qualitative data analysts) relates to the area of sampling. Although external generalizability (or external validity) is typically not a concern when interpreting qualitative data, internal generalizability usually is (Maxwell, 1992).[5] Yet, surprisingly, the assumptions associated with internal generalizability have received scant attention in the qualitative literature. Recently, however, Onwuegbuzie (2001) contended that the justification for generalizing qualitative findings within the setting, group, or individual studied should never be taken for granted. This is because words arising from a person, group of individuals, or observations within a particular setting are equivalent to sample units of data from those sources. Such samples can be representative—or not—of the total number of words/observations arising from that person, group of individuals, or setting.

A common goal of qualitative researchers, especially when interviewing and focus techniques are used, is to capture the voice of the person(s) being studied. Regardless of the number of interviews conducted (single vs. multiple), the length of each interview, the type of interviews (unstructured, partially structured, semistructured, structured, or totally structured), and the format of interviews (formal vs. informal), words collected represent a mere *sample* of the interviewee's voice or the "truth space." Thus, when undertaking thematic analyses, *inferences* are made from the sample of words to the interviewee's truth space. Just as quantitative researchers hope that their sample is representative of the population, qualitative researchers hope that their sample of words is representative of the truth space. However, if the sample of words collected is not representative of the interviewee's total truth space, then the voice sampling error will be large. Consequently, any subsequent analyses of the sample of words likely will lead to untrustworthy findings. Thus, one way of checking the assumption that the truth space has been adequately sampled is by assessing the degree to which *persistent observations, prolonged engagement* and/or *triangulation* underlie the qualitative data to be analyzed. Lincoln and Guba (1985) acknowledged the importance of these three facets for maximizing understanding of the underlying phenomenon.

One analytical assumption that is unique to mixed methods data analyses comes to the fore when data are quantitized, particularly when qualitative data are binarized. Some qualitative researchers contend that quantitizing data does not honor adequately the reality from which the original qualitative data were extracted. Some qualitative researchers contend that binarizing themes represents an oversimplification of emergent themes that does not capture the complexity of the meaning conveyed by the unit. However, as stated by Sechrest and Sidani (1995), the individual making the statement or action that characterizes each theme "would have to have shared understanding of all those additional meanings, in which case the binary code would include them all, or else the statement would have to be accompanied by a set of additional descriptors/modifiers that could themselves be coded" (p. 79).

Nevertheless, as Miles and Huberman (1994) admonished, quantitizing data "is not an operation to be taken lightly. Rather, it should be a self-conscious procedure with clear decision rules" (p. 214). Similarly, as noted by Sandelowski (2001),

researchers should avoid the problems associated with verbal counting, overcounting, misleading counting, and acontextual counting. Indeed, counting is not appropriate for some types of qualitative data and contexts.

DECISION 7: SOURCE OF TYPOLOGY DEVELOPMENT

According to Caracelli and Greene (1993), typology development is one of the four major mixed methods analytic strategies. Typology development involves the analysis of one data type that yields a set of substantive categories or themes (i.e., typology) that is subsequently "applied to an analysis of the other data type, the results of which could, in turn, be used to refine and elaborate the typology" (p. 199). In creating a typology, at least five sources can be used. These five loci of origination are *investigative* (constructed directly by the researcher), *participants* (participants themselves identify categories), *literature* (derived from findings and conclusions documented in the extant literature), *interpretative* (constructed from a preexisting set of analytical concepts), and *programs* (constructed from a set of goals or objectives stated in a program manifesto) (Constas, 1992). The mixed methods data analyst should decide beforehand where the responsibility or authority for the typology development resides.

In the AREP evaluation discussed earlier (Teddlie, 1999), both participants and programs were used as sources for typology development. The data found in Table 13.2 were derived from the program participants (the 10 AREP coordinators), who listed all of the activities that they had undertaken during their previous funding cycle. An earlier analysis had used the program objectives stated in each of the 10

AREP proposals to the U.S. Fish and Welfare Service as the data source.

DECISION 8: NOMINATION SOURCE FOR TYPOLOGY DEVELOPMENT

Mixed methods data analysts also should decide on the source of the names used to identify a given category, theme, or typology. As is the case for loci of origination, the source of names used to identify a category include the following: *investigative* (provided directly by the researcher), *participants* (participants themselves name the categories), *literature* (existing theories from the literature lead to the naming of categories), *interpretative* (names derived from a preexisting set of analytical concepts), and *programs* (derived directly from programmatic objectives).

In the AREP example, investigators provided the category names based on the constant comparative method (Lincoln & Guba, 1985). Two different investigators produced sets of categories, which were then reconciled.

DECISION 9: VERIFICATION SOURCE FOR TYPOLOGY DEVELOPMENT

Once a typology has been constructed from a mixed methods analysis, the analyst should attempt to justify its creation. According to Constas (1992), there are at least six sources of justification: *rational* (using reasoning and logic to justify a given typology), *empirical* (verifies a typology by examining the coverage, distinctiveness, and exclusivity of the categories that underlie it), *technical* (employs language and concepts used by quantitative researchers to verify a typology such as interrater reliability), *participative* (participants are asked to review and then to verify or modify one or more catego-

ries), *referential* (using research findings or theoretical frameworks to justify, through corroboration, a particular typology), and *external* (using a panel of experts not connected to the study to verify and substantiate a given typology). Clearly, the analyst can use more than one of these sources simultaneously to verify a typology.

DECISION 10: TEMPORAL DESIGNATION FOR DATA-ANALYTICAL PROCEDURES

Temporal designation refers to the temporal characteristics of the data analysis process. Here, the analyst decides whether typology development will occur a posteriori, a priori, or iteratively (Constas, 1992). In the a posteriori case, categories are created after all data have been collected. In the a priori context, categories are created before data are collected. Finally, in the iterative scenario, categories are created at different phases of the mixed methods research process.

DECISION 11: DATA ANALYSIS TOOLS

Another important decision for the analyst to make is whether to use a computer to conduct the mixed methods analysis. Obviously, the larger the sample and the more complex the analysis, the more essential a computer will be. Unless the sample size for the quantitative portion of the mixed methods analysis is very small, a computer likely will be needed.

Whereas the use of computers by quantitative researchers has been standard practice for decades, computer software has been underused by qualitative researchers (Creswell, 1998). Yet, as noted by Creswell (1998), when the text database is large, computers offer many advantages over manual data analysis. These benefits include the fact that qualitative computer programs provide electronic file systems that can be retrieved quickly and easily. However, the computer program should not serve as a substitute for a thorough reading of the text so as to maximize meaning. Choice of the type of qualitative software depends on the experience of the analyst with computers, whether the data source is single or multiple, whether single or multiple cases are used, whether the data are fixed or evolving, whether the data are structured or unstructured, and the size of the database (Miles & Huberman, 1994). As noted by Miles and Huberman (1994), choice of qualitative software also depends on whether the intended data analysis is exploratory or confirmatory, whether the coding scheme is fixed or evolving, whether single or multiple coding is being used, whether the data analysis is iterative, the specificity of the analysis, the level of interest in the context of the data, and the level of sophistication needed for the data display.

Interestingly, by quantitizing qualitative data, computer software associated with numerical data can be used. For example, Witcher et al. (2001) used the Statistical Analysis System (SAS Institute, 1990) to correlate the quantitative and qualitative data. Bazeley (Chapter 14, this volume) summarizes various computer analysis techniques for mixed methods studies.

DECISION 12: PROCESS OF LEGITIMATION

Once data interpretation begins, it is imperative that the analyst verifies any inferences that evolve before making any final conclusions. Threats to internal and external validity should be assessed for inferences that emerge from the quantitative data. Building on Campbell and Stanley's (Campbell, 1957; Campbell & Stanley, 1963) framework of sources of invalidity, Onwuegbuzie (in press-a) presented 49 threats to internal and external validity that occur at the data collection, data analysis, and/or data collection stages. Such frameworks can be used as part of the overall mixed methods legitimation process.

Onwuegbuzie (2000b) proposed a Qualitative Legitimation Model that attempts to integrate many of the types of validity identified by qualitative researchers and describes 24 methods for assessing the truth value of qualitative research interpretations. These techniques are prolonged engagement, persistent observation, triangulation, leaving an audit trail, member checking/informant feedback, weighting the evidence, checking for representativeness of sources of data, checking for researcher effects/clarifying researcher bias, making contrasts/comparisons, theoretical sampling, checking the meaning of outliers, using extreme cases, ruling out spurious relations, replicating a finding, referential adequacy, following up surprises, structural relationships, peer debriefing, rich and thick description, the modus operandi approach, assessing rival explanations, negative case analysis, confirmatory data analyses, and effect sizes.

Mixed methods data analysts should consider using one or more of these methods to assess the legitimacy of their interpretations. Such a legitimation process will involve *eliminative induction*, which is a systematic attempt to eliminate rival hypotheses until only the one hypothesis remains as a viable explanation (e.g.,

Manicas & Kruger, 1976). As noted by Miller (Chapter 15, this volume), eliminative induction is extremely appropriate for mixed methods studies.

◆ A Model for the Mixed Methods Data Analysis Process

Once the mixed methods data analyst has made the 12 sets of decisions presented in the previous section, he or she is ready to analyze the data. Figure 13.1 provides a model of the mixed methods research process. It can be seen from this diagram that data analysis is part of a four-component, interactive, cyclical research process involving data collection, data analysis, data interpretation, and legitimation. These four components are represented in Figure 13.1 by ellipsoids.

Once data have been collected and the 12 aforementioned sets of decisions have been made, the mixed methods data analysis begins. Data analysis consists of the following seven stages: data reduction (Stage 1), data display (Stage 2), data transformation (Stage 3), data correlation (Stage 4), data consolidation (Stage 5), data comparison (Stage 6), and data integration (Stage 7). These data analysis stages are represented in Figure 13.1 by rectangles and are defined in Table 13.4.

It should be noted, however, that while these seven stages are somewhat sequential, they are not linear. For example, to proceed from the data analysis stage to the data interpretation step, an analyst may undergo only two of these steps (e.g., from data reduction to data display to data interpretation). The arrows in Figure 13.1 indicate the possible paths available for the researcher. Each of these seven stages is described in this section.

STAGE 1: DATA REDUCTION

The analysis stage first involves reduction of whatever forms of data were gathered at the data collection stage. For quantitative data, data reduction includes computation of descriptive statistics (e.g., measures of central tendency, measures of dispersion/variability). Other ways of reducing numerical data are presented in Table 13.3 in the exploratory data analysis column (e.g., exploratory factor analysis, cluster analysis). Ways of reducing qualitative data include exploratory thematic analysis and profile analysis. Other techniques are presented in Table 13.3 under the exploratory qualitative data analysis column. At a more micro level, qualitative data reduction includes writing summaries, coding, writing memos, making clusters, and making partitions. Reducing the data, whether they be quantitative or qualitative, "sharpens, sorts, focuses, discards, and organizes data in such a way that 'final' conclusions can be drawn and verified" (Miles & Huberman, 1994, p. 11). However, in reducing the data, it is important that the analyst retain the context in which these data occur.

STAGE 2: DATA DISPLAY

The data reduction stage is followed by the data display stage, which involves reducing the information into appropriate and simplified "gestalts or easily understood configurations" (Miles & Huberman, 1994, p. 11). For numerical data, tables (e.g., intercorrelation matrices) and graphs (e.g., histograms) are the two most popular ways to display data. Qualitative data displays include matrices, charts, graphs, networks, lists, rubrics, and Venn diagrams. It is possible for the data display to

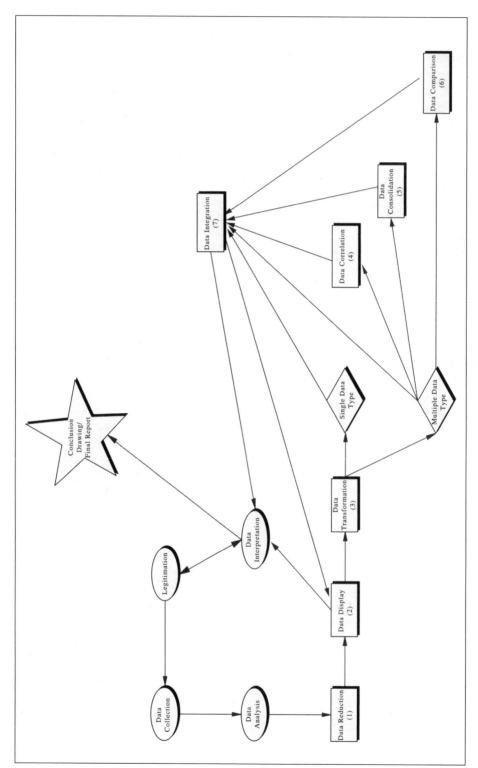

Figure 13.1. Mixed Methods Research Process

TABLE 13.4   Stages of Mixed Methods Data Analyses Process

Stage	Definition
1. Data reduction	Reducing quantitative data (e.g., descriptive statistics, exploratory factor analysis) and qualitative data (e.g., exploratory thematic analysis, memoing)
2. Data display	Reducing quantitative data (e.g., tables, graphs) and qualitative data (e.g., matrices, charts, graphs, networks, lists, rubrics, Venn diagrams)
3. Data transformation	Qualitizing and/or quantitizing data (e.g., possible use of effect sizes, exploratory factor analysis)
4. Data correlation	Correlating quantitative data with qualitized data
5. Data consolidation	Combining both data types to create new or consolidated variables or data sets
6. Data comparison	Comparing data from different data sources
7. Data integration	Integrating all data into a coherent whole or two separate sets (i.e., quantitative and qualitative) of coherent wholes

be so compelling that data interpretation can immediately begin without advancing to the other four data analysis stages.

STAGE 3: DATA TRANSFORMATION

The data display stage in mixed methods analyses often is followed by the data transformation stage in which the data types are *qualitized* and/or *quantitized* (Tashakkori & Teddlie, 1998). If the collected data are qualitized, then effect sizes may provide more meaning to the data. Onwuegbuzie (2001) advocated conducting traditional exploratory factor analysis on the emergent themes at this stage, once these themes have been binarized. That is, an exploratory factor analysis can be un-

dertaken on an interrespondent matrix (i.e., Participant × Theme matrix) or an intrarespondent matrix (i.e., Participant × Unit matrix) so as to determine the hierarchical structure of the themes. Onwuegbuzie calls the factors emerging from this analysis *meta-themes*, which represent themes at a higher level of abstraction than the original emergent themes.

According to Onwuegbuzie (2001), the manner in which the emergent themes cluster within each factor (i.e., meta-theme) facilitates identification of the interrelationships among the themes. Once the meta-themes have been determined, an interrespondent meta-theme matrix (i.e., Participant × Meta-theme matrix) and an intrarespondent thematic matrix (i.e., Unit × Meta-theme matrix) can be

constructed comprising a combination of
0s and 1s. These matrices can then be used
to determine frequency (manifest) effect
sizes and intensity (manifest) effect sizes
for the meta-themes (see Table 13.1).

For example, in the Witcher et al.
(2001) study described earlier in which
preservice teachers' perceptions of characteristics of effective teachers were examined, the researchers found that the six
emergent themes (student-centeredness,
enthusiasm for teaching, ethicalness,
classroom and behavior management,
teaching methodology, and knowledge of
subject) subdivided into the following
four meta-themes: classroom atmosphere,
subject and student, ethicalness, and
teaching methodology. Both the latent effect sizes (proportions of variance explained) and manifest effect sizes (endorsement proportion) associated with
these meta-themes were moderate to
large. The thematic structure is displayed
in Figure 13.2. In this figure, the latent effect sizes pertain to the proportion of variance explained by each meta-theme,
whereas the manifest effect size indicates
the proportion of units identified per
meta-theme.

It should be noted that caution should
be exercised when conducting a factor
analysis on a set of dichotomous items,
such as that representing inter- and intrarespondent matrices, because spurious
results may emerge. Indeed, as demonstrated by Bernstein and Teng (1989), categorization can spuriously influence apparent dimensionality inferred from (a)
principal components analyses, (b) exploratory maximum likelihood factor
analyses, and (c) confirmatory factor
analyses. However, two points are worth
mentioning here. First and foremost, dichotomous variables are the hallmark
of cognitive tests, particularly, multiple
choice examinations, where factor analysis has been used to develop a myriad of

theory throughout the social and behavioral sciences (Onwuegbuzie, 2001). In
any case, if it is inappropriate to conduct factor analyses on inter- and intrarespondent matrices, then it is also inappropriate to conduct factor analyses on
scores representing cognitive and affective
measures. Second, according to Bernstein
and Teng (1989), dichotomous items are
less likely to yield artifacts using factor-
analytical techniques than are multi-
category (e.g., Likert-type) items.

STAGE 4: DATA CORRELATION

If only one type of data is collected,
then the data transformation leads to the
data integration stage in which all data are
integrated into a coherent whole. However, if both types of data are collected,
then the next step might be the data correlation stage. As described earlier (e.g.,
Witcher et al., 2001), this stage involves
correlating the quantitative data with the
quantitized (qualitative) data. The ability
to undertake a correlation exists if both
data types are collected for each sample
member. The data correlation stage is appropriate if the purpose of the mixed
methods research is triangulation (Greene
et al., 1989).

STAGE 5: DATA CONSOLIDATION

Instead of trying to correlate the two
types of data, the analyst may prefer to
combine both data forms to create new
or consolidated variables or data sets
(Caracelli & Greene, 1993). For example,
in a study to determine students' and parents' attitudes toward school climate, a researcher might administer a 5-point Likert
format scale (i.e., quantitative data) to a
group of students and conduct an interview with each participating student's par-

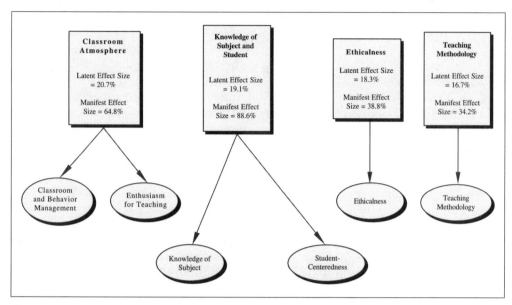

Figure 13.2. Thematic Structure Pertaining to Preservice Teachers' Perceptions of the Characteristics of Effective Teachers

SOURCE: Witcher, Onwuegbuzie, and Minor (in press).

ent (i.e., qualitative data). The researcher could then obtain an overall family index of attitudes toward school climate (range = 1-5) by first quantitizing each parent's open-ended responses to a 5-point scale (1 = *strong negative attitude toward school climate,* 5 = *strong positive attitude toward school climate*) and then averaging the parent's quantitized response (range = 1-5) and the child's mean item response (range = 1-5) for each family. This overall index would then represent consolidated data that can be used in subsequent analyses. The data consolidation stage is appropriate if the purpose of the mixed methods research is development (Greene et al., 1989).

STAGE 6: DATA COMPARISON

The researcher might not be able (or might choose not) to correlate or consoli-

date the two types of data. Instead, the analyst might decide to compare these data. This data comparison stage involves comparing data from different data sources. This step may be used if the purpose of the mixed methods research is either triangulation, initiation, or complementarity (Greene et al., 1989).

STAGE 7: DATA INTEGRATION

If the purpose of the mixed methods research is expansion (Greene et al., 1989), then the researcher may bypass the data correlation, consolidation, and comparison stages and proceed directly to the data integration stage, which is the last link in the data analysis chain. In this stage, all data are integrated into a coherent whole or two separate sets of coherent wholes (quantitative and qualitative). Data integration leads to an initial data interpretation, whereby inferences are made. As noted by Miller (Chapter 15, this volume),

> The nature of the implicit process of mixed methodology lies along at least four dimensions: the inferences assumed for the quantitative portion of the analysis, the inferences assumed for the qualitative portion of the analysis, the inferential relationship between the two, and the possibility for an *overall* pattern or type of inferential process when one is claiming to engage in doing mixed methods research.

The data interpretation stage is then subjected to legitimation, which might necessitate the collection of more data and subsequent analyses that lead to a modified data interpretation (either directly or indirectly) through a combination of the data reduction, display, transformation, correlation, consolidation, comparison, and integration stages.

Once the analyst believes that the interpretation represents the most plausible explanation of the underlying data (i.e., legitimation), conclusions are made and a final report is written. The chain is then completed via follow-up studies in which research questions are reformulated based on these conclusions.

◆ Model for Selecting Mixed Methods Data-Analytical Designs

The previous section outlined the various stages of the mixed methods data analysis process. As can be seen, the mixed methods data analysis process is a continuous iterative endeavor. However, the model in Figure 13.1 does not identify the exact combination of quantitative and qualitative data analysis. Such a taxonomy is presented in Figure 13.3.

As can be seen in Figure 13.3, the purpose of the mixed methods data analysis is the starting point. Just as the purpose of the research study initiates the research study (see Newman et al., Chapter 6, this volume), so too does the data analysis purpose begin the data analysis process. As noted by Newman and Benz (1998), theory has an important place for both quantitative and qualitative researchers. Although some inquiries are atheoretical (e.g., purely descriptive studies), in the majority of studies, researchers seek either (a) to generate/expand theory or (b) to test/confirm theory. The former case leads to exploratory data analysis techniques (as do atheoretical analyses), whereas theory testing leads to confirmatory data analysis techniques.

Once a decision has been made about whether an exploratory or a confirmatory data analysis approach is more appropriate (assuming that both data types will be analyzed), the mixed methods analyst next decides whether a concurrent mixed analysis, a sequential mixed analysis, or a parallel mixed analysis is more appropriate. In Figure 13.3, the analysis that is undertaken first appears first, the uppercase letters denote priority, the plus (+) sign represents a concurrent relationship, the arrow (↓) represents a sequential relationship, and the slash (/) indicates a parallel track. Again, the data analysis leads to data interpretation, legitimation, and internal inferences (i.e., inferences made within the setting or group studied) and/or external inferences (i.e., inferences made beyond the group, setting, context, or time).

As can be seen from the taxonomy in Figure 13.3, we do not agree with Miller's (Chapter 15, this volume) recommendation that mixed methods researchers should begin with a quantitative perspective. That is, contrary to Miller's assertions, mixed methods and mixed models should not give primacy to quantitative

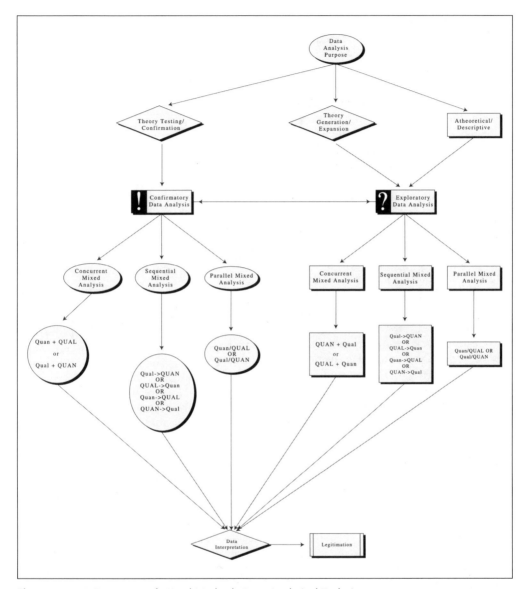

Figure 13.3. A Taxonomy of Mixed Methods Data-Analytical Techniques

analyses. Nor should the quantitative design and analysis supervene on the qualitative design and analysis. Rather, the purpose of the mixed methods data analysis, which stems from the overall research purpose, should determine the relationship of the quantitative and qualitative data-analytical techniques in the mixed methods framework.

◆ Summary and Conclusion

Mixed methods research remains a controversial approach to doing research in the social and behavioral sciences. Thus, researchers undertaking mixed methods techniques should seek to defend explicitly the approaches they are employing. As noted by Miller (Chapter 15, this volume), "If mixed methods as a field of study is to survive deeper scrutiny, it needs a framework where *some* consistent justification can be made in terms of the issues of inference, logic-of-choice, supervenience, and rules."

We have attempted to provide a framework for conducting mixed methods data analyses in this chapter. This framework includes preanalysis considerations for mixed methods investigations, a model of the mixed methods data analysis process, and a taxonomic classification of various possibilities for combining quantitative and qualitative data analyses—a form of "logic-of-procedures," as recommended by Miller (Chapter 15, this volume).

We are aware that the views and recommendations presented in this chapter represent only a portion of the larger body of meta-thinking and appraisal in the field of mixed methods research. In providing this framework for mixed methods data analyses, we encourage the reader either to endorse our recommendations or to point out errors in our logic. At the very least, we hope that we have provided a framework for promoting dialogue.

■ Notes

1. It should be noted that triangulation often involves the testing of hypotheses because triangulation of data methods requires quantitative data, and quantitative data are often generated in an effort to assess the validity of alternative hypotheses.

2. Teddlie, Kirby, and Stringfield (1989) described a process similar to binarizing that they called "simple valence analysis." They converted more than 10,000 open-ended classroom observation responses into three categories: The response contained evidence of effective teaching behavior regarding this teaching component (value of +1), the response contained evidence of contradictory teaching be-

havior regarding this component (value of 0), and the response contained evidence of ineffective teaching behavior regarding this component (value of –1). These data were converted further to a 3-point scale (3, 2, or 1) and subjected to statistical analysis.

3. This tendency to emphasize results, rather than their interpretation, was recently criticized by the American Psychological Association Task Force on Statistical Inference, which stipulated that "interpreting effect sizes is essential to good research" (Wilkinson & Task Force on Statistical Inference, 1999, pp. 10-11). This article criticized quantitative researchers for failing to report this information, which is essential for the proper interpretation of their findings.

4. One way of implementing condition-seeking methods is via qualitative follow-up interaction analyses. Here, interactions that emerge from statistical analyses are investigated by determining whether qualitative differences exist (via interviews, focus groups, etc.) between high- and low-scoring groups at different levels of the other variable(s) that are involved in the interaction.

5. A caveat regarding the external validity of qualitative research is required. Some authors (e.g., Lincoln & Guba, 1985; Tashakkori & Teddlie, 1998) have referred to the "transferability" of results from a sending context to a receiving context. They contend that results for a qualitative study in a specific setting (the sending context) may be generalized to another specific setting (the receiving context) to the degree that the two contexts are similar. Tashakkori and Teddlie (1998) concluded that "some degree of generalizability (whether labeled 'external validity' or 'transferability') of conclusions/inferences is important to all researchers" (p. 66).

■ References

Becker, H. S. (1970). *Sociological work: Method and substance*. New Brunswick, NJ: Transaction Books.

Becker, H. S., Geer, B., Hughes, E. C., & Strauss, A. L. (1977). *Boys in white: Student culture in medical school.* New Brunswick, NJ: Transaction Books. (Original work published 1961)

Bernstein, I. H., & Teng, G. (1989). Factoring items and factoring scales are different: Spurious evidence for multidimensionality due to item categorization. *Psychological Bulletin, 105,* 467-477.

Boyatzis, R. E. (1998). *Transforming qualitative information: Thematic analysis and code development.* Thousand Oaks, CA: Sage.

Campbell, D. T. (1957). Factors relevant to the validity of experiments in social settings. *Psychological Bulletin, 54,* 297-312.

Campbell, D. T., & Stanley, J. C. (1963). *Experimental and quasi-experimental designs for research.* Chicago: Rand McNally.

Caracelli, V. W., & Greene, J. C. (1993). Data analysis strategies for mixed-method evaluation designs. *Educational Evaluation and Policy Analysis, 15,* 195-207.

Cohen, J. (1968). Multiple regression as a general data-analytic system. *Psychological Bulletin, 70,* 426-443.

Collins, K. M. T. (2000, October). *Implementing mathematics curricula standards: Effective instruction for "all" students?* Paper presented at the annual meeting of the Midwestern Educational Research Association, Chicago.

Constas, M. A. (1992). Qualitative analysis as a public event: The documentation of category development procedures. *American Educational Research Journal, 29,* 253-266.

Creswell, J. W. (1994). *Research design: Qualitative and quantitative approaches.* Thousand Oaks, CA: Sage.

Creswell, J. W. (1998). *Qualitative inquiry and research design: Choosing among five traditions.* Thousand Oaks, CA: Sage.

Crone, L., & Teddlie, C. (1995). Further examination of teacher behavior in differentially effective schools: Selection and socialization processes. *Journal of Classroom Interaction, 30*(1), 1-9.

Daley, C. E., & Onwuegbuzie, A. J. (in press). Attributions toward violence of male juvenile delinquents: A concurrent mixed methods analysis. *Journal of Psychology.*

Denzin, N. K. (1978). *The research act: A theoretical introduction to sociological methods.* New York: Praeger.

Derry, S. J., Levin, J. R., Osana, H. P., Jones, M. S., & Peterson, M. (2000). Fostering students' statistical and scientific thinking: Lessons learned from an innovative college course. *American Educational Research Journal, 37,* 747-773.

Dey, I. (1993). *Qualitative data analysis: A user-friendly guide for social scientists.* London: Routledge.

Gay, L. R., & Airasian, P. W. (2000). *Educational research: Competencies for analysis and application* (6th ed.). Englewood Cliffs, NJ: Prentice Hall.

Glaser, B. G., & Strauss, A. L. (1967). *The discovery of grounded theory.* Chicago: Aldine.

Greene, J. C., Caracelli, V. J., & Graham, W. F. (1989). Toward a conceptual framework for mixed-method evaluation designs. *Educational Evaluation and Policy Analysis, 11,* 255-274.

Greenwald, A. G., Pratkanis, A. R., Leippe, M. R., & Baumgardner, M. H. (1986). Under what conditions does theory obstruct research progress? *Psychological Review, 93,* 216-229.

Hallinger, P., & Murphy, J. (1986). The social context of effective schools. *American Journal of Education, 94,* 328-355.

Halpern, E. S. (1983). *Auditing naturalistic inquiries: The development and application of a model.* Unpublished doctoral dissertation, Indiana University.

Johnson, B., & Christensen, L. (2000). *Educational research: Quantitative and qualitative approaches.* Boston: Allyn & Bacon.

Keselman, H. J., Huberty, C. J., Lix, L. M., Olejnik, S., Cribbie, R. A., Donahue, B., Kowalchuk, R. K., Lowman, L. L., Petoskey, M. D., Keselman, J. C., & Levin, J. R. (1998). Statistical practices of educational researchers: An analysis of their ANOVA, MANOVA, and ANCOVA analyses. *Review of Educational Research, 68,* 350-386.

Knapp, T. R. (1978). Canonical correlation analysis: A general parametric significance testing system. *Psychological Bulletin, 85,* 410-416.

Lazarsfeld, P. F., & Barton, A. (1955). Some functions of qualitative data analysis in sociological research. *Sociologica, 1,* 324-361.

Li, S., Marquart, J. M., & Zercher, C. (2000). Conceptual issues and analytical strategies in mixed-method studies of preschool inclusion. *Journal of Early Intervention, 23,* 116-132.

Lincoln, Y. S., & Guba, E. G. (1985). *Naturalistic inquiry.* Beverly Hills, CA: Sage.

Manicas, P. Z., & Kruger, A. N. (1976). *Logic: The essentials.* New York: McGraw-Hill.

Maxwell, J. A. (1992). Understanding and validity in qualitative research. *Harvard Educational Review, 62,* 279-299.

Miles, M., & Huberman, M. (1994). *Qualitative data analysis: An expanded sourcebook* (2nd ed.). Thousand Oaks, CA: Sage.

Minor, L., Onwuegbuzie, A. J., & Witcher, A. E. (in press). Preservice teachers' perceptions of characteristics of effective teachers: A multi-stage mixed methods analysis. *Journal of Educational Research.*

Newman, I., & Benz, C. R. (1998). *Qualitative-quantitative research methodology: Exploring the interactive continuum.* Carbondale: Southern Illinois University Press.

Onwuegbuzie, A. J. (1997). Writing a research proposal: The role of library anxiety, statistics anxiety, and composition anxiety. *Library and Information Science Research, 19,* 5-33.

Onwuegbuzie, A. J. (2000a, November). *On becoming a bi-researcher: The importance of combining quantitative and qualitative research methodologies.* Paper presented at the annual meeting of the National Academy of Educational Researchers, Ponte Vedra, FL.

Onwuegbuzie, A. J. (2000b, November). *Validity and qualitative research: An oxymoron?* Paper presented at the annual meeting of the Association for the Advancement of Educational Research, Ponte Vedra, FL.

Onwuegbuzie, A. J. (2001, April). *Effect sizes in qualitative research: A prolegomenon.* Paper presented at the annual meeting of the American Educational Research Association, Seattle, WA.

Onwuegbuzie, A. J. (in press-a). Expanding the framework of internal and external validity in quantitative research. *Research in the Schools.*

Onwuegbuzie, A. J. (in press-b). Positivists, post-positivists, post-structuralists, and post-modernists: Why can't we all get along? Towards a framework for unifying research paradigms. *Education.*

Onwuegbuzie, A. J., & Daniel, L. G. (in press). Typology of analytical and interpretation errors in quantitative and qualitative educational research. *Current Issues in Education.*

Onwuegbuzie, A. J., & Daniel, L. G. (2002). Uses and misuses of the correlation coefficient. *Research in the Schools, 9*(1), 73-90.

Onwuegbuzie, A. J., & DaRos-Voseles, D. A. (2001). The role of cooperative learning in research methodology courses: A mixed-methods analysis. *Research in the Schools, 8,* 61-75.

Patton, M. Q. (1990). *Qualitative evaluation and research methods* (2nd ed.). Newbury Park, CA: Sage.

Sandelowski, M. (2001). Real qualitative researchers don't count: The use of numbers in qualitative research. *Research in Nursing & Health, 24,* 230-240.

SAS Institute. (1990). *SAS/STAT user's guide* (Version 6.12). Cary, NC: Author.

Sechrest, L., & Sidani, S. (1995). Quantitative and qualitative methods: Is there an alternative? *Evaluation and Program Planning, 18,* 77-87.

Sheumaker, M. F. (2001). *Technology integration in middle school classrooms: The influence of staff development on the beliefs of teachers and administrators.* Unpublished doctoral dissertation, Valdosta State University.

Smith, M. L., & Glass, G. V. (1987). *Research and evaluation in education and the social sciences.* Englewood Cliffs, NJ: Prentice Hall.

Tashakkori, A., & Teddlie, C. (1998). *Mixed methodology: Combining qualitative and quantitative approaches* (Applied Social

Research Methods, No. 46). Thousand Oaks, CA: Sage.

Taylor, D. L., & Tashakkori, A. (1997). Toward an understanding of teachers' desire for participation in decision making. *Journal of School Leadership, 7,* 1-20.

Teddlie, C. (1999). *A description and comparison of the AREPs in ten southeastern states, including an analysis of the programs' subcomponents and activities.* Baton Rouge, LA: K. T. Associates.

Teddlie, C., Kirby, P., & Stringfield, S. (1989). Effective versus ineffective schools: Observable differences in the classroom. *American Journal of Education, 97,* 221-236.

Teddlie, C., & Stringfield, S. (1993). *Schools make a difference: Lessons learned from a 10-year study of school effects.* New York: Teachers College Press.

Teddlie, C., Stringfield, S., & Reynolds, D. (2000). Context issues within school effectiveness research. In C. Teddlie & D. Reynolds (Eds.), *The international handbook of school effectiveness research* (pp. 160-185). London: Falmer.

Thompson, B. (1998, April). *Five methodological errors in educational research: The pantheon of statistical significance and other faux pas.* Paper presented at the annual meeting of the American Educational Research Association, San Diego.

Wilkinson, L., & Task Force on Statistical Inference. (1999). Statistical methods in psychology journals: Guidelines and explanations. *American Psychologist, 54,* 594-604.

Witcher, A. E., Onwuegbuzie, A. J., & Minor, L. C. (2001). Characteristics of effective teachers: Perceptions of preservice teachers. *Research in the Schools, 8*(2), 45-57.

14

COMPUTERIZED DATA ANALYSIS FOR MIXED METHODS RESEARCH

◆ Pat Bazeley

Changes in analysis software have opened up new possibilities for working with mixed data types and analysis methods. Boundaries between numerically and textually based research are becoming less distinct; data may be readily transformed from one type to another, making achievable integration of data types and analysis methods. This chapter considers these new possibilities and the opportunities they present for answering questions asked in the social and behavioral sciences. Unashamedly, it approaches the task more from the point of view of "doing methods" (seeing what one can get the software to do in relation to generic analytical problems) than from that of "doing research" (beginning with a substantive problem that needs solving).[1]

Software programs for statistical analysis and for qualitative data analysis (QDA) can be used side by side for parallel or sequential analyses of mixed form data. In so doing, they offer simply greater convenience and efficiency in data handling. More exciting is the capacity of QDA software to incorporate quantitative data into a qualitative analysis and to transform qualitative coding and matrices developed from qualitative coding into a format that allows statistical analysis. The application of these techniques for exploratory, comparative, and predictive analyses is explained and illustrated with reference to a number of published and ongoing studies. The "fusing" of analysis then takes the researcher beyond blending of different sources to the place where the same sources are used in different but interdependent ways so as to more fully understand the topic at hand.

The emphasis of this handbook is on the mixing of qualitative and quantitative approaches to research. The potential for integration of data types and analysis methods using software goes beyond these bounds, however. Brief consideration is therefore given also to the integration of bibliographic software with data analysis software, the contribution of various strategies for mapping data, and nonstatistical approaches to analysis of dichotomized data.

Use of these techniques for manipulation and analysis of data raises both technical and epistemological issues. On the technical side, there are issues of sampling and appropriate choice of statistical tools. The meaning of codes, themes, and variables raises both epistemological and technical issues as data are transformed from one form to another. Each of these issues needs to be viewed within the framework set by the goals of the analysis but also with an understanding of the limitations imposed by technology. Finally, it is noted that traditional methods of presenting research studies are generally inappropriate for mixed methods analyses of these types.

◆ *Analysis Software: Blurring the Boundaries*

Since Tesch (1990) first reviewed software for the qualitative analysis of text, there has been a rapid expansion in the number, capacity, flexibility, and popularity of computer programs available for both qualitative data analysis and quantitative content analysis of text. The past few years have also seen increasing acceptance of the use of QDA software to assist interpretive analysis of text and other nonnumerical sources, particularly as pro-

gramming developments have removed some of the earlier restrictions on what could be achieved with a computer using "messy" textual data. Statistical analysis of numerical data, by contrast, has been possible since the earliest introduction of computers, and the better known programs (e.g., Statistical Package for the Social Sciences [SPSS]) have been available for more than 25 years. The issue of whether use of software changes the process of analysis has arisen with QDA rather than computationally oriented statistical software, although recent developments in statistical processing made possible by high-speed computers (e.g., the application of genetic algorithms and other data mining procedures) could change that.

In response to user demand, a number of programs that were initially designed for either quantitative *or* qualitative analysis are now being extended or developed to make analytical use of both textual and numerical data. From the statistical side, for example, in mid-1997 SPSS Corporation released Text Smart, to facilitate categorization of text responses to open-ended questions, as an add-on to their popular SPSS. Similarly, Sphinx Survey has released a Lexica edition that provides simple tools for content analysis of open-ended text. Both of these programs allow integration of statistical analysis of the results obtained from the content/lexical analysis with the statistical analysis of other variable data. Improvements in computing speed and power have allowed the development of a number of new programs specifically for quantitative content analysis of text (Alexa & Zuell, 2000; Roberts, 2000), some with in-built dictionaries designed to automate the process as much as possible. On the qualitative side, most programs now have tools for incorporating demographic and other categorical data into a qualitative analysis (with varying degrees of sophistication)—some for inclusion of interval data—and several provide for export of coded information from the qualitative database to SPSS or related statistical programs. While Kuckartz (1995, 1998) deliberately set out to provide for integration of variable data with his text analysis program (MAX, now winMAX Pro), this development was initially less intentional for, but has now been fully embraced by, Qualitative Solutions and Research (QSR), the developers of NUD*IST[2] and NVivo.

Software developers respond to user demand; these quite recent developments reflect the growing acceptance of the integration of qualitative and quantitative data and analyses as a legitimate approach to handling data. These developments also offer exciting new possibilities for researchers wishing to explore the limits of what can be achieved with computer software as a tool. From a methods point of view, integrating different approaches has largely regained acceptability following the "paradigm wars" of the 1970s and 1980s; from a technical point of view, integrating qualitative and quantitative data is no longer difficult provided that one is reasonably comfortable with computers and with moving among a range of software packages. Yet there are surprisingly few published studies reporting results from projects that make more than very elementary use of the capacity to integrate data and analyses using computers.

In this chapter, an outline of the ways in which computers can be used to facilitate a mixed methods analysis is provided, and issues that arise in using computers for mixed methods analyses are explored. Discussion focuses on the principles involved and the features of different classes of analysis software rather than on individual computer programs and what they can do. Necessarily, however, specific programs may be referred to in providing illustrations or where they have distinct features.

MIXED METHODS OR MIXED DATA?

Most social scientists think of mixed methods as the concurrent or sequential use of qualitative and quantitative approaches to data collection and analysis, while the more adventurous refer also to integration of these approaches. Those with a broader view of mixed methods might also consider the application of differing methods within the same broad approach, as occurred in the multitrait-multimethod study credited with originating the concept of "triangulation" in social research (Campbell & Fiske, 1959). Different methods of statistical analysis or modeling may be applied to the same data set to answer a particular question (e.g., Marsh & Bazeley, 1999), or different methodological approaches may be taken to qualitative analysis of the same interview or focus group data (cautioned by Barbour, 1998; illustrated by Creswell, 1998). The integration of data and methods from quite different disciplinary traditions, such as the use of social science research methods within the biophysical domain (in, say, environmental or natural resources research) or in the integration of historical and sociological methods (Trom, 2000), also falls within the broad domain of mixed methods. Conversely, a study might use mixed data (numerical and text) and alternative tools (statistics and text analysis) but apply the same method, for example, in developing a grounded theory.

Much of the confusion about what constitutes mixed methods and the legitimacy of doing it arises from loose application of the terms *qualitative* and *quantitative*. Because these terms have been applied to everything from data, to methods, to methodologies, to paradigms, some clarification is necessary. The term *quantitative* implies something that can be quantified or measured, and in that sense it might be applied to those things that involve counting such as numerical data and the use of some statistical procedures. The term *qualitative* implies making an assessment or judgment that involves interpretation. It might therefore be applied to both certain types of data (those that involve making judgments) and interpretive analysis, with the latter typically involving text or other non-numerical material but potentially also numerical data or statistical output. The terms *qualitative* and *quantitative*, seen in this way, are therefore applicable with respect to type of data and analytical activity only—and even then without an assumption that the type of analysis depends on the type of data; it makes no sense to apply the term *qualitative* or *quantitative* at the level of methodology, perspective, or paradigm.

Software generally does not prescribe a particular method of analysis (within its broad domain) but rather provides tools for application to the researcher's chosen method of analysis. While recognizing the range of possibilities for mixing methods within a quantitative or a qualitative analysis, my focus in this chapter is on the use of computers in combining qualitative and quantitative data and in integrating textual analyses (taken here to include analyses of pictorial, audio, and video material) and statistical analyses within the same project.

DESIGN POSSIBILITIES AND QUESTIONS

Mixed methods may be employed at different stages in the research process, from design and sampling through to final analysis (Tashakkori & Teddlie, 1998). When researchers propose a mixed methods study, they are typically thinking of using a design where qualitative and quantitative aspects both are present but where they remain as two separate elements of the project, with the lack of integration of these elements often extending into the final report or dissertation. Writing about mixed methods design has tended to focus on the relative importance of the quantitative or qualitative components (leading to use of terms such as QUAN, quan, QUAL, and qual) and the sequencing of those components to give, for example, qual-QUAN designs (e.g., Creswell, 1994; Morgan, 1998; Morse, 1991). Again the implication is that the quantitative and qualitative components are largely separate elements of the study. The "mixing" may serve to confirm, corroborate, or elaborate interpretation, or it may serve to develop and/or initiate new ideas and understanding (Rossman & Wilson, 1994). The rationale behind the use of mixed methods may be pragmatic, seeking to ensure that data are "situationally responsive and relevant," or dialectical, seeking to "understand more fully by generating new insights" (Greene & Caracelli, 1997, p. 10).

Integration of mixed data can occur on a number of levels and is particularly facilitated by the use of computer software. The simplest forms of integration involve the transfer of one kind of data for use in conjunction with another. This might involve the inclusion of demographic or other categorical information in a qualitative database to provide context or facilitate making comparisons, or it might involve the inclusion of individual respondent coding information derived from qualitative data as additional variables in a statistical analysis. The integration of analytical strategies adds a further dimension to the mix. More complex integrated designs are likely to involve a number of strategies for moving back and forth between the qualitative and quantitative material. Not only is there linking of data, but also analyses in one mode inform analyses in the other in holistic, iterative, embedded, or transformative designs (Caracelli & Greene, 1997).

It should be the nature of the research question that leads to a choice to use mixed methods—never the reverse. A combination of research strategies has been particularly common in evaluative and community-based studies, where purpose-designed (single-source) data are often not accessible, and the researcher must make the most of whatever information can be obtained while maintaining an ethical approach to working with human subjects (Datta, 1997; Patton, 1988). Increasingly, however, mixed methods studies are being deliberately designed to employ and work with data in forms and ways that recognize the complexity of the human subject and the inadequacy of any one approach to developing knowledge and understanding of the human condition (Jick, 1979; Rossman & Wilson, 1985).

Table 14.1 outlines some of the design possibilities and questions that might be answered when using computers for mixed methods research. That the organization of this table, like the organization of this chapter, is based on technical possibilities rather than on questions is not meant in any way to imply the primacy of technique over question; it is intended simply to avoid the repetition that would occur if the material were organized around the kinds of questions that lead to a choice to employ mixed methods.

A PRAGMATIC APPROACH

Paradigms have been variously described as "formal philosophical systems, born and nurtured in the armchair . . . abstract, generalized, and logically consistent" (Smith, 1997, p. 74) and as "social constructions, just historically and culturally embedded discourse practices" (Greene & Caracelli, 1997, p. 11). Prior to the 1970s, the issues raised with respect to methods were more technical than philosophical, and some would argue that mixing methods has remained more technically than epistemologically possible (e.g., Bryman, 1988). It is now generally agreed that the paradigmatic approach taken by the researcher does not preclude particular types of data or necessarily particular tools for data analysis. Nor does the use of particular data or tools necessarily imply adoption of a particular paradigm. The researcher's paradigmatic approach can, however, greatly influence the way in which those tools are used and the method and style of interpretations derived from the data.

The approach taken to research design and data analysis in this chapter is a pragmatic one (Datta, 1997; Greene & Caracelli, 1997; Smaling, 1994), a "shamelessly eclectic" approach (Rossman & Wilson, 1994) in which any data or approaches to analysis that contribute to an understanding of the issues at hand are seen as worthy of consideration (Patton, 1988). After noting arguments for seeing everything as 0 or 1 and, alternatively, for viewing everything as ultimately having a qualitative background, Miles and Huberman (1994) asserted that "at bottom, we have to face the fact that numbers and words are *both* needed if we are to understand the world" (p. 40, italics in original). In this handbook, Teddlie and Tashakkori (Chapter 1) and Maxcy (Chapter 2) both provide philosophical justification for the use of pragmatism as an epistemological underpinning for the use of mixed methods.

◆ Strategies for Integrating Data and Programs

Analysis software is primarily designed either for quantitative (statistical) analysis of numerical data (or descriptive data converted into a numerical format) or for qualitative (interpretive) analysis of text

TABLE 14.1   Questions to Answer Using Mixed Computer Software

Type of Data/Action	Example of Research Question
Parallel/sequential (nonintegrated) analyses:	
Analyze quantitative and qualitative data separately.	Are the conclusions generated from the two analyses the same? If not, is there a methodological or substantive reason why not?
	Is one needed to prepare for use of the other?
	Can data from one source complete, or elaborate on, the picture created from the other source?
Incorporating quantitative data into a qualitative analysis:	
Incorporate demographic and other quantitative information (e.g., scores on scaled variables) into a qualitative analysis of interview or other unstructured material.	Is the way in which respondents talk about Y, or answer this question, differentially associated with their gender (or age, education, etc.), their score on X, or the way in which they answered another question?
Or,	If a score on X differentiates ways of talking about Y or responses to a question, do these differences validate the scaled measure? Or, what does it mean experientially to be at a certain point as measured by a quantitative scale?
Incorporate demographic and other quantitative information (e.g., scores on scaled variables) into an analysis of text responses to structured topics or questions.	What new dimensions are revealed for this concept by examining differences across subgroups of the sample?
Include responses to open-ended questions in an analysis of questionnaire data.	As above, but also:
	What are the kinds of examples or comments provided by people who gave different responses to precategorized questions? Do these support and/or illuminate the quantified responses? Do these show that all respondents were interpreting the question in the same way?
Exporting quantitative data from a qualitative project:	
Extract variable information from open-ended or unstructured data, for export to a statistical program.	How do these concepts cluster?
	Does mention of this factor influence the outcome?
	What combination of variables best predicts Y?

(Continued)

TABLE 14.1 (Continued)

Type of Data/Action	Example of Research Question
Integrated analysis: Multidirectional transfers of data:	
For example, import or re-import variables created from the statistical analysis of the quantitative or qualitative data so as to review the qualitative data in the light of that statistical analysis.	Does the statistical analysis reveal new dimensions for consideration in the qualitative material? Is there support for the statistical outcomes in the qualitative data? Does it change the way in which one might view the statistical analysis?

or other non-numerical material. No programs provide a comprehensive set of tools to cover both applications. Use of software for mixed methods analyses might not require any special use or integration of statistical or text analysis programs as, for example, when different data sources or methods are used side by side for validation or elaboration of findings. Integrative analyses are, however, likely to require the transfer of quantitative data (perhaps from a spreadsheet, database, or statistical program) into a qualitative program or the transfer of quantitative data generated by a qualitative program into a statistical program.

There are also programs that apply quantitative analytical procedures to text data. Whether these content analysis programs might be defined as employing mixed methods is a moot point; clearly, some are designed purely for quantification, while others are designed more to take the hard work out of qualitative coding. Perhaps an analysis technique should be described as mixed only if the analysis takes into account both forms of the data and an integrated interpretation is derived.

Furthermore, there are strategies employing links from quantitative or qualitative programs to other types of software. These may fall under the general rubric of mixed methods, depending on how they are used. For example, references and notes from bibliographic software may be exported to a qualitative program; data used in graphical programs, such as those for mapping social networks, can be linked to both quantitative and qualitative databases; and semantic and/or concept mapping tools may be part of or link to qualitative analysis programs. These possibilities are reviewed only briefly given that the primary focus of the discussion in this chapter is on linking qualitative and quantitative data.

While the technical procedures involved in combining or transforming data are not especially complex, sometimes they can be annoyingly "fiddly" or tedious as, for example, when exports from various programs use nonmatching fields, sort orders, terms for respondent identification, or criteria for naming variables. But the issues that arise in using statistical and QDA software together are much more to do with purposes and concepts than with technicalities; the latter can usually be solved by a "workaround" if not directly. That SPSS exports numerical codes rather than labels for values of variables wanted for inclusion in a qualitative analysis, for example, can be easily solved using a spreadsheet or database as an intermediary program; what variables in the quantitative database warrant transfer to the qualitative database is the more important theoretical issue.

A NOTE REGARDING ILLUSTRATIVE STUDIES

The strategies described are illustrated with examples of completed or "in progress" studies drawn from a variety of published and unpublished sources. The recency of some software developments, combined with publication lags and the dispersion of methodological literature, has made it difficult to rely solely on published sources.

One study in particular, conducted by the author, is used to illustrate a number of the strategies described. A brief background and methodological description of this study is therefore given here. It is referred to in later text simply as the "Research Performance study."

Research Performance: An Integrated Study. Changes in higher education in Australia (and globally) have brought about an increased emphasis on accountability and on measurement of research performance. The response of researchers in Australia to the proposal to use dollars won and simple counts of refereed publications was a loud complaint that quality of research work would be sacrificed for quantity of output, with those in the social sciences and humanities feeling particularly aggrieved. This study was conceived as an attempt to construct an alternative

perspective on the dimensions and properties of research performance by considering researchers' descriptions of those known to them (i.e., "real" people) who perform at a high level. It was designed as a cross-sectional survey involving a single collection of mixed form data (nominal, numerical, and text) to be analyzed using both statistical and QDA procedures and software.

Academics were asked to think of and describe someone they knew who could be characterized as having ability in research, someone who was a productive researcher, someone who found satisfaction in research, someone whose research had benefit, someone who undertook quality research, someone who was approachable as a researcher, someone who gained recognition, and someone who was an active researcher (the order of presentation of these eight characteristics was varied across respondents to control for response set). They were also asked to distribute 100 points among the eight characteristics (randomly listed) to indicate their relative importance for *doing* research and again for *assessing* research performance. Demographic data, in addition to university, included highest level of qualification, level of appointment, gender, and primary discipline. Level of interest and involvement in research were assessed using two 100-millimeter visual analog scales.

The survey was mailed to the 2,000 academic staff listed at three quite different universities. No follow-up was attempted. Out of 320 returns, 297 usable responses to the open-ended questions were obtained[3] along with 274 responses to the quantitative (distributional) questions. Responses to the visual analog scales suggest a bias toward those who are more interested/involved in research among those who responded to the survey as compared with the general academic population.

Quantitative data were entered into SPSS for analysis using standard statistical techniques including *t* tests, analysis of variance (ANOVA), and correlations to assess relationships between and within demographic and scaled variables. Responses to open-ended questions were typed and then imported into NUD*IST using one document per respondent, with each response being typed under a subheading indicating the characteristic it was describing. Because the questions were structured, it was possible, first of all, to "autocode" each response for the characteristic it was describing. Categories were then generated as needed to capture the specific ideas or descriptors being presented; these were periodically reorganized (moved, combined, or expanded) during the coding process. The descriptor categories that were so developed referred to the circumstances under which researchers operate, their personal characteristics, their research competence/style, their intellectual approach to research, the outcomes of their research, and interpersonal aspects of their work.

Demographic and scaled data were imported into NUD*IST via a table generated from SPSS. Each document was therefore also coded for each of the demographic and scaled variables, allowing comparison of qualitative responses on the basis of those variables. Two main types of quantitative reports were generated from NUD*IST and exported back to SPSS for additional statistical analyses. The first of these was a matrix of 47 descriptors by the eight prompt characteristics in which the cell counts represented the frequency with which each descriptor was used in relation to each characteristic (partially illustrated later in Table 14.2). The second was a table of coding output indicating simply whether an individual respondent had or had not used a particular descriptor. For more recent analyses,

the qualitative database has been imported into NVivo, where fewer steps are required for production of quantified versions of individual coding and matrix data and where more detailed breakdowns of the quantified data are possible (Bazeley, in press). Given the exploratory nature of the techniques, the amazing wealth of data generated from such a short survey, and the evolving capacity of the programs to capture new elements of the data, analysis of the data is a continuing and evolving process.

PARALLEL OR SEQUENTIAL USE OF PROGRAMS

The majority of mixed methods studies employ parallel or sequential use of different methods rather than an integration of data or analyses. Researchers employing mixed methods in this way are usually seeking to confirm, elaborate, or generalize findings from one method using another or seeking to use one method as a basis for sampling or to develop instrumentation for another. Analysis software may or may not be used for the separate components, but where it is used, computer-related issues specific to mixed methods do not generally arise because the data derived from different methods are not integrated—and therefore neither is the software. The advantages of using computer programs in this context are therefore generally those that apply in single method analyses—the ability to manage the data, the ability to return to the data and explore them in more detail, and the ability to ask different questions of the data.

Parallel Use of Text and Statistics for Confirmation. In the classic understanding of methodological triangulation (Denzin, 1978; Greene, Caracelli, & Graham,

1989), the researcher seeks to confirm his or her conclusions by using two or more different methods to study the same phenomenon, just as the surveyor sights a point from different directions to confirm its location. Unlike surveying, however, the different processes of research are likely to become iterative and cyclical. In the Research Performance study, qualitative and quantitative analyses offered different yet confirmatory angles on the multiple dimensions of research performance. The shapes of the dimensions were pursued in further analyses involving more integrated methods.

Respondents reported that they quite commonly referred to the same person when thinking about quality and ability in research (confirming our preanalysis assumption that these belonged to the same broad dimension, i.e., in contrast to quantity). In the qualitative data, descriptors used for quality and ability had more in common with each other than with descriptors for more quantitatively oriented characteristics such as activity and productivity. There were, nevertheless, some significant differences in the pattern of descriptors used for quality and ability, and even where these descriptions were assigned the same code, qualitative analysis of coded text revealed that it could be expressed in subtly different ways depending on whether it was in relation to quality or ability. The difference between these two characteristics, seen in both choice of descriptors and ways of expressing those descriptors, could be understood as a difference in focus rather than in substance. When describing *ability* in research, respondents focused more on qualities of the researcher (e.g., their capacity to ask questions and think deeply and creatively), while for *quality* in research they focused on (often parallel) evidence about the research (e.g., its originality and the production of new ideas and new knowledge).

Thus, while the qualitative data generally supported the presence of a quality versus quantity dimension, they also demonstrated a necessity to distinguish between the performer and the performance.

Similar patterns in the characteristics needed to *do* and *assess* research were demonstrated in the statistical analysis of the quantitative data. Quality was considered of highest priority for both doing and assessing research; activity, recognition, and approachability were rated low for both. Quality and ability were rated as the two most needed characteristics to undertake highly rated research, but while quality was assigned even higher priority for assessing research, ability was rated here as less of a priority than were benefit and productivity. These statistical results confirmed that undertaking research (where the focus is on the researcher) is seen as similar to yet different from assessing research (where the focus is on the research itself). Performer and performance are thus related but distinguishable facets of the whole issue being investigated.

The use of qualitative software in this exploration of the data first opened up the similarities and differences between quality and ability and the importance of distinguishing between the qualities of the researcher and the qualities of their research (which were somewhat confused in the responses given). The statistical analysis confirmed a distinction between performance and assessment. Each confirmed and added clarity to the other—and also confirmed researchers' views that indicators used to assess performance might not necessarily identify the best researchers.

Exploring Discrepant Findings. Using different methods for confirming findings increases the risk of generating conflicting results. Yet resolving an apparent conflict may produce a key to understanding an underlying process (Jick, 1979), even where there is a straightforward methodological reason for the differences (Rossman & Wilson, 1994). Dealing with conflicting results may involve further data collection (e.g. Mark, Feller, & Button, 1997), or it may simply involve being able to ask further questions of the existing data sets to assist interpretation and find an explanation (Jick, 1979). The flexibility of computers in allowing for extensions to data analysis potentially provides a real advantage here: Once data are entered and coded (be they quantitative or qualitative), possibilities for complex sorting and/or further manipulation of the data in the search for answers become limited more by imagination than by the available tools.

Where data from the different sources can be matched (as when categorical survey data are linked with qualitative responses through a common respondent identifier), further possibilities arise for exploring discrepancies in the data. In a study of women working within a male-dominated science (conducted by the Australian Institute of Physics and analyzed by the author), respondents were asked whether they had experienced harassment, discrimination, and/or different treatment at various stages through the development of their careers and to provide examples to illustrate their answers. Categorical responses were exported from the statistical database into the qualitative program (as described later) so that they could be linked to the text of the examples and comments. Discrepancies between their assessments of the situations described (given in their responses to the precategorized questions) and the illustrations they provided were noted for some respondents. These were able to be identified from the qualitative database and then compared with others in relation to other demographic and experiential variables using the statistical database. It was

found that those who passed off such things as "occasional sexist remarks," being patronized, and others' questioning of their technical ability were older and married, in contrast to the younger unmarried respondents who were much more likely to report such events as harassment or discrimination. Such a finding can be interpreted within the sociology of modern feminism and its impact on workplace relations.

Sequential Methods for Sampling or Question Design. Preliminary interviews and, more recently, focus group discussions are a standard source from which questions for structured interviews and questionnaires are derived (Creswell, 1994; Morgan, 1998; Morse, 1991). Conversely, quantitative data collection may be used as a basis for selecting a sample for qualitative interviewing with the secondary benefit of allowing comparison of the final list of interviewees with a larger (and potentially more representative) sample of the population. Sadly, few make more than cursory use of the preliminary data generated, and even fewer integrate both sources in a computerized analysis.

Nickel, Berger, Schmidt, and Plies (1995) used cluster analysis on their random sample of 1,500 juveniles to identify interviewees representing varying attitudes and experience for a study of sexual behavior. Once clusters were determined (eight for each of the sexually active and sexually inactive subgroups), those clusters containing members most relevant to the aims of the study were identified (those exhibiting most and least "at risk" attitudes and behaviors). The most typical case was selected for each cluster, and cases that did not really fit were eliminated. From those that remained, SPSS was used to generate a random selection of 50 respondents. The 38 of these who had indicated preparedness to be interviewed were followed up. Nonresponse forced a repeat of the selection procedure until a sufficient number of respondents could be found. The initial quantitative data were able to be used also to analyze patterns of nonresponse to requests for an interview. Despite problems caused by nonresponse, selection of potential interviewees on the basis of a preliminary, large-scale, randomly distributed survey is likely to have been both more targeted and broader in its sweep than if such a survey (to define a population of interest) had not been conducted.

TRANSFERRING QUANTITATIVE DATA TO A QUALITATIVE PROGRAM

Inclusion of demographic data for cases (e.g., respondents or sites typically represented in a qualitative program by documents) where the primary data sources are qualitative is one of the most common forms of integration of quantitative with qualitative data. The assumption is that a person's gender, age, or role (or whatever it is that has been included) is relevant to everything he or she might say. In a simple extension of this principle, responses to precategorized questions (e.g., yes/no, often/sometimes/never) or scaled measures (e.g., level of satisfaction, scores on a measure of social alienation) can also be incorporated into the interpretive analysis of the qualitative data.

Programs designed to facilitate inclusion of variable data (including NUD*IST, NVivo, and winMAX) allow for the data to be imported directly from a table such as might be prepared in a spreadsheet, database, or statistical package. The file is saved in a specified (tab-delimited text or dBase) format to be read and applied to documents or cases by the qualitative program. Other alternatives are to interactively code one document at a time with

demographic or other categorical information (imposing severe limitations on the amount of data one might therefore include) or to enter key words in the documents to allow autocoding of whole or part documents using text search (as with, e.g., Atlas.ti and HyperResearch).

Comparative Analysis. The primary purpose of importing demographic and other categorical information into a qualitative database is to allow for comparative analysis of the responses of subgroups within the sample of participants with respect to themes, concepts, or issues raised in the qualitative material. It becomes possible to ask how those, say, in their 30s report an experience and then to determine whether this differs from the experience of those who are older or younger. Or it becomes possible to ask whether an issue is gendered—do males and females have similar or different views?

Such comparative analysis can reveal unexpected differences pointing to new dimensions in the qualitative data. One of the clearest examples in my own experience arose when I examined the text of responses regarding reasons for supporting organ donation given by people who had been in the situation of having to decide whether or not to allow donation. Those rated as having different levels of grief resolution (a categorical variable derived from a quantitative database) and who expressed an altruistic attitude did so in surprisingly different ways. Continuing expression of unresolved grief was associated with speaking in absolute terms about living and dying, while those who had resolved their grief spoke in relative terms, for example, of improving life and regaining normality. The absolute-relative dimension was not associated with altruism as a reason for donation (there were equal numbers of absolute and relative altruistic responses), even though it was revealed through that analysis. Rather, it could be interpreted more broadly as a conversational guide about those to whom staff might need to direct particular help in managing and resolving grief in traumatic situations.

Some QDA software will also allow data to be filtered using the values of a categorical variable so that, for example, it becomes possible to analyze the pattern of relationships occurring within a subgroup of the total sample. This facility is particularly relevant where case studies are being carried out—perhaps of different companies, in different geographic locations, or around particular target individuals. Using the categorical variable (for company, location, or target person) as a filter allows the analysis to be scoped to a particular case or, alternatively, allows for cross-case comparisons.

Validation of Measures. Mixed methods can contribute to the process of validating quantitative scales. Validity testing of quantitative scales is traditionally carried out using confirmatory factor analysis to examine data clusters for conceptual integrity. Blasius and Thiessen (1998) proposed the use of multiple correspondence analysis as a tool for verifying that different points on a scale are actually measuring progressively different levels of the same entity (i.e., they plot in a consistent direction across the same dimension). Further assessment of the meaning of different scores on a scale can be sought from qualitative data, where coded text relating to the concept being measured can be sorted by scores on the quantitative measure to determine whether differences in scores are reflected by comparable differences in the text. This procedure simply requires matching of quantitative and qualitative sources within a qualitative program and the ability to review text of a coded concept for subgroups defined by points on the quantitative scale (or, where it is available in the program, using a matrix intersection search to generate sorted text). For example, narrative data regarding the experience of depression might be examined in relation to scores on a depression inventory as a way of determining the meaning of such scores and validating that they do indeed signify different degrees of depression.

TRANSFERRING QUALITATIVE DATA TO A QUANTITATIVE PROGRAM

Most qualitative researchers are prepared to allow the occasional count into a report of their analyses, although even that is unacceptable to some. Less commonly, categorized or quantified coding information (often referred to as "quantitized" data) is transferred from a qualitative program to a quantitative program for statistical analysis. This may be in the form of 0/1 coding to indicate presence or absence in the text of a coded category for each document/primary text or case, numerical form expressing volume of text coded at the selected categories for each document or case, scales representing the "weight" assigned to each code, or ratings based on an interpretation of the text. For all code and retrieve programs used to generate quantitized coding information, the supporting text is available for review and verification or further interpretation.

Information about coding for individual respondents is produced in a variety of file formats by different qualitative programs and is achieved with greater or lesser convenience for different purposes by the different programs. Programs vary in whether they export coding data for whole documents (NUD*IST and NVivo) or for each separately coded segment of text within each document (Atlas.ti and winMAX), whether they will export for all codes at one time (Atlas.ti, winMAX, NVivo) or a limited selection at any time (NUD*IST), the format in which codes are exported (SPSS syntax, dBase format, or tab-delimited text), and what filtering can be applied to production of the data. Codes can be weighted in both winMAX (on a 100-point visual analog scale) and Atlas.ti (at nine levels of subcategories treated as a "family") to represent the strength of the concept being coded. Programs exporting data for coded segments rather than whole cases necessitate an additional step of aggregating data for documents within the statistical or database program if links are to be made on a case-by-case basis with other (i.e., quantitative) sources of data or if cross-tabulations are to be constructed. NUD*IST and NVivo have the additional facility of being able to export matrix data derived from "qualitative cross-tabulations" conducted within the program.

Exported coding, once transferred to a statistical package, allows for a different type of examination of regularities and complex relationships in the data. Nonparametric statistical techniques, including use of medians rather than means, use of correspondence and cluster analysis, and use of logistic rather than linear regression models, are generally likely to be more appropriate than procedures that assume a large, probabilistic, normally distributed sample.

Using Individual Document Coding. The quantification of qualitative data makes it possible to include variables derived from a qualitative analysis in the same analysis as variables derived from quantitative data. The advantage of using a computer to achieve this over manual categorization of the qualitative data is likely more complete and greater accuracy of categorization (or quantification) and, more particularly, the ability to retrieve supporting text

to increase the interpretability of the results or to verify coding. Examples follow of the extended analyses made possible through the combination of quantitized coding data with other quantitative data.

Strategies for managing mood states employed by 36 caregivers to adults with disabilities or dementia were compared with scores derived from the Profile of Mood States (POMS) by Ayres (1998). Nominal codes based on whether the interviewees primarily used positive or negative management strategies were derived from the qualitative database and transferred to the statistical database, where t tests were used with subscales of the POMS as "dependent" variables. Three of the six subscales (depression, fatigue, and tension) were scored differently in relation to caregiver use of positive or negative mood strategies, with effect sizes ranging from 0.97 to 1.24. These three scales at least were therefore seen as being potentially useful as an outcome measure in a study to evaluate caregiver interventions. Furthermore, reference to the coded text allowed Ayres to understand lack of discrimination on other subscales. For example, "simmering annoyance" could energize caregivers who used blame as a (negative) mood management strategy, and so they did not differ on the vigor subscale from those using positive strategies.

Predictive models are usually built using regression techniques—standard multiple regression for models predicting a continuously measured outcome, logistic regression where the outcome is dichotomous, or discriminant function analysis where group membership is being predicted. Analysis of legal judgments to predict an outcome is one type of study to benefit from use of a quantitizing strategy in that no quantitative database is kept of the facts pertaining to the case and, in particular, of those facts *and issues* that the judge takes into consideration in arriving at his or her judgment.

The Justice Research Centre of New South Wales, Australia, is currently undertaking a large-scale review of the issues a judge (or an arbitrator) takes into account when determining the amount to award the plaintiff in a motor vehicle accident compensation case (a matter of great interest to the insurance companies). Available categorical information is of a procedural nature such as the level of court where the hearing is taking place. All other information has to be determined from the judgment itself. This is of three broad types: "facts" such as the nature and location of the injury; issues raised by the judge regarding, say, the character of the plaintiff or the reliability of witnesses; and legal issues considered, for example, previous cases referred to in the case. Outcome measures include subtypes of payment (e.g., for loss of quality of life) as well as the total amount awarded as compensation. The amounts paid out are, of course, interval measures. These are entered directly into an SPSS database along with the procedural data. Coding derived from the qualitative database (in this case, NUD*IST) is exported in 0/1 format to indicate presence or absence of the category in the text for each case and then imported into the existing SPSS database as additional variables. Even on very preliminary data (using a series of *t* tests or their nonparametric equivalent), it is possible to see, for example, that having an "obvious" injury, such as an orthopedic injury or a disfigurement, will rate a higher level of compensation, while arguing pain or psychological distress will, by comparison, reduce the level of compensation. When the final database is built using a large, consecutively drawn sample of cases, it will be possible to build a model showing the additive contribution (within certain confidence limits) of various factors, separately and in combination, in determining the actual amount of money awarded. Data from such a model can be used in two ways: to determine which factors may be more critical than others in presenting a case and to determine the likely level of compensation that will be awarded given the facts of the case (based on the regression equations). The latter could facilitate making out-of-court settlements and so reduce costs.

Predicting health outcomes can be built in a similar way, although these will typically have a 0/1 outcome and so will be based on logistic modeling. Most epidemiological studies rely on quantitative measures, but there is increasing recognition of the role of social factors in disease, particularly where attitudes and customs affect lifestyle, and so there is an increasing role for the inclusion of qualitative data in epidemiological studies.

Exploration of Coding Patterns Using Matrix Displays. Survey analysts routinely run all variables against one or two key grouping variables in an initial search for a patterning of responses, using either contingency table analyses or comparisons of means. In a qualitative analysis, coding information generated from text data and displayed in a matrix can provide a basis for analysis of patterns in the data (Morgan, 1993; Richards, 2000). Data for a matrix display might be entered directly into a spreadsheet in summary form (e.g., the formats recommended by Miles & Huberman, 1994) or extracted from content analysis or QDA software.

Knafl and Ayres (1996), studying family response to chronic childhood illness, used The Ethnograph for initial coding of a large volume of text data and for exploration of concepts and then transferred summaries from retrieved codes to a database management program so as to view individual family patterns of response—

something that had been difficult to see using the QDA program. Use of the database allowed instantaneous reordering of the summary data based on categories used in a selected column, which facilitated the detection of associated patterns in the data. A sort based on family management style, for example, revealed a typical (albeit not uniform) association of that variable with the constellation of family members' views of the child's illness.

A similar technique was used to assess patterns of provision for the development of early career researchers in academic departments (Bazeley et al., 1996). Brief summaries (sometimes including pithy quotes) about various circumstances and strategies were derived from interviews with department heads and entered into Excel. Each row represented a department, and each column represented a strategy or circumstance. Data in rows could then be sorted on the basis of the discipline of the department (these were limited to six representative disciplines), the type of university, or both. Sorting facilitated further data reduction through creation of summaries for subgroups where consistent patterns were revealed, for example, in the provision of resources for new researchers across a particular discipline group or the degree to which teaching was linked to research interests. From this analysis, it was also possible to see that varying patterns of provision were more easily detectable when the data were sorted by discipline than when they were sorted by type of university; when the primary sort was by university, a subsort by broad disciplinary orientation (social science/science) was necessary to see any pattern in responses.

Use of Computer-Generated Matrix Data. Computers can be used to "reduce" and view data in matrix displays, working directly from counts derived from qualitative coding of the data. A matrix showing where codes (or variables and codes) intersect or otherwise co-occur in the text is constructed. A report of numbers of respondents/cases or density of text represented by each cell in the matrix then reveals overall patterns of response, providing a basis for interpretation. Most often, cross-tabulations are used by the researcher simply to illustrate a trend in association between categories or to demonstrate a comparison between groups that is also being discussed in prose form. For example, one might construct a matrix of the gender (or role, experience, or age) breakdown of who does what in some setting of interest. This can be examined for patterns (e.g., males talk more often than females about research as discovery but much less often than females about how it helps people) as well as for content (e.g., whether males express a particular viewpoint differently from females). Or, at a more theoretical level, one might produce a matrix display showing the association among, say, types of experiences, the settings in which the experiences occur, and responses to those experiences.

If more than a simple numerical display is required, cross-tabulated (matrix) coding can be exported to a statistical (or mathematical) database for further analysis using techniques such as cluster and correspondence analysis. Much depends on the way in which data are coded and analyzed within the qualitative program in determining whether and what statistical techniques can be appropriately applied. Much depends also on the researcher's purpose in using these statistical techniques, for example, whether it is for exploration or confirmation. Exploratory techniques involving graphical displays of relationships between codes (variables) are likely to be used to assist interpretive analysis of this type of data rather than its being subject to rigorous hypothesis testing.

In the Research Performance study, a Boolean matrix intersection search was used in NVivo to produce a table showing the frequency with which respondents used any of 47 descriptors (codes) for each of the eight characteristics used to elicit the descriptions (partially shown in Table 14.2). The (complete) table was exported to SPSS, where cluster analysis was first used to identify homogeneous groupings within the eight characteristics based on the similarity of frequency with which various descriptors were used. The 47 descriptors were also clustered based on the characteristics to which they were applied. The goal of this analysis was to reduce the numbers of characteristics and descriptors used to describe high-level research performers into a meaningful set of key elements for research performance. Clustering, most easily interpreted when displayed as a dendrogram (Figure 14.1), confirmed that despite earlier discussed differences between ability and quality, these were nevertheless more closely related to each other than either was to other characteristics but that productivity and activity were even more closely associated with each other. Overall, these data support a broad quality-quantity divide, with approachability being seen as something entirely different from the other characteristics being described. Clustering of the 47 descriptors used for coding, while far from definitive given the small number of "cases" (eight) on which it was based, suggested the following as elements of high-level research performance: a disciplined approach, quiet confidence, focused activity, a commitment to soundly based yet innovative work, generosity, producing work that advances the discipline, producing knowledge with a practical application, and volume of output.

Correspondence analysis is a further exploratory technique that summarizes categorical data held in a two-way contingency table. Relationships between the categories, both within and across the variables, plotted along a number of dimensions (along with statistical summaries) allow the researcher to determine whether there are meaningful underlying dimensions in the data. When codes based on qualitative data are analyzed in this way, dimensions underlying the choice and expression of ideas by respondents may be revealed or, alternatively, revealed dimensions may be interpreted with the assistance of the qualitative text.

Again using the descriptor by characteristic matrix generated in the Research Performance study, correspondence analysis was applied in the continuing search for ways of understanding and describing research performance. Results were less than clear-cut in that an undesirably large number of dimensions were needed to summarize the data and therefore were suggestive rather than definitive in their usefulness. First, the correspondence analysis confirmed the "outlier" status of approachability and descriptors closely related to approachability, as suggested already by the cluster analysis. These stood in strong contrast to all others to define the first dimension in the data, and this accounted for 32% of the variability in responses. The second dimension, strongly influenced by benefit, was about whose interest the research served (self-other); the third dimension described content (substance vs. appearance); and the fourth was about process (intrinsic-performer vs. extrinsic-performance), with these together explaining a further 50% of variance. The use of correspondence analysis plots to aid in interpretation of this type of data is illustrated in Figure 14.2.

While correspondence analysis requires coding for two or more variables (to provide a cross-tabulation), cluster analysis can be applied also to individual coding data. For statistical reasons, however,

TABLE 14.2 Research Performance: Matrix Showing the Numbers of Respondents Providing Particular Descriptors for Researchers Demonstrating Various Characteristics (Partial Display Only)

Descriptor	Characteristic							
	Ability	Quality	Activity	Productivity	Recognition	Satisfaction	Benefit	Approachability
Opportunity	11	1	16	7	11	7	1	3
Funding	14	12	28	34	45	6	5	1
Commitment	73	8	56	23	13	18	2	5
Confident	18	1	0	1	6	5	1	24
Self-seeking	1	0	5	7	71	14	2	
Good organization	41	1	17	10	3	2	0	
Interest, passion	19	4	28	7	3	95	4	
Can communicate	15	12	6	3	16	6	6	
Humility	5	2	1	3	3	12	2	
Focused	30	2	64	19	5	12		
Problem solving	7	3	10	3	0	29		
Careful	21	35	2	5	5	5		
Open mind	13	0	4	3	1	2		
Innovative	79	56	9	5	16	12		
Can think	67	23	4	2	4	4		
Questions	63	12	23	10	3	23		
Substantive knowledge	47	50	21	15	20			
Long term	1	9	1	5	6			
Applied	1	12	6	13	4			
Theoretical	26	21	1	1	2			
Strong methods	85	72	8	8	12			
Breadth	29	11	23	14				
Writes well	17	22	2	1				
Relevant to academy	6	45	9	15				
Relevant to society	5	6	2	6				
Relevant to practice	2	8	2	7				
Interested in others	4	0	1					
Networker	1	0	12					
Collaborator	10	3	10					
Inspirational	12	5	11					
Reputation	7	29						
Shares ideas	3	0						
Produces	6	4						
Has new ideas	4	16						
Reaches goals	16	2						
Publishes volume	4	0						
Publishes quality	3							
Publishes—other	11							
New knowledge	7							

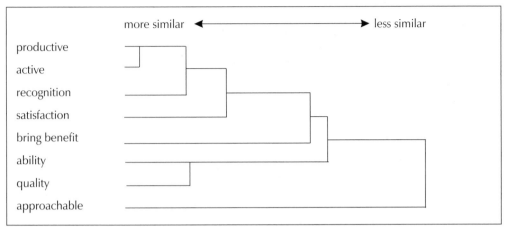

Figure 14.1. Research Performance: Clustering of Characteristics of Researchers

NOTE: The dendrogram uses average linkage (between groups) based on squared Euclidean distances calculated from similarities in the frequency with which up to 47 descriptors were used by 297 respondents for researchers

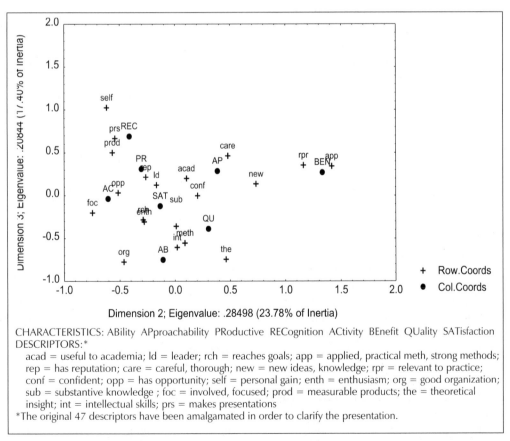

CHARACTERISTICS: ABility APproachability PRoductive RECognition ACtivity BEnefit QUality SATisfaction
DESCRIPTORS:*
   acad = useful to academia; ld = leader; rch = reaches goals; app = applied, practical meth, strong methods;
rep = has reputation; care = careful, thorough; new = new ideas, knowledge; rpr = relevant to practice;
conf = confident; opp = has opportunity; self = personal gain; enth = enthusiasm; org = good organization;
sub = substantive knowledge ; foc = involved, focused; prod = measurable products; the = theoretical
insight; int = intellectual skills; prs = makes presentations
*The original 47 descriptors have been amalgamated in order to clarify the presentation.

Figure 14.2. Research Performance: Correspondence Analysis Plot Showing Coordinates of Eight Characteristics and 20 Descriptors for Dimension 2 (Interest) × Dimension 3 (Content)

when using individual coding data it may be preferable to base clustering on density or strength of coding references rather than on the simple presence or absence of coding at the category being considered.

QUANTITATIVE ANALYSIS OF QUALITATIVE DATA (CONTENT ANALYSIS)

Content analysis has been defined as "any technique for making inferences by objectively and systematically identifying specified characteristics of messages" (Holsti, 1969, p. 14). It emerged as a technique used primarily in communication research following World War II (Morgan, 1993). It became viewed as a quantitative method (Berelson, 1952; Krippendorff, 1980), albeit one that was applied to qualitative (text) data (although the inappropriately loose use of the term by many qualitative researchers has tended to cloud that meaning). Increasing capacity of computers to handle large-scale and complex processing tasks has allowed a relatively recent expansion in the availability of software for automated content coding of language-based materials.

Software for content analysis searches text records for words, phrases, expressions, or statements that are considered by the researchers to reflect the domain of interest of the research question. They vary as to whether they include internal dictionaries of terms and expressions for searching, rely on user-defined dictionaries, or allow some combination of these (Alexa & Zuell, 2000). The more sophisticated programs examine co-occurrences of terms and include complex syntactical rules to determine relationships between the concepts that are embodied within statements (Carley, 1994). Counts are then analyzed statistically to provide sum-

maries of content and for comparative analyses, for example, to compare media reports of different political events (Schrodt, 2000) or to reveal the psychological states associated with different experiences (Gottschalk & Bechtel, 1995). The advantage of these programs is that once the dictionaries have been developed for a particular topic or measure, coding is very rapid and totally standardized, especially when compared with earlier hand-coding methods. This makes it possible to design projects based on larger volumes of text material and, together with the standardization of coding, allows for more reliable statistical inference. The obvious disadvantage is that such coding cannot readily take account of unusual expressions or latent meaning in the text.

There is a significant start-up time incurred in the development of the dictionaries; between 100 and 500 concepts are needed to code knowledge on a specific topic within a specific sociolinguistic environment (Carley, 1993), but a general dictionary to analyze media reports of international political events (based on lead sentences) using sparse parsing techniques requires some 5,000 terms to compare events statistically (Schrodt, 2000). Once such dictionaries have been developed, however, costs are greatly reduced. Schrodt (2000) reported automatic coding of up to 3,000 events per second (on a 650-MHz computer) as compared with 40 events per day by human coders.

Comparative analysis is often the primary purpose for undertaking content analysis. The desire to compare reports of international events lies behind the development of the KEDS and TABARI databases (Schrodt, 2000). Berth and Romppel (2000) applied standardized psychological scales based on content analysis (using the German-language program CoAn) to compare the levels of dogmatism and anxiety expressed by East and West German newspapers around the period of German reunification (1989-1990). They found that East German newspapers demonstrated higher levels of both dogmatism and anxiety, reflecting the greater impact of these events on the East than on the West. The higher levels of dogmatism were interpreted as the journalists' way of attempting to reduce the people's insecurity during those politically turbulent times. Temporally based graphs were used to associate fluctuations in the two indexes for each set of newspapers with the progression of events.

Qualitative Content Analysis. It can be argued that unless further qualitative analysis is undertaken to extend or expand the results of the content analysis, it cannot really be considered a mixed method; rather, it is a quantitative method that happens to be applied to qualitative data. There are those who employ variants of content analysis that retain the rigor of quantitative analysis but modify or add to it to create "qualitative content analysis." These approaches vary in whether the more interpretive elements of the approach come before or after the more automated component.

Mayring (2000) described as qualitative content analysis a procedure in which categories to be used in the analysis are first derived inductively from the material to be analyzed and are formulated as much as possible in terms of that material. This contrasts with the "given" categories of quantitative content analysis (which are generally derived a priori from theory). In outcome, this procedure does not appear markedly different from that of quantitizing a qualitative analysis (as described earlier), with the probable exception that the procedures for categorizing the text are likely to become much more rigor-

ously defined during the development of the project.

Classic content analysis techniques may be used to find dominant patterns and co-occurrences, followed by the use of qualitative retrievals to complete a "fine-grained" analysis of frequent and rare responses—a procedure defined as hermeneutic-classificatory content analysis by Roller, Mathes, and Eckert (1995). Alternatively, content analysis may be applied to qualitatively selected subtexts.

Programs used for qualitative content analysis typically include those used for qualitative analysis more generally, such as Atlas-ti, NUD*IST, and winMAX, rather than specialist content analysis software. Each of these allows for interactive coding as well as "automated" coding by text search, for retrieval of text associated with codes, and for generation of total and comparative frequencies that can be exported in file format. The command file language available in NUD*IST permits repetitive running of a set of (multiple) searches over different sets of documents with minimal effort, with text of finds stored for later review as needed. A "search swarm" (e.g., a group of synonyms) can be saved in Atlas.ti for repetitive running as further primary texts are imported into a project. Atlas.ti has also recently introduced a "word-cruncher" feature. This lists each word in a document—ordered alphabetically or by frequency of use—with the number of times it is used and what percentage of the whole it is.

Two programs—Concordance and NVivo—were used concurrently by Seale (2001) to study the use of "struggle" language and sporting metaphors in media stories about people with cancer. NVivo was used to code and retrieve, separately for each gender, 358 texts specifically depicting a person with cancer. Concordance

TABLE 14.3   Counts of Selected Words Used to Convey Creativity in Describing Researchers Who Demonstrate Ability and/or Quality

Word	Ability	Quality
Creative	29	9
Imaginative	11	1
Lateral	8	0
Innovative	14	15
Original	14	19
Novel	2	3
N words used	606	519

was then used on this text to create a profile of words used, from which linguistic terms associated with military, sports, and other metaphors were identified. Further coding in NVivo drew on this sensitization to language to provide a review of the different ways in which struggle language was applied, with and without sporting connotations, in reports of people experiencing different types of cancer and in differing situations. Subsets of the text were further analyzed with Concordance to provide a quantification of terms used in those different situations. This iterative procedure, drawing on the strengths of both (interpretivist) discourse analysis and (objectivist) content analysis, enabled Seale to dispute previous theory and argue that the language used to describe people's experience with cancer was more sporting than militaristic in orientation.

In the Research Performance study, creativity/innovation was one of those categories that was used in describing both ability and quality in research but not for other characteristics. A count of key words used to express creativity, however, strengthened the growing understanding of the difference between ability and quality (Table 14.3). The words used primarily for ability focused more on the quality of mind of the researcher, while those used for quality were more oriented to describing a product.

QUALITATIVE ANALYSIS OF QUANTITATIVE DATA

Where sample size or the method of sampling is inadequate to allow statistical testing of inferences from data, numerical data may still be used in a "qualitative" way. Counts generated from either quantitative or qualitative sources are used to summarize patterns rather than for statistical inference—an activity sometimes referred to as "qualitizing" (Tashakkori & Teddlie, 1998). Morgan (1993) argued, "The fact that numbers are necessary for [generalization to larger populations or tests of statistical inference] certainly does not preclude their descriptive use for more qualitative purposes" (p. 116). In the study of juvenile sexual behavior referred to earlier, Nickel et al. (1995) generated useful descriptive summaries of subgroups in their target population based on clustering of data in a quantitative survey. Writing of case studies routinely includes summaries of statistical information and interpretation of those data in a situation where no statistical testing can take place.

Summary statistics are produced by most, if not all, qualitative analysis programs, allowing for an interpretive summary of the characteristics of an individual case or of statistical patterns across cases. The ability to use quantitative data of this type to draw comparisons with a known population or to compare with established norms can make an important contribution to a qualitative study where samples are rarely random and are usually comparatively small. In many situations, researchers have scaled or other quantitative data that they have gathered as part of their study—data that also allow them to locate their sample within a larger population and that then assist in determining the extent to which they might generalize conclusions drawn from their qualitative study.

Directly importing statistical databases and statistical reports as raw data, where those reports include graphs, tables, or equations, is not possible in any QDA software (with the exception of importing variable data for matched cases as outlined earlier). Statistical reports can, however, be included in a project in pictorial form (e.g., Atlas.ti, HyperResearch) or proxy format (e.g., NVivo with hyperlinks to the original files where these are available). This allows for qualitative coding of segments of the report and hence inclusion of it in the interpretive analysis of the entire data set. Annual reports from companies and government reports are most likely to be used in this way.

When one considers the steps taken in producing an exploratory factor analysis or even a regression model, the blurring of the boundaries between qualitative and quantitative data and analysis becomes markedly evident. Right from the commencement of the process—the writing and selection of items and the assessment of those items by the respondent—to the manipulation of the analysis procedure to find a workable solution, interpretation is involved and a largely inductive process is being used. Arrival at a "satisfactory" final solution (involving method of factoring, choice of rotation, and number and naming of factors) relies heavily on the theoretical and contextual knowledge and interpretive ability of the researcher. Thus, although the data are in numerical form and statistics are used as an analytical tool, it can be argued that the process involved is largely qualitative.

WORKING WITH MIXED TYPE SURVEY DATA

Data collected using a survey form often include a mix of categorical, numerical, and text data. Rudimentary analysis of survey data can occur within the spreadsheet or database program typically used for initial data entry. Descriptive and simple bivariate statistics can be calculated, and the contents of text fields can be sorted by categories of variables within the database in the search for patterning of responses. If sophisticated statistical analysis of the data is required, the variable-based data will need to be transferred to a statistical program for further processing; likewise, if more sophisticated analysis of the qualitative material is required, the analyst will benefit from transferring the data to a qualitative analysis program. The former is usually a straightforward process, with a direct transfer of data from one program to the other being possible; the latter is less straightforward.

There are at least two programs available that are designed specifically to analyze both quantitative and qualitative survey data in ways other than the usual simple sorting of responses: Sphinx Survey (Lexica edition) and SPSS with Text Smart. Specific tools provided by each of these programs for handling the text in open-ended questions are based on content analysis. While Sphinx Survey focuses on counts of words or user-defined phrases and viewing these in context, Text Smart categorizes texts based on clusters of regularly co-occurring words (or user-modified clusters). Both programs link output from the textual data analysis with existing quantitative variables in further statistical analyses. Searching for specific terms used in open-ended responses is also possible in EpiInfo, a freeware statistical and survey analysis program provided by the Center for Disease Control in Atlanta, Georgia.

A number of QDA programs have tools (other than interactive text searches) that facilitate sorting of responses to each open-ended question by using a code to identify the question asked. This is achieved through use of command language in NUD*IST, the text preprocessor in winMAX, or the section coder in NVivo. A word processor template can be used to prepare standardized documents, or a form letter can be designed to appropriately format responses held in a spreadsheet or database for autocoding in this way. Combined with the ability in each of these programs to import variable data from tabular format, this facility allows immediate sorting of qualitative responses to particular questions according to values of selected variables— as well as interactive coding of the text content.

The introduction, as recently as 1997, of a live "Node Browser" in NUD*IST 4 made for a further revolution in the way in which mixed form survey data can be processed. The ability in NUD*IST and also NVivo to directly "code-on" (Richards, 1999) already coded text means that coding and analysis can proceed via each question (or group of questions) as an alternative to working through all questions, document by document, that is, using a variable-oriented rather than a case-oriented analysis (see Onwuegbuzie & Teddlie, Chapter 13, this volume). The analyst can thus concentrate on each issue, work with and think about a reduced set of categories at any one time (while all the time adding to a general set of content categories), become aware of emerging patterns as he or she works, and consequently design the analysis for that issue while the data relating to it are exclusively in his or her field of attention—without losing the ability to immediately retrieve the broader context or to generate respondent-based information.

ALTERNATIVE FORMS OF DATA TRANSFER AND MANIPULATION

Exploiting the transferability of data between programs that allow for different kinds of use or analysis of data in research is, of course, not limited to statistical and text analysis programs. Software developers have, for some time, been building data transfer procedures into their products. People now typically work with a suite of more general applications (e.g., Microsoft Office, Corel Suite), while output from specialized data analysis software can be directly exported to word processing packages, spreadsheets, or other specialized software allowing complementary approaches to analysis.

Analysis of Bibliographic Material

Researchers reading the literature on or around their topic benefit enormously from using a bibliographic database to store reference information as well as the notes they make when reading. With programs such as EndNote and ProCite, reference information can be downloaded directly from CD-ROM databases such as MedLine and SocioLit. Once data are entered, reference lists, formatted to user preference, can be automatically generated from citation information inserted into a manuscript (using the "cite while you write" functions provided), simplifying the final production (or editing) of articles and dissertations.

In the current context, it is useful (but rarely done) to view literature (or notes from literature) as data, to be integrated and analyzed along with other available material. Understanding of concepts or processes could well be enriched by drawing on the imagination, thoughts, and discoveries of others as well as on the responses of current research participants. Indeed, literature might not be just academic writing on a topic but rather might include items from the popular press, company or departmental reports, brochures, and the like. For example, a study of family caregiving by Poirier and Ayres (2002) used the following as sources of data:

◆ Novels and short stories about families and care

◆ Feminist theories of care

◆ Nursing theories that put care in the forefront

◆ Interviews with family caregivers

◆ Autobiographies of caregivers

Ayres reports,

> We used the novels and interviews to investigate the theories, to see how the theories worked out in practice. Novels and short stories give us more permission to "pry into secrets," to know about the underlying beliefs and motives of the characters, something we're not allowed to do with interviews. Autobiographies are a kind of combination—they are like interviews in that they "really happened," and yet they are crafted like novels and short stories. (personal communication, September 26, 2000)

Output from bibliographic programs can be imported directly into NVivo (as a Microsoft Word rich text file) or converted to plain text for importing into other qualitative software. In the latter case, where the qualitative program allows for sectioning of documents, it is useful to first apply some formatting to the output file so that, for example, each reference becomes a discrete section of the imported document. This formatting can be incorporated into the configuration of the output file so that it is automatically applied when the bibliography is generated. In NVivo, if the file has not been preconfigured with headings, author and date information can be converted to a heading style (to create a section for each reference) while the material is being coded.

Once they are imported and coded, being able to instantly retrieve any notes relevant to a particular subtopic along with author and date information greatly facilitates writing a review of the literature. Alternatively, at any stage of the project, what is said in the literature about any particular topic or issue can be compared with data from other sources, again facil-

410 ◆ METHODOLOGICAL AND ANALYTICAL ISSUES

itating critical review, analysis, and writing up.

Bibliographic material, of course, forms the major data source for quantitative meta-analysis procedures. Meta-analysis does not involve direct transfer of data between programs; rather, it involves recording of results from original research reports (either directly or involving interpretation and summary) in such a way that further analysis of the trends in those results can take place using statistical software (Glass, McGaw, & Smith, 1981; Schmidt, 1992).

"Mapping" and Mixed Methods Analysis

Programs that create a visual representation of links in data through network or concept maps provide a powerful extension to text or numerical descriptions of those data.

Social Network Analysis. It is difficult to say whether social network analysis, involving the use of both graphs and indexes to describe the network (Scott, 2000; Wasserman & Faust, 1994), is a quantification of qualitative information or a qualitative interpretation of quantitative information. Really, it is both. The raw data, generated from reports of specified types of contacts among members of the network, is entered into a simple text file to be read by both statistical and graphical programs. Mathematical indexes for centrality, density, and connectivity (among others) for networks or for the individuals within them can be calculated using, for example, UCINet; Krackplot allows direct interpretation of a graphical representation of the network. Few studies compare more than a few networks, however, so that statistical hypothesis testing is unlikely, at least at the whole network level,

and interpretation is often of a more "qualitative" nature.

Social network analysis is being used by the author in a study of the structure of research groups to determine whether research productivity is related to structural relations within the group. Within-case and cross-case analysis can be applied at the group level based on the pattern of networks that exist and their related indexes and measures of joint and total productivity, along with general information about regularity of meetings and other activities and qualitative comments made by group members about group functioning. These case analyses are necessarily qualitative in nature given that just eight groups were studied. At an individual level, however, respondents' performance ratings can be statistically related to indexes describing their positions in their networks, taking into account the characteristics of their group as a whole.

Mapping Semantic Networks. Mapping of concepts derived through content analysis involves recording codes for the relationships among those concepts such as strength, sign, direction, and (possibly) type as well as their frequency (Carley, 1993). These maps may be analyzed graphically or statistically, giving both qualitative and quantitative views of, for example, the degree to which both concepts and meanings are shared across two (or more) bodies of text—with interesting results particularly when concepts are shared but meanings are not. There is considerable overlap between the principles of social network analysis and those of semantic network analysis; coding for mapping in the latter case can be particularly complex, but once it is achieved, "it is relatively easy to extract vast quantities of empirical information" (p. 116).

Simpler, more interactive forms of mapping of concepts derived from coding of qualitative data are provided within Atlas.ti and NVivo. These programs provide the opportunity to bring codes into a "semantic network" (Atlas.ti) or a "model" (NVivo) and to show conceptual or theoretical links among those codes or concepts. Atlas.ti provides a greater range of types of links from which to select, while NVivo allows for labeling of links, layering of models, and grouping of concepts within models. Both programs allow for inclusion of submodels within models. For regular coding and searching/querying purposes in these programs, concepts are listed alphabetically (Atlas.ti) or taxonomically (NVivo). The benefit of developing these types of semantic models, therefore, derives from arranging the concepts so as to reflect on theoretical relationships among them.

Cognitive Mapping and Qualitative Analysis. Yet another approach to mapping has been taken by the developers of Decision Explorer (Banxia Software). Concepts generated through qualitative analysis using NUD*IST or NVivo can be directly exported to Decision Explorer, where they can be displayed as a hierarchical tree (i.e., as arranged in the original program) or, more usefully, further manipulated to develop concept maps—perhaps to illustrate elements contributing to a process or to explore or demonstrate a theory being developed using those concepts. All manipulation of concepts in the program is interactively managed by the researcher rather than being the result of an automated process (unlike maps based on content analysis). The maps generated in Decision Explorer may be analyzed further in ways not possible within the qualitative application, for example, to reveal the most direct path between two points in the map,

to show all of the indirect paths, to show dead ends, to identify the density of links or the potency of concepts, and to cluster concepts based on their relationships.

Alternatively, concepts (and in some cases the memos attached to them) created within Decision Explorer maps can be exported to other applications, including NUD*IST and NVivo, for further qualitative analysis, or they can be output as text files that can be copied and pasted into a variety of other applications. Decision Explorer also has dynamic data exchange (or DDE) capabilities that are exploited by some users to customize the exchange of information with other Windows applications. This requires some programming skills but means that the analyst can develop his or her own "add-ons" to Decision Explorer to expand the modeling capability. Virtually all of the information in Decision Explorer is accessible in this way so that the analyst can create and edit concepts and links from external applications, such as databases, from which he or she may want to draw source information or to which he or she may want to export results.

Algebraic Analysis of Qualitative Data

The combination of qualitative data and algebraic processing provides an alternative approach to cross-case analysis for small samples. In qualitative comparative analysis (Ragin, 1995), each case is dichotomously scored (0/1) to reflect the presence or absence, in the data available for that case, of selected descriptors, conditions, or themes as well as for an outcome variable (these data could be exported from a qualitative program based on the presence or absence of coding therein). Boolean algebra is then applied to the data to identify, through an iterative process, the minimum set of configurations of codes needed to cover each of the cases in the sample. A "truth table" is constructed listing this set of configurations, the number of cases with each configuration, and the values of the outcome variable for these cases, leading to the derivation of one or more logical equations that summarize the revealed relationships. Algebraic processing, in contrast to regular statistical processing, allows the analyst to focus on patterns of covariation across cases, rather than on the characteristics of individual cases, and to see causal factors as conjunctural rather than additive (Ragin, 1995), that is, as working together to create an outcome rather than being potentially masked by an associated variable in a multivariate model. The ultimate goal of such analysis is the construction of typologies to describe the cases studied.

MULTIDIRECTIONAL INTEGRATION OF PROGRAMS

Few published articles as yet have reported projects in which there are fully integrated quantitative and qualitative analyses of mixed form data involving the integrated use of computer programs, although the possibility of doing such has been discussed for some years (Bazeley, 1999; Tashakkori & Teddlie, 1998).

An integrated mixed methods project— or, as defined by Tashakkori and Teddlie (1998), a mixed model study—is one that may involve the gathering of both qualitative and quantitative data and that involves both statistical and textual analysis. Different types of data and methods of analysis are used to develop, extend, or otherwise inform each other in a holistic, iterative, or dialectical way at various stages through the data gathering and analysis processes. Data of one type may be included in the analysis of data of a different type, some or all data may be trans-

formed from one type to another, and statistical and textual analyses occur in cycles informed by previous transformations and analyses. Where both textual and statistical analyses are applied to the same data sources in a mutually informing way (as in the Research Performance study), I have referred to this as a "fused" analysis (Bazeley, 1999).

Perhaps one or another line of analysis is not revealing a full picture, creating dilemmas for interpretation. Kemp (1999) was struggling to understand the apparent arbitrariness of service provision for the spinal-injured population of New South Wales and the ambivalence of those for whom the services were provided. Her solution involved taking coding generated from qualitative data, reflecting a range of feelings about services, into an existing statistical database based on survey data. There she combined it with the availability of, desire for, and satisfaction with services as experienced by the same people, making a new composite variable. When the new variable was imported for inclusion back into the qualitative analysis, understandable patterns in the text became identifiable. These revealed the critical nature of the plans of life of spinal-injured persons (to be "ordinary") and the consequences for access to services where those plans were on a collision course with expectations of service providers (to be "different"). Kemp (2001) drew an analogy between this process of analysis and the mutations that occur in the sense and antisense strands of DNA so as to build a functionally cohesive organism.

A quite different approach to integration of methods is being taken by West (West & Tulloch, 2001). In a study of domestic violence within lesbian relationships, West is using conditional and posterior probability scores generated from a discriminant function analysis of survey data (categorical and scaled) to characterize respondents as "predictable" or not. She is then choosing to interview those who "should" self-define as abused (on the basis of power negotiation and/or behavioral experience) but who do not and those who do self-define as abused while not fitting the pattern of most abused women (where self-definition is the grouping variable) or, alternatively, those who are correctly predicted on one measure—either power or behavior—but not on the other. From these women, a deeper understanding of the nature of abuse, its causes, and its relationships to power and violence is being gained. The discriminant function analysis is also contributing to her choice of questions and issues to follow up so that she is selecting those issues that best discriminated her two groups as the prompts for discussion. And in turn, the discussions are being used to generate questions that are hoped will improve the discriminating power of the survey for a second round of data collection. Preparation for interview includes being aware of the respondent's answers to various questions on the initial survey, some of which are directly addressed by West when the interview is conducted. Background information from and responses to the surveys are also informing the analysis of the interview data. Integration of data and methods is therefore occurring at all stages—from sample selection, to data design and collection, to analysis.

It is possible to follow many different leads through data and analyses in the Research Performance study, given that this was an exploratory study with a rather descriptive goal, so as to build a rich picture of what makes for high-level research performance. Text and numerical data used interactively showed, for example, that those who viewed approachability as having some relevance to performance (the 30 who allocated it 10% or more)[4] were more likely than those who did not (giving it

0%) to see it in terms of two-way rather than downard-only communication. The combination of statistical and textual analyses revealed both overt and subtle differences in criteria for assessing research performance by those from different disciplinary groups (e.g., different emphasis on and views of the role of theory in research), differences that may need to be expressed in terms of content and weighting in any eventual performance indicators. And again, the use of exploratory statistical techniques such as clustering and correspondence analysis, in combination with analyses of the actual texts, is building an understanding of constellations of skills, orientations, and personal characteristics that will make it possible to model research performance in a way that can also provide guidance for contextually relevant assessment of performance.

Without the availability of modern computer software, the incorporation of these types of interactive techniques within an integrated mixed methods design becomes, at the least, tedious and, at the most, nearly impossible. Just as the ready availability of statistical software facilitated the application of multivariate techniques to analysis of, say, epidemiological data, it can be expected also that increased fluency in using software for integrated analyses may allow researchers to better deal with and understand the complexity of troublesome social (and other) issues.

◆ Issues Arising From Integration of Qualitative and Quantitative Computing

The primary issues that are specific to use of computers when mixing methods revolve around the nature of codes and variables and the potential conflicts in approaches to and methods of analysis. Other issues relating to the combination of qualitative and quantitative data and methods of analysis that are not specifically a consequence of using computers are discussed in other sections of this handbook.

CODES, THEMES, AND VARIABLES

No matter what approach is taken, coding or categorizing of data is an essential component in nearly any system for analysis of data. Statisticians working with quantitative data talk of variables and codes; interpretive researchers working with text talk of themes and concepts—but text is "coded." Codes—the way they are generated, what they stand for, and the way they are used—lie at the heart of differences between quantitative and qualitative data and analysis tools.

Researchers using a statistical program need to define their variables "up front" and have little leeway for change. Categories developed through a qualitative analysis may also be defined a priori but generally are not (and typically need to be changed if they are). QDA software allows for generation of new codes as analysis is progressing, for rearrangement of codes, and (depending on the program) for recoding from existing codes into new categories. These differences will become an issue only if a researcher is determined to have a common coding system across data types so as to force comparability of conclusions from the different data sources.

What codes are used for or stand for is more of an issue. In qualitative programs, codes have typically been used for multiple purposes, blurring the distinction between variable- and theme-oriented coding. Codes are used for demographic information (e.g., values of gender), categorical or scaled data (e.g., an answer of

often/sometimes/never, a score or point on a scale, categorization of an attitude as positive or negative), project-based information (e.g., who the interviewer was, what kind of data), and classifying multiple sources of data into cases as well as for the topic themes, or concepts, that are being extracted from the data. Even the latter might be of multiple types, from substantive concepts (e.g., a view of research as discovery; cooperation in community) to codes that indicate how these concepts are being expressed (e.g., as opinion/ expectation/experience). Themes or concepts might also be coded in descriptive (or representational) categories such as wages and organizational structure; interpretive (or instrumental) categories such as worry and stimulation; or even more abstract analytical categories such as identification, social loss, and hidden caregiving. Quantitative variable sets cover a similarly wide range of variable types, from demographics to scores on underlying constructs.

Differences between the two broad classes of program lie, then, not so much in the range of things that have come to be represented by codes as in the specificity and/or directionality of those codes—referred to by Sivesind (1999) as a distinction between single-dimensionality and singularity. Because codes are the only medium for communicating information in a quantitative data set, they are necessarily precise in what they are conveying, including whether it is being expressed, say, positively or negatively. Qualitative coding, by contrast, is often conceptually based and multidirectional in that all text about a particular issue, idea, or experience will be assigned the same code, regardless of the way in which it is expressed (the latter may be picked up in a second code applied to the same text). The analyst is then able to explore the concept as a whole by reviewing that collection of text segments. Different dimensions within the concept may be determined directly from that review or may be revealed through pattern or comparative analyses. These dimensions are not predetermined by the coding system and may provide a whole new perspective on the meaning of the concept (or something related to it).

Given these differences in the way in which codes and coding are managed, the critical issue from the point of view of mixed methods computing becomes the meaning of the code that is exported from one type of analysis program to another, principally from QDA software to a statistical database. In practical terms, coding involving negatives compounds the problem. When a theme code is quantitized, its meaning becomes fixed and single-dimensional (Sivesind, 1999). For example, in the study of legal judgments referred to earlier, two kinds of data were exported to the statistical database. Even injury data, which have the appearance of being factual, are tempered by the consideration that only those injuries (and facts pertaining to them) that were mentioned by the judge could be included, with no guarantee as to the comprehensiveness of or lack of bias in what was included. Second, coding related to a number of issues was also exported, including issues relating to the character of the plaintiff, the truthfulness of the plaintiff's statements, and experience of previous or subsequent injuries. In each of these, it was possible that the judge had made either a favorable or an unfavorable determination with respect to the plaintiff but that directionality was not embodied in the coding. Statistical analysis involving these variables must therefore be carefully interpreted to reflect that what was exported was a record of simply whether the issue had been raised or not in the final judgment, not of how it was dealt with. If directional coding is required for exporting purposes, it can, of course, be

carried out that way in the qualitative program—either in the first instance or by coding-on from the broader concept (where the program allows). The critical issue, then, is to be fully aware of what kind of concept or variable is being exported and the contingencies surrounding the generation of those concepts or variables and to take that into account in the interpretation of subsequent analyses.

ISSUES RELATED TO SAMPLING AND THE GOALS OF ANALYSIS

Inferential statistics cannot be applied to small purposive samples such as might be used for textual analysis, and fine hermeneutic analysis cannot be applied to textual data from large random samples such as would be sought for a statistical analysis. For an integrated analysis, then, there may have to be a "trade-off" between extensiveness and intensiveness (Prein & Kuckartz, 1995). The typical goal for sampling in qualitative analysis is to reach "theoretical saturation" regarding the topic or process being investigated, having purposively explored and accounted for variations in the experience and discourse of the target group. The goal of sampling in statistical analysis, however, is to generate results that can be generalized to a larger population with a minimum of error—error that may be contributed either by biased selection of participants/respondents or by high levels of variability (standard error) in scores on measures used.

Sampling issues are related to issues around the goals of the analysis—whether the researcher wants to understand the details of a process or to understand the extent of a phenomenon, for example. Mixed methods often are used precisely because both goals are present, but each goal requires different analytical processes. Sampling arises as a critical issue primarily where the analysis is truly integrated, or fused, rather than where one method is used to lead to, compare with, or complement the other.

Difficulties arise when the researcher wants to apply statistical procedures to coding information obtained from a small sample. For example, it is considered inappropriate by statisticians to report percentages where the total N is less than 20, and few inferential statistical procedures can be applied to such small samples. The chi-square statistic cannot be validly used to test a relationship between variables where there are small expected frequencies, and samples in the range of 10 to 20 cases per variable are required for multivariate analyses. When qualitative programs can provide statistical summaries, there is a temptation to overinterpret small numbers (frequency or cross-tabulated data) generated through coding texts, especially in comparative studies or those involving pattern analysis.

At the other end of the spectrum lies the danger that researchers will expect or need to handle much larger volumes of unstructured data because the computer can do it. Whereas previously researchers might have been content with, say, 20 to 30 interviews, now they might seek 100, 200, or even more. Purposive sampling gives way to stratified random sampling or quota sampling so as to meet expectations for generalization of results—and the nature of the qualitative enterprise is changed in the process. The software will assist in managing large data sets, but large amounts of time are still needed to work through the text in detail for a satisfactory interpretive analysis; alternatively, the data are "processed" in a somewhat more superficial way. One option provided by the computer to manage analysis for larger numbers of documents and achieve breadth, while still satisfying require-

ments for fine-grained analysis, is to begin analysis using a small random sample of documents and then purposively sample from within the pool of documents, undertake detailed analysis until theoretical saturation is reached (typically around 20-25 cases), and then use rapid reading combined with text search procedures to verify conclusions and check for deviance in the remaining cases. An alternative approach is to apply the automated coding procedures of content analysis (or exploratory text searches) to the larger corpus and then to identify a targeted sample of cases to follow through for a more detailed analysis of the complete texts. The adequacy of these solutions, particularly if quantification of codes is required for transfer back into a statistical database, will be dependent on the capacity of text searches or content analysis to locate and code the desired concepts in the remaining data.

SEGMENTATION OF TEXTS AND EXPORTED CODING

The way in which (qualitative) texts are segmented, especially the way in which overlapping codes are dealt with, has implications for analysis and for the generation of counts both for content analysis (Roberts, 2000) and for QDA. Even for simple thematic analysis, programs vary in how they count coding references (each distinctively coded string of text), in how overlapping coding is translated into statistical records where each row in the database represents a segment of text, and in whether or not (as a consequence of the former factor) intersections in coding are recognized and counted in cross-tabulations based on exported coding references (and if they are, under what circumstances, what is being counted, and how many times it is counted). Researchers using exported coding data therefore need to test out and become familiar with the transfer syntax used by their selected software.

ISSUES FOR STATISTICAL ANALYSIS

Sample selection and sample sizes affect statistical inferences given that most inferential statistics are based on an assumption of random or representative selection of cases and that error rates in derived estimates of population characteristics are proportional to sample size. This limits the kind of statistical procedures that might be legitimately used where quantitized qualitative data are involved and/or the capacity to generalize to a larger population.

The manner in which coding information is transferred between programs has implications for statistical analyses based on quantitized data as well. Some programs generate a row of data for each coding reference of each document, while others generate a single row for each document, thus affecting the number of "cases" in the analysis and hence the probability estimates that will be generated from that analysis.

The researcher may have a choice in exporting (or aggregating) binary codes indicating presence or absence of a concept, counts giving raw frequency of mention, or proportions indicating the relative volume of text coded particular ways in a document. While use of any one of these consistent with statistical assumptions of the procedure used is not an issue, the meaning of the "measure" might be; for example, counts of coding references within documents are influenced by the verbosity of the particular respondent. Content analysis techniques typically control for this by carefully defining units of text to be coded and applying correction

factors for length of document, but counts may be less precise for other forms of QDA given the possible variation in lengths of coded segments as well as in length of documents overall.

All statistical techniques carry certain assumptions that must be met for appropriate use of those techniques; particular assumptions vary depending on the technique to be employed. Where coding is exported for a semantic network (rather than a simple matrix of counts of words or themes), there is likelihood of error (e.g., multicollinearity) arising from lack of independence in the observations (Roberts, 2000). Similarly, chi-square analysis carries an assumption that categories on the same axis are mutually exclusive. Cluster and correspondence analysis can be applied to quantitized data where conditions of normality and randomness are not necessarily met. Even these exploratory techniques, however, contain methodological assumptions that can affect the process of analysis (Prein & Kuckartz, 1995).

WRITING MIXED METHODS

Integrated analyses need to be written up in an integrated way. All too often, an attempt is made to present first the results and conclusions from one type of data or analysis and then the results and conclusions for the other before attempting to draw them together (if the latter is done at all). This may be appropriate for a study where different methods were selected with a view to seeking convergence of results or perhaps where the different methods were applied to quite different aspects of the general problem being researched. But assuming that both sets of data and analyses are components in a path to a common understanding or a common conclusion, the various elements that go to make up the overall analysis are best presented as a logical chain of evidence leading to that conclusion, regardless of source of data or method of data analysis for those particular elements. In taking this approach, it also becomes impossible to separate the presentation of results from the interpretation of those results; to do so typically leads to unnecessary repetition of findings as they are first simply presented and then repeated as the interpretation is discussed.

Exploratory mixed methods research may well be depicted as a journey of discovery, while research that sets out to support or refute a proposition progressively unveils the evidence that builds toward the conclusion. Literature is brought in as it becomes relevant, as is other data and evidence from analyses. In qualitative work, and often also in mixed methods studies, validity arises less from correlation with some external criterion than from the potency of the arguments presented and the clarity and completeness of the audit trail that shows how the conclusions were derived.

"FOR EVERYTHING THERE IS A SEASON"

This chapter has necessarily focused on the application of computers in analysis of both qualitative and quantitative data, with an emphasis on manipulation of data as the researcher moves across types of data and methods of analysis. The danger of focusing on techniques and technology is to give a distorted view of what is desirable in data analysis, undermining the craftsmanship involved in analysis and interpretation of data (Sandelowski, 1995). To focus on techniques is also to risk placing method before question and, with the techniques described, to invite a "fishing expedition" rather than exploration of data to answer deliberate questions.

One does not therefore automatically choose to use mixed methods or to combine programs as a matter of course. Mixed methods of data handling and analysis must be appropriate to the questions being asked, the goals of the research, and the data that can be sought or are available. Under those conditions, selectively employing specialized computer programs either singly or in combination can powerfully enhance the researcher's ability to analyze and interpret data.

This chapter has illustrated something of the extent of that enhancement and how it can occur. Exploratory analyses, where hermeneutic techniques are dominant, can benefit, for example, from statistical clustering and dimensionalizing of concepts derived from the data. Predictive analyses may be better informed when quantitized qualitative data are added to existing quantitative data sets. The meaning of scores on statistical scales or results of statistical inference testing are clarified when directly linked with alternative data forms. Computer-based mixed methods of analysis are less commonly employed for corroborative data analyses, perhaps because these are largely parallel rather than integrated in form. The role of computers nevertheless supports both major rationales for use of mixed methods—representation and legitimation—as outlined by Onwuegbuzie and Teddlie (Chapter 13, this volume).

These developments have been facilitated largely by the development of QDA programs that allow researchers to successfully integrate different data forms as well as to transform data types. Undoubtedly, the technology available (and the inventiveness of analysts' minds) will continue to develop. But while the technology may develop, the role of the researcher remains paramount in deciding issues relating to the meaning of codes, the appropriateness of samples, the choice of techniques for manipulating data and methods of analysis, and the interpretation of the data tables and displays produced using the computer.

■ Notes

1. I am indebted to Lioness Ayres, at the University of Wisconsin–Madison, for making this distinction and for her many thoughtful comments on an early draft of this chapter.

2. With the release of N6, there are now several versions of the NUD*IST software in common use (N6, N5, and N4 Classic). Although QSR has dropped the use of NUD*IST in the names of its products, I have retained it for this article to avoid having to refer to multiple programs and because the software is still best known by this name.

3. At approximately 15% of the original sample, this is not an unusual response rate for an anonymous mail survey of this type. Because the research was designed to explore concepts and arrive at an operationalization of those concepts rather than to estimate population characteristics, the low rate of response and the likely biases in who did respond do not cause particular problems for the analysis.

4. Approachability was included as a prompt characteristic because my role at the time made for an awareness of how important it was that those with skills be prepared to share these with colleagues who were new researchers and, of course, with students. Clearly, other researchers did not generally share my view that this was a relevant, let alone important, feature of research performance.

■ References

Alexa, M., & Zuell, C. (2000). Text analysis software: Commonalities, differences, and limitations—The results of a review. *Quality and Quantity, 34*, 299-321.

Ayres, L. (1998, March). *"I just say 'Help me Lord'": Family caregivers' strategies to manage emotional distress.* Paper presented at the meeting of the Midwest Nursing Research Society, Columbus, OH.

Barbour, R. S. (1998). Mixing qualitative methods: Quality assurance or qualitative quagmire? *Qualitative Health Research, 8,* 352-361.

Bazeley, P. (1999). The *bricoleur* with a computer: Piecing together qualitative and quantitative data. *Qualitative Health Research, 9,* 279-287.

Bazeley, P. (in press). The evolution of a project involving an integrated analysis of structured qualitative and quantitative data: From N3 to NVivo. *International Journal of Social Research Methodology: Theory & Practice.*

Bazeley, P., Kemp, L., Stevens, K., Asmar, C., Grbich, C., Marsh, H., & Bhathal, R. (1996). *Waiting in the wings: A study of early career academic researchers in Australia* (National Board of Employment Education and Training, Commissioned Report No. 50). Canberra: Australian Government Publishing Service.

Berelson, B. (1952). *Content analysis in communication research.* Glencoe, IL: Free Press.

Berth, H., & Romppel, M. (2000, October). *Measurement of anxiety and dogmatism using computer aided content analysis.* Paper presented at the 5th International Conference on Logic and Methodology for the International Sociological Association, Cologne, Germany.

Blasius, J., & Thiessen, V. (1998, July). *Exploring response structures.* Paper presented at the 14th World Congress of Sociology, Montreal.

Bryman, A. (1988). *Quantity and quality in social research.* London: Routledge.

Campbell, D. T., & Fiske, D. (1959). Convergent and discriminant validation by the multitrait-multimethod matrix. *Psychological Bulletin, 56,* 81-105.

Caracelli, V. J., & Greene, J. C. (1997). Crafting mixed-method evaluation designs. In J. C. Greene & V. J. Caracelli (Eds.), *Advances in mixed-method evaluation: The challenges and benefits of integrating diverse paradigms* (pp. 19-32). San Francisco: Jossey-Bass.

Carley, K. (1993). Coding choices for textual analysis: A comparison of content analysis and map analysis. *Sociological Methodology, 23,* 75-126.

Carley, K. (1994). Content analysis. In R. E. Asher et al. (Eds.), *The encyclopedia of language and linguistics* (pp. 725-730). New York: Pergamon.

Creswell, J. W. (1994). *Research design: Qualitative and quantitative approaches.* Thousand Oaks, CA: Sage.

Creswell, J. (1998). *Qualitative inquiry and research design: Choosing among five traditions.* Thousand Oaks, CA: Sage.

Datta, L. (1997). A pragmatic basis for mixed-method designs. In J. C. Greene & V. J. Caracelli (Eds.), *Advances in mixed-method evaluation: The challenges and benefits of integrating diverse paradigms* (pp. 33-46). San Francisco: Jossey-Bass.

Denzin, N. K. (1978). *The research act: A theoretical introduction to sociological methods* (2nd ed.). New York: McGraw-Hill.

Glass, G. V., McGaw, B., & Smith, M. L. (1981). *Meta-analysis in social research.* Beverly Hills, CA: Sage.

Gottschalk, L. A., & Bechtel, R. (1995). Computerized measurement of the content analysis of natural language for use in biomedical and neuropsychiatric research. *Computer Methods and Programs in Biomedicine, 47,* 123-130.

Greene, J. C., & Caracelli, V. J. (1997). Defining and describing the paradigm issues in mixed-method evaluation. In J. C. Greene & V. J. Caracelli (Eds.), *Advances in mixed-method evaluation: The challenges and benefits of integrating diverse paradigms* (pp. 5-18). San Francisco: Jossey-Bass.

Greene, J. C., Caracelli, V. J., & Graham, W. F. (1989). Toward a conceptual framework for mixed-method evaluation designs. *Educational Evaluation and Policy Analysis, 11,* 255-274.

Holsti, O. R. (1969). *Content analysis for the social sciences and humanities.* Reading, MA: Addison-Wesley.

Jick, T. D. (1979). Mixing qualitative and quantitative methods: Triangulation in action. *Administrative Science Quarterly, 24,* 602-611.

Kemp, L. A. (1999). *Charting a parallel course: Meeting the community service needs of persons with spinal injuries.* Unpublished doctoral dissertation, University of Western Sydney.

Kemp, L. A. (2001, May). *The DNA of integrated methods.* Paper presented at the meeting of the Australian Association for Social Research, Wollongong, New South Wales.

Knafl, K. A., & Ayres, L. (1996). Managing large qualitative data sets in family research. *Journal of Family Nursing, 2,* 350-364.

Krippendorff, K. (1980). *Content analysis: An introduction to its methodology.* New York: Plenum.

Kuckartz, U. (1995). Case-oriented quantification. In U. Kelle (Ed.), *Computer-aided qualitative data analysis: Theory, methods, and practice* (pp. 158-176). Thousand Oaks, CA: Sage.

Kuckartz, U. (1998). *winMAX user's guide.* Thousand Oaks, CA: Scolari.

Mark, M. M., Feller, I., & Button, S. B. (1997). Integrating qualitative methods in a predominantly quantitative evaluation: A case study and some reflections. In J. C. Greene & V. J. Caracelli (Eds.), *Advances in mixed-method evaluation: The challenges and benefits of integrating diverse paradigms* (pp. 47-60). San Francisco: Jossey-Bass.

Marsh, H., & Bazeley, P. (1999). Multiple evaluations of grant proposals by independent assessors: Confirmatory factor analysis evaluations of reliability, validity, and structure. *Multivariate Behavioral Research, 34*(1), 1-30.

Mayring, P. (2000). Qualitative content analysis. *Forum: Qualitative Social Research, 1*(2). [Online]. Available: www.qualitative-research.net/fqs-texte/2-00/2-00mayring-e.htm

Miles, M. B., & Huberman, A. M. (1994). *Qualitative data analysis: An expanded sourcebook.* Thousand Oaks, CA: Sage.

Morgan, D. L. (1993). Qualitative content analysis: A guide to paths not taken. *Qualitative Health Research, 3,* 112-121.

Morgan, D. L. (1998). Practical strategies for combining qualitative and quantitative methods: Applications to health research. *Qualitative Health Research, 8,* 362-376.

Morse, J. M. (1991). Approaches to qualitative-quantitative methodological triangulation. *Nursing Research, 40,* 120-123.

Nickel, B., Berger, M., Schmidt, P., & Plies, K. (1995). Qualitative sampling in a multimethod survey. *Quality and Quantity, 29,* 223-240.

Patton, M. Q. (1988). Paradigms and pragmatism. In D. M. Fetterman (Ed.), *Qualitative approaches to evaluation in education: The silent scientific revolution* (pp. 116-137). New York: Praeger.

Poirier, S., & Ayres, L. (2002). *Stories of family caregiving: Reconsiderations of theory, literature, and life.* Indianapolis, IN: Sigma Theta Tau International.

Prein, G., & Kuckartz, U. (1995). Computers and triangulation: Introduction—Between quality and quantity. In U. Kelle (Ed.), *Computer-aided qualitative data analysis: Theory, methods, and practice* (pp. 152-157). Thousand Oaks, CA: Sage.

Ragin, C. C. (1995). Using qualitative comparative analysis to study configurations. In U. Kelle (Ed.), *Computer-aided qualitative data analysis: Theory, methods, and practice* (pp. 177-189). Thousand Oaks, CA: Sage.

Richards, L. (1999). *Using NVivo for qualitative analysis.* London: Sage.

Richards, L. (2000, October). *Integrating data: Can qualitative software do it?* Paper presented at the 5th International Conference on Logic and Methodology for the International Sociological Association, Cologne, Germany.

Roberts, C. W. (2000). A conceptual framework for quantitative text analysis. *Quality and Quantity, 34,* 259-274.

Roller, E., Mathes, R., & Eckert, T. (1995). Hermeneutic-classificatory content analysis: A technique combining principles of quantitative and qualitative research. In U. Kelle (Ed.), *Computer-aided qualitative data analysis: Theory, methods, and practice* (pp. 167-176). Thousand Oaks, CA: Sage.

Rossman, G. B., & Wilson, B. L. (1985). Numbers and words: Combining quantitative

and qualitative methods in a single large-scale evaluation study. *Evaluation Review, 9,* 627-643.

Rossman, G. B., & Wilson, B. L. (1994). Numbers and words revisited: Being "shamelessly eclectic." *Quality and Quantity, 28,* 315-327.

Sandelowski, M. (1995). On the aesthetics of qualitative research. *Image: The Journal of Nursing Scholarship, 27,* 205-209.

Schmidt, F. L. (1992). What do data really mean? Research findings, meta-analysis, and cumulative knowledge in psychology. *American Psychologist, 47,* 1173-1181.

Schrodt, P. A. (2000, October). *Automated coding of international event data using sparse parsing techniques.* Paper presented at the 5th International Conference on Logic and Methodology for the International Sociological Association, Cologne, Germany.

Scott, J. (2000). *Social network analysis: A handbook.* London: Sage.

Seale, C. F. (2001). Sporting cancer: Struggle language in news reports of people with cancer. *Sociology of Health and Illness, 23,* 308-329.

Sivesind, K. H. (1999). Structured, qualitative comparison: Between singularity and single-dimensionality. *Quality and Quantity, 33,* 361-380.

Smaling, A. (1994). The pragmatic dimension: Paradigmatic and pragmatic aspects of choosing a qualitative or quantitative method. *Quality and Quantity, 28,* 233-249.

Smith, M. L. (1997). Mixing and matching: Methods and models. In J. C. Greene & V. J. Caracelli (Eds.), *Advances in mixed-method evaluation: The challenges and benefits of integrating diverse paradigms* (pp. 73-86). San Francisco: Jossey-Bass.

Tashakkori, A., & Teddlie, C. (1998). *Mixed methodology: Combining qualitative and quantitative approaches* (Applied Social Research Methods, No. 46). Thousand Oaks, CA: Sage.

Tesch, R. (1990). *Qualitative research: Analysis types and software tools.* London: Falmer.

Trom, D. (2000, October). *Ethnographic enquiry and the historicity of action.* Paper presented at the 5th International Conference on Logic and Methodology for the International Sociological Association, Cologne, Germany.

Wasserman, S., & Faust, K. (1994). *Social network analysis: Methods and applications.* Cambridge, UK: Cambridge University Press.

West, E., & Tulloch, M. (2001, May). *Qualitizing quantitative data: Should we do it, and if so, how?* Paper presented at the meeting of the Australian Association for Social Research, Wollongong, New South Wales.

■ *Computer Software*

Atlas.ti: www.atlasti.de

CoAn: www.coan.de

Concordance: www.concordance.ukgateway. net/

Decision Explorer: www.banxia.com

EndNote: www.endnote.com

EpiInfo: www.cdc.gov/epiinfo/

Ethnograph: www.QualisResearch.com

HyperResearch: www.researchware.com

KEDS/Tabari: www.ukans.edu/~keds/

Krackplot: www.contrib.andrew.cmu.edu/~krack/

NUD*IST and NVivo: www.qsrinternational. com

ProCite: www.procite.com

Sphinx Survey: www.lesphinx-developpement. fr/en/

Statistical Package for the Social Sciences (SPSS): www.spss.com

UCINet: http://eclectic.ss.uci.edu/~lin/ucinet. html

winMAX Pro: www.winmax.de

15

IMPACT OF MIXED METHODS AND DESIGN ON INFERENCE QUALITY

◆ Steven Miller

The motivation for this chapter stems from the seminal work of Tashakkori and Teddlie (1998) in attempting to, in effect, develop and justify the parameters of inquiry for the emerging field of mixed methodology. While comprehensive in its scope, the Tashakkori and Teddlie volume has, I believe, also left room for the development and clarification of a number of related issues. The two that I have identified, and wish to comment on, are the use of the term *inference* and the application of the term to one of Tashakkori and Teddlie's classifications (p. 127) concerning alternative mixed methods data analysis strategies. The specific one I have in mind was labeled by them as "Sequential Quan-Qual analysis: Quantitative data analysis followed by qualitative data collection and analysis"

(p. 127, Table 6.3). Their first subheading [labeled (a)] under this classification was defined as "Forming groups of people/settings on the basis of Quan data (e.g., cluster analysis), comparing the groups on Qual data." The authors included an asterisk with this classification and noted, "These two strategies need further development in the future. They are presented here tentatively and are not discussed in the text" (p. 127).

Finding this reference struck me because it was the area within mixed methods that I was independently working on but also the one that would permit me to integrate the problems and issues associated with the term *inference* as they apply not only to this case but more generally to this whole emerging field. Thus, my purpose here is to say something more about

◆ 423

the central role of inference in understanding what it means to *do* mixed methods and then to use the preceding classification as a backdrop to illustrate these ideas and outline some related issues as well. One issue that I attempt to develop more fully, and which is directly related to the request indicated by Tashakkori and Teddlie in the note just cited, is what I call the *placeholder theory.* This is at least a beginning step in trying to address what I consider to be one of the central issues in trying to justify *how* one can combine Quan and Qual approaches without just simply saying one is going to do so.

The overall structure of the chapter, then, includes a series of issues that I believe are central to understanding the nature and purpose of mixed methods. While these issues are not exhaustive, they constitute a framework that is somewhat different from what is normally involved in methodological debates. Thus, in the first section, I discuss the nature of inference itself. This is followed by a discussion of *supervenience theory* as an overall framework for situating the nature of inference as it applies to mixed methods. Next, the ideas of inference and supervenience are further developed by what I refer to as the *placeholder theory.* This is followed by a discussion of whether and how specific *rules* for mixed methods can be developed that would include the topics previously mentioned. I then conclude with a brief analysis of the way I view the *epistemological* and *ontological* debate surrounding the justification of mixed methods designs and approaches. Here, I argue that the position of "minimal realism" may be the ontology of choice for mixed methods. I conclude with some broad recommendations for practicing researchers.

Finally, I should mention that I am approaching these topics from my role both as a qualitative and (to a lesser extent)

quantitative methodologist and as a philosopher of social science. This may explain some of my reasons for choosing these topics and what I intend to say about them.

◆ What Is an Inference?

Before I address the issue of inference and try to show its significance to mixed methodology, I briefly want to mention, and dismiss, the "problem" of mixed methodology as being incompatible with certain epistemological and ontological stances. I do not wish to review the rather tired debates of the past concerning the so-called "paradigm wars" between quantitative and qualitative research perspectives or the aftermaths of the "death" of logical positivism (Phillips, 1987; Smith, 1983; Smith, 1994; Smith & Heshusius, 1986). While Tashakkori and Teddlie (1998) did nicely lay out some of these issues (pp. 22-29) and opted for what they called a "cautiously optimistic pragmatism" (p. 29), two additional distinctions can be mentioned here that are often overlooked in these discussions. The first is that while the ontological issue (in my view) is the central one, it is often linked with the epistemological one in a way that gives primacy to it. However, it is often overlooked that ontological theories do not entail epistemological ones and, especially, so-called methods that are (also often wrongly) associated with a given epistemological theory. There is nothing, in principle, that says that the holding of a particular ontological position (e.g., "realism") commits one to a given methodology. Thus, if I can adjust the old biological maxim here, one could say, "Ontology does not recapitulate epistemology (methodology)." The second point is that even if we wish to start with methodological issues, differences here do not necessarily imply differences in ontology (e.g., the crude labels often attached to "idealism" and "realism"). Indeed, as Lynch (1998) recently showed in a very convincing manner, a "minimal realist" (but still realist) position is compatible and defensible with many versions of "pluralism" and, by extension, with various methodological approaches including mixed methods. Although it may be retained, even the "cautiously optimistic pragmatism" of Tashakkori and Teddlie need not be, given that mixed methods could be defended adequately, I believe, from a (minimal) realist position. Indeed, doing so may be desirable because it could avoid some difficult problems associated with pragmatism itself such as the possibility that although beliefs are "useful," they can also be false (Schmitt, 1995).

While this brief foray into philosophical issues may seem irrelevant to the topic at hand (i.e., inference), it is not, given that inferential processes are, after all, the way we ultimately, if indirectly, make our ontological claims. For example, if I am correctly inferring by way of some mixed methodological strategy, I am also saying that the (social) world is somehow the way I am saying it is. But having said this, we still need to know what the term *inference* actually is. One problem is that the term is used so frequently in quantitative, qualitative, and mixed methodological discussions that its meaning alone or within a specific context is seldom brought to consciousness. For instance, Tashakkori and Teddlie (1998), in trying to address the importance of the issue of internal validity for different research approaches (pp. 67-71), cited one type of internal validity developed by Krathwohl (1993, pp. 271-280) called the "inferential consistency audit" and defined (by them) as "determining the degree to which inferences and interpretations are consistent with the

analysis of obtained data/information and also determining the degree to which different inferences and conclusions that are made in the same study do not contradict each other" (Tashakkori & Teddlie, 1998, p. 70).

I am not arguing for or against the nature or utility of the inferential consistency audit as a legitimate means for establishing some notion of internal validity. Rather, I am only interested in pointing out that in the title and the definition, the term *inference* is prominent. However, it is not clear how the term is being used. Again, this may be due to the fact that its use is simply so well-known by the research community that defining it would be superfluous. Or, it may be that indeed it should be defined in some way. If we look at the definition of the inferential consistency audit cited earlier, there is the phrase "inferences and interpretations are consistent with . . ." It appears as if inferences and interpretations may be two different things or processes, but in fact the very act of interpretation would presume some inferential process.

What, then, is an inference or the process of inference? If put in this way, as Audi (1999) noted, there is an interesting "process-product" ambiguity associated with the term. If inference is a process, then it is something one does or applies in some way; if it is a product, then it is the end result or something that has been produced. While the distinction is probably not of crucial importance in the conduct of mixed methodology research, it is worth mentioning because it highlights the need to be clear on this term. In terms of the inferential consistency audit example, for instance, it would seem that the validity of the audit itself would be tied to the *process* of inference. Yet this is not certain; more important, even if it were certain, how one would go about *applying* the inferential process is not. The need for understanding the possibility of how inference works in mixed methods is especially crucial because we must determine whether it is present in both and, if so, whether it can take on different forms. If this is a possibility, then the conclusions of mixed methodological studies might not have the degree of internal validity—assuming that inference is an important criterion of internal validity—that one would hope for. Conversely, perhaps mixed methodological studies can be shown to have one similar way of assessing the nature of inference, whether of the process or the product variety. Audi defined inference as "the process of drawing a conclusion from premises or assumptions, or, loosely, the conclusion so drawn" (p. 427).

Basically, this is what inference is about. In mixed methods approaches, inference would consist of claiming that conclusions based on findings are indeed credible, warranted, or valid and are even possibly "true." Whatever term is used, the point is that we come to *believe* the findings because presumably our inferences are correct. But what makes an inference correct (we may notice here a "product" sense)? In general, the *process* of inference is thought to involve a set of beliefs that become premises so that a conclusion about these beliefs can be shown to follow. The process of inference sounds close to engaging in *deductive reasoning*, and so it is. Philosophers, however, have put a few additional "spins" on inference that at least are worth mentioning in passing because they may have some bearing on understanding the term's use in regard to mixed methodological research. For instance, we often associate (correctly) the idea of deductive reasoning with a *deductive argument*. But strictly speaking, an argument of this type can simply consist of premises and a conclusion. Here, no inference is involved. What makes a deductive

argument an example of inference is our *belief* in the premises and the conclusion (Audi, 1999, p. 427). Likewise, the terms *infer* and *imply* often get confused. Strictly speaking, as Mautner (1999) indicates in the *Dictionary of Philosophy,* when we *infer* that Q follows from P, we are *showing* how our beliefs lead to drawing *that* conclusion; in *implying,* we let the audience "infer" that Q follows from P.

For most purposes, however, we may associate the "doing" of inference as the doing of (valid) deductive reasoning. If this is the case, then why these other fine-grained distinctions? I mention them to illustrate that, as researchers, we often use terms in rather loose ways. There is nothing too wrong in doing this if such terms are understood conventionally. That is, if as mixed methodologists we all pretty much know and use the term *inference* in the same way, all the better. But I think this is not the case. What makes it an important issue is that a term such as *infer* critically underpins our justification of what we are attempting to do as proponents of the area of mixed methodology. Not only are the inferences crucial, but they are often latent or implicit. This fact makes the realization even more problematic. Although I analyze this in more depth later, the nature of the implicit inference process of mixed methodology lies along at least four dimensions: the inferences assumed for the quantitative portion of the analysis, the inferences assumed for the qualitative portion of the analysis, the inferential relationship between the two, and the possibility for an *overall* pattern or type of inferential process when one is claiming to engage in doing mixed methods research. It is these issues of inference and their analysis that are central to this chapter. But there are some additional things about inference that need to be mentioned.

INFERENCE AND INDUCTION

Although the term *inference* is used ambiguously and vaguely in the literature (Eisner, 1998), it generally is taken to mean, I believe, something like "deductive reasoning." That is, if we are making inferences, then we are constructing (valid) arguments by which our conclusions can be known to logically follow from our premises. At least that appears to be the implied model. However, in much of the literature (especially on the qualitative side of mixed methods), the term *inference* is most likely associated with the term *induction*. There is often a conflation of the two terms, resulting in masking the deeper significance to the research process of both. What occurs is that some rough notions of both deduction and induction are acknowledged as being important to the research process, but then the point that they *both* are types of inference is lost. What I am suggesting is that their central role as ways of *making* inferences is diluted by forgetting that deduction and induction both are types of inference-making machines, but different kinds for different purposes. What results, however, is a confusion of what inference and induction really are and a tendency to view induction as the only meaning of inference. Moreover, the lack of clear distinctions leads to confusion about how, in terms of methods, terms are to be applied. Returning to the previous example of the inferential consistency audit, should one interpret *inferential* as being equivalent to *induction*? Most likely it is, but it is not clear that it is or, if so, how induction would clearly apply to it.

The problems of reference to deduction and induction without clarifying the underlying notion of inference can be seen in Strauss and Corbin's (1998) discussion of these terms:

> The concept of induction often is applied to qualitative research. Our position on the matter is as follows. Although statements of relationship or hypotheses do evolve from data (we go from the specific case to the general), whenever we conceptualize data or develop hypotheses, we are interpreting to some degree. To us, an interpretation is a form of deduction. We are deducing what is going on based on data but also based on our readings of that data. (pp. 136-137)

Strauss and Corbin (1998) were rather typical of many researchers in acknowledging the importance of the process of inference use to the research act but not explicating how it works or why it is important. Deduction and induction, as processes of inference, remain vague in the qualitative literature because, I suspect, we do not clearly understand their respective purposes or roles. Or perhaps more accurately, we are not as clear as we should be on the application of the rules governing each. These facile descriptions of deductive and inductive mask the importance of the inferential processes underlying both. Thus, for deduction, the preceding passage is suggestive but vague. What does it mean to say that "interpretation is a form of deduction"? There is, for instance, the issue of equivalence; can we also say that deduction is a form of interpretation? Assuming that it is not, there still remains the problem of what constitutes deduction. For example, according to Strauss and Corbin, when one engages in interpretation, one is doing some form of deduction. This implies some knowledge of and conscious application of a former rule of deduction. But what should it (or they) be? Is it, for instance, the application of some rule of deductive logic such as the *conditional* $p > q$ or perhaps the use of some other specific rule of (deductive) inference such as *distribution* where $p(q \lor r) = (pq \lor pr)$? Now, if the conditional form were chosen (for whatever reasons), then of course one is committed to its use as a means of establishing the validity of its conclusion. For example, given p and $p > q$, one can *infer q* (*modus ponens*). But is something like this what Strauss and Corbin had in mind? Left open is whether they believe that either "interpretation" is the *result* of the application of deductive reasoning to data or whether interpretation is a "species" of deduction. My guess is that, as researchers, we often sense the potential benefit of deductive reasoning to the research act itself (e.g., in drawing valid inferences), but the term *deduction* is often rather loosely counterposed to *induction* in terms of what we are about. However, our knowledge of induction as a type of inference is at times in need of additional clarification. Let me continue with some examples in what follows.

TYPES OF INDUCTIONS

Within the emerging field of mixed methodology, but also in qualitative and quantitative analysis separately, the term *induction* is used with such frequency that it often (especially for qualitative analysis) takes on a life of its own. Induction becomes a type of reified or super-principle that defines and underpins the research act itself. Although, as mentioned earlier, induction is more openly appealed to in qualitative research writings (Miles & Huberman, 1994), it should be noted that it is in principle as relevant to quantitative and mixed methodology approaches. As with inference in general, an interesting question is whether mixed methodology approaches can *as a whole* be character-

ized as inductive. I return to this later. But for the issue at hand, I want to claim that induction is often as clearly misunderstood as is deduction. Skipping the parallels between inference in general and deduction and induction on the "process-product" ambiguity issue, the first thing to be noted is that induction *is*, of course, a type of inference. But it is a type of inference that goes beyond simple descriptions such as a process that proceeds "from the specific to the general."

As a form of inference, induction or, more precisely, *inductive logic* is characterized as a form of inquiry that is concerned with the evaluation of what is known as *ampliative* inference. Ampliative inference was defined by Audi (1999) as "any inference where the claim made by the conclusion goes beyond the claim jointly made by the premises" (p. 425). Types of inductive inferences include arguments by analogy, predictive inference, and causes and confirmation of scientific laws and theories. An inductive argument, then, is one in which the premises provide some, but not conclusive, evidence for the conclusion—unlike a valid deductive argument in which the conclusion must necessarily follow from the premises (Manicas & Kruger, 1976, p. 481). Inductions come in different varieties such as the following:

> *Enumerative induction*: a type of induction in which what is observed as true of a number of individuals is then claimed as true of all such individuals in a class. Also called an inductive generalization. (Manicas & Kruger, 1976, p. 481)
>
> *Inductive analogy*: Reaching a conclusion about a single case on the basis of a similarity between that case and other previously observed cases. (Barker, 1989, pp. 260-261)

Perfect induction: A case in which the premises assert something true about each of the observed individuals, so that what is true of each is (then) true of all. Because the conclusion does not go beyond the evidence, the reasoning is actually deductive. (Manicas & Kruger, 1976, p. 481)

Eliminative induction: A process of induction where there is a systematic attempt to eliminate rival or alternative claims to an hypothesis. The idea is that the remaining alternative is probably the "cause" of the hypothesis. Mill's Methods of Induction are varieties of eliminative induction. (Manicas & Kruger, 1976, pp. 253-254)

We can now see that the term *induction* is not as simple as it appears. What is at stake for mixed methodology approaches in terms of induction is, in a sense, its very justification. By this, I mean that the entire process of doing this type of research, as Tashakkori and Teddlie (1998, pp. 13-19) suggested, is more than some type of "mixing" of quantitative and qualitative methods. This can be done, of course, but as this chapter will continue to attempt to show, there must be a "logic" to combining methods or models. I believe that this logic is basically an inductive one. However, I also believe that its explicit formulation of how it ought to apply has not been formulated in enough depth. Without it, how can mixed methods ever be truly justified? Even more practically, if we say we are at least partially about doing induction, then there is some necessity to do it if only to establish a case for the validity of our findings. One reason for the tendency to use the term *induction* so loosely is that we do not have a clear model of what is involved. While there are many forms of induction (as noted previously), the gen-

eral structure may be depicted, following Rappaport (1996), as follows:

> The observed data are such and such. Hypothesis H is the likeliest of the competing potential explanations of these data. So (probably) H is true. (p. 67)

One thing to notice is that this model is similar to *eliminative induction*. I believe that eliminative induction is the correct one not only for qualitative analysis but also for mixed methodology approaches. The advantage lies in the fact that eliminative induction encourages the researcher to suggest more than one plausible interpretation for a phenomenon but then also to defend a particular one. A part of knowing how to suggest that one inductive model may be more efficacious than another is to first realize that more than one type of induction exists and to then argue for a given one. For example, we could contrast eliminative induction with *enumerative induction*. This form of inductive strategy is also known as an *inductive generalization* and has the following form:

a, b, c . . . Each has been observed to be S and P.

Nothing has been observed to be S without being P.

Therefore, probably, all S are P. (Baker, 1989, p. 186)

As with all inductions, the conclusion is not certain (in the deductive sense) but rather probabilistic. The contrast between eliminative and enumerative induction, and what this may indicate for the interpretation of findings, can now be seen. Enumerative induction is a variety of a basic form of *confirmation* theory where one makes a claim for a hypothesis by citing the accumulation of positive instances—the more, the better. The aim is to eventually derive at least a partial (but credible) generalization. Eliminative induction, on the other hand, aims toward the elimination of competing hypotheses until only one remains as a credible alternative. In this sense, it is very generally a type of *falsification theory* advocated by Popper (1959). Both forms retain the probabilistic nature of the conclusion and so are inductive in nature, albeit with highly different aims.

In contrasting these two types of induction, I am trying to suggest not only the importance of induction to the overall purpose of doing mixed methodology research but also the need to be clearer about our central terms. The question, however, is "How clear is clear?" There seem to be at least two opposing views on this matter. The first is, roughly, the position holding that it is sufficient to use or mention certain terms and that, once having done so, there is no longer any need to clarify or draw distinctions. This position was held by Eisner (1998), for instance, as indicated in his discussion of structural collaboration:

> To point this [procedural objectivity] out is not to sanction or justify the intentional neglect of evidence contrary to one's vested interests or educational values. On the contrary, because qualitative methods are vulnerable to such effects, *it is especially important not only to use multiple types of data, but also to consider disconfirming evidence and contradictory interpretations or appraisals* when one presents one's own conclusions. In saying this, I do not mean that educational critics are obliged to provide readers with every possible interpretation and appraisal of a situation they write about;

> such a procedure would not only be cumbersome and graceless, it would not have much utility. I do mean that it is both prudent and important to consider those alternative interpretations and appraisals that one considers reasonably credible. There is no measure for determining such credibility; it too is a matter of judgment. The issue is one of fairness, of considering reasonable alternative interpretations. It does not mean relinquishing one's own view. (p. 111, italics added)

While Eisner (1998) was not specifically denying the importance of thinking about what one is doing methodologically, he downplayed its utility because it may produce graceless writing and, more important, such activities are still "matters of judgment" in any case. At a more implicit level, what may be operating here is a reluctance to have researchers acknowledge that the justification of what they are doing is often lacking. I believe exactly the opposite; not only should researchers be clear about what they are doing in terms of what concepts they use, they should explicitly be able to write about and defend what they are doing. If we use key terms such as inference and induction too casually, our interpretations suffer in turn. In regard to the mixed methodological case, there is a dual and different obligation on the part of the researcher. Moreover, the obligation is asymmetrical in that the qualitative aspect traditionally is the one that is more in need of explicit justification. For example, if we have a mixed methodological study in which we first begin with a correlational strategy and then follow up with a qualitative interviewing technique, the underlying inferential assumptions of the correlational part are simply assumed as being valid. That is, even though correlational analysis is based on inductive inference (i.e., enumerative generally, eliminative if hypotheses are involved), it is more readily presumed both that the researcher is aware of this and that the inference assumptions are appropriate and correct. On the qualitative side, there is a latent or lingering suspicion that the need for inference justification is more pressing. And indeed, it may be. It may be so because, as I have been trying to show, basic terms are often used in ambiguous ways, and the nature of the inferential process is seldom clearly articulated.

Although the relationship in the mixed methodological case especially highlights this asymmetry, this very condition can be used to identify the need to examine *related* issues, common to both and unique to mixed methods. For example, in terms of the first, both quantitative and qualitative approaches are ultimately directed to how methods generate data that, in turn, become *evidence* for some claim. What is crucial here is some reflection on the nature of evidence itself—a clearer vision of what is at stake when we conduct research (Miller, 1994). What is at stake, ultimately, is the truthfulness of the statements we make. The field of law gives a sense of this relationship through its use of phrases such as "beyond a reasonable doubt" and "preponderance of the evidence." Although ambiguous, the phrases hint at what is finally crucial: how what we *take* to be evidence relates to what is being claimed. Thus, the "weight of the evidence" is some type of inferential relationship between statements of one kind in relationship to one or more statements (e.g., hypotheses, research questions) of another kind. What we often fail to understand here is that the relationship itself, as well as its assessment, is primarily a *logical* one.

From the quantitative side, this idea can be illustrated by the logic of hypothesis testing (Nachmias & Nachmias, 1981, pp. 448-451). Let us say that we have some theory (T), and from it we predict some

type of phenomenon (P). This is the familiar conditional "if-then" form of deductive logic. It has a number of valid and invalid forms. For instance, a valid form is called *affirming the antecedent*: If T, then P, T, therefore P; that is, "If my theory is correct, then I believe the following prediction(s) will hold true." In other words, the theory entails (i.e., certain things can be validly deduced from it) certain outcomes or consequences. If this is the case, then if I affirm the truthfulness of the theory, the consequences necessarily have to follow. However, our theories in the human sciences are seldom very strong, so we must try to give them support through credible *evidence*. The evidence is generated by testing the predictions of the theory to see whether they support or refute the theory. The problem is that by simply testing the predictions, even if we think they are giving us truthful evidence, we cannot be sure the theory is supported. The reason is again logical, for in proceeding in this way, we may be committing a logical fallacy associated with conditional (if-then) statements, namely the fallacy of affirming the consequent. Consider our notation: If T, then P, P, therefore T. This is an *invalid* form of reasoning because it is still possible for our theory to be incorrect in spite of our "confirming" evidence in terms of testing the predictions. The logical fallacy can be seen by way of this simple example. If I claim, "If this test is valid (in the research sense), then it is reliable (in the research sense)." I show that the test is reliable (i.e., this is my evidence), but can I conclude that it is valid? No. The test may be reliable (affirming the consequent), but this does not guarantee its validity.

To avoid the fallacy of affirming the consequent, we try to substitute another valid form of reasoning called *denying the consequent*. It has this form: If T, then P, not P, therefore not T. Thus, a test's consistent nonreliability will cast doubt on its validity. Now, in testing the so-called null hypothesis, for instance, we are caught in a type of dilemma. On the one hand, we want positive confirming instances of our predictions (the confirmationist position), but doing this may lead to the fallacy of affirming the consequent. On the other hand, falsification of the predictions (the falsificationist position) may lead to a rejection of our theory, something we do not want to do, although (logically speaking) this is a valid form of reasoning. Again, we try to substitute the valid form of reasoning called denying the consequent: If T, then P, not P, therefore not T. Thus, a test's consistent nonreliability will cast doubt on its validity. Now, in testing the so-called null hypothesis, for instance, we are caught in a type of dilemma. On the one hand, we want positive confirming instances of our predictions (the confirmationist position), but doing this may lead to the fallacy of affirming the consequent. On the other hand, falsification of the predictions (the falsificationist position) may lead to a rejection of our theory, something we do not want to do, although once more (logically speaking) this is a valid form of reasoning. From an empirical perspective, what we do, of course, is specify how much risk we want to take in rejecting the null hypothesis (i.e., the levels of significance) given that it might be true. In other words, we are saying this: We will accept the confirmability of our positive instances only under rather stringent conditions; we do not want to reject our theory, but we also do not want to believe it if it is false.

To return to our theme, what I am suggesting is that even quantitative analysis is premised on very basic inference assumptions that are often overlooked. The result is the dismissal of the importance of these assumptions in determining how research findings become evidence for our (hopefully truthful) claims about the social world. In the preceding example, for instance, we can see the interplay of both deductive and inductive inference rules. We seldom fully appreciate the fact that hypothesis testing is an attempt to reason in deductively valid ways but that in doing so we attempt to use forms of enumerative and eliminative induction in specific ways.

The qualitative perspective is often even less specific and aware of the need to clarify what inferential processes are being assumed or used. I shortly specify some of the reasons I believe are responsible for this "inferential inadequacy," but a few additional examples here may clarify the situation. Tashakkori and Teddlie (1998, pp. 89-93), for instance, specified a rather long list of techniques and perspectives that are commonly known in the qualitative research literature. They titled the section "Quality of Data and Inferences: Qualitative Perspective" (p. 89) and directed their attention to how these perspectives may enhance the qualitative counterpart of internal validity. Here, I want to look at only one of these, randomly chosen, to illustrate some aspects of inference and induction.

PEER DEBRIEFING

Lincoln and Guba (1985) defined this as a process of "exposing oneself to a disinterested peer in a manner paralleling an analytic session and for the purpose of exploring aspects of the inquiry that might otherwise remain only implicit within an inquirer's mind" (p. 308). Tashakkori and Teddlie (1998) went on to indicate that "this [peer debriefing] is clearly relevant to the quality of researchers' *inferences/conclusions*" (p. 91, italics added). I assume that peer debriefing is some type of inductive inference-making process. But this is exactly the point; we do not know what it is *as* an inference process.

There is, again, a certain type of process-product ambiguity operating here. Even given that it is some type of induction, it is unclear whether the process itself of doing peer debriefing is where the inference takes place or whether the *conclusion* of the process represents some type of inference type.

If you "peer debrief" what I have done in my research study, and assuming that it is directed toward my findings (although this is not clear), what exactly is it that you are doing? If you look back at Lincoln and Guba's (1985) definition, there is some mention of doing this "debriefing" as a way of exploring aspects of inquiry that otherwise would remain implicit in my mind. I am not sure what this really means. Is it that your job is to probe my latent mental states given that it is even possible to know, a priori, what they are? Or, do you see real mistakes in what I have done, and your job is to tell me what I have done incorrectly and possibly also correct it? Moreover, what is likely to be an adequate indicator of "success" of this debriefing? In both of the preceding cases, it would appear to involve some agreement on my part that your assessment of my mental state and/or pointing out a mistake is correct. But what if I disagree with you on one or both of these things? Is it then a "failure" of peer debriefing or a stimulus to keep at it—whatever it is?

These are the kinds of issues that obfuscate those areas of the qualitative research paradigm that need the most clarity. It is not that a perspective such as peer debriefing is unworthy of use or even central to use, it is just that one does not know precisely *how* it works. The idea that it is some type of inference process, most likely inductive, would be a valuable insight or justification for its use if only the idea of inference could be specified or described more clearly, even in a general sense.

Thus, an example such as peer debriefing has good potential for applying inductive inference techniques in terms of qualitative research. However, currently these techniques are not clearly articulated enough. We may legitimately ask whether such a case can even *be* made, that is, an explicit case for inference that attempts to explain what is at stake in the use of a particular perspective. There is no need, following Eisner here, to require detailed and unwieldy excursions attempting to justify every technique and perspective used. What I am advocating, however, is a deeper awareness of what constitute the basic assumptions of what we attempt to do, whether it be qualitative, quantitative, or mixed methodological.

One argument is that we cannot even make known our inferential practices because our minds find it difficult, or perhaps impossible, to define or describe what such practices look like. So, for example, if I want you to actually describe what *inferential* means in "inferential audit," or the logic of changing the *phenomenon* in classic analytical induction or the term *induction* generally as it is used in qualitative research methods, this position says that a detailed definition is either not possible or, in any case, not desirable. Now, it may be difficult to do so for a variety of reasons such as simply not having thought about the issue in this way before and perhaps having some, but not sufficient, background knowledge for the topic. A third reason may be that the topic is so difficult that even if we are well-acquainted with what is at issue, a simple or elegant application or solution is not available.

While these are all possibilities, I do not believe we want or need to become skeptical about finding some acceptable common ground. Or, perhaps trying to find a "minimal" common ground for our inductive practices would be a better way of stating it. For quantitative approaches, the inferential practices are *potentially* better known, although at the level of the research practitioner, in many instances I do not believe they are thought about, although they are in some sense "known." In other words, in quantitative analysis generally, there is a clearer way to "index" the assumptions of the nature of underlying inferences. The case is different in qualitative approaches. Here, the language referring to either latent or manifest inferential processes is in need of further clarification.

Another way of putting this concern is to look at a distinction employed in philosophy called the use-mention distinction (Audi, 1999, p. 942). It is also, importantly, a fallacy in terms of reasoning. The idea is that we often (unwittingly) confuse the "use" and "mention" characteristics of language. For example, assume that I ask, (1) "Does the inferential consistency audit increase internal validity?" or (2) "Does the 'inferential' consistency audit increase internal validity?" In the first case, "inferential" is being *used*. In the second, it is being *mentioned*. The result of confusing the two may lead to drawing false conclusions. If I mean it in the sense of (1), then if I conclude that it *does* increase internal validity, I may be correct. If I view it in the sense of (2), however, with the same conclusion, I may still be correct but I also may be wrong. I may still be wrong in (1), of course, but in (2) I am implying that there may be other kinds of consistency audits and that I am claiming *this* type to be the correct one in increasing internal validity. What I am suggesting, then, is that in trying to discern inferential processes on the qualitative side especially, we seem to often confuse the use (1) sense with the mention (2) sense. Or, put differently, we need to pay more attention to the possibility that statements such as "Grounded theory is a highly inductive

process" and "Grounded theory is a highly *inductive* process" can make a crucial difference in understanding what we are ultimately trying to accomplish as researchers.

◆ Inference to the Best Explanation and Supervenience

All of these considerations bring us to the issue of the nature of the inference process in relation to mixed methods approaches beginning with a discussion of the mixed methods approach in the context of *supervenience theory*.

To begin with, I believe that the major obstacle in justifying the mixed methods approach as a separate and legitimate form of inquiry is its (for now) lack of a clear "logic-of-choice." By logic-of-choice, I do not mean the use of either formal deductive or inductive methods; rather, I mean something closer to a "rationale-for-proceeding" in a particular way. If such a rationale is not developed, then whatever mixed methods are chosen may appear ad hoc or arbitrary. This, in turn, may lead to a perception that there is really no justification for arguing for the uniqueness or utility of mixed methods as a research approach.

There seem to be currently two ways of addressing the logic-of-choice issue, although I am not aware of systematic discussion that this is what underpins the doing of mixed methods. The first approach appears to be a type of *taxonomic* classification where all of the possibilities for combining quantitative and qualitative techniques (and possibly others, e.g., historical analysis) are considered. This in itself may be a very useful (and possibly needed) device as a new field is trying to determine its parameters. Tashakkori and Teddlie (1998) were, of course, leading figures here. I cite some of their classificatory types as examples:

◆ *Equivalent status designs:* sequential (QUAN/QUAL and QUAL/QUAN) and parallel/simultaneous (QUAN + QUAL and QUAL + QUAN)

◆ *Dominant-less dominant designs:* sequential (QUAN/qual and QUAL/quan) and parallel/simultaneous (QUAN + qual and QUAL + quan).

The first type was defined as follows: "In sequential mixed method designs, the researcher conducts a qualitative phase of a study and then a separate quantitative phase, or vice versa" (Tashakkori & Teddlie, 1998, p. 46), while "in parallel/ simultaneous mixed method designs, the quantitative and qualitative data are collected at the same time and analyzed in a complementary manner" (p. 47). It should be noted that a complete and historically developed taxonomy was given by Tashakkori and Teddlie in their Table 1.1 (p. 15). Likewise, lowercase letters indicate a "dominant-less dominant" mixed methods design, where a given paradigm and its methods are dominant, with the other taking on a lesser role. As I indicate later, I believe that a certain version of the dominance idea may be important overall in justifying mixed methods approaches.

But even here, in terms of an adequate taxonomic development, the picture is further complicated by the fact that Tashakkori and Teddlie (1998) made a distinction (and rightfully so) between *methods* and *models* (pp. 52-58). The "model" conception was a refinement of Patton's (1990) earlier work, but in the case of model designs, the terminology and focus changed from experimental versus naturalistic to *confirmatory* (qualitative case studies, experimental designs,

and nonexperimental studies) versus *exploratory* studies (naturalistic inquiry and surveys) (p. 139). The various taxonomic classifications from including *model* designs were given in Table 3.1 (p. 57) of Tashakkori and Teddlie's text. To give a brief example here, the authors used the classification Type I ("confirmatory investigation, qualitative data, and statistical analysis" [pp. 139-140]) as a model design that parallels Patton's idea of experimental design, qualitative data, and statistical analysis. Basically, participants are randomly assigned to experimental and control groups, qualitative pre- and posttests are employed, and a panel of judges then rate the interviews on a predetermined scale relating to "outcomes."

Now, what all of these examples illustrate in terms of the logic-of-choice issue is that while the taxonomic classifications are necessary for understanding the emerging field of mixed methods, they are not sufficient. By this, I mean that the *choice* of either a mixed or models approach is, of course, a *type* of choice but one that is not constrained in any way beyond this. Thus, even if I choose to conduct a "confirmatory" study, I *need not* proceed in this way, and even if I do, the options of various quantitative and qualitative combinations are still there. Moreover, the *content* of the topic does not (and perhaps should not) limit the choice of possible strategies. Thus, if I want to study the relationship between, say, socioeconomic status (SES) and school achievement, my choices could be confirmatory or exploratory, quantitative or qualitative, in several combinations.

One implication of this logic-of-choice issue is that there seems to be a type of *equivalence* or "parity of type." That is, if there are not prima facie reasons or criteria for saying *this* mixed method or model, and if there are not a priori reasons for choosing based on content, then at least in some weak sense, all approaches are equivalent. The point is not that any given mixed methods/models approach is "wrong" or is "better" than another, but if they are somehow equivalent, the rationale for using any one over another is *indeterminate*. If this is so, the extreme position would be to return to separate methods/models.

I do not believe that extreme position is warranted, but its avoidance depends on at least two issues: (1) the notion of inference and (2) the recognition of the possible importance of the supervenience thesis. In terms of the first issue, there is a theory in the philosophical and research literature that goes by the technical name of *inference to the best explanation* (IBE; Lipton, 1993). An IBE consists of proposing and justifying a framework that, all things considered, gives a person good reasons for a belief. This framework centers on the term *explanation*, of course. Leaving aside the fact that the term *explanation* is itself quite complex (Martin, 1997), the general idea is to *say* that one has "explained" something by reference to what one has "done." In other words, one gives a "how" response to a given form (whatever it may be) of an explanation. The "how" response is, of course, intimately connected to the "why" response. So, if I ask you why you chose a Type II (confirmatory investigation and qualitative analysis) mixed model design (Tashakkori & Teddlie, 1998, p. 139), you might respond that you believed it was (the "why") the best way to explain the given phenomenon. If I then pressured you further on the matter, you might want to refer to the inference process(es) you employed. We are once more at the point where we started; we need to be aware of, and to some extent "explain," our own inferences. In turn, they become "best" to the extent we know of them, how they work, and why we chose them. Thus, as to the "indeterminate" issue discussed previously, an acceptable response would be grounded in the ability of the researcher to justify his or her version of IBE by *both* the choice of the mixed model design and an explication of the inference process(es) used. A "strong" version of the IBE applied to our example would require the researcher to, in effect, employ two designs where, concerning the same phenomenon, all aspects (save one) would be the same and then (supposedly) one version would supply the "better" explanation.

However, this "strong" version of IBE is not necessary and is very unlikely in any case. This does not settle the logic-of-choice issue but at least suggests that this type of indeterminacy need not be pernicious. In other words, if more *explicit* attention is given to the inferential process(es) we do use, a fairly strong "within" methods/models case can be made. A further way of viewing the logic-of-choice issue, as well as perhaps clarifying the taxonomies currently in use, is through the idea of *supervenience*.

The concept of supervenience in its most basic formulation is directed toward understanding the possibility of *reductionism* (Kim, 1992). Reductionism here means the possibility that something at one level of analysis can be "reduced" to another more basic level of analysis. The terms *higher* and *lower* are often used in discussions of reductionism, but they are used in a special way. For instance, as applied to disciplines, *sociology* would be considered a "higher level" discipline because many of its theories and concepts are "abstract" in the sense of being highly general, abstract, and not governed by well-known and rigorous laws. Conversely, *physics* would be considered a "lower level" science for exactly the opposite reasons; its explanations are well-established, general, rigorously derived, and in these ways simply more *basic*. This is not to say that the theories of sociology are false; rather, they are simply not well-established at this time. However, reductionism would assert that whatever these laws turn out to be in sociology, they can (and will) be better explained by physics—always.

Sober (1999) gave a helpful illustration of the hierarchical and nesting principles associated with reductionism:

> The distinction between higher and lower of course requires clarification, but it is meant to evoke a familiar hierarchical picture; it runs (top to bottom) as follows—the social sciences, individual psychology, biology, chemistry, and physics. Every society is composed of individuals who have minds; every individual with a mind is alive; every individual who is alive is an individual in which chemical processes occur; and every system in which chemical processes occur is one in which physical processes occur. The domains of higher-level sciences are subsets of the domains of lower-level sciences. Since physics has the most inclusive domain, immaterial souls do not exist and neither do immaterial vital fluids. In addition, since the domains are (properly) nested, there will be phenomena that lower-level sciences can explain, but that higher-level sciences cannot. (p. 543)

Such a reductive hierarchy is logically possible, but what it means in practice is an issue that must be further analyzed. For example, reductionism in its strong form *requires* that a lower level explanation be a necessary condition for a higher level one. Thus, any concept from sociology, say "ethnocentrism," would have to be explained from an individual psychology level. Yet many constructs cannot be re-

duced in such simple ways. Furthermore, if we invoke some type of principle of transitivity between the highest and lowest levels, it is difficult to see how some principle or theory from physics could be used to explain the concept of ethnocentrism.

As Little (1991, pp. 192-195) indicated, a weaker form of the reductionist argument has evolved to keep the possibility (and possible importance) of the notion in place, but without some of its undesirable consequences. Thus, the idea of reductionism has been replaced with that of supervenience. As Little stated the thesis,

> Supervenience is a doctrine about the relations that obtain between the systems of regularities and facts in a pair of domains. It absorbs the truth of the ontological thesis [that higher-level] entities are constituted by lower-level [entities] but rejects the doctrines of meaning reduction or explanatory reduction. To say that one level of description supervenes on another is to assert that all distinctions and variations among phenomena at the higher level depend on distinctions and variations among phenomena at the lower level. (p. 193)

The basic idea of supervenience, then, is a type of "dependency" relation, but one that does not imply the reduction of one level into another. One advantage of the supervenience concept is that it encourages us to think differently about notions such as inference, explanation, and causality. It is also important in suggesting the possibility of what is known as the *multiple realizability thesis*. The multiple realizability thesis is a claim that a higher level statement, generalization, or assertion may be explained by noting that while its meaning is in some way dependent on a lower level condition, the lower level condition does not necessarily provide the *only* explanation for the higher level generalization. To use an example from Little (1991, pp. 194-195), while the concept of "bureaucracy" supervenes on the idea of individual persons, this level does not necessarily explain bureaucracy in general or a bureaucracy having some particular defining characteristic (e.g., it is highly coercive). A further dimension of multiple realizability is that it is *asymmetrical*. This condition basically means that while the higher level supervenes on the lower level, the lower level may have many properties, any of which could be used to explain the higher level generalization. Following an example given by Sober (1999, pp. 544-545), if we have a higher level generalization of the (conditional-type) form, "If P, then Q," there may be many instances at the lower level for both P ($A_1, A_2, A_3, \ldots, A_n$) and Q ($B_1, B_2, B_3, \ldots, B_n$) that individually may bring about P or Q or in a particular combination (e.g., a_1, b_1). In this characterization, the asymmetry occurs because P and Q are what they are in consequence of what particular A and B are involved. As Sober stated,

> Because the higher-level properties are multiply realizable, the mapping from lower to higher is many-to-one. You cannot tell which of the A properties is exhibited by a system just from knowing that it has property P, and you cannot tell which of the B properties the system has just from knowing that it has Q. (p. 514)

The idea of supervenience itself, then, is a construct that focuses our attention (hopefully) in a unique way. It suggests that the very idea of mixed methods or mixed designs, or more precisely their better understanding, may lie in examining how their *taxonomic* classifications may

be varieties of the supervenience thesis. Likewise, if the multiple realizability thesis is possible, we may be able to better understand the range, domain, and inference types associated with this emerging field. I want to turn now to a further development of some of these issues.

MIXED METHODS
AND SUPERVENIENCE

I do not try to argue here that the supervenience idea can be readily applied to all cases of mixed methods and mixed models. However, I do believe that it can serve as a useful preliminary attempt to bring some additional clarity to the taxonomic variations. I do not examine all of these, but I examine what I believe to be some central and representative ones.

Sequential Mixed Methods Designs: QUAN/QUAL or QUAL/QUAN. Most basically, this approach uses two *separate* or distinct phases to conduct the study. They are supposed to be distinct, but in one example given by Tashakkori and Teddlie (1998, p. 47), this might not be the case because the authors stated that the QUAL/QUAN may imply that the QUAN (e.g., survey) is premised on the QUAL (e.g., interviews) first having been completed. However, in general, it would seem that the sequential mixed methods design would *not* be an instance of a supervenience relationship because by definition they are distinct.

Parallel/Simultaneous Mixed Methods Designs: QUAL + QUAN or QUAN + QUAL. The idea is that "quantitative and qualitative data are collected *at the same time* and analyzed in a complementary manner" (Tashakkori & Teddlie, 1998, p. 47, italics in original). It seems that because the data are collected simultaneously, there appears to be no direct type of supervenience present. But there is some ambiguity as to whether the data are then analyzed separately or a final analysis (i.e., comparison between the two data sets) is done either qualitatively or quantitatively. If the latter is possible, then there may be a type of supervenience at work here.

Dominant-Less Dominant Designs (Across Both Paradigms/Methods): QUAL/quan or QUAN/qual (Sequential) and QUAL + quan or QUAN + qual (Parallel/ simultaneous). In this alternative, we basically keep the sequential-parallel distinction, but now one paradigm and its methods are dominant, while the less dominant aspect constitutes a smaller or minor part of the study. For example, an experimental hypothesis testing design predominates, while an open-ended postexperimental interview is also conducted but not as an integral part of the study.

The dominant-less dominant designs, whether sequential or parallel, have at least a semblance of the supervenience concept. In these cases, it would appear that the less dominant would supervene on the dominant. That is, the less dominant strategy is in some way "dependent" on the dominant one. However, if the sequential-parallel/simultaneous distinction is kept, it is not clear how the supervention would work. It may be, using the preceding example, that a postexperimental interview supervenes on the experimental design, but only to the extent that a case could be made that it does so (i.e., *if* qualitative data are sought, then the postexperimental interview *is* the way to proceed). Cases such as this could loosely be called *second-order* supervenience, with a case of *first-order* supervenience being a clear-cut case where we can argue that a given method or model depends on another method or model.

As we can see, the supervenience idea is linked with the logic-of-choice notion mentioned previously. That is, the logic-of-choice issue is highlighted, I believe, in its importance by the supervenience one. Put differently, if we *could* make a clear case for supervenience, we could justify our logic-of-choice better; not only would the taxonomic classifications constitute the *logically possible* combinations, but also their "internal structure" would be better understood.

Tashakkori and Teddlie (1998, chap. 6) did, however, refine their basic classifications in a variety of interesting ways, and one such example is mentioned next.

AN ALTERNATIVE STRATEGY

Sequential QUAL-QUAN Analysis and Sequential QUAN-QUAL Analysis. In the first variety, qualitative data analysis forms the basis of similar groups. These groups "are then compared *either* on the QUAN data that are available *or* on the data that are collected following the QUAL analysis" (Tashakkori & Teddlie, 1998, p. 133, italics added). Tashakkori and Teddlie (1998, pp. 133-134) gave the example of teachers being divided into "effective" and "ineffective" groups (labeled as "typology" development), and then *further* information about them was analyzed. These additional data, using their example, are gathered by survey instruments or (more indirectly) on performance tests taken by their students. If we look more closely at this example, the supervenience seems to be as follows: The direct survey data supervenes on the qualitative categories, while the quantitative data, as reflected by the students' performance tests, *indirectly* supervenes on the original qualitative categories. We can reverse the sequence here—QUAN-QUAL—but the same considerations would apply.

In any case, what we have, by way of the supervenience thesis, is a "weak" but plausible form. That is, in some of these instances, the particular pattern does suggest a dependence relation; however, it is not strong enough to give a completely satisfactory explanation on the logic-of-choice matter. The multiple realizability thesis might suggest not only a taxonomic classification but also a closer examination of the reasons for choosing *any* given type. I would again suggest that the answer must lie in the arguments we make for a given type as fulfilling some notion of inference to the best explanation *as* a unique type. The supervenience idea is then a *focal point* to begin additional reflection on the logic-of-choice question in relation to the IBE concern. Put differently, the emerging area of mixed methods and mixed models is in need of making a transition from its *descriptive phase* to its *justification phase* or, to use the traditional distinction somewhat analogously, from the *context* (or logic) *of discovery* to the *context* (or logic) *of justification*.

My aim here is to suggest the importance of this "shift" in purpose and to try to establish a rough outline of its parameters. At this stage, however, I believe that more work still needs to be done on simply trying to get a better understanding of what is involved in the context of discovery stage. Tashakkori and Teddlie (1998), in their distinction between mixed methods and models, did (I believe) further illustrate the complexities involved in trying to accurately map the context of discovery stage. In the next subsection, I briefly examine the idea of models.

MODELS AND SUPERVENIENCE

Tashakkori and Teddlie (1998, esp. chap. 7) attempted to expand and refine the emerging field by looking not only at methods but also what they called "models." The idea of a model is a more inclusive category that for them includes *confirmatory* (including qualitative case studies, experimental designs, and non-experimental studies) and *exploratory* (including naturalistic inquiry and quantitative exploratory studies such as surveys) designs (p. 139). These classifications are extensions and refinements of Patton's (1990) original categories of "experimental versus naturalistic" designs. A full typology of models developed by Tashakkori and Teddlie was given in their Table 3.1 (p. 57).

In the following analysis, however, I wish to look at only one illustration of the models to see their possible implications for the supervenience thesis.

Type I: confirmatory investigation, qualitative data, and statistical analysis

An example of Type I (and following Patton's classification of experimental design, qualitative data, and statistical analysis [Tashakkori & Teddlie, 1998, p. 140, Box 7.1) would be a random assignment of participants into experimental and control groups and pre- and postqualitative interviews and then "quantitizing" several "outcome dimensions" on a predetermined and operationalized scale. The intent here was to assess how a *program* of some type (exposure vs. not exposure) was judged by the participants.

It would appear that the "model" characterization is broadly useful as a means of forming further taxonomic classifications. At a minimum, it shows that "typing" studies as "confirmatory" and "exploratory" does *not* rule out the possibility of "mixed" analyses. The issue of supervenience, however, remains ambiguous, as it did with "methods."

To summarize, I believe that the major "paradigm" issues facing the acceptability of the field of mixed methodology lie in the interrelated areas of inference making in general, IBE (specifically, the logic-of-choice in knowing how and why to proceed in a particular research study), and the need to keep thinking about these issues from the point of view of supervenience. Again, the supervenience issue, while an important one connected with justification in its own right, is (I believe) especially crucial in mixed methodology because it highlights the others. Thus, if we had a clear idea of direct supervenience, we would have a better grasp on these other areas.

In the next section, I attempt to present some additional ways of looking at these issues. Specifically, I want to propose a model of mixed methods that, while appearing to be narrow and with a number of constraints, will at least propose a different aspect of this developing area. Then, I will again look at this proposal within the context of inference making.

◆ *Mixed Methods and Placeholding*

I begin with the following radical proposal: Mixed methods/models should give primacy to quantitative perspectives and analyses. Proposing this does no harm to the "pure" varieties of either qualitative or quantitative research. It does, however, remove those mixed methods/models that emphasize the qualitative perspective. As I try to explain throughout, I believe that the issue of inference can be more clearly addressed by this approach, mostly because the inference assumptions of quantitative analysis are more systematic and complete. If this is the case, then inferences to the "best" explanation become more

feasible. However, these ideas should be considered as preliminary and a source for further analysis, debate, and even possible rejection.

To show some of my thinking here, I begin with a basic framework and then comment and expand on it as I go along.

Let us suppose, as an example, that we are interested in a study looking at the possible relationship of SES and school achievement. While such a study could be either confirmatory (i.e., hypothesis testing) or exploratory (i.e., simply seeing whether the two variables are possibly related), we decide on the exploratory category. Let us further assume that the rationale for this choice is based on the fact (presumably) that not much is known about this topic theoretically or empirically.

Furthermore, let us assume that the variables involved have been satisfactorily operationalized and a representative sample has been drawn. Methodologically, we will use a measure of association, χ^2 (chi-square), that is appropriate here, although others could certainly be used. And, finally, let us assume that the association between the variables is statistically significant at $p < .05$.

The issue at this point is to consider whether anything else needs to be said and, if so, how to say it. In other words, the "logic" of integrating a *qualitative* perspective needs to be thought out, hopefully as a part of the total study, before it is undertaken. But what should such a rationale be, and where and how should it be included within the quantitative analysis? In a very basic sense, the qualitative analysis must be directed to some part of the quantitative analysis so that something

		SES		
		H	M	L
	H	(a)	(b)	(c)
School Achievement	L	(d)	(e)	(f)

Figure 15.1. Hypothetical Cross-Tabulation

more, different, or novel may be discovered and analyzed. That is, there must be the presumption that there is something more to the "story" than what is given by the quantitative portion of the study.

But what more is there to the story? Here, the researcher may encounter a dilemma. If the quantitative portion is conducted *because* it is believed to shed insight into the research question, then the qualitative is not needed or, at best, is artificially appended. However, if the qualitative is chosen in addition to the quantitative as a commitment to the *mixed methods* enterprise, then it must in some sense "compliment" the other. If it did not, then there would be no sense in doing it. Or, if it was done to somehow refute, disconfirm, or intentionally show the weakness of the other, then either there would be no point in doing mixed methods or its overall purpose would be drastically altered; it would now become a way of *falsifying* claims.

Operating here is already one version of the logic-of-choice problem. It is not so much a question of choosing among the large number of classifications as of asking "Why?" and "Why in *this* situation?" The choice for using the qualitative perspective must be thought through rather carefully. For example, is the qualitative analysis to serve some confirmatory or exploratory function? In the first, the qualitative analysis is a way of supporting the

original quantitative relationship, while the second suggests that there is *another* dimension beyond the quantitative that *ought* to be explored. A third dimension here may be called "emergent" and describes a situation in which a given statistical analysis is *not* statistically significant, but one then pursues the qualitative in some sense to "explain" why there was no statistical significance.

These and other related ideas can be illustrated further through Figure 15.1. This figure depicts the preceding example. Again, let us assume the chi-square relationship between the two variables is statistically significant and that we have decided to employ an open-ended interview schedule based on the assumption that beliefs children hold about schooling may be influenced by their perceptions of their own setting, situation, or environment (i.e., SES). It is also assumed that the interview schedule has been determined to possess validity (e.g., face, content, some form of construct) and that the *findings* will further be subject to "interpretive" validity checks (Maxwell, 1996).

In the form of analysis I am proposing, the qualitative design and analysis *supervenes* on the quantitative, with the further stipulation that it will do so (overall) only if the quantitative analysis is statistically significant. I will assume, then, that Figure 15.1 depicts this. The problem now becomes one of determining what to further analyze and why. That is, in chi-square analysis, an overall relationship is given, but *where* it is depends on the researcher's ability to examine the various "cells" of the table, that is, (a) through (f). But before this, the specific point I wish to make is how this design illustrates what I call the *placeholder effect.*

The placeholder effect uses the quantitative analysis not only to say something about the overall relationship of the variables but also as a specific *sample sorting* device to identify subgroups for further qualitative analysis. What I am trying to do is further specify and elaborate what Tashakkori and Teddlie (1998, p. 127, Table 6.3) labeled as "Forming groups of people/settings on the basis of QUAN data (e.g., cluster analysis), comparing the groups on qualitative data." Again, they included an asterisk indicating that this strategy needs further future development. My intent here is to illustrate not only how it can be developed further as a research strategy but, more important, how it can be used as a paradigm case for illustrating and discussing some of the broader issues that have been the subject of this chapter.

To return to the placeholder concept, the statistical strategy serves *most basically* as a means of dividing the sample into further subcategories for qualitative analysis. What is desired through the qualitative analysis is a deeper understanding of how and why the variables indicate what they do. The analysis is then basically one of forming *comparison groups.*

The qualitative analysis can also be viewed as a type of *second-order supervenience* on the comparison groups themselves. In other words, our qualitative analysis depends on how and why we form the comparison groups. The groups are "placeholders" in the sense that their *primary* function is simply to identify people on the "intersection" of selected attributes

they possess. The question of whether the placeholder effect can ultimately also be a type of causal effect is not pursued here.

When Figure 15.1 is further examined, one central issue becomes the determination of which comparison groups and why. Again, the logic-of-choice issue asserts itself, which comes down to the possibility of formulating rational "decision rules." I discuss the rules problem later in more depth, but one can already see it operating in the relatively simple diagram in Figure 15.1. The idea is to give due consideration, a priori, to what comparisons *ought* to be made, and this may translate into a "rule" saying that they *all* should be made. On the other hand, the rule may be one that directs the researcher to look at only those cells where, for instance, the percentage differences between observed and expected values appears to be large. I leave it to the readers to figure out all of the possible combinations (permutations?). A few are mentioned here just to illustrate what is involved.

◆ Perhaps (c) [low SES, high achievement] versus (d) [high SES, low achievement] to compare "extreme" cases

◆ Or (a) versus (d), or (a) versus (b) versus (c) to see possible variation by SES, but only for high achievement kids

Along with these logic-of-choice scenarios, there is also the continuing need to give some attention to *inference* issues. These may be more complex than originally thought. In general, from the qualitative perspective alone, it would seem most likely that some type of *enumerative induction* was being used here; we want to make a case that (hopefully) the students would be responding consistently to the questions asked and that differences in responses would reflect placeholder effect

		Self-Concept						
		H			SES	L		
		H	M	L		H	M	L
School Achievement	H	(a)	(b)	(c)		(g)	(h)	(i)
	L	(d)	(e)	(f)		(j)	(k)	(l)

Figure 15.2. Hypothetical Elaboration

differences. On the other hand, the IBE issue may present a different set of problems, but again, problems that should be thought about by the researcher as part of the overall mixed methods design. We basically want to explain why the relationship occurred between SES and school achievement. We are further assuming that in a mixed methods design of this type, a clearer picture may be obtained if we look qualitatively at placeholder comparison groups. The problem, however, is determining what comparisons are sufficient, and possibly necessary for explaining, to make the "best" inference case.

If, in trying to do this, we *claim* to be using some form of *eliminative induction,* it might imply that *all* placeholder combinations be examined and evaluated. Those remaining, or possibly the *one* remaining, would in principle be the IBE we are searching for. Of course, *how* this should be done is unclear, but it possibly could be accomplished, for example, by a series of interrater reliability judgments. Alternatively, the eliminative induction may consist of an a priori rule whereby the category (or categories) showing the largest percentage difference will be the deciding factor in making the IBE. The complexity of the emerging field of mixed methodology lies, I believe, in trying to handle some of these issues.

What happens, on the other hand, to our example of mixed methods when we include a third variable? Of course, *why* we would want to add one would depend on theoretical and other reasons. Let us assume that we have those reasons and decide to add the variable "self-concept" simply operationalized as "high" and "low." Figure 15.2 shows the relevant categories and subcategories.

I make the assumption that self-concept is an "intervening" variable. That is, one's SES may influence self-concept, which in turn may affect school achievement. We proceed by controlling for self-concept (e.g., percentage differences, chi-square, partial correlation), and indeed, when we do, the original relationship between SES and school achievement disappears or, at least, is significantly reduced. So, it would appear that the third variable is truly intervening. Now, as before, we are still claiming the supervenience condition and the same type of qualitative approach and analysis.

However, our placeholders have now doubled and with them all of the issues mentioned in reference to Figure 15.1. Notice the complexities involved in trying to decide what "comparison" groups should be chosen for further analysis. The qualitative methods are still supervening on the quantitative methods that generated the placeholder comparison groups, but now, while the supervenience claim is still (I believe) correct and the enumerative and eliminative strategies are at least possible in principle, the meaningfulness of the enterprise comes into question.

All of this may suggest that we need to start thinking more carefully about some type of possible "threshold effect" where either QUAN-QUAL or QUAL-QUAN, of whatever taxonomic type, should or should not be pursued. Here, it would seem that given the primacy of the quantitative to even begin doing mixed methods analysis, and even assuming a very basic quantitative model, one should not go beyond the two-variable case. Of course, as Tashakkori and Teddlie (1998) pointed out, all kinds of "add-on" or "ad hoc" possibilities can be (and often are) pursued. But neither those authors nor I believe that this is the way to pursue the emerging field. Again, to anticipate and prevent these types of ad hoc add-ons, a basic starting point remains, in my opinion, the supervenience notion. It is not a perfect notion and is one that is often difficult in its application, but its value lies in its function as a *focal point* in identifying and addressing the fundamental and basic issues of mixed methods approaches and designs.

INFERENCE REVISITED

While the issue of inference making in the field of mixed methods may seem far removed from the concerns of practicing researchers, there are fundamental issues of credibility and justification at stake. The type of inference structure used is reflected in the types of conclusions we make, which in turn is the very heart of *doing* research. The inference issue is of special interest in the mixed methods or models case simply because we are *using* a "mixed" approach. The question becomes

one of trying to discern what types of inference are taking place. Initially, three possibilities come to mind: (a) the inferences are different because the methods/models are different, (b) one method/model takes precedence in terms of inference, and (c) a new type of inference structure comes about from the very fact that we are using a new way of conducting research.

In the first option, the taxonomic classifications might include sequential mixed method, parallel/simultaneous mixed method, and equal status mixed method designs. As best as I can understand these approaches, they all involve or permit the application/use of separate types of analysis. The question is whether the interpretation of the findings is in some sense "equivalent." For example, in the parallel/simultaneous mixed methods example given by Tashakkori and Teddlie (1998, p. 47), teachers were given a closed-ended survey about their perceptions concerning the extent of school restructuring, while administrators' data were gathered through an open-ended interview format. The authors then stated that each data set was examined for instances of agreement or disagreement between the two samples.

Here we are faced with a number of inference issues. First, from the QUAN side, we would need to know something more about the usual issues of sampling and the validity and reliability of the survey items. Let us assume that the items produce "good" (e.g., .70 or above) reliability estimates. On the QUAL side, let us assume that a "credible" case has been made for the open-ended schedule by piloting it and arguing for some type of *judgmental validity* (Boyatzis, 1998).

But now the issue of inference becomes problematic. In the example, we are looking for agreement or disagreement between the two samples *on* the respective items, assuming that there is a correspondence between a given survey and an open-ended item. Although not perfectly clear, I assume that the inference is to the agreement by both approaches. If there is such agreement, then logically one could suggest that whatever the mode of inference associated with both methods, they are in some sense "equivalent" or "equally weighted" here. Of course, other complexities are possible; for instance, on the QUAL side, the justification for *saying* that a given item is so-and-so is to suggest that it is so because some *inductive* inference process (e.g., "member checks") has been applied.

The second possibility is that a given model or method has "inferential precedence" over another. Again, something like this seems to be implied in the dominant-less dominant method designs. And again, one example may be when a classical experimental design is the dominant strategy followed by a postexperimental interview. The term *dominance* could be understood, however, as "inferentially dominant" or simply as "stipulatively dominant." If it is the former, then indeed the researcher is claiming that the validity of the interpretation of the findings lies squarely with the superior inference-making procedure underlying the method. If it is the latter, then no real claim about inference dominance can be made. And in both instances, the less dominant is, by implication, the less inferentially powerful.

In my own notion of placeholder effects, for example, because I am assuming that all mixed methods efforts should begin with the QUAN side, I am giving priority to whatever inference forms belong to this perspective (or these perspectives).[1] The supervenience notion further reflects my belief that the QUAL "depends," in the preceding sense, on the inference process(es) of the QUAN perspective. In other words, the QUAN inferential process(es) "set the stage" for the subsequent QUAL

analysis. However, the "stage setting" is of a particular type; it sets the overall pattern, boundaries, and constraints of *where* the QUAL analysis is to take place. However, it does not rigidly set limits to what types of analyses *can* take place. To use an analogy from quantitative analysis, the placeholder effect does set the "degrees of freedom" for the qualitative analysis, but there is more than one degree of freedom available.

The placeholder idea, although proceeding in a given way (QUAN to QUAL), does not have the negative implication of "dominance." Importantly, the inference process(es) of both QUAN and QUAL have to be viewed as being in a particular relationship to one another. To use another analogy from the quantitative portion of the analysis, the placeholder effect sets the *boundaries* of the qualitative analysis but is then "held constant," with the expectation that the qualitative analysis can then "do its own thing."

Put this way, the inference process(es) on the qualitative side is (are) "dominant" in the sense that the inferences made and the *process* of making them have front stage. As mentioned, there are many approaches using the words *inference* and *induction*. In any case, the overall analysis will be richer and more complex; it will be *elaborated*.

These considerations bring us to the third possibility of trying to *uniquely* define the nature of inference for the mixed methods approaches. That is, given the overall *intent* of mixed methodology, which is rooted in the idea of *combination* itself, can there be an inference process or inference *type* that separately and uniquely characterizes the mixed methods case? I do not believe this is possible. But having said this, I do not mean to suggest that either the topic of inference itself or the continuing need to refine our thinking about how specific forms of inference shape our practices should be abandoned.

Returning to the *inference* issue itself, the *form* of the inference, based on Figures 15.1 and 15.2, may be as follows: (a) to the inspected category itself, for example, "Given the qualitative methods that I have used, I will infer that such-and-such is the interpretation of the high-achievement, low-SES, low-self-concept case"; (b) to another category comparison, for example, "Given that I have used qualitative techniques to compare the low-SES, high-achievement, low-self-concept case with the low-SES, high-achievement, high-self-concept case, I will infer such and such"; and (c) to the original hypothesis or to the original hypothesis with the third variable controlled, both determined quantitatively, for example, "Given my qualitative analysis of the high-achievement category with both the high- and low-SES categories, I can infer that in terms of the original hypothesis, such-and-such." As we can see, the inference type possibilities are complex and complicate the interpretation of the possibility of a *unique* type of inference by this process for a mixed methodology analysis.

The "interaction"-type inference process for mixed methods (of the preceding variety) is based on the premise that the particular type of qualitatively based inference "interacts" with, and only with, the subcategories generated by the QUAN process given *its* underlying inference assumptions. Thus, the term *interacts* refers to the fact that the qualitative analysis depends on and is constrained by the subcategories.[2]

There may be much more to say about the inference issues in mixed methods approaches, but I think the discussion here at least identifies some of the major problems and issues. However, another issue is still problematic and cuts across inference, logic-of-choice, and supervenience con-

cerns. That is the possibility of procedural rules.

RULES AND MIXED METHODS

Much of the preceding discussion has actually implied that one of the major issues in mixed methods and models is the lack of explicit selection and procedure rules. By this, I mean that it is difficult to determine how to *choose* a given taxonomic classification and, even if a choice is made, how to proceed from there. As Wittgenstein indicated in his famous question, "What is it to follow a rule?" (Kripke, 1982, pp. 90-91), the very idea of a rule and its "following" often raises deeper philosophical issues. For example, rule following implies that there *is* something to "follow." But what is being followed may range from arbitrary regulative-type rules (e.g., "Do not drive, here, on the left side of the road), which are imposed from without, to "constitutive" rules (e.g., chess, baseball playing), which "set" the rules by the very fact that the game is played in a certain way. And there are issues such as how and which "communities" form rules and how rules should be followed so as to "count" (Searle, 1995). Although the very idea of a rule is complex, for our purposes let us just stipulate the following: A rule consists of some rationally derived and applied set of procedures directed toward a rational explanation of some state of affairs.

The definition is only a rough guideline at best. However, in terms of what we are trying to analyze by way of mixed methods and models, it does suggest the need to use (or appeal to) *standards* by which to proceed and then to justify a given taxonomic *choice*. But what are these rules for the mixed methods case? Are they (if they even do exist) implicit or explicit? And in any case, what is their range of applica-

		Type	
		Substantive	Procedural
Mode	Implicit	(a)	(b)
	Explicit	(c)	(d)

Figure 15.3. Rule Classifications

tion; that is, does a given rule apply only to the "more dominant/less dominant" option or to all options in the same way? I do not pretend to have full and complete answers to these questions. What I am suggesting, however, is that they need to be given some thought.

One criticism of such an enterprise is that any such attempt is ad hoc; that is, definitions for rules are developed after the fact. However, this is not bad so long as the formulations are not arbitrary and unreasonable. At times, we can only proceed in this way given the amount of information and level of conceptualization existing at a particular time. Another criticism may be that the task is too difficult given that we are dealing with the supposed synthesis of different methods and models. Again, my view is that determining complexity is a first step in trying to sensibly critique the issues at stake.

What I would like to do in addressing these concerns is to first attempt some basic distinctions and then refer to my own example of placeholder effects for further analysis in terms of rules. Figure 15.3 illustrates some of these distinctions.

We have mentioned all along that in mixed methods approaches there appear to be factors that are implicit and explicit (or latent and manifest) in terms of different types and levels of analysis. For example, to use a previous example, Tashakkori and Teddlie's (1998, p. 93) use of the phrase *inferential consistency audit* (as modified from Lincoln & Guba's [1985]

confirmability audit) suggests that some types of inferential rules are implied here. The very use of the term *inferential* would be an *explicit* mention of this possibility, while the *implicit* would suggest that the type of inference might be either inductive or deductive. In Figure 15.3, I am simply saying that the implicit-explicit dimension seems to be relevant in an initial understanding of "rules" for the mixed methods case. Such implicit rules also seem to be more prevalent in the QUAL domain.

Figure 15.3 also suggests that rules may be described as "substantive" and "procedural." Of course, there are many other ways to describe rules, but this division at least seems relevant to mixed methods. Roughly, by a substantive rule, I mean a rule (i.e., a statement) that is fairly well-known, or can come to be known, by a variety of communities; directs thought or action in a particular way; and can include a range of other types such as "regulative" and "constitutive" at various levels of abstraction. I grant that this definition is fraught with all kinds of potential difficulties, but by the term *substantive* I mean something like the rules of inference (especially deductive) in logic, rules of grammar and syntax in natural languages, and rules of law such as the "hearsay" rule. Substantive rules are basic, generally imply a more abstract level of understanding, and have a fairly large domain of applicability.

Procedural rules, on the other hand, are more specific, are more limited, and *pri-*

marily focus on some notion of giving "directions" or "steps" to accomplish a task or arrive at a goal. Of course, a completely sharp distinction is often not possible because a procedural rule may be premised on a substantive one, and a substantive one may require procedural elements to arrive at its meaning. However, from the perspective of mixed methods or the conduct of research in the human sciences generally, what I have in mind is something like giving step-by-step (procedural) directions for computing the chi-square statistic versus the rules of inference underlying any statistical procedure or the underlying ideas of a "normal distribution" (substantive)—or, to use a related example, the difference between computing and looking up a statistical level of significance (procedural) and understanding the rules underlying the logic of hypothesis testing (substantive). In a rough sense, then, substantive rules tend to be *explanatory*, whereas procedural rules tend to be *descriptive*.

For the current purpose, however, I simply want to examine whether these distinctions may or may not be useful in the mixed methods case. If we return to Figure 15.3, Cell (a) (substantive implicit), would on the face seem to apply to quantitative analysis, whether of the QUAN-QUAL or QUAL-QUAN variety. I believe that the substantive rule case could be more persuasively made for QUAN in general. However, it seems that in the mixed methods approaches, these are implicit. It would seem, as a reasonable possibility, that they are implicit *because* there is a greater likelihood that they can be *retrieved* and made *explicit* if need be. The pure or mixed QUAL case seems closer to Cell (b) (implicit procedural). Our previous discussion of how the term *induction* is used in qualitative approaches would seem to indicate this. A strong version here would be to suggest that they are implicit *because* they are unsystematic on the pro-

cedural aspect. This may be too strong a claim, with a more plausible one being that they are mostly implicit because they are *procedurally diverse*.

In addition, Figure 15.3 points out *borderline* cases of various kinds. For example, in Cell (d) (explicit procedural), I would place, from the qualitative side alone, grounded theory (Strauss & Corbin, 1998). In grounded theory, there are many procedural aspects that appear to be, overall, systematic and explicit. On the other hand, Cell (c) (explicit substantive) does not seem to be characteristic of QUAN or QUAL, individually or in combination. As Figure 15.3 points out, for mixed methods analysis, the problem is similar to one of the inference types; namely, can mixed methods or designs be uniquely characterized *because* they are mixed methods or designs? In terms of *rules*, the issue is analogous; can there be a *unique* rule characterization of mixed methods and models designs? As mentioned in connection with supervenience, for example, consistently clear-cut examples are hard to find.

PLACEHOLDERS REVISITED

In the placeholder concept, I tried to make a case for a particular type (or option) of mixed methods. My claim was that the emerging field of mixed methods should be delineated by a primary focus on quantitative approaches followed by qualitative ones. I suggested that this procedure was more defensible than others because a somewhat more unique case could be made for supervenience and that this feature, in turn, would provide for a better procedural and interpretive rationale.

Having said this, however, is there a way to characterize this design from a rule-related point of view? And if so, could it be *uniquely* characterized in terms of rules? From the standpoint of rules, my choice of a QUAN approach, and specifically chi-square contingency analysis, would suggest Cell (a) (implicit substantive) and also Cell (d) (explicit procedural) in Figure 15.3. Because both Cells (a) and (d) can be laid out clearly, I believe they provide a better justification than for a QUAL approach.

I also argued for a specific supervenience approach, the qualitative supervening on the quantitative. However, because the supervenience relationship is, at least partially, a "dependence" one, I would suggest that the qualitative aspect must make a clear case for its quantitative counterpart in terms of Cells (a) and (d) in Figure 15.3. That is, the case for the *uniqueness* of a mixed methods rule-related justification should lie in its "matching" between the quantitative and the qualitative. The matching need not be in type but may be in kind; that is, for Cell (a), the qualitative component must be shown to possess, or be able to possess in principle, a "substantive" rule. In general, whatever combination (in Figure 15.3) is given by QUAN needs to be followed up in an analogous way by QUAL.

Because implicit procedural rules seem to be the norm at this time, it may be that we need to more fully develop such rules in a similar way as, and as a compliment to what, Tashakkori and Teddlie (1998) have done. Put differently, the existing taxonomic classifications might suggest corresponding *explicit* procedural rules. I would like to explore this possibility briefly.

MIXED METHODS AND PROCEDURAL RULES

Although the logic-of-choice issue remains for the field of mixed methodology, it perhaps can be reconfigured to some degree under the title *logic-of-procedures*. As mentioned previously, the logic-of-choice involves the determination, among an extensive and large number of taxonomic possibilities, of how a researcher should choose any particular one. Can this be done?

To do so would require a narrowing of the idea of a procedural rule to a series of very specific "steps" one follows to undertake the research design. If these procedural rules have a "logic" built into them, as implied by their name, then they can be at least partially justified on criteria that are not completely ad hoc. The downside is that the degree of specificity may be so great that the "rules" become tedious and perhaps trivial. What I am suggesting is some type of explicit approach that guides the researcher as to how to proceed given any particular mixed methods or models choice.

How would such procedural rules work? Again, it is a matter of trying to impose some type of "rational constraint" so that the element of choice is preserved without sacrificing the need for rigor. Without some notion of rational constraint, the problem of justification for any chosen mixed method or model combination becomes problematic. As I indicated previously, the justification *could* come (especially for qualitative analysis) in the form of "explanatory narratives" discussing why a particular application was chosen and how it works in a given research situation. I still believe this should be done, especially in thinking through inference issues—particularly IBE issues—in either a *public* or a *private* format, with the former being directed toward explanations within the research study itself and the latter being capable of being accessed "on call" if so required.

The current discussion, however, concerns the possibility of an *initial constraint*, or an *initial rationale*, for engaging in mixed methodological analysis. It is difficult to specify such constraints completely, but a few are put forth here for additional discussion. Starting from all of those possibilities that begin with a QUAN emphasis (and this remains my personal preference), and generally for both confirmatory and exploratory approaches, two constraints would be sampling and statistical significance.[3] A strong constraint on sampling would be to require an appropriate *probability* sampling strategy. Another constraint (and I believe it is an important one) would be to *require* statistical significance (e.g., at the "conventional" .05 level) as a *precondition* for continuing the mixed methods process. This constraint, in effect, sets a threshold that must be met, and meeting it implies that a presumed important relationship has been established beyond chance. It is a signal to the researcher to "go ahead" with the mixed methods analysis. What happens after that, qualitatively, does need additional and separate justification; but this stage does not occur in the absence of statistical significance.

In those cases where the QUAL perspective predominates, the constraints are minimal. This may or may not be desirable depending on the nature of the research. However, when the quantitative aspect is added, there are generally no rules to assist here. For example, if the qualitative data are to be transformed *into* quantitative representations, then some of the very uniqueness of the qualitative-as-qualitative aspect is lost; so then, as mentioned earlier, why even bother with the qualitative? It seems that a specific logic-of-procedure faces similar problems as does the logic-of-choice. Again, my own feeling is that a minimally acceptable procedural rule case can be made only in those instances where mixed methods approaches make a clear and overt commitment to the primacy of the quantitative.

This position does not diminish the importance of the qualitative in any way. What it does say is that if mixed methods as a field of study is to survive deeper scrutiny, it needs a framework where *some* consistent justification can be made in terms of the issues of inference, logic-of-choice, supervenience, and rules. Currently, I believe that the quantitative gives us a better grasp of a minimal threshold that we have to reach. But these "constraints" *are* rather minimal, if necessary. As I described earlier in the placeholder effects discussion, once the categories for analysis are set, the possibilities for qualitative analysis are broad and potentially far-reaching. The more important overall point, however, is the need for the field itself to ask and discuss what I consider to be these very basic and fundamental questions.

I would like to conclude this chapter by returning to some of the *ontological* issues raised by mixed methodological approaches. I mentioned earlier that such approaches could find some justification in the *minimal realist* position, but some additional clarification is needed. The issue is important because mixed methods are positing a new and different epistemological stance or "paradigm." Even if, as I mentioned previously, a given ontological stance does not entail a given epistemological position, the mixed methods paradigm does say something about both. What I think it "says" is briefly discussed in what follows.

CAUTIOUSLY OPTIMISTIC PRAGMATISM

In their comprehensive overview of the epistemological and ontological issues that relate to mixed methods and models, Tashakkori and Teddlie (1998, pp. 26-30) concluded that some form of pragmatism may be the most credible *epistemological* justification for this field. I think that they labeled their position "cautiously optimistic" because they sensed that it is difficult to make definitive judgments about different and competing epistemological positions. On the other hand, the term *cautious* may suggest that mixed methods and models *do* give us alternatives to viewing what *research* as a form of epistemological enterprise attempts to do—give us plausible interpretations of behaviors and actions (Cherryholmes, 1992).

There are difficulties and complexities with all theories of "truth" (this is what epistemology is about), theories of "existence" (ontology), and the relationship between the two. As I mentioned in the beginning of this chapter, one very general defense for mixed methods and models would lie in the observation that, first, minimal realism would be a plausible possibility for this field and, second, that (in any case) the ontological position would not imply (and therefore not rule out) some type of epistemological stance.

There is not sufficient space here to assess the many ontological and epistemological arguments that might apply to mixed methods and models. For instance, on the epistemological side, there are many objections to the viability of pragmatism as a theory of truth but also some possibilities for a type of limited acceptability with some versions of "correspondence" theories (Schmitt, 1995, pp. 78-97). Ontologically, besides the minimal realism possibility (Lynch, 1998, esp. chap. 5), there is the important related issue of the status of "social facts" or the kinds of "things" we attempt to study in the human sciences. Here, the ontological issue concerns the "reality" of such entities. Moser (1993, pp. 21-24), for instance, indicated that there is a "strong" and a "weak" position concerning which features of "reality" are "conceiving-independent." The strong realist position on the conceiving-independent feature would be the claim that there is reality that exists independently of us. The weak position would be that there are other features of reality (i.e., social facts) that exist independently of us in virtue of the fact that while "we" formulate them, we do not have to constantly refer back to this condition.

I mention these points to illustrate that there are other issues of ontological and epistemological significance that are related in complex ways to the mixed methods and models case. One way to view this complexity is to notice, for example, that the ideas of a research question, methodology, and possible ontology are often conflated. That is, while these factors are related, they are often not seen as individual elements that then become parts of an interactive process. In saying this, I am not arguing for a strict form of "constructivism" that would hold that all of our notions of reality are simply "constructed" by us (for criticisms of this position, see Bunge, 1996; Goldman, 1999; Searle, 1995). Rather, I want to point out that mixed methods and models *do* involve us in ontological issues and commitments of various kinds.

What may be such commitments? To begin with, we often forget the important relation of a *research question* to some (often implicit) type of ontological commitment. For instance, in our earlier example where we claimed some possible relation between SES and school achievement, our beliefs include the "existence" of such entities and that they "correspond" in some way to an independently existing reality. The important point often overlooked is that the research question posits not only the possible existence of these entities individually but also that they "exist" in a unique way—as a relation that may be associational and possibly causal and also consisting of a possible "strength." That is, our *research methods* are the epistemological claims we make concerning not only the possibility of a "reality" but also a particular way in which reality can be configured and described. The research question, then, is a way of configuring an "ontological landscape" in a particular way and then arguing that it is, is not, or is to a certain degree or extent the way we believe it to be. Our notions about "statistical significance" illustrate this; we assume not only that our ontological landscape is the way we say it is but also that there is a pretty good chance it *is* in this particular way.

Now, when we come to mixed methods and models, we can see that they are involved in potentially quite complex epistemological and ontological claims. The major issue is whether the *findings* of mixed methods approaches constitute a *unique* ontological claim. Do they characterize "reality" in a way that is truthful yet different from other ways of coming to know? In my view, this is the central underlying claim of mixed methods and models; otherwise, what would be the point of engaging in such a practice?

There are a number of ways of thinking about this issue. Contrary to what one might initially believe, it is *not* the range of taxonomic classifications that is central. For example, in principle, one may equally choose to begin with a QUAN/QUAL as with a QUAL/QUAN approach. I have given my reasons for preferring the former, but this does not necessarily mean that my construal of the ontological landscape is "better" than the former. I may believe it to be, and hopefully it is, but it may be some other way. Thus, for instance, an analysis of variance design cannot in principle be said to represent reality better than a correlational one, nor can a grounded theory approach be said to represent reality better than an analytic inductive one.

However, the implied uniqueness of mixed methods and models lies in the fact that they *do*, presumably, give us in some

sense both a different and a more unique ontological picture. Again, for various mixed methods and models versions, one can argue that a given version is "stronger" or "weaker" because of some issue such as "inferential adequacy," the implication being that if a given mixed option is stronger in terms of type and clarity of its inferential process(es), then it may be more ontologically credible as well. And indeed it may be, but the point is as follows: Does any mixed method or model become more "credible" in virtue of its *being* a mixed method or model?

At this stage in the development of this emerging field, I do not believe that a clear answer can be given. However, a clear answer perhaps can never be given, not because it is impossible for mixed methods or models to do so but rather because this (ontological) issue is one that characterizes the nature of social science research in general.

In conclusion, I believe that among all of the issues I have tried to address here, the *central* one for mixed methods and models remains this ontological one. At this time, a partial but broadly satisfactory response to it may lie in the acceptance of two assumptions: first, that an external independent (social) reality exists and can in principle be accessed by mixed methods and, second, that this reality may be consistent with the idea that it may have *multiple characterizations*. This is, after all, why we are doing, for pragmatist or other reasons, mixed methods and models research.

■ *Notes*

1. To clarify this point somewhat more, the *process* of making inferences permeates the whole enterprise of mixed methods approaches and designs. First, in terms of the placeholder concept, I am suggesting that the inferential processes associated with QUAN approaches

be acknowledged as central because they are better developed in terms of methods that display these processes. Second, once the initial case is made for the placeholder, the inference process takes two additional forms. First, given the inference process underlying the legitimacy of the finding that, in the example, SES and achievement *are* related, we can *infer* further that the categories associated with the two variables are "valid." Second, the inference processes associated with the QUAL must (now) come into play as those associated with methods and those associated with the relationship of data to findings.

2. Another way of putting this would be to say that the qualitative perspective "interacts" with those subcategories generated by the quantitative perspective.

3. Of course, parallel designs might not apply here, especially those that conduct *separate* QUAN/QUAL analyses on data subsets. My point, however, is that I believe in only those mixed methods approaches that give priority to the QUAN in a QUAN-QUAL supervenience relationship.

■ *References*

Audi, R. (Ed.). (1999). *The Cambridge dictionary of philosophy* (2nd ed.). Cambridge, MA: Cambridge University Press.

Barker, S. F. (1989). *The elements of logic* (5th ed.). New York: McGraw-Hill.

Boyatzis, R. E. (1998). *Thematic analysis and code development: Transforming qualitative information.* Thousand Oaks, CA: Sage.

Bunge, M. (1996). *Finding philosophy in social science.* New Haven, CT: Yale University Press.

Cherryholmes, C. C. (1992). Notes on pragmatism and scientific realism. *Educational Researcher, 21*(6), 13-17.

Eisner, E. W. (1998). *The enlightened eye: Qualitative inquiry and enhancement of educational practice.* Upper Saddle River, NJ: Prentice Hall/Merrill.

Freeman, D. (1983). *Margaret Mead and Samoa: The making and unmaking of an anthropological myth.* Cambridge, MA: Harvard University Press.

Goldman, A. I. (1999). *Knowledge in a social world.* Oxford, UK: Clarendon.

Kim, J. (1992). Multiple realization and the meta-physics of reduction. *Philosophy and Phenomenological Research, 52,* 1-26.

Krathwohl, D. R. (1993). *Methods of educational and social research.* New York: Longmans.

Kripke, S. A. (1982). *Wittgenstein: On rules and private language.* Cambridge, MA: Harvard University Press.

Lincoln, Y. S., & Guba, E. G. (1985). *Naturalistic inquiry.* Beverly Hills, CA: Sage.

Lipton, P. (1993). *Inference to the best explanation.* London: Routledge.

Little, D. (1991). *Varieties of social explanation: An introduction to the philosophy of social science.* Boulder, CO: Westview.

Lynch, M. P. (1998). *Truth in context: An essay on pluralism and objectivity.* Cambridge, MA: MIT Press.

Manicas, P. Z., & Kruger, A. N. (1976). *Logic: The essentials.* New York: McGraw-Hill.

Martin, R. M. (1997). *Scientific thinking.* Toronto: Broadview.

Mautner, T. (Ed.). (1999). *Dictionary of philosophy.* London: Penguin.

Maxwell, J.A. (1996). *Qualitative research designs: An interpretive approach.* Thousand Oaks, CA: Sage.

Miles, M., & Huberman, M. (1994). *Qualitative data analysis: An expanded sourcebook* (2nd ed.). Thousand Oaks, CA: Sage.

Miller, S. I. (1994). Evidence as an idealized cognitive model. *Social Epistemology, 8*(2), 163-165.

Moser, P. K. (1993). *Philosophy after objectivity: Making sense in perspective.* New York: Oxford University Press.

Nachmias, D., & Nachmias, C. (1981). *Research methods in the social sciences* (2nd ed.). New York: St. Martin's.

Patton, M. (1990). *Qualitative evaluation and research methods* (2nd ed.). Newbury Park, CA: Sage.

Phillips, D. C. (1987). *Philosophy, science, and social inquiry: Contemporary methodolog-*

ical controversies in social science and related applied fields of research. New York: Pergamon.

Popper, K. R. (1959). *The logic of scientific discovery.* New York: Basic Books.

Rappaport, S. (1996). Inference to the best explanation: Is it really different from Mills' methods? *Philosophy of Science, 63,* 65-80.

Schmitt, F. F. (1995). *Truth: A primer.* Boulder, CO: Westview.

Searle, J. (1995). *The construction of social reality.* New York: Free Press.

Smith, J. K. (1983). Quantitative versus qualitative research: An attempt to clarify the issue. *Educational Researcher, 12,* 6-13.

Smith, J. K. (1994). An opportunity lost? In L. Heshusius & K. Ballard (Eds.), *From positivism to interpretivism and beyond: Tales of transformation in educational and social research* (pp. 161-168). New York: Teachers College Press.

Smith, J. K., & Heshusius, L. (1986). Closing down the conversation: The end of the quantitative-qualitative debate among educational researchers. *Educational Researcher, 15,* 4-12.

Sober, E. (1999). The multiple realizability argument against reductionism. *Philosophy of Science, 66,* 542-564.

Strauss, A., & Corbin, J. (1998). *Basics of qualitative research: Techniques and procedures for developing grounded theory.* Thousand Oaks, CA: Sage.

Tashakkori, A., & Teddlie, C. (1998). *Mixed methodology: Combining qualitative and quantitative approaches* (Applied Social Research Methods, No. 46). Thousand Oaks, CA: Sage.

16

MAKING INFERENCES IN MIXED METHODS: THE RULES OF INTEGRATION

◆ **Christian Erzberger**
Udo Kelle

The purpose of this chapter is to discuss different ways in which the outcomes of qualitative and quantitative studies may be related to each other in a meaningful way and to derive crucial "rules of integration" for qualitative and quantitative research results from these considerations. Questions concerning the relation between qualitative and quantitative outcomes often arise in research projects in which mixed methods designs are applied by gathering and analyzing qualitative and quantitative data separately. As a consequence of ongoing "paradigm wars," researchers often have difficulties

in finding advice in the methodological literature about how logical relations between qualitative and quantitative research results can be developed and how theoretical propositions can be based on a synthesis of the outcomes of qualitative and quantitative research. Social scientists who write methodological texts often have strong ties with and loyalties to a certain methodological "camp"; sometimes they are even "paradigm warriors" (for this term, see Tashakkori & Teddlie, 1998) who regard the different epistemological positions that they see as the foundations of qualitative and quantitative

AUTHORS' NOTE: Many thanks go to Vicki May for revising our English.

research methods as fully incompatible (see Blaikie, 1991; Lincoln & Guba, 1985; Smith, 1983).

Although since the 1930s a considerable number of social studies, among them the "Hawthorne Study" (Roethlisberger & Dickson, 1939) and the *Marienthalstudie* (an investigation of Austrian unemployed workers shortly after the Great Depression [Jahoda, Lazarsfeld, & Zeisel, 1933/1982]), have been carried out combining qualitative and quantitative methods, it is still difficult to obtain methodological advice on how qualitative and quantitative findings can be related to each other so as to allow valid inferences. This may be due to the fact that paradigm warriors often restrict their arguments to general epistemological ideas on the nature of reality (emphasizing, e.g., that there are "multiple realities"), whereas "pacifists" or "integrationists" (e.g., Brannen, 1992; Bryman, 1988; Creswell, 1994; Tashakkori & Teddlie, 1998) have mainly developed methodological guidelines for method integration and regard theoretical and substantive aspects as a matter to be decided according to the requirements of each respective research project.

Any serious methodological consideration within the context of any science should examine the nature of the phenomenon under investigation first and only then address the question as to which method may adequately describe, explain, or understand this phenomenon. This is especially true so far as the relation between qualitative and quantitative research results is concerned, for in order to understand the specific logic of reasoning that has to be applied when theoretical concepts are developed or tested by combining qualitative and quantitative results, one would have to link *methodological* and *epistemological* arguments to *theoretical* considerations concerning the social domain in question. Rather than holding

methodological discussions on a purely abstract level, it is more helpful to link methodological with substantial considerations by examining the usefulness of methodological concepts with the help of examples from research practice.

We shall, therefore, evaluate a general methodological concept for the integration of research results, known as "triangulation," with the help of several examples from empirical social research practice. We first summarize some of the discussions surrounding this notion, thereby demonstrating that the term, initially borrowed from the field of trigonometry for use in quantitative psychological research, carries systematic ambiguities when applied in the realm of method integration. We then discuss different understandings of the triangulation metaphor: triangulation in its original trigonometrical sense and its use in the methodological debate in the social sciences, where triangulation is understood by some authors as an attempt at mutual validation, while it is seen by others as a means to combine different theoretical perspectives on a phenomenon under investigation. Each of these understandings has its own merit, showing different possibilities for relating qualitative and quantitative results to each other. However, none of these concepts may serve as a general methodological model for this purpose. In the third section, we try to specify certain aspects of the triangulation metaphor so as to achieve a more precise understanding of how different research results can be related to each other. In the fourth section, we use these specifications to describe and discuss outcomes from three empirical studies that combined qualitative and quantitative panels. Each of these examples represents a certain "paradigm"[1] for the relation between qualitative and quantitative research results; such results may either *converge, supplement, or contradict* each other. These three possibilities are discussed in detail, and on this basis in the fifth section we describe the basic forms of logical inference that play a role in triangulating convergent, complementary, and divergent findings from qualitative and quantitative research. In the sixth section, we try to develop some more general methodological and logical rules for the integration of qualitative and quantitative research results from the previous discussion.

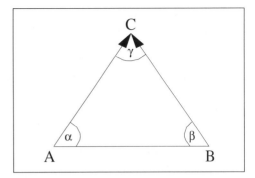

Figure 16.1. Triangulation in Land Surveying

◆ Triangulation: A Methodological Metaphor

Since the 1970s, *triangulation* has been a popular term in the methodological debate surrounding mixed methodology (see Denzin, 1978; Fielding & Fielding, 1986; Flick, 1991, 1992, 1998; Lamnek, 1995). If one takes a closer look at its original meaning in navigation and land surveying, one soon realizes that this notion loses much of its clarity when transferred to the realm of social science methodology; there it changes from a distinct mathematical concept with a clear meaning to a metaphor with a broad semantic field. In its original meaning, triangulation is a method for determining the yet unknown position of a certain spatial point (C) through measurement operations from two known points, A and B. Using well-known trigonometrical laws for the calculation of the angles and sides of a triangle, it is easily possible to determine the spatial position of C if other quantities are given (see Figure 16.1).[2]

To calculate the distances AC and BC, by which the spatial position of the point C can be determined, one first has to measure the distance AB. After that, one must determine the angle α that originates from drawing a line from the end point A of the

leg AB to the point C as well as the angle β that originates from drawing the line between B and C. Because the sum of angles in a triangle amounts to 180 degrees, one can easily determine the angle γ by calculating the residual $180 - (\alpha + \beta)$ and afterward calculating the lengths of AC and BC, respectively, with the help of the known mathematical sine laws.

In the methodological debate in the social sciences, the term *triangulation* has acquired two different meanings—both of them remote from its original trigonometrical understanding. During the 1950s, the term was used for the first time to describe a research strategy that employs different measurement operations or empirical results to answer a certain research question. In the context of a theory of psychological testing, Campbell and Fiske (1959) proposed to supplement or to further test empirical results by the use of different instruments. According to these authors, "multitrait-multimethod matrices" should be constructed using correlation coefficients between scores obtained through different tests. These matrices should then serve as a means to determine the degree of convergence as an indicator for the validity of research results: "Validation is typically convergent, a confirmation by independent measurement procedures" (p. 81).

In their book about unobtrusive measures, Webb and his colleagues picked up Campbell and Fiske's idea and transferred it to a broader methodological framework (see Webb, Campbell, Schwartz, & Sechrest, 1966), arguing that the collection of data from different sources and their analysis using different strategies would improve the validity of results: "Ideally, we should like to converge data from several different data classes, as well as converge with multiple variants from within a single class" (p. 35). This idea was picked up by a dedicated advocate of qualitative methods in social research. In his famous monograph *The Research Act*, Denzin (1978) used the argument of Webb and colleagues that a hypothesis that had survived a series of tests with different methods could be regarded as more valid than a hypothesis tested only with the help of a single method. Because different methods entail different weaknesses and strengths, Denzin opted for "methodological triangulation," which consists of a "complex process of playing each method off against the other so as to maximize the validity of field efforts" (p. 304), leading to a reduction of "threats to internal and external validity" (p. 308).

The idea of supplementing qualitative research by the application of statistical methods so as to further validate findings was certainly not new. As early as 1928, Thomas and Thomas (1928/1970), two of the founding parents of the qualitative tradition, had maintained,

We are of the opinion that verification, through statistics, is an important process in most of the fields of study of human behavior. . . . What is needed is continual and detailed study of case-histories and life-histories . . . along with the available statistical studies, to be used as a basis for the inferences drawn. (p. 570) . . . Statistics becomes, then, the continuous process of verification. As it becomes possible to transmute more and more data to quantitative form and apply statistical methods, our inferences will become more probable and have a sounder basis. But the statistical results must always be interpreted in the confirmation of the as yet unmeasured factors and the hypothesis emerging from the study of cases must, whenever possible, be verified statistically. (p. 571)

The idea that the convergence of the results of different measurement operations would enhance the validity of research findings led to the adoption of the term *triangulation* in the methodological debate in the social sciences. Such a meaning was clearly not implied by the usual trigonometrical understanding of this word, which was that two operations of measurement (to establish the angles α and β) and one known quantity (the leg AB) are necessary for the localization of the point C. With one of these components of triangulation missing, it would no longer be possible to find the position of C. After determining the angle α, the second operation of measurement providing knowledge about β could be regarded not as a verification or validation of the first measurement operation but rather as one of the necessary prerequisites for determining the spatial position of C. In contrast to methodological triangulation in social research, one single measurement operation would not lead to a certain (either true or false) result that could then be subjected to verification through further measurement; it would not yield any useful result whatsoever (apart from the size of a certain angle that itself does not provide any information about the quantities in question—the lengths of AC and BC).

The concept of triangulation as a means of verification or mutual validation has also been criticized as being inadequate by many authors (see, e.g., Fielding & Fielding, 1986; Flick, 1991, 1992, 1998; Lamnek, 1995; Rossman & Wilson, 1985, 1994). With the growing reputation of qualitative methods during the 1980s, the idea gained acceptance that different methods of social research can be based on different epistemological concepts and can relate to different empirical phenomena and that it thus may be difficult to simply compare research results acquired by means of different methods so as to check their validity. Fielding and Fielding (1986), for example, emphasized that researchers may misinterpret commonalties and differences between data collected using incompatible methods by falsely assuming "a common epistemic framework among data sources" (p. 31). Consequently, "using several different methods can actually increase the chance of error" (p. 31).

Also, other critics of Denzin's (1978) approach (e.g., Bryman, 1988, p. 133; Hammersley & Atkinson, 1983, p. 199) have rejected the assumption that a mere convergence of research results has to be interpreted as a sign of validity. This problem was already relevant for Campbell and Fiske's (1959) original concept of triangulation through multitrait-multimethod matrices. Although there may be strong correlations between the results of tests, these may occur because the tests are biased in a similar way, so that the convergence between two research results can be the result of the fact either that both results are *right* or that they are *wrong in the same way*. Research methods are often developed within differing research traditions, each with its own epistemological and theoretical assumptions. Thus, the combination of methods may add "breadth or depth to our analysis" (Fielding & Fielding, 1986, p. 33) but might not lead to more valid results. A potential *complementarity* of qualitative and quantitative research methods has been empha-

sized by others, among them Flick (1998), who came to the following conclusion: "Triangulation is less a strategy for validating results and procedures than an alternative to validation . . . which increases scope, depth, and consistency in methodological proceedings" (p. 230).

This view stimulated a further understanding of triangulation: The use of different methods to investigate a certain domain of social reality can be compared with the examination of a physical object from two different viewpoints or angles. Both viewpoints provide different pictures of this object that might not be useful to validate each other but that might yield a fuller and more complete picture of the phenomenon concerned if brought together. To use another metaphor: Empirical research results obtained with different methods are like the pieces of a jigsaw puzzle that provide a full image of a certain object if put together in the correct way.

As with the concept of triangulation as a means of mutual validation, the idea of combining methods to produce a "fuller" or "more complete" picture also differs from the original mathematical understanding of triangulation. The trigonometrical context from which the term *triangulation* comes would suggest a far more restrictive understanding of method integration. Because the location of a certain point requires different measurement operations, one single observation (determining, e.g., only the angle α) would lead not only to an incomplete or partial result but to no result at all if the aim were to establish the length of the distances between C and A and between C and B.

Hence, the transfer of the notion of triangulation from trigonometry to the realm of mixed methods research seemed to have transformed it into a somewhat fuzzy idea with a variety of possible meanings. Whereas the term represents a straightforward concept in its initial frame of reference, it carries a systematic ambiguity when transferred to the domain of social research methods. Triangulation may be considered for the *mutual validation* of methods and research results so as to identify "threats to validity," or it may be seen as a means to produce a more complete and "fuller" picture of the social phenomena under study. Furthermore, if one wishes to retain the original meaning used in land surveying and navigation for the term *triangulation,* then one could regard triangulation of qualitative and quantitative methods even as a necessary prerequisite for any theoretical explanation based on empirical data given that, in trigonometrical triangulation, the result of a single measurement operation is useless if no further calculations are carried out.

At least a part of this terminological confusion may be due to the fact that the term *triangulation* has been transferred from one frame of reference to another without defining the meaning of its different components within the new framework. To compare the process by which a certain point in a landscape is determined through different measurement operations with the process by which results obtained using different sociological methods are related to each other, it first has to be clarified how terms such as "spatial position of a point" and "distance between two points" can be understood within the context of empirical social research.

◆ Triangulation Between the Theoretical and the Empirical Level of Reasoning

From the preceding discussion, it should have become clear that triangulation cannot be considered as a single unique method but instead should be considered as a methodological metaphor with different possible meanings that can be related to a variety of problems and tasks. To make use of such a metaphor within the discipline of social sciences, one has to specify the meaning of the geometrical figure of a triangle within our special frame of reference (which is theoretical reasoning based on the results of empirical social research). To retain the trigonometrical image of measuring angles, one would at least need an idea about what the points of a triangle and its sides may stand for in the context of social research. To describe different possible consequences of method triangulation, we define the components of the triangulation triangle in the following way: The *points* of the triangle shall represent *propositions* or *statements,* whereas the *lines* between points—the sides of the triangle—shall stand for *logical relations* between these propositions.

With regard to the propositions or statements, it will be necessary to differentiate between general theoretical propositions, on the one hand, and empirical observation statements ("basic sentences" in the sense that Karl Popper used the term [see Popper, 1934/1989, p. 17 ff.]), on the other. Empirical observation statements may be the results of empirical investigations of all kinds and relate to different types of social phenomena. They may represent single events (e.g., a certain couple splitting up, a certain person losing his or her job) or statistical phenomena (e.g., the divorce rate among people of a specific social group in a certain year, an unemployment rate). Theoretical statements are all kinds of abstract propositions that are formulated within a certain scientific community so as to understand and/or explain such empirical phenomena. The whole set of all theoretical statements of a science, on the one hand, and the whole set of empirical observation statements formulated on the basis of methodologically controlled research, on the other, can be regarded as two distinct levels of knowledge that can be logically related to each other. To make use of the triangulation metaphor, it will be helpful to imagine these two levels—the level of theories and the level of empirical knowledge—as "maps" that should under no circumstances be confused with the real "landscape" they represent. Like geographical maps produced with the help of land surveying, "scientific maps" (whether empirical or theoretical) may contain errors and inconsistencies, they may be imprecise in many regards, and they have to be constantly revised so as to keep track of the various changes that take place in the real world.

As Popper has maintained in a famous and impressive figurative idea, the bold constructions of scientific theory do not rest on a firm and solid empirical rock but instead rest on pillars that are lowered from above into swampy ground (see Popper, 1934/1989, p. 75 ff.). Every part of scientific knowledge—not only theoretical ideas but also "basic sentences" formulated on the basis of direct empirical observations—is falsifiable and thus a potential starting point for further investigation. Consequently, the empirical as well as the theoretical level of scientific knowledge consists of more or less secure knowledge and insights that may be rejected or modified (leading to the "redrawing" of the corresponding parts of the map).

The currently accepted scientific knowledge (the parts shaded gray in Figure 16.2) nevertheless serves as a starting point for new scientific inquiries and discoveries. However, the production of such scientific knowledge always requires the connection between theoretical and empirical knowledge. Using the proposed model, one would have to establish links between the theoretical and empirical "maps." Figure 16.2 illustrates this process: Two statements about empirical phenomena (the two points at the base of the triangle) are linked through a logical relation (marked by a line) and are also logically connected with the theoretical level.

Following an idea of Hempel, one may say that the theoretical level "hangs" above the level of empirical observation (see Hempel, 1952, p. 36) and at the same time is connected with this level through various "strings of interpretation." Starting from certain empirical data, it is possible to go up to a certain point of a theoretical network using such a string. One can reach further points of the theoretical network by using definitions and hypotheses, and one can descend to the level of empirical observation by another string of interpretation.

The triangle displayed in Figure 16.2, of course, represents only one single way of illustrating such relations between the two levels of knowledge. However, to keep our model as straightforward as possible, we stay with these simple geometrical figures for the illustration of the relations between theoretical and empirical statements. To illustrate some of the basic problems of theory formulation, we define the "strings of interpretation" mentioned by Hempel more precisely as *logical relations* or *logical inferences* between propositions. Since the times of Aristotle, philosophers have distinguished between two central modes of logical inference:[3]

◆ Logical inferences by which general theoretical statements are formulated on the basis of empirical observation statements are called *inductions* or *inductive inferences*. Social scientists may, for instance, inductively infer from a certain statistical phenomenon, such as a high divorce rate among members of a certain minority observed in a national survey, a general sociological rule that members of stigmatized or oppressed groups stand a higher risk of experiencing stressful family relations.

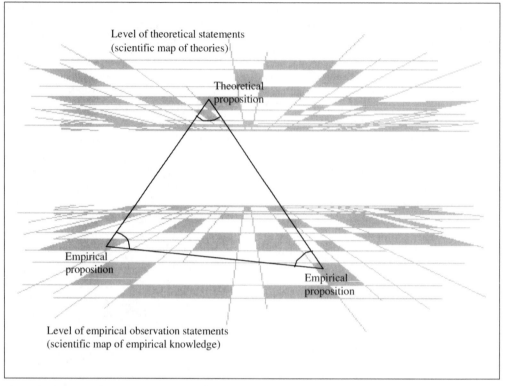

Level of theoretical statements
(scientific map of theories)

Theoretical
proposition

Empirical
proposition

Empirical
proposition

Level of empirical observation statements
(scientific map of empirical knowledge)

Figure 16.2. Connections Between the Theoretical and Empirical Levels of Knowledge in Empirical Sciences

◆ Logical inferences by which statements about single empirical phenomena are derived from general rules or theoretical statements are called *deductions* or *deductive inferences*. A social scientist may, for instance, deduce from a general theory of class conflict certain events that she or he expects to take place in societies with certain attributes without having information about any empirical data whatsoever.

Following the differentiation between inductive and deductive reasoning, two general methodological models of research processes can be identified that are usually connected with two different strands or camps in epistemology (see Kelle, 1998, pp. 111-114). *Inductivist models* regard research in the empirical sciences as an inductive process that starts with the collection of empirical observations and then proceeds by developing general rules out of the patterns or structures found in the empirical material. This model of the process of empirical research was popular in the early days of modern natural sciences during the 17th and 18th centuries. The idea that the only legitimate theories were those that could be inductively derived by simple generalization from observable data was originally developed by empiricist philosophers such as Locke and Bacon. Later, during the 19th and 20th centuries, modern forms of inductivism, such as the "logical positivism" of the Vienna Circle, were criticized as representing a naive tabula rasa concept of human knowledge. Beginning with Kant, rationalist philosophers have argued that a researcher is capable of structuring the chaos of sense data only if a certain theoretical framework is already available before empirical observations are made. This crucial epistemological problem of inductivism has been discussed during recent decades under the heading of the so-called "*theory-ladenness of observation*" (see Hanson, 1952/1965). Nowadays, one of the most crucial and widely accepted insights of contemporary epistemology is the fact that "there are and can be no sensations unimpregnated by expectations" (Lakatos, 1982, p. 15). This philosophical critique of inductivism highlights the role of prior theoretical knowledge that provides researchers with the necessary categorical tools for structuring their observed data (see Laudan, 1977).

> Both historical examples and recent philosophical analysis have made it clear that the world is always perceived through the "lenses" of some conceptual network or other and that such networks and the languages in which they are embedded may, for all we know, provide an ineliminable "tint" to what we perceive. (p. 15)

These obvious limitations of inductivist models motivated many philosophers of science and methodologists to propose and accept a strict form of deductivism. Following the *hypothetico-deductive approach*, which is based on the works of philosophers such as Popper, Hempel, and Braithwaite and which is popular in quantitative social research methodology, the researcher has to first formulate theoretical concepts and explanations for the phenomena under investigation and must

then deduce hypotheses from these concepts that are subsequently tested with the help of empirical data. This model of the empirical research process also has serious shortcomings, however, reducing as it does the role of empirical research to the mere testing of already formulated theoretical propositions. Following deductivist models, the actual process of construction and development of theoretical statements (which in practice often makes use of empirical observations) remains in the dark; the *context of discovery* is considered as a domain of research psychology but not as a subject for serious methodological reflection.

This sharp distinction between the context of discovery and the context of justification, culminating in a view that banned discovery from methodology, has been questioned over the past two decades through a host of case studies into the history of the sciences. These investigations show that the process of discovery always entails moments of logical and rational reasoning that can be made subject to methodological reflections (see Kirschenmann, 1991; Nersessian, 1989; Nickles, 1980, 1985, 1990). These investigations led to a methodological attention to discovery and creativity that considers empirical results as an important source of inspiration and refutation. Contrary to assumptions on which the hypothetico-deductive approach is based, the development of new theoretical ideas is often based on empirical data and is only incompletely understood if seen as a domain of sudden and irrational insights and intuitions. Inductivist models, however, also do not adequately grasp the process of discovery; truly novel discoveries are never the result of simply applying some standardized procedure. Furthermore, any process of scientific discovery is linked to problem solving based on heuristic rules guiding innovative research where strong problem-solving methods are missing. In the ongoing discussion in the philosophy of science, certain models have been developed to explain discoveries and creative processes and to address the question of how rational researchers should proceed when confronted with problems for which there is no standard procedure.

These concepts are remote from naive inductivist approaches. The "logic of discovery" cannot be primarily based on induction, as Hanson showed in his groundbreaking monograph, *Patterns of Discovery*. An inductivist position is correct, as Hanson stated, to a certain extent to claim that empirical phenomena are the starting point of scientific discoveries. But it is wrong to suggest that theories are only a *summary* of the data rather than being what they have to be, that is, an *explanation* of the data (see Hanson, 1952/1965, p. 71).

Both classical models of the research process thus fail in their attempts to explain the generation of theoretical and empirical knowledge. Inductivist models neglect the theory-ladenness of any empirical observation and do not take into account the fact that inductive inferences may generalize empirical observations but cannot *explain* them. Deductivist models completely exclude processes of (empirically based) theory generation from the domain of methodological discourse, processes that do in fact take place in the empirical sciences.

These models obviously cannot grasp the complex interplay between the theoretical and empirical levels that leads to the generation of new knowledge. To fill the gaps and the "white spots" on the empirical and theoretical maps of the social sciences, it usually does not suffice to simply connect a theoretical statement (a "hypothesis") with empirical data by means of simple induction or deduction. Furthermore, a process is necessary that resembles several aspects of triangulation techniques employed in land surveying or navigation; empirical results of qualitative and quantitative social research have to be related to each other and to statements on the theoretical level as shown in Figure 16.2. Using this form of "between-method triangulation" (as Denzin [1978] called it), qualitative and quantitative data are collected and analyzed separately, and the results are related to each other.

If qualitative and quantitative methods are combined to answer a specific research question, in principle one of the following three outcomes may arise (see Erzberger & Prein, 1997; Erzberger, 1998; Kelle & Erzberger, 1999; Kelle, 2001):

1. Qualitative and quantitative results may *converge*; in this case, these results lead to the same conclusions.

2. Qualitative and quantitative results may relate to different objects or phenomena but may be *complementary* to each other and thus can be used to *supplement* each other.

3. Qualitative and quantitative results may be *divergent* or *contradictory*.

Each of these possibilities requires a different method of triangulation; that is, in each of these cases, propositions on the theoretical level have to be linked in a specific way to statements on the empirical level. This is done by using different forms of reasoning and logical inference (i.e., induction, deduction, and a third type of inference called "abduction" or "retroductive inference" in the literature [for details, see section titled "Triangulation and Logical Inference" later] and combining them in such a way as to establish meaningful connections between the empirical data and the theoretical concepts.

◆ Triangulation in Research Practice

We have already argued that the debate about qualitative and quantitative methods is overburdened with abstract methodological and empirical arguments that often lack any connection to research practice. Following Reichenbach (1938/ 1983) and Kaplan (1964), we now attempt to enrich the methodological debate with rational reconstructions of practical research experience and its "logics-in-use." For this purpose, we give examples in this section for the *convergence, complementarity,* and *divergence* of qualitative and quantitative research results, and we discuss their methodological consequences for the different possible links between the theoretical and empirical levels of knowledge. The examples are taken from sociological life course research carried out in the Special Collaborative Center 186 ("Status Passages and Risks in the Life Course").[4] The work of this research center focuses on the relationship among social structures, social change, life course patterns, and individual biographies during the modernization process in Germany.

Within this framework, a variety of quantitative and qualitative studies were carried out that are related to specific trajectories and risks in the life course, thereby investigating, for instance, transitions between the educational system and the labor market or between the employment sector and the pension system. In many of the research projects of the Special Collaborative Center 186, qualitative and quantitative methods of data collection and data analysis were combined, mainly by combining standardized panel studies with large data sets, on the one hand, with small samples of open-ended interviews, on the other. The integration of research methods and results thereby posed a variety of methodological and theoretical challenges that can be related to the discussions on triangulation described previously.

CONVERGENCE OF QUALITATIVE AND QUANTITATIVE RESULTS

The search for concurrent or convergent results by means of different methods represents the classical concept of triangulation. As has been described already, this idea gave rise to the whole methodological debate over the integration of qualitative and quantitative methods. Here, a mutual verification of research results and a potential increase of validity produced by such a verification was regarded as the primary goal of triangulation (see Denzin, 1978, pp. 301-304).

Using our terminology, we may describe the general methodological strategy which has to be applied for this purpose as follows. In the first step, one has to deductively establish a relation between one or more statements on the theoretical level and empirical observation statements. That means, from the perspective of research practice, that a theoretical assumption (a "hypothesis") has to be formulated first, after which empirical evidence for this assumption has to be sought by the collection of empirical data. In case this empirical investigation leads to the formulation of empirical observation statements that support the initial theoretical assumption, triangulation would mean the search for *further empirical evidence* using *another research method*. Through this procedure, the trustworthiness of the theoretical statement, as well as of the empirical data initially collected, is increased. Concurrence or convergence of empirical results is regarded as an indicator for their validity and strengthens the initial assumptions and the theoretical framework that was used to structure the research process.

A research project about life course patterns of males who at the time of this retrospective study had already left the labor market may serve as a good example here. These men had passed through the status passage to retirement and thus were capable of having a view of their whole working lives (see Krüger, 2001). The project collected standardized data on the occupational life courses of a sample of males from the birth cohort of 1930 ($n = 74$). These data referred to the starting and end points of employment and self-employed work as well as the starting and end points of periods of unemployment, training, illness, and so forth. At the same time, open-ended qualitative interviews were conducted with a subsample ($n = 37$) where the males reported on their own views, their subjective interpretations, and their personal stock taking over their occupational lives.

West Germany's postwar period, namely the 1950s and 1960s (often called the "era of the economic miracle" [*Wirtschaftswunder*]), was a phase of extraordinary economic growth leading to a prosperous economy and full employment for many years (see Lutz, 1984). The men who took part in the study experienced a large proportion of their working lives during this period, which was also characterized by a dominance of traditional normative orientations and gender role patterns with regard to the tasks, obligations, and rights of husbands and wives in their marital relations and the division of labor in family work and waged work (see Nave-Herz, 1988).

Consequently, the researchers expected the occupational life courses of the investigated males to show a high stability without major breaks or interruptions and a clear division between male breadwinning and female housekeeping roles in their families. Furthermore, the assumption was formulated that these structures of occupational life courses were accompanied and stabilized by gender-stereotyped attitudes and normative orientations of the males, who saw themselves as the sole breadwinners responsible for the economic well-being of their whole families.

These theoretical assumptions were first examined with the help of quantitative data that were collected to study the succession of different phases and forms of employment and nonemployment over the life course. Empirical observation statements that could be made on the basis of statistical analyses of these standardized data provided evidence for the initial theoretical assumptions; a great majority of the males in the sample were in full employment nearly all of the time during their life courses. Apart from some short periods of joblessness and sickness, there were no further interruptions in their occupational careers.

These results from the quantitative part of the study were further validated by the analysis of the qualitative data material. In extended in-depth interviews, the respondents answered questions about subjective interpretations of their occupational biographies, their own perceptions concerning their breadwinner role, and their participation in household and family work. The qualitative findings demonstrate the high significance that paid labor had for the respondents who regarded it as their "fair share" of their and their spouses' joint efforts for their whole families. Over the whole life course, the respondents considered breadwinning as the husband's central moral obligation and as fulfillment of his family work duties (see Braemer, 1994). Given this background of normative orientations, the respondents' continuing participation in the labor market is of crucial significance for their self-perception and self-esteem as loyal spouses

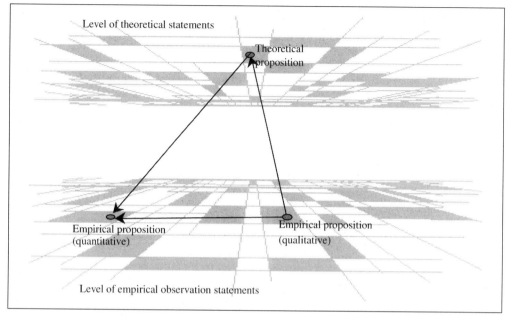

Figure 16.3. Convergence of Research Results

and responsible fathers. And due to the favorable economic conditions during the era of the Wirtschaftswunder, these personal orientations, cultural beliefs (*Leitbilder*), and role expectations found their expression in the dominant patterns of male occupational careers. Consequently, no inconsistencies could be found between the actions of respondents related to their occupational life courses (empirically described by the records produced with standardized questionnaires), on the one hand, and subjective interpretations of these actions (made visible through the qualitative data material), on the other.

Figure 16.3 illustrates this process of establishing convergence. After formulating the basic theoretical assumptions for the investigated domain of social reality (i.e., after drawing a "theoretical map" for the landscape in question), the theoretical statements were first tested deductively through quantitative empirical data. A second empirical study using qualitative methods provided additional evidence for the theoretical hypotheses and thus helped to further validate these assumptions as well as the empirical observation statements developed on the basis of the standardized data.

COMPLEMENTARY RESULTS

The search for complementary results corresponds with the complementarity model of triangulation. As discussed earlier, the underlying idea of this model is that the investigated phenomenon itself is (at least partly) constructed by the applied methods and that different methods highlight different aspects of it or may even constitute different phenomena (see Erzberger, 1998; Fielding & Fielding, 1986; Flick, 1992; Kelle & Erzberger, 1999). Thus, the varying perspectives opened up by different methods may supplement each other so as to produce a fuller picture of the empirical domain under study, which would not be the case if only one single method were applied.

The complementarity model can be meaningfully applied in all cases where one single research method does not suffice to collect adequate and/or enough empirical data to support the initial theoretical assumptions. Qualitative or quantitative methods alone may often be able to relate only a small part of the theoretical framework to empirical observation statements. In particular, empirical studies where theoretical propositions are exclusively based on sociodemographic data may serve as good examples of such a situation; in such studies, social researchers often tend to explain correlations between sociodemographic data with additional theoretical explanations that are not sufficiently grounded in empirical data.

To illustrate this point, a well-known sociological fact can be used, that is, an association between *social background* (in terms of social stratification) of pupils and their *school-level attainment* that is reported in numerous empirical studies about inequality in the educational system (see Brauns, 1999; Henz & Maas, 1995; Shavit & Blossfeld, 1993). Pupils of parents who have a high socioeconomic status usually attain a higher formal educational achievement than do pupils from a lower class background. In this connection, the data of a study done by a research project on occupational careers of young adults[5] shows that 31% of the children of higher grade professionals, administrators, managers, or civil servants attained the *Abitur*—the highest school-level attainment in Germany—as compared with 7.5% of children of unskilled or semi-skilled manual workers. Children with this class background most often acquire the lowest level of school exam (*Hauptschule*, 43%) or a medium-level school exam (*Realschule*, 41%) (see Heinz,

Kelle, Witzel, & Zinn, 1998; Kelle & Zinn, 1998). Because the highest school-level attainment (Abitur) is the necessary prerequisite for being admitted to university in Germany, children of working-class families are clearly underrepresented at universities.

These data thus describe a key mechanism of the intergenerational reproduction of social inequality. The socioeconomic status of parents exerts an influence on the education their children get and thus provides the children with different opportunities and constraints. It is important to realize the underlying rationale that is (almost intuitively) applied if one tries to sociologically understand such empirical facts. Sociodemographic data are then interpreted by postulating a relation between two variables:

1. One of these variables, *the level of school education*, describes social actions or the results of social actions. (Clearly, the actors are not only those individuals whose data had been collected but also actors in their social environment given that school attainment is not only the result of the pupils' actions but also the result of their parents' actions, the decisions of teachers, examination boards, etc.)

2. The second variable, *sociodemographic status of the father*, is used as an indicator ("proxy") for structural influences on individuals.

In the usual manner of sociological reasoning, the second variable is regarded as an *independent variable* and the first as a *dependent variable*; it is claimed that a specific class origin *influences, leads to*, or even *causes* specific events, in this case attending specific schools and passing specific exams. This idea is usually expressed in terms of a mathematical model that assumes a *functional relation* between these variables. It is of the utmost importance thereby to note the difference between the functional relation of these two variables and the sociological explanation for it.

To model the association between school-level attainment and class origin as a (mathematical) *functional relation* simply means that one assumes a regularity between these kinds of events; to look for a *sociological explanation* means to identify such institutional processes or rules that constitute these regularities. Following current theories of class structure and social inequality (see Rossides, 1997), a variety of explanations may be formulated:

1. Members of the upper class and upper-middle class invest more into the human capital of their children by motivating and supervising them steadily and thus monitoring their progress in school.

2. Children from upper-middle-class backgrounds develop more *cultural capital* by learning specific modes of language and behavior at home.

3. Children from working-class families experience an atmosphere at home that is indifferent (or even hostile) toward educational achievements.

4. Or one could claim that a subtle form of class exclusion takes place in schools. Middle-class teachers tend to (subconsciously) discriminate against children from working-class families.

The function of such an explanation is to link the observed empirical phenomenon to general sociological theories, which could be a rational choice approach, an approach in the tradition of structural functionalism, social exchange theory, or conflict theory, to name a few examples. Using an approach in the functionalist tradition, for instance, one would postulate the existence of a specific sociocultural environment that imposes a certain normative order that influences the normative orientations and thus the preferences and goals of the actors. However, sociodemographic data do not necessarily contain evidence concerning all aspects covered by these theoretical explanations. The data from the preceding example, for instance, contain no information about the atmosphere in the families of respondents and whether it was positive or negative about educational achievements. That means that empirical information about the concrete normative order in the social environment of the actors or about their normative orientations is not available.

Thus, an important part of the theoretical assumptions used to explain such empirical findings is itself not "empirically grounded"; *additional assumptions* have to be devised. Such additional assumptions can relate to the contents of a normative order, for instance, or to the preference structures of certain groups of actors. Here, social researchers often use a strategy that can be called the *heuristics of commonsense knowledge*; they construct such additional assumptions by drawing on their own personal commonsense knowledge about the norms, preferences, and goals that the people in the empirical field under investigation ordinarily have and the means they use to achieve their goals (see Kelle & Lüdemann, 1995). Information about normative orientations needed for the additional assumptions usually form an integral part of culturally or subculturally specific stocks of everyday knowledge and, therefore, represent a fundamental and unavoidable prerequisite for the actors to cope with their given life world. In many cases, the heuristics of commonsense knowledge causes no major problems, especially if research takes place within the researcher's own culture

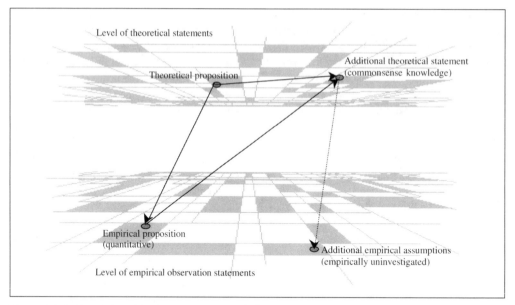

Figure 16.4. Heuristics of Commonsense Knowledge

or subculture where he or she has easy access to its stocks of everyday knowledge. But because a great deal of this knowledge is self-evident or implicit, the application of this heuristic strategy is usually not discussed explicitly by social researchers; instead, it serves as a "shadow methodology" of theory construction.

Now, the hazards of such a shadow methodology for the investigation of foreign cultures or unfamiliar domestic subcultures are obvious. Not being a member of such cultures, researchers do not possess sufficient knowledge to formulate hypotheses about the actors' preferences, norms, and goals. In these cases, the heuristics of commonsense knowledge can exert harmful results, seducing the researcher into deriving hypotheses that might completely fail to account for the norms, preferences, and goals the actors in the empirical field really have and the means they use to attain these goals.

Figure 16.4 illustrates such a shadow methodology of commonsense knowledge that is often applied in the analysis of

sociodemographic data. After formulating theoretical assumptions about the empirical domain under study with a relatively narrow scope and limited explanatory power, the associations between the independent and dependent variables are determined empirically. The researcher then draws on additional theoretical assumptions that increase the explanatory power of his or her theoretical framework but that are empirically supported by commonsense knowledge alone.

To avoid the pitfalls of such a shadow methodology, those additional theoretical assumptions that are developed to further substantiate empirical findings have to be grounded empirically. The additional information relates to the subjective interpretations, personal preferences, norms, preferences, goals, and the like of the actors in the domain under study and can, therefore, often be acquired only with the help of *qualitative* data. Consequently, the triangulation of qualitative and quantitative methods is an important alternative to the heuristics of commonsense knowledge here. In such cases, quantitative and qualitative methods serve different purposes and help to illuminate different aspects of the sociological phenomenon under study; quantitative methods help to describe the actions of (large numbers of) individuals, whereas qualitative methods provide information about possible reasons for these actions in terms of the actors' interpretations of situations and their goals and preferences. Thus, qualitative and quantitative methods help to answer different questions; the results of statistical analyses show *what kinds of actions* social actors typically perform (e.g., attending certain schools, achieving certain school exams), while the analysis of qualitative data helps to answer *why* questions (e.g., "For what purposes do actors attend schools of certain levels?," "How do they perceive and define their situation?," "Which norms do they acknowledge?"). Here, qualitative and quantitative results are not interchangeable. It is not possible to analyze the aggregated results of social actions (e.g., the overall rate of school-leavers of a certain school type) with the help of qualitative interview data, whereas local knowledge about norms, preferences, and definitions of situations typical for a certain culture or life world often cannot be investigated using standardized questionnaires because the researchers do not usually have sufficient knowledge to construct such research instruments. In such cases, qualitative studies have to be carried out to explore stocks of local knowledge in the corresponding life worlds so as to avoid misinterpretations of quantitative data due to misguided commonsense knowledge. Thus, empirical results from qualitative studies help to build the necessary theoretical framework to understand the empirical results of statistical analyses and "to enrich the bare bones of statistical results," as Rossman and Wilson (1985, p. 636) put it.

This specific strategy of triangulation is based on a certain (meta)theoretical view of social phenomena that was developed in and defended by a variety of classical and modern theoretical writings in sociology (especially in the works of Weber, Mead, Parsons, and Giddens) but is not shared by all theoretical approaches in sociology. This view assumes that social actions are not adequately understood if the intentions of social actors are not taken into account. Starting from this theoretical standpoint, the integration of qualitative and quantitative methods can prove necessary to produce valid and meaningful theoretical explanations in all such domains where knowledge about the typical intentions of actors is not immediately available to the researcher.

This may quite often be the case, as made clear by the following example, which comes from a research project that dealt with unemployment in relation to delinquency during adolescence. A longitudinal study with qualitative and quantitative panel data was carried out to analyze the dynamics of the occupational life course of teenagers and adolescents as well as its dependency on delinquent behavior over time. Young German schoolleavers from the lowest possible level of education were interviewed from 1989 onward in subsequent waves by means of standardized questionnaires and openended qualitative interviews. The respondents were asked about their labor market participation and their delinquent behavior during the past years, and qualitative material from individual court records was used as an additional data source (see Prein & Seus, 2000).

Statistical analyses of the quantitative data showed that many young people were successful and highly motivated in their jobs, on the one hand, but were highly criminal during their leisure time, on the other, which led to numerous encounters with the police and the criminal justice system. Two questions arose out of these facts. First, why and on what terms can delinquency during leisure time become socially accepted and compatible with high adjustment to social norms during working hours? Second, under what conditions does a delinquent's job loss reinforce the punitive reaction of the criminal justice system? These questions could not be answered on the basis of the statistical material alone because (not very strong) correlations among employment status, frequency and type of delinquency, and the intensity of penalties imposed by the criminal justice system were the only information the quantitative data provided. An explanation of these findings had to be formulated on the basis of the qualitative material contained in the delinquents' individual court records.

These records were analyzed so as to reconstruct substantial reasons for the type and intensity of punishment for all cases of the respondents' criminal offences that had become known to the court. The data showed that both representatives of the criminal justice system, on the one hand, and actors responsible for the vocational training, on the other, concurred strongly in their endeavors to avoid successful and motivated trainees being severely penalized and, as a consequence, socially marginalized. Furthermore, unemployed delinquents were often only mildly punished for their offenses if they could convince the court magistrates that they were undertaking serious efforts to get jobs. Consequently, the working morale of the delinquents (as perceived by judges or trainers as agents of social control) turned out to be more relevant for the judgment of delinquent behavior than their current occupational status.

Figure 16.5 illustrates this example in which a complementarity of empirical results was achieved. In terms of the triangulation metaphor, two triangles are gen-

erated that then interconnect. Starting from Theoretical Statement 1 (assuming a causal relation among employment status, deviant behavior, and sanctions imposed by the criminal justice system), quantitative methods were applied to collect empirical data that support these assumptions. However, the empirical data analyzed by statistical means provided only limited evidence (in the form of weak correlations) for Statement 1. To further explain and understand these findings, the role of the intentions of different actors in the investigated domain was theoretically substantiated (Theoretical Statement 2). This statement served as a starting point for a second empirical inquiry. Qualitative data contained in court records were analyzed and used to further elaborate Theoretical Statement 2 and its relation to the first theoretical statement. Here, it was possible to show that the initially assumed relation among employment status, delinquency, and severity of punishment was far more complex than expected—an insight that would not have been acquired using one single (either qualitative or quantitative) method.

DIVERGENCE OF QUALITATIVE AND QUANTITATIVE FINDINGS

In the previous example, qualitative and quantitative methods served to provide *complementary findings*. Qualitative or quantitative data alone did not yield sufficient information to allow us to understand fully the social processes under scrutiny, and qualitative and quantitative methods had to be combined to allow adequate explanations of the phenomena under study. Nevertheless, the complementarity model is not a good *general* methodological concept for the integration of qualitative and quantitative methods because the triangulation of research

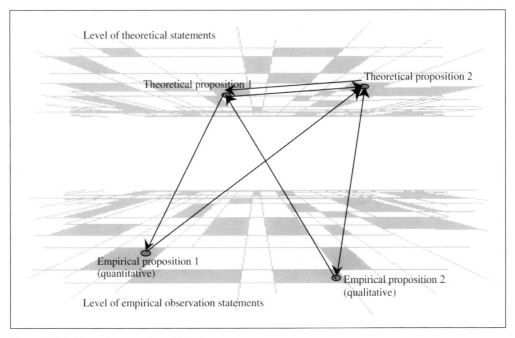

Figure 16.5. Complementarity of Results

results often leads to a situation in which the different findings do not fit. In many cases, outcomes of qualitative and quantitative research may at first sight even contradict each other, which means that the statements on the theoretical level fail as explanations for the divergent empirical results.

This possibility leads us back to the concept of triangulation for the mutual validation of research results. If different methods are used to investigate the same phenomenon, then the results produced with one method may invalidate findings produced with the other. Such an instance can be regarded as one in which the Popperian falsification concept of theory modification is applied to triangulation. The purposeful search for divergences can be used to find new and better explanations for the phenomena under investigation, or, in the words of Rossman and Wilson (1985), "Searching for areas of

divergent findings may set up the dissonance, doubt, and ambiguity often associated with significant creative intellectual insights" (p. 633). Thus, divergent empirical findings should not always be considered as an indicator of a poor research design; instead, they may be considered as a pointer to new theoretical insights. However, before theoretical concepts are revised, changed, or even rejected for the sake of new concepts, it should be checked first whether the research methods were adequately applied. In principle, inconsistencies between qualitative and quantitative findings can be explained in one of two ways:

◆ As results of mistakes made in the application of the data collection or data analysis methods

◆ As a consequence of the inadequacy of the applied theoretical concepts

To exclude the first possibility, a methodological examination of all important aspects of the qualitative and quantitative investigation (including the sampling, the research instruments, and the process of data analysis) is necessary. The operationalization procedures used to construct the quantitative research instrument have to be scrutinized, as does the development of categories and concepts on which the qualitative findings were based. Only if no obvious methodological mistakes can be identified should the initial theoretical assumptions be checked further.

Once the methodological soundness of the observed empirical facts is established, these facts may be considered as starting points for the development of new hypotheses (see also Erzberger, 1998; Erzberger & Prein, 1997; Fielding & Fielding, 1986; Kelle, 2001). It may, therefore, be necessary to revise and modify the initial theoretical assumptions and to draw on further theoretical concepts that have not yet been related to the domain in question.[6] Before discussing further the generation of new theoretical assumptions on the basis of unexpected empirical data, we first illustrate this process with another example from research practice.

The example comes from a project of the Special Collaborative Center 186 that deals with the status passage between the educational system and the employment sector in the German Democratic Republic (GDR), the part of Germany that was under Communist rule until 1989.

In current discussions over possible reasons for an often-cited efficiency gap between the western part of reunified Germany and the former GDR, it is often claimed that East German employees lack adaptability to the new Western economic system due to their specific experiences under Communist rule (for an exposition and a critique, see Weymann, Sackmann, & Wingens, 1999). One of the basic tenets of the Communist system was that every aspect of life was political, which implied that the state was also responsible for the solution of various individual problems. This ideological politicization of the life world was accompanied by attempts to exert extensive social control over individual life courses. Consequently, one important assumption in so-called "transformation research" was that socialization experienced under the conditions of state socialism leads to a lack of individual autonomy, which may explain a sociopsychological "modernization deficit"—an inability to cope actively in certain situations combined with pretentious and submissive attitudes toward state authorities.

One focus of the previously mentioned research project lay on the interplay between bureaucratic regulation and individual action strategies in the transition between education and work (Wingens, 1999). In official government sources, it was emphasized that East Germany had established a highly formalized transition system between education and employment. The central idea behind this was that the output of the educational system had to be regulated in accordance with the requirements of the national economy. For this purpose, rough productivity and economic growth targets were defined at the top level of the planning administration, and on the basis of these targets a governmental planning commission calculated how many university graduates and employees were required. To meet these requirements, a highly bureaucratized career guidance system was set up. The status passage between graduation and work, for instance, was supervised at each university by a graduate allocation bureau that had to assign jobs to school-leavers.

The research project conducted a quantitative survey ($n = 551$), interviewing academics who had experienced the transition from education to employment before and during the transformation of the political system. According to these data, the system of state control over individual career paths and trajectories worked very well. Around 60% of university graduates from the cohort that had experienced the transition from university to work under the conditions of the socialist economy named the official allocation authority as the source of information for their job-seeking activities. Personal networks were important for only 17%, and direct information from the factories was important for only 18%, of the respondents. If one takes the quantitative data as the sole information source, one would easily come to the conclusion that the system of rigid control over individual careers promoted by the official ideology of the governing party was rather successful.

As with the other projects described previously, qualitative interviews were then carried out with the members of a subsample drawn from the larger quantitative sample ($n = 21$). Most interestingly, this material provided a totally different picture of the transition process under investigation from that of the data collected using standardized questionnaires, and it revealed that individual actors were indeed able to influence their individual careers to a remarkable extent if they were creative enough. For instance, it was possible to strategically use the formal procedures developed for the delegation of employees to universities by their companies to fulfill individual career plans. The bureaucratic allocation of graduates to their workplaces—the core of the system of state control over individual life courses—turned out in many cases to be nothing more than a legitimization for individual job seeking; graduates looked for companies that were interested in employing them (which often turned out to be rela-

tively easy because in nearly every sector of the East German economy there was an urgent demand for skilled personnel). After the graduates and the companies had come to agreements, the companies reported the vacancies to the allocation bureau where the graduates asked for positions they themselves had helped to establish. The function of the allocation bureaus thus changed from that of bringing together graduates and vacancies to that of legitimizing the individual actions of the graduates. The interviewees maintained that this procedure was not an exception but rather the usual way to get a job. Allocation, the official function of the bureau, became an exception and a second-rate procedure. Only graduates who were unable to find jobs by themselves were guided by the bureaucratic allocation structure.

Without the detailed accounts about the status passages between education and work given by the respondents in qualitative interviews, it would have been nearly impossible to uncover this interplay between structural constraints and individual action. The qualitative data thereby revealed that the simple and straightforward picture produced by quantitative data was incorrect and misleading; the obvious tendency of respondents to conform to the norms of "double-speak" even after the collapse of the socialist system produced a "Potemkin village" in the quantitative survey (see Erzberger, 2000). Only with the help of qualitative material were the researchers able to gain insight into the empirical reality behind the facades of ideology. At the same time, the qualitative material also helped to examine and revise the leading hypothesis of the project. The divergent results of the quantitative analysis that supported the image of bureaucratic allocation, on the one hand, and the qualitative research that emphasized the role of individual job seeking, on the other,

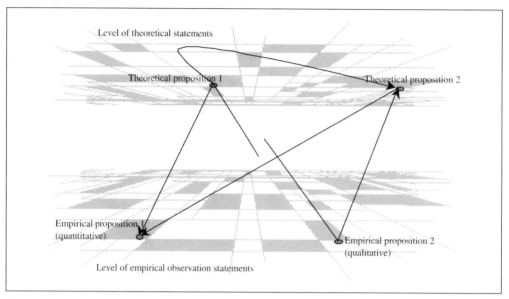

Figure 16.6. Divergence of Findings

could be reconciled by a theoretical redefinition of the sociological function of the allocation bureau. It was no longer seen as a distribution agency; instead, it was seen as an institution for the legitimization of individual action within a system that was ideologically based on a collectivist rhetoric. Thus, the empirical data provided serious counterevidence for the thesis that the bureaucratic allocation structure gave rise to a specific lack of adaptability to capitalist economy as some kind of inherent personality trait in East German academics. At least the researcher found good reasons to assume that the causes for such an alleged incapacity to adapt, if it indeed exists, do not lie in a lack of self-initiative in job seeking (see Wingens, 1999).

Such a reconciliation between divergent findings of qualitative and quantitative research may be illustrated with a triangulation figure (Figure 16.6) similar to those used to depict the triangulation of convergent or complementary results.

The example from transformation research describes a strategy often used to solve conceptual problems posed by divergent findings within the framework of a multimethod design; the initial theoretical concepts and assumptions have to be modified and adapted to account for the empirical results.[7] As with the other two forms of triangulation, the whole process begins with an assumption on the theoretical level (Theoretical Statement 1 in Figure 16.6 regarding the lack of personal autonomy of individual actors brought about by socialization processes in an authoritarian political system). Although first investigations, carried out with the help of quantitative methods, led to empirical results that supported the initial assumption (Empirical Statement 1, representing evidence for the hypothesis that the official system of allocation was accepted and used by the majority of respondents), the analysis of further (qualitative) data revealed inconsistencies when evidence was found that job seeking was an individualized and creative process even under the conditions of a state economy (Empirical Statement 2). In contrast to the complementarity model, the collection and analysis of qualitative data in this case did not supplement the quantitative findings, giving a fuller picture of the phenomenon under investigation, but produced counterevidence to the first hypothesis. To explain the inconsistent and divergent findings, it is then necessary to seek theoretical concepts and statements that can change the divergence of results to convergence or complementarity. In the example, this was achieved by developing a new theoretical understanding of the institutional function of the allocation bureau; contrary to the official semantics, it was not so much an institution for the governing of individual life courses as a mere device for the legitimization of individual job-seeking behavior (Theoretical Statement 2).

This kind of reasoning cannot be sufficiently described as either deduction or induction. Furthermore, it represents a different mode of logical inference that is discussed in detail in the following section.

◆ Triangulation and Logical Inference

The development of relations between the level of theoretical propositions and the level of empirical observation statements can rest on different forms of logical inference. It was already mentioned earlier that *deduction* and *induction* are modes of inference discussed frequently in methodological textbooks. Deduction is a type of reasoning usually applied if a link is drawn from an already formulated theoretical statement to a statement about observable empirical facts, a link that can be generalized in the following term: "If A (a theoretical statement) is true, then we would expect the fact C to happen." Such a linkage represents a specific *empirical hypothesis* (in contrast to a more general theoretical

assumption or *theoretical hypothesis* that is part of a theoretical map).

If the development of a relation between the empirical and theoretical levels starts with a point on the empirical map, then the situation is more complicated. Only in rare cases does such a relation take the simple form of an inductive inference, which means a generalization of an empirical fact (which can be generalized as follows: "Because these objects of Class X have the attribute Y, it is reasonable to assume that all X are Y"). Usually, linking an empirical observation to the level of theoretical knowledge does not simply mean *generalizing* the corresponding fact but also *explaining* and *understanding* it in theoretical terms. Consequently, an inference from a single observation to a theoretical statement is not primarily based on induction, as one might think, given that theories are not merely *summaries* of data but also *explanations* of data. Such logical inferences are neither inductive nor deductive but represent a special kind of logical reasoning whose premises are a set of empirical phenomena and whose conclusion is an explanatory hypothesis. This kind of inference has been given different labels by mathematicians, logicians, and philosophers of science. In the literature, one finds the terms *abduction, retroduction, retroductive inference, reduction,* and *inference to the best explanation* (see also Miller, Chapter 15, this volume) to describe this specific mode of reasoning. Retroductive inference (as this mode of inference had been called by Norwood Hanson, who described it using illuminating reconstructions of various scientific discoveries [Hanson, 1952/1965]) converts the process of deductive reasoning; a retroductive inference starts with what would be the conclusion of a deduction and infers from that to the premises. The notion of "reduction," which was developed by the logician Bochenski, represents the same form of reasoning that can also be called *hypothetical reasoning,* a term that reflects more clearly its role in the research process; retroductive, reductive, or hypothetical inferences serve to find a *hypothesis* that can explain certain empirical findings.

The earliest concepts of hypothetical reasoning were developed by the pragmatist philosopher Charles Peirce. According to Peirce, hypothetical reasoning represents a third form of inference apart from deduction and induction (Peirce, 1974 [hereafter CP] 2.621; see also Maxcy, Chapter 2, this volume)[8]; deductive reasoning is the application of general rules to specific cases to infer a result. Induction is an inversion of this deductive syllogism; by induction, one generalizes from a number of cases where a certain result is observed, and one infers from it a general rule claiming that these results can be observed in all cases of a class to which the observed cases belong. For example, if one draws at random a handful of beans from a bag and, finding that two thirds of the beans in that handful are white, concludes that about two thirds of those in the bag are white, one conducts an inductive inference. But this kind of inference is not the only way of inverting a deductive syllogism.

> Suppose I enter a room and there find a number of bags, containing different kinds of beans. On the table there is a handful of white beans; and after some searching, I find one of the bags contains white beans only. I at once infer as a probability, or as a fair guess, that this handful was taken out of that bag. This sort of inference is called *making a hypothesis.* It is the inference of a *case* from a *rule* and a *result.* (CP, 2.623, italics in original)

If one wants to use the terminology of deductive reasoning, then one can describe hypothetical inference as follows: The inference begins with the conclusion, and the researcher looks for a general statement that might serve—in the context of a deductive inference—as a major premise and thereby explain the observed phenomenon.

It is useful here to distinguish between two types of hypothetical inference depending on whether one has the general rule applicable to the specific case at hand or whether this rule has yet to be found. According to Reichertz (1991), these two forms can already be distinguished in the works of Peirce. If the researcher already has a general rule that can explain the observed phenomena at his or her disposal, then the outcome of a hypothetical inference is a hypothesis about the minor premise. That means that a specific empirical phenomenon is described or explained by subsuming it under an already existing rule or scientific law. In his later writings, Peirce has called this form of hypothetical inference *induction by characters* or *qualitative induction.* By qualitative induction, the process is described by which the researcher explains an observed phenomenon on the basis of his or her previous knowledge.

This is a kind of hypothetical reasoning often applied when qualitative data material is analyzed. Empirical phenomena are observed and subsumed under already known theoretical concepts. The social researcher identifies certain aspects of investigated events as instances of adjusted or deviant behavior of social actors, as instances of stigmatization through institutions of social control, and so forth. This type of reasoning often plays an important role in the context of the convergence or complementarity model of triangulation. Without having formulated a specific theoretical assumption that anticipates a certain empirical finding in advance, either the researcher using qualitative methods discovers empirical phenomena that support theoretical assumptions that formed the starting point for a quantitative study and thus reaches a convergence of results, or he or she finds empirical facts that can be related to theoretical statements that supplement the initial theoretical assumptions and thus achieves complementary findings that help to produce a more complete picture of the investigated domain.

However, if the simultaneous application of quantitative and qualitative methods leads to inconsistent or divergent findings representing counterevidence for previous theoretical assumptions, then a *second form* of hypothetical reasoning comes into play that Peirce has called *abduction* or *abductive inference*. Whereas qualitative induction helps to explain a certain event by subsuming it under an already existing concept or rule, abductive inference serves as a means to discover new and still unknown concepts or rules. The starting point of an abductive inference is a surprising anomalous event that cannot be explained on the basis of previous knowledge. Peirce described the process of abductive inference as follows:

The surprising fact C is observed.

But if A were true, [then] C would be a matter of course.

Hence there is a reason to suspect that A is true. (CP, 5.189)

An abductive inference helps to find a possible explanation for a surprising fact A by generating a new rule C that is applicable to this fact. In conducting a qualitative induction, the researcher looks for an already existing rule (the major premise of a deductive inference), while through abductive inferences such a rule can be newly developed. Confronted with an anomalous event, "we turn over our recollection of observed facts; we endeavor so

to rearrange them, to view them in such new perspective that the unexpected experience shall no longer appear surprising" (CP, 7.36).

This is, of course, a creative endeavor that sometimes "comes to us like a flash" (CP, 5.182). Nevertheless, the researcher's creativity is limited by certain constraints. The originality of the newly developed hypotheses is limited by the facts that must be explained (see Anderson, 1987, p. 44). Furthermore, an abductive inference not only must lead to a satisfactory explanation of the observed facts but also must be related to the previous knowledge of the researcher—"the different elements of the hypothesis were in our minds before," as Peirce put it (CP, 5.181). An abductive inference always requires an integration of previous knowledge and new experience. For this purpose, theoretical preconceptions have to be revised; often, assumptions and beliefs taken for granted for a long time have to be abandoned or at least modified.

However, this mode of reasoning carries certain methodological and epistemological risks. If an explanation gap resulting from divergent empirical results is closed in this way, then the danger of eclecticism is imminent if one draws on theoretical approaches that have not yet been used to explain such facts. Furthermore, researchers can easily abuse this mode of inference for the development of arbitrary ad hoc explanations, and they may be tempted to invent unstable auxiliary assumptions that serve the immunization of already falsified theoretical assumptions. Yet methodological rules to countervail such *threats to validity* can be formulated on the basis of *models of rational theory transition* developed by Imre Lakatos and Larry Laudan in their attempts to further develop Popper's concept of theory generation (Lakatos, 1982; Laudan, 1977). Their models are based on a differentiation between "progressive" and "degenerating" problem shifts that can take place if one theory is replaced by another after the discovery of empirical counterevidence.

According to Lakatos (1982), a *degenerating problem shift* occurs when an existing theory is immunized through ad hoc hypotheses that reduce its empirical content. A *progressive problem shift* requires an increase of empirical content; the new theory not only must be able to explain the empirical phenomena that were explained by its predecessor together with the anomalous facts that led to its falsification, it also must predict new empirical phenomena. Laudan (1977) proposed a further criterion for the progressivity of a problem shift: that the modification of a theory may also be admissible if the new theory contains less conceptual problems than its predecessor. Conceptual problems of a theory are normally generated by logical inconsistencies between parts of the theory itself, or they are the result of a lack of compatibility with already well-established theoretical approaches. Thus, two further strategies (apart from the invention of ad hoc hypotheses that reduce the empirical content of the theory) may also lead to a degenerating problem shift: first, the use of auxiliary hypotheses, which are simply "glued" onto a theory without having any further substantive relation to it, and second, the use of assumptions, which lead to contradictions to other well-established theories.

To induce a progressive problem shift, a new hypothesis must fulfill at least one of the following three criteria:

1. It must lead to an increase of empirical content. That means that the theory, when modified with the help of the new hypothesis, must be able to explain additional empirical phenomena or predict further empirical facts.

2. It must lead to a reduction of internal conceptual problems through an increase of logical coherence, internal consistency, or parsimony.

3. It must increase the adaptability of the theory; that is, crucial assumptions of the theory, when modified with the help of the new hypothesis, can be consistently related to other well-established theories about the empirical domain.

It is important to avoid increasing one of these three attributes—*empirical content, consistency,* or *adaptability*—at the expense of the others. This means, for instance, that the increased empirical content of a theory must not be achieved by means of reducing theoretical consistency.

◆ Rules of Integration

On the basis of the previous considerations, a set of rules can be formulated that may be helpful in drawing inferences from the results of qualitative and quantitative studies in mixed methods designs. These rules should be understood not as recipes to be followed exactly in a step-by-step manner but rather as general guidelines whose significance varies according to the research question at hand and the empirical domain under investigation and depending on the specific methods employed.

1. The selection of adequate methods should not be made mainly on the basis of sympathies toward a certain methodological camp or school. Methods are tools for the answering of research questions and not vice versa. Consequently, decisions about the applied methods should not be made before the research questions are formulated

2. Each method is well-suited to specific empirical domains, while there are other empirical fields of interest where

the same method will not yield meaningful results.

3. One should always look for a sufficient empirical basis for one's theoretical propositions. That means that additional assumptions, which cannot be examined with the help of empirical data for the interpretation of empirical data and of relations between these data, should be avoided.

4. There is no single methodological model of method integration available (that claims, e.g., that qualitative and quantitative empirical investigation must always lead to convergent or complementary results). The model of triangulation for mutual validation and the complementarity model both have strengths and weaknesses depending on the research questions posed and the empirical domains under investigation. Consequently, the aim of method integration, be it the mutual validation of data and methods or the complementarity of research results, has to be determined on the basis of theoretical and substantive considerations for each research project.

5. If method integration is carried out with the purpose of mutual validation, then convergence of research results may provide good arguments for their validity but can never fully prove this validity, for it is always possible that all of the convergent results are biased for the same reason and in the same direction.

6. The crucial function of method integration performed for the purpose of complementary results is to provide additional empirical material in an empirical research domain where one single method is insufficient for the investigation of the full empirical basis of a theoretical assumption.

7. If the qualitative and quantitative methods applied simultaneously lead to divergent results, then in principle two explanations are possible. Either the divergence is the result of mistakes made when applying one method (or both methods) and thus represents a methodological artifact, or the initial theoretical assumptions have to be modified and revised.

8. The modification and revision of theoretical assumptions as a consequence of divergent findings is based on hypothetical inferences and thus is a risky endeavor. In this process, ad hoc hypotheses have to be formulated on the basis of already collected empirical data that may tempt researchers into immunizing their initial theories as well as formulating far-reaching speculations that lack a sound empirical basis. Therefore, either the newly developed hypotheses must increase the empirical content of the initial theory without diminishing its consistency, or they must improve the consistency of the initial theory without leading to a loss of empirical content. Furthermore, the newly developed hypotheses should be empirically examined with new empirical data as soon as possible. Finally, the newly developed hypotheses should be adaptable to other well-established theories about the empirical domain under investigation.

◆ Conclusions

Due partly to the ongoing controversies between methodological camps, recent methodological discussions have provided only sparse material for the solution of problems surrounding the theoretical integration of research results in a mixed methods design. The term *triangulation* represents one of the more promising concepts here, although it carries certain systematic ambiguities when transferred to the realm of method integration in social research. The different understandings of the triangulation metaphor outlined in this chapter—triangulation as a means of mutual validation, triangulation for the integration of different perspectives, and triangulation in its original trigonometrical meaning—stress different possibilities for relating qualitative and quantitative results. However, although each of these concepts is helpful in gaining a deeper insight into different aspects of method integration, none of them can be considered as a methodological model suitable for all aspects of method integration.

The most serious problem of the methodological discussions concerning triangulation is that epistemological and methodological concepts are often not sufficiently linked to theoretical considerations about the nature of the empirical phenomena under investigation. In this chapter, we have tried to fill this gap by depicting the processes of relating qualitative and quantitative research results as processes of relating two "maps" representing the level of theory and the level of empirical observation, respectively, to each other. It is of the utmost importance to pay attention to the fact that theoretical concepts or ideas (whether elaborated hypotheses or vague assumptions) always play a central role in any combination of qualitative and quantitative data and methods, regardless of which triangulation model is applied.

The *mutual validation model* regards the search for convergent findings that are deemed to be indicators of validity as the most important purpose, if not the sole purpose, of triangulation. By claiming that empirical results produced with the help of a certain method are supported through the application of another method,

this concept represents a verification strategy in the tradition of empiricist epistemology. Although such verificationist ideas have earned legitimate criticism in methodological debates where it has been emphasized that methods often not only help to describe but also help to construct their empirical domains, the mutual validation model should not be fully discarded; under certain circumstances, given the domain under study and the research question posed, its application can yield fruitful results. Regardless of whether one tries to further examine qualitative findings through quantitative methods or vice versa, however, it should not be forgotten that such an attempt requires a common theoretical framework for the employment of qualitative and quantitative data collection and analysis.

In contrast to the mutual validation model, the *complementarity model* draws our attention to the fact that different methods may relate to different aspects of the domain in question because certain methods have been developed within different theoretical traditions and thus serve the investigation of different phenomena. From this perspective, one would expect not convergent or divergent findings but rather supplementary findings that—like pieces of a jigsaw puzzle—produce a full picture of a certain domain if put together in the correct way. However, it will be always necessary to draw a rough theoretical outline of this picture beforehand; as with the convergence model, complementarity can be achieved only if empirical results can be understood within a common theoretical framework.

Like the mutual validation model of triangulation, the complementarity model is applicable in many, but not all, situations. The limits of the complementarity model soon become clear if divergent results arise within a mixed methods design (quantitative and qualitative). Again, with divergent qualitative and quantitative findings, the role of theory comes into play because divergence can be meaningfully defined only within a certain theoretical framework. To solve the problems posed by contradictory findings, this framework has to be modified and revised. Quite often, this will be carried out by drawing on parts of the "theoretical map" to which the divergent empirical findings have not been related so far. In other cases, huge parts of the map have to be drawn anew. The search for new explanations that can account for anomalous findings is based on processes of *hypothetical reasoning* that help to construct new theoretical ideas and concepts on the basis of already available empirical data material. This can be a risky endeavor and requires certain methodological precautions. For example, great attention has to be paid to the empirical content and to the consistency of the newly developed theoretical concepts, as well as to their adaptability to already established theories, if one truly wishes to avoid the invention of immunizing auxiliary assumptions.

Whether certain empirical results can be regarded as convergent, complementary, or divergent clearly depends on the chosen theoretical framework. Here, the limits of our metaphorical concept become evident. Using triangulation in navigation or land surveying means determining the length of the sides of a triangle by applying clearly defined measurement operations and by carrying out clearly defined calculations with the help of well-known mathematical laws. If we triangulate in social research, we do not wish to determine the spatial position of a given point; rather, we wish to identify the nature of a certain social phenomenon. Contrary to trigonometry, where well-established mathematical concepts and clearly defined rules can be used to relate certain empirical data to each other, the

social sciences often provide a confusing multiplicity of theoretical approaches that give different meanings to the observed phenomena and to their possible relations. This situation has no analogy, at least in classical Euclidean trigonometry; only our imaginations can help us to envisage a situation in which a multitude of triangles can be meaningfully constructed using the same three points. In this way, the notion of triangulation will remain a metaphor with clear boundaries in the field of social research methodology. As with any other metaphor, it may pave the way for serious misunderstandings of real-world processes as well as allow illuminating insights.

■ *Notes*

1. It does so in the original sense of that word, meaning a "leading" or "crucial example" for a theoretical concept.

2. "Triangulation" belongs to the realm of "trigonometry"—"measurement of three angles."

3. In the following figures, we use arrows for the sides of the triangles to clarify in each case the kind of logical inference (inductive or deductive) to which the example in question refers.

4. It was established in 1988 at the University of Bremen and financed mainly by the German Research Foundation (DFG or *Deutsche Forschungsgemeinschaft*).

5. These young adults come from 6 different occupational fields in the technical and service sector from the list of the 10 fields chosen most often by young people for vocational training: bank employees, office workers, industrial mechanics, car mechanics, retail sales personnel, and hairdressers.

6. It has sometimes been emphasized in the corresponding methodological literature that divergences between qualitative and quantitative findings may be regarded as starting points for new theoretical insights. Bryman (1988) suggested, as a solution to the problem

of divergent findings, "treat[ing] the two sets of results as indicative of different aspects of the phenomenon in question and . . . search[ing] for a hypothesis which would help to explain their inconsistency" (p. 166). Rossman and Wilson (1985) defined this kind of integration as "initiation": "Initiation is the analytic function that turns ideas around. It initiates new interpretations, suggests areas for further exploration, or recasts the entire research question" (p. 637).

7. In Figure 16.6, the curved arrow stands for the search for a theoretical statement that can explain the quantitative as well as the qualitative empirical results. The broken line shows that the Empirical Proposition 2 does not support the Theoretical Proposition 1.

8. When quoting Peirce, we have adhered to the convention of quoting the paragraph numbers to be found in the *Collected Papers* (Peirce, 1974, p. 79).

■ *References*

Anderson, D. R. (1987). *Creativity and the philosophy of C. S. Peirce.* Dordrecht, Netherlands: Martinus Nijhoff.

Blaikie, N. W. (1991). A critique of the use of triangulation in social research. *Quality & Quantity, 2,* 115-136.

Braemer, G. (1994). *Wandel im Selbstbild des Familienernährers? Reflexion über vierzig Jahre Ehe-, Erwerbs-, und Familienleben.* Arbeitspapier 29 des Sfb 186, Bremen, Germany.

Brannen, J. (Ed.). (1992). *Mixing methods: Qualitative and quantitative research.* Aldershot, UK: Avebury.

Brauns, H. (1999). Soziale Herkunft und Bildungserfolg in Frankreich. *Zeitschrift für Soziologie, 3,* 197-218.

Bryman, A. (1988). *Quantity and quality in social research.* London: Routledge.

Campbell, D. T., & Fiske, D. W. (1959). Convergent and discriminant validation by the multitrait-multimethod matrix. *Psychological Bulletin, 2,* 81-105.

Creswell, J. W. (1994). *Research design: Qualitative and quantitative approaches.* Thousand Oaks, CA: Sage.

Denzin, N. K. (1978). *The research act: A theoretical introduction to sociological methods.* New York: McGraw-Hill.

Erzberger, C. (1998). *Zahlen und Wörter: Die Verbindung quantitativer und qualitativer Daten und Methoden im Forschungsprozess.* Weinheim, Germany: Deutscher Studien Verlag.

Erzberger, C. (2000, October). *What can we learn from Potemkin? Qualitative results as optical illusions.* Paper presented at the 5th International Conference on Social Science Methodology, Cologne, Germany.

Erzberger, C., & Prein, G. (1997). Triangulation: Validity and empirically based hypothesis construction. *Quality & Quantity, 2,* 141-154.

Fielding, N. G., & Fielding, J. L. (1986). *Linking data* (Qualitative Research Methods, Vol. 4). London: Sage.

Flick, U. (1991). Triangulation. In U. Flick, E. von Kardoff, H. Keupp, L. von Rosenstiel, & S. Wolff (Eds.), *Handbuch qualitative Sozialforschung* (pp. 432-434). Munich, Germany: Psychologie Verlags Union.

Flick, U. (1992). Triangulation revisited: Strategy of validation or alternative? *Journal of the Theory of Social Behaviour, 2,* 175-197.

Flick, U. (1998). *An introduction to qualitative research.* Thousand Oaks, CA: Sage.

Hammersley, M., & Atkinson, P. (1983). *Ethnography: Principles in practice* (2nd ed.). London: Routledge.

Hanson, N. R. (1965). *Patterns of discovery: An inquiry into the conceptual foundations of science.* Cambridge, UK: Cambridge University Press. (Original work published 1952)

Heinz, W. R., Kelle, U., Witzel, A., & Zinn, J. (1998). Vocational training and career development in Germany: Results from a longitudinal study. *International Journal of Behavioral Development, 1,* 77-101.

Hempel, C. G. (1952). *Fundamentals in concept formation in empirical science.* Chicago: University of Chicago Press.

Henz, U., & Maas, I. (1995): Chancengleich-heit durch die Bildungsexpansion? *Kölner Zeitschrift für Soziologie und Sozialpsychologie, 4,* 605-633.

Jahoda, M., Lazarsfeld, P. F., & Zeisel, H. (1982). *Die Arbeitslosen von Marienthal.* Frankfurt, Germany: Suhrkamp. (Original work published 1933)

Kaplan, A. (1964). *The conduct of inquiry: Methodology for behavioral science.* San Francisco: Chandler.

Kelle, U. (1998). *Empirisch begründete Theoriebildung: Zur Logik und Methodologie interpretativer Sozialforschung.* Weinheim, Germany: Deutscher Studien Verlag.

Kelle, U. (2001). Sociological explanations between micro and macro and method triangulation. In N. Fielding & M. Schreier (Eds.), *Qualitative und quantitative Forschung: Übereinstimmungen und Divergenzen* [Online]. Available: www. qualitative-research.net/fqs/fqs.htm

Kelle, U., & Erzberger, C. (1999). Integration qualitativer und quantitativer Methoden. *Kölner Zeitschrift für Soziologie und Sozialpsychologie, 3,* 509-531.

Kelle, U., & Lüdemann, C. (1995). "Grau, teurer Freund, ist alle Theorie . . .": Rational Choice und das Problem der Brückenannahmen. *Kölner Zeitschrift für Soziologie und Sozialpsychologie, 2,* 249-267.

Kelle, U., & Zinn, J. (1998). School-to-work transition and occupational careers: Results from a longitudinal study in Germany. In T. Lange (Ed.), *Understanding the school-to-work transition* (pp. 71-90). New York: Nova Science.

Kirschenmann, P. P. (1991). Logic and normative rationality of science: The content of discovery rehabilitated. *Zeitschrift für allgemeine Wissenschaftstheorie, 22,* 61-72.

Krüger, H. (2001). Social change in two generations: Employment patterns and their costs for family life. In V. W. Marshall, W. R. Heinz, H. Krüger, & A. Verma (Eds.), *Restructuring work and the life course* (pp. 401-423). Toronto: Toronto University Press.

Lakatos, I. (1982). *Die Methodologie der wissenschaftlichen Forschungsprogramme.* Brunswick, Germany: Vieweg.

Lamnek, S. (1995). *Qualitative Sozialforschung, Band 1: Methodologie.* Weinheim, Germany: Psychologie Verlags Union.

Laudan, L. (1977). *Progress and its problems: Towards a theory of scientific growth.* London: Routledge & Kegan Paul.

Lincoln, Y. S., & Guba, E. G. (1985). *Naturalistic inquiry.* Beverly Hills, CA: Sage

Lutz, B. (1984). *Der kurze Traum immerwährender Prosperität: Eine Neuinterpretation der industriell-kapitalistischen Entwicklung im Europa des 20. Jahrhunderts.* Frankfurt, Germany: Campus.

Nave-Herz, R. (1988). Zeitgeschichtlicher Bedeutungswandel von Ehe und Familie in der Bundesrepublik Deutschland. In R. Nave-Herz & M. Markefka (Eds.), *Handbuch der Familien und Jugendforschung, Band 1: Familienforschung* (pp. 211-222). Frankfurt, Germany: Luchterhand.

Nersessian, N. J. (1989). Scientific discovery and commensurability of meaning. In K. Gavroglu, Y. Goudarolis, & P. Nicolacopoulos (Eds.), *Imre Lakatos and theories of scientific change* (pp. 323-334). Dordrecht, Netherlands: Kluwer Academic.

Nickles, T. (Ed.). (1980). *Scientific discovery, logic, and rationality* (Boston Studies in the Philosophy of Science, Vol. 56). Dordrecht, Netherlands: Reidel.

Nickles, T. (1985). Beyond divorce: Current status of the discovery debate. *Philosophy of Science, 52,* 177-206.

Nickles, T. (1990). Discovery logics. *Philosophica, 45,* 732.

Peirce, C. S. (1974). *Collected papers* (C. Hartshore, P. Weiss, & A. Burks, Eds.). Cambridge, MA: Belknap Press of Harvard University Press.

Popper, K. R. (1989). *Logik der Forschung* (9th ed.). Tübingen, Germany: J. C. B. Mohr. (Original work published 1934)

Prein, G., & Seus, L. (2000). "The devil finds work for idle hands to do": The relationship between unemployment and delinquency. In N. G. Fielding, A. Clarke, & R. Witt (Eds.), *The economic dimensions of crime* (pp. 193-209). New York: Macmillan.

Reichenbach, H. (1983). *Erfahrung und Prognose* (Gesammelte Werke, Bd. 4, A. Kamlah

& M. Reichenbach, Eds.). Brunswick, Germany: Vieweg. (Original work published 1938)

Reichertz, J. (1991). *Aufklärungsarbeit. Kriminalpolizisten, und teilnehmende Beobachter bei der Arbeit.* Stuttgart, Germany: Enke.

Roethlisberger, F. J., & Dickson, W. J. (1939). *Management and the worker.* Cambridge, MA: Harvard University Press.

Rossides, D. W. (1997). *Social stratification: The interplay of class, race, and gender.* Upper Saddle River, NJ: Prentice Hall.

Rossman, G. B., & Wilson, B. L. (1985). Numbers and words: Combining quantitative and qualitative methods in a single-scale evaluation study. *Evaluation Review, 5,* 627-643.

Rossman, G. B., & Wilson, B. L. (1994). Numbers and words revisited: Being shamelessly eclectic. *Quality & Quantity, 3,* 315-327.

Shavit, Y., & Blossfeld, H. P. (Eds.). (1993). *Persistent inequality.* Boulder, CO: Westview.

Smith, J. K. (1983). Quantitative versus qualitative research: An attempt to clarify the issue. *Educational Researcher, 12*(3), 6-13.

Tashakkori, A., & Teddlie, C. (1998). *Mixed methods: Combining qualitative and quantitative approaches* (Applied Social Research Methods, No. 46). Thousand Oaks, CA: Sage.

Thomas, W. I., & Thomas, D. S. (1970): *The child in America: Behavior problems and programs.* New York: Knopf. (Original work published 1928)

Webb, E. J., Campbell, D. T., Schwartz, R. D., & Sechrest, L. (1966). *Unobtrusive measures: Nonreactive research in the social sciences.* Chicago: Rand McNally.

Weymann, A., Sackmann, R., & Wingens, M. (1999). Social change and the life course in East Germany: A cohort approach to inequalities. *International Journal of Sociology and Social Policy, 19,* 90-114.

Wingens, M. (1999). Der "gelernte DDR-Bürger": Biographischer Modernisierungsrückstand als Transformationsblockade? Planwirtschaftliche Semantik, Gesellschaftsstruktur, und Biographie. *Soziale Welt, 50,* 255-280.

Applications and Examples of Mixed Methods Research Across Disciplines

17

MIXED METHODS IN EVALUATION CONTEXTS: A PRAGMATIC FRAMEWORK

◆ Sharon F. Rallis
Gretchen B. Rossman

The past two decades have witnessed an increasing frustration with methodological purism[1] and its attendant claims that a particular methodological choice is superior to others. Purists argue that various research methods are grounded in distinct, incommensurate paradigmatic assumptions; combining or mixing them represents an egregious form of methodological miscegenation. Calls for methodological purity echoed in aca-demic journals and the hallways of university buildings (for a historical perspective, see Rossman & Wilson, 1985; for a more current one, see Greene & Caracelli, 1997). Many who witnessed this debate (and participated from the sidelines) took a more pragmatic stance. Working in applied fields such as business, health care, social services, and education, researchers and evaluators went about their work seeking to design and conduct studies that

AUTHORS' NOTE: This chapter was prepared with assistance from Natalia Kovalyova, Silva Kurtisa, and Fulgence Swai at the University of Massachusetts. We also thank Valerie Caracelli, Jennifer Greene, David Fetterman, Marsha Mueller, Jim Riccio, Deb Rog, Rikki Savaya, and Mark Waysman for reviewing this work and making valuable comments.

relied on multiple methods to understand complex social phenomena. Articles in journals and books began to appear that explicated methodological pluralism. General treatises include the work of Bamberger (2000), Brewer and Hunter (1989), Bryman (1988), Creswell (1994), Fielding and Fielding (1986), Newman and Benz (1998), and Taylor (2000), all helpful for guiding the principles and practice of mixing research methods in a single study.

In the field of evaluation, combining methods has a long-standing history, albeit not without sometimes fractious debate about the merits and challenges of such practice. As Riggin (1997) noted, "Mixed-methods evaluations have advanced to the point of being obsolete as a distinct type of evaluation. Evaluators have learned that *combining quantitative and qualitative information is not only advisable but inevitable*" (p. 87, italics added). Guides for combining methods in evaluations include Caracelli and Greene (1993); Cook and Reichardt (1979); Datta (1997a, 1997b); Greene and Caracelli (1997); Greene, Caracelli, and Graham (1989); Mark and Shotland (1987); Reichardt and Rallis (1994); and Rossman and Wilson (1985, 1994). As a quintessentially applied field, evaluation must serve the information needs of those who have contracted for the evaluation—the stakeholders. This demand for high-quality useful information characterizes the evaluation enterprise and sets it apart from research conducted for more theoretical or "pure" purposes (see Patton, 1990). Because of this information demand, evaluators are generally pragmatists (at least those who continue to receive evaluation contracts); they understand that evaluation research is a series of decisions that are compromises based on logistics, feasibility, stakeholder interests, the value stance of the evaluator, time, and other resources. Mixed methods designs have been used in evaluations for "more than three decades" to answer "formative, process, descriptive, and implementation questions" (Datta, 1997a, p. 347). This pragmatic approach to answering evaluative questions is integral to evaluation practice.

Datta (1997b) defined pragmatism in evaluation to mean that "*the essential criteria for making design decisions are practical, contextually responsive, and consequential*" (p. 34, italics in original). Pragmatism, however, does not imply a shameless disregard for the assumptive worlds from which specific methods derive; instead, it serves as a reminder that the overall purpose of evaluation is to make judgments about the merit and worth of social programs and to do so with integrity, rigor, and ethics. Grounding design decisions in assumptions about epistemology—how we come to know the social world as inquirers—provides what Greene and Caracelli (1997) called "a paradigmatic anchor" that keeps the evaluator from being "too readily buffeted by the sociopolitical influences of the context" (p. 11).

Evaluation theorists have long suggested that design and methods decisions are grounded in the paradigmatic assumptions of the evaluators, the key stakeholders, or the programs—or some mix of these. Paradigms are, however, constructs that are not logically required in the real world of practice (see Patton, 1988). The term *paradigm*, moreover, has been seriously challenged as a useful basis for guiding decisions, in large part because the construct has been trivialized into what Newman and Benz (1998) called "a false dichotomy" (p. 9). That is, the complex world of social science inquiry has been bifurcated into qualitative or quantitative assumptions and methodologies. An alternative is to view research strategies along a continuum that privileges the research or evaluation questions over assumptive worlds. In fact, most real-world evaluations pose multiple and diverse questions that cross paradigmatic boundaries, so evaluators tend to be pragmatic in drawing on methods. This methodological pragmatism and the resulting pluralism serve to enhance the practice of evaluation. Evaluators can choose from a variety of designs and methods when conceptualizing and conducting a study. Ideally, they choose relevant and rigorous data collection methods and analytical strategies that will answer the evaluation questions.

Given a potentially wide array of choices, one strategy to anchor important design questions is for the evaluator to continuously consider the purposes of the evaluation as well as the purposes for combining methods. For example, Chelimsky (1997) identified three main purposes of evaluation: accountability to promote "good management" (p. 5), development to foster "institutional learning and outreach among people" (p. 5), and the building of knowledge about specific recurring social problems. Rossman and Rallis (2000) named learning as the purpose of evaluation. D. M. Fetterman (personal communication, January 27, 2001) argued that mixing methods strengthens any of these purposes.

In this chapter, we argue that evaluation entails three primary activities: description, comparison, and prediction. Undergirding these three is evaluation's demand to make value judgments about the merit and worth of that which is being evaluated. This chapter explicates a pragmatic framework and provides examples of how mixed methods evaluations meet them to varying degrees. As primary examples, we draw on four evaluations deemed "exemplary" by the American Evaluation Association; these are supplemented by an illustrative example from an international context. In using these examples, we categorize them into different mixed methods designs, applying the typology developed by Caracelli and Greene (1997).

◆ The Evaluation Context

As suggested in the introduction, evaluation is a specialized form of social science research. While employing the methods of social science, evaluation has the fundamental purpose of making judgments about the merit and worth of programs and policies. As Scriven (1991) noted, "What distinguishes evaluation from other applied research is at most that it leads to evaluative conclusions, and to get to them requires identifying standards and performance data, and the integration of the two" (pp. 143-144). In a more colloquial style, he noted that "evaluation is what distinguishes food from garbage, lies from truth, and science from superstition" (pp. 139-140). Evaluation is less concerned than other social science research with general truths because it focuses on specific programs and practices. Weiss's (1998) definition is both elegant and simple: "Evaluation is the *systematic assessment* of the *operation* and/or the *outcomes* of a program or policy, compared to a set of *explicit* or *implicit standards*, as a means of contributing to the *improvement* of the program or policy" (p. 4, italics in original).

The construct of *program theory* has been widely used in evaluation theory and practice as one mechanism for understanding a social program's goals and how it is designed to achieve those goals. Thus, program theory can serve as a basis for evaluation design. Weiss (1998) described a program theory as "the set of beliefs that underlie action" (p. 55), "a set of hypotheses upon which people build their program plans" (p. 55), and "an explanation of the causal links that tie program inputs to expected program outputs" (p. 55). Bickman (1987) defined program theory as "a plausible and sensible model of how a program is supposed to work" (p. 5), while Wholey (1987) noted that program theory identifies "program resources, program activities, and intended program outcomes, and specifies a chain of causal assumptions linking program resources, activities, intermediate outcomes, and ultimate goals" (p. 78).

Key ideas are descriptions of linkages among program activities, comparisons to program goals and other standards, and hypothesized causal links between attributes and outcomes that allow for judgments, recommendations, and predictions. Implicit throughout is the act of *valuing*. Defined as the working logic about how the program will bring about preferred results (predictive judgments), this embedded logic model—the program's implicit theory—guides fundamental decisions about project design and is often linked to evaluation goals (for further details, see Chen, 1990, 1997).

Evaluations take many forms and adhere to differing theoretical perspectives. Some concentrate on one program implemented at one site; others are much more broad, assessing the effectiveness of multiple instances of a program; and yet others make cross-national evaluative judgments. Evaluations also differ in design complexity. Some rely on a single measure or descriptor, while others use multiple methods to ensure rich and detailed assessments of complex programs. Some consider a single instance in time—a snapshot—while others are longitudinal.

Because this chapter is devoted to evaluations that combine multiple methods, some clarification of what we mean by *combining methods, multiple methods,*

and *mixing methods* is in order. As research methodologists, we understand *methods* as referring to two types of research activities: data collection and data analysis. Thus, the word *methods* refers to ways, techniques, or tools for generating thoughtful, accurate, and ethical data about a program *and also* to ways, techniques, or strategies for manipulating those data. We believe there is some confusion about this distinction in the literature. That is, when many authors refer to *multiple methods*, they seem to conflate data collection and analysis, assuming that these processes are the same. We see the two as separable conceptually. Thus, an evaluation can gather data in the form of words (e.g., through document review or interviews) and then manipulate those data statistically. Alternatively, another evaluation may gather data in the form of numbers (e.g., frequencies, percentages) that are seen as qualities to be manipulated conceptually (e.g., "Most of the families in this group are low income"). In this way, evaluators naturally use a mix of methods. Thus, we avoid lumping methods into the large and meaningless categories of qualitative or quantitative and instead try to state precisely what we are doing with the data.

Methods are mixed quite naturally because the inquiry process that is evaluation is an iterative learning process; one phase informs another and then loops back to reframe an earlier phase. For example, we begin with questions that shape data collection, but data collected inform and modify the questions. Like learning, data collection and analysis pervade both the design and doing stages of evaluation. Learning begins as the

> researcher plays with ideas, poses research questions, and constructs conceptual frameworks. As the research questions are refined, methods [are]

chosen to respond to them, and data are gathered, the researcher becomes fully engaged in learning about the phenomenon. These processes and decisions preclude some ways of thinking about the phenomenon and highlight others. (Rossman & Wilson, 1994, p. 315)

In evaluation, learning about the phenomenon often requires more than one way of thinking. These divergent ways of thinking lead the evaluator to multiple methods.

◆ Exemplary Evaluations

To illustrate the pragmatic framework for mixed methods evaluations, we have selected four recent evaluations that have received one of the American Evaluation Association's awards as well as one mixed methods evaluation from an international context. Over the past few years, the association has solicited nominations for various awards, committees have reviewed them, and the awards have been announced at the association's annual meetings. Our sole criterion in selection was that the evaluations demonstrated the use of multiple methods; given that they have received such outstanding awards, we assumed that the evaluations are of high quality. We have also included the evaluation of SHATIL, the capacity-building branch of the New Israel Fund, because it serves as a useful illustration.

A MIXED METHODS TYPOLOGY

In describing the evaluations, we categorize them using the typology presented by Caracelli and Greene (1997). This typology clusters mixed methods designs into *component designs* and *integrated designs*. In component designs, methods are used as "discrete aspects of the overall inquiry and remain distinct throughout the inquiry" (p. 22), and they include triangulation, complementarity, and expansion designs. Integrated designs, by contrast, combine methods from "disparate paradigms and have the potential to produce significantly more insightful, even dialectically transformed, understandings" of the program (p. 23). Included here are iterative, embedded or nested, holistic, and transformative designs. This typology is quite useful for understanding the underlying logic of the evaluation to ascertain the intent of the evaluator in mixing methods. While we do not apply this typology exhaustively, we do use some of its categories for explicating the exemplary evaluations used in the remainder of this chapter (see Table 17.1).

In what follows, we offer brief descriptions of the exemplary evaluations. These are presented in Table 17.2. The program and the evaluation design are presented, followed by references that readers can use to learn more about the evaluations. Each outstanding evaluation was briefly described in the *American Journal of Evaluation* (formerly *Evaluation Practice*), followed by an in-depth interview with the evaluator. We draw on both sources to illustrate the pragmatic framework.[2]

THE GAIN EVALUATION

GAIN, created by the California legislature as a welfare-to-work program for recipients of Aid to Families With Dependent Children (AFDC), provided welfare recipients with job search assistance, basic education, vocational training, postsecondary education, and unpaid work experience. The goals of GAIN were to increase employment and reduce reliance on

TABLE 17.1   A Typology of Mixed Methods Designs

Design	Key Features
Component	Data gathering methods implemented as separate aspects of the evaluation and remain distinct throughout
Triangulation	Findings from one method used to corroborate findings generated through other methods
Complementarity	Findings from one dominant method enhanced or elaborated through findings from another method
Expansion	Different methods implemented to generate results for distinct components of the evaluation; results presented "side-by-side" (p. 23)
Integrated	Methods integrated throughout the evaluation
Iterative	Dynamic interplay of findings generated through different methods throughout the evaluation
Embedded or nested	One method located within another method; framework of "creative tension" (p. 24)
Holistic	Simultaneous integration of methods throughout the evaluation, building toward one integrated explanation of results
Transformative	Mixing methods to capture differing value commitments that can lead to "reconfiguring the dialog across ideological differences" (p. 24)

SOURCE: Caracelli and Greene (1997).

welfare. Counties had flexibility in implementing the program.

The evaluation, conducted by James Riccio and his colleagues at the Manpower Demonstration Research Corporation (MRDC), had four goals: (a) to learn about the counties' experiences in implementing the program and about recipients' participation and experiences, (b) to determine GAIN's effects, (c) to assess how different program strategies influence those results, and (d) to determine costs and benefits. The evaluation used an array of data, including employment and welfare administrative records, case file data, surveys of both staff and program recipients, field research, and fiscal data from agencies. The impact analysis was a large-scale experiment that randomly assigned welfare recipients to GAIN or to a control group. Impacts were assessed using administrative records and survey results. A cost-benefit analysis estimated overall financial gain or loss to welfare recipients, government budgets, taxpayers, and society overall. Given the discrete questions and sources of data used in this evaluation, it appears to fall under the *component expansion design* category where "results are characteristically

TABLE 17.2 The Exemplary Evaluations

Evaluation	Evaluator	Scope	Design	Sample Size	Data Collection
GAIN	Riccio/ Manpower Demonstration Research Corporation	State	Component expansion	13 counties 6 intensive 33,000 recipients	Review of administrative records Review of case file data Surveys Field research Review of fiscal data
ECFE	Mueller	State	Integrated iterative	14 districts 409 recipients 150 intensive	Enrollment surveys Parent interviews Videotaped observations Stimulated response parent interviews
STEP	Fetterman	Organization	Integrated holistic	1 program	Faculty and student interviews Classroom observations Review of curricula and reports Review of financial records
HFP	Rog (VIPPS)	National	Integrated iterative	9 cities 3 comparison sites 1,300 recipients	Review of program documents Family, individual, and staff focus group interviews Observations Review of administrative records
SHATIL	Waysman & Savaya	National	Component expansion and integrated iterative	233 organizations	Focus group interviews Individual interviews Surveys

offered in a side-by-side fashion" (Caracelli & Greene, 1997, p. 23). These side-by-side results indicated that program recipients did increase employment and earnings, that they did reduce reliance on welfare, and that effects increased over time. For further information, see Riccio and Orenstein (1996); Riccio, Friedlander, and Freedman (1994); and Riccio and Hasenfeld (1996). A brief summary of the evaluation and an interview with Riccio appeared in *Evaluation Practice*; see Riccio (1997) and Fitzpatrick (1997).

THE EARLY CHILDHOOD FAMILY EDUCATION PROGRAM EVALUATION

The Early Childhood Family Education (ECFE) Program, a voluntary public school program for all Minnesota families with children up to kindergarten age, aims to strengthen families through education and support to provide an optimal environment for healthy growth and development of children. The evaluation of the ECFE Program sought to learn what outcomes lower-income families involved in the program demonstrate and to build capacity within the organization to evaluate its own programs.

Conducted by Marsha Mueller and the ECFE staff, the evaluation questions were as follows. To what extent are lower-income families entering the programs, and what are their characteristics? What knowledge and skills do lower-income families bring to the ECFE Program? To what extent and in what ways are lower-income families involved in the ECFE Program? How do families assess their ECFE experience? How do parents change their knowledge and skill? The evaluation design emphasized staff participation in all phases of the study. Data collection techniques included surveys, interviews, video-

taped observations, stimulated response interviews, and participant record reviews. Given the interplay of data gathering and the extensive interaction between evaluators and staff regarding the design and results of the evaluation, the ECFE study appears to be an *integrated iterative* design where there is a "dynamic and ongoing interplay over time between the different methodologies" (Caracelli & Greene, 1997, p. 23).

Results indicated that the ECFE Program made a positive difference in the parenting knowledge, skills, and specific behaviors of low-income families. For further information, see Mueller (1994, 1995, 1996a, 1996b). A brief description of the evaluation and an interview with Mueller appeared in the *American Journal of Evaluation;* see Mueller (1998) and Fitzpatrick (1998).

THE STANFORD UNIVERSITY TEACHER EDUCATION PROGRAM EVALUATION

The Stanford University Teacher Education Program (STEP), a 12-month teacher education program offering both a master's degree and a secondary school teaching credential, was evaluated to inform program improvement and to provide an overall assessment of the program. Conducted by David Fetterman and his associates at Stanford, the evaluation focused on the following areas: unity of purpose and mission, curriculum, research, alumni contact, professional development, school/university school partnerships, faculty involvement, excellence of teaching, and length of the program. Data collection was conducted through interviews, observations, surveys, and digital photography in classrooms and Web surveys. Weekly evaluation team meetings and frequent database sorts facilitated data analysis.

Furthermore, the evaluation team wrote frequent reports to facilitate formative thinking about the teacher education program. This interplay of data gathering, intensive meetings to discuss emergent findings, and the elaborated conceptual framework guiding the evaluation suggests that it represents an *integrated holistic design* in which there is "interdependence of different methodologies" and "a simultaneity of the integration of methods in these designs rather than a sense of taking turns" (Caracelli & Greene, 1997, p. 24).

Results suggested that the STEP (and other teacher education programs) lacked a unity of purpose, a disjuncture between theory and practice was confusing for students in the program, teachers in the program did not reflect on their practice systematically, and the program did not maintain contact with alumni. The evaluation made recommendations consistent with these results. For further information, see Fetterman et al. (1999); Fetterman, Connors, Dunlap, Brower, and Matos (1998); and Fetterman, Dunlap, Greenfield, and Yoo (1997). Information is also available at Stanford's Web site (www.stanford.edu/~davidf/step. html). A brief description of the evaluation and an interview with Fetterman appeared in the *American Journal of Evaluation;* see Fetterman (2000) and Fitzpatrick (2000a).

THE HOMELESS FAMILIES PROGRAM EVALUATION

The Homeless Families Program (HFP), a joint demonstration effort of the Robert Wood Johnson Foundation and the U.S. Department of Housing and Urban Development, sought to (a) create systems change in health and support services for homeless families and (b) develop and test a model of services-enriched housing for homeless families that have multiple problems. Conducted by Debra J. Rog and her associates at the Vanderbilt Institute for Public Policy, the cross-site evaluation was designed to learn more about the needs of the families; how services and systems might be better organized to meet those needs; and how housing might be delivered to foster stability, service use, and progress toward self-sufficiency.

Data collection had two major components: (a) case studies of the project sites and three comparison sites and (b) collection of extensive family data gathered by each family's case manager. The case studies included reviews of key documents, on-site interviews, and observations and tours of facilities and activities. The family-level data were gathered at intake, as well as monthly, quarterly, and at exit from the program, and provided standardized information about the needs and characteristics of the participating families. Given the interrelated elements of this design and its exploratory nature, it appears to illustrate the *integrated iterative design* where data gathered through the various methods lead to "a progressive reconfiguration of substantive findings and interpretations in a pattern of increasing insight and sophistication" (Caracelli & Greene, 1997, p. 23).

The study tracked the web of deep structural and personal challenges that homeless families face and provided critical guidance for developing initiatives for impoverished families. The evaluators concluded that homelessness can be ameliorated when families receive housing subsidies. For further information, see Rog (1994) and Rog, Holumpka, and McCombs-Thornton (1995). A brief description of the evaluation and an interview with Rog appeared in the *American Journal of Evaluation;* see Rog (1999) and Fitzpatrick (1999).

THE SHATIL EVALUATION

SHATIL is the capacity-building branch of the New Israel Fund, a philanthropic foundation that helps to fund local nongovernmental organizations active in achieving social change. SHATIL provides individualized direct assistance to nonprofit community-based social change organizations in the following areas: organizational consultation, fund-raising and finances, advocacy and media/public relations, and volunteer recruitment and management. SHATIL also provides nonindividualized or indirect services such as professional training and workshops for groups of organizations, and it also establishes and maintains coalitions of organizations that work together to further common goals. Conducted by Mark Waysman and Rikki Savaya at the Center for Evaluation of Human Services, the evaluation objectives were to (a) map the characteristics of the organizations that apply to SHATIL, (b) map the services provided to these organizations, (c) assess the perceived contribution of SHATIL to the development and goal attainment of these organizations, and (d) evaluate the satisfaction of these organizations with the services provided to them by SHATIL.

The evaluation consisted of three phases. Phase I examined the program's aims, characteristics of client organizations, and their needs and experiences with SHATIL. Data were collected through structured personal interviews with senior SHATIL staff and through a series of four focus groups with representatives of client organizations. Data were analyzed to learn about the components and aims of the services provided by SHATIL and to learn issues of relevance and significance to SHATIL's client organizations. Phase II used questionnaires to explore client perceptions of services as well as analysis of an existing database to learn more about client characteristics and types, amounts, and frequency of services provided. Phase III identified two focus groups (those most satisfied with SHATIL services and those least satisfied) to explore sources of satisfaction and dissatisfaction. The three phases were implemented sequentially, with each subsequent phase building on the previous one(s). Given this phased design, the evaluation does not fit neatly into the Caracelli and Greene (1997) typology; it offers some characteristics of a *component expansion* design in which specific methods are implemented to generate findings for one component (phase). In fact, the evaluators stipulated, "The main aim of using mixed-methods in this study was *expansion,* which occurs when researchers mix methods in order to extend the scope, breadth, and range of inquiry" (Greene et al., 1989, cited in Waysman & Savaya, 1997b, p. 233). We argue that the evaluation also fits into the *integrated iterative design* where there is an interplay of methods over time. Further information about this evaluation is found in Waysman and Savaya (1997a).

In the next section, we develop a framework for pragmatic mixed methods designs in evaluation and use the exemplary evaluations to illustrate the framework.

◆ A Pragmatic Framework

Certain activities are integral to the evaluation process. First, an evaluation *describes* the following. What is this program we are evaluating? What are its attributes? How are these features or characteristics of the program organized into patterns? An evaluation also *compares* the following. How are the patterns of this program similar to or different from the patterns of similar programs? How does this program differ from others? How does this program measure up against a standard? The comparison activity is especially important in evaluation because the worth of a program is typically judged in relation to another program or standard. Finally, to meet the information needs of stakeholders, an evaluation *predicts* the following. What features of this program make a difference? If the program includes a particular intervention, will we reach the desired outcome? These predictions become recommendations that inform future plans.

Description, comparison, and prediction contribute to making value judgments about a program or policy. They are complex, interrelated cognitive activities that are seldom performed in a linear process. Usually, all three activities are related and used iteratively in an evaluation. We must describe and understand so as to compare and predict; similarly, comparisons and testing predictions yield richer descriptions and deeper understandings. At one time or another during an evaluation, one activity will receive a relatively stronger emphasis. In fact, all of our exemplars begin with descriptive data collection; they need to know about the program. Some begin with building logical models or a theory base, but others build the logical model or generate the theory as they learn about the program. The model or theory then shapes both the design and the analysis as the process continues. Ultimately, the model becomes part of the prediction.

These three activities, while present in all social inquiry, are crucial to making the judgments required in evaluation. According to Patton (1997), "Program evaluation is the systematic collection of information about the activities, characteristics, and outcomes of programs to make judgments about the program, [to] improve program effectiveness, and/or to inform decisions about future programming" (p. 23). Judgments about the program lead to recommendations for improvement, and they inform decision making.

Evaluators do not choose methods to collect and analyze data, then, according to a qualitative and quantitative distinction; rather, they do so according to the questions being asked. The goal is to learn so as to make judgments about the program. Given the program goals, objectives, and context, and given the available resources, what are the best methods to help us understand the program's merit, to make the most useful comparisons that reveal merit, and/or to predict worthy outcomes?

Because evaluations have these multiple purposes that result in learning and judging, many evaluators draw from the multiple methods for data collection and analysis that are available to them. Among these methods appear new and innovative ways to supplement the traditional interviews, observations, document reviews, surveys, test scores, and demographic data. We see videotapes that capture interactions, digital photography, and Web-based surveys. We do not label a specific method as either qualitative or quantitative but simply introduce it as a technique to collect and/or analyze data for description, comparison, or prediction. We offer this framework for explicating the use of mixed methods in evaluation as an alternative to the traditional qualitative and quantitative paradigms. We use the exemplary evaluations to illustrate methodological choices.

DESCRIPTION

Fundamentally, an evaluation describes so as to understand and appreciate the various aspects of the program or intervention. What do we do when we describe? We provide details on characteristics, activities, events, and attitudes. We ask the following questions. What happens in the program to whom and how often? What services are provided? What activities occur? Who is involved? How do they experience the activities or services? How is the program working? What is working? What is not working? What outcomes are achieved? We use words or numbers to draw a picture of the program.

How, then, does description contribute to the judgment function of evaluation? The details of the picture reveal the program's inherent goodness or quality—as well as its shortcomings or weaknesses. The *Oxford English Dictionary* (Brown, 1993) defines *merit* as "a point of intrinsic quality; a commendable quality, an excellence, a good point" (p. 1748). Scriven (1991) defined merit as "the 'intrinsic' value of evaluands, as opposed to extrinsic or system-related value/worth" (p. 227). Merit is revealed in the attributes—or intrinsic qualities—of the program or intervention. Thus, judgments of merit depend on detailed—or "thick" (Geertz, 1973)—descriptions of these characteristics and attributes, that is, descriptions that allow stakeholders to interpret activities and events.

As evaluators, then, our first task is to provide those details so that the program's quality—its merit—is evident. We can examine the attributes and decide if we value them. The scope of the judgment is self-contained; it is made on and within the program or service itself. Does this service have value on its own merit, not in relation to others? The merit of the program—or of its components—is apparent to readers in the description of the program's attributes. These judgments are typical of the determinations evaluators are contracted to provide.

Because we want the most revealing picture—the fullest and thickest description—we draw from the plethora of methods available to collect, analyze, and display data. Descriptions may be entirely qualitative; portraits, for example, reveal details about a program that enable stakeholders to judge merit (Lawrence-Lightfoot & Davis, 1997). Or descriptions may be entirely quantitative; tables of demographics or frequencies, for example, reveal details for interpretation. However, evaluators recognize that descriptions can be more complete if a mix of methods is used, so evaluation designs commonly use a variety of ways to describe the phenomenon.

Obviously, using a mix of methods for collection and analysis yields more and different data to produce a more comprehensive description. The mix provides elaboration of detail that is less likely if only one method is used. "Data from one source extend, clarify, illuminate, or help interpret data from another method" (Rossman & Wilson, 1994, p. 321). The mix also serves to corroborate a description emerging from one source or method with that emerging from another (Rossman & Wilson, 1994). An evaluator can explicate the merits of a "phenomenon more accurately by sighting in on it from different methodological viewpoints" (Brewer & Hunter, 1989, p. 17).

The exemplary evaluations draw their details for description from many sources. The evaluators of GAIN, the ECFE Program, the HFP, and SHATIL all emphasize their need to understand the program characteristics and implementation. Describing and understanding was especially challenging in these programs because of their complexity and the multiple sites of implementation. The STEP evaluation employed a variety of data collection methods that included some innovative techniques.

The GAIN evaluation sought to understand the different counties' experiences implementing the welfare-to-work legislation, asking the following questions. How are different players in the system interpreting and operationalizing their work? What are staff doing? Who is participating? For how long? What are participants' experiences? How much are the activities costing? The data were collected from employment and welfare administrative records, program case files, staff and recipient surveys, and fiscal records. Field researchers went to the counties to observe meetings, workshops, and other aspects of day-to-day operations. These researchers also interviewed staff at GAIN and welfare offices and at agencies that provided services. Staff surveys asked case managers about program practices and staff-resident interactions. Surveys questioned recipients' views of the program. The evaluators analyzed data to reveal patterns of delivery and participation as well as relationships between aspects of delivery and participation. The evaluators were trying to "get inside the black box" to learn about different program strategies and program impacts (Fitzpatrick, 1997, p. 243).

The principal investigator, Riccio, was explicit about the use of multiple methods:

> We had to proceed on both these tracks at the same time. We did not have the luxury of doing field research first and surveys next. However, the results of the two different methods did produce consistent findings. . . . Together, all the different sources of data provided us with a rich picture of GAIN in each of the counties. (Fitzpatrick, 1997, p. 247)

The merit of GAIN is especially apparent in the case study of Riverside County that reveals the breadth, magnitude, and consistency of program effects.

The evaluation of the HFP was primarily descriptive. Rog, the director of the evaluation, noted,

> We used a mix of methodologies and addressed many different content areas. The whole topic of homelessness among families was a new, emerging issue at that time. Homelessness was ill-defined. . . . There was especially little known about homeless families—who they were, how many there were, what their needs were, how they became homeless. . . . Therefore, in our evaluation, it was critical that we try to obtain some of this information, focusing more on describing the participants in the program than we might otherwise, to help increase our understanding of these families. (Fitzpatrick, 1999, p. 562)

Rog admitted that "we did err on the side of collecting more detail than one might do in a more controlled study" (p. 565). The evaluators used interviews, focus groups, and document reviews to get at questions such as the following. What does the system of service delivery look like at each site? How does the system deliver services? How do the staff and participants view the system? They reviewed and analyzed case records and documents and surveyed participants to describe family characteristics and needs and outcomes. In total, the multiple sources yielded descriptive data about the families that were "very rich" (p. 568) and useful. Rog commented on how one set of information "helped us to understand" (p. 570) another set of information. Analysis of the details contributed to building a theory for serving homeless families.

The evaluation of Minnesota's ECFE Program aimed to learn about the families that participated and the outcomes from their participation, so the data collection methods were chosen to provide details from multiple perspectives. Surveys collected demographic characteristics and tapped parents' perceptions of the program and of their participation. Program records were reviewed. Parents were interviewed to capture the knowledge and skills they brought to the program and, later, their perceptions about the changes in this knowledge and these skills. Parent-child interactions were videotaped in several locations, and parents participated in stimulated response interviews. Analysis sought patterns among the families but instead illustrated the diversity both in the families and in their experiences. The evaluation allowed the agencies involved to *see*, and thereby judge, the children's environments for growth and development.

The evaluators of the STEP relied on multiple sources to describe the program. Data were drawn from interviews of faculty and students, observations of classroom activity, focus groups with students and alumni, and Web surveys. To elaborate the picture, data also came from reviews of curricular, financial, and accreditation records. Findings were displayed both through narratives and numerically. Digital photography elaborated the data on classroom activity. The result is a picture of a program that stakeholders can judge for intrinsic quality. One discovery of the evaluation, for example, that the program lacked a common mission, illustrates the value of a descriptor for judging inherent merit.

The first phase of the SHATIL evaluation was devoted to collecting descriptive data to understand the many components of the program and its clients. To learn about the client organizations and their needs and about SHATIL services and clients' experiences with the services, the evaluation conducted structured interviews with senior staff as well as a series of focus groups with representatives of the client organizations. This descriptive phase allowed the evaluators to learn about the range and variety of clients' characteristics, needs, and experiences with SHATIL (Waysman & Savaya, 1997b). Inherent in the descriptions were strengths and weaknesses. This qualitative phase of description was followed by a second quantitative phase that consisted of two parts: (a) a comprehensive survey of all SHATIL client-organizations that was designed based on the findings of the first phase and (b) an analysis of computerized data from the SHATIL management information system. The analysis of these data provided a representative picture of client characteristics and the types and amounts of services they received from SHATIL; it also depicted their levels of satisfaction with and perceptions of SHATIL's effectiveness in helping them to develop their organizations and achieve their organizational goals.

Finally, another evaluation that was chosen as "outstanding" by the American Evaluation Association but that is not included in our exemplars because it does not use mixed methods is the Georgia Council for School Performance annual School and System Performance Reports. The council collects, stores in a database, and analyzes school performance measures. We point out this evaluation because, while the figures in the resulting report cards do provide a detailed numerical picture of the schools in Georgia, the council's director has noted that description and understanding of the schools' performances would be enhanced by adding narrative based on data from additional sources (Fitzpatrick, 2000b).

COMPARISON

Evaluations seldom end with the self-contained judgments that derive solely from attributes intrinsic to the program. Evaluation moves beyond description to use comparisons for judging merit in relation to another service or intervention or to a standard. The comparison activity is more salient with data analysis than with data collection. In the descriptive activity, analyses search for patterns and correlations, asking the following questions. Into what categories do the attributes fall, and how are these attributes related to each other? What do these patterns of relationship tell us about how and why the program operates as it does? What is this program an example of?

Then, the analysis moves outside the program itself to ask comparative questions. How does this program differ from others? How are the patterns of this intervention similar to or different from the patterns of other interventions? Is this intervention or service better than another? How does this program measure up against a standard? The comparison activity is especially important in evaluation because judgments about a program's merit in relation to a standard—either a relative or an absolute—are often more powerful to stakeholders than judgments based on intrinsic quality.

Comparisons can be made across many dimensions, including time (does performance improve over time in the program?), cost (what is the benefit of the program in relation to its costs?), components within a program (does training produce better results than mentoring?), and results between programs (which program has the better outcomes?). In these evaluations, merit is relative.

Comparisons are also made against an absolute standard. The standard may be professional, theoretical, or practical. Whenever possible, evaluators conduct literature reviews to build logical models or to identify indicators or benchmarks from theory against which to measure the program components. Sometimes, the ideal model exists (at least on paper) to use as a comparison with the program. Other times, the standard derives from practice; it emerges from the description of the program itself and its components. We see what is working and generate our own models or rubrics. In all of these comparisons, merit is based on whether the program measures up to the standard or ideal.

The exemplars provide illustrations of using mixed methods in a variety of comparative analyses. The GAIN evaluation compared the effects of different strategies on results within counties, and cross-case analyses compared, on a variety of dimensions, the experiences of recipients with those in different counties. Because this was a multisite, multimethod design—a component expansion design—the evaluators "were able to test through systematic site comparisons some different assumptions—theories, really—about what approaches worked best" (Fitzpatrick, 1997, p. 243). Riccio noted how the various components of the evaluation strengthened one another: "The staff surveys gave us an opportunity to compare counties more rigorously and systematically than we could have with field research data alone . . . [and] the field research complemented the survey data in important ways" (Fitzpatrick, 1997, p. 247).

The STEP evaluators used several different comparative analyses. First, stakeholders articulated their normative model: This was a Stanford program; did it measure up to Stanford standards? Two indicators of Stanford's standards used to measure the program's merit were a common vision and curricular connections between theory and practice. The evaluators also reviewed the literature associated with teacher education to introduce a theory-based model, consistent with an integrated holistic design. They asked what aspects of the program coincided with the model. For example, theory states that students should be given chances to teach classes and that mentor teachers should stay in the classroom to observe, so interviews and observations as well as surveys were designed to reveal answers to these questions.

Comparisons were also made across results from different collection methods in the STEP, providing new questions and additional data for analysis. For example, if courses were evaluated solely on the survey, then the results would be all positive because no course was rated below satisfactory. However, class observations revealed a full spectrum of instructional quality, and in interviews "the variability in the assessments of teaching quality went from 0 to absolutely stellar" (Fitzpatrick, 2000a, p. 243). This discrepancy stimulated further probing and question refinement that would not have been possible without this integrated holistic mixed methods design.

The HFP evaluation design included case studies of the project sites and three comparison sites where the project was not in place. For each case study, data were sufficient to allow comparisons of services and outcomes at specific intervals and longitudinally within that case. The integrated, iterative mixed methods design also allowed cross-case analysis within the project as a whole. A logical model evolved as data were collected and analyzed. The evaluators looked backward and "catalogued what [the sites] were doing under the rubric of systems change activities" (Fitzpatrick, 1999, p. 571). Analysis of each activity examined "how it fit within the framework of what you would want an ideal system to achieve" (p. 571). Program merit was clarified when held up to the absolute standard of this model.

For judging merit, the ECFE evaluation compared activities with professional standards from the literature on child de-

velopment and parenting. For example, the evaluation used experts and staff to rate the videotapes according to a rubric of appropriate knowledge of child development and parenting skill. They also used time comparisons when they reported percentages to compare changes across time from pre-program measures to post-program measures. The integrated iterative design helped to foster the interplay of data gathered through various methods, which strengthened the credibility and usefulness of the findings.

The integrated, iterative mixed methods design of SHATIL supported normative or relative comparison. The interviews and focus groups conducted during Phase I generated a framework of variance among client organizations that guided further data collection to identify issues of significance to the organizations. This information served as a basis for the questionnaire survey of Phase II. The survey results produced a representative picture of the organizations and their levels of satisfaction with services, allowing the evaluators to compare and judge satisfaction of client organizations and perceived effectiveness of SHATIL's services. These were assessed according to stage of organizational development, amount and types of services received, and consultant characteristics such as task versus process orientation and directive versus nondirective (see Waysman & Savaya, 1997a, 1997b).

PREDICTION

Inherent in evaluation is the notion of making predictive statements about what could be done to improve or extend a program. In the research literature, the concept of prediction has a specialized meaning; one designs studies to make probabilistic (statistical) predictions about outcomes or results of particular interventions. We argue that the term has a more general meaning in evaluation. Statements about what is working well or poorly, as well as specific recommendations, have connotations for the future—predictions. The *Oxford English Dictionary* (Brown, 1993) notes that *prediction* comes from the Latin *praedicere—pre* (before) plus *dicere* (speak)—meaning to speak before or mention previously in speech or writing. To predict is to "announce as an event that will happen in the future; . . . [to] have as a deducible consequence; [to] imply" (p. 2328). By the same reasoning, a prediction is "the action of predicting future events; . . . a forecast" (p. 2328).

As noted earlier in the definitions of evaluation, evaluations are intended to "improve program effectiveness and/or inform decisions about future programming" (Patton, 1997, p. 23). The implicit logic in this definition is that, through systematic inquiry (evaluation data gathering and analysis), the evaluator comes to make judgments about the program that then lead to recommendations about what *could* work better. This orientation toward the future (of the program or policy) is predictive in nature. We caution that our use of the term *predictive* does not mean "crystal ball forecasting"; instead, it means best guesses or working hypotheses—the kind of cognitions that we all undertake when planning actions and weighing consequences and reasonable outcomes for those actions.

Prediction is based, in part, on a judgment of worth. Evaluators express worth when they make judgments about the overall value of the program to some group of constituents or to society in general, including recommendations about future programming and funding. A program's worth considers its extrinsic value—how it is assessed and valued by others. Scriven (1991) noted that worth "usually refers to the value to an institution or col-

lective [program or service]," in contrast to intrinsic value (p. 382). He went on to note, "When people ask 'what something is worth,' they are usually referring to *market value,* and market value is a function of the market's (hypothesized) behavior toward it, not of the thing's intrinsic virtues" (pp. 382-283, italics in original). Do we as a society value the program sufficiently to invest further resources in it? The program may have merit (intrinsic value), but does it have worth (extrinsic value)?

Moreover, stakeholders and policy makers want evaluations to be predictive; their responsibilities include making decisions about program improvement, extending (to other sites or locales), increasing funding, and terminating. To make these decisions, they need evaluative information to support this planning process. What attributes of the program are related to desired outcomes, how are they related, and what changes in the program (recommendations) would improve program operations? These individuals want to know enough to judge the program's worth. They want information to plan programs and policies for the future.

When evaluators engage in this predictive thinking, what do they do? Several activities of evaluation illustrate and reflect this type of thinking. Assessing what is working well and what is not suggests that if the program were modified in the direction of what is working well, then it would work better—a prediction. Determining the overall merit of a program implies that the program is worth further investment (by legislators or other funders); if continued (in the future), the program will continue to yield results valued by society— also a prediction. Making recommendations (about future programming) is fundamentally oriented toward the future, and here the evaluator explicitly owns this predictive function. Recommendations contain predictive notions; if you do this, then the program will be better, more effective, or cost-effective, or it will reach more. If you terminate the program, then another better program could be developed in its stead.

Each of the exemplars illustrates the use of mixed methods in this predictive activity to a greater or lesser extent. The GAIN evaluation is an especially useful example of how making predictive judgments was integral to the mixed methods design. The study was commissioned by a legislative body to assess a key, and very expensive, piece of legislation. Policy makers needed to know what impact the program was having as well as if and how it should be modified to better achieve desired results and to inform planning. The California legislature and governor were key audiences for the evaluation. Key legislative staff strongly advocated for a rigorous independent evaluation of the policy. As Riccio noted,

> They did this because they cared about making good public policy. . . . They wanted to ensure that *in the future* the legislature would be in a position to decide whether GAIN was worth continuing, or how it could be strengthened, on the basis of facts and not have to rely just on ideology and anecdotes. (Fitzpatrick, 1997, p. 244, italics added)

The evaluation's use of a component expansion mixed methods design strengthened the credibility of both preliminary and final results. Riccio noted that early and frequent involvement of key stakeholders helped to foster use of the findings "even before the final results were in" (p. 245). Early preliminary results were used by legislators to argue that major modifi-

cations in the program should be held off until the final results were available.

The ECFE evaluation was much less concerned with linking directly back to policy making than was the GAIN evaluation. Mueller noted that this was the second outcome study of the ECFE Program, and therefore the focus was on "what we can learn rather than responding to a legislative mandate" (Fitzpatrick, 1998, p. 90). This *enlightenment* use of evaluation has become acceptable within the evaluation enterprise. Funding for this evaluation came from an independent foundation— the McKnight Foundation—to the organization conducting the evaluation, whereas the GAIN evaluation was funded directly by the legislature. The ECFE evaluation resulted in a set of policy and program recommendations; results were disseminated quite widely. Embedded in these recommendations were, of course, predictive statements about future policy to support the program as well as modifications in organization and implementation that could lead to more consistent and valued outcomes. However, the major purpose of this evaluation was to describe, in greater depth than previously, the life circumstances of low-income families that participated in this family support program, and thus the use of an integrated iterative design enhanced its descriptive power (as discussed earlier).

The HFP evaluation also focused more on description and comparison than on predictive statements. As noted previously, this evaluation was of one of the first large-scale initiatives to try to address the problem of family homelessness. The foundation that funded the evaluation was, according to Rog, interested in "an evaluation to understand the variation across sites [comparison] and to examine how the funding affected systems changes as well as outcomes for families"

(Fitzpatrick, 1999, p. 563). The integrated, iterative mixed methods design of comparative case studies that gathered family-level data as well as service and outcome information at regular intervals provided "greater explanatory power [prediction]" (p. 565) to the evaluation than a monomethod design would have.

The STEP evaluation focused on the traditional evaluation purpose of describing and making judgments about whether the program was achieving its goals and objectives from, as Fetterman noted, "a consumer perspective" (Fitzpatrick, 2000a, p. 243). The evaluation included several sets of recommendations that have received national attention from other universities' teacher education programs. These recommendations can be seen as predictive statements about how to improve not only the STEP but also teacher education programs in general. For example, one major STEP recommendation was that those involved in the program "need to agree on a unity of purpose in a program" (p. 245). Embedded in this recommendation is the implicit logic that *if* there is greater unity in the program, then there will be greater _____ (fill in the blank: success, completion rates, satisfaction, comradeship, etc.). The integrated, holistic mixed methods design supports this predictive activity, lending greater credence to findings than would reliance on a single evaluation research method.

The SHATIL evaluation was implemented specifically for the purposes of "look[ing] back and plan[ning] ahead, based on feedback from client organizations" (Waysman & Savaya, 1997b, p. 229). The use of an integrated, iterative mixed methods design was critically important to generate information useful for future planning. This design encouraged the expression of divergent opinions about SHATIL's effectiveness. As the eval-

uators noted, "Participants raised several issues that neither the evaluators nor the staff of SHATIL had thought to address in the study" (p. 235). These findings were then incorporated into the second-phase questionnaire, and subsequently some were confirmed as widely held views, while others were found to reflect the experiences of only a few organizations, sometimes with specific common characteristics (e.g., minority groups such as Arabs and immigrants from Ethiopia). The interview data, corroborated through the questionnaire responses, "resonated strongly among SHATIL staff," who were not always aware of the issues raised by their client-organizations, and "several meetings were held to develop procedures to cope with this issue" (p. 235). Thus staff used the results of the mixed methods evaluation directly to plan new directions for the future of the organization.

◆ Conclusion

This chapter has illustrated the use of mixed methods designs in exemplary evaluations. We argued that each evaluation, while designed somewhat differently and with differing scopes and purposes, demonstrates the fundamental evaluation activities of description, comparison, and prediction. These activities are central to the evaluation enterprise; mixing methods enhances these activities by providing greater depth, detail, and clarity than would monomethod designs. However, mixed methods designs are time-consuming to implement and demand a level of methodological sophistication not often found in one individual. We note, therefore, that many evaluations implementing mixed methods designs rely on teams that represent the expertise necessary to rigorously, ethically, and sensitively conduct the evaluations.

■ Notes

1. The very use of the term *purism* invokes its opposite—impure or tainted. Those of us who are committed to mixing methods enjoy the scandalous messiness of this impure activity.

2. When quoting from interviews with the evaluators, bibliographic references are made to Fitzpatrick, the editor of the Outstanding Evaluation series, who conducted the interviews.

■ References

Bamberger, M. (Ed.). (2000). *Integrating quantitative and qualitative research in development projects.* Washington, DC: World Bank.

Bickman, L. (Ed.). (1987). *Using program theory in evaluation* (New Directions for Program Evaluation, No. 33). San Francisco: Jossey-Bass.

Brewer, J., & Hunter, A. (1989). *Multimethod research: A synthesis of styles.* Newbury Park, CA: Sage.

Brown, L. (Ed.). (1993). *The new shorter Oxford English dictionary.* Oxford, UK: Clarendon.

Bryman, A. (1988). *Quality and quantity in social research.* London: Unwin.

Caracelli, V. J., & Greene, J. C. (1993). Data analysis strategies for mixed-method evaluation designs. *Educational Evaluation and Policy Analysis, 15,* 195-207.

Caracelli, V. J., & Greene, J. C. (1997). Crafting mixed-methods evaluations designs. In J. C. Greene & V. J. Caracelli (Eds.), *Advances in mixed-method evaluation: The challenges and benefits of integrating diverse paradigms* (New Directions for Evaluation, No. 74, pp. 19-32). San Francisco: Jossey-Bass.

Chelimsky, E. (1997). The coming transformation in evaluation. In E. Chelimsky & W. R. Shadish (Eds.), *Evaluation for the 21st century: A handbook* (pp. 1-26). Thousand Oaks, CA: Sage.

Chen, H. T. (1990). *Theory-driven evaluation.* Newbury Park, CA: Sage.

Chen, H. T. (1997). Applying mixed methods under the framework of theory-driven evaluations. In J. C. Greene & V. J. Caracelli (Eds.), *Advances in mixed-method evaluation: The challenges and benefits of integrating diverse paradigms* (New Directions for Evaluation, No. 74, pp. 61-72). San Francisco: Jossey-Bass.

Cook, T. D., & Reichardt, C. S. (Eds.). (1979). *Qualitative and quantitative methods in evaluation research.* Beverly Hills, CA: Sage.

Creswell, J. W. (1994). *Research design: Qualitative and quantitative approaches.* Thousand Oaks, CA: Sage.

Datta, L. (1997a). Multimethod evaluations: Using case studies together with other methods. In E. Chelimsky & W. R. Shadish (Eds.), *Evaluation for the 21st century: A handbook* (pp. 344-359). Thousand Oaks, CA: Sage.

Datta, L. (1997b). A pragmatic basis for mixed-method designs. In J. C. Greene & V. J. Caracelli (Eds.), *Advances in mixed-method evaluation: The challenges and benefits of integrating diverse paradigms* (New Directions for Evaluation, No. 74, pp. 33-46). San Francisco: Jossey-Bass.

Fetterman, D. M. (2000). Summary of the STEP evaluation. *American Journal of Evaluation, 21,* 239-241.

Fetterman, D. M., Connors, W., Dunlap, K., Brower, G., & Matos, T. (1998). *Stanford Teacher Education Program 1997-98 evaluation report.* Stanford, CA: Stanford University, School of Education.

Fetterman, D. M., Connors, W., Dunlap, K., Brower, G., Matos, T., & Paik, S. (1999). *Stanford Teacher Education Program 1997-98 evaluation.* Stanford, CA: Stanford University, School of Education.

Fetterman, D. M., Dunlap, K., Greenfield, A., & Yoo, J. (1997). *Stanford Teacher Education Program 1997 summer school evalua-*

tion report. Stanford, CA: Stanford University, School of Education.

Fielding, N. G., & Fielding, J. L. (1986). *Linking data* (Qualitative Research Methods, No. 4). Beverly Hills, CA: Sage.

Fitzpatrick, J. (1997). Dialogue with James Riccio. *Evaluation Practice, 18,* 243-252.

Fitzpatrick, J. (1998). Dialogue with Marsha Mueller. *American Journal of Evaluation, 19,* 87-99.

Fitzpatrick, J. (1999). Dialogue with Debra J. Rog. *American Journal of Evaluation, 20,* 562-575.

Fitzpatrick, J. (2000a). Dialogue with David Fetterman. *American Journal of Evaluation, 21,* 242-259.

Fitzpatrick, J. (2000b). Dialogue with Gary Henry. *American Journal of Evaluation, 21,* 108-117.

Geertz, C. (1973). *The interpretation of cultures: Selected essays.* New York: Basic Books.

Greene, J. C., & Caracelli, V. J. (1997). Defining and describing the paradigm issue in mixed-method evaluation. In J. C. Greene & V. J. Caracelli (Eds.), *Advances in mixed-method evaluation: The challenges and benefits of integrating diverse paradigms* (New Directions for Evaluation, No. 74, pp. 5-17). San Francisco: Jossey-Bass.

Greene, J. C., Caracelli, V. J., & Graham, W. F. (1989). Toward a conceptual framework of mixed-method evaluation design. *Educational Evaluation and Policy Analysis, 11,* 255-274.

Lawrence-Lightfoot, S., & Davis, J. H. (1997). *The art and science of portraiture.* San Francisco: Jossey-Bass.

Mark, M. M., & Shotland, R. L. (Eds.). (1987). *Multiple methods in program evaluation* (New Directions for Program Evaluation, No. 35). San Francisco: Jossey-Bass.

Mueller, M. R. (1994). *Changing times, changing families II—Fall evaluation guide.* St. Paul, MN: Department of Children, Families, and Learning.

Mueller, M. R. (1995). *Changing times, changing families II—Spring evaluation guide.* St. Paul, MN: Department of Children, Families, and Learning.

Mueller, M. R. (1996a). *Immediate outcomes of lower income participants in Minnesota's universal access Early Childhood Family Education.* St. Paul, MN: Department of Children, Families, and Learning.

Mueller, M. R. (1996b, August). *Observations: Second year follow-up—Changing times, changing families, Phase II.* Unpublished report to Family Education Resources of Minnesota, Minneapolis.

Mueller, M. R. (1998). The evaluation of Minnesota's Early Childhood Family Education Program. *American Journal of Evaluation, 19*(1), 80-86.

Newman, I., & Benz, C. R. (1998). *Qualitative-quantitative methodology: Exploring the interactive continuum.* Carbondale: Southern Illinois University Press.

Patton, M. Q. (1988). Paradigms and pragmatism. In D. M. Fetterman (Ed.), *Qualitative approaches to evaluation in education: The silent scientific revolution* (pp. 116-137). New York: Praeger.

Patton, M. Q. (1990). *Qualitative evaluation and research methods* (2nd ed.). Newbury Park, CA: Sage.

Patton, M. Q. (1997). *Utilization focused evaluation: The new century text* (3rd ed.). Thousand Oaks, CA: Sage.

Reichardt, C. S., & Rallis, S. F. (1994). *The qualitative-quantitative debate: New perspectives* (New Directions for Program Evaluation, No. 61). San Francisco: Jossey-Bass.

Riccio, J. (1997). MDRC's evaluation of GAIN: A summary. *Evaluation Practice, 18,* 241-242.

Riccio, J., Friedlander, D., & Freedman, S. (1994). *GAIN: Benefits, costs, and three-year impacts of a welfare-to-work program.* New York: Manpower Demonstration Research Corporation.

Riccio, J., & Hasenfeld, Y. (1996). Enforcing a participation mandate in a welfare-to-work program. *Social Services Review, 70,* 516-542.

Riccio, J. A., & Orenstein, A. (1996). Understanding best practices for operating welfare-to-work programs. *Evaluation Review, 20*(3), 3-28.

Riggin, L. J. C. (1997). Advances in mixed-method evaluation: A synthesis and comment. In J. C. Greene & V. J. Caracelli (Eds.), *Advances in mixed-method evaluation: The challenges and benefits of integrating diverse paradigms* (New Directions for Evaluation, No. 74, pp. 87-94). San Francisco: Jossey-Bass.

Rog, D. J. (1994). *The Homeless Families Program: Interim benchmarks.* Washington, DC: Vanderbilt Institute for Public Policy Studies.

Rog, D. J. (1999). The evaluation of the Homeless Families Program. *American Journal of Evaluation, 20*(3), 558-561.

Rog, D. J., Holumpka, C. S., & McCombs-Thornton, K. L. (1995). Implementation of the Homeless Families Program. *American Journal of Orthopsychiatry, 63,* 502-513.

Rossman, G. B., & Rallis, S. F. (2000). Critical inquiry and use as action. In V. J. Caracelli & H. Preskill (Eds.), *The expanding scope of evaluation use* (New Directions for Evaluation, No. 88, pp. 55-69). San Francisco: Jossey-Bass.

Rossman, G. B., & Wilson, B. L. (1985). Numbers and words: Combining quantitative and qualitative methods in a single large-scale evaluation study. *Evaluation Review, 9,* 627-643.

Rossman, G. B., & Wilson, B. L. (1994). Numbers and words revisited: Being shamelessly eclectic. *Quality and Quantity, 28,* 315-327.

Scriven, M. (1991). *Evaluation thesaurus* (4th ed.). Newbury Park, CA: Sage.

Taylor, G. R. (2000). *Integrating quantitative and qualitative methods in research.* Lanham, MD: University Press of America.

Waysman, M., & Savaya, R. (1997a). Differential assessment of the consultation needs of volunteer organizations, according to stage of development. *Organization Development Journal, 15*(4), 61-70.

Waysman, M., & Savaya, R. (1997b). Mixed method evaluation: A case study. *Evaluation Practice, 18,* 227-237.

Weiss, C. H. (1998). *Evaluation* (2nd ed.). Upper Saddle River, NJ: Prentice Hall.

Wholey, J. S. (Ed.). (1987). *Organizational excellence: Stimulating quality and communicating value.* Lexington, MA: Lexington Books.

18

RESEARCH METHODS IN MANAGEMENT AND ORGANIZATIONAL RESEARCH: TOWARD INTEGRATION OF QUALITATIVE AND QUANTITATIVE TECHNIQUES

◆ Steven C. Currall
  Annette J. Towler

M anagement and organizational research exhibits a rich diversity of qualitative and quantitative methodological approaches. This diversity of methods is advantageous for three reasons. First, methodological diversity is beneficial to the field because it mirrors the variety of research questions posed by management and organizational researchers. For example, management and organizational research ranges from investigating personality differences in predicting employee job performance to identifying organizational factors (e.g.,

technology, organizational design, human capital) that create a competitive advantage for companies. These different research questions, of course, require different methods. Second, heterogeneity of research methods is required because management and organizational research draws on numerous theoretical paradigms, including psychology, anthropology, sociology, economics, and political science. Third, management and organizational research is characterized by investigations that involve multiple levels of analysis (individual, dyad, group, or organization); therefore, different methods are necessitated depending on a study's level of analysis (House, Rousseau, & Thomas-Hunt, 1995; Klein, Dansereau, & Hall, 1994).

Organizational and management researchers often acknowledge that neither qualitative nor quantitative methods are inherently superior. The dictum is that one's research objectives must determine the appropriate method(s). Indeed, McCall and Bobko (1990) advocated balance between qualitative and quantitative methods by arguing that no method has "superiority over the others." They added, "There is no advantage to limiting our thinking about research methods to the procedures used in statistical analyses and verification processes. Doing whatever needs to be done to enhance discovery is also a critical part of methodology" (p. 412). Recently, some progress toward balance has been made. For example, Bartunek, Bobko, and Venkatraman (1993) observed that the methodological pendulum has swung slightly in the direction of greater appreciation for qualitative methods.

Nevertheless, most management and organizational researchers have adopted the positivist stance of the natural sciences. This is signified in the attempt to define organizational and management research within a scientific paradigm emphasizing theory testing through quantitative analyses. The positivist stance explains why, historically, qualitative methods have been seen by some as techniques of ill repute, while quantitative techniques have been embraced to a fault (McCall & Bobko, 1990). Bouchard (1976) captured this point by stating that the context of theory development has hardly been mined, while the context of theory testing has been overburdened with trivial investigations.

Despite some movement toward greater balance, qualitative and quantitative methods have largely continued to operate on separate tracks. In particular, procedures for linking qualitative and quantitative techniques within a single study have received little attention. So, despite the attractive aspects of methodological heterogeneity, qualitative and quantitative methods remain bifurcated; most published studies use purely qualitative or quantitative techniques. This bifurcation is understandable to the extent that researchers' specialization in qualitative or quantitative methods results in technically coherent and paradigmatically pure findings. Yet we believe that methodological bifurcation has many drawbacks. For instance, qualitative research typically fails to draw on the strengths of quantitative methods (e.g., theory testing through the use of statistical inference), and quantitative research normally fails to use the advantages of qualitative methods (e.g., theory development through the use of detailed observation of organizational phenomena). In this chapter, we argue in favor of combining qualitative and quantitative methods to examine management and organizational phenomena.

◆ Aims and Scope of the Chapter

The aims of the chapter are threefold. First, we compare the characteristics of qualitative and quantitative methods in terms of realism, access to participants, detail, measurement precision, control, statistical conclusion validity, and generalizability. Although much of what we discuss has applicability across the social science disciplines, we focus our discussion exclusively on management and organizational research literature. Our second aim is to suggest that the integration of qualitative and quantitative methods maximizes the "knowledge yield" of research (McCall & Bobko, 1990). A study's knowledge yield is enhanced when a range of intriguing new hypotheses are formulated, precise hypothesis tests are conducted, detailed explanations for the phenomenon being studied are provided, alternative explanations for relationships among variables are eliminated, and other researchers can build on the study's findings in a cumulative manner. We provide examples of empirical studies that integrate qualitative and quantitative methods. Third, we propose an agenda for promoting integration of qualitative and quantitative methods. In addition to advocating "triangulation" (i.e., use of multiple methods or data sources) to maximize knowledge yield, the agenda we propose includes combining "etic" and "emic" methodological traditions, increasing the breadth of graduate research methods training, expanding collaboration among qualitative and quantitative researchers within professional associations, establishing promotion and tenure policies that reward methodological breadth, and instituting journal editorial policies that support the combination of methods.

◆ Relative Strengths of Qualitative and Quantitative Methods Used in Management and Organizational Research

In this section, we lay the groundwork for the remainder of the chapter by providing an overview of strengths and weaknesses of qualitative versus quantitative methods. After the overview, we provide additional detail regarding the merits of specific methods. In addition to our chapter's overview focusing on management and organizational research, interested readers may wish to consult other comparisons of qualitative and quantitative methods such as Jick (1979), Larsson (1993), Lee (1999), McCall and Bobko (1990), Miles and Huberman (1994), and Stevenson and Cooper (1997).

"Typically, 'qualitative observation' identifies the presence or absence of something, in contrast to 'quantitative observation,' which involves measuring the degree to which some feature is present" (Kirk & Miller, 1986, p. 9). Qualitative methods have several advantages for investigating organizations. First, qualitative data (e.g., data obtained via participant observation or interviews) are rich in detail about interactions among organizational participants. That is, qualitative techniques often involve "sustained interaction with the people being studied in their own language and on their own turf" (p. 12). Second, the qualitative methodologist's intimate knowledge of organizational history and norms provides an interpretive framework with which to decipher the actions of organizational participants (Adler & Adler, 1994); without such a framework, their actions would be frequently misconstrued. It is worth noting that, despite stereotypes about qualitative researchers, they routinely go beyond simple use of categorical data by applying quantitative techniques such as odds ratios analyses (Lee, 1999).

Qualitative techniques, however, suffer from several methodological disadvantages. First, the cognitive information processing limitations of an observer dictate that the behaviors of some organizational participants may go unrecorded. Second, although observers often provide explicit descriptions of techniques used to record fieldnotes (e.g., Whyte, 1973), it is nearly impossible for other researchers to see exactly how the observer makes interpretations from the fieldnotes. A third disadvantage is that, traditionally, fieldnotes have not been used to test hypotheses using statistical inference techniques. Observational findings often have been limited to the observer's "thick description" of events and behaviors (Strauss, 1987). Thus, although observation can yield a wealth of fine-grained information about what happens inside an organization (or between organizations), in raw form the fieldnotes do not lend themselves to hypothesis testing using statistical inference.

Historically, quantitative methods have been the techniques of choice by organizational and management researchers. These methods use standardized measures of variables (via experiments or surveys) that allow the researcher to state with precision the strength and direction of relationships between variables (Pedhazur & Schmelkin, 1991). Standardized measures pave the way for the use of inferential statistics (e.g., correlations, regression coefficients) that can be compared across studies. Moreover, statistical inference allows the researcher to make estimates concerning the probability that a relationship between variables was detected by chance. Therefore, quantitative studies lend themselves to the development of cumulative findings based on the use of standardized statistical indexes.

Quantitative methods, however, also have their disadvantages. For example, correlational studies (e.g., surveys) provide limited information about causation between variables. Another quantitative method, the laboratory study, typically is a one-shot enterprise; experiments are rarely used to conduct longitudinal research. In addition, the central strength of experiments, maintaining rigorous control, can undermine the value of experimental findings because, in the process of seeking control, the researcher may create highly artificial situations (Forsyth, 1990). Overall, quantitative studies, conducted in the laboratory or in the field, permit extensive statistical analyses yet are sometimes criticized for being "sanitized" and lacking in contextual realism. Moreover, Van Maanen (1979) pointed out that quantitative procedures run the risk of becoming so ritualized that the organizational researcher loses touch with the necessary connection between a concept and its measure. Finally, there is some distrust and skepticism that conventional data collection techniques (e.g., sample surveys, interviews, laboratory experiments) actually distort and falsely portray the phenomena that such methods seek to study (Van Maanen, 1979).

Table 18.1 provides a summary of qualitative and quantitative methods used by management and organizational researchers. Johnson and Turner (Chapter 11, this volume) provide detailed descriptions of quantitative and qualitative methods, so here we provide a general overview. Although the table lists a range of qualitative and quantitative methods, it should be noted that management and organizational researchers have historically used a somewhat restricted set of qualitative techniques (Lee, 1999), namely participant observation and interviewing. Quantitative researchers rely less on their own personal observation and more on standardized measurement instruments. Table 18.1 characterizes methods in terms of several features (Scandura & Williams, 2000; Weingart, 1997): (a) realism, (b) access to participants, (c) detail, (d) measurement precision, (e) control, (f) statistical conclusion validity, and (g) generalizability. We characterize each method with respect to its relative strength (low, moderate, or high) in comparison with

TABLE 18.1 Characteristics of Qualitative and Quantitative Methods

Methods Used in Management and Organizational Research

	Realism	Access to Participants	Detail	Measurement Precision	Control	Statistical Conclusion Validity	Generalizability
Participant observation	High	High	High	Low	Low	Low	Low
Nonparticipant observation	High	Moderate	High	Low	Low	Low	Moderate
Interviewing	High	High	Moderate	Moderate	Low	Low	Moderate
Document analysis	Low	Low	Moderate	Moderate	Low	Low	High
Formal theory/literature reviews	Low	Low	Moderate	Low	Low	Low	High
Sample survey	Low	Moderate	Low	Moderate	Moderate	High	Moderate
Laboratory experiment	Low	High	Moderate	High	High	High	Low
Experimental simulation	Moderate	High	Moderate	High	High	High	Low
Field study: Primary data	High	High	Moderate	Moderate	Moderate	Low	Low
Field study: Secondary data	Moderate	Moderate	Moderate	Moderate	Low	Moderate	Moderate
Field experiment	Moderate	Moderate	High	Moderate	High	High	Low
Judgment task	Moderate	High	High	High	Moderate	Moderate	Moderate
Computer simulation	Moderate	High	Low	Low	Moderate	Moderate	Low

other methods. It is worth emphasizing that Table 18.1 describes each method as having *relative* strengths and weaknesses in comparison with other methods.

In addition to describing the features of various methods, an implication of Table 18.1 is that combining research strategies can leverage the strengths of various methods. For example, a combination of observational methods with field or laboratory experiments maximizes various features, namely realism of context and richness in detail with precision in measurement. A combination of both qualitative and quantitative research strategies enables researchers to have greater faith in their findings and make greater contributions to the field.

◆ Illustrative Studies That Integrate Qualitative and Quantitative Methods

We believe that a new methodological approach lies neither in the qualitative nor the quantitative domain exclusively but rather in how the two techniques can be interwoven to maximize the "knowledge yield" (McCall & Bobko, 1990) of a research endeavor. The advantage of using both qualitative and quantitative methods is the accomplishment of both *discovery* and *justification* within a single research project. McCall and Bobko (1990) defined discovery or exploratory as "anything related to the creation of new theories or interpretive applications, including anything related to adopting novel approaches to measurement, inventing or uncovering new constructs, or inventing or uncovering original theoretical perspectives from which to view organizational phenomena" (p. 382). They defined

justification as "the empirical evaluation and confirmation of theory" (p. 382).

Unlike much management and organizational research that focuses either on discovery (i.e., most qualitative research) or justification (i.e., most quantitative research), studies that combine qualitative and quantitative methods have the potential to make an even greater contribution through dual emphasis on *both* discovery and justification. Uses of qualitative research methods are particularly well-positioned to generate hypotheses, hunches, and speculations from which theory can be built. Quantitative research that uses experimental or statistical control techniques can complement qualitative investigation by limiting threats to internal validity and by isolating causal relationships (Yin, 1989).

In an example of a study that combined qualitative and quantitative methods, Currall, Hammer, Baggett, and Doniger (1999) mixed the richness of detail that is characteristic of qualitative data collection with the hypothesis testing advantage of statistical inference techniques. Qualitative data came from a 5-year participant observation study of a corporate board of directors. Quantification of the participant observer's qualitative field-notes was achieved by using content analysis to code directors' verbal behaviors. Based on counts of directors' verbal behaviors, Currall et al. tested illustrative hypotheses concerning group process within the board using nonparametric statistical techniques such as log Poisson regression. Taken separately, none of the study's individual methodological elements (e.g., content analysis) was novel. Yet the study was unusual because it used both "discovery" (i.e., theory development) and "justification" (i.e., theory evaluation) to foster a "discovery-justification-discovery cycle" that was useful for understanding group processes within the corporate board.

THREE TYPES OF INTEGRATIVE DESIGNS

To further articulate how qualitative and quantitative techniques can be combined, we now turn to Creswell's (1994) three types of research designs that combine both methods. We also provide several examples of studies from the management and organizational literature that employed these designs.

Dominant-Less Dominant Design. In the *dominant-less dominant design*, the researcher presents a study based largely on a single method with small components drawn from alternative methods. Sutton and Hargadon's (1996) study of brainstorming groups in organizations is an example of a dominant-less dominant design. Their study relied on qualitative ethnographic data, yet they used quantitative survey data as a supplement. To investigate managers' use of punishment, Butterfield, Trevino, and Ball (1996) employed a qualitative interview approach to gather accounts from managers regarding incidents when they had punished subordinates. They used a statistical test, as the less dominant element, to estimate the proportion of incidents managers deemed as being effective or ineffective. This inductive approach allowed the researchers to develop "a model of punishment from a managerial prospective."

In another example, a recent cross-cultural study used a combination of qualitative and quantitative methods to examine the culture of transnational teams in organizations (Earley & Mosakowski, 2000). In particular, the investigators were interested in the effects of heterogeneity of team member composition. One qualitative study and two laboratory studies were conducted. To develop their theory, they first conducted a field study collecting data from five transnational teams. The investigators directly observed team meetings, obtained company records of demographic information, and conducted open-ended and structured on-site interviews with key team personnel. The second and third studies, which were laboratory experiments, made up the bulk of the research project. These studies built on the first study by rigorously testing those variables that mediated the effects of team heterogeneity on team effectiveness.

Two-Phase Designs. In *two-phase designs*, the researcher proceeds sequentially, for example, a qualitative phase followed by a quantitative phase (or vice versa). The presence of both paradigms are well-delineated and separate. Many examples of two-phase designs are found in the management and organizational research literature. Ancona and Caldwell's (1992) study of ways in which groups interacted with their external environments was an example of a two-phase design. The authors used qualitative interview data to describe groups' external activities and used those data to generate hypotheses about external activities, group performance, and internal group processes. Quantitative survey data were then collected for hypothesis testing.

Sutton and Rafaeli (1988) used a two-phase design to test the hypothesis that store sales would increase with the frequency of positive emotions displayed by clerks in transactions with customers. The researchers used a random sample of 576 convenience stores selected from 18 corporate divisions in the United States and Canada. Incognito participant observers visited each store twice and recorded a total of 11,805 clerk-customer transactions. Scores measuring the display of positive emotion were an index of the mean level of greeting, thanking, smiling, and eye contact observed. The second phase involved application of multiple regression analyses using these variables. The results concerning positive emotion scores, control variables, and total store sales were unexpected, as positive emotion scores were negatively correlated with store sales. A follow-up study revealed that store sales reflect store pace, which influences the expression of emotions.

Mixed Methods Design. The *mixed methods design* signifies the greatest extent of integrating methods. Here, aspects of qualitative and quantitative methods are used at all or many steps in the study. The mixed methods design represents the greatest challenge for the researcher because it requires extensive knowledge of both qualitative and quantitative methods. Moreover, the mixed methods design is challenging because it requires the researcher to describe a combination of techniques that may be unfamiliar to many readers (Creswell, 1994). Jick (1979) used a mixed methods design in his research on the effect of a merger on employee anxiety. He used triangulation of multiple sources of both qualitative data (e.g., unobtrusive observation, archival data) and quantitative data (e.g., surveys, behavioral incidents) to study employee anxiety. As another example, Webster and Hackley (1997) employed both quantitative and qualitative information in a mixed methods design to investigate teaching effectiveness in distance learning. The quantitative information came from a questionnaire designed to study the factors affecting outcomes of technology-mediated distance learning. Multiple types of qualitative information were collected to help "triangulate" findings, including observation of at least one class

meeting in each course, informal interviews with students and instructors before and after classes and during breaks, and feedback from instructors that was obtained through electronic mail.

◆ Current Trends in Management and Organizational Research and the Use of Integrative Models

Our review suggests that when organizational researchers used a combination of qualitative and quantitative methods to investigate organizational phenomena, this research yielded greater information than can be achieved through reliance on single methods. Although researchers are coming to recognize the benefits of using a combination of methods, many are still reticent to combine methods on a regular basis. A perusal of the management literature over the past 10 years suggests that a combination of methods is still rare. Mixed model designs, in particular, appear quite infrequently. In fact, many researchers who combine qualitative and quantitative methods tend to collect qualitative data only to quickly condense it through use of quantitative methods. To quote Langley (1999), "There is a certain irony in the idea that researchers who give themselves the trouble of collecting rich qualitative data in real organizations are so uncomfortable with this richness that they immediately rush to transform it . . . into a much thinner data set" (p. 698).

There are studies, however, that preserve the strengths of various methods. For example, one recent study demonstrated the insights that can be achieved from integrating methods by retaining qualitative data as well as subjecting the data to statistical analysis. Gersick, Bartunek, and Dutton (2000) employed both qualitative and quantitative methods in examining the importance of social networks for individuals' careers within academia. They conducted 37 in-depth interviews with faculty from six management schools. As part of the study, interviewees told stories about an individual (past or present) of importance to them in their working life. The stories were coded and grouped to create a set of categories. The researchers then conducted statistical analyses to uncover the association between stories and variables such as gender. Therefore, this article presented evidence from both interviews and statistical analyses on the importance of social networks and how experiences can differ as a function of gender.

A combination of qualitative and quantitative techniques is more frequently used in some research areas than in others. Several journals (e.g., *Journal of Management, Journal of Organizational Behavior*) receive relatively few manuscripts that employ both qualitative and quantitative method (Hemingway, 2001). In contrast, journals focusing on research on group dynamics, organizational change, and international management tend to receive more manuscripts employing both methods (Hemingway, 2001).

Although we believe that a combination of quantitative and qualitative methods is useful for all research areas, the perception among many researchers is that a mixture of methods is suitable only when particular questions are raised. For example, mixed methods are considered appropriate when research questions concerning process and dynamic phenomena, such as innovation and change, are addressed (Langley, 1999; Van de Ven & Huber, 1990). In general, in management and organizational research, process explanations are commonly used to explain reciprocal causation between independent and dependent variables. This area of work has generated considerable debate concerning useful methods and strategies

to tackle such questions of process (Langley, 1999; Van de Ven, 1992). One method that implicitly uses both qualitative and quantitative methods is the synthetic strategy in which the researcher initially gains information on the organizational process involved and then constructs measures from the data to describe the process (Langley, 1999). Eisenhardt (1989; see also Eisenhardt & Bourgeois, 1988) has used this method when examining decision-making environments in high-velocity (i.e., fast-changing) organizations. For example, in one study examining the linkages among power, politics, and performance, data were collected from eight microcomputer firms (Eisenhardt & Bourgeois, 1988). To gain insight into political behavior, every member of each top management team was interviewed. Then, quantitative data on political patterns within each group were obtained from questionnaires introduced during interviews. The results of the study focused on the complex interplay of independent and dependent variables involved in decision making.

A combination of qualitative and quantitative methods also appears to be employed when researchers wish to validate nascent theory. A recent special edition of a top-ranked management journal (*Academy of Management Journal*) focused on the management of organizations in the natural environment (Stark & Marcus, 2000). This special edition included several empirical studies that combined qualitative and quantitative methods in an effort to refine and test theoretical models (Andersson & Bateman, 2000; Bansal & Roth, 2000; Egri & Herman, 2000). For example, Bansal and Roth (2000) investigated factors that induced corporate ecological responsiveness. To examine why companies "go green," they collected data to test and challenge emerging hypotheses and to refine theory. To test inferences, they drew on multiple sources, including in-depth interviews, participant observations, and archival documents. All interviews were coded, and these data were used to determine the organization's motivation to be ecologically responsive. Furthermore, archival data and literature reviews were used in an iterative process to refine and formulate hypotheses.

◆ Proposals for Enhancing Integration of Qualitative and Quantitative Methods in Management and Organizational Research

Looking forward, we call for a reduction in purely qualitative or quantitative research designs in management and organizational research. Instead, we urge researchers to design their studies in a way that draws on appropriate qualitative and quantitative techniques within a single research endeavor. Our field will benefit from fewer incremental studies that rely exclusively on qualitative methods to develop a theory without testing it. Moreover, fewer studies should rely exclusively on quantitative methods that test a sliver of a theory or provide a modest methodological tweak on established techniques without having a direct and qualitative understanding of the phenomenon under study. In short, we argue for more dominant-less dominant designs, two-phase designs, and (if possible) fully mixed methods designs.

COMBINING ETIC AND EMIC APPROACHES

We believe that an increase in the use and appreciation of combined research methods will facilitate collaboration among qualitative and quantitative researchers.

Despite the progress that has been made in theory development and verification of findings, different approaches to understanding human behavior and thinking have exacerbated divisions between methodological "camps." For example, two long-standing traditions for understanding social systems are the etic and emic approaches. *Etic* refers to a trained observer's analysis of "raw" data, whereas *emic* refers to how those data are interpreted by an "insider" to the system or organization (Pike, 1967). Etic and emic approaches traditionally have been associated with differing research methods (Morris, Leung, Ames, & Lickel, 1999), with a reliance on qualitative research methods among emic researchers and a preference for quantitative methods in the etic tradition. Emic researchers tend to use observational techniques within a single organization and immerse themselves in the setting while developing relationships with the informants (Morris et al., 1999). They rely on, for example, content analysis of text to interpret their findings. Etic researchers rely on surveys from a wide range of organizations and make inferences based on quantitative data. When emic and etic approaches are combined, researchers can conduct both exploratory and confirmatory research.

In addition to their methodological advantages, combining etic and emic approaches can aid in the implementation of managerial interventions in organizations (Morris et al., 1999). For example, if proposed through a solely etic perspective, an organizational change such as decentralization of organizational decision making is likely to meet resistance from shop floor workers because interventions may be based on survey findings from other firms with little insight into the day-to-day experience of lower level employees. In contrast, a solely emic perspective is likely to encounter resistance from senior management (Morris et al., 1999) because of emphasis on the phenomenological experience of employees at the expense of the quantitative benchmarking information from other competing firms within the industry that top executives often use. Yet an intervention plan that incorporates both perspectives is likely to be met with less resistance from employees across levels. For example, a recent study investigating reactions to a peer rating system collected qualitative data to consider changes that might improve the peer review system (Fedor, Bettenhausen, & Davis, 1999). Quantitative data were also collected to test research hypotheses on which implementation was then based.

BREADTH OF GRADUATE RESEARCH METHODS TRAINING

We believe that the merits of combining qualitative and quantitative methods make a compelling argument for greater breadth of methods training for future management and organizational researchers. In addition to traditional training regarding theory testing using statistical inference techniques, it is appropriate for doctoral programs in management or organization studies to place an emphasis on tools that facilitate the theory development process, namely creating new approaches to measurement, uncovering new constructs, and creating novel theoretical viewpoints from which to see organizations. This suggestion parallels McCall and Bobko's (1990) belief that the question of "what to study" has received insufficient attention in our training (see also Campbell, Daft, & Hulin, 1982). Coupled with traditional statistics coursework, training concerning the discovery process (e.g., qualitative observational techniques, case studies) has the advantage of enabling researchers to think fully

about what types of research questions are innovative, interesting, and practically relevant.

But is it feasible for doctoral students in management and organization studies to learn both qualitative and quantitative techniques? We believe that it is. Indeed, many doctoral programs are heavy on coursework in content areas (e.g., theories of management and organization, special topic courses) but light on methods training. Many doctoral programs require only two or three methods courses. One possible curriculum for doctoral training would be a five-course methods sequence that consists of two courses on qualitative techniques, one course on measurement and psychometrics, and two courses on data analysis (statistics). There is an additional reason for emphasizing a comprehensive research methods course sequence during doctoral training, namely, that once one begins his or her academic career, it is difficult to strengthen one's research methods training because of other time demands (e.g., teaching). Thus, typically it is only during a doctoral program that one can devote significant time and energy to deepening research methods skills.

PROMOTION AND TENURE POLICIES: THE "NUMBERS GAME"?

One factor that contributes to researchers' use of purely qualitative or quantitative techniques is the relentless push to author a high number of refereed journal articles. Although the emphasis on publishing in refereed publications is well-placed, the problem is in the "numbers game." Because some members of promotion and tenure committees might not be sufficiently knowledgeable of a candidate's field, committee members have been known to resort to the simplest possible index of research activity, namely a count of the number of journal articles on a candidate's curriculum vitae. Therefore, in light of the emphasis by many promotion and tenure committees on number of publications as opposed to overall impact of research, some researchers develop narrow specialization in either qualitative or quantitative techniques and then aim to maximize the number of publications in one or two journals that cater to specialists. This narrow specialization contributes to bifurcation of the field into qualitative and quantitative divisions. Promotion and tenure committees should be composed of those who are sufficiently knowledgeable to fairly evaluate the overall contribution and impact of a candidate's research. Committee members also must have the sophistication to understand publications that use or integrate both qualitative and quantitative techniques.

REEVALUATION OF JOURNAL EDITORIAL POLICIES

Last, we urge a reevaluation of journal editorial policies in favor of greater appreciation of the value of integrating methods. In particular, we urge editors and editorial boards to consider deemphasizing purely qualitative or quantitative studies and, instead, to emphasize broader and more ambitious studies that use qualitative methods to develop new theory and hypotheses as well as quantitative methods to rigorously test theories. We believe that integrative studies that use both qualitative and quantitative techniques will have a greater impact on our field as compared with studies that are purely qualitative or quantitative. Indeed, we note that some of the most highly regarded journals in our field (e.g., *Administrative Science Quarterly*) show significant breadth in that they publish both qualitative and

quantitative studies as well as studies that draw on both methods.

In studies that integrate methods, journal editors should require authors to fully explicate the qualitative and quantitative methods used within a study. Full explication is required for readers to adequately evaluate the methods used and to replicate the procedures if desired. Moreover, such detailed explication has the benefit of conveying the methodological challenges involved in integrating qualitative and quantitative methods as well as the judgment calls (McGrath, Martin, & Kulka, 1982) necessary to address those challenges (Currall et al., 1999). Full explication also can stimulate future researchers to consider innovative ways of combining qualitative and quantitative techniques.

◆ Conclusion

Quantitative and qualitative research methods are complementary rather than opposed approaches (Lee, 1991; Morris et al., 1999). A combination of research methods can serve mutual purposes. Indeed, the relative strengths of qualitative and quantitative methods enable management and organizational researchers to address important questions at different stages of a research inquiry. Thus, a combination of techniques can enhance and enrich current knowledge by "filling in the gaps" that studies adopting a singular approach are unable to do. Therefore, we advocate that researchers embrace these complementary approaches in their research. Such a combination of research approaches will maximize knowledge yield and widen the scope of research contributions by management and organizational researchers.

■ *References*

Adler, P. A., & Adler, P. (1994). Observational techniques. In N. K. Denzin & Y. S. Lincoln (Eds.), *Handbook of qualitative research* (pp. 377-392). Thousand Oaks, CA: Sage.

Ancona, D. G., & Caldwell, D. F. (1992). Bridging the boundary: External activity and performance in organizational teams. *Administrative Science Quarterly, 37,* 634-665.

Andersson, L. M., & Bateman, T. S. (2000). Individual environmental initiative: Championing natural environmental issues in U.S. business organizations. *Academy of Management Journal, 43,* 548-570.

Bansal, P., & Roth, K. (2000). Why companies go green: A model of ecological responsiveness. *Academy of Management Journal, 43,* 717-736.

Bartunek, J. M., Bobko, P., & Venkatraman, N. (1993). Toward innovation and diversity in management research methods. *Academy of Management Journal, 36,* 1362-1373.

Bouchard, T. J. (1976). Field research methods: Interviewing, questionnaires, participant observation, systematic observation, and unobtrusive measures. In M. D. Dunnette (Ed.), *Handbook of industrial and organizational psychology.* Chicago: Rand McNally.

Butterfield, K. D., Trevino, L. K., & Ball, G. A. (1996). Punishment from the manager's perspective: A grounded investigation and inductive model. *Academy of Management Journal, 39,* 1479-1512.

Campbell, J. P., Daft, R. L., & Hulin, C. L. (1982). *What to study: Generating and developing research questions.* Beverly Hills, CA: Sage.

Creswell, J. (1994). *Research design: Qualitative and quantitative approaches.* Thousand Oaks, CA: Sage.

Currall, S. C., Hammer, T. H., Baggett, L. S., & Doniger, G. M. (1999). Combining qualitative and quantitative methodologies to study group processes: An illustrative study of a corporate board of directors. *Organizational Research Methods, 2,* 5-36.

Earley, P. C., & Mosakowski, E. (2000). Creating hybrid team cultures: An empirical test of transnational team functioning. *Academy of Management Journal, 43,* 26-49.

Egri, C. P., & Herman, S. (2000). Leadership in the North American environmental sector: Values, leadership styles, and contexts of environmental leaders and their organizations. *Academy of Management Journal, 43,* 571-604.

Eisenhardt, K. M. (1989). Making fast strategic decisions in high velocity environments. *Academy of Management Journal, 31,* 543-576.

Eisenhardt, K. M., & Bourgeois, L. J. (1988). Politics of strategic decision making in high-velocity environments. *Academy of Management Journal, 31,* 737-770.

Fedor, D. B., Bettenhausen, K. L., & Davis, W. (1999). Peer reviews: Employees' dual roles as raters and recipients. *Group & Organization Management, 24,* 92-120.

Forsyth, D. R. (1990). *Group dynamics* (2nd ed.). Pacific Grove, CA: Brooks/Cole.

Gersick, C. J. G., Bartunek, J .M., & Dutton, J. E. (2000). Learning from academia: The importance of relationship in professional life. *Academy of Management Journal, 43,* 1026-1044.

Hemingway, M. (2001). Qualitative research in I-O psychology. *The Industrial-Organizational Psychologist, 38*(3), 45-51.

House, R., Rousseau, D., & Thomas-Hunt, T. (1995). The meso paradigm: A framework for the integration of micro and macro organizational behavior. In L. Cummings & B. Staw (Eds.), *Research in organizational behavior* (Vol. 17, pp. 71-114). Greenwich, CT: JAI.

Jick, T. D. (1979). Mixing qualitative and quantitative methods: Triangulation in action. *Administrative Science Quarterly, 24,* 602-611.

Kirk, J., & Miller, M. L. (1986). *Reliability and validity in qualitative research.* Beverly Hills, CA: Sage.

Klein, K. J., Dansereau, F., & Hall, R. J. (1994). Levels issues in theory development, data collection, and analysis. *Academy of Management Review, 19,* 195-229.

Langley, A. (1999). Strategies for theorizing from process data. *Academy of Management Review, 24,* 691-710.

Larsson, R. (1993). Case survey methodology: Quantitative analysis of patterns across case studies. *Academy of Management Journal, 36,* 1515-1546.

Lee, A. S. (1991). Integrating positivist and interpretive approaches to organizational research. *Organization Science, 2,* 342-365.

Lee, T. (1999). *Using qualitative methods in organizational research.* Thousand Oaks, CA: Sage.

McCall, M. W., & Bobko, P. (1990). Research methods in the service of discovery. In M. D. Dunnette & L. M. Hough (Eds.), *Handbook of industrial and organizational psychology* (2nd ed., Vol. 1, pp. 381-418). Palo Alto, CA: Consulting Psychologists.

McGrath, J. E., Martin, J., & Kulka, R. A. (1982). *Judgment calls in research.* Beverly Hills, CA: Sage.

Miles, M. B., & Huberman, A. M. (1994). *Qualitative analysis: An expanded sourcebook.* Thousand Oaks, CA: Sage.

Morris, M. W., Leung, K., Ames, D., & Lickel, B. (1999). View from inside and outside: Integrating emic and etic insights about culture and justice judgment. *Academy of Management Review, 24,* 781-796.

Pedhazur, E. J., & Schmelkin, L. P. (1991). *Measurement, design, and analysis: An integrated approach.* Hillsdale, NJ: Lawrence Erlbaum.

Pike, K. L. (1967). *Language in relation to a unified theory of the structure of human behavior.* The Hague, Netherlands: Mouton.

Scandura, T. A., & Williams, E. A. (2000). Research methodology in management: Current practices, trends, and implications for future research. *Academy of Management Journal, 43,* 1248-1264.

Stark, M., & Marcus, A. A. (2000). Introduction to the special research forum on the management of organizations in the natural environment: A field emerging from multiple paths, with many challenges ahead. *Academy of Management Journal, 43,* 539-547.

Stevenson, C., & Cooper, N. (1997). Qualitative and quantitative research. *The Psychologist: Bulletin of the British Psychological Society, 10,* 159-160.

Strauss, A. (1987). *Qualitative analysis for social scientists.* Cambridge, UK: Cambridge University Press.

Sutton, R., & Hargadon, A. (1996). Brainstorming groups in context: Effectiveness in a product design firm. *Administrative Science Quarterly, 41,* 685-718.

Sutton, R. I., & Rafaeli, A. (1988). Untangling the relationship between displayed emotions and organizational sales: The case of convenience stores. *Academy of Management Journal, 31,* 461-487.

Van de Ven, A. H. (1992). Suggestions for studying strategy process: A research note. *Strategic Management Journal, 13,* 169-188.

Van de Ven, A. H., & Huber, G. P. (1990). Longitudinal field research methods for studying processes of organizational change. *Organization Science, 1,* 213-219.

Van Maanen, J. (1979). Reclaiming qualitative methods for organizational research: A preface. *Administrative Science Quarterly, 24,* 520-526.

Webster, J., & Hackley, P. (1997). Teaching effectiveness in technology-mediated distance learning. *Academy of Management Journal, 40,* 1282-1309.

Weingart, L. R. (1997). How did they do that? The ways and means of studying group processes. In L. L. Cummings & B. M. Staw (Eds.), *Research in organizational behavior* (Vol. 19, pp. 361-404). Greenwich, CT: JAI.

Whyte, W. F. (1973). *Street-corner society* (3rd ed.). Chicago: University of Chicago Press.

Yin, R. K. (1989). *Case study research: Design and methods.* Newbury Park, CA: Sage.

STATUS OF MIXED METHODS
IN THE HEALTH SCIENCES

♦ Melinda S. Forthofer

Just as the emergence of mixed methods approaches to evaluation research was described by Rallis and Rossman (Chapter 17, this volume) as driven by pragmatism, so has been the emergence of mixed methods research in the health sciences. The health sciences are, in general, applied disciplines in which utility for decision-making purposes increasingly overshadows paradigmatic loyalties. Qualitative methods historically have enjoyed greater acceptance in public health, nursing, and allied health disciplines than in medicine. Likewise, mixed methods research remains somewhat more common in public health, nursing, and allied health disciplines than in medicine. Nonetheless, the use of mixed methods is growing exponentially across most, if not all, areas of research in the health sciences.

This chapter provides an overview of top priorities in our nation's health sciences research agenda and corresponding trends in the foci of health sciences research endeavors. Then, the contributions of mixed methods approaches relative to monomethod approaches for addressing these priorities are discussed in terms of overall research design, measurement, and data analysis. Examples are provided to illustrate the distinctions between the utility of inferences drawn from mixed methods approaches and the utility of those drawn from monomethod approaches. The chapter concludes with a discussion of challenges and next steps related to the use of mixed methods approaches in the health sciences.

The chapter is organized around four dominant themes in the current state of health sciences research: (a) the study of individual behaviors or "lifestyle" factors in health, (b) the study of social determinants of health, (c) the study of more patient-focused health care delivery, and (d) the responsibility of researchers to accelerate the translation of research into practice. In each area, some of the unique methodological challenges associated with research in that area are identified, along with a discussion of the contribution of mixed methods for addressing those challenges and examples from previous research.

The evolution of methodological approaches in the social and behavioral sciences, from monomethod approaches to more pragmatic mixed method and mixed model approaches, has paralleled an evolution in the substantive foci of health sciences research. Conceptualizations of health have come to recognize growing evidence that health has multiple causes, many of which are social and behavioral, rather than biological, in origin. This trend in health sciences priorities began with a shift from a focus on the biological to a focus on individual behavior patterns or "lifestyles." Now, after years of focusing on individual responsibility for health, health scientists are also investigating the role of the environment, including both social systems and the organization of health and social services, as an important factor in health outcomes.

In gatherings of health sciences researchers, remarks that "the easy health problems have all been solved" are virtually commonplace. These remarks allude to the fact that improvements in areas such as sanitation and immunization therapy have had tremendous impacts on population health, whereas most of the most significant health problems today (e.g., lung cancer, cardiovascular disease, diabetes, osteoporosis) have multiple complex causes—often indirect causes with effects mediated by individual behaviors. Recog-

nition of the centrality of health behavior for advances in the health sciences has led to programs of research devoted entirely to understanding mechanisms for changing individual behaviors and promoting "healthy lifestyles." Consequently, the methodologies of the social and behavioral sciences have garnered widespread use in the health sciences.

As the body of evidence regarding determinants of individual health behaviors has grown, the role of environment as a determinant of individual health outcomes has been realized. Increasingly, health sciences researchers are aware that no individual is an island—that individual health is influenced by the surrounding context.

Research on use of and satisfaction with health services has also undergone a transition during recent decades, from an emphasis on provider directives for treatment to an emphasis on more patient- and family-focused services. We now recognize the need for health care providers to tailor their behaviors, recommendations, and the like to the needs and perspectives of patients and their families. With this transition, new areas of research and new methodological challenges have arisen.

In all areas of the health sciences, we are increasingly concerned with a rapid translation of research into practice. Health sciences research is by nature applied, and with applied research comes a pressure to account for benefits of research. The concern for a rapid translation of research into practice has spawned research that examines promising approaches for accelerating that process, especially approaches that include community collaboration. This movement has brought the science of community collaboration and partnership development, as well as their corresponding methodological uniquenesses, into the realm of the health sciences.

◆ *Using Mixed Methods to Study Individual Lifestyle Factors in Health*

Early attempts by health sciences researchers to promote health through individual behavior change were primarily directed toward educating individuals about the behaviors they should be enacting through "top-down" prescriptive approaches (Petersen & Lupton, 1996). Admittedly, education about recommended dietary practices, exercise patterns, and screening behaviors may be all that is needed to change the behavior of some health consumers. However, for most individuals, behavior change is much more difficult to facilitate and requires an understanding of a wide range of factors that influence behaviors. Mounting evidence of the role that such factors play in the production of health disparities has fueled philosophical debates about the roles of human agency and personal responsibility in individual health promotion (Minkler, 1999). A critical balance between emphasis on individual responsibility for health and emphasis on supporting the capacity of individuals and communities to respond to needs and challenges underlies the frameworks through which mixed methods are often employed to study individual health promotion.

With appreciation of the need for this balance, approaches have emerged that focus on the need to understand the desired health behavior changes from the perspective of the target populations or consumers. Conceptual frameworks used frequently in health behavior research are the PRECEDE model, the transtheoretical model, and social marketing. All of these frameworks incorporate consumers' perspectives into their models of the behavior change process, although the specific terms and conceptualizations of change

mechanisms vary from one model to another, resulting in some variation in how mixed methods are used to better understand individual health behaviors.

The PRECEDE model is an epidemiological and ecological model that was designed to guide the development of outcome-based approaches to health education programs (Green & Kreuter, 1999). The model considers behavioral factors and environmental factors (including societal, community, organizational, and interpersonal contexts) as well as the actual determinants for such patterns. These determinants are conceptualized as "predisposing" (i.e., preexisting characteristics of individuals associated with motivation to engage in a particular behavior), "enabling" (i.e., characteristics of the environment or available resources that facilitate engaging in a particular behavior), and "reinforcing" (i.e., expected consequences of behavior change that are perceived as either rewards or punishments for that behavior change).

In the transtheoretical model, changes in individual behaviors are conceptualized around two basic concepts: (a) that most change is believed to occur through incremental stages and (b) that the processes or mechanisms through which change occurs vary from one stage to another (Prochaska, DiClemente, & Norcross, 1992). Stages of change are conceptualized in terms of intentions to enact target behaviors and/or the actual enactment of those behaviors. Individuals are thought to begin in a precontemplation stage in which they have no intention of enacting target behaviors. Then, effective change processes would lead to a transition from the precontemplation to the contemplation stage in which individuals would be thinking about enacting the target behaviors in the foreseeable future (i.e., the next 6 months). As individuals begin to plan concretely for behavior changes in the short term (i.e., 1 month), they are viewed as being in the preparation stage. Those who have enacted the behaviors recently are viewed as being in the action stage, and those who sustain the behaviors over a period of 6 months or more are considered to be in the maintenance stage. In each transition from one stage to another, change strategies would be tailored to the specific characteristics of those stages. For example, strategies aimed at encouraging a transition from precontemplation to contemplation might focus on increasing individuals' awareness of the risks associated with not enacting a desired behavior change, whereas strategies aimed at encouraging a transition from action to maintenance might focus on supporting individuals in sustaining behavior change by preparing them to deal with obstacles and affirming their initial success at maintaining the behavior change. Research using the transtheoretical model to understand determinants of behavior changes often employs mixed methods to delineate the specific change processes that apply to stage transitions for particular health behaviors.

Similar to commercial marketing, social marketing emphasizes consumer-driven research so as to understand consumers' needs and expectations (Andreason, 1995). However, while commercial marketers apply this information to design and sell products or services that will benefit their companies, social marketers use this information to encourage people to adopt practices voluntarily that will benefit them and the societies in which they live. In the implementation of research based on this consumer orientation, marketing serves as the organizing concept and provides analytical techniques for segmenting market audiences, product development, pricing, testing, and distribution. Marketing conceives the consumer to be the center of a process involving four variables: product

(commodity, idea, or health practice), price, place (channels of communication and distribution points for products), and promotion. The social and behavioral sciences provide methodologies and constructs relevant to the explanation of individual knowledge, beliefs, attitudes, and behaviors.

By designing studies to understand the factors that facilitate or deter behavior change as well as individuals' trusted sources of influence, health scientists have been able to develop interventions with greater promise for producing behavior change. Designs for studying the factors associated with behavior change from consumers' perspectives often benefit from the use of mixed methods. First, the notion of understanding behavior change from the perspective of consumers implies that we understand that behavior change in the terms that are meaningful for those consumers. Mixed methods designs are often vastly preferred over monomethod designs for obtaining such an understanding because the former enable the strengths of some methods to compensate for the limitations of other methods. Thus, the most comprehensive research on consumers' perspectives of desired behavior change and related factors uses a combination of qualitative and quantitative approaches, often in a sequential design that allows each phase of research to build on the knowledge gained in previous phases.

Frequently, this research begins with qualitative in-depth interviews of individuals and focus group discussions using nonprobability samples. In-depth interviews are used to develop a preliminary understanding of the factors relevant to the desired behavior change and to discover the language that individuals in the target population use to discuss these issues. Focus group discussions are designed to capitalize on small-group dynamics to generate additional insights into attitudes and the factors that influence the desired behavior change. Then, the results of this qualitative research are used to develop more standardized—usually quantitative—methods such as standardized survey research on probability samples of the target population. Occasionally, the quantitative research is followed by another phase of qualitative research, primarily to aid in interpretation of previous findings.

For example, in our research on the determinants of breast and cervical cancer screening among underserved women in Florida, we combined focus group and survey research methods to develop a consumer-based understanding of the determinants of mammography use (Bryant, Forthofer, McCormack Brown, Alfonso, & Quinn, 2000). This research was based on a social marketing framework; consequently, considerable attention was devoted to identifying what consumers might see as "benefits" of routine breast cancer screening as well as what they see as "barriers" to routine breast cancer screening. Florida's population of medically underserved and underinsured women includes a great deal of cultural diversity; thus, the validity of methodologies aimed at standardized, population-based assessments was threatened by the possibility of varying conceptualizations of common terms related to mammography use.

As we attempted to address the need for generalizable, population-based research while minimizing the threats to the internal validity of such research, mixed methods seemed to be a necessary feature of the research design. We carried out a sequential mixed methods study with three phases. The first phase was in-depth qualitative research (via individual interviews and focus groups) with members of population subgroups defined by age and indicators of cultural background such as ethnicity and the language most often spoken in the home. As might be expected, these interviews and focus group discussions revealed variations in conceptualizations of cancer etiology and risk as well as in conceptualizations of individual responsibility and control over cancer. For example, we learned from our focus group research that women in certain cultural groups regarded cancer prevention and control as not within the power/control of an individual. Rather, they viewed whether a woman experienced breast cancer as a decision made by God. Variations among population subgroups' views of such issues could potentially have an enormous impact on the pattern of responses to questions about individual risk perception. From a theoretical standpoint, the focus group results allowed us to estimate, albeit subjectively, the magnitude of the variation in these conceptualizations of breast cancer as a disease; methodologically, the magnitude of variation in conceptualizations of breast cancer represented an estimate of the potential severity of the threat to internal validity described previously.

In the second phase of this research, we used the existing literature and our own focus group results to develop a survey instrument for use in more standardized population-based research throughout Florida. This development process was itself iterative, with early iterations using in-depth individual interviews to elicit open-ended responses to potential survey questions and later iterations gradually progressing toward a more closed-ended, standardized tool. At each step, our work was focused either on representing the diversity of cultural perspectives in our survey language or on identifying language that was culturally nonspecific in our target population. Because constraints imposed by collaborative sponsorship of the research required that the final survey be appropriate for both telephone and face-to-face interviews, this survey development phase also included piloting of late iterations of the instrument in both face-to-face and telephone formats.

The third and final phase of the research was itself characterized by a combination of methods in terms of the sampling methods and data collection format. Telephone surveys and face-to-face household interviews were conducted in 13 Florida counties. Telephone interviewers made three attempts to interview women selected for participation in the study. Face-to-face interviewers made two attempts to interview women living in the homes selected for the study. If an eligible participant was not at home during the second attempt, a survey formatted for self-administration in English or Spanish, instructions for self-administration, and a self-addressed stamped return envelope were left at the house with an invitation to participate in the study. In the final sample of 2,373 women, 37% were interviewed by telephone, 50% were interviewed face-to-face, and the remaining 13% returned surveys by mail. Given the diversity of the study population and the diversity of data collection formats imposed by the research sponsor, the sequential use of mixed methods in this study was invaluable to our ensuring a high level of confidence in both the internal and external validity of our study findings.

A second methodological challenge associated with health sciences research on individual behavior change is that, to evaluate the effectiveness of intervention strategies designed to change individuals' behaviors, we often must obtain measures of individuals' behaviors. Often, behavior change objectives are phrased in terms of population-level indicators but interventions are implemented at the level of communities or individuals. Few health behavior change interventions have a scope sufficient to produce rapid evidence of shifts in population-level indicators. Thus,

health scientists are often faced with a need to combine measurements and even combine methodologies to accumulate indirect evidence of intervention impact.

For example, when a breast cancer screening program for uninsured and underinsured women (i.e., coverage of mammography at less than recommended frequency) was funded by Florida's state legislature, renewal funding was determined on an annual basis. The objectives of the program were to reduce breast cancer morbidity and mortality by 25% and to significantly reduce the ethnic disparities in breast cancer morbidity and mortality. Certainly, data from existing breast cancer surveillance programs might provide the most direct evidence of progress toward meeting these objectives. Yet even in a highly effective program, any expectation that one would see clear evidence of such impact after only 1 year of implementation would be extremely unrealistic. At the same time, the state legislature expected some examination of program progress on which to base renewal funding decisions.

The team of researchers assigned to evaluate the program's impact chose a quasi-experimental design that triangulated indirect evidence from multiple parallel measurement methods. The program's screening sites provided data on clients' self-reported first-time breast cancer screening rates, clients' self-reported repeat breast cancer screening rates, and site-specific breast cancer detection rates at regular intervals for comparison of pre-program and post-program indicators. Concurrently, a random sample of program clients were interviewed by independent evaluation staff to obtain separate self-reports of breast cancer screening behaviors along with knowledge, attitudes, and future intentions for rescreening. These program clients were also asked for consent to access their medical claims data so that self-reported screening could be verified against paid claims. Collectively, these indirect indicators provided the program with evidence of program impact that was strengthened by the use of multiple and complementary measurement methods.

◆ Using Mixed Methods to Study the Social Determinants of Health

As our knowledge base regarding factors that influence health outcomes grows, the importance of ecological factors in health is underscored. Consequently, health sciences research increasingly includes the study of ecological influences. This work has included a variety of challenges that, although perhaps not new to the social sciences, are relatively new to health sciences research. These include (a) selecting the level of measurement in studies of ecological influences on health, (b) capitalizing on the relative merits of "objective" and "subjective" measures of ecological factors, and (c) balancing analysis of diverse experiences in measures of ecological factors.

Researchers who investigate ecological influences on health are faced with a great deal of ambiguity when it comes to operationalizing ecological factors. Whereas social and ecological theories posit environmental factors and social systems as having direct influences on individuals, direct measurement of macro-level environmental factors and social systems is not always feasible. To directly measure macro-level influences, researchers much make critical decisions about the ecological scope of their studies. That is, should one measure the characteristics of neighborhoods, school districts, or metropolitan areas? Moreover, when individual mo-

bility makes it possible for individuals to live within multiple ecologies, must one measure the characteristics of all such ecologies?

Obviously, there is no single answer to these questions. Thus, mixed methods, with their natural applicability to the gathering of multiple perspectives, enable researchers to make some thoughtful compromises in the measurement of ecological influences. For example, the use of publicly available records to document structural issues (e.g., income inequality, population density, ethnic diversity, age integration) can enable understanding of the most macro-level ecological factors. Standardized quantitative tools can be an effective means of capturing situational information from individuals about their specific social systems. Then, for capturing information about perceived inequalities or discrimination, open-ended qualitative interviews provide a view that is grounded in context. Direct observational methods take measurement of ecological factors to another level—the measurement of physical environmental characteristics (Sampson & Raudenbush, 1999).

As an example of the wide range of approaches available to researchers attempting to study the social determinants of health, recent research on the role of collective efficacy in health promotion is discussed. Collective efficacy is defined as group members' perceptions about the group's ability to (a) work together in a well-coordinated, organized manner to achieve an objective; (b) work together to create desirable short-term and long-term changes in the community; and (c) access and use resources in the community to help achieve an objective. Group members' perceptions about collective efficacy influence how well resources are used, how much effort is put into group endeavors, the degree of persistence when collective efforts meet opposition or fail to produce quick results (Bandura, 1995), members' motivation to work on behalf of the group (Gist, 1987; Shamir, 1990), members' commitment to goals, and the level of group cohesion (Zaccaro, Blair, Peterson, & Zazanis, 1995). Therefore, the stronger the collective efficacy, the greater the belief that individuals working together can have an impact (e.g., influencing social change), which then motivates individuals to engage more actively in collective efforts to achieve the desired impact (Bandura, 1995).

One of the most difficult decisions in research on collective efficacy relates to the frame of reference for collective efficacy measurement. Some research on collective efficacy employs measures of individual general perceptions of communities (Sampson, Morenoff, & Earls, 1999; Sampson, Raudenbush, & Earls, 1997), whereas other research is focused on describing trends in members' perceptions of the collective efficacy of community groups formed to address specific community needs (Eaton, Forthofer, & McDermott, 2001). Each approach offers a unique and valuable perspective on the social processes that support individual and community-level health promotion. An opportunity exists for integration of the two approaches using mixed methods to examine the concordance of community group collective efficacy and community-wide or neighborhood collective efficacy.

One notable aspect of the measurement strategies outlined here is their variation in reliance on subjective versus objective approaches. Perhaps the area of health sciences research where this distinction is most palpable is research on the effects of socioeconomic disparities in health outcomes. In this research, socioeconomic disparities may be measured as "objectively" as median household incomes across neighborhoods or communities or "subjectively" as variation in perceptions of financial strain among individuals.

A growing list of studies of the effects of socioeconomic status (SES) on health illustrates the unique relative contributions of the views afforded by objective and subjective measurements of SES. In general, SES, however measured, has been negatively associated with health outcomes for decades (for a comprehensive review, see Wagstaff & von Doorslaer, 2000). Furthermore, some recent evidence suggests that the magnitude of socioeconomic inequality in a population (as measured by the range of SES in the population) as well as subjective perceptions of deprivation or unfavorable social comparisons may have a unique impact on health status, above and beyond objectively defined SES (Hagerty, 2000; Kessler, Mickelson, & Williams, 1999).

Perhaps due to the complexity of studying individual health and disease processes in the context of social systems, multilevel mixed methods research (Tashakkori & Teddlie, 1998, p. 18) is steadily gaining in popularity among health sciences researchers. An excellent example of multilevel mixed methods research on the social determinants of individual health is described in an article published by Kegler, Rodine, McLeroy, and Oman (1998) on a community-wide adolescent pregnancy prevention initiative in Oklahoma City, Oklahoma. Kegler et al. employed mixed methods in a parallel or simultaneous fashion across multiple levels in two phases of their work: the phase focused on community assessment for program planning purposes and the phase focused on program evaluation. In the community assessment phase, observational methods (via windshield tours of neighborhoods), individual- and group-level qualitative methods, and population-based quantitative methods were used in combination to develop extremely rich descriptions of the neighborhoods selected for inclusion in the pregnancy prevention program. Similarly, the program evaluation phase featured an integration of several methodological approaches, including case studies, process logs, content analysis of program records, surveys of program staff, surveys of prospective program clients, and vital statistics records. The study's contribution to the field is integrally linked to its use of mixed methods in that it represents a comprehensive attempt to study directly the very environmental and social contexts that the program aims to modify.

Another methodological challenge inherent in studies of the social determinants of health relates to the tremendous mobility that many individuals have in today's communities. With a huge array of transportation options, individuals are no longer forced to live in the communities in which they work. School-age children now frequently attend schools at considerable distance from their homes. Moreover, widespread use of the Internet enables virtual social ties with persons all over the world (Wellman, Salaff, & Dimitrova, 1996). Collectively, these patterns present an enormous challenge for researchers aimed at "measuring" social environments in that any one individual may, quite plausibly, engage in a whole myriad of social systems. Currently, few studies take this complexity into account; nonetheless, this challenge represents yet another opportunity for creative application of mixed methods.

◆ Patient- and Family-Focused Health Care

The focus of research on health care delivery and health services use has also shifted considerably during recent decades. Where previous research concentrated on the need for patients to comply with the recommendations and treatment regimens of health care providers and to adapt to existing models of health care delivery, research is now informed by a more patient- and family-centered approach to health care. Within this new approach, research on changes in provider behaviors and adapting health care delivery to the needs of patients is not out of the question; it is, in fact, the focus of numerous programs of research (e.g., Roter & Hall, 1993; Ruckdeschel, Albrecht, Blanchard, & Hemmick, 1996). Also, evidence regarding the importance and complexity of social networks, especially social support from family members, for patient outcomes has grown immeasurably during recent decades (e.g., Cohen, Underwood, & Gottlieb, 2000; Glasser, Prohaska, & Roska, 1992; Rook, 1998).

With the rise of patient-centered perspectives of health service delivery, health scientists have gained a heightened awareness of the importance of the therapeutic alliance for patient outcomes. Put simply, the term *therapeutic alliance* refers to a collaboration between patients and their health care providers, one that values the perspectives of both partners as equals in the decision-making process. Thus, an entirely new area of research has emerged—one of understanding that which fosters an effective therapeutic alliance.

Much research on health care delivery examines the factors associated with the use of health services and with delivering services in a way that directly addresses patients' needs. Traditionally, this research has been monomethod in nature, employing quantitative methods to identify predictors of health care use and subsequent health outcomes. Mixed methods approaches, particularly multilevel mixed methods approaches (Tashakkori & Teddlie,

1998), represent a tremendous opportunity to advance this area of research as a vehicle for illuminating contextual issues surrounding health care use. Just as research on individual behavior change has used mixed methods to enhance our understanding of consumer perspectives, research on health care use and health care delivery can employ qualitative methods to gather contextual information that enhances our understanding of health outcomes. Such a broadened understanding of health outcomes can serve as a springboard for promising multidisciplinary collaborations to enhance patient outcomes.

This comprehensive approach to improving health outcomes through system-wide improvements forms the bedrock of the *friendly access* approach to improving the health outcomes of low-income mothers and their children (Albrecht, 1999; Albrecht, Eaton, & Rivera, 1999). Friendly access represents a configuration of health and social systems to ensure that what

> the mother receives enables her to obtain regular care, what happens to her physically, cognitively and emotionally during actual visits, the auxiliary services that are available to help prepare for delivery and newborn care, the anticipation and early screening for medical complications, the psychological support received at home and professionally, and the provision of services for early childhood and for subsequent pregnancies. (Albrecht et al., 1999, pp. 33-34)

Like the research by Kegler et al. (1998) described previously, our research (aimed at further development and evaluation of friendly access) will make use of a diverse array of methodologies at several levels, including content analysis of media and program records, in-depth interviews with clients and service providers, analyses of service delivery networks, tracking of community and service sector collaboration for improved service delivery, tracking of service use, and surveillance of maternal and infant outcomes.

As noted previously, the fact that social support is associated with health outcomes has been documented extensively. Research in this area is now focused directly on explicating the mechanisms through which social support influences health, and it is in this work that the use of mixed methods poses numerous advantages over monomethod approaches. One example of an innovative use of mixed methods to study the mechanisms through which social support influences health is found in thesis research conducted by Alfonso (2000). Alfonso's study included parallel use of focus group methods, in-depth individual interviews, and standardized survey research with adolescent girls and their mothers to examine their conceptualizations of problematic support in the mother-daughter dyad. The study was based on an interactivity between methods and data sources such that the notion of constant comparison, popular in the literature on qualitative methods, characterized Alfonso's work at several levels.

◆ Translation of Research Findings Into Practice

As evidence mounts that health is influenced by multiple factors (many of which relate to entire community systems), and as public health priorities adopt a focus on disparities in health status, health scientists are decreasingly attuned to interventions *on* individuals residing in communities and increasingly focused on collaborating *with* communities of individuals to bring about social change. Available evidence from a broad literature on partnership-based approaches to improving community health suggests that collaborative approaches have been moderately effective at changing a variety of health behaviors and that these approaches show particular promise for producing changes in community-level processes and health practices (Roussos & Fawcett, 2000).

The speed with which the field of public health has embraced community-based approaches overshadows the challenges and tensions inherent in academic-community partnerships. The most pervasive tensions revolve around balances between "insiders" and "outsiders" and between "products" and "processes" (Roundtable on Comprehensive Community Initiatives for Children and Families, 1997).

The success of academic-community partnerships is dependent on their ability to incorporate the values, norms, and language of community members. Cultural values of a population or its subgroups related to health issues must be expressed and understood by academic partners. Similarly, the values, norms, and language of faculty researchers must be made accessible to community partners. Without a free exchange of cultural expertise among academic and community partners, partnerships cannot overcome histories of exploitation of communities by academic researchers. Adhering to established principles for academic-community collaboration ensures that the unique contributions of each partner can be understood and valued (Baker, Homan, Schonhoff, & Kreuter, 1999).

Another challenge related to insider-outside distinctions is that community advisory groups vary considerably in the extent to which their members actually represent the entire community. Community leaders might not understand issues of importance beyond their individual areas of responsibility, and they might not share the life experiences of the community members they serve. Attention to the inclusion of all perspectives in the community is critical if the knowledge created through the partnership is to reflect all relevant truths in the community.

Members of community organizations and academic institutions often differ significantly in their use of time and their focus on time constraints, with community organizations focused on addressing immediate community needs and academicians accustomed to research that may take years to produce usable results (McWilliam, Desai, & Greig, 1997). Also critical is allowing sufficient time for community members to become comfortable participating in the partnership prior to implementing and evaluating interventions (Brownson, Riley, & Bruce, 1998). Without adequate time, evaluations may generate false negative results.

In academic-community partnerships, the balance between process and product is extremely delicate, primarily because the relationship between processes and products is almost invariably symbiotic. That is, a focus on developing good processes early in the partnership is critical for the development of the empowerment, ownership, and capacity that characterizes the most productive partnerships. Yet visible products early in the partnership are often necessary for stimulating and maintaining community members' participation and commitment to the collaborative process. Thus, as one participant in a comprehensive community initiative stated, "Every objective stands for two things: an end in and of itself, and a stage of development, a means to a later end" (Roundtable on Comprehensive Community Initiatives for Children and Families, 1997, p. 23).

All too frequently, evaluations of community-based initiatives are focused on documenting the products of the initiative, often strictly in terms of population-level health status indicators, to the exclusion of tracking process indicators and intermediate outcomes. Then, regardless of whether evaluation results support resounding claims of success, little is understood about why an initiative produced the observed results. This convention in evaluation research places the field of public health at risk for discarding promising interventions when the outcome measures employed are not sensitive enough to track the actual change produced by the intervention and for applauding interventions as effective when little is understood about what is required to implement them effectively in other contexts.

◆ The Climate for Mixed Methods Research in the Health Sciences

This chapter has summarized some of the key challenges in health sciences research in terms of four areas: (a) the study of individual behaviors or lifestyle factors in health, (b) the study of social determinants of health, (c) the study of more patient-focused health care delivery, and (d) the responsibility of researchers to accelerate the translation of research into practice. The section on lifestyle factors discussed the unique contributions of mixed methods approaches for carrying out consumer- or participant-based research and the value of mixed methods in the measurement of the short-term impact of behavioral interventions. The section on the social determinants of health discussed variations in the unit of analysis and variation in the use of objective versus subjective measures across studies of social

determinants and opportunities for integrating these strategies through the use of mixed methods. The section on patient- and family-focused health care described the contributions of mixed methods to understanding the impact of changes in service delivery changes and for understanding dyadic or family influences. Last, the section on the translation of research findings into practice discussed the current emphasis on academic-community partnerships in the health sciences and the value of mixed methods approaches to building and sustaining these partnerships.

Certainly, this chapter's focus has been on the advantages of employing mixed methods in health sciences research. We would be remiss, however, if we did not include some mention of the costs or barriers to the use of mixed methods in health sciences research. Perhaps the most significant cost for researchers associated with the use of mixed methods is the amount of time required for the design and implementation of studies that truly take advantage of what mixed methods offer above and beyond what monomethod approaches offer. Mixed methods designs are inherently more complex, and those that attempt any integration or synthesis of results across methodologies require an additional phase of "meta-interpretation." This cost is compounded by the fact that the incentive structures of most academic institutions continue to place more emphasis on the quantity of products than on the quality of products. Efforts to promote the unique value of mixed methods research are part of the solution, but appreciation of the costs and sincere reviews of incentives and disincentives related to mixed methods research are also needed.

Another cost or barrier associated with attempting to carry out mixed methods research in the health sciences relates to the organization of funding mechanisms for research in the health sciences. The vast majority of health sciences research funding is distributed categorically through disease- or risk factor-specific mechanisms. Moreover, few funding mechanisms allow researchers the flexibility in time lines and project length needed to truly facilitate the expansion of mixed methods approaches. The result is a funding structure better equipped to facilitate the use of mono-method approaches at a time when health sciences research could be more than ever advanced by the use of mixed methods approaches. Again, advocacy to increase the familiarity of funding agencies with mixed methods approaches will help to put these issues on agendas when funding priorities are being set.

■ *References*

Albrecht, T. L. (1999, November). *The "friendly access model": Research/conceptual framework and evaluation.* Paper presented at the meeting of the National Perinatal Association, Milwaukee, WI.

Albrecht, T. L., Eaton, D. K., & Rivera, L. (1999, February). *Portal to portal: Friendly access healthcare for low-income mothers and babies* (technical report prepared for the Lawton and Rhea Chiles Center for Healthy Mothers and Babies). Paper presented at the meeting of the Friendly Access Advisory Board, Orlando, FL.

Alfonso, M. L. (2000). *Problematic support: An exploration of supportive and unsupportive coping assistance within mother-daughter relationships.* Unpublished master's thesis, University of South Florida.

Andreason, A. (1995). *Marketing social change.* San Francisco: Jossey-Bass.

Baker, E. A., Homan, S., Schonhoff, R., & Kreuter, M. (1999). Principles of practice for academic/practice/community research partnerships. *American Journal of Preventive Medicine, 16*(3), 86-93.

Bandura, A. (1995). Exercise of personal and collective efficacy in changing societies. In A. Bandura (Ed.), *Self-efficacy in changing societies.* New York: Cambridge University Press.

Brownson, R. C., Riley, P., & Bruce, T. A. (1998). Demonstration projects in community-based prevention. *Journal of Public Health Management and Practice, 4*(2), 66-77.

Bryant, C. A., Forthofer, M. S., McCormack Brown, K., Alfonso, M., & Quinn, G. (2000). A social marketing approach to increasing breast cancer screening rates. *Journal of Health Education, 31,* 320-328.

Cohen, S., Underwood, L. G., & Gottlieb, B. H. (2000). *Social support measurement and intervention: A guide for health and social scientists.* New York: Oxford University Press.

Eaton, D. K., Forthofer, M. S., & McDermott, R. J. (2001). *Development of a task-specific measure for group collective efficacy.* Unpublished manuscript, University of South Florida.

Gist, M. E. (1987). Self-efficacy: Implications for organizational behavior and human resource management. *Academy of Management Review, 12,* 472-485.

Glasser, M., Prohaska, T., & Roska, J. (1992). The role of the family in medical care-seeking decisions of older adults. *Family & Community Health, 15,* 59-70.

Green, L., & Kreuter, M. (1999). *Health promotion planning: An educational and ecological approach* (3rd ed.). Mountain View, CA: Mayfield.

Hagerty, M. R. (2000). Social comparison of income in one's community: Evidence from national surveys of income and happiness. *Journal of Personality and Social Psychology, 78,* 764-771.

Kegler, M. C., Rodine, S., McLeroy, K., & Oman, R. (1998). Combining quantitative and qualitative techniques in planning and evaluating a community-wide project to prevent adolescent pregnancy. *International Electronic Journal of Health Education, 1,* 39-48.

Kessler, R. C., Mickelson, K. D., & Williams, D. R. (1999). The prevalence, distribution, and mental health correlates of perceived discrimination in the United States. *Journal of Health and Social Behavior, 40,* 208-223.

McWilliam, C. L., Desai, K., & Greig, B. (1997). Bridging town and gown: Building research partnerships between community-based professional providers and academia. *Journal of Professional Nursing, 13,* 307-315.

Minkler, M. (1999). Personal responsibility for health? A review of the arguments and the evidence at century's end. *Health Education & Behavior, 26,* 121-140.

Petersen, A., & Lupton, D. (1996). *The new public health: Health and self in the age of risk.* London: Sage.

Prochaska, J. O., DiClemente, C. C., & Norcross, J. C. (1992). In search of how people change: Applications to addictive behaviors. *American Psychologist, 47,* 1102-1114.

Rook, K. (1998). Investigating the positive and negative sides of personal relationships: Through a lens darkly? In B. H. Spitzberg & W. R. Cupach (Eds.), *The dark side of close relationships* (pp. 369-393). Mahwah, NJ: Lawrence Erlbaum.

Roter, D., & Hall, J. (1993). *Doctors talking to patients, patients talking to doctors: Improving communication in medical visits.* Westport, CT: Auburn House.

Roundtable on Comprehensive Community Initiatives for Children and Families. (1997). *Voices from the field: Learning from the early works of comprehensive community initiatives.* Washington, DC: Aspen Institute.

Roussos, S. T., & Fawcett, S. B. (2000). A review of collaborative partnerships as a strategy for improving community health. *Annual Review of Public Health, 21,* 369-402.

Ruckdeschel, J. C., Albrecht, T. L., Blanchard, C., & Hemmick, R. M. (1996). Communication, accrual process to clinical trials, and the physician-patient relationship. *Journal of Cancer Education, 11,* 73-79.

Sampson, R. J., Morenoff, J. D., & Earls, F. (1999). Beyond social capital: Spatial dynamics of collective efficacy for children. *American Sociological Review, 64,* 633-660.

Sampson, R. J., & Raudenbush, S. W. (1999). Systematic social observation of public spaces: A new look at disorder in urban neighborhoods. *American Journal of Sociology, 105,* 603-652.

Sampson, R. J., Raudenbush, S. W., & Earls, F. (1997). Neighborhoods and violent crime: A multilevel study of collective efficacy. *Science, 277,* 918-924.

Shamir, B. (1990). Calculations, values, and identities: The sources of collectivistic work motivation. *Human Relations, 43,* 313-332.

Tashakkori, A., & Teddlie, C. (1998). *Mixed methodology: Combining qualitative and quantitative approaches* (Applied Social Research Methods, No. 46). Thousand Oaks, CA: Sage.

Wagstaff, A., & von Doorslaer, E. (2000). Income inequality and health: What does the literature tell us? *Annual Review of Public Health, 21,* 543-567.

Wellman, B., Salaff, J., & Dimitrova, D. (1996). Computer networks as social networks: Collaborative work, telework, and virtual community. *Annual Review of Sociology, 22,* 213-238.

Zaccaro, S. J., Blair, V., Peterson, C., & Zazanis, M. (1995). Collective efficacy. In J. E. Maddux (Ed.), *Self-efficacy, adaptation, and adjustment: Theory, research, and application* (pp. 305-328). New York: Plenum.

20

STATUS OF MIXED METHODS RESEARCH IN NURSING

◆ Sheila Twinn

Nursing research has been defined as "a systematic search for and validation of knowledge about issues of importance to the nursing profession" (Polit & Hungler, 1999, p. 3). Issues of importance have been determined by the research traditions of the discipline as well as by practitioners working within nursing. Indeed, practitioners within the discipline of nursing cover the spectrum of an individual's health status, with practice interventions ranging from the promotion and maintenance of health to the facilitation of a peaceful death. An understanding of human experiences is fundamental to the process of nursing across this spectrum and therefore plays an implicit role in the development of nursing knowledge. Yet until quite recently, nursing research has frequently not acknowledged the significance of this process to the research agenda, with designs grounded in the more distinct traditional paradigms of positivism (or postpositivism) and interpretivism.

This chapter raises questions about the status of mixed methods design in nursing research, particularly because a strength of this design in its ability to contribute to an understanding of human experiences and the outcome of nursing interventions. Examining the status of this design in nursing raises some important questions that include the following:

◆ What is the contribution of the historical development of nursing research to the current status of mixed methods design?

◆ How does the mixed methods design contribute to the development of nursing knowledge and practice?

◆ What are the issues arising from attempts to develop this design within the context of nursing research and practice?

This chapter attempts to address these questions by focusing on five particular issues:

◆ The traditions of nursing research: Implications for developing mixed methods design

◆ The contribution of research designs in explicating and developing nursing knowledge and clinical interventions

◆ An analysis of the development and application of mixed methods design in nursing

◆ An evaluation of the contribution of mixed methods design to nursing research

◆ Issues emerging from the application of mixed methods design in nursing research

◆ The Traditions of Nursing Research: Implications for Developing Mixed Methods Design

Authors such as Millor, Haber, Feldman, Hott and Jacobson (1992) suggest that knowledge of the historical developments that have shaped nursing knowledge and nursing research help to explain the traditions of research in nursing. The first of these is that nursing research, although

now well-established, is still perceived as relatively inexperienced compared with other professions and disciplines. Despite the early work of Florence Nightingale during the 1860s in the use of epidemiological data to determine factors influencing the mortality and morbidity affecting soldiers in the Crimean War (Harkness, 1995), further research was limited until the 1950s. Early research focused on the education of nurses rather than on the processes involved in nursing. It was not until the 1960s, with an increasing number of nurses with advanced academic degrees (generally in the United States), that research moved away from the education and attitudes of nurses to nursing practice. The establishment of organizations such as the American Nurses Foundation, with its particular emphasis on promoting research, and the availability of more funding for research acted as stimuli to the development of nursing research programs and to the growth in the number of nurse researchers. The historical development also contributed to the traditions of research found in nursing, particularly in determining the growth in research activity during the past four decades.

A consistent finding in the literature is the influence of doctoral programs in determining the specific research approach undertaken by nurses (Millor et al., 1992). Leininger (1985), in describing the growth of nursing in the United States, highlighted this factor as one of four influencing the prevailing research tradition. Other factors included the following:

◆ The perceived need for research to be accepted and respected by other scientific disciplines

◆ The availability of funding

◆ The publishing preference of available nursing journals

Such factors focused the early research in clinical practice toward the positivist paradigm, leading to the development of specific patient outcome measures such as the measure of social support developed by Jane Norbeck during the 1980s (Millor et al., 1992). Developments such as these, considered indicative of the maturation of nursing as an academic discipline, provide support for the idea that the prevailing tradition was one borrowed from other disciplines. Other authors writing at this time argued that the emphasis on a positivist research paradigm meant that strategies were not available to study the complex and dynamic constructs relevant to nursing (Mitchell, 1986). More recently, the incongruence between the empiricist domain and commitment to a holistic approach to care has been highlighted (Foster, 1997).

There were, however, other influences in the development of the traditions of nursing research that may be seen as opportunities to address issues such as those just described. The women's movement of the 1970s provides an example of a stimulus that encouraged nurse researchers to go beyond an emphasis on knowledge confined to scientific reasoning to one that included the study of the role of intuition and clinical judgment in the development of nursing practice. This contributed to a growing interest in qualitative research as a method of developing the originality in thought required to reflect the true nature of nursing. This was considered particularly important in developing nursing practice because nursing questions frequently arise from complex social situations.

The development of an alternative paradigm in research contributed to a lengthy and lively debate in the nursing literature about the most appropriate paradigm from which to answer nursing research questions and develop the discipline of nursing (e.g., Brink & Wood,

1998; Morse, 1991). It was clear that there was little consensus among researchers as to the research paradigm that would best develop nursing knowledge. Indeed, the debate lent support to the notion that nursing had a history of divided opinion as to the most appropriate research paradigm to answer nursing questions. This debate led several writers (from the early 1980s onward) to state that multiple and mixed methods designs provided nursing with the opportunity to propel nursing into the visionary stage of wisdom.

The work of nurse academics, such as that by Carper (1978) on the development of nursing knowledge, contributed to this view by positing that all patterns of knowing were of equal importance. Discussions such as these added to a growing consensus that not only was neither paradigm superior, but a combination of the two might be most appropriate in creating a new tradition to underpin the development of nursing knowledge (e.g., Foster, 1997; Sohier, 1988).

◆ *The Contribution of Research Designs in Explicating and Developing Nursing Knowledge and Clinical Interventions*

A major purpose of nursing research is to develop and test theory so as to develop a body of nursing knowledge that will then allow practitioners to understand the processes and patterns of human health behavior within the health-illness continuum as well as inform the development and implementation of therapeutic nursing interventions (Foster, 1997). Such a definition highlights the importance of both theoretical knowledge and clinical practice to the development of the discipline of nursing. The development of nursing knowledge is implicitly linked with research and the pursuit of knowledge. Within nursing, the pursuit of knowledge has been determined in part by borrowing assumptions, theories, and concepts from other disciplines (Hogan & DeSantis, 1991). This approach initially contributed to a focus on scientific knowledge without acknowledging the influence of human experience on the phenomenon in question. Indeed, the recognition that perceptions of health, illness adjustment, participation, and care fit uneasily within this approach to the interpretation of nursing knowledge has been significant in refocusing understandings of nursing knowledge and approaches in the pursuit of knowledge (Corner, 1991; Fish, 1998).

THE CONTEXT OF CARE

The assumptions that nurses are part of the context in which health care occurs and that this context is significant to the process of nursing and nursing interventions have also influenced the development of nursing knowledge and theory (Hogan & DeSantis, 1991). Such assumptions highlight the significance of the practice environment and the social context of care. Im and Meleis (1999), in a study of Korean immigrant women's menopausal transition, highlighted the significance of context to the understanding of the theory of transition on women's health behavior patterns. Such evidence contributes to an increasing understanding among practitioners that the research question, rather than a particular research paradigm, determines the approach and methods used to explicate the problem. In addition, the context in which practice occurs is becoming increasingly complex, making further demands on the development of nursing knowledge.

Another issue that must be considered within the context of practice and the implications for nursing research is that of

the increasing demands for the justification of resources that has contributed to a focus on outcomes research (e.g., Koehler, Miller, Vojir, Hester, & Foster, 1997). The use of evidence-based nursing care has implications for the development of nursing research because within this approach to practice, intervention studies based within a positivist paradigm are considered the strongest evidence from which to develop clinical guidelines. However, although randomized control trials are considered the gold standard in developing clinical guidelines, growing debate among researchers questions the extent to which this approach to clinical research provides guidance for practitioners in understanding why outcomes occur. Resolving this issue is essential to the development of nursing practice.

A consequence of the recognition of the complexity of the practice world has led nurse researchers to acknowledge that clear definitions between research paradigms become "less well defined at the social and technical level of research practice" (Proctor, 1998, p. 75). Indeed, the complex research questions facing practitioners frequently require a number of research perspectives to be considered to successfully contribute to the body of nursing knowledge. It is this recognition that has contributed to the development and implementation of mixed methods research in nursing practice. It is interesting to note that since the early 1980s, mixed methods research has been described as a possible strategy to facilitate the development of a methodology for nursing from which to answer nursing-specific research questions (Mitchell, 1986). It has also been described as holding much promise for nursing research (Banik, 1993). The extent to which this has been achieved in nursing, and the implications for the development of nursing research, provides the focus for the next sections of the chapter.

◆ An Analysis of the Development and Application of Mixed Methods Design in Nursing

A review of the published nursing literature from 1982 to late 2000, using the Medline and CINAHL databases, identified 112 English-language articles using or describing mixed methods research design. It is significant to note, however, that the majority of these articles were identified using the term *triangulation* rather than *mixed methods* or *multimethod* design, with no articles identified prior to 1985. The emphasis on triangulation studies in mixed methods design in nursing research has implications for the status of this design within nursing and is explored in more detail later in the chapter.

An analysis of the literature identified three major categories outlining the use of the research design in nursing:

◆ Theoretical discourses on the development of the research design

◆ A critique of the contribution of the design to nursing research

◆ Empirical studies using the design

THEORETICAL DISCOURSES ON THE DEVELOPMENT OF THE RESEARCH DESIGN

The development of mixed methods design provides an important starting point for the analysis. Nurse researchers continue to appear divided in their acknowledgment of the use of the design in nursing. Brink and Wood (1998), in editing a new edition of a textbook of advanced design in nursing research, made no reference to mixed methods design. The frequently cited nursing research textbook written by Polit and Hungler (1999), however, described the integration of qualitative and quantitative designs as a trend that emerged during the 1980s as a result of an increasing acceptance of methodological pluralism. Although earlier editions of the book included some discussion about the design gaining momentum in the future, the most recent edition has much greater coverage of the design. A similar trend was identified in the most recent edition of the nursing research textbook authored by Burns and Grove (1997). They limited a rather brief discussion of the design to that of triangulation, however, and cautioned readers about the complexity of the design when used rigorously in empirical studies.

The interpretation of mixed methods design (as being synonymous with triangulation) was also apparent in the published articles identified in the literature review. The earliest reference to the design found through this review was an article by Mitchell (1986) in which the use of multiple triangulation as a methodology for nursing science was examined. She argued that nursing requires "methodological strategies that promote the study of [a] complex and dynamic phenomenon like human health behavior" (p. 18). She went on to argue that the lack of such strategies has contributed to the lack of advancement in nursing science. This early article on the development of the mixed methods design in nursing highlights the need for researchers to consider the application of four principles fundamental to triangulation:

◆ The need for a clearly focused research question

◆ The complementary nature of the strengths and weaknesses of the chosen methods

◆ Relevance of the methods to the nature of the phenomenon

◆ The need for continued evaluation of the chosen methodological approach

Other articles published later in the decade also focused on the positive contribution of triangulation to nursing research. Authors such as Sohier (1988) described triangulation as having the power to demonstrate the holistic nature of the process of nursing. It was also during the mid-1980s that the first empirical nursing studies using triangulation were reported. The study undertaken by Smith (1987) in the United Kingdom of the relationship between the quality of care received by patients and the quality of the ward as a learning environment for student nurses provides an example of mixed methods research. It is interesting to note that the focus of this study was on nursing education, thereby reflecting the initial stages in the development of nursing research.

It was during the 1990s, however, that the major developments in the use of triangulation emerged from the literature. Morse (1991), in her work on methodological triangulation, proposed a taxonomy to consider the key issue of whether the theory driving the research was developed inductively or used deductively. The significance of the theoretical drive of the design to the findings of the study in both mixed methods and multimethod designs is examined in this handbook (see Morse, Chapter 7). Knafl and Breitmayer (1991) contributed to an understanding of the mixed methods design by combining a theoretical discussion with the presentation of an empirical study. Knafl and Breitmayer described the purpose of triangulation as a method for describing and conceptualizing the multifaceted complexity of human response to illness and health care, using a study of how families defined and managed their children's chronic illnesses to illustrate the issues involved in the design. They discussed the issue of the different applications of triangulation in nursing studies, debating whether each application is one of completeness or confirmation. They described completeness as a process whereby different theoretical and substantive components come together to ensure that all aspects of the phenomenon are examined. Confirmation was described as a verification strategy, using multiple approaches to data collection in which the strengths and weaknesses of the methods are known and counterbalanced, to address threats to validity. The discussion of these concepts by Knafl and Breitmayer generated further debate in the nursing literature (e.g., Nolan & Behi, 1995; Norman, Redfern, Tomalin, & Oliver, 1992; Sandelowski, 1995).

A CRITIQUE OF THE DESIGN IN NURSING RESEARCH

The theoretical articles written during the mid-1990s generally examined the contribution of triangulation as a research design within the context of the complexity of nursing interventions and practice. Indeed, acknowledgment of the complexity of the design contributed to a series of debates about the contribution of triangulation to nursing research in both the United States and the United Kingdom. In the United States, Sandelowski (1995), in her discussion of the contribution of triangulation to nursing research, provided an impressive list of authors' positive responses to the technique. She went on, however, to express concern that the design had become popular as a kind of "misplaced ecumenism aimed at reducing conflict by minimizing and even trivializing differences amongst modes of enquiry" (p. 569). The rationale underpinning such concern, in particular the use and misuse of terms (e.g., the overuse of *triangulation*), is examined in more detail in Sandelowski's chapter in this handbook (Chapter 12). This concern was also reflected in an editorial written in the journal *Research Nursing and Health* in which the editor described her concern about the "misuse of complex theoretical perspectives," particularly in the use of triangulation (Oberst, 1993). In the United Kingdom, an article by Corner (1991) highlighted some of the complexities and practical issues encountered by researchers when using triangulation as a methodology.

These concerns highlight another issue within the development of the design that relates to confusion not only about the definition and concepts underpinning triangulation but also about the implementation of the different types of triangulation. Letters appearing in a 1990 edition of the journal *Nursing Research* from Judith Kimchi and Shirley Murphy provided an illustration of the diverse perceptions of nurse researchers regarding different types of triangulation (Kimchi & Murphy, 1990). More recent literature suggests that confusion remains about the interpretation of the different types of triangulation (Davidhizar, 1997), with authors continuing to have different perceptions regarding the complexity of the design. Some authors continue to present a rather simple interpretation of the design by encouraging future researchers to uncritically adopt multiple types of triangulation so as to accomplish the twin goals of completeness and confirmation (e.g., Begley, 1996). Other authors, recognizing the complexity of the design, raise both epistemological and practical issues about the rigorous use of triangulation in research studies (e.g., Barbour, 1998; Coyle & Williams, 2000; Foster, 1997).

EMPIRICAL NURSING STUDIES USING MIXED METHODS DESIGN

Polit and Hungler (1999) described mixed methods research as addressing a wide range of research purposes. These included the following:

◆ Instrument development

◆ Explicating and validating constructs

◆ Understanding relationships and causal processes

◆ The illustration of constructs and relationships

◆ Theory development, in particular potential disconfirmation of a theory

When considering the articles in the current review of nursing, the greatest application for mixed methods is in instrument development. Mixed methods were frequently used in testing the validity of instruments, which ranged from screening tools for family effectiveness (Friedemann & Smith, 1997), to nursing quality assessment instruments (Redfern & Norman, 1995), to the development of nursing minimum data sets (Goossen et al., 2000). The method of triangulation adopted in the development of the instrument varied in the different types of studies. An article examining the application of the multitrait-multimethod technique (developed to evaluate construct validation through the assessment of convergent and discriminant validity of measures) was also identified (Lowe & Ryan-Wenger, 1992).

The application of triangulation methodology in describing and explaining the processes and outcomes of a disaster project provided an early illustration of the application of this methodology in nursing research. Murphy's (1989) complex longitudinal study provided an example of using this methodology to understand both relationships and causal processes. More recently, the mixed methods design has frequently been used in health promotion and public health research in an attempt to understand the processes and outcomes in different but equally complex human health behavior (Baum, 1995; Milburn, Fraser, Secker, & Pavis, 1995). Cigno and Gore (1999) used the methodology to evaluate a multidisciplinary approach to the care provided for families with children with disabilities. Other studies illustrate the use of the design in transcultural nursing (Davidhizar, 1997) and cultural perspectives in health care (Callister, Venvilainen-Julkunen, & Lauri, 1996).

Triangulation has also been used to illustrate and attempt to understand the complex processes through which health care takes place. Barbour (1998) described the application of a mixed methods design to study the effects of changed management arrangements for community nursing staff working in a variety of primary health care teams. The data sources consisted of quantitative workload data, semistructured interviews with 152 participants, focus group discussions, and observational fieldwork in which the researcher accompanied practitioners on home visits to clients and patients. Barbour argued that a pragmatic decision led to the selection of this methodology in an attempt to obtain a complete understanding of the effects of change. A major aim of the article, however, was described as challenging the assumption that within-methods triangulation provides researchers with less of an epistemological challenge.

The review also identified studies using triangulation to explicate and validate constructs. Studies relating to vigor in heart failure (Fontana, 1996) and to social support in childhood cancer (Murray, 1999) were identified. Other studies examined the construct of hope from the perspective of homeless families (Herth, 1996) and sleep patterns as perceived by healthy older adults (Floyd, 1993). In addition, studies were identified that related to the outcomes of care; for example, Verhoef, Scott, and Hilsden (1998) used a multimethod study to examine the use of complementary therapies among patients with inflammatory bowel disease.

This review clearly highlights the breadth of the application of the research design in nursing, raising issues about the contribution of the design to the development of nursing research as well as about the perceived status of the design within the discipline.

◆ An Evaluation of the Contribution of Mixed Methods Design to Nursing Research

Evaluation of the contribution of the mixed methods design to the development of nursing research implicitly involves judging the outcome and quality of the research informed by the design as well as the perceived status of the design within the discipline of nursing. Tashakkori and Teddlie (1998, p. 14), in a discussion of the evolution of the use of mixed methods design in the behavioral and social sciences, identified three points for consideration in the process:

1. The acceptance of the use of mixed methods

2. The application of the distinctions that emerged during the "paradigm wars" to all phases of the research process

3. The ever increasing pace of evolution

This evolutionary process provides a useful framework from which to consider the perceived status of mixed methods research in nursing research. The rest of this chapter first reviews the status of mixed methods in nursing research using these three approaches. This is followed by a discussion of the contributions of mixed methods to nursing knowledge and practice.

ACCEPTANCE OF MIXED METHODS IN NURSING RESEARCH

The nursing literature generally has accepted the idea of mixed methods research. As noted earlier, the design has been described and discussed in the nursing literature since the mid-1980s. An obvious increase in available literature, both about the methodology and about empirical studies informed by the design, was apparent during the 1990s, perhaps mirroring events found during the 1980s in the social and behavioral sciences (Tashakkori & Teddlie, 1998, p. 15). In addition, the authors of two popular nursing research textbooks positively acknowledged the contribution of the design to nursing research, despite expressing some concern about the phenomenon of joining a "popular bandwagon" (Burns & Grove, 1997; Polit & Hungler, 1999).

PARADIGM ISSUES IN NURSING RESEARCH

The second point relates to distinctions in the paradigm wars and is, of course, more complex and therefore more difficult to assess. There is little doubt that the paradigm wars have been resolved within nursing. In general, there has been acceptance for several years of the need for both the positivist and constructivist paradigms in addressing nursing questions. Discussion about the emergence of the pragmatist paradigm provides an illustration of the thinking among some nurse researchers (Proctor, 1998). There has, however, been very little debate about the distinctions among different designs within mixed methods. Although this is rather a different point, it is equally significant to the status of mixed methodology in nursing. One important illustration is provided by the use of the term *triangulation*. As described previously, in completing the literature review to write this chapter, it was necessary to use *triangulation* as a key word for the search. Tashakkori and Teddlie (1998) indicated that triangulation techniques are common to all mixed methods designs and therefore have limited use as a method of identifying distinctions within designs unless they are used within the context of component design as described by Greene and Caracelli (1997, cited in Polit & Hungler, 1999, p. 264). Indeed, Polit and Hungler (1999) provided one of the few references in the nursing literature to distinctions in mixed methods design by referring readers to the work of Greene and Caracelli (1997; see also Greene & Caracelli, Chapter 3, this volume).

Other authors writing in the nursing literature have attempted to consider the distinctions within mixed methods design but have done so within the context of triangulation. As described earlier, Morse (1991) developed a taxonomy of methodological triangulation, while Knafl and Breitmayer (1991) defined the distinct purposes of triangulation studies within nursing, thereby informing the work of other nurse researchers (Norman et al., 1992). Foster (1997), in an article considering the epistemological and practical issues emerging from a study using conceptual triangulation as an approach to mixed methods research, highlighted the lack of practical advice available to nurse researchers in carrying out such studies. The tendency of nurses to publish articles about a complex area of research with little research training or experience, however, may have contributed to the lack of debate and understanding about the distinctions in triangulation or, indeed, mixed methods research (Dootson, 1995). More recently, authors such as Barbour (1998) and Coyle and Williams (2000) have attempted to consider the epistemological distinctions and complexities in developing and implementing mixed methods design.

PREVALENCE OF MIXED METHODS IN NURSING RESEARCH

The third point in the process of evolution relates to its increasing pace. Evidence from the literature search suggests that although there is an increasing interest and focus on the use of mixed methods design, it is difficult to accurately assess the extent to which the pace is increasing. Indeed, evidence also indicates a continuing emphasis on the use of qualitative studies in nursing research (Cullum, 2001). Evidence such as this has implications in determining the contribution of mixed methods design to nursing, particularly in assessing and understanding the outcomes of practice interventions.

◆ Contribution of Mixed Methods to Nursing Knowledge and Practice

One approach to evaluating the status of mixed methods design in nursing involves an assessment of the contribution to nursing knowledge of the findings of empirical studies informed by the design. In general,

it appears that there are two areas of practice where this design is of particular relevance. The first relates to assessing the impact of nursing interventions and the outcomes of those interventions. This is an important issue for nursing research because many intervention studies are multidimensional and are therefore difficult to make attributions from regarding the relationship of cause and effect. The second relates to the need to develop an understanding of complex health behaviors to facilitate the development of appropriate nursing interventions to meet identified health needs.

The literature search resulted in approximately 80 empirical studies, which covered a wide range of practice settings, and consequently health behaviors and nursing interventions, published in a variety of nursing journals. This finding raised questions about the appropriate criteria to assess the contribution of these studies. The majority of these studies used triangulation techniques, suggesting that the application of the principles of methodological triangulation, identified by Mitchell (1986), should contribute to an understanding of the status of the design in nursing research. The comprehensive application of these principles outlined earlier in the chapter, however, was not possible. This was generally due to lack of detail concerning the research designs in many of the articles, which may have been the result of the different content requirements of the wide range of journals identified in the literature review.

After careful consideration, a pragmatic approach was considered the most appropriate one. This approach involved a review of the description of the research design presented in each article in an attempt to assess the extent to which distinctions in the mixed methods design could be identified. Interestingly, an important finding from this review was the lack of any attempt to identify distinctions in the mixed methods design. In general, authors described the study design as using some form of triangulation, with the majority of studies using methodological triangulation.

A study by Burr (1998) provides an illustration of a design using multiple triangulation to address the "complexity and uniqueness of human needs and responses when faced with the experience of having a critically ill family member" (p. 163). The design used family members and intensive care nurses as data sources and used both quantitative and qualitative methods of data collection. Data collection with both nurses and family members involved the completion of a scale to measure family needs as well as semistructured interviews with a different sample of participants from those respondents who had completed the questionnaire. Burr indicated that this approach was undertaken to ensure both confirmation and completeness of data, but description of the findings provided little evidence to demonstrate how this was achieved. It was also difficult to assess whether the study had achieved both completeness and confirmation, generally considered as two distinct approaches to triangulation (Knafl & Breitmayer, 1991).

An interesting finding emerging from the review was the tendency of many authors to present some detail about general triangulation techniques, in particular the different types of techniques, rather than focusing on the designs used for their particular studies. The findings from the studies, however, appear to provide some contribution to the development of nursing knowledge, particularly within the context of instrument development. Indeed, this review of available literature indicates that mixed methods design provides an increasingly important methodology for nursing research. In particular, the review provided evidence of acceptance of the

methodology and an increasing interest in the design in an attempt to address a range of nursing issues and questions. The review, however, also raised some important issues to consider in the application of the design in nursing research.

◆ Issues Emerging From the Application of Mixed Methods Design in Nursing Research

In general, it appears that the issues emerging from the application of the mixed methods design in nursing can be divided into two categories. The first category relates to substantive issues, and the second relates to practical issues. It is interesting that these issues reflect those identified by Mitchell (1986) in her article on methodological issues related to triangulation, perhaps indicating the limited progress that has been made in the development of the design in nursing. The substantive issues appear to be the most significant to the status of the research design and therefore are considered first. Within the substantive issues, there are three major concerns that can be denoted as follows:

◆ Description of the design

◆ Complexity of design

◆ The "inherent good" of mixed methods design

SUBSTANTIVE ISSUES

Description of the Design. The description of the design raises two different points for consideration. The first of these relates to the language used by researchers, and the second relates to the specific description of the design. *Triangulation* is used nearly universally throughout the nursing literature as the term to describe the methodology employed in mixed methods design. In mixed methods design, this term appears to be used to describe either techniques or one particular approach to mixed methods design, which is that of convergence of data (Tashakkori & Teddlie, 1998). It is interesting to note that even those authors in nursing research who attempt to describe the different types of mixed methods design use the terms *triangulation* and *multimethod* interchangeably (Polit & Hungler, 1999, p. 271). It may be argued that terminology is not a major issue influencing the use of the research design. It does appear, however, to hinder the development of a research design and the levels of sophistication at which it can be applied if researchers are unclear about the concepts and terminology underpinning the design.

The specific description of the research design has also been highlighted as an issue of concern. Sandelowski (1995) described triangulation as coming to mean "virtually any more-than-one instance of one or more elements of the research process within a study" (p. 571). Breitmayer, Ayres, and Knafl (1993) also highlighted issues of description. They particularly related this issue to the failure of researchers to provide evidence in their study of how the use of triangulation contributed to either completeness or confirmation of the data set. Although this failure may, as implied earlier, be a result of publication constraints, such description is important to the development of the design and an understanding of its contribution to nursing research.

Complexity of Design. Complexity of design is another issue that is apparent from the review of the literature. Epistemological and methodological issues are two

factors contributing to this complexity. Epistemological issues focus on assumptions, which include both bias and incompatibility, and appear to be implicitly linked together. Some authors continue to express concern regarding the extent to which apparently incompatible assumptions can be overcome to develop a rigorous research design (e.g., Barbour, 1998; Coyle & Williams, 2000). Other authors, acknowledging the eclectic nature of nursing research and researchers, suggest that this issue might not be pertinent to the use of mixed methods design within the discipline (Polit & Hungler, 1999). Interestingly, there was very little evidence in the literature of any reference to the development of different paradigms (e.g., pragmatism) underpinning research designs (Proctor, 1998).

Epistemological assumptions were, however, also linked to methodological issues influencing the complexity of the design. Sim and Sharp (1998) highlighted the implicit link between the method of data collection and the nature of the phenomenon. Other authors have highlighted the challenge of data analysis as an important factor determining the rigor of mixed methods design (Corner, 1991; Polit & Hungler, 1999). The concepts of completeness and convergence have also been highlighted as contributing to the complexity of data analysis. Issues such as complexity of design have important implications when considering the rigor of mixed methods design in nursing research.

The "Inherent Good" of Mixed Methods Design. The final issue is implicitly linked with that of rigor and relates to the perception, among some researchers, that triangulation is an "inherent good" (Knafl & Breitmayer, 1991). Indeed, Sim and Sharp (1998), in their critical appraisal of the role of triangulation in nursing research, raised some interesting issues about whether research that combines methods should be considered superior to research that uses a single method, particularly when considering how the additional data will contribute to an understanding of the research question or phenomenon. Anecdotal evidence, indicating the requirement for novice researchers to include triangulation in developing research strategies at the master's degree level, supports the importance of this cautionary note. There is also evidence in the published literature of possible oversimplification of the use of triangulation as a research design (Begley, 1996).

There is little dispute about the design providing a method of examining the complexity of human health behavior and the context in which nursing care is provided. Questions remain, however, regarding the extent to which researchers consider alternative research strategies before joining what might be perceived as a "popular bandwagon." Indeed, although the perception of the inherent good of triangulation provides evidence for the acceptance of some types of mixed methods research in nursing, it fails to take account of the complexity of the design and the practical issues involved in undertaking such research.

PRACTICAL ISSUES RELATED TO THE RESEARCH DESIGN

The practical issues identified by researchers when undertaking triangulation studies also have implications for the status of mixed methods design. The first of these relates to investigator demands, particularly in the research training undertaken by the researcher. There is general acknowledgment that one investigator will often not have the required skills to successfully complete a mixed methods study, thereby requiring at least two investigators with complementary research skills to complete the study. This highlights another important issue, which is that of the high costs frequently incurred by mixed methods studies in terms of both time and resources. The funding bodies for nurse research need to recognize the contribution of mixed methods research in developing nursing knowledge and must be prepared to fund such studies.

◆ Conclusions

It appears that despite the range of issues influencing the status of mixed methods research in nursing, there is growing acceptance that the design provides an appropriate methodology to address the complex health problems frequently faced by the nursing discipline. This acceptance has been influenced by the historical development of nursing research, which has acknowledged the need to move away from the more traditional paradigms of positivism and interpretivism to address the complexity of many nursing research questions. It is also possible, however, to critically describe the influence of the historical development of the design in terms of its nearly exclusive emphasis on triangulation and the difficulties this has caused in assessing the contribution of mixed methods research to the field of nursing.

This review of mixed methods research in nursing also has highlighted some important issues that contribute to the current status of the design. The first of these relates to the application of mixed methods design and highlights the significance of careful consideration of the research question and whether it lends itself to the design. The indiscriminant use of any research design limits the potential of that design to contribute to the development of nursing research and nursing knowledge. The second issue relates to the need for greater understanding of the different approaches available in mixed methods design. In developing a greater understanding of the different approaches to design, distinctions among them need to be identified. These design differences will then inform inferences drawn from the findings of the study. The final issue relates to the epistemological assumptions underpinning the design and highlights the importance of further exploration and debate about the paradigms informing the research design. Although in nursing the paradigms of both positivism and interpretivism are considered equally significant to the development of nursing knowledge and practice, there has been little debate about the development of alternative paradigms such as pragmatism. Such debate is essential to the development and application, and implicitly the status, of mixed methods design in nursing.

■ *References*

Banik, B. J. (1993). Applying triangulation in nursing research. *Applied Nursing Research*, 6, 47-52.

Barbour, R. S. (1998). Mixing qualitative methods: Quality assurance or qualitative quagmire? *Qualitative Health Research*, 8, 352-361.

Baum, F. (1995). Researching public health: Behind the qualitative-quantitative methodological debate. *Social Science and Medicine*, 40, 459-468.

Begley, C. M. (1996). Using triangulation in nursing research. *Journal of Advanced Nursing*, 24, 122-128.

Breitmayer, B. J., Ayres, L., & Knafl, K. A. (1993). Triangulation in qualitative research: Evaluation of completeness and confirmation purposes. *Journal of Nursing Scholarship*, 25, 237-243.

Brink, P., & Wood, M. (1998). *Advanced designs in nursing research* (2nd ed.). Thousand Oaks, CA: Sage.

Burns, N., & Grove, S. (1997). *The practice of nursing research* (3rd ed.). Philadelphia: W. B. Saunders.

Burr, G. (1998). Contextualizing critical care family need through triangulation: An Australian study. *Intensive and Critical Care Nursing*, 14, 161-169.

Callister, L. C., Venvilainen-Julkunen, K., & Lauri, S. (1996). Cultural perceptions of childbirth. *Journal of Holistic Nursing*, 14(1), 66-78.

Carper, B. A. (1978). Fundamental patterns of knowing in nursing. *Advances in Nursing Science*, 1(1), 13-23.

Cigno, K., & Gore, J. (1999). A seamless service: Meeting the needs of children with disabilities through a multi-agency approach. *Child and Family Social Work*, 4, 325-335.

Corner, J. (1991). In search of more complete answers to research questions: Quantitative versus qualitative research methods—Is there a way? *Journal of Advanced Nursing*, 16, 718-727.

Coyle, J., & Williams, B. (2000). An exploration of the epistemological intricacies of using qualitative data to develop a quantitative measure of user views of health care. *Journal of Advanced Nursing*, 31, 1235-1243.

Cullum, V. (2001, Summer). Scholarship in nursing practice. *Sigma Theta Tau International Honor Society of Nursing Newsletter*, p. 2.

Davidhizar, R. (1997). Use of triangulation in transcultural nursing research. *Journal of Nursing Science*, 2, 3-4.

Dootson, S. (1995). An in-depth study of triangulation. *Journal of Advanced Nursing*, 22, 183-187.

Fish, D. (1998). *Appreciating practice in the caring professions*. Oxford, UK: Butterworth Heinemann.

Floyd, J. A. (1993). The use of across-method triangulation in the study of sleep concerns in healthy older adults. *Advanced Nursing Science, 16*(2), 70-80.

Fontana, J. (1996). The emergence of the person-environment interaction in descriptive study of vigor in heart failure. *Advanced Nursing Science, 18*(4), 70-82.

Foster, R. L. (1997). Addressing epistemologic and practical issues in multimethod research: A procedure for conceptual triangulation. *Advances in Nursing Science, 20* (2), 1-12.

Friedemann, M. L., & Smith, A. A. (1997). A triangulation approach of testing a family instrument. *Western Journal of Nursing Research, 19*, 364-378.

Goossen, W. T. F., Epping, P. J. M. M., Van den Heuvel, W. J. A., Feuth, T., Frederiks, C. M. A., & Hasman, A. (2000). Development of nursing minimum data set for the Netherlands (NMDSN): Identification of categories and items. *Journal of Advanced Nursing, 31*, 536-547.

Greene, J. C., & Caracelli, V. J. (Eds.). (1997). *Advances in mixed method evaluation: The challenges and benefits of integrating diverse paradigms.* San Francisco: Jossey-Bass.

Harkness, G. (1995). *Epidemiology in nursing practice.* St. Louis, MO: C. V. Mosby.

Herth, K. (1996). Hope from the perspective of homeless families. *Journal of Advanced Nursing, 24*, 743-753.

Hogan, N., & DeSantis, L. (1991). Development of substantive theory in nursing. *Nurse Education Today, 11*, 167-171.

Im, E. O., & Meleis, A. I. (1999). A situation-specific theory of Korean immigrant women's menopausal transition. *Journal of Nursing Scholarship, 31*, 333-338.

Kimchi, J., & Murphy, S. A. (1990). Letters. *Nursing Research, 39*, 217.

Knafl, K., & Breitmayer, B. (1991). Triangulation in qualitative research: Issues of conceptual clarity and purpose. In J. Morse (Ed.), *Qualitative nursing research* (pp. 226-239). Newbury Park, CA: Sage.

Koehler, J. A., Miller, K. L., Vojir, C. P., Hester, N. O., & Foster, R. L. (1997). Multisite clinical research: A challenge for nursing

leaders. *JONA, 27*(7-8), 42-48. (*Journal of Nursing Administration*)

Leininger, M. M. (1985). Nature, rationale, and importance of qualitative research methods in nursing. In M. M. Leininger (Ed.), *Qualitative research methods in nursing* (pp. 1-25). Orlando, FL: Grune & Stratton.

Lowe, N. K., & Ryan-Wenger, M. (1992). Beyond Campbell and Fiske: Assessment of convergent and discriminant validity. *Research in Nursing & Health, 15*, 67-75.

Milburn, K., Fraser, E., Secker, J., & Pavis, S. (1995). Combining methods in health promotion research: Some considerations about appropriate use. *Health Education Journal, 54*, 347-356.

Millor, G. K., Haber, J. E., Feldman, H. R., Hott, J. R., & Jacobson, L. (1992). What is nursing research? Evolving approaches to methods and content. *Journal of the New York State Nurses Association, 23*(3), 4-9.

Mitchell, E. S. (1986). Multiple triangulation: A methodology for nursing science. *Advances in Nursing Science, 8*(3), 18-26.

Morse, J. M. (1991). Approaches to qualitative-quantitative methodological triangulation. *Nursing Research, 40*, 120-123.

Murphy, S. A. (1989). Multiple triangulation: Applications in a program of nursing research. *Nursing Research, 38*, 294-297.

Murray, J. S. (1999). Methodological triangulation in a study of social support for siblings of children with cancer. *Journal of Pediatric Oncology Nursing, 16*, 194-200.

Nolan, M., & Behi, R. (1995). Triangulation: The best of all worlds? *British Journal of Nursing, 4*, 829-832.

Norman, I., Redfern, S., Tomalin, D., & Oliver, S. (1992). Applying triangulation to the assessment of quality of nursing. *Nursing Times, 88*(8), 43-46.

Oberst, M. T. (1993). Possibilities and pitfalls in triangulation [editorial]. *Research in Nursing & Health, 16*, 393-394.

Polit, D. F., & Hungler, B. P. (1999). *Nursing research principles and methods* (6th ed.). Philadelphia: J. B. Lippincott.

Proctor, S. (1998). Linking philosophy and method in the research process: The case for realism. *Nurse Researcher, 5*(4), 73-90.

Redfern, S. J., & Norman, I. J. (1995). Quality assessment instruments in nursing: Towards validation. *International Journal of Nursing Studies, 32*(2), 115-125.

Sandelowski, M. (1995). Focus on qualitative methods: Triangles and crystals—On the geometry of qualitative research. *Research in Nursing & Health, 18,* 569-574.

Sim, J., & Sharp, K. (1998). A critical appraisal of the role of triangulation in nursing research. *International Journal of Nursing Studies, 35,* 23-31.

Smith, P. (1987). The relationship between quality of nursing care and the ward as a learning environment: Developing a methodology. *Journal of Advanced Nursing, 12,* 413-420.

Sohier, R. (1988). Multiple triangulation and contemporary nursing research. *Western Journal of Nursing Research, 10,* 732-242.

Tashakkori, A., & Teddlie, C. (1998). *Mixed methodology: Combining qualitative and quantitative approaches* (Applied Social Research Methods, Vol. 46). Thousand Oaks, CA: Sage.

Verhoef, M. J., Scott, C. M., & Hilsden, R. J. (1998). A multimethod research study on the use of complementary therapies among patients with inflammatory bowel disease. *Alternative Therapies, 4*(4), 68-71.

21

MIXED METHODS IN PSYCHOLOGICAL RESEARCH

◆ Cindy Waszak
  Marylyn C. Sines

Although psychological research has relied heavily on experimental and quasi-experimental techniques to test theory using quantitative data, these are not the only means by which psychologists have answered questions about human behavior. This chapter presents an overview of research using mixed methods designs in psychology, following more or less the historical trends in the discipline moving from experimental methodology to qualitative research and then to more recent applied work using mixed methods.

The reason for psychology's reliance on quantitative methods is that psychology, like other behavioral disciplines, has been dominated by a positivist/postpositivist paradigm. A criticism of this paradigm by constructivist researchers has been that it is guided by the belief in a single objective reality: that human behavior is predictable from its antecedents and that every behavior has a distinct cause. However, as discussed by Tashakkori and Teddlie (in press), psychological research during the past few decades rarely has fit the profile just presented; prediction of behaviors is probabilistic at best and only at an aggregate level (Tashakkori & Teddlie, 1998), and relativity of perceptions has been a major component of psychological theory and research (e.g., attribution theory, social cognition, social comparison theory). Furthermore, behavior has often been assumed to have multiple causes, often affected by differential perceptions of the environment.

Several subdisciplines within psychology have been more accepting of a constructivist approach. One of these is clinical psychology, where qualitative data from case studies, clinical interviews, observations, and projective techniques have long been used inductively to generate theory. They often are used in conjunction with personality inventories, standardized tests, and other quantitative data. Experimental methods are often used to evaluate various forms of treatment that are designed based on qualitative information.

Another line of psychological research conducive to mixed methods has been in the interface between psychology and culture that is studied by cross-cultural psychologists and psychological anthropologists. Driven by the types of questions under study, often involving the qualitative concept of "culture," cross-cultural psychology and psychological anthropology have long used mixed methods, although they are not often identified as such. After a detailed review of research and data collection techniques in cross-cultural psychology, psychological anthropology, and comparative psychology, Berry (1980) noted,

> In cross-cultural psychology particularly it is important to obtain cross-validating evidence using ethnographic and observational techniques that will exhibit consistency with, for example, test results. If there is contradiction between the cultural and the test sources, then the problem must be resolved, perhaps with the use of yet another method. Moreover, ethnographic and archival methods may be important in the selection of field sites, in the development of hypotheses, and in the interpretation of data usually collected by interviewing or testing with field samples. Thus, it is clear that a combination of methods not only

increases empirical coverage, but becomes indispensable to developing a more complete theory. Reliance upon a single (cultural or psychological) method takes psychologists only halfway to their goal. (p. 23)

With the application of psychological explanations to social problems comes additional opportunities for other types of interdisciplinary research requiring a pragmatic approach to problem solving that the use of mixed methods offers. Taking psychological theory outside of the lab allows for the possibility of uncontrollable factors (e.g., cultural norms) being introduced into the study that are not well-understood by the researcher ahead of time. The collection of qualitative data becomes a necessary adjunct to quantitative data. One area of application that is discussed in this chapter is the study of psychological constructs as they are related to reproductive health. Begun as population psychology, the scope has widened from a relatively narrow interest in motivations for fertility to include a number of questions related to sexuality that have an impact on reproductive health more generally.

The purpose of this chapter is to describe how qualitative and quantitative methodologies have been used in combination to study psychological phenomena. The chapter begins with a discussion of how qualitative data have been used to augment quantitative experimental data and then describes a more recent emphasis by some psychologists on qualitative work and how some qualitative researchers have explored the use of quantitative techniques for a richer exploration of qualitative data. To illustrate more applied uses of mixed methods, we discuss research focusing on one applied area—sexuality and fertility behavior—in a number of cultural settings. These settings require multiple methodologies to capture the complexities of the behaviors of interest. The definition of *psychological research* becomes somewhat fuzzy, however, as a result of the interdisciplinary nature of much of this research. What these applied studies do have in common, however, is the inclusion of psychological constructs as dependent or independent variables in their implicit or explicit conceptual frameworks.

While we have not used the Tashakkori and Teddlie (1998) typology of mixed methods to organize our discussion, it should be noted here that most of the mixed methods research in psychology falls within a few categories. By and large, most mixed methods psychological research is sequential, usually involving a qualitative phase followed by a quantitative phase (qual-QUAN or QUAL-QUAN), although at least a couple of examples illustrate the opposite sequence (quan-QUAL or QUAN-QUAL). Sometimes the qualitative phase is less dominant than the quantitative phase (this is not surprising given psychology's historical reliance on positivism), but often the two components are equally weighted in the contributions they make to answering the research question. Table 21.1 is provided to help guide the readers as to how the examples discussed in this chapter map onto the typology.

Psychological research has employed concurrent mixed strategies to a lesser extent than it has employed sequential strategies. A notable exception to this is the quantitizing of qualitative data, often occurring in studies using content analysis techniques. A couple of parallel studies are described in which two types of data are collected within the same data collection activity and provide complementary data.

Mixed methods are often categorized according to which phase is exploratory and which phase is confirmatory. The iterative nature of mixed methods research often makes the distinction dependent on which slice of the researcher's work one happens to be reviewing. Any one piece of research, regardless of its qualitative or quantitative nature, is likely to be both confirming earlier generated hypotheses and generating new ones for later testing. This is amply illustrated in the examples offered.

◆ *Generating and Testing Theory: Augmenting Experimental Methods With Qualitative Data*

In a review of the use of qualitative methods with psychological experiments, Fine and Elsbach (2000) argued that although experimental methodologies have dominated the field of social psychology, a number of researchers actually have used qualitative data in creative ways to generate and test theory. They described two types of tactics that have been used in combining qualitative and quantitative data in social-psychological theory building: sequential tactics and merged tactics.

SEQUENTIAL TACTICS

The first of these are *sequential tactics* in which one type of research follows another. Fine and Elsbach (2000) described three sequential tactics: (a) participant observation followed by an experimental test, (b) in-depth interviews followed by an experimental test, and (c) an experimental test followed by systematic non-participant observation. These tactics cycle between induction and deduction, which allows for both the expansion and the refinement of theory. Cycling also empha-

TABLE 21.1 Illustrative Psychological Studies Categorized by Mixed Methods Typology

Sequential Qual-Quan	Sequential Quan-Qual	Concurrent Qualitizing Quantitative Data	Concurrent Parallel Data Collection	Complex
Charitable giving (Cialdini & Schroeder, 1976; Cialdini et al., 1978) Foot-in-the-door (Freedman & Fraser, 1966; Schein, 1956) Cognitive dissonance (Festinger et al., 1956) Construction of maternal role (Flanagan et al., 1995) Cross-cultural occurrence of Oedipal complex (Johnson & Price-Williams, 1996) Gender differences in sexual motivation in Cameroon (Calves et al., 1996)	Unmet need in Egypt (National Population Council & Macro International, 1997) Gender norms in Jamaica (Eggleston et al., 1999) Adolescent dating aggression in United Kingdom (Hird, 2000)	Spontaneous self-concept (McGuire & McGuire, 1981; McGuire & Padawar-Singer, 1976)	Obedience Study (Milgram, 1974) Robber's Cave Experiment (Sherif et al., 1961)	Deindividuation (Zimbardo, 1969)

sizes the dynamic characteristic of social systems central to social-psychological theory. Fine and Elsbach noted Cialdini's (1980) essay on "full-cycle" research, which suggests that social psychologists should begin theory building through real-world (qualitative) observations, proceed to lab experiments (quantitative), and then cycle back to real-world observations (qualitative or quantitative) again for further refinement. This process encompasses Fine and Elsbach's first and third sequential tactics.

Cialdini's own work on charitable giving is an example of the first sequential tactic. His initial theory grew out of a personal experience with the United Way. Based on his own behavior, Cialdini developed a lab test of two competing theories to explain this behavior and was able to confirm one and discard the other (Cialdini, Cacioppo, Bassett, & Miller, 1978; Cialdini & Schroeder, 1976).

The second sequential tactic was illustrated by work on the "foot-in-the-door" technique. A series of in-depth interviews with former U.S. prisoners of war led Schein (1956) to describe the process of brainwashing used by Koreans in which small requests were used to achieve compliance with larger ones. While in-depth interviewing was critical to describing the process, the theory that complying with a small request will lead to compliance with a larger one was tested by a lab experiment by Freedman and Fraser (1966).

The third sequential tactic was exemplified by Zimbardo's (1969) experiments on deindividuation in which he went from a set of observations about violence and collective behavior, to experiments on anonymity and aggression, and then back to field observations. Worried that his field observations may have been biased by his lab findings, he followed up with a field experiment to confirm his six-stage theory of vandalism.

MERGED TACTICS

Fine and Elsbach (2000) also identified experimental studies that used *merged* tactics. These are means of collecting both qualitative and quantitative data within the same experimental setting. They described combined data collection from (a) laboratory experiments, (b) field observations with independent variables arranged and manipulated by the experimenter, and (c) field observations with naturally occurring independent variables.

With regard to the first of these, Fine and Elsbach (2000) noted that there often are potential sources of qualitative information available in the experimental situation that are rarely treated as data. He cited an exception in Stanley Milgram's Obedience Study (Milgram, 1974) in which transcripts from the laboratory experience were examined in more detail than usual and were provided as additional evidence for the validity of his quantitative results.

The second merged tactic, triangulation of qualitative and quantitative data in a field experiment, is exemplified by Sherif, Harvey, White, Hood, and Sherif's (1961) study known as the Robber's Cave Experiment. While this type of field experiment is not extremely unusual, what made this study noteworthy for Fine and Elsbach (2000) was the use of qualitative data generated through participant observation to explain the quantitative participant responses measuring dependent variables such as stereotype ratings, friendship choices, and judgment of the performances. The activities assigned to the participants were the experimental manipulations necessary to create the independent variables of note such as isolation, the pressure to compete, and the need to cooperate. The qualitative data recorded by the participant observers provided a context for the relationship between independent and dependent variables—a cultural context, even though this was a created culture. Fine and Elsbach stated,

> The power of the analysis derives from the fact that one can simultaneously see the boys' reactions to the camp structure through the objective measures and through cultural responses. The tactic of triangulating one's findings using quantitative and qualitative data provides confidence in the reliability of the conclusions and confidence in their validity. (p. 71)

The third merged tactic described by Fine and Elsbach (2000) was the transformation of qualitative data collected in ethnographic research into an experimental test. They used as an example Festinger's study of a small group of believers called "The Seekers" who believed in an end-of-the-world prophecy (Festinger, Riecken, & Schacter, 1956). Festinger and his colleagues observed the group's behavior when the prophecy failed, looking for evidence for a set of hypotheses about what would happen after belief disconfirmation. While the data for this study actually were all qualitative, Fine and Elsbach (2000) argued that the naturally occurring "experiment" that provided the opportunity to test a set of cognitive dissonance hypotheses provided the "quantitative" aspect of the research. Three categorical independent variables were identified (conviction, commitment to conviction, and social support during times of disconfirmation) that were thought to predict the dependent variable (proselytizing) given the situation.

This view of Festinger's work may stretch the categorization of "merged" tactics a bit; we also could view this as the qualitative phase of a sequential tactic given that it inspired numerous laboratory experiments related to dissonance theory. Nevertheless, it does exemplify the willingness of certain psychologists to creatively examine a social situation not constrained by the rigors of the experimental condition and to do so in as scientific a manner as possible. The researchers did not reject valuable information because they were not able to quantify attitudes and behaviors using standard psychological scales. This ethnography did differ from classic ethnographies, however, because it tested a priori hypotheses rather than merely explore a phenomenon. The qualitative data, however, allowed researchers to learn more about context than they might have otherwise.

FUTURE OF USING QUALITATIVE DATA WITH EXPERIMENTS

It is interesting that the examples provided by Fine and Elsbach (2000) for their typology of mixed methods were studies conducted more than two decades ago. We may wonder whether the maturing discipline became more rigid in its methodology or whether social psychologists became less willing to expose the qualitative aspects of their work to public scrutiny. It is not likely that real-life events became less of a stimulus to theory development. Fine and Elsbach presented these examples as an argument for the feasibility and utility of qualitative data collected in conjunction with experimental methodologies in developing and testing theory.

◆ Qualitative Data Collection as a Primary Technique to Generate and Test Theory

The examples provided by Fine and Elsbach (2000) all used experiments as a reference point from which all data were generated, albeit in different forms. The experiments differed by location (field or lab), but the methodologies were essentially similar. While not mainstream, there are research psychologists who use non-experimental methodologies to collect qualitative data almost exclusively (Hayes, 1997) in the process of generating and testing theory. One qualitative approach in psychology is that of "grounded theory" (Pidgeon & Henwood, 1997). Grounded theory is based on inductive processes and uses mostly qualitative data (although inductive processes by no means require qualitative data). Another qualitative approach in psychology is found in feminist research.

GROUNDED THEORY RESEARCH

Grounded theory research was borne out of a constructivist approach to epistemology that reverses the relationships of object and scientific knowledge (Glaser & Strauss, 1967). According to this view, objects cannot be known directly but are constructed through the perceptual field of the observer. Radical constructivism argues that there may not be any one true representation of an object. At least four factors define how an object is perceived: participants' own understandings, researchers' interpretations, cultural meaning systems that inform both researchers' and participants' understandings, and acts of judging particular interpretations as valid. Qualitative methodologies are used by researchers to study psychological and sociological phenomena from a constructivist point of view because this point of view allows for greater interpretation from participants and researchers and avoids imposing external objective systems of meaning.

Grounded theory is one approach to qualitative research. Glaser and Strauss developed this approach to theory generation that is "grounded" in a close inspection of qualitative data gathered from concrete settings. Grounded theory not only refers to the theory generated through an inductive method but also refers to a system of analysis and to a standard of quality for this type of research. Grounded theory alone does not ensure the reflection of a constructivist approach to research, but the use of qualitative methodologies does allow for multiple points of view to be generated from the research—for "truth" to be subjective and complex.

COGNITIVE DEVELOPMENT AND CONSTRUCTION OF MATERNAL ROLE

An example of a psychological grounded theory study that used qualitative data to generate hypotheses for subsequent validation by quantitative data was conducted by Flanagan, McGrath, Meyer, and Garcia (1995) to examine the relationship between adolescent cognitive development and the concept of maternal role among young mothers. Data from group and individual interviews with 42 teenage mothers were analyzed using the constant comparative method. Each line, phrase, sentence, and paragraph from the transcribed interviews was analyzed during a 2-year period. The data were coded for descriptions of the adolescents talking about themselves, their children, and their mothering roles after the researchers listened to, read, and reflected on the interview data.

Five topic categories of adolescent self-development and motherhood emerged: (a) descriptions of the self, (b) discussions of goal behavior, (c) discussions of how life had changed since the birth of their children, (d) descriptions of the qualities of motherhood, and (e) descriptions of their children. Within each of these topics, clear developmental themes were found.

The qualitative data gave Flanagan et al. (1995) insight into the experience of motherhood for adolescent girls and the role that adolescent development plays in their experience of motherhood. The hypothesis generated from these data was that a young woman's conceptualization of motherhood and her maternal role would correlate with her level of cognitive and psychological development. A standardized five-item interview was constructed, as was a paradigm for scoring the developmental complexity of each response.

The five questions were as follows:

1. Please describe yourself to me. Tell me who you are.

2. What do you see yourself doing in 5 years?

3. How has your life changed since the birth of your child?

4. What are the qualities that make a good mother? Describe for me a good mother.

5. Please describe your baby for me. Tell me who he or she is.

A total of 25 adolescent mothers ages 14 to 18 years were interviewed; interviews were audiotaped and transcribed. Each question was coded separately from the others on a 5-point scale for level of developmental complexity. Interrater reliability based on a 20% subset was 92%. The responses to questions about "self" (1 and 2) were correlated to questions about motherhood (3-5).

Responses to all of the interview questions spanned the range of developmental complexity. There was a positive correla-

tion between each mother's response to the self-related questions and the developmental complexity of her response to the motherhood-related questions. A regression of the sum of the motherhood questions onto the sum of the self questions found an r^2 value of .81. No relationship was found between these scores and the narrow range of chronological age.

Flanagan et al. (1995) concluded that adolescent mothers are "adolescents first" and that motherhood does not necessarily increase the speed of developmental progression. Findings from this study indicate that it is important for clinicians working with adolescent mothers to understand that their cognitive skills might not match their reproductive capacities. Health providers cannot take for granted that young mothers understand certain things about pregnancy or their own babies' development, and young mothers should be counseled accordingly.

Results from the qualitative and quantitative components of this study seem to "weigh in" equally in terms of the goals of the study. The extensive analysis of the qualitative study provided a detailed framework for the quantitative component. The raw data for the quantitative component were themselves "qualitative," but with scaled numbers assigned to responses based on a rich developmental framework developed from the first stage of research. The numbers allowed for a statistical analysis and verification of what researchers already believed to be true.

The Flanagan et al. (1995) study was an outgrowth of previous research on the cognitive aspects of maternal identity formation. It applies to the context of adolescent motherhood where cognitive processes themselves are still under development. The use of grounded theory allowed for full exploration of a new context for previous research findings while it also allowed for an estimation of the magnitude of the effect. The in-depth information collected through this study provides concrete examples of varying levels of cognitive development as it applies to young mothers' conceptions of the maternal role that can be used in practical applications of the research results.

FEMINIST PSYCHOLOGY

Feminist approaches to research also are characterized by a concern with presenting multiple realities and participants' own interpretations of their lives (Ulin, Robinson, Tolley, & McNeill, 2002). Special attention is given to exploring realities about women's lives that are not based on patriarchal assumptions. A defining feature of feminist research is that it is not value-neutral. Feminist research is driven by the belief that the influence of power relations on social organization and behavior has not been given the consideration it deserves in the social sciences. Feminist research highlights the invisibility of women and minorities that has characterized much previous scholarship. Even in an applied area such as family planning research, where much of the research is about women, until recently women's voices have rarely been heard.

Qualitative methodologies are critical means by which to listen to the voices of women. This methodology is seen as one that will empower women to talk about their lives. Collecting data means guiding the participants to answer questions in their own words without constraining their answers by standardized instruments. Researchers become partners with study participants.

While qualitative methods figure prominently in feminist research, they are not the only methods used. Tolman and Szalacha (1999) described a fierce debate in psychology about whether mixed methodologies should—or even *can*—be used to answer the same research question. They identified two approaches to understanding feminist methodology and the role of methods in feminist transformation of psychology. The first is the use of traditional psychological methodology to answer questions of relevance to feminist theory. Proponents of this approach believe that this research will be more easily accepted into the discipline and thus will have more influence in transforming it. The second approach abandons the use of traditional methods of objective experimental and survey methods because feminist methods should be participant-centered, which is necessarily qualitative. Proponents of this approach believe that these methods are necessary to generate knowledge about women's lives not previously generated through traditional methods.

These two positions often are posed in opposition to each other within the larger poststructuralism and postmodern debates about research paradigms. Qualitative and quantitative approaches are considered by many to be different research paradigms with "radically differing assumptions, requirements, and procedures that are rooted in completely different epistemologies" (Tolman & Szalacha, 1999, p. 9).

While some psychologists believe that it is impossible to combine these methodologies because they represent different worldviews, others believe that they *should* be combined because these concerns "should be superseded in importance by political goals about how research findings should be used" (Tolman & Szalacha, 1999, p. 9). Still others take a more pragmatic approach to the whole question, understanding that different methodologies have grown out of different disciplines for historical reasons but that researchers who can understand and use both have an advantage in having more effective means available to them to answer their research questions.

DIMENSIONS OF DESIRE

Tolman and Szalacha's (1999) own research perspective is self-identified as a feminist one. They believe that mixed methods can be used, but they are careful to consider the possible implications of method choice as they do their work. They studied adolescent girls' experiences of sexual desire by combining qualitative and quantitative analysis methods in a sequential integration. Responding to "an acute absence of acknowledgment in psychological research of sexual desire as a normative aspect of female adolescent development" (p. 7), they designed a study to explore the "missing discourse of desire in adults' discussions of girls' sexuality" (p. 8).

Using girls' voices as a starting point, they collected narrative data during individual interviews with 30 girls from urban and suburban areas and then analyzed these data in three ways. They began with an exploratory analysis of voiced experience of sexual desire. Their research question was "How do girls describe their experience of sexual desire?"

Data were analyzed using a method of narrative analysis called "The Listening Guide." Using this feminist interpretive method, each narrative was read or "listened to" several distinct times to identify four voices associated with girls' sexual desire. These voices were the voice of the self, an erotic voice, a voice of the body, and a voice of response to one's own desire.

About two thirds of the girls said they felt desire, and the rest said they were confused about this. All of the girls acknowl-edging desire described it in terms of physical experience, although many girls questioned their entitlement to their own sexual feelings and whether it was right to act on their feelings. Differences emerged between the urban and suburban girls, however, in their descriptions of their responses to their desire. Tolman and Szalacha (1999) wrote, "Urban girls describe an agency in the service of protection, and suburban girls tell of an agency in service of pleasure" (p. 15).

With the identification of these general patterns, two additional research questions emerged that required a quantitative analysis: "What is the size and significance of the difference between urban and suburban girls' experience of their own sexual desire?" and "Is there an interaction between social location and reported experience of sexual abuse or violence in whether urban and suburban girls associate their own desire with pleasure, vulnerability, or both?"

Tolman and Szalacha (1999) said of their techniques for using narrative data to answer these questions, "Our challenge was to choose or develop a feminist approach to data reduction so that our interview data could be analyzed statistically" (p. 17). Specifically, they did not want to lose the complexity achieved through their qualitative analysis in the process of testing hypotheses about social location.

To accomplish this, they used the 128 "narratives" told by the 30 participants as the unit of analysis and coded each one according to whether it was predominantly about "vulnerability" or "pleasure," although none of the girls' narratives was a story exclusively of one or the other. No differences were found in the numbers of narratives told by girls in the urban and suburban groups. Sexual violation was measured by the answer to the question "Has anything bad ever happened to you that has to do with sex that you would like to tell me about?" About half of the girls from each location (urban and suburban) reported sexual violation.

About half of the narratives were predominantly about vulnerability, nearly a third were about pleasure, and a quarter were about both. More narratives of urban girls focused on vulnerability as compared with those of suburban girls. More narratives of urban girls were equally about vulnerability and pleasure as compared with those of suburban girls. About twice as many suburban narratives focused on pleasure as compared with urban narratives. Suburban girls told about equal numbers of stories about pleasure and vulnerability, while urban girls told about three times as many stories of vulnerability as stories of pleasure.

An interaction was found between social location and sexual violation. Suburban girls who had experienced sexual violation told many more narratives of vulnerability than of pleasure, as did both groups of urban girls. It was the suburban girls with no sexual violation who told the greatest number of narratives where pleasure was the predominant theme. This interaction among social location, experience of sexual violation, and the theme of pleasure in sexual narratives was supported and confirmed through a series of statistical tests, concluding with three fixed-effects logistic regression models that could control for possible problems associated with a lack of independence of each narrative and therefore possible overestimation of the independent degrees of freedom.

The researchers then went through the data a third time for a second qualitative analysis to determine how suburban girls who had not experienced sexual violation differed in their narratives from the other three groups of girls. Supporting the quantitative findings, strong differences were found between the suburban girls who

had not experienced sexual violation and the other groups of girls. These suburban girls spoke about their desire as profoundly physical experiences that were positively integrated into their emotional lives. Both emotional and physical feelings contributed to feelings of desire. For the other three groups, there was a split between mind and body as well as descriptions of how their minds offered a type of control over their desire, associated with fear of trouble and negative consequences.

The Tolman and Szalacha (1999) study is a very creative approach to integrating methodologies in a way that speaks to their ethical and philosophical concerns. The authors described their work as a feminist study, beginning with the voices of girls instead of patriarchal assumptions about their experiences. They viewed their methodological approach as emerging from this feminist perspective, which requires the identification of "complexities in women's and girls' experiences and potential that have been difficult to know within the traditional practice of psychology" (p. 34). This echoes much of the rationale for grounded theory research, and indeed, this work can be viewed as grounded theory as well. Their work is noteworthy for its flexibility and willingness to quantify certain aspects of their qualitative analysis for hypothesis testing given the ongoing feminist debate.

◆ Content Analysis

Content analysis is somewhat of a hybrid as we discuss research in terms of experiments versus more qualitative methods. Content analysis uses qualitative data generated from study participants or archival sources and quantitizes them for use in confirming hypotheses. Two very different uses of content analysis are described in this section. In the first, two sets of archival sources are used to determine the cross-cultural nature of the Freudian concept of the Oedipal complex. In the second, researchers explore a new way of conceptualizing self-concept using both qualitative and quantitative analysis of participant-generated answers to the item "Tell me about yourself."

PSYCHOLOGICAL ANTHROPOLOGY AND THE OEDIPAL COMPLEX

Following Malinowski's (1923, 1927) early work on the nature of the Oedipus complex, Johnson and Price-Williams (1996) conducted a study that began with a detailed qualitative study of classic myths and folktales from around the globe to determine the universality of Freud's theory. They stated,

> On the basis of our examination of the stories in the collection, we concluded that the tales that have an "Oedipal feel" are usually Oedipal at core, even when they lack specific Oedipal content of the story. Several kinds of transformation tend to mask or dilute the Oedipal content of the story. These variously affect the three protagonists: son, father, and mother. (p. 43)

Johnson and Price-Williams identified different types of roles a father takes in these stories and also concluded that "the relationship between mother and father is often ignored in these tales" (p. 44).

Further analysis of the folktales revealed different patterns (also called "models") of relationships among father, mother, son, and daughter. Finally, a "general model of the family complex" was developed to account for "the great diversity of folktales of incest and aggression" (p. 69).

The second phase of Johnson and Price-Williams's (1996) study consisted of a quantitative analysis to further investigate the association between different features of the family complex in folktales. A total of 164 folktales were coded on a number of dimensions in the stories (e.g., prior awareness of the partners that they were committing incest, aggressive acts such as abandonment at birth) as well as on the attributes of societies from which the stories originated (e.g., political stratification, patrilineality). Chi-square tests of significance were used to test hypotheses about the association between story dimensions and societal attributes. For example, the core Oedipal content of folktales differed for politically stratified and unstratified societies. Tales from stratified societies showed much greater evidence of repression than did tales from unstratified societies.

Based on the results of the two phases of the study, a detailed review of previous literature, and their own cultural observations, Johnson and Price-Williams (1996) drew two primary conclusions: "Family-complex folktales are universal and tend strongly to depict Freud's masculine Oedipus complex, but not a feminine one" and "The core content of most of these tales reflects aspects of mental life that have been repressed" (p. 89).

SPONTANEOUS SELF-CONCEPT

A series of studies by McGuire and his colleagues (McGuire & McGuire, 1981; McGuire, McGuire, & Winton, 1979; McGuire & Padawar-Singer, 1976) are examples of theory development and testing through the quantitizing of qualitative data. In most of these studies, the qualitative data generated the data for quantitative analysis. McGuire criticized the state of research on self-perceptions for its insensitivity to individuals' "phenomenological musings about themselves" (McGuire & McGuire, 1981, p. 147). He argued that previous quantitative measures of self-perceptions were actually measures of the "reactive self." In the words of McGuire and McGuire (1981), "The reactive self-concept is seriously deficient in that it provides no information on the more interesting question of what are the dimensions in terms of which people tend spontaneously to think of themselves, what the aspects of self are" (p. 149).

McGuire's measure of "spontaneous self-concept" consisted of responses to a single open-ended (qualitative) item: "Tell me about yourself." These qualitative responses were content-analyzed. The results indicated that self-perceptions included physical, intellectual, moral, and emotional evaluations. However, an interesting finding was that, contrary to the assumption of purely quantitative studies, the combination of all of these self-evaluations accounted for a small proportion (7%) of the statements generated in response to this item (McGuire & McGuire, 1981).

Based on an exploratory content analysis, a "distinctiveness postulate" was formulated to explain the spontaneous self-concept. To test the postulate, a series of two-phase studies, each with similar quan-QUAL formats, tested statistical hypotheses on the quantitized data collected and analyzed through content analysis. Qualitative data consisting of unstructured essays were content-analyzed by judges unfamiliar with the hypotheses. They read essays and recorded all occurrences of reference to personal attributes (e.g., weight, hair color, eyeglasses). The data were quantitized by counting the number of occurrences in each emerging category, as well as by recording the length of self-referent statements, and were analyzed statistically to test the hypotheses.

Quantitizing qualitative data enabled McGuire and his colleagues to formulate an inductive theory of spontaneous self-concept and to test the predictions of the theory through a transformation of the original qualitative data.

◆ Mixed Methods in Applied Research

There is a large body of research using mixed methods research that is applied, interdisciplinary, and often atheoretical. The motivation for using mixed methods has come from a need for greater understanding of results derived from traditional methods of data collection that do not make sense to the researcher. An example of this comes from the field of population and family planning, where years of intensive interventions have had varying results in countries around the world. Many of these interventions were based on a Western notion of development; that is, if family planning services were offered to women, then the population rate would be reduced. However, there are a number of countries where family planning programs exist but where contraceptive rates have not increased.

Using mixed methods has involved the addition of qualitative methods in conjunction with more traditional quantitative methods. Another way of looking at this is that researchers are taking a more constructivist view when data derived from positivist-oriented studies do not yield useful results. This mix has been an uneasy one because the dominant methodologies understood by researchers in the field have been demographic and epidemiological.

There is a common misconception that qualitative research can be done by anyone with minimal training. The qualitative "add-ons" are often done by people who have no formal training in qualitative techniques, with resulting lower quality research. A vicious cycle occurs in perceptions of qualitative research quality because there have been so few qualitatively trained researchers doing field-driven family planning research. Those who are skeptical in the first place rarely are exposed to high-quality qualitative research that would alter their negative opinions. One solution to this is to work in interdisciplinary teams so that those who have been trained in qualitative research can do the qualitative components of the study (for details regarding the formation and functioning of these teams, see Shulha & Wilson, Chapter 25, this volume). While this is ideal, it often is difficult to implement because people who have different worldviews seldom work together on joint research projects given that they are situated in different disciplines or fields of study. Very often, they have very different research goals and different underlying assumptions about research.

In spite of these difficulties, grasping for answers not provided through demographic or epidemiological studies, the use of mixed methods has been more or less institutionalized in population research. It is very common to read an article that starts out with the following or similar wording: "A mix of qualitative and quantitative methods was used for this study." This usually means that focus groups were conducted at the beginning of the study, followed by a survey. The focus groups were conducted to generate questions to be used on the survey. Often, there is a program-related problem to be solved such as determining how to improve the quality of care in clinical settings or determining why there is an unmet need for family planning. In general, but not always, the quantitative data are primary in the analysis, with illustrative focus group discussion quotes inserted.

Sometimes, focus groups are conducted after rather than before the survey as a way of verifying, explaining, or following up on the survey results. For example, focus groups are sometimes conducted after demographic and health surveys have been analyzed to obtain more data on puzzling or seemingly inconsistent data. For example, focus groups were conducted after the Egyptian demographic and health survey in 1996 to help donors understand why so many women said they did not want to be pregnant now but were not using a family planning method (National Population Council and Macro International, 1997). Through the focus groups, it was found that the three most serious barriers to using family planning services for those *who did not want to get pregnant* were concerns about side effects, concerns about a pelvic examination, and difficulty in paying for the services.

Recently, some of these studies have become interdisciplinary. Population and family planning has been a topic of scholarly pursuit primarily by sociologists and public health specialists, so many of the outcomes have focused on macro- rather than micro-level outcomes. To the extent that psychologists have become involved in this research, their interests were primarily related to attitudes toward contraception and fertility and control.

For example, adoption of contraceptive practices was an interesting application of theoretical work on attitude-behavior consistency and the model of reasoned action (Fishbein, 1972; Fishbein & Jaccard, 1973). Developmental psychologists have been involved to some extent as they examined the reasons for unwanted adolescent pregnancies within the context of social learning theory (Bandura, 1977). In general, this research was limited to U.S.

populations; international research has focused more on macro-level outcomes such as fertility rate and contraceptive prevalence rate.

This focus on macro-level indicators has changed, however, as researchers seek answers that fall outside the realm of supply and demand. Individual and cultural characteristics have been recognized as part of the picture. Sporton (1999), a population geographer promoting the use of qualitative methods in population research, stated, "The implication for fertility research is that to develop a deeper understanding of reproductive behavior, we need to tap into this discursive consciousness and encourage self-reflexivity on the part of respondents which rigid census and survey designs conventionally deny" (p. 71).

Therefore, family planning research has recently brought psychologists and anthropologists more into the mainstream of their work. While the behavioral theories are often being tested exclusively using quantitative methods, there also is more of an interest in the cultural context of family planning adoption as well as measures of psychological well-being that accompany it (or do not) (Barnett & Stein, 1999), which requires mixed methods.

Three examples of mixed methods research that consider psychological factors as dependent or independent variables are described here. All are on related topics (gender norms and adolescent sexual behavior) but in different countries. They illustrate two ways in which qualitative and quantitative methods are combined to answer the research question.

GENDER NORMS IN JAMAICA

The first is a study of sexual attitudes and behavior among adolescents in Ja-

maica (Eggleston, Jackson, & Hardee, 1999). A school-based survey of 945 Jamaican adolescents, ages 11 to 14 years, was conducted as part of an evaluation of a sexuality education program targeting younger adolescents. Data from the survey demonstrated a wide discrepancy between boys and girls with regard to sexual experience. Fully 64% of the males, as compared with 6% of the females, said they had experienced sexual intercourse.

Focus groups were conducted after the survey data were analyzed to provide the researchers and program managers with a better understanding of these results. These focus groups consisted of eight single-sex groups for a total of 64 12-year-old respondents. Eggleston et al. (1999) believed that focus groups would elicit richer and more detailed information than would be possible from young adolescents with limited literacy skills on a written survey. Also of concern on the survey was the validity of self-report for behaviors of ambiguous social sanctions. Focus group participants did not report their own behavior in the discussions, but focus groups did offer an opportunity to learn more about normative behavior, thus getting some insight into the validity of the survey results and the norms themselves. The discussions focused on a story about two fictional students, "Nell" and "Ted," who become romantically involved and face decisions about sex, family planning, pregnancy, and parenthood. It is through the participants' elaboration of the story that these norms emerge.

The focus of the follow-up focus groups themselves was on how these norms of sexual behavior are influenced by gender. In the focus groups, boys and girls expressed differing opinions about the acceptability of premarital sex. Boys were divided on the issue, with some believing that young people should wait until they are older but others not disapproving. Girls generally found more consensus, with most disapproving of girls their age engaging in sex and very cognizant of the possible negative consequences, including getting a bad reputation.

Focus group participants were asked about their understanding of sexual intercourse, and it was found that everyone knew what it meant. When questioned about the likely age ranges for having sex, boys were insistent in all groups that having sex at 8 or 9 years of age was not uncommon, while girls believed that sex at that age was unlikely but could happen. With regard to motivations to have sex, girls talked mostly about love and about wanting to keep their boyfriends happy. Boys looked at sex as a means of physical pleasure and of demonstrating their manhood.

Findings from both the survey and focus group discussions also included peer and parental attitudes toward sex, family planning behavior and attitudes, and attitudes on pregnancy and parenthood. The combined findings from the two study components presented a more complete picture of students' beliefs and behavior than either would have provided alone. From this picture, Eggleston et al. (1999) concluded,

> The clearly defined gender norms regarding sexual behavior perceived by the 12-year-olds in the focus groups, the inaccurate knowledge revealed in both focus groups and survey findings, and the number of adolescents who reported having had sex suggests that family life education must be introduced among younger children, not just those entering puberty. (p. 83)

This study is an example of a sequential use of mixed methods. Results from the survey and the focus group discussions were given more or less equal weight in their presentation, and an integrated analysis demonstrated the consistencies and inconsistencies found between the two sources.

◆ Gender Differences in Sexual Motivation and Strategies in the Cameroon

A second example of research on a similar topic, gender differences in motivations and strategies in sexual behavior among adolescents in the Cameroon, also used a sequential strategy, albeit in reverse order from the first example. In this study by Calves, Cornwell, and Envegue (1996), four focus group discussions were conducted to explore the sexual experience and strategies and motivations of males and females, followed by a two-stage random sample survey. The survey results were reported as validation of the focus group results, providing information on the prevalence of attitudes and behaviors found in the focus group discussions and offering an opportunity to test hypotheses about differences between males and females.

The results from this study are presented in parallel for each subtopic. That is, they were presented separately, but the results are very consistent and the survey results basically provided numbers to support the qualitative results.

Some of the interesting study findings are as follows:

◆ Premarital sex is very common among young people in urban areas of the Cameroon. Males are more likely to be sexually active than are females at younger ages, but after 20 years of age there is virtually no difference.

◆ Having multiple partners is quite common in this age group. Males are more likely to have multiple partners than are females. The most common reason given by both males and females for having multiple partners was to protect against emotional disappointment.

◆ The motivations underlying female sexual activity included acquiring financial support, establishing social and economic networking, and looking for a spouse. Males also have financial concerns motivating sexual relationships, but they mostly are looking for sexual experience, sexual satisfaction, and social status.

In a way, the two types of data in the Calves et al. (1996) study are "weighted" equally in the analysis of the Cameroon data. In the Jamaican study (Eggleston et al., 1999), results were highly integrated as well, although the focus group results were presented as an explanation for the survey results. One wonders how each might have been different if the sequence had been reversed. Would different questions have been asked in the Jamaica survey?

Both of these studies are characteristic of much of mixed methods research conducted in the field of population, family planning, and reproductive health. Although some of this research is guided by theory, it is rarely theory *driven*. Rather, it is driven by pragmatic questions about the extent of a social problem and how it can be addressed. The use of mixed methods has allowed researchers to explore personal and cultural factors related to fertility behavior that were largely missing from the more quantitative macro-level analyses of earlier times. Interestingly, it is this interest in the personal that is encouraging more psychological research, and

this in turn is necessitating more qualitative research because of the lack of good cross-cultural measures of many psychological outcomes. While the marriage of methodologies still meets with resistance on various levels, the hope is that eventually there will be the right mix of expertise and flexibility to conduct studies using the most effective methodology to answer the research questions.

One further study on a similar topic is described here as an example of a sequential mixed methods (QUAN-QUAL) study in which the conclusions drawn from the quantitative phase are altered by the information gathered during the later qualitative phase.

ADOLESCENT DATING AGGRESSION IN THE UNITED KINGDOM

A study conducted by Hird (2000) in the United Kingdom to investigate the level of aggression experienced by girls and boys in heterosexual dating situations and to test the "symmetry of aggression" theory began with a self-administered survey that was followed by focus group discussions and interviews. The results from the survey indicated that, overall, about half of both girls and boys had experienced psychological, physical, or sexual aggression in their dating relationships. The results confirmed a symmetry of aggression between girls and boys with respect to psychological and physical aggression; however, a gender asymmetry was found with respect to sexual aggression.

The purpose of the qualitative phase was to explore the meaning and context of the aggression reported in the survey. The qualitative results found less support for symmetry of aggression. It was found that much of the girls' reported physical aggression was actually self-defense against their boyfriends' use of physical and/or sexual aggression. Girls viewed aggressive acts against them by boys as "worse" because of the boys' greater strength and the greater likelihood of their causing more harm. Girls discussed male dating aggression within the larger context of gendered power relations. Hird (2000) concluded,

> Meaning and context are crucial to understanding the multidimensionality of adolescent dating aggression. . . . The meaning that the adolescents in this study attributed to aggressive behavior and the context of heterosexual dating relationships within which this aggression takes place suggest that it is male-defined normative behavior which governs relations of unequal power. (p. 77)

◆ Conclusions and Future Directions

Psychological research, developing out of a positivist perspective, has been a highly quantitative field. There have been uses of qualitative data in psychological research—clinical case studies, transcripts from experimental situations, participant observation—but historically it was not used as the primary source of information. Over the past several decades, however, there has been more interest in using other research paradigms to study psychological phenomena. Two examples of these, grounded theory and feminist research, have developed out of the constructivist approach, studying phenomena from the perspective of research participants. The development of psychological theory, however, requires a cycling between approaches. Although not mainstream, a number of psychologists are attempting to combine methods, either sequentially or simultaneously, to generate, expand, or refine theory as needed.

In applied fields, the research questions are often interdisciplinary, measuring outcomes that may be psychological, sociological, and anthropological. A mix of methods often is necessary to generate the appropriate questions to ask and then to determine the extent to which a situation exists and/or the magnitude of relationships among possible causes. The challenge is to (re)socialize researchers to believe in the equal value of both paradigms, to understand the strengths and weaknesses of each for specific research questions and situations, and to have the wisdom to know what is appropriate and when.

■ References

Bandura, A. (1977). Self-efficacy: Toward a unifying theory of behavior change. *Psychological Review, 84,* 191-215.

Barnett, B., & Stein, J. (1999). *Women's voices, women's lives: The impact of family planning.* Research Triangle Park, NC: Family Health International.

Berry, J. W. (1980). Introduction to methodology. In H. C. Triandis & J. W. Berry (Eds.), *Handbook of cross-cultural psychology: Methodology* (Vol. 2, pp. 1-28). Boston: Allyn & Bacon.

Calves, A., Cornwell, G., & Envegue, P. (1996). *Adolescent sexual activity in Sub-Saharan Africa: Do men have the same strategies and motivations as women?* Population Institute Working Papers in African Demography, No. AD96-04, Pennsylvania State University.

Cialdini, R. (1980). Full-cycle psychology. In L. Bickman (Ed.), *Applied social psychology annual* (Vol. 1, pp. 21-47). Beverly Hills, CA: Sage.

Cialdini, R. B., Cacioppo, J. T., Bassett, R., & Miller, J. A. (1978). Low-ball procedure for producing compliance: Commitment then cost. *Journal of Personality and Social Psychology, 36*, 463-476.

Cialdini, R. B., & Schroeder, D. A. (1976). Increasing compliance by legitimizing paltry contributions: When every penny helps. *Journal of Personality and Social Psychology, 34*, 599-604.

Eggleston, E., Jackson, J., & Hardee, K. (1999). Sexual attitudes and behavior among young adolescents in Jamaica. *International Family Planning Perspectives, 25*, 78-84, 91.

Festinger, L., Riecken, H. W., & Schacter, S. (1956). *When prophecy fails.* Minneapolis: University of Minnesota Press.

Fine, G., & Elsbach, K. (2000). Ethnography and experiment in social psychological theory building: Tactics for integrating qualitative field data with quantitative lab data. *Journal of Experimental Social Psychology, 36*, 51-76.

Fishbein, M. (1972). Toward an understanding of family planning behaviors. *Journal of Applied Social Psychology, 2*, 214-227.

Fishbein, M., & Jaccard, J. (1973). Theoretical and methodological considerations in the prediction of family planning intentions and behaviors. *Representative Research in Social Psychology, 4*, 37-52.

Flanagan, P., McGrath, M., Meyer, E., & Garcia, C. (1995). Adolescent development and transitions to motherhood. *Pediatrics, 96*, 273-277.

Freedman, J. L., & Fraser, S. C. (1966). Compliance without pressure: The foot-in-the-door technique. *Journal of Personality and Social Psychology, 4*, 195-202.

Glaser, B. G., & Strauss, A. (1967). *The discovery of grounded theory: Strategies for qualitative research.* New York: Aldine.

Hayes, N. (Ed.). (1997). *Doing qualitative analysis in psychology.* East Sussex, UK: Psychology Press.

Hird, M. (2000). An empirical study of adolescent dating aggression in the U.K. *Journal of Adolescence, 23*, 69-78.

Johnson, A. W., & Price-Williams, D. (1996). *Oedipus ubiquitous: The family complex in world folk literature.* Stanford, CA: Stanford University Press.

Malinowski, B. (1923). The psychology of sex and the foundations of kinship in primitive societies. *Psyche, 4*, 98-128.

Malinowski, B. (1927). *Sex and repression in savage society.* London: Routledge.

McGuire, W. J., & McGuire, C. V. (1981). The spontaneous self-concept as affected by personal distinctiveness. In M. D. Lynch, A. Norem-Hebeistein, & K. Gergen (Eds.), *The self-concept* (pp. 147-171). New York: Ballinger.

McGuire, W. J., McGuire, C. V., & Winton, W. (1979). Effects of household sex composition on the salience of one's gender in the spontaneous self-concept. *Journal of Experimental Social Psychology, 15*, 77-90.

McGuire, W. J., & Padawar-Singer, A. (1976). Trait salience in the spontaneous self-concept. *Journal of Personality and Social Psychology, 33*, 743-754.

Milgram, S. (1974). *Obedience to authority: An experimental view.* New York: Harper & Row.

National Population Council and Macro International. (1997). *Egypt in-depth study on the reasons for nonuse of family planning.* Cairo, Egypt: Author.

Pidgeon, N., & Henwood, K. (1997). Using grounded theory in psychological research. In N. Hayes (Ed.), *Doing qualitative analysis in psychology* (pp. 245-273). East Sussex, UK: Psychology Press.

Schein, E. H. (1956). The Chinese indoctrination program for prisoners of war: A study of attempted "brainwashing." *Psychiatry, 19*, 149-172.

Sherif, M., Harvey, O. J., White, B. J., Hood, W. R., & Sherif, C. W. (1961). *Intergroup conflict and cooperation: The Robber's Cave Experiment.* Norman: University of Oklahoma Institute of Intergroup Relations.

Sporton, D. (1999). Mixing methods in fertility research. *Professional Geographer, 51*, 68-76.

Tashakkori, A., & Teddlie, C. (1998). *Mixed methodologies: Combining Qualitative and Quantitative Approaches* (Applied Social Research Methods, No. 46). Thousand Oaks, CA: Sage.

Tashakkori, A., & Teddlie, C. (in press). Issues and dilemmas in teaching research methods courses in social and behavioral sciences: A U.S. perspective. *International Journal of Social Research Methodology.*

Tolman, D., & Szalacha, L. (1999). Dimensions of desire: Bridging qualitative and quantitative methods in a study of female sexuality. *Psychology of Women Quarterly, 23,* 7-39.

Ulin, P., Robinson, E., Tolley, E., & McNeill, E. (2002). *Qualitative methods: A field guide for applied research in sexual and reproductive health.* Research Triangle Park, NC: Family Health International.

Zimbardo, P. G. (1969). The human choice: Individuation, reason, and order versus de-individuation, impulse, and chaos. In W. T. Arnold & D. Levine (Eds.), *Nebraska Symposium on Motivation* (Vol. 17, pp. 237-307). Lincoln: University of Nebraska Press.

22

MULTIMETHOD RESEARCH IN SOCIOLOGY

◆ Albert Hunter
John Brewer

ociology is a discipline strategically poised within the network of the social sciences to be able both to contribute to and benefit from methodological innovation. As one of the younger disciplines, it has been able to draw eclectically from the distinctive methodologies of other disciplines such as the fieldwork of anthropology, the experiments of psychology, the voting and public opinion polls of political science, and the archival sources of history. Moreover, it has remained unwedded to any singular method, open instead to all that show promise and accommodating within the discipline practitioners of virtually all of the various methods of social research. Sociologists are also very methodologically self-conscious and often contentious, noted for debating not only the substance and

theories of their research but its methods as well. This critical self-scrutiny means that the different methods have been poked and probed with appropriate scientific skepticism. As a result, different methods' comparative strengths and limits have been exposed, leading many sociologists to adopt a multimethod perspective on research.

Multimethod research may be briefly defined as the practice of employing different types, or styles, of data-collecting methods within the same study or research program, for example, measuring variables with both survey and archival data, testing hypotheses with both experimental and nonexperimental methods, or employing qualitative fieldwork to develop a theoretical interpretation of a quantitative survey's findings. As we have written previously,

Methods differ both in the kinds of data that they afford and in their vulnerability to different kinds of error. The multimethod approach is a strategy for overcoming each method's weaknesses and limitations by deliberately combining different types of methods within the same investigations. The methods used in multimethod studies are, for the most part, the standard methods of contemporary social research. In that respect, there is little new in the multimethod approach. What is new is the planned, systematic synthesis of these different research styles, purposefully aimed at improving social science knowledge. (Brewer & Hunter, 1989, p. 11)

◆ A Brief History of Multimethod Research in Sociology

Sociology in the United States has been a methodologically diverse enterprise from the beginning. But this diversity is far better known—perhaps rightly so—for creating divisions and controversies than for encouraging the kinds of methodological synthesis and collaboration that multimethod research implies. Even during the first decades of the 20th century, before sociologists in the United States had really done much research, "statistics" versus "case studies" was a heated issue, foreshadowing the quantitative versus qualitative divide that continues to this day. And by the late decades of the century, the divisions had become yet more numerous and the controversies had become more complex. Survey research versus fieldwork, experimentation versus observational and quasi-experimental work, and nonreactive versus reactive methods were by then all at issue.

But division and controversy are certainly not the whole story. From the early days of sociology in the United States until now, there have been efforts to reconcile methodological differences and to exploit the advantages that a variety of methods might afford. For instance, Ernest W. Burgess, writing during the 1920s, urged,

The methods of statistics and of case study are not in conflict with one another; they are, in fact, mutually complementary. Statistical comparisons and correlations may often suggest leads for research by the case study method, and documentary materials as they reveal social processes will inevitably point the way to more adequate social indices. (Burgess, 1927/1974, p. 373)

He went on to predict that "the interaction of the two methods is certain to prove fruitful" (p. 373).

Burgess's prediction of fruitful interaction between the quantitative and qualitative research styles must often have appeared to be overly optimistic. For example, during the 1950s field-workers and survey researchers squared off in a now famous debate over the relative merits of their methods (e.g., Becker & Geer, 1957; Trow, 1957). But during the 1970s, Sieber's (1973) article, "Integrating Fieldwork and Survey Methods," confirmed the fruitful interaction that Burgess predicted. Sieber demonstrated that the two apparently antagonistic styles of research had in fact often been profitably integrated in the design, data collection, and analysis phases of single research projects. He concluded that "one could almost say that a new style of research is born of the marriage of survey and fieldwork methodologies" (p. 1337).

Moreover, despite the early establishment of competing research styles, many of the classic sociological studies of that era (such as the Middletown, Yankee City, and Hawthorne studies) in fact employed what appears today to be an eclectic mix of qualitative ("case study") and quantitative ("statistics") methods and what would now be considered multimethod studies. Similarly, Sieber (1973) found on close analysis that some classics of survey research (e.g., Lipset, Trow, & Coleman's [1966] *Union Democracy*) actually also made significant use of information derived from fieldwork and vice versa.

Studies using multiple methods before multimethod research came to be recognized as a distinctive research style compose an important part of the multimethod research tradition. But they have so far been only very partially and selectively studied, and they need to be much more fully sampled and examined (Brewer & Hunter, 1989). For example, Reinharz (1992), in her study of feminist research, called attention to the work of Margaret Hagood, who in her research on fertility patterns of southern White women decided (in her own words)

> to be both more realistic and comprehensive in a sort of attempt to get away from the restricted statistical treatment and stereotyped "case studies," and yet to combine as far as possible some features of the statistical, case, and survey methods. (quoted in Reinharz, 1992, pp. 197-198; see also Hagood, 1939)

The tentative, but deliberate, tone of Margaret Hagood's remark suggests the daring, and the resolve, that it takes to depart from recognized research styles.

The emergence of multimethod research as a research style arguably began in 1959 with the publication of Donald T. Campbell and D. W. Fiske's now well-known article on multiple operationalism

(Campbell & Fiske, 1959). The article introduced the idea of triangulation and the technique of multitrait-multimethod measurement validation, from which the multimethod approach derives its name. Later work by Webb, Campbell, Schwartz, and Sechrest (1966, 2000) provided a compelling rationale for extending the approach beyond measurement validation to the testing of causal hypotheses and theories. They argued persuasively that additional methods are not just helpful adjuncts at various stages of research but are in fact crucial, especially during the validation phase, because of the ever present threat of monomethod bias.

By the 1970s, the idea of multimethod research, often referred to simply as triangulation, had spread widely and been accepted by many sociologists and others as a potentially valuable research option. But along with this acceptance came the common complaint that the advocates of multimethod research rarely told how to do it (e.g., Jick, 1979). This, of course, assumed that multimethod research was completely new, with few if any existing exemplars. However, as we have already suggested here (and elsewhere), this was not necessarily the case (see also Brewer & Hunter, 1989). The conventional wisdom concerning the divisive nature of methods in sociology fosters that false impression.

◆ Major Methods in Sociology

Methodological diversity in a discipline is obviously a necessary condition for multimethod research, and sociology clearly has that. There are now at least four major styles of sociological research: fieldwork, survey research, experimentation, and nonreactive research. Each of these four methods, or styles, of research involves a different strategy for collecting data and a purpose for which it is particularly well-suited. Field-workers observe people and events in natural social settings to achieve a full firsthand view of social phenomena. Survey researchers either interview or administer questionnaires to samples of respondents drawn statistically from populations to generalize about the distribution of attitudes, opinions, and reported behaviors as well as the relationships among those kinds of variables. Experimentalists study phenomena under controlled conditions, deliberately established by the experimenter, to test particular causal hypotheses. Nonreactive researchers either employ unobtrusive observational techniques or study artifacts, archives, official records, and other naturally occurring by-products of past social life, with the aim of reducing the risk of reactive error (e.g., guinea pig effects) and the need for participants' cooperation in the research.

The classical quantitative versus qualitative distinction crosscuts the four styles just described and may produce variants and offshoots of each of these styles. That is, fieldwork includes both qualitative participant observation and quantitative case studies. Survey research similarly employs both statistical sampling surveys and qualitative focus groups. Nonreactive research includes not only quantified unobtrusive measurement and statistical analysis of records but also narrative historical research and textual analysis of documents. And there is even qualitative experimentation of a sort, for example, ethnomethodologists' "breaching experiments."

But diversity by itself is not a sufficient condition for multimethod research. Researchers must also be convinced that their research problems raise more, or more complex, questions than any single type of method can handle. A case in point is Campbell's (1957) often-cited conclusion with respect to the external versus internal validity of even true experimental designs: "Both criteria are obviously important, although it turns out that they are to some extent incompatible, in that the controls required for internal validity often tend to jeopardize representativeness" (p. 297). The message is that researchers, who are concerned with both the external and the internal validity of their experimental findings, may need to investigate their hypotheses with non- or quasi-experimental methods as well. As we have suggested elsewhere, similar caveats are associated with each type of research method (Brewer & Hunter, 1989). But fortunately, methods differ both in their vulnerability to particular kinds of error and in the kinds of information to which they give access.

Finally, we have noted that much recent writing on mixed methods research chiefly contrasts quantitative and qualitative methods (much as early sociologists did with statistics and case studies) rather than considering the fuller range of research methods discussed here. The distinction between quantitative and qualitative styles is certainly important, but to focus on it exclusively ignores a wider range of methodological problems and opportunities to solve them. The multimethod strategy calls for the use of multiple methods with complementary strengths and different weaknesses in relation to a given set of research problems. But these criteria do not imply that one must always employ a mix of qualitative and quantitative methods in each project. This may sometimes be the case, but some research problems might be better served by combining two different types of quantitative methods (e.g., a survey and an experiment) or qualitative methods (e.g., a field study and a textual analysis of archival documents). In short, the multimethod strategy focuses more on the problem's demands than on some particular set of methods.

◆ *Methodological Questions, Multimethod Answers*

Multimethod research is, we maintain, a widely practiced activity in sociology, although often done unsystematically and at times unconsciously. A more systematic use of multimethod can be used to solve a number of recurrent methodological questions that researchers often confront. In short, multimethod research can reduce the inevitable limitations inherent in any single method. We address five of these questions:

1. How does one increase measurement reliability and validity?

2. How does one sequence the stages of research?

3. Should one pursue breadth versus depth?

4. What is the goal of research—inductive theory construction or deductive hypothesis testing?

5. How does one resolve ethical dilemmas of research?

RELIABILITY AND VALIDITY

The two qualities most central to assessment of the "goodness" of a measurement are its reliability and its validity. Briefly, *validity* refers to the question of whether or not one's measurement of a phenomenon is true; that is, does it measure what it purports to measure? *Reliability*, on the other hand, refers to the degree to which a measurement can be replicated; that is, do repeated measurements of the same phenomenon produce consistent results from one time to the next? A number of sophisticated techniques have been developed within the so-cial sciences to assess the statistical validity and reliability of measurements beyond the preliminary crude assessment of "face validity"; that is, does the measurement on its surface—"on the face of it"—look like it is measuring what the researcher says it is measuring? The multitrait-multimethod strategy of Campbell and Fiske (1959) referred to earlier is one example of these more sophisticated techniques.

Finer and finer distinctions are made with respect to both validity and reliability such as internal validity versus external validity or construct validity/predictive validity/instrument reliability versus researcher reliability. The key element in all of these is that one measurement is being compared with some other measurement in some fashion. For both reliability and validity, in short, multiple measurements are required. Reliability emphasizes the repeated use of a single measurement, while validity implies different measurements. Multimethods, then, have built into them almost by definition the very essence of what is needed to assess the validity of research. The more diverse the methods, the more likely one is to sense that similar results increase the validity of the research findings. If very similar methods are used and the results are similar, then validity is increased somewhat. If the same method is used and results are similar, then one has an assessment of reliability. From the multimethod perspective, reliability and validity are a continuum for the assessment of the quality of one's measurement and research results, and where one is on that continuum is a function of the degree of similarity or difference in the research methods used.

It should be noted that the lack of agreement in the use of multimethods need not necessarily be equated with invalid measurement. Different methods might simply be tapping different dimensions, qualities, or aspects of a given phenomenon. These differences might be as theoretically and substantively important to consider as are methodologically generated differences. As one example, Lever (1981) noted how the gender differences in certain aspects of children's play depended on whether one was using a diary versus observation versus interviews of the children. It is not simply that one method was "valid" and the others "invalid"; rather, these differences reflected "meaningful" substantive differences in perception and normative expectations. Above all, it is clear that the multimethod strategy has much to contribute to the continuing concern over the reliability and validity of measurement.

Elsewhere (Brewer & Hunter, 1989, pp. 167-175), we have discussed these issues at length in terms of the concept of multitest validity—confidence in a hypothesis based on multiple empirical test results. We considered several different types of multiple tests, especially same-method and multimethod extensions (as opposed to exact replications). We considered how the interpretation of converging and diverging test results varies depending on the types of tests employed. Our discussion raised a number of complex issues requiring additional analysis. But our general conclusion was that multitest validation of hypotheses requires multimethod tests. These avoid the possibility of spurious convergence between findings resulting from monomethod bias. And in the event of divergence, multimethod tests may lead to important specifications of the hypothesis being tested and to improvements in the methods of testing.

STAGES OF RESEARCH

The stages of social research are usually defined as a sequence that moves from problem definition to research design, to data collection, to analysis, and finally to write-up and publication. Different research styles involve distinct ways of dealing with each of these stages. For example, survey research may stress careful operationalizing of concepts through questionnaire design and testing as well as careful and systematic sampling procedures, concerns that might not be raised in the same manner (or in similar detail) at this stage of research by other methods such as field research. In contrast, field research in its analysis stage may be very concerned with directly observing and establishing a temporal and processual order to events, while survey research extracts these at a cross-sectional single point in time. Different methods emphasize, expend energy and resources on, and hold up to careful scrutiny different aspects and stages of the research process. To contend that all stages are equally important is an ideal that cannot be argued with, but the reality is that given stages are considered more important in some methods than in others. By using a multimethod strategy, one tends to decrease the likelihood that certain stages of the research will be slighted or merely run through by rote procedures with relatively less conscious deliberation. Even in the write-up stage, survey and experimental researchers are more likely to use more "generic" formats than are field ethnographers, who must more consciously think about how to organize data and discussion into coherent narratives.

The different stages of research also have different costs in time, energy, effort, and money connected with different methods. Experimental and survey researchers again have much greater research design costs than do field ethnographers, and sampling and data collection costs are much less for experimentalists than for survey researchers. Archivists and field researchers often have high analysis costs, while experimentalists have the least analysis costs. In short, different methods have different costs at different stages. In a multimethod strategy, one can combine methods and stretch costs more uniformly across the stages of the research.

BREADTH VERSUS DEPTH

One of the enduring dilemmas of all research is that between breadth of coverage, meaning the number of units (or human subjects) studied, and depth or the amount of data that one will be able to collect about any given unit (or human subject). One of the ways of envisioning this dilemma is to picture a data matrix that consists of rows that represent different units and columns that represent different variables about each of the units. If one focuses on only one row, then that is one unit of observation, and one may collect many different variables on that unit. This is what field researchers are fond of referring to as a "richness" of data, that is, studying one case in great depth. In contrast, one may focus on many different rows, or units of observation, but collect many fewer variables—in the extreme, only one, two, or three about each of these many units. That is, one has increased one's breadth of coverage (many units) but reduced the depth of knowledge (number of variables) about these units.

This distinction parallels that early debate in the discipline between the case study versus statistics, but today the two methods that best exemplify it are participant observation of a single case versus survey research, which allows one to use statistical inference to generalize from a sample to a much larger population. This dilemma of breadth versus depth need not involve a necessary trade-off if one uses multimethods that allow one to explore

both. Multimethods allow one to collect breadth of data about a population of units and also allow one to explore a much smaller set of selected units in greater detail. Multimethods are an ideal resolution to this dilemma and in the process produce a more complete set of research results.

THEORY: INDUCTIVE CONSTRUCTION VERSUS DEDUCTIVE TESTING

All good social science research has some relationship to theory; social science is seldom significant just for reporting the facts. One of the great divides in science, and the social sciences to a degree, is that between empiricists and theorists. To be sure, both contribute to the great division of labor within the sciences, but their foci and the assessment of their contributions are often based on quite different criteria. The relationship between theory and method is, however, inextricable. Robert Merton long ago noted the ways in which theory guides research and how research enlightens theory (Merton, 1957). Too often, however, a methodological distinction is drawn between those methods that are used to suggest, develop, or construct new theory and those that are considered to be better at testing or validating theory. The distinction often equates field research with the former inductive social construction of theory and equates surveys (or especially experimental designs) with the latter deductive testing of theory.

The multimethod strategy reveals two important insights with respect to this distinction: first, that theory testing and theory construction can occur in each of the methods, and second, that by combining the methods, one can both create or construct new theory and test it in the same piece of research (for excellent examples of the discovery and use of grounded theory, see Glaser & Strauss, 1967; Strauss & Corbin, 1998). Innovative strategies may shift back and forth between methods at different stages of the research process, with all contributing to a more comprehensive and satisfying piece of research on both methodological and theoretical grounds.

ETHICS

Ever since a number of notorious examples of major lapses in ethical considerations by researchers (see, e.g., Milgram's [1963] "obedience to authority" experiments, Humphries's (1970) clandestine study of bisexual males, or a number of medical experiments such as the Tuskegee study of syphilis in prisoners [Reverby, 2000] and the Department of Defense's study of the effects of proximity of soldiers to atomic bomb tests), the federal government and professional social science associations have established codes of ethics to protect the welfare of human subjects. Most institutions, or at least those receiving federal funds for research, have set up institutional review boards that are responsible for evaluating the costs/benefits of research proposals, and they are specifically charged with protecting human subjects against risks and must balance these against possible benefits of the research. The operating phrase for making such assessments is that potential human subjects for research must exercise "voluntary informed consent."

There is no doubt that such ethical considerations produce additional limits or constraints for different research methods in a given study. At this point, multimethods enter again. By using alternative research methods, one may sidestep or circumvent the limits that exist on one's preferred method. To be sure, the data may be slightly different, and the questions one can answer may have to be altered as well, but through a combination of less than optimal methods, one may approximate the results one would have attained by using the ethically questionable method. For example, experimental manipulation might not prove ethically feasible in a given situation, so one could hunt for natural experiments that may be buried in the archival record, and these data, in conjunction with some in-depth interviewing of participants, may allow one to explore closely related propositions. As with other kinds of limits, ethical considerations are a challenge to investigators to open their repertoire of styles and to consider using previously overlooked methods.

◆ Three Classic Exemplars

Examples of multimethod research are, we suggest, more frequently found in the sociological literature than even their authors are aware. The debriefing interview from an experiment, the extensive number of interviews in a field study that approach that of a sample survey, the insightful quote from a curator of archives—all of these exemplify ways in which a second method can often unwittingly inform a primary piece of research. We are suggesting, however, that for the multimethod strategy to take full advantage of its strengths, it should ideally become a consciously planned practice from the inception of a piece of research and incorporated into one's research design from the very beginning. Fortunately, there are a number of classical sociological studies that exemplify this multimethod strategy.

Kuhn (1970) argued that "exemplars" play a crucial role in scientific research as the ideal type of training vehicles for socializing neophytes into not just the substance but also the style of good research. We offer a brief look at three sociological studies as exemplars of the use of multi-method strategies: Roethlisberger and Dickson's (1939) famous experiments from the "Hawthorne Studies," Warner and his associates' studies of "Yankee City" (Warner & Lunt, 1941), and Lipset et al.'s (1956) investigation of "union democracy." These three works are sufficiently part of the sociological core to be identified as important landmark studies, and they are works that have stood the test of time required to earn the sobriquet "classics."

THE HAWTHORNE STUDIES

In 1924, the management of the Hawthorne Works of the Western Electric Company near Chicago began a series of experiments to test the possible effects of different levels of illumination on their workers' morale and productivity. What they discovered instead, of course, is the famous "Hawthorne effect." Their experimental variations in lighting conditions apparently had far weaker effects than did the workers' awareness of being seriously studied. For example, output increased with improved illumination but failed to decline when the usual illumination was restored or even reduced below its original levels. Intrigued by these findings—so the story goes—the Hawthorne management turned to the recently founded Harvard University Department of Industrial Relations. In 1927, 5 years of research began. The research, as reported by Roethlisberger and Dickson (1939), comprised a series of three major investigations: the relay assembly test room study, the interview project, and the bank wiring observation room study. Each of the investiga-

tions was designed to help interpret and expand on the findings of the preceding phase. The relay test assembly room study was designed to help understand better the Hawthorne management's first experimental findings. The researchers set up a very small-scale experimental study consisting of six women whose work was typical of the factory's general work in important ways (i.e., essentially a microcosm). The women were then studied for several years under experimentally varied working conditions, and as in the earlier experiments, their productivity generally rose. But looked at now, this study appears less like a classic experimental design and more like a field study of an experiment to determine how a particular effect is produced. For example, there was a "test room observer" present in the room, and the women were interviewed and tested in various ways individually, including collection of some life history data. And their research led Roethlisberger and Dickson (1939) to reconceptualize their research problem drastically. They summarized this first phase of the work as follows:

> No longer were the investigators interested in testing for the effects of single variables. In place of a controlled experiment, they substituted the notion of a social situation which needed to be described and understood as a system of interdependent elements. . . . The situation included not only the external events but the meaning which individuals assign to them and their preoccupations about them. Rather than trying to keep these "psychological factors" constant, the investigators had to regard them as important variables in the situation. As much attention had to be given to these psychological factors as to output in assessing

the external changes which took place. (pp. 183-184)

Roethlisberger and Dickson's (1939) reconceptualization led them simultaneously in two different methodological directions, both of which they followed. The emphasis on "psychological factors" just mentioned led to the interviewing program, which involved some 1,600 employees with whom more than 10,000 interviews were conducted. The interviews at first followed a schedule of questions about working conditions and the like. Later, however, they took a more nondirective form, and the program itself began to take on a counseling, as well as a data gathering, function.

Their emphasis on "the social situation" led in another direction—to the establishment of the Bank Wiring Observation Room. This was a completely nonexperimental field site in which the researchers, using standard fieldwork techniques, could observe firsthand the work and everyday social relations of workers. Their observations, of course, provided the beginnings of our present-day understanding of the interplay of formal and informal behavior and structure in organizations.

YANKEE CITY

Newburyport, Massachusetts, may seem an unlikely place to locate a study that would purport to represent the nature of community life in the United States. But like Lynd and Lynd's (1927) research in "Middletown," W. Lloyd Warner, trained as an anthropologist, was most interested in capturing the full round of day-to-day life and the structure of activities of a community whose institutions and residents could in some way represent broader issues of social life in the United States (Hunter, 1990a, 1990b). This meant that the community should have an industrial economic base, have diversity with respect to social class and ethnicity, and be of a size to permit a limited number of researchers to fully observe and document the community's varied social life. Given this broad agenda, Warner drew together a research team that employed a variety of methods that would allow him to capture more specifically the history of the community, its stratification system and class structure, the structure of its major institutions (including economic and religious life), and the cultural meanings and symbolism of the whole. To study these diverse topics, as well as the different questions they posed, would require an openness to a variety of research strategies and methods to get at the different data sets necessary to answer them.

It is worth quoting at length the diverse methods that were used and the researchers' sensitivity to the fact that different methods have different strengths and weaknesses to answer different questions:

The fundamental and most important technique we used to gather material in the field was the interview. . . . In addition to the interview, various types of sustained observations were made; a great variety and number of printed documents were collected; case histories, biographies, autobiographies, and other intimate histories were gathered from our informants; photographs were made of houses and other objects of significance; and an aerial survey was made. Many other surveys were also pursued, and the newspapers were systematically used. The distribution of various kinds of phenomena [was] mapped. Each of these separate techniques will be described in detail, and the use of some of them in the Yankee City research will be evaluated according to the tests of (1) reliability; (2) time required; (3) area of social relations covered; (4) insight into the social behavior which use of the technique gives to the investigator; (5) comparative depth or superficiality; (6) value at various periods in the research and not at others; (7) special uses, such as quantification of behavior already defined and isolated and prepared for measurement; (8) availability for the isolation and definition of social behavior at that time unknown or not yet sufficiently understood to define; and (9) special uses associated with particular techniques. (Warner & Lunt, 1941, pp. 44-45)

More specifically, Warner and Lunt (1941) described how they located a "key informant"—a leader in the community who would introduce them to others—and how quantitative questionnaires supplemented interviews. They detailed the archives and records that included local police crime reports, school records, and health department records and statistics, among others. It is very clear in their analysis that they gave different weights to different methods at different points, but in general they spoke to the power of combining these multimethods to achieve their primary purpose of documenting the full round of social life in this community. They clearly bridged dichotomous choices that are often falsely held up today by "methodological ideologues" such as quantitative versus qualitative or inductive versus deductive. Focused on substance, the Yankee City researchers spoke to a conscious pragmatic, but systematic use of eclectic methods to achieve their objectives.

UNION DEMOCRACY

Philosophers have debated for millennia the ideal form of government, and having settled in our day on democracy as the form that most closely adheres to the central values of our culture, the next question is an empirical one: How does one construct and maintain a democratic political system? This is the question that Lipset et al. (1956) attempted to answer in their landmark study of the International Typographical Union in North America.

The researchers quickly recognized that to explore these issues thoroughly required distinguishing among three different levels or units of analysis: the union as a whole, the intermediate units of the union locals, and the individual union members themselves. They quickly recognized that strategic choices and trade-offs must be made between depth and breadth with respect to the amount of data to be collected from the different levels. They wrote the following about the survey sampling strategy among the three levels: "Interviewing more men in each shop would have meant interviewing each man less thoroughly or else covering fewer shops, thus gaining knowledge about shops at the expense of knowledge about either individuals or the union as a whole" (p. 473).

Using three distinct levels in their analysis required that Lipset et al. (1956) clearly identify the different types of data appropriate to each level. In a concise chart that arrayed "types of data gathered" by "types of units," they presented a clear picture of their multimethod strategy (p. 474). For the "total system" (the union as a whole), they indicated the wide use of records and archival material: "issues; data on occupation; union laws; policies; historical data; convention reports." For the "intermediate units," they used "local histories and voting records; issues on local level; size of locals." Finally, for the "individual" level, they had "interviews with leaders; interviews of the sample of men." In short, they drew on a variety of data sets generated by different methods—archives and records, sample surveys, and interviews. And most significantly, they integrated the data sets in an innovative analysis that allowed them to explore the "structural effects" that larger units had on their constituent units and, in turn, the way in which constituent units aggregated to produce unique structural features of the larger, more inclusive units.

One of the important lessons to be learned from *Union Democracy* (Lipset et al., 1956) is that combining different methods in the same investigation opens up whole new theoretical questions to investigation that previously remained unexplored. In this case, it was the structural features of the union that promoted democratic participation by its members (e.g., an independent union newspaper) and certain characteristics of the members that promoted structural characteristics (e.g., the high literacy rate of members). Clearly, multimethod research has implications far beyond the methodological questions of increased validity and reliability, and it can directly contribute to broader theoretical advances in the field. In the next section, we explore some of the more recent developments that reflect an extension beyond the classical multimethod exemplars into the postmodern positivism.

◆ From Modern to Postmodern Multimethod Research

Within the past few decades, the positivist and modernist methods of the social sciences have come under increasing criticism and outright attack on a number of grounds. Many of these criticisms center on some variant of the charge that the social sciences are engaged in a "naive empiricism." Core assumptions of the positivist tradition (e.g., an uncritical acceptance of assumptions about the positing of an external objective world of social phenomena, the validity of quantitative measurement of those phenomena, and the capacity to make empirical generalizations and formulate theoretical propositions of increasing abstraction) are now called into question. The critiques themselves have taken a number of forms, and we touch on only three of the more significant of these: the ideas of narrative, rhetoric, and the social construction of scientific facts.

NARRATIVE

The first critique of classical positivism is what may be called the narrative framing of social phenomena. In part stemming from a hyper historicism, this perspective argues in a somewhat ideographic manner that the relatively static, synchronic, or cross-sectional nature of most social science research may generate internally consistent theories (e.g., theories composed of logically interrelated testable hypotheses) that still leave one begging for more in the way of explanation of the phenomena under investigation. In its most simplistic formulation, the narrative critique is a call for taking time seriously. A narrative approach argues for the need to elucidate a concatenated set of temporal factors that may have small, distinct, and separate origins that over time come together or coalesce to create the conditions that produce the phenomena being studied. The narrative approach stresses ideas such as "contingency," "path dependency," and "sequence" that speak to a potential multiplicity of outcomes rather than a mechanical determinism often contained in positivist explanations. It is a call for sociologists to stop overgeneralizing about reified phenomena that have been wrenched from their spatiotemporal context.

The most recent positivist attempt to capture "time" in some manner is through techniques such as "event history analysis," which (in spite of its name) attempts to analyze "events" as autonomous "units" existing apart from their embeddedness in a rich and complex historical context. The narrative critique would call for a more discursive and nuanced verbal rendering of events, while the event history analysis would stress the sophisticated quantitative statistical controls that render history and time as but a variable, not as an intrinsic property of the very idea of "explanation" itself. Narrative is, in short, not variable-based linear regression but rather linear unfolding of concatenated reciprocal paths.

All good narratives have a beginning, a middle, and an end. They tell a story, and more often than not, there is a moral to the story—a lesson to be learned.

One variant of narrative is biography, or in today's parlance "life history," which may be construed as constructing a life narrative. And to paraphrase C. Wright Mills's classic definition, "sociology" is the intersection of biography and history—the playing out of two different scales of narrative time (Mills, 1959). Methodologically, life histories may be considered a form of in-depth interviewing or, if the participants write out their own life histories, a form of archival document. Life histories have become significant at the intersection of history and sociology as "social history" has emerged as distinct subdiscipline. Social history is the study of the lives of ordinary folks during different historical periods, not simply a concern with kings, generals, and other rulers and elites. Early sociologists brought to the fore life histories such as

the early Chicago School's studies of The Jackroller, The Wayward Girl, and The Hobo (Anderson, 1923/1961; Cressey, 1953; Thomas & Znaniecki, 1918/1958). As Bennett (1981) noted, often these "biographies" were a complex methodology that were produced as an amalgam of a number of different life histories. As to their veracity, the claim could be maintained that "nothing in this has been made up."

Life histories speak to a further critique of positivism with its search for more or less determinist theories. This critique concerns the role of "agency" or the ability of individuals to rise above their social and historical conditions and, by exercising will, to alter the course of their own lives, the course of events, and ultimately the course of history. The idea of agency is a deeply rooted philosophical assumption in modern Western thought that directly confronts the assumptions of a predictive science of society focused on the behavior of objectified participants.

RHETORIC

The art of rhetoric, according to Aristotle, was one of the three key modes of speech acts, with the other two being dialectic and commemorative speech. Rhetoric was concerned with persuading others of the truth of one's assertions. Sir Francis Bacon's development of the logic of modern science during the 16th century can be seen as a reaction to the degenerate place of rhetoric as "mere rhetoric," for as he said, he took the questions that the scholastic rhetoricians of the Middle Ages posed to one another and then turned and posed them to nature itself. The scholastic dialogue was now a scientific dialogue between empirical researchers and the natural world. Nonetheless, the reporting of the research was still a rhetorical exercise in which scientists had to convince peers and others of the truth of their assertions. The scientific method was, in this sense, a "tool" or a set of rules such that if they were used properly, others would more likely be convinced that they had produced valid results.

The rhetorical view of science critiques this naive positivism for masking or rendering the rhetorical elements invisible. Scientists use the passive voice, for example, to render the individual scientist transparent and to highlight the central role of the method itself—not "I found . . ." but rather "It was found that . . ." The rhetorical critique calls for a greater consciousness of what is being done in scientific research and, above all, more truth and accuracy in reporting what it is that scientists actually do in their research. The format of the modern scientific report in its standardized form, a genre of writing that some attribute to Newton himself, contributes to this unconscious unreflective masking of numerous decisions, compromises, and outright serendipity that is part-and-parcel of the messy conduct of most scientific investigations. Most research is in fact pragmatically eclectic.

This rhetorical critique has been applied to a number of the social sciences such as McCloskey's (1985) *The Rhetoric of Economics* and Brown's (1977, 1987) *A Poetic for Sociology* and *Sociology as Text*. The question becomes the following: How does this rhetorical aspect directly affect the nature of research methods, and more specifically, what might it contribute to a multimethod approach? We suggest that its major contribution lies in seeing the process of research not only as a question of the search for truth in some objectified positivist sense but also as a concern about the variety of tools that might be employed to better convince others of the truth of one's assertions. Different audiences with different substantive interests and, above all, different method-

ological predilections are more likely to be convinced if research findings are the result of their specific preferred styles. The outcome is both a broader audience of support and a deeper, more staunch commitment and intense agreement with one's assertions. From a rhetorician's viewpoint, the more arguments (methods), the better.

THE SOCIAL CONSTRUCTION OF SCIENTIFIC FACTS

To view science as a social process, and the institutions of science as but one more institutional sphere ripe for sociological investigation, is a further extension of the narrative and rhetorical critiques of the positivist modernist conception of science. In its extreme, the postmodern social constructionist view asserts that all truth is but a "social agreement" and places less emphasis on the empirical and positivist notion of truth that lies in the "agreement" between hypotheses (theory) and data from a real objectified world (research)—Bacon's classic "dialogue." Even the seemingly unequivocal and mundane question of what is a "fact" is held up to detailed scrutiny and seen to be the outcome of a complex social process wherein sometimes ambiguous and contradictory research results are subjected to debate and deliberation (Latour & Woolgar, 1979). Facts, the basic building blocks of an empirical science, are the product of social negotiation and all that this implies. Differences in power, prestige, and positions in social networks—and not simply the truth as defined by unambiguous and reliable measurement—are highlighted as determining the acceptance of a given fact.

The implications of this for the multimethod strategy are, first, the heightened awareness that allows one to be sensitive to how it is that the social processes involved in one's research (from the largest structural features of inequality to the most quotidian nuance of approbation) may be influencing the nature of the research results. Second, this awareness can lead to a proactive research strategy that, through the use of different styles of research, may mitigate, but never obliterate, the social embeddedness of the research process. Where face-to-face contact may result in biased measurement, for example, archives far removed from direct interpersonal contact with participants may counter these biases. Arguments with peers about the purity of one's research techniques should be tempered with a healthy skepticism about the inevitable threats to validity that may have been unanticipated when initially developing one's research design. Consciously using more than one method allows one, first, to answer threats to validity oneself internally within the research process itself and, second, to broaden the dialogues with others who are involved in the constructing of scientific facts.

SOME CONTEMPORARY EXAMPLES

The preceding discussion of postmodern social research has emphasized three concerns: narrative, rhetoric, and the social construction of scientific facts. Let us now consider some contemporary research examples in which the multimethod approach has been employed to address these concerns as they impinge on survey research, often more conventionally depicted as naively positivist.

The first example, a study conducted by Dykema and Schaeffer (2000), asked "how the patterning of experiences in the lives of respondents leads to errors in understanding survey questions and in recalling the experiences they ask about" (p. 619). The narrative (our term here, not theirs) variables that they considered were "complexity (how frequent, regular, and similar the payments are), clarity (how distinct the payments are from like events), and the intensity of affect about exchanging child support" (p. 619). They hypothesized that reports "should be less accurate when events are complex, indistinct from like events, and emotionally neutral" (p. 619). In sum, the recall of significant events is dependent on the nature of their embeddedness in a meaningful narrative that orders and routinizes the flux of everyday life. Dykema and Schaeffer tested their hypotheses by comparing the results of two telephone surveys of divorced parents asking for self-reports of child support payments with actual court records of child support payments. They concluded that survey "instruments that take the patterning of events into account may substantially increase the accuracy of reports" (p. 628).

The second example, a study conducted by Krysan (1999), considered some surprising survey findings dealing with attitudes toward racial equality. The findings were that in surveys over time, the U.S. population appears to be becoming more liberal on the issue of residential integration but not on the issue of equal employment opportunities. Krysan hypothesized that this may in fact be due to differences between survey researchers' and survey respondents' understandings of the questions being asked. To explore her hypothesis, she conducted individual qualitative interviews with 14 respondents from a large-scale survey in Detroit concerning their earlier questionnaire responses to items about open housing and fair employment. Her findings suggested to her that differences in understandings might well explain the surprising findings, and they led her to recommend more regular follow-ups to surveys of this qualitative sort. She concluded, "Our survey answers will mean very little to us if we do not understand what they mean to respondents" (p. 217). This is clearly a rhetorical problem, at least in part: how to open research to competing rhetorics, including the rhetoric of the research participants, which may be very different from that of the researcher, as the following exchange suggests:

Respondent: What do you mean by fair treatment in jobs?

Interviewer: Whatever it means to you.

Respondent: Oh, come on! (Respondent 14, p. 217)

The third example consists of a much-publicized series of studies bearing on the apparently high rate of church attendance in the United States as compared with similar nations. The first of these studies is Hadaway, Marler, and Chaves's (1993) research titled "What the Polls Don't Show: A Closer Look at U.S. Church Attendance." Polls had generally shown that about 40% of the people in the United States attend church weekly. Hadaway et al. challenged this with an archival, head count, and limited survey study that suggested the rate of attendance was far less. Their results were both challenged and supported by later research reported in a 1998 symposium published in the *American Sociological Review* (*ASR*) ("Symposium," 1998). Various aspects of their multimethod study were severely criticized. But redesigned surveys based on their analysis suggested that in fact church attendance in the United States had been overestimated. The earlier editor of the *ASR* had introduced Hadaway et al.'s work as a study of "the social construction of stylized facts." Clearly, the social construction perspective is amenable to multimethod exploration and elaboration.

Finally, Gioia and Thomas (1996) used a multimethod strategy to explore an interesting organizational issue of concern to most academics: the strategy of academic administrators in pursuing a move up in academic rankings. Specifically, they explored how administrators symbolically perceive or define certain issues as either (a) routine and maintenance oriented and thereby not affecting prestige rankings or (b) strategic and likely to affect such rankings. They combined an initial qualitative case study of a single university with a quantitative regression analysis based on a sample of more than 300 universities. Gioia and Thomas showed how "identity" and "image" are distinct, with the former referring to self-perception and the latter referring to others' perceptions and with the two showing distinct patterns of differential attention on the part of administrators as they label different types of issues as either routine or strategic. The qualitative case study lays out a detailed narrative of how administrators think about, classify, and act on different types of issues, while the quantitative analysis supports and generalizes these findings to a larger universe. In short, this explicitly multimethod study epitomized the best of subjective and objective insights. The researchers showed nicely the way in which the social construction of "issues" and the "identity" question of symbolic interaction can be explored using the strengths of both qualitative in-depth case studies and survey research as well as the value both have for understanding the hard-nosed reality of organizational change and decision making.

◆ The Future

The practice of what we now call multimethod research, as we have tried to show here through our emphasis on history and classic research examples, emerged early in sociology in the United States. But its potential as a deliberately employed research strategy was slow to be recognized and even slower to be systematically explored and analyzed as a strategy in its own right. However, the sociological experience with multiple methods has shown that research employing this approach requires such attention. It has its own special properties and presents its own special problems and opportunities throughout the research process (Brewer & Hunter, 1989).

Postmodern critiques of empirical inquiry, accompanied by a proliferation and growing interest in qualitative research styles (Denzin & Lincoln, 1994, 2000) as well as the continuing development of sophisticated quantitative research techniques, virtually ensure that sociology in the foreseeable future will be at least as methodologically diverse and contentious as it has been in the past. In an important way, this continuing methodological diversity and contentiousness is a healthy sign. Skepticism is, of course, an essential aspect of scientific inquiry, and contending methodologies obviously represent important critical perspectives on one another and on social reality. Equally important, however, is the fact that newer emerging methodologies may also offer solutions not yet conceived for existing methodological problems and present surprising opportunities to increase the depth and scope of social inquiry. The key requirement is perhaps that we conduct and think about social research in (to borrow Gouldner's [1966] words) a sociologically self-reflexive manner.

■ *References*

Anderson, N. (1961). *The hobo: The sociology of the homeless man.* Chicago: University of Chicago Press. (Original work published 1923)

Becker, H. S., & Geer, B. (1957). Participant observation and interviewing. *Human Organization, 16,* 28-32.

Bennett, J. (1981). *Oral history and delinquency: The rhetoric of criminology.* Chicago: University of Chicago Press.

Brewer, J., & Hunter, A. (1989). *Multimethod research: A synthesis of styles.* Newbury Park, CA: Sage.

Brown, R. H. (1977). *A poetic for sociology.* Cambridge, UK: Cambridge University Press.

Brown, R. H. (1987). *Sociology as text: Essays on rhetoric, reason, and reality.* Chicago: University of Chicago Press.

Burgess, E. W. (1974). Statistics and case studies as methods of sociological research. Reprinted in D. J. Bogue (Ed.), *The basic writings of Ernest W. Burgess* (pp. 367-373). Chicago: University of Chicago, Community and Family Study Center. (Original work published 1927)

Campbell, D. (1957). Factors relevant to the validity of experiments in social settings. *Psychological Bulletin, 54,* 295-312.

Campbell, D., & Fiske, D. W. (1959). Convergent and discriminant validation by the multitrait-multimethod matrix. *Psychological Bulletin, 54,* 297-312.

Cressey, D. R. (1953). *Other people's money: A study in the social psychology of embezzlement.* Glencoe, IL: Free Press.

Denzin, N. K., & Lincoln, Y. S. (1994). *Handbook of qualitative research.* Thousand Oaks, CA: Sage.

Denzin, N. K., & Lincoln, Y. S. (Eds.). (2000). *Handbook of qualitative research* (2nd ed.). Thousand Oaks, CA: Sage.

Dykema, J., & Schaeffer, N. C. (2000). Events, instruments, and error reporting. *American Sociological Review, 65,* 619-629.

Gioia, D. A., & Thomas, J. B. (1996). Identity, image, and issue interpretation: Sensemaking during strategic change in academia. *Administrative Science Quarterly, 41,* 370-403.

Glaser, B. G., & Strauss, A. L. (1967). *The discovery of grounded theory: Strategies for qualitative research.* Chicago: Aldine.

Gouldner, A. (1966). *The coming crisis of Western sociology.* New York: Macmillan.

Hadaway, C. K., Marler, P. L., & Chaves, M. (1993). What the polls don't show: A closer look at U.S. church attendance. *American Sociological Review, 58,* 741-752. (Gerald Marwell, Editor's Comment, in the same issue, pp. iii-iv)

Hagood, M. (1939). *Mothers of the South: Portraiture of the White tenant farm woman.* Chapel Hill: University of North Carolina Press.

Humphries, L. (1970, January). Tearoom trade: Impersonal sex in public places. *Trans-Action,* pp. 11-25.

Hunter, A. (1990a). Introduction: Rhetoric in research, networks of knowledge. In A. Hunter (Ed.), *The rhetoric of social research: Understood and believed* (pp. 1-22). New Brunswick, NJ: Rutgers University Press.

Hunter, A. (1990b). Setting the scene, sampling, and synecdoche. In A. Hunter (Ed.), *The rhetoric of social research: Understood and believed* (pp. 111-128). New Brunswick, NJ: Rutgers University Press.

Jick, T. D. (1979). Mixing qualitative and quantitative methods: Triangulation in action. *Administrative Science Quarterly, 24,* 602-611.

Krysan, M. (1999). Qualifying a quantifying analysis on racial equality. *Social Psychological Quarterly, 62,* 211-218.

Kuhn, T. S. (1970). *The structure of scientific revolutions* (2nd ed.). Chicago: University of Chicago Press.

Latour, B., & Woolgar, S. (1979). *Laboratory life: The social construction of scientific fact.* Beverly Hills, CA: Sage.

Lever, J. (1981). Multiple methods of data collection: A note on divergence. *Urban Life, 10,* 199-213.

Lipset, S. M., Trow, M., & Coleman, J. (1956). *Union democracy.* Garden City, NY: Anchor Books.

Lynd, R. S., & Lynd, H. M. (1927). *Middletown.* New York: Harcourt, Brace.

McCloskey, D. (1985). *The rhetoric of economics.* Madison: University of Wisconsin Press.

Merton, R. K. (1957). *Social theory and social structure.* Glencoe, IL: Free Press.

Milgram, S. (1963). Behavioral study of obedience. *Journal of Abnormal Social Psychology, 67,* 371-378.

Mills, C. W. (1959). *The sociological imagination.* New York: Oxford University Press.

Reinharz, S. (1992). *Feminist methods in social research.* New York: Oxford University Press.

Reverby, S. M. (Ed.). (2000). *Tuskegee's truths: Rethinking the Tuskegee Syphilis Study.* Chapel Hill: University of North Carolina Press.

Roethlisberger, F. J., & Dickson, W. J. (1939). *Management and the worker.* Cambridge, MA: Harvard University Press.

Sieber, S. D. (1973). Integrating fieldwork and survey methods. *American Journal of Sociology, 78,* 1335-1359.

Strauss, A., & Corbin, J. (1998). *Basics of qualitative research: Techniques and procedures for developing grounded theory* (2nd ed.). Thousand Oaks, CA: Sage.

Symposium: Surveys of U.S. church attendance. (1998). *American Sociological Review, 63,* 111-154.

Thomas, W. I., & Znaniecki, F. (1958). *The Polish peasant in Europe and America.* New York: Dover. (Original work published 1918)

Trow, M. (1957). Comment on participant observation and interviewing: A comparison. *Human Organization, 16,* 33-35.

Warner, W. L., & Lunt, P. S. (1941). *The social life of a modern community* (Yankee City, Vol. 1). New Haven, CT: Yale University Press.

Webb, E. J., Campbell, D. T., Schwartz, R. D., & Sechrest, L. (1966). *Unobtrusive measures: Nonreactive research in the social sciences.* Chicago: Rand McNally.

Webb, E. J., Campbell, D. T., Schwartz, R. D., & Sechrest, L. (2000). *Unobtrusive measures* (Rev. ed.). Thousand Oaks, CA: Sage.

23

THE PRAGMATIC AND DIALECTICAL LENSES: TWO VIEWS OF MIXED METHODS USE IN EDUCATION

◆ Tonette S. Rocco
Linda A. Bliss
Suzanne Gallagher
Aixa Perez-Prado
Cengiz Alacaci
Eric S. Dwyer
Joyce C. Fine
N. Eleni Pappamihiel

Greene and Caracelli (1997) argued that "using multiple and diverse methods is a good idea, but is not automatically good science" (p. 5). This chapter provides a discussion of the ways in which mixed methods are approached in education. Mixed methods proponents across the wide field of education share the goal of conducting good social science. Good research design ad-

dresses the intertwined political, philosophical, and technical levels of decision making (Greene & Caracelli, 1997).

Greene and Caracelli (1997) pointed out that the "qualitative-quantitative debate" on social inquiry is often framed by positioning the two major research paradigms as oppositional: "the interpretivist, constructivist paradigm (exemplified by Lincoln and Guba, 1985) and the postpositivist, or postempiricist, paradigm (exemplified by Campbell, 1969; Cook, 1985)" (Greene & Caracelli, 1997, p. 6). However, as Maxwell and Loomis (Chapter 9, this volume) point out, the history of social science research reveals a pattern of using both qualitative and quantitative "techniques and approaches without deliberately drawing attention to this." They further note that some of the more recent studies have used these methods both "implicitly" and "self-consciously."

We connect these two ways of using mixed methods with Greene and Caracelli's observation that mixed methods inquiry may be conducted from either a pragmatic or a dialectical position. The *pragmatic position* implicitly calls for choosing a paradigm and a method by what will "work best" to meet the practical demands of a particular inquiry (Patton, 1988) and thereby help to answer the research question. Any philosophical assumptions about paradigms of inquiry are deemed to be logically independent of these decisions. Paradigmatic philosophical assumptions are less important than the myriad "practical demands" of the particular research problem when making choices about data collection and interpretation. In this research frame, therefore, any potential contradictory ontological (the nature of reality) or epistemological (the nature of truth) assumptions are less important than "situational responsiveness and a commitment to an empirical perspective" (Greene & Caracelli, 1997, p. 9).

Individuals' pragmatic decisions to mix qualitative and quantitative methods either sequentially or simultaneously within their research projects are leading to a number of "mixed methods" educational studies, although as some researchers from other disciplines report in this handbook about studies in their fields, this label is not always applied in educational research. Tashakkori and Teddlie (1998) have been prominent among those social scientists calling for more clarity in delineating the characteristics of these studies and conducting more qualitatively-quantitatively integrated mixed model studies. Their underlying philosophical assumption is that these two practices will enhance the quality of educational research and make it more accurate and useful. Addressing technical-level concerns in detail, Tashakkori and Teddlie's mixed model typology is driven by each study's exploratory or confirmatory purpose. Model designations are based on the particular qualitative and/or quantitative nature of research components or stages. The authors identified three especially relevant stages: data collection, analysis, and inference.

The *dialectical position* self-consciously calls for a "synergistic" use of methods deliberately "shaped by both interpretivist and postpositivist paradigms in an integrative manner" (Greene & Caracelli, 1997, p. 10). The term is traced to Geertz (1979), who argued for a continuous "'dialectical tacking' between experience-near (particular, context specific, idiographic) and experience-distant (general, universal, nomothetic) concepts, because both types of concepts are needed for comprehensiveness and meaningful understanding" (Greene & Caracelli, 1997, p. 10). Therefore, if in a research project issues such as particularity and generality are purposefully addressed from within each of these paradigms, then in the end more can be known about both specific participants and the larger social context they share with others. Consciously going back and forth between qualitative interpretation and quantitative analysis is explicitly seen as yielding important insights concerning the phenomena under study. Maxwell and Loomis (Chapter 9, this volume) note the "interactive" networked nature of dialectical research. In this research frame, this integration of multiple perspectives is seen as being better able to reflect social realities.

We found these two lenses, the pragmatic and dialectical, to be helpful in clarifying the technical data collection and interpretation decisions made by recent educational researchers. Specifically, we looked at Greene, Caracelli, and Graham's (1989) framework for discerning research decisions made for the purposes of triangulation, complementarity, development, initiation, and expansion. These purposes, driven by the researchers' search for convergence and/or elaboration, are further explained in Onwuegbuzie and Teddlie (Chaper 13, this volume). Initiation, or the seeking of new perspectives about the phenomenon under study, may arise during the evolution of the study. It is the purpose most open to the dialectical "self-conscious" use of mixed methods (see Maxwell & Loomis, Chapter 9, this volume).

Tashakkori and Teddlie's (1998) pragmatic framework for the mixed model typology is also purpose driven. Methods are chosen for exploratory or confirmatory purposes and lead to their six types of mixed methods studies and two types of multiphasic mixed model studies. Study type designations are based on the particular qualitative and/or quantitative nature of research components or stages (see Onwuegbuzie & Teddlie, Chapter 13, this volume).

It is interesting to note that, within the field of research in education, we have found that various researchers have understood the nature of the dialectical lens in different ways. For example, Onwuegbuzie and Teddlie (Chapter 13, this volume) find that the dialectical lens

has a sequential linear nature, contrary to the interactive nature seen by Maxwell and Loomis (Chapter 9, this volume). We find Maxwell and Loomis's vision to be closer to our own concerning what characterizes dialectical integration of the components of a mixed methods research project. We also find that mixed methods employed dialectically can best be seen as connected in, as Maxwell and Loomis state, a "network or web rather than a linear or cyclic sequence." The remainder of this chapter examines the status of mixed methods research in education today. We also direct interested readers to Chapters 9 and 13 in this handbook for other views of mixed methods research in education. Our exploration of the literature that follows uses these two lenses, the pragmatic and the dialectical, to bring some clarity to the current state of mixed methods research in education today.

The remainder of the chapter is divided into two sections. The first section examines research from four specific fields. In these fields, we found examples of researchers conducting research using both the pragmatic and dialectical lenses. Our analysis was guided by two questions: "What rationale do educational researchers provide for using mixed methods in their projects?" and "In the absence of explicit rationales, what justifications are evident for using mixed methods?" Each subsection is divided into these segments: a description of the field, current trends in research methodology, and examples of mixed methods studies.

In the second section of the chapter, we look through the dialectical lens at a national reading study and the repertory grid technique—a way of understanding knowledge construction. These examples illustrate research that contains explicit discussions of mixed methods use. The chapter concludes with observations and

TABLE 23.1   Studies Reviewed in First Section of Chapter

Content Area	Sample Study	Lens Used in Sample Study
HRD	Callahan (2000)	Pragmatic
HRD	May (1999)	Dialectical
HRD	Nurmi (1999)	Dialectical
HRD	Stein et al. (2000)	Pragmatic
HRD	Wentling & Palma-Rivas (2000)	Pragmatic
AE	Boshier (1991)	Pragmatic
AE	Cervero et al. (1986)	Pragmatic
AE	Courtenay et al. (2000)	Pragmatic
AE	Gordon & Sork (2001)	Pragmatic
AE	Shipp & McKenzie (1981)	Pragmatic
FLE	Govoni & Feyten (1999)	Dialectical
FLE	Kubota (1999)	Dialectical
FLE	Pappamihiel (1999)	Pragmatic
DE	Hillman (1999)	Pragmatic
DE	Kanuka & Anderson (1998)	Dialectical
DE	Kitchen & McDougall (1998-1999)	Pragmatic
DE	McIsaac et al. (1999)	Pragmatic

NOTE: HRD = human resource development; AE = adult education; FLE = foreign language education; DE = distance education.

suggestions to enhance mixed methods use in education.

◆ A View Through the Pragmatic and Dialectical Lenses

A view through the pragmatic and dialectical lenses focuses on how methodological decisions are described in research studies. We reviewed studies looking for explicit evidence of researchers making conscious decisions to mix methods. One purpose for mixing methods is to respond in a pragmatic way to the research question by using what works. Another purpose for mixing methods includes research design choices made with the specific intent to dialectically integrate both quantitative and qualitative methods. The four fields examined in this section are human resource development, adult education, foreign language education, and distance education. Table 23.1 indicates which studies are reviewed in this section.

HUMAN RESOURCE DEVELOPMENT

Human resource development (HRD) is an applied field primarily concerned with identifying and implementing interventions in the workplace. Interventions can occur at individual, group, and organizational levels to increase workplace learning and productivity. In HRD, mixed methods studies are rarely supported by literature from the mixed methods field. This lack of acknowledgment extends to meta-analyses of research practice. For example, Williams (2001) conducted a review of research methods to determine whether the field of HRD was following a similar developmental pattern to management science. Even though she clearly stated an interest in statistical methods only, her analysis noted the use of qualitative methods. Strikingly, there was no mention of mixed methods. Hixon and McClernon (1999) examined a wide range of HRD literature published in 1997, classifying the literature by using four types of research and "two tools (i.e., qualitative and quantitative)" (p. 899). Hixon and McClernon placed all of the articles and papers into one of two categories, qualitative or quantitative, and ignored the possibility of a category of mixed methods.

Hardy (1999) examined the methodological appropriateness of papers presented at the 1997 and 1998 Academy of Human Resource Development conferences. After setting the stage for the inclusion of mixed methods studies through his discussion of hybrid designs, he discussed his findings only in terms of the dichotomy of qualitative and quantitative categories, ignoring the continuum possible when mixing methods.

Hardy (1999) stated that qualitative and quantitative methods "are not mutually exclusive but can be viewed as interdependent" (p. 880). For Hardy, the role of qualitative methods is to develop new theory, expand conceptual frameworks, and enhance understanding of social realities, while quantitative methods should be used to test and generalize theory. The qualitative-quantitative linkage though a hybrid (mixed) design demonstrates the interactivity and interdependence of these

components of reflective inquiry. Hybrid designs use the strengths of both types and "can supplement and [complement] the strength of design and general robustness of the findings" (p. 881). He stated that the ultimate usefulness of hybrid designs is dependent on the comparative relationships of the results, conclusions, and contributions to the field, yet he advocated the use of multivariate studies to mature the field.

These reviews revealed that a general lack of awareness of mixed methods and the literature base that supports them are common in the field of HRD. In a related example, in the HRD research handbook there is no mention of mixed methods (Swanson & Holton, 1997). The chapter on qualitative methods includes a discussion of appropriate uses of qualitative methods that includes explaining statistical findings, developing quantitative instruments, and strengthening quantitative studies (Swanson, Watkins, & Marsick, 1997). These technical uses for mixing methods are not explored. The chapter on quantitative methods is not concerned with the appropriate use of quantitative methods but does mention that both methods are powerful when used together (Holton & Burnett, 1997). Political, philosophical, and technical rationales for using mixed methods (Greene & Caracelli, 1997) are missing from the research inquiry literature of HRD. The research studies discussed in this segment include two papers using mixed methods literature and three articles using mixed methods without regard to the mixed methods literature.

May (1999) and Nurmi (1999) used the mixed methods literature to support their research design decisions. May (1999) advocated using qualitative methods in transfer of training research. The study developed and tested a theory-based practice protocol and its effect on learning and transfer of learning. The quantitative component included a pretest-posttest control group design. Data on dependent measures were collected using a free-recall test, rating videotaped role-plays using a criterion checklist, and using a multirater 360-degree survey instrument to measure listening in the workplace. Analysis of covariance (ANCOVA) conducted on each dependent measure indicated significant differences between groups. Learning in both groups did not meet acceptable levels in terms of practical significance. The qualitative component included semistructured interviews of 36 of the 38 participants. The responses were coded and categorized according to underlying concepts. May's purpose was to pragmatically use the qualitative data to "illuminate quantitative data" (p. 1108).

Nurmi (1999) used mixed methods to evaluate an industrial development program in Finland. The research design decision making is philosophically based, using the work of Greene and Caracelli (1997), among others, to support mixing paradigms as well as methods. Nurmi (1999) wrote, "These paradigms were seen as complementary choices rather than competing methodological schools" (p. 554). An HRD program for new hires in a paper mill was evaluated using postpositivist quantitative surveys and multivariate analysis and naturalistic methods such as interviews and journals. Nurmi's study demonstrated complementarity (Greene et al., 1989) and consciously used mixed methods "to reach a deeper understanding" (Nurmi, 1999, p. 556).

Wentling and Palma-Rivas (2000) surveyed multinational organizations on the status of diversity initiatives, the dimensions of the initiatives, and the dynamics of corporate responses. Data collection used semistructured interviews and document analysis with a sample of eight randomly selected diversity managers. Inter-

views were content-analyzed, with emergent themes ranked by their frequency. Wentling and Palma-Rivas used quantitative data "to provide basic research evidence, while qualitative data were used to round out the picture and provide examples" (p. 40). Qualitative data were used for statistical inference as in a Type IV design (Tashakkori & Teddlie, 1998).

Stein, Rocco, and Goldenetz (2000) conducted an instrumental case study using the embedded single case study design to examine the phenomenon of aging workers in a university setting. Qualitative and quantitative data were collected. Structured interviews were used to enhance descriptive statistics obtained from documents produced and maintained by the human resource and training departments. The demographic information provided by the descriptive statistics was used to see whether increases in older workers meant that organizational policies were developed to address the needs of returning and remaining older workers. Interviews were conducted "to provide insights into the effects of the policies and procedures on older workers' lives" (p. 65). Without reference to the mixed methods literature, the authors identified triangulation as the rationale for using quantitative and qualitative data sources (Patton, 1990; Yin, 1994). Data analysis used two qualitative methods: grounded theory and comparative analysis by question.

Callahan (2000) conducted a case study of nonprofit organization members' purposes for managing their experience and expression of emotion. Data were collected using individual interviews, observations, surveys, and document analysis. Multiple methods of data collection were used for validity through triangulation (Patton, 1990). Callahan identified the study as "primarily qualitative . . . based on a naturalistic design" (p. 251). Data analysis of the interviews and correspondence used codes constructed from theory as the primary coding scheme. Within a primary code, open coding was used to arrive at broad concepts within a constructed code. Themes emerged within the primary coded categories. Analyses of variance (ANOVAs) were conducted on the survey data to ensure that the larger surveyed sample was not significantly different from the interviewed and surveyed sample. This is an example of a Type IV mixed method model (Tashakkori & Teddlie, 1998) or naturalistic inquiry that collects qualitative data and statistically analyzes it. In addition, colleagues familiar with the theory being explored coded a data set to establish internal validity. Seven scholars reviewed the findings and interpretations for consistency. Four participant researchers reviewed the final document for accuracy of interpretation. Even though Callahan described this study as primarily qualitative, she took many quantitative steps to ensure reliability and validity of the data.

Of the five studies examined here, only two (May, 1999; Nurmi, 1999) used the theoretical framework provided by the field of mixed methods. The other three studies used mixed methods to enhance evidence (Wentling & Palma-Rivas, 2000), for triangulation (Stein et al., 2000), and for triangulation and to ensure integrity (Callahan, 2000). The decisions to use mixed methods were both dialectical and pragmatic.

ADULT EDUCATION

Adult education has been defined as "activities intentionally designed for the purpose of bringing about learning among those whose age, social roles, or self-perception define them as adult" (Merriam & Brockett, 1997, p. 8). Knowles identified adult education as "the process of adults learning" and identified the combination of efforts toward this end as "a movement or field of social practice" (quoted in Merriam & Brockett, 1997, p. 8). Other terms such as *lifelong learning, continuing education,* and *nontraditional education* are associated with adult education.

Nearly two decades ago, Brookfield (1984) issued a challenge to adult education researchers to examine their "methodolatory" processes of generating knowledge. He criticized researchers for their overreliance on "the adoption of strictly defined and tightly administered quantitative measures in the investigation of self-directed learning" (p. 65). The principal text on adult education research reflects the momentum gained by qualitative research designs. Merriam and Simpson (2000) included one chapter on quantitative research, two chapters on qualitative research, and no chapters on mixed methods in their second edition of *A Guide to Research for Educators and Trainers of Adults.* They affirmed that "both types of data [quantitative and qualitative] are useful in the process of systematic inquiry related to adult education and training" (p. 147). They suggested that content analysis can be approached using both quantitative and qualitative methods. Merriam and Simpson, however, were silent on how quantitative and qualitative data collection and data analysis can be meaningfully mixed in the same study.

An examination of articles from the *Adult Education Quarterly* provides evidence of mixed methods in adult education research and a silence on rationales for their use. It is striking to note that very few authors identify their work as mixed methods in either the abstracts or the method sections of their articles. For example, Cervero, Rottet, and Dimmock (1986) indicated that they used both qualitative and quantitative data to evaluate a nursing continuing education program, but they did not identify a rationale for the use of historically polarized approaches. The authors cited in this subsection reflect the pragmatic approach in using both quantitative and qualitative research methods. As Tashakkori and Teddlie (1998) wrote, "Most researchers now use whatever method is appropriate for their studies instead of relying on one method exclusively" (pp. 5-6).

Identifying the pragmatic research design according to the mixed methods typology delineated by Tashakkori and Teddlie (1998) can enhance adult education research by locating the research within a pragmatic paradigm, justifying the use of mixed methods, and clarifying their use in the various stages of research (e.g., sampling, data collection, data analysis, inference). This reduces the conceptual confusion associated with mixing qualitative and quantitative approaches, as evidenced in the following examples.

Gordon and Sork (2001) replicated an earlier study about adult education practitioners' views on the need for a code of ethics. The survey methodology they employed included both closed-ended and open-ended questions. The answers to the closed-ended questions were statistically analyzed using descriptive statistics, chi-square tests, and one-way ANOVA tests. "Responses to open-ended questions were categorized and frequency counts made for each category" (p. 206). The results of the study included both findings of statistical significance and descriptions of ethical situations encountered by practitioners. This study is a parallel mixed model or Type VII study. Two stages of the investigation, data collection and data analysis, used both qualitative and quantitative approaches.

Cervero et al. (1986) tested a framework for the relationship between nursing continuing education and job perfor-

mance. Cervero et al. used quantitative and qualitative data collection and analysis. The quantitative data collection used a survey. A 74-item quality assurance review was used to score the dependent variable, and rating scores for the independent variables were taken. A hierarchical ANOVA was conducted at 1 week and 6 months to explain the variance in nursing performance. The three independent variables were attitudes toward nursing practice, intent to implement program goals, and program evaluation index. The attitude variable was the strongest at 1 week (25% of variance). At 6 months, all of the variables together, including mentors' performance, accounted for only 21% of the variance. The qualitative data collection "asked the nurses in the hospital to give [their] explanations for the [statistical] findings" (p. 82). Three themes emerged and were supported by the data from questionnaires and groups. This sequential mixed model study (Tashakkori & Teddlie, 1998) had two distinct phases: one with quantitative inquiry and operations and one with qualitative inquiry and analysis.

Boshier (1991) tested the validity of a motivation scale using both qualitative and quantitative data collection. Quantitative data were collected and statistically analyzed to determine predictive validity of the Education Participation Scale (Form A). The author gave no references for including the qualitative component and did not justify its insertion into the study. The use of qualitative data collection (i.e., interviewing) assisted Boshier in developing additional motivational test items that he later validated and used to predict outcomes. The study clearly used "what worked" to answer the question without an articulated theoretical framework.

A study by Courtenay, Merriam, Reeves, and Baumgartner (2000) was a subtle variation of a Type II mixed method study that was driven by research questions. In this study, the authors interviewed members from a sample they studied 2 years earlier to see whether their perspective transformation was stable and to identify ways in which they continued to make meaning in their lives. The authors identified the follow-up study of adults with HIV as qualitative and "primarily inductive"; however, one part of their study was to test Mezirow's (1991) theory that perspective transformation was stable. They used Glaser and Strauss (1967) to justify the insertion of a quantitative approach (Courtenay et al., 2000, p. 106).

Some of the articles reviewed predate the literature on mixing methods yet show evidence of the use of mixed methods to answer research questions. Shipp and McKenzie (1981) used both quantitative and qualitative designs in their study of demographic and psychographic characteristics of adult learners and nonlearners. Quantitative data were collected through structured indirect interviews and were statistically analyzed. A qualitative summary or demographic profile was written for the learner and the nonlearner. This study reversed the usual trend of quantifying qualitative data and qualitatively analyzed quantitative information. The authors did not identify their use of mixed methods in either the abstract or the method section. Shipp and McKenzie used quantitative data to create profiles of adult learners and nonlearners. They effectively answered the question about similarities and differences of adult learners and nonlearners as well as characteristics for program planning. The quantitative information established demographic characteristics of learners and nonlearners. From this information, qualitative profiles were compiled to illustrate the similarities and differences (Tashakkori & Teddlie, 1998).

These examples of adult education research highlighted the silent use of the mixed methods design to answer research questions. The studies reviewed here successfully addressed their research questions by using "what works." Articulating the mixed methods design and clarifying the various stages in which mixed methods were used can strengthen the power of studies, inferences, and conclusions.

FOREIGN LANGUAGE EDUCATION

Foreign language education (FLE) is concerned with the learning of languages after the primary language has been acquired. This broad field of study includes second language acquisition, bilingual education, teaching English to speakers of other languages, and applied linguistics.

Edwards (1985) argued that educational research must not only investigate the cognitive aspects of learning but also explore the affective issues related to education. Some FLE researchers have responded to this call by combining qualitative and quantitative methods so as to provide a more accurate multidimensional view of education and the learner. In the field of FLE, Johnson (1992) noted a preference for research that links numbers to "highly personal meanings . . . depending on [the participants'] experiences, background knowledge, [and] current interests" (p. 213). FLE has begun to turn to mixed methods so as to both measure and understand culturally and individually grounded learner differences.

Bilingual education advocates are insisting on a more complete description of classrooms so as to conduct adequate program evaluations (Horst et al., 1980). Mixed methods could be used to meet this need by producing a more complete description through the "use [of] whatever method is appropriate" to answer research questions (Tashakkori & Teddlie, 1998, p. 5).

An important SLA textbook by Larsen-Freeman and Long (1991) discussed qualitative and quantitative research paradigms and methods. It argued that there is no "neat separation" between qualitative and quantitative paradigms, nor should the typical attributes and methods associated with each be regarded as exclusive to that paradigm. A study's purpose or research question should determine the method to be used. "There is no reason why the attributes could not be interchanged so that combination or hybrid methodologies result" (p. 23).

Some foreign language educators have expressed concern about the inadequacy of their training in statistical procedures (Lazaraton, Riggenbach, & Ediger, 1987). Nevertheless, FLE does not advocate a complete turn to qualitative methods, especially when qualitative methods are used as a substitute for quantitative methods. Mixing methods that bring together the strengths of both quantitative and qualitative methods will enhance research in the field. According to Tarone (cited in Cumming, 1994), "Researchers typically agree, in theory, that both qualitative and quantitative methodologies are essential to the accurate description and analysis of learner language" (p. 676). In response, many journals have chosen to print more articles that take advantage of mixed methods designs. Lazaraton (2000) reviewed the four principal journals in the language learning field and found that more than one tenth of all articles reflected mixed methods practices. While still small, this represents a great increase in the number of qualitative and mixed methods studies found through 1985.

In FLE, we have seen that the singular implementation of either quantitative or qualitative processes can on occasion leave a researcher wishing for more comprehen-sive results. A review of recent mixed methods studies in FLE reveals that decisions to mix reflect Greene and Caracelli's (1997) technical-level concerns.

Pappamihiel (1999) found that language anxiety did have a measurable effect on learners of English, but she was not able to adequately investigate that effect until she introduced qualitative methods. This is an example of a dominant-less dominant sequential mixed methods design (Tashakkori & Teddlie, 1998). For the first phase, she adapted a Likert scale survey that measured anxiety in college students' language learning. Using ANCOVA and factor analyses on the survey data revealed the presence of a difference in the source of language anxiety of English-as-a-second-language and mainstream Mexican high school students. Focus groups were conducted to better understand this difference in anxiety. Students wrote responses to five questions, which formed the basis of the focus group discussions. A thematic analysis of the focus group transcripts was conducted. The quantitative analysis pointed broadly to a difference, while the qualitative data enabled the researcher to discern the nature of the difference. ANCOVA and factor analyses provided a description of participants' anxiety levels, and the focus groups provided the participants' rationales for why and when such anxiety occurred.

Complementarity (Greene et al., 1989) helps to explain Kubota's (1999) decision to combine quantitative data and analysis with qualitative data informally gathered and analyzed. Pre- and post-study questionnaires were used to assess anxiety, desire to learn, and perceived usefulness of computers in learning Japanese. A *t* test was used to examine whether the change in scores for each statement was significant. Students provided written comments on their learning experience and kept journals. The researcher recorded observations and reflective notes. Kubota specifically indicated that the qualitative information echoed and elaborated on the questionnaire results, bringing out other aspects (e.g., student motivation) that she had not expected. This use of mixed methods allowed for an elaboration of the questionnaire results (Greene et al., 1989).

Govoni and Feyten (1999) used an experimental design collecting quantitative and qualitative data during the pre- and posttreatment phases. The purpose of the study was to confirm whether training resulted in increased teacher awareness of proficiency-oriented curriculum. A purposeful sample of teachers was selected based on qualitative data collected through a pre-study questionnaire. Data were collected from teachers' self-evaluations and interviews, students' questionnaires, exams, and observations of classrooms. Quantitative data were analyzed using ANOVA. Qualitative analysis was not discussed. In this case, the combination of methods allowed the researchers to triangulate data collection.

Currently, there seems to be little explicit discussion of the theoretical basis applied for the combined use of qualitative and quantitative methods in FLE. Few researchers have overtly stated that they chose a mixed methodology over singularly qualitative or quantitative analyses. In fact, they usually described their studies as a use of the two rather than as a combination.

DISTANCE EDUCATION

Distance education has evolved from a multitude of disciplines, including education, educational technology, computer science, sociology, economics, and psychology. It is also a field that is in a continuous rapid state of change with the advent of increasingly sophisticated technology that demands alterations in teaching practices and learner experiences. Currently, there is more of a focus on asynchronous learning using computer-mediated communication (CMC) systems and virtual classrooms. Traditional classrooms incorporate both teaching and learning roles within one environment, whereas students who participate in distance learning must construct their own learning environment separate from a teacher.

Research in distance education demands an acknowledgment of the environmental factors that exist separating teacher and students. Fraser (1998) stated,

> The assessment of learning environments and research applications [has] involved a variety of quantitative and qualitative methods, and an important accomplishment within the field has been the productive combination of quantitative and qualitative research methods. (p. 7)

Gunawardena, Lowe, and Carabajal (2000) critically reflected on both the models and methods used by researchers to evaluate online learning. They suggested that the use of a single technique for analyzing online learning experiences is inadequate and that a mixed methods approach is called for in studying online learning networks.

A large number of the articles that have been published in distance education either are developmental in nature or espouse the virtues of one particular instructional program or software tool rather than reporting on experimental research studies. Those experimental studies that have been conducted and published are a small percentage of the articles found in international and online academic journals from 1997 to 1999 (for an annotated bibliography, see www.ed.psu.edu/acsde/annbib/annbib.asp). Nevertheless, a review of the literature in the field of distance education reveals that a great majority of the experimental studies use either a quantitative or a qualitative method of data collection and analysis. This pattern continues, with very few studies currently using both qualitative and quantitative methods.

Theoretical frameworks that guide distance education research, and specifically online and virtual learning, revolve primarily around constructivist thinking and pedagogy (Feyten & Nutta, 1999). This includes a Vygotskyan understanding that knowledge is actively constructed through the relationship between teacher and learners. Knowledge construction depends on what is already known, the experiences of individual learners, and the interpretation of those experiences by individuals and groups. Garrison (1989) described the importance of examining and giving value to the perspectives, ideas, and knowledge bases of both teachers and learners. The idea that knowledge is generated through social intercourse and that learners actively construct meaning is central to the kinds of research questions that distance education researchers are currently pursuing.

The great majority of these issues demand an understanding of contextual factors and in-depth analysis of noncountable data. This has led to an increase in the number of studies in which qualitative methodology has become the methodology of choice. Thorough examinations are needed of distance students using computer interactions through the use of qualitative data that "thickly describe" these students' perspectives (Eastmond, 1995, p. 189). However, some researchers have chosen to include both quantitative and qualitative measures in their studies so as to enhance their research findings and provide more thorough explanations of their data. Several of these studies that

have deliberately used mixed methods are discussed next.

Kitchen and McDougall (1998-1999) conducted a study that examined graduate students' perceptions of the educational value of collaborative learning while taking part in an online course. This study used a survey questionnaire designed to capture information on demographics, user skills, satisfaction, perceptions, and learning styles for quantitative analysis. The survey was conducted through semistructured interviews that provided insights into users' perceptions of the usefulness of collaborative learning strategies, thus helping to interpret survey findings. This survey was quantitatively analyzed, and the results were used in conjunction with subsequent qualitative data collection and analysis of students from two of the small groups studied. Data from the interviews were also compared with other data sources such as a reflective paper and computer conference transcripts. The researchers stated that they used both methods of data analysis in the tradition of triangulation of data so as to strengthen their findings.

Kanuka and Anderson (1998) conducted an exploratory multimethod evaluation study of an online forum. Methods used in the study included a survey, a Likert scale questionnaire, forum postings, and telephone interviews. A constructivist interaction analysis model developed by Gunawardena, Lowe, and Anderson (1997) provided the phases by which the forum transcriptions were analyzed producing the codes. The researchers discussed discrepancies in their coding and determined a single code for each message. Grounded theory was used to explore the observed patterns of interactions among study participants. This allowed researchers to reassess and recategorize postings as needed. Interviews were used to support the coded transcript findings.

Quantitative data were derived from the coded transcripts and the questionnaire. Both types of analyses reveal important data on the nature and structure of online formats, reflecting a complementarity research goal (Greene et al., 1989). This study also appears to be one of the few within the field that explicitly brought both constructivist and postpositivist paradigms together within a single study. As Greene and Caracelli (1997) pointed out, this response to philosophical-level decision making is on the cutting edge of mixed methods research.

Hillman (1999) developed a software coding system to analyze interaction patterns in face-to-face (FTF) and CMC courses. Public interactions occurring within the courses were recorded and transcribed. A total of 52,681 sentences were recorded. After each sentence was coded, the numbers of sentences from each course were standardized by percentages and plotted on graphs to reveal differences between the FTF and CMC interaction patterns. The researcher expressed dissatisfaction with interaction studies that merely count words or characters in interactions and provide purely quantitative data. The data were analyzed through a system that both counts interactions and qualitatively codes these according to purpose, means, and content. This study used qualitative data analysis to reveal additional information regarding quantified interaction information. As discourse analysis begins to be used to examine asynchronous interaction, qualitative methods bring a fresh perspective to the research. This reflects Greene et al.'s (1989) initiation purpose for mixed methods studies.

McIsaac, Blocher, Mahes, and Vrasidas (1999) conducted a study that compared student and teacher perceptions of interaction in CMC. Doctoral students engaged in collaborative research projects using CMC were the study participants, and their engagement along with faculty in educational research was explored. Quantitative data on user interaction statistics, such as numbers of postings, were collected in this study. A software package was used that provided statistical data in the form of ASCII text files. A review of the quantitative data by the doctoral students led to additional research questions; "about social context and interaction, [they] recognized that qualitative data analysis would be necessary" (p. 124). Qualitative data, including message archives and logs of student-instructor chats and participant interviews, were collected. The qualitative data in this study provided for a deeper exploration and understanding of quantitative results. This sequential study is an example of using mixed methods for the purpose of development (Greene et al., 1989).

It seems clear that the sorts of research questions and topics of interest that researchers in the field of distance education, and particularly online learning, are pursuing lend themselves to a mixed methods approach in data collection and analysis. This type of an approach generates a broad view of the topic while allowing for a more thorough and comprehensive analysis of study data. Furthermore, studies that use both qualitative and quantitative data inevitably lead to more questions and further investigations in the field.

◆ Narrowing the Focus

As we reviewed studies looking for explicit evidence of researchers making conscious decisions to mix methods, we found that some research contained explicit discussion of the intent of the researchers in choosing both qualitative and quantitative methodologies. Unlike pragmatists who argue that method and paradigm can properly be considered separately, Greene and Caracelli (1997) explicitly argued, "The various methods *are* linked to different inquiry paradigms" (p. 7, italics in original). In describing research where the researchers have used this dialectical lens to make research decisions, they argued that the decision is based on the "underlying premise" that "each paradigm offers a meaningful and legitimate way of knowing and understanding" (p. 7). We now turn to studies in education where the explanation for mixing methods includes a discussion of the benefits of mixing paradigms.

Several of these investigations were small-scale studies undertaken to elicit and represent "personal content knowledge" that individuals had about various aspects of mathematics. One was an ongoing national study undertaken to assess the quality of instruction in beginning teachers' classrooms. The International Reading Association (IRA) initiated this study for the purpose of documenting the nature and quality of the teaching of reading that was occurring in the classrooms of recent graduates of teacher education programs that the IRA identified as having "high-quality programs." This study was undertaken in 1998, a time when claims were being made in the public sphere that teacher preparation was inadequate and that teaching reading was substandard. As the national political spotlight was turned on children's reading achievement, the board of directors of the IRA launched this study in part to establish the profession's position as to what constitutes effective and exemplary practice in reading instruction. Greene and Caracelli's (1997) research decision framework described political-level decisions as those concerned with the broad-based purposes of specific research projects. The social context of this large-scale study speaks to an overarching political-level decision by the

IRA researchers. We believe that this study also illustrates an implicit philosophical-level decision through the claim—being made from within the field of reading—to legitimate knowledge about what constitutes good teacher preparation and practices for teachers of reading. For this professional association, both the interpretivist and postpositivist paradigms grounded this knowledge.

By this claim, we mean that quantitative data gathered, analyzed, and used to draw inferences in ways generally connected with the postpositivist paradigm are being integrated with data gathered, interpreted, and used to draw interpretivist inferences. A committee of experts selected eight elementary education sites of excellence in reading preparation (based on a vigorous application process). Then, in the first stage of this multiphase study, aspects of reading programs were identified and rated. Beginning teachers from these programs were interviewed at multiple times during their first year. During the second year, researchers from these sites of excellence in reading teacher education (SERTE) collected classroom observation data on both these beginning teachers and matched teachers in the same school from other preparation programs. Quantitative data are being gathered through observations of student interactions with text, interviews with students and beginning teachers, and teachers and researchers inventorying the texts present in the classrooms. The third stage will conclude with assessments of the students' reading abilities and behaviors.

A more sharply focused look at one aspect of this study will reveal the way it "tacks" between paradigms. Common crucial features of reading teacher education programs were ascertained through the collaborative efforts of the SERTE representatives. Their knowledge claims were emic. As reading specialists, they brought together their particular insights, observations, and analyses of their own and each other's programs so as to construct a theoretical framework for further study of the features that characterize good programs for preparing teachers of reading. While this aspect of the study may be seen as following constructivist guidelines, other aspects display a more postpositivist influence.

The results of text inventories, as well as interview and observation protocols, call for gathering both quantitative and qualitative data. For example, observers will be asked to use an observation protocol with a list of 17 different types of texts to count and a prescribed rubric to categorize the number and quality of materials found in the classroom. The quantitative data will be statistically analyzed, looking at patterns and correlational analyses between the major components. There are plans to use hierarchical regression models to explore the impact of the variables under study and the context variables (e.g., the socioeconomic status of students) on students' achievement. This analysis is guided more by the search for generality, representativeness, and causality that characterizes the postpositivist paradigm. The "values and interests" (Greene & Caracelli, 1997, p. 13) of the two traditions both are clearly present in this study.

This is not surprising given that within the field, reading itself is viewed as situated cognition. Therefore, assessment of individuals and research into the reading process must be multidimensional. Historically, by the 1970s the field of reading instruction and reading research began to change its theoretical perspective from behaviorism to cognitive science. As psycholinguistics came into being, concepts such as schemata (the knowledge structures in one's mind) and metacognition (thinking about one's own thinking) changed

research and practice in reading. During the 1980s, sociocultural considerations (Gaffney & Anderson, 2000) started to change the field through the influence of social constructivists such as Vygotsky. Since then, reading researchers have focused on studying reading as a multifaceted complex process of constructing meaning in context. The context includes the physio-, socio-, and/or psycholinguistic background of the reader.

Schema theory offers research in education a firm theoretical basis for mixing methods and paradigms. Its psychological grounding is especially valuable to educational researchers concerned with ascertaining the nature and level of people's knowledge. The related tool of *repertory grid technique* (RGT) has roots in both constructivist and postpositivist paradigms. Researchers using RGT are making a philosophical-level decision to integrate methods of data gathering, analysis, and inference from both paradigms. RGT has the potential to be used more extensively across educational fields because it so clearly addresses basic epistemological concerns about what it means to know something.

Knowledge as recorded in external means (e.g., books) and knowledge as a psychological entity (i.e., as stored in human memory) are two different things. The tension between the inherent subjective nature and the need for intersubjective representation of human knowledge resembles the distinction between empiricist/positivist and constructivist paradigms in education as described by Tashakkori and Teddlie (1998). Purely qualitative attempts of eliciting human knowledge (e.g., using *interview* or *think-aloud* techniques) have been criticized as being limited in utility because there is an unavoidable interpretive gap between readers and the data. Quantitative attempts (e.g., standardized tests) have been criticized for not being able to tap into the structural complexity of human knowledge (Loef, 1990). RGT provides a technique for combining the relative strengths of qualitative and quantitative methods of knowledge elicitation while minimizing the respective disadvantages.

Although some variations exist, typically RGT involves eliciting an individual's constructs by presenting triplets of events (termed *elements*) and inviting the individual to indicate the similarities and differences among the elements. RGT can be thought of as producing a map of an individual's knowledge construction system (Loef, 1990).

After the constructs are elicited, the individual rates the elements for each construct by using a Likert-type scale to indicate how much the construct characterizes the element. This provides a measure of the distance between each element and others in relation to a construct. A two-dimensional matrix of rankings formed by elements in one dimension and constructs in the other can be used for a variety of quantitative statistical methods of clustering such as *additive tree structures* (Sattath & Tversky, 1977). Clustering methods can provide visual representations of how an individual organizes various constructs in relation to the elements supplied.

Examples of RGT studies will make this process clearer. Loef (1990) used this technique to represent elementary school teachers' knowledge in teaching mathematics, and Alacaci (1998) used it to represent the knowledge that expert and novice statisticians used to statistically model applied research situations. In the latter study, Alacaci found that there were no significant differences between experts and novices in the extensiveness of the knowledge they used. However, the organization of the constructs elicited from experts and novices showed interesting dif-

ferences; the constructs that are important for facilitating statistical modeling of applied problem situations were situated in higher levels of the hierarchical organization of experts' knowledge as compared with those of novices. The superior performance of experts was attributed to this difference in knowledge organization.

In her study of teacher knowledge, Loef (1990) attempted to understand elementary school teachers' knowledge of arithmetic problems and how this knowledge relates with their pedagogical actions. The purpose was to compare and contrast teachers' knowledge with different levels of success in implementing an innovative program drawing on children's knowledge in solving arithmetic problems.

Drawing on recent cognitive research on teacher knowledge, Loef (1990) started with the assumption that teachers' knowledge is composed of constructs, these constructs are organized into systems, and there are relationships indicated among the constructs. She designed 12 arithmetic problems of addition and subtraction involving different semantic situations (compare, part-part-whole, separate, and join [see Carpenter, Fennema, Peterson, & Carrey, 1988]) and 11 teaching-learning scenarios using arithmetic problems that varied along certain dimensions. Loef interviewed eight teachers, four of whom were successful in implementing an innovative program that drew on students' thinking and four of whom were less successful. She interviewed the teachers three times. In the first interview, the teachers were asked to compare and contrast (triads of) the arithmetic problems from the point of view of "how their students would solve them and view them differently." In the second interview, the teachers were asked to compare and contrast the problems "in regards to their teaching of addition and subtraction and the actions taken in teaching them." In the third interview, the participants were given dyads of scenarios involving classroom situations in addition and subtraction and were asked to compare and contrast them. The three interviews aimed to elicit teachers' content knowledge, pedagogical content knowledge, and knowledge in action, respectively. The teachers filled in rating matrices in the second phase of the interviews. Loef then performed cluster analyses on the matrices to reveal the organization of constructs elicited for each type of teacher knowledge as well as the clusters of problems and scenarios. She then applied fuzzy logic to each of the grids to show the strength and direction of relationships of implications among the constructs (Gaines & Shaw, 1986).

Loef (1990) found systematic differences between the knowledge bases of teachers who are successful in implementing the innovative program and those of teachers who are less successful. The researcher was able to describe differences between the ways in which more and less successful teachers both identified the problems and perceived the scenarios. Her inferences were made possible by a careful classification of the elicited constructs, by an interpretive analysis of the organization of constructs and elements, and by the implicational relations among the constructs.

RGT is a flexible and powerful tool that combines the relative strengths of the qualitative interview technique with the rigor of the quantitative cluster analysis and additive tree structure techniques. It enables researchers to elicit and represent an individual's knowledge and to aggregate across individuals along parameters of knowledge. As such a research tool, RGT clearly demonstrates how employing constructivist and postpositivist paradigms dialectically within a single research project can obtain sound interpretations of multifaceted data (Greene & Caracelli,

1997). When the purpose is *development* of the topic (Greene et al., 1989), educational researchers seeking to better understand the knowledge held by both learners and teachers may quantitize the qualitative data they collect through using the RGT. RGT represents rational choices about the deliberate use of both paradigms. This sound philosophical-level decision making illustrates an integral aspect of conducting research that is an example of good social science.

◆ Implications for Education Research

Little explicit discussion of research design decision making or theoretical support for design components was observed in the examples used in this chapter. This lack of seemingly informed decision making often included a lack of information on what qualitative analysis techniques were being used in a study. The authors may have had sound rationales for their choices, but this level of detail did not make it into the method sections of their articles. This has larger implications for education as a field as we strive to have our research taken seriously by other disciplines. So long as our journal editors and manuscript reviewers do not hold all work to a higher standard, the rigor of educational research will continue to be questioned.

Many research questions and topics of interest lend themselves to mixed methods approaches. Yet we lack training in using mixed methods in all but the most rudimentary ways (e.g., triangulation). There is a need for research courses that demonstrate quantitative and qualitative data collection and analysis techniques, followed by instruction in how and when to mix methods in the various stages of a research design. We hope that this will lead to a greater sophistication when making thoughtful design decisions at the technical level and will encourage design decisions to be made at the philosophical and political levels.

In conclusion, many of the educational research reports we reviewed did not discuss the broader philosophical- and political-level decisions that ultimately shape research agendas. They confined their discussions concerning research design and data interpretation to descriptions of technical-level decisions about "methods and procedures" (Greene & Caracelli, 1997, p. 6). These discussions were often cursory, and they seldom extended into discussions of how qualitative data were analyzed.

At the same time, however, evidence that some researchers are beginning to seriously address educational research's larger philosophical- and political-level decisions encourages us. We support Greene and Caracelli's (1997) admonition that to be doing good science, researchers using mixed methods must begin to more thoughtfully address the broader level decisions. To use Greene and Caracelli's term, on the political level, these researchers should be seeking the development of a body of strong *defensible* research about education. Mixed methods advocates should be leading the academic discussions about the ontological and epistemological issues of what can be known about "the social world and our ability to know" (p. 5). As Greene and Caracelli pointed out, "The underlying rationale for mixed-method inquiry is to understand more fully, to generate deeper and broader insights, [and] to develop important knowledge claims that respect a wider range of interests and perspectives" (p. 7). Mixed methods research that emerges from this discourse has the potential to be more use-ful to people making policy decisions about education and society.

■ References

Alacaci, C. (1998). *Understanding knowledge structures in inferential statistics.* Unpublished doctoral dissertation, University of Pittsburgh.

Boshier, R. (1991). Psychometric properties of the alternate form of the Education Participation Scale. *Adult Education Quarterly, 41*(3), 150-167.

Brookfield, S. (1984). Self-directed adult learning: A critical paradigm. *Adult Education Quarterly, 35*(2), 59-71.

Callahan, J. L. (2000). Emotion management and organizational functions: A case study of patterns in a not-for-profit organization. *Human Resource Development Quarterly, 11*, 245-267.

Campbell, D. T. (1969). Reforms as experiments. *American Psychologist, 24*, 409-429.

Carpenter, T., Fennema, E., Peterson, P., & Carrey, S. (1988). Representation of addition and subtraction word problems. *Journal for Research in Mathematics Education, 19*, 345-357.

Cervero, R. M., Rottet, S., & Dimmock, K. H. (1986). Analyzing the effectiveness of continuing professional education at the workplace. *Adult Education Quarterly, 36*(2), 78-85.

Cook, T. D. (1985). Postpositivist critical multiplism. In R. L. Shotland and M. M. Mark (Eds.), *Social Science and Social Policy.* Thousand Oaks, CA: Sage.

Courtenay, B. C., Merriam, S., Reeves, P., & Baumgartner, P. (2000). Perspective transformation overtime: A 2 year follow-up study of HIV-positive adults. *Adult Education Quarterly, 50*(2), 102-119.

Cumming, A. (1994). Alternatives in TESOL research: Descriptive, interpretive, and ideological orientations. *TESOL Quarterly, 21*, 263-277.

Eastmond, D. E. (1995). *Alone but together: Computer conferencing in adult education.* Cresskill, NJ: Hampton Press.

Edwards, J. (1985). *Language, society, and identity.* New York: Basil Blackwell.

Feyten, C. M., & Nutta, J. W. (1999). *Virtual instruction: Issues and insights from an international perspective.* Englewood, CO: Libraries Unlimited.

Fraser, B. J. (1998). Classroom environment instruments: Development, validity, and applications. *Learning Environments Research, 1,* 1-5.

Gaffney, J. S., & Anderson, R. C. (2000). Trends in reading research in the United States: Changing intellectual currents over three decades. In M. L. Kamil, P. B. Mosenthal, P. D. Pearson, & R. Barr (Eds.), *Handbook of reading research* (Vol. 3, pp. 53-74). Mahwah, NJ: Lawrence Erlbaum.

Gaines, B. R., & Shaw, M. L. G. (1986). Induction of inference rules for expert systems. *Fuzzy Sets and Systems, 18,* 315-328.

Garrison, D. R. (1989). Distance education. In S. B. Merriam & P. M. Cunningham (Eds.), *Handbook of adult and continuing education* (pp. 221-232). San Francisco: Jossey-Bass.

Geertz, C. (1979). From the native's point of view: On the nature of anthropological understanding. In P. Rabinow & W. Sullivan (Eds.), *Interpretive social science.* Berkeley: University of California Press.

Glaser, B. G., & Strauss, A. L. (1967). *The discovery of grounded theory: Strategies for qualitative research.* Chicago: AVC.

Gordon, W., & Sork, T. J. (2001). Ethical issues and codes of ethics: Views of adult education practitioners in Canada and the United States. *Adult Education Quarterly, 51*(3), 202-218.

Govoni, J. M., & Feyten, C. M. (1999). Effects of the ACTFL-OPI-type training on student performance, instructional methods, and classroom materials in the secondary foreign language classroom. *Foreign Language Annuals, 32*(2), 189-204.

Greene, J. C., & Caracelli, V. J. (1997). Defining and describing the paradigm issue in mixed-method evaluation. In J. C. Greene & V. J. Caracelli (Eds.), *Advances in mixed-method evaluation: The challenges and benefits of integrating diverse paradigms* (New Directions for Evaluation, No. 74, pp. 5-17). San Francisco: Jossey-Bass.

Greene, J. C., Caracelli, V. J., & Graham, W. D. (1989). Toward a conceptual framework for mixed-method evaluation designs. *Educational Evaluation and Policy Analysis, 11,* 255-274.

Gunawardena, L., Lowe, C., & Anderson, T. (1997). Interaction analysis of a global online debate and the development of a constructivist interaction analysis model for computer conferencing. *Journal of Educational Computing Research, 17,* 395-429.

Gunawardena, C., Lowe, C., & Carabajal, K. (2000). Evaluating online learning models and methods. In *Society for Information Technology and Teacher Education: International conference—Proceedings of SITE 2000.* San Diego: Society for Information Technology and Teacher Education.

Hardy, C. R. (1999). A discussion of the methodological appropriateness of research presented in the AHRD proceedings: A strategic perspective for journey management. In K. P. Kuchinke (Ed.), *Academy of Human Resource Development 1999 conference proceedings* (pp. 880-887). Baton Rouge, LA: Academy of Human Resource Development.

Hillman, D. (1999). A new method for analyzing patterns of interaction. *American Journal of Distance Education, 13*(2), 37-47.

Hixon, J. A., & McClernon, T. R. (1999). The status of HRD research literature in 1997. In K. P. Kuchinke (Ed.), *Academy of Human Resource Development 1999 conference proceedings* (pp. 897-902). Baton Rouge, LA: Academy of Human Resource Development.

Holton, E. F., & Burnett, M. F. (1997). Quantitative research methods. In R. A. Swanson & E. F. Holton (Eds.), *Human resource development research handbook: Linking research and practice* (pp. 65-87). San Francisco: Berrett-Koehler.

Horst, D. P., Douglas, D. E., Friendly, L. D., Johnson, D. M., Luber, L. M., McKay, M., Nava, H. G., Peistrup, A. M., Roberts, A. O. H., & Valdez, A. (1980). *An evaluation of project information packages as used for the diffusion of bilingual projects* (Vol. 2, Report No. VR-460). Mountain View, CA: RMC Research Corporation. (ERIC Document Reproduction Service No. ED 193 955)

Johnson, D. (1992). *Approaches to research in second language learning.* New York: Longman.

Kanuka, H., & Anderson, T. (1998). Online social interchange, discord, and knowledge construction. *Journal of Distance Education, 13*(2), 57-74.

Kitchen, D., & McDougall, D. (1998-1999). Collaborative learning on the Internet. *Journal of Educational Technology Systems, 27,* 245-258.

Kubota, R. (1999). Word processing and WWW projects in a college Japanese language class. *Foreign Language Annals, 32*(2), 205-218.

Larsen-Freeman, D., & Long, M. (1991). *An introduction to second language research.* New York: Longman.

Lazaraton, A. (2000). Current trends in research methodology and statistics in applied linguistics. *TESOL Quarterly, 34,* 175-181.

Lazaraton, A., Riggenbach, H., & Ediger, A. (1987). Forming a discipline: Applied linguistics' literacy in research methodology and statistics. *TESOL Quarterly, 21,* 263-277.

Lincoln, Y. S., & Guba, E. G. (1985). *Naturalistic inquiry.* Beverly Hills, CA: Sage.

Loef, M. M. (1990). *Understanding teachers' knowledge about building instruction on children's mathematical thinking: Applications of a personal construct approach* (AAC 9033785). Unpublished doctoral dissertation, University of Wisconsin–Madison.

May, G. L. (1999). Mixed methods: The value of the qualitative perspective in transfer of training research. In K. P. Kuchinke (Ed.), *Academy of Human Resource Development 1999 conference proceedings* (pp. 1108-1115). Baton Rouge, LA: Academy of Human Resource Development.

McIsaac, M. S., Blocher, J. M., Mahes, V., & Vrasidas, C. (1999). Student and teacher perceptions of interaction in online computer-mediated communication. *Educational Media International, 36*(2), 121-128.

Merriam, S. B., & Brockett, R. G. (1997). *The profession and practice of adult education.* San Francisco: Jossey-Bass.

Merriam, S. B., & Simpson, E. L. (2000). *A guide to research for educators and trainers of adults* (2nd ed.). Malabar, FL: Krieger.

Mezirow, J. (1991). *Transformative dimensions of adult learning.* San Francisco: Jossey-Bass.

Nurmi, V. (1999). The mixed-method evaluation in HRD: A description of methods applied in the industrial development program. In K. P. Kuchinke (Ed.), *Academy of Human Resource Development 1999 conference proceedings* (pp. 554-561). Baton Rouge, LA: Academy of Human Resource Development.

Pappamihiel, N. E. (1999). *The development of an English language anxiety assessment instrument for Mexican middle school English language learners.* Unpublished doctoral dissertation, University of Texas at Austin.

Patton, M. Q. (1988). Paradigms and pragmatism. In D. M. Fetterman (Ed.), *Qualitative approaches to evaluation in education: The silent scientific revolution* (pp. 116-137). New York: Praeger.

Patton, M. Q. (1990). *Qualitative evaluation and research methods* (2nd ed.). Newbury Park, CA: Sage.

Sattath, S., & Tversky, A. (1977). Additive similarity trees. *Psychometrica, 42,* 319-345.

Shipp, T., & McKenzie, L. R. (1981). Adult learners and non-learners: Demographic characteristics as an indicator of psychographic characteristics. *Adult Education Quarterly, 31*(4), 187-198.

Stein, D., Rocco, T. S., & Goldenetz, K. A. (2000). Age and the university workplace: A case study of remaining, retiring, or returning older workers. *Human Resource Development Quarterly, 11,* 35-60.

Swanson, B. L., Watkins, K. E., & Marsick, V. J. (1997). Qualitative research methods. In R. A. Swanson & E. F. Holton (Eds.), *Human resource development research handbook: Linking research and practice* (pp. 88-113). San Francisco: Berrett-Koehler.

Swanson, R. A., & Holton, E. F. (Eds.). (1997). *Human resource development research handbook: Linking research and practice.* San Francisco: Berrett-Koehler.

Tashakkori, A., & Teddlie, C. (1998). *Mixed methodology: Combining qualitative and quantitative approaches* (Applied Social Research Methods, No. 46). Thousand Oaks, CA: Sage.

Tarone, E. (1994). Analysis of learners' language. In A. Cumming (Ed.), "Alternatives in TESOL Research: Description, Interpretive, and Ideological Orientations." *TESOL Quarterly, 28*(4, Winter), 676-678.

Wentling, R. M., & Palma-Rivas, N. (2000). Current status of diversity initiatives in selected multinational corporations. *Human Resource Development Quarterly, 11,* 35-60.

Williams, H. A. (2001). A critical review of research and statistical methodologies within *Human Resource Development Quarterly, Academy of Management Journal,* and *Personnel Psychology,* 1995-1999. In O. A. Aliaga (Ed.), *Academy of Human Resource Development 2001 conference proceedings* (pp. 841-847). Baton Rouge, LA: Academy of Human Resource Development.

Yin, R. K. (1994). *Case study research: Design and methods* (3rd ed.). Thousand Oaks, CA: Sage.

SECTION FOUR

Conclusions
and Future Directions

24

TEACHING MIXED METHODS RESEARCH: PRACTICES, DILEMMAS, AND CHALLENGES

◆ John W. Creswell
Abbas Tashakkori
Ken D. Jensen
Kathy L. Shapley

During the past 15 years, interest in mixed methods research has developed at a steady pace. With the decreased emphasis on the "paradigm wars" (Datta, 1994; Guba & Lincoln, 1994), the emerging discussions about procedures of conducting mixed methods studies (Creswell, 1999; Morgan, 1997; Tashakkori & Teddlie, 1998), the publication of major books (e.g., Brewer & Hunter, 1989; Greene & Caracelli, 1997), and the numerous published mixed methods studies being evaluated and chronicled (Creswell, Goodchild, & Turner, 1996; Datta, 1994; Greene, Caracelli, & Graham, 1989), attention now needs to turn to the teaching of courses devoted to mixed methods research. Although extensive discussions now exist about teaching qualitative research (e.g., Webb & Glesne, 1992), no thorough writings have been collected on the pedagogy of mixed methods research and the nature of such courses in the social science curricula.

AUTHORS' NOTE: We appreciate the time and effort contributed by colleagues who completed our questionnaire and responded in other ways.

While mixed methods courses have appeared in graduate programs, current faculty are discovering that there is very little information available to help them design and plan courses (Tashakkori & Teddlie, 2000). To the best of our knowledge, very few courses are currently available specifically on mixed methods research. One example that we were able to locate is a course by Richard Schmertzing (with Marsha Reed) at Valdosta State University on Advanced Mixed Methodology (RSCH 9860). This Web-based course, taught during the summer of 2000, offered assignments, a syllabus, communications between students and instructors, and a discussion board in an electronic format (http://thumper.valdosta.edu:8001/rsch9860/). As suggested by Tashakkori and Teddlie (2000, in press), professors of research methodology either are teaching both qualitative and quantitative methods in single courses but in a sequential manner or are teaching them totally separate from each other.

Unquestionably, as Tashakkori and Teddlie (2000, in press) suggested, there are many challenges and dilemmas that confront the "first generation" of faculty who desire to offer a course in mixed methods research. Despite numerous papers and journal articles on mixed methods research, there is a minimal amount of material available on teaching mixed methods research courses or introductory courses with a mixed methods approach. Perhaps this is due to the emerging nature of mixed methods, presenting researchers with issues such as ambiguous terminology, diverse worldviews, different assumptions, and an undefined procedural model (Creswell, 1999; Morgan, 1997). Other factors confronting faculty who are creating new courses in mixed methods research include determining how much information should be included in a one-semester class, who might contribute as a speaker or an expert in this area, and what pedagogical style would best serve student learning.

To provide an extensive framework for creating a course in mixed methods, we have surveyed 11 current practitioners who have taught mixed methods courses or workshops. Responses from this e-mail survey included issues such as prerequisites, learning objectives/outcomes, pedagogical styles, course readings, reasons why students enroll in their courses, and views of mixed methods research by colleagues. The responses from these educators serve to construct a general idea of the teaching of mixed methods research and the potential dilemmas and challenges. The intent of this chapter is to present an overview about the teaching and pedagogy of a mixed methods course, to base our observations on responses from faculty who are presently teaching such a course, and to sketch the potential dilemmas and challenges for faculty who may seek to design and teach such a course.

◆ Practices Used by Mixed Methods Instructors

We developed an e-mail survey that was sent during the spring of 2001 to 31 individuals affiliated with a mixed methods Web site (www.fiu.edu/~bridges/) developed by Abbas Tashakkori at Florida International University. This survey consisted of nine open-ended questions addressing topics such as their experiences in teaching mixed methods; information about their syllabi, prerequisites, textbooks and journal articles, pedagogical style, and learning objectives; and their thoughts about the acceptance of such courses in their college curricula. Of the 31 individuals receiving the survey, 11 provided information about their mixed methods courses.

Responses to our questions regarding the teaching of mixed methods research included scenarios in which qualitative instruction was the major component of the course, while quantitative research occupied a smaller segment of the semester curriculum. Another scenario gave *equal time* to qualitative and quantitative research, with each segment taught separately. Other respondents taught qualitative and quantitative research separately but then integrated the methodologies into an end-of-semester project. We learned that some faculty presented qualitative and quantitative research at the same time, pointing out differences and similarities as the semester progressed. An interesting finding from their answers was that most respondents said that they would change several aspects of their courses before teaching the same courses in the future. This observation may reflect the state of mixed methods today and its continuing emerging nature.

However, it is important to develop a profile of current courses so that changes and improvements can be made in the future. Accordingly, we present here respondent views on learning objectives, important books and articles to read, prerequisites for a mixed methods course, topics typically addressed during such a course, and overall instructor's comments about the teaching of mixed methods and the integration of mixed methods into the graduate curricula of their schools and colleges.

LEARNING OBJECTIVES

As a reflection of the diverse style of teaching a mixed methods course, the learning objectives of courses currently being taught were extensive. Most objectives stated a basic awareness such as to "understand the differences between qualitative and quantitative research" and to "become familiar with the various types of mixed methodology designs." Charles Teddlie's "Advanced Seminar in Educational Research Methodology: The Application of Mixed Methodology to Dissertation and Other Educational Research" (personal communication, March 5, 2001) was more specific when he commented about the following objective: "Familiarize the students with the use of mixed methodology in educational research, including the issue [of] the paradigms and politics of educational research, focusing on pragmatism as the philosophical underpinning for conducting mixed method and mixed model studies."

It might be helpful to summarize some of the learning objectives of mixed methods courses identified by our respondents:

◆ Produce written works that integrate qualitative and quantitative methods.

◆ Understand the modes of qualitative and quantitative inquiry and the subsequent techniques for collecting, analyzing, and interpreting data.

◆ Interpret past empirical studies.

◆ Determine appropriate data analysis techniques.

◆ Present research data in a professional American Psychological Association format.

◆ Develop a sound understanding of the process of research in education and other behavioral/social disciplines.

◆ Develop the necessary skills and the knowledge to identify and use different types of research designs and methods.

◆ Develop the critical skills necessary to become an informed consumer of research literature.

◆ Develop the skills necessary to present research findings to peers and other professionals.

◆ Understand the role of triangulation in research.

As displayed in this list, the objectives are partly related to general research methods. They are also based on obtaining a general overview of mixed methods research and the application of mixed methods ideas.

IMPORTANT BOOKS AND ARTICLES TO READ

Resource materials dealing with mixed methodology are gradually becoming more available. Faculty who teach mixed methods courses need to include the latest literature on this design as well as articles and studies that have led to the current practices. The reading materials might include major texts as well as select journal articles from studies reported in varied social science journals. At the outset, it is helpful to chronicle the complete books written about mixed methods research, the chapters devoted to the topic, and the journal articles often cited by instructors teaching mixed methods courses.

Table 24.1 presents books, book chapters, and journal articles specifically devoted to mixed methods research spanning the period from 1979 to 1998. They cover research methods in a variety of disciplines such as evaluation, sociology, psychology, and education. Also, a course on mixed methods research might also include specific manuscript and journal article readings that convey the content of the area, including discussions about triangulation, the purpose of mixed methods research, the paradigm debate, data analysis strategies, and models and designs for mixed methods studies.

PREREQUISITES

Students wishing to enroll in established mixed methods courses must have attained at least a graduate student status, according to responses from our survey. However, the placement of mixed methods courses within the graduate programs varied. Many faculty required a working knowledge of qualitative and quantitative methodology for students before enrolling in classes. Another program requested that graduate students be at the doctorate level before registering for a mixed methods research class. The doctoral status meant that the students had covered both quantitative and qualitative research in other coursework such as during the master's degree program. Another program offered the mixed methods model as part of the introductory research class in the graduate program. There were no universal standards with regard to prerequisites for a mixed methods course; as with graduate work in any discipline, there was not a consensus as to "where" to place a mixed methodology course in the curriculum.

INSTRUCTIONAL ACTIVITIES

A degree of consensus was present in the survey results regarding instructional activities typically included in a mixed methods course. The mixed methods courses often involved lectures along with vigorous student participation. Several in-

TABLE 24.1   Chronology of Books, Chapters, and Journal Articles on Mixed Methods Research

Books:

Cook, T. D., & Reichardt, C. S. (Eds.). (1979). *Qualitative and quantitative methods in evaluation research.* Beverly Hills, CA: Sage.

Bryman, A. (1989). *Quantity and quality in social science research.* London: Routledge.

Brewer, J., & Hunter, A. (1989). *Multimethod research: A synthesis of style.* Newbury Park, CA: Sage.

Reichardt, C. S., & Rallis, S. F. (Eds.). (1994). *Qualitative-quantitative debate: New perspectives* (New Directions for Program Evaluation, No. 61). San Francisco: Jossey-Bass.

Greene, J. C., & Caracelli, V. J. (Eds.). (1997). *Advances in mixed-method evaluation: The challenges and benefits of integrating diverse paradigms* (New Directions for Evaluation, No. 74). San Francisco: Jossey-Bass.

Newman, I., & Benz, C. R. (1998). *Qualitative-quantitative research methodology: Exploring the interactive continuum.* Carbondale: University of Illinois Press.

Tashakkori, A., & Teddlie, C. (1998). *Mixed methodology: Combining qualitative and quantitative approaches.* Thousand Oaks, CA: Sage.

Book Chapters:

Smith, M. L. (1986). The whole is greater: Combining qualitative and quantitative approaches in evaluation studies. In D. D. Williams (Ed.), *Naturalistic evaluation* (New Directions for Evaluation, No. 30, pp. 37-54). San Francisco: Jossey-Bass.

Creswell, J. W. (1995). Combined quantitative and qualitative designs. In J. W. Creswell, *Research design: Qualitative and quantitative approaches* (Chapter 10). Thousand Oaks, CA: Sage.

Reynolds, D., Creemers, B., Stringfield, S., & Teddlie, C. (1998). Climbing an educational mountain: Conducting the International School Effectiveness Research Project (ISERP). In G. Walford (Ed.), *Doing research about education* (pp. 111-124). London: Falmer.

Creswell, J. W. (1999). Mixed-method research: Introduction and application. In C. Ciznek (Ed.), *Handbook of educational policy* (pp. 455-472). San Diego: Academic Press.

McMillan, J. H., & Schumacher, S. (2001). *Research in education: A conceptual introduction.* New York: Longman.

Creswell, J. W. (2002). Mixed method designs. In J. W. Creswell, *Educational research: Planning, conducting, and evaluating quantitative and qualitative research* (Chapter 17). Upper Saddle River, NJ: Merrill Prentice Hall.

Journal Articles:

Jick, T. D. (1983). Mixing qualitative and quantitative methods: Triangulation in action. In J. Van Maanen (Ed.), *Qualitative methodology* (pp. 135-148). Beverly Hills, CA: Sage.

Greene, J. C., & McClintock, C. (1985). Triangulation in evaluation: Design and analysis issues. *Evaluation Review, 9,* 523-545.

(Continued)

TABLE 24.1   (Continued)

Journal Articles (Continued)

Rossman, G. B., & Wilson, B. L. (1985). Numbers and words: Combining quantitative and qualitative methods in a single large-scale evaluation study. *Evaluation Review, 9,* 627-643.

Howe, K. R. (1988). Against the quantitative-qualitative incompatibility thesis or dogmas die hard. *Educational Researcher, 17*(8), 10-16.

Greene, J. C., Caracelli, V. J., & Graham, W. F. (1989). Toward a conceptual framework for mixed-method evaluation designs. *Educational Evaluation and Policy Analysis, 11,* 255-274.

Laurie, H., & Sullivan, O. (1991). Combining qualitative and quantitative methods in the longitudinal study of household allocations. *Sociological Review, 39,* 113-139.

Caracelli, V. W., & Greene, J. C. (1993). Data analysis strategies for mixed-method evaluation designs. *Educational Evaluation and Policy Analysis, 15,* 195-207.

Morse, J. (1996). Is qualitative research complete? *Qualitative Health Research, 6,* 3-5.

Morgan, D. L. (1998). Practical strategies for combining qualitative and quantitative methods: Application to health research. *Qualitative Health Research, 3,* 362-376.

structors organized their mixed methods classes in a seminar-type environment. Faculty emphasized student participation as essential for the success of their courses. Student participation encompassed informal discussion, working in small groups, presenting a chapter or a concept to the class, critical analysis of research models, and field-based data collection. In addition, student participation sometimes included journaling outside of class time. When the journals were collected at a predetermined phase in the course, the instructor amended the course schedule to discuss issues raised in the student journals.

To give an example of how an instructor might address instructional activities, the following excerpts are from the syllabus for the course "Mixed Methods in Program Evaluation" by Jennifer Greene (personal communication, May 29, 2001):

Write a mixed-method paper. The major work for this course will be a paper to be crafted as a publishable article. Students may choose to work in groups for this paper. The class as a whole will discuss all intended papers. Several groups may team up to propose a panel at a conference, featuring our work in this course. In other words, a significant amount of interaction in generating these papers is expected and desired.

Find empirical examples of mixed-method work in your domain of interest. Throughout the semester, our conceptual discussions will be grounded in and tested by empirical examples. Then, the third part of the course will focus on a review of empirical work. For these purposes, students will be responsible for locating and contributing examples of "good" mixed-method practice in their own area of interest. Students may also contribute their own research or evaluation work for this purpose.

Lead a seminar. Alone or with a partner, each student will be responsible for planning and then leading a "practical applications" discussion component of one class meeting during Parts 1 and 2 of the course. This discussion should focus on practical implications of the conceptual ideas being discussed. This "practical applications" discussion could engage the class with an empirical example, with alternative designs of a study, with values and politics as relevant domains of practice, or with other "so what?" questions. Students will work with the instructor in planning and implementing these discussions.

Another suggestion our survey respondents gave for class activities was dyadic dialogue. This involved discussing the pros and cons of a mixed methods study in relation to research topics or student projects. Student doctoral research proposals and critiques of current mixed methods studies would also be excellent topics for a course.

Donna Mertens (personal communication, May 16, 2001) uses writing exercises to facilitate the development of professional competencies that are established in the course "Advanced Research Design II." As shown in Box 24.1, Mertens's syllabus included activities related to both the design and presentation of a research proposal in a mixed methods class.

Sharon Rallis (personal communication, May 9, 2001) offered an additional, and perhaps fundamental, perspective on

class activity. For the course "Inquiry and Decision Making for School Leaders," Rallis stated in her course syllabus,

Discussion will be most useful to you and others if you can maintain a stance of openness and respect, whether the class is considering one of the readings, someone's viewpoint, a field experience, or a written assignment. The best time to inquire, paradoxically, may be when you think you know the most.

COURSE TOPICS

Topics varied from one class syllabus to another in the information we received from mixed methods teachers. A recurring theme in coursework was the emphasis on the historical perspective of the paradigm wars of mixed methodology. While there was a great deal of editorializing about the paradigm wars, journal articles have now begun to focus on "when" and "why" one might choose mixed methodology research.

Many of our survey respondents used several class periods for "empirical review and discussion." Class sessions were devoted to discussion concerning the past and present research of mixed methodology. Coinciding with these analytical discussions, class time and resources addressed the topic of triangulation. Some syllabus topics included how to use the computer for online searches. John Creswell (personal communication, November 16, 2001) used a skill-based orientation to the topics he addressed in the "Mixed Method Seminar" offered one semester each academic year. These skills include the following:

◆ Learning how to identify a mixed methods research study in a published journal article study

BOX 24.1
Proposal Development Activities in Mertens's Course

1. Write an initial statement of your personal position in terms of the major paradigms of research. It should be about three or four double-spaced pages and reflect your own ideas regarding where you stand in terms of the alternative paradigms of research. You will be learning about several different paradigms in this course. Do you find yourself more intrigued by or comfortable with one than another? Do you find yourself somewhat in the middle? Are you withholding judgment until you know more? Use the words epistemology, ontology, and methodology in your explanation. Discuss your position and give your reasons for that.

2. Write an initial draft of your research problem based on your literature review in EDF 810 [the previous research course] (or you may select another topic). Draft a set of research questions to go with the research problem.

3. For each of the following types of research,

   (a) Identify one research article that exemplifies that approach.

   (b) Draft a short paper explaining how you would use this type of design to conduct a research study of your research problem.

      Experimental/quasi-experimental

      Causal comparative/correlational designs

      Survey qualitative designs

      History

   In your paper, you should explain how the researchers in the identified article implemented the design, specifically answering questions of critical analysis for each study, and then explain how you would use the design, again explaining how you would address the questions for critical analysis to ensure that your design is strong.

4. Prepare a research proposal that follows Gallaudet University's Guidelines for Dissertation Proposals (including a more refined statement of your paradigmatic perspective). Select one of the research approaches to include in your proposal and add sections related to sampling, ethics, data collection, and data analysis and interpretation.

5. Make a presentation to the class on your proposal. After receiving feedback from Donna Mertens and the other class members, revise the proposal and submit your final draft.

◆ Using appropriate search terms for locating mixed methods research studies in computerized databases

◆ Writing a rationale for the need to "mix" quantitative and qualitative data in a single research study

◆ Writing a purpose statement and research questions for a mixed methods research study

◆ Summarizing the types of data that are often collected in mixed methods research and being able to distinguish between quantitative and qualitative types

◆ Transforming quantitative data into qualitative data and vice versa

◆ Combining or triangulating quantitative and qualitative data to reach conclusions

◆ Identifying the basic procedures of computer programs that allow for the analysis of both quantitative and qualitative data

◆ Drawing a visual model of a mixed methods research design

◆ Identifying the criteria that distinguish among the different types of mixed methods designs

◆ Comparing the strengths and weaknesses of the different types of designs as they relate to the research problem under study

◆ Evaluating a mixed methods study in terms of criteria

◆ Applying the steps in the design of a mixed methods study to a proposed project

As an instructor of mixed methods research, one should address several questions when deciding on topics for a mixed methods course. Is the objective to introduce mixed methods research? Is the objective to present an advanced course with in-depth discussion on specific models? How should the more philosophical issue of multiple methodologies relate to the more procedural issue of how to conduct a study? Other topics introduced in mixed methods courses, as mentioned by respondents to our survey, included the following:

◆ Focus principally on qualitative and make comparisons with quantitative research.

◆ Include the paradigm question of the relationship between epistemology and methods.

◆ Review data collection strategies.

◆ Discuss pragmatism as a philosophical approach to research and the choice of research strategy.

◆ Address research design issues (i.e., how to collect both quantitative and qualitative data, analyze them, and report them in a study).

◆ Share examples of mixed methodology designs.

◆ Discuss advancements in mixed methods evaluation.

SYLLABI

Faculty who responded to our mixed methods survey included in their responses a variety of course syllabi. Many course outlines were also accessible through Web sites. To provide one example for current mixed methodology coursework, in Appendix 24.1 we include the syllabus for "Combining Qualitative and Quantitative Methods." This course is taught by David Morgan (personal communication, May 25, 2001). The course begins with history and then moves to the paradigm question, addresses data collection, reviews models for designs, and considers future directions for mixed methods research.

FACULTY REACTIONS

In the survey, we asked instructors to give us their thoughts about the popularity of mixed methods courses at their institutions, how peers perceived this "new" type of research, how students responded to these classes, and any other thoughts they might want to share. The following are some excerpts from these responses:

◆ "Because qualitative and quantitative methods have different strengths, there is an intuitive appeal to research designs that combine what they each have to offer. Yet, social scientists often encounter severe problems when they attempt to do research that brings these different methods together. This class addresses this gap by considering practical strategies for combining qualitative and quantitative methods."

◆ "It is an exciting experience, as I always learn through my students. It is challenging, as many students have limited views of what it means to do such research. That is, because such methods are not necessarily mainstream, it is important to exercise considerable rigor in the use of mixed methods and care in analysis and reporting."

◆ "I think . . . these [are] important courses for students in making connections between research and practice. . . . For doctoral students, who often come with the baggage of the quantitative/qualitative distinction, it helps them see that multiple/mixed methods, data and analysis approaches lead to significant advances in theory and practice. I don't know that my colleagues really understand what I do in my teaching and research related to mixed methods, as it is often alien to their own thinking and what constitutes good research."

◆ "This course is really meant to introduce students to inquiry. My purpose is to move away from the qual-quan paradigms—that is, to teach researchers to ask: What is knowledge? . . . How is it produced? Methods are presented as tools to inform the research questions."

◆ "I will teach this course on a 'demand' basis; when enough doctoral students want to take it, I will offer it."

◆ "The course is accepted in my department and is very popular among graduate students in other departments as well."

◆ "Students liked the course, and I have been asked to teach it again. This seems to be a very popular topic. . . . I recently gave an open lecture on practical approaches to combining multiple methods, and several professors brought their classes."

◆ Dilemmas and Challenges

During the past decade, the positivists and interpretive-constructivists have found some common ground in an area known as mixed methods (Brewer & Hunter, 1989) or the mixed model approach (Tashakkori

& Teddlie, 1998). Research in the areas of education and psychology no longer follows a strict QUAL-QUAN dichotomy (Currall, Hammer, Baggett, & Doniger, 1999; Donmoyer, 1999; Miles & Huberman, 1994; Miller & Crabtree, 2000). During the 1970s and 1980s, researchers were faced with teaching themselves and their students qualitative research. Today, the challenge for both traditionally trained quantitative researchers and qualitative researchers is learning mixed methods research. The "first generation" of social and behavioral researchers who are beginning to master and teach mixed methods research face many dilemmas, including those related to professional development and teaching issues.

PROFESSIONAL DEVELOPMENT ISSUES

Self-Study. While the opportunities for professional development in the area of mixed methods research are more common today than they were 5 years ago, many professors use a "self-study" approach to learn about this methodology. For example, it may be beneficial to recruit a colleague or graduate students to participate in a mixed methods seminar. One such seminar took place during the fall of 2000 at a large midwestern university (John Creswell, personal communication, March 11, 2001). The professor conducting the seminar invited to two sessions faculty members who were interested in conducting a mixed methods study but did not have time to participate in the entire seminar. These two presented their research ideas to the faculty and students who were participating in the seminar. After hearing the ideas and types of data collection that were proposed, the students suggested the "best" mixed methods design, noted possible obstacles that might be encountered, and developed a visual or concept map of the research project.

The exercise proved to be valuable to both the researchers and the students. Another seminar project might include having the students conceptualize a group project and collect pilot data during the semester. Recommendations for additional activities include the following:

◆ Designate a brief amount of time for the paradigm debate; it is important to understand the issues, but do not allow the group to fixate on this topic.

◆ Become familiar with at least the three basic mixed methods designs: triangulation, complementary, and sequential.

◆ Read published mixed methods studies and identify the designs used and also examine the writing style.

◆ Examine completed quantitative or qualitative research projects and discuss whether or not a mixed methods design would have enhanced the studies.

◆ Draw concept maps of the potential mixed methods designs, including the type of data that will be collected for both the qualitative and quantitative sections.

As with any self-study project, the instructor should have a designated amount of time for study, set a time line to avoid lengthy debates, and set realistic short- and long-term goals. This self-study approach is not impossible but requires some discipline.

Textbooks. Once a professional has dedicated a set amount of time to learn this new research method, his or her first roadblock may be finding appropriate text-books on the subject. Research methodology textbooks have gone through an evolutionary change since the 1970s. Once strictly quantitative in nature with little discussion of qualitative research (e.g., Ary, Jacobs, & Razavieh, 1972; Bordens & Abbott, 1988; Durso & Mellgren, 1989), textbooks have recently begun to include a minimal discussion about qualitative research (e.g., Leary, 1995; Liebert & Liebert, 1995; Miller & Salkind, 2002; Rosnow & Rosenthal, 1996). Finally, recent methodology books are emerging that provide a more "balanced" treatment to both quantitative and qualitative research but clearly separate the two (e.g., Johnson & Christensen, 2000; Mertens, 1998; Neuman, 1998). Fortunately, despite a continuation of the dichotomy between quantitative and qualitative research, an increasing number of authors are now adding mixed methods designs to their textbooks. For example, McMillan and Schumacher (2001) dedicated a part of a chapter to "mixed methods evaluation," and Creswell's (1994, 2002) textbooks have contained entire chapters on mixed methods designs.

Mentoring/Support. In addition, professionals who seek to broaden their expertise might not find ready collaborators in their learning experiences of mixed methods research. Some researchers are reluctant to explore mixed methods research, and those who do might not have opportunities to collaborate with other researchers at their institutions. The very nature of being the first generation implies that there are not well-established support systems of colleagues from which to draw. However, those learning mixed methods research are able to take advantage of the advances in technology. E-mail, discussion boards, and phone calls may help to decrease the feelings of isolation and to

bridge the gap between those who are interested in mixed methodology and those who have conducted mixed methods studies.

The labor-intensive stages of mixed methods research, such as data collection and data analysis, may reduce less experienced researchers' enthusiasm for using them in their research. Furthermore, students who wish to complete theses or dissertations using a mixed methods approach may be discouraged by their committee members and directed to use either a quantitative or a qualitative approach but not both. In some instances, students may find themselves in the position of having to educate or teach their committee members about mixed methodology. As suggested by Newman and Benz (1998) and Tashakkori and Teddlie (in press), this educational need is largely a result of the fact that in the past (and even currently) graduate programs have prepared students "with a monolithic perspective. Either they become well-trained statisticians, or they become cultural anthropologists, methodologically weak in asking research questions in justifying one or the other set of strategies" (Newman & Benz, 1998, pp. 7-8).

Inconsistent Terminology. Another challenge researchers face is the inconsistent terminology that is used in mixed methods research. The confusion exists in all aspects of mixed methods inquiry, from the typology of mixed methods designs (see Teddlie & Tashakkori, Chapter 1, this volume) to the criteria for evaluating the quality of inferences drawn from mixed methods research (Tashakkori & Teddlie, 1998, in press). For example, Greene and Caracelli (1997) referred to three basic designs as triangulation, complementary, and expansion. They indicated that these three designs fall into a larger group called mixed method component designs.

Creswell (2002) referred to these same three basic designs as triangulation, explanation, and exploration without a broader classification of mixed method component design. Field and Morse (1985) referred to them as "several types of methodological triangulation." They indicated that triangulation can be simultaneous or sequential. An examination of the chapters in the current handbook reveals the need for creating a more agreed-on typology of mixed methods designs (see chapters in this volume by Morse [Chapter 7] and Creswell, Plano Clark, Gutmann, & Hanson [Chapter 8] as well as the Glossary).

PEDAGOGICAL INFLUENCES

Personal Bias. Epistemological views shape an instructor's preference for a paradigm or worldview perspective they bring to research. Acknowledged paradigm perspectives, such as positivist, postpositivist, constructivist, critical, participatory, and pragmatic (see Maxcy, Chapter 2, this volume), influence knowledge claims and ultimately affect an instructor's preferences for methodologies and methods (see these knowledge claims in Cherryholmes, 1992; Lincoln & Guba, 2000; Mertens, 1998; Neuman, 1998). Most researchers are trained extensively in one paradigm perspective, such as postpositivist or constructivist, with just a surface understanding of the other types of paradigms. Although they may show an interest in learning this combined approach, they may unconsciously favor or give more emphasis to their primary methodology. A challenge in mixed methods research for both the instructor and students in the class is to learn multiple paradigm perspectives and remain open to possibilities.

Anxieties/Misconceptions. Teaching a course with a mixed methods approach presents a unique challenge to professors. Because this methodology is composed of both quantitative and qualitative methods, students bring all of the challenges and frustrations associated with each individual type of method to one class. It has been documented that students experience varying degrees of anxiety while taking quantitative research classes; although students may have less fear in general methods courses, anything that emphasizes quantitative analysis may aggravate the students' level of anxiety (Bridges, Pershing, Gillmore, & Bates, 1998). In addition, many students have misconceptions and are not prepared for the intense concentration and amount of work needed to conduct qualitative research (Webb & Glesne, 1992).

Students may also lack interest in fully understanding the research process. Students have been conditioned to memorize theories and "right" answers to questions throughout their academic training. They often approach research in a similar manner. The problem with this type of approach is that research is not necessarily smooth and linear, there may be more than one "right" answer to a research question, and "wrong" answers may prove to be important as well (Harris, 1975; Webb & Glesne, 1992). McBurney (1995) pointed out that two researchers may design a particular study in different ways and that there is not one perfect design for a study. While these issues may pose challenges for the seasoned researcher, they may overwhelm a student just learning the process of research.

As discussed previously, the issue of what type of student should take a course in mixed methods research needs to be addressed. Instructors must decide whether they will allow only students who have had previous research experience or methodology coursework so that they have little anxiety about the process of research. However, these students may have already constructed a worldview that is not consistent with the idea of mixing different paradigms. If professors open their "advanced research" classes to novice researchers, the anxiety and lack of application of these new inquirers may be apparent, but these students may also fully accept the idea of mixing the two traditional methods without getting caught up in the paradigm debate.

Design and Data Analysis. Perhaps the biggest challenge instructors face when teaching mixed methods research is teaching students how to decide which design to use and how to analyze the data once they have been collected. Deciding which design to use for a mixed methods study may direct how and where the "mixing" will occur. During the mixed methods seminar mentioned earlier, it was suggested that mixed methods researchers should clarify their designs with concept maps. The visual displays of their research projects clarified the process not only for the researchers but also for other individuals involved in their projects such as graduate advisers, funding sources, and research assistants (see Creswell et al., Chapter 8, this volume).

Given the discussions about integrating different types of data, transforming data, and building from one data set to another (Caracelli & Greene, 1993; Tashakkori & Teddlie, 1998), students need to learn how to mix quantitative and qualitative data and obtain a familiarity with the basic procedures. One activity would be to provide students with both types of data and have them work through each type of mixing. For example, "mock" interviews may be collected. Some students could be directed to answer the questions in a particular way that would cause their themes to

be different from those of the rest of the group. Students could collect, transcribe, and code the interviews and then decide what additional data they will collect on the extreme case(s). Another mock scenario might include providing the students with results from a survey that, when analyzed, will identify four clusters/groups. Students could work in small groups and develop a qualitative research piece (e.g., research questions, interview questions and probes) that might be used with the subgroups identified from the quantitative data.

As with many aspects of mixed methods research, there are many choices in the process. What type of design should one use? Where should one mix the methods? What type of data analysis should one use? To address these questions, we make the following suggestions for teachers of mixed methods research:

◆ Introduce the basic designs such as triangulation, explanatory, and exploratory.

◆ Stress the value of a visual or concept map as an aide for both the researcher and others involved in the research project.

◆ Understand that the mixing can occur at any/all phases of the process of research; however, it may be easiest for first-time researchers to mix at just one phase (e.g., interpretation).

◆ Provide examples of the different types of data analysis strategies, but suggest implementing only one strategy initially to develop comfort when handling both types of data (see Onwuegbuzie & Teddlie, Chapter 13, this volume).

◆ Familiarize yourself and your students with the numerous software packages available for data analysis—SAS, SPSS, NUD*IST, NVivo, ATLAS.ti (see Bazeley, Chapter 14, this volume).

◆ Conclusion

With the increased interest in and publication of many mixed methods studies, our attention needs to turn to pedagogical approaches that instructors might teach and students might learn in mixed methods courses. Unfortunately, no discussions are available that address this subject. Accordingly, we surveyed 31 faculty members who are interested in or teach mixed methods courses, and we obtained responses from 11 of these individuals. Their approaches varied considerably from course to course, but we were able to learn about their learning objectives, important books and articles to use in a course, their expectations in terms of prerequisites for a course, and their instructional activities. Course topics varied as well, and we included a complete syllabus for review of the topics typically included in a mixed methods course. Overall, faculty believed that mixed methods courses were well-accepted in their graduate programs.

With this information, we further explored some of the dilemmas and challenges facing the mixed methods instructor today. Some faculty might need to embark on a self-study program to learn mixed methods research because it was not available when they were trained as methodologists. A series of strategies for this self-study were identified. Then, we reviewed the various textbooks available that provide a quantitative orientation and a minor qualitative component as well as those that provide a better "balance" between quantitative and qualitative research. We noted the "new" research method texts that integrate both forms of

research and include specific chapters on mixed methods designs. In addition, the support and mentoring needed for faculty to teach a mixed methods course meant that they might be working on their own without natural collaboration from others. It is important for individuals who accept the challenge of teaching a mixed methods course to recognize that the study and teaching of mixed methods is unfamiliar territory to most faculty in the social sciences. We also indicated that the terminology may also present a challenge to mixed methods researchers who find many different terms for designs and the difficulty of locating mixed methods studies in the scholarly literature. Another challenge is that individuals may bring to mixed methods research personal biases toward paradigm perspectives and may unintentionally favor one over the other. How to provide equal balance, or a balance in a two-phase sequence, is a challenge to mixed methods instructors. Finally, for students who may be anxious about only *one* form of inquiry, their anxieties may be enhanced when faculty introduce *two* forms as in mixed methods research.

From this survey and review of several dilemmas and challenges, what needs to be further studied? In this chapter, we have touched on many issues and approaches used by mixed methods instructors. As more courses become available, a larger survey is needed to record important topics such as the content being introduced, the readings used, and the faculty and student experiences with a mixed methods course. As new and more complicated designs are introduced into the literature, we need to know how best to teach these designs and how students can practice them to effectively become good mixed methods researchers. With the increased attention to computer programs that mix quantitative and qualitative data, such technical issues will undoubtedly demand more attention from mixed methods instructors, and we need to know what programs they are using, how they are introducing students to applications, and the student experiences in running and using the programs.

These are but a few of the possible new developments in teaching (and learning) mixed methods research. To begin the conversation and highlight the experiences of a few instructors here, and to signal potential dilemmas and challenges, provides a useful starting point in the discussion about the pedagogy of mixed methods research.

◆ Appendix 24.1: Condensed Version of Syllabus

COMBINING QUALITATIVE AND QUANTITATIVE METHODS USP 510/610, F '97

David L. Morgan	Office Hours:
Institute on Aging	Tues. 1-3
725-5146	Wed. 1-3
morgand@pdx.edu	Room 121-A, UPA

Because qualitative and quantitative methods have different strengths, there is an intuitive appeal to research designs that combine what they each have to offer. Yet social scientists often encounter severe problems when they attempt to do research that brings these different methods together. This class addresses this gap by considering practical strategies for combining qualitative and quantitative methods.

The class will emphasize a set of existing research designs for combining qualitative and quantitative methods that (a) have reasonably well-understood benefits and (b) can be implemented in a relatively straightforward fashion.

We will also investigate new extensions to this existing set of "practical" research designs. Although most of our attention will be on the practicalities of designing workable research projects, we will also consider the broader epistemological or "paradigm" issues involved in efforts to combine qualitative and quantitative methods.

The assignments for the class will emphasize mastering the existing methodological literature on combining qualitative and quantitative methods as well as producing written work that integrates these readings with each student's own research interests. Because this course emphasizes research design, it will not require the collection or analysis of data (nor is it intended to support projects that are already at advanced stages of data collection or analysis).

The course will be interdisciplinary in nature, with a goal of creating connections across the widely scattered fields that have contributed to both qualitative and quantitative methods. In particular, the course will use e-mail and other Internet technologies to create a high level of ongoing exchanges among the students throughout the quarter. Although the course will meet in a standard evening time slot, it will carry 4 units due to the amount of reading, writing, and Internet usage that will be required. Much of the Internet portion of the course will rely on a Web page that is currently located at http://odin.cc.pdx.edu/~psu06847/index.htm.

Grades

Most of the grade for this course will come from a series of short papers that you will also edit into a final course paper. The goal is for you to create a research design that uses a combination of qualitative and quantitative methods to investigate your own substantive research interests. The four papers that go together to make up this series are described on a separate page; in total, they represent 70% of the final grade.

In addition to the cumulative series of papers, there is a separate assignment to produce three annotated abstracts of published articles that combine qualitative and quantitative methods. Each of these three abstracts is worth 5% of the grade. This part of the grading is also discussed on a separate page.

The final component of the grade involves participation in the electronic (Internet) aspects of the course. This aspect of the class will be limited to the use of e-mail and connection to a Web page supporting this class. There will be technical support available to assist any students who need help with this part of the coursework. Unlike most grades for "class participation," the use of e-mail will allow direct monitoring of the extent to which each student contributes to the electronic class discussion. In addition, several of the assignments will request that you submit class materials via e-mail. As a general rule, if you fulfill the class assignments that require the use of e-mail and the Web page, you will receive the 15% of the grade that is tied to electronic participation. Once again, this portion of the grading is described in more detail on a separate page.

10% initial statement of interests (1 p; due before Week 2)

15% expanded statement of interests plus methods (3 pp; due Week 4)

15% your methods and current procedures in your field (3 pp; due Week 6)

30% final research design (10 pp; due Week 10)

15% abstracts (3 @ 5% each; due Weeks 3, 5, and 7)

15% electronic participation

Readings and Assignments

All of the readings for this course are contained in a course pack available through Clean Copy (1732 S.W. 6th). There are no textbooks. For Week 4 on "The paradigm question," there are several optional readings.

These will be available both at the Institute on Aging main office in Room 122 UPA and at the reserve desk in the main library. There may also be additional optional readings added for later weeks of the course. Any of these optional readings are truly optional; they are simply meant to be a resource for students who wish to pursue additional background in a particular area.

Week 1. "Introduction: Who is taking this course and why?"

Week 2. "My basic framework"

Week 3. "History and background of work in this area"

Week 4. "The paradigm question"

Week 5. "Cell #1: Principally quantitative with preliminary qualitative"

Week 6. "Cell #2: Principally qualitative with preliminary quantitative"

Week 7. "Cell #3: Principally quantitative with follow-up qualitative"

Week 8. "Cell #4: Principally qualitative with follow-up quantitative"

Week 9. "Triangulation reconsidered"

Week 10. "Career paths and future directions"

■ References

Ary, D., Jacobs, L. C., & Razavieh, A. (1972). *Introduction to research in education.* New York: Holt, Rinehart & Winston.

Bordens, K. S., & Abbott, B. B. (1988). *Research design and methods: A process approach.* Newbury Park, CA: Sage.

Brewer, J., & Hunter, A. (1989). *Multimethod research: A synthesis of style.* Newbury Park, CA: Sage.

Bridges, G. S., Pershing, J. L., Gillmore, G. M., & Bates, K. A. (1998). Teaching quantitative research methods: A quasi-experimental analysis. *Teaching Sociology, 26,* 14-18.

Caracelli, V. J., & Greene, J. C. (1993). Data analysis strategies for mixed-method evaluation designs. *Educational Evaluation and Policy Analysis, 15*, 195-207.

Cherryholmes, C. H. (1992). Notes on pragmatism and scientific realism. *Educational Researcher, 21*(6), 13-17.

Creswell, J. W. (1994). *Research design: Qualitative and quantitative approaches.* Thousand Oaks, CA: Sage.

Creswell, J. W. (1999). Mixed-method research: Introduction and application. In J. W. Creswell (Ed.), *Handbook of educational policy* (pp. 455-472). San Diego: Academic Press.

Creswell, J. W. (2002). *Educational research: Planning, conducting, and evaluating quantitative and qualitative approaches.* Upper Saddle River, NJ: Merrill/Pearson Education.

Creswell, J. W., Goodchild, L. F., & Turner, P. H. (1996). Integrated qualitative and quantitative research: Epistemology, history, and design. In J. C. Smart (Ed.), *Higher education: Handbook of theory and research* (Vol. 11, pp. 90-136). New York: Agathon.

Currall, S. C., Hammer, T. H., Baggett, L. S., & Doniger, G. M. (1999). Combining qualitative and quantitative methodologies to study group processes: An illustrative study of a corporate board of directors. *Organizational Research Methods, 2*, 5-36.

Datta, L. (1994). Paradigm wars: A basis for peaceful coexistence and beyond. In C. S. Reichardt & S. F. Rallis (Eds.), *The qualitative-quantitative debate: New perspectives* (New Directions for Program Evaluation, No. 61, pp. 53-70). San Francisco: Jossey-Bass.

Donmoyer, R. (1999). Paradigm talk (and its absence) in the second edition of the *Handbook of Research on Educational Administration. Educational Administration Quarterly, 35*, 614-641.

Durso, F. T., & Mellgren, R. L. (1989). *Thinking about research.* St. Paul, MN: West.

Field, P. A., & Morse, J. M. (1985). *Qualitative nursing research: The application of qualitative approaches.* Rockville, MD: Aspen.

Greene, J. C., & Caracelli, V. J. (Eds.). (1997). *Advances in mixed-method evaluation: The challenges and benefits of integrating diverse paradigms* (New Directions for Evaluation, No. 74). San Francisco: Jossey-Bass.

Greene, J. C., Caracelli, V. J., & Graham, W. F. (1989). Toward a conceptual framework for mixed-method evaluation designs. *Educational Evaluation and Policy Analysis, 11*, 255-274.

Guba, E. G., & Lincoln, Y. S. (1994). Competing paradigms in qualitative research. In N. K. Denzin & Y. S. Lincoln (Eds.), *Handbook of qualitative research* (pp. 105-117). Thousand Oaks, CA: Sage.

Harris, L. J. (1975). Teaching a research methods course in developmental psychology: Some principles, methods, and problems. *Teaching of Psychology, 2*(4), 171-175.

Johnson, B., & Christensen, L. (2000). *Educational research: Quantitative and qualitative approaches.* Boston: Allyn & Bacon.

Leary, M. R. (1995). *Introduction to behavioral research methods.* Pacific Grove, CA: Brooks/Cole.

Liebert, R. M., & Liebert, L. L. (1995). *Science and behavior: An introduction to methods of psychological research.* Englewood Cliffs, NJ: Prentice Hall.

Lincoln, Y. S., & Guba, E. G. (2000). Paradigmatic controversies, contradictions, and emerging confluences. In N. K. Denzin & Y. S. Lincoln (Eds.), *Handbook of qualitative research* (2nd ed., pp. 163-188). Thousand Oaks, CA: Sage.

McBurney, D. H. (1995). The problem method of teaching research methods. *Teaching of Psychology, 22*(1), 36-38.

McMillan, J. H., & Schumacher, S. (2001). *Research in education: A conceptual introduction* (5th ed.). New York: Longman.

Mertens, D. M. (1998). *Research methods in education and psychology: Integrating diversity with quantitative and qualitative approaches.* Thousand Oaks, CA: Sage.

Miles, M. B., & Huberman, A. M. (1994). *Qualitative data analysis* (2nd ed.). Thousand Oaks, CA: Sage.

Miller, D. C., & Salkind, N. J. (2002). *Handbook of research design and social measurement* (6th ed.). Thousand Oaks, CA: Sage.

Miller, W. L., & Crabtree, B. J. (2000). Clinical research. In N. K. Denzin & Y. S. Lincoln (Eds.), *Handbook of qualitative research* (2nd ed., pp. 607-631). Thousand Oaks, CA: Sage.

Morgan, D. (1997). *Practical strategies for combining qualitative and quantitative methods.* Unpublished manuscript, Portland State University.

Neuman, W. L. (1998). *Social research methods: Qualitative and quantitative approaches* (4th ed.). Boston: Allyn & Bacon.

Newman, I., & Benz, C. R. (1998). *Qualitative-quantitative research methodology: Exploring the interactive continuum.* Carbondale: Southern Illinois University Press.

Rosnow, R. L., & Rosenthal, R. R. (1996). *Beginning behavioral research: A conceptual primer.* Englewood Cliffs, NJ: Prentice Hall.

Tashakkori, A., & Teddlie, C. (1998). *Mixed methodology: Combining qualitative and quantitative approaches* (Applied Social Research Methods, No. 46). Thousand Oaks, CA: Sage.

Tashakkori, A., & Teddlie, C. (2000, November). *Pedagogical issues and dilemmas for the "first generation" of professors teaching mixed methods.* Paper presented at the meeting of the Association for the Advancement of Educational Research, Pointe Verda Beach, FL.

Tashakkori, A., & Teddlie, C. (in press). Issues and dilemmas in teaching research methods courses in social and behavioral sciences: A U.S. perspective. *International Journal of Social Research Methodology.*

Webb, R. B., & Glesne, C. (1992). Teaching qualitative research. In M. LeCompte, W. Milroy, & J. Preissle (Eds.), *The handbook of qualitative research in education* (pp. 771-814). San Diego: Academic Press.

25

COLLABORATIVE MIXED METHODS RESEARCH

♦ Lyn M. Shulha
Robert J. Wilson

Collaboration has become so ubiquitous a term that it is rarely defined. It is common for policy makers, program planners, practitioners, and researchers to use collaborative to mean any degree of coordinated, cooperative, or consultative effort. Yet the increasing appearance of collaboration as a criterion in the adjudicating of human and social science research proposals suggests that collaboration is gaining credibility as a feature of investigation. Indeed, many research agendas can and do benefit from even nominal amounts of joint effort. For example, research teams engaged in various forms of mixed methods research described in this handbook, demanding many forms of expertise, are themselves creating the conditions for collaborative approaches to inquiry.

One frequent concomitant of collaborative research effort is a difference in perception about what evidence will count, what indicators are worth pursuing, and what designs will yield the most fruitful and powerful data. When the purpose of collaboration is to further mixed methods research, disputes around these various perceptions can easily lead to debilitating epistemological debates. It is our contention that energy spent attempting to convert collaborators to a particular vision of worthwhile inquiry is energy wasted.

♦ Introduction

By collaborative mixed methods research, we mean the purposeful application of a multiple person, multiple perspective approach to questions of research and evaluation. Decisions about how methods are combined and about how analyses are conducted are grounded in the needs and emerging complexity of each project rather than in preordinate methodological conventions.

Within this context, methods can be "mixed" in a variety of ways. Sometimes, one method serves another in validating and explicating findings that emerge from a dominant approach. On other occasions, different methods are used for different parts of the issues being investigated and in an independent way. In more complex cases, the methods and perspectives are deliberately mixed from the beginning of the process. The resulting interaction of problem, method, and results produces a more comprehensive, internally consistent, and ultimately more valid general approach. What sets the most complex forms of collaborative mixed methods research apart from other forms of inquiry is that findings depend as much on the researchers' capacities to learn through joint effort and to construct joint meaning as on their expertise in conventional data collection and analysis techniques.

One current problem is that the influence of collaboration in research is relatively unknown. When collaborative inquiry yields desirable outcomes, success is often attributed to the design, be it single method or mixed methods. Any critical examination of the collaborative process itself appears unnecessary. No matter how collaboration was enacted, the assumption is that the process was both appropriate and effective. Only when intended outcomes are not achieved or projects break down does there appear to be an obvious need to examine the characteristics of collaboration. It is rare, however, for participants or funders of unproductive research

projects to invest even more resources into examining an inquiry process that has proven unsatisfactory. Thus, our understanding of collaboration in inquiry, whether it results in featured, functional, or forgettable outcomes, remains largely unstudied.

Currently, it is possible to label research collaborative without clarifying who has been involved in the inquiry or how decisions concerning design, data collection, data analysis, and reporting have been made. Obfuscation of such details while continuing to label the inquiry collaborative may leave the impression that research findings are more participatory, more coherent, more broadly applicable, or more politically relevant than is actually warranted.

Designers and consumers of research alike can benefit from clarity about what constitutes the various forms of collaborative inquiry. Only with this groundwork in place can assumptions and findings attributed to these practices be tested. What is of critical importance to this chapter is how notions of collaboration not only shape mixed methods research but also transform it. We begin with an example of how collaboration and mixed methods actually played out in a program of research on teachers' assessment practice.

CASE 1: CAVE CANEM

How do preservice teachers make sense of the tasks of marking and grading? This question motivated the current authors to design their first collaborative mixed methods study. It was a question that followed naturally from Wilson's efforts over the previous decade to better understand and guide theory development in classroom assessment (Wilson, 1990, 1992) and from Shulha's experiences of inviting teachers to be collaborators in research that would focus on their own assessment practices (Shulha & Wilson, 1995). What brought us together in this study was a shared hypothesis that the student evaluation strategies recommended by measurement specialists were not particularly useful in the preparation of classroom teachers and in the formulation of assessment policies. Recommending alternative strategies was problematic in part because both the implicit and explicit logic underpinning teachers' actual decision making remained unclear.

Because this problem was equally important to both researchers, the concern with methods was subsumed under the discussion of ways in which to produce evidence that would be defensible. Such evidence may have been framed by Wilson in terms of reliability and validity and by Shulha in terms of trustworthiness and transferability, but the constructs underlying these value-laden standards were discovered to be the same. Consequently, decisions about which were the most important questions to address were made on their merits in furthering the research and not on which approach would be used to answer them.

This approach of focusing on the problem sidestepped an issue that can bedevil attempts to mix methods. When researchers have been successful in using one particular research approach, they will be more inclined to define problems they investigate in terms that lend themselves to that approach. When faced with limitations, they may feel forced to deal with those who have other methods. If the starting point for this type of collaboration is debate about what counts as knowledge, then the result may be irreconcilable conflict. Waszack and Sines (Chapter 21, this volume) describe an example from the field of population and

family planning where this kind of blockage ensued.

The judgment that needs to be made in collaborative approaches to mixed methods research is not so much how well each approach agrees with or supports the other but, more generally, to what extent the application of mixed methods contributes to results that will stand up to serious scrutiny by informed critics. In our case, there were many stakeholders who would critique our efforts—teachers, administrators, measurement specialists, teacher educators, and researchers. Phillips and Burbules (2000) labeled this approach to conceptualizing and conducting research nonfoundationalist. A nonfoundationalist approach to human knowledge

> rejects the view that knowledge is erected on absolutely secure foundations—for there are no such things; postpositivists accept fallibilism as an unavoidable fact of life. . . . In short, postpositivists see knowledge as conjectural. These conjectures are supported by the strongest (if possibly imperfect) warrants we can muster at the time and are always subject to reconsideration. (pp. 29-30, italics in original)

This approach led naturally to the addition of meaningfulness and utility as criteria we would impose on our efforts.

The typology introduced by Greene and Caracelli (1997) and expanded on in this handbook by Maxwell and Loomis (Chapter 9) provides a useful tool for understanding the mixed methods approach that shaped this case. Our research design was integrated by a "portfolio study"[1] that required each of the participating preservice teachers to grade products that represented the work of one fictitious eighth-grade student over a single term. At the end of that time, these teachers submitted the portfolio and the student's final grade for that term. The task was designed to be as ecologically valid as possible. We would learn about teachers' implicit notions of grading by testing out how a set of controlled variables influenced the construction of the student's final grade (Wilson & Martinussen, 1999). This understanding was to be supplemented with responses from open-ended questions administered once the final grade was submitted.

If the research had unfolded precisely as planned, it would have already met the minimum criterion of a collaborative mixed methods design: two academics engaged in joint inquiry using both quantitative and qualitative methods to investigate a problem. The unique feature of this study was how it evolved as both a collaborative and a mixed methods design. These transformations are attributable to the behaviors of the study's participants and to the variety of research questions that the researchers were willing to entertain as the findings emerged.

In the initial instructions, each teacher was asked to give the student he or she was tracking a grade on each of the products submitted to a portfolio. When the portfolios were collected, we discovered that these teachers not only had graded each product with a number but also had provided a median of three comments on each product as feedback to their hypothetical student (Shulha, 1999b). These comments, when combined with the mark, gave us new insights into preservice teachers' thinking about assessment as it was happening. The research had evolved from an integrated design consisting of two self-contained studies to an embedded one. The teacher feedback data were now nested in the collection of quantitative data.

The second transformation occurred during the data analysis. As findings from both marks and teacher feedback were being accumulated, it occurred to us that the relationships that existed among the variables might be working together in ways that could be specified using a structural equation model (SEM). At that time, neither of us was particularly experienced in using an SEM statistical program. This led us to approach a colleague who willingly brought this skill to the analysis (Anderson, 1999).

It was after our first joint presentation of the study that we began to seriously discuss what form the publication of our findings might take. Wilson had taken the lead in conducting the descriptive and regression analyses of the quantitative findings. Shulha had structured the qualitative analyses. Anderson had built the SEM. Each of us could work relatively independently on summarizing one piece of the analysis and link his or her own findings to the work of the other two.[2]

A cursory glimpse at the first products would suggest that three researchers with differing analytical skills had each carved out an independent study related to a common research problem. In practice, the meaning of collaboration and mixed methods research was much more complex. The focus for Shulha and Wilson from the early discussions of design to the fine-tuning of interpretations was on each other's understandings of the study's aims and what the data meant within the context of those aims. In the end, we spent well over a year negotiating the design of the study and its instruments and a second year examining the raw data and testing out the power of differing interpretations.

While it is true that Anderson worked more independently and only on the structural modeling piece, this had more to do with geography and differences in time zones (a separation of more than 2,500 miles) than with his interest in the work. At the point when Anderson joined as a collaborator, there was even some sense that an independent analysis of the data would be useful in checking the veracity of our own findings.

A companion piece to the three empirical reports (Shulha, Wilson, & Anderson, 1999) was created to make transparent the complex processes that had shaped the collaborative mixed methods design and its final claims. It described some of the intimate back-and-forth testing, critiquing, and syntheses that had occurred. In making "the good case" for our work (Phillips, 1992, pp. 74-93), no one form of data took on a solely supportive role. It turned out that beyond triangulating the data, a valid feature of mixed methods, this series of studies allowed audiences with various perspectives on the complexities of assessment and grading to view the logic, warrants, and evidence for the integrated set of claims that emerged.

When some common perceptions of our findings were reached, our final test was to vet these not only with each other but also with the several audiences we had identified as stakeholders in the research. The questions and challenges generated through this process allowed us to analyze what Hutchins (1991) labeled the constraints of these early descriptions and to adjust these so that the logic of the overall interpretation was more coherent and transparent. This final phase helped us to avoid at least one hazard that is inherent in collaborative mixed methods research, namely the tendency to develop unwarranted confidence that method had created meaning.

While understandable, it is restricting for methodologists of various persuasions to presume that effective collaborative mixed methods research requires a work-ing knowledge of each other's languages and paradigms. Such a starting point is more likely to focus the energies of participants away from their primary reason for forming a work team—a more complete understanding of the issues underpinning the inquiry—and into debates about epistemology and methodological adequacy. Rather than attempting to educate each other on the power of our preferred methodological approaches, we worked to clarify our differing views and identify how these might contribute to an expanded sense of the problem and its solutions. In methodological terms, it was not the "shared" variance alone that was of most interest; rather, it was the combination of "shared" and "unique" variance that led to our final understanding of the issues investigated.

One of the lessons of this and the two other studies we describe in this chapter is that when the goal is to produce defensible valid responses to important questions, the relationship between collaboration and mixed methods is not straightforward. When collaboration and mixed methods both are employed in a single study—with all of the variations that are possible in both—the meanings of the constructs themselves may be transformed in the process.

CHAPTER OVERVIEW

We open by situating the concept of collaboration within more general theories of cognitive development and decision making. Notions of collaboration are then expanded and grounded in current forms of inquiry and evaluation as these are being practiced both within the academic community and between academics and practitioners. This review of theory and use provides a framework for considering the merit, worth, and significance of collaborative research and is the background for an in-depth look at two additional cases in which the authors purposefully constructed collaborative mixed methods designs. The examples differ in context, process, and outcomes. In each case, we pay special attention to the features that motivated us to call the research collaborative and attempt to answer the question, "What is being 'mixed' in this form of research?"

Finally, we introduce a rubric for collaborative action. This instrument allows collaborators to create a profile of their joint effort and assess the likelihood that the collaboration itself is contributing to learning about the research problem. We hope that this will be a useful tool in the practical activities of forming collaborative teams and monitoring collaborative inquiry. We conclude by reviewing the warrants that shape the practice of human and social science research as well as the relevance of these standards to collaborative mixed methods designs.

◆ Conceptions of Collaboration

Elliott and Woloshyn (1997) offered as a general definition of *collaboration* "co-laboring or working equitably with at least one other person on the same project or task" (p. 24). At a very minimum, then, collaboration involves purposeful and joint effort. When describing a work strategy, this definition alone may be sufficient. Later in this chapter, however, we link the quality of our research findings to the nature of our collaboration. To support this stance, we need to have in place evidence that joint effort creates unique and productive ways for individuals to gather, manage, and interpret data. We also need

a framework for understanding the essential dimensions of collaboration and how they interact.

An integrative theory of collaboration is still a work in progress. Those providing rich descriptions and syntheses of their collaborative experiences are forwarding this goal.[3] This literature has helped us a great deal to understand our own work, and some is referenced here. To understand the potential for collaborative mixed methods research, however, we rely primarily on sources that attempt to understand the phenomena of collaboration in theoretical terms.

LEARNING AND DEVELOPMENT THROUGH COLLABORATION

Joint effort attracts individuals interested in pursuing "a project that they each individually could not produce at all, a more creative product than each could produce alone, or an opportunity to be in a collegial, less isolating intellectual situation" (Baldwin & Austin, 1995, p. 58). These rewards have made collaboration, whether named or unnamed, a long-standing feature of many professional, artistic, scientific, and academic endeavors.

John-Steiner (2000) studied the critical features of more than 15 famous collaborative partnerships (e.g., Jean-Paul Sartre and Simone de Beauvoir, Albert Einstein and Marcel Grossman, Aaron Copeland and Leonard Bernstein, Marie Curie and Pierre Curie). One of her stated purposes was to analyze the key features and processes of each partnership so as to construct a grounded theory of collaboration. An understated but significant impetus for this work was the author's interest in determining whether the processes and outcomes readily attributed to "creative people" might be equally appropriate to more mainstream "thought communities" (p. 187).

John-Steiner (2000) observed that significant and meaningful collaborations were built on a shared passionate interest in a new problem, art form, or societal challenge. If the focus for joint effort had importance on a personal level, individuals seemed willing to invest the time and energy required to set the partnership in motion. In a limited partnership, this interest alone may be sufficient to sustain joint effort long enough to achieve desired goals. In her examples of collaboration, however, the partnerships developed and extended over time. This occurred in part because individuals made early and favorable informal assessments about their "complementarity" (pp. 40-56). The more individuals' experiences, work styles, personal values, and general temperaments fit, the more likely the joint work continued.

For John-Steiner (2000), what distinguished collaboration from other forms of partnership was its dynamics—the reciprocal ways in which individual behavior and relationship influenced each other. While the creative activities of the disciplines varied within and across collaborations, the activities around relationship were quite similar. They featured risk taking—testing out the worth of ideas, being playful in ways that stimulated imaginative leaps, expressing belief in a partner's capabilities, challenging the ideas of the other(s), appropriating values or ideas of the other(s), and deepening each other's contributions to the product or task. "Collaboration is complex; it is charged both cognitively and emotionally" (p. 124). Collaboration, at least within John-Steiner's data set, contributed not only to developments within specialized fields but also to the personal growth of these individuals.

Personal development is possible, John-Steiner (2000) argued, when the collaboration becomes a "functional dynamic system" (p. 102), an expression introduced by Vygotsky (1978). Such a system emphasizes risk taking, supports individuals who challenge conventional wisdom and dichotomies within the disciplines, and urges those within the system to reconfigure knowledge and ideas in ways that tender more powerful explanations and predictions. In short, such systems represent a social context capable of stimulating higher cognitive functioning. For adults working in equitable partnerships, "collaboration can be a mirror for each partner—a chance to understand one's habits, styles, working methods, and beliefs through the comparison and contrast with one's collaborator." In Vygotskyan terms, then, collaborators create "zones of proximal development for each other" (John-Steiner, 2000, p. 189).

The zone John-Steiner (2000) was referring to is part of the sociocultural framework that Vygotsky created to account for the development of higher psychological processes in children (Wertsch, 1991). His theory is grounded in the assumption that being human is by nature developmental (Cole & Scribner, 1978) and that the catalyst for this development is learning. Learning relationships invoke the use of psychological tools, and these tools help individuals to bridge the gap between established frameworks for thinking and novel, more complex psychological processes that may be demanded by the task. Symbol systems for counting, writing, and drawing all are part of the psychological tool kit that mediates this learning. Of all available tools, however, the most important is language—and in particular speech. "Speech is the mechanism common to both social behavior and the psychological processes that are unique to human beings" (Minick, 1996, p. 31). Particular forms and patterns of talk within the collaborative relationship can stimulate individuals to behave differently and experiment with newer patterns of mental functioning. If these newer processes become internalized, they can be activated in contexts other than those in which the learning has occurred. When this happens, it reflects the presence of a more advanced profile of development.

> Learning is not development; however, properly organized learning results in mental development that would be impossible apart from learning. Thus, learning is a necessary and universal aspect of the process of developing culturally organized, specifically human, psychological functions. . . . The development process lags behind the learning process; this sequence then results in zones of proximal development. (Vygotsky, 1978, p. 90)

John-Steiner (2000) argued that in each of the partnerships she studied, complementarity crafted a foundation of trust and mutual regard suitable to sustain learning about the essential elements of both the discipline and the collaboration. This learning process, without exception, featured extended interaction and purposeful dialectic and is credited with stimulating the formation of new psychological systems, that is, "new relationships between mental functions" (Minick, 1996, p. 29) or schemata (Hutchins, 1991). If Vygotsky's framework holds, then particular forms of collaborative learning have the potential to rouse new psychological structures that help individuals not only to think creatively about the task at hand but

ultimately to construct a permanently enhanced capacity to think about the world.

COLLABORATION AS SOCIALLY SHARED COGNITION

It is appealing to apply Vygotsky's theory of the sociocultural origins of higher mental functioning in children to the context of adult learning as John-Steiner and Minnick have done. The empirical work of scholars in the field of socially shared cognition makes such linkages increasingly credible. The working assumptions of this branch of cognitive psychology are largely constructivist. In treating social process as cognition, the challenge becomes one of analyzing "the ways in which people jointly construct knowledge under particular conditions of social purpose and interaction" (Resnick, 1991, p. 2). The use of language again appears as a significant mediator in the creation and reorganization of knowledge structures.

> Directly experienced events are only part of the basis for that construction. Our daily lives are filled with instances in which we influence each other's constructive processes by providing information, pointing things out to one another, asking questions, and arguing with and elaborating each other's ideas. (p. 2)

Emerging facets of socially shared cognition have been discussed in a collection of conceptual and empirical studies (Resnick, Levine, & Teasley, 1991). Most pertinent in its implications for this chapter is Hutchins's (1991) study of the stability of confirmation bias in the formation of collaborative interpretations of data.

Confirmation bias is "a propensity to affirm interpretations and to discount, ignore, or reinterpret evidence counter to an already formed interpretation. It is a bias to confirm an already held hypothesis about the nature of the world" (p. 286). On the surface, any strategy that might help researchers to limit the influence of bias would have utility. In collaborative mixed methods research, the bias may be as subtle as an overdeveloped sense of confidence in one's ability to interpret findings generated by a particular method.

Hutchins's (1991) question was whether the combined efforts of individuals could produce decisions unattainable by any individual alone. If it could be shown that the cognitive properties of the group could differ from those of the individuals who constituted the group, then there would be evidence of cognitive processes unique to collaborative contexts, a phenomenon he referred to as distributed cognition.

To investigate this hypothesis, Hutchins (1991) built a problem suitable for computer analysis that would monitor the behavior of a connectionist system called a constraint satisfaction network. The purpose of this network was to provide a rough model of how individuals form interpretations of evidence. Hutchins programmed the individual units within the network with common properties. The effect was the equivalent to forming a group by selecting people who have similar qualities and characteristics. Such a group would have more complementarity than would likely to be found in even a well-established collaborative mixed methods research team.

Hutchins (1991) was interested in what, if anything, might induce individuals working collectively to construct an interpretation of data that would be different from any independent analysis. In practice, a logical and coherent interpreta-tion of phenomena requires that the individual construct a number of hypotheses about the data being experienced. Some hypotheses work to support each other, while others work to exclude or inhibit each other. The linkages constructed between the parts of an argument are called the constraints. The quality of the logic used at each constraint will determine the overall quality of the interpretation. "A good interpretation is one that is both internally consistent and in agreement with the available data" (p. 289).

Hutchins's (1991) findings revealed that even when the individual units were programmed to have similar schemata for phenomena, equal access to environmental evidence, comparable predispositions, and similar beliefs, the various groups he formed using subsets of individual units displayed different cognitive properties. Differences were attributed to the collective qualities of the individuals, the group's functioning, and the group's strategies for communication. Specific findings from this study that have implications for collaborative mixed methods research include the following:

◆ More intensive distribution of data to group members does not always lead to better communication. This finding appeared when the structures for communication led group members to assume that everyone had equal access to all of the data. Under these conditions, there appeared to be less motivation to track the development of others' thinking.

◆ Space for interpretation is more likely when the group members vary on individual parameters. Even subtle individual differences contributed to the construction of unique group profiles. These differences among individuals made the exploration of a wider range of interpretations more likely so long as communication patterns were not too dense.

◆ A hierarchy of authority may influence the consideration of alternative interpretations of data. When the cognitive labor related to a task was distributed, many individual interpretations resulted. These interpretations were not examined when one individual was invested with the authority for interpretation. Alternatively, when the role for the authority was to act as "a special kind of cognitive apparatus, one that tracks the center of gravity of the entire community in conceptual space" (p. 301), dialogue about the interpretations occurred. An authority in this instance is pulled to one interpretation or another and may even have a change of mind about which is the better interpretation based on the quality of the logical constraints being generated.

◆ High levels of persuasiveness for the purpose of consensus building may create conflict among individuals. This is especially true when individuals have a bias to confirm their own interpretations. Under these circumstances, the only meaningful way in which to dislodge the established logic was to give individuals direct access to evidence that would contradict their interpretations.

◆ High levels of persuasiveness for the purpose of consensus building may lead to an interpretation that is not a good fit with the data. When the number of units willing to occupy a particular conceptual space determined the final interpretation of evidence, the quality of the interpretation often suffered. In practice, expending energy on consensus building rather than on building

quality constraints may shortcut communications that are critical to a good interpretation.

A limitation associated with these findings is that they emerged from a simulation and therefore do not represent actual behavior in a social context. For cultural psychologists, this constraint is especially problematic. Researchers such as Cole (1988) would argue that cognition is inseparable from its indigenous context. It would be reasonable for Hutchins (1991) to counter that culture in his study could be loosely defined by the parameters he set for the individual unit responses and by the various patterns of group process and communication he tested.

Beyond this criticism, Hutchins's (1991) study challenges those interested in collaborative mixed methods research to pay special attention to the way in which group processes and communication within the group are structured. Familiarity with all forms of relevant data appears to be the best predictor of a strong interpretation and for overcoming confirmation bias. For this reason, collaborative researchers must be cautious of any propensity to be easily satisfied with one individual's interpretation of evidence, no matter how experienced that person might be. A second hazard would be to assign quality to an interpretation simply because it is supported by a majority of the research team members. One way in which to avoid these pitfalls is for the research team members to develop, a priori, some criteria for deciding whether they have had adequate access to a full range of relevant data.

So far, we have observed that collaboration, at its most powerful, has the capacity to foster creativity in the form of new schemata for understanding and resolving human and social problems. It can do so in three ways:

1. Collaboration can craft a cognitive space, characterized by freedom to think outside of existing frameworks and within the security of a relationship. It is inside this space that individuals explore their understandings, making both fine adjustments and cognitive leaps.

2. Through a dynamic relationship that includes sustained interactivity, extended iterative dialogue, and a dialectic, collaboration can elevate the psychological processes that can be applied to the problem at hand (for a more in-depth discussion of these processes, see the work of Huberman [1999] and Greene & Caracelli [Chapter 3, this volume]).

3. Collaboration can promote learning that, in turn, permanently transforms individual cognitive structures. When this occurs, newer forms of reasoning extend beyond the context of the original learning.

◆ Collaborative Research

If collaborative work has the power to enhance inquiry, then we should be able to observe growing acceptability and use of collaboration in academic contexts. In this section, we examine collaborative research as it is being adopted among academics and between academics and practitioners. A look at collaborative inquiry in both of these contexts sets the stage for other examples of our own work.

Our first task was to identify who, in the academy, was pursing collaborative research.

> Recent work has shown that no hard and fast dichotomy exists between researchers who conduct strictly applied or collaborative research (or orient their activities toward this type of research) and others who conduct only basic research. As could be expected, it is generally the same researchers who engage in both types of research activity. . . . Researchers take part in collaborative research because of the advantages they can get, such as access to new areas of research, instruments, unpublished data, or additional sources of funding. (Goudin & Gingras, 1999, p. 9)

COLLABORATIVE INQUIRY AMONG ACADEMICS

By the early 1990s, there was considerable interest in collaborative research within universities (Goodlad & Keating, 1990; Lieberman, 1992). Efforts to generate grounded theory for this practice were evident in a number of contexts. Baldwin and Austin (1995), for example, studied 18 scholars working in various interdisciplinary activities. All of the participants in this study had reputable research and publishing records and were known by others as successful collaborators. The programs of research represented by this group ranged from 2 to 7 years in length. Baldwin and Austin conducted interviews of 1 to 2½ hours with each of the researchers in their study. Their interview protocol consisted of seven questions, four of which were particularly salient for understanding collaboration in mixed methods research. These four related to the roles that collaborators constructed for themselves and their partners, the problems or challenges that developed within the collaboration, the strategies for resolving collaborative problems, and the perceived positive and negative outcomes of collaborative inquiry.

Similar to the collaborators studied by John-Steiner (2000), the participants in

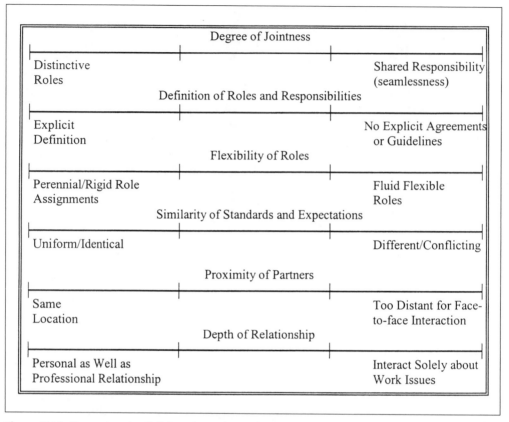

Figure 25.1. Dynamics of a Collaborative Relationship

SOURCE: Baldwin and Austin (1995, p. 60).

this study were able to continuously negotiate the relationships that would ground their work. Baldwin and Austin (1995) recognized this as being consistent with the views of negotiated order theorists who contend that individuals invest considerable effort to establish ways of relating and interconnecting (e.g., Gray, 1989; Strauss, 1978). As such, collaborations can be viewed as negotiated orders. Based on their data, Baldwin and Austin were able to identify six different dynamics within collaborative inquiry that required negotiation (see Figure 25.1).

These scales alert collaborators to the many decisions inherent in establishing a collaborative work group. Baldwin and Austin (1995) concluded that some unique mix of individual attributes of the collaborators and contextual circumstances surrounding the research will ultimately determine how these dynamics are enacted. The individual differences they identified were gender, race, cultural heritage, career stage, geographic location, and professional status. The contextual circumstances are presented in Table 25.1.

The work of Baldwin and Austin (1995) helps to clarify how difficult it would be to standardize collaborative activity. Yet the fact that collaboration can take so many different forms may partially

TABLE 25.1   Contextual Circumstances Affecting Academic Collaborations

Features of Academic Institutions	*Features of Academic Disciplines*
Values and priorities	Modes of operation
Evaluation criteria	Theory base/paradigm development
Reward system	Resources
Incentives for collaboration	Technological base
Resources for collaboration	Collaboration policies and conventions
Policies on collaboration	

SOURCE: Adapted from Baldwin and Austin (1995, p. 63).

account for the growing popularity of the practice and the increase in jointly published articles across the disciplines (see also Goudin & Gingras, 1999; Hafernik, Messerschmitt, & Vandrick, 1997).

This increase in joint effort, however, has not necessarily reshaped the values of the academic community. Hafernik et al. (1997) depicted collaborative research as a practice that remains at best confusing, especially for those who must either assess or demonstrate individual intellectual contributions to the products. More often, they argued, attitudes toward collaborative research, especially in the humanities while less so in the social sciences and the natural sciences, can be disparaging. Here, they quoted colleagues Ervin and Fox (1994): "Collaborative work . . . is frequently interpreted as intellectual weakness. . . . Critics may conclude that one or both contributors couldn't handle the work alone" (p. 54). As we noted previously, it may be quite accurate to observe that the products generated through collaboration might never have emerged from one person's independent research agenda. The fallacy may be only in attributing the impetus toward collaboration to intellectual weakness.

In reporting on their own collaborative work, Hafernik et al. (1997) reported the same benefits as those predicted by theories of sociocultural learning and socially shared cognition. They discussed an enhanced motivation and willingness to risk, opportunities to encounter multiple perspectives, the availability of feedback that advances their own thinking, and ultimately products they indicated reflect more creativity and quality than would be anticipated in independent work.

What Hafernik et al. (1997) added is more insight into collaborative process. John-Steiner's (2000) collaborators demonstrated that prolonged effort across months and even years is a common feature of successful collaborations. These authors claimed that their collaboration was productive in part because contact time and responsibilities remained variable over the course of the relationship. They emphasized not being overly regimented or committed to exact schedules and divisions of labor but rather being open to needs and opportunities as they arise. "Much of what we have done and are doing grows very organically" (Hafernik et al., 1997, p. 34). This caution may appear to contradict the principles of design in academic research. In our own example of teachers' assessment practices, however, if we had not been open to redefining what data we each were prepared to look at and when, then we would have missed an opportunity to include information about "assessment-in-action" in our more general understanding of marking and grading.

Our discussion in this subsection has focused on collaboration among academics as it has evolved both within the disciplines and in interdisciplinary research. It is worth noting that there are now disciplines that focus significant attention on the processes and products of collaboration. "Both cultural historical theory and feminist theory share the belief that it is important to go beyond the narratives of individualism when studying human activity"[4] (John-Steiner, 2000, p. 6). These literatures are not examined here because of their overlap with the sociocultural arguments already used to establish the potential of collaboration to further inquiry. What these additional literatures reinforce is how dialogue and decision making vary depending on the gender mix of the work group (Baldwin & Austin, 1995; Clark & Watson, 1997).

COLLABORATION AS ACADEMIC-PRACTITIONER INQUIRY

Academics not yet experienced in this form of research may have some concerns about the quality and utility of its products. Goudin and Gingras (1999) traced the impact of collaborative studies conducted by Canadian university researchers working with partners outside the university sector. Because these studies were published primarily in "applied" journals, the question posed by Goudin and Gingras was whether such research was useful in the development of basic scientific knowl-

edge. The impact measure Goudin and Gingras selected was one already established by the Institute for Scientific Information: the average number of citations an article receives in 1 year across all journals of the Science Citation Index. The authors found that articles published by cross-organizational collaborators and those published by university authors only did not differ in their ability to influence and support subsequent writings in the field.

The utility of academic-practitioner collaborative research is of special interest to many engaged in evaluative inquiry. The emergence of practical participatory evaluation (Cousins & Earl, 1992, 1995) was the logical extension of successive efforts to make program evaluation more useful for program personnel and their organizations (Shulha & Cousins, 1997). As an approach to problem solving, this form of evaluative inquiry features the joint efforts of program practitioners and one or more trained evaluators. "In the participatory model, the evaluator is the coordinator of the project with responsibility for technical support, training, and quality control, but conducting the study is a joint responsibility" (Cousins & Earl, 1992, p. 400). Defining the scope of the evaluation; preparing data collection instruments; and collecting, analyzing, and reporting data are thus a collaborative undertaking.

The specific nature of these collaborative participatory processes is of interest because they determine the extent to which participants are able to engage in the social construction of knowledge. Such knowledge has proven to be most useful in decisions concerning program processes and outcomes (adaptive) while providing the basis for more informed and complex thinking about the program and its processes (generative).[5]

Using a collection of eight studies that featured participatory evaluation, Cousins and Earl (1995) presented empirical support for a theoretical framework that could account for the variability often observed in collaborative participatory processes. In summary, they demonstrated that the quality of the inquiry and the resulting knowledge was shaped by

1. the roles and responsibilities taken on by practitioner collaborators;

2. the meaning and importance that the evaluator(s), the practitioners, and their organizations ascribed to the inquiry; and

3. the extent to which the specialized knowledge and skills of both the practitioners and the evaluators were allowed to influence the evaluation process.

What is apparent from this framework is that the essential skills of the evaluator are not confined to those studied in methods courses. Consistent with Hutchins's (1991) findings, a participatory evaluator must have an ability to communicate effectively, enact the role of evaluation authority with sensitivity, and know when to be a facilitator and when to be a participant in group processes.

Having constructed this framework, Cousins and Earl (1995) cautioned that *greater* involvement, *deeper* levels of participation, and *more* control over the research by practitioners do not necessarily signify *better* collaboration. For example, if spending time on data collection limits the opportunity for partners to be involved in the interpretation of data, then negotiating a greater role for university personnel in data collection may be desirable.

In a recent book chapter, Cousins (in press) refined this framework. The three dimensions, now labeled *stakeholder selection, depth of participation,* and *control of the evaluation process,* were the basis of instruments used to assess the quality of collaborative participatory processes. The instruments proved powerful enough in field tests to distinguish between collaborative and noncollaborative evaluation designs. Cousins then examined his supposition that partners in a truly participatory and collaborative process would be more likely to carry their learning beyond the evaluation context. A total of 29 evaluation studies, largely American and Canadian conducted between 1996 and 2000, were reviewed. Of these, 17 were "reflective essays," meaning narratives grounded in experience. The remainder reported empirical findings in ways that were more conventional.

Cousins's (in press) analysis of this literature led him to argue that, given certain contextual and policy conditions, collaborative participatory practice shaped the production of knowledge in ways that directly influenced the utility of that knowledge for individuals, groups, and their organization (process use) as well as for the program itself. When both types of evaluation use were evident, there was a greater propensity for individuals to transform the knowledge constructed within the evaluation setting and to apply it in other contexts. This was especially true when individuals went on to deal with issues of liberation, emancipation, enlightenment, empowerment, and self-determination.

Cousins's (in press) work supports John-Steiner's (2000) contention that when adults are immersed in challenging contexts where learning is supported by a social structure such as a collaborative partnership, the conditions are ripe for the development of knowledge structures that transcend that task. In the context of social program evaluation, collaborative inquiry has demonstrated the ability to inspire participants to think and act in new and proactive ways.

The field of evaluation is also developing an increased sensitivity to the role of dialogue in collaborative partnerships.[6] O'Sullivan and O'Sullivan (1998), in their evaluation of a dropout prevention program, argued for extensive dialogue between the evaluator and members of the program community. Dialogue was presented as the tool most effective in tapping the implicit notions of the program so that these could be taken into account throughout the evaluation. It was equally important, they argued, that partners' implicit understandings of the inquiry get the same airing.

This process of checking assumptions and clarifying meanings, whether these are public or more obscure, can introduce stress into partnership development. At such times, Schwandt (1997) directed researchers to be especially conscious of keeping the dialogue reasoned and ethically informed.[7] In more complex forms of collaborative inquiry, this responsibility is dispersed throughout the work group. It would be important, therefore, for collaborators to periodically explore the features of productive dialogue and how these can be supported during highly charged interactions. Owen (1998) was also interested in the quality of dialogue and its role in promoting reasoned inquiry. His call was for a theory of negotiation. Formally integrating stages of negotiation into the inquiry was forwarded as one way in which collaborators could reach agreement not only about the direction and scope of the inquiry but also about the values that would dominate their interactions and subsequent judgments.

The past decade has seen concerted efforts by evaluators and some researchers to understand the effects of building collaborative features into academic-practitioner investigations. Insights from these endeavors effectively complement findings that have been garnered over decades from the field of education.

COLLABORATION IN EDUCATIONAL RESEARCH

The history of collaborative research in education can be traced to the efforts of John Dewey. In his work, Dewey (1938) promoted teacher-researcher partnerships because they proved to be a useful tool in helping teachers to think about and conduct their practice (King, 1995). When Lewin coined the phrase action research in 1944 (Gold, 1999), a body of literature began to formalize around a specific form of inquiry facilitated by the joint actions of teachers and researchers.[8]

Today, collaboration within an action research context typically focuses on the needs of practitioners in their own classrooms and is shaped by a cycle of observation, reflection, and action. The knowledge generated is often highly valued by those who have constructed it. Findings are formalized when there is enough evidence to facilitate localized action and understanding. This outcome usually signals closure of the collaborative activity for both practitioners and researchers. While modern action researchers encourage university-school collaborators to test out the efficacy of their efforts and outcomes by subjecting them to public criticism (Ahar, Holly, & Kasten, 2001), the validating process does not often occur. King and Lonquist (1992) were the first to observe this phenomenon. In a more recent analysis of action research studies listed in the Education Resources Information Center (ERIC) between 1992 and 1999, a bare 10% of entries ($n = 35$) had been refereed for publication (Shulha, 1999a). This inattention to a broader audience may contribute to the low profile sometimes accorded collaborative action research in other research communities.

A great deal of collaborative inquiry in education, however, is no longer classical action research. Currently, we are seeing more collaborative inquiry intended to inform both program and policy development. It is a transformation that is likely a response to many conditions: the failure of conventional top-down models of knowledge dissemination (Brookhart & Loadman, 1992); the snail's pace of traditional models of research, development, and implementation (Tikunoff & Ward, 1983); and an emerging interest in new contexts for educational theory building and testing (Wilson & Shulha, 2001).

Involvement in a collaborative theory-building project focusing on teachers' classroom assessment practices motivated Lee and Shulha (1999) to review 54 studies and opinion pieces related to collaborative practice in education. Their questions were concerned with the responsibilities of collaborators and the potential of collaboration to contribute to knowledge construction. This review was limited in that only readily available books, journal articles, and conference papers published or distributed between 1985 and 1999 were used.

An unexpected finding of the review was the difference in emphasis between the conceptual and empirical literatures. The empirical studies consistently accentuated the goals of collaboration and the roles that partners might play to pursue such goals. Collaboration was essentially defined as a collection of behaviors to be implemented throughout a partnership. Done effectively, these behaviors would lead to mutually beneficial outcomes. For example, Feldman (1992) talked about the need to minimize the power differential that can exist between teachers and researchers, recommending role-switching

with teachers as a way to accomplish this goal.

The conceptual literature, by contrast, described collaboration as a series of cognitive and cultural interactions. Brookhart and Loadman (1992), for example, reasoned that because schools and universities represent different cultures, teachers and researchers carry different values and bring different cognitive conceptions to the inquiry process. The challenge, they argued, is to generate some mutual understanding of the focus, tempo, rewards, and power relations implicit in each other's practices. Collaboration is portrayed as joint meaning making. This mutual construction of meaning is facilitated by an abundance of shared experiences and quality dialogue over time (Cole & Knowles, 1993).

> The physical and interpersonal contextual elements of collaboration are the building blocks of culture and can be seen to impinge upon cognitive processes utilized by collaborators. Consequently, a consideration of collaboration cannot be divorced from an understanding of cultural and cognitive process. (Lee & Shulha, 1999, p. 5)

Frameworks offered by the conceptual literature accounted for many of the successes and frustrations reported by teachers, researchers, and evaluators in the reviewed studies. This led Lee and Shulha (1999) to argue that when the focus within a partnership remains at the level of distinguishing or promoting different roles and goals alone, partners fail to understand the importance of their work. A critical feature of collaboration in conceptual literature, but not well attended to in practice, was the extent to which partners facilitated the clarification of language and the values embedded in that language. Clarifying goals, taking on the other's role, engaging in shared activities, and structuring joint efforts all served collaborative purposes, but when these strategies were not purposefully linked to meaning making, efforts were sometimes wasted.

It was not uncommon for collaborators in the empirical studies to report dissatisfaction with collaborative activities and disappointment when apparent understandings broke down under stress (see Shulha & Wilson, 1995). These accounts confirmed that overly structured learning experiences and traditional consensus activities were not highly functional elements of collaborative inquiry. Activities such as formal instruction by a more capable member of the collaboration and consensus building are purposefully designed to change the stance of the other. Collaborative activities work to illuminate each individual's stance and the purpose it serves. In a collaborative context, only the individual holding a position has the authority to modify it. When this begins to occur, it is evidence of a reframing process (Huberman, 1990) rather than a capitulation to the authority of a facilitator or group.

SUMMARIZING THE NATURE OF COLLABORATION IN RESEARCH

We have referenced the work of social, cognitive, and cultural psychologists as well as the grounded theories of interdisciplinary researchers, educational researchers, and evaluators to make the following argument: Collaboration is simultaneously an individual and social pattern of interaction with the potential to stimulate ways of thinking that are normally inaccessible to any individual working on her or his own. In the field of research, this unique method of learning can result in a depth of understanding about phenomena that is more complex and less vulnerable to individual confirmation bias. There is also growing evidence that more in-depth collaborative partnerships—ones that yield insights into both the object of inquiry and the learning processes that gave rise to these insights—leave their participants more capable of extending their understandings into new problem contexts.

Collaboration is recognizable through a full range of behaviors. These behaviors help with learning about self, others, and the problem or task at hand. This learning is facilitated if there are both individual differences and complementarity within the group. The utility of collaboration in research is twofold; it has the potential to facilitate both imaginative investigations of problems and the reasoned deliberation about contradictions and conflicts as these appear within individuals, within the group, and across the margins of individual and organizational cultures.

We have also gathered evidence that to advance unique learnings, collaborators must have a high degree of sensitivity to the conversational interplay that supports joint effort. This includes being able to monitor and shape the quality of the dialogue (i.e., the extent to which there is mutual exchange, active listening, probing, clarifying, and/or risk taking) and of the dialectic (i.e., the art and practice of logical discussion). It follows that researchers wishing to make claims about their findings based on collaborative designs must be able to provide evidence about the depth and quality of interaction among participants, including the process of meaning making.

The literature reviewed in this section demonstrates that the interests of many types of research are well-served when an appropriate collaborative component is built into the inquiry. This holds whether the research is basic or applied, university or field based, conceptual or empirical. It is reasonable to expect, therefore, that if the purposes for joint effort fit the nature of the problem to be investigated, then mixed methods inquiry can also benefit from collaborative approaches.

◆ Collaborative Mixed Methods Research

The two studies documented in this section both feature collaborative mixed methods research involving the authors and others. Having established the importance of individual characteristics in shaping the quality of collaborative activity and findings, it seems appropriate that we provide a brief introduction of who we are. Shulha is currently a midcareer female academic whose doctoral work in educational evaluation has led her to work and conduct research in the areas of program evaluation, collaboration, and student assessment. Her work in evaluation necessitated the use of mixed methods approaches. Wilson is a male senior professor in educational measurement. He has designed and conducted numerous program evaluations and has participated extensively in the design, implementation, and analysis of large-scale provincial, national, and international educational assessments. He continues doing research in classroom assessment practices and research methods.

Our impressions of each other's values and beliefs about teaching and research, and our propensity to challenge each other's thinking about theory and practice, originated during our work as instructors of different sections of a common preservice education course. Over the past decade, our collaborative work has been marked by intellectual play,

space for independent projects, support from our spouses, and quizzical looks from colleagues and clients who, on hearing our verbal banter, wonder how we could possibly work together. While there are enough differences in academic background, research background, gender, experience, and professional status to create differing capabilities and perspectives in our collaborative efforts, we also have found a significant degree of complementarity (John-Steiner, 2000). This foundational relationship shaped the variations on collaborative mixed methods research described in this section.

CASE 2: PROFESSIONAL DEVELOPMENT INTERNATIONAL

Should teachers and academics form a learning partnership? In an effort to support professional work of both academics and practitioners, administrators from Queen's University in Kingston, Canada, and Colegio Bolivar in Cali, Colombia, proposed a 3-year learning partnership. A unique feature of this project was that teachers and faculty were given the authority to determine the viability of this proposal. The final decision to establish the partnership was grounded in the results of a university-school evaluative inquiry session that was conducted at the school. For 2 extended days at the beginning of summer vacation, 18 teachers worked collaboratively with us to synthesize data and construct findings about the feasibility and utility of a learning partnership.

"The challenge was to design [a process] that would be powerful enough to actively engage us all in collaborative inquiry, prepare us for decision making, and leave us with new understandings of professional learning" (Shulha, 2000, p. 45). We decided to structure the orienting inquiry in ways consistent with the model of collaborative participatory evaluation described by Cousins and Earl (1992). Our joint task was to understand the notions of teaching and learning that shaped individual, department, and school-based behaviors and to see how these might be supported by a learning partnership. All teachers at the school completed a survey comprising of both qualitative and quantitative items.

Our participatory approach required that teachers, as primary users of the data, take on the central role in analyzing it. Our responsibility was to determine the appropriateness of a learning partnership from a university perspective. Given our evaluation backgrounds, we were also charged with ensuring quality control during the instrument design, data gathering, and analysis phases of the inquiry. To facilitate the qualitative analysis, we instructed teachers in the techniques of constant comparative analysis. Their interest and responsiveness to the task freed us up to do a concurrent analysis of the quantitative data. While our tasks were different, we worked together in the same space.

In the beginning, we held primarily tacit understandings of how the group process we were orchestrating was shaping the quality of the data analysis. Our priority was to facilitate full and productive participation of teachers in the inquiry. This task was particularly complex because it was orchestrated in a cross-cultural context. Not only did our inquiry process require the joint effort of a unique mix of school and university people, it required that the dialogue be conducted in both English and Spanish, and we were by no means fluent in the latter language.

It was an early and somewhat surprising realization that data relevant to our decision about a partnership was being gleaned not only from the surveys but

also from the ways in which we were currently working as a group. We found ourselves carefully monitoring the teachers' behaviors.

> Their questions and comments as they proceeded with the assigned tasks provided important feedback about the quality of their learning and their commitment to the task. At times, [these] data came from breakout discussions and lunchtime conversations. These more informal interactions were significant because they provided additional "spaces" where individuals could connect what they were learning about their colleagues and their school with their own emerging ideas of what a partnership might look like. Regular, formal debriefings of "where are we now" made it possible to integrate talk from both the formal and informal contexts into our ongoing work. (Shulha, 2000, p. 46)

What we all acknowledged in subsequent discussions was that the orientation inquiry had always been done with "one eye on the other." Both groups collected and analyzed observational data. Of particular interest was evidence that represented a commitment to learning, sensitivity to individual differences, openness to new ideas, risk taking, and student-centeredness.

The survey findings, both qualitative and quantitative, allowed us to draft a description of the current state of teaching and learning at Colegio Bolivar and the current constraints to optimal learning. It also gave us an indication of teachers' aspirations for students and the professional learning activities that were a priority for teachers at the school (Shulha & Wilson, 1996). These values and needs did indeed match the values and expertise of our university. These findings, however, played a far smaller role in decision making than might have been predicted.

> By the end of the needs assessment, it was apparent that our joint inquiry had fostered interdependence and a sense of anticipation for the first fall module. This is no doubt what Preskill and Torres (1999) are referring to when they describe evaluative inquiry as having the potential to be "self renewing." Teachers, administrators, and evaluators were now "in relationship," and as time would attest, it was a relationship that would remain significant over the life of the partnership and beyond. (Shulha, 2000, p. 49)

We left Colombia with a strong sense that a partnership would be beneficial for members of both organizations. The group had been able to draft a structure for the learning and a set of nine indicators that would help assess the workings of partnership over time.

In our opening example of collaborative mixed methods research, the collaboration was especially influential in shaping the design of the instruments and in resolving the meanings of data generated at different times by different methods. In this example, the collaboration shaped the way in which our work group was able to make sense of data generated in different ways, from different sources, and in different languages. The formal survey data (both qualitative and quantitative) had been supplemented with observations and a unique form of mutual interviewing. These latter two sources of data came directly out of the collaborative activities that ranged in formality from structured summarizing exercises to group lunches.

The decision to commit to a learning partnership was based on a blend of formal findings and informally derived evidence of complementarity. The learnings and personal insights that fed into the final decision were a product of the collaboration that our work group had enacted.

This case introduces the notion that collaborative inquiry may do more than support the formal activities and mental processes that are normally identified as research methods. The conversations, behaviors, and observations that take place during collaborative inquiry may actually become useful data in addressing the research problem. Our final case explores this hypothesis further.

CASE 3: CLASSROOM PRACTICES—NATIONAL

What can we learn about classroom assessment practices by tracking teachers' efforts to resolve an authentic assessment dilemma? Three teachers (two elementary school and one secondary school), two doctoral students, and the authors identified this question as part of a larger collaborative cross-provincial study of classroom assessment. It was a collaboration that was active for 4 years and formally ended only when there were no more resources available to support it. (Informally, much collaboration continues.) Closure was marked by presentations of processes and findings at both academic and practitioner conferences. Six of the seven members of our group remained active until the end.

The program of research was launched around dilemmas of classroom assessment as identified by the teachers. As the collaboration evolved, the researchers, reflecting on their teacher roles, contributed dilemmas as well. Over the course of the partnership, we addressed concerns such as the following:

- My students need to become more independent and self-regulating.

- My parents need a better understanding of what and how their children are learning, and the children need to understand this better as well.

- The government has just imposed large-scale standardized assessment in mathematics, and I do not know how this fits with my teaching of math.

- My students focus more on passing tests than on learning.

- I hate marking.

- I am not sure when I am actively assessing and what it looks like.

- I want to integrate students' interests into what is taught and learned.

The design of this study, particularly the methods we would use to collect and analyze data, was not easily conceptualized (Wilson & Shulha, 2001). We reviewed the assumptions underpinning quasi-experimental research and realized that many were problematic for this context. In its conventional uses, this form of research is powerful in testing out predictions about phenomena of interest. When we listened to our teachers talk about their dilemmas, we realized that we had no predictions about either why the dilemmas existed or how they could be resolved. After just meeting these practitioners, we were in no position to identify for them the variables that might be contributing to their dilemmas, nor were we prepared to design an intervention that might test how

certain practices would work to address the dilemmas. Such an approach would constitute an intrusion into their regular classroom routines and practices and would defeat the purpose of understanding the theories and beliefs that guide assessment-in-action. It would also turn our focus more toward the accurate measurement of variables and less on understanding how decision making about assessment occurs.

The obvious alternative was a design that was more interpretive, but this direction would also have constraints. A case study approach, for example, begins with a question that often can be linked to emerging grounded theory. This method would have us gather rich and thick descriptions of the teachers' behaviors and actions within the classroom. Some of these data would be our own observations, others would be the communication patterns used in the classroom, and still others would be the self-reports of the teachers reflecting on their practices and planning interventions.

Typically, however, researchers construct the meaning of these data. Certainly, we could make considerable efforts to represent the study from our teachers' viewpoint. This could be done by involving them in aspects of the data collection and analysis, by using their language in the analysis, and by checking our interpretations against theirs. These strategies, however, would not have altered our ultimate responsibilities to determine what aspects of self-reported thinking and behavior were most credible as data, to make decisions about how to reduce the data, to establish the codes and categories for analysis, to identify the patterns in the data, and to propose their meaning.

Our quandary was that we also had theories about what kinds of assessment might work in classrooms and how those outside the classroom were shaping teachers' assessment practices. As we began the research, we had no clear idea about how our values and beliefs might be woven into our own actions and interpretations. Our assumption was that teachers' "logic-in-theory" and "logic-in-action" (and the discrepancy between the two) was best understood when teachers had the freedom to select and investigate, with support, issues of personal relevance. The method problem we faced was that no conventional form of inquiry, mixed or otherwise, could be imposed on our teachers. As researchers, we had no methodological way to control the inquiry.

> The absence of preset criteria or even questions for investigation means that these studies can examine dilemmas selected by teachers which are then open to negotiation with the investigators. Issues that emerge during the inquiry are tested against what is already practiced and the principles enunciated by the participants themselves. The discussions within this paradigm most often focus on discovery. The goal is to see emergent understandings facilitate improvement in practice. Because no dilemma remains static during the course of the inquiry, it is often necessary to revisit and reestablish the focus as the study progresses. (Wilson & Shulha, 2001, p. 4)

Even with many of the method issues unresolved, we proceeded. We began to call our method of inquiry collaboration. The desired outcome of this method, beyond any that could be applied to improving classroom practice, was the joint construction of meaning around particular facets of classroom assessment. This is not the same as a quest for a common meaning of classroom assessment practice. Efforts at meaning making required us to partici-

pate in constant iterative dialogue. It was primarily through such dialogue that each of us was able to access the implicit assumptions and tacit knowledge that shaped our individual as well as our group's understandings, beliefs, and practices. We set out to learn together, and we used as the grist for this learning our various dilemmas. What we mixed in this method were our individual attributes and expertise.

We reviewed literature, observed and commented on each other's practices, became active listeners, and supported a dialectic in both formal and informal settings. All of these activities helped to build trust and establish complementarity. Authority within the group was distributed, and leadership during any particular meeting was invested in the person willing to be a conceptual leader around the issue being discussed.

We deconstructed popular and conventional models of assessment practice and rebuilt them using a combination of examined research findings and evidence from our own practices. For some models of practice (e.g., rubric building, portfolio development), particular dimensions of the model became accepted as "true," while other dimensions remained variable. When there were differences in our thinking, it was a signal for either more dialogue or more data. The issue of interest determined whether these data were qualitative or quantitative. Differences in understanding, then, were not problematic and in need of resolution; rather, they were generative and in need of testing.

As the collaboration continued, it did become possible to summarize new learnings about classroom assessment (Wilson, 2000). It was also the case that more people became interested in these emergent understandings. Our team members, both individually and in various groupings, were regularly invited to work with teachers and administrators in the analysis and construction of assessment practices.

The two teachers, who remained in collaboration with us for 2 years beyond our formal agreement, have been recognized as leaders in thinking about assessment. They have led professional development activities for their colleagues both within and outside their own schools. One of our teachers was given a district award for the quality of his teaching practices; the other was conscripted by provincial education officials to develop guidelines for helping teachers to focus on the quality of their students' learning. These post-research developments are consistent with the form of knowledge use that Cousins (in press) argued would be a logical extension of quality collaboration and the kind of development that Vygotsky theorized would follow significant learning within the zone of proximal development.

The notion of collaboration as mixed methods research is not without merit. As collaborators, we brought to the inquiry varied, complex, and at times tacit knowledge structures related to assessment practice. We each used our own understandings to sense and make sense of each other's ideas and work. In so doing, we not only made the implicit explicit but also analyzed the underlying assumptions that shaped reasoning and behavior—our own and others'. We were, in practice, six different instruments working in different ways to generate and analyze data about problems that interested us.

The task of each individual in the group was to bring forward observations and meanings as these were being formed. The task of the work group was to expose contradictions and constraints in meaning making. The continuous enactment of these forms of data collection and analysis shaped the individual and collaborative understandings that we were to report. As in Hutchins's (1991) experiment, our individual contributions (the utility of persons

as instruments) were mediated by the nature of the group process and our normative patterns of communication. This understanding spurred us to report on the features of our collaboration as well as on our findings.

In this final example, collaboration was the primary method of inquiry. As such, the procedures used needed to be made as explicit and comprehensible as any of the companion quantitative or qualitative approaches. While a reference to constant comparative and regression methods communicates precise and accepted practices, researchers have yet to establish standards of behavior for particular forms of collaboration. The conceptual literature and empirical examples cited in this chapter can provide a foundation for distinguishing these forms.

◆ A Rubric for Understanding Collaboration

No one way of collaborating is necessarily better than another. A collaboration in which the scope and limitations of inquiry and analysis are at least partially defined by established paradigms (Case 1) does not require the same degree of mutual learning as a collaboration that is used to generate new data and promote cross-cultural understandings (Case 2). The variation in our three cases supports our contention that judgments about the appropriateness of collaboration cannot be made independent of the expressed purpose for the inquiry itself. The more findings are attributed to collaborative inquiry, the more important it is that a profile of that collaboration be transparent to those with a stake in the findings.

Frameworks such as the ones offered by Baldwin and Austin (1995; see Figure 25.1 and Table 25.1) and Cousins (in press) are first steps in helping collaborators to see their work as complex and dynamic. But for those examining the contribution of joint effort to the outcomes of inquiry, it is the quality rather than the quantity of such effort that is important to discern.

In contrast to scales, growth rubrics offer distinct advantages for measuring complex behavior (Fostaty Young & Wilson, 2000). They can (a) act as a guide for learning the behavior, (b) distinguish among various types and progressively more complex forms of the behavior, (c) provide feedback about progress toward a desired form of the behavior, and (d) offer explicit criteria for judging expertise. If collaboration is undertaken as one of the methods of inquiry, then the behavior that defines the collaboration must be scrutinized at various points during the inquiry. Only then can the importance of collaboration within the research process be understood. The use of rubrics supports such scrutiny.

To construct such a rubric (see Table 25.2), we reviewed the factors and dimensions identified by the various literatures and then tested these against our own experiences. As a set, the five elements we constructed for our rubric do the best job of explaining the variability in learning that can occur during collaborative research. Our elements are *motivation for involvement* (Baldwin & Austin, 1995; Cousins & Earl, 1995), *depth of participation* (Baldwin & Austin, 1995; Cousins & Earl, 1995; John-Steiner, 2000), *quality of the dialogue* (Hutchins, 1991; John-Steiner, 2000; Minick, 1996; O'Sullivan & O'Sullivan, 1998; Owen, 1998), *authority in decision making* (Baldwin & Austin, 1995; Huberman, 1990; Hutchins, 1991), and *joint meaning making* (Cole & Knowles, 1993; Cousins, in press).

Our next challenge was to develop qualitative descriptors of what these elements would look like as they became integral to learning. In its simplest form,

collaboration and learning are distanced independent activities. As behavior within each of these elements becomes more complex, collaboration and learning become more related and ultimately integrated. When this final stage occurs, it becomes virtually impossible to separate collaboration from learning; the whole point of the collaborative activity—the motivation for engaging in the process at all—is learning.

An early version of this rubric was used to assess the quality of collaboration in our third study (Shulha, 2000). In the resulting profile, the elements were assessed as primarily, but not totally, *integrated*. Our motivation for involvement, the depth of our participation, and the authority we shared in decision making contributed most to our claim of collaborative learning. The other two elements, while also contributing to a sophisticated profile, showed room for growth. The fact that this pattern of collaborative learning was distributed across two levels of complexity and was still sufficient to contribute to the study's overall findings supports this subsequent claim: No single set of behaviors can adequately identify "best collaborative practices." Rather, the optimal form of collaboration will always depend on the purpose of the joint effort. When collaboration is purposefully added as a method of inquiry (thus creating a new form of mixed methods design), the responsibility is on the research team to make the case that its behaviors were sufficient to support a unique form of learning.

LEARNINGS FROM THREE CASES OF COLLABORATIVE MIXED METHODS RESEARCH

Each of the three case studies presented in this chapter demonstrates a different way in which to conceptualize and enact collaborative mixed methods research. The more an inquiry relies on conventional

TABLE 25.2   A Growth Model of Collaborative Learning

Elements of Collaboration	Distanced	Related	Integrated
Motivation for involvement	• To represent the interests of a group • To represent a self-interest • To serve colleagues or an employer • To avoid the consequences of noninvolvement	• To achieve an otherwise unattainable goal(s) • To work in a less isolated context • To fulfill a role as a stakeholder in the outcomes of joint work	• To explore a complex dilemma/problem of personal or professional interest • To experience personal or professional growth • To fulfill a role as a primary user of the processes and outcomes of joint work
Depth of participation	• Describes joint effort as a series of routines • Focuses on meeting the expectations of others • Is constrained by opportunities for interaction • Is constrained by current level of communication skills	• Supports extended interactions • Participates in both formal and informal collective activities • Participates in the formal gathering, analysis, and interpretation of data • Takes an interest in the roles, goals, ideas, and values of others in the work group	• Initiates activities that advance joint effort • Expresses values and ideas that nurture a dynamic relationship • Contributes vigor and playful energy in support of joint activities • Risks unconventional approaches to problem solving
Quality of the dialogue	• Advances primarily self-interests • Focuses on efficiency in decision making and problem solving • Proposes ideas that fit with the perceived aims and needs of external authorities	• Welcomes divergent ideas • Features listening, clarifying, and reframing the ideas of others • Demonstrates trust and mutual regard • Inserts reasoned responses into highly charged deliberations	• Questions and probes the values and behaviors of self and others • Works to make explicit the assumptions shaping ideas and actions • Focuses on data and the logic of the argument • Inserts reasoned and creative, but untested, ideas into deliberations

(Continued)

TABLE 25.2 (Continued)

Elements of Collaboration	Distanced	Related	Integrated
Authority for decision making	• Assumed based on roles in current or other contexts • "Purchased" in exchange for time and effort on behalf of the group	• Allocated based on a fit between specific expertise of individual and the current task/challenge	• Invested in particular individuals depending on context • Dispersed over all members of the group
Meaning making	• Understandings of the joint effort are additive • Understandings represent the "majority," "authority," or "consensus" view • Next steps and summary accounts reflect individual perspectives	• Individual meanings and uses of terms are clarified and honored • Understandings of joint effort, past and present, evolve • Understandings are a product of extended iterative dialogue • Next steps and summary accounts acknowledge alternative views	• Partners are joint theorists in constructing meaning of information and behavior • Individuals attribute outcomes to both personal and joint effort • Next steps and summary accounts are grounded in data and are a logical consequence of a transparent dialectic • Learnings are individual and collective • Learnings are extended and make contributions in other contexts

quantitative and qualitative methods to define what is being mixed, the more important it is for collaborators to assess the unique observations that these differing lenses provide the inquiry as a whole. This process is likely facilitated when participants see collaboration and learning as primarily related (see Table 25.2).

As new understandings become more dependent on the meanings that research team members construct in interaction with each other (as was partly the case during our work in Colombia and as was entirely the case in our final example), the more the participants themselves become the instruments of data collection and the mediators of design and analysis procedures. In a context where the quality of the inquiry is dependent on researchers' tacit and explicit understandings of the research problem and its context, it is critical that collaboration and learning be mostly integrated (see Table 25.2).

Ultimately, a case needs to be made that the behaviors within the work group served the purpose of the inquiry. This is a different process from proving that an inquiry was collaborative. The elements and individual cells of the rubric for collaborative learning found in Table 25.2 make it possible for those engaged in joint effort to construct a profile of their efforts and to use this profile both formatively and summatively.

◆ Warrants for New Understandings About Collaborative Mixed Methods Research

In preparing this exploration, we took our case-specific understandings and connected them to each other and to related theoretical frameworks. In so doing, we discovered that collaborative mixed methods research could be more than the joint effort of researchers using conventional qualitative and quantitative paradigms. We documented how collaboration itself can transform the nature of data collection and analysis. In seeking to identify how this restructuring of methods can arise and, furthermore, why it can be successful, we revisit the nature of the inquiry.

At the root of academic inquiry are the twin pillars of the persuasiveness of rationality and of evidence. Making the "good case" for a form of mixed methods inquiry (and for other methods, for that matter) involves trustworthiness, logic of argument, consistency across multiple lines of evidence, transparency of assumptions, clarity of expression, consistency with expectations of audience, and some evidence of concept scope. By focusing on

these warrants rather than on methods, we are required to critique each step in the process leading to findings and interpretations.

Collaborative mixed methods research may be more likely to persuade (in appropriate settings) when it broadens the evidence base and the boundaries of discussion. What is created with this approach is a unique web of argument to support conclusions about particular problems or phenomena. By bringing contrasting views together to focus on an issue and on evidence, including the ways in which the evidence was amassed, mixed methods research can result in advances not possible with a single method. In this sense, when mixed methods are also collaborative, in any form, the potential exists for learning that is more than additive. Indeed, when the focus is squarely on the learning that collaborative activity will bring into being, methods of whatever kind and in whatever combination are subordinate to the overall goal of understanding more about the phenomena that gave rise to the research in the first place.

■ Notes

1. For the full description, see Wilson and Martinussen (1999).

2. You will notice that the Wilson and Martinussen (1999) article is also joint work. Martinussen was a master's student at the time and contributed to a portion of the data analysis but not in the writing of the article.

3. For a more complete delineation of the styles, purposes, and philosophical underpinnings to collaborative research, particularly in the field of education and participatory evaluation, see Cousins (in press), Lee and Shulha (1999), and Levin (1993).

4. John-Steiner (2000) referenced her previous work in this claim (see John-Steiner, 1999).

5. The value of participating in evaluation is a feature of "process use" and is described in detail in Patton (1997, 1998).

6. To sample various authors in this area, see Hopson (2000).

7. For additional guidance in ethics of working with collaborators, see the Propriety Standards developed by the Joint Committee on Standards for Educational Evaluation (1994).

8. The traditions, popularity, and complexities of action research are thoroughly explored by King and Lonquist (1992).

■ *References*

Ahar, J. M., Holly, M. L., & Kasten, W. C. (2001). *Action research for teachers: Traveling the yellow brick road.* Upper Saddle River, NJ: Merrill Prentice Hall.

Anderson, J. O. (1999). Modelling the development of student assessment. *Alberta Journal of Educational Research, 45,* 267-277.

Baldwin, R. G., & Austin, A. E. (1995). Toward greater understanding of faculty research collaboration. *Review of Higher Education, 19*(1), 45-70.

Brookhart, S. E., & Loadman, W. E. (1992). School-university collaborations: Across cultures. *Teaching Education, 4*(2), 53-68.

Clark, C. M., & Watson, D. B. (1997). *Women's experience of academic collaboration* [Online]. Available: www.edst.educ.ubc.ca/aerc/1997/97clark.htm

Cole, A., & Knowles, J. (1993). Teacher development partnership research: A focus on method and issues. *American Educational Research Journal, 30,* 473-495.

Cole, M. (1988). Cross-cultural research in a socio-historical tradition. *Human Development, 31,* 137-157.

Cole, M., & Scribner, S. (1978). Introduction. In M. Cole, V. John-Steiner, S. Scribner, & E. Souberman (Eds.), *Mind in society: The development of higher psychological processes* (pp. 1-14). Cambridge, MA: Harvard University Press.

Cousins, J. B. (in press). Understanding participatory evaluation for knowledge utilization: A review and synthesis of current research-based knowledge. In D. Nevo & D. Stufflebeam (Eds.), *International handbook of educational evaluation.* Boston: Kluwer Academic.

Cousins, J. B., & Earl, L. M. (1992). The case for participatory evaluation. *Educational Evaluation and Policy Analysis, 14,* 397-418.

Cousins, J. B., & Earl, L. M. (Eds.). (1995). *Participatory evaluation in education: Studies in evaluation use and organizational learning.* London: Falmer.

Dewey, J. (1938). *Experience and education.* New York: Macmillan.

Elliott, A. E., & Woloshyn, V. E. (1997). Some female professors' experiences of collaboration: Mapping the collaborative process through rough terrain. *Alberta Journal of Educational Research, 43,* 23-36.

Ervin, E., & Fox, D. (1994). Collaboration as political action. *Journal of Advanced Composition, 14*(1), 53-71.

Feldman, A. (1992, April). *Models of equitable collaboration between university researchers and school teachers.* Paper presented at the meeting of the American Educational Research Association, San Francisco.

Fostaty Young, S., & Wilson, R. J. (2000). *Assessment and learning: The ICE approach.* Winnipeg, Manitoba: Portage & Main.

Gold, M. (1999). *The complete social scientist: A Kurt Lewin reader.* Washington, DC: American Psychological Association.

Goodlad, J., & Keating, P. (1990). *Access to knowledge: An agenda for our nation's schools.* New York: College Entrance Examination Board.

Goudin, B., & Gingras, Y. (1999). The impact of collaborative research on scientific production. *Research, 3*(3). (Ottawa: Association of Universities and Colleges of Canada)

Gray, B. (1989). *Collaborating: Finding common ground for multiparty problems.* San Francisco: Jossey-Bass.

Greene, J. C., & Caracelli, V. J. (1997). Defining and describing the paradigm issues in mixed-method evaluations. In J. C. Greene & V. J. Caracelli (Eds.), *Advances in mixed-method evaluation: The challenges and benefits of integrating diverse paradigms* (New Directions for Evaluation, No. 74, pp. 5-17). San Francisco: Jossey-Bass.

Hafernik, J. J., Messerschmitt, D. S., & Vandrick, S. (1997). Collaborative research: Why and how? *Educational Researcher, 26*(9), 31-36.

Hopson, R. K. (Ed.). (2000). *How and why language matters in evaluation* (New Directions for Evaluation, No. 86). San Francisco: Jossey-Bass.

Huberman, M. (1990). Linkage between researchers and practitioners: A qualitative study. *American Educational Research Journal, 27,* 363-391.

Huberman, M. (1999). *The mind is its own place: The influence of sustained interactivity with practitioners on educational researchers.* Harvard Educational Review, 69, 289-319.

Hutchins, E. (1991). The social organization of distributed cognition. In L. Resnick, J. Levine, & S. Teasley (Eds.), *Perspectives on socially shared cognition* (pp. 283-307). Washington, DC: American Psychological Association.

John-Steiner, V. (1999). Sociocultural and feminist theory: Mutuality and relevance. In S. Chaiklin, M. Hedegaard, & U. J. Jensen (Eds.), *Activity theory and social practice* (pp. 201-224). Arhus, Denmark: Arhus University Press.

John-Steiner, V. (2000). *Creative collaboration.* New York: Oxford University Press.

Joint Committee on Standards for Educational Evaluation. (1994). *The Program Evaluation Standards* (2nd ed.). Thousand Oaks, CA: Sage.

King, J. (1995). Involving practitioners in evaluation studies: How viable is collaborative evaluation in schools? In B. Cousins & L. Earl (Eds.), *Participatory evaluation in education: Studies in evaluation use and organizational learning* (pp. 86-102). London: Falmer.

King, J. A., & Lonquist, M. P. (1992). *A review of writing on action research (1944-present).* Madison, WI: Office of Educational Research and Improvement. (ERIC Document Reproduction Service No. ED 355 664)

Lee, M., & Shulha, L. M. (1999, June) *The emergence, anatomy, and implications of teacher/researcher collaboration.* Paper presented at the meeting of the Canadian Society for Studies in Education, Sherbrooke, Quebec.

Levin, B. (1993). Collaborative research in and with organizations. *Qualitative Studies in Education, 6,* 331-340.

Lieberman, A. (1992). The meaning of scholarly activity and the building of community. *Educational Researcher, 21*(6), 5-12.

Minick, N. J. (1996). The development of Vygotsky's thought: An introduction to thinking and speech. In H. Daniels (Ed.), *An introduction to Vygotsky* (pp. 28-52). New York: Routledge.

O'Sullivan, R. G., & O'Sullivan, J. (1998, April). *Model dropout prevention program at Reidsville Middle School: A case study evaluation.* Paper presented at the meeting of the American Council on Rural Special Education and the National Rural Small Schools Consortium, Tucson, AZ.

Owen, J. M. (1998, December). Towards a theory of negotiation. *Evaluation News and Comment,* pp. 32-35.

Patton, M. Q. (1997). *Utilization-focused evaluation: The new century text* (3rd ed.). Thousand Oaks, CA: Sage.

Patton, M. Q. (1998). Discovering process use. *Evaluation, 4,* 225-233.

Phillips, D. C. (1992). *The social scientist's bestiary: A guide to fabled threats to, and defenses of, naturalistic social science.* New York: Pergamon.

Phillips, D. C., & Burbules, N. C. (2000). *Postpositivism and educational research.* Totawa, NJ: Rowan & Littlefield.

Preskill, H., & Torres, R. (1999). *Evaluative inquiry for learning in organizations.* Thousand Oaks, CA: Sage.

Resnick, L. (1991). Shared cognition: Thinking as social practice. In L. Resnick, J. Levine, & S. Teasley (Eds.), *Perspectives on socially shared cognition* (pp. 1-22). Washington, DC: American Psychological Association.

Resnick, L., Levine, J., & Teasley, S. (Eds.). (1991). *Perspectives on socially shared cognition*. Washington, DC: American Psychological Association.

Schwandt, T. A. (1997). The landscape of values in evaluation: Charter terrain and unexplored territory. In D. J. Rog & D. Fournier (Eds.), *Progress and future directions in evaluation: Perspectives on theory, practice, and methods* (New Directions for Evaluation, No. 76, pp. 25-39). San Francisco: Jossey-Bass.

Shulha, L. M. (1999a, November). *Evaluators as partners in school/university collaborations*. Paper presented at the meeting of the American Evaluation Association, Orlando, FL.

Shulha, L. M. (1999b). Understanding novice teachers' thinking about assessment. *Alberta Journal of Educational Research, 45,* 288-303.

Shulha, L. M. (2000). Evaluative inquiry in university-school professional learning partnerships. In V. Caracelli & H. Preskill (Eds.), *The expanding scope of evaluation use* (New Directions for Evaluation, No. 88, pp. 39-54). San Francisco: Jossey-Bass.

Shulha, L. M., & Cousins, J. B. (1997). Evaluation use: Theory, research, and practice since 1986. *Evaluation Practice, 18*(3), 195-208.

Shulha, L. M., & Wilson, R. J. (1995). Inviting collaboration: Insights into researcher-school community partnerships. In B. Cousins & L. Earl (Eds.), *Participatory evaluation in education: Studies in evaluation use and organizational learning* (pp. 115-139). London: Falmer.

Shulha, L. M., & Wilson, R. J. (1996). *Developing a learning partnership in teacher professional development and research: A technical report*. Kingston, Ontario: Queen's University, Faculty of Education.

Shulha, L. M., Wilson, R. J., & Anderson, J. O. (1999). Exploratory, non-foundationalist mixed-method research. *Alberta Journal of Educational Research, 45,* 304-314.

Strauss, D. (1978). *Negotiations, varieties, contexts, processes, and social order.* San Francisco: Jossey-Bass.

Tikunoff, W. J., & Ward, B. A. (1983). Collaborative research on teaching. *Elementary School Journal, 83,* 453-468.

Vygotsky, L. S. (1978). *Mind in society.* Cambridge, MA: Harvard University Press.

Wertsch, J. V. (1991). A sociocultural approach to socially shared cognition. In L. B. Resnick, J. M. Levine, & S. D. Teasley (Eds.), *Perspectives on socially shared cognition.* Washington, DC: American Psychological Association.

Wilson, R. J. (1990). Classroom practices in evaluating student achievement. *Alberta Journal of Educational Research, 36*(1), 4-17.

Wilson, R. J. (1992). The context of classroom procedures in evaluation of students. In D. L. Bateson (Ed.), *Classroom testing in Canada* (pp. 3-10). Vancouver: University of British Columbia, Center for Applied Studies in Evaluation.

Wilson, R. J. (2000, May). *Toward an integrated model of assessment-in-practice.* Paper presented at the meeting of the Canadian Educational Researchers Association, Edmonton, Alberta.

Wilson, R. J., & Martinussen, R. L. (1999). Factors affecting the assessment of student achievement. *Alberta Journal of Educational Research, 45,* 267-277.

Wilson, R. J., & Shulha, L. M. (2001, April). *Effects of methods on conclusions about teachers' assessment practices.* Paper presented at the meeting of the American Education Research Association, Seattle, WA.

26

THE PAST AND FUTURE OF MIXED METHODS RESEARCH: FROM DATA TRIANGULATION TO MIXED MODEL DESIGNS

♦ Abbas Tashakkori
  Charles Teddlie

Here we are, at the end of our journey through mixed methods, or is it the beginning? While putting together this handbook has been a long and arduous endeavor, it has also been an exciting one that included working with some of the best authors currently writing on mixed methods.

The contributors to the handbook examined a diverse array of concepts, issues, and practices in mixed methods. We identified several controversial areas in Chapter 1 and provided an overview of those issues there. Contributors addressed these issues in greater detail throughout the handbook, providing both convergent and divergent viewpoints. These contributors have provided us with fertile ground on which to develop a more comprehensive and systematic framework for mixed methods research.

With few exceptions (mainly due to presentation style), we edited the handbook chapters as lightly as possible so that the diverse "voices" of the contributors could be heard. For example, at least four distinct voices were expressed regarding mixed methods design typologies: Morse in Chapter 7; Creswell, Plano Clark, Gutmann, and Hanson in Chapter 8; Maxwell and Loomis in Chapter 9; and our contribution in Chapters 1 and 26. We hope that the juxtaposition of these differing typologies will eventually create greater consistency in the area. To facilitate this goal, we have suggested hybrid terms that incorporate the QUAL and QUAN traditions. These terms are intended to be descriptive of the QUAL and QUAN counterparts in multiple strands of a mixed methods study.

The handbook was written by a diverse and accomplished group of authors. We purposefully selected some authors who had already made major contributions to the field (e.g., Creswell, Greene & Caracelli, Hunter & Brewer, Maxwell, Morse, Newman, Rallis & Rossman, Sandelowski) so that their unique viewpoints could be heard. We also selected other scholars relatively new to the field who we believed would make interesting contributions (e.g., Bazeley, Johnson & Turner, Onwuegbuzie). Finally, we selected individuals to write chapters related to specific disciplines, and these seven chapters demonstrated the breadth of appeal that the field of mixed methods has.[1]

This diverse group of authors has demonstrated the major point of this handbook: Mixed methods research is a distinct third methodological movement in the social and behavioral sciences. This third methodological movement rejects the "either-or" of the quantitative or qualitative approaches. It has its own nomenclature, paradigm orientations, designs, and practices that are different from the other two movements.

In Chapter 1, we pointed to six controversial areas in the literature related to mixed methods. We identified six major unresolved issues and controversies in the use of mixed methods in social and behavioral research:

1. The nomenclature and basic definitions used in mixed methods research

2. The utility of mixed methods research (why do we do it)

3. The paradigmatic foundations for mixed methods research

4. Design issues in mixed methods research

5. Issues in drawing inferences in mixed methods research

6. The logistics of conducting mixed methods research

These issues were discussed throughout the handbook, and this chapter contains some final words regarding each of them. While there are still unresolved aspects of each of these issues, we now have the material for creating consistencies and bridges within the field.

◆ The Nomenclature and Basic Definitions Used in Mixed Methods Research

We discussed several nomenclature and definition issues in Chapter 1. Probably the most important decision regarding nomenclature in mixed methods concerns the following two options:

1. Should we develop or select two sets of bilingual terms (one set of terms for QUAN constructs and another set of terms for similar QUAL constructs) and then use them interchangeably as we move from descriptions of QUAN to QUAL research processes (and vice versa)? As noted in Chapter 1, Lincoln and Guba (1985) did this for validity (QUAN) and trustworthiness (QUAL) criteria.

2. Should we develop new mixed methods terms to replace the traditional QUAN and QUAL terms? We did this in Chapter 1 when we suggested replacing various QUAN and QUAL validity terms with a new mixed methods terminology that includes inference, inference quality, design quality, interpretive rigor, inference transferability, and so on.

Some authors have expressed concern that if we develop a whole new set of terms, this would confuse the already overly complex language of research methodology. We are suggesting that there are in fact three languages of research methodology:

◆ One well-developed language for the QUAN tradition with many terms consistently defined

◆ One fairly well-developed language for the QUAL tradition with a number of terms defined differently depending on the particular paradigms in use

◆ One developing language for mixed methods research

The mixed methods research language will consist of the following:

◆ Bilingual terms that describe similar processes from the QUAL and QUAN traditions

◆ Terms unique to the QUAL tradition that have no analogs in the QUAN tradition but may be expanded or slightly modified to incorporate some of the concepts in that area

◆ Terms unique to the QUAN tradition that have no analogs in the QUAL tradition but may be expanded or slightly modified to incorporate some of the concepts in that area

◆ New mixed methods terms

These options are not mutually exclusive and singular (i.e., they might be combined). For example, the new mixed methods terminology related to inference consists of terms from QUAL and QUAN literature, combinations that are unique to mixed methods (e.g., ecological transferability), and new terms (e.g., inference quality). In Chapter 1, we concluded that there are three basic conditions under which new mixed methods terms may be developed to replace traditional QUAN and QUAL terms: (a) when the described QUAN and QUAL processes are highly similar, (b) when the existing QUAL and QUAN terms have been overly used or misused, and (c) when appropriate terminology exists. These conditions existed with regard to the various validity terms, and we then proposed the substitution of the inference terminology.

Differences in mixed methods terms used across disciplines was another area discussed in Chapter 1. These cross-disciplinary differences were illustrated in Chapters 17 to 23. We believe that many of these differences will disappear as a common mixed methods research language develops.

One interesting difference alluded to in Chapter 1 of the handbook was the overuse of the term triangulation in the field of nursing, as noted by both Sandelowski (Chapter 12) and Twinn (Chapter 20). Sandelowski makes this point very clearly:

p.328

> When any kind of research combination is designated as triangulation, there is no inquiry that is not triangulated. Having too much meaning, the word triangulation has no meaning at

all. . . . Triangulation appears as a "near-talismanic method" (Miles & Huberman, 1994, p. 266) for democratizing inquiry and resolving conflicts between qualitative and quantitative inquiry.

Triangulation is a veritable "magical" word in mixed methods research, having been developed through a series of insightful works (e.g., Campbell & Fiske, 1959; Denzin, 1978; Jick, 1979; Patton, 1990). Triangulation is a word that most researchers, regardless of their own methodological orientation, associate with mixed methods. We would not want to discard a word with "near-talismanic" meaning, so what do we do when it appears to be overused to the point where it means nothing? Can the term be rehabilitated, or does it carry too much baggage? Only time will tell.

In the Glossary, we have defined triangulation as "the combinations and comparisons of multiple data sources, data collection and analysis procedures, research methods, and/or inferences that occur at the end of a study." This definition was made quite broad to cover the most important aspects of research that have been associated with triangulation. Data sources, data collection and analysis procedures, and research methods have been tied to triangulation techniques in seminal articles and chapters on the topic (e.g., Denzin, 1978; Patton, 1990). Creswell et al. (Chapter 8, this volume) used triangulation in their typology of design (e.g., "concurrent triangulation design"). Inferences were also included because Erzberger and Kelle (Chapter 16, this volume) used the term to refer to agreement between inferences (e.g., rules of integration). While we have broadened the definition of the term triangulation to make it more consistent with the literature, it is

unclear whether the term has any meaning when it is so broadly defined. Despite the popularity of the term, we encourage mixed methodologists to refrain from using it unless they specify how it was specifically defined in their research context. Also, we leave it up to the readers to decide whether the term has become so broad as to mean nothing.

◆ The Utility of Mixed Methods Research

In Chapter 1, we concluded that there were three reasons to conduct mixed methods research:

- ◆ Mixed methods research can answer research questions that the other methods cannot.

- ◆ Mixed methods research provides better (stronger) inferences.

- ◆ Mixed methods research provides the opportunity for presenting a greater diversity of views.

There are examples of research throughout the handbook that illustrate these three characteristics of mixed methods research. We briefly review three of these research projects in this section.

MIXED METHODS RESEARCH CAN ANSWER RESEARCH QUESTIONS THAT OTHER METHODS CANNOT

The GAIN evaluation described by Rallis and Rossman (Chapter 17, this volume) is an excellent example of a mixed methods research study that answered confirmatory and exploratory questions simultaneously. GAIN was a welfare-to-work program created by the California legislature that provided welfare recipients with job search assistance, basic education, vocational training, and so on. GAIN's goals were an increase in employment and a reduction in reliance on welfare. Three of the four goals of the evaluation (Riccio, 1997) can be restated as questions:

1. What are GAIN's effects on employment and on the number of individuals on welfare?

2. What can we learn about the California counties' experiences in implementing GAIN and the recipients' participation and experiences?

3. How did different program strategies influence the results?

The first question is a confirmatory one because the evaluators (or at least their funding agency) expected GAIN to have a positive effect on employment and on welfare roll figures. This question was answered by statistical analysis of quantitative data generated by a large-scale experimental study in which welfare recipients were randomly assigned to GAIN or a control group.

The second and third questions were exploratory ones aimed at describing the counties' experiences in implementing GAIN, the recipients' experiences, and how various strategies influenced results. A variety of data sources were used to answer these questions: field research, case file data, surveys of both staff and program recipients, and so on. These exploratory questions were vital to the evaluation because without them the evaluators would not know how the program's effects occurred.

MIXED METHODS RESEARCH PROVIDES BETTER (STRONGER) INFERENCES

The occupational life study described by Erzberger and Kelle (Chapter 16, this volume) is a good example of a study whose inferences were stronger because they resulted from both quantitative and qualitative data. This project had two major sources of data (Krüger, 2001):

1. Standardized questionnaire data on the occupational life courses of a sample of males (birth cohort of 1930), including starting and end points of employment, of periods of unemployment, of illnesses, and so on

2. Open-ended qualitative interviews in which the males discussed their interpretations and perceptions of their occupational and domestic lives

The researchers expected great stability in the occupational life courses of the cohort because the respondents had worked during West Germany's postwar period (i.e., the 1950s and 1960s), often called the "era of the economic miracle." The study cohort members experienced a large part of their working lives in this "economic miracle," which was characterized by traditional orientations and norms, including gender role patterns with regard to the tasks, obligations, and rights of males and females.

The quantitative data indicated that the great majority of the men in the cohort were fully employed nearly all of their lives except for short periods of joblessness or sickness. There were few interruptions in their work careers.

The qualitative data confirmed the results from the analysis of the quantitative data. The in-depth interviews included questions about the males' interpretations of their work biographies, their perceptions of their role as "breadwinners," and their participation in household and family work. Paid labor had a high importance for the males in the study, who perceived it as their fair share of the total work effort for the family. They considered "breadwinning" as the husband's central moral obligation and as fulfillment of his family work duties.

The consistency between the experiences of the respondents related to their occupational life courses (quantitatively described through the standardized questionnaires) and their subjective interpretations of these experiences (qualitatively determined through their responses to the open-ended questions) made the inferences from the study much stronger. Having both sources of data also made the reporting of the results much more interesting.

MIXED METHODS PROVIDES THE OPPORTUNITY FOR PRESENTING A GREATER DIVERSITY OF DIVERGENT VIEWS

The evaluation of the federal housing subsidy program described by Maxwell and Loomis (Chapter 9, this volume) is a good example of a mixed methods research study that provided the opportunity for presenting divergent views. This study, conducted by Trend (1978), involved the concurrent, but separate, collection of quantitative and qualitative data on a federal housing subsidy program. The data sources were as follows:

1. Quantitative data gathered mainly by surveys on agency activities, expenses, demographic characteristics of clients, and housing quality

2. Qualitative case studies of each site written by anthropologists using field observations, interviews, and documents

The quantitative data were expected to determine the success of the program, while the case studies were to be used to provide a picture of program process. Divergent views emerged, however, when the conclusions from one observer in one site directly contradicted the results of the quantitative analysis of the program effect at that site. Part of the reason for this divergence in results involved values; the observer advocated the position of the agency staff and clients, while the quantitative analysts tended to represent the views of the program managers and the funding agency.

A series of actions then occurred. The funding agency sided with the quantitative analysts and told the observer to rewrite his case study to agree with the quantitative results. Trend (the author of the evaluation report) and the observer reexamined the quantitative and qualitative data and eventually came up with a coherent process explanation that went beyond the initial quantitative and qualitative analyses. This mixed methods analysis pointed out shortcomings in both the initial qualitative and initial quantitative analyses.

If only the quantitative data had been analyzed, then an inaccurate (too positive) picture of the federal housing subsidy program would have resulted. Similarly, if only the case study had occurred, then an inaccurate (too negative) picture of the program would have emerged. When the data were mixed, a more accurate picture developed. In this evaluation, mixed methods first allowed the opportunity for divergent views to be voiced and then served as the catalyst for a more balanced evaluation.

◆ The Paradigmatic Foundations for Mixed Methods Research

Six different positions were described in Chapter 1 concerning the use of paradigms in mixed methods research. The three most viable ones (i.e., the three that have been advocated the most in this handbook) are as follows:

1. The "dialectical" stance regards mixed methods research as intentionally engaging multiple sets of paradigms and does not advocate one paradigm above others (e.g., Greene & Caracelli, 1997; Chapter 3, this volume). To think dialectically means to examine the tensions that emerge from the juxtaposition of these multiple diverse perspectives.

2. The single paradigm thesis is popular for those mixed methodologists who prefer a consistent worldview. The two most popular paradigms presented in this handbook are pragmatism (e.g., Maxcy, Chapter 2) and the transformative-emancipatory paradigm (Mertens, Chapter 5).

3. The multiple paradigm position proposes that the researcher engage the paradigm that is most appropriate for the particular design that is undertaken (e.g., Creswell et al., Chapter 8, this volume).

There is no need to rehash the similarities and differences among these three positions given that they were spelled out in detail in Chapter 1 and throughout the handbook. Nevertheless, there are two questions that require some further consideration. First, how could pragmatism and the transformative-emancipatory paradigm be used as alternative worldviews for studies employing mixed methods? Second, why is pragmatism the paradigm of choice for so many mixed methodologists?

PRAGMATISM AND TRANSFORMATIVE-EMANCIPATORY PARADIGMS AS ALTERNATIVE WORLDVIEWS FOR THE USE OF MIXED METHODS

As noted in Chapter 1, scholars are now explicitly acknowledging that multiple paradigms may be associated with the use of mixed methods designs. Creswell and his colleagues (Chapter 8, this volume) gave several examples in which multiple paradigms were applied to six different mixed methods designs introduced in that chapter. This multiple paradigm stance may be employed to justify the use of both pragmatism and the transformative-emancipatory paradigm as alternative worldviews for the use of mixed methods.[2]

Probably the most basic difference between these two points of view is axiology or the role of values in research. Pragmatists believe that the values of the researcher play a large role in the selection of research topics and in the interpretation of results. Advocates of the transformative-emancipatory viewpoint posit social justice and democracy, especially for oppressed groups, as the goal of research.[3] Cherryholmes (1992) further elucidated the role of axiology for pragmatists:

> For pragmatists, values and visions of human action and interaction precede a search for descriptions, theories, explanations, and narratives. Pragmatic research is driven by anticipated consequences. Pragmatic choices about what to research and how to go about it are conditioned by where we want to

go in the broadest of senses. . . . Beginning with what he or she thinks is known and looking to the consequences he or she desires, our pragmatist would pick and choose how and what to research and what to do. (pp. 13-14)

In our opinion, these two axiological positions are not in conflict; rather, they describe research programs that may be quite different from one another. A scholar working in the transformative-emancipatory tradition seeks topics that may directly help an oppressed member of the society. A pragmatist selects topics that are of special interest to him or her but that quite often also involve aspects of social relevance.

Consider the school effectiveness research area as an example of the use of both points of view. There are three major strands of school effectiveness research (Reynolds & Teddlie, 2000, p. 3):

◆ "School effects" research: Studies of the scientific properties of school effects evolving from economically driven input-output studies to current research using multilevel statistical models

◆ "Effective schools" research: Research concerned with the processes of effective schooling evolving from case studies of outlier schools through contemporary studies using mixed methods in the simultaneous study of classrooms and schools

◆ School improvement research: Examining the processes whereby schools can be changed using increasingly sophisticated models that have gone beyond simple applications of school effectiveness knowledge to sophisticated "multiple lever" models

School effects research is conducted within the tradition of postpositivism. Researchers working in this area use quantitative analyses of large-scale databases to determine the scientific properties of school effects such as the percentage of variance in students' learning that is attributable to the school.

Effective schools research is concerned with determining the "processes" of effective schooling, which are the behavioral patterns that distinguish more effective schools from less effective schools. Many effective schools researchers are pragmatists (Teddlie & Reynolds, 2001), and they use mixed methods to answer their research questions.

What constitutes the belief system of pragmatists conducting effective schools research? First, they believe that some schools are more effective in educating their students than are other schools serving the same general population of students (e.g., more effective and less effective schools serving students from primarily middle-class backgrounds). Thus, these pragmatists believe that there is a school effect. Second, these pragmatic researchers believe that there are discernible practices that distinguish more effective schools from less effective ones.

Third, these researchers believe that mixed methods are most appropriate for answering their research questions because these methods provide the broadest array of techniques to answer those queries. Fourth, pragmatists believe that the results from their research should be written up in a manner that highlights the effective schools processes; that is, researchers focus on results that they think will best illuminate the processes whereby schools become more effective. Pragmatists typically write the results for a broad educational audience. The anticipated consequences of pragmatists' research might include that the audience will be more convinced that there is such a phenomenon as a school effect, the audience will learn ways to improve schools in general, the audience will learn ways to improve their own schools, and so on.

School improvement research is typically conducted by individuals who want to make schools, and therefore the educational system, better. These researchers often have a particular group of students they want to help (e.g., lower socioeconomic status students, African American students, dyslexic students). Researchers conducting school improvement research specifically for one of these "oppressed" groups of students are working in the transformative-emancipatory tradition.

Some school effectiveness researchers have first conducted effective schools research and then used the information from that research to establish a school improvement program (e.g., Stringfield, 1995). Such a researcher would be using the pragmatist approach in the effective schools research studies and the transformative-emancipatory approach in the school improvement studies, especially if the latter studies focused on particular groups of students.

From a sampling perspective, the researcher's attentions turned from the general population of students to oppressed subgroups or minorities as his or her research program evolved from effective schools research to school improvement research. The researcher's viewpoint would be pragmatic when it focused on the entire population of students. The researcher's viewpoint would more accurately be called transformative-emancipatory at the point where his or her research focused on a specific group of oppressed students.

Popularity of Pragmatism Among Mixed Methodologists. Pragmatism is the paradigm most often mentioned in the mixed methods literature and in this handbook; sources advocating the pragmatist position include Bazeley (Chapter 14, this volume), Datta (1997), Forthofer (Chapter 19, this volume), Howe (1988), Maxcy (Chapter 2, this volume), Patton (1988, 1990), Rallis and Rossman (Chapter 17, this volume), Rossman and Wilson (1994), Rocco et al. (Chapter 23, this volume), Smaling (1994), Tashakkori and Teddlie (1998), and Teddlie and Tashakkori (Chapter 1, this volume). Because this paradigm is mentioned most often in the mixed methods literature, there are some further points to be briefly addressed in the remainder of this section.

Why is pragmatism such a popular position among so many mixed methodologists? One major reason is that mixed methods are often employed in applied settings where practical decisions stress the utility of multiple data sources for decision-making purposes. Several of the chapters written by individuals from applied fields in this handbook (e.g., education, evaluation, health sciences) were written from the pragmatic viewpoint. Such fields often require multiple methods to understand complex social phenomena.

Pragmatic researchers also consider the research question to be more important than either the method they use or the paradigm that underlies the method (the "dictatorship of the research question"). This stance is very appealing to many researchers throughout the social and behavioral sciences. Pragmatists also reject the forced choice between the positions of the QUALs and QUANs on a number of dimensions, and this acceptance of aspects of both orientations is popular among many researchers.

Lingering Criticisms of Pragmatism. Despite the popularity of pragmatism, there are still critics who assume that pragmatism is inappropriate as a worldview for conducting mixed methods research. For instance, Mertens (Chapter 5, this volume) stated,

> The value of pragmatics that drives the desire to adopt a mixed methods stance in research is seen as inadequate and unexamined because it does not answer the question "Practical for whom and to what end?" (House & Howe, 1999). Transformative-emancipatory scholars recommend the adoption of an explicit goal for research to serve the ends of creating a more just and democratic society that permeates the entire research process, from the problem formulation to the drawing of conclusions and the use of the results (Mertens, 1998).

We have several reactions to this statement. First, as noted previously, we believe that pragmatism and the transformative-emancipatory model can be used as alternative worldviews associated with the use of mixed methods, depending on the type of research that is being done. Of course, other paradigms might also be appropriate, but at this point in time these are the two most widely advocated, at least in this handbook.

Second, stating that one paradigm is the best one, and that others are inferior because they do not employ the correct value system, seems to put us back into the type of atmosphere that characterized the "paradigm wars." Why do we want to take that step backward when even the old-time warriors now adopt the multiple paradigm viewpoint?

Third, we believe that the transformative-emancipatory orientation might be better conceptualized as a purpose of a research project (see Newman, Ridenour, Newman, & DeMarco, Chapter 6, this volume). Researchers often have goals that are different from "creating a more just and democratic society." These goals might include simple curiosity about why any given phenomenon occurs. Or they could include an examination of the effect of a new reading program for all third-graders (not just third-graders from certain oppressed groups). These alternative goals of research are as acceptable as the goal of creating a more just and democratic society within the transformative-emancipatory paradigm.

◆ Design Issues in Mixed Methods Research: Toward an Integrated Typology of Mixed Methods Designs

Determining a typology of mixed methods designs (i.e., identifying the basic procedures for using both QUAL and QUAN strands in a single study) is among the most complex and controversial issues in mixed methodology. There are numerous types of mixed methods designs in the literature. For example, we have identified nearly 40 types of mixed methods designs in this handbook or elsewhere in the literature, including triangulation, transformative, integrated, component, sequential, parallel, concurrent, simultaneous, branching, nested, explanatory, exploratory, confirmatory, developmental, decomposed, embedded, mixed method, mixed model, hierarchical, monomethod, multimethod, multimethods (plural), equivalent-status, dominant-less dominant, multilevel, two-phase, methodological triangulated design, sequential triangulation, simultaneous triangulation, and Design Types II through VIII of Tashakkori and Teddlie.

Although this list is not exhaustive, it clearly demonstrates the need for creating a consistent system or typology that would incorporate many of the diverse designs described in the literature. Someone needs to create an integrated typology of

TABLE 26.1   A Dynamic Conceptualization of Mixed Methods Research

	Quantitative <------------- Mixed Methods -------------> Qualitative	
Sphere of concepts (abstract operations) Purposes Questions	Deductive questions <----------------------------> Inductive questions Objective purpose <----------------------------> Subjective purpose Value neutral <----------------------------> Value involved Politically neutral <----------------------------> Transformative	
Experiential sphere (concrete observations and operations) Data Observation	Numerical data <----------------------------> Narrative data Structured process <----------------------------> Emergent process Statistical analysis <----------------------------> Content analysis	
Sphere of inferences (abstract explanations and understandings) Theories Explanations Inferences	Deductive logic <----------------------------> Inductive logic Objective inference <----------------------------> Subjective inference Value neutral <----------------------------> Value involved Politically neutral <----------------------------> Transformative	

mixed methods research designs. We present our expanded typology (from that initially presented in Chapter 1) later in this section.

A CONCEPTUAL MODEL FOR MIXED METHODS RESEARCH

Before we present our classification of mixed methods research designs, we briefly present a simplified conceptual model for mixed methods research. Table 26.1 presents this model in which three spheres represent three general stages of research (conceptualization, method, and inference). This tripartite division of the research process is a modified form of the three dimensions (type of investigation, type of data collection and operations, and type of analysis and inference) used in

our earlier work (Tashakkori & Teddlie, 1998).

For each sphere, three or four areas (attributes) are presented that traditionally have been assumed to distinguish QUAN and QUAL approaches (e.g., "objective" vs. "subjective" inference). Mixed methods designs are characterized by one of the following two conditions:

1. They have multiple positions along each attribute in Table 26.1 (e.g., they have both confirmatory and exploratory questions).

2. They are near one end of the continuum on one attribute (e.g., inductive question) and near the other end on another attribute (e.g., statistical analysis). The switching ends of the continuum across attributes may be present within spheres or between them.

To reduce the chaotic terminology associated with mixed methods designs, a new typology should be developed that is relatively simple and consistent but that also meets the needs of scholars from many fields. This is an ambitious task, but it is possible to do. We believe that we are at a point in the history of mixed methods that we can (collectively) create a common design typology that incorporates the many convergent and divergent viewpoints that have been voiced.

In our opinion, such an integrated typology is possible only if it is developed hierarchically on the basis of the importance of decisions that the investigator has to make in choosing a particular design for doing a study. The highest level of classification in the typology should include the most important decisions that the investigator needs to make so as to conceptualize his or her research design. The second level consists of less common or more specialized issues.

To construct this integrated typology, we use three decision points for the first level of the hierarchy: (a) how many strands (single or multiple) the study will require, (b) what sort of procedure will be employed to create the mixing (sequential, concurrent, or data conversion), and (c) at what stage the mixing will occur (only in method of study or in all stages). The distinction between single strand (monostrand) and multiple strand (multistrand) designs is used instead of terms using phase so as to create commonality in language with Maxwell and Loomis (Chapter 9, this volume) as well as with Greene and Caracelli (Chapter 3, this volume).

We also suggest that a second classification level might be added to any of the design types that resulted from the first level of the hierarchy. The second level might further classify each research design on the basis of "purpose of the study" (e.g., transformative, exploratory, confir-

matory) (see chapters in this volume by Mertens [Chapter 5] and Newman et al. [Chapter 6]) or on the basis of "priority" (e.g., dominance, supervenience) (see Creswell, 2002; Creswell et al., Chapter 8, this volume; Morgan, 1998; Morse, Chapter 7, this volume; Miller, Chapter 15, this volume). For the "dominance" dimension, three subtypes are possible (equal status, predominantly QUAL, and predominantly QUAN).

We should also note here that the design typology presented throughout this section incorporates a wide array of ideas and design types presented by others. However, it is mainly based on the procedures of the study (as represented in the first level of the hierarchy) rather than on purpose or expected/unexpected results or priority (as represented in the second level of the hierarchy). As discussed by Erzberger and Kelle (Chapter 16, this volume), research outcomes such as complementarity, expansion, triangulation, confirmation, and "dissonance" of inferences in mixed methods studies are not predictable beforehand. Furthermore, any of these conditions might be present at the end of any mixed methods design, regardless of type. Therefore, we consider them to be either the purpose of the mixed methods studies (e.g., "transformative-emancipatory" purpose or "generate new ideas" purpose in Newman et al., Chapter 6, this volume) or the expected/unexpected results of the studies (e.g., confirmation or expansion in Erzberger & Kelle, Chapter 16, this volume).

Although we have incorporated most of the underlying dimensions of other classifications, we are not suggesting that the typology proposed in this chapter should replace them. We are hoping that other scholars will use our logic to expand/modify their own current typologies of designs. For example, we have incorporated/modified two dimensions (stage of integration and sequence) from Creswell and colleagues' (Chapter 8, this volume) typology. Within each type of design presented later in this section, subcategories may also be created based on Creswell and colleagues' third dimension (theoretical framework or what we call political ideology or purpose).

CONNECTION WITH THE TYPOLOGY PRESENTED IN CHAPTER 1

In Chapter 1, we outlined the relationship among multimethods and mixed methods designs. In this chapter, we present an expanded version of that typology based on criteria to be described later in this section. It seems useful to present a more detailed outline at this point as an advanced organizer. This detailed outline presents where the designs described in this chapter fit within the overall typology of designs presented in Chapter 1. Traditional monomethod (QUAL or QUAN) designs are not placed in this outline because they do not have more than one method or more than one worldview.

I. Multiple Method Designs (more than one method or more than one worldview)

A. Multimethod designs (more than one method but restricted to within worldview (e.g., QUAN/QUAN, QUAL/QUAL)

1. Multimethod QUAN studies— multimethod QUAN designs

2. Multimethod QUAL studies— multimethod QUAL designs

B. Mixed methods designs (use of QUAL and QUAN research methods or data collection/analysis procedures)

1. Mixed method research (occurs in the methods stage of a study)—

concurrent mixed method designs, sequential mixed method designs, conversion mixed method designs

2. Mixed model research (can occur in all stages of a study)— monostrand mixed model designs, concurrent mixed model designs, sequential mixed model designs, conversion mixed model designs, fully integrated mixed model designs

MONOSTRAND DESIGNS

We presented a classification of monostrand designs in Chapter 1 (Table 1.2) based on our earlier work (Tashakkori & Teddlie, 1998). Monostrand mixed methods designs (also known as single phase designs) have not been well-articulated in mixed methods research; therefore, there is no other systematic typology to integrate at this time. These designs use a single research method or data collection technique (QUAL or QUAN) and corresponding data analysis procedures to answer research questions. By contrast, multistrand designs use more than one research method or data collection procedure. Nearly all typologies of mixed methods in the literature (including the ones in this handbook) are multistrand in nature. We present a detailed typology of both groups of designs (monostrand and multistrand) in the remainder of this section.

There are two basic types of monostrand designs:

1. Monostrand (Monomethod) QUAL or QUAN Design. This is the traditional qualitative or quantitative design, depicted in Figure 26.1, in which the investigator has either exploratory or confirmatory questions, uses a qualitative or quantitative research method to answer

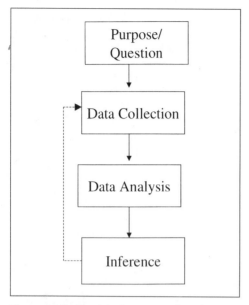

Figure 26.1. Graphic Depiction of Traditional QUAL or QUAN Designs

them, and accordingly makes inferences that are either QUAL (e.g., subjective, constructivist) or QUAN (e.g., objective, value-neutral) in nature (see also Table 26.1 for a summary of these QUAL and QUAN attributes).

2. *Monostrand Mixed Designs.*[4] In these designs, only one research method (QUAL or QUAN) is used to answer research questions that are exploratory/QUAL and/or confirmatory/QUAN. Mixing occurs across stages of the research process. We depicted these stages in Table 26.1 in terms of three spheres: sphere of concepts (abstract operations), experiential sphere (concrete observations and operations), and sphere of inferences (abstract explanations and understandings). Mono-strand mixed model designs shift ends of the continuum (QUAL or QUAN) from one attribute/line to another within or across these three spheres. Two specific

types of this design are identified on the basis of the stage at which this shift occurs:

◆ Designs that switch ends of the continuum from the first sphere (i.e., conceptualization, question) to the second sphere (i.e., method, concrete operations)

◆ Designs that switch ends of the continuum in the middle sphere (i.e., method, concrete operations)

The first case is conceptually mixed (e.g., a confirmatory question is answered through using a qualitative research method or data collection and analysis). Detailed examples of this design may be found in Tashakkori and Teddlie (1998) and in Patton (1990, pp. 191-193). We suggest naming it conceptually mixed monostrand design.

Figure 26.2 depicts this type of design. Please note that in this figure and all subsequent ones, geometric shapes (rectangle or oval) may represent either a QUAL or a QUAN approach. In other words, each figure presents two variations; in one the rectangle shape is defined as QUAL, and in the other it is defined as QUAN. Also, please note that the broken line between "inference" and "data collection" indicates an iterative or "interactive" relationship (see Maxwell & Loomis, Chapter 9, this volume) in which the inferences might point to the necessity of further data collection.

The second general category of monostrand mixed model designs involves exploratory or confirmatory questions that are answered through an analysis of transformed data (i.e., when either narrative data are quantitized and analyzed statistically or numerical data are qualitized and analyzed qualitatively). These studies are mixed because they switch approach in the method of study (see Table 26.1).

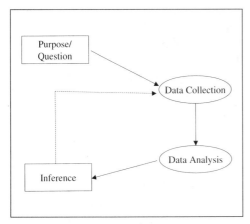

Figure 26.2. Graphic Presentation of Conceptually Mixed Monostrand Design

NOTE: Geometric shape (rectangle or oval) represents either a QUAL or a QUAN approach. The broken line between "inference" and "data collection" indicates an iterative or "interactive" relationship.

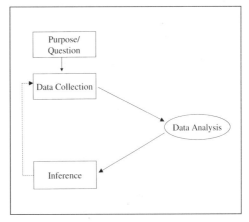

Figure 26.3. Graphic Presentation of Monostrand Conversion Design

Figure 26.3 depicts this type of design. We suggest naming this type monostrand conversion design.

An interesting attribute of the monostrand conversion design is that it has been used extensively throughout the history of social and behavioral research (in both qualitative and quantitative traditions) without being recognized by researchers as "mixed" (see, e.g., chapters in this volume by Maxwell & Loomis [Chapter 9], Waszack & Sines [Chapter 21], and Hunter & Brewer [Chapter 22]).

MULTISTRAND DESIGNS

Multistrand designs use more than one research method or data collection procedure. Multistrand designs are distinguished on three dimensions: (a) having single or multiple approaches (i.e., having two QUAL or two QUAN strands vs. having both QUAL and QUAN strands), (b) stage of integration (i.e., across all stages vs. within method only), and (c) procedures for linking the strands (e.g., sequential vs. concurrent).

a. *Single or Multiple Approach Dimension.* In Chapter 1, we distinguished multimethod from mixed methods designs. Multimethod designs use more than one research method or data collection procedure that are restricted to a single "worldview" (i.e., two QUAL or two QUAN strands) (see Sandelowski, Chapter 12, this volume). They are differentiated into multimethod QUAN and multimethod QUAL studies. This type of design is depicted in Figure 26.4. The multimethod QUAN design was employed by Campbell and Fiske (1959) in their pioneering work on the multitrait-multimethod matrix.

Multistrand mixed methods designs are the main focus for the classification typology in this chapter because they are the most widely used and innovative mixed methods designs. They use two methods of study (e.g., ethnography and survey) or

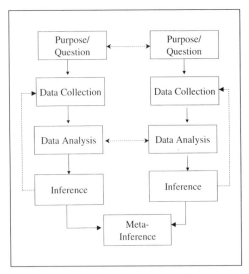

Figure 26.4. Graphic Presentation of Traditional Multimethod Qualitative or Multimethod Quantitative Designs

two data collection techniques (e.g., qualitative observations and closed-ended questionnaires) to answer exploratory and/or confirmatory research questions. For simplicity, we refer to them as multistrand mixed designs (as compared with monostrand mixed designs) throughout the remainder of this chapter.

The other two dimensions of classification apply to this type of design.

b. *Stage of Integration Dimension.* We have differentiated multistrand mixed designs into those that incorporate two types of data (QUAL and QUAN), thereby using mixed methods only, as compared with those that are mixed across all three spheres presented in Table 26.1, thereby using mixed models.

c. *Procedures for Integration Dimension.* As noted earlier in this section, there are three possible procedures for mixing methods: concurrent,[5] sequential, and conversion procedures.

The result of this two-dimensional classification of multistrand mixed designs (i.e., stage of integration and the procedures for integration) is six types of research designs presented in Table 26.2. A final design (fully integrated mixed model design), consisting of two or more of the other types, is not presented in Table 26.2 and is discussed separately later.

TYPES OF MULTISTRAND DESIGNS

1. Concurrent Mixed Designs

In the concurrent mixed design, there are multiple questions (QUAL and QUAN), and each is answered by collecting and analyzing corresponding data (QUAL or QUAN). The inferences are pulled together to reach a meta-inference (see next section on inferences). Concurrent mixed designs are often identified as parallel designs because two preplanned and relatively independent procedures are employed to answer the research questions either simultaneously or with a time lag (i.e., the data for the two strands might be collected in different time periods). In either case, the inferences from one phase do not determine the questions and/or procedures of the other phase. There are two types of this design:

a. *Concurrent Mixed Method Design.* In this type of study, one kind of question is simultaneously addressed by collecting and analyzing both QUAN and QUAL data, and then one type of inference is made on the basis of both data sources (see Figure 26.5). This design incorporates Creswell's (2002, p. 565) triangulation mixed method design.

b. *Concurrent Mixed Model Design.* In this type of design, there are two strands of research with both types of questions,

TABLE 26.2   A Two-Dimensional Framework for Conceptualizing Multistrand Mixed Designs

Procedure	Mixed Method Study	Mixed Model Study
Concurrent	Concurrent mixed method design (Figure 26.5)	Concurrent mixed model design (Figure 26.6)
Sequential	Sequential mixed method design (Figure 26.7)	Sequential mixed model design (Figure 26.8)
Conversion	Conversion mixed method design (Figure 26.9)	Conversion mixed model design (Figure 26.10)

NOTE: *Mixed method* designs involve the mixing of the QUAN and QUAL approaches only in the methods stage of a study. *Mixed model* designs involve the mixing of the QUAN and QUAL approaches in several stages of a study.

both types of data and analysis, and both types of inferences that are pulled together at the end to reach a meta-inference (see Figure 26.6). This design seems to incorporate McMillan and Schumacher's (2001, p. 342) simultaneous forms and Creswell and colleagues' (Chapter 8, this volume) concurrent triangulation design. As discussed previously, it is possible to further subdivide this design on the basis of purpose (e.g., political ideology) or priority (dominance or supervenience of one strand [see Miller, Chapter 15, this volume]). The first case would include the concurrent transformative design from Creswell's (2002) classification scheme.

2. Sequential Mixed Designs

The distinguishing attribute of the sequential mixed design is that the second phase (strand) of the study (e.g., the qualitative phase) emerges as a result of, or in response to, the findings of the first phase. There are two varieties of these designs based on the stage of integration:

a. *Sequential Mixed Method Design.* This design involves one type of question (exploratory or confirmatory, QUAL or QUAN), two types of data (QUAL and QUAN) that are collected in sequence (with one being dependent on the other, e.g., selecting extreme cases) and analyzed accordingly, and one type of inference at the end (see Figure 26.7). The second strand of the study emerges as a response to or during the data analysis of the first strand. In other words, this design is mixed in its data collection and analysis phase only. This design incorporates McMillan and Schumacher's (2001, p. 342) sequential forms.

b. *Sequential Mixed Model Design.* In this type of study, questions for the second strand of the study emerge from the inferences of the first strand (see Figure 26.8). In other words, the research questions of the second strand (e.g., QUAN) are based on the inferences that were made in the first strand (e.g., QUAL).

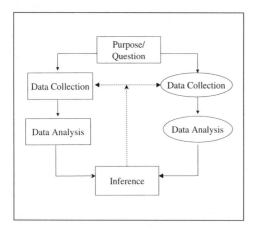

Figure 26.5. Concurrent Mixed Method Design

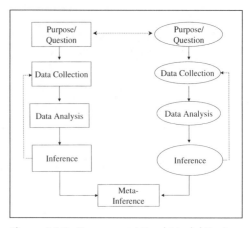

Figure 26.6. Concurrent Mixed Model Design

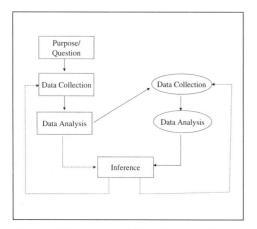

Figure 26.7. Sequential Mixed Method Design

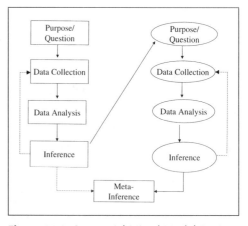

Figure 26.8. Sequential Mixed Model Design

The first strand of the study is often an exploratory study, while the second strand is often a confirmatory study. The first strand of the study includes data collection, data analysis, and inference in one approach (e.g., QUAN). The second strand of the study involves new data, their analysis, and inferences in the other approach (e.g., QUAL). The final meta-inferences are made on the basis of the confirmatory or disconfirmatory nature of the inferences in the two strands of the study (see Figure 26.8). This design incorporates

Creswell's (2002, p. 265) explanatory mixed method design and exploratory mixed method design.[6] It also incorporates Creswell and colleagues' (Chapter 8, this volume) sequential exploratory, sequential explanatory, and sequential transformative designs.

3. Multistrand Conversion Mixed Designs

In multistrand conversion mixed designs, there is only one method of study

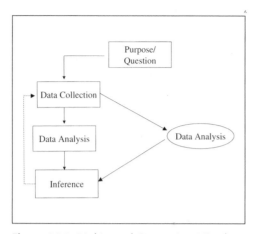

Figure 26.9. Multistrand Conversion Mixed Method Design

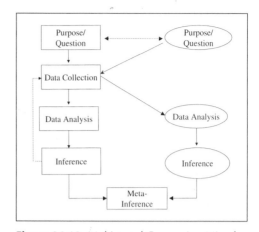

Figure 26.10. Multistrand Conversion Mixed Model Design

and one type of data (QUAL or QUAN). Nevertheless, multistrand conversion mixed designs emulate two strands by converting the data from QUAL to QUAN, or from QUAN to QUAL, and reanalyzing them accordingly. Inferences are made on the basis of both sets of analyses. There are two cases of such designs:

a. *Multistrand Conversion Mixed Method Design.* One type of question (exploratory or confirmatory, QUAL or QUAN) is asked, one type of data is collected and also transformed (qualitized/quantitized) and analyzed again accordingly, and one type of inference is made on the basis of all results (see Figure 26.9). This design represents a predominantly QUAL or QUAN study in which the data are transformed and reanalyzed in another approach to aid in final inferences.

b. *Multistrand Conversion Mixed Model Design.* In this type of design, multiple approach questions are asked. One type of data is collected and analyzed and is then transformed to another data type (qualitized/quantitized) and analyzed ac-

cordingly. Two types of inferences are made on the basis of each set of results and are pulled together at the end to generate meta-inferences (see Figure 26.10). This design is different from the previous one in that it is also mixed in the conceptualization stage (e.g., questions) as well as in the inference stage.

4. Fully Integrated Mixed Model Designs

Fully integrated mixed model designs are the most advanced, and most dynamic, of all mixed model designs, and they incorporate two or more of the previous types. In this type of study, multiple approach questions are asked and answered through the collection and analysis of both QUAL and QUAN data (see Figure 26.11). The two types of data might also be converted (qualitized/quantitized) and analyzed accordingly. Inferences are made on the basis of the QUAL and QUAN results of data analyses and are combined together at the end to form a meta-inference. Because it incorporates concurrent and sequential possibilities, this type is an "inter-

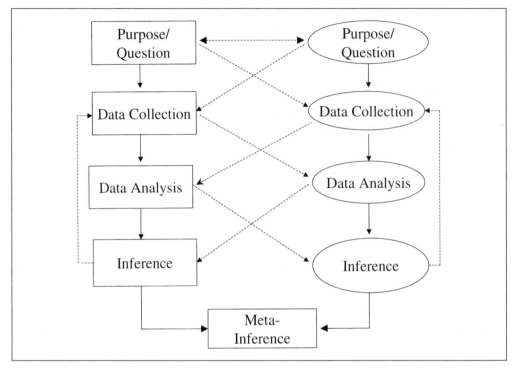

Figure 26.11. Fully Integrated Mixed Model Design

active design" (Maxwell & Loomis, Chapter 9, this volume). In other words, at every stage, there is a possibility of modifying one of the approaches based on the other (e.g., changing the type of QUAL data based on the QUAN analysis).

The following are a few notes regarding the classification typology depicted in Table 26.2 and Figures 26.1 to 26.11:

1. The proposed classification is based on the procedures of the study rather than on the purpose of the study (e.g., exploratory, explanatory, transformative). In most cases, it is not possible to decide beforehand whether the inferences will agree with each other (triangulate), complement each other, or need to be subsumed under a meta-inference

(dissonant inferences [e.g., Erzberger & Kelle, Chapter 16, this volume]).

2. In applied settings, a research project might combine components of more than one type of design in a dynamic manner. In other words, at any stage, based on the progress made in reaching the goals of the study (i.e., answering specific questions), the investigator might feel the need to change the design of the study by adding components. The most comprehensive type of mixed model study (using the fully integrated mixed model design) incorporates features from the other types.

3. Several controversies exist regarding the use of the designs in this typology. For example, according to Sandelowski (Chapter 12, this volume), there are

some designs in the mixed methods literature that are assumed to be mixed but in reality are not. According to Sandelowski, "Not all . . . transformations are appropriately called mixed methods studies. . . . Most studies in the social and behavioral sciences, as well as in the practice disciplines, entail the use of more than one of something (e.g., investigators, participants, sites) for data collection. The mere use of more than one of some research entity in a study does not constitute a mixed methods study and might not even constitute a multimethods study."

4. Transformations in this context meant quantitizing or qualitizing the data. Following Sandelowski's point of view, the monostrand conversion design (Figure 26.3), and perhaps even the multistrand conversion mixed method design (Figure 26.9), might be considered marginally mixed. This, however, does not apply to the multistrand conversion mixed model design (Figure 26.10) in which a more comprehensive level of integration exists at all stages.

◆ *Issues in Drawing Inferences in Mixed Methods Research*

We argued in Chapter 1 that inference (e.g., interpretation of the results, conclusions, making sense of the findings) is the most important aspect of a research project. Many of the authors in the handbook agree with this assertion, at least to a certain degree. Inferences not only are answers to research question but also provide a fertile ground for developing new understandings and new explanations for events, phenomena, and relationships. Despite their importance, the literature of research methodology has not discussed

inferences in any detail until this handbook. For example, the process of reaching inferences on the basis of the results from a study and the procedures for evaluating the outcome of such a process are usually absent from research methods textbooks.

At least four questions should be asked in this respect:

1. What is inference?

2. How does one integrate inferences in mixed methods research (i.e., what are the rules for integration)?

3. How does one evaluate the quality (e.g., internal validity, credibility) of inferences in mixed methods research (i.e., what are standards for evaluation)?

4. How does one improve the quality of inferences in mixed methods research (i.e., what are the strategies for ensuring high-quality inferences)?

The remainder of this section provides some partial answers to these questions.

THE DEFINITION OF INFERENCE

In Chapter 1, we presented an inclusive definition of inference that included the processes of both induction and deduction. Some other authors in this handbook discuss the process and the outcome of inferences. For example, Miller (Chapter 15) suggested that inference is both a process ("something one does or applies in some way") and an outcome ("something that has been produced"). We discussed inference as an outcome (i.e., the end result of interpretations of the findings). Because we discussed this issue in great detail in Chapter 1, there is no need to repeat it here.

692 ◆ CONCLUSIONS AND FUTURE DIRECTIONS

In an earlier section of this chapter, we placed inferences in the sphere in which we create an understanding (e.g., "gestalt" or whole) on the basis of all results. Such a gestalt, which here refers to the theory that an organized whole is perceived as more than the sum of its parts, has been labeled theory, grounded theory, abstraction, and so on by other scholars. In this chapter, it is referred to as inference.

Inference is a researcher's construction of the relationships among people, events, and variables as well as his or her construction of respondents' perceptions, behaviors, and feelings and how these relate to each other in a coherent and systematic manner. Inferences are integrated and internally consistent sets of statements about the phenomena, events, people, and/or constructs under study. The "evidence" on which these inferences are based should be clearly delineated in the research report so that other scholars can review and judge the adequacy of the researcher's representations and conclusions. Social, behavioral, and health researchers and program evaluators often make policy recommendations on the basis of these constructions.

In an earlier section of this chapter, we distinguished inferences that are obtained from each strand of a mixed methods study from meta-inferences that are obtained by integrating these initial inferences. The rules of integration for such meta-interpretations (Forthofer, Chapter 19, this volume) are discussed in what follows.

PROCEDURES FOR FORMING INFERENCES IN MIXED METHODS RESEARCH

Erzberger and Kelle (Chapter 16, this volume) discussed inference as a process

(i.e., rules of integration), although they also paid some attention to the outcomes of the process (triangulated inferences, complementary inferences, and expanded inferences). They developed eight very useful rules of integration that detailed how the results from different data sources should be assimilated. We recap some of them here, but readers are urged to read Chapter 16 to get the full logic behind these rules.

Erzberger and Kelle (Chapter 16, this volume) warned that the selection of methods should not be made before the research questions are formulated because they drive the selection of the methods. This is another aspect of what we have called the "dictatorship of the research question" (Tashakkori & Teddlie, 1998). Erzberger and Kelle also noted that each method is suited to certain empirical domains but that none is suited to all domains. This implies that researchers must learn several methods if they want to explore a wide range of research topics.

Erzberger and Kelle (Chapter 16, this volume) concluded that there is no single methodological model for method integration available, pointing out issues with triangulation and proposing some other methods for integration. They also detailed what to do in cases where there are complementary results and where there are divergent results. Their discussion of the rules of integration for divergent results is particularly insightful.

STANDARDS FOR EVALUATING THE QUALITY OF INFERENCES

We have suggested before (Tashakkori & Teddlie, 1998, in press; see also Teddlie & Tashakkori, Chapter 1, this volume) that there is a need for separating standards for evaluating the quality of data/

observations from those that are required for evaluating the quality of inferences. Table 26.3 delineates this distinction and some of the questions that are pertinent to each of the two components (data and inference). Note that these are only examples. More detailed questions were presented in Chapter 1.

STRATEGIES FOR IMPROVING THE QUALITY OF INFERENCES

Quantitative research literature has detailed descriptions of strategies for reducing the threat of "extraneous" variables to the internal validity of the conclusions. A detailed description of these strategies is beyond the scope of this chapter (see Polit & Hungler, 1999; Punch, 1998). These strategies range from random assignment of participants to experimental groups to statistical control of nuisance variables through partial correlation and analysis of covariance.

Unfortunately, many of these strategies are, in one form or another, linked to experimental and quasi-experimental designs. Some (e.g., double blind procedures) might be applicable to both QUAL and QUAN designs. QUAL literature, on the other hand, has a wide variety of strategies for improving the quality of inferences that may be applied to both qualitative and some quantitative designs. Examples of these are audit trail, peer debriefing (to make sure that there is consensus in interpretation), method and investigator triangulation, prolonged engagement, negative case analysis, and thick description. We have presented details of some of these strategies elsewhere (Tashakkori & Teddlie, 1998, pp. 84-93).

◆ The Logistics of Conducting Mixed Methods Research

As noted in Chapter 1, logistical issues in mixed methods research involve both pedagogy and collaboration. The collaboration issue was reviewed comprehensively in the handbook in both Chapter 1 (with the presentation of three distinct collaborative models) and Chapter 25 (Shulha & Wilson). Further consideration of collaboration issues is not necessary in this chapter.

Therefore, this section examines some of the unresolved pedagogical issues in mixed methods research. In Chapter 1, we referred to the "failure of pedagogy" in mixed methods research and noted that the first two articles on teaching mixed methods have just appeared in 2002 (Creswell, Tashakkori, Jensen, & Shapley, Chapter 24, this volume; Tashakkori & Teddlie, in press). Both of these articles address several important issues in pedagogy (e.g., course content), but there are at least three questions that require further elucidation:

◆ In what sequence should courses from the three methodological movements be presented in graduate school?

◆ How many courses are required to be trilingual (i.e., minimally literate in the QUAL, QUAN, and mixed research languages)?

◆ What sort of projects should a mixed methods research course include, and what activities should students conduct?

Sequence is an interesting issue. Should students take a mixed methods course

TABLE 26.3 Criteria and Questions Distinguishing Data Quality From Inference Quality

Component Being Evaluated	Definition/ Question Asked	Components/ Aspects of Evaluation	Evaluation Question	Evaluation and Improvement Strategy
Data quality	Do the data, records, observations, etc., meet the minimum criteria to be acceptable/trustworthy?	Validity, trust-worthiness	Did we indeed capture the phenomenon or attribute that we intended to (or we believe we captured)	Consistency within aspects of the same measurement or observation procedure; method (data collection procedure) triangulation
	Does the data adequately represent the theoretical phenomena or the attributes under study?	Reliability, dependability	Did we accurately capture/ represent the phenomenon or attribute under investigation?	Consistency between different procedures for measurement/ observation of the same phenomenon or attribute; audit trail, data triangulation
Inference quality	Does the inference meet the minimum criteria to be defensible/ credible?	Design quality	Were the procedures implemented with quality and rigor? Is there "within-design consistency"?	Was the method of study appropriate for answering the research question(s)? Was the method capable of capturing the answers/ effects/relationships? Were the components of the design (measurement, sampling, etc.) implemented adequately?
		Interpretive rigor	Are the results/findings interpreted in a defensible manner? • Cross-inference consistency • Theoretical consistency • Interpretive agreement • Interpretive distinctiveness	Does the inference follow the findings? Are the interpretations consistent with theory and state of knowledge in the field? Are the inferences consistent with each other? Do the global inferences adequately incorporate the inferences made from QUAL and QUAN strands of the study?

before taking QUAL and/or QUAN courses, or should they take a mixed methods course after they have taken at least one QUAL and one QUAN course? We (Tashakkori & Teddlie, in press) stated recently that we do not believe that students have to take QUAL and QUAN courses before taking a mixed methods course. We argued that the first methods course taken by graduate students should be a mixed methods course so that they develop an understanding of the similarities between the two orientations from the beginning of their graduate careers.

Others would argue with this, stating that students must have a firm grounding in each of the traditional methodologies (as separate entities) before they consider mixing them. This argument is an extension of the discussion from Chapter 1 regarding different paradigmatic positions. The "complementary strengths" thesis (e.g., Brewer & Hunter, 1989; Morse, 1991; Morse, Chapter 7, this volume) states that mixed methods research should keep the QUAN and QUAL methods as separate as possible so that the strengths of each paradigmatic position (e.g., postpositivism, constructivism) can be realized. This is not a popular position in current theoretical and applied work in mixed methods research, as indicated in several chapters of this handbook. For example, Maxwell and Loomis (Chapter 9) do not believe in uniform, purely QUAL and purely QUAN research paradigms; therefore, because the two research paradigms are not "pure" to begin with, the researcher loses little when he or she mixes them up in a variety of often creative ways.

Actually, this issue of sequence could be reduced in significance if all research methods courses were taught in a manner that emphasized the importance of the research question in conducting studies. Elsewhere, we (Tashakkori & Teddlie,

1998) referred to this as "the dictatorship of the research question (not the paradigm or method)." If students were taught in each research course that the methods learned in that class are part of a broad assortment of techniques that can be used to answer their research questions, then sequence of classes would not be that important. A mixed methods curriculum would emphasize both approaches (QUAL and QUAN) and would encourage the use of both approaches (if appropriate) for answering research questions.

How many courses are required to be trilingual (i.e., minimally literate in the QUAL, QUAN, and mixed research languages)? In some respects, this is an unanswerable question because it depends so much on contextual norms of the graduate program under consideration and on the competence of the research staff to deliver the courses. We concluded in Chapter 1 that the minimum educational requirement for doing mixed methods research is to have taken courses in both the QUAL and QUAN research traditions or to be self-taught (which requires years of experience). Many graduate programs in education require at least two courses in a given tradition (QUAL or QUAN) to be on that "track." Certainly, if a graduate program required at least five research methods courses, then two courses in QUAL, two courses in QUAN, and one mixed methods course (as an introduction or a capstone) would be appropriate.

What if a graduate program required only three research methods courses? Is one course in each of the three methodological movements enough? Certainly not, from our perspective, but having a mixed methods course as one of the three requirements is certainly better than not having one at all.

The issue of class projects is tied to the sequence issue. If the mixed methods course were the first in the research sequence, then projects would need to be tightly monitored by the instructor and would probably be team projects. If the mixed methods course were the capstone for the research sequence, then greater independence would be expected. The project in the course could indeed serve as a pilot study for the dissertation if the student were committed to a specific topic.

These pedagogical issues may seem a bit "nitty-gritty" for a handbook, but we are in a situation where we have an increasingly important imperative to train our students to be trilingual because more institutions and funding agencies are requiring that new employees have more than one set of skills. We need to teach our students to be comfortable in using techniques from any of the three methodological movements so that they will be competitive in the academic and industrial job markets.

◆ *Some Fundamental Principles of Mixed Methods Research*

Johnson and Turner (Chapter 11, this volume) presented the fundamental principle of mixed methods, which states, "Methods should be mixed in a way that has complementary strengths and nonoverlapping weaknesses." As we have edited the handbook, a variety of other principles of mixed methods research have emerged that we recount in this section. Newman et al. (Chapter 6, this volume) also presented four major principles associated with mixed methods that had been developed earlier (Newman & Benz, 1998).

The following are five additional principles of mixed methods research that we have gleaned from the chapters in this handbook:

◆ Mixing may occur in any stage of a study, from purpose/questions to data collection procedures, data analysis techniques, and the final inferences. (second principle of mixed methods)

◆ Research design determines data collection procedures in mixed methods but is also independent of those procedures. Multiple data collection procedures might be used in both QUAN and QUAL strands of a mixed methods study (e.g., focus group interview and observation). (third principle of mixed methods)

◆ Data collection procedures are independent of data analysis techniques (e.g., data collected through observation may be analyzed two ways: QUAL and QUAN). Collected data may be transformed at any point in a mixed methods study and may be analyzed both quantiatively and qualitatively. (fourth principle of mixed methods)

◆ If the data do not represent the theoretical phenomena or the attributes under study, then nothing else in the design of the study matters. (fifth principle of mixed methods) (This was also referred to in Chapter 1 as the fundamental principle of data quality in mixed methods research.)

◆ Data quality is a necessary condition for inference quality but is not a sufficient condition for it. The criteria for evaluating the quality of the data and the quality of the inferences are not the same. (sixth principle of mixed methods) (Quality of inferences and quality of data/observations are largely independent of each other [i.e., bad conclusions may be made on the basis of good results], with one exception: Poor data lead to poor inferences.)

◆ The Future for Mixed Methods: The Third Methodological Movement

The emergence of mixed methods as a third methodological movement in the social and behavioral sciences began during the 1980s. The evidence of this major shift in methodology is apparent in many ways (e.g., the publication of this handbook and numerous other seminal sources), and its impact should continue to increase over the next couple of decades.

While the conditions are ripe for the emergence of mixed methods, this methodological movement is not on as firm ground as was qualitative methods when the first edition of Denzin and Lincoln's (1994) Handbook of Qualitative Research came out 8 years ago. Qualitative research had the following advantages in 1994 that mixed methods does not as this handbook goes to press:

◆ Qualitative research had a long intellectual history, going back to the early part of the 20th century in sociology and anthropology.

◆ The paradigm wars had led to a widespread recognition of the stance of the QUALs on paradigms, methods, and so on.

◆ The qualitative research movement had an aura of mystique because it was presented by many authors as a revolutionary movement intended to sweep away the "received" tradition of the quantitatively oriented tradition.

◆ Several of the QUALs were zealots in their orientation, and they proudly spread the word of the "rightness" of their orientation.

◆ A number of textbooks, journals, and research monographs concerned solely with qualitative methods came out during the decade or so preceding the publication of the first edition of Denzin and Lincoln's (1994) Handbook of Qualitative Research.

◆ A number of universities were offering courses in qualitative research methods, and that number was rapidly increasing.

Mixed methods research has the following characteristics at this point in time:

◆ Mixed methods research has a much shorter history (going back only to the 1980s) as a distinct methodological movement, although some of the most famous and influential research of the 20th century could be accurately referred to as mixed methods.

◆ The paradigm wars were between the QUALs and the QUANs, with little participation by mixed methodologists, although the field did emerge in response to the incompatibility thesis.

◆ Indeed, neither the QUALs nor the QUANs have recognized mixed methods to any large degree in their writings, nor have either engaged in serious discussion with the mixed methods community.

◆ The mixed methods movement is a "quiet" revolution in that its orientation has been to resolve conflicts between qualitative and quantitative inquiry.

◆ Some influential books and articles have been written about mixed methods.

◆ Textbooks have grudgingly begun to introduce mixed methods as a separate topic, and a couple of journals devoted to mixed methods have emerged.

◆ Only a handful of graduate programs offer courses in mixed methods.

The lack of engagement between the two more established traditions and mixed methods research is illustrated by the fact that a noted "bible" of postpositivism (Cook & Campbell, 1979) mentioned mixed methods only when discussing the monomethod bias. Similarly, the first edition of the Handbook of Qualitative Research (Denzin & Lincoln, 1994) had only one chapter (on clinical research methods) that directly addressed mixed methods.

When will we know that mixed methods has gained wider acceptance and that the third methodological movement is recognized as such? The following would be some signs:

◆ When mixed methods are discussed as a separate research movement, not just a fusion of the QUAL and QUAN approaches, in basic methods textbooks

◆ When research textbooks are more integrated instead of being artificially divided into QUAL and QUAN on every topic

◆ When professors and students stop referring to themselves as QUANs and QUALs and begin thinking more about how to address their research questions

◆ When graduate students are not expected to declare themselves as either QUALs or QUANs

◆ When graduate programs require courses in mixed methods

◆ When graduate students are expected to be trilingual (i.e., knowing the QUAL, QUAN, and mixed methods languages and being able to translate across them)

◆ When there are more journals exclusively publishing mixed methods articles

◆ When authors writing in the QUAL or QUAN tradition refer to mixed methods as a third methodological movement

We see some movement in the direction of these "signs." While textbooks generally reflect the current state of an academic field, they are also good indicators of where that field is going. We see a gradual shift in the research methods textbooks in the direction of mixed methods. Increasingly, new textbooks in research methodology, or most recent editions of the current texts (e.g., Creswell, 2002; Johnson & Christensen, in press; McMillan & Schumacher, 2001) include either chapters or substantial discussions of mixed methods. Given the current state of the field, inconsistencies are naturally expected among these texts, but that is part of the process toward generating greater consistency over time.

In addition to the textbooks, there are a few journals that devote some space to mixed methods (e.g., *Quality & Quantity, International Journal of Social Research Methodology Theory and Practice*). We are aware of at least one other publisher (Sage) that is planning to publish a journal devoted entirely to mixed methods and mixed methods studies.

We hope that the increasing popularity of mixed methods will have an impact on what we called the residue of the paradigm wars in Chapter 1. The negative results of those wars have included a great deal of confusion, contradiction, and inconsistency in the methods, terminology, and standards of quality in the social and behavioral sciences. Journals, funding agencies, and tenure and promotion committees have struggled to integrate these inconsistent models.

The worst residue of the paradigm wars has been their impact on students. Many of our students are suffering from a fractured "dual-lingualism," which represents a split personality in methods of study and ways of thinking. At any given moment, they are asked to be either QUAL or QUAN and while in each mode to forget that the other exists. This is evident in textbooks, which typically have two sections: one devoted to the qualitative perspective and the other devoted to the quantitative point of view. The residues are also evident in our programs of study in graduate schools, where some students take the QUAL route, while others take the QUAN route. They are evident in the mentoring style in universities and professional organizations, where the QUALs and QUANs each speak their own language, do not interact with the other group, and proclaim the inferiority of the other group's orientation and methods. Many graduate programs either have a split personality or take on the position of one of the major orientations.

The mixed methods research movement is a positive reaction to this split personality and to the excesses of both the QUAN and QUAL camps. We believe that mixed methods will eventually pave the way for more commonality in research language that will benefit both the QUAL and QUAN camps. As the authors in this handbook demonstrated repeatedly, our methodological forebears in the social and behavioral sciences tried to lay the foundation for an eclectic mixed methods research approach (e.g., Waszack & Sines's chapter on psychology [Chapter 21], Hunter & Brewer's chapter on sociology [Chapter 22]).

We are aware of the threat that this new (or, as some of the chapter authors skillfully demonstrated, not so new) research methodology will pose to some scholars and graduate research programs. Nevertheless, change is inherent in research, and the third methodological movement has emerged as a legitimate alternative to the excesses of the other two traditions. The challenge of solving problems, creating new ideas, and establishing bridges between seemingly incompatible ideas is certainly rewarding to all of us. We hope that this handbook facilitates that challenge and provides insights for a new generation of more adaptable scholars.

■ Notes

1. An unexpected diversity among the authors occurred with regard to nationality. While most chapters were written by individuals from the United States, there were contributors from five other countries: Australia, Canada, Germany, Hong Kong, and the United Kingdom. Further internationalization of the field will be a welcome trend.

2. These two worldviews are used because they are the two that were the most frequently mentioned in this handbook as paradigms associated with mixed methods.

3. It could be argued that the transformative-emancipatory paradigm is not a true paradigm because the primary emphases in the orientation are (a) the sampling procedure (i.e., sampling underrepresented or marginalized groups such as people with disabilities, women, ethnic/racial minorities, members of the lesbian and gay communities, and people in poverty) and (b) an emphasis on a particular set of values that promotes social justice and equity for marginalized groups. The transformative-emancipatory perspective focuses on the degree to which research results in greater social justice and equity for these marginalized groups. We leave it to the readers to decide whether this is a research purpose (end point) or a paradigm.

4. Because mixed method designs (as compared with mixed model designs) require both QUAL and QUAN research methods or data collection procedures (i.e., they require more than one strand), a monostrand mixed method design is not conceivable. Therefore, it is not included in the classification. This also renders model unnecessary as a distinguishing term.

5. We are abandoning the term parallel to create consistency with Creswell and colleagues' (Chapter 8 in this volume) typology.

6. Please note that Creswell (2002) used mixed method as a generic term as compared with the classification presented here. As he explained, these two designs are mixed in more than method of study.

■ *References*

Brewer, J., & Hunter, A. (1989). *Multimethod research: A synthesis of styles.* Newbury Park, CA: Sage.

Campbell, D., & Fiske, D. W. (1959). Convergent and discriminant validation by the multitrait-multimethod matrix. *Psychological Bulletin, 54,* 297-312.

Cherryholmes, C. C. (1992). Notes on pragmatism and scientific realism. *Educational Researcher, 21*(6), 13-17.

Cook, T. D., & Campbell, D. T. (1979). *Quasi-experimentation: Design and analysis issues for field settings.* Boston: Houghton Mifflin.

Creswell, J. W. (2002). *Educational research: Planning, conducting, and evaluating quantitative and qualitative research.* Upper Saddle River, NJ: Merrill Prentice Hall.

Datta, L. (1997). A pragmatic basis for mixed-method designs. In J. C. Greene & V. J. Caracelli (Eds.), *Advances in mixed-method evaluation: The challenges and benefits of integrating diverse paradigms* (pp. 33-46). San Francisco: Jossey-Bass.

Denzin, N. K. (1978). The logic of naturalistic inquiry. In N. K. Denzin (Ed.), *Sociological methods: A sourcebook.* New York: McGraw-Hill.

Denzin, N. K., & Lincoln, Y. S. (Eds.). (1994). *Handbook of qualitative research.* Thousand Oaks, CA: Sage.

Greene, J. C., & Caracelli, V. J. (Eds.). (1997). *Advances in mixed-method evaluation: The challenges and benefits of integrating diverse paradigms* (New Directions for Evaluation, No. 74). San Francisco: Jossey-Bass.

House, E. R., & Howe, K. R. (1999). *Values in evaluation and social research.* Thousand Oaks, CA: Sage.

Howe, K. R. (1988). Against the quantitative-qualitative incompatibility thesis or dogmas die hard. *Educational Researcher, 17*(8), 10-16.

Jick, T. D. (1979). Mixing qualitative and quantitative methods: Triangulation in action. *Administrative Science Quarterly, 24,* 602-611.

Johnson, B., & Christensen, L. (in press). *Educational research: Quantitative and qualitative approaches* (2nd ed.). Boston: Allyn & Bacon.

Krüger, H. (2001). Social change in two generations: Employment patterns and their costs for family life. In V. W. Marshall, W. R. Heinz, H. Krüger, & A. Verma (Eds.), *Restructuring work and the life course* (pp. 401-423). Toronto: Toronto University Press.

Lincoln, Y. S., & Guba, E. G. (1985). *Naturalistic inquiry.* Beverly Hills, CA: Sage.

McMillan, J. H., & Schumacher, S. (2001). *Research in education: A conceptual introduction* (5th ed.). New York: Longman.

Mertens, D. M. (1998). *Research methods in education and psychology: Integrating diversity with quantitative and qualitative approaches.* Thousand Oaks, CA: Sage.

Miles, M., & Huberman, M. (1994). *Qualitative data analysis: An expanded sourcebook* (2nd ed.). Thousand Oaks, CA: Sage.

Morgan, D. (1998). Practical strategies for combining qualitative and quantitative methods: Applications to health research. *Qualitative Health Research, 8,* 362-376.

Morse, J. M. (1991). Approaches to qualitative-quantitative methodological triangulation. *Nursing Research, 40,* 120-123.

Newman, I., & Benz, C. R. (1998). *Qualitative-quantitative research methodology: Exploring the interactive continuum.* Carbondale: Southern Illinois University Press.

Patton, M. Q. (1988). Paradigms and pragmatism. In D. M. Fetterman (Ed.), *Qualitative approaches to evaluation in education: The silent scientific revolution* (pp. 116-137). New York: Praeger.

Patton, M. Q. (1990). *Qualitative evaluation and research methods* (2nd ed.). Newbury Park, CA: Sage.

Polit, D. F., & Hungler, B. P. (1999). *Nursing research principles and methods* (6th ed.). Philadelphia: J. B. Lippincott.

Punch, K. F. (1998). *Introduction to social research: Quantitative and qualitative approaches.* Thousand Oaks, CA: Sage.

Reynolds, D., & Teddlie, C., with Creemers, B., Scheerens, J., & Townsend, T. (2000). An introduction to school effectiveness research. In C. Teddlie & D. Reynolds (Eds.), *The international handbook of school effectiveness research* (pp. 3-25). London: Falmer.

Riccio, J. (1997). MDRC's evaluation of GAIN: A summary. *Evaluation Practice, 18,* 241-242.

Rossman, G. B., & Wilson, B. L. (1994). Numbers and words revisited: Being "shamelessly eclectic." *Quality and Quantity, 28,* 315-327.

Smaling, A. (1994). The pragmatic dimension: Paradigmatic and pragmatic aspects of choosing a qualitative or quantitative method. *Quality and Quantity, 28,* 233-249.

Stringfield, S. (1995). Attempting to enhance students' learning through innovative programs: The case for schools evolving into high reliability organizations. *School Effectiveness and School Improvement, 6*(1), 67-96.

Tashakkori, A., & Teddlie, C. (1998). *Mixed methodology: Combining the qualitative and quantitative approaches* (Applied Social Research Methods, No. 46). Thousand Oaks, CA: Sage.

Tashakkori, A., & Teddlie, C. (in press). Issues and dilemmas in teaching research methods courses in social and behavioral sciences: A U.S. perspective. *International Journal of Social Research Methodology.*

Teddlie, C., & Reynolds, D. (2001). Countering the critics: Responses to recent criticisms of school effectiveness research. *School Effectiveness and School Improvement, 12*(1), 41-82.

Trend, M. G. (1978). On the reconciliation of qualitative and quantitative analyses: A case study. *Human Organization, 37,* 345-354. (Reprinted in T. D. Cook & C. S. Reichardt (Eds.), *Qualitative and quantitative methods in evaluation research.* Newbury Park, CA: Sage)

GLOSSARY

There are four general sources for the terms and definitions in this Glossary:

1. *Terms taken directly from chapters in this handbook and noted by chapter numbers and authors' names.* There are typically no quotation marks around these definitions (although some do have them) because the chapter numbers denote the authors of the definitions. Some of these definitions have been expanded to fit the format of this Glossary (e.g., complete sentences have replaced sentence fragments).

2. *Terms from other authors writing in the field of mixed methodology (or research methodology in general).* The authors' names, the dates of publication, and the page numbers for the definitions are given in these Glossary entries.

3. *Terms constructed by the editors of this volume or modified by the editors to include components of the definitions of other authors.* These definitions are marked with an asterisk (*). They include terms from Chapters 1 and 26.

4. *Terms with multiple sources.* These multiple sources are noted in the definitions and often result in terms with alternative definitions.

Abduction (or abductive inference): (Erzberger & Kelle, Chapter 16, this volume) Whereas qualitative induction helps to explain a certain event by subsuming it under an already existing concept or rule, abductive inference serves as a means to discover new, and still unknown, concepts or rules. The starting point of an abductive inference is a surprising anomalous event that cannot be explained on the basis of previous knowledge. Peirce (1974) described the process of abductive inference as follows: The surprising fact C is observed; but if A were true, then C would be a matter of course; hence, there is a reason to suspect that A is true. See also **retroductive inference** and **inference.**

A priori themes analysis (or preplanned themes analysis): See **content analysis.**

Axiology: This refers to the role of values in inquiry (Lincoln & Guba, 1985, p. 37).

Binarize: (Onwuegbuzie & Teddlie, Chapter 13, this volume) This means converting qualitative data to scores of 1 or 0.

Breaching experiments: (Hunter & Brewer, Chapter 22, this volume) This refers to unusual situations created and presented to participants by ethnomethodologists so as to investigate how people reconstruct everyday social reality when it has been disrupted.

*Causal comparative design:** This is a group comparison ex post facto design in which relationships (especially tentative causal ones) are inferred through comparing groups that are known to have been different in the past either in the dependent variable or in the independent variable.

Collaboration: (Shulha & Wilson, Chapter 25, this volume) This means "co-laboring or working equitably with at least one other person on the same project or task" (Elliott & Woloshyn, 1997, p. 24). At a very minimum, then, collaboration involves purposeful and joint effort.

Collaborative mixed methods research: (Shulha & Wilson, Chapter 25, this volume) This method invokes the purposeful application of a multiple person, multiple perspective approach to questions of research and evaluation. Decisions about how methods are combined and how analyses are conducted are grounded in the needs and emerging complexity of each project rather than in any preordinate methodological convention. Researchers work to synthesize understandings that arise when a variety of methods, practical expertise, and implicit understandings of the problem domain are invoked.

Comparative analysis: (Bazeley, Chapter 14, this volume) This refers to importing demographic and other categorical information into a qualitative database to allow for comparison of the responses of subgroups within the sample of participants with respect to themes, concepts, or issues raised in the qualitative material. Such analysis can reveal unexpected differences pointing to new dimensions in the qualitative data.

*Complementary inference:** This is when the results of two strands of a mixed methods study provide two different but nonconflicting conclusions or interpretations.

Completeness: (Twinn, Chapter 20, this volume) This is a process whereby different theoretical and substantive components come together to ensure that all aspects of the phenomenon being researched are examined. The term was introduced into the nursing literature by Knafl, Breitmayer, Gallo, and Zoeller (1996).

Conceptual (or inferential) consistency: This refers to the degree to which the inferences are consistent with each other and with the known state of knowledge and theory.

Conceptual framework: (1) (Maxwell & Loomis, Chapter 9, this volume) "The conceptual framework for a study consists of the theory (or theories) relevant to the phenomena being studied that inform and influence the research. . . . A mismatch between the conceptual framework and the research questions or methods used can create serious problems for the research; a variance theory can't adequately guide and inform a process-oriented investigation and vice versa." *(2) This is a consistent and comprehensive theoretical framework emerging from an inductive integration of previous literature, theories, and other pertinent information. A conceptual framework is usually the basis for reframing the research questions and for formulating hypotheses or making informal tentative predictions about the possible outcome of the study.

*Concurrent mixed method design:** This is a multistrand design in which both QUAL and QUAN data are collected and analyzed to answer a single type of research question (either QUAL or QUAN). The final inferences are based on both data analysis results. The two types of data are collected independently at the same time or with a time lag.

*Concurrent mixed model design: This is a multistrand mixed design in which there are two relatively independent strands/phases: one with QUAL questions and data collection and analysis techniques and the other with QUAN questions and data collection and analysis techniques. The inferences made on the basis of the results of each strand are pulled together to form **meta-inferences** at the end of the study. See also **rules of integration**.

Concurrent nested design: This is a concurrent mixed model design classified on the basis of (conceptual or paradigmatic) dominance or priority of the study. In this design, a quantitative strand/phase is embedded within a predominantly qualitative study (quan + QUAL) or vice versa (QUAN + qual). QUAL and QUAN approaches are used to "confirm, cross-validate, or corroborate findings within a single study" (Creswell, Plano Clark, Gutmann, & Hanson, Chapter 8, this volume).

Concurrent triangulation design: This is a concurrent mixed model design classified on the basis of purpose of the study. In this design, QUAL and QUAN approaches are used to "confirm, cross-validate, or corroborate findings within a single study" (Creswell et al., Chapter 8, this volume).

Confirmation: (Twinn, Chapter 20, this volume) This is a verification strategy, using multiple approaches to data collection, in which the strengths and weaknesses of the methods are known and counterbalanced to address threats to validity.

*Construct validity: See **convergent validity, data quality**, and **discriminant validity**.

Constructivism: (Maxcy, Chapter 2, this volume) The constructivist/phenomenological approach (also interpretivism or naturalism) is the view that observation cannot be pure in the sense of altogether excluding the interests and values of individuals; investigations must employ empathic understanding of those being studied; the paradigm supports qualitative methods (Howe, 1988).

*Content analysis: (1) This refers to a method of data analysis for narrative data (e.g., texts, transcriptions) in which the segments of the text are systematically categorized such that segments within each category are similar to each other and are different from segments in other categories (see **similarity-contrast principle**). Categories might be preplanned on the basis of theory and conceptual framework (**a priori themes**) or might emerge during the analysis (**emergent themes analysis**). (2) This refers to "any technique for making inferences by objectively and systematically identifying specified characteristics of messages" (Holsti, 1969, quoted in Bazeley, Chapter 14, this volume).

*Contrast principle: See **similarity-contrast principle**.

*Convergent inference: This is when the conclusions or interpretations of two strands of a mixed methods study are consistent with each other (i.e., agree with each other).

*Convergent validity: (1) This is the degree to which the data collection procedure (e.g., instrument, test, observational protocol) shows similarity between groups that are theoretically expected to be similar on the construct or attribute under investigation. (2) This is when the results of data collection procedure are highly correlated with the other ways of measuring the attribute (e.g., other methods of data collection, other tests). (3) This is when the results of measurement are consistent with the indicators of the construct under investigation or other constructs that are theoretically expected to be highly related to it. It is synonymous with data triangulation in qualitative research. See also **data quality** and **similarity-contrast principle.**

*Conversion mixed model design: This is a multistrand concurrent design in which mixing of QUAL and QUAN approaches occurs in all components/stages, with data transformed (qualitized or quantitized) and analyzed both qualitatively and quantitatively.

Culture: (Moghaddam, Walker, & Harré, Chapter 4, this volume) This refers to a normative system, integral to which are norms, rules, and other indicators of how people in particular roles and in particular places should "behave."

Cultural distance: (Moghaddam et al., Chapter 4, this volume) This refers to a gap between researchers, who are for the most part White, middle-class Western males living in affluent urban centers of industrial societies, and the majority of the people in non-Western societies, who are relatively more rural, illiterate, materially poor, and religious.

*Data consolidation: This means combining qualitative and quantitative data to create new or consolidated variables or data sets.

*Data conversion/transformation: Collected quantitative data types are converted into narratives that can be analyzed qualitatively (i.e., qualitized), and/or qualitative data types are converted into numerical codes that can be statistically analyzed (i.e., quantitized).

*Data quality: This is the degree to which the collected data (results of measurement or observation) meet the standards of quality to be considered valid (trustworthy) and reliable (dependable). This term was used by Punch (1998) to represent "quality control of data . . . in terms of procedures in the collection of the data and . . . in terms of three technical aspects of quality of the data: reliability, validity, and reactivity" (p. 257). (1) **Data/measurement validity:** Do the results of data collection truly represent the construct or phenomenon that they are expected to capture (measure or represent)? How well do the data represent the phenomena for which they stand (Punch, 1998, p. 258)? See also **convergent validity** and **discriminant validity**. (2) **Data/measurement reliability:** Do the obtained results of measurement or observation accurately reflect the magnitude, intensity, or quality of the attribute or phenomenon that is being measured or observed?

*Deductive inference (in research cycle): This is a process in which hypotheses or predictions are formed on the basis of (1) a conceptual framework that is constructed from the literature, (2) the inferences of a previous strand of a mixed methods study, or (3) an existing theory. See also **inference** and **inference quality**.

Deductive logic: (Erzberger & Kelle, Chapter 16, this volume) (1) This refers to the application of general rules to specific cases. For example, from the general rule that all men are mortal, it can be deduced that if Socrates is a man, then he will be mortal. (2) This refers to a type of reasoning usually applied if a link is drawn from an already formulated theoretical statement to a statement about observable empirical facts, a link that can be generalized in the following term: "If A (a theoretical statement) is true, then we would expect the fact C to happen."

*Design quality: See **inference quality**.

Dialectical position: (1) (Greene & Caracelli, Chapter 3, this volume) To think dialectically is to invite the juxtaposition of opposed or contradictory ideas, to interact with the tensions invoked by these contesting arguments, or to engage in the play of ideas. The arguments and ideas that are engaged in this dialectical stance emanate from the assumptions that constitute philosophical paradigms—assumptions about the social world, social knowledge, and the purpose of science in society. (2) (Rocco et al., Chapter 23, this volume) This means self-consciously calling for a "synergistic" use of methods deliberately "shaped by both interpretivist and postpositive paradigms in an integrative manner" (Greene & Caracelli, 1997, p. 10). The term is traced to Geertz (1979), who argued for a continuous "'dialectical tacking' between experience-near (particular, context specific, idiographic) and experience-distant (general, universal, nomothetic) concepts, because both types of concepts are needed for comprehensiveness and meaningful understanding" (cited in Greene & Caracelli, 1997, p. 10).

Discovery: (Currall & Towler, Chapter 18, this volume) This refers to any technique related to the creation of new theories or interpretive applications, including anything related to adopting novel approaches to measurement, inventing or uncovering new constructs, or inventing or uncovering original theoretical perspectives from which to view organizational phenomena (McCall & Bobco, 1990, p. 382). See also **theoretical perspective.**

*Discriminant validity: (1) This is the degree to which the data collection procedure (e.g., instrument, test, observational protocol) shows differences between groups that are theoretically expected to be different on the construct or attribute under investigation. (2) This is when the results of data collection procedures are uncorrelated with the measures or indicators of the attribute that are theoretically expected to be unrelated to the attribute or phenomenon that is being measured/observed. See also **similarity-contrast principle.**

Divergent inference: (Erzberger & Kelle, Chapter 16, this volume) This is when the

inferences made on the basis of the two strands of a mixed methods study are inconsistent or dissonant (Rossman & Wilson, 1985); that is, they do not agree with each other. Inconsistencies between qualitative and quantitative findings might be a consequence of the inadequacy of the applied theoretical concepts. It might, therefore, be necessary to revise and modify the initial theoretical assumptions and to draw on further theoretical concepts that have not yet been related to the domain in question.

Dominant-less dominant design: (Currall & Towler, Chapter 18, this volume) This is a mixed methods study based largely on a single method with additional components drawn from alternative methods. This type of research design has been discussed by many authors (sometimes by different names), including Morse (1991; Chapter 7, this volume).

*Ecological transferability: This refers to generalizability or applicability of inferences obtained in a study to other settings or contexts. It subumes the QUAN terms *ecological validity* and *ecological external validity* as well as the QUAL term *transferability*. See also **inference transferability.**

Ecological validity (or ecological external validity): See **ecological transferability.**

*Effect size: This refers to the intensity, magnitude, or practical significance of an obtained result (e.g., relationship, difference) in the QUAL or QUAN strands of a mixed methods study. Onwuegbuzie and Teddlie (Chapter 13, this volume) explicitly relate this historically QUAN term to QUAL research, naming several new terms, including manifest effect size, frequency (manifest) effect size, and intensity (manifest) effect size.

Eliminative induction: (Miller, Chapter 15, this volume) This is a process of induction where there is a systematic attempt to eliminate rival or alternative claims to a hypothesis. The idea is that the remaining alternative is *probably* the "cause" of the hypothesis. John Stuart Mills's methods of induction are varieties of eliminative induction (Rappaport, 1996).

Emergent themes analysis: See content analysis.

Emic: (Currall & Towler, Chapter 18, this volume) This refers to interpretation of information or data by an insider within an organization.

Enumerative induction: (Miller, Chapter 15, this volume) This is a type of induction in which what is observed as true of a number of individuals is then claimed as true of all such individuals in a class. This is also called an inductive generalization.

Epistemology: (Erzberger & Kelle, Chapter 16, this volume) (1) This is a branch of philosophy concerned with questions about whether and how valid knowledge about reality can be achieved. (2) This is the relationship of the knower to the known (Lincoln & Guba, 1985, p. 37).

*__Ethnography:__ This is the social scientific study of a people and their culture. This also refers to a qualitative research method in which data are collected through different procedures such as participant observation, interviews, and examination of artifacts and records.

Ethnomethodology: (Hunter & Brewer, Chapter 22, this volume) This is the study of the "methods," or social procedures, by which people construct reality and make sense of events in everyday life.

Etic: (Currall & Towler, Chapter 18, this volume) This refers to a trained observer's analysis of uninterpreted "raw" data or information.

External validity: This is defined by Cook and Campbell (1979, p. 37) as follows: "the approximate validity with which we can infer that the presumed causal relationship can be generalized to and across alternate mea-

sures of the cause and effect and across different types of persons, settings, and times" (p. 37). See **inference transferability.**

Focus group (or focus group interview): (Johnson & Turner, Chapter 11, this volume) This refers to an interactive interview setting in which a small number of respondents (preferably six to eight) engage in discussion in response to a moderator's questions. Johnson and Turner define these groups as follows: "Focus group sessions generally last between 1 and 3 hours and allow in-depth discussion. During the conduct of a focus group, the group moderator typically facilitates group discussion on a series of about 5 to 10 open-ended items written on the moderator's 'focus group interview protocol'; all of the items on the protocol are related to the focus topic."

*__Fully integrated mixed model design:__ This is a multistrand concurrent design in which mixing of QUAL and QUAN approaches occurs in an interactive (i.e., dynamic, reciprocal, interdependent, iterative) manner at all stages of the study. At each stage (e.g., in formulating questions), one approach (e.g., QUAL) affects the formulation of the other (e.g., QUAN). See also **interactive model.**

Fundamental principle of mixed methods research: (Johnson & Turner, Chapter 11, this volume) Johnson and Turner define this principle as follows: "Methods should be mixed in a way that has complementary strengths and nonoverlapping weaknesses. . . . It involves the recognition that all methods have their limitations as well as their strengths. The fundamental principle is followed for at least three reasons: (a) to obtain convergence or corroboration of findings, (b) to eliminate or minimize key plausible alternative explanations for conclusions drawn from the research data, and (c) to elucidate the divergent aspects of a phenomenon. The fundamental principle can be applied to all stages or components of the research process."

Generalizability: See **external validity** and **inference transferability**.

*Gestalt principle: This refers to the whole or the totality. Gestalt psychology is known for the principle (among many others) stating that the whole is bigger than the sum of its parts. The Gestalt principle is applied to mixed methods in Chapter 1 of this handbook to demonstrate that global inferences made at the end of mixed methods studies are more than the simple sum of the inferences gleaned from QUAL and QUAN strands.

Grounded theory: Strauss and Corbin (1994) defined grounded theory as "a general methodology for developing theory that is grounded in data systematically gathered and analyzed" (p. 273).

Hypothetical inference: (Erzberger & Kelle, Chapter 16, this volume) This is a mode of inference, also called abduction or retroduction, whereby a certain empirical phenomenon is explained ex post facto either by drawing on an already known general rule (qualitative induction) or by finding a new rule that would explain the phenomenon (abduction).

Inductive analogy: (Miller, Chapter 15, this volume) This means reaching a conclusion about a single case on the basis of a similarity between that case and other previously observed cases . See also **inductive inference (in research cycle)** and **inductive logic.**

*Inductive inference (in research cycle): This refers to a process of creating meaningful and consistent explanations, understandings, conceptual frameworks, and/or theories by integrating (a) the current knowledge gleaned from the literature, (b) concrete observations or facts, and (c) results of data analysis in a research project (Tashakkori & Teddlie, 1998).

Inductive logic: (Erzberger & Kelle, Chapter 16, this volume) This refers to a mode of logical inference whereby a general rule is inferred from a number of cases where a certain result is observed, thereby claiming that these results can be observed in all cases of a class to which the observed cases belong. See also **eliminative induction, enumerative induction, inductive analogy, inductive inference (in research cycle),** and **perfect induction.**

*Inference: (1) This is an umbrella term referring to a final outcome of a study. The outcome may consist of a conclusion about, an understanding of, or an explanation for an event, a behavior, a relationship, or a case. (2) This is "a conclusion reached" where there is either (a) a "deduction from premises that are accepted as true" or (b) an "induction" by "deriving a conclusion from factual statements taken as evidence for the conclusion" (Angeles, 1981, p. 133). See also **deductive inference (in research cycle), deductive logic, inductive inference (in research cycle), inductive logic, meta-inference (or integrated mixed inference),** and **retroductive inference.**

*Inference quality: (1) This is proposed as a mixed methods term to incorporate the QUAN term *internal validity* and the QUAL terms *trustworthiness* and *credibility* of interpretations (Tashakkori & Teddlie, 1998, in press). The definition of the term is as follows: the degree to which the interpretations and conclusions made on the basis of the results meet the professional standards of rigor, trustworthiness, and acceptability as well as the degree to which alternative plausible explanations for the obtained results can be ruled out. Inference quality consists of design quality (**within-design consistency**) and interpretive rigor (**conceptual [or inferential] consistency, interpretive agreement [or interpretive consistency],** and **interpretive distinctiveness**).

Inference to the best explanation: (Miller, Chapter 15, this volume) This refers to the theory that attempts to discover and evaluate which criterion, among possibly competing ones, offers the most credible (i.e., "best") explanation for a phenomenon.

*Inference transferability: This refers to generalizability or applicability of inferences obtained in a study to other individuals or entities (see **population transferability**), other settings or situations (see **ecological transferability**), other time periods (see **temporal transferability**), or other methods of observation/measurement (see **operational transferability**). It subsumes the QUAN terms *external validity* and *generalizability* as well as the QUAL term *transferability.*

Interactive continuum of research: Newman and Benz (1998) proposed the perspective that the field of research is holistic, that the qualitative-quantitative dichotomy is a false one, and that the point at which the researcher intervenes on the continuum with a research purpose and research question helps to clarify assumptions and methods decisions.

Interactive model: (Maxwell & Loomis, Chapter 9, this volume) Applied to mixed methods research, this model indicates that "the different components of actual mixed methods studies are . . . connected in a network or web rather than a linear or cyclic sequence."

Internal validity: This term is defined by Cook and Campbell (1979) as follows: "the approximate validity with which we infer that a relationship between two variables is causal or that the absence of a relationship implies the absence of cause" (p. 37). See also **inference quality.**

Interpretive agreement (or interpretive consistency): This refers to consistency of interpretations across people (e.g., consistency among scholars, consistency with participants' construction of reality).

Interpretive distinctiveness: This is the degree to which the inferences are distinctively different from (and superior to) other plausible interpretations of the results and the rival explanations are ruled out (eliminated).

Interpretivism: (Maxcy, Chapter 2, this volume) See **constructivism.**

Joint meaning-making: (Shulha & Wilson, Chapter 25, this volume) This is a process anchored by dialogue and a dialectic that makes explicit how and where evolving understandings among participants diverge as well as converge. This knowledge is eagerly sought after in collaborative designs. As collaboration and learning become more integrated, joint meaning making becomes a more prominent feature within the inquiry process and in shaping the findings.

*Justification: This refers to the empirical evaluation, testing, or confirmation of theory.

Legitimation: See **inference quality.**

Measurement validity: See **data quality.**

*Meta-inference (or integrated mixed inference): This is an inference developed through an integration of the inferences that are obtained on the basis of QUAL and QUAN strands of a mixed methods study.

Meta-interpretation: (Forthofer, Chapter 19, this volume) Forthofer describes this term as follows: "Mixed methods designs are inherently more complex, and those that attempt any integration or synthesis of results across methodologies require an additional phase of 'meta-interpretation.' " See also **inference.**

Methodological triangulated design: (Morse, Chapter 7, this volume) This is a project that is composed of two or more subprojects, each of which exhibits methodological integrity. While complete in themselves, these projects fit to complement or enable the attainment of the overall programmatic research goals.

Mixed method design: (1) *This is a design that includes both QUAL and QUAN data collection and analysis in parallel form (concurrent mixed method design, in which two types of data are collected and analyzed), in sequential form (sequential mixed method design, in which one type of data provides a basis for collection of another type of data), or where the data are converted (qualitized or quantitized) and analyzed again (conversion mixed method design). (2) (Bazeley, Chapter 14, this volume) This design includes studies that "use mixed data (numerical and text) and alternative tools (statistics and text analysis) but apply the same method, for example, in developing a grounded theory." See also **mixed model design.**

Mixed methods: (1) *This is a type of research design in which QUAL and QUAN approaches are used in type of questions, research methods, data collection and analysis procedures, and/or inferences. (2) (Creswell et al., Chapter 8, this volume). This is a "collection or analysis of both quantitative and qualitative data in a single study in which the data are collected concurrently or sequentially, are given a priority, and involve integration of the data at one or more stages in the process of research." (3) (Morse, Chapter 7, this volume) This is "when *strategies* derived from qualitative and quantitative methods are used within a single project." (4) (Morse, Chapter 7, this volume) This is when QUAN data collection strategies are used in a QUAL study or vice versa: "when research strategies are used that are *not normally* described as a part of that design."

Mixed methods sampling: (Kemper, Stringfield, & Teddlie, Chapter 10, this volume) This is simultaneous selection of units of study through both probability (to increase generalizability/transferability) and purposive sampling strategies (to increase inference quality).

*Mixed model design:** This is a design in which mixing of QUAL and QUAN approaches occurs in all stages of the study (formulation of research questions, data collection procedures and research method, and interpretation of the results to make final inferences) or across stages of the study (e.g., QUAL questions, QUAN data). In multistrand designs, either the strands are parallel (concurrent mixed model design) or sequential (sequential mixed model design, in which inferences of one strand lead to questions of the next strand) or the data are converted and analyzed again to answer different questions (conversion mixed model design).

Monomethod design: See **monostrand design.**

*Monostrand design:** These designs use a single research method or data collection technique (QUAL or QUAN) and corresponding data analysis procedures to answer research questions. They are also known as single-phase designs.

*Multilevel mixed method design:** This is a design in which QUAL data are collected at one level (e.g., child), and QUAN data are collected at another level (e.g., family) in a concurrent or sequential manner to answer different aspects of the same research question. Both types of data are analyzed accordingly, and the results are used to make inferences. Because the questions and inferences all are in one approach (QUAL or QUAN), this is a predominantly QUAL or QUAN study with some added components. In practice, because research questions and the inferences that are made at the end of the study are usually both QUAL and QUAN (using mixed models), this design is not common. See also **multilevel mixed model design.**

*Multilevel mixed model design:** This is a design in which QUAL data are collected at one level (e.g., child) and QUAN data are collected at another level (e.g., family) in a concurrent or sequential manner to answer interrelated research questions with multiple approaches (QUAL and QUAN). Both types of data are analyzed accordingly, and the results are used to make multiple types of inferences (QUAL and QUAN) that are pulled together at the end of the study in the form of "global inferences." See also **multilevel mixed method design.**

Multilevel mixed sampling: (Kemper et al., Chapter 10, this volume) This is sampling strategy in which probability and purposive sampling techniques are used at different levels of the study (e.g., student, class, school, district).

Multimethods design: (1) *This refers to designs in which the research questions are answered by using two data collection procedures or two research methods, both with either the QUAL or QUAN approach. See also **multimethods QUAL study** and **multimethods QUAN study.** (2) (Hunter & Brewer, Chapter 22, this volume) The term has also been used synonymously with *multiple methods* designs: "use of multiple methods with complementary strengths and different weaknesses in relation to a given set of research problems." (3) (Morse, Chapter 7, this volume) The term has been used to identify "two or more interrelated studies" (rather than a single project). Morse describes them as follows: "qualitative and quantitative projects that are relatively complete but are used together to form essential components of one research program."

*Multimethod QUAL study:** This refers to designs in which the research questions are answered by using two QUAL data collection procedures or two QUAL research methods.

*Multimethod QUAN study:** This refers to designs in which the research questions are

answered by using two QUAN data collection procedures or two QUAN research methods.

*Multiple methods design:** This refers to designs in which more than one research method or data collection and analysis technique is used to answer research questions (Hunter & Brewer, Chapter 22, this volume). They include **mixed methods designs** (QUAL + QUAN) and **multimethods designs** (QUAN + QUAN or QUAL + QUAL).

*Multistrand design:** This refers to designs that use more than one research method or data collection procedure. See also **multimethods design.**

Multitrait-multimethod matrix: This is a matrix of correlations between multiple methods of measuring each of a set of attributes. The diagonal values indicate the reliability of each measure/method. The off-diagonal values indicate the **convergent validity** and **discriminant validity** of each procedure/instrument. This method was introduced by Campbell and Fiske (1959) to evaluate the quality of data obtained from measurement instruments.

Ontology: This term refers to the nature of reality (Lincoln & Guba, 1985, p. 37).

*Operational transferability:** This is the degree to which the inferences that are made on the basis of the results of the study are generalizable to other methods of observing/measuring the entities or attributes that the inference is about. It subsumes the QUAN terms *external validity of operations* and *operational external validity* (see Ary et al., 2002).

Paradigm: (1) (Mertens, Chapter 5, this volume) This is a conceptual model of a person's worldview, complete with the assumptions that are associated with that view. (2) (Greene & Caracelli, Chapter 3, this volume) This is a social construction, a historically and culturally embedded discourse practice, and therefore is neither inviolate nor unchanging.

Parallel mixed model design: See **concurrent mixed model design.**

Perfect induction: (Miller, Chapter 15, this volume) This is a case where the premises assert something true about *each* of the observed individuals so that what is true of each is (then) true of all. Because the conclusion does *not* go beyond the evidence, the reasoning is actually deductive. See also **inductive inference** and **inductive logic.**

Phase (of a mixed methods study): See **strand.**

Placeholder theory: (Miller, Chapter 15, this volume) This is a rationale for explaining mixed methods that holds that one domain (QUAL or QUAN) supervenes on the other and in so doing sets a "threshold" effect on the other in terms of what can be further explained.

*Population transferability: This refers to generalizability or applicability of inferences obtained in a study to other individuals or entities. It subsumes the QUAN terms *population validity* and *population external validity* as well as the QUAL term *transferability.* See **inference transferability.**

*Population validity (or population external validity): See **inference transferability.**

Positivism: (Maxcy, Chapter 2, this volume) The positivist/empiricist approach (also logical positivism, logical empiricism, or postpositivism) is the view, according to Atkinson and Hammersley (1994), that "social research should adopt scientific method, that this method is exemplified in the work of modern physicists, and that it consists of the rigorous testing of hypotheses by means of data that take the form of quantitative measurements" (p. 251). Postpositivism revised positivism by addressing several of the more widely discredited tenets of positivism (Tashakkori & Teddlie, 1998).

*Pragmatism: This is a deconstructive paradigm that debunks concepts such as "truth" and "reality" and focuses instead on "what works" as the truth regarding the research questions under investigation. Pragmatism rejects the either/or choices associated with the paradigm wars, advocates for the use of mixed methods in research, and acknowledges that the values of the researcher play a large role in interpretation of results.

Priority (of an approach in mixed methods studies): See **theoretical perspective.**

*Probability sampling: This means selecting a relatively large number of units from a population, or from specific subgroups (strata) of a population, in a random manner where the probability of inclusion for every member of the population is determinable. Examples of this type of sampling are simple random, cluster (groups of individuals), and stratified (selecting from subpopulations).

*Purposive sampling: This means selecting specific units (e.g., events, people, groups, settings, artifacts), or types of units, based on a specific purpose rather than randomly. Examples of such sampling include quota, snowball, extreme case/group, and sampling for maximum variation (heterogeneity).

qual: (Morse, Chapter 7, this volume) This term refers to the qualitative methodology used in a study. When lowercase, this means that the qualitative methodology was less dominant. The term was coined by Morse (1991).

QUAL: (Morse, Chapter 7, this volume) This term refers to the qualitative methodology used in a study. When uppercase, this means that the qualitative methodology was dominant. The term was coined by Morse (1991).

*Qualitizing: This is the process by which quantitative data are transformed into data that can be analyzed qualitatively.

*QUALs: This term refers to qualitatively oriented social and behavioral scientists.

quan: (Morse, Chapter 7, this volume) This term refers to the quantitative methodology used in a study. When lowercase, this means that the quantitative methodology was less dominant. The term was coined by Morse (1991).

QUAN: (Morse, Chapter 7, this volume) This term refers to the quantitative methodology used in a study. When uppercase, this means that the quantitative methodology was dominant. The term was coined by Morse (1991).

*QUANs: This term refers to quantitatively oriented social and behavioral scientists.

Quantitizing: This means converting qualitative data into numerical codes that can be statistically analyzed. The term was initially coined by Miles and Huberman (1994).

Reliability (data reliability or measurement reliability): See data quality.

Repertory grid technique: This involves eliciting an individual's constructs by presenting triplets of events (termed *elements*) and inviting the individual to indicate the similarities and differences among the elements. The term can be thought of as producing a map of an individual's knowledge construction system (Loef, 1990). After the constructs are elicited, the individual rates the elements for each construct by using a Likert-type scale to indicate how much the construct characterizes the elements. This provides a measure of the distance between each element and others in relation to a construct. A two-dimensional matrix of rankings formed by elements in one dimension and constructs in the other can be used for a variety of quantitative statistical methods of clustering such as *additive tree structures* (Sattath & Tversky, 1977). Clustering methods can provide visual representations of how an individual organizes various con-

structs in relation to the elements supplied (Rocco et al., Chapter 23, this volume).

Representation: (Sandelowski, Chapter 12, this volume) This is a domain of study of linguistic, visual, or other strategies used to represent (render or portray) persons, objects, or experiences.

Retroductive inference: (1) (Miller, Chapter 15, this volume) This is a mode of inference also called **abduction.** This occurs when a certain empirical phenomenon is explained ex post facto either by drawing on an already known general rule (qualitative induction) or by finding a new rule that would explain the phenomenon (abduction). (2) (Erzberger & Kelle, Chapter 16, this volume) This is also called *abduction, retroduction, reduction,* or **inference to the best explanation** are other terms used to describe this specific mode of reasoning. The process starts with what would be the conclusion of a deduction and infers from that to the premises, a form of reasoning that can also be called *hypothetical reasoning,* a term that reflects more clearly its role in the research process; retroductive, reductive, or hypothetical inferences serve to find a hypothesis that can explain certain empirical findings.

Rhetoric: (Sandelowski, Chapter 12, this volume) This is a domain of study of the effective use of language and discursive strategies used for persuasion.

Rubric: This is an assessment tool to demonstrate how the elements of a complex multifaceted skill (e.g., collaborative learning) will be performed differently depending on the acquired expertise of the performer. The value of a growth rubric is that it allows individuals to develop a profile of their current behavior while providing guidance in "next steps" if a more sophisticated performance is desired.

Rules of integration: (Erzberger & Kelle, Chapter 16, this volume) A set of rules can be formulated that may be helpful for drawing inferences from the results of qualitative and quantitative strands of mixed methods designs. These rules should be understood as general guidelines whose significance varies according to the research question, the empirical domain under investigation, and the specific methods employed. Erzberger and Kelle list eight rules of integration. See also **inference**.

*Sampling: This means selecting units (e.g., events, people, groups, settings, artifacts) in a manner that maximizes the researcher's ability to answer research questions that are set forth in a study. The term is broadly categorized into **probability sampling** and **purposive sampling**.

Secondary data: (Johnson & Turner, chapter 11, this volume) Johnson and Turner describe these data as follows: "Secondary data (sometimes called 'existing or available data') are data that were originally recorded or 'left behind' or collected at an earlier time by a different person from the current researcher, often for an entirely different purpose from the current research purpose. . . . There are several common types of secondary data that researchers can 'go find' such as personal documents, official documents, physical data, and archived research data."

Sequential explanatory design: (Creswell et al., Chapter 8, this volume) According to Creswell et al., this design "is characterized by the collection and analysis of quantitative data followed by the collection and analysis of qualitative data. Priority is typically given to the quantitative data, and the two methods are integrated during the interpretation phase of the study."

Sequential exploratory design: (Creswell et al., Chapter 8, this volume) According to Creswell et al., this design "is characterized by an initial phase of qualitative data collection and analysis followed by a phase of quantitative data collection and analysis. Therefore, the priority is given to the qualitative aspect of the study."

Sequential mixed method design: (Onwuegbuzie and Teddlie, Chapter 13, this volume) This is a design in which one type of data (e.g., QUAN) provides a basis for the collection of another type of data (e.g., QUAL). It answers one type of question (QUAL or QUAN) by collecting and analyzing two types of data (QUAL and QUAN). Inferences are based on the analysis of both types of data. This term subsumes *sequential study, two-phase design, sequential QUAL-QUAN analysis,* and *sequential QUAN-QUAL analysis.*

Sequential mixed model design: This is a multistrand mixed (QUAL-QUAN or QUAN-QUAL) design in which the conclusions that are made on the basis of the results of the first strand (e.g., a QUAN phase) lead to formulation of questions, data collection, and data analysis for the next strand (e.g., a QUAL phase). The final inferences are based on the results of both strands of the study. The second strand/phase of the study is conducted either to confirm/disconfirm the inferences of the first strand or to provide further explanation for unexpected findings of the first strand.

*Similarity-contrast principle: This is a principle underlying data analysis in both qualitative and quantitative research. It governs the process of grouping of units of analysis (e.g., statements, items of a test) into categories (e.g., themes, factors, components, clusters) that are similar to each other and distinctly different from other groups of such units. See also **convergent validity** and **discriminant validity**.

*Single phase design: This refers to a study with either a qualitative phase or a quantitative phase. See also **monostrand design**.

*Stage (of a study): This refers to a step or component of a strand/phase of a mixed methods study (e.g., conceptualization, method, inference).

*Strand: This is a phase of a mixed methods study in which a QUAL or a QUAN approach is used in the method of study, in data collection procedures, or in data analysis. Phases/stands might be concurrent (parallel or simultaneous) or sequential, or they might include conversion of one type of data to another for analysis (conversion). See also monostrand design and multistrand design.

Supervenience theory: (Miller, Chapter 15, this volume) This is a theory that holds that certain facts or properties exist and can be explained by a type of "dependency" relationship they have to each other. Thus, social facts "depend" (or supervene) on the existence of individuals but cannot be completely explained by this relation.

Supplemental data: (Morse, Chapter 7, this volume) This refers to data that are collected to enrich or confirm the original data.

*Temporal transferability: This refers to generalizability or applicability of inferences obtained in a study to other time periods. It subsumes the QUAN terms temporal validity and temporal external validity (see Ary, Jacobs, & Razavieh, 2002) and the QUAL term transferability. See inference transferability.

Temporal validity (or temporal external validity): See inference transferability.

Theoretical drive (or theoretical thrust): (Morse, Chapter 7, this volume) This is the overall direction of the project, as determined from the original questions or purpose, and is primarily inductive or deductive. While quantitative inquiry may be placed within a project with an inductive quantitative drive, the theoretical drive remains inductive. The converse is also true for a deductive theoretical drive.

Theoretical perspective: (Creswell et al., Chapter 8, this volume) At an informal level, this perspective reflects researchers' personal stance toward the topics they are studying, a stance based on personal history, experience, culture, gender, and class perspectives. At a more formal level, social science researchers bring to their inquiry a formal lenses through which they view their topics—lenses such as gendered perspectives (e.g., feminist theory), cultural perspectives (e.g., racial/ethnic theory), lifestyle orientation (e.g., queer theory), critical theory perspectives, and class and social status views.

Transferability: This term was used by Lincoln and Guba (1985, p. 300) as a qualitative analog to external validity. See also inference transferability.

Transformative-emancipatory perspective: (Mertens, Chapter 5, this volume) Mertens (1999) described this perspective in the following way: "Transformative scholars assume that knowledge is not neutral but is influenced by human interests, that all knowledge reflects the power and social relationships within society, and that an important purpose of knowledge construction is to help people improve society" (p. 4). In this volume, she adds, "The transformative paradigm is characterized as placing central importance on the lives and experiences of marginalized groups such as women, ethnic/racial minorities, members of the gay and lesbian communities, people with disabilities, and those who are poor. The researcher who works within this paradigm consciously analyzes asymmetric power relationships, seeks ways to link the results of social inquiry to action, and links the results of the inquiry to wider questions of social inequity and social justice."

Transformative mixed methods design: (Creswell et al., Chapter 8, this volume) This refers to a research project that Creswell et al. describe as follows: "In both perspective and outcomes, it is dedicated to promoting change at levels ranging from the personal to the political. Furthermore, it is possible to conduct any quantitative, qualitative, or mixed methods study with a transformative or advocacy purpose." These designs "give primacy to the value-based and action-oriented dimensions of different inquiry traditions" (Greene & Caracelli, 1997, p. 24). According to Creswell et al., "These purposes may be to promote equity and justice for policies and practices so as to create a personal, social, institutional, and/or organizational impact (as addressed by Newman, Ridenour, Newman, & DeMarco in Chapter 6 of this volume) or to address specific questions related to oppression, domination, alienation, and inequality."

*Triangulation: This refers to the combinations and comparisons of multiple data sources, data collection and analysis procedures, research methods, and/or inferences that occur at the end of a study. Denzin (1978) used the terms *data triangulation, theory triangulation,* and *methodological triangulation.* Erzberger and Kelle (Chapter 16, this volume) use the term to refer to agreement between inferences. See also **rules of integration.**

Two-phase design: (Currall & Towler, Chapter 18, this volume) This refers to a study with a qualitative phase followed by a quantitative phase or vice versa. See also **multistrand design.**

Typology of research purposes: (Newman et al., Chapter 6, this volume) This is a systematic classification of types of purposes for conducting mixed methods research.

Validity (design validity or inferential validity): See **inference quality.**

Validity (measurement validity or data validity): See **data quality.**

*Warrants: These are the justifications for claims resulting from research. A warrant may include "consistency with other findings" or "internal consistency of argument." All warrants exist outside the internal workings of any particular study and must be acceptable to all who would use the research. Much argument over research results is not about the results themselves but rather about the warrants put forth for why the results should be persuasive.

Within-design consistency: This refers to the consistency of the procedures of the study from which the inferences emerged. See also **inference quality.**

■ *References*

Angeles, P. A. (1981). *Dictionary of philosophy.* New York: Barnes & Noble.

Ary, D., Jacobs, L. C., & Razavieh, A. (2002). *Introduction to research in education.* Belmont, CA: Wadsworth.

Atkinson, P., & Hammersley, M. (1994). Ethnography and participant observation. In N. K. Denzin & Y. S. Lincoln (Eds.), *Handbook of qualitative research* (pp. 248-261). Thousand Oaks, CA: Sage.

Campbell, D., & Fiske, D. W. (1959). Convergent and discriminant validation by the multitrait-multimethod matrix. *Psychological Bulletin, 54,* 297-312.

Cook, T. D., & Campbell, D. T. (1979). *Quasi-experimentation: Design and analysis issues for field settings.* Boston: Houghton Mifflin.

Denzin, N. K. (1978). *The research act: A theoretical introduction to sociological methods.* New York: McGraw-Hill.

Elliott, A. E., & Woloshyn, V. E. (1997). Some female professors' experiences of collaboration: Mapping the collaborative process through rough terrain. *Alberta Journal of Educational Research, 43,* 23-36.

Geertz, C. (1979). From the native's point of view: On the nature of anthropological understanding. In P. Rabinow & W. Sullivan (Eds.), *Interpretive social science.* Berkeley: University of California Press.

Greene, J. C., & Caracelli, V. J. (1997). Defining and describing the paradigm issue in mixed-method evaluation. In J. C. Greene & V. J. Caracelli (Eds.), *Advances in mixed-method evaluation: The challenges and benefits of integrating diverse paradigms* (New Directions for Evaluation, No. 74, pp. 5-17). San Francisco: Jossey-Bass.

Holsti, O. R. (1969). *Content analysis for the social sciences and humanities.* Reading, MA: Addison-Wesley.

Howe, K. R. (1988). Against the quantitative-qualitative incompatibility thesis or dogmas die hard. *Educational Researcher, 17*(8), 10-16.

Knafl, K., Breitmayer, B., Gallo, A., & Zoeller, L. (1996). Family response to childhood illness: Description of management styles. *Journal of Pediatric Nursing, 11,* 315-326.

Lincoln, Y. S., & Guba, E. G. (1985). *Naturalistic inquiry.* Beverly Hills, CA: Sage.

Loef, M. M. (1990). *Understanding teachers' knowledge about building instruction on children's mathematical thinking: Applications of a personal construct approach* (AAC 9033785). Unpublished doctoral dissertation, University of Wisconsin–Madison.

McCall, M. W., & Bobko, P. (1990). Research methods in the service of discovery. In M. D. Dunnette & L. M. Hough (Eds.), *Handbook of industrial and organizational psychology* (2nd ed., Vol. 1, pp. 381-418). Palo Alto, CA: Consulting Psychologists.

Mertens, D. M. (1999). Inclusive evaluation: Implications of transformative theory for evaluation. *American Journal of Evaluation, 20*(1), 1-14.

Miles, M., & Huberman, M. (1994). *Qualitative data analysis: An expanded sourcebook* (2nd ed.). Thousand Oaks, CA: Sage.

Morse, J. M. (1991). Approaches to qualitative-quantitative methodological triangulation. *Nursing Research, 40*(2), 120-123.

Newman, I., & Benz, C. R. (1998). *Qualitative-quantitative research methodology: Exploring the interactive continuum.* Carbondale: Southern Illinois University Press.

Peirce, C. S. (1974). *Collected papers* (C. Hartshore, P. Weiss, & A. Burks, Eds.). Cambridge, MA: Belknap Press of Harvard University Press.

Punch, K. (1998). *Introduction to social research: Quantitative and qualitative approaches.* London: Sage.

Rappaport, S. (1996). Inference to the best explanation: Is it really different from Mills' methods? *Philosophy of Science, 63,* 65-80.

Sattath, S., & Tversky, A. (1977). Additive similarity trees. *Psychometrica, 42,* 319-345.

Strauss, A., & Corbin, J. (1994). Grounded theory methodology: An overview. In N. K. Denzin & Y. S. Lincoln (Eds.), *Handbook of qualitative research* (pp. 273-285). Thousand Oaks, CA: Sage.

Tashakkori, A., & Teddlie, C. (1998). *Mixed methodology: Combining the qualitative and quantitative approaches* (Applied Social Research Methods, No. 46). Thousand Oaks, CA: Sage.

Tashakkori, A., & Teddlie, C. (in press). Issues and dilemmas in teaching research methods courses in social and behavioral sciences: A U.S. perspective. *International Journal of Social Research Methodology.*

GLOSSARY

NAME INDEX

Abbott, B. B., 630
Abraham, I. L., 345
Achilles, C. M., 173, 174
Addams, J., 56, 80
Adler, P. A., 515
Agar, M., 149, 153, 154, 155, 156, 157
Aguilar-Gaxioler, S., 280
Ahar, J. M., 654
Airasian, P. W., 354
Alacaci, C., 610
Albrecht, T. L., 535, 536
Alcoff, L., 139
Alderete, E., 280
Alexa, M., 386, 404
Alexander, T. M., 80, 83, 84
Alfonso, M. L., 531, 536
Altheide, D. L., 172
Alvesson, M., 85
Amann, K., 339
American Psychological Association, 8, 147, 331, 332
Ames, D., 522, 523, 524
Anastasi, A., 311
Ancona, D. G., 519
Anderson, C. A., 122
Anderson, D. J., 129
Anderson, D. R., 481
Anderson, J. O., 642, 643

Anderson, K. B., 122
Anderson, N., 589
Anderson, R. C., 609
Anderson, T., 598, 606
Andersson, L. M., 521
Andreason, A., 530
Angeles, P. A., 35, 709
Annells, M., 325
Apel, K., 54, 67, 85
Aristotle, 463, 589
Aronson, N., 328
Ary, D., 630, 712, 716
Asch, S., 242
Asmar, C., 404
Atkinson, P., 325, 461, 713
Audi, R., 425, 426, 428, 434
Auerback, C. F., 283
Austin, A. E., 644, 649, 650, 651, 652, 662, 663
Ayres, L., 192, 337, 338, 339, 340, 398, 399, 409, 552

Babbie, E., 301
Bacon, F., 464, 589, 590
Baggett, L. S., 518, 524, 629
Bailey, D., 341
Bain, R., 64

de Visser, R. O., 283
Dewey, J., 20, 52, 53, 54, 55, 56, 57-58, 59, 60, 63, 64, 68, 70, 71, 72, 73, 74, 75, 78, 79, 80, 82, 83, 84, 85, 177, 178, 654
Dey, I., 328, 355
Dickerson, S. S., 315
Dickson, W. J., 6, 458, 585, 586
Dickstein, M., 53, 86
DiClemente, C. C., 529
Dillon, W. R., 311
Dimitrova, D., 535
Dimmock, K. H., 598, 601, 602
Doan, H., 202
Dockery, G., 137
Doniger, G. M., 518, 524, 629
Donmoyer, R., 629
Dootson, S., 550
Dordick, G. A., 314
Douglas, D. E., 603
Du Bois, W. E. B., 83
Dunkel, F., 283
Dunlap, K., 499
Durso, F. T., 630
Dutton, J. E., 520
Dykema, J., 591
Dzurec, L. C., 345

Earl, L. M., 652, 653, 658, 663
Earley, P. C., 519
Earls, F., 534
Eastmond, D. E., 606
Eaton, D. K., 534, 536
Eckert, T., 405
Edgerton, S. Y., 332, 333, 334
Ediger, A., 604
Edwards, J., 603
Edwards, R., 137
Eggleston, E., 560, 571, 572, 573
Egri, C. P., 521
Einstein, A., 644
Eisenberg, N., 314
Eisenhardt, K. M., 521
Eisner, E. W., 321, 331, 332, 427, 430, 433
Ellingson, S. A., 313
Elliott, A. E., 644, 704

Elsbach, K., 559, 561, 562
Emerson, R. W., 57
English, B., 153
Envegue, P., 560, 572, 573
Epping, P. J. M. M., 547
Ervin, E., 651
Erzberger, C., 15, 16, 34, 41, 466, 469, 476, 477
Escher, M. C., 326
Etzioni, A., 267
Evers, C., 60, 76
Ezzy, D. M., 283

Family Health International, 565
Farley, J., 140
Faust, K., 410
Fawcett, S. B., 537
Fay, B., 77, 98
Fazio, F., 131
Fedor, D. B., 523
Feldman, A., 655
Feldman, H. R., 542, 543
Feller, I., 395
Fennema, E., 610
Fenton, N., 17
Festinger, L., 6, 242, 260, 261, 262, 263, 266, 267, 268, 560, 562
Fetterman, D. M., 493, 497, 498, 499, 509
Feuth, T., 547
Feyten, C. M., 598, 605, 606
Field, P. A., 200, 631
Fielding, J. L., 212, 459, 461, 469, 476, 492
Fielding, N. G., 212, 459, 461, 469, 476, 492
Fine, G., 192, 559, 561, 562
Fine, M., 139, 251
Finn, J. D., 173, 174
Firestone, W., 108
Firtle, N. H., 311
Fisch, M. H., 53, 67
Fischer, P. J., 263, 264, 266, 267, 268
Fish, D., 544
Fish, S., 321
Fishbein, M., 570
Fisher, R. A., 78
Fishman, M. C., 122

SUBJECT INDEX

ABOUT THE CONTRIBUTORS

Cengiz Alacaci is Assistant Professor of Mathematics Education in the Department of Curriculum and Instruction at Florida International University. He received his doctoral degree in mathematics education from the University of Pittsburgh. He regularly teaches courses on methods of teaching mathematics. His areas of research include mathematical reasoning and problem solving in K-12 mathematics curriculum. He is also interested in expert reasoning in statistical modeling of applied social research and methods of knowledge elicitation in knowledge-rich domains.

Pat Bazeley (Ph.D., Macquarie University) provides research training and consulting through her company, Research Support P/L, to academics, graduate students, and practitioners from a wide range of disciplines in universities and government departments in Australia and internationally. Since graduating with a degree in psychology, she has worked in community development, project consulting, and academic research development. In consequence, she has had experience with research design and methodology broadly across the social sciences. Her particular expertise is in helping researchers to make sense of both quantitative and qualitative data and the use of computer programs for management and analysis of data.

Linda A. Bliss (Ph.D., University of North Carolina at Greensboro) teaches courses in Foundations of Education and Qualitative Research at Florida International University. Her research has focused on issues of cultural identity. She is the author of "Teaching and Learning in a Multicultural World: Who We Are" (in Shapiro's [1999] edited *Strangers in the Land: Pedagogy, Modernity, and Jewish Identity*). Before moving to South Florida, she participated in an Upward Bound program evaluation in the mountains of rural North Carolina, interviewing Appalachian high school students about their perceptions of program benefits. Her current research concerns Cuban American identity.

John Brewer is Professor of Sociology Emeritus at Trinity College in Hartford, Connecticut. Previously, he taught at the University of California, Los Angeles, York University, and Wesleyan University. He received his B.A., M.A., and Ph.D. degrees from the University of Chicago, where he was a Woodrow Wilson Fellow. He is coauthor (with Albert Hunter) of *Multi-*

method Research: A Synthesis of Styles (Sage, 1989). He has studied formal organizations, written about problems in organizational research and theory, and served as secretary of the American Sociological Association's section on Organizations and Occupations. His current interests include collegial administration, organizations and the law, strategies (e.g., multimethod research) for encouraging and assessing the growth of social scientific knowledge, and the sociology of art and architecture.

Valerie J. Caracelli, Ph.D., is Senior Social Science Analyst in the Center for Evaluation Methods and Issues Within Applied Research and Methods at the U.S. General Accounting Office. She serves as chair for the Topical Interest Group on Evaluation Use. Her research work focuses on the quality of evaluations and multiplist forms of inquiry.

John W. Creswell (Ph.D., University of Iowa) is Professor of Educational Psychology in the Graduate Program of Quantitative and Qualitative Methods in Education at the University of Nebraska–Lincoln. He specializes in research methods and design, qualitative inquiry, and mixed methods research, and he has authored eight books and numerous chapters and journal articles. His most recent three books address quantitative and qualitative research design, qualitative inquiry, and educational research.

Steven C. Currall (Ph.D., Cornell University) is the William N. and Stephanie Sick Professor of Entrepreneurship and Associate Professor of Management, Psychology, and Statistics in the Jones Graduate School of Management at Rice University. He also is the founding director of the Rice Alliance for Technology and Entrepreneurship. His research focuses on (a) interpersonal and interorganizational trust, (b) conflict and power within corporate boards of directors, and (c) research designs for integrating qualitative and quantitative research methods. He has published in *Organizational Behavior*

and Human Decision Processes, Organizational Research Methods, and *Industrial and Labor Relations Review.*

George Mario Paul DeMarco, Jr., Ed.D., is Coordinator of the Physical Education Teacher Preparation Program at the University of Dayton, where he teaches courses in curriculum, instruction, and research methodology and supervises community-based physical education programs. He completed his doctorate in physical education at the University of Georgia, his master's degree in physical education at Ithaca College, and his bachelor's degree in health and physical education at Bridgewater State College in Massachusetts. He joined the University of Dayton faculty in August 1997. His research interests include teacher-coach effectiveness, expertise, and behavior, areas in which he has presented and published at state, national, and international levels.

Eric S. Dwyer (Ph.D., University of Texas at Austin) is Associate Professor of Modern Language Education and Teachers of English to Speakers of Other Languages at Florida International University. He has taught foreign language in the United States, Mexico, and Japan. He has also done language education consulting work in Korea, Russia, and Peru.

Christian Erzberger (Ph.D., University of Bremen) is Senior Researcher at the Institute for Innovative Social Research and Social Planning (GISS) in Bremen, Germany, with research projects in various fields of social planning and social research. From 1991 to 2001, he worked as a research fellow at the Special Research Center ("Status Passages and Risks in the Life Course," founded by the German Research Foundation) at the University of Bremen. His main fields of interest in teaching and research cover the methodology of social research, especially the problems surrounding the integration of qualitative and quantitative data and methods and statistical methods for the exploratory analysis of longitudinal life course data (e.g., optimal matching techniques).

Joyce C. Fine, Ed.D., is Associate Professor of Reading/Language Arts at Florida International University. She focuses on literacy interventions and teacher education. As a reading researcher, she serves on the International Reading Association's National Commission on Excellence in Reading Teacher Preparation. She is the author of numerous articles and publications and has served on the editorial boards and as an officer of professional organizations. Her work involves the design and implementation of Project READS, a collaborative reading master's program with the Miami-Dade County Public Schools, and Project LIFT: Literacy Intervention for Teens, with the Miami-Dade County Juvenile Assessment Center.

Melinda S. Forthofer (Ph.D., University of Michigan) is Assistant Professor in the Department of Community and Family Health in the College of Public Health at the University of South Florida. She teaches courses in research methodology and the social determinants of health in the College of Public Health. Her research program is focused on mixed methods evaluation of community-based disease prevention and health promotion programs. She is co-principal investigator of the Florida Prevention Research Center and serves as director of the center's Methods and Evaluation Unit. She is also principal investigator of the Florida Health Literacy Study, director of evaluation for the Central Hillsborough Healthy Start Initiative, and director of evaluation for the National Friendly Access program.

Suzanne Gallagher is pursuing her doctorate in adult education/human resource development at Florida International University. She currently holds an administrative position in a nonprofit organization serving individuals with developmental disabilities. The focus of her work is on human resource development in human service organizations.

Jennifer C. Greene is Professor of Educational Psychology at the University of Illinois, Urbana-Champaign. She has been an evaluation scholar-practitioner for more than 25 years. Her theoretical work has focused on the intersections of evaluation and politics and includes developments in qualitative, participatory, and mixed methods evaluation approaches. Her evaluation practice has concentrated on public programs for children and families.

Michelle L. Gutmann (M.S., C.C.C.-S.L.P.) is a speech-language pathologist with 10 years of clinical experience in augmentative and alternative communication. Throughout this time, she has worked with both adults and children across a variety of settings. She is currently pursuing her doctorate in speech pathology and is interested in outcome measures and in-depth study of specific clinical populations.

William E. Hanson (Ph.D., Arizona State University, M.A., University of Minnesota) is Assistant Professor in the Department of Educational Psychology at the University of Nebraska–Lincoln. He teaches in the Counseling Psychology Program. He specializes in psychological assessment, psychotherapy process and outcome research, and counselor training/supervision.

Rom Harré (M.A., B.S., B.Phil., D.Litt.) is Emeritus Fellow of Linacre College in Oxford, United Kingdom; Professor of Psychology at Georgetown University; and Adjunct Professor of Philosophy at American University. He studied mathematics and physics and then philosophy and anthropology. His published work includes studies in the philosophy of the natural sciences such as *Varieties of Realism* and *Great Scientific Experiments.* He has been among the pioneers of the "discursive" approach in the human sciences. In *Social Being, Personal Being and Physical Being,* he explored the role of rules and conventions in various aspects of human cognition, while in *Pronouns and People,* he and Peter Mühlhäusler developed the thesis that grammar and the sense of self are intimately related. His most recent work, *One Thousand Years of Philosophy*, follows the philosophical enterprise in India, China, Islam, and Europe since A.D. 1000. He holds honorary doctorates from the universities of Helsinki, Brussels, Arhus, and Lima.

Albert Hunter is Professor of Sociology at Northwestern University. He has taught previously at the University of Chicago, Wesleyan University, and the University of Rochester, and he has had visiting appointments at Yale University, the London School of Economics, the University of Paris, and the University of Edinburgh. His major work is in urban sociology and the question of community. He is the author of *Symbolic Communities: The Persistence and Change of Chicago's Local Communities*. His work on research methods is exemplified in two books, *Multimethod Research: A Synthesis of Styles* (1989, with John Brewer) and *The Rhetoric of Social Research: Understood and Believed* (1990). He is currently working on a number of comparative community case studies on gangs and suburban politics as well as a comparative study of civil society in the United States and the United Kingdom.

Ken D. Jensen is a Ph.D. candidate in instructional technology in Teachers College at the University of Nebraska–Lincoln. He is Director of the university's Instructional Design Center, a technology-based support service for students, faculty, and staff of the university community.

Burke Johnson is Associate Professor in the College of Education at the University of South Alabama. He is the coauthor of *Educational Research: Quantitative and Qualitative Approaches* and has published in journals such as *Evaluation Review, Evaluation and Program Planning, Educational Researcher,* and the *Journal of Educational Psychology*.

Udo Kelle, Ph.D., is Lecturer in (quantitative and qualitative) Social Research Methods at the University of Vechta in the northwest region of Germany. He received his master's degree in psychology and his doctorate in sociology at the University of Bremen and worked there between 1989 and 1997 as a senior research fellow at the Special Research Center of the German National Science Foundation. He has written several books and numerous articles in English and German, mostly about methodological issues in the social sciences, including *Computer Aided Qualitative Data Analysis* (Sage, 1995) and *Vom Einzelfall zum Typus* (1999, with Susann Kluge). He has also done empirical work in the fields of life course research and social gerontology. His research interests cover the methodology of social research and its philosophical underpinnings, especially of qualitative methods, sociological and philosophical theories of action, and the sociology of aging.

Elizabeth A. Kemper (Ph.D., Louisiana State University) is Assistant Professor in the Department of Education Research, Leadership, and Counselor Education at North Carolina State University. Her research interests focus on school reform implementation and policy issues, specifically their impact on economically disadvantaged students. She is currently the series co-editor of *Readings on Equal Education* and was a guest co-editor for a recent issue of the *Journal of Education for Students Placed at Risk* investigating the impact of the Direct Instruction school reform model.

Diane M. Loomis is a doctoral candidate in the Graduate School of Education at George Mason University. Her professional background includes special education administration and arts education for deaf students. Her current interests include research methodology and the spiritual development of children through education.

Spencer J. Maxcy (Ph.D., Indiana University) is Professor of Education and a John Dewey Specialist at Louisiana State University. He has authored eight books that apply pragmatism to problems and issues in contemporary education, including *Ethical School Leadership* (2002); *Democracy, Chaos, and the New School Order* (1995); *Postmodern School Leadership: Meeting the Crisis in Educational Administration* (1995); and *Educational Leadership: A Critical Pragmatic Perspective* (1991). His latest work is an edited three-volume series, *John Dewey and American Education*, that introduces first-edition reprints of three seminal works on pragmatism and education by Dewey.

Joseph A. Maxwell is Associate Professor in the Graduate School of Education at George Mason University. He is the author of *Qualitative Research Design* (Sage, 1996) and of publications in qualitative methods, anthropology, and education. He has worked in both academic and applied settings, and he has been an invited speaker at conferences and universities in the United States, Europe, Puerto Rico, and China. The focus of his current work is on the intersection among philosophy, sociocultural theory, and research methodology. He has a Ph.D. in anthropology from the University of Chicago.

Donna M. Mertens is Professor in the Department of Educational Foundations and Research at Gallaudet University. She teaches research methods, program evaluation, and educational psychology to deaf and hearing students at the undergraduate and graduate levels. She is a past president and current board member of the American Evaluation Association, providing leadership for its Building Diversity Initiative and International Committee. She has authored or edited several books, including *Parent Experiences With Young Deaf or Hard of Hearing Children* (2002, with Kay Meadow Orlans and Marilyn Sass Lehrer), *Research and Inequality* (2000, with Carole Truman and Beth Humphries), *Research Methods in Education*

and Psychology: Integrating Diversity (Sage, 1998), and *Research Methods in Special Education* (Sage, 1995, with John McLaughlin). She has also published in journals such as the *American Journal of Evaluation, American Annals of the Deaf*, and *Educational Evaluation and Policy Analysis*.

Steven Miller, Ph.D., is Professor of Educational Policy Studies in the School of Education at Loyola University of Chicago. He also has an adjunct professor appointment in the Department of Philosophy. His major research interests lie at the intersection of educational research methods and issues in the philosophy of the social sciences. His interests in the emerging field of mixed methods are centered on trying to understand the specific inference processes that inform these perspectives. He is the author of several textbooks in the sociology of education and research methods and related areas, and he has also published in journals such as *The Educational Researcher, Philosophy of Science, Philosophy of Social Science, Social Epistemology, Qualitative Health Research*, and *Synthese*. His current research involves the role of educational research methods in forming and perpetuating the idea of social kinds.

Fathali M. Moghaddam is Professor of Psychology at Georgetown University. His endeavor to develop a normative science of human behavior is reflected in his most recent books, *The Individual and Society: A Cultural Integration* (2002), *Social Psychology: Exploring Universals Across Cultures* (1998), and *The Specialized Society: The Plight of the Individual in an Age of Individualism* (1997). He is currently exploring alternative qualitative methods.

Janice M. Morse (Ph.D. [Nurs.], Ph.D. [Anthro.], D.Nurs. [Hon.], F.A.A.N.) is Director of the International Institute of Qualitative Methodology and Professor in the Faculty of Nursing at the University of Alberta as well as Adjunct Professor in the School of Nursing at

The Pennsylvania State University. She has an interest in developing qualitative methods and has published more than 200 articles and 13 books on clinical nursing research and research methods. Her more recent books include *Qualitative Research Methods for Health Professionals* (1995, with Peggy Anne Field), *Qualitative Nursing Research: A Contemporary Dialogue* (1991), *Critical Issues in Qualitative Research* (1994), *Completing a Qualitative Project* (1997), *The Nature of Qualitative Evidence* (2002, with Janice Swanson and Tony Kuzel), and *Read Me First: A User's Guide to Qualitative Methods* (2002, with Lyn Richards). She is the editor of *Qualitative Health Research*.

Carole Newman, Ph.D., is Associate Professor in the Department of Curricular and Instructional Studies at the University of Akron. Since 1990, she has taught graduate and undergraduate courses in teacher education, served on many dissertation committees, and guided classroom research. She teaches a graduate course in action research. She is known for her successful grant writing, and she presents workshops on a range of topics such as assessment, mentoring, curriculum mapping, instructional strategies, and grant writing. For the past 10 years, she has worked at the state and local levels to design programs that support entry-level teachers.

Isadore Newman, Ph.D., is Distinguished Professor at the University of Akron, where he has been teaching research courses since 1971. Specializing in mixed methodology and the general linear model, he has served on more than 300 dissertation committees and has authored approximately 100 articles and 9 books and monographs. He is an adjunct professor at North East Ohio Universities College of Medicine, associate director of the Institute for Life-Span Development and Gerontology, and scientific director of the Cardiovascular Research and Wellness Institute at Akron City Hospital.

He also has been editor and on the editorial boards of a number of journals.

Anthony J. Onwuegbuzie is Associate Professor in the Department of Human Development and Psychoeducational Studies at Howard University. He earned his Ph.D. in educational research at the University of South Carolina. His research topics primarily involve disadvantaged and underserved populations such as minorities, learning-disabled students, and juvenile delinquents. During the past 6 years, he has secured more than 100 publications in national and international journals and made more than 200 presentations at the international, national, regional, and university levels. He has a forthcoming book titled *Library Anxiety: Theory, Research, and Applications.*

N. Eleni Pappamihiel (Ph.D., University of Texas at Austin) is Assistant Professor in the Multilingual/Multicultural Education Program at Florida State University. She has also been an instructor at the University of Texas at Austin and the University of Texas at San Antonio. Her research interests include preservice teacher training and affective factors in second language acquisition. She has published in the *Bilingual Research Journal* and *Research in Teaching English,* and she has presented papers at the National Association of Bilingual Education and American Council of Teachers of Foreign Languages.

Aixa Perez-Prado is Assistant Professor in the College of Education at Florida International University. Her doctoral degree in social science and education is from Florida State University, where she was a Title VII Bilingual/Bicultural Fellow. She has worked internationally in teaching English as a second language as well as in teacher preparation and curriculum design. Her current research interests are in the areas of distance education and learning partnerships with populations of linguistic and cultural minority students.

Vicki L. Plano Clark (M.S., Michigan State University) is Laboratory Manager in the Department of Physics and Astronomy, as well as a doctoral candidate in quantitative and qualitative methods in education, at the University of Nebraska–Lincoln. In addition to her doctoral work, which emphasizes mixed methods research, she has focused on curriculum development that incorporates computer-based technologies into introductory physics teaching laboratory courses. She has been a co-principal investigator on three National Science Foundation grants as well as the leader of numerous faculty development workshops at regional and national professional society meetings.

Sharon F. Rallis is Professor of Education in the Neag School of Education at the University of Connecticut, where she teaches courses on inquiry, qualitative methods, and educational policy. For more than 20 years, she has conducted evaluations of educational, medical, and social programs and has taught about evaluation. She has been a lecturer at the Harvard Graduate School of Education and has directed a major school reform initiative for a federal educational laboratory. Her books include *Principals of Dynamic Schools: Taking Charge of Change* (2nd ed., Corwin, 2000, with Ellen Goldring) and *Learning in the Field: An Introduction to Qualitative Inquiry* (Sage, 1998, with Gretchen Rossman). She has also published extensively in education and evaluation journals. Currently, she is serving her second term on the board of directors of the American Evaluation Association.

Carolyn S. Ridenour is Professor in the Department of Educational Leadership at the University of Dayton, where she teaches qualitative and quantitative research methods to graduate students and works with doctoral candidates. Her most recent publications address school policy issues related to urban schools, school choice, and cultural diversity. She is the coauthor of *Qualitative-Quantitative Research*

Methodology (1998, with Isadore Newman) and has published in numerous education journals (prior to 1998 as Carolyn R. Benz).

Tonette S. Rocco, Ph.D., is Assistant Professor of Adult Education and Human Resource Development at Florida International University. She is the Qualitative Methods editor for Volumes 12 to 15 of the *Human Resource Development Quarterly* and is a member of the fifth group of Cyril O. Houle Scholars in Adult and Continuing Education Program funded by the W. K. Kellogg Foundation and administered by the University of Georgia.

Gretchen B. Rossman (Ph.D., University of Pennsylvania) is Professor of Education at the University of Massachusetts at Amherst. Her research has focused on the local impact of changes in federal, state, and local policies. She has served as methodological consultant to projects focusing on professional development programs for personnel serving children with disabilities; the impact of welfare reform, immigration reform, and the changing workplace on adult learners; and professional development programs for adult basic education teachers. Her books include *Change and Effectiveness in Schools: A Cultural Perspective* (1988, with Dick Corbett and Bill Firestone), *Mandating Academic Excellence: High School Responses to State Curriculum Reform* (1993, with Bruce Wilson), *Dynamic Teachers: Taking Charge of Change* (Corwin, 1996, with Sharon Rallis), *Designing Qualitative Research* (3rd ed., Sage, 1999, with Catherine Marshall), and *Learning in the Field: An Introduction to Qualitative Research* (Sage, 1998, with Sharon Rallis).

Margarete Sandelowski is Professor and Director of the Annual Summer Institutes in Qualitative Research in the School of Nursing at the University of North Carolina at Chapel Hill. She is the author of more than 100 publications in the areas of infertility and childbearing, gender and technology, and qualitative methodology, including the award-winning book *With Child in Mind: Studies of the Personal Encounter With Infertility* (1993). Her most recent book is *Devices and Desires: Gender, Technology, and American Nursing* (2000). She is currently principal investigator of a 5-year study, funded by the National Institute of Nursing Research, National Institutes of Health, to develop the analytical and interpretive techniques to conduct qualitative meta- syntheses.

Kathy L. Shapley is a doctoral student in the Department of Communication Disorders at the University of Nebraska–Lincoln. She is also working on a master of arts degree in educational psychology with an emphasis on quantitative and qualitative methods in education. Her research interests include early communication development in children with motor speech disorders and the use of mixed methodology to examine aspects of family access to and satisfaction with early intervention services.

Lyn M. Shulha (Ph.D., University of Virginia) is Associate Professor in Educational Evaluation, Planning, and Assessment at Queen's University in Kingston, Ontario. Her general interest is in the nature and complexity of inquiry, particularly evaluative and collaborative inquiry. This supports her teaching and research in program evaluation, classroom assessment practices, and professional learning. She has served as executive officer of the Canadian Educational Researchers Association and as associate editor for the *American Journal of Evaluation,* and she is currently chair of the Professional Development Committee of the American Evaluation Association.

Marylyn C. Sines (Ed.S., University of Georgia) is currently a school psychologist in Naples, Florida. Previously, she has been a school psychologist in Baton Rouge, Louisiana; Tampa, Florida; and Orlando, Florida. Her professional experiences include a practicum at the Texas Children's Hospital (Houston) and a 1-year internship at the University of New Mexico School of Medicine. Her research experiences and presentations have involved program evaluation and alternative/bilingual assessment. Her professional interests are in the areas of attention deficit hyperactivity disorder and pediatric neuropsychology. Her research in progress includes a comparison of the psychological profiles of Mexican American and non-Hispanic sexually abused children. She has published in *The Clinical Neuropsychologist.*

Sam Stringfield (Ph.D., Temple University) is Principal Research Scientist in the Center for the Social Organization of Schools at Johns Hopkins University. He serves as co-director of the Systemic Supports for School Improvement section of the Center for Research on Education of Students Placed at Risk. He co-directs the Program on Integrated Reform in the Center for Research on Education, Diversity, and Excellence at the University of California, Santa Cruz. He is a founding editor of the *Journal of Education for Students Placed at Risk* and a member of the New Board of School Commissioners in Baltimore, Maryland. He has authored more than 100 articles, chapters, and books. His research focuses on designs for improving schools and for improving systemic supports for schools serving disadvantaged schools in the United States and around the world.

Abbas Tashakkori (Ph.D., University of North Carolina at Chapel Hill) is Professor of Educational Psychology and Research Methodology in the Department of Educational and Psychological Studies at Florida International University. He has been a postdoctoral fellow at the Carolina Population Center and the University of North Carolina at Chapel Hill as well as a visiting scholar at Texas A&M University. He has extensive experience as an educational program evaluator, and he has taught research methods for more than two decades in undergraduate and graduate programs at the University of North Carolina, Shiraz University (Iran), Stetson University, Louisiana State University, and Florida International University. In addition to research methodology, his published work covers a wide spectrum of research and program evaluation in cross-cultural and multicultural contexts, including self-perceptions, attitudes, and gender/ethnicity. He is the coauthor of *Mixed Methodology: Combining the Qualitative and Quantitative Approaches* (Sage, 1998, with Charles Teddlie) and the coeditor of *Education of Hispanics in the U.S.: Politics, Policies, and Outcomes* (1999, with Hector Ochoa).

Charles Teddlie (Ph.D., University of North Carolina at Chapel Hill) is the Jo Ellen Levy Yates Distinguished Professor of Education at Louisiana State University. He has also taught at the University of New Orleans and has been a visiting professor at the University of Newcastle-upon-Tyne and the University of Exeter (both in the United Kingdom). He also served as assistant superintendent for research and development at the Louisiana Department of Education. His major writing interests are social science research methodology and school effectiveness research. He has taught research methods courses for more than 20 years, including statistics and qualitative research methods. He has been awarded the Excellence in Teaching Award from the College of Education at Louisiana State. He has published more than 100 chapters and articles and is the coauthor or coeditor of nine books, including *Schools Make a Difference: Lessons Learned From a 10-Year Study of School Effects* (1993, with Sam Stringfield), *Forty Years After the Brown Decision: Social and Cultural Implications of School Desegregation* (1997, with Kofi Lomotey), *Mixed Methodology: Combining the Qualitative and Quantitative Approaches* (Sage, 1998, with Abbas Tashakkori), and *The International Handbook of School Effectiveness Research* (2000, with David Reynolds). He has lectured on school effectiveness research

and educational research methodology in several countries, including the United Kingdom, the Republic of Ireland, the Netherlands, Norway, Denmark, Russia, the Ukraine, and Belarus.

Annette J. Towler (Ph.D., Rice University) is currently Assistant Professor in Industrial Organizational Psychology at the University of Colorado at Denver. Her chapter in this handbook was completed when she was a doctoral student at Rice University. Her current research issues include training and development and charismatic leadership. She has published in the *Journal of Applied Psychology* and worked in industry for several years as a management trainer.

Lisa A. Turner, Ph.D., is Associate Professor in the Department of Psychology at the University of South Alabama. She has recently published in the *American Journal of Mental Retardation* and the *Journal of Educational Psychology.*

Sheila Twinn, Ph.D., P.G.C.E.A., R.N., R.S.C.N., R.H.V., is Professor in the Nethersole School of Nursing at the Chinese University of Hong Kong. Since joining that school in 1992, she has continued to develop her work in health promotion and public health, in particular women's health issues. Her research work in women's health and the development of health promotion strategies has mainly focused on Hong Kong Chinese women's experiences of screening for cervical cancer, particularly factors influencing uptake rates and re-attendance rates for further screening. Mixed methods design has provided the research methodology for several of these studies.

Benjamin R. Walker is Assistant Professor in the Department of Psychology at Georgetown University, where he teaches neuropsychology courses and conducts research on the autonomic control of limbic motor seizures and autism. He received his Ph.D. in psychology from the University of Virginia, where he specialized in the neuroanatomy of sensory system organization. He held a postdoctoral fellowship position with Dr. Karen Gale in the Department of Pharmacology and the Interdisciplinary Program for Neuroscience at Georgetown University Medical Center from 1996 to 2000.

Cindy Waszak (Ph.D., M.A., University of North Carolina at Chapel Hill) is Senior Scientist for Family Health International (FHI) conducting research on the social and psychological aspects of reproductive health in diverse countries such as Cameroon, Egypt, Jamaica, Kenya, Uganda, Vietnam, Zambia, and Zimbabwe. Previously, she worked for FHI from 1980 to 1986 and then left for a brief time to return to the University of North Carolina to get a Ph.D. in social psychology and to work as research director at the Center for Population Options in Washington, D.C., before returning to FHI in 1991. During the past 15 years, much of her work has focused on adolescent reproductive health, and currently she is part of the research team for FHI's recently awarded YouthNet project.

Robert J. Wilson has been on the faculty of Queen's University in Kingston, Ontario, since 1972. He is past president of the Canadian Educational Researchers Association and is one of two Canadian members of the Joint Committee on Evaluation Standards. He holds a Ph.D. in educational psychology from the University of Washington. His current main area of research is teachers' assessment practices, focusing particularly on how teachers actually assess students in their classrooms. Collaborative research methods dominate his approach in this field. In addition, he consults frequently with large-scale assessment organizations on technical matters relating to their work.

Department of Social Policy and Social Work
University of Oxford
Barnett House
32 Wellington Square
Oxford OX1 2ER
England